W9-BKG-380
RUSSIA
MONGOLIA
MONGOLIAN PLATEAU
GOBI DESERT
YIN MTS.
ORDOS DESERT
GREATER KHINGAN RANGE
NORTHEAST CHINA PLAIN
NORTH CHINA PLAIN
LÜLIANG MTS.
QIN LING
DABIE MTS.
WUYI MTS.
Lake Baikal
Amur
Heihe
Hailar
Qiqihar
Jiamusi
Harbin
Baicheng
Changchun
Jilin
Xilinhot
Xar Moron
Liao
Tumen
Shenyang
Fushun
Anshan
Benxi
Yalu
Baotou
Datong
Beijing
Tangshan
Tianjin
Dalian
Korea Bay
Bo Hai
Baoding
Shijiazhuang
Taiyuan
Handan
Jinan
Qingdao
Shandong Peninsula
Yellow Sea
Yellow (Huang)
Xianyang
Wei
Xi'an
Zhengzhou
Xuzhou
Yancheng
Nanjing
Wuxi
Suzhou
Shanghai
Hangzhou Bay
Hangzhou
Ningbo
Three Gorges Dam
Yichang
Wuhan
Yangzi (Chang)
Changde
Nanchang
Changsha
Fuzhou
Taibei
Taiwan Strait
TAIWAN
Guilin
Shaoguan
Zhangzhou
Hongshui
Xi
Guangzhou
Shantou
Shenzhen
Hong Kong (Xianggang)
Kaohsiung
Nanning
Qinzhou
Yangjiang
Gulf of Tonkin
Haikou
Hainan Island
South China Sea
Luzon Strait
Babuyan Islands (PHILIPPINES)
NORTH KOREA
SOUTH KOREA
Jeju I. (S. KOREA)
Tsushima (JAPAN)
Korea Strait
JAPAN
East Sea (Sea of Japan)
Tsugaru Strait
La Perouse Strait
Tatar Strait
Lake Khanka
Ussuri
Songhua
East China Sea
Ryukyu Islands (JAPAN)
Philippine Sea
Tropic of Cancer
110°E
120°E
130°E
40°N
30°N
20°N
0 100 200 300 400 500 miles
0 100 200 300 400 500 km

Encyclopedia of Modern China

Encyclopedia of Modern China

VOLUME 2

F–M

David Pong

EDITOR IN CHIEF

CHARLES SCRIBNER'S SONS

A part of Gale, Cengage Learning

Detroit • New York • San Francisco • New Haven, Conn • Waterville, Maine • London

Encyclopedia of Modern China

David Pong, Editor in Chief

For product information and technology assistance, contact us at
Gale Customer Support, 1-800-877-4253.
For permission to use material from this text or product,
submit all requests online at **www.cengage.com/permissions.**
Further permissions questions can be emailed to
permissionrequest@cengage.com

Library of Congress Cataloging-in-Publication Data

Encyclopedia of modern China / David Pong, editor in chief.
p. cm. --
Includes bibliographical references and index.
ISBN 978-0-684-31566-9 (set : alk. paper) -- ISBN 978-0-684-31567-6 (v. 1 : alk. paper) -- ISBN 978-0-684-31568-3 (v. 2 : alk. paper) -- ISBN 978-0-684-31569-0 (v. 3 : alk. paper) -- ISBN 978-0-684-31570-6 (v. 4 : alk. paper) -- ISBN 978-0-684-31571-3 (e-book)
1. China--Civilization--1644-1912--Encyclopedias. 2. China--Civilization--1912-1949--Encyclopedias. 3. China--Civilization--1949---Encyclopedias. I. Pong, David, 1939-.

DS755.E63 2009
951.003--dc22 2009003279

Gale
27500 Drake Rd.
Farmington Hills, MI 48331-3535

ISBN-13: 978-0-684-31566-9 (set) ISBN-10: 0-684-31566-1 (set)
ISBN-13: 978-0-684-31567-6 (vol. 1) ISBN-10: 0-684-31567-X (vol. 1)
ISBN-13: 978-0-684-31568-3 (vol. 2) ISBN-10: 0-684-31568-8 (vol. 2)
ISBN-13: 978-0-684-31569-0 (vol. 3) ISBN-10: 0-684-31569-6 (vol. 3)
ISBN-13: 978-0-684-31570-6 (vol. 4) ISBN-10: 0-684-31570-X (vol. 4)

This title is also available as an e-book.
ISBN-13: 978-0-684-31571-3 ISBN-10: 0-684-31571-8
Contact your Gale sales representative for ordering information.

Printed in the United States of America
1 2 3 4 5 6 7 13 12 11 10 09

Editorial Board

Contents

List of Maps

F

FALUN GONG

The Falun Gong (the discipline of the dharma wheel), also known as Falun Dafa (the great way of the dharma wheel), is a school of *qigong* founded by Li Hongzhi. The Falun Gong is best known for the ongoing campaign against it by Chinese authorities, prompted by a massive peaceful Falun Gong demonstration outside of Communist Party headquarters in Beijing in late April 1999.

ORIGINS AND TEACHINGS

The Falun Gong emerged in 1992 toward the end of the *qigong* boom, and can only be understood in the context of the larger *qigong* movement. Like other *qigong* masters, Falun Gong founder Li Hongzhi taught basic *qigong* movements, described in his first book-length publication, *China Falun Gong* (1993). Between 1992 and the end of 1994, he organized national lecture tours in which he spoke to thousands of enthusiastic practitioners. Li was celebrated as a rising star in the *qigong* movement, and the Falun Gong was welcomed into the China Qigong Scientific Research Association. The Falun Gong quickly became one of the largest *qigong* organizations in China, consisting at its height in the mid-1990s of 28,263 base-level practice centers, 1,900 midlevel training stations, and thirty-nine main stations, which coordinated the network under Li's orders.

From the beginning, Li Hongzhi was scornful of flashy *qigong* masters who touted their supernormal powers, and he promised to teach *qigong* "at a higher level," by which he meant moral and spiritual cultivation rather than the pursuit of miracle cures. Li offered to cleanse practitioners' bodies (surely a claim to a supernormal power) so that they could proceed directly to high-level cultivation, consisting of the Falun Gong regime of exercises and Li's spiritual teachings, which emphasize traditional moral behavior and the abandonment of all attachments, be they material, sentimental, or sensual. By maintaining a high moral standard in their workaday lives, Falun Gong practitioners were to burn off karma (a cumulative debt incurred through immoral behavior in past and present lives) and accumulate virtue. The transformation was physical as well as moral; the practitioner who remained steadfast in the face of suffering would see his molecular matter change from black (the color of karma) to white (the color of virtue). For the same reason, Falun Gong practitioners were not to take medication when ill, because medication would reduce suffering and slow the burning away of karma. Li reinforced his calls to moral fundamentalism with traditional millenarian messages, often mentioning the imminent end of the world.

Li left China in early 1995 and established himself in the United States, subsequently spending more time among practitioners in the Chinese diaspora in North America, Europe, and Australia than with the mass of his following in China. Although Li's departure was motivated by fears of impending political problems, the Falun Gong continued to flourish in China, despite increasing media criticism. In his absence, Li accorded increasing importance to his chief scripture, *Zhuan falun* (The Revolving Dharma Wheel), a transcription of his lectures published on the eve of Li's departure from China, and he demanded that repeated study of this masterwork constitute the core of practitioners' cultivation activities. This emphasis on scripture, added to Li's focus on morality and suffering, lent the Falun Gong a religious character less obvious in other *qigong* groups, even if other *qigong* masters also talked about morality and published *qigong* books.

Falun Gong follower meditating outside government offices in Hong Kong, August 24, 2001. *A blend of spiritual and meditative teachings, Falun Gong gained a large number of followers in the 1990s. Alarmed Chinese government officials banned the movement by decade's end, enacting a fierce campaign against adherents that alarmed many international human rights organizations.* © REUTERS/CORBIS

Between 1996 and 1999, Falun Gong practitioners within China reacted to media criticism by organizing frequent peaceful protests, demanding equal time to refute what they saw as slanderous charges against them. Chinese government sources claim that there were some three hundred such incidents during this period, stunning testimony of practitioners' organizational acumen and sense of self-righteousness. Although the Falun Gong appears to have prevailed in most of these instances, media criticism continued. The outcome was the spectacular Falun Gong demonstration in Beijing in April 1999, once again sparked by media attacks—backed up by police truncheons—on the Falun Gong in the neighboring city of Tianjin.

GOVERNMENT SUPPRESSION AND FALUN GONG RESPONSE

The Chinese government's response to the demonstration was swift and decisive. Secretly declaring the Falun Gong to be the greatest danger to China since the student demonstrations of 1989, President Jiang Zemin directed a campaign of suppression against the movement, henceforth condemned as a dangerous cult like Aum Shinrikyo in Japan or the Branch Davidians in the United States. The effectiveness of the campaign was blunted by the surprisingly vigorous reaction of Falun Gong practitioners in the Chinese diaspora, particularly in North America. These practitioners, most of whom were recent emigrants from China, successfully brought pressure on Western governments and media, depicting the issue as one of freedom of speech and religious belief, at the same time encouraging their copractitioners in China to continue to protest the crackdown. Diaspora practitioners also began to construct an impressive network of Web sites and other media, which continued to champion the Falun Gong cause.

After publicly defending the April demonstration in the spring of 1999, Li Hongzhi went into hiding and said little between the summer of 1999 and the fall of 2000. When he resumed speaking at practitioner-organized "experience-sharing conferences" in late 2000, he depicted the government's campaign of suppression as a test that practitioners had to pass. In his New Year's Day message of 2001, Li called on followers to "go beyond forbearance" ("truth, benevolence, and forbearance" is a central Falun Gong slogan), apparently attempting to mobilize them to active resistance. In February 2001, Chinese television showed grisly film of several alleged Falun Gong practitioners who had set themselves on fire in Tiananmen Square in central Beijing. Although Falun Gong spokespeople disputed the claim that these were indeed practitioners, the incident marked a turning point in public opinion toward the Falun Gong, particularly in China, but to some extent worldwide.

Falun Gong activists, especially in the diaspora, have continued their efforts to bring attention to the persecution of practitioners in China, hacking into cable and even satellite broadcasts in China, serving legal papers on Chinese leaders traveling outside of China (charging them with genocide and other crimes against humanity), multiplying Web sites, and even founding a television station, the New Tang Dynasty Television, and a newspaper, *The Epoch Times*, that is available in both online and print editions. The Falun Gong also organizes Chinese New Year spectaculars outside of China, performances that use traditional forms of Chinese music and dance to denounce the persecution of Falun Gong practitioners in China. Inevitably, the orientation of the Falun Gong has become increasingly political, accusing the Chinese Communist Party of any number of crimes and calling on party members to surrender their membership. Although human rights organizations agree that claims of persecution of Falun Gong practitioners in China are real, the efforts of Falun Gong practitioners to call attention to that persecution are increasingly viewed as exaggerated and hence have lost much of their original effectiveness.

SEE ALSO *Qigong.*

BIBLIOGRAPHY

Li Hongzhi. *China Falun Gong.* Rev. ed. Englewood, NJ: Universe Publishing, 1999.

Ownby, David. *Falun Gong and the Future of China.* New York: Oxford University Press, 2008.

Palmer, David A. *Qigong Fever: Body, Science, and Utopia in China.* New York: Columbia University Press, 2007.

Penny, Benjamin. The Life and Times of Li Hongzhi: Falun Gong and Religious Biography. *China Quarterly* 175 (2003): 643–661.

Tong, James. An Organizational Analysis of the Falun Gong: Structure, Communications, Financing. *China Quarterly* 171 (2002): 636–660.

David Ownby

FAMILY

This entry contains the following:

OVERVIEW

From earliest times, the Chinese stressed the family as the most important unit in society. The individual counted, but his or her principal role was to strengthen and perpetuate the family. By contrast, in contemporary urbanized societies, the function of the family is much more to raise the individual to maturity and independence.

Chinese rice farmers sharing a meal, 1951. *Traditional Chinese culture placed greater priority on the family rather than the individual, with male family members superior to female ones. Multiple generations generally lived together under one roof, with married sons remaining with their father and daughters joining their husband's parents.* © HORACE BRISTOL/CORBIS

RELATIONSHIPS IN THE FAMILY

The basic relationship upon which all others were modeled was that between father and son. It was axiomatic that the father was superior to the son and could expect absolute obedience, respect, and service from him. This was in principle true throughout their lives, though stories of a ninety-year-old father beating his seventy-year-old son for disobedience are probably apocryphal.

A father was, of course, of a higher generation than his son. On the same generational principle, a grandfather was superior to a grandson, and an uncle to his nephew. The father was also older than his son, and on this age principle an elder brother must be superior to a younger, and an older cousin to a younger. A father's relationship with his daughter echoed that with his son, and implicit in this was the principle that a male was superior to a female, so a husband was superior to his wife, and a brother to his sister.

The father-son relationship embodied the three major features (generation, age, and gender) that were central to the ordering of family hierarchy. By reference to them, each member of the family knew his or her position vis-à-vis every other member, and since the system produced no equals (even in the case of twins, one was born before the other), all relationships were clearly stratified. Theoretically, there could be no arguments or lack of harmony within the group, not because of natural affection, but thanks to the restraints that the duty of obedience and subservience imposed.

In practice, families did not hold slavishly to the system. Even if the accident of distribution of strong and weak personalities within the group were not enough to make a nonsense of formal hierarchy, there were inbuilt contradictions. Perhaps most notable was the tension in the mother-son relationship, where the mother was clearly superior in generation and age, but inferior in gender—who should control whom?

THE FAMILY UNIT

A simple family of father, mother, and unmarried children was not unusual, but it was not considered ideal, because such a group would disintegrate when the children married and the parents died. The ideal family was an everlasting corporation where the personnel came and went but the unit remained. To achieve this it was necessary that married children should stay with the family and raise grandchildren there, and that they in turn should stay. The elderly would die, but membership would be continually replenished from below.

Of course it was not possible for all families to retain all their children—the system could not work. The answer lay in the principle of superiority of males over females. Families kept their sons at home but allowed daughters to leave on marriage. A woman became part of her husband's family, and her children bore his name and were brought up in his home. The family, whether perpetual or not, traced its descent through males. Surname, property, and title all went down the male line.

There was no theoretical limit to family size. If more than one son survived in successive generations, each of them marrying and having children, the family could be dozens-strong within decades. In practice, high mortality, lack of economic opportunity or physical space to expand, and the prohibitive cost of marrying were among the reasons why few families managed to grow into the ranks of the ideal superfamily. A large-scale survey of farm households conducted in the mid-1930s revealed that average household size then was no more than a little over five people.

The family lived, ate, and worked together. The common purse was controlled by the family head (usually a male), and he and senior members of the family arranged marriages for the children.

MARRIAGE AND DIVORCE

Until the mid-twentieth century, it was rare for an individual to have free choice of spouse, and often the bride and groom would not have even met before their wedding day. The interests of the individual were subordinated to the family. The intricacies of negotiation and the social advantage to be harvested from a long-term connection with another family made it far too weighty a matter for the young to be allowed to make decisions.

For the same reasons, divorce was rare. Incompatibility of temperament on the part of the spouses was unimportant, because marriage was seen in terms of family duty rather than of conjugal affection. And the consequences of unraveling the web of relationships were too great for most families to contemplate. Where divorce occurred, it was the husband who divorced his wife. Grounds included adultery (risk of contamination to the descent line), failure to bear a son (primary purpose of marriage), persistent ill health (interfering with the wife's duty of service to the family), and talking too much (a wagging tongue could ferment disharmony in the family). Any children remained with the husband.

A sonless wife was in danger of divorce, but a man could take as many secondary wives (concubines) as he wanted or could afford, and he might do so in the hope of begetting an heir. His wife might well agree to this, because she was considered the formal mother of any son born to a concubine, and that strengthened her position. The couple might also adopt a son, though by law the adoptee had to be a male of the same surname as the husband.

ANCESTOR WORSHIP

Central to the idea of the family was the notion of an ongoing line of descent that passed unbroken from remote antiquity to the eternal future. Living family members were the channels through which this line passed, but they were neither more nor less important to it than were their ancestors and their descendants yet unborn.

The religion of the family was ancestor worship. Family members must worship their own dead only, and failure to do so was thought to bring down the ancestors' wrath on the living. In turn, the living could expect to be worshipped in due course. Confucian thinkers stressed the wrongness of exposing oneself to danger: Ancestors and descendants only existed through the living, taking risks was to endanger more than the self alone.

THE FAMILY AND THE STATE

The state taxed the family as a unit, and treated it as a mutual responsibility group under the control of the family head. Any member of the family could be charged for a crime committed by another member. For a serious crime, the whole family might be punished.

In order to bolster the head's position, the state would severely punish a son who usurped his father's authority, or cursed, or struck, or injured his father. Murder of one's father automatically called down the extreme form of capital punishment (death by slicing). A son should not report his father for committing a crime, and if he did so he would be punished as if he himself had perpetrated it. But a father could beat his son with impunity, only suffering mild punishment if he went too far and caused serious injury or death. In acknowledgement of the importance of the family, crimes within it merited punishment in a different degree from crimes against outsiders.

The Confucian state strove to strengthen the family as an instrument of social control, holding that the relationship of a subject to the ruler was analogous to that of a son to his father. The common people also valued the family, though their belief was tempered by a pragmatic accommodation to the realities of everyday life.

An ethnic Tibetan farmer with her son, Jiuzhaigou, Sichuan province, September 3, 2007. *Under imperial rule in China, laws promoted the primacy of the family, with the oldest male considered the head of the household. With the rise to power of the Communist Party in the mid-twentieth century, rights shifted to favor the individual, male or female, though the traditional preference for sons persists throughout much of Chinese society.* © DIEGO AZUBEL/EPA/CORBIS

THE CONTEMPORARY FAMILY

With the end of imperial rule, Chinese governments began to bring in laws to reform the family system. The Civil Code of the Republic of China of 1931 gave equal inheritance rights to males and females, did away with arranged marriage, and made it possible for either party to institute divorce proceedings. It failed to deal with concubinage, but in any case the code probably had little effect other than in major cities.

The Marriage Law passed by the People's Republic in 1950 was backed by effective political power. It gave individuals freedom from family domination, and it made arranged marriage, concubinage, betrothal of children, and sexual discrimination within the family illegal. The 1970s saw the implementation of the one-child-family policy, which was directly contrary to old ideas of the extended family.

The weight of popular tradition has acted as a drag on reform. Preference for sons has been slow to disappear, and imbalances in the birth ratio indicate that female infanticide may sometimes have been practiced. "Clannism" and nepotism remain as problems. Change has been slowed by the state's need to preserve the family in order to supply the welfare functions not yet provided by society. But it is clear that the emphasis has swung away from the group and toward the individual. The Chinese family is rapidly coming to resemble families in other parts of the developed world.

SEE ALSO *Adoptions; Domestic Violence; Life Cycle: Birth; Life Cycle: Marriage; Lineage; Marriage Laws; Popular Religion; Population Policy: Birth-Planning Policy; Women, Status of.*

BIBLIOGRAPHY

Baker, Hugh D. R. *Chinese Family and Kinship*. London: Macmillan; New York: Columbia University Press, 1979.

Buck, John L. *Land Utilization in China: A Study of 16,786 Farms in 168 Localities, and 38,256 Farm Families in Twenty-two Provinces in China, 1929–1933*. Nanjing: University of Nanjing, 1937. Reprint, New York: Paragon, 1964.

Buxbaum, David C., ed. *Chinese Family Law and Social Change in Historical and Comparative Perspective*. Seattle: University of Washington Press, 1978.

Wolf, Arthur, and Huang Jieshan (Chieh-shan Huang). *Marriage and Adoption in China, 1845–1945*. Stanford, CA: Stanford University Press, 1980.

Hugh D. R. Baker

RITUALS

Traditional Chinese family life had a strongly religious character. Not only did family rituals often involve prayers to gods, but in a sense every traditional Chinese home was a religious shrine, the centerpiece of which was the altar to the ancestors (*ci*), with ancestors' spirit tablets (*lingpai*) prominently displayed. Other household deities included those especially important to the well-being of the household: the door gods (*men shen*) for protection, the Kitchen God (Zaojun) to ensure prosperity and health, and the Earth God (Tudi Shen) for harmony. Among these the Kitchen God occupied pride of place. The Kitchen God, with oversight of the space where food was stored and prepared, is distinct in that he was worshiped not in temples but in the kitchen. On the first and fifteenth day of each month, family members made offerings to him. Before the Lunar New Year, more elaborate sacrifices were presented in the hope that he would put in a good word for the family when he returns to Heaven.

ANCESTOR WORSHIP

Central to family ritual is the worship of ancestors. Most homes have a family altar. It usually stands in the central hall, facing the main entrance, to protect against evil spirits and influences that may try to enter the house. Ancestors' spirit tablets, placed on this altar, are the focus of family ritual activities.

In Chinese funeral rituals, when a person is near death, all family members are summoned and gather around the bedside to await this person's death. Upon death, the living room is cleared of all furniture, and a white banner is placed on the transom of the entrance to the home to signify that a death has occurred in the family. Family members put on special garments as a sign of mourning. Traditionally, there are five grades of mourning, with garments of different colors to denote the relationship of the mourners to the deceased. This is followed by ritually washing, clothing, and coffining the deceased. The coffin is then set before the family altar for the funeral wake, which usually lasts from three to seven days. During the wake, daily offerings of food, incense, and joss paper money are placed before the coffin.

On the final night of the wake, religious specialists (Buddhist monks or Taoist priests) are engaged to conduct funerary rites. These rituals serve the important function of leading the soul of the deceased through the netherworld and assisting in the transformation from a ghost into an ancestor of the family. After these rituals, the deceased is buried in the family or lineage graveyard. And after the burial, an ancestral spirit tablet is set up for the deceased on the family altar. Every morning and evening, family members offer food and ritual prayers and burn joss sticks. On the first and fifteenth of each lunar month, a slightly more elaborate ritual is performed. On a few occasions each year, such as the birth and death anniversaries of the ancestor, there are elaborate rituals accompanied by a large offering of food, with all family members gathered in the home, kneeling before the family ancestral altar to pay ritual obeisance, and burning joss paper money, to commemorate the ancestors (Tong 2004).

Ancestral rituals aid in integrating and perpetuating the family unit. Embedded in family rituals are ethical values important to maintaining the family unit, such as filiality and perpetuating the family name. These values define behavior expected of the individual or family.

LIFE-EVENT RITUALS

Gods and ancestors are present and invoked at important family events, such as a birth, marriage, or death, as well as at important calendrical occasions, including Chunjie

(Spring Festival or Chinese New Year), Qingming (Chinese All Souls' Day), and Dongzhi (Winter Solstice Festival). On these occasions, offerings of meat, chicken, fruits, or flowers are made to ancestors and gods on the family altar. The family, as a group and with joss sticks in hand, pay ritual obeisance to the gods and ancestors, requesting blessings and protection.

The most important life events—birth, marriage, and death—have a central place in family rituals. In birth rituals, the most important event is the full-month celebration (*manyue*). On the morning of the first full month after birth, the family, as a group, makes food offerings and burns incense on the family altar to inform the ancestors, as well as the deities, of the new addition to the family and to appeal to the spirits to protect the child. Special gifts are presented to relatives and family friends. In addition to cakes and sweets, red eggs (hard boiled eggs dyed red) are given. The eggs symbolize the renewal of life, and the round shape is traditionally associated with family harmony and unity.

Marriage rituals also occupy a central place in Chinese-family-ritual life. The six classical marriage rites (matchmaking, consulting the fortune teller, betrothal, sending gifts, fixing the date of the wedding, and greeting the bride) have been diluted over time, but are evident in some form in most Chinese weddings. Two central features of contemporary marriage are the *pinli* (gifts for the bride to confirm the union) and *nacai* (an exchange of gifts). The *nacai* takes place a few days before the wedding, usually on an auspicious day chosen with the aid of a Chinese almanac (*tongshu*). The prospective groom sends an assortment of gifts, including red packets containing cash (*hongbao*), two pairs of long red candles with the wedding symbols of a phoenix and dragon, pieces of gold jewelery, a whole roasted pig, and fruits such as oranges and sugarcane. On the day of the wedding, the bride's hair is symbolically combed in a hair-styling ritual (*shangtou*). This signifies that the bride will have a good fate and will bear many children. Another important ritual is the offering of food to the ancestors of the groom's family (*baitang*), to inform the ancestors of the addition of a new family member. Finally, the centerpiece of the marriage ceremony is the tea ceremony (*chali*), in which the bridal couple offers cups of tea to senior members of the groom's family, including the ancestors of the groom's family, to seek their blessings. The tea offering signifies acceptance of the bride as a family member.

COMMUNISM AND RITUAL LIFE

In traditional times, rituals underscored the family hierarchy and male dominance in that hierarchy. To create a more egalitarian society, during the Communist era, family rituals, along with religious practices, were branded as feudal superstitions and were suppressed (Yang 1961). Yet as Fan (2003, p. 450) notes, in the reform era since the late 1970s, there has been a renaissance of popular religion, with temple cults and temple festivals becoming ever popular. Ancestor-worship halls (*jiamiao*) have sprung up in almost every town in southeast China. Such life events as weddings, funerals, and births have all become vibrant, with the ritual economy spawning whole new occupations: ritual experts, fortune tellers, geomantic surveyors, and lineage managers (Yang 2000, p. 493).

Families spend lavishly on paper replicas of modern luxury goods such as cars and houses for the deceased to use in the spirit world, and on extravagant banquets at funerals and weddings (Yang 2000, p. 479). Such rituals are expressions of filial piety and sacrifice and are perceived as the glue that holds family members together. The importance of these rituals for social cohesion and stability is also recognized by the Chinese government, which in 2008 authorized a national holiday for the Qingming Festival, when families have traditionally visited the graves of their ancestors.

SEE ALSO *Confucianism; Life Cycle: Infancy and Childhood; Popular Religion.*

BIBLIOGRAPHY

Chao, Paul. *Chinese Kinship*. London: Kegan Paul International, 1983.

Dean, Kenneth. *Taoist Ritual and Popular Cults of Southeast China*. Princeton, NJ: Princeton University Press, 1993.

Fan Lizhu. Popular Religion in Contemporary China. *Social Compass* 50, 4 (2003): 449–457.

Feuchtwang, Stephan. *Popular Religion in China: The Imperial Metaphor*. Richmond, Surrey, U.K.: Curzon Press, 2001.

Tong Chee Kiong. *Chinese Death Rituals in Singapore*. New York: Routledge Curzon, 2004.

Yang, C. K. *Religion in Chinese Society: A Study of Contemporary Social Functions of Religion and Some of Their Historical Factors*. Berkeley: University of California Press, 1961.

Yang, Mayfair Mei-hui. Putting Global Capitalism in Its Place. *Current Anthropology* 41, 4 (August–October 2000): 477–510.

Tong Chee Kiong

ROLES OF THE ELDERLY

Respect for the elderly has long been a Chinese tradition. In the family, older persons, especially males, were figures of authority. According to the teachings of Confucius (551–479 BCE), filial piety meant obeying and respecting parents and putting parents' needs and wishes above one's own. Adult children, specifically sons, were expected to live with and care for their parents in old age. Daughters had the same obligations until they married; after that, their filial obligations transferred to their parents-in-law.

Multigenerational households were the ideal family form in which the older generation was revered and cared for by the younger generation. The elderly had a responsibility to pass on knowledge and wisdom to the young; more importantly, they should ensure that there were male offspring to carry on the family name.

In spite of being denounced by Mao Zedong and other leaders, Confucianism continued to color the social fabric of the society governed by the Communist Party (Whyte 2004). In the late 1970s, China began transforming from a planned socialist economy to a market-oriented economy. These reforms have led to an improvement in the standard of living, as well as other social changes that have reshaped intergenerational relationships and the role of the elderly in the family.

Percentages of persons aged sixty and older living in intergenerational households: 1990 and 2000

	Two-generation	Three-generation	Skip-generation	Intergeneration households
1990	24.0	48.5	2.2	74.7
2000	12.4	22.8	22.3	57.5

SOURCE: Wu Xiaolan, 2004.

Table 1

Percentages of older persons living in different types of intergenerational households in 2000, by rural and urban residence

	Two-generation	Three-generation	Skip-generation	Intergenerational households
Urban	14.7	36.2	7.3	58.2
Rural	10.2	10.2	36.5	56.9

SOURCE: Wu Xiaolan, 2004.

Table 2

LIVING ARRANGEMENTS

Family living arrangements constitute one area of significant change. During the era of the planned socialist economy, urban housing was distributed by work unit and was in tight supply; most adult children had no choice but to live with their parents. Housing reforms that began in late 1980s and accelerated in the mid-1990s included subsidies to encourage tenants to purchase their apartments (Ikels 2006). Concomitantly, there was a rapid expansion of urban housing projects. With increased housing supply and higher incomes resulting from the new market economy, more young married couples opted to purchase their own homes.

Changes in living arrangements have also been occurring in the countryside. While the policy to decollectivize agriculture has allowed peasant families to farm their own land and make economic decisions, it has also provided an opportunity for married adult sons to request family division and set up their own households.

The percentage of older Chinese living in intergenerational households (i.e., with adult children and/or grandchildren) has decreased from 74.7 percent in 1990 to 57.5 percent in 2000 (Table 1). The decrease would have been more dramatic if not for the increase in skip-generation households, defined as grandparents living with grandchildren without the middle generation.

Skip-generation households are a rural phenomenon. Table 2 shows the difference in the type of intergenerational households between rural and urban areas. Whereas three-generation households (i.e., grandparents living with adult children and grandchildren) were the majority among urban elders, older people in the countryside were more likely to live in skip-generation households.

Separate households are not only preferred by adult children but also some aging parents (China Research Center on Aging 2000). Although they may live apart, parents and children typically live in close proximity, have frequent face-to-face interaction, and exchange help on a regular basis.

Many parents, in fact, help their adult children establish their own homes. It is not uncommon for urban parents to financially support their sons to purchase a new home in preparation for marriage. In the countryside, parents build new houses for sons who are engaged to be wed. Additionally, parents incur expenses related to sons' weddings. Such financial obligations require significant savings, and reflect the importance of continuing the family lineage.

CHILD CARE

Older persons also assist adult children with the demands of daily life, particularly child care. In cities, many young couples have to juggle work and family. Some urban elders take over the care of their young grandchildren full time; most, however, prefer to be a part-time caregiver.

In the countryside, many elderly persons have to take up the role of parenting their grandchildren. Since the economic reforms, many able-bodied men and women in rural areas have left for cities to find jobs, leaving their children to live with their elderly parents; hence the prevalence of skip-generation households in rural areas (Table 2). Migrant workers return to their home villages only once or twice a year; thus grandparents are the primary caregivers of the young.

Regardless of whether or not elderly people provide direct care to their grandchildren, in both the city and countryside, grandparents usually have frequent interactions with grandchildren. Most derive great satisfaction from the relationship.

RETIREMENT AND HEALTH

Age obviously makes a difference in what older persons can do for younger generations. In cities, the retirement age is fifty-five for women and sixty for men. Most are quite healthy in the first decade after retirement, and also financially secure because of pensions. Some older persons take advantage of these golden years to attend college, pursue personal interests, or actively participate in the residents' committee of their neighborhood. Although rural elders do not have pensions, they have land that they continue to farm until they cannot do so for health reasons. Parents and adult children help each other during busy farming seasons.

Health problems associated with age are the major challenge to older Chinese and to Chinese society as a whole. This challenge is growing as the number of older persons, particularly the oldest (eighty years old or more), keeps rising (Table 3). For instance, in 2000 about twelve million, or 0.9 percent of the Chinese population, were eighty or more years old. This number is predicted to more than double in twenty years, reaching almost twenty-nine million, or 2.0 percent of the population, by 2020. The rapid growth in the percentage of elderly in the Chinese population is due to an increase in life expectancy and to a decline in fertility rates resulting from the one-child birth policy introduced in 1979.

Illnesses can lead to financial hardship for older persons and their adult children. The cost of medical care has skyrocketed because of privatization (Wong et al. 2006). Even though older persons in the cities have medical insurance, full coverage is rare and copayments are often required. Urban elders, nonetheless, are much better off than their counterparts in the countryside. The vast majority of rural elders have no health insurance. Medical care is sought only when an illness is very serious, which can result in high medical costs that deplete family assets.

Elderly population in China: Selected years between 1990 and 2030

	Age sixty and older		Age eighty and older	
	Number	Percentage	Number	Percentage
1990	63,031,383	5.5	7,679,559	0.7
2000	87,538,308	6.9	12,041,226	0.9
2010	111,282,073	8.3	18,615,045	1.4
2020	169,602,648	11.9	28,724,014	2.0
2030	239,480,149	16.4	44,463,436	3.0

SOURCE: U.S. Census Bureau.

Table 3

Additionally, most of the health problems of older people are chronic and disabling, requiring long-term care (Wang et al. 2005). Adult children play an important role in such times of need, helping their elderly parents financially, instrumentally, and emotionally. In most instances, all adult children, including daughters, share the parent-care responsibility. The wife of the oldest son is often obligated to be the primary caregiver when the parent is widowed, or she is expected to play a key assisting role when parents are married. While the current cohort of older persons usually have several children, the coming cohorts are likely to have only one child. These demographics do not bode well for a care system based on the traditions of filial piety. Balancing the responsibility of elder care between the state and the family will surely be an important task of the Chinese government in the coming decades.

SEE ALSO *Leisure and Culture for the Elderly; Life Cycle: Old Age.*

BIBLIOGRAPHY

China Research Center on Aging. *Survey of the Elderly Population in Urban and Rural China.* Beijing: China Official Printing, 2000.

Ikels, Charlotte. Economic Reform and Intergenerational Relationships in China. *Oxford Development Studies* 34, 4 (2006): 387–400.

U.S. Census Bureau. International Data Base. http://www.census.gov/ipc/www/idb/.

Wang Longde, Kong Lingzhi, Wu Fan, et al. 2005. Chronic Diseases 4: Preventing Chronic Diseases in China. *The Lancet* 366 (2005): 1821–1824.

Whyte, Martin K. Filial Obligations in Chinese Families: Paradoxes of Modernization. In *Filial Piety: Practice and Discourse in Contemporary East Asia*, ed. Charlotte Ikels, 106–127. Stanford, CA: Stanford University Press, 2004.

Wong Chack-Kie, Lo Vai Io, and Tang Kwong-leung. 2006. *China's Urban Health Care Reform: From State Protection to Individual Responsibility.* Oxford: Lexington, 2006.

Wu Xiaolan. 2004. Living Arrangements of Older People in China: Urban-Rural Differences and Historical Changes. *Market and Demographic Analysis*, Supp. (2004): 119–123.

Lydia Li
Yujie Sui

INFANTICIDE

Infanticide has long been observed worldwide in preindustrial societies as a means to limit family size and check population growth. Yet the practice of infanticide in Chinese society was strongly associated with the Chinese patrilineal and patrilocal family system. In this family system, sons were highly valued, as they would carry on the family name and ensure an unbroken line of descent. They also contributed labor, wealth, and glory to the family, and provided for their parents in old age and after death. Daughters, in contrast, were considered a useless economic drain on their natal families. They would leave their natal home upon marriage, reproduce offspring for their husband's patriline, and provide care for their in-laws rather than their own parents. In times of adversity, families would resort to female infanticide to reserve limited resources for male children. According to Lee (1981, p. 167), the earliest reference to the practice of female infanticide was recorded in *Han Feizi* in the Warring States Period (403–221 BCE):

> Parents' attitudes to children is such that when they bear a son they congratulate each other, but when they bear a daughter they kill her. Both come from the parents' love, but they congratulate each other when it is a boy and kill it if it is a girl because they are considering their later convenience and calculating their long-term interests.

Increasing pressure to provide a dowry in Ming (1368–1644) and early Qing (1644–1912) is also linked with the practice of female infanticide. Dowering a daughter first became prominent during the Song (960–1279) among upper-class families. By the eighteenth century the practice became common even among families of modest means. The pressure of adequately dowering a daughter and preparing her to be an ideal wife was particularly strong among elite families. A rich dowry reflected well on the status of the bride's family and could attract a husband of higher social standing, thus enabling the bride's family to forge important social and political links. But the pressure created by this practice may well have led some families to kill girl babies just to avoid the sacrifices that adequately dowering them would entail (Waltner 1995). Even as many as one-tenth of the daughters born into the imperial lineage from 1700 to 1830 were victims of infanticide. "Some Qing nobles were almost as likely as high Qing peasants to kill their daughters" (Lee and Wang 1999, p. 60).

In general, the primary cause of female infanticide was poverty. Among peasants born between 1774 and 1873 in Liaoning Province in Northeast China, an estimated 20 to 25 percent of all females died from infanticide (Lee and Campbell 1997). In a Jiangsu village in East China in the mid-1930s, because of small land holdings and population pressure, the usual survival strategy was to limit the number of children through infanticide, more likely of girls. This was evidenced by an unusually high male sex ratio in the age group of 0 to 5: 135 boys to 100 girls (Fei 1939, p. 33). The Chinese inheritance system, which gave all sons an approximately equal share, tended to diminish landholdings with each passing generation and confronted most Chinese farm families with the threat of downward mobility and perennial poverty, which rendered them doubly vulnerable to famine, rebellions, and social chaos.

According to Lee, there was a gradual decline in the practice of female infanticide from the Republican period (1912–1949), which she attributed to an increase in the demand for female labor: "There was a demand for children's and women's labor in the new factories and more girls were being used in the domestic industry, and the fact that some families were beginning to see girls as an economic asset undoubtedly increased their chances of survival" (1981, p. 176). Using two large retrospective fertility surveys, Coale and Banister (1994) found that the sex ratio of births averaged 1.13 from 1936 to 1942, suggesting high rates of female infanticide, and declined steadily to 1.093 by 1949.

But it was in Maoist China (1949–1978) when the incident of female infanticide declined precipitously. After the Communists took over power in 1949, the government outlawed such practices as infanticide, child brides, purchase marriages, and prostitution, and advocated women's emancipation and gender equality by mobilizing women into the work force. The importance attached to women's role in the work force and the new emphasis on gender equality greatly increased the economic value of daughters in the home and to the society at large. Collectivization in the countryside and nationalization of industry in urban China not only eliminated extreme poverty but also placed all families under the strict surveillance of the state—facts that made it both unnecessary and impossible to resort to female infanticide as a strategy for family survival. An indication that female infanticide was all but eliminated during the Maoist era can be seen in the sustained normal sex ratio at birth, averaging 107 boys per 100 girls from the 1950s to the 1970s (Coale and Banister 1994).

However, since China launched its stringent one-child policy in 1980 to curb population growth, which by then was considered a hindrance to China's new modernization drive, the incident of female infanticide and abandonment has been on the rise. Caught between the state's intrusive policy to limit births and the desire and need of Chinese families, especially rural families, to have a son, desperate parents killed or abandoned their baby girls in order to have a son. The sex ratio at birth began to rise dramatically from 108.5 boys for every 100 girls in 1982 to 114.1 in 1990, 117.1 in 1995, and 119.2 in 2000 (Wang 2005). Three factors have contributed to the rising skewed sex ratio in the last two decades: underreporting of baby girls; excess female infant deaths through deliberate neglect, abandonment, and infanticide; and frequent use of sex-selective abortions (Chu 2001; Johnson 1996; Li, Zhu, and Feldman 2004). Although it is difficult to pinpoint the relative contribution of these factors to the rising skewed sex ratio at birth, what is clear is that the stringent state birth policy has inadvertently intensified the preference for sons in Chinese culture and put infant girls at risk as rural parents who want a son for eldercare and continuing the family line revive the age-old practice of female infanticide or resort to the new technology of sex-selective abortions.

SEE ALSO *Gender Relations; Sex Ratio; Women, Status of.*

BIBLIOGRAPHY

Chu, Junhong. Prenatal Sex Determination and Sex-Selective Abortion in Rural China. *Population and Development Review* 27, 2 (2001): 259–281.

Coale, Ansley J., and Judith Banister. Five Decades of Missing Females in China. *Demography* 31, 3 (1994): 459–479.

Fei, Hsiao-Tung (Fei Xiaotong). *Peasant Life in China: A Field Study of Country Life in the Yangtze Valley.* London and Henley: Routledge & Kegan Paul 1980 (1939).

Johnson, Ann K. The Politics of the Revival of Infant Abandonment, with Special Reference to Hunan. *Population and Development Review* 22 (1996): 77–98.

Lee, Bernice J. Female Infanticide in China. In *Women in China: Current Directions in Historical Scholarship*, ed. Richard W. Guisso and Stanley Johannesen, 163–177. Youngstown, NY: Philo Press, 1981.

Lee, James, and Cameron Campbell. *Fate and Fortune in Rural China: Social Organization and Population Behavior in Liaoning, 1774–1873.* Cambridge, U.K.: Cambridge University Press, 1997.

Lee, James, and Feng Wang. *One Quarter of Humanity: Malthusian Mythology and Chinese Realities.* Cambridge, MA: Harvard University Press, 1999.

Li, S., C. Zhu, and Marcus W. Feldman. Gender Differences in Child Survival in Contemporary Rural China: A County Study. *Journal of Biosocial Science* 36 (2004): 83–109.

Waltner, Ann. Infanticide and Dowry in Ming and Early Qing China. In *Chinese Views of Childhood*, ed. A. B. Kinney, pp. 193–217. Honolulu: University of Hawaii Press, 1995.

Wang, Feng. Can China Afford to Continue Its One-Child Policy? *Asian Pacific Issues* 77 (2005): 1–12.

Hong Zhang

ONE-CHILD POLICY

The one-child policy was introduced in 1979 as the Chinese government was embarking on an ambitious program of market reform following the economic stagnation of the Cultural Revolution. At this time, the Chinese comprised a quarter of the world's population but were occupying just 7 percent of the world's arable land, two-thirds of the population was under thirty years old, and the baby boomers of the 1950s and 1960s were about to enter their reproductive years. The government saw strict population containment as essential to the economic reform process and to improvement in living standards, so the one-child policy was introduced.

HOW DOES IT WORK?

The policy consists of a set of regulations governing the approved size of Chinese families. The regulations involve family size, late marriage, and childbearing, and stipulate spacing of around five years after which second children are permitted. The State Family-Planning Bureau sets the overall targets and policy direction, while local family-planning committees devise strategies for implementation.

Despite its name, the one-child rule applies to a minority of the population. For urban residents and government employees, who comprise around 40 percent of the population, the one-child rule is strictly enforced with few exceptions. Exceptions are made for multiple births, for couples whose first child has a disability or chronic disease, for workers in high-risk occupations such as mining, and in some areas for couples in which both the husband and the wife are themselves only children. In rural areas, a second child is generally allowed five years after the birth of the first child, but this exception sometimes applies only if the first child is a girl, clearly acknowledging the traditional preference for boys. Some ethnic minorities are allowed to have a third child.

The policy is underpinned by a system of rewards and penalties, which are largely at the discretion of local officials, and hence vary widely. These include economic incentives for compliance, and substantial fines, confiscation of belongings dismissal from work and loss of access to subsidized schooling for noncompliance. The policy depends on virtually universal access to abortion and contraception, with a heavy reliance on long-term methods, such as intrauterine devices and sterilization.

THE IMPACT OF THE ONE-CHILD POLICY

Discussion about the impact of the policy has centered on its effects on population growth, the sex ratio, the increasing proportion of elderly dependents, and the emergence of a "spoiled" generation of only children. The Chinese authorities claim that the policy has prevented 250 to 300 million births, and has helped to lift over 200 million people out of poverty. The fertility rate, or the average number of children born to each woman of reproductive age, decreased from 2.9 in 1979 to 1.7 in 2004, with a fertility rate of 1.25 in urban areas and 1.98 in rural areas in 2004. This has created a pattern of predominantly one-child urban families and predominantly two-child rural families.

Most worrying perhaps is the impact of the policy on the sex ratio. The sex ratio at birth is defined as the proportion of male live births to female live births, and ranges between 1.03 and 1.07 male births for each female birth across human populations. In China, there has been a steady increase in the sex ratio from 1.06 in 1979, to

Government billboard promoting China's one-child policy, Shanghai, China. *Fearing a baby boom as families earned higher wages after the Cultural Revolution, China's leaders enacted a strict limit on the number of offspring a married couple could produce, reasoning the country would be more prosperous with fewer citizens to support.* © WOLFGANG KAEHLER/CORBIS

1.11 in 1988, and to 1.17 in 2001. There is a marked gradient across birth order: in rural areas, the sex ratio for the first birth is 1.05, which is within normal limits, but the ratio rises steeply for second and third births. In urban areas, the sex ratio is 1.13 for first birth. The picture that emerges is that some urban Chinese make the choice to sex-select with the first pregnancy, since they are allowed only one child. In rural areas, most are permitted to have a second child, especially if the first is female. So if the second (or subsequent) pregnancies are female, they "disappear," allowing the couple to conceive another child.

It is widely believed that the main cause of the missing females is sex-selective abortion. Although this is officially illegal, it is known to be widely practiced. Nonregistration of female births also occurs, and although female infanticide is probably rare now, less aggressive management of sick infant girls is known to occur. This imbalance in sex ratio means that by 2020 there will be at least 20 million excess males of marriageable age, with poor, uneducated men most likely to have difficulty finding a wife. In China today there are growing numbers of young men in the lower echelons of society who are marginalized because they lack family prospects and who have little outlet for sexual energy. A number of commentators predict that this will lead to increased levels of antisocial behavior and violence and will ultimately present a threat to the stability and security of society.

The one-child policy is not, however, the only cause of the imbalance in the sex ratio. Many other Asian countries with declining fertility rates and traditional preference for males are seeing gender imbalances: In 2005 the sex ratio at birth in Taiwan was 1.16, Singapore 1.15, South Korea 1.11, and parts of northern India 1.20.

The rapid fall in the birth rate combined with improving life expectancy has led to an increasing proportion of elderly people in China. The proportion of the population over sixty-five was 5 percent in 1982; by 2007 it was 7.5 percent, but the proportion is expected to rise to over 15 percent by 2025. While these figures are lower than in most industrialized countries, a lack of adequate pension provision in China means that financial dependence on offspring is still necessary for over 60 percent of elderly people. With only one or two children per couple, this can represent a considerable burden. Partly to address this problem, the one-child policy has been relaxed in urban areas, so that couples who are both only children are allowed to have more than one child. As the cohorts of only children reach reproductive age, many couples will meet these criteria.

Finally, there has been much speculation about the societal and personal impacts of a generation of only children in Chinese cities, the so-called spoiled generation. However, the weight of evidence suggests that, while these only children may be indulged when they are young, the highly competitive academic environment leads parents to put great pressures on their child. This has resulted in high levels of depression and anxiety among the many only children born during the policy, especially in the academically intense teenage years.

THE FUTURE OF THE ONE-CHILD POLICY

The Chinese government is facing a dilemma: the need to balance the basic human right of reproduction with a population that, despite the policy's successes, was still growing at a rate of 10 million people per year (equivalent to the population of Belgium) by 2008. In making decisions about the future, several factors must be taken into consideration.

First, relaxation of the policy can only be considered if the fertility aspirations of the reproductive generation are low. There is now good evidence that China *is* becoming a small-family culture and that a relaxation of the one-child policy would almost certainly not result in a baby boom. Secondly, what was appropriate and acceptable in 1979 may not be so some three decades later. China has undergone massive socioeconomic change since the policy was first implemented, with far greater freedom resulting from wealth and globalization, making the one-child policy seem increasingly anachronistic. This increased wealth and freedom also makes it harder to enforce the policy. Economic disincentives are not a deterrent to many wealthier individuals, and increased freedom of movement has made it difficult for family-planning authorities to track individuals if they choose to flout the regulations. Finally, the evidence of slowing in population growth, the high sex ratio, and the aging population all suggest that a relaxation of the policy would be desirable.

A number of different options for the future have been suggested. One possibility is that everyone should be allowed to have up to two, but *only* two, children, with a space of at least five years between them. It has been predicted that this option would give a total fertility rate of 1.7 over the next two decades, and would be acceptable to the overwhelming majority of people.

But the government feels that vigilance is still essential. It is feared that any wavering in policy implementation, while not leading to a baby boom, may compromise the goal of keeping the population below 1.4 billion by 2010, which in turn could threaten economic growth and stability. There is already some relaxation: Couples are to be allowed choice in contraceptive methods as part of so-called client-centered family-planning services. Furthermore, couples no longer need to obtain permission to have a first child, spelling the end of the very unpopular system of local birth quotas. The government is particularly concerned about the consequences of the skewed sex ratio and has developed a strategic plan called "Care for Girls" to address attitudes toward girl children and to try to enforce legislation banning prenatal sex determination. These changes, together with declining fertility aspirations, are having the important effect of reducing (though not eliminating) tensions between the one-child policy and society, thus allowing the government to adopt a cautious approach to the relaxing of the policy.

SEE ALSO *Family: Infanticide; Life Cycle: Infancy and Childhood; Population Policy: Birth-Planning Policy; Sex Ratio.*

BIBLIOGRAPHY

Hesketh, Therese, and Zhu Wei Xing. The One Child Family Policy: The Good, the Bad, and the Ugly. *BMJ* 314 (1997): 1685–1687.

Hesketh, Therese, Li Lu, and Zhu Wei Xing. The Effect of China's One Child Family Policy after 25 Years. *New England Journal of Medicine* 353, 11 (2005): 1171–1176.

Hudson, Valerie M., and Andrea Den Boer. A Surplus of Men, A Deficit of Peace: Security and Sex Ratios in Asia's Largest States. *International Security* 26, 4 (2002): 5–39.

Winkler, Edwin A. Chinese Reproductive Policy at the Turn of the Millennium: Dynamic Stability. *Population and Development Review* 28, 3 (2002): 379–418.

Therese Hesketh

FAMINE SINCE 1800

Famines were a major part of China's historical experience in the nineteenth and twentieth centuries. Most were the result of natural disasters—principally droughts and floods. The shifting of the course of the Yellow River several times, but most dramatically in 1855, caused great human devastation. Between 1876 and 1879, a drought of epic proportions struck all of North China, costing an estimated thirteen million lives. Another major famine occurred in North China in 1920 to 1921, taking a half million lives. Yet another famine occurred in North and Northwest China from 1928 to 1930, with a toll of an estimated ten million lives. The flooding of the Yangzi River in 1931 affected many provinces in Central China and caused homelessness, devastation of fields and houses, and widespread disease. About 422,000 people lost their lives. Between 1942 and 1943, hunger and famine in Central China may have taken as many as three million lives. In the Mao Zedong era, the Great Leap Famine (1959–1961) cost at least thirty million lives (Xia Mingfang and Kang Peizhu 2001; Li Wenhai et al. 1994).

Other natural disasters, such as earthquakes, also resulted in high mortality, but not necessarily in famine. The huge earthquake at Tangshan in 1976 took 240,000 lives according to official figures; the actual toll may have been much greater. Epidemics were another type of disaster, causing high mortality. Although epidemics were not directly related to bad harvests, malnutrition could make a population more susceptible to disease. Locust infestations, by contrast, were a type of natural disaster, like major droughts or floods, that resulted in crop failure and hunger.

In the Chinese terminology, all major catastrophes were, and are still, called *zaihuang*—whether or not they were caused by, or resulted in, hunger or in high mortality. Floods and droughts were the most common events affecting the harvest, so the term *huang* itself literally means a lost harvest or crop failure. In a predominantly agricultural society, the harvest was the main focus of concern, and not human mortality as such. In the Western concept, by contrast, elevated mortality due to hunger and starvation is the defining characteristic of *famine*, regardless of the cause. In China, only some natural catastrophes were recorded as *jihuang*, where starvation was explicitly mentioned. The North China famines of 1876 to 1879, 1920 to 1921, 1928 to 1930, and 1942 to 1943 were major examples. In contrast, the shifting of the Yellow River caused devastation, including hunger and deaths, but it was not described as a *jihuang*, probably because its principal cause was not a crop failure.

DROUGHTS AND FLOODS

Droughts and floods were the most frequent and worst enemies of good harvests. From ancient times, chronicles spoke of their threatening nature, and the need for wise rulers to act to prevent them when possible or to act swiftly to minimize the damage. Droughts were particularly threatening in North China, where annual rainfall is often insufficient. Millet and sorghum, crops that were drought resistant, were the principal subsistence crops of the north before the twentieth century. Wheat was also widely grown in the north, but it required more water than millet or sorghum, and was more sensitive to deficiencies in rainfall. It was more of a luxury crop, and sometimes a cash crop for farm families. In the twentieth century, wheat was more widely grown because of the expansion of irrigation. In North China, drought in one season or year was a hardship that could be endured, but two or more successive years of drought would be disastrous. The major North China famines of 1876 to 1879, 1920 to 1921, and 1928 to 1930 were all the result of successive years of drought. In Central and South China, years of drought were also experienced, but sustained, multiyear events were less frequent.

Flooding was such a common phenomenon in ancient times that the legendary ruler Yu was said to have shown his merit by taming the rivers. There is no question, however, that flooding became a more frequent and extensive phenomenon in the nineteenth century and in the first half of the twentieth. This was not because more rain fell in recent centuries, but rather that the manmade engineering intended to contain the rivers became increasingly vulnerable to even small excesses of rainfall. Increased silting, due to intense land use and deforestation upstream, had raised the bed of the Yellow River so that it was higher than the level of the surrounding countryside. When the long levees or dikes were not properly maintained, even a small amount of excess rainfall could topple them, causing widespread flooding. Other smaller rivers in the north, notably the Yongding River near Beijing and Tianjin, were also subject to intense engineering, heavy siltation, and frequent inundations. The Yangzi River, China's most important river, had a deeper bed, but over the centuries the Yangzi had also been subject to much diking, damming, and diversions. Intense use of wetlands for farming made the river more likely to overflow its banks, and the population and farmland adjacent to the river more vulnerable to disaster.

FOOD AND POPULATION

The greater number of natural disasters in the nineteenth and twentieth centuries was thus partially due to the intensification of human settlement on the land. Population growth is usually considered to be one of the major causes of famines in the modern period. China is considered to be the major example of the dictum of Thomas R. Malthus (1766–1834), who wrote in the late eighteenth century that "the increase of population is necessarily limited by the means of subsistence." When population outstrips the ability of land to produce food, "famine seems to be the last, the most dreadful resource of nature" ([1798] 1976, p. 56). This Malthusian equation dominated thinking about population growth in the twentieth century, but in the field of Chinese history, it is controversial. Some have proclaimed Malthusianism to be a myth (James Lee and Feng Wang 1999), but most popular and scholarly opinion sees population growth as the major burden on the agricultural economy and the natural environment. One view cautions against assuming that population growth necessarily has a Malthusian outcome (Lillian M. Li 2007).

There is no doubt that China experienced two population booms, one in the eighteenth century, when the

Chinese famine ticket blaming the British for food shortages, Shanghai, 1927. *During the famine years of the 1920s, Communists in China tried to gain support by blaming the crisis on the British government, appealing to anti-imperialist sentiment among the hungry.* KEYSTONE/HULTON ARCHIVE/GETTY IMAGES

population may have doubled from 150 million to 300 million in a century, and a second in the late twentieth century, when the population grew from about 600 million to one billion in half a century. Between these two booms, from the early nineteenth century until the mid-twentieth century, the population size grew, but at a slower rate than before or after, probably due to internal rebellions, Japanese invasion, and civil war. Although the productivity of the land improved in the eighteenth century and again in the late twentieth century, the margin of self-sufficiency became thinner and thinner. Under the People's Republic, rationing of grain and other staples was enforced from the late 1950s until the early 1990s. Population policy in the Mao era and afterward was highly controversial, but the one-child policy in the late twentieth century was a response to the specter of an ever-expanding population pressure on limited resources, even in the age of economic reform and development.

In the post-Mao era, the alleviation of hunger was no longer considered to be a straightforward matter of expanding food supply to match population size. As China's population became increasingly urbanized, and the economy increasingly nonagricultural, the key variable in a family's adequate nutrition became economic. Higher-income families could purchase the food they needed; an economically vibrant China in turn no longer needed to grow all of its own food, but could purchase grain and other foods from overseas. There was still hunger and malnutrition in China, but it was due to regional disparities and income distribution, not absolute scarcity.

"NATURAL DISASTER AND HUMAN CALAMITY"

While famines were overwhelmingly associated with natural disasters, in the nineteenth century, public opinion, as it emerged, saw that the incidence of famine was closely tied to political events. Such catastrophes have been described as *tianzai renhuo*, "natural disaster and human calamity." The horrific famine in Henan Province in 1943 was caused not simply by poor harvest, but principally by the blockade that contending military factions imposed on the shipment of grain into the province. This event was famously described by American writers Theodore White and Annalee Jacoby in their wartime report, *Thunder Out of China* (1946). In general, the Japanese invasion and occupation resulted in grave deprivation in North China, where the Japanese army commandeered local grain supplies to feed themselves.

FAMINE PREVENTION AND RELIEF IN THE QING PERIOD

In the face of recurrent natural disasters, rulers and local elites in China had been charged with the responsibility for both the prevention and the relief of disasters. China's ancient ideology clearly stated that a ruler who failed in this responsibility no longer deserved to hold the mandate of heaven and could be replaced. In the Song dynasty (960–1279), major thinkers advanced ideas about local responsibility. In the late Ming (1368–1644) and early Qing (1644–1912) period, numerous treatises served to guide local leaders in discharging such responsibilities. In the Qing period, especially during the reigns of Kangxi (r. 1661–1722), Yongzheng (r. 1723–1735), and Qianlong (r. 1736–1796), state policies, institutions, and funding became very substantial. Enormous sums were spent to control the Yellow River and also the smaller river systems near the capital, including the Yongding River. Policies to expand agriculture, empirewide reporting of weather and grain prices, grain storage, below–market price grain sales (*pingtiao*), and famine-relief campaigns were among the major practices of the central government. Each step was carefully documented; a voluminous record survives. These state measures were not applied evenly over all provinces. In the wealthier central and southern provinces, less grain was stored, and local communities were expected to play a larger role. Central government measures were sometimes controversial because of their costs and other unintended consequences. Recent academic studies, however, have demonstrated the overall efficacy of such measures for the eighteenth century (Will 1990; Will et al. 1991; Lillian M. Li 2007).

In the nineteenth century, not only were the problems of river control increasingly difficult, but the Qing government's resources were greatly constrained. The Opium War (1839–1842), the Treaty of Nanjing (1842), and the opening of treaty ports were only the beginning of China's foreign challenges, while the Taiping Uprising (1851–1864) was the greatest but certainly not the last of the internal calamities. Yet the structure and practices of state famine-relief measures were continued until the end of the dynasty, but with far less funding and effectiveness (Edgerton-Tarpley 2008; Lillian M. Li 2007). As in the past, the state encouraged local elites to assume responsibility for river control, grain storage, and famine relief, but the large-scale problems of the Yellow River and North China famines could not be met adequately through decentralized and local efforts.

FAMINE RELIEF, 1870s–1930s

Starting with the North China famine of 1876 to 1879, famine relief became a national public effort that included international assistance as well. In China even the large-scale famines were confined to one region or locality. Because there had been no means of modern communication, comprehensive information about a disaster was limited to the court and high-ranking officials. From the 1860s, however, newspapers were introduced into the major cities. News of the North China famine spread to Shanghai and the other treaty ports, where a new public consciousness developed. Contributions for famine relief were raised, and private famine-relief associations formed. Some southerners traveled to the north to participate in the distribution of relief. This public consciousness was part of a new sense of nationalism that became more visible during the reform and revolutionary movements beginning in the 1890s. Famine was seen to be a national problem, not just the experience of one region or the responsibility of imperial or local officials.

International famine-relief efforts also began in the 1870s under the leadership of Timothy Richard (1845–1919), a Welsh missionary reformer. Numerous different relief societies were formed to collect donations but also to work inland in the difficult terrain of Shanxi Province, where the famine was the most severe. Following this, subsequent famines saw the involvement of foreign relief workers. In the extensive 1917 flood that inundated virtually all of Zhili Province (around Beijing), numerous foreign and Chinese relief organizations worked under the coordination of a committee organized by the new central government. In the 1920–1921 North China drought, there was an even larger infusion of foreign funds, collected from churches in the United States and Europe, and an even greater number of foreign relief workers. In 1921 the various foreign groups organized themselves under an umbrella organization called the China International Famine Relief Commission. For almost two decades, this private voluntary organization coordinated the work of foreign and Chinese members. Its mission was not simply famine relief, but also the building of public-works projects, such as roads, bridges, dikes, and dams, which served the purpose of flood prevention.

After the Nanjing government was established in 1928, it sought to gain political control over the China International Famine Relief Commission. In the 1931 megaflood of the Yangzi River, the new authorities exercised control of the relief and reconstruction program. The National Flood Relief Commission asserted the government's sovereignty, but also employed many foreigners: Its director-general was British, and several Americans with long experience in the China International Famine Relief Commission were on the staff of the Nationalist organization.

THE GREAT LEAP FAMINE, 1959–1961

The greatest famine in Chinese history, and indeed in world history, was that of the Great Leap Forward. Lasting for

Chinese converging at government station to purchase rice, July 18, 1948. *As civil war in China followed World War II, Communists provided affordable foodstuffs for the hungry in hopes of earning their support. Ironically, after the Communists defeated the Kuomintang, millions of citizens died of starvation stemming from Mao Zedong's Great Leap Forward campaign to transform agrarian China into an industrialized communist society.* © BETTMANN/CORBIS

three years, 1959 to 1961, it was the unintended, and largely unacknowledged, consequence of the Great Leap Forward, launched in 1958 to fulfill Mao's utopian vision of catching up to Great Britain and advanced industrialized countries in a few years. The organization of rural society into communes was to provide the foundation for the Great Leap. The communes not only organized rural work into teams, brigades, and communes, but also attempted to displace the way of life of farm families. Communal dining halls were to relieve each farm family from the traditional task of preparing its own meals. Although intended to be a more efficient way to allocate time and resources, the communes became a source of waste. In addition to an "eat as much as you can" policy, there was pilferage and leakage of supplies. Some scholars see the communal dining halls as a major factor in the famine (Yang 1996).

On the broader scale, however, the practice of false reporting of harvests probably played a larger role. Under intense political pressure to fulfill and exceed production targets, local cadres often reported inflated harvest figures. Such figures permitted higher authorities to claim a larger than expected portion of the harvest as procurement (tax), leaving the commune a smaller share for local consumption. This process was later described as *fukua*, or exaggeration. Some provinces suffered more seriously than others because of corrupt and cruel party leaders, who resorted to physical torture of those who failed to comply. The provinces that suffered the highest rates of mortality—such as Anhui and Sichuan—were those where leadership abuse was the most egregious (Becker 1996). The total loss of lives in China attributed to the Great Leap policies is admitted by the government to have been thirty million over three years. Some demographers estimate even greater losses.

In historical perspective, the Great Leap Famine is unique not only for its huge scale, but also for its causes. For many years, it was known simply as "the three difficult years," and was first attributed to bad weather, secondly to the need to repay Soviet loans, and, later, to the phenomenon of *fukua*. Even after the demographic data were officially revealed, Chinese authorities and historians almost never referred to it as a famine or *jihuang*. The clearest reason for this anomaly was that full political blame had not yet been assigned. Top party leaders knew of great suffering in the rural areas as early as 1959, and Mao Zedong was about to call a halt or modification to the Great Leap Forward at the Lushan Plenum of that year, but changed his mind when he felt that his authority was being challenged by Peng Dehuai. It thus appears that the immense mortality of the Great Leap might have been avoided in 1959 but for Mao's personal and individual decision. Nevertheless, a full accounting for the famine was not made, and very little was written about the event. Only around 2008, fifty years after the Great Leap Forward, did some witnesses to, and survivors of, the famine start to record their memories and to analyze the event.

HISTORICAL SIGNIFICANCE

The causes of famines, particularly the Great Leap Famine, will always remain controversial. Whether they were due to long-term climatic forces or to short-term cycles; whether they were due to overpopulation; whether they were due to failed imperial leadership or to authoritarian dictators; whether they were due to secrecy and lack of public scrutiny; whether they were due to imperfect markets and economic trends; or whether they were due to unequal distribution of wealth or to poor transportation and distribution—are all significant and relevant questions.

The historical significance of famines, and the social and political impact of frequent famines and widespread hunger, are much clearer. Famine mortality was a large component of low life expectancy in China before 1949. Hunger, disease, and a low standard of living contributed to social unrest and political disorder. Next to bringing peace, the promise to feed the people was the most potent political ideology of the twentieth century.

SEE ALSO *Agricultural Production; Poverty; Richard, Timothy.*

BIBLIOGRAPHY

Becker, Jasper. *Hungry Ghosts: Mao's Secret Famine*. New York: Free Press, 1996.

Edgerton-Tarpley, Kathryn. *Tears from Iron: Cultural Responses to Famine in Nineteenth-Century China*. Berkeley: University of California Press, 2008.

Lee, James Z., and Feng Wang. *One Quarter of Humanity: Malthusian Mythology and Chinese Realities, 1700–2000*. Cambridge, MA: Harvard University Press, 1999.

Li, Lillian M. *Fighting Famine in North China: State, Market, and Environmental Decline, 1690s–1990s*. Stanford, CA: Stanford University Press, 2007.

Li Wenhai et al., eds. *Zhongguo jindai shi da zaihuang* [The ten big famines in modern China]. Shanghai: Renmin, 1994.

Malthus, Thomas Robert. *An Essay on the Principle of Population*. Ed. Philip Appleman. Norton Critical Edition of 1798 edition. New York: Norton, 1976.

Will, Pierre-Étienne. *Bureaucracy and Famine in Eighteenth-century China*. Trans. Ellborg Forster. Stanford, CA: Stanford University Press, 1990.

Will, Pierre-Étienne, and R. Bin Wong, with James Lee. *Nourish the People: The State Civilian Granary System in China, 1650–1850*. Ann Arbor: University of Michigan, Center for Chinese Studies, 1991.

Xia Mingfang. *Minguo shiqi ziran zaihai yu xiangcun shehui* [Natural disasters and village society in the Republican Period]. Beijing: Zhonghua Shuju, 2000.

Xia Mingfang and Kang Peizhu, eds. *Ershi shiji Zhongguo zaibian tushi* [Pictorial history of disasters in twentieth-century China]. Fuzhou, PRC: Fujian Jiaoyu, 2001.

Yang, Dali L. *Calamity and Reform in China: State, Rural Society, and Institutional Change since the Great Leap Forward*. Stanford, CA: Stanford University Press, 1996.

Lillian M. Li

FAN CHANGJIANG

1909–1970

Fan Changjiang (Fan Xitian) was a prominent journalist who first became famous in the 1930s for his coverage of the little-known northwest China. He later became a leading Communist reporter, holding important posts at party news-propaganda organs such as *Xinhua She* (New China News Agency), *Renmin Ribao* (People's Daily), and *Jiefang Ribao* (Liberation Daily). In his early years Fan was instrumental in elevating the status and standards of Chinese journalists, making news reporting a respectable vocation in modern China.

Born into a waning gentry family in Neijiang County, Sichuan Province, Fan Changjiang did not aim to become a journalist. He received no formal education in journalism; instead he was trained on the job, in the old-style method of most veteran journalists. Fan was involved in politics early on. He was a student activist in middle school at Chengdu and was forced to leave the city in 1927 after participating in student demonstrations against Sichuan warlords. He was admitted to the Central Political Institute in Nanjing in 1928, and then left for Beiping (Beijing) in 1931, discontented with the Guomindang's soft resistance to Japanese aggression. As a student of philosophy at National Beijing University, Fan freelanced for several newspapers, including Beiping's *Chenbao* and Tianjin's *Yishi Bao* to help pay for tuition.

In 1934, Fan began to work as a reporter for the Tianjin-based *Dagong Bao* (Impartial Daily), arguably the most influential daily of that time. Despite receiving support from Chiang Kai-shek (Jiang Jieshi) and the Guomindang, *Dagong Bao* maintained its advocacy for press independence and practiced nonpartisanship until 1941 when its editor-in-chief Zhang Jiluan died. Fan's experience at *Dagaong Bao* from 1934 to 1938, during which he worked as a war correspondent, sending home eyewitness accounts about the realities of the war, established him among a new generation of journalists in China. As the historian Hung Chang-tai noted, Fan's importance lies in "his role as an involved, patriotic journalist" (Hung 1991, p. 429).

Fan's rare sensitivity to overlooked subjects set him apart from reporters of previous generations. He was among the first reporters who paid attention to the issue of ethnic inequality—in Fan's case, the suppression of Mongolians and Muslims that he witnessed during his famous expedition to remote areas of northwest China. His reports on the disappearing cultures of the minorities were collected and published in 1936 as *Zhongguo de xibei jiao* (The northwest corner of China), an extremely popular book that was reprinted seven times within its first few months. At the beginning of the War of Resistance against Japan (1937–1945), Fan was assigned to report on the Marco Polo Bridge incident, the fall of Beiping, and the fight at the Nankou Pass in northwestern Heibei in 1937. His wartime reportages were characterized by acute, detailed observations and vivid descriptions conveyed in a simple, straightforward language.

Fan also was the first journalist in the world to report on the Long March, the Chinese Communist Party's (CCP) retreat to the remote northwest of China in 1934 and 1935. These reports were extremely rare at that time, given the Guominang restricted any publications on the Chinese Communists. Nonetheless, journalists ventured to the CCP's wartime headquarters at Yan'an Shannxi, among whom Edgar Snow was the most famous. Fan was the first native Chinese reporter to visit Yan'an, in early 1937. He wrote about his night-long interview with Mao Zedong and his experience in witnessing how the Red Army defeated its enemies with few resources. These reports later appeared in the book, *Saishang Xing* (Journeys on the Frontier), published in 1937, the same year Snow published his book, *Red Star over China*. Both journalists wrote favorable accounts on the CCP, describing it as a rising power, the hope for China's future. Fan's firsthand contact with the CCP and its leaders probably sowed the seeds for his future conversion to Communism when he became disillusioned with the Guomindang's ineffective and corrupt rule.

As a powerful advocate for the professionalization of Chinese journalists, Fan helped establish the Zhongguo Qingnian Xinwen Jizhe Xuehui (Chinese Young Journalists Society), the first professional journalists' association, in Hankou (now Wuhan) on March 30, 1938. Fan became increasingly pro-Communist during the early phase of the war, and eventually joined the CCP in May 1939. Fan's conversion marked his transformation from an engaging reporter to a fervent propagandist who used his expertise in journalism to champion for the cause of the CCP. By the time Fan became a Communist convert, he was already a seasoned newsman. Fan helped found the CCP's first two official papers: the *Jiefang Ribao* (Liberation Daily) and the *Renmin Ribao* (People's Daily). In the early years of the People's Republic of China, he was the vice chancellor of the China Information Agency and the president of the Beijing School of Journalism. He was, however, purged and forced to live in solitude at the beginning of the Cultural Revolution in 1966. He committed suicide in 1970, and his reputation was not restored until eight years after his death.

SEE ALSO *Journalism; Long March; Snow, Edgar.*

BIBLIOGRAPHY

Boorman, Howard L., ed. *Biographical Dictionary of Republican China*. Vol.1. New York: Columbia University Press, 1967.

Fang Meng. *Fan Changjiang zhuan* [Biography of Fan Changjiang]. Beijing: Zhongguo Xinwen Chubanshe, 1989.

Hung Chang-tai. Paper Bullets: Fan Changjiang and New Journalism in Wartime China. *Modern China* 17, 4 (October 1991): 427–468.

Eliza Ho

FANG LIZHI
1936–

Born on February 12, 1936, in Beijing, Fang Lizhi is an astrophysicist who became well known for the impassioned speeches he delivered during the 1980s in front of enthusiastic Chinese students.

While studying modern physics at the Science Institute of the Chinese Academy in Beijing from 1952 to 1956, Fang was approached by the Chinese Communist Party (CCP) in 1955 to join the Youth League, but he was publicly expelled from the party in 1957 because of a paper he had written decrying the intrusion of Marxism in education, especially in scientific matters. Fang nevertheless pursued his scientific career, doing research on solid-state and laser physics.

During the Cultural Revolution, Fang suffered several setbacks when he was confined for a year in 1966 and then sent to a communal farm for "reeducation." He also spent a year in a coal mine in Huainan in 1970. During this period, Fang began studying astrophysics, which became his main field of research.

At the start of the post-Mao era, Fang's party membership was restored, and he was allowed to attend conferences abroad and to resume a successful career. He was appointed vice president of the University of Science and Technology of Hefei, in Anhui Province. When the political climate relaxed during Hu Yaobang's presidency of the CCP from 1982 to 1987, Fang gained fame, in and outside of China, for his outspoken criticism of the Communist system.

Influenced and encouraged by the temerity of their professor—and such declarations as "Whatever you study, you must raise questions. But authorities in Communist countries do not like you to raise questions," and "Democracy does not come from the top down. It is never bestowed"—students demonstrated for freedom of speech and an independent press in Hefei during the winter of 1986 to 1987. Their movement spread quickly around the country, but ended on January 17, 1987, when Deng Xiaoping ordered Hu Yaobang, Fang Lizhi, and two other intellectuals to be expelled from the party.

Fang Lizhi later played an important role in preparing the ground for the student demonstrations of 1989 in Beijing when he published an open letter to Deng Xiaoping in January 1989, asking for Wei Jingsheng's liberation. (Wei had been active during the democratic movement of winter 1978 and was sentenced to fifteen years in jail in 1979.) Fang's letter triggered a number of petitions and was instrumental in creating the political upheaval known as the Tiananmen Incident of May and June 1989.

Because Deng Xiaoping again held Fang Lizhi responsible for the demonstrations, Fang and his wife Li Shuxian took refuge in the U.S. embassy in early June 1989. They were finally able to leave the country a year later, and Fang subsequently conducted research in Britain and the United States. He remains active in the Chinese democratic movement abroad and has not been permitted to return to China as of 2009.

SEE ALSO *Dissidents; Hundred Flowers Campaign; Prodemocracy Movement (1989).*

BIBLIOGRAPHY

Béja, Jean-Philippe. *A la recherche d'une ombre chinoise: Le mouvement pour la démocratie en Chine (1919–2004).* Paris: Seuil, 2004.

Buruma, Ian. *Bad Elements: Chinese Rebels from Los Angeles to Beijing.* New York: Random House, 2001.

Lilley, James R. *China Hands: Nine Decades of Adventure, Espionage, and Diplomacy in Asia.* New York: Public Affairs, 2004.

Marie Holzman

FASCISM

In the 1930s, an allegedly fascist movement flourished for a time within the then-ruling political party, the Chinese Nationalist Party (Guomindang, or GMD). Called the Blue Shirt Society (Lanyi She) by outsiders, especially the Japanese, the movement identified itself as the Chinese Renaissance Society (Zhonghua Fuxing She). What precipitated the founding of the society was Japan's invasion of China's northeastern provinces, known as Manchuria. Convinced that the very survival of China was imperiled, twenty young men—all GMD members and graduates of the Whampoa Military Academy—founded the society on March 1, 1932, in Nanjing in order to "save the nation." The movement was organized as a series of concentric circles. Within the innermost ring was the 300-member Three People's Principles Earnest Action Society (Sanmin Zhuyi Lixing She), charged with policy making. Mass organizations constituted the outermost ring, the largest of which was the Chinese Renaissance Society, with a membership of about 100,000.

The Renaissance movement was animated by a resolve to modernize China through the realization of the ideological program (Three People's Principles) of Sun Yat-sen (Sun Yixian or Sun Zhongshan), the founder of the precursor to the GMD. The movement believed that only through an aggressive program of economic and political development could China be revitalized. Economic development would begin with land reform, which included the equalization of land rights, the reallocation of land to the tillers, and collective farms. Rapid industrialization would be promoted through a mixed economy that combined state capital with private initiative. The economic program required a fundamental political restructuring that would begin with the instauration of a strong central government that could wield effective authority over the national territory without being compromised by foreign imperialists or domestic rivals, whether Communist or warlord. At the same time, a sense of nationalism would be inculcated among the people, whom Sun had long lamented as resembling "a tray of loose sand." All this would be undertaken by a single party led by a charismatic leader—an authoritarian rule thought necessary because of Japan's invasion. But one-party rule would be an emergency and transitional measure, the necessary means toward the ends of national defense, rapid industrialization, and eventual self-government—all of which were consistent with Sun's Three Principles. The Renaissance movement believed that the GMD would be that party, but only if it reformed itself by renewing its commitment to Sun's ideology, purifying itself of corrupt and elitist practices, and mobilizing grassroots support among the people.

Its commitment to Sun's ideology of developmental nationalism made the Chinese Renaissance Society one of many similar movements and ideologies of delayed industrialization of the nineteenth and twentieth centuries. Others arose in Meiji Japan, fascist Italy, and countries that embraced Marxism-Leninism, Kemalism, Gandhiism, and Nasserism. Unlike Italian fascism, however, the one-party authoritarian rule advocated by both Sun and the Renaissance Society was to be strictly transitional—as the necessary means toward the abiding end of democratic government. Although short-lived, the Renaissance movement counted among its achievements four mass campaigns in the 1930s: the New Life movement, the National Voluntary Labor movement, the National Economic Reconstruction movement, and the National Military Education movement. In March 1938, in an effort at party unity, the Renaissance Society was dissolved by an Extraordinary National Conference of the GMD and merged with two other intraparty factions to form the Three People's Principles Youth Corps.

BIBLIOGRAPHY

Chang, Maria Hsia. *The Chinese Blue Shirt Society: Fascism and Developmental Nationalism.* Berkeley: University of California, Institute of East Asian Studies, 1985.

Eastman, Lloyd E. *The Abortive Revolution: China under Nationalist Rule, 1927–1937.* Cambridge, MA: Harvard University Press, 1974.

Maria Hsia Chang

FASHION

Fashion in China changed dramatically during the twentieth and twenty-first centuries due to political and social transformation and the attendant rise of modernity and consumerism. Historically, fashion trends have represented either liberalization or suppression for Chinese women, and have had strong connotations in their representations of gender in a cultural and political context.

MODERNITY IN A CHINESE CONTEXT

By the early twentieth century, Chinese society had experienced immense political and social upheaval that had led to the rise of the domestic fashion industry (Finnane 2005, p. 588). After the fall of the Qing dynasty in 1912 women's fashion evolved parallel to society; footbinding was outlawed, for example, and the government sought to prescribe an appropriate dress code. Courtesans and prostitutes had been the fashion trendsetters whose styles were emulated by other women, but by the 1930s the leading fashion icons of China were popular actresses (Finnane 2007, p. 95).

By the 1920s "modernity" was equated with Westernization (Lee 1999, p. 45). As Antonia Finnane notes, the switch to Western style of dress was believed by anti-Qing political reformers to be a prerequisite for the formation of a democratic political system (Finnane 1999). Consequently, Chinese dress started to display traces of Western influence. Styles evolved rapidly, fueled by a volatile political climate. People were identified as citizens of the Republic by their changes in attitudes, attire, and customs (Harrison 2000, p. 75). Foreign dress was worn for its exotic appeal, its ostentatious nature, and the shock it generated; Western fashion represented liberty and equality (Harrison 2000, p. 54). Middle-class women in particular "were susceptible to the effects of life in the modernizing cities," and "what they wore assumed a transcendental importance, signifying the hegemony of the modern" (Finnane 1996, p. 111).

It was evident that domestic fashion trends were shaped by international and cross-cultural communications (Finnane 2005, p. 588). For example, spectacles were worn by some for aesthetic rather than practical reasons, simply because they were perceived as a symbol of modernity. Despite the seemingly blind mimicking of Western culture, clothing style was usually a hybrid that incorporated both Western and Eastern elements (Chang 2003, p. 434).

In the 1920s Shanghai matured into a cosmopolitan city, and its booming fashion industry was a sign of the city's dynamism. Shanghai's first fashion show was held in 1926 by Whitelaw's Department Store in the Nanjing Road under the direction of a Chinese graphic artist, Ye Qianyu (1907–1995), whose role was to promote Western material and the store's new products. Chinese dress in Shanghai in the 1930s was a mix of "indigenous as well as cosmopolitan" (Finnane 2007, p. 102).

THE RISE OF NATIONALISM

Political, economic, and social forces soon affected domestic fashion culture. Nationalistic sentiments, in reaction to the Nationalist movement as well as mounting Japanese encroachments in China in the 1930s, began to counteract the notion of modernity, and the adoption of Western-style dress eventually sparked concern about the corruption of Chinese integrity. Fears that the populace was "more motivated by modernity than by nationalist considerations" led to calls for action by local textile guild leaders; the alleged threat to the domestic commercial sector was a strong factor (Carroll 2003, p. 445). Consequently, nationalist campaigns such as the Anti-foreign National Goods movement were implemented to encourage patriotism and popular support for domestically produced textiles. Karl Gerth (2003, p. 4) asserts that efforts to create a nationalistic consumer culture had innumerable social manifestations, making the consumption of domestic goods an essential part of Chinese nationality.

Cantonese couple in Western-style dress, Guangzhou, Guangdong province, September 5, 1935. *After the end of the Qing dynasty in 1912, many Chinese threw off imperial styles of dress in favor of modern ones, including jacket and trousers for men and form-fitting* cheongsams *for women. These fashions again changed as the Communists took power nearly four decades later, with jackets similar to Mao Zedong's becoming popular and Western-style dress prohibited by government authorities.* GENERAL PHOTOGRAPHIC AGENCY/HULTON ARCHIVE/GETTY IMAGES

The climate of nationalism in the 1920s sparked a resurgence in the popularity of older garments such as the *qipao*. The *qipao* was inspired by the *changyi*, a long, one-piece garment worn by Manchu women that looked like the *changpao* worn by male scholars. The *qipao* was a common form of attire for politically active women, especially those who followed Madam Sun, a trendsetter of the "anti-imperialist" new look (Edwards 2006, p. 7). Western style of dress was now viewed with suspicion and interpreted as antinationalist. It was during this time that the *qipao* attained "weighty political, social, and moral meanings" (Finnane 2007, p. 4).

Nationalistic sentiment was not the only reason behind the revival of the *qipao*. Women's fashion was sensitive to change because the period was dominated by freedom of expression and the emancipation of women in the social sphere (Roberts 1997, p. 20). Finnane attributes the rise in popularity of *qipao* to the trend toward androgyny, arguing that it was a rejection of womanhood in its 1911 guise (1996, p. 113); similarly, Eileen Chang posits that the decision to wear *qipao* was not a display of allegiance to the Qing dynasty or support for its restoration, but a reflection of women's desire to look like men (2003, p. 434). This ideological change was due in part to the 1920s literary renaissance that attacked Confucian teachings for their neglect of women's rights (Finnane 1996, p. 114).

For men, there was a shift from the traditional long gowns to a military-style suit. The Sun Yat-sen suit became the signature suit, a symbol of independence, modernization, and nationalism during the Nationalist revolution (Finnane 2007, p. 176; Roberts 1997, p. 19). The country was divided in two groups: the Nationalists wearing Sun Yat-sen military look-alike uniforms, showing their party allegiance, and the successful businessmen from the city wearing Westernized suits that signified modernity as well as wealth (Finnane 2007, pp. 178–179).

THE INFLUENCE OF COMMUNISM

Nationalist sentiment, revolution, and ideology continued after the establishment of the People's Republic of China in 1949 under Mao Zedong. Stringent rules were enforced; although clothes were personal artifacts, they could be used to "emphasize ideological agendas" (Wilson 1999, p. 173). Western-style attire was no longer perceived as modern, and even local style of dress such as the *qipao* came under fire as being "counterrevolutionary" or "un-Chinese." Mao inspired a new wave of militarized fashion, including a variation of the Sun Yat-sen suit (*Zhongshan zhuang*) referred to as the "Mao suit" (*Mao zhuang*), which appeared during the Yan'an period, and women began wearing suits called "cadre suits" or "Lenin suits" (*Lenin zhuang*), which were extremely popular with the female revolutionaries of the time. The suits for both sexes were most popular in blue, green, or gray. Most women dressed similarly to the proletariat, in loose-fitting unisex clothing, dull in color and lacking ornamentation (for merely practical reasons). The unisex uniform was meant to alleviate gender discrimination and promote equal rights in the workforce and in the political sphere; for women, wearing military dress meant identifying with the Maoist revolution (Finnane 2007, p. 235). At the time, the frugality and simplicity of this style of dress were celebrated as supporting the revolutionary cause (Wilson 1999, pp. 173–177). In spite of the enforced homogeneity, though, instances of subtle variation in women's attire were apparent (Roberts 1997, p. 22).

Because cotton harvests were low and textiles were costly, recycling of old clothes—including the *qipao*—was encouraged. In 1956 Yu Feng (1916–2007) launched a new dress reform campaign designed to refresh the national look for women. She attempted to rescue the folk customs of ethnic minorities and a romantic rural tradition in designing a woman's dress for the masses—a dress that would convey Chinese identity and legacy with a deep meaning of identification. But politics militated against the success of the Dress Reform movement, and other campaigns such as the Hundred Flowers movement took precedence in the social sphere. Eventually it was decided by the central government, with Russian influence, that Chinese women should wear skirts because they were cheaper than trousers to make, as well as practical and aesthetically pleasing (Finnane 2007, pp. 206–207, 220).

The Cultural Revolution bought with it another change in fashion, which this time was enforced strictly by the government. Approved clothing included imitations of the military uniforms; colorful or fashionable clothing was seen as bourgeois. Women who paid too much attention to appearance were subject to public humiliation. Rationing and limited income hindered people's consumption during Mao's reign, and of necessity, clothes were replaced only when they were beyond repair (Roberts 1997, p. 23). In the 1970s the Gang of Four member Jiang Qing designed a dress to represent Chinese femininity that was inspired by the Tang dynasty; it had a low neckline offset by a band and a pleated skirt. However, the dress never did catch on with the common people (Finnane 2007, p. 253).

FASHION IN THE REFORM ERA

After Mao's death, in the era of reform and opening, China became more accepting of Western fashion, but fashion's return to the social sphere after 1978 was a gradual process. According to Roberts (1997, pp. 22, 97), dress was one of the first areas to benefit from the government's more relaxed attitude toward social behavior. Women, who had been unable to express their femininity and individuality through dress, began to adorn themselves with colorful, printed clothing with a notable absence of patriotic phrases, which had been printed on clothing previously.

Foreign fashion trends were once again seen as cutting edge. There was also a reawakening of femininity, though the *qipao* was still perceived as the attire of old-fashioned minorities and prostitutes; it was only in the 1990s that the *qipao* became the national dress of China. Despite the newfound desire for modernity, Finnane argues that during the 1980s people's limited spending power posed a constraint to their desire to "break with the immediate past" and to be "up-to-date by international standards." As a result, they wore what "was available, affordable and conventional" (Finnane 2005, p. 591).

From 1979 to 1981 there were debates with regard to Westernization versus the "goal of building a strong socialist nation" and the right to express one's individuality (Steele and Major 1999, p. 65). Globalization began to affect the Chinese market as people were allowed to travel more freely and foreign mass media became more accessible. Indeed, the growth of the global economy in the 1980s spurred the development of "world fashion" (Eicher 1995, p. 300). Major economic reform introduced China to the benefits of capitalism, and in this new climate of openness, people began to embrace the international community and the fashion trends it promoted. During the early years of the twenty-first century American icons such as "jeans, sweatshirts, T-shirts, and sneakers" were the clothing choice of global youth (Taylor 2005, p. 602). American brands such as Levi Strauss and Nike became popular among the Chinese youth.

This development was triggered by "exploitative mechanisms of the globalization of clothing manufacture, distribution, and retailing, and by new technologies, global commodity advertising of branded leisure clothing, and the cultural and political domination of the United States" (Taylor 2005, p. 603). Lou Taylor maintains that these clothes signified youth, modernity, and the eagerness to belong to a globalized, capitalist world (Taylor 2005, p. 603). Capitalism and globalization brought new wealth, and created a new materialistic culture in China.

In 1978 the fashion designers Hanae Mori (b. 1926) and Pierre Cardin (b. 1922) visited China, marking the opening of China to the outside fashion world. Major style influences came from Japan, Korea, Taiwan, and Western nations (Finnane 2007, pp. 260–261, 271–272, 290). Clothing styles worn by the general populace changed slowly, helped along by media of popular culture. China's first fashion magazine, *Zhizhuang* (Fashion), appeared in 1979 featuring items on beauty, culture, and fashion. International women's fashion magazines such as *Vogue* also became popular, reflecting the high interest in personal appearance, beauty, and consumer culture.

CHINESE FASHION DESIGNERS

Institutional signs of change were strong. Universities and technical schools incorporated programs in clothing design, and graduates were hired by big companies. In the 1990s many new designers emerged, including Zhou Guoping, Liu Yang, and Zhang Zhaoda, who introduced professional modeling to China. Zhang's elegant and individual designs, which draw inspiration from Chinese history, made him the most successful and famous Chinese designer at home and abroad. In 1985 he established his own brand, Mark Cheung (Finnane 2007, p. 264). The designer Feng Ling combines the *qipao* with the Mao suit and army uniforms, using silks and satins to reference China's Chinese past, yet Chinese have difficulty recognizing her retro designs as fashion, and up to 70 percent of her customers are foreigners. Another important designer is Ma Ke (Coco Ma), whose designs have a Korean theme. One of China's most popular designers, the Milan-based Guo Pei (b. 1967), is clearly influenced by European fashion. Mao Jianguo from Shanghai Garment Group Limited and their label T & A (Technology & Art) target profitable youth markets. Jimmy Choo (b. 1961) is known worldwide for his fashionable women's bags and shoes. Other important contemporary Chinese designers include Sun Jian (b. 1967) and William Tang (b. 1959), who started their careers by working for foreign designers and international labels before setting out to create their own labels. Designers such as Liu Yang, Li Keyu, Xu Wenyuan, Jing Jinrui, Feng Ling, Shi Lin and Lu Yue have presented collections abroad, showing that Chinese fashion can compete on the international stage. Similarly, the success of the Chinese menswear label LiLang at the 2007 Milan Fashion Week demonstrated that a Chinese-designed clothing line could make an important contribution to the global fashion industry. Chinese designers produce a culturally distinctive and internationally recognized and respected brand of fashion that refers to their history for inspiration, underlining the importance of historical clothing to their identity (Finnane 2007, pp. 278, 289).

The Hong Kong textile industry also helped to launch many Chinese fashion designers. Peter Lau's (b. 1955) experience in the textile, knitwear, and manufacturing industry complemented his education at the Polytechnic University in Hong Kong. Lau established his own business in 1982 targeting the female market, and in 1990 he started a new label, XC VIII Ninety-Eight, using vivid colors, patterns, and textures. Lau's designs incorporate traditional Chinese colors and patterns with Western tailoring. Pacino Wan, another graduate of the Hong Kong Polytechnic University, launched his own brand, He & She Limited, which focuses on casual wear, accessories, and bags for young women (Roberts 1997, p. 94).

Many aspects of the modern fashion industry that had been present in the West for decades, such as modeling, fashion magazines, and international recognition of designers, were introduced to China only in the late 1970s and developed throughout the 1980s. There are not many Chinese models on the international catwalks, but one of the most famous in China is Lu Yan. Despite the modernization and development of the Chinese fashion industry, Chinese designers in the twenty-first century generally have not garnered the same international prestige as Western and Japanese designers, and China is still considered to be an export goods country rather than a fashion design empire. Nevertheless, China's impact on the global fashion industry was realized during the Ninth Asia-Pacific Economic Cooperation Summit in October 2001, when all the heads of the member nations wore Tang-style clothes.

A woman modeling clothing designed by Mark Cheung during Beijing Fashion Week, November 7, 2007. *Designers display their creations to the international fashion industry while competing for awards during Beijing Fashion Week.* © JASON LEE/REUTERS/CORBIS

THE FUTURE OF FASHION IN CHINA

In 2006 China's economy grew 10.7 percent, resulting in an increase in overall wealth and a popular change in attitude toward luxury. The rise of the middle class and their search for modernity and symbols of affluence brought an increased demand for designer goods. The effects of this were evident in Fendi's decision to stage a fashion show on the Great Wall of China in 2007 (Reuters 2007).

The symbiotic relationship between social climate and dress in China is evident from the effects of social, economic, and political events such as Westernization, modernity, globalization, and nationalism. These factors have influenced social attitudes, and therefore fueled fashion trends in twentieth- and twenty-first-century China. The Chinese state has had an enormous influence and impact in the development of fashion, which it has employed as a means of social control; it is only since the 1980s that the state has loosened its grip, allowing fashion to function as a means of personal expression. Chinese designers have tried to promote individuality and change, but they will be embraced by the international fashion network only after they are freed from the symbolic meanings in their creations.

SEE ALSO *Clothing since 1800; Footbinding; Hairstyles; Textiles.*

BIBLIOGRAPHY

Carroll, Peter. Re-fashioning Suzhou: Dress, Commodification, and Modernity. *Positions* 11 (2003): 445.

Chang, Eileen. A Chronicle of Changing Clothes. *Positions* 11 (2003): 434.

Economist. Luxury's New Empire: Conspicuous Consumption in China. June 19, 2004.

Edwards, Louis. Dressing for Power: Scholars Robes, School Uniforms, and Military Attire in China. *IIAS Newsletter* 46 (2006): 6–7.

Eicher, Joanne B., ed. *Dress and Ethnicity: Change across Space and Time.* Oxford, U.K.: Berg, 1995.

Finnane, Antonia. What Should Chinese Women Wear?: A National Problem. *Modern China* 22 (1996): 99–131.

Finnane, Antonia. Military Culture and Chinese Dress in the Early Twentieth Century. In *China Chic: East Meets West*, ed. Valerie Steele and John S. Major, 119–132. New Haven, CT: Yale University Press, 1999.

Finnane, Antonia. China on the Catwalk: Between Economic Success and Nationalist Anxiety. *China Quarterly* 183 (2005): 588, 591.

Finnane, Antonia. *Changing Clothes in China: Fashion, History, Nation.* New York: Columbia University Press, 2007.

Gerth, Karl. *China Made: Consumer Culture and the Creation of the Nation.* Cambridge, MA: Harvard University Press, 2003.

Harrison, Henrietta. *The Making of the Republican Citizen: Political Ceremonies and Symbols in China.* New York: Oxford University Press, 2000.

Lee, Leo Ou-Fan. In Search of Modernity: Reflections on a New Mode of Consciousness in Modern Chinese Literature and Thought. In *Ideas across Cultures: Essays in Honor of Benjamin Schwartz*, ed. Paul A. Cohen and Merle Goldman, 110–111. Cambridge, MA: Harvard University Press, 1990.

Lee, Leo Ou-Fan. *Shanghai Modern: The Flowering of a New Urban Culture in China, 1930–1945.* Cambridge, MA: Harvard University Press, 1999.

Reuters. China's Great Wall Gets First Fashion Show. October19, 2007. http://in.reuters.com/article/lifestyleMolt/idINPEK 1387120071019?pageNumber=1.

Roberts, Claire, ed. *Evolution and Revolution: Chinese Dress, 1700s–1990s.* Sydney, Australia: Powerhouse, 1997.

Steele, Valerie, and John S. Major, eds. *China Chic: East Meets West.* New Haven, CT: Yale University Press, 1999.

Taylor, Lou. Dress. In *New Dictionary of the History of Ideas*, vol. 2, ed. Maryanne Horowitz, 596–605. Detroit, MI: Charles Scribner's Sons, 2005.

Wilson, Verity. Dress and the Cultural Revolution. In *China Chic: East Meets West*, ed. Valerie Steele and John S. Major, 167–186. New Haven, CT: Yale University Press, 1999.

Lai Chi-kong

FEDERALISM

Since the unification of China by the Qin dynasty in 221 BCE, the ideal has been a unified and centralized China. Despite this, the Han (206 BCE–220 CE) and Tang (618–907) dynasties were followed by extended periods of disintegration. Following the death of strongman Yuan Shikai in 1916, another period of fragmentation occurred. Called the *warlord era* and named after the brutal soldiers who dominated it, it lasted until the nominal reunification of China in 1928 by the Guomindang.

During this period, military men, politicians, and intellectuals suggested that a federal system might be the answer to China's distress. Although federal systems in Europe and the United States were mentioned by Chinese scholars as early as the mid-nineteenth century, serious discussions of federalism in China can be traced back to the 1890s, with such major figures as Sun Yat-sen (Sun Yixian), Liang Qichao, and Zhang Jian advocating a federal government along the lines of the U.S. and Swiss models. Given the vast area of China and its diverse provinces, federalism seemed a logical answer to rampant regionalism and an impotent central government in the late Qing (1644–1912). Moreover, in an age of increasing provincial power during the late Qing, federalism reflected the desire of provinces to control local taxes, administration, and defense. In the wake of the 1911 Revolution, the republican provisional government and several provinces called for a federal system. During his time in power (1912–1916), Yuan Shikai rejected the idea of federalism, both because he was a proponent of centralization and because his opponents, such as the Progressive Party (Jinbudang), used federalism to challenge his rule. Thus, until Yuan's death, federalism was overshadowed by pressure for centralization.

The heyday of federalism, both as an idea and an experiment, came in the early 1920s. Federalism experienced a surge in popularity, and numerous articles debating its suitability appeared in magazines and newspapers. Hu Shi took up the federalist cause, arguing that the cure for warlordism was the strengthening of civil society by shifting more power to the local level. In 1918 a former premier of the republic, Xiong Xiling (1870–1942), called for federalism as a way to eliminate civil war and restore peace. The idea was that a balance of power between the center and the provinces might lessen power struggles. Chinese Communist Party leader Chen Duxiu countered that expansion of the local self-rule that was an integral part of federalism would only strengthen the warlords and thus prolong the disunity of China. In fact, some provincial military men did take up federalism as a means of holding on to their local bases of power. Although a supporter of federalism in its early years, by 1923 Sun Yat-sen stressed national unification.

The first strongman to come out in favor of federalism was Hunan military governor Tan Yankai (1879–1930), who in 1920 supported self-government in his province and called for a federation of self-governing provinces (*liansheng zizhi*). He was supported by Xiong and Liang Qichao, who, emulating the American federal system, advocated that Hunan and other provinces create constitutions providing for provincial self-rule. Tan's initiative won support from warlords all over south and southwest China, and thus the federalist movement of the early 1920s flourished. Although co-opted by warlords as a means to preserve their local control, it also was used to oppose warlords. Thus, in 1924, a federation of the lower Yangzi provinces was proposed as a way to resist warlord Sun Chuanfang (1885–1935).

Federalism's influence was not limited to the provinces. Two national constitutions drafted in 1923 both contained strong federalist elements. Nevertheless, disparaged by nationalists as a cover for the warlords' desire for provincial autonomy and thus an obstacle to national unity, the federalist movement petered out.

SEE ALSO *Regionalism.*

BIBLIOGRAPHY

Chen Dingyan (Chen, Leslie H. Dingyan). *Chen Jiongming and the Federalist Movement: Regional Leadership and Nation Building in Early Republican China.* Ann Arbor, MI: Center for Chinese Studies, University of Michigan, 1999.

Chesneaux, Jean. The Federalist Movement in China, 1920–1923. In *Modern China's Search for a Political Form*, ed. Jack Gray, 96–137. London: Oxford University Press, 1969.

Duara, Prasenjit. *Rescuing History from the Nation: Questioning Narratives of Modern China.* Chicago: University of Chicago Press, 1995.

Waldron, Arthur. Warlordism Versus Federalism: The Revival of a Debate? *China Quarterly* 121 (1990): 116–128.

Roger B. Jeans

FEDERATION OF LITERARY AND ART CIRCLES

On January 31, 1949, the Communists took Beijing, and after their swift victory over the Nationalists in the following months, the Chinese Communist Party (CCP) was soon faced with transforming itself from an oppositional force into a national government. Since the CCP had developed its party structure while in remote rural exile over the previous decades, administration of China's urban areas and rule of the entire nation presented new challenges.

Exhausted by eight years of war with Japan and disappointed during the four postwar years by the corruption of the Nationalist regime, the Chinese public yearned for a peaceful, honest, and effective government to rebuild the country. The new Communist regime thus enjoyed enthusiastic support and bore the weight of high expectations from rural and urban citizens alike. It eagerly sought support from the full diversity of China's people, reaching out to members of many different political forces and social groups, thus differentiating itself from the defeated Nationalist government, which it criticized as dictatorial. For this purpose, the new regime organized the Chinese People's Political Consultative Committee (Zhongguo Renmin Zhengzhi Xieshang Huiyi, CPPCC) as a public relations foundation for the new civilian government. Prominent individuals were chosen as delegates of major political parties and social groups, thus presenting a broadly representative and unified public face for the government under the rubric of the New Democracy.

As one of the founding organizations within the CPPCC, the China Federation of Literary and Art Circles (Zhongguo Wenxue Yishu Jie Lianhehui) was established in July 1949 to represent intellectuals in the literary and artistic fields. Many left-wing intellectuals who had been active since the 1920s, especially in China's major urban centers, were called to serve as leaders in this organization. The first All-China Congress of Literary and Art Workers (Zhonghua Quanguo Wenxue Yishu Gongzuozhe Daibiao Dahui) was held from June 30 to July 28, 1949, in Beijing, the future capital of the People's Republic of China. At this meeting, on July 19, the All-China Federation of Literary and Art Circles (Zhonghua Quanguo Wenxue Yishu Jie Lianhehui) was founded, laying claim to a national territory that was not yet entirely under Communist control. The veteran left-wing writer Guo Moruo was elected as its chairman, and Mao Dun and Zhou Yang as vice chairmen. At the beginning, the function of the organization was to reach a wide range of influential non-Communist intellectuals and to inspire their confidence in the potential of the CCP to establish an effective government.

Four years after the official founding of the new government, during the second Congress of Literary and Art Workers, held in Beijing from September 23 to October 26, 1953, the organization changed its name to the China Federation of Literary and Art Circles (CFLAC) to reflect the reality of the regime's control, and to make a strong statement for its legitimacy as the only government of China. The new organization was strongly influenced by Soviet practices. From that time forward, CFLAC was devoted primarily to helping the CCP implement its evolving ideological goals and was under the direct supervision of the party's Central Propaganda Department. By organizing writers and artists to participate in research trips, conferences, performances, and exhibitions, and by granting awards and funding, CFLAC helped carry out party policies as they related to literature and the arts. In that period, when all China's arts were subject to the constraints of the centrally planned socialist economy, CFLAC and its member organizations played a significant role as one of the few sources of funding for literary and artistic activities. CFLAC and its member organizations also tightly controlled the access of artists and writers to publication venues, exhibition galleries, and performance spaces, as well as offering special privileges and prestige to favored individuals within the cultural world. Many of the intellectuals who were members of professional associations under CFLAC's umbrella spoke out when their opinions were sought during the Hundred Flowers campaign of 1957, and some of those individuals were condemned and suffered greatly in the Anti-Rightist campaign that followed.

The third congress, held July 22 to August 13, 1960, retained the leadership team established in 1949, with Guo Moruo, Zhou Yang, and Mao Dun occupying the top posts, but strengthened control of and communication to the subordinate or local societies by expanding the vice chairmanship to include such prominent leaders in drama, art, literature, music, and film as Mei Lanfang, He Xiangning, Ba Jin, Ma Sicong, Tian Han, Lao She, and Xia Yan. This structural change of the leadership reflected Liu Shaoqi and Deng Xiaoping's expansion of the bureaucracy to create a more effective administration after Mao's Great Leap Forward failed.

The fourth congress was not held until October 30, 1979, after the Cultural Revolution. Most members of CFLAC had been targets during the Cultural Revolution, and those who survived had suffered greatly. Although these senior figures did not directly criticize Mao Zedong at the meeting, they did so by implication in their strong criticism of the literary and arts policies of the Cultural Revolution. With an assumption established under Mao of the primacy of ideology in all party decisions, changes and conflicts in the cultural world had extraordinary symbolic power in the 1979. This meeting, which provided a platform in literature and arts fields for this criticism, thus stimulated a sympathetic and supportive attitude and provided ideological preparation for changes that would soon be announced in the economic and administrative sphere. As one of the first high-level public expressions of such opinions, this meeting was an important component of the ideological opening that laid the groundwork for the thirty year "reform period" since 1979, with its liberalization of literary and arts policies, as well as its economic boom. Four congresses have been held since that time; the eighth took place in November 2006.

Since it was founded in 1949, CFLAC membership has consisted of organizations representing different cultural fields. In 2009 it comprised fifty-two organizational members, including such professionally based institutions as the China Writers Association, China Theater Association, China Film Association, China Musicians Association, China Artists Association, China Dancers Association, China Photographers Association, and China Calligraphers Association, along with thirty-one provincial-level literary and art organizations and eight industry-specific cultural organizations. These organizations publish more than thirty journals and newspapers and run seven publishing firms. CFLAC funding comes largely from direct governmental allocations, from membership fees, and from donations. CFLAC continues to serve as the voice of the CCP and government within the cultural sphere. It also serves as a source of funding for activities falling under its purview, and organizes international exchange opportunities for Chinese and foreign creative artists and writers. With the economic expansion since the 1980s, however, private sources of funding and professional legitimization, both domestic and foreign, are now far more important to China's writers, filmmakers, and artists. As CFLAC's financial impact has dwindled, its ideological influence has also waned.

SEE ALSO *Art, Policy on, since 1949; Ba Jin; Cultural Revolution, 1966–1969; Guo Moruo; Influences Abroad: Maoism and Art; Lao She; Mao Dun; Mei Lanfang; Zhou Yang.*

BIBLIOGRAPHY

Andrews, Julia F. *Painters and Politics in the People's Republic of China, 1949–1979.* Berkeley: University of California Press, 1994.

China Federation of Literary and Art Circles. http://www.cflac.org.cn/english.htm.

Goldman, Merle. Hu Feng's Conflict with the Communist Literary Authorities. *China Quarterly* 12 (1962): 102–137.

Liushinian wenyi dashiji, 1919–1979 [Sixty-year record of major events in literature and art], ed. Disici wendaihui choubeizhu qicaozu [Drafting Group of the Preparation Group for the Fourth Congress of Literary and Art Workers]. Beijing: Wenhuabu Wenxue Yishu Yanjiuyuan Lilun Zhengce Yanjiushi [Theory and Policy Research Center of the Ministry of Culture's Literature and Art Research Institute], 1979.

Kuiyi Shen
Julia F. Andrews

FENG GUIFEN
1809–1874

Feng Guifen was a native of Suzhou, a major center of learning and commerce in southern Jiangsu Province. Situated between Nanjing and Shanghai, Suzhou was one of the southernmost cities along the Grand Canal, China's major north-south water route. Feng's career began and ended in the Jiangnan region, but his highly developed local knowledge of administration, taxation, education, and other topics informed the advice he gave high government officials and the essays he wrote.

CAREER IN GOVERNMENT

Feng Guifen advanced through the civil service examinations, winning his *juren* degree in 1832 and his *jinshi* in 1840. During this period Feng served as a private secretary for Jiangsu officials, beginning with a county magistrate and including Jiangsu governor Lin Zexu. Here he saw the depredations of yamen clerks and runners, and the effects of the crushing taxes borne by the peasants. Feng's ascent continued in 1840, with his receipt of one of the most coveted positions, that of Hanlin compiler in Beijing. Feng's growing reputation—his essays on waterways, the salt tax, and military organization demonstrated his knowledge of current affairs and economics—led to his being recommended to the Xianfeng emperor in 1850 as an able official.

Feng's metropolitan career was cut short when he returned home to mourn his father's death—an occasion to refocus his attention on Suzhou and its survival in the midst of the Taiping Rebellion. In 1853 Feng helped organize a local militia in Suzhou, and this military service received imperial recognition. But the Taiping attack on Suzhou in 1860 forced Feng to flee to Shanghai in 1861. Feng, along with other officials concerned about Suzhou, finally convinced Zeng Guofan to dispatch Li Hongzhang to Jiangsu in hopes of suppressing the Taiping rebels. Feng joined Li's staff in April and immediately put his local knowledge to work. Feng knew that some long-suffering Jiangsu peasants had welcomed the Taiping rebels in hopes of escaping heavy taxation and corrupt officials. Fiscal reform was sorely needed—in three areas in Jiangsu, including Suzhou, a mere 1 percent of China's population were required to provide 33 percent of a special type of rice levy. Li heard from Feng and others who agreed that this quota was exorbitant. Li and Zeng Guofan, in a joint memorandum informed in part by Feng's advice, gained imperial support; Feng became a member of the tax-reduction board that was established in Shanghai in August 1863. (In 1865, a year after Li Hongzhang's forces had suppressed the Taipings in the Jiangnan area, the tax burden Feng had criticized was finally lightened.)

In 1864 Li Hongzhang appointed Feng to head the Zhenjiang Academy in Suzhou. Until his death in 1874 Feng headed this academy, continued to advise the government, and edited a new local gazetteer for his native Suzhou Prefecture.

ESSAYS OF PROTEST

In the midst of the Taiping crisis, Feng completed a collection of essays that would enhance his reputation even further. These forty *Essays of Protest* (*Jiaobinlu kangyi*), with a preface dated November 1861, were sent to Zeng Guofan in 1862. There were two types of proposals: one aimed at improving government administration in areas like water control and fiscal reform, and the other called for a rebalancing of power and status within the bureaucracy and between officials and the people. The former reminded readers of reform ideas in the statecraft (*jingshi*) tradition dating to the 1820s and 1830s, when Feng's first high-level patron, Lin Zexu, had held provincial-level posts. The latter, however, was clearly influenced by Western ideas and included radical proposals that Feng would later leave out of his collected works. His son published part of *Essays of Protest* a few years after Feng's death. The complete work was published in 1884.

Feng's essays and ideas were recommended to the Guangxu emperor, first in 1889 by the emperor's tutor, Weng Tonghe (1830–1904), who believed Feng's ideas were "appropriate to the times," and again during the Hundred Days Reform in 1898, by Sun Jia'nai (1827–1909), a government official who suggested to the emperor that the government print copies of the work for distribution to high officials for comments about the feasibility of implementing Feng's ideas. Within a week, one thousand copies were printed and ready for distribution.

In this way, Feng's ideas, based on his detailed local experience in Jiangnan and a lifetime of study of the works of statecraft thinkers like Gu Yanwu (1613–1682), achieved national prominence and influence. For example, the provincial official Zhao Erxun (1844–1927) drew, as had Feng, on the compact anthology of statecraft essays and documents *Collected Writings on Statecraft* (*Jingshi Wenbian*), published in 1826. Both men looked to Gu Yanwu's essays on subcounty administrative reform for inspiration as they grappled with one of the central statecraft distinctions, the one between centralized bureaucratic monarchical rule (*junxian*) and feudalism (*fengjian*). Feng, in his essay "A Proposal to Restore Local Rule," used the principle of "imbuing *junxian* with the essence of *fengjian*" in order to legitimize and exploit existing power relationships in local society, while decreasing reliance on predatory unofficial hierarchies. In doing so, however, Feng juxtaposed his classical knowledge of China's ancient dynasties with proposals, such as local elections for officials, that betrayed his knowledge of the West. For officials like Zhao, also well-versed in the classics, experienced in local administration, and curious about Western and Japanese approaches to these questions, Feng's essays could provide valuable arguments to use in persuading conservatives, many of whom felt threatened by Western ideas and institutions, to consider new ideas in the context of more familiar statecraft theory.

Feng's career exemplified the channels by which reformist ideas of local literati percolated upward to levels of national power through the patronage of eminent officials, such as Li Hongzhang, who employed Feng in his personal staff (*mufu*). He merits special notice because of his flexible blending of native Chinese statecraft learning and western political culture, seemingly without a sense of incongruity.

SEE ALSO *Li Hongzhang; Qing Restoration.*

BIBLIOGRAPHY

Deng Siyu (Ssu-yü Teng) and John K. Fairbank. *China's Response to the West: A Documentary Survey, 1839–1923*. Cambridge, MA: Harvard University Press, 1954.

Kuhn, Philip A. Reform on Trial. In *Origins of the Modern Chinese State*, 54–79. Stanford, CA: Stanford University Press, 2002.

Lojewsky, Frank. Local Reform and Its Opponents: Feng Kuei-fen's Struggle for Equality in Taxation. In *Reform in Nineteenth-century China*, eds. Paul A. Cohen and John E. Schrecker, 128–136. Cambridge, MA: Harvard University Press, 1976.

Min Tu-gi. The Theory of Political Feudalism in the Ch'ing Period. In *National Polity and Local Power: The Transformation of Late Imperial China*, ed. Philip A. Kuhn and Timothy Brook, 89–136. Cambridge, MA: Council on East Asian Studies, Harvard University: Harvard-Yenching Institute: Harvard University Press, 1989.

Momose, Hiromu. Feng Kuei-fen. In *Eminent Chinese of the Ch'ing Period (1644–1912)*, vol. 1, ed. Arthur W. Hummel Jr. 241–243. Washington, DC: U.S. Government Printing Office, 1943–1944.

Polachek, James. Gentry Hegemony: Soochow in the T'ung-chih Restoration. In *Conflict and Control in Late Imperial China*, eds. Frederic Wakeman Jr. and Carolyn Grant, 211–256. Berkeley: University of California Press, 1975.

Thompson, Roger R. *China's Local Councils in the Age of Constitutional Reform, 1898–1911*. Cambridge, MA: Council on East Asian Studies, Harvard University: Harvard University Press, 1995.

Roger R. Thompson

FENG XIAOGANG
1958–

Feng Xiaogang, the most popular contemporary film director in the People's Republic of China (PRC), has demonstrated the viability of profitable domestic film production in a globalizing market. Born in Beijing in 1958, Feng was apprenticed in set design at the Song and Dance Ensemble of the Beijing Military Region. In 1985 he started working at Beijing TV Art Center and contributed to a number of well-received TV series. Feng gained a reputation for his witty script for *Stories from the Editorial Board* (*Bianjibu de gushi*, 1992, with Wang Shuo) and the unadorned directing style in *Beijinger in New York* (*Beijing ren zai niuyue*, 1993, with Zheng Xiaolong). The immense success of these TV series led to Feng's directing debut in *Lost My Love* (*Yong shi wo ai*, 1994) and to his breakthrough in *The Dream Factory* (*Jiafang yifang*, 1997).

The Dream Factory, together with the subsequent *Be There or Be Square* (*Bu jian bu san*, 1998) and *Sorry Baby* (*Mei wan mei liao*, 1999), introduced a new form of filmmaking. Rather than relying on either government subsidies or recognition in art-house theaters abroad, Feng made entertaining movies with small budgets and garnered large and loyal audiences in China. Feng perfected the formula sought by slightly older directors of the Fifth Generation such as Xia Gang (b. 1953), Zhang Jianya (b. 1951), and Huang Jianxin (b. 1954), who also were producing urban comedies. It was perhaps to Feng's advantage that unlike those directors, he did not graduate from the prestigious Beijing Film Academy and was not beholden to purported standards of film art. The popular appeal of Feng's films owed to a blend of street-smart wit, in line with Wang Shuo's "hoodlum literature" that inspired the films, and the protagonists' reiterated faith in social responsibility. Viewers readily identified with the combination of con-artist cool and good-hearted naïveté. Feng was also the first to adopt the Hong Kong marketing ploy of releasing his films for the holiday season, as New Year's movies.

Feng's commercial success gave a boost to an industry in decline. In the mid-1990s the Chinese film market was in crisis and undergoing a major restructuring. In 1992 only 10.5 billion tickets were sold in the PRC, a historical low and roughly one-third of movie attendance in 1979. In January 1994 the Ministry of Radio, Film, and Television responded by delegating China Film to import ten foreign films each year. Although attendance shot up, domestic film producers were not prepared for the exposure to Hollywood blockbusters, which immediately dominated the market. Feng's New Year's movies responded to the threat of Hollywood's takeover, just as Han Sanping, the president of Beijing Film Studio, had hoped when he invited Feng to make *The Dream Factory*.

In his second decade as a filmmaker, Feng experimented with new genres and themes. *A Sigh* (*Yisheng tanxi*, 2000) and *Cell Phone* (*Shouji*, 2003) are more somber psychological dramas, addressing marital infidelity. *Big Shot's Funeral* (*Da wan'r*, 2001) continues Feng's focus on benevolent slickers and comments on the tense relations between domestic filmmakers and foreign investors; ironically, the movie lost its local flavor to the casting of international actors, dictated by the collaboration with Columbia Pictures. Feng returned to his element with another thief-overcome-by-goodwill flick, *A World without Thieves* (*Tianxia wu zei*, 2004). *The Banquet* (*Ye yan*, 2006) combines gravity, as an adaptation of *Hamlet*, and popular appeal as a martial arts flick (with scenes choreographed by Yuen Woo-ping of *Crouching Tiger, Hidden Dragon* [*Wo hu cang long*] fame). *Assembly* (*Jijie hao*, 2007) is a war film revolving around an old battleground mystery, in the vein of Clint Eastwood's *Flags of Our Fathers* (2006). These recent productions, as well as Feng's TV commercials and cameo appearances in other directors' films, are evidence of Feng's desire to increase his exposure beyond his base in northern China and even to other countries, where he is practically unknown.

SEE ALSO *Film Industry: Fifth Generation Filmmakers; New Year's Movies; Wang Shuo.*

BIBLIOGRAPHY

Feng Xiaogang. *Wo ba qingchun xiangei ni* [I dedicate my youth to you]. Wuhan, China: Changjiang Chubanshe, 2003.

McGrath, Jason. *Postsocialist Modernity: Chinese Cinema, Literature, and Criticism in the Market Age.* Stanford, CA: Stanford University Press, 2008.

Wang, Ting. Hollywood's Crusade in China Prior to China's WTO Accession. *Jump Cut: A Review of Contemporary Media* 49 (spring 2007). http://ejumpcut.org/archive/jc49.2007/TingWang/index.html.

Zhang Rui. *Cinema of Feng Xiaogang: Commercialization and Censorship in Chinese Cinema after 1989.* Seattle: University of Washington Press, 2008.

Yomi Braester

FENG ZIKAI
1898–1975

Born about three years after the first Sino-Japanese War and passing away during the decade of the Cultural Revolution, the artist, illustrator, cartoonist, and designer Feng Zikai, like China itself, confronted great political chaos and shocks from the impact of the West and Japan. Born in Shimenwan, Zhejiang Province, Feng received a classical Chinese education, followed by a Western one. Like many May Fourth intellectuals, Feng, in his youth, stood at a crossroads in the development of modern China, and his particular humanistic vision was the result.

In 1914 Feng entered Hangzhou First Normal School, where he met the most influential mentor in his life, the Japanese-educated artist and educator Li Shutong (1880–1942), whose decision to become a Buddhist monk in 1918 powerfully affected Feng Zikai. Following Li Shutong, later known as Master Hongyi, Feng embraced Buddhism and undertook a lifelong artistic project, the creation of six volumes of illustrations, *Husheng huaji* (Paintings to protect life), based on Buddhist poems by Hongyi and his followers.

Feng visited Japan in 1921, where he was inspired by the illustrations, prints, and paintings of Takehisa Yumeji (1884–1934), which synthesize Western and Eastern trends and possess strong humanistic concerns. The flat colors and striking compositions of Feng's artworks may have been inspired by Japanese woodblock landscapes, such as those of Katsushika Hokusai (1760–1849) and Andō Hiroshige (1797–1858). Influenced also by Chen Shizeng (1876–1923) and Omura Seigai (1868–1927), Feng believed that China should take what was enviable from the West while retaining the essence of indigenous culture. His personal style successfully combined his humanistic concerns, Western painting methods, and Chinese lyricism.

In the middle of the 1920s, Feng, who was one of the earliest Chinese artists to adopt the term *manhua* (in Japanese, *manga*) to describe his art, created a great many cartoons of the behavior and character of children. The success of Feng's cartoons of and for children lies in his aim to convey a child's mode of perception. He admired the creative imagination and ingenuity of children, and believed that the pure heart of a child is what adults should value and emulate.

Feng reached the peak of his creativity in drawing cartoons in the 1920s and 1930s. His works of the time, in black and white, possessed qualities of forcefulness and urgency, yet most of them were relatively intimate in size. He did not do many large-scale paintings until the late 1930s. In the late 1930s and 1940s, Feng began painting more expansive landscape paintings, to which he added color.

Japan's invasion of China in 1937 forced Feng Zikai, along with many Chinese artists living near the coast, to flee their studios and travel inland to unfamiliar parts of the country, surroundings that greatly changed the style of his works. Feng's landscape paintings, such as *Huoran kailang* (Gazing at the lake) and *Jingbao zuo meiren* (Air-raid alarm plays the role of a go-between), communicate the exhilaration of exploration and discovery and a keen sense of curiosity about his physical surroundings.

The spontaneity and humor found in his artwork ensure Feng's position as a well-loved master of twentieth-century Chinese art. In addition to producing, in the 1930s and 1940s, many illustrations for magazine articles and stories, publications of fairy tales, and the like, Feng was also a pioneering designer of Chinese book covers, with a signature style that combined art nouveau and his version of the cartoon. With a combination of whimsy, sympathy, and creativity, Feng used cover design to stimulate readers' interest and help them to understand the contents of publications to which he contributed, particularly during his years at the progressive Kaiming Book Company (Kaiming Shudian).

Feng is best remembered for his role in the modern Chinese cartoon *(manhua)* movement. Yet he was equally accomplished as a writer, calligrapher, musician, translator, and painter. His surviving artistic works include Chinese painting (*guohua*), calligraphy, woodblock prints, cartoons, illustrations, and cover designs.

SEE ALSO *Chinese Painting (guohua); Commercial Art: Cartoons, Comics, and Manhua.*

BIBLIOGRAPHY

Barme, Geremie. *An Artistic Exile: A Life of Feng Zikai (1898–1975).* Berkeley: University of California Press, 2002.

Barme, Geremie. An Artist and His Epithet: Notes on Feng Zikai and the Manhua. *Papers on Far Eastern History* 39 (March 1989): 17–43.

Bi Keguan and Huang Yuanlin. *Zhongguo manhua shi* [A history of Chinese cartoons]. Beijing: Wenhua Yishu Chubanshe, 1986.

Feng Yiyin. *Xiaosa fengshen: Wo de fuqin Feng Zikai* [A natural and refined air: My father Feng Zikai]. Shanghai: Huadong Shifan Daxue Chubanshe, 1998.

Feng Yiyin. *Baba de hua* [My father's paintings]. 4 vols. Shanghai: Huadong Shifan Daxue Chubanshe, 1999.

Feng Zikai. *Husheng huaji* [Paintings to protect life]. 6 vols. Shanghai: Haitian Chubanshe, 1993.

Nishimaki Isamu. Hō Shigai no Chūgoku bijutsu yūiron to Nihon [Feng Zikai on the superiority of Chinese art and Japan]. *Hikaku bungaku* 39 (1996): 52–66.

Nishimaki Isamu. Manga to bunka: Hō Shigai to Takehisa Yumeji o megutte [Cartoons and culture: Feng Zikai and Takehisa Yumeji]. *Hikaku bungaku* 36 (1993): 92–103.

Su-hsing Lin

FENGSHUI

Fengshui is the name given to various techniques that supposedly bring good fortune to people when their homes and graves are properly oriented to the flow of *qi*. In Chinese cosmology, the human anatomy is a microcosm of the earth, and the veins and nodes of one correspond to the rivers and lakes of the other. When the ground is broken for a new house, or when a grave is dug, such action influences the earth just like the acupuncture needle taps the *qi* meridians of the body. Regardless of the type of fengshui, all site-orientation methods seek to locate this energy or life force. When *qi* is directed toward the tomb, it invigorates the bones of the ancestor buried there, whose spirit then bestows good fortune on the descendents. When the house is properly oriented according to the disposition of *qi* in the surrounding environment, the good fortune of the inhabitants will be enhanced.

Two different procedures for locating *qi* began to develop by the Han dynasty (206 BCE–220 CE). The first was based on the geophysical nature of *qi*. The fourth-century *Book of Burial*, based on a lost Han dynasty *Classic of Burial*, was the earliest Chinese text to discuss the physical environment of fengshui: "Where the earth takes shape, *qi* flows accordingly; thereby things are born. For *qi* courses within the ground, its flow follows the contour of the ground, and its accumulation results from the halt of terrain. For burial, seek the source and ride it to its terminus." There is also an important meteorological element in the physical description of the site, portrayed in another passage from the *Book of Burial*: "*Qi* rides the wind (*feng*) and scatters, but is retained when encountering water (*shui*). The ancients collected it to prevent its dissipation, and guided it to assure its retention. Thus it was called *fengshui*. According to the laws of fengshui, the site that attracts water is optimal, followed by the site that catches wind."

Wind and water are the means by which *qi* is controlled. Wind captures *qi* and scatters it, so its ingress should be blocked. Water captures *qi* and concentrates it, so its presence should be encouraged. This will ensure that sufficient *qi* surrounds the tomb. Since this theoretical system is based on the landscape features of a given locale, it eventually became known as the "forces and features" or Form school of fengshui.

The Compass or "directions and positions" school also relies on the disposition of *qi* in the cosmos, but on its metaphysical qualities rather than its geophysical characteristics. While the theories of fengshui are of ancient origin, the early history of their practice is unclear at best. It was not until the medieval period that records become numerous enough to give scholars a good picture of its development. Yang Yunsong, purportedly the fengshui master to Tang dynasty emperor Xizong (r. 873–888), is recognized as the patriarch of Form school fengshui, while the father of Compass school fengshui is Wang Zhaoqing of the southern Song dynasty (1127–1206). It was Wang who popularized the use of the *luopan*, or the fengshui compass. The techniques of both schools are still utilized in contemporary China, while the latter is almost exclusively used in the West.

The most popular form of fengshui practiced in the United States is the Eight-House or Nine-Star system of Compass school fengshui. Practitioners of this system analyze *qi* as a force that progresses through five elemental processes called the "five phases." In the productive phase, earth harbors metal, metal condenses water, water nourishes wood, wood feeds fire, and fire burns to earth. In the destructive phase, earth dams water, water quenches fire, fire melts metal, metal cuts wood, and wood saps earth. These phases are correlated with the eight directional trigrams of the *Yijing* or *Book of Changes*, and a person's year of birth also corresponds to a particular trigram. By orienting dwellings or arranging rooms in productive directions with regard to an individual's natal *qi*, it is thus

A fengshui practitioner orientating a coffin with a compass. *Many Chinese adhere to the principles of fengshui, a set of beliefs that look to improve one's good fortune through the strategic placement of objects. Fengshui adherents suggest that proper alignment of important items, such as family graves, allow the deceased's spirit to benefit the surviving family.* © CHRISTOPHE BOISVIEUX/CORBIS

possible to avoid *sha*, which is the *qi* generated by destructive directions. Another form of Compass school fengshui, Flying Star, takes the passage of time into account, assuming that the flow of energy in the universe is not static but changes with the flow of time. The stars of both Nine-Star and Flying-Star fengshui are not asterisms in the astronomical sense, but are names of auspice based on five-phase conjunctions. Whereas the stars of Eight-House fengshui are static throughout a person's life, those of Flying Star move through a fixed sequence of temporal changes based on a cycle of twenty years.

Fengshui first became known to the English-speaking world in 1873, when the German missionary Ernest Eitel (1838–1908) published his landmark study, *Feng-shui: or, The Rudiments of Natural Science in China*. However, after the founding of the People's Republic of China in 1949, fengshui was branded as superstition and its practice was prohibited. Although not officially rehabilitated, fengshui is now openly practiced in China and, while still vilified by many intellectuals, it is the subject of some scholarly study.

During the half century of prohibition, the practice flourished in Taiwan, Hong Kong, and Singapore, as well as among other communities of Chinese overseas. Many of the purported masters in the West were born and trained in these Chinese communities. One of the earliest proponents of fengshui was Thomas Yun Lin, who founded a temple in the United States for American Black Sect Tantric Buddhism in 1986. Lin's brand of fengshui capitalized on the popularity of New Age religion by relying on intuition and mystical knowledge at the expense of traditional practices. Every major city in the United States now has its own community of fengshui consultants, many of them trained by Lin or his disciples. However, the popularity of Lin's Black Sect school has slowly been eclipsed by the spread of so-called traditional fengshui—those institutions teaching Eight-House and Flying-Star theories.

SEE ALSO *Medicine, Traditional; Popular Religion.*

BIBLIOGRAPHY

Aylward, Thomas F., trans. *The Imperial Guide to Feng Shui & Chinese Astrology: The Only Authentic Translation from the Original Chinese*. London: Watkins, 2007.

Bennett, Steven J. Patterns of Sky and Earth: A Chinese System of Applied Cosmology. *Chinese Science* 3 (1978): 1–26.

Field, Stephen. The Numerology of Nine Star Fengshui: A *Hetu, Luoshu* Resolution of the Mystery of Directional Auspice. *Journal of Chinese Religion* 27 (1999): 13–33.

Field, Stephen. In Search of Dragons: The Folk Ecology of Fengshui. In *Daoism and Ecology: Ways Within a Cosmic Landscape*, ed. N. J. Girardot, James Miller, and Liu Xiaogan, 185–197. Cambridge, MA: Harvard University Center for the Study of World Religions, 2001.

Field, Stephen. *Ancient Chinese Divination*. Honolulu: University of Hawai'i Press, 2008.

Guo Pu. The *Zangshu*, or *Book of Burial*. Trans. Stephen Field. 2003. http://www.trinity.edu/sfield/Fengshui/Zangshu.html.

Wong, Eva. *Feng-shui: The Ancient Wisdom of Harmonious Living for Modern Times*. Boston and London: Shambhala, 1996.

Stephen L. Field

FESTIVALS

Festival life in contemporary China is highly eclectic, and includes birthday and Christmas celebrations, as well as a range of national and local festivals, many of which have seen new interest in recent years as the reformist government has revived some cultural practices that were abandoned during the Mao years (1949–1976). The festivals that the Chinese themselves would call traditional are tied closely to the agricultural rhythms of social life dating back at least to the Zhou dynasty (c. 1046–256 BCE). The most significant festivals in the Chinese calendar remain those connected to the spring planting and autumn harvest.

The Chinese agricultural (and festival) year is traditionally divided between six *yang* months, as cold turns slowly to the warmth of spring and the heat of summer, and six *yin* months, as summer heat gives way to cooler weather. Chinese almanacs to this day subdivide these units into twenty-four seasonal nodes of approximately fifteen days each. These periods have been celebrated in Chinese music and verse for many centuries. More than a way to organize the calendar, these twenty-four "joints and breaths" (*jieqi*) of the calendar lie at the heart of Chinese festival observances.

FESTIVALS OF THE SOLAR YEAR

The lunar and solar calendar rhythms overlap to create a rich combination of Chinese festivals. Of the solar holidays, only one can claim a long heritage stretching back to agricultural origins in early China. The Qingming (Pure and Bright) Festival marks the fifth seasonal node and was originally a celebration of spring in which communities came together to bring hopes for a successful farming season. Over the course of centuries, the celebration tended to focus more on the extended family network and dedication to the departed. Today the holiday is also known as Tomb-Sweeping Day, an opportunity for families to come together to tidy the ancestral graves, pay respects, and share meals.

The solar New Year on January 1 is not nearly as widely observed in China as it is in other parts of the world, but some people in urban centers who do business with the world have begun to take notice. Other prominent solar calendar holidays in the Chinese-speaking world include Women's Day on March 8, International Labor Day on May 1, and Children's Day on June 1. A cluster of holidays (some with time off from work and school) in the spring and summer commemorate important events in modern Chinese history or significant institutions in Chinese society. Youth Day on May 4 honors students and workers who demonstrated in 1919 against Japan's colonization attempts in Shandong Province. The Chinese Communist Party's "birthday" is observed with editorials and government pronouncements on July 1, and Army Day on August 1 has traditionally been a time for fostering ties between the army and the civilian population. Teacher's Day is observed in the People's Republic on September 10; in Taiwan it is celebrated as a commemoration of Confucius' birthday on September 28.

China's National Day commemorates the founding on October 1, 1949, when Mao Zedong stood in Tiananmen Square and proclaimed the birth of the People's Republic after a four-year battle with Nationalist forces, who retreated to Taiwan. The Republic of China continues to celebrate the Double Tenth holiday, which hearkens back to the end of imperial rule in China and the founding of the Republic in October 1911. Rounding out the solar year, the Winter Solstice Festival ushers in a transitional period between the end of one year and the beginning of another. Since the late twentieth century, celebrations of the Christmas holiday have become increasingly popular.

FESTIVALS OF THE LUNAR YEAR

The lunar festivals have always been by far the most important in the Chinese tradition. Of these the most important is the Spring Festival, which begins the year by marking the new moon that falls between mid-January and mid-February. It is difficult to understand life in China without having a sense of the greetings, family gatherings, and activities (prescribed and proscribed) associated with the days of the festival. Traditionally, public and commercial life in China shuts down for more than two weeks of feasting, visiting, and relaxation. In the late twentieth and early twenty-first centuries the celebrations have been significantly shortened, but most people still expect to have the opportunity to go home during the festival.

The New Year celebrations begin with preparations that have traditionally included settling accounts from the previous year, writing poetic couplets, and cleaning the household—activities that would be considered unlucky should they occur early in the New Year. New Year's Eve has always been a time for family observances, and the noise of fireworks has been prominent for many centuries. New Year's Day is a quiet time for family gatherings to wish one another well in the New Year, as well as for giving children red envelopes (*hongbao*) with small amounts of money. Beginning on the second day, people visit friends and more distant kin. They also send greetings to a wide array of friends, relatives, and colleagues.

The New Year's celebration ends with the Lantern Festival, celebrating the first full moon of the year. Traditionally, whole families would go out to admire exquisitely decorated lanterns and show off their best spring clothing. Chinese literature over the centuries is filled with descriptions of teeming crowds, brimming markets, and public celebrations during the Lantern Festival, which in earlier times lasted four or five days. It remains one of the highlights of the Chinese year, marked by lion and dragon dances and consuming special sweet rice dumplings. The Lantern Festival is especially important in China's rural areas, but urban celebrations have for much of the last millennium offered spectacles on a monumental scale.

Other significant lunar festivals dot the calendar, the most significant of which take place in the fifth, seventh, and ninth moons of the year. The Dragon Boat Festival (the fifth day of the fifth month) commemorates Qu Yuan (c. 340–278 BCE), a minister of the state of Chu who drowned himself in the Miluo River to protest the actions of his ruler. Tradition has it that people flocked to the river to try to save him. Unsuccessful, they then threw silk-wrapped dumplings into the river to feed the fish and thus keep them away from Qu Yuan's body. Today, the Dragon Boat Festival is marked by the consumption of *zongzi*, a bamboo-wrapped rice dumpling very popular in southern China. Dragon boat races are held in Asia, Europe, and the Americas.

Two months later, many Chinese celebrate the most significant holiday of what is commonly known as Ghost Month. The seventh day of the seventh month marks the reuniting of the herdboy and the weaving maiden, who, in stories dating back at least to the Zhou dynasty, were separated from each other and able to reunite only once a year. Sometimes called Chinese Valentine's Day, the traditional holiday has diminished in significance as the Western Valentine's Day has assumed enormous importance as a marriage date and time for exchange of gifts. The story behind the original festival, however, is familiar to everyone through tales, poems, and plays.

The last of the lunar double festivals is celebrated on the ninth day of the ninth moon. The Double Yang Festival is a time to gather with friends and family, recite poetry, and distribute certain foods. The number nine is significant in Chinese thought, since odd numbers are said to be *yang* and even numbers *yin*. Doubling any number gives it added prestige, and double nine is perhaps the most auspicious of all. Traditionally, the Double Yang Festival was thought to be a good time to climb to a high spot and look out over the countryside. Pilgrimages to China's sacred mountains, especially Mount Tai in Shandong Province, have remained common during this period.

Although it actually takes place a few weeks before Double Yang, the year that began with the Spring Festival is brought to its agricultural conclusion with the celebration on the fifteenth day of the eighth month—the harvest moon—of the Mid-Autumn Festival. It is often said that the moon is completely round at this time. Families enjoyed the short period between what in most parts of China was the end of the summer harvest and the beginning of the autumn harvest. Although the roots of the festival are in the agricultural rhythms and marriage alliances of early China, the festival quickly came to be associated with a range of moon legends, the most prominent of which tells the story of Chang E and her husband, the archer Hou Yi. Today, families sit together and view the full moon, enjoy a snack known as moon cakes, and tell variations of the Chang E story.

The final months of the year are marked by the October National Days and several minor festivals. As the *yin* months turn colder, the calendar notes days for the sending off of winter clothes, the Winter Solstice, and the exit of the kitchen god as he makes his way to heaven (so the story goes) to report on the family's conduct over the past year.

SEE ALSO *Calendar; Food since 1800; New Year's Movies.*

BIBLIOGRAPHY

Aijmer, Göran. *New Year Celebrations in Central China in Late Imperial Times.* Hong Kong: Chinese University Press, 2003.

Bodde, Derk. *Festivals in Classical China: New Year and Other Annual Observances during the Han Dynasty, 206 B.C.–A.D. 220.* Princeton, NJ: Princeton University Press, 1975.

Granet, Marcel. *The Religion of the Chinese People.* Ed. and trans. Maurice Freedman. New York: Harper & Row, 1975.

Tun Li-ch'en. *Annual Customs and Festivals in Peking as Recorded in the Yen-ching Sui-shih-chi.* 2nd rev. ed. Trans. Derk Bodde. Hong Kong: Hong Kong University Press, 1965.

Robert André LaFleur

FILIAL PIETY

Filial piety, emphasizing the importance of respect, obedience, and reverence that children (especially sons) owed their parents both in life and death, is a virtue long exalted in Chinese history. The Chinese written character for filial piety (*xiao*)—which pictorially represents an old man being supported by a child, and remains in use today—first appeared on ritual bronze vessels dating from about 1000 BCE. Worship of ancestors was already an important ritual at this time. The meaning of *xiao* in the bronze inscriptions, however, although principally referring to piety expressed toward one's *dead* parents, also implied a duty of respect and reverence toward the living (parents as well as relatives senior to one's generation).

In the teachings of both Confucius (551–479 BCE) and Mencius (c. 372–289 BCE), the practice of filial piety—referring specifically to devout acts of reverence by children in honor of parents living and dead (which included the obligation to continue the patrilineal line by having sons)—was considered a perfectly natural aspect of human behavior that possessed a moral value of virtually universal significance. Later canonical texts valorized by Confucian thinkers and the state and constituting the core of the educational curriculum throughout imperial times, such as the *Xiaojing* (Classic of filial piety, compiled between the fourth and third centuries BCE), also drew a direct parallel between filial piety exhibited toward parents and the loyalty and obedience subjects and ministers owed their rulers.

Later dynastic histories invariably included heroic tales of stoical and selfless individuals who performed near mythical acts of devotion and self-sacrifice to honor, succor, or heal elderly parents (one such act included the slicing of a person's flesh in order to make medicinal broth for an ailing parent). Over time, stories of especially filial daughters-in-law increasingly figured in morality tracts and popular literature.

As historian Donald Holzman has noted (1998, p. 198), a tradition of near fanatical behavior associated with filial piety was not dissimilar to that of Christian saints in the West engaging in extreme acts of self-abnegation in order to demonstrate their absolute devotion to god. Such a tradition is evident in the elaborate mourning rituals prescribed in various texts and which constituted an important element of filial piety (and which were satirized brilliantly in Zhang Yimou's 1991 film, *Ju Dou*). Thus, after a parent's death, a son or daughter was expected to undergo a period of extreme asceticism for up to three years (dressing frugally and foregoing meat, alcohol, and sex). In imperial times, these mourning requirements were even applied to the bureaucracy, with officials expected to "retire" temporarily to their home districts after the death of a parent for a period of about two years (such rules were gradually loosened during the eighteenth and nineteenth centuries, when the Qing dynasty allowed officials to carry out "private" mourning while still on the job).

UNDER ATTACK IN THE EARLY TWENTIETH CENTURY

Beginning in the late nineteenth century, growing external and internal crises prompted scholars to question traditional values. A gradual process of "desacralization" of Confucian learning began. The process—accelerated no less by the Qing government's own education reforms, which abolished the Confucian-based civil service examinations in 1905 and created modern schools in which the study of the Confucian classics was gradually reduced—culminated in the New Culture or May Fourth movement (1915–early 1920s)

A number of radical intellectuals, such as Chen Duxiu (1879–1942), Lu Xun (1881–1936), and Hu Shi (1891–1962), argued that the political change of 1912 (when the monarchy had been replaced by a republic) had not brought about fundamental social and cultural change, a situation they attributed to the continuing influence of the Confucian tradition. As a core Confucian value, filial piety, with its denial of individualism and stress on unquestioning obedience to elders, was blamed for preventing the emergence of a dynamic and democratic society (ironically, not a few of these radical intellectuals had themselves entered into arranged marriages in accordance with their parents' wishes).

An abortive attempt was made to resurrect Confucian values during the neotraditionalist New Life movement (1934) promoted by Chiang Kai-shek's (Jiang Jieshi's) Nationalist regime to ward off the growing threat from Chinese Communists. The link between filial piety and loyalty to the state was once again emphasized when students were enjoined to think of the state as their own family.

THE FALL AND RISE OF FILIAL PIETY SINCE 1949

The Communist revolution of 1949, with its ideological attack on the feudal tradition and its insistence that loyalty and commitment to the Chinese Communist Party (CCP) and to the socialist state overrode everything else, seemed to sound the death knell for filial piety as an admired virtue. Furthermore, early radical measures, such as the Marriage Reform Law (1950), reduced parental authority over children by insisting on free-choice marriage. However, political, demographic, and social developments since 1976 have led to greater state toleration (and even valorization) of core Confucian values such as filial piety.

The market-oriented reform since the early 1980s has generated much social and political tensions. Widening gaps in wealth and opportunity as well as noticeable upsurge in official corruption were directly linked to the Tiananmen student and worker protests of 1989. In response the CCP promotes a "new conservatism," which embodies a strong nationalistic element, enlisting traditional cultural values such as harmony, respect for elders, loyalty, and discipline to ensure political and social stability, and to fill the ideological vacuum bequeathed by the declining importance of socialism (both ideologically and in practice). Filial piety and related values are further touted as uniquely Chinese, and thus a source of national pride. In the process, the CCP also hopes to harness nationalist feelings to buttress its legitimacy.

The recent valorization of filial piety is also the result of demographic change and the chronic lack of welfare provision, particularly in the countryside, where conditions have been exacerbated by the dismantling of the collectives. Decreasing fertility rates as a result of the state's one-child policy since 1979 has meant that the elderly (those aged sixty-five and over) constitute an ever-increasing proportion of the population; in 1998 they made up 6.6 percent of the total population, but it is estimated that by 2025 this figure will be 13 percent. This growing elderly population will only be able to rely on the support of one child. However, due to changing social mores and the increasing financial independence of the young, many newly married sons (especially in urban areas) choose not to live with their parents—a far cry from the Confucian ideal of the multigenerational household.

For the state, therefore, filial piety is primarily associated with the care of elderly parents (the state continues to discourage the practice of lavish funerals), a compulsory duty for both sons and daughters that has been enshrined in the revised Marriage Law of 1980 and in legislation during the 1990s. Recent investigations reveal, however, that much of this responsibility is devolving to daughters (in contrast to imperial times, when parental care was seen primarily as a son's duty), a situation that parents themselves seem to prefer because they perceive daughters as more caring and often complain publicly about the poor treatment meted out to them by sons.

SEE ALSO *May Fourth Movement.*

BIBLIOGRAPHY

Chan, Alan, and Sor-hoon Tan, eds. *Filial Piety in Chinese Thought and Society*. London: Routledge, 2004.

Deutsch, Francine M. Filial Piety, Patrilineality, and China's One-Child Policy. *Journal of Family Issues* 27, 3 (2006): 366–389.

Holzman, Donald. The Place of Filial Piety in Ancient China. *Journal of the American Oriental Society* 118, 2 (1998): 185–199.

Ikels, Charlotte, ed. *Filial Piety: Practice and Discourse in Contemporary East Asia*. Stanford, CA: Stanford University Press, 2004.

Kipnis, Andrew. Within and Against Peasantness: Backwardness and Filiality in Rural China. *Comparative Studies in Society and History* 37, 1 (1995): 110–135.

Whyte, Martin K. The Fate of Filial Obligations in Urban China. *China Journal* 38, 1 (1997): 1–31.

Zhan, Heying Jenny, and Rhonda Montgomery. Gender and Elder Care in China: The Influence of Filial Piety and Structural Constraints. *Gender and Society* 17, 2 (2003): 209–229.

Paul J. Bailey

FILM INDUSTRY

This entry contains the following:

OVERVIEW

The trajectory of the development of Chinese film over the last century can best be evaluated against the backdrop of actual historical events, through a sometimes amorphous institutional setting, and especially by the contribution of an outstanding group of individuals. Accordingly, this discussion will chronologically examine the work of six generations of filmmakers (and their institutional settings) in eight definitive historical eras.

WARLORDS, TREATY PORTS, AND A NASCENT NATIONAL FILM CULTURE, 1916–1927

A dichotomous beginning marked both the production and presentation sides of Chinese cinema. In 1905 the photographer Ren Qingtai produced a documentary short on Beijing opera, and in 1916 the director-writer Zhang Shichuan (1889–1953) produced the feature-length anti-imperial *Hei ji yuan hen* (*Victims of Opium*), which enjoyed a seven-year theater run after its release. Most theaters were foreign-owned, located in treaty port cities, and showed imported Hollywood films. Meanwhile, domestic production initially copied Hollywood's preference for romantic entertainment films. Yet with domestic production, distinctly Chinese genres also emerged, such as martial-arts or god-spirit films. Such films were often made in response to historical events. Drawing on specific legends, they served as both a catharsis and an escape for urban audiences in the warlord era and the early days of Chiang Kai-shek's white terror (1927–1931).

With visionary capital and film pioneers, Chinese cinema also progressed by tapping into popular demand for more socially responsible films. Trendsetting Shanghai companies like Tianyi (est. 1925) and Mingxing (est. 1926) helped lend respectability to film through their recruitment of important film artists (see table 1).

Notable filmmakers and their films, 1916–1949

Filmmaker	Representative films
Zheng Zhengqiu (1889–1935), writer-director	*Zimei hua* (*Twin Sisters*; 1933)
Zhang Shichuan (1889–1953), producer-director	*Hei ji yuan hen* (*Victims of Opium*; 1916)
Dan Duyu (1897–1972), writer-director	*Hai shi* (*Sea Oath*; 1921)
Bu Wancang (1903–1974), producer-director	*Sange modeng nüren* (*Three Modern Women*; 1933)
Chen Bugao (1898–1966), director	*Chun cao* (*Spring Silkworms*; 1933)
Xia Yan (1900–1995), administrator-writer	*Kuang liu* (*Wild Torrents*; 1933)
Cai Chusheng (1906–1968), writer-director	*Yuguang qu* (*Song of the Fisherman*; 1934)
Jin Yan (1910–1983), actor	*Dalu* (*The Big Road*; 1934)
Sun Yu (1900–1990), writer-director	*Dalu* (*The Big Road*; 1934)
Yuan Muzhi (1909–1978), administrator-writer	*Taoli jie* (*Plunder of Peach and Plum*; 1934)
Ruan Lingyu (1910–1935), actress	*Xin nüren* (*New Woman*; 1935)
Jin Shan (1911–1982), writer-director	*Songhuajiang shang* (*Along the Sungari River*; 1947), *Wuya yu maque* (*Crows and Sparrows*; 1949)
Zheng Junli (1911–1969), writer-director	*Yijiang chunshui xiangdong liu* (*The Spring River Flows East*; 1947)
Chen Liting (b. 1910), director	*Yaoyuan de ai* (*Love Far Away*; 1947)
Fei Mu (1906–1951), director	*Xiao cheng zhi chun* (*Spring in a Small Town*; 1948)
Shen Fu (1905–1994), director	*Wanjia denghuo* (*A Myriad of Lights*; 1948)

Table 1

THE NANJING DECADE, 1928–1937: NATIONALIST CENSORSHIP AND A FLOURISHING LEFT-WING MOVEMENT

A relatively tranquil filmmaking environment in Shanghai shifted with historical events. The Northern Expedition to unify the country raised expectations everywhere. The new government gained international standing, people displayed a higher political consciousness and growing nationalism, and film audiences pushed for films that addressed social concerns. With worldwide economic depression and the first Japanese invasion (1931–1932), consolidation and a reduction in the number of film companies took place. The invasion in fact brought about the destruction of the Mingxing Studios in Shanghai's Zhabei district.

China's film industry became more bifurcated than before. American sound films dominated, achieving a 90 percent market share in Shanghai's best theaters in 1929. Yet the confluence of a new generation of filmgoers and filmmakers and a growing domestic film culture with a newly established government censorship committee produced a remarkable Chinese film movement that was at least autonomous if not fully underground. It functioned continuously until 1952 despite strenuous efforts by successive political regimes—Nationalist, Japanese, and Communist—to dictate film themes and content. Previously mentioned first-generation filmmakers all remained active and were joined by a younger cohort of second-generation directors and writers, who collectively made up the left-wing film movement (*zuobang dianying*) that began in 1931 (see table 1).

THE ANTI-JAPANESE WAR, 1937–1945: PROPAGANDA, WAR, SOFT FILM, AND AMBIGUOUS LEGACIES

Japan's full-scale invasion in the summer of 1937 did not eliminate China's film industry, although important Shanghai studios were seized (Mingxing), dissolved (Lianhua), or moved to Hong Kong (Tianyi). Film artists scattered to far-flung points south, west, and east. The industry relied wholly on imported film stock and equipment (China reached self-sufficiency in these only in 1960), especially in the Nationalist wartime capital of Chongqing. Elsewhere, Shanghai, Manchuria, and Hong Kong churned out impressive numbers of films and documentaries, many of which differed from the previous leftist era.

Chongqing was the most traditional wartime film producer, with themes of nationalism and resistance dominating, especially as leftist directors continued their attempts to redefine acceptable boundaries of government censorship. Hong Kong also briefly became a refuge for politically active Chinese filmmakers, at least until it fell into Japanese hands in December 1941. During the "orphan island" (*gudao*) period (1937–1941), when Chinese films, unfettered by Japanese jurisdiction, could be made in the international settlement, Shanghai opted largely for entertainment films removed from contemporary politics. Most difficult to assess is the legacy of Japan's Manying Studio. The largest film studio in East Asia when it opened in Changchun in 1938, Manying produced more than 200 films over the next seven years. Predictably, many were fictional entertainment films, and the vast majority of them were written and directed by Chinese recruited from Shanghai (although most if not all Manying cameramen were Japanese).

THE CIVIL WAR, 1945–1949: THE UNLIKELY GOLDEN AGE OF CHINESE CINEMA

The postwar period saw a great increase in anti-Japanese films. However, heightened political tensions and ruinous inflation during the civil war thoroughly disrupted the Chinese economy. Nonetheless, widespread disillusionment, fear, anxiety, and war-weariness inspired remarkable cinematic achievements in these four years (see table 1).

At the war's end the Nationalist government seized control of many studios, theaters, and film distributors, and dissatisfied artists left their employ to form the influential private Kunlun and Wenhua companies. Nationalist film censors continued to restrict the now more openly subversive left. Of 162 films made in the three years after October 1945, 48 were substantially revised, cut, or shelved. Still, on the whole the era's films are notable for their hardscrabble quality, apparent in inverse proportion to the strength of Nationalist government authority.

MAOIST CINEMA, 1949–1966: THE HEYDAY OF WORKER-PEASANT-SOLDIER FILMS

Establishment of the new People's Republic in 1949 gave hope to three generations of filmmakers scarred by war, inflation, and Nationalist incompetence. The Maoist party-state further defined and clarified national cinema after taking over the largest film studios in Shanghai, Beijing, and Changchun. Chairman Mao Zedong declared that film artists and their work should serve first the workers, peasants, and soldiers. With that, and because of geographic peculiarities and the civil war, Changchun remained China's film capital until 1957.

Many first- and second-generation filmmakers accepted Mao's dictum and even echoed his sentiments. Cai Chusheng said, "A film industry must be created for China that serves the interests of all its people and speaks clearly and truthfully on the burning issues of the day" (Leyda 1972, p. 182). These veteran film artists anticipated fulfilling the promise of the left-wing movement begun twenty years before. However, a nationwide campaign to criticize the Kunlun studio's *Wu Xun zhuan* (*The Life of Wu Xun*, 1950), directed by Sun Yu, effectively ended private film production in China and brought feature filmmaking to a standstill for more than a year.

Third-generation filmmakers plied their trade in a state-sponsored system that promoted "socialist realism" (*shehuizhuyi xianshizhuyi*) and "revolutionary romanticism" (*geming langmangzhuyi*), as opposed to the petit-bourgeois Hollywood style popular in pre-1949 Shanghai films. These artists came from divergent backgrounds, including the army, and though some learned how to make films either in Moscow or from Soviet filmmakers, their films with worker-peasant-soldier (*gongnongbing*) themes reflected distinctive aspects of Chinese history and culture (see table 2).

Precipitous political shifts beginning in 1957 sent shock waves through China's film industry. The anti-rightist campaign sidelined dozens of top directors, writers, performers, and critics and caused a number of pioneering films to be withdrawn. Yet with the Great Leap Forward the next year, film production quadrupled (with the help of five new provincial studios). Although many productions rated as hastily made collectivist propaganda, half a dozen bona fide classics were completed for the tenth anniversary of the People's Republic (1959).

Notable filmmakers and their films, 1949–2008

Filmmaker	Representative films
Shi Hui (1915–1957), actor-director	*Wo zhe yi beizi* (*This Life of Mine*; 1950)
Shui Hua (1916–1995), director	*Bai mao nü* (*The White-Haired Girl*; 1951)
Tian Hua (b. 1928), actress	*Bai mao nü* (*The White-Haired Girl*; 1951)
Lu Ban (1913–1976), director	*Liu hao men* (*Gate #6*; 1953)
Sun Daolin (1921–2007), actor	*Dujiang zhencha ji* (*Reconnaissance across the Yangzi*; 1954)
Tang Xiaodan (b. 1910), director	*Dujiang zhencha ji* (*Reconaissance across the Yangzi*; 1954)
Ke Ling (1905–1996), writer	*Bu ye cheng* (*The City that Never Sleeps*; 1957)
Wang Ping (1916–1990), director	*Liu Bao de gushi* (*The Story of Liu Bao Village*; 1957)
Zhao Dan (1915–1980), actor	*Lin Zexu* (1959)
Su Li (1919–2005), director	*Liu san jie* (*Third Sister Liu*; 1960)
Xie Jin (b. 1923), director	*Hongse niangzi jun* (*The Red Detachment of Women*; 1960), *Furong zhen* (*Hibiscus Town*; 1986)
Li Zhun (b. 1916), writer	*Li Shuangshuang* (1962)
Zhang Ruifang (b. 1918), actress	*Li Shuangshuang* (1962)
Xie Tieli (b. 1925), director	*Zao chun Eryue* (*Early Spring in February*; 1963)
Wu Yonggang (1907–1982), director	*Bashan yeyu* (*Evening Rain*; 1981)
Wu Yigong (b. 1938), director-administrator	*Chengnan jiushi* (*Memories of Old Beijing*; 1983)
Chen Kaige (b. 1952), director	*Huang tudi* (*Yellow Earth*; 1984)
Liu Shaoqing (b. 1951), actress	*Furong zhen* (*Hibiscus Town*; 1986)
Jiang Wen (b. 1963), actor-director	*Hong gaoliang* (*Red Sorghum*; 1987)
Zhang Yimou (b. 1950), director	*Qiu Ju da guansi* (*The Story of Qiu Ju*; 1992)
Gong Li (b. 1966), actress	*Bawang bie ji* (*Farewell My Concubine*; 1993)
Tian Zhuangzhuang (b. 1952), director	*Lan fengzheng* (*The Blue Kite*; 1993)
Jia Jiangke (b. 1970), director	*Xiaowu* (*Pickpocket*; 1997)
Wang Xiaoshuai (b. 1966), director	*Shiqisui de danche* (*Beijing Bicycle*; 2001)
Li Yang (b. 1959), director	*Mangjing* (*Blind Shaft*; 2003)

Table 2

The failure of the Great Leap Forward coincided with an unexpected flowering of Maoist cinema during the so-called thermidorean interregnum (1961–1964). In a famous June 1961 speech, Premier Zhou Enlai called for themes beyond simply workers, peasants, and soldiers, and for giving greater attention to quality and treatment. He thus implicitly signaled that directors should go beyond slavishly filming the screenplay. Unfortunately, what followed was the Cultural Revolution (1966–1969).

MAOIST CINEMA, 1966–1976: AN UNFORGETTABLE STRUGGLE

Feeling that the governing apparatus and ideology of the People's Republic was straying from its revolutionary origins, Mao issued a momentous clarion call, urging

Chinese film director Wang Feng (right), with actors Shum Lo and Au Yeung Sha Fei in Hong Kong, April, 1976. *During the early part of the twentieth century, a small but thriving film industry existed in China, as filmmakers portrayed traditional stories as well as contemporary politics on film. Many of these companies fled mainland China for Hong Kong, however, after the Japanese invasion of 1937, establishing a prolific film industry in the British colony.* DIRCK HALSTEAD/TIME & LIFE PICTURES/GETTY IMAGES

youths nationwide to carry out a revolution of the proletariat. In film, Mao's wife Jiang Qing did more than anyone else to frame a strict orthodoxy that turned the industry upside down. As early as 1964, the former Shanghai actress labeled ten films as "poisonous weeds." Not surprisingly, six of them came from the thaw period after the Great Leap Forward. By the onset of the Cultural Revolution two years later, nearly all Chinese feature films dating back to the silent era, more than 650 films, were similarly labeled. Along with the elitist petit-bourgeois Shanghai style of the 1930s, the entire previous seventeen years of Maoist cinema was condemned. Only three films continued to be shown through the decade of the Cultural Revolution (1966–1976), and feature-film production shut down for nearly seven years (1966–1973).

In place of feature films came filmed performances of eight model operas (*yangban xi*), beginning with *Hongdeng ji* (*The Red Lantern*) in 1970. Interestingly, these elaborately staged, exaggerated portrayals of moral uprightness and heroism were directed, often without credit, by prominent third-generation film artists whose previous works had been denounced. The sixty-four films made in Shanghai, Beijing, and Changchun between 1973 and 1976 amalgamated various talents. These included veteran filmmakers, the academically trained fourth-generation (whose careers had been in hiatus between 1966 and 1973), and an influx of newly recruited amateurs.

THE REFORM PERIOD, 1978–1989: CHINESE CINEMA REACHES THE WORLD STAGE

The "second liberation of thought" (*dierci sixiang jiefang*) after the Cultural Revolution ushered in a remarkable decade of angst, exploration, catharsis, and ultimately, internationally recognized cinematic achievements. The atmosphere in Deng Xiaoping's China was more open than even during the early 1960s. With liberalization came a desire to open up to the West, which brought unprecedented numbers of Western films and the powerful influence of Western culture.

Three generations of Chinese filmmakers operated in this freer atmosphere almost simultaneously. Several films from the third generation scrutinized recent Chinese history and politics in ways thought not possible before. Much has been written of the deprivations experienced by fifth-generation artists, who absorbed the fury of the Cultural Revolution in their youth, but many fourth-generation filmmakers waited twenty years before directing their first films. Schooled at the Beijing Film Academy (Beijing Dianying Xueyuan), they lived as students through the extreme hardship of the Great Leap Forward and began their careers in the exhilaration of the thermidorean period of relaxation. They also made stories critical of contemporary life (see table 2).

The fifth generation built on the successes of their predecessors even as they vowed to reject the "false history" (*wei lishi*) portrayed in Maoist cinema. To be sure, they were less tradition-bound and less willing simply to faithfully film scenarios as written. Their formative experiences caused them to question the Communist Party and government perspective. Unlike previous generations of filmmakers, few joined the Communist Party. They were also the first Chinese film artists to formally study film theory and aesthetics, and to immerse themselves in a study of U.S. and European cinema in place of the socialist realism of the Soviet bloc.

Many in the fifth generation, avoiding film centers that would have restricted their autonomy, began outside the studio system. The Guangxi Film Studio in South China and especially the Xi'an Film Studio in the Northwest proved crucial for their early successes. Yet rather than confronting contemporary issues directly, the new filmmakers typically grounded their films in the "old society" (*jiu shehui*) before 1949.

AFTER TIANANMEN, 1990–2008: POLITICS, FINANCIAL CRISIS, AND THE RISE OF THE SIXTH GENERATION

After being acknowledged internationally, top fifth-generation film artists sought to combine their distinctive aesthetics with more transparent social commentary, particularly after the traumatic June Fourth incident of 1989 (the Tiananmen Square massacre). Yet a persistent financial crisis plaguing Chinese cinema from 1987 generally dampened the innovativeness that made the fifth generation famous. Film attendance in China fell nearly 50 percent in a decade. Studios such as the Shanghai Film Corporation embraced new opportunities, chiefly in the form of popular television serials, but others, most notably the Changchun Film Studio, did not and as a consequence found themselves without capital to make films. Under these circumstances, fifth-generation filmmakers increasingly relied on supplemental financing from abroad to make their films, which predictably became more entertainment- and profit-oriented.

As the fifth generation evolved from using new artistic models to explore China's collective memory of history to simply making attractive entertainment films, a new group of Beijing Film Academy graduates emerged. Born during or even after the active phase of the Cultural Revolution (1966–1969), these film artists showed little curiosity for the political tribulations of the Maoist past or for the exotic, allegorical Chinese westerns popularized by the fifth generation. Perhaps because they were not connected to the studio system, they could focus, far more critically than any before them, on contemporary urban life, and especially on the unsettling effects of rapid modernization.

Often making feature films on shoestring budgets of less than US$100,000, the sixth generation relied hardly at all on literature for their film source material. Believing their visual images would be more powerful than the written words that former filmmakers had depended upon, they instilled in their films an edgy, documentary-like quality, with hand-held cameras, few dramatic or glamorous plot turns, and nonprofessionals cast even in leading roles. Iconoclastic protagonists in these films were silent, unrepentant individuals, but not extraordinary or heroic.

The earliest generation of filmmakers produced distinct Chinese film genres and emphasized themes of national resistance and sovereignty. Third- and fourth-generation filmmakers, active after the Anti-Japanese War (1937–1945), accepted the dictates of the Maoist revolution and so became the bridge linking the people to communist ideology. Finally, post-Mao era filmmakers of the last two generations carved out a rugged individualism and set new standards for film aesthetics. Yet the challenges facing Chinese cinema in the early twenty-first century are as much a product of the contemporary global economy as any previous domestic ills carried forward: increased competition for the entertainment dollar, higher capital-investment risks, and shrinking audiences.

SEE ALSO *New Year's Movies.*

BIBLIOGRAPHY

Chen Huangmei, ed. *Dangdai Zhongguo dianying* [Contemporary Chinese cinema]. 2 vols. Beijing: Zhongguo Shehui Kexue Chubanshe, 1989.

Cheng Jihua, Li Shaobai, and Xing Zuwen, eds. *Zhongguo dianying fazhanshi* [The historical development of Chinese cinema]. 2 vols. Beijing: Zhongguo Dianying Chubanshe, 1963.

Clark, Paul. *Chinese Cinema: Culture and Politics since 1949.* New York: Cambridge University Press, 1987.

Clark, Paul. *Reinventing China: A Generation and Its Films.* Hong Kong: Chinese University Press, 2005.

Hu Chang. *Xin Zhongguo dianying de yaolan* [The cradle of new China's cinema]. Changchun: Jilin Wenxue Chubanshe, 1986.

Hu Chang. *Manying: Guoce dianying mianmian guan* [Manying Studio: A look at all aspects of state-controlled films]. Changchun: Jilin Wenxue Chubanshe, 1989.

Leyda, Jay. *Dianying: An Account of Films and the Film Audience in China*. Cambridge, MA: MIT Press, 1972.

Li Suyuan and Hu Jubin. *Zhongguo wusheng dianying shi* [A history of Chinese silent films]. Beijing: Zhongguo Dianying Chubanshe, 1996.

Yin Hong and Ling Yan. *Xin Zhongguo dianying shi* [A history of new China's cinema, 1949–2000]. Changsha: Hunan Meishu Chubanshe, 2002.

Zhang Junxiang and Cheng Jihua, eds. *Zhongguo dianying da cidian* [Encyclopedia of Chinese cinema]. Shanghai: Shanghai Cishu Chubanshe, 1995.

Zhang Yingjin and Xiao Zhiwei, eds. *Encyclopedia of Chinese Film*. London: Routledge, 1998.

Zhongguo Dianyingjia Xiehui [Chinese Film Artists Association]. *Zhongguo dianyingjia liezhuan* [Biographies of Chinese film artists]. 7 vols. Beijing: Zhongguo Dianying Chubanshe, 1982–1986.

Gregory Lewis

FIFTH GENERATION FILMMAKERS

"Fifth generation" refers specifically to the 1982 graduating class of the Beijing Film Academy (Beijing Dianying Xueyuan), the first class to emerge from China's only film academy when it reopened in 1978, after being shut down for a decade during the Cultural Revolution. The end of the Maoist era brought a period of relative ideological openness, which, together with generous funding from the state, created the conditions for an unprecedented art-cinema movement. Taking stylistic cues from European art cinema, fifth-generation filmmakers used the opportunity to produce China's own new wave, a movement that culminated in the mid-1980s with the arrival of internationally acclaimed films like *One and Eight* (*Yige he bage*, Zhang Junzhao, 1984), *Yellow Earth* (*Huang tudi*, Chen Kaige, 1985), and *Horse Thief* (*Daomazei*, Tian Zhuangzhuang, 1985).

EMERGENCE OF THE NEW WAVE

In its infancy, the fifth generation did not have a clear group identity for distinctive cultural and stylistic aspirations. Though sharing the leitmotif of antitradition in its challenge of the established norms of Chinese cinema, the fifth generation's awareness of its group identity came only after critics called for the arrival of a new wave. What became the Chinese new wave was the overriding style and leitmotif of early fifth-generation films that challenged the norms of socialist-realist cinema and the Communist myth manufactured within the confines of such norms. All new-wave films have utilized, to varying degrees, the principles of art-cinema narration. From *One and Eight* to *Horse Thief*, there is a progression toward dedramatizing.

Prominent among this group of filmmakers, Chen Kaige, Tian Zhuangzhuang, Zhang Junzhao, and Zhang Yimou became famous for making experimental art films that challenged both the socialist-realist tradition of the Mao era and the classical, Hollywood-informed conventions of China's prerevolutionary cinema. The achievements of this small circle of filmmakers won global recognition for Chinese cinema in the mid to late 1980s.

The fifth generation initially engaged in highbrow formalist experimentation, seeking to divorce cinema from the melodramatic dramaturgical traditions of Chinese cinema and shadowplays. By the late 1980s the fifth generation's willful self-marginalization by its fascination with film form was taken by some critics as an attempt to conceal or compensate for a fundamental inability to construct classical narratives. Though they endeavored to leave the past behind in their creative practice, the fifth generation's very earnestness about art owed something to the edifying purposefulness of the socialist cinema of the 1930s and beyond, and they were still affected by the closely related admonishing film criticism and idealistic film practice of that didactic tradition. Sensitive in this way, the more the fifth generation was charged with narrative impotence, the more compelled filmmakers like Zhang Yimou felt to demonstrate otherwise. Zhang, a cinematographer before he emerged as a leading director, was eager to make a film that would combine formal experimentation with a classical plot structure. His directorial debut, *Red Sorghum* (*Hong gaoliang*, 1987), deliberately employed a popular narrative structure defined by goal-oriented characters who actively seek to solve a clear-cut problem. This was successfully coupled with an erotic display of richly colored props and ethnographic details. The resulting product, an art film with box-office potency, established a new direction for fifth-generation film.

COMMERCIALIZATION

A new coproduction approach utilizing international capital, global distribution networks, and multicultural audiences allowed fifth-generation filmmakers to produce a hybrid cinema that was still received as art film internationally even as it began to perform as commercial cinema domestically. Tian Zhuangzhuang's 1985 film *Horse Thief*, a nearly dialogue-free meditation on the remoteness of a place (Tibet) and its people, was highly regarded by film aficionados around the world, but nearly universally rejected by the popular audience at home. His next film, *The Blue Kite* (*Lan fengzheng*, 1993) was one of several fifth-generation films dealing with a subject closer to popular concerns in China (the Cultural Revolution and its historical antecedents), and featured a rich narrative gorgeously realized in supporting images. Meanwhile, the

Scene from* Curse of the Golden Flower, *2006. *The year 1982 marked the first graduating class of filmmakers from the Beijing Film Academy after a ten-year hiatus imposed during the Cultural Revolution. Known collectively as the Fifth Generation, these directors have earned international regard for their efforts, including Zhang Yimou's epic drama* Curse of the Golden Flower, *pictured above.* BEIJING NEW PICTURE FILM CO./SONY PICTURES CLASSICS/THE KOBAL COLLECTION/THE PICTURE DESK, INC.

director Chen Kaige traveled a similar route from films like *Yellow Earth* and *King of the Children* (*Haizi wang*, 1988) to *Farwell My Concubine* (*Bawang bie ji*, 1993), another treatment of the Cultural Revolution. The last film, which shared the Palme d'Or award (with Jane Campion's *The Piano*) at the 1993 Cannes Film Festival, was banned in China for its treatment of homosexuality and the brutality of the Cultural Revolution, but after it was unbanned, the popular reception was positive.

As China's film industry made the transition from state-supported institution to commercial practice in the early 1990s, other fifth-generation filmmakers made the same transition from sparse narrative, meditative pace, and thematically ambiguous experimentation to a more audience-driven hybrid cinema.

Cultural authorities—concerned with ideology, public morality, China's image abroad, and the ruling party's legitimacy—have at various times and for various reasons banned (and later unbanned) many fifth-generation films and/or blacklisted the filmmakers. International criticism has often treated fifth-generation films as political allegories primarily, and has assumed that political content accounted for most of the run-ins with the censors. The filmmakers themselves, however, have not always agreed with this critical emphasis.

In the twenty-first century, Zhang Yimou and Chen Kaige have led the way in a new trend toward creating big-budget, Hollywood-style Chinese blockbusters for international consumption. Zhang's *Hero* (*Yingxiong*, 2002), *House of Flying Daggers* (*Shimian maifu*, 2004), and *Curse of the Golden Flower* (*Man cheng jin dai huangjin jia*, 2006), and Chen's *The Promise* (*Wuji*, 2005) are the most expensive productions ever mounted in China. Each is a historical epic, similar to popular Chinese-television period serials and in the mold of the Taiwanese director Ang Lee's *Crouching Tiger, Hidden Dragon* (*Wo hu, cang long*, 2000). Each is also an attempt to employ big budgets, star power, sophisticated special effects, and major promotional campaigns to achieve blockbuster results, after the Hollywood blockbuster model. All have been favored by the state, which has actively encouraged the development of Chinese cinema along these lines at least since the stunning box-office success of Hollywood's *Titanic* (1997) in China.

As a result of varying degrees of state support and domestic and international recognition, the practice and position of fifth-generation filmmakers has shifted. Succeeded by a less homogeneous sixth generation, they are no longer China's cinematic avant-garde. In fact, figures like Zhang Yimou, Chen Kaige, and Tian Zhuangzhuang constitute something like a film establishment in China. Zhang Yimou in particular has become a kind of semi-official cultural ambassador to the world, traveling to Italy and the United States to direct major operas on stage, serving on international-film-festival juries, and directing China's 2008 Summer Olympics Opening Ceremonies, even as he continues to make movies.

SEE ALSO *Chen Kaige; Feng Xiaogang; Zhang Yimou.*

BIBLIOGRAPHY

Berry, Chris, ed. *Perspectives on Chinese Cinema.* London: BFI Publishers, 1991.

Rayns, Tony. Screening China. *Sight and Sound* 1, 3 (July 1991): 26–28.

Zhang, Yingjin. *Chinese National Cinema.* New York: Routledge, 2004.

Zhu, Ying. *Chinese Cinema during the Era of Reform: The Ingenuity of the System.* Westport, CT: Praeger Publishers, 2003.

Ying Zhu

SIXTH GENERATION FILMMAKERS

Most of the sixth generation filmmakers are 1985 or 1987 graduates from Beijing Film Academy (Beijing Dianying Xueyuan), who started to make independent films in the 1990s. Emerging in the reform era, in which marketization and globalization dominate the contemporary sociopolitical scene, they present, as Yingjin Zhang has pointed out, "different configurations of cultural production, artistic pursuit, political control, ideological positioning, and institutional restructuring" (Yingjin Zhang 2007). Representative sixth generation filmmakers include Lou Ye, Zhang Yuan, Wang Xiaoshuai, Jia Zhangke, Lu Xuechang, Guan Hu, Wu Wenguang, Jiang Wen, He Jianjun, Zhang Ming, and Li Yang, and their films include:

Guan Hu: *Toufa luanle* (*Dirt*), 1994

He Jianjun: *Youchai* (*Postman*), 1995

Jia Zhangke: *Xiao Wu* (*Xiao Wu*), 1998; *Zhantai* (*Platform*), 2000; *Ren xiaoyao* (*Unknown Pleasures*), 2002

Lou Ye: *Zhoumo qingren* (*Weekend Lover*), 1994; *Suzhou he* (*Suzhou River*), 2000

Wang Xiaoshuai: *Jidu hanleng* (*Frozen*), 1995; *Biandan guniang* (*So Close to Paradise*), 1998; *Shiqishui de danche* (*Beijing Bicycle*), 2000

Zhang Yuan: *Beijing zazhong* (*Beijng Bastards*), 1992; *Donggong xigong* (*East Palace, West Palace*), 1996

Sixth-generation cinema is sometimes designated as "post–fifth generation cinema," "Chinese underground/independent film," "dissident film," and "urban-generation cinema" (Dai 2000, p. 74). These various labels have generated intense discussions on the accuracy of their uses. Many critics think that sixth generation directors are not "underground" filmmakers. Chen Mo and Zhiwei Xiao remind us that "many underground filmmakers are employed in the mainstream film industry and have done well within the conventional film establishment" (Pickowicz and Zhang 2007, p. 144). Many scholars prefer to label films by these young filmmakers as "independent," rather than "underground," as they are politically uncontroversial, technically poorly made, and thematically rooted in individual values (Pickowicz and Zhang 2007, p. 148).

Many critics claim that the popularity of Chinese underground cinema in the West resulted from its status as an alternative to Zhang Yimou's films, which have become all too familiar (Dai 1997, p. 380). Some argue that the "underground" label in Western discourse about newborn-generation film betrays an ideological agenda (Chen and Shi 2003, p. 390). Underground filmmakers in China are suspected of making politically dissident films for Western viewers (Pickowicz and Zhang 2007, p. 13).

SIXTH GENERATION FILMS VERSUS FIFTH GENERATION FILMS

The sixth generation's films depart remarkably from those of the fifth generation's, both in film language and artistic vision. The sublime landscape and glorious colors of fifth generation films are replaced by raw and grainy images in the sixth generation's films. In contrast to the fifth generation's desire to tell good stories professionally, the sixth generation often employs nonprofessional actors and allows improvisations to create a documentary-like narrative of everyday life.

Sixth generation films also differ from the fifth generation's in terms of their cinematic treatment of space, gender relationships, and political issues. Fifth generation films, (such as Chen Kaige's *Yellow Earth* (*Huang tudi*) and Zhang Yimou's *Raise the Red Lantern* (*Da hong denglong gaogaogua*), are usually set in traditional rural China and are depoliticized on the surface. In contrast, sixth generation films usually are set in cities and depict ordinary citizen's lives, for example He Jianjun's *Postman*

Movie Still from* Beijing Bicycle*, directed by Wang Xiaoshuai. *Departing from the colorful films of the Fifth Generation, China's Sixth Generation of graduates from the Beijing Film Academy have earned notice for their gritty, documentary-type films examining socioeconomic changes in the country.* © COLUMBIA PICTURES/COURTESY EVERETT COLLECTION

(*Youchai*) and Wang Xiaoshuai's *So Close to Paradise* (*Biandan guniang*), or openly go against mainstream ideologies by filming marginal lives and providing alternatives to mainstream culture, for instance Guan Hu's *Dirt* (*Toufa luan le*), Zhang Yuan's *Beijng Bastards* (*Beijing zazhong*), and Wang Xiaoshuai's *Frozen* (*Jidu hanleng*). Fifth generation films are usually allegorical tales exhibiting many aspects of "ethnic" Chinese culture in exotic and often erotic forms (Lu 1997, p. 113). In contrast, Chinese independent filmmakers often deal directly with their subjects by openly embracing sexuality. Heterosexuality and homosexuality are openly represented and explored in such sixth generation films as Zhang Yuan's *East Palace, West Palace* (*Donggong xigong*). Fifth generation films still reflect a sense of common culture, while sixth generation films are very individual and personal, each with its own style.

LOU YE

The sixth generation filmmaker Lou Ye was born in Shanghai in 1965, and later attended Beijing Film Academy. Lou Ye's graduation film, *Weekend Lover* (*Zhoumo qingren*, 1994), won the Rainer Werner Fassbinder Prize for Best Director at the Mannheim-Heidelberg Film Festival in 1996. This film, a forerunner of sixth generation films, depicts the lives of a group of discontented young people in Shanghai during the 1980s and early 1990s. Eschewing the loaded historical and cultural themes in films made by the fifth generation, *Weekend Lover* shifts the focus from traditional rural China to contemporary urban lives and individuals. The film marvelously captures restless Chinese urban youth, full of energy and unsatisfied with reality.

Lou Ye later made *Suzhou River* (*Suzhou he*, 2000), winner of the VPRO Tiger Award at the 29th Rotterdam Film Festival 2000. This film is structured around the Suzhou River, which runs through Shanghai. River scenery and the lives of people who live by the river are all captured by a shaky camera, which produces an aesthetic effect similar to impressionistic paintings. Rather than the splendorous images of most movies set in Shanghai, *Suzhou River* presents the rather dark and decrepit aspects of the city: unemployed youth, suicides, lawless businessmen, adultery, kidnapping, and murder. This chaotic situation somewhat reflects social reality in the post-Mao era. The nostalgic, critical monologue of the film is representative of the aesthetic tendencies of sixth generation films.

ZHANG YUAN

Zhang Yuan, a primary figure of the sixth generation, highlights the vibrant underground cultural scene in his works. For instance, in *East Palace, West Palace* he represents and explores homosexuality, and in *Beijing Bastards*, he features Cui Jian, the father of Chinese rock. As Yingjin Zhang points out, "By featuring Cui Jian as both a star in and a producer of *Beijing Bastards*, Zhang Yuan was quick to forge an alliance between rock music and cinematic rebellion in China" (Zhang Zhen 2007, p. 61).

WANG XIAOSHUAI

Wang Xiaoshuai, a 1989 graduate from Beijing Film Academy, is one of the better-known sixth generation filmmakers in film festival audiences. He tends to feature marginal characters in his films, such as the artist Qi Lei in *Frozen*, and the young migrants in *So Close to Paradise. Beijing Bicycle* (*Shiqisui de danche*, 2000) juxtaposes and intertwines the lives of two teenage protagonists: Gui, a rural migrant, and Jian, a Beijing teenager. Despite obvious differences between Gui and Jian—such as class, fate, and rural/urban origins—both of them live in back alleys (Gui lives with a fellow countryman, and Jian lives with his reassembled family), and their fates are linked by a bicycle, once a necessity in Beijing, now a symbol of wealth for urban youth. By telling the story of these two teenagers, *Beijing Bicycle* grapples with the social issues stemming from China's fast-paced urbanization, commercialization, and globalization.

JIA ZHANGKE

Jia Zhangke's films, which have garnered numerous international awards, address the changing social landscape of China, treating themes of alienated youth, urban development, and globalization. Jia uses nonprofessional actors and on-location improvisation of dialogues to portray marginal characters and alienated youth. Many of his earlier films—such as *Xiao Wu* (1998), *Platform* (*Zhantai*, 2000), and *Unknown Pleasure* (*Ren xiaoyao*, 2002)—are set in Shanxi Province, Jia's home region, and are often thick with nostalgia. The images in these earlier films are often raw and grainy as a result of his use of hand-held cameras. *The World* (*Shijie*, 2004), a later film, was his first made with official government approval. The film depicts the lives of displaced migrants in Beijing's World Park (a theme park featuring important landmarks from all over the world). The relationship between the subjects and the place is temporal, opportunistic, commercial, and staged. On the one hand, they are "global" beings living in "globalized surroundings"; on the other, they are trapped in this "prison" of make-believe (the World Park).

BIBLIOGRAPHY

Chen Xihe and Shi Chuan. *Duoyuan yujing zhong de xinshengdai dianying: Zhongguo xinshengdai dianying lunwenji* [Newborn-generation films in multiple contexts: Essays on Chinese newborn-generation film]. Shanghai: Xuelin Chubanshe, 2003.

Dai Jinhua. *Wu zhong fengjing* [A scene in fog]. Beijing: Beijing Daxue Chubanshe, 2000.

Lu, Sheldon, ed. *Transnational Chinese Cinema: Identity, Nationhood, Gender*. Honolulu: University of Hawaii Press, 1997.

Pickowicz, Paul G., and Yingjin Zhang, eds. *From Underground to Independent: Alternative Film Culture in Contemporary China*. Lanham, MD: Rowman and Littlefield, 2007.

Yingjin Zhang. Rebel without a Cause? China's New Urban Generation and Postsocialist Filmmaking. In *The Urban Generation: Chinese Cinema and Society at the Turn of the Twenty-first Century*, ed. Zhang Zhen, 52–53. Durham, NC: Duke University Press, 2007.

Jing Nie

HONG KONG

Since the advent of talking pictures, Hong Kong cinema has exerted such an influence far beyond its borders that it earned the title "Hollywood of the East." There was some filmmaking during the silent era, but on a far more modest scale. A Shanghai-based film company shot what is reportedly the colony's first short, *Tou shaoya* (*Stealing the Roast Duck*), in 1909. Four years later, the first wholly Hong Kong–produced dramatic short film, *Zhuangzi shi qi* (*Zhuangzi Tests His Wife*), was produced and directed by Lai Man-wai (Li Minwei), today acknowledged as the father of Hong Kong cinema. After World War I, he cofounded China Sun (Minxin), Hong Kong's first full-fledged film studio, and produced Hong Kong's first feature-length dramatic film, *Yanzhi* (*Rouge*; 1924).

But the film industry did not really take off till the mid-1930s and the establishment of the British colony as the main producer of Cantonese-dialect motion pictures, due in part to the Chinese government's discouragement of dialect-cinema production in Guangzhou. An important export market to the Chinese diaspora in Southeast Asia and North America accelerated Hong Kong's annual output to nearly 100 features by the early 1940s. With the Japanese invasion of December 1941, however, production came to a total halt that lasted for four years.

After World War II, Hong Kong's primacy as greater China's number one filmmaking center was cemented by the civil-war disruption of the Mandarin commercial movie business in Shanghai and the emigration to Hong

Movie still from* Bullet in the Head, *directed by John Woo, 1990. *In the 1990s, the Hong Kong movie industry began to receive greater recognition for its contributions to filmmaking. Actors such as Jackie Chan and Jet Li became stars in Hollywood productions, and directors such as John Woo earned greater recognition among a new audience of moviegoers.* **© TAI SENG/COURTESY EVERETT COLLECTION**

Kong of a large number of its leading producers, directors, and stars. By the early 1960s, over 250 features were produced annually in the colony, with Cantonese the primary dialect, followed by the Mandarin, Chaozhou (Teochow), and Xiamen (Amoy) dialects. The film industry was further divided by pro-Communist and pro-Nationalist ideologies. Features produced by left-wing studios, such as *Changcheng* (*Great Wall*) and *Feng Huang*, were eligible for release in mainland theaters and banned in Taiwan, with the opposite situation prevailing for Hong Kong's right-wing film companies, which were in the majority.

Hong Kong cinema embraced a wide variety of genres, from Cantonese opera, Western-style musicals, and costume dramas to contemporary comedies and Chinese martial arts. Changing trends led to the virtual extinction of traditional Cantonese movie-making by 1970 and the dominance of Mandarin as the dialect of choice throughout much of the decade. By the 1980s the language issue had become moot, as films were no longer shot with synchronized sound but were primarily dubbed, with Cantonese versions released in Hong Kong and Mandarin versions exported to markets such as Singapore and Taiwan.

From the 1950s to the 1980s, Hong Kong's largest studio was Shaw Brothers (Shao Shi Xiongdi), a sprawling filmmaking complex whose product was released in its own multinational theater chain. In the late 1960s the Shaws helped develop a new style of martial-arts adventure that redefined the popular nature of Hong Kong cinema. Chief rival in this genre was Golden Harvest (Jiahe), a studio that came to prominence in the 1970s with the kung fu pictures of Bruce Lee (Li Xiaolong) and Jackie Chan (Cheng Long), Hong Kong's first bona fide international superstars.

In the 1970s and 1980s, new life was breathed into the film industry by the Hui Brothers (Xu Shi Xiongdi), Michael and Sam, and their fresh approach to purely local

WONG KAR-WAI

Wong Kar-wai (Wang Jiawei), born in 1958, and whose family came to Hong Kong from Shanghai in 1961, went from writing and directing for commercial television to world fame as a film director. His postmodern style reflects the insubstantiality of Hong Kong as a colony: culturally autonomous but politically dependent. Throughout his career Wong used the prize-winning avant-garde cinematographer Christopher Doyle to provide a distinctive look and feel for his films. He also used such popular stars as Leslie Cheung, Maggie Cheung, Tony Leung, Brigette Lin, and Takeshi Kaneshiro.

His only commercial hit was his first feature film, *As Tears Go By* (*Wangjiao kamen*, 1988), an epic of family loyalty among small-time mobsters. *Days of Being Wild* (*A Fei zhengzhuan*, 1991), starring Leslie Cheung as a moody Hong Kong playboy, was a box-office disappointment but also a transition into the global art-house genre, in which the plot is less striking than ambience and character. *Ashes of Time* (*Dong xie xi du*, 1994; reissued as *Ashes of Time Redux*, 2008) is a reinvention of the martial arts film. The characters brood introspectively on their fates, and the sequence of action is nonlinear. In a break from shooting *Ashes of Time*, Wong used the cast to make *Chungking Express* (*Chongqing senlin*, 1995), which became a critical favorite. The film comprises two aleatory, almost improvised vignettes of nightlife in Hong Kong's Kowloon district, each centered on a romance, which, by implication, is just as ephemeral as the British lease on Hong Kong set to expire in 1997. *Fallen Angels* (*Duoluo tianshi*, 1995) is a sequel. *Happy Together* (*Chunguang zhaxie*, 1997) features Tony Leung and Leslie Cheung as an ill-fated Hong Kong gay couple in vibrant Brazil. *In the Mood for Love* (*Huayang nianhua*, 2000) and *2046* (2004), set in a hotel room with that number, intertwine characters and portents from *Days of Being Wild* to form a Hong Kong trilogy. In Wong's work, Hong Kong film found a distinctive native product which transcended commercialism and entered the international art world.

BIBLIOGRAPHY

Bordwell, David. *Planet Hong Kong: Popular Cinema and the Art of Entertainment.* Cambridge, MA: Harvard University Press, 2000.

Brunette, Peter and Kar-wai Wong. *Wong Kar-wai.* Urbana: Univsersity of Illinois Press, 2005.

Teo, Stephen. *Wong Kar-wai: Auteur of Time.* London: British Film Institute, 2005.

Charles W. Hayford

comedy. A new wave of young filmmakers such as Allen Fong (Fang Yuping), Tsui Hark (Xu Ke), and Lawrence Ah Mon (Liu Guochang), many of them graduates from overseas film schools who served their apprenticeship in Hong Kong television, made movies that attempted to break away from mainstream conventions.

By the early 1990s, Hong Kong cinema had entered a new golden age in terms of productivity and popularity, both at home and throughout East Asia. Hollywood took note, and top directors such as John Woo (Wu Yusen) and stars like Chow Yun-fat (Zhou Runfa), Jet Li (Li Lianjie), and Jackie Chan became the first members of Hong Kong's film community to find acceptance with mainstream American audiences in mainstream American films.

On the home front, Stephen Chow (Zhou Xingchi) and his brand of *moleitau* (*wulitou*) screwball farce, was number one at the box office, while on the art-film circuit, movies by Wong Kar-wai (Wang Jiawei) enjoyed unprecedented critical acclaim.

Such successes could not stave off the depression that engulfed the Hong Kong film industry by the mid-1990s and continued unabated over a decade later. It was created by a confluence of factors, including escalating ticket prices, the rise of digital home entertainment, the Internet, the prevalence of digital piracy, and the public's growing apathy toward relatively lackluster new productions and the dearth of new stars. Since the 1997 return of Hong Kong to Chinese sovereignty, there has been a gradual opening up of the China market and greater cooperation between producers and artists on both sides of the border—factors that bode well for the industry as a whole. While vast mainland Chinese audiences may be a potential savior in financial terms, catering to them is another matter. Issues of censorship and access aside, the kind of big-budget Pan-Asian spectacles that found box-office favor in the early twenty-first century threaten to so nullify the local character of Hong Kong cinema that it is in real danger of eventually becoming just another homogenous cog in the nation's vast filmmaking apparatus.

SEE ALSO *Hong Kong.*

BIBLIOGRAPHY

Fonoroff, Paul. *Silver Light: A Pictorial History of Hong Kong Cinema, 1920–1970.* Hong Kong: Joint Publishing Company, 1997.

Fonoroff, Paul. *At the Hong Kong Movies: 600 Reviews from 1988 Till the Handover.* Hong Kong: Film Biweekly Publishing House, 1998.

Paul Fonoroff

TAIWAN

Taiwan's volatile history and complex colonial experience has had a marked effect on the film industry. The commercial sector in Taiwan's film industry has not been

Film still from* Yi Yi, *directed by Edward Yang, 2000. *As film production slowed in mainland China, Taiwan's film industry thrived during the 1960s and 1970s, distributing films to the Chinese diaspora in the region. While fewer movies have been made since then, Taiwanese films continue to earn international attention, as evidenced by Edward Yang's best director award at the Cannes Film Festival for* Yi Yi.

buoyant, and film production has been supported primarily by the state. The most important film producer in postwar Taiwan has been Central Motion Pictures Company (Zhongyang Dianying Gongsi), run until 2005 by the Guomindang (Nationalist Party). This company was regarded as the cradle of Taiwanese New Cinema of the 1980s and 1990s, and since 1990, government film subsidies have been the most important source of funding for producing art films and developing new talent.

Film was introduced into Taiwan by the Japanese around 1900–1901. Early Japanese production in Taiwan served propaganda purposes. The first locally made feature film, *Shei zhi guo* (Whose fault is this?), was released in 1925. After the Guomindang took over Taiwan, the local film industry remained inactive, and it was not until 1950 that the first postwar Taiwanese film, *Alishan fengyun* (Storm on Mount Ali), was released. In the mid-1950s the production of films in the Taiwanese dialect effectively launched Taiwan's film industry, although the popularity of these films began to decline in the 1960s as Mandarin films came to dominate film production. During this period, Central Motion Pictures embarked on the production of healthy realist (*jiankang xieshi*) films, which emphasized positive postwar developments and offered moral lessons for an increasingly modernized society.

Taiwan's film industry boomed in the 1960s to the mid-1970s, since the Chinese market on the mainland was closed, and the need for Chinese films in the global market was huge. Taiwanese film production reached its peak in 1968, when the island boasted the second biggest film industry in the world (second to Japan). Two genres became increasingly dominant during this time: kung fu films and romantic melodramas. Directors such as Li Xing (Lee Hsing), Bai Jingrui (Pai Ching-jui), Hu Jinquan (King Hu), and Li Hanxiang came to be regarded by some as the founding fathers of early postwar Taiwanese cinema.

When the Republican government encountered a series of diplomatic setbacks in the 1970s, there emerged a wave of anticommunist propaganda films condemning communism and advocating patriotic sentiments. However, audiences in the 1970s did not respond positively to propaganda films. By the end of the decade, the survival of this once prosperous industry seemed in question. The market was dominated by Hollywood films, and the increasing popularity of video also affected cinema attendance.

In the early 1980s Central Motion Pictures sought to reenergize the film industry by investing in new talent and making two portmanteau films: *Guangyin de gushi* (*A Story in Our Time*) in 1982 and *Erzi de da wan'ou* (*The Sandwich Man*) in 1983. These two low-budget productions comprised several short films by different young directors and won both critical acclaim and box-office success. This success encouraged Central Motion Pictures to increase production of similar films. From this first wave of New Cinema emerged such important directors as Hou Xiaoxian (Hou Hsiao-hsien), Yang Dechang (Edward Yang), Chen Kunhou (Chen Kun-hou), and Wan Ren (Wan Jen), who drew significant international attention.

In contrast to the unrealistic or patriotic films of the past, New Cinema reflected the lives of ordinary people in Taiwan. The works of these directors generally depicted a gradually opening industrial society in a variety of aesthetic styles, with a shared philosophy close to that of Italian neorealism. Because it engaged with Taiwan's transition to modernity, this body of work played an important role in the development of contemporary Taiwanese identity.

In addition to Central Motion Pictures' support of new talent, the state also started subsidizing art films in 1990. As a result, a second generation of New Cinema emerged to deal with such contemporary issues as urbanization, industrialization, and sexuality. Prominent directors of this period include Li An (Ang Lee), Cai Mingliang (Tsai Ming-liang), and Lin Zhengsheng (Lin Cheng-sheng). During the same period, the documentary emerged as a new medium and an alternative forum for new talent.

The emergence of New Cinema in the early 1980s gave the Taiwanese film industry an injection of energy and international recognition. Directors such as Hou Xiaoxian, Yang Dechang, Cai Mingliang, and Li An won major awards at international film festivals. Yet the international and critical success of New Cinema was not mirrored in the domestic market, where audiences preferred entertainment to art cinema. Taiwan's film industry in the late 1980s was torn between producing art films and providing entertainment, a tension never resolved.

Despite government investment, the film industry has not developed significantly. Between 1996 and 2007, Taiwanese-made films never accounted for more than 11 percent of the local market, and since Taiwan joined the

HOU HSIAO-HSIEN

Hou Hsiao-hsien (Hou Xiaoxian), a Taiwan filmmaker who, starting in the early 1980s, built a global reputation for Taiwan arthouse film along with Edward Yang (Yang Decheng) and Tsai Ming-liang (Cai Mingliang). Hou's films of Taiwan everyday life and history are restrained and meditative but deeply emotional, original but grounded in world film. Born in Meixian, Guangdong, in 1947 to a Hakka family that moved the following year to Taiwan, Hou studied at the National Taiwan Academy of the Arts but did not start to make feature films until he was nearly forty.

His early releases are autobiographically based chronicles of the smothered ambitions of energetic youth in small-town Taiwan, reminiscent of films by the Italian neorealist directors and the Japanese director Ozu Yasujirō. He is best known for his Taiwan trilogy: *A City of Sadness* (*Beiqing chengshi*, 1989) displays with chilling calm the destruction of a family during the White Terror of 1945–1949, including the February 28 incident of 1947, as the Nationalist Government ruthlessly established control; *The Puppet Master* (*Ximeng rensheng*, 1993) stars an actual puppet master portraying his own life under Japanese colonial rule; and *Good Men, Good Women* (*Haonan haonü*, 1996) follows Communist cell members who fought the Japanese on the mainland in the 1940s but were suppressed in the 1950s in Taiwan.

In other work, *Goodbye South, Goodbye* (*Nanguo zaijian, nanguo*, 1996) returns to the theme of working-class village youth migrating to the city. *Flowers of Shanghai* (*Haishang hua*, 1998) is an exquisitely composed film set in 1880s Shanghai "flower houses" (houses for sing-song girls). Hou's later films reprise and elaborate his earlier themes. *Millennium Mambo* (*Qianxi Manbo*, 2001) is set in the demimonde of present-day Taibei. *Café lumière* (2003) was made in Japan as a tribute to Ozu. In *Three Times* (*Zui hao de shiguang*, 2005), two lovers appear in a 1911 episode, then return in 1966 and 2005. *Le voyage du ballon rouge* (2006) is an homage to the 1956 French film *Ballon rouge*.

Charles Hayford

World Trade Organization in 2001, Hollywood films have further come to dominate in Taiwan.

SEE ALSO *Lee, Ang.*

BIBLIOGRAPHY

Berry, Chris, and Feii Lu, eds. *Island on the Edge: Taiwan New Cinema and After.* Hong Kong: Hong Kong University Press, 2005.

Chen, Ruxiu. *Taiwan xin dianying de lishi wenhua jingyan* [The historical and cultural experience of Taiwan's New Cinema]. Taibei: Wanxiang Tushu, 1993.

Davis, Darrell William, and Ru-shou Robert Chen, eds. *Cinema Taiwan: Politics, Popularity and State of the Arts.* Abingdon, U.K.: Routledge, 2007.

Lu Feiyi. *Taiwan dianying: Zhengzhi, jingji, meixue, 1949–1994* [Taiwan cinema: Politics, economy, aesthetics from 1949 to 1994]. Taibei: Yuanliu, 1998.

Lu, *Tonglin. Confronting Modernity in the Cinemas of Taiwan and Mainland China.* Cambridge, U.K.: Cambridge University Press, 2007.

Yeh, Emilie Yueh-yu, and Darrell William Davis. *Taiwan Film Directors: A Treasure Island.* New York: Columbia University Press, 2005.

Bi-yu Chang

FINANCIAL MARKETS

China's financial markets have been developing rapidly since 1978, when the country's economic transition began. A financial market is a mechanism for buying and selling financial instruments, including cash, securities (e.g., stocks and bonds), and commodities (e.g., agricultural goods and precious metals). Sociologists also use the term *financial markets* to refer more generally to the structure of ongoing exchange ties among buyers and sellers of financial resources. During economic transition, China's banking system has changed dramatically, and the government's role in banking has been altered in ways that affect both banks and their customers. Two stock markets have also emerged in China, providing a forum for buying and selling corporate equities much like Western stock exchanges.

Restructuring relations among the state, banks, and firms to increase the efficiency of capital allocation has been central to the reform of China's financial markets. As a result, changes in the structure and functioning of state-owned enterprises and the development of the financial markets are intertwined. While the scale and availability of financial resources for Chinese firms; the transformed relationship of the state, banks, and firms; and inequalities arising as the financial markets evolve are discussed here, more comprehensive treatments of issues such as bond, futures, and derivatives markets; venture capital; mortgage; insurance; investment; foreign-exchange-rate policy; and the entry of foreign financial institutions are available for those who want more detail (see Calomiris 2007, Neftci and Ménager-Xu 2007).

THE CHANGING ROLE OF BANKS

In pre-reform China, there were no financial markets and no central bank. Rather, the state controlled the entire banking system. The State Council issued currency and administered loans to enterprises. Banks existed as state agencies responsible for enacting and enforcing government monetary policy. State-owned enterprises and banks operated on a transfer system of credit controlled by the government bureaus (Keister 2002, 2004). Bargaining for scarce capital was common, and financing was highly uncertain because funding varied with state political whims and the personal allegiances of high-ranking officials. While firms depended on the state for all inputs, the state also depended on firms to provide scarce resources to other enterprises and to provide employees with jobs, housing, medical care, and other social services. The interdependence between the state and enterprises created soft budget constraints for firms (Kornai 1986); that is, when state-owned enterprises spent over their budget limits, the state could (and often did) grant them additional funds. This practice rewarded and encouraged inefficiency and waste. State bureaus attempted to monitor many enterprise activities to prevent waste and to curtail budget problems. However, the need to monitor a large number of firms made it difficult for bureaucrats to monitor enterprises effectively, and informational asymmetries favoring enterprises allowed managers to hoard resources and bargain for favorable treatment (Walder 1992).

In 1978 Chinese state reformers began to implement extensive economic reforms, including reform of firm finance and the banking system. The People's Bank of China was separated from the Ministry of Finance and became the central bank in 1984 (Keister 2002, 2004). It gradually assumed control of the money supply and began to set monetary policy and regulate exchange rates. Under the People's Bank of China, four large state-owned commercial banks—the Agricultural Bank, the Bank of China, the Construction Bank, and the Industrial and Commercial Bank—emerged as financial intermediaries and gradually began to accept deposits and to lend capital independently of government intervention. Firms applied for funds, and their requests were increasingly evaluated on the merit of the firm and the application. By the end of the 1980s, Chinese firms begun to acquire capital from a variety of sources: banks, other firms, public debt, and foreign sources.

Since the mid-1990s, the state has accelerated banking-system reform to further separate commercial and policy financing and reduce the ratio of nonperforming loans in the four state-owned commercial banks. Three policy banks—the China Development Bank, the Agricultural Development Bank of China, and the Export-Import Bank

An investor examining stock market activity at day's end, Shanghai, January 23, 2008. *After over fifty years of inactivity, the Shanghai Stock Exchange resumed trading in China in 1990, followed by the formation of the Shenzhen Stock Exchange one year later. As interest rates issued by the People's Bank of China remain low, many citizens have opted to invest in the stock market, leading to a large demand for scarce shares of stock.* © NIR ELIAS/REUTERS/CORBIS

of China—were established in 1994. After the policy banks took over the function of providing policy financing, the state-owned commercial banks were allowed to focus on commercial lending. Four asset-management companies were established in 1999, and each was partnered with one of the four state-owned commercial banks to absorb their nonperforming loans. The state-owned commercial banks also received new capital injection from the China Development Bank (Brandt and Zhu 2007). However, the state-owned commercial banks remained state-owned, and their lending at times reflected state policy more than the financial objectives of the banks (Branstetter 2007).

THE EMERGENCE OF STOCK MARKETS

The emergence of stock markets has also been an important part of the development of financial markets in China. China now has two active, internationally recognized stock exchanges: the Shanghai Stock Exchange (reopened in 1990), and the Shenzhen Stock Exchange, established in 1991 (Chan, Fung, and Thapa 2007). Since the 1990s initial public offerings in stock markets have played an important role in the partial privatization of large state-owned enterprises (Hu 2007). By 2005 the two exchanges had more than 1,300 firms listed. Although the development of stock markets is intended to increase firm access to external capital, listing on the exchanges is tightly controlled. Only a small number of firms are listed on the exchanges each year, and those are carefully selected. Perhaps even more important, the state retains a controlling stake in most publicly traded firms in key industries, and such shares are not traded on the market. The Chinese government has also selected some of the best assets of the best-performing state-owned enterprises to be listed on the Hong Kong Stock Exchange (called H shares) or foreign stock markets.

IMPACTS AND INEQUALITIES

China's market transition has been state-initiated, regional, and experimental. The pace and scope of financial-market reform has been largely controlled by the state, and increasing the efficiency of state-owned enterprises has been a primary motive of the reforms. The financial system remains dominated by state-owned banks, with the state-owned commercial banks still controlling about 60 percent of banking assets in China. State dominance and the priority given to state-owned enterprises may exacerbate regional and sectoral disparities and increase social inequalities.

From early in the reform, the state encouraged markets to develop in certain regions before others. Coastal regions benefited disproportionately from these measures and have since developed more rapidly than other areas. The development of financial markets was fairly typical. Special economic zones and special trade regions allowed markets for certain financial instruments to develop more quickly in those areas. Coastal areas developed first, with other regions lagging behind. In addition, firms in poorly developed regions borrow differently from firms in more developed regions, and hence may adapt more slowly to reform. Their being slow to adapt may in turn result in long-term inequalities in firm well-being and related inequalities in worker well-being. The result of China's plan to introduce reforms gradually by region may be that long-term regional inequalities become even more extreme.

The coexistence of various types of firm ownership has been a hallmark of China's reform. State-owned banks are obliged to grant loans to state-owned enterprises (usually for political rather than economic reasons), even though of the bank loans to state-owned enterprises in the 1990s, more than half, it is estimated, turned into nonperforming loans (Brandt and Zhu 2007). This is potentially problematic because limited access to capital may hinder the growth of private firms. Fearing discrimination in capital allocation, many private firms chose a vague property-right arrangement to minimize the costs of raising external funds (Nee 1992, Chen 2007).

Household income inequality has grown since the start of reform (Nee 1991, Keister forthcoming), and some byproducts of financial market development have the potential to exacerbate income and wealth inequality. Although China's household saving rate has been high, ordinary savers have benefited little, because the People's Bank of China has kept interest rates low (Brandt and Zhu 2007). Stock-market investing, including speculation by households with limited capital, has become common. The limited supply of stocks and the lack of other investment venues have led to an overheated stock market with irrational pricing, rampant insider trading, and high volatility that has the potential to harm households with limited savings (Green and Liu 2005). Households with significant capital may be able to weather dramatic fluctuations in stock prices, but ordinary households may suffer as a result of these extremes.

FUTURE DEVELOPMENT

China's financial markets, even in transition, "have still managed to function effectively enough to power one of economic history's great development successes" (Branstetter 2007, p. 66). Yet inefficient capital allocation remains a central issue to financial-market reform and may become increasingly critical. Financial market reformers also need to allow state-owned enterprises and private firms to compete on more level ground for bank loans and access to the stock markets, and to give domestic investors alternative investment venues in the domestic and international market. Moreover, economic planners need to coordinate uneven developments across regions and sectors, and to balance growth, stability, and social equality.

BIBLIOGRAPHY

Brandt, Loren, and Xiaodong Zhu. China's Banking Sector and Economic Growth. In *China's Financial Transition at a Crossroads*, ed. Charles W. Calomiris, 86–136. New York: Columbia University Press, 2007.

Branstetter, Lee. China's Financial Markets: An Overview. In *China's Financial Transition at a Crossroads*, ed. Charles W. Calomiris, 23–78. New York: Columbia University Press, 2007.

Calomiris, Charles W., ed. *China's Financial Transition at a Crossroads*. New York: Columbia University Press, 2007.

Chan, Kam C., Hung-Gay Fung, and Samanta Thapa. China Financial Research: A Review and Synthesis. *International Review of Economics and Finance* 16, 3 (2007): 416–428.

Chen, Wenhong. Does the Colour of the Cat Matter? The Red Hat Strategy in China's Private Enterprises. *Management and Organization Review* 3, 1 (2007): 55–80.

Green, Stephen Paul, and Guy Shaojia Liu, eds. *Exit the Dragon? Privatization and State Control in China*. Malden, MA: Blackwell, 2005.

Hu, Fred. The Effects of Stock Market Listing on the Financial Performance of Chinese Firms. In *China's Financial Transition at a Crossroads*, ed. Charles W. Calomiris, 290–306. New York: Columbia University Press, 2007.

Keister, Lisa A. Capital Structure in Transition: The Transformation of Financial Strategies in China's Emerging Economy. *Organization Science* 15, 2 (2004): 145–158.

Keister, Lisa A. Financial Markets, Money, and Banking. *Annual Review of Sociology* 28 (2002): 39–61.

Keister, Lisa A. Market Transition: Process and Outcomes. In *Handbook of Rational Choice Sociology*, ed. Rafael Wittek, Victor Nee, and Thomas Snijders. New York: Russell Sage, forthcoming.

Kornai, János. The Soft Budget Constraint. *Kyklos* 39, 1 (1986): 3–30.

Nee, Victor. Organizational Dynamics of Market Transition: Hybrid Forms, Property Rights, and Mixed Economy in China. *Administrative Science Quarterly* 37, 1 (1992): 1–27.

Nee, Victor. Social Inequalities in Reforming State Socialism: Between Redistribution and Markets in China. *American Sociological Review* 56, 3 (1991): 267–282.

Neftci, Salih N., and Michelle Yuan Ménager-Xu, ed. *China's Financial Markets: An Insider's Guide to How the Markets Work*. Burlington, MA: Elsevier, 2007.

Walder, Andrew G. Property Rights and Stratification in Socialist Redistributive Economies. *American Sociological Review* 57, 4 (1992): 524–539.

Lisa A. Keister
Wenhong Chen

FINANCIAL REGULATION

The regulatory bodies of China's financial markets are the People's Bank of China (PBOC), the China Banking Regulatory Commission (CBRC), the China Securities Regulatory Commission (CSRC), and the China Insurance Regulatory Commission (CIRC). The historical development of these institutions can be traced as follows:

Prior to 1983: People's Bank of China (PBOC) was the sole regulatory body of the financial markets, as well as a specialized bank.

1983: PBOC assumed the responsibilities of the central bank.

1992: The Securities Committee of the State Council (SCSC) and the China Securities Regulatory Commission (CSRC) were established.

1998: CSRC merged with SCSC as the only regulatory authority of securities and futures markets. China Insurance Regulatory Commission (CIRC) was established.

2003: China Banking Regulatory Commission (CBRC) was established, assuming the regulatory functions of PBOC.

PBOC AND MONETARY POLICY

The PBOC acts as the central bank, performing the following functions under the Law of the People's Bank of China (1995, amended in 2003): (1) formulating and implementing monetary policy; (2) preventing and mitigating financial risks; and (3) maintaining financial stability. Its main function is to formulate monetary policy. In 1997 it established the Monetary Policy Committee, a consultation and advisory body, and China's monetary policy changed. Rather than directly controlling credit, a number of measures—for example, capital adequacy ratio, a central-bank-based interest rate, rediscounting, central-bank lending, open-market operation, and other measures taken by the State Council—have been implemented.

China's interest rate is regulated by the PBOC. Since 1996 the reform process of interest-rate marketization has begun. In 1999 the Regulations on Renminbi (RMB) Interest-Rate Management were promulgated, providing the scope of the interest rate administrated by the PBOC and interest rates set by individual financial institutions. The PBOC also assumes the function of a foreign-exchange administration. The State Administration of Foreign Exchange (SAFE) is responsible for supervising the foreign-exchange market under the PBOC. The foreign-exchange system is governed by the Regulations on the Foreign-Exchange System (1996, amended in 1997).

Between 1979 and 2007, reforms were implemented in the foreign-exchange rate regime. In July 2005 a managed floating exchange-rate regime, based on market supply and demand with reference to a basket of currencies, was implemented. The RMB is no longer pegged to the U.S. dollar, providing greater flexibility.

CBRC AND THE REFORM OF THE BANKING SECTOR

The CBRC is responsible for the regulation and supervision of China's banking institutions and their business operations. It was established in April 2003 and is regulated by the Law of Banking Regulation and Supervision (2003, amended in 2006).

The commercial banks are the core of China's banking sector. They are regulated by the Company Law (1993, amended in 2004 and 2005) and the Law of Commercial Banks (1995, amended in 2003). Since 1979 China has been transforming its banking institutions from policy banks to commercial banks, especially the four state-owned commercial banks: the Agriculture Bank of China (ABC), the Bank of China (BOC), the Industry and Commercial Bank of China (ICBC), and the China Construction Bank (CCB). By 2007 the BOC, ICBC, and CCB had completed their reorganization and were listed on the stock exchanges of the Hong Kong Special Administrative Region or the mainland. The historical developments of these banks can be traced as follows:

1983: Four special banks (Agriculture Bank of China, Bank of China, Industry and Commercial Bank of China, and China Construction Bank) were established or reestablished.

1993: Three policy banks—China Development Bank, the Export–Import Bank of China, and the Agricultural Development Bank of China—were established, taking over policy loans transferred from the four special banks.

1995: The Law of Commercial Banks provided that commercial banks should be fully responsible for their own risks, profits and losses, and self-restraint.

2003: The State Council approved the Shareholding System Reform of State-owned Commercial Banks.

CHINA SECURITIES REGULATORY COMMISSION

The regulatory body of China's securities and futures markets is the China Securities Regulatory Commission (CSRC), established in 1992. The CSRC performs the following functions under the Securities Law (1998, amended in 2004 and 2005). First, the CSRC supervises the securities and futures business—that is, stock and futures-exchange markets, listed companies, fund-management companies investing in securities, securities and futures investment consulting firms, and other intermediaries involved in the securities and futures business. Second, the CSRC supervises the disclosure of information in connection with the offering and trading of securities. Third, the CSRC organizes the drafting of laws and regulations for securities and futures markets, formulating the principles, policies, and rules related to securities and futures markets, as well as the qualification criteria and code of conduct for persons engaged in the securities business. And fourth, the CSRC performs any other functions delegated to it by the State Council.

The CRSC has 16 functional departments or offices, 3 subordinate centers within its headquarters, as well as thirty-six local offices in thirty-one province-level administrative regions and five cities (Dalian, Qingdao, Ningbo, Xiamen, and Shenzhen). The development of the CSRC may be outlined as follows:

1992: The Securities Committee of the State Council (SCSC) and CSRC were established. The SCSC was the authority responsible for regulating the securities market, and the CSRC worked under the SCSC as an enforcement arm. The uniform regulatory body for the securities market had been formed.

1995: The futures market began to be regulated by the SCSC and CSRC.

1997: The CSRC began to regulate the Shenzhen and Shanghai stock exchanges. Meanwhile, the regulation of securities-trading institutions was transferred from the People's Bank of China to the CSRC.

1998: The SCSC and CSRC were merged to form one ministry. The CSRC became an enterprise unit directly under the State Council and the authorized department for governing securities and futures markets.

BIBLIOGRAPHY

China Securities Regulatory Commission. http://www.csrc.gov.cn/.

Li Huang. Wo Guo Zheng Quan Jian Guan Ti Zhi De Fa Zhan Yu Wan Shan [The development and improvement of China Securities Regulatory System]. *Journal of Yangtze University (Social Science)* 29, 2 (2006): 175–176.

Berry F. C. Hsu
Lifen Pu

Under China's World Trade Organization (WTO) commitments, the Regulations of the Administration of Foreign-funded Banks were promulgated in 2006 to liberalize the country's financial markets. The regulations abolished all non-prudential limitations for entrance and other restrictions on foreign-funded banks registered in China.

CSRC

The regulatory body of China's securities and futures markets is the CSRC, which operates under the Securities Law (1998, amended in 2004 and 2005) and the Securities Investment Fund Law (2003). The Securities Law provides the principles and framework for securities and futures markets, and the Securities Investment Fund Law regulates activities related to investment funds. There are further rules promulgated by the State Council and CSRC regulating public offerings, markets, institutions, futures, overseas issuance, and accounting.

CIRC

The CIRC administers, supervises, and regulates the insurance market in China under the Insurance Law (1995, amended in 2002). Insurance companies operate under the Insurance Law, the Company Law, and the Administration Provisions on Insurance Companies (2004). Foreign-funded insurance companies are mainly governed by the Regulation of the Administration of Foreign-funded Insurance Companies (2001), promulgated by the State Council. Besides the Insurance Law, insurance contracts in China are also regulated by the Contract Law of the People's Republic of China (1999).

BIBLIOGRAPHY

Li Yifu (Yi-Fu Lin), Li Yongjun (Yong-Jun Li), and Lu Lei (Lei Lu). *Zhong guo jin rong ti zhi gai ge de hui gu he zhan wang* [Review and prospect of China financial system reform]. China Center for Economic Research Working Paper Series (No. C2000005), April 2000.

Lü Jinzhong (Jin-Zhong Lü). *Zhong guo wai hui zhi du bian qian* [The development of China exchange system]. Beijing: China Financial Publishing House, 2006.

Jin rong ti zhi gai ge fa zhan hui fang [Retrospection of the development of financial system reform]. *China Finance* 18 (2006): 50–60.

Zhong guo jin rong gai ge de ji ben hui gu [Review of China financial reform]. Beijing: China Commerce and Trade Press, April 2003. http://www.china.com.cn/chinese/zhuanti/305838.htm.

Zhong Ying. Zhong gong zhong yang dui jin rong wen ti de ren shi yu zhong guo jin rong ti zhi gai ge jin cheng [The Central Committee of the Communist Party of China's understanding of financial issues and the financial system reform of China]. In *Zhong guo gong chan dang yu xin zhong guo jian she* [The Communist Party of China and the construction of New China], ed. Zhang Qihua (Qi-Hua Zhang), 638–659. Beijing: Modern China Publishing House, 2003.

Berry F.C. Hsu
Lifen Pu

FIVE-YEAR PLANS

Five-year plans (usually referred to in Chinese by an abbreviation—for example, *jiu wu*, "nine five," meaning the Ninth Five-Year Plan) were a pivotal coordinating mechanism in China's long-term central planning and have been an important organizing feature of Chinese economic policies and development since 1949. Following the pace and direction of economic reforms since 1978, the nature of five-year plans shifted from being frameworks for yearly material plans to general statements of sectoral economic policies and development goals. This shift was recognized when the Eleventh Five-Year Plan (2006–2010) was called a "development guideline" (*fazhan guihua*), so that today the mandatory claims of five-year plans no longer exist. In the past, five-year plans were embedded into longer-term development plans, such as ten-year plans or long-range plans.

Typically, five-year plans take several years to prepare. Preparations for the Eleventh Five-Year Plan for the 2006–2010 period, for example, started in 2003. Furthermore, given the sometimes abrupt crises and turns in Chinese politics, shifts of emphasis have to be implemented during preparation, as occurred in the transition from the Fifth Five-Year Plan (1976–1980) to the Sixth Five-Year Plan (1981–1985), which coincided with the launch of economic reforms. These preparations frequently send strong signals to subordinate organizations to adapt their ongoing work. Thus, it is appropriate to say that the preparations for a five-year plan are as important as the eventual implementation.

Final approval of a five-year plan marks the end of an intensive intragovernmental bargaining process across all levels of government, thus fixing balances of interest between the regions and the center, as well as between different ministries in terms of their impact and significance in the national policy framework. In this process, the collection and assessment of economic data play a crucial role. Under the auspices of socialist central planning, the balance between production potentials and material production targets was a central concern. Today, interests are defined in a much more complex way, solving multiple trade-offs, for example, between environmental policy, infrastructure development, and regional aspirations for growth. Thus, the guidelines of today may be best interpreted as focal points in a complex and ongoing strategic interaction between different governmental units and powerful actors in the enterprise sector.

The changing nature of five-year plans in the new millennium was reflected in the abolishment of the State Planning Commission, which had been in charge of drafting five-year plans since 1952. In 1998 this body was renamed the State Development Planning Commission, which was merged with the State Council Office for Restructuring the Economic System and became a part of the State Economic and Trade Commission in 2003. This new organization was dubbed the National Development and Reform Commission (NDRC). The NDRC is responsible for coordinating national industrial policies and for designing and overseeing national developmental projects, such as the western development strategy or the national strategy for energy security.

In the past, the sequence and duration of five-year plans was heavily influenced by political events. The launch of the State Planning Commission in 1952, for example, was overshadowed by the so called Gao-Rao affair, when the

Five-Year Plans, 1953–2010

Five Year Plan	1	2	3	4	5	6	7	8	9	10	11
Period	1953–1957	1958–aborted	1966–1970	1971–1975	1976–1980	1981–1985	1986–1990	1991–1995	1996–2000	2001–2005	2006–2010

Table 1

commission's first chairman, Gao Gang (1905–1954), together with Rao Shushi (1903-1975), then Director of the Central Committee's organization department, conspired against Liu Shaoqi and Zhou Enlai to take their position in the CCP power hierarchy. Both were ousted in 1954.

The First Five-Year Plan (1953–1957) centered on the implementation of a Soviet-style system of central planning and the launch of an industrialization strategy that built on heavy industry. However, the Second Five-Year Plan, launched in 1958, was quickly superseded by the Great Leap Forward and its sudden switch to a rural industrialization strategy. Thus, Mao's voluntarism and the breakdown of the cooperation with the Soviet Union left the Second FYP as an irrelevant document. The ensuing human catastrophe in the countryside revealed a fatal weakness in the Chinese planning system—that is, the low reliability of statistical information and the lack of organizational standardization in the statistical system. This weakness was further exacerbated during the five-year plans of the Cultural Revolution (1966–1969), which was accompanied by a sweeping decentralization of the country's industrial organization. Leftist ideologists strongly criticized the use of economic indicators in economic organization, which was seen as a doorway to the revival of capitalist drives. As a result, the central planning apparatus was severely curtailed in the 1970s, leaving only a few hundred staff members in the central statistical system. In fact, the Third Five-Year Plan (1966–1970) and the Fourth Five-Year Plan (1971–1975) were only drafts that were adapted to the economic realities in the course of time.

The transition to economic reform provides a clear example how five-year plans served to redefine power balances across levels of governments. Economic reforms were introduced through a clear reinstatement of central control in the economy and, hence, a strengthening of national targets issued by the State Planning Commission. In this movement, the political goal of stabilizing central power harmonized with the need to impose macroeconomic control after the eruption of severe imbalances between 1977 and 1981, which resulted from the massive attempts to import modern technology and revive the economy via an investment push under Hua Guofeng (1921–2008), again resulting from a mistaken estimation of capacities in the energy and industrial sector. Similarly, political and economic determinants converged in austerity policies after the 1989 Tiananmen incident, preparing the ground for the fiscal recentralization of 1994.

In the new millennium, five-year plans mainly serve to communicate the strategic concerns and goals of the central government. Thus, the transition to the Hu Jintao and Wen Jiabao leadership was marked by the Tenth Five-Year Plan (2001–2005), which put special emphasis on addressing regional imbalances, expanding investment into education, and launching new initiatives in social policy. At the same time, five-year plans continue to include specific strategies for core national industries, thus building a synthesis between political targets and corporate strategy.

SEE ALSO *Central Planning.*

BIBLIOGRAPHY

Lardy, Nicholas. Economic Recovery and the 1st Five-Year Plan. In *The Cambridge History of China*, Vol. 14: *The People's Republic*, eds. Roderick MacFarquhar and John K. Fairbank, Pt. 1: *The Emergence of Revolutionary China, 1949–1965*, 144–184. Cambridge, U.K.: Cambridge University Press, 1978–.

Naughton, Barry. *The Chinese Economy: Transitions and Growth.* Chaps. 3 and 4. Cambridge, MA: MIT Press, 2007.

Carsten Herrmann-Pillath

FOLK ART

Much of what is now classified as folk art in China is of great antiquity. However, the term *folk art* (*minjian meishu*), referring to visual arts, was not commonly used until the 1930s. A new intellectual interest in folk culture developed in the 1910s and 1920s. Scholars and writers such as Liu Fu (Liu Bannong, 1891–1934) and Gu Jiegang (1893–1980), looking for alternatives to elite traditions, became fascinated with folk songs, and promoted the study of folklore and folk literature. Activists in rural reform efforts (such as those led by James Yen [Yan Yangchu, 1890–1990] and the National Association of Mass Education Movements) also studied local songs, plays, and crafts in hopes that this would help them better understand and communicate with rural people.

While folklorists and rural reformers saw folk arts as a valuable resource, others saw them as expressions of dangerously outmoded values and beliefs. Activists in the Guomindang-supported antisuperstition campaigns of the late 1920s and early 1930s, for example, destroyed temples and idols despite their value as art. But although intellectuals regarded folk art with ambivalence, they recognized its influence within Chinese culture. In the 1930s, art magazines introduced the idea of folk art to urban readers, and the renowned writer Lu Xun (1881–1936) referred to folk New Year pictures as sources of inspiration for new art.

WHAT IS FOLK ART?

In China as elsewhere, the definition of folk art is notoriously imprecise. Under the broadest definition, it is art

A puppeteer performing during the Tianqiao Folk Art Festival, Beijing, September 15, 2007. *Many forms of Chinese folk art have been preserved for hundreds of years. During China's economic boom at the turn of the twenty-first century, increased tourism opportunities have fostered a new audience for many regional forms of folk art, raising awareness about conserving important cultural traditions.* CHINA PHOTOS/GETTY IMAGES

produced and consumed in the lower classes of stratified societies. Folk art is also often defined in terms of ideal traits: It might be said, for example, that folk art is essentially traditional rather than innovative; that it expresses the tastes and values of communities, rather than the individual; that folk artists are untrained and intuitive; and that folk art is naive, simple, and pure. In practice, the diversity of things categorized as folk art defies such idealizations. Materials socially placed as "folk" often turn out to be complex, sophisticated, and responsive to technological and social change. In many cases, what makes an art "folk" is often simply its exclusion from the canons of fine art.

In China, folk art encompasses a wide array of art forms, from weaving to architecture. These diverse art forms share an association with lower-class or rural people, and often share subject matter and aesthetic concepts, but are not always made and used by the same people or in the same way. Nor are they always exclusive to the lower classes. Two of the most popular folk art forms, New Year pictures (*nianhua*) and paper cuts (*jian zhi*), serve as examples.

Folk New Year pictures are colorful woodcut prints, used in both decoration and religious rituals. Their varied subjects include auspicious images of fat babies, scenes from the opera, and gods and spirits. Such pictures were already sold in New Year markets by the Song dynasty (960–1279), if not earlier, and they enjoyed tremendous popularity through the nineteenth century and into the twentieth. Most of these prints were made by male craftsmen in commercial workshops. Large-scale production made prints inexpensive enough for even poor families, though wealthier families also bought them. Especially large and lavish New Year pictures were made for the imperial household and hung in the Forbidden City.

Paper cuts, are, as the name suggests, designs cut from paper with scissors or knives. Chinese paper cutting is ancient: despite their fragile nature, a few paper cuts survive from as early as the sixth century. Paper cuts might show auspicious symbols, scenes from daily life, or the same stories found in New Year pictures. Like New Year pictures, they are widely used as holiday decorations, their bold silhouettes pasted on windows or lanterns or hung from doorways. Unlike New Year pictures, however, paper cuts are usually (although not always) produced by women within the home. Paper cuts were also used as embroidery patterns, laid directly on a piece of cloth and covered with stitches, by both lower- and upper-class women.

FOLK ART IN A CHANGING SOCIETY

War further damaged an already weakened woodcut New Year picture industry. During the Anti-Japanese War (1937–1945), however, many urban, educated artists (including the cartoonist Huang Yao [1917–1987] and the printmaker Hu Yichuan [1910–2000]) used styles and motifs drawn from folk art in works intended to build national morale and encourage support of the war effort. Although the use of "old forms" was controversial, its value in propaganda made it widely accepted. Communist Party artists continued making propaganda art based on folk art during the civil war.

The cultural policies of the new state promoted reform, control, and preservation of folk art. Independent creative activities of all kinds were limited, but scholarly research on folk arts increased, and, in the art academies, young artists were encouraged to use folk elements in new art. The government also promoted new-style machine-printed New Year pictures. The remaining private woodcut New Year print workshops were shut down by the end of the 1950s; but in many cases, folk printmakers (and other folk artists) continued to practice their crafts in state-run workshops.

During the Cultural Revolution (1966–1969), folk art was attacked as a manifestation of traditional culture. However, at the same time, the call to "serve the people" and the forced relocation of many educated urbanites to the countryside created a social interchange that set the stage for a new intellectual appreciation of folk art. The phenomenon of "peasant painting" also gained prominence in the later years of the Cultural Revolution. In peasant painting, rural people tutored by professional artists created images of an ideally prosperous countryside, using an idealized folklike aesthetic of brightness, flatness, and busy detail. Peasant paintings were among the first Chinese artworks sent abroad for exhibition as China reopened contacts with the West the 1970s, presenting a reassuringly colorful and cheerful vision of Chinese society.

THE REFORM PERIOD: FOLK ART IN THE FREE MARKET

China's rapid economic development in recent decades has further eroded folk art's original social contexts, but the growth of markets and tourism has given it new economic importance, and both artists and scholars have enjoyed greater freedom. Contemporary fine artists such as Lü Shengzhong have continued to use folk forms and motifs, but with aesthetic and emotional effects very different from that of earlier folk-based art. The 2004 Shanghai Biennale featured paper cuts by artists active in one northern Shaanxi county, collected by the independent contemporary art group the Long March Project. The Fan Xiaomei, a Shaanxi paper cutter who learned from her mother and grandmother, promotes her craft with books and teaching. From the mid-1990s, the novelist Feng Jicai, spurred by damage to his native Tianjin's historic cityscape, has called for the preservation of folk art and architecture, with mixed success. The government has also begun to look at the place of folk art in Chinese culture, and the problem of preservation, in new ways. In recent years, the State Administration of Cultural Heritage has embraced the UNESCO-inspired concept of "intangible cultural heritage," and has given many forms of folk art official status under this heading.

SEE ALSO *Lu Xun.*

BIBLIOGRAPHY

Berliner, Nancy. *Chinese Folk Art: The Small Skills of Carving Insects*. Boston: Little, Brown, 1986.

Doar, Bruce G., and Geremie R. Barmé. A Tale of Two Lists: An Examination of the New Lists of Intangible Cultural Properties. *Chinese Heritage Quarterly* 7 (September 2006). http://chinaheritagenewsletter.org/.

Flath, James. *The Cult of Happiness: Nianhua, Art, and History in Rural North China*. Vancouver University of British Columbia Press, 2004.

Jin Zhilin. *Chinese Folk Arts*. Beijing: China Intercontinental Press, 2004.

Laing, Ellen Johnston. *Art and Aesthetics in Chinese Popular Prints: Selections from the Muban Foundation Collection*. Ann Arbor: Center for Chinese Studies, University of Michigan, 2002.

Lu Jia and David Tung, eds. *The Great Survey of Paper-cutting in Yanchuan County*. Beijing: 25000 Cultural Transmission Center, 2004.

Felicity Lufkin

FOOD SINCE 1800

In their mythical view of primordial times, the Chinese, longtime grain farmers, see themselves as consumers of cereals and cooked foods. The sovereign's role as intermediary between heaven and earth, and provider of food for his people, is also part of this social myth. The classic texts add that "from the prince to the mere commoner, everyone consumes grains and soup." According to his disciples, Confucius (551–479 BCE) enjoyed eating good-

Bean paste sauce with noodles. *While traditional Chinese foods such as rice and noodles continue to be consumed by the majority of the population, many urban areas now feature Western-style fast food restaurants in additional to the standard local cuisine.* © STUDIO EYE/CORBIS

quality rice with finely sliced meat, but he never allowed the latter to exceed the grain in quantity. The sage thus established a norm that made starches the core of the meal, while founding an ethic of moderation between the need to live on grains and the pleasure of eating meat and the dishes that accompany it. This model meal, which has persisted throughout Chinese history, is still valid today for a great majority of Chinese people. However, what is understood as "cooking," *pengtiao*, refers only to side dishes (*cai*), that is, the flavorful elements of a meal, considered as additional and even superfluous, whose purpose is to "get the starchy *fan* [rice] down."

In normal times, nearly 90 percent of the Chinese population lived simply on a diet consisting largely of starch, while the remaining 10 percent could enjoy great dietary affluence based on the richest products. Despite this numerical imbalance, the Chinese shared the same dietary ideal, although the specific way they fulfilled it obviously varied according to their region and climate. Even the poorest thought of indulging their weakness for good food when their basic needs had been satisfied by consuming enough starch. They then enriched the side dishes or gave themselves a little treat at a restaurant or a street merchant's stall. But when food emergencies arose, as they did repeatedly during this period, the poor were the ones who suffered most. This was the case during the severe famines of 1876 to 1879 and 1920 to 1922.

NECESSITY AND PLEASURE

While it is always difficult to establish an exact idea of the diet of populations at the bottom of the social hierarchy in the past, the available accounts and rare studies of the period being examined in this entry give the impression that Chinese "workers" lived precariously from day to day. They subsisted almost exclusively on grains or tubers (depending on their region) with a few salted vegetables, soy sauce, sometimes a little sesame oil, and, on rare occasions, small quantities of meat. This is true of the boatmen who worked for British ambassador Lord George Macartney (1737–1806) just before 1800, of the people who traveled with Scottish botanist Robert Fortune (1812–1880) during the 1840s, and of the rickshaw pullers of Beijing around 1920. If the novel *The Gourmet* (1986) by Lu Wenfu (1928–2005) can be believed, the Suzhou rickshaw puller of the 1950s was better off: He ate his rice with tofu and braised goose, but only until the dietary reform imposed around 1955 deprived him of his meat dish. In 1973 the typical meal for the little tailor who kept a shop near the Beijing Institute of Foreign Languages consisted of one or two steamed whole wheat flour buns with a bowl of vegetable soup. Today, in 2008, this is still the diet of the migrant laborers working on construction projects in Beijing, who eat out of lunchboxes.

However, everyone agrees that this frugal diet was broken the instant an occasion to do so presented itself: family celebrations or official holidays, a visit by a relative from the provinces, a student's success in an examination, and so forth. The public holidays were, and have once again become, important times for social mixing; they are times when people meet in parks or temples to be entertained by various shows and to taste the specialties of the day. This "outdoor food" service was provided by a range of small restaurants and mobile street vendors, since street food has always been a characteristic of life in China. Still today, for their daily meals, construction workers in Shanghai can sometimes have a mobile vendor come right onto the building site and prepare sautéed noodles or garnished pancakes on demand for a few cents.

THE GASTRONOMY OF THE ELITE

At the opposite end of the social hierarchy, the imperial court was the supreme place for dietary abundance and haute cuisine. Not only did the court meet the needs of the emperor and his family, it also controlled the taxation of agricultural surpluses, monitored the administration of tributes, particularly the tribute paid in grain (rice), and assumed the management of any famines that arose. In addition, the Imperial Household was responsible for the food and beverage service to the emperor and his family, for the official meals offered to the courtiers and associates closest to the emperor and to the various vassals of the empire, and for the great sacrifices that were held periodically, with their highly elaborate ritual and important symbolic role. Several hundred people attended to the imperial family's daily menus, which required the marshaling of considerable resources. The quality of the food was ensured by a supply of select products from the tribute, imperial farms, and the markets of Beijing. Service protocol was so burdensome that the last emperor, Puyi (1906–1967), preferred to be served only a few dishes that were specially concocted for him in the private kitchens of certain princes assigned to his court.

Imperial cuisine was, nonetheless, considered the very best, and worthy of imitation. It left a heritage in the gastronomical tradition of Beijing of several small cakes and milk-based desserts that are still popular today. Several imperial cooks, left jobless by the fall of the dynasty, were hired by the famous Fangshan Fanzhuang restaurant, founded in 1925, whose name appropriately means "restaurant imitating imperial cuisine." The restaurant is still in operation today in Beijing.

The only cuisine in a position to rival that of the imperial court was produced by the Kong family, direct-line heirs of Confucius. Thanks to the opening of their archives, it is now known that at their immense, magnificent residence at Qufu in Shandong, the Kongs had maintained a high-flying culinary tradition whose only beneficiaries, besides themselves, were the members of the imperial family and a few high dignitaries.

These prestigious cuisines were considered a benchmark by the men of letters of the Lower Yangzi, even if a few of them sometimes made fun of the munificence of the courtiers' way of life. During the late Ming dynasty (1368–1644), in fact, a culture of good taste developed among the cultivated circles of the small villages in the southern Yangzi, with its lovers of art and exquisite food. This refined society devoted much of its time to feasting, mixing music and poetry with the enjoyment of excellent meals, drinking sessions, or tastings of the rarest and most exquisite teas. The phenomenon grew under the Qing dynasty (1644–1912), involving increasingly lavish spending throughout the nineteenth century. In 1792 the great poet Yuan Mei (1716–1798) set the tone for the following century by publishing, along with a considerable body of work, a treatise on cuisine titled *Suiyuan shidan* (Menus of Suiyuan). Composed of more than three hundred recipes, this text established a veritable southern culinary aesthetic. Yuan Mei became a model for his successors, who were, like him, authors of culinary works. His treatise, which went through many editions, is still appreciated, and is the most famous book of Chinese cooking. The hedonism of Yuan Mei, or of his predecessor Li Yu (c. 1611–1680), would be proclaimed by certain writers of the 1920s and 1930s, such as Lin Yutang (1895–1976), the popular leader of a politically neutral essayistic literature whose themes taken from daily life award a preferential place to epicurean enjoyment and fine dining.

COMMERCIAL FOOD SERVICE AND GASTRONOMY

With Yuan Mei and his friends, gastronomy was private, nearly secret, and reserved for a tiny elite. It could not be compared to the commercial gastronomy of the Chinese cities where, during the nineteenth and twentieth centuries, restaurants and small inns of every style and quality proliferated. The towns, regional trade centers, and provincial examination centers were bustling with a highly diversified clientele. Merchants were welcomed at their guild headquarters, which periodically organized banquets, but also frequented the town restaurants, as did traveling literati in search of a place to amuse themselves and enjoy a tasty delicacy. These select circles hardly mixed in the Beijing of the 1850s; each group had its regular places for fun and culinary delights. The *Dumen jilüe* (A glimpse of the capital gates), a guide to the city's best spots compiled in 1845 and reissued many times, enabled them to vary their pleasures. And then there was the clientele of well-heeled individuals who could more or less regularly afford to treat themselves to something extra, or to drink a few glasses of rice wine accompanied by the local specialties while contemplating, for example, the beautiful landscape of the shores of West Lake at Hangzhou.

Between 1843 and 1860, more than fifteen ports were opened to international trade, and the establishment of foreign concessions in many of those cities profoundly changed their configuration and neighborhood life. Western cooking and dietary practices first made their appearance in the homes of foreigners living in China. It was to make the training of their Chinese household servants easier that the Shanghai Presbyterian mission presses issued, in 1866, the first Western cookbook in the Chinese language: *Zao yangfan shu* (Treatise on the preparation of Western meals). Its author was Martha Foster Crawford (1830–1909), an American Baptist missionary who lived in China with her husband for fifty years.

Western cooking, generally of British inspiration, spread quickly beyond the foreign families thanks to the establishment of a great many restaurants between 1860 and 1870, especially in Shanghai, a city that was emblematic of this trend. But if Western cuisine aroused more curiosity than genuine liking when it was first introduced in China, it ended up converting tastes and becoming a fashionable trend. Until 1937, it would be a captivating part of the hectic lives of businessmen and of the activities of a mixed leisure society that was open to all pleasures. The taste for red meat reflected by the rich menus of Western cuisine surprised the Chinese, but they very quickly grew accustomed to it, just as they learned to appreciate bread, pastries, coffee, lemonade, cognac, whiskey, champagne, and so on. The specific supplies needed for Western cooking would, moreover, give rise to the creation of slaughterhouses and small agri-food industries. Shanghai was home to the first brewery, before the Harbin or Qingdao establishments were founded. But it was the beer made in Qingdao, founded in 1903 by Germans who had annexed Shandong in 1897, that was to achieve the greatest renown. Shanghai, however, would maintain its reputation as a center of Western cuisine, and particularly as a producer of fine pastries, until beyond the 1970s.

NEW CULINARY REGIMES

After the shortages imposed by the war, the establishment of the Communist regime in 1949 enabled a sort of return to the prewar dietary order for a few years. Those with the means to do so were able to continue eating well in the restaurants of China's cities. In 1955, with rations imposed on staple foods, dietary practices changed on a national scale. In 1958, during the Great Leap Forward, the situation became harsher with the widespread imposition of the canteen system in people's communes and at work sites. Restaurants were also gradually transformed into refectories, and chefs demoted to mere cooks.

The canteen system, abandoned in 1961, was defined as "a practice that enables productivity to be increased and working peoples' forces to be stimulated on a grand scale." It inspired a "canteen culture" based on eating as morality, whose cardinal virtues were austerity and frugality. Food was actually considered as playing a merely functional role: allowing the workforce to reproduce. This direction became more pronounced during the Cultural Revolution (1966–1969), and would last until the end of the 1970s.

The canteen culture was updated in 1966 with the appearance of the only cookbook available in China for ten years, *Dazhong shitang caipu* (Canteen recipes for the working masses), a collection of nearly three hundred simple recipes furnished by the official regional organs charged with feeding the people, certain canteens, and people's restaurants. The book went through several subsequent editions under the revised title *Dazhong caipu* (Recipes for the working masses), and the last edition, in 1985, ran to more than two million copies. Due to the disaster it caused, some analysts blame the canteen system for a major part of the famine that descended upon the Chinese countryside between 1959 and 1961. Today it is known that the victims numbered in the tens of millions.

The chronic, insidious shortages that ravaged the country from 1958 to the end of the 1970s helped the Chinese internalize the dogma of austerity. Their lives were tied to the rhythm of seasonal vegetables, since they had very few other ingredients to accompany their starches, and these were obtained in exchange for rationing coupons. The few gourmet restaurants that remained open were patronized only by foreigners, diplomats, merchants, and a restricted number of very highly placed Chinese officials, who could enjoy high-quality traditional cuisine in such establishments. The few restaurants offering midlevel cuisine opened during heavily restricted hours, and received only officials on special assignment whose expenses were paid by their work unit. Bars disappeared completely, as did the small-scale street vendors, who were probably considered a source of disorder and useless activity. After the Cultural Revolution, young city dwellers who had been sent en masse to rural areas, where getting enough to eat was a struggle, had to manage on their own to find a source of subsistence.

RUPTURE AND REVIVAL: 1980

The beginning of the 1980s marked a deep ideological break from the dietary policy pursued up to that point. In

Female members of a Chinese family preparing dumplings, Yantai, March 19, 1993. *Although increased incomes have afforded many Chinese the opportunity to try new foods offered in restaurants, home-prepared meals remain focused on traditional elements, such as the dumplings being made by several generations of Chinese women in the above photo.* © REUTERS/CORBIS

just a few years, the Chinese would move from the harsh condemnation of eating well, which had been branded a decadent bourgeois passion, to the all-out promotion of Chinese haute cuisine, and of gastronomy in general. The revival of the agri-food sector and the Chinese food-service industry was clearly not due to chance. Nor was it the consequence of deregulation giving uncontrolled private enterprise a free hand. Rather, it was a voluntary initiative on the part of the Chinese government. Beginning in December 1980, the magazine *Zhongguo pengren* (Chinese cuisine) was published and aimed at the professional sector. Its objectives were clearly educational and cultural: The reader can easily see that one of its aims is to restore the image of a profession that had suffered a disaster thirty years earlier. Its appearance, under the auspices of the Ministry of Commerce, and its immediately permitted distribution abroad, are further signs of an appeal to the Chinese communities in foreign countries to arouse their interest and stimulate their future investments. A year later, the State Council issued a directive for the "awareness of the heritage represented by the classic texts." The presses of the Ministry of Commerce responded by creating a small collection of ancient Chinese culinary treatises, quite clearly aimed at Chinese chefs.

This movement to reclaim a tradition would result, within less than twenty years, in an unprecedented boom in the Chinese agri-food industry, in an opening to foreign dietary and culinary worlds with the establishment in 1987 of the KFC chain, and in the wildly successful opening of McDonald's in the heart of Beijing in 1992. All over China, "private" restaurants sprang up like mushrooms, and the traditional street food reappeared in certain districts, along with some street vendors of traditional delicacies. An extraordinary craze for food and consumption took hold of city dwellers open to all trends, wherever they might come from. A considerable effort was made to improve the food-supply system, especially after 1989. In 1993 rationing coupons were finally eliminated.

Since then, food products imported from all over the world can be found in the major cities of China.

The "nutritional transition"—that is, the progression from a model of meals based on starches to a freer model including a greater proportion of meat-based proteins and dairy products—is about to be completed in many urban-dwelling families. The same process took nearly a century in Europe. These very fast transitions, which have not always been followed by the indispensable creation of regulation mechanisms and control authorities, particularly in questions of safety, hygiene, and nutritional recommendations, have begun producing harmful effects. Childhood obesity is now a public health problem, and reports of food contamination are front-page news, such as the case of tainted powdered formula milk, that caused the deaths of a number of infants and seriously affected the health of hundreds of thousands of other children. China continues to wrestle with difficulties similar to those affecting major industrialized countries in the realm of public health for the urban fringe of its population.

SEE ALSO *Agricultural Production; Leisure; Lin Yutang.*

BIBLIOGRAPHY

Darrobers, Roger. Théâtre et convivialité à Pékin au XIXè siècle: Évolution du goût [Theater and conviviality in nineteenth-century Peking: The evolution of taste]. In *Savourer, Goûter*, eds. Flora Blanchon and Centre de recherche sur l'Extrême-Orient de Paris-Sorbonne (CREOPS), 341–356. Paris: Presses de l'Université de Paris-Sorbonne, 1995.

Deng Li and Li Xiusong, eds. *Zao yangfan shu*. Beijing: Zhongguo Shangye Chubanshe, 1986.

Jun Jing. *Feeding China's Little Emperors: Food, Children, and Social Change*. Stanford, CA: Stanford University Press, 2001.

Leppman, Elizabeth. J. *Changing Rice Bowl: Economic Development and Diet in China*. Hong Kong: Hong Kong University Press, 2005.

Lu Wenfu. *Vie et passion d'un gastronome chinois* [Life and passion of a Chinese gastronome]. Trans. Annie Curien and Feng Chen. Preface: "Avant-goût," by Françoise Sabban. Paris: Picquier-Unesco, 1988.

Sabban, Françoise. Art et culture contre science et technique: Les enjeux culturels et identitaires de la gastronomie chinoise face à l'Occident [Art and culture versus science and technique: Issues of culture and identity in Chinese gastronomy compared to the West]. *L'Homme* 137, 1 (1996): 163–194.

Spence, Jonathan. Ch'ing. In *Food in Chinese Culture: Anthropological and Historical Perspectives*, ed. K. C. Chang (Zhang Guangzhi). New Haven, CT: Yale University Press, 1979.

Waley, Arthur. *Yuan Mei: Eighteenth Century Chinese Poet*. London: Allen and Unwin, 1956.

Watson, James L., ed. *Golden Arches East: McDonald's in East Asia*. 2nd ed. Stanford, CA: Stanford University Press, 2006.

Will, Pierre-Étienne. *Bureaucracy and Famine in Eighteenth-Century China*. Trans. Elborg Forster. Stanford, CA: Stanford University Press, 1990.

Yuan Mei. *Suiyuan shidan* [Menus of Suiyuan]. Beijing: Zhongguo Shangye Chubanshe, 1984.

Françoise Sabban

FOOTBINDING

The centuries-old practice of footbinding reached its peak in the Qing dynasty (1644–1912), when the majority of Han women bound their feet in a ritual begun when a young girl was five to six years old, with the aim of securing her a good husband. A bandage approximately 4 inches wide and 13 feet long was wrapped from behind the ankle and used to force the four small toes under the sole of the foot. The bandage was continually tightened until the girl stopped growing, stunting the growth of her feet to the ideal length of 3 inches. Critics, including Yuan Mei (1716–1798), Li Ruzhen (c. 1763–1830), and Yu Zhengxie (1775–1840), spoke out against this practice in the late eighteenth and early nineteenth centuries. It was not until the late nineteenth century, however, that bound feet were transformed from the highest form of female social capital to a cultural embarrassment, from a marker of Han civilization to an emblem of China's national backwardness. And it was not until the first decades of the twentieth century that the practice was gradually eradicated.

The demise of footbinding was partly a result of foreign opposition to and foreign representations of bound feet. Western Protestant missionaries first addressed the topic in 1874 in Amoy (Xiamen). By the 1890s, missionary publications such as the *Wanguo gongbao* (The Chinese global magazine) condemned the practice as un-Christian. In 1895 ten Western women, including Alicia Little (1845–1926), the wife of a British merchant, organized the Natural Foot Society (Tianzu Hui) in Shanghai. The Japanese also expressed disdain for the practice at the turn of the twentieth century. They featured footbinding as a signpost of China's underdevelopment both at the Tokyo Imperial Household Museum and in a display booth planned for the Races of Man Pavilion at the 1903 Osaka Exposition.

The primary motivation for the interdiction of footbinding was, however, China's indigenous reform movement—itself a response to foreign military and cultural humiliation—and most specifically the reformers' promotion of female education. A number of late-nineteenth-century scholars, including Song Shu (1862–1910) and Zheng Guanying (1842–1922), highlighted the link between footbinding and restrictions on female education. From 1883, when Kang Youwei (1858–1927) established the first Chinese-initiated anti-footbinding association, the movements for natural feet and women's public schooling were intimately linked both to one another and to Chinese nationalism. Yan Fu (1853–1921) tied natural feet to the social Darwinian notion of survival of the fittest. Kang's disciple, Liang Qichao (1873–1929), who was active in an anti-footbinding society founded in 1897, associated unbound feet with women's learning and national strengthening in his influential essay "On Female Education" (Lun nüxue).

Elderly woman bathing her bound foot, 1998. *The practice of intentionally deforming a young girl's foot to stunt its growth began in earnest in tenth-century China, first among wealthy families before filtering down to the lower classes. While footbinding became illegal after the fall of the Qing dynasty, living examples of the procedure continue to exist into the twenty-first century among a few remaining elderly Chinese women.* JODI COBB/NATIONAL GEOGRAPHIC/GETTY IMAGES

While the Qing government banned footbinding in 1902, it was this link between education and natural feet that was the most effective means of ending the practice (similar prohibition edicts that had not been tied to broader programs of social and educational reform had failed in 1636, 1638, and 1664). The earliest schools for Chinese girls and women in both China and Japan followed the lead of the reformers and made natural or unbound feet a prerequisite for enrollment. They included the Chinese Women's School (Zhongguo Nü Xuetang), established in Shanghai in 1898 by Liang among others, and Shimoda Utako's (1854–1936) Jissen Women's School (Jissen Jogakkō) in Tokyo, which accepted Chinese students from 1901. When the Qing government finally sanctioned public education for girls and women in 1907, the Education Board's regulations for government schools explicitly forbade the practice.

Late Qing textbooks written explicitly for girls and women reinforced these developments. They promoted women's physical education and condemned footbinding for physically weakening women and impeding their ability to escape from natural disasters or human assailants. The textbooks' overriding argument against footbinding and the mantra of the natural foot movement in the early twentieth century, however, was that women with bound feet could not mother strong citizens. The textbooks asserted that the strength or weakness of the male body was directly related to the strength or weakness of the female body: Bound-footed women debilitated the Han race. Some textbooks even included detailed instructions on how to unbind the feet.

Early-twentieth-century Chinese women writing in the new media of the period offered a passionate personal perspective on the practice. They used some of the harshest language to condemn it as a form of physical mutilation responsible for women's status as secluded, ignorant playthings. The female writers also documented their own experience of unbinding in order to encourage more women to liberate their feet. They described using carbolic acid and warm water to wash their tender and swollen feet several times a day before wrapping them in cotton.

A study from Dingxian near Beijing in 1929 gives a sense of the effectiveness of these various anti-footbinding measures. It recorded that 99.2 percent of women born in this community before 1890 had bound feet, while only 59.7 percent of those born between 1905 and 1909, and 19.5 percent of those born between 1910 and 1914 did. There were no reported cases among those born after 1919. The last assembly line of the last Chinese factory that produced shoes for bound feet finally closed in late 1999 (Ko 2005).

SEE ALSO *Education: Women's Education; Kang Youwei; Liang Qichao; Little, Alicia; Women, Status of; Yan Fu.*

BIBLIOGRAPHY

Chen Yan'an. Quan nüzi liuxue shuo [Exhortation for female overseas study]. *Jiangsu* [Jiangsu journal] 3 (June 1903): 155–156 [0585–0586].

Fang Liusheng. *Nüzi guowen duben* [Chinese reader for girls]. Shanghai: Shangwu Yinshuguan, 1905.

Guang Zhanyun, Guang Yiyun, and Chen Yuxin, comps. *Zuixin funü guowen duben* [Newest Chinese reader for women]. 10 vols. (8 extant: vols. 1, 4–10). Fuzhou, PRC: Jiaoyu Pujishe, 1908.

Judge, Joan. *The Precious Raft of History: The Past, the West, and the Woman Question in China*. Stanford, CA: Stanford University Press, 2008.

Ko, Dorothy. *Cinderella's Sisters: A Revisionist History of Footbinding*. Berkeley: University of California Press, 2005.

Pao Tao Chia-lin. The Anti-footbinding Movement in Late Ch'ing China: Indigenous Development and Western Influence. *Jindai Zhongguo funü shi yanjiu* [Research on women in modern Chinese history] 2 (1994): 141–178.

Wang Lian. Tongxiang hui jishi: Hubei zhi bu [Record of same-place association meeting: Section on Hubei]. *Hubei xuesheng jie* [Students of Hubei] 2 (February 1903): 113–116 [0287–0290].

Xia Xiaohong. Wan-Qing funü shenghuo zhong de xin yinsu [New elements in the lives of late Qing women]. In *Wan-Qing shehui yu wenhua* [Late Qing society and culture], 249–310. Wuhan, PRC: Hubei Jiaoyu Chubanshe, 2000.

Xie Chongxie. *Chudeng xiaoxue nüzi xiushen jiaokeshu* [Lower-level elementary female ethics textbook]. Shanghai: Zhongguo Jiaoyu Gailiang Hui, 1906.

Joan Judge

FORBIDDEN CITY

The Forbidden City (Zijin cheng), the principal official (if not always actual) seat of government throughout most of the Ming (1368–1644) and Qing (1644–1912) dynasties, is generally taken to consist of the great walled compound in central Beijing now managed by the National Palace Museum (Gugong Bowuyuan). However, these Outer and Inner Courts (Da Nei, or "Great Within") of the old imperial palace historically formed just one part of a larger complex that extended to the north and west, encompassing the Lake Palaces around Beihai and Zhongnanhai. The latter is the site of what many regard as the current Great Within, housing residences and offices for the top leadership of the party-state.

CONSTRUCTION AND DESIGN

Construction of the Forbidden City was undertaken from 1406 to 1420 by the Ming emperor Yongle (r. 1402–1424), who after usurping the throne had decided in 1406 to move his capital from Nanjing to his northern power base in Beiping (renamed Beijing, or "northern capital").

His palace, like that of the Mongol rulers of the preceding Yuan dynasty (1279–1368) (on which it was largely modeled), adhered closely to the ideal outlined in the *Zhou li* (Rituals of Zhou). (The Yuan edifice, on the later site of the Lake Palaces, was demolished on completion of Yongle's replacement.) The dictates of geomancy, or fengshui, were closely followed; these involved strict orientation along a north-south meridian, propitiously sited water features, and an artificial hill (Jing Shan) to the north of the palace. The main audience halls, designed to inspire awe and reverence for imperial might, were originally constructed from the rare timbers *zitan* and *nanmu* (consequently rendered practically extinct by the late Ming). Shortly after its completion, the new palace was ravaged by fire in 1421—an occurrence repeated many times over the centuries. The structure also underwent considerable reconstruction or alteration under the Kangxi emperor (r. 1661–1722) and the Qianlong emperor (r. 1736–1796) of the Qing dynasty.

FALL INTO DISREPAIR AND CONVERSION INTO A MUSEUM

As contact with various Western powers intensified over the course of the nineteenth century, the Forbidden City (along with the Great Wall) came to be regarded as a metaphor for qualities of exoticism, mystique, and inscrutability associated with a China widely perceived as vainly attempting to seal itself off from the forces of progress and modernity. Stereotypes of obscurantism and decadence were particularly associated—both by Western observers and early Chinese reformers—with the tenure of the much-vilified empress dowager Cixi (a dominant influence over state affairs for several decades prior to her death in 1908), whose ascendancy witnessed the sacking and looting of the Forbidden City by Western and Japanese forces in the aftermath of the Boxer Uprising of 1899 to 1900.

At the fall of the Qing dynasty in 1912, much of the palace was falling into disrepair—and its condition worsened during the early Republican period. The deposed Xuantong emperor (r. 1909–1912), Puyi, was initially permitted to continue living in the Inner Court of the palace, while the president of the new Chinese Republic, Yuan Shikai (r. 1912–1916), made the Lake Palaces the new seat of government. Yuan attempted to proclaim himself emperor in 1915, but died in 1916, and his planned enthronement in the Hall of Supreme Harmony (Taihe Dian) never took place.

In 1917 the warlord Zhang Xun (1854–1923) attempted to restore the Qing dynasty, and Puyi was briefly reenthroned, but in the face of national opposition (including a somewhat desultory air attack on the Forbidden City itself), he abdicated after twelve days. The ex-emperor and his eunuchs meanwhile competed in the pilfering of the imperial collections with a view to profiting from a thriving antiques market. Following Puyi's announcement that he intended to hold an inventory of the Qianlong emperor's collection, many valuable items were destroyed in a mysterious fire on June 27, 1923, that gutted the Palace of Established Happiness (Jianfu Gong). Most remaining eunuchs were evicted by Puyi from the Forbidden City the next day, but the entire imperial family was to follow them within little over a year.

A Gallery of Antiquities (Guwu Chenlie Suo) had been opened in the Hall of Martial Valor (Wuying Dian) as early as 1913, but the vacating of the Forbidden City's Inner Court in 1924 allowed a new Palace Museum (Gugong Gongli Bowuyuan) to open its doors to the public on National Day (October 10) in 1925. Despite government proposals as early as 1926 for a merger of the Gallery of Antiquities with the Palace Museum, such a move was resisted until 1948. The new museum initially displayed the imperial apartments in the disordered state in which they had been left by the departing court of Puyi, the better to illustrate for public edification the decadent lifestyle of China's former Manchu rulers. Whereas the Gallery of Antiquities aimed to display select national treasures to elite visitors, and levied exorbitant admission charges calculated to exclude the unwashed masses, the Palace Museum from an early stage adopted a more democratic mission, and charged far more affordable entry fees.

THE FORBIDDEN CITY UNDER NATIONALIST CONTROL

In 1928 the new Nationalist regime based in Nanjing established control over Beijing, stripping the city of its status as national capital, and restoring its early Ming title of Beiping (the north pacified). The Palace Museum came under control of the national government, while the Gallery of Antiquities, whose management had enjoyed close ties to the city's former warlord rulers, fell into decline. The Zhongnanhai compound, no longer required for government use, was meanwhile partially opened to the public, and a swimming pool opened there in 1933.

From 1931, Beijing was threatened by invasion from the Japanese in Manchuria (where Puyi was installed in 1934 as emperor of the puppet regime of Manchukuo), and this prompted the evacuation of many of the museum's most valuable treasures. These were transported first to the new capital in Nanjing, and then, shortly before the Japanese occupation of that city in 1937 (the same year they occupied Beiping), southwest to the Nationalists' wartime capital of Chongqing. With defeat in the civil war against the Communists imminent, the Nationalist regime in 1948 shipped about 600,000 of the choicest objects to Taiwan, where they were to form the basis of the collection of Taibei's own National Palace Museum.

THE FORBIDDEN CITY IN THE PEOPLE'S REPUBLIC OF CHINA

The fabric of the Forbidden City meanwhile suffered little serious damage during the Japanese occupation of Beiping between 1937 and 1945, but persisted in a condition of stately decay. From 1949, however, the restoration of Beijing's status as national capital under the new Communist regime heralded a period of more dramatic transformation for the old imperial palace and, more especially, for the city around it. Tiananmen, or the Gate of Heavenly Peace, to the south of the Meridian Gate (the entrance to the Forbidden City proper), was the site of the declaration of the founding of the People's Republic, and became the stage from which party leaders would greet the masses, or review the troops, on occasions of particular national importance.

In 1952 a scheme that would have preserved much of the old imperial city from the ravages of revolutionary progress was rejected, and the remodeling of the capital proceeded apace. A vast area south of Tiananmen was flattened to provide space upon which the masses could congregate to hail their leaders (or occasionally, as in 1989, to excoriate them), while on either side monumental Soviet-style public buildings were erected. The broad Chang'an Boulevard cut from east to west across the city, to the south of Tiananmen and the leadership's base in Zhongnanhai, bisecting the meridian of the imperial city. In 1956 the Upper Northern Gate, the northern entrance of the Forbidden City, was demolished to make way for another road-building program. During the Great Leap Forward (1958–1960), as part of plans for a complete remodeling of Beijing (including demolition of the city's walls), a project to build yet another east-west highway passing in front of the Meridian Gate was announced—but this was abandoned during the period of austerity following the Great Leap.

Inside the Forbidden City itself, meanwhile, museum workers proceeded to catalog those objects not removed to Taiwan by the Nationalists (about ten thousand crates of

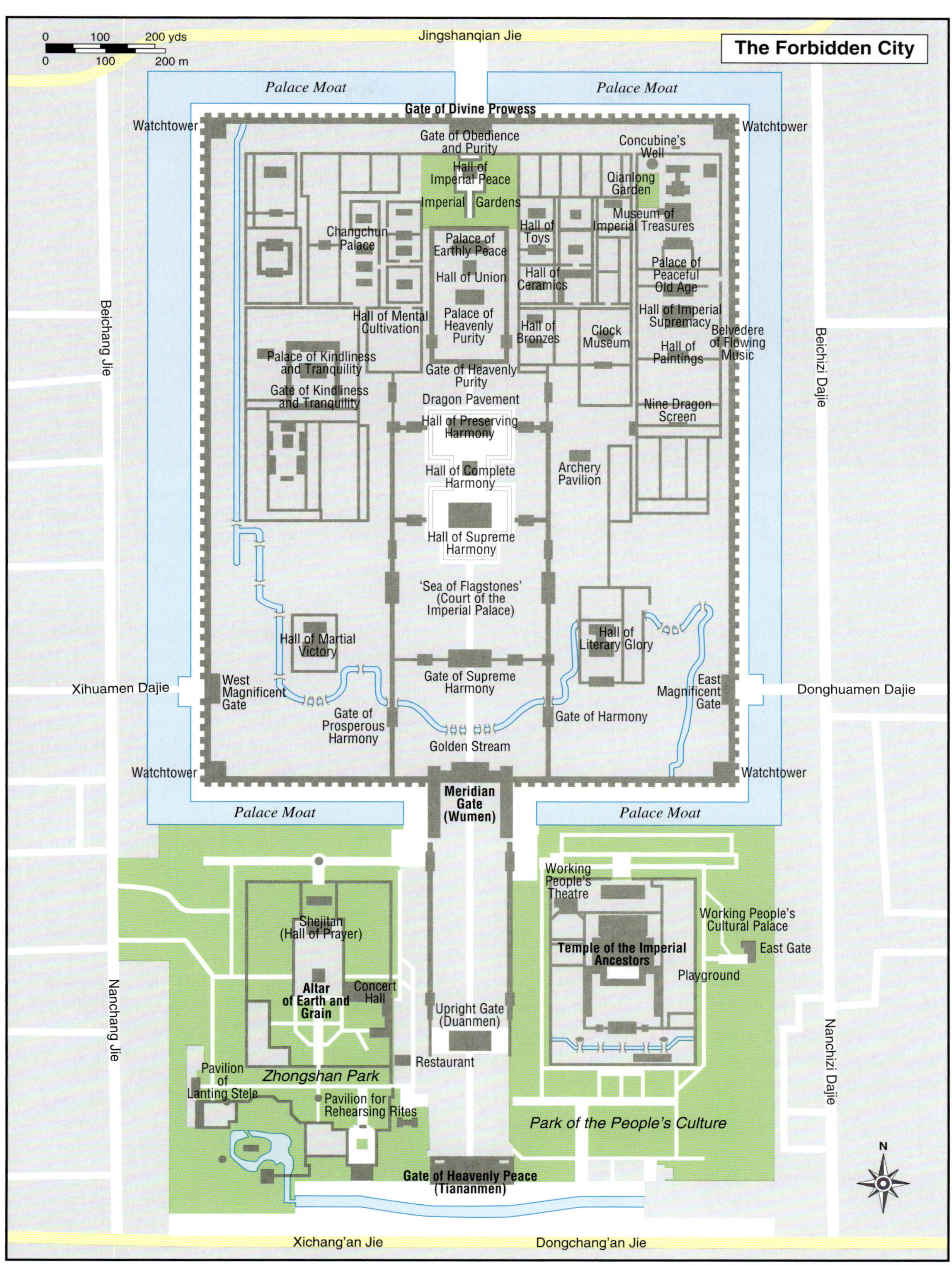
The Forbidden City
0 100 200 yds
0 100 200 m
Jingshanqian Jie
Palace Moat
Palace Moat
Gate of Divine Prowess
Watchtower
Watchtower
Gate of Obedience and Purity
Concubine's Well
Hall of Imperial Peace
Qianlong Garden
Imperial Gardens
Museum of Imperial Treasures
Changchun Palace
Hall of Toys
Palace of Earthly Peace
Palace of Peaceful Old Age
Hall of Union
Hall of Ceramics
Hall of Imperial Supremacy
Hall of Mental Cultivation
Palace of Heavenly Purity
Hall of Bronzes
Clock Museum
Belvedere of Flowing Music
Hall of Paintings
Palace of Kindliness and Tranquility
Gate of Heavenly Purity
Gate of Kindliness and Tranquility
Dragon Pavement
Nine Dragon Screen
Hall of Preserving Harmony
Hall of Complete Harmony
Archery Pavilion
Hall of Supreme Harmony
Beichang Jie
Beichizi Dajie
'Sea of Flagstones' (Court of the Imperial Palace)
Hall of Literary Glory
Hall of Martial Victory
Xihuamen Dajie
West Magnificent Gate
Gate of Supreme Harmony
East Magnificent Gate
Donghuamen Dajie
Gate of Prosperous Harmony
Gate of Harmony
Golden Stream
Watchtower
Watchtower
Meridian Gate (Wumen)
Palace Moat
Palace Moat
Working People's Theatre
Working People's Cultural Palace
Shejitan (Hall of Prayer)
Temple of the Imperial Ancestors
East Gate
Playground
Altar of Earth and Grain
Concert Hall
Nanchang Jie
Upright Gate (Duanmen)
Nanchizi Dajie
Restaurant
Pavilion of Lanting Stele
Zhongshan Park
Pavilion for Rehearsing Rites
Park of the People's Culture
N
Gate of Heavenly Peace (Tiananmen)
Xichang'an Jie
Dongchang'an Jie

View from the side door at the Forbidden City's Hall of Supreme Harmony, Beijing, 2003. *During both the Ming and Qing dynasties, the Forbidden City served as the seat of government for China's emperors. Initially rejected by Communist leaders as a symbol of traditional Chinese culture, the Forbidden City earned renewed appreciation at the end of the twentieth century for its historical significance to the country.* © REDLINK/CORBIS

artifacts were returned to Beijing from Nanjing after 1949), and an aggressive program of acquisitions was embarked upon, both to restore items from the original collection, and to extend it. The palace also served as the venue for work preparatory to the establishment of a Central Museum of the Revolution, the first exhibition of which was held in the Hall of Martial Valor in 1950. However, exhibition space within the Forbidden City was to remain very limited, particularly when set against the enormous size of the Palace Museum's collection. In addition to paintings and artifacts, the palace also continued to house a portion of the old imperial archives, though many documents were removed to the National Archives of China. During the first three decades of the People's Republic, the Forbidden City's Ancestral Temple also served a ceremonial function—as the venue for state funerals of important party leaders. Since the 1980s, however, it has housed an exhibition of clocks.

The Palace Museum was spared the worst ravages of the Cultural Revolution and its aftermath (1966–1976), although Red Guards attempted to storm the Forbidden City in August 1966, and the staff of the museum was "revolutionized" in a manner similar to that witnessed in other work units (thus the old museum head was subjected to ritual humiliation at the hands of his workers). From 1967 to 1970, the museum remained closed and, at the order of Premier Zhou Enlai, under guard by a battalion of military troops. Meanwhile, in 1969 and 1970, the Gate of Heavenly Peace (Tiananmen) was entirely reconstructed, its old timbers having been infested by ants. Subtle alterations were made to its architectural detail, with the imperial dragon motif on the roof tiles replaced with sunflowers, representing the masses turning to their sun, Chairman Mao, and paintwork on the eaves adjusted to include motifs previously reserved exclusively for palace halls. The rebuilt gate was to be the site of Mao's last public appearance, in 1971.

In 1970 Zhou ordered the museum staff to prepare for reopening, and in 1971 the palace welcomed an American ping-pong team, in advance of the visit by President Richard Nixon (1913–1994) the following year. Visits to the Forbidden City and the Great Wall were subsequently to form an obligatory feature of the itineraries for all major state visits. Nevertheless, Chairman Mao was to deliver one final posthumous (if on his part unintended) insult to the Forbidden City when his mausoleum was constructed in Tiananmen Square right across the north-south meridian, on the site of the former Great Qing Gate.

POPULAR VIEWS OF THE FORBIDDEN CITY

The early decades of the People's Republic had witnessed considerable ideological antagonism on the part of radical leftists, including Mao himself, to the Forbidden City and the hidebound "old culture" that it was perceived to embody. For many die-hard post-1949 revolutionaries, as for some radicals during the earlier Republican period, the old imperial palace represented all the forces of tradition and conservatism from which a "New China" would need to liberate itself. However, during the decades of "reform and opening" since 1978, and particularly since the early 1990s, celebration of China's traditional heritage and "five thousand years of glorious history" have become central to state propaganda, as well as reflecting growing popular triumphalism over China's economic and political resurgence.

Amid a mood of growing reverence for the symbols of the imperial past, the Forbidden City has formed the backdrop to, or setting for, a number of popular films, such as Bernardo Bertolucci's *The Last Emperor* (1987), and the 2003 television series *Towards the Republic* (*Zou xiang Gonghe*), which featured a revisionist portrayal of Empress Dowager Cixi and other late imperial figures. During the presidency of the opera-loving Jiang Zemin, Giacomo Puccini's *Turandot* (1926) was performed live at the Ancestral Temple in 1998, with stage sets designed by the film director Zhang Yimou, and in June 2001 the Three Tenors (Plácido Domingo, José Carreras, and Luciano Pavarotti) performed in front of the Meridian Gate.

Fear of damage to the fabric of the palace complex means that it is unlikely to be used again to stage such large-scale performances. Since 2005, a major program of restoration of the Forbidden City has been underway, and is scheduled to continue until 2020 (the six hundredth anniversary of its construction). Meanwhile, the new mood of patriotic fervor, encouraged if not always directed by the regime, has fueled a drive to purge the Palace Museum of inappropriate "foreign" influences, resulting in the replacement of a discreetly located branch of the American chain Starbucks with a Chinese-owned cafeteria serving Yunnan coffee.

Ironically, the period since the early 1990s, during which the Forbidden City and its late-imperial residents have increasingly been touted by China's Communist regime as positive symbols of a national identity newly rooted in tradition, has also witnessed the rapid destruction of most of what remained of old Beijing outside the palace walls. In the early twenty-first century, the Forbidden City is an incongruous island of ancient exotica amid an ocean of ultramodern glass and concrete. However, following efforts to spruce up the capital in advance of the 2008 Beijing Olympic Games, the Forbidden City once again found itself central to a revived north-south axis, stretching from a rebuilt (though half-size) Yongdingmen (Eternally Fixed Gate) directly to the south, to the Olympic Stadium, the "Bird's Nest" (Niao Chao), in the north.

SEE ALSO *Beijing; Imperial Palaces; Museums; Yuan Shikai.*

BIBLIOGRAPHY

Barmé, Geremie R. *The Forbidden City.* Cambridge, MA: Harvard University Press, 2008.

Holdsworth, May. *The Forbidden City.* Oxford, U.K.: Oxford University Press, 1998.

Na Zhi Liang. *Dian shou gu gong guobao qishi nian* [Seventy years of preserving the national treasures of the palace museum]. Beijing: Zijin Cheng Chubanshe, 2004.

Edward Vickers

FOREIGN CONCESSIONS, SETTLEMENTS, AND LEASED TERRITORIES

Foreign concessions and settlements were areas established within sixteen of the ninety-two treaty ports that existed in China at the height of the treaty port system. Concessions were leased in perpetuity to particular foreign governments. Settlements, by contrast, were not leased to the foreign power, but simply set aside by treaty for foreign residence and trade. In concessions, the relevant consul held the lease for the whole territory, and individual foreigners obtained subleases to their property through him. This was the arrangement, for example, for individual concessions in Tianjin, Hankou, and Guangzhou (Canton). In the Shanghai settlements, it was the Chinese authorities who issued title deeds to the foreigners who bought land.

The third form of foreign-controlled area was the leased territory, in which Chinese sovereignty was extinguished for the duration of the lease. All five leased territories in China were established in 1898 in a period of intense competition between the imperialist powers, and represented their attempts to gain exclusive control of mineral resources and communications. Jiaozhou Bay in Shandong Province was leased to Germany, the Liaodong Peninsula in northeast China to Russia, Guangzhou Bay in the south to France, and what became the New Territories of Hong Kong and the port of Weihaiwei in Shandong to Great Britain.

Though some foreign enclaves were more important and lasted longer than others, all of the concessions, settlements, and leased territories developed as mini-colonies governed, policed, and taxed by foreign powers. They allowed the emergence of a modernized urban Chinese culture. At the same time, though, they were a blatant affront to China's sovereignty, and an obvious symbol of

China's semicolonial status. No wonder that most Chinese felt profoundly ambivalent about them.

GOVERNMENT OF THE FOREIGN SETTLEMENTS

Foreign consuls were at first in charge of administration as well as public order in concessions and settlements. Increasingly elaborate institutions developed in the major settlements to take control of administration and the police. The most sophisticated—and best studied—was the Shanghai Municipal Council (SMC) (*gongbuju*) of the International Settlement (Shanghai gonggongzujie), which began as an executive committee of ratepayers but gradually accumulated what were in effect the powers of government, exercising jurisdiction over both foreign and Chinese residents and going far beyond the legal basis derived from the treaties. Only foreigners were allowed to vote for SMC members, and the property qualification was high. Chinese gained representation on the SMC and most other municipal councils after 1928. The foreign settlements certainly did not offer a model of democracy. They were controlled in effect by nationals of the dominant foreign power—Great Britain in the case of Shanghai's International Settlement—in the interest of business and trade. In cities such as Tianjin, where seven nations held concessions, and Hankou, where there were five, relations between the different foreign administrations were complex and time consuming.

Despite their differing legal statuses, the concessions, settlements, and leased territories foreign enclaves all developed societies and institutions with points of similarity. Law and order, sanitation, and planning were in the hands of foreign authorities. Because the enclaves were designed to offer expatriate residents the amenities of home, they were dominated by Western-style buildings, and had utilities, street lighting, shopping areas, and leisure facilities modeled on those of Western cities. Seaboard settlements such as Weihaiwei and Qingdao in the north and Shamian in the south also developed as holiday resorts for foreigners seeking to escape the oppressive heat.

CHINESE IN THE FOREIGN SETTLEMENTS

Although the government of these enclaves was foreign, they did not exclude Chinese residents; indeed, the majority of their populations was Chinese. Chinese residents included not only the poorer classes working to serve the foreigners and their enterprises in various capacities but also the new Chinese middle class. Spacious Western-style housing and shops, tapped water, sanitation, electricity, and the other comforts of foreign settlement life were all attractive to Chinese with money. Even more important was the security offered by the foreign enclaves. The foreign authorities consistently denied Chinese troops the right to enter the enclaves. Their residents were largely protected from the civil disturbances, rebellions, and civil wars that were a feature of the period. Prosperous traders could shelter their money and their property from the demands of Chinese governments, warlord armies, and rebels. Warlords also often maintained bank accounts in foreign enclaves, as well as residences to which they could retreat in defeat or retirement.

Wealthy Chinese were second-class citizens within the foreign enclaves. They paid taxes but were disenfranchised. In the settlements they had no legal right to own land, although many did so through foreign proxies. Social life in the apparently cosmopolitan societies of the foreign enclaves was in fact highly segmented along national and racial lines. At the bottom of the racial hierarchy, Chinese were excluded from foreign clubs and associations. Nevertheless, a modern urban Chinese culture developed. The settlements increasingly hosted new Chinese social institutions such as chambers of commerce, modern schools, clubs, trade unions, and charity and political associations. A major Chinese-language newspaper and publishing industry developed comparatively free of censorship and played an important part in building new political, commercial, and aesthetic cultures.

By the time of the early Republic, the Chinese middle class based in the foreign settlements was made up not only of merchants and traders but also of professionals such as journalists, teachers, doctors, lawyers, writers, and people involved in theater and film. Lu Xun, Mao Dun, Ba Jin and many lesser writers chose to live in Shanghai, which also developed a vibrant cinema culture. Song Qingling lived in a house in Shanghai's French concession; she was one of many opposition figures to use the shelter offered by the foreign settlements in Chiang Kai-shek's China. Young Chinese educated in the schools and colleges of the foreign settlement acquired foreign-languages skills and knowledge of the outside world that they needed to work in business or in the professions in China or in the outside world.

The foreign settlements created a space in which a modernized urban Chinese society was able to flourish for a time. Historians disagree about the importance of its legacy. Some argue that the foreign settlements created both economic and cultural duality in China. For them, the modernity of the treaty ports could not transform the "real China" of the interior, from which it was so profoundly different. For others, the vibrancy and heterogeneity of the culture that developed in the shelter of foreign enclaves lives on in modernizing trends in contemporary Chinese society.

SEE ALSO *Extraterritoriality; Imperialism; Shanghai; Shanghai Mixed Court.*

BIBLIOGRAPHY

Bergère, Marie-Claire. The Chinese Bourgeoisie, 1911–1937. In *Republican China, 1912–1949, Part 1*. Vol. 12 of *Cambridge History of China*, ed. John K. Fairbank, 722–826. Cambridge, U.K.: Cambridge University Press, 1983.

Feuerwerker, Albert. The Foreign Presence in China. In *Republican China, 1912–1949, Part 1*. Vol. 12 of *Cambridge History of China*, ed. John K. Fairbank, 128–208. Cambridge, U.K.: Cambridge University Press, 1983.

Lu Hanchao. *Beyond the Neon Lights: Everyday Shanghai in the Early Twentieth Century*. Berkeley: University of California Press, 1999.

Pye, Lucien. How China's Nationalism Was Shanghaied. In *Chinese Nationalism*, ed. Jonathan Unger, 86–112. Armonk, NY, and London: M. E. Sharpe, 1996.

Delia Davin

FOREIGN CURRENCY RESERVES

The currencies of different countries are traded in an active market that circles the globe and operates around the clock. Under the rules of the International Monetary Fund (IMF), which the People's Republic of China joined in 1980, a country is free to choose either to permit its currency to fluctuate against other currencies or to peg its currency to another currency. In the years since 1971, when President Nixon unilaterally cancelled the link between the U.S. dollar and gold, many central banks have permitted their currencies to fluctuate against the dollar. However, as can be seen in Figure 1, following a period of fluctuation and a major devaluation in 1994, the Chinese currency (which is referred to as both the *renminbi* and the *yuan*) was firmly pegged to the U.S. dollar for about a decade, at the rate of about 8.28 *yuan* to the dollar. During these years, China had a balance-of-payments surplus with the United States, which meant that normally the value of the *yuan* would have risen against the dollar. To offset this pressure, the Chinese monetary authorities used *yuan* (of which they have effectively an infinite supply, since they can always print more) to buy up dollars in the international currency market.

This policy intervention had at least four consequences: (1) it maintained a stable exchange rate, which facilitated international business transactions by reducing the foreign exchange risk—a result that had widespread benefits; (2) it led the Chinese monetary authorities to accumulate ever-growing reserves of foreign currencies, especially U.S. dollars, as graphed in Figure 2—a result that, in and of itself, was arguably of little importance; (3) it made Chinese products cheaper for American consumers—a result that benefited American consumers but worried

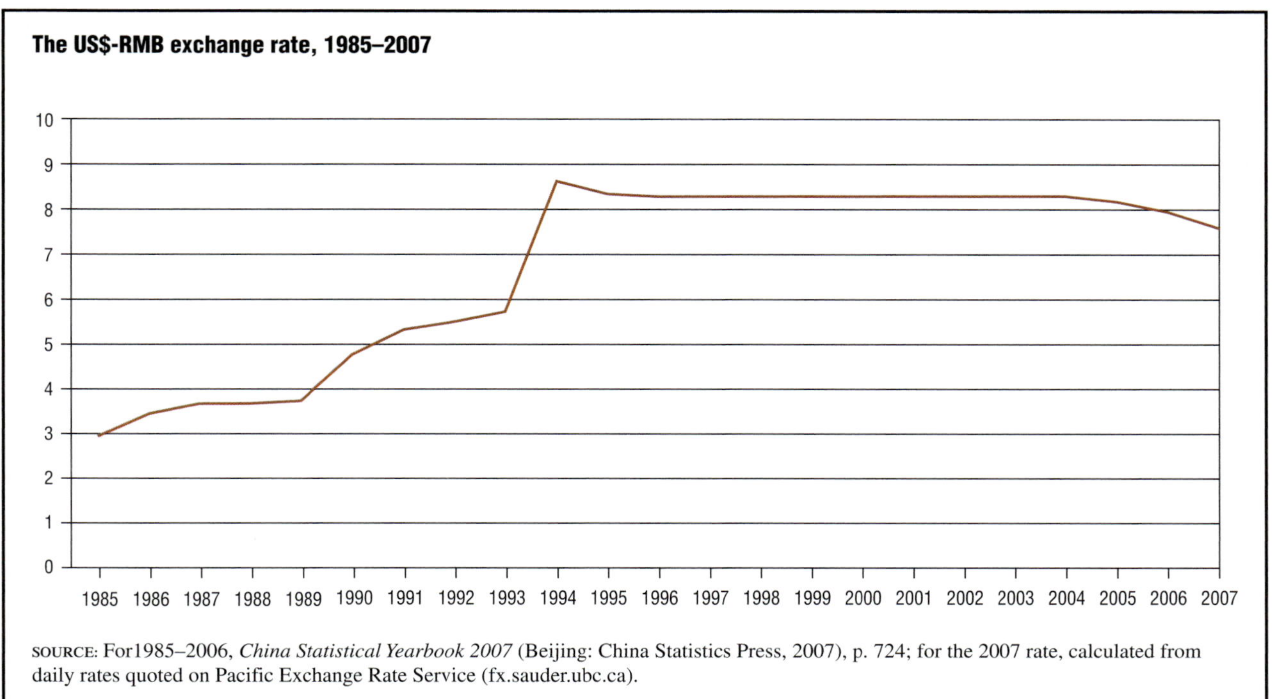

SOURCE: For1985–2006, *China Statistical Yearbook 2007* (Beijing: China Statistics Press, 2007), p. 724; for the 2007 rate, calculated from daily rates quoted on Pacific Exchange Rate Service (fx.sauder.ubc.ca).

Figure 1

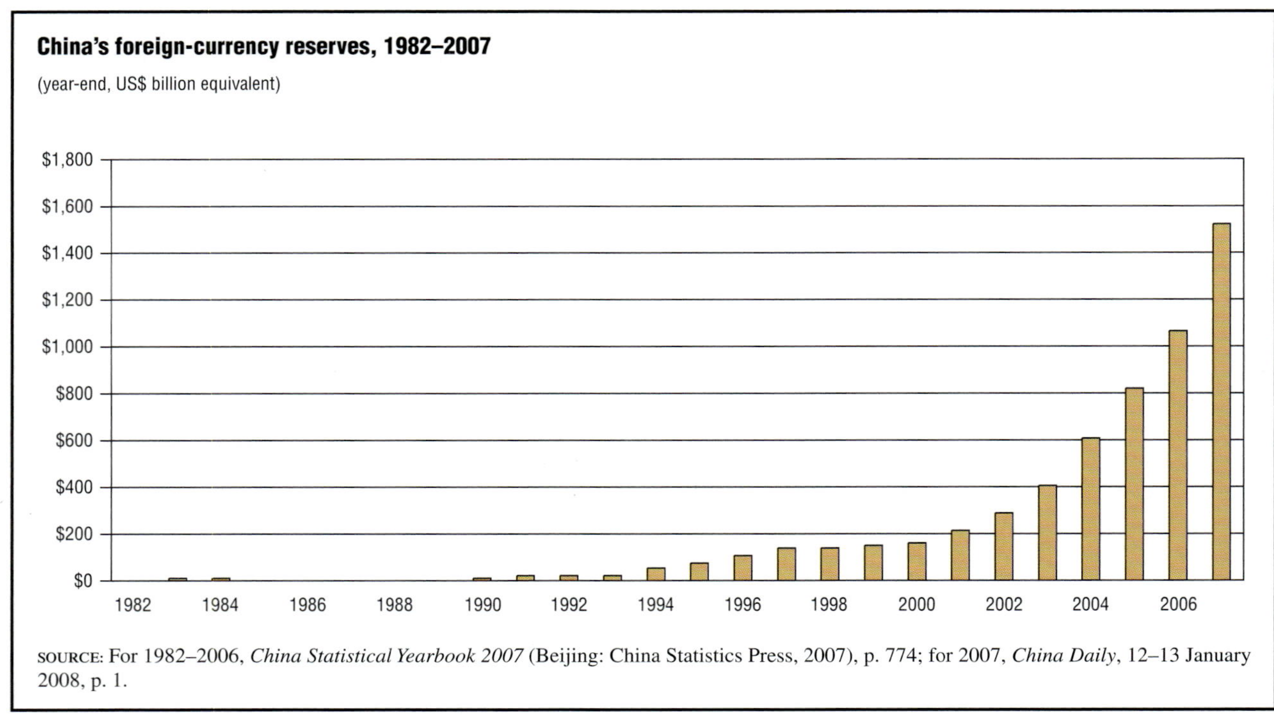

SOURCE: For 1982–2006, *China Statistical Yearbook 2007* (Beijing: China Statistics Press, 2007), p. 774; for 2007, *China Daily*, 12–13 January 2008, p. 1.

Figure 2

American workers; and (4) it increased the domestic money supply in China (the number of *yuan* in circulation), thereby feeding inflationary pressures—a result that worried the Chinese authorities greatly, because in China political instability has often been triggered by periods of price inflation.

As China's trade surpluses with the United States expanded, the U.S. government became increasingly vocal in criticizing the Chinese policy of a pegged exchange rate, and in 2005 the Chinese announced that they would permit the *yuan* to appreciate against the dollar. As can be seen from Figure 1, the *yuan* has indeed appreciated gradually since 2005. But, as can be seen from Figure 2, the Chinese authorities are still intervening actively in the foreign currency market to prevent this change from occurring too quickly (from their point of view), which has led to American complaints that the adjustment, while welcome, has been too slow.

To an economist, these American complaints are puzzling, since they are based on a simple misunderstanding. It is true that since the mid-1990s the United States has experienced a massive deficit in its international trade, and it is also true that a significant portion of these imports come from China (about 31% in 2006). However, it does not follow that an appreciation of the *yuan* would reduce the U.S. trade deficit, though it probably would cause a shift away from China and toward other foreign suppliers—in Canada, Germany, Vietnam, or wherever. For any country, it is necessarily true that a shortfall in total domestic savings (the amount by which household, corporate, and government spending exceeds the savings and taxes available to finance such spending) will be matched by a deficit in international trade. What this unavoidable truth means is that, so long as American households and governments engage in deficit spending (which they did to the tune of about US $800 billion in 2006), the American economy will exhibit a trade deficit (which, predictably, was also about US $800 billion in 2006). In brief, an appreciation of the *yuan* exchange rate will not—cannot—solve the U.S. trade deficit.

SEE ALSO *European Union, Relations with; Financial Regulation; Foreign Trade since 1950; United States, Relations with.*

BIBLIOGRAPHY

State Administration for Foreign Exchange. http://www.safe.gov.cn.

U.S. Department of Commerce, Bureau of Economic Analysis. http://www.bea.gov.

Ralph W. Huenemann

STATE ADMINISTRATION OF FOREIGN EXCHANGE (SAFE)

Under the control of the People's Bank of China (PBOC), the State Administration of Foreign Exchange (SAFE) regulates the foreign-exchange market and manages the bulk of China's foreign-exchange reserves. It is headed by Hu Xiaolian, who also serves as deputy governor of the PBOC. SAFE's Reserve Management Department maintains subsidiaries in Hong Kong, Singapore, London, and New York. In order to ensure the PBOC's ability to protect the value of the renminbi in the case of a currency crisis, to honor foreign debt obligations during a capital account crisis, and to cover imports during a current account crisis, SAFE invests China's foreign-exchange reserves in secure and liquid asset classes that only achieve a modest return.

SAFE does not disclose the composition of its portfolio. It is estimated that up to 70 percent of the reserves under SAFE's management are invested in U.S. dollar-denominated securities. The remaining part is believed to be mainly invested in securities denominated in euros and, to a smaller extent, Japanese yen and British pounds. More than a quarter of the foreign-exchange reserves under SAFE's management are invested in U.S. Treasury bonds. A slightly smaller amount is invested in U.S. agency bonds. However, with rapidly growing foreign-exchange reserves, a shift in China's investment strategy is under way, as only a small portion of its reserves would be needed to intervene in the case of a crisis.

While interest rates in China were lower than in the U.S., the PBOC was making a profit by investing China's foreign exchange reserves in U.S. Treasury and agency bonds while issuing local currency bills for the purpose of sterilization. However, due to the reversal in monetary cycles, the PBOC is now paying more on the renminbi-denominated central bank bills than it gets on its Treasury and agency bonds. Therefore, there is a need to diversify into riskier and less liquid asset classes in order to achieve higher returns. In addition, a diversification away from the depreciating U.S. dollar is necessary to prevent a further decline in the value of China's reserves measured in renminbi. SAFE has already started diversifying its portfolio. In January 2008, it was revealed that SAFE's Hong Kong based subsidiary SAFE Investment Company had acquired stakes of less than one per cent in three of Australia's largest banks. In the following months, SAFE acquired a 1.6 percent stake in the French energy company Total and a stake of less than one percent in the British energy company BP. It also invested 2.5 billion dollars in a fund run by the US private equity firm TPG. However, these investments came as a surprise, as investments in riskier and less-liquid asset classes were supposed to be carried out by the China Investment Corporation. It is believed that SAFE is trying to demonstrate its ability to achieve higher returns in order to prevent further transfers of reserves to the China Investment Corporation. The competition between SAFE and the China Investment Corporation reflects a rivalry between the PBOC, which controls SAFE, and the Ministry of Finance, which exerts significant influence over the China Investment Corporation.

Sandra Heep

FOREIGN INVESTMENT, 1800–1949

The infusion of foreign capital into China began after the first Opium War (1839–1842). In the early stages of this process, most foreigners invested only in the treaty ports, because the Qing government itself, in the interest of "self-strengthening," was focused on building military arsenals, dockyards, coal mines, a cotton mill, and inland telegraph lines. After China signed the Treaty of Shimonoseki with Japan in 1895, both foreign direct investment and indirect investment in China increased dramatically. The major reason was China's need to raise funds from abroad to pay off its huge indemnity debts. In addition, the Treaty of Shimonoseki allowed Japan, as well as other major foreign powers, to build factories in China. The profitability of direct investment in China at the time was high, about 5 to 20 percent, and the figure for foreign direct investment was never less than indirect investment. In 1931 no less than 78 percent of total foreign investment was direct investment. By the 1930s, Britain, Japan, Russia, and the United States held the largest investments in China (France and Germany dropped out of the leading positions after World War I [1914–1918]). About 46 percent of their investments were located in Shanghai, with 36 percent in Manchuria and 18 percent in the rest of China.

CHINA INVESTMENT CORPORATION

The China Investment Corporation (CIC, Zhongguo Touzi Youxian Zeren Gongsi) was formally established in September 2007. It is mandated to invest a portion of China's foreign-exchange reserves. By investing in riskier asset classes than treasury and agency bonds and by diversifying away from the U.S. dollar, it is hoped that the CIC will increase the return on China's reserves and prevent a further decline in the value of its reserves measured in renminbi.

The CIC has ministry status and reports directly to the State Council. The agencies that are represented in the leadership of the CIC are the Ministry of Finance, the National Development and Reform Commission, the People's Bank of China, the State Administration of Foreign Exchange, the Ministry of Commerce, and the China Banking Regulatory Commission. The CIC's chairman, Lou Jiwei, formerly served as vice minister of finance. Its president, Gao Xiqing, was vice chairman of China's National Council for Social Security Fund. The CIC is financed through the issuance of renminbi-denominated special treasury bonds by the Ministry of Finance, which uses the proceeds to purchase a portion of the foreign-exchange reserves from the central bank. This procedure is intended to help withdraw excess liquidity from the Chinese economy. The debt service on the special treasury bonds is covered by the CIC.

The CIC has US $200 billion under management. It used $67 billion to take over the Central Huijin Investment Company, which will continue to recapitalize state-owned financial institutions and to foster the reform of the financial sector. At the end of 2007, Huijin invested RMB $20 billion in China Everbright Bank and $20 billion in China Development Bank. It will recapitalize Agricultural Bank of China with an estimated $20 billion. Therefore, the CIC has only an estimated $90 billion to invest in international capital markets. A large part of this sum will be given to external managers to invest in equities and fixed-income products, as well as private equity funds and hedge funds. The amount of capital that is directly managed by the CIC will be mainly used for portfolio investments. The CIC invested $3 billion in the private equity firm Blackstone, $5 billion in the investment bank Morgan Stanley, and $3.2 billion in a fund run by the private equity firm JC Flowers that will target financial institutions.

Despite the CIC's claim that it will operate on a purely commercial basis, there has been a debate within government and academic circles on strategic investments that could secure the supply of raw materials, contribute to the stabilization of China's economy, and help finance the overseas expansion of state-owned enterprises.

BIBLIOGRAPHY

Altbach, Eric G., and Cognato, Michael H. "Understanding China's New Sovereign Wealth Fund." *NBR Analysis* 19, 1 (2008).

Heep, Sandra. Chinas neuer Staatsfonds: Organisation, Finanzierung und Investitionsstrategie der China Investment Corporation [China's new sovereign wealth fund: Organization, financing, and investment strategy of the China Investment Corporation]. *Asien*, no. 108 (2008): 51–66.

Sandra Heep

IMPACT OF FOREIGN INVESTMENT

The role of foreign capital in China's economic development has been controversial: Did foreign capital oppress Chinese-owned enterprises by retarding their growth? There have been two schools of thought in answering the question. One view stresses the "imperialist" character of investments that were protected by extraterritorial rights, leased areas, treaty ports, railroad zones, foreign troops, and other "unequal" terms provided by treaties. The other view highlights the "innovative" impact of the foreign enterprises: China's leading shipping company, the China Merchants' Steam Navigation Company; the first modern Chinese bank, the Imperial Bank of China; and many other modern enterprises were modeled on Western counterparts trading in China. Yet, the amount of foreign investment per capita in China, $7 (U.S. dollars) in 1936, was small compared with that in other underdeveloped regions—for example, $20 in India and $86 in Latin America in 1938.

CHINESE PARTICIPATION IN FOREIGN INVESTMENT

Generally, foreign enterprises in China had a high ratio of reinvestment. About one-third of the enterprises reinvested

Foreign investments in China

[unit: U.S. millions]

	1902	1914	1931	1936
Britain	260.3 (33%)	607.5 (37.7%)	1189.2 (36.7%)	1220.8 (35%)
Japan	1.0 (0.1%)	219.6 (13.6%)	1136.9 (35.1%)	1394.0 (40%)
Russia	246.5 (31.3%)	269.3 (16.7%)	273.2 (8.4%)	0
U.S.	19.7 (2.5%)	49.3 (3.1%)	196.8 (6.1%)	298.8 (8.6%)
France	91.1 (11.6%)	171.4 (10.7%)	192.4 (5.9%)	234.1 (6.7%)
Germany	164.3 (20.9%)	263.6 (16.4%)	87.0 (2.7%)	148.5 (4.3%)
Others	5.0 (0.6%)	29.6 (1.8%)	167.0 (5.1%)	187.0 (5.4%)
Total	787.9 (100%)	1610.3 (100%)	3242.5 (100%)	3483.2 (100%)

Table 1

half of their profits, both in their established businesses and in related lines of business. The British company Jardine Matheson, for example, started as a small trading firm in the 1830s, but by the 1930s it had grown into a transnational enterprise with multiple branches in trading, banking, insurance, and manufacturing. Chinese collaborators, such as the compradors and agents who served as middlemen, accounted for the success of these early foreign enterprises. The foreign companies' reliance on Chinese employees varied from firm to firm. For example, the Hongkong and Shanghai Banking Corporation employed compradors from the 1860s up to the 1960s, whereas its Japanese counterpart, Mitsui, insisted on training its own Japanese staff to replace all of its Chinese compradors in the 1920s.

In contrast to Japan, British investment in China was mostly in finance, insurance, transport, and all tertiary sectors. Japanese investment comprised both light and heavy industries, ranging from agricultural plantations and mining in Manchuria to cotton-textile manufacturing in Shanghai. During the 1920s and 1930s, Japanese products—particularly in labor-intensive industries, such as matches, cotton, and glass—were the major competitors of Chinese products. Overseas Chinese sent huge amounts of money back to China, particularly in the 1930s when silver in China depreciated against most foreign currencies. This money helped China's balance of payment in terms of foreign trade, but it was not counted as foreign investment.

CONCLUSION

The liberation of Shanghai in May 1949 did not end foreign investment in China. The foreign community in Shanghai, particularly the British, did not retreat until 1956. Jardine Matheson was still conducting business with Communist China in the early 1950s. However, the Korean War (1950–1953), the American embargo, and other measures authorized by the United Nations against China had a major impact on foreign investment. Tax liabilities and labor compensation became issues of negotiations between foreign businesses and the new Chinese government. Because normal business operations could not be maintained, foreign businesses in China came to a standstill. National City Bank paid a liquidation tax of $233,000 (U.S. dollars) before it left China in 1950. Nevertheless, a few British firms, such as Jardine Matheson and the Hongkong and Shanghai Banking Corporation, never closed their offices in China.

SEE ALSO *China Merchants' Steam Navigation Company; Comprador; Foreign Loans, 1800–1949.*

BIBLIOGRAPHY

Allen, G. C., and Audrey G. Donnithorne. *Western Enterprise in Far Eastern Economic Development: China and Japan*. London: Allen and Unwin, 1954.

Cochran, Sherman. *Encountering Chinese Networks: Western, Japanese, and Chinese Corporations in China, 1880–1937*. Berkeley: University of California Press, 2000.

Goto-Shibata Harumi. *Japan and Britain in Shanghai, 1925–31*. Basingstoke, U.K.: Macmillan, 1995.

Hou Chi-ming (Hou Jiming). *Foreign Investment and Economic Development in China, 1840–1937*. Cambridge, MA: Harvard University Press, 1965.

Keswick, Maggie, and Clara Weatherall, eds. *The Thistle and the Jade: A Celebration of 175 Years of Jardine Matheson*. Rev. ed. London: Frances Lincoln, 2008.

King, Frank H. H. *The Hongkong Bank in the Period of Development and Nationalism, 1941–1984: From Regional Bank to Multinational Group*. Cambridge, U.K.: Cambridge University Press, 1991.

Remer, C. F. *Foreign Investments in China*. New York: Macmillan, 1933.

Shai, Aron. *The Fate of British and French Firms in China, 1949–1954: Imperialism Imprisoned*. Basingstoke, U.K.: Macmillan, 1996.

Starr, Peter. *Citibank: A Century in Asia*. Singapore: Editions Didier Millet, 2002.

Lee Pui-tak

FOREIGN INVESTMENT SINCE 1949

Prior to 1949, foreign direct investment (FDI) in China was confined mostly to a few enclaves in the coastal area, with most of the Chinese territory beyond reach for foreign investors. Great Britain and Japan (after seizing Manchuria in 1931) were by far the largest investors before World War II, representing 75 percent of total FDI in 1936 (Feuerwerker 1983, p. 117). Great Britain invested mostly in foreign trade (50% of the total), real estate (21%), and manufacturing (18%), whereas Japanese

FDI, concentrated in the northeast of the country, was mostly in transport, foreign trade, textile, and mining. But on the whole, FDI had little impact on the Chinese economy.

EARLY YEARS UNDER COMMUNISM

After the Chinese Communist Party seized power in 1949, a radical change occurred in FDI policy. Doors closed abruptly for foreign ownership in Chinese territory. Factories owned by Western countries or Japan were expropriated in the first years of the Communist regime, and until 1979, technical cooperation without foreign investment remained the rule. Despite this ban, China was in great need of foreign technologies to implement its ambitious industrialization plan. Between 1951 and 1960 the Soviet Union became the biggest provider of foreign capital and technology and played a critical role in helping a takeoff in various sectors of Chinese industry. During the First Five-Year Plan (1953–1958), half of all capital construction investment was channelled to Soviet aid projects, and 10,800 Soviet and 1,500 East European technicians were sent to China to design and build 156 big factories and infrastructure projects (Riskin 1987, p. 74). Among them, seven giant iron and steel plants, twenty-four electric power stations, and sixty-three machinery plants were completed thanks to the Soviet aid. After the recall of all Soviet experts and aid in July 1960, China remained nearly closed until 1978. Only a few "turnkey" factories were purchased by China between 1960 and 1978, without any foreign capital control in the operation.

OPEN DOORS, 1978

The crucial turning point occurred in December 1978 when economic reform was officially launched by Deng Xiaoping. In 1979 foreign ownership was once again authorized, in four special economic zones (SEZs) in coastal areas in southern China. FDI was restricted to light industry and real estate and had to be established through joint ventures (JVs) where foreign investor capital control could not exceed 49 percent. Soon after, the Chinese government decided to extend this open-door policy to fourteen coastal port cities (in May 1984), and to five big SEZs (in February 1985), in the Yangzi River Delta, Pearl River Delta, Xiamen-Zhangzhou-Quanzhou triangle in south Fujian Province, Jiaodong Peninsula, and Liaodong Peninsula. After three years of interruption following the Tiananmen massacre in June 1989, the pace of reform in FDI legislation accelerated. Foreign investors were granted the right to raise their stake in JVs beyond 49 percent, and in certain sectors to set up wholly owned factories. The open-door policy also was extended to the hinterland in the biggest cities, in land border area and along major rivers of the country. Finally, after China joined the World Trade Organization (WTO) in 2001, its foreign trade and investment legal framework was deeply revised by the Chinese government in order to comply with the commitments it made with its main trading partners during the negotiation period (United States and Europe mostly). With some exceptions (e.g., land, public utilities, energy, automobile, telecommunication, and military) all sectors of the economy are today officially open to FDI. Previous restrictions on FDI, such as geographical restrictions, minimum local-content production provisions, and limits on access to domestic market and imposed technology transfer, have been withdrawn in the new legislation.

NEW REFORM, 1992

From 1979 to 1992 the volume of FDI remained modest, averaging $1.7 billion per year. A turning point occurred in 1992, after Deng Xiaoping's decision to restart economic reform. According to the Ministry of Commerce of the People's Republic of China (MOFCOM), FDI jumped from $4.3 billion in 1991 to $11 billion in 1992, and then to $27.5 billion in 1993, and from 1995 to 2007 an average of $51.7 billion per year ($83 billion in 2007) have been invested by foreign investors in China. (These figures include profit made by foreign investors and reinvested in China, and represent between 20% and 30% of total FDI figures.) The coastal area has absorbed most of FDI since 1979—82 percent of the total, with 28 percent in Guangdong Province alone. After rules on wholly owned foreign investment were relaxed in the mid-1990s, it became the most preferred form of investment by foreigners, representing 78 percent of total FDI in 2007; only 20 percent of investment was made through JVs (MOFCOM at U.S.–China Business Council). Investors from Asian countries are by large the most important contributors to FDI. Of the total FDI accumulated between 1979 and 2003, Hong Kong accounted for nearly half, Taiwan and Japan 8 percent each Singapore 5 percent, and South Korea 4 percent. The United States and the European Union accounted for 9 percent and 8 percent respectively. Recent years have witnessed a large increase in foreign investment coming from the British Virgin Islands (19% of total FDI in 2007), the Cayman Islands (3%), Western Samoa (3%), and Mauritius (1.6%). MOFCOM believes that this foreign investment, along with FDI from Hong Kong (which represents as much as 25% of total of FDI in China), is the result of "round-tripping" investment, whereby firms and individuals of Chinese origin first invest abroad and then bring their investments back to China to benefit from the tax and other preferential rules given to foreign investors (UNCTAD 2007). Concerning the sectors, 60 percent of the total FDI accumulated since 1979 went to manufacturing, 25 percent into real estate, and 15 percent into services. But with the relaxation on foreign investment rules in services after China's entry to the WTO, FDI in the financial sector and real estate both have been growing rapidly in recent years.

On the whole, the open-door policy of thirty years ago that paved the way for a massive FDI influx after 1992 had a positive impact on China's economic development. Despite some massive labor-rights violations that occurred in foreign-funded companies (especially in Hong Kong, Taiwan, and South Korea JVs), the open policy gave China access to a vast amount of capital to fund its industrial development and to develop new manufacturing capabilities. It also enabled a big part of the coastal area and thousands of domestic enterprises to integrate into the world economy by subcontracting for foreign-funded companies operating in China. Although some have criticized the high degree of openness of the Chinese economy to foreign capital (Yasheng Huang 2003), China so far has avoided the main pitfall of FDI in developing countries, by implementing strict rules on foreign investments and progressively opening its domestic market to foreign companies. Until 2002, foreign investors could invest only in long-term industrial projects for export; the domestic market was protected by important tariff and nontariff barriers. This policy gave domestic producers sufficient time to boost their competitiveness with foreign investors. The absence of short-term FDI in portfolio investment protected China from the rapid movement of capital that has devastated other developing nations. Over the years, by changing FDI policies the Chinese government has been able to maintain a "fine tuning" between domestic needs (access to capital, to technology, and to foreign markets) and foreign pressures (access to domestic market and preferential tax and financial incentives). The government's new objectives in economic development (high technology industry and investments abroad by Chinese companies), as well as pressing demands from foreign companies (lower nontariff barriers, potential acquisition of Chinese firms, opening of new sectors for investment) may trigger another evolution of Chinese policy in terms of FDI.

SEE ALSO *Industrial Development since 1949.*

BIBLIOGRAPHY

Feuerwerker, Albert. Economic Trends, 1912–49. In *Republican China, 1912–1949*. Part 1, Vol. 12 of *The Cambridge History of China*, ed. John K. Fairbank and Denis Twitchett, 28–127. Cambridge, U.K.: Cambridge University Press, 1983.

Howell, Jude. *China Opens Its Doors: The Politics of Economic Transition*. Hertfordshire, U.K.: Harvester Wheatsheaf, 1993.

Naughton, Barry. *The Chinese Economy: Transitions and Growth*. Cambridge: Massachusetts Institute of Technology Press, 2007.

Riskin, Carl. *China's Political Economy: The Quest for Development Since 1949*. Oxford, U.K.: Oxford University Press, 1987.

Studwell, Joe. *The China Dream: The Elusive Quest for the Greatest Untapped Market on Earth*. London: Profile Books, 2002.

United Nations Conference on Trade and Development (UNCTAD). Rising FDI into China: The Facts Behind the Numbers. Investment Brief no. 2, 2007. http://www.unctad.org/en/docs/iteiiamisc20075_en.pdf.

U.S.–China Business Council. FDI in China. http://www.uschina.org/statistics/fdi_cumulative.html.

Yasheng Huang. *Selling China: Foreign Direct Investment during the Reform Era*. Cambridge, U.K.: Cambridge University Press, 2003.

Zweig, David. *Internationalizing China: Domestic Interests and Global Linkages*. Ithaca, NY: Cornell University, 2002.

Jean-François Huchet

FOREIGN LOANS, 1800–1949

Foreign loans were a new phenomenon in public finance in the latter half of the nineteenth century. They were floated to fund the costs for suppressing rebellions, the amortization of war indemnities, and China's nascent industrial and commercial enterprises. Historians disagree as to the date and nature of China's first foreign loan. Some have traced it to a modest 71,342 *taels* advanced by foreign merchants in 1853 to help suppress the Taiping Rebellion. Other historians, however, have argued that this was an advance against import duties payable to the Shanghai customs intendant and therefore a local arrangement (although it did require a memorial to the throne). Beijing did not incur its first sovereign-risk loan until 1865; it amounted to 1,431,664 pounds, and was borrowed from Britain to repay czarist Russia for arms and supplies delivered to Chinese forces in Xinjiang. Even then, that loan was also a "private" placement, in contrast to the first public issue guaranteed by the Qing dynasty government in 1874.

The "Chinese Imperial Government Fuzhou 8 percent loan" for 627,615 pounds (or 2 million *yangping taels*) to meet defense expenses was floated in 1874 by the Hongkong and Shanghai Bank in London. The loan was repayable over ten years with a nominal interest rate of 8 percent at 95 percent firm, and thus an effective interest rate of close to 8.5 percent. As further assurance for subscribers, the loan was secured on customs revenue by an imperial edict. The issuing price to the foreign subscribing public thus commanded a premium, making the issue highly profitable for the foreign banks. In addition to commissions and service charges, banks generated more profits by arbitrating the exchange rates between silver and gold in Shanghai and London. Such terms and operations became regular elements for foreign loans of the period.

The floating of loans on the international market underwritten by the foreign banks and guaranteed by

Foreign loans by period

Number	Total	
1853–1911	208	1,336,802,375 taels*
1912–1927	633	1,556,000,000 yuan**
1928–1949	108	45,000,000,000 yuan**
1928–1937		2,838,000 British pounds 33,299,108 U.S. dollars 450,000,000 francs 2,331,443 custom gold unit 92,500,000 fabi
1938–1949		14,427,649 British pounds 1,083,200,000 U.S. dollars*** 33,523,418 Canadian dollars 740,000 fabi

SOURCE: *Zhongguo renmin yinhang cangshishi, comp. *Zhongguo Qingdai waizhaishi ziliao* [Historical materials on foreign debt during the Qing dynasty]. Beijing: Zhongguo jinrong chubanshe, 1991; **Xu Yi, ed. *Beiyang zhengfu waizhai yu fengjian fupi* [Foreign debts of the northern warlord government and feudal restoration]. Beijing: Jingji chubanshe, 2000; *** U.S. Department of State. Disbursed Economic and Military Credits. In *United States Relations with China*. 2 vols., I: 1043–1053. Stanford, CA: Stanford University Press, 1967.

Table 1

Uses for foreign loans by period

	Indemnity	Government administration/ military/defense	Industrial/ railroad
1853–1911	62	9	29
1911–1927	1	64	35
1928–1946	0	71.8	27.4**

SOURCE: **Adapted from Mi Rucheng. "Zhongguo jindai waizhaishi lunyao." In *Jindai Zhongguo jingjishi yantaohui, 1999 lunwenji* [Proceedings of Symposium on Modern Chinese Economic History, 1999]. Hong Kong: Xinya yanjiusuo, 1999, p. 260.

Table 2

the Chinese government became a common means for the raising of funds (see Table 1).

HOW FOREIGN LOANS WERE USED

Regularized borrowing from foreign sources reflected the worsening fiscal condition of China. As the White Lotus, Taiping, and Nian rebellions drained the imperial treasury, local officials as well as the central government began to borrow ever larger amounts to meet mounting needs. Condemned to modernize the country's military, the increase in defense spending was largely met by short-term foreign loans. Conflicts with foreign powers incurred more expenses. Defeats were settled with humiliating, if not debilitating, indemnities—especially following the First Sino-Japanese War (1894–1895) and the Boxer Uprising (1900)—necessitating long-term borrowing from abroad. The bulk of foreign loans during the Qing period thus went to pay for indemnities, but approximately one-third of the loans financed state-run enterprises, public works, mines, and especially railroads, which provided the initial impetus for China's early industrialization (see Table 2).

Historians, whether of the nationalistic or communist persuasion, nevertheless made a case for the inefficient use of these loans. An estimated half of the railroads remained incomplete, with the funds diverted to other uses. As part of their "spheres of interest," foreign powers attached stringent terms to these railroad and mining concessions, including the right of first refusal for future loans and the hiring of their respective nationals as engineers and managers, further compromising China's sovereignty.

FOREIGN EXPLOITATION?

Historians also pointed to the negative impact of silver-gold exchange trends as an additional burden, if not quite exploitation of the country. Many of the loans were delivered in silver, while both interest and principal had to be repaid in gold over the life of the loan. Because gold appreciated throughout the period (with the exceptions of the 1904–1907 and 1916–1920 periods), more silver was needed to service the loans. The Boxer indemnities thus required an additional loan of one million pounds in 1905 to service loans from the Hongkong and Shanghai Bank. Disputes also arose as to whether repayments should be made using the exchange rate quoted in the loan agreement or the exchange rate that stood when payments became due, and if the latter, the rate "fixed" by the servicing bank or by the market (Shanghai, London, or New York) rate of the day.

Government income provided primary and secondary surety to many of these loans. As the number of foreign loans to China increased, a combination of customs revenue as well as surplus, provincial income, commercial taxes (*lijin*), title-deed fees, and finally the *gabelle* (salt tax) became sureties for loan repayment. To ensure that the Chinese government could service the mounting debt, Great Britain and other countries insisted on appointing their own nationals to modernize the collection and audit of such revenues. The Maritime Customs and the Salt Administration thus became "synarchies" run by Sino-foreign bureaucracies, with appointments to key positions a matter of contentious diplomacy among the powers of the day.

Political banking thus became part of the game. While such institutions as the Hongkong and Shanghai Bank might have wished that their loan decisions could be commercially driven, competition among banks in England (including Chartered Bank) and with European, American, and Japanese bank consortiums for a share of profits, not to mention national prestige and strategic interests, rendered such loans and the banks an extension of diplomacy. Seeking the support of their respective governments, bank syndicates often conducted negotiations through their respective foreign ministries. Loan offers and "synarchy" thus combined to give the powers immense control over successive Chinese governments.

As China's finances in the 1920s disintegrated, negotiations and conferences were held to address defaults and renegotiation of interest rates and payments. In addition to partial releases of "loans" converted from the Boxer indemnities, limited success was achieved as other loans were settled with cancellation of interest in arrears, reduced interest rates, and repayment of principal by installment. However, the onset of World War II (1937–1945) resulted in the suspension of all debt service in 1939 and another round of predominately war-related loans that dwarfed previous periods in scale. By August 1948, the Nationalist government reported outstanding foreign loans (principal only) totaling 659,818,143 U.S. dollars, 49,092,136 British pounds, 33,523,418 Canadian dollars, and 740,000 Chinese *fabi.*

SEE ALSO *Foreign Trade, 1800-1950; Imperialism.*

BIBLIOGRAPHY

Bank of China Research Department, comp. *Chinese Government Foreign Loan Obligations*. Shanghai: Bank of China, 1935.

King, Frank H. H., with Catherine E. King and David J. S. King. *The History of the Hongkong and Shanghai Banking Corporation*. 4 vols. Cambridge, U.K.: Cambridge University Press, 1987–1991.

Lu Yangyuan et al. *Minguo shehui jingjishi* [A social and economic history of Republican China]. Beijing: Zhongguo Jingji Chubanshe, 1991.

MacMurray, John V. A., comp. *Treaties and Agreements with and Concerning China, 1894–1919*. 2 vols. New York: Oxford University Press, 1921.

Mi Rucheng. Zhongguo jindai waizhaishi lunyao. In *Jindai Zhongguo jingjishi yantaohui, 1999 lunwenji* [Proceedings of Symposium on Modern Chinese Economic History, 1999], pp. 251–266. Hong Kong: Xinya Yanjiusuo, 1999.

U.S. Department of State. Disbursed Economic and Military Credits. In *United States Relations with China*, vol. 1: 1043–1053. Stanford, CA: Stanford University Press, 1967.

Xu Yi, ed. *Beiyang zhengfu waizhai yu fengjian fupi* [Foreign debts of the Northern warlord government and feudal restoration]. Beijing: Jingji Chubanshe, 2000.

Xu Yisheng. *Zhongguo jindai waizhaishi tongji ziliao* [Statistical materials on modern China's foreign debt]. Beijing: Zhonghua Shuju, 1962.

Young, Arthur. *China's Nation-building Effort, 1927–1937: The Financial and Economic Record*. Stanford, CA: Hoover Institution Press, 1971.

Zhongguo renmin yinhang cangshishi, comp. *Zhongguo Qingdai waizhaishi ziliao* [Historical materials on foreign debt during the Qing dynasty]. Beijing: Zhongguo Jinrong Chubanshe, 1991.

Kwan Man Bun (Guan Wenbin)

FOREIGN POLICY FRAMEWORKS AND THEORIES

This entry contains the following:

OVERVIEW

In general, Chinese foreign policy since 1949 has scored high marks from most international scholars who have written on the subject. In its first three or four decades, the People's Republic of China had limited economic and military capabilities. Yet since the Geneva Conference in 1954, China has managed to maintain its major-power status and has enjoyed considerable influence in international affairs. Until the early 1990s, Chinese leaders formulated China's foreign policy according to their worldview and their analysis of global contradictions. Discussions of China's national interest only emerged in the early 1990s. With the exception of the "leaning to one side" policy in the first half of the 1950s, China largely pursued an independent foreign policy. The Taiwan question, though regarded as a domestic issue, is very significant in the Chinese foreign policy framework because it is related to the legitimacy of the Chinese Communist regime as well as the recognition and status of China in the international community.

"LEANING TO ONE SIDE"

In spring 1949, the Chinese Communist leadership proposed its basic positions on China's foreign relations: (1) "setting up a new stove," meaning that New China had to cultivate a new breed of diplomats; (2) "cleaning up the house first before receiving guests," meaning that the legacy and influence of imperialist powers in China had to be removed; and (3) "leaning to one side," meaning that China would become part of the united front against anti-imperialism led by the Soviet Union.

The "leaning to one side" position was forced upon China. In the final years of World War II (1937–1945) and in the early postwar years, the Chinese Communist leadership sought contact and cooperation with the United States. But the U.S. government closed its doors and continued to support the Guomindang regime. At the beginning of the Korean War (1950–1953), the United Nations imposed an embargo against China, while the administration of Harry S. Truman (1884–1972) perceived China as a follower of the Soviet Union and attempted to "contain" China through alliances with its neighbors. The Sino-Soviet alliance was instrumental in preventing the Korean War from spreading to mainland China. The Soviet Union also became an important source of economic assistance and guidance in building China's planned economy in its imposed isolation.

Chinese leaders soon realized the limitations of "leaning to one side." They attempted to establish friendly relations with China's neutral neighbors, including India and Burma (Myanmar), on the basis of the "five principles of peaceful coexistence." The Bandung Conference in 1955 provided an excellent opportunity for Premier Zhou Enlai to promote this policy.

Relations with the Soviet Union, however, began to deteriorate in 1956. Mao Zedong disagreed with Nikita Khrushchev's (1894–1971) efforts at "de-Stalinization" and his foreign policy of "peaceful co-existence, peaceful competition, and peaceful transition" while reducing support for national liberation movements. These differences spread to conflicts that finally led to the withdrawal of Soviet aid in 1960. Ideological differences were publicized with open polemics between the two Communist parties in 1963 and 1964.

"THEORY OF THE THREE WORLDS"

Mao believed that the world was in the midst of "great turmoil, great divisions, and great reorganizations" in the 1960s as the two camps led by the United States and the Soviet Union became weakened with internal divisions, thus giving developing countries more room to maneuver. In 1964 Mao outlined his concept of the two intermediate zones between the two superpowers: the first involving Asia, Africa, and Latin America, and the second including Western Europe, Canada, Australia, and so forth. Collusion and struggles characterized the relationship between the two superpowers, and they concentrated on competition in the intermediate zones.

The Soviet invasion of Czechoslovakia reduced the Soviet Union from a revisionist state to a social-imperialist power. To the Chinese leadership, the two superpowers had become equally evil, and China was justified in playing one against the other. On this basis, Mao articulated his "theory of the three worlds." The two imperialist powers were designated the first world, the developed countries (the second intermediate zone) the second world, and the developing countries (the first intermediate zone) the third world. The Soviet Union was perceived to be the more dangerous because it was a latecomer and had to rely more on military means to expand. The Soviet military threat was highlighted by the bilateral armed conflict on the Ussuri (Wusuli) River in March 1969.

When Soviet expansionism reached its peak in the late 1970s, China formed a pseudo-alliance with the United States and Japan after they agreed in principle to combat hegemonism. The Chinese leadership's policy of economic reforms and opening to the external world obviously meant a continuous strengthening of economic ties with the Western world.

MODERNIZATION DIPLOMACY

China adjusted its foreign policy in 1982 and 1983 to emphasize independence and peace, implying a more even-handed approach toward the two superpowers. Deng Xiaoping wanted to concentrate on China's modernization, and Chinese foreign policy was designed to promote a peaceful international environment to facilitate China's efforts to catch up with the advanced countries and to maintain the Communist regime's legitimacy by improving the people's living standards. This diplomacy of modernization has remained consistent since the early 1980s. Chinese leaders accord priority to strengthening the country's "comprehensive national power," with substantial weight given to the economy and advanced technology. They realize that China needs many decades to catch up.

China's success in its modernization process implies that it has been satisfied with the existing international political and economic order. It intends to adapt to the existing rules of the game and to strengthen its influence to adjust the rules to its advantage. In many ways, modernization diplomacy has transformed China into a status quo power. Ideology is no longer an important factor in foreign policy as China embraces the market economy.

CONTAINMENT AND PEACEFUL EVOLUTION

The Tiananmen incident in 1989 was a severe setback for Chinese foreign policy. China suffered sanctions from the Western world, and the arms embargo imposed by the European Union was still in effect almost two decades later. More important still, the breakup of the Soviet Union in 1991 and significant political changes in Eastern Europe left China as the only major socialist country in the world.

Beijing felt threatened by the Western world's attempts to "contain" China and to engineer "peaceful evolution" in China, that is, to bring about regime change through the promotion of democracy and other Western liberal values.

Deng Xiaoping's response was to further open up China and deepen economic reforms, leading to impressive economic achievements that have greatly strengthened China's international influence. Elements of major-power diplomacy and nationalism enter into considerations of Chinese foreign policy. The Chinese people and their leaders believe that China is a major power and that its interests as a major power should be respected. Nationalist sentiments especially affect Sino-Japanese relations. There is also suspicion that the United States and the Western world do not want to see a strong China.

Chinese leaders appreciate the adverse impact of the perception of a "China threat," that is, the potential danger that China will engage in expansionism as it becomes strong economically and militarily. China as "the international workshop" and "the black hole for foreign investment" is seen as a threat by developing countries too. Since the end of 2003, Chinese leaders have been articulating the theme of China's "peaceful rise" or "peace and development" to dispel this perception. They argue that China accepts the role of a "responsible stakeholder" in the international community. China also practices multilateral diplomacy, and assumes an increasingly active role in international organizations.

China's economic growth prompts Chinese leaders to pursue "resource diplomacy," similar to that of Japan since the 1970s. China's substantial foreign-exchange reserves enable it to give foreign aid and invest in developing countries to open up markets, build manufacturing bases, and secure a reliable supply of raw materials, including oil. Investment in developed countries, on the other hand, is designed to acquire advanced technology and modern management, as well as establish sales networks.

BIBLIOGRAPHY

Goldstein, Avery. *Rising to the Challenge: China's Grand Strategy and International Security*. Stanford, CA: Stanford University Press, 2005.

Johnston, Alastair Iain, and Robert S. Ross, eds. *New Directions in the Study of China's Foreign Policy*. Stanford, CA: Stanford University Press, 2006.

Van Ness, Peter. *Revolution and Chinese Foreign Policy: Peking's Support for Wars of National Liberation*. Berkeley: University of California Press, 1970.

Yahuda, Michael B. *China's Role in World Affairs*. New York: St. Martin's Press, 1978.

Zheng Yushuo (Joseph Y. S. Cheng). The Evolution of China's Foreign Policy in the Post-Mao Era: From Anti-Hegemony to Modernization Diplomacy. In *China: Modernization in the 1980s*, ed. Joseph. Y. S. Cheng, 161–201. Hong Kong: Chinese University Press, 1989.

Joseph Y. S. Cheng (Zheng Yushuo)

ONE-CHINA POLICY AND "ONE COUNTRY, TWO SYSTEMS"

For the Chinese Communist Party (CCP) leadership, the Republic of China (ROC) was abolished and therefore disappeared from the map when the People's Republic of China (PRC) was established in 1949. This one-China principle has never been questioned, even when in the 1960s the U.S. government toyed with a two-China policy. The one-China principle was then shared by the ROC authorities, who continued to claim that they constituted the only legal and legitimate government representative of China. This unrealistic policy eased the PRC's entry into the United Nations in 1971 and the ROC's ipso facto exclusion from this organization. Since then, Beijing has stuck to this principle and requested all the countries that set up diplomatic relations with the PRC to abide by the one-China policy, according to which Taiwan is part of China (if not always formally the PRC).

In December 1978, Deng Xiaoping launched a peaceful reunification policy toward Taiwan. In September 1981, Marshal Ye Jianying (1897–1986) made a nine-point proposal to Taibei (Taipei) that would allow Taiwan to keep a high degree of autonomy, and even part of its armed forces, after its reunification with the mainland. To legalize this new policy, the PRC's December 1982 constitution included an article designing the establishment of "special administrative regions" (Art. 31).

Six months later, in June 1983, Deng Xiaoping summed up this new policy in a formula that would later become famous: "one country, two systems" (*yi ge guojia, liangge zhidu* or *yiguo liang zhi*). Then, in a statement regarded as "Deng's Six Principles," he said:

> The most important issue is the reunification of the motherland. After reunification with the motherland, different systems may be practiced in Taiwan, but it must be the People's Republic of China alone that represents China internationally. Taiwan will enjoy certain powers of its own that the other provinces, municipalities, and autonomous regions do not possess, provided the national interests are not impaired. Taiwan may maintain its own army, provided it does not threaten the mainland. (*Deng Xiaoping wenxuan,* 1985.)

At the time, Deng's new formula was clearly targeting Taiwan rather than Hong Kong or Macau. However, since Taibei's reaction to this formula has always been very negative, it has only been so far implemented, on the whole successfully, in the former British and Portuguese colonies, after 1997 and 1999 respectively.

In the 1980s, ROC president Jiang Jingguo (Chiang Ching-kuo) was still proposing to reunify China under

Sun Yat-sen's (Sun Yixian's) "three principles of the people" (nationalism, democracy, and people's livelihood). After Taiwan democratized, Li Denghui (Lee Teng-hui), Jiang's successor, advocated in 1991 a gradual unification process that would allow China's two political entities (*zhengzhi shiti*) to coexist on an equal footing on the international stage for a long time. Moreover, this new policy was criticized by the newly formed opposition and independence-leaning Democratic Progressive Party (DPP).

In 1999 Li embarked on a new mainland policy, qualifying Taiwan's relation to the PRC as "quasi state-to-state relations." Then approved by the majority of the Guomindang (GMD) and acclaimed by the DPP, this new policy triggered a harsh reaction from Beijing as well as criticism from Washington, Taiwan's only protector. In 2000 Chen Shuibian (Chen Shui-bian), Li's successor, accepted the freezing of this policy, but two years later he described Taiwan's relation with the PRC as "one country on each side of the Taiwan Strait" (*yibian yiguo*), confirming Taiwan's fierce opposition to the "one country, two systems" formula.

Since Ma Yingjiu's (Ma Ying-jeou's) election in March 2008, relations across the Taiwan Strait have improved. Nevertheless, a large majority of Taiwanese remain opposed to such a formula and to unification policy (between 70 and 80 percent according to opinion surveys regularly conducted).

For this reason, Beijing has quietly moved away from this formula, although not from the one-China principle. Since 2004, after Hu Jintao succeeded Jiang Zemin, the PRC's top leaders have refrained from invoking it, and there is no mention of this formula in China's 2005 antisecession law. And in June 2008, Beijing accepted the resumption of talks with Taibei after the GMD re-endorsed the verbal compromise reached in 1992 by both sides of the strait about the one-China principle without defining it, in other words, allowing Taiwan—and as a consequence Beijing—to keep its own interpretation (*yi ge zhongguo, ge zi biaoshu*). Qualified by the GMD and then the CCP after 2000 as the "1992 consensus" (*jiu'er gongshi*), this ambiguous compromise underscores the difficulties ahead for both Beijing and Taibei. Although the GMD has accepted the revival of its old principle—there is officially one China, the ROC—the legal and actual realities are different: one China is the PRC for most countries, and on the ground there are two Chinas, or, for the Taiwanese opposition, in particular the DPP, one China and one Taiwan. In other words, Taiwan is not Hong Kong or Macau: It is a de facto sovereign state that must be treated on an equal footing and cannot be dissolved into or subordinated to the PRC.

SEE ALSO *Deng Xiaoping; Hong Kong; Macau; Taiwan, Republic of China.*

BIBLIOGRAPHY

Cabestan, Jean-Pierre. Taiwan's Mainland Policy: Normalization, Yes; Reunification, Later. *China Quarterly* 148 (1996): 1260–1283.

Cabestan, Jean-Pierre. China-Taiwan: Integration without Reunification. *Cambridge Review of International Affairs* 15, 1 (2002): 95–103.

Cabestan, Jean-Pierre. The Taiwan Conundrum. In *Charting China's Future: Political, Social, and International Dimensions*, ed. Jae Ho Chung, 165–190. Lanham, MD: Rowman & Littlefield, 2006.

Deng Xiaoping. An Idea for the Peaceful Reunification of the Chinese Mainland and Taiwan (June 18, 1983). In *Build Socialism with Chinese Characteristics*, 18–19. Beijing: Foreign Languages Press, 1985.

Deng Xiaoping. *Deng Xiaoping wenxuan* [Selected works of Deng Xiaoping]. Beijing: Renmin Chubanshe, 1985, p. 30.

Henckaerts, Jean-Marie, ed. *The International Status of Taiwan in the New World Order: Legal and Political Considerations*. The Hague, Netherlands: Martinus Nijhoff, 1996.

Steve Yui-Sang Tsang (Zeng Ruisheng) and Hung-mao Tien (Tian Hongmao), eds. *Democratization in Taiwan: Implication for China*. Hong Kong: Hong Kong University Press, 1999.

Zagoria, Donald S. ed. *Breaking the China-Taiwan Impasse*. New York: Greenwood, 2003.

Jean-Pierre Cabestan

FOREIGN TRADE, 1800–1950

The Qing government allowed private foreign merchants to trade with China under the system called *hushi*, which required foreign merchants to do business only with licensed Chinese merchants, who were obliged to pay foreign trade tax to the government. Chinese exports such as tea, silk, and porcelain were in strong demand in other parts of the world, and were paid for mainly in silver, before Chinese imports of opium significantly increased.

THE TREATY PORT SYSTEM

China's defeat in the Opium War (1839–1842) and the consequent development of the treaty-port system changed institutional settings for China's foreign trade, but during its first two decades the treaty-port system did not work well for either China or its foreign counterparts. On the one hand, once licensed Chinese merchants ceased to make transactions exclusively with foreign merchants, the Qing government lacked any institution to collect trade tax. On the other hand, in spite of the high expectations on the part of the foreign powers, China's imports of foreign goods, including British machine-made textiles, increased slowly, even after the opening of the treaty ports.

In 1853 the Taiping rebels occupied Shanghai and the customhouse was closed. To deal with the collection

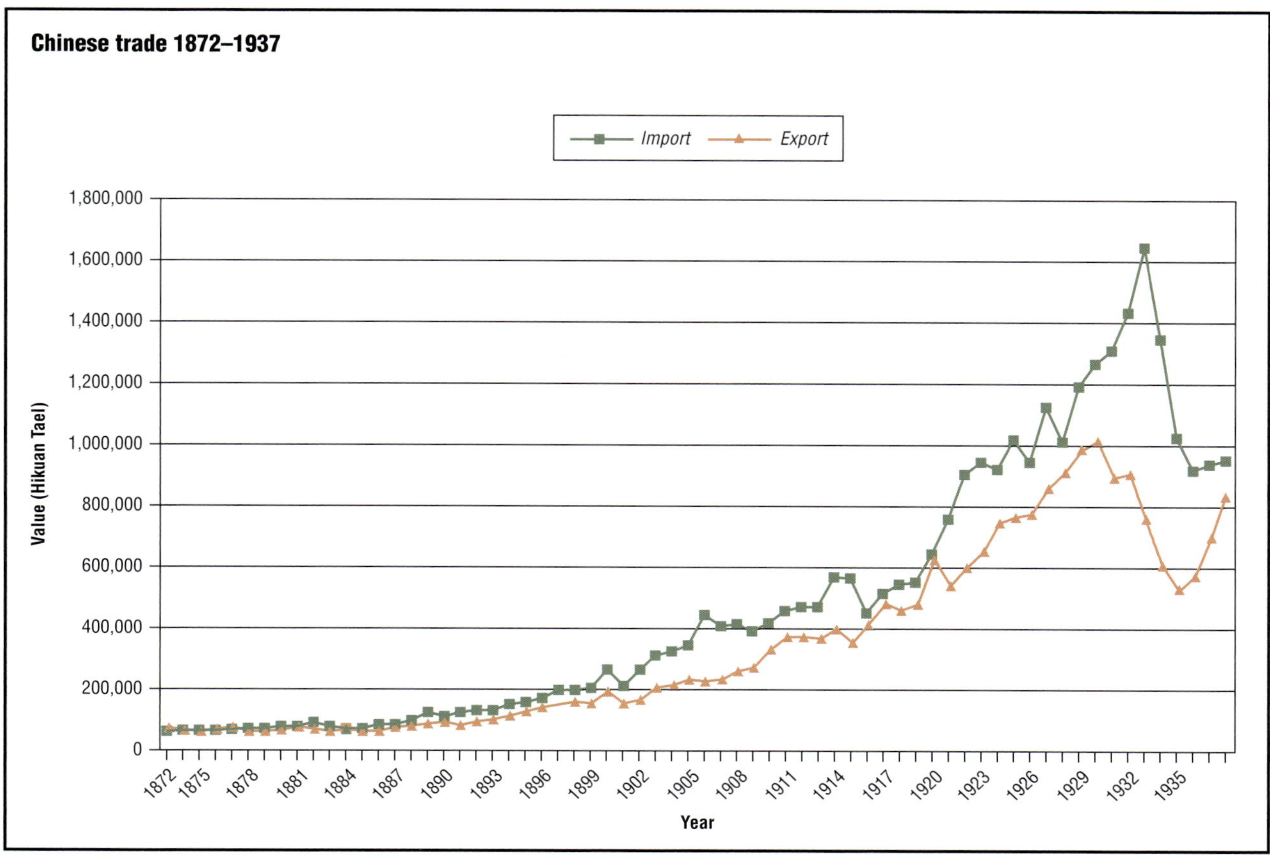

Figure 1

of customs tax, the British, French, and U.S. consuls there established the Inspectorate General of Customs, a board of three foreign inspectors nominated by local Chinese officials. The system successfully reduced corruption and increased custom revenue, and it was adopted by the other ports as well. In 1863 an Ulsterman, Robert Hart (1835–1911), was appointed the inspector-general of Customs, and all customs at treaty ports came to be governed by foreign staffs.

THE LATE NINETEENTH CENTURY TO 1936

Beginning in 1864 the inspectorate published annual reports on the returns of China's trade, covering all treaty ports open to foreign trade.

From 1868, the first year for which complete trade return commodities are available, to 1913, a year before World War I erupted, in terms of silver-standard currency, China's total exports and imports increased about seven and one-half times, from 125.108 million Haikwan taels to 973.468 million Haikwan taels. Although the introduction of steamships along the coast and the Yangzi River in the mid-nineteenth century contributed to the growth of trade, the opening of Manchuria and the completion of China's major railway line after the turn of the century were the most important factors in the increase; indeed, the trade increase in the last thirteen years (1901–1913) was twice of that of the preceding thirty-two years (1868–1900). The devaluation of silver in relation to gold also greatly inflated the increase of trade: When the trade values are converted into U.S. dollars, the increase was about three and one-half times.

Silk and tea were the two major exports from China, although their relative importance gradually declined. In 1868 tea and silk together accounted for 94 percent of China's exports; that percentage declined to 64 percent in 1890, 46 percent in 1900, and 34 percent in 1913. Beans and bean cakes from Manchuria became the leading export, and other important export items included eggs and egg products, hides, leather and skins, and ores and metals. Among the imports, opium ranked first until the 1890s, when cotton goods and yarns surpassed it.

During World War I Western countries could not supply the Chinese market with industrial manufactures, and international demand for Chinese exports increased. Against this background, industrialization in China accelerated, changing the composition of China's foreign trade. The cotton textile industry, for example, was greatly affected. Before 1913 the imports of cotton manufactured goods and cotton yarns consisted of almost one-third of China's total imports. After World War I the relative importance of imports of textile products declined, and from 1920 China increased imports of raw cotton as well as exports of cotton yarn to India, Hong Kong, and Dutch Indies. Overall, as modern manufacturing industries developed, producer goods such as machinery, chemicals, fuels, and related commodities increased considerably in their import values.

The direction of trade also changed. Before World War I the United Kingdom and its colonies and commonwealths (India, Singapore, and Australia) were China's primary trading partners for both imports and exports; after the war, the United States and Japan emerged as China's major trade partners. The volume of Sino-American trade increased in the 1920s, and by the 1930s the United States had the greatest share of China's trade. In contrast, Japan's share, which had accounted for about one-third of China's exports and imports right after the war, shrank to less than 20 percent in 1930s, partly because of China's boycott of Japanese goods in protest against Japanese acts of aggression such as the Mukden incident of September 18, 1931.

The 1932 establishment of Manchukuo, the Japanese puppet state in Manchuria, was another important factor. Before 1931, nearly 55 to 65 percent of Manchuria's imports were from Japan and 35 to 60 percent of exports were to Japan (Remer 1926, pp. 45–46). Once Manchuria was detached from the Chinese republic the region's key exports, such as beans and bean cakes, dropped abruptly. Japan increased its exports, particularly of machinery and materials for constructing public infrastructures, and its imports, not only of bean products but also of mineral ores and metallic products.

It is important to keep in mind the depreciation of the silver-standard Chinese currency when analyzing Chinese trade statistics, especially those from the late 1920s to the early 1930s because of the sharp decline in the international price of silver and the consequent drop in the value of the Chinese currency. China's foreign trade suffered during the Great Depression, particularly after the second half of 1931. When China's major trade partners left the gold standard and depreciated their currencies to inflate their economies, the Chinese exchange rate against them rose. The higher exchange rate hampered China's exports, which already had been hit by the sluggishness of the world market, and failed to stimulate imports. When income from commercial exports, foreign investments, and overseas Chinese all decreased during the worldwide economic slump, Chinese consumption could not grow. It was not until November 1935, when the Chinese government abandoned the silver standard, that China's foreign trade started to recover, particularly its exports to the United States, Europe, and Southeast Asia.

WAR AND THE END OF TREATY-PORT SYSTEM (1937–1945)

The Anti-Japanese War erupted in July 1937, disrupting Chinese trade. Shanghai was most severely hit; its trade value dropped 71 percent from the previous year. For China as a whole (both Japanese-occupied China and free China), from 1937 to 1941 imports more than doubled, increasing from US$279.9 million in 1937 to US$605.5 million in 1941, but exports decreased, from $279.9 million in 1937 to $154.3 million in 1941. Occupied China's share was much larger than free China's during that period—on average, 81 percent compared to 19 percent (Remer 1926, pp. 123–127). In terms of imports into occupied China, the United States was the most important trade partner, supplying raw cotton, tobacco leaves, chemicals, and iron and steel manufactures for factories in coastal China, and wheat flour, kerosene oil, and other necessities for the area's residents. Regarding exports, the United States and Europe, historically China's most important markets, continued to purchase major commodities such as raw silk and silk goods. Import and export trade with Southeast Asia and India also recorded remarkable growth, as commercial ties with their European mother countries were loosened during the war. In free China, the United States, Southeast Asia, and India were the most important importers. In terms of exports, it is difficult to form a clear picture of their final destinations: Although direct trade with the West declined because of the war, Chinese customs records show that the shares of Hong Kong and Southeast Asia increased, casting some doubt on the final destinations of Chinese commodities.

Until the outbreak of the Pacific War in December 1941, Chinese Maritime Customs maintained tariff administration and continued to publish trade reports and returns covering both occupied and free China. The Japanese military forces in China took over the Inspectorate General of Chinese Customs at Shanghai in December 1941, disrupting the continuity of its nationwide administration. Later, the unequal treaties settling institutional arrangements for China's trade were abrogated in the course of the war early in 1943. Although maritime customs were newly established in both occupied China and free China, their records are incomplete. According to other sources, the total volume of trade in occupied China, both imports and exports, sharply declined after 1941. In 1944 imports and exports shrank to less than 13 percent of their 1941 value, then declined further in the first eight months of 1945. Because of limited air and land transportation capacities after 1941, the trade of free China's trade declined during the period, too. In 1944 import value amounted to only 41.5 percent of 1942's value, and export value, only 57.1 percent (Remer 1926, pp. 139–147).

POSTWAR DEVELOPMENT (1946–1948)

Postwar China saw an import surplus: US$411.7 million in 1946, $235.3 million in 1947, and $40.6 million in 1948. The Chinese government encouraged imports of consumer goods to tide against inflation, and paid for the import excess with its reserve in foreign exchange and gold. Another significant factor during this period was the United Nations Relief and Rehabilitation Aid (UNRRA) supplies of 1946 and 1947 and U.S. commodity aid valued at US$433.1 million, which comprised 22 to 36 percent of total import value. (Remer 1926, pp. 170–177).

Export trade value ranged from US$149 million to $216 million. In addition to raw products such as raw silk, mineral ores, and leather and hides, the export of Chinese cotton products increased in importance, comprising 27 percent of China's total exports in 1947 and 39 percent in 1948. Southeast Asia was the major consumer of Chinese cotton products (Remer 1926, pp. 180–185).

SEE ALSO *Great Depression; Hart, Robert; Silk since 1800; Tea since 1800.*

BIBLIOGRAPHY

Cheng, Yu-Kwei. *Foreign Trade and Industrial Development of China: An Historical and Integrated Analylsis through 1948.* Washington, DC: University Press of Washington, D.C., 1956.

Fairbank, John King. *Trade and Diplomacy on the China Coast: The Openings of the Treaty Ports, 1842–1854.* Cambridge, MA: Harvard University Press, 1953.

Hsiao, Liang-lin. *China's Foreign Trade Sstatistics, 1864–1949.* Cambridge, MA: Harvard University Press, 1974.

Remer, Charles Frederick. *The Foreign Trade of China.* Shanghai: Commercial Press, 1926.

Tomoko Shiroyama

FOREIGN TRADE SINCE 1950

China's trade recovered when order returned in 1950 to an economy ravaged by war since 1937. However, normal trade growth was interrupted by China's entry into the Korean War in late 1950. Under the U.S.–led trade embargo against China, China had to "lean to one side." China reoriented its trade from the West to the Soviet bloc.

PRE-REFORM TRADE

Before the Sino-Soviet rift of 1960, China was quite open to Soviet trade, aid, and even Soviet foreign direct investment (FDI). To support rapid industrialization, China imported Soviet factories and equipment, and exported textiles and foodstuffs in return. The Soviet bloc accounted for two-thirds of China's trade. The rest of the trade was mainly with Hong Kong and Southeast Asia.

During the Great Leap Forward (1958–1960), China combined political mobilization with accelerated industrialization. China advocated a "walking on two legs" policy in which simple indigenous technology was combined with advanced industrial technology mostly imported from the Soviet Union. This led to an unsustainable spurt in output and trade that collapsed in the subsequent economic crisis. Imports of machinery stopped with economic retrenchment, and scarce foreign exchange was diverted for grain imports to relieve China's famine. In the turbulent years of the Cultural Revolution (1966–1969), China was completely isolated, and the Maoist strategy of "self-reliance" made virtue out of necessity. China had to reorient its trade from the Soviet bloc to Japan and Europe. However, China did not have the expertise to sell in the world market. Hong Kong was the mainland's largest market from the 1960s to the early 1980s.

Mainland China also relied on Hong Kong for its trade links with market economies. Trade fairs have been held in Guangzhou in spring and autumn every year since 1957 because businessmen can easily travel from Hong Kong to Guangzhou. The fair is reminiscent of foreign trade in the Qing dynasty, when foreign trade was restricted to the Hongs in Canton: It is no accident that the fair is popularly known as the "Canton Fair."

In the pre-reform era, China insulated the domestic economy from the world economy to preserve China's artificial domestic price structure, characterized by low prices for agricultural goods and high prices for manufactures. The structure was designed to depress consumption and extract a surplus for investment and defense. Insulation operated through two "airlocks": state monopoly of foreign trade through about ten state-owned foreign trade corporations (FTCs), and foreign exchange controls. All imports had to be handled by the FTCs, and all uses of foreign exchange were rationed by the state. As expected, state-administered trade was inefficient and cumbersome. China traded very little and lost many benefits of trade.

OPENING SINCE 1979

As the dust of the Cultural Revolution settled with the arrest of the Gang of Four in 1976, China was able to

Value of China's foreign trade, 1950–2007

	Export								
Year	USD 100 million	% of China's GDP	% of world exports	Imports USD 100 million	Trade balance USD 100 million	World export (USD 100 million)	GDP (RMB 100 million)	Exchange rate*	Export (RMB 100 million)
1950	5.5	4.10	0.89	5.8	−0.3	62,000	—	3.6594	20.2
1951	7.6	4.21	0.90	12.0	−4.4	84,000	—	3.1842	24.2
1952	8.2	3.92	1.00	11.2	−3.0	82,000	692	3.3049	27.1
1953	10.2	4.17	1.21	13.5	−3.3	84,000	834	3.4118	34.8
1954	11.5	4.55	1.32	12.9	−1.4	87,000	878	3.4783	40
1955	14.1	5.21	1.48	17.3	−3.2	95,000	935	3.4539	48.7
1956	16.5	5.39	1.57	15.6	0.9	105,000	1,034	3.3758	55.7
1957	16.0	4.95	1.40	15.1	0.9	114,000	1,102	3.4063	54.5
1958	19.8	5.19	1.80	18.9	0.9	110,000	1,291	3.3838	67
1959	22.6	5.38	1.92	21.2	1.4	118,000	1,451	3.4558	78.1
1960	18.6	4.20	1.43	19.5	−0.9	130,000	1,508	3.4032	63.3
1961	14.9	3.75	1.10	14.5	0.4	136,000	1,275	3.2081	47.8
1962	14.9	4.00	1.04	11.7	3.2	143,000	1,176	3.1611	47.1
1963	16.5	3.87	1.05	12.7	3.8	157,000	1,293	3.0303	50
1964	19.2	3.84	1.09	15.5	3.7	176,000	1,442	2.8854	55.4
1965	22.3	3.87	1.17	20.2	2.1	190,000	1,629	2.8296	63.1
1966	23.7	3.61	1.14	22.5	1.2	208,000	1,827	2.7848	66
1967	21.4	3.44	0.98	20.2	1.2	218,000	1,708	2.7477	58.8
1968	21.0	3.37	0.87	19.5	1.5	242,000	1,709	2.7429	57.6
1969	22.0	3.22	0.79	18.3	3.7	277,000	1,858	2.7182	59.8
1970	22.6	2.57	0.71	23.3	−0.7	317,000	2,207	2.5133	56.8
1971	26.4	2.86	0.75	22.1	4.3	354,000	2,393	2.5947	68.5
1972	34.4	3.38	0.82	28.6	5.8	419,000	2,454	2.4099	82.9
1973	58.2	4.38	1.00	51.6	6.6	580,000	2,670	2.0086	116.9
1974	69.5	5.09	0.83	76.2	−6.7	840,000	2,739	2.0058	139.4
1975	72.6	4.85	0.83	74.9	−2.3	877,000	2,950	1.9697	143
1976	68.6	4.54	0.69	65.8	2.8	992,000	2,968	1.9650	134.8
1977	75.9	4.41	0.67	72.1	3.8	1,128,000	3,166	1.8406	139.7
1978	97.5	4.60	0.75	108.9	−11.4	1,307,000	3,645	1.7190	167.6
1979	136.6	5.23	0.82	15.8	120.8	1,659,000	4,063	1.5549	211.7
1980	181.2	5.97	0.89	200.2	−19.0	2,034,000	4,546	1.4984	271.2
1981	220.1	7.67	1.10	220.2	−0.1	2,010,000	4,892	1.7050	367.6
1982	223.2	7.93	1.19	192.9	30.3	1,883,000	5,323	1.8925	413.8
1983	222.3	7.37	1.20	213.9	8.4	1,846,000	5,963	1.9757	438.3
1984	261.4	8.44	1.34	274.1	−12.7	1,956,000	7,208	2.3270	580.5
1985	273.5	8.91	1.40	422.5	−149.0	1,954,000	9,016	2.9366	808.9
1986	309.4	10.40	1.45	429.1	−119.7	2,138,000	10,275	3.4528	1,082.1
1987	394.4	12.17	1.57	432.1	−37.7	2,516,000	12,059	3.7221	1,470
1988	475.2	11.76	1.66	552.7	−77.5	2,869,000	15,043	3.7221	1,766.7
1989	525.4	11.64	1.70	591.4	−66.0	3,098,000	16,992	3.7651	1,956
1990	620.9	15.91	1.80	533.5	87.4	3,449,000	18,668	4.7832	2,985.8
1991	719.1	17.57	2.05	637.9	81.2	3,515,000	21,781	5.3233	3,827.1
1992	849.4	17.40	2.26	805.9	43.5	3,765,000	26,923	5.5146	4,676.3
1993	917.4	14.96	2.43	1,039.6	−122.2	3,782,000	35,334	5.7620	5,284.8
1994	1,210.1	21.64	2.80	1,156.1	54.0	4,326,000	48,198	8.6187	10,421.8
1995	1,487.8	20.44	2.88	1,320.8	167.0	5,164,000	60,794	8.3510	12,451.8
1996	1,510.5	17.64	2.80	1,388.3	122.2	5,403,000	71,177	8.3142	12,576.4
1997	1,827.9	19.19	3.27	1,423.7	404.2	5,591,000	78,973	8.2898	15,160.7
1998	1,837.1	18.02	3.34	1,402.4	434.7	5,501,000	84,402	8.2791	15,223.6
1999	1,949.3	17.99	3.41	1,657.0	292.3	5,712,000	89,677	8.2783	16,159.8
2000	2,492.0	20.79	3.86	2,250.9	241.1	6,456,000	99,215	8.2784	20,634.4
2001	2,661.0	20.09	4.30	2,435.5	225.5	6,191,000	109,655	8.2770	22,024.4
2002	3,256.0	22.40	5.02	2,951.7	304.3	6,492,000	120,333	8.2770	26,947.9
2003	4,382.3	26.71	5.78	4,127.6	254.7	7,585,000	135,823	8.2770	36,287.9
2004	5,933.2	30.72	6.44	5,612.3	320.9	9,220,000	159,878	8.2768	49,103.3
2005	7,619.5	33.95	7.27	6,599.5	1,020.0	10,485,000	183,868	8.1917	62,648.1
2006	9,689.4	36.45	8.00	7,914.6	1,774.8	12,113,000	211,924	7.9718	77,594.6
2007	12,180.1	37.12	8.73	9,559.5	2,620.6	13,950,000	249,530	7.6040	—

*Exchange rate from 1950–1978 was estimated from the ratio of export in USD & RMB dollar

SOURCE: GDP for 1950–1977 are from China Compendium of Statistics 1949–2004. World exports are from The World Trade Organization. The rest are from the China Statisticsl Yearbook, various issues.

Table 1

export more light manufactures as well as oil from the Daqing oil field. The ambitious 1977 plant import program of Hua Guofeng (Great Leap Outward) was based on a projection of increasing oil exports, which failed to materialize. China's leadership realized that economic reforms, including reform of state-administered trade, would be essential for China's modernization. Opening to the outside world and domestic economic reforms proved to be complementary, as epitomized by the slogan of the reform era: "Reform and Opening" (*gaige kaifeng*).

China practiced gradualism in its reform strategy, and foreign trade reform was no exception. State-administered trade gradually shrank, giving more scope to above-plan trade. The power to import and export was progressively decentralized. In addition to the centrally administered foreign exchange market, a secondary "swap" market was established. The official exchange rate was devalued to more realistic levels, allowing market forces to influence trade and production. By the mid-1980s, China had moved to a partially reformed trading system, in which market forces were circumscribed by government intervention in the form of tariffs, quotas, and administrative controls.

More significantly, China created a separate export processing (EP) regime that bypassed the planned system of "ordinary trade" (OT). In the EP regime, foreign invested enterprises (FIEs) were allowed to bypass China's planned trading system. Parts and components used in exports could be imported duty free. The EP regime allowed international production networks, especially those from Hong Kong and Taiwan, to expand into the Chinese mainland, helping China to realize her comparative advantage in labor-intensive exports. Processed exports soared from nothing in 1979 to around half of China's total exports in (and since) 1995.

On January 1, 1994, China ended its two-track exchange rate system by devaluing the official exchange rate to a level around that of the secondary swap market. Current-account convertibility was achieved around mid-1995. Besides export promotion, China started to liberalize imports aggressively in the 1990s. China's average tariff rate dropped gradually from 56 percent in 1982 to 15 percent in 2001 on the eve of China's entry to the World Trade Organization (WTO). China's WTO entry in December 2001 after fifteen years of hard bargaining underlined the success of China's reforms. China's WTO commitments were the most liberal among developing economies. China lowered average tariffs on industrial products to 9.4 percent in 2004, one year ahead of its WTO commitments. By 2007 China had implemented most of its commitments to liberalize services as well.

China's opening since 1979 has been a stunning success. In the reform era, China's share of world trade has risen faster than that of any other country. China's rank in the world as an exporter rose from twenty-fourth in 1979 to third in 2004, just after Germany and the United States. China is projected to become the world's number one exporter around 2010. Since 1992 China also has become the number one host of foreign direct investment (FDI) among developing countries.

China's trade expansion has led to frictions with trading partners because of the speed and scale of China's entry to the world market. China has also been running a sizable current account surplus since 2003, a sign that the nation has not liberalized imports fast enough. To cope with such problems, China has appreciated the renminbi by more than 15 percent from mid-2005 to mid-2008. China has also been promoting outward foreign investment aggressively, and has become an important source of FDI among developing countries.

With import liberalization, China is rapidly becoming a world market in addition to being a "world factory." China has concluded numerous free trade agreements with its neighbors. China signed the "ten plus one" agreement with the ten nations of the Association of South East Asian Nations (ASEAN) in November 2001 to implement free trade by 2010. A "ten plus three" agreement that includes Japan and South Korea is under negotiation as of 2009. With the rise of China, a China-centered trade bloc is likely to emerge in a tripolar world economy dominated by North America, the European Union, and East Asia.

SEE ALSO *ASEAN, Relations with; Foreign Investment since 1949; International Relations: Since 1949.*

BIBLIOGRAPHY

Bergsten, C. Fred, Bates Gill, Nicholas R. Lardy, and Derek Mitchell. China in the World Economy: Opportunity or Threat? In *China: The Balance Sheet: What the World Needs To Know Now about the Emerging Superpower*, 73–117. New York: Public Affairs, 2007.

Lardy, Nicholas R. *Integrating China into the Global Economy.* Washington D. C.: Brookings Institution Press, 2002.

Naughton, Barry. China and the World Economy. In *The Chinese Economy: Transitions and Growth*, 375–423. Cambridge: Massachusetts Institute of Technology Press, 2007.

Sung, Yun-Wing. An Appraisal of China's Foreign Trade Policy, 1950–1992. In *Agriculture and Trade in China and India*, ed. T. N. Srinivasan, 109–153. San Francisco: International Center for Economic Growth, 1994.

Yun-Wing Sung

FOUR MODERNIZATIONS

The Four Modernizations program was an ambitious national project to reinvigorate the Chinese economy so that the country could become an advanced industrial nation by the start of the twenty-first century. It aimed to modernize four sectors: agriculture, industry, science and technology, and national defense. The program was intended to lay the foundation for China to become a strong socialist state in the form of a national economic system with a comprehensive industrial base approaching that of the advanced industrial economies.

The program was first unveiled by Premier Zhou Enlai in his report to the Third National People's Congress held on December 21 and 22, 1964. The program was soon derailed, however, by the Great Proletarian Cultural Revolution (1966–1969). A decade later, Zhou reintroduced the program at the Fourth National People's Congress in 1975, a move that signified that China was moving away from class struggle and toward economic development during the final phase of the Cultural Revolution. However, the program remained in limbo as it was soon sabotaged by the Gang of Four.

Mao Zedong's appointed successor, Hua Guofeng, had the Gang of Four arrested on October 6, 1976, shortly after the death of Mao. The Chinese Communist Party (CCP) could then pull itself together to focus on economic development. Hua, while relying on Maoist dogmatism, was forced to accept the precepts of the Four Modernizations, which represented the economic policies promoted by Zhou Enlai and Deng Xiaoping between 1973 and 1976. At the first session of the Fifth National People's Congress in February 1978, Hua presented a ten-year economic development plan to implement the first part of the Four Modernizations. The same congress also incorporated the Four Modernizations into the state constitution, following its incorporation into the party constitution at the Eleventh Party Congress in August 1977. Such a move is not surprising when seen from a historical perspective. China has always wanted to pursue the twin goals of wealth and power (*fuqiang*) after suffering defeat and humiliation at the hands of foreign powers. The Four Modernizations program is a concentrated expression of such sentiment: "If there was such a thing as a national consensus in China, it focused on the commitment to the Four Modernizations" (Xu Zhongyue 2000, p. 803).

Initially, the policies consisted of targeted investments through the state planning system; that is, they were largely conventional economic measures with the added element of bringing in advanced foreign technology, although they violated the voluntarist dogma of mass mobilization and self-sufficiency. The initial failure of the large investment programs (including the major importation of foreign technology, for example, for Baoshan Iron and Steel Mill), was made up for gradually during the 1980s.

A change came during the Third Plenum of the Eleventh Central Committee in December 1978, when Hua was eclipsed by Deng Xiaopeng. To Deng, self-reliance was not a sacred principle and could be discarded if it did not serve practice. He argued that the political focus of the CCP should be the Four Modernizations and not class struggle. Gone too was the slogan of continuance of revolution under the dictatorship of the proletariat. Deng argued that Marxist principles must be adapted to meet the needs of concrete conditions in order to "build socialism with Chinese characteristics." Even though the Four Modernizations policy was de facto abandoned with Deng's rise to power in 1978, it was not denounced—it became a central element of the statement of the reform—and for a while it was used as a slogan to justify the reform policies (even though these involved totally different approaches), suggesting a continuation from Zhou Enlai's legacy.

After the launch of the Four Modernizations, the Chinese leadership gradually realized that the program's goals could not be accomplished by the turn of the century. The leadership therefore decided to increase the volume of trade by opening up China's market and adopting export-oriented growth, access to advanced technology, and management know-how. At the Twelfth Party Congress in September 1982, there was a change in the sequence of the four components: Industrial modernization was given priority over agricultural modernization (*China Daily* 2007). The reasoning was that industrialization formed the material basis for the entire modernization program. After the Thirteenth Party Congress in 1987, the term *Four Modernizations* was seldom used. Instead, the vocabulary evolved toward the use of such terms as *reform, opening up*, and *socialist modernization*, reflecting the move from a planned economy to a market economy.

Deng shrewdly propounded the idea of "seeking truth from facts," and he argued that "practice is the sole criterion of truth." This view implies that practice rather than Mao's words should be the standard when deciding on the merits of a policy. Social reality and facts, rather than ideology, should form the basis of truth. Such thinking is very much in line with Deng's remark that a cat should be judged on its ability to catch mice rather than its color.

With economic modernization as the national goal, profit incentives and bonuses took the place of revolutionary slogans. The people's communes were dismantled and replaced by the responsibility system. Peasant households had more freedom to decide what to produce and how to sell their harvest. And factory managers were granted flexibility to negotiate terms with both domestic and foreign companies.

SEE ALSO *Agricultural Production; Economic Development: Overview; Economic Reform since 1978; Foreign Trade since 1950; Industrial Policy since 1949; Science and Technology Policy.*

BIBLIOGRAPHY

China Daily. The 12th Party Congress. 2007. http://chinadaily.com.cn/china/2007-07/10/content_6142010.htm.

Hsü, Immanuel C. Y. (Xu Zhongyue). *The Rise of Modern China*. 6th ed. Oxford, U.K.: Oxford University Press, 2000.

Zhao Enlai. Zai disanjie Quanguo Renmin Daibiao Dahui diyici huiyi shang zhengfu gongzuo baogao [Government report presented to the First Session of the Third National People's Congress]. 1964. http://news.xinhuanet.com/ziliao/2004-10/15/content_2093452.htm.

Zhao Enlai. Zai disijie Quanguo Renmin Daibiao Dahui diyici huiyi shang zhengfu gongzuo baogao [Government report presented to the First Session of the Fourth National People's Congress]. 1975. http://www.people.com.cn/item/lianghui/zlhb/rd/4jie/newfiles/a1070.html.

Michael Heng Siam-Heng (Wang Zhaoxing)

FRANCE, RELATIONS WITH

Contrary to official statements, France was not the first Western country to recognize the People's Republic of China (PRC)—the United Kingdom, Switzerland, and several countries in northern Europe had opened the way in January 1950, before the outbreak of the Korean War (1950–1953). At that time, France could not consider establishing official ties with the PRC due to the support given by Beijing to nationalist groups such as the Vietminh in Vietnam and the Algerian Front de libération nationale (FLN). But with these obstacles eliminated, France, unlike most other countries of the Western camp, did not wait for the first signs of a Sino-American normalization, and established diplomatic relations with the PRC on January 27, 1964, prompting the Taibei (Taipei) government to sever its ties with Paris.

However, French president Charles de Gaulle's (1890–1970) political gesture did not produce substantial exchanges until the adoption by the PRC of the reform and open-door policy at the end of the 1970s. During this time, nearly all other Western states normalized their relations with Beijing. Moreover, ever since diplomatic relations were established between the European Community (EC) and the PRC in 1974, with political dialogue instituted from 1994, a growing number of issues, such as China's entry into the World Trade Organization (WTO) or the smuggling of illegal immigrants, have been tackled at the European level. Yet, there is a continuity in France's China policy that rests on equating de Gaulle's 1964 move to an alleged privileged France-China relationship, leading to a strong consensus among French political parties. Occasional political disagreements over France's China policy primarily reflect an instrumentalization of this policy for domestic—and more precisely electoral—purposes, rather than any basic cleavage between right-wing and left-wing parties.

SWAPPING THE CENSORSHIP POSTURE

After the Tiananmen crackdown on June 4, 1989, France and other members of the Group of Seven (G7) industrialized nations imposed sanctions on China: state guarantees and most credits were frozen, high-level contacts were suspended, and an embargo was imposed on arms sales. Among Western countries, France was particularly concerned for three reasons: France was about to take over the EC presidency, host the annual G7 summit, and commemorate the bicentenary of its 1789 revolution. Many Chinese dissidents found refuge in France, while Chinese students in mourning garb were placed by the French authorities at the head of the parade commemorating the French Revolution, which passed in front of more than thirty heads of state and government, as well as banks of television cameras. The economic sanctions, however, did not last long: as early as October 2, 1990, the EC member states lifted the economic embargo, even though there had been no noticeable shift in the political stance of the Chinese regime, and bilateral contacts resumed. France's minister of foreign affairs, Roland Dumas, visited China in April 1991.

But the Chinese government itself imposed sanctions because of two major arms deals between France and Taiwan: one in the autumn of 1991 involving La Fayette frigates, the other a year later involving sixty Mirage 2000-5 fighter jets. Although the French government insisted that these sales were exclusively commercial deals and reaffirmed the position that France recognized the government of the PRC as the sole legal government of China, and though the Mirage deal was concomitant with the sale to Taiwan by the United States of F-16 fighter jets, only France became the target of sanctions imposed by China in December 1992. The Chinese government ordered the French consulate and the French Trade Commission in Guangzhou to be closed, and French firms were excluded from some contract tenders, including the one for Guangzhou's rapid-transit system. These sanctions were aimed not only at punishing France, but also at deterring other European countries from selling arms to Taiwan, since both German and Dutch firms were contemplating similar deals.

The celebration of the thirtieth anniversary of the establishment of Sino-French diplomatic relations provided the opportunity to put an end to this crisis. A joint communiqué issued by Paris and Beijing on January 12, 1994, stated that the "French government commits itself not to authorize French firms in the future to participate in the armament of Taiwan," while "the Chinese side declares that French firms are welcome to compete, on an equal footing, in the Chinese market."

A publishing house employee reviews a Chinese translation of French President Nicolas Sarkozy's autobiography, November 25, 2007. *Giving diplomatic recognition to the People's Republic of China in 1964, France established strong ties with the Communist government, using this early contact to strengthen trade relations at the end of the century.* MARK RALSTON/AFP/GETTY IMAGES

SEEKING A PRIVILEGED BILATERAL RELATIONSHIP

After a short transitional period, during which an increasing number of official visits were studded with diplomatic incidents, the French authorities in the spring of 1997, under Jacques Chirac's presidency, ostentatiously changed their approach to the human rights issue in China, which was France's first step toward the institution of a global partnership. On April 15 of that year, France (followed by Germany, Spain, Italy, and Greece) for the first time refused to support the annual United Nations Commission for Human Rights' resolution condemning China. In fact, in the Sino-French joint declaration announcing the global partnership signed on May 16, 1997, in Beijing by Jiang Zemin and Jacques Chirac, the two sides emphasized that "efforts promoting and protecting human rights must respect the aims and the principles of the UN charter, as well as the universality of human rights, while taking into account the particularities of each."

In 2003 President Chirac and the French government initiated the issue of lifting the European embargo on arms sales to China, responding to a demand from Chinese authorities that this decision should not be linked to the issue of human rights. During the 2004–2005 winter, a consensus among European Union member states was emerging, the nature of the necessary accompanying measures being the only remaining divergence. But American pressure convinced French and other European enterprises that the rewards of the Chinese market would be lower than the cost generated by American retaliatory measures. In addition, the passing in March 2005 of the Chinese "antisecession law," which sanctions military action should Taiwan declare independence or postpone talks on reunification, blocked the lifting of the embargo. It must be noted that this embargo results from a decision of the then twelve member states adopted by the European council on June 27, 1989, that is prior to the implementation of the Common Foreign and Security Policy. Each member state being thus free to determine its mode of enforcement, France does not consider that the embargo covers sales of non lethal arms, and French firms have sold to China materials that are banned by some other European countries.

As far as the Taiwan issue is concerned, France has concomitantly sided with the Chinese government. Chirac publicly condemned the antimissile defense referendum organized in Taiwan in March 2004, and French prime minister Jean-Pierre Raffarin, while visiting China in April 2005, stated that the antisecession law was compatible with France's view of "one China." President Nicolas Sarkozy's stance is in line with his predecessors.

DISAPPOINTING ECONOMIC REPERCUSSIONS FOR FRANCE

French exports to China have long benefited from favorable terms of payment. From 1985, when the first financial agreement was signed, to 1996, China was the country to benefit most from France's export credits; more than three-quarters of this aid benefiting four companies (Alcatel Alsthom, Lyonnaise des Eaux, Peugeot SA, and Technip). But this aid has been decreasing due to the tightening of Organization for Economic Cooperation and Development (OECD) constraints, among other reasons.

Yet, France's trade deficit with China has been steadily worsening and China remains France's number one trade deficit, increasing from 8 billion euros in 2002 to 16.2 billion euros in 2006. In terms of market share, in

2006 France ranked second among European countries, enjoying less than 1.5 percent as a supplier of the Chinese market, far behind Germany, which held about 5 percent. Moreover, France's exports to China are highly dependent upon the fulfillment of large-scale deals of civil equipment goods supported by the state, and not upon ordinary trade. Bilateral trade mainly concentrates in the nuclear, aerospace, communications, and telecom sectors. Hence, the hypothesis often put forward of a strategic trade-off between key contracts for China's foreign partners and political advantage for China, such as the lifting of the arms embargo. But it must be disregarded as Chinese authorities have often demonstrated—whatever their rhetoric—that they are not aiming at establishing a privileged relationship with one supplier.

SEE ALSO *European Union, Relations with; Foreign Trade since 1950; International Relations.*

BIBLIOGRAPHY

Guiheux, Gilles. France-China Economic Relations since 1979: Assessment, Policies, Debates. *East-West Dialogue* 6, 2 and 7, 1 (2002): 166–196.

Mengin, Françoise. La politique chinoise de la France: Du mythe de la relation privilégiée au syndrome de la normalisation. *Critique Internationale* 12 (2001): 89–110. Published in English as France's China Policy: From the Myth of a Privileged Relationship to a Syndrome of Normalisation. *East-West Dialogue* 6, 2 and 7, 1 (2002): 99–125.

Mengin, Françoise. A Functional Relationship: Political Extensions to Europe-Taiwan Ties. *China Quarterly* 169 (2002): 136–153.

Françoise Mengin

FUJIAN

With a population of 36 million in 2006 and land area of 121 million square kilometers, Fujian is one of China's smaller provinces. Chosen as one of the first provinces for economic reform in the 1980s, at the beginning of the twenty-first century it has become one of the wealthiest. Much of Fujian's distinctiveness derives from its geography. Situated on the southeast coast, Fujian has strong ties to Taiwan and to overseas Chinese, and its mountainous topography has led to considerable internal linguistic and cultural diversity.

FUJIAN

Capital city: Fuzhou
Largest cities (population): Quanzhou, Fuzhou (6,230,000 [2006]), Xiamen
Area: 121,400 sq. km. (46,900 sq. mi.)
Population: 35,580,000 (2006)
Demographics: Han, 98%; She, 1.1%; Hui, 0.3%
GDP: gross, CNY 761.4 billion (2006)
Famous sites: Song Dynasty shipwreck and Qingjing Mosque in Quanzhou; rammed earth buildings (Tulou) of southern Fujian; treaty port architecture of Gulangyu Island, Xiamen

GEOGRAPHY AND HISTORY

Fujian, often referred to by its ancient name Min, is bordered by Zhejiang to the north, Jiangxi to the west, and Guangdong to the south. On the east Fujian lies on the coast, facing Taiwan. The climate is subtropical. Arable land makes up only about 10 percent of Fujian's territory, and most of the province is mountainous. Two main ranges run north-south across the province, the Daiyun range in the center of Fujian and the higher Wuyi range in the western part along the border with Jiangxi. Historically, human settlement and development have been concentrated in the valleys and plains along the eastern coast, in particular along four main river valleys. These are the sites of Fujian's four main urbanized areas: Fuzhou on the Min River, Putian on the Mulan, Quanzhou on the Jin, and Xiamen and Zhangzhou on the Jiulong.

Although formally a part of the Chinese empire for two thousand years, Fujian was long considered a peripheral region. Inhabitants mostly claim to be descended from immigrants from the central regions of China who moved to Fujian in a series of large-scale migrations. Yet it seems more likely that the current population results from the immigrants' intermarriage with and gradual assimilation of indigenous peoples whose presence predated these migrations. Some legacies of this assimilation process survive in folklore and in the She minority, the main ethnic minority in Fujian. About half of the total She population of 700,000 live in Fujian. While not recognized as a national minority by the government, the other distinctive group in Fujian is the Hakka (Kejia), who number several million and are concentrated in southwestern Fujian. There are many contradictory legends about the origins of the Hakka. The current scholarly consensus is that they descend from migrants from central China who settled in mountainous areas of the province rather than on the coastal plains, and their distinctiveness arises from their long history of interaction with and attempts to distinguish themselves from the She around them. There is also a small population of Hui, or Chinese Muslims, living in the Quanzhou area and descended from early Arab traders who married local women.

Traditional Hakka earth houses, Longyan, Fujian Province, October, 2002. *A small province located on the southeast coast, Fujian remains known for the large concentration of* tulou, *or earthen-walled houses, dotting the region. Built several stories high, these defensive structures have traditionally provided shelter for large collections of families, with inhabitants sometimes numbering in the hundreds.* © CHEN ZHONGHE/XINHUA PRESS/CORBIS

By the Song dynasty (960–1279), Fujian was fully incorporated into the empire and had become a major center of classical scholarship. It was closely tied into national and international trade networks, and Quanzhou was China's largest port. While rice agriculture remained attractive in the coastal plains, especially after the introduction of new strains that could produce multiple crops in a single year, the favorable climate and commercial opportunities led local farmers to turn increasingly to commercial crops, such as fruit, sugarcane, and later tobacco. Fujian has long been famous as the source of the finest lychees, oranges, and other fruits. Other important commercial crops include timber, paper, and especially tea, all produced in the western parts of Fujian.

TAIWAN AND FUJIAN'S OVERSEAS CHINESE

The island of Taiwan was part of Fujian Province from its formal incorporation into the Qing empire in 1683 until 1877. Originally inhabited by Austronesian aboriginal groups, Taiwan was settled by migrants from Fujian and northern Guangdong beginning in the Ming dynasty (1368–1644), and in 2006 much of the population of Taiwan claims descent from migrants from Fujian, in roughly equal proportions from Quanzhou and Zhangzhou. Across the Taiwan Strait there remain close linguistic and cultural ties. Because of its rapid development, Taiwan was made a separate province in 1877 before being ceded to Japan in 1895 as a result of the Sino-Japanese War (1894–1895). At the beginning of the twenty-first century, the Republic of China on Taiwan still controls two small island groups on the Fujian coast, Jinmen (Quemoy) and Mazu (Matsu), which have historically been part of Fujian Province. For this reason, the Republic of China on Taiwan also has a Fujian provincial government, whose territory is limited to these islands.

Besides Taiwan, Fujian was also the sending region for large numbers of emigrants to southeast Asia. Emigration is usually ascribed to the high population of Fujian relative to arable land. But since emigration from Fujian is highly localized to a few places, more persuasive arguments must include the long history of involvement in overseas commerce and the importance of a few early migrants in creating channels for subsequent ones. In 2006 about 10 million overseas Chinese traced their roots back to Fujian. There are large communities of overseas Chinese of Fujian origin in Indonesia, Malaysia, Singapore, and the Philippines. More recently, a new wave of legal and illegal emigrants from the Fuzhou region, numbering several hundred thousand, have emigrated to North America. Places that have sent a large number of migrants abroad are known as *qiaoxiang* (overseas-Chinese homeland communities). Many such communities have benefited from remittances to individual families, contributions to village welfare such as schools and other public works, and investment. More broadly, overseas Chinese and Taiwanese with ties to Fujian have played an important role in economic development since the 1980s, as discussed below.

The growing tea trade in the nineteenth century aroused European interest in the province, and after the first Opium War (1839–1842), Fuzhou and Xiamen (Amoy) became treaty ports opened to foreign trade. This led to the growth of missionary activities in the province and to substantial Christian populations. (From several centuries earlier there were already small communities of Catholics in northeastern Fujian.) Foreign and overseas Chinese investment was responsible for much of Fujian's early industrial development. Its strategic position also explains the location of one of China's earliest shipyards at Fuzhou.

After the 1911 Revolution, Fujian was in the hands of a succession of military warlords before the Guomindang's Northern Expedition brought the province back under the control of the central government in the mid-1920s. A secessionist movement briefly held power in 1933–1934 before being violently suppressed—an indication that a certain sense of local independence persisted into the twentieth century. A few years later, during World War II, the Japanese occupied portions of the coast, including the largest cities.

FUJIAN IN THE REFORM PERIOD

Since 1949 the basic pattern of economic development in Fujian has mirrored that of the People's Republic as a whole, with two main exceptions. First, because of ongoing antagonism across the Taiwan Strait, there was little construction in coastal areas during the Maoist period (1949–1976). Instead, much industrial development was relocated to a "second front" and "third front" in the interior of the province, where it would be safe in the event of an attack or invasion. Second, from 1978 Fujian, together with Guangdong, was selected as the site for experiments in economic reform. It was precisely Fujian's ties with Taiwan and overseas Chinese that led to its selection. Investment in Fujian, largely by these two groups, led to rapid economic growth and also rapid integration into the regional and global economies. Internally, such development has intensified regional disparities and restored the traditional pattern of relative prosperity on the coast and poverty in the interior. This is somewhat offset by the flow of migrant labor from the poor uplands to the coastal cities. At the beginning of the twenty-first century, coastal Fujian is home to huge numbers of small export-processing factories, as well as the large factories of multinationals and their subcontractors. In 1980, Xiamen became one of the original four Special Economic Zones created to promote economic development, and it has grown into the main regional metropolis. In 2006 the per capita gross domestic product of the province was CNY 21,471 ($2,985), ranking it sixth among China's provinces and ninth among all administrative regions, including major cities.

SOCIETY, CULTURE, AND INTERNAL DIVERSITY

One of the distinguishing aspects of Fujian culture in the past was the high degree of lineage organization. From the Ming dynasty onward, in many parts of the province, communities claimed descent from a common ancestor, compiled genealogies to demonstrate this, and worshipped their ancestors in elaborate ancestral halls. Considerable

property was corporately owned by lineages. Sometimes these groups engaged in violent feuds with one another. In recent years there have been efforts to revive the lineage organizations, which were destroyed after the Communists came to power in 1949.

While various stereotypes about Fujian are held outside the province, people within the province generally stress internal differences. For example, residents of each of the four geographic quadrants of the province are thought to share a set of distinctive characteristics. Fuzhou residents and Quanzhou residents are also thought to differ in character. Such assumptions are, of course, stereotypes and ignore the substantial immigration from other parts of China from the 1980s, but they do reflect some real historical differences.

The most striking difference is linguistic. The three main linguistic regions in Fujian—the north and east, the south, and the southwest—are home to mutually unintelligible dialects. The southern dialect, known as Southern Min (Minnanhua), is also the chief dialect on Taiwan. Probably because of the mountainous topography, Fujian has considerable linguistic variation even within these three groups, and in some parts of the province people separated by only a short distance cannot understand one another.

There are other significant cultural differences as well, for example in traditional architecture and religion. Perhaps because of the long history of ethnic and subethnic tension in the region, in some parts of southwestern Fujian are found *tulou*, large fortified communal dwellings that may house several hundred inhabitants. In the realm of popular religion, some important cults are confined largely to a single region. Thus people in the Zhangzhou region strongly venerate Kai-Min Shengwang (the Sagely King Who Opened Up Fujian), the deified spirit of an early Chinese official, while he has only a marginal cult in other regions. The partial incorporation of other cults, such as that of Mazu, the patron goddess of seafarers, into a state-sanctioned religious hierarchy may in the past have played a role in the integration of local cultures into national culture. From the 1980s, religious ties have been part of the larger reintegration of Taiwan and Fujian. For example, temples to Mazu on Taiwan send delegations on pilgrimages to her home temple in Fujian. The ties were further strengthened in 2001 with the introduction of direct ferry links between Jinmen and Xiamen and other coastal cities, the first direct personal-travel links between territory under Taiwanese control and the mainland.

SEE ALSO *Chinese Overseas.*

BIBLIOGRAPHY

Dean, Kenneth. *Taoist Ritual and Popular Cults in Southeast China*. Princeton, NJ: Princeton University Press, 1993.

Gardella, Robert. *Harvesting Mountains: Fujian and the China Tea Trade, 1757–1937*. Berkeley: University of California Press, 1994.

Hook, Brian, ed. *Fujian: Gateway to Taiwan*. Oxford: Oxford University Press, 1996.

Ng Chin-keong. *Trade and Society: The Amoy Network on the China Coast, 1683–1735*. Singapore: Singapore University Press, 1983.

Rubinstein, Murray, ed. *Taiwan: A New History*. Armonk, NY: Sharpe, 1999.

Yeung, Y. M., and David K. Y. Chu, eds. *Fujian: A Coastal Province in Transition and Transformation*. Hong Kong: Chinese University Press, 2000.

Zhongguo Guojia Tongji Ju (National Bureau of Statistics of China), ed. *Zhongguo tongji nianjian* [China statistical yearbook 2007]. Hong Kong: Xianggang Jingji Baodao She, 2007.

Michael Szonyi

FURNITURE

The furniture traditions of China are long and varied. *Jiaju* (literally, household implements), though suggesting a much broader range of gear for the home than tables, chairs, and beds, is the term that has come to be used for furniture. This includes the classical, hardwood furniture associated with the Ming (1368–1644) and early Qing (1644–1912) dynasties, lacquered furniture, and vernacular furniture. While numerous furniture examples from the sixteenth century on have survived, the continuities and changes within this category of household furnishings have benefited from archeological finds, evidence from paintings dating to the Tang (618–907) and Song (960–1279) dynasties, textual sources, literature, and woodblock prints.

Scholars and collectors have long admired the hardwood pieces of the Ming and Qing periods, characterized by an aesthetic that valued simplicity of design and superiority of craftsmanship. Limited to wealthy households, such classical furniture continued to be made and valued for centuries following the Ming dynasty, and is today reproduced in a range of qualities, whether acknowledged or spuriously represented as genuine.

Lacquer furniture, often considered an aesthetic opposite of its unadorned hardwood cousin, has a long and distinguished history. Excavated examples of Chinese lacquer tomb furnishings dating to the second century BCE suggest the importance of lacquer for furniture and decorative and ritual accessories throughout much of Chinese history. Constructed of less costly softwoods, lacquer furniture requires a laborious application of layers of lacquer varnish, which can be colored red or black, painted, carved, or inlaid. Early surviving examples of lacquer furniture are rare, but evidence suggests that lacquer furniture has been in continuous production for millennia.

If fine lacquer furniture and hardwood furniture were made to serve the relatively small number of wealthy households, vernacular furniture was a vaster, more encompassing tradition. Made of less expensive materials—softwoods and bamboo—vernacular furniture tended to be locally produced and used. Forms can be utilitarian and simple, can be decorated with auspicious symbols, or can imitate the styles of more valuable hardwood types. As utilitarian objects, vernacular-furniture pieces have had limited value and appeal to collectors, but have been increasingly appreciated by contemporary scholars of material culture.

METHODS AND MATERIALS

Chinese furniture shares with architecture common materials and methods of construction. As with architecture, Chinese furniture is traditionally constructed without benefit of nails or glue, relying instead on a sophisticated system of interlinking parts and pieces. The mortise-and-tenon joinery means that pieces fit together like a jigsaw puzzle, making disassembly easy and thereby increasing a piece's portability. This method of production requires great precision and technical skill, and remains one of the distinctive features of Chinese furniture.

Furniture and architecture are the shared theme of the *Lu Ban jing* (Classic of Lu Ban), a carpenter's manual compiled in the fifteenth century. Lu Ban, a fifth-century master craftsman, came to be known as the patron saint of builders and woodworkers. The work that bears his name includes measurements and instructions for individual pieces of furniture, from tables and benches, to chairs and beds and boxes. The book, which includes sections on rituals and magic in addition to the technical aspects of construction, continued to be sought after by tradesmen into the twentieth century.

The materials of furniture include hardwoods, softwoods, lacquer, and bamboo, all of which were domestically available within China in the past. A number of the hardwoods, such as the highly desirable *huanghuali* (a rosewood) and *zitan* (a sandalwood), which were originally obtainable from subtropical areas of China, were depleted and replaced by sources in Southeast Asia.

Furniture of all types (wooden, lacquer, bamboo) has been produced across China in regional and local centers. During the Ming dynasty, Suzhou was the center of fine furniture production. In the early twentieth century, Guangzhou became renowned for the workmanship of its furniture makers. Furniture of a range of quality, types, and styles to serve the everyday and special-occasion needs of all classes of society has been manufactured throughout China to the present day. Regional furniture is an area of study that continues to be explored. Early research suggests a certain consistency of forms and types, with differences expressed in materials and decoration. Guangdong, for instance, has a tradition of lacquer furniture, while furniture made in Chengdu is characterized by ornate carving. Tibet boasts of its own identifiable decorative style of furniture, with subregional styles within Tibet and western Sichuan expressed in variations in motifs and fittings.

FURNITURE MAKERS

Prior to the twentieth century, little was known about the identity of individual furniture makers, who worked as anonymous craftsmen. No signed pieces of furniture, account books, catalogs of designs, or working sketches have survived. Sources suggest that individual pieces were the responsibility of a single woodworker whose tasks encompassed each step in the process of assembling the piece.

Organized guilds for furniture makers came late among trade groups. While other crafts established trade associations centuries earlier, woodworking guilds seem to be a development of the nineteenth century. In 1810 the Guild of Fine Woodwork was established in Suzhou, and by 1850 the Sacred Society of Lu Ban, an organization of woodworkers and cabinetmakers, was established in Beijing. These organizations continued into the early decades of the twentieth century. Prior to the late Qing dynasty, it seems that woodworkers sold their goods without benefit of intermediaries. Shops specializing in the sale of furniture appeared only late in the Qing. An association of retail shopkeepers of furniture, the Guild of Tables and Chairs was established in Beijing in the late nineteenth century, coinciding with the emergence of specialty furniture shops in the capital.

Information about furniture making, gleaned from various sources in the early modern period, emerges anew during the twentieth century. A level of detail unknown from earlier centuries appears in such unexpected works as Mao Zedong's series of rural investigations. Conducted in the late 1920s and early 1930s as Mao developed his theory of revolution, these include detailed accounts of everyday life away from the major metropolitan centers. In Xunwu County, a remote area of Jiangxi, Mao spent part of 1930. His *Xunwu diaocha* (Xunwu investigation) includes a section on the local cabinetmaker in Xunwu City, a man named Hu Donglin. Mao identified Hu as the leading maker of furniture and other wooden items in Xunwu City, and listed nineteen items that Hu Donglin's workshop produced, ranging from tables and chairs, to buckets and signage. His clientele was drawn from the landlords and rich peasants throughout the county, as well as Western missionaries resident in Xunwu. Hu's furniture was considered quality woodwork in Xunwu, too expensive for most peasants, with the exception of those who purchased furniture for bridal dowries. Hu Donglin's business prospered until 1928, when economic dislocations caused by revolutionary changes in land redistribution led to its downturn. All of the furniture sold to the more prosperous residents of Xunwu was, as Mao described, in the "old style." From this unconventional source comes information as disparate as details on patronage, inventory, and style.

SCHOLARSHIP AND CONNOISSEURSHIP

Scholarship on furniture, collecting, and connoisseurship is quite rare until the twentieth century. In addition to *Lu Ban jing*, there are several other Ming-dynasty sources, for example Tu Long's *Kao pan yu shi* (Desultory remarks on furnishing the abode of the retired scholar, 1607) and Wen Zhenheng's *Zhangwu zhi* (Treatise on superfluous things, around 1620). Westerners dominated modern scholarly interest in Chinese furniture in the early decades of the twentieth century. Their works reflect the ready availability of antique classical furniture in Beijing during

Chinese furniture makers, c. 1933–1946. *Much of the furniture available for purchase in China during the early twentieth century continued to be made by hand, using traditional techniques. Wealthy customers often sought finely crafted lacquered and hardwood furniture, while poorer Chinese looked to own more functional pieces, generally made from softer, cheaper woods.* HARVARD COLLEGE LIBRARY

the Republican period (1912–1949). Gustav Ecke, a German sinologist who taught in China, was an enthusiastic collector of Ming-style hardwood furniture, with which he furnished his Beijing home. A serious scholar as well as a collector, Ecke's collection and passion for Chinese furniture was fueled by Chinese acquaintances who shared his interest and helped him with his research and acquisitions. Ecke's research resulted in the publication in 1944 of *Chinese Domestic Furniture*, published in a limited edition with photographs and detailed drawings. Relying heavily on pieces in his own collection for illustrations and drawings, *Chinese Domestic Furniture* was a pioneering work, the first serious modern monograph on any aspect of China's furniture traditions. It was reprinted in 1963 and continues to be available. Four years after Ecke, George Kates, an American resident of Beijing, documented his furniture experiences in *Chinese Household Furniture* (1948). It was based on furniture collected by Western residents in Beijing in the late 1930s.

The strong interest in Chinese furniture among the foreign community in Beijing was reflected in the scholarship of authors like Ecke and Kates. Private Western collections of Chinese furniture outside China were also assembled during the early decades of the twentieth century. These, in turn, led to exhibitions of Chinese furniture at Western museums by the 1940s. The nucleus of a number of important museum collections of Chinese furniture dates to this same period, including the collection formed by Laurence Sickman for the Nelson-Atkins Museum in 1946.

In the post-1949 period, many furniture dealers in China went out of business. Indeed, the furniture district in Beijing known as Lu Ban Guan had been renowned for the many shops that had sold antique and new furniture since the early Qing period. Through the twentieth century, shops there were remodeled, moved, or destroyed until the entire district was demolished in 2002, part of the massive rebuilding and expansion sweeping Beijing. Nevertheless, the interests of committed scholars and collectors within China continued unabated, despite the political movements and economic changes that marked the post-1949 period. The fruits of Wang Shixiang's decades of research, for example, were finally published in the 1980s, as the constraints of the Cultural Revolution became a more distant memory and the accepted spheres for scholarly inquiry more relaxed. Wang's research resulted in numerous articles and two seminal books, *Mingshi jiaju zhenshang* (1985; published as *Classic Chinese Furniture* in 1986) and *Mingshi jiaju yanjiu* (1989; *Connoisseurship of Chinese Furniture*).

FURNITURE AND IDENTITY

By the late twentieth century, public and private collections flourished, as did scholarly associations and interest groups, which published research, hosted symposia and conferences, and advanced this growing field of inquiry. A new generation of scholars around the world has published scholarship and curated exhibitions on traditions for imperial furniture, classical furniture, and vernacular furniture.

In early modern China, Ming and Qing sources indicate that furniture served as a marker of status, taste, and class identity. By the late twentieth century, furniture became an object valued by Chinese and Western collectors, connoisseurs, and scholars for its aesthetic, social, and monetary value. As part of the material culture of traditional China, household furniture was often featured in paintings, woodblock prints, and fiction—sources that continue to provide valuable clues about its function and value. In the decades since the Cultural Revolution, furniture has come to be appreciated for new reasons. In the heated, rapidly changing social and economic world of post–Deng Xiaoping China, artists began to question their identity and role both within China and in the transglobal world and its market. One means of doing this was by considering aspects of traditional culture in defining modern China. Furniture has increasingly become a vehicle for these considerations.

Furniture as a means of creative expression is not restricted to furniture makers. In fact, contemporary artists and designers of many backgrounds and styles have found China's furniture tradition fruitful. Ai Weiwei (b. 1957), an avant-garde artist who made his reputation in the stars movement of 1979, works in a variety of media, frequently with the goal of confronting authority and unsettling the viewer. In the late 1990s he began to reengineer pieces of antique Qing furniture, mostly tables and chairs. Two tables might be rearranged into a single X-shaped piece, or a table top split and rejoined at a 90-degree angle to make a less than functional L-shaped object with two legs on the floor and two on the wall—the past reconfigured and rendered useless.

Tian Jiaqing (b. 1953) and Shao Fan (b. 1964) found their own ways of making the tradition of Chinese furniture making relevant to themselves and their works. Tian, himself a scholar of traditional furniture, has studied all the intricacies of furniture design and construction. His furniture is known for quality of materials and exquisite attention to craftsmanship, with designs that are modern in taste but sensitive to the aesthetic ideals of his Ming predecessors. Shao Fan's furniture shows a similar reverence for the past. In Shao's works, though, historical designs are deconstructed and then reconceived in a recognizable but totally altered form. A table and stool, for example, closely resemble their Ming counterparts in all details, but have been contorted into unusual U-shaped arrangements unknown in the Ming dynasty.

Sa Benjie (b. 1948) prefers calligraphy as his expressive medium. In 1994 he wrote a series of furniture calligraphies that were inspired by Wang Shixiang's detailed histories of individual pieces of furniture. Wang's stories moved Sa to imagine furniture as imbued with personalities and life stories. One series of images uses chairs and stools to recreate familial relationships. Sa's furniture calligraphy combines three traditions: painting, calligraphy, and furniture in a new dynamic, one that embraces the past but uses it in a gently satirical way. Clever in combination, the images gesture toward the past, but use traditional forms of art and references to material culture to question the relevance of that past and the ideals it endorses in the context of the Chinese present and the shifting global order.

FURNITURE MAKING IN CONTEMPORARY CHINA

With increased interest in the field, fine-furniture making is no longer anonymous in contemporary China, and a new generation of artists, designers, furniture makers, and sculptors have emerged to refocus attention on this ancient craft. Contemporary works, commissioned and exhibited in museum collections, have increased the visibility of this venerable tradition and reversed millennia-long traditions of obscurity. Even vernacular furniture has been the subject of museum attention. In addition, exhibitions, symposia, and publications continue to expand the field. Materials, methods, and conventions of the past have been honored, copied, and reinterpreted, and scholars continue to unravel the past. All the while, a new tradition of Chinese furniture making and scholarship is taking form.

SEE ALSO *Architecture, History of: Architecture to 1949; Architecture, History of: Architecture, 1949–1979; Sculpture and Public Art.*

BIBLIOGRAPHY

Barrass, Gordon. *The Art of Calligraphy in Modern China.* Berkeley: University of California Press, 2002.

Berliner, Nancy, and Edward S. Cooke Jr. *Inspired by China: Contemporary Furnituremakers Explore Chinese Traditions.* Salem, MA: Peabody Essex Museum, 2006.

Berliner, Nancy, and Sarah Handler. *Friends of the House: Furniture from China's Towns and Villages.* Salem, MA: Peabody Essex Museum, 1995.

Bruce, Grace Wu. *Chinese Classical Furniture.* Oxford: Oxford University Press, 1995.

Clunas, Craig. *Chinese Furniture.* London: Victoria and Albert Museum, 1988.

Ecke, Gustav. *Chinese Domestic Furniture.* Beijing: H. Vetch, 1944. Reprint. Rutland, VT: Tuttle, 1962.

Ellsworth, Robert Hatfield. *Chinese Furniture: Hardwood Examples of the Ming and Early Ch'ing Dynasties.* New York: Random House, 1970.

Handler, Sarah. *Austere Luminosity of Chinese Classical Furniture.* Berkeley: University of California Press, 2001.

Kates, George. *Chinese Household Furniture.* New York: Harper, 1952.

Mao Zedong. *Report from Xunwu.* Trans. Roger Thompson. Stanford, CA: Stanford University Press, 1990.

Ruitenbeek, Klaas. *Carpentry and Building in Late Imperial China: A Study of the Fifteenth-Century Carpenter's Manual "Lu Ban jing."* Leiden: Brill, 1993.

Wang Shixiang. *Classical Chinese Furniture: Ming and Early Qing Dynasties.* Hong Kong: Joint Publishing Co., 1986.

Wang Shixiang. *Connoisseurship of Chinese Furniture: Ming and Early Qing Dynasties.* 2 vols. Hong Kong: Joint Publishing Co., 1990.

Melissa J. Walt

FUZHOU

The administrative center and largest city of Fujian Province, Fuzhou is strategically located on the lower reaches of the Min River in eastern Fujian. The city enjoys a favorable subtropical climate, with an annual mean temperature of 66 degrees Fahrenheit. It is historically renowned for its hot springs, jasmine, and banyan trees (from which it acquired the name Rongcheng [City of the Banyan]). Surrounded by hills, this riverine port city is located some 56 miles from the East China Sea. The greater city, which covers an area of 4,693 square miles, comprises five districts, six counties, two county-level municipalities, and one economic zone, with an estimated residential population of 6.6 million at the end of 2004. The city proper, covering 403 square miles, then had an estimated population of 1.7 million. The city administration is located in the city's Gulou District, and Greater Fuzhou borders the municipalities of Ningde, Nanping, Sanming, Quanzhou, and Putian.

HISTORY

Fuzhou was designated by the State Council in 1986 as one of China's ancient cultural cities. Archaeologists and historians trace an urban polity back to the Minyue Kingdom. An administrative Chinese identity was established through the Minzhong Prefecture of the Qin dynasty (221–206 BCE), which eventually replaced the Minyue Kingdom. The first city wall of Fuzhou was constructed in 202 BCE, when Liu Bang, who became the founding emperor of the Han dynasty (206 BCE–220 CE), gave permission to King Wuzhu of Minyue to establish his capital Ye on the site of what would become Fuzhou. Its designation as the Fuzhou Area Military Commandery dates from the Kaiyuan period (713–741) of the Tang dynasty, and by the Song dynasty (960–1279) the city was actively involved in foreign trade. The city was reportedly visited by Marco Polo at the end of the thirteenth century, when it housed a sizeable community of foreign traders from South Asia, some of whom were Nestorian Christians. Fuzhou was a major center of Buddhism, and the city today boasts of a number of ancient temples, including Hualin, Dizang, Xichan, and Yongquan temples, as well as two ancient pagodas, Wu Ta and Bai Ta. Theater was also highly developed in and around Fuzhou. The man generally regarded as traditional China's greatest playwright, Tang Xianzu (1550–1616), was a native of Linchuan (Fuzhou), and various local theatrical genres of the Fuzhou region had a wide influence.

Fuzhou's modern history began with its designation as one of China's five treaty ports in the 1842 Treaty of Nanjing, which concluded the First Opium War (1839–1842), and its opening marked the beginning of the city's prosperity. A major modernization project of the late-Qing Self-strengthening movement, the Fuzhou Naval Yard, dubbed "the cradle of China's modern navy," was established at Mawei in 1867. The Naval Yard continues today, engaging in construction of container vessels and other craft. The naval academy attached to the shipyard became a center for the study of Western technology and European languages. Yan Fu (1854–1921), a key figure in the introduction to China of Western knowledge, including Darwinian thinking, was trained at the academy. Fuzhou remained a commercial center and trading port until the 1950s, and after 1958 its pace of industrialization accelerated. Its current status as a prosperous investment zone was enhanced in early 2004 by the passage of provincial legislation calling for the establishment of a special economic zone on the western side of the Taiwan Strait and a large and powerful provincial center.

FUZHOU AS A REGIONAL HUB

The city is a hub of land and water transportation and is strategically located close to Guangdong and Jiangxi provinces, which will be brought even closer with the completion of the major Xiangtang-Putian railroad in 2010. Direct flights from Fuzhou's Changle International Airport connect Fuzhou with Beijing, Shanghai, Guangzhou, Wuhan, Nanchang, Xiamen, and Hong Kong, and direct flights to Taiwan are still under discussion. Connecting the city with the rest of the country are a rail network and highway system, the latter extensively upgraded in the 1990s with the completion of the Nanchang-Xiamen, Beijing-Fujian, and Shanghai-Ruijin highways. Construction continues on the Fuzhou-Ji'an and Jinan-Guangzhou expressways, and a new central railway station was under construction in the city's Cangshan District as of 2009. There are regular daily bus services to Guangzhou and Shenzhen, and foreign passenger ships can berth in Mawei Harbor. Although Fuzhou itself is no longer accessible to oceangoing vessels, Greater Fuzhou includes some 706 miles of coastline and boasts of a number of deepwater ports, including Fuqing Bay. Fuzhou also once served as headquarters of the strategic Fujian Military District, which commanded the Taiwan Strait, but this was dismantled around 1985, and the area is now subsumed within the much larger Nanjing Military Command. Fuzhou's close historical, cultural, and linguistic links with Taiwan are underscored by the policy of encouraging investment from businessmen from Taiwan. Designated in 1984 as one of China's open cities following the introduction of the Reform and Opening policy, Fuzhou boasts of the Fuzhou Economic and Technological Development Zone, one of China's earliest, which was approved by the Fujian Provincial People's Congress in December 1986. Cross-strait investment has made Fuzhou one of China's most prosperous cities, and the city continues to offer favorable investment conditions, now aimed primarily at attracting investment from Taiwan for the city's high-tech industries. Agriculture, forestry, animal husbandry, and handicrafts all remain important pillars of Fuzhou's economy, but the chemical, pharmaceutical, electronic, textile, and machine industries now form the focus of development.

DIALECT AND FOOD

The dialect of Fuzhou (sometimes written Hokchiew) is regarded by linguists as having a substratum based on the language of the ancient Minyue people and is one of the eastern Min dialects, with some well-preserved elements of archaic and ancient Chinese. Migration from Fujian Province in the nineteenth and twentieth centuries took Fuzhou dialect speakers to Southeast Asia and other parts of the world, and the dialect is alive in a number of centers, such as Sibu in Sarawak, Malaysia. Mandarin has replaced the Fuzhou dialect in schools in Fuzhou, and although the Fujian provincial government has expressed the wish to reverse the decline of the dialect, there are few calls for preserving the dialect in its native place. Ironically, the Nationalist government in Taiwan has taken active steps to preserve the Fuzhou language, spoken by 10,000 people on the Mazu (Matsu) Islands.

The Min cuisine of Fuzhou is regarded as one of China's eight major cuisines. It is noted for its exquisite ingredients, fresh seasonings, and meticulous methods of preparation.

SEE ALSO *Fujian.*

BIBLIOGRAPHY

Dunch, Ryan. *Fuzhou Protestants and the Making of a Modern China, 1857–1927.* New Haven, CT: Yale University Press, 2001.

Fuzhou. http://www.fuzhou.gov.cn. The municipal government Web site.

Fuzhou-shi Renmin Zhengfu [Fuzhou Municipality People's Government], ed. *Fuzhou Nianjian, 2005* [Fuzhou Yearbook, 2005]. Beijing: Zhongguo Tongji Chubanshe, 2006.

Pong, David. *Shen Pao-chen and China's Modernization in the Nineteenth Century.* Cambridge, U.K.: Cambridge University Press, 1994.

Yeung, Y. M., and David K. Y. Chu, eds. *Fujian: A Coastal Province in Transition and Transformation.* Hong Kong: Chinese University Press, 2000.

Bruce Doar

G

GAMES AND PLAY

Like art, ritual, language, and politics, games structure human experience. Some games in China possess immense historical depth, and others are proof of the busy traffic of material and ideas in both directions across the country's borders. Historical evidence of these conditions emerges from literature, representational arts, material artifacts, and ethnographic surveys.

Early writing and art concerning games, which date back two millennia, stress mostly the play of the elite. None of it was concerned with, say, the forms of gambling that barge-haulers preferred on a rare day off. The history of games over the last two hundred years is at least socially broader. One vital late aid to understanding ancient and modern forms of play followed the rise of newspapers and illustrated news during the nineteenth century. Images created by illustrators such as Wu Youru (d. 1893) provide crucial comment on the integration of games with contemporary religion, politics, and family life. Games, it appears, became a major category of social knowledge among growing numbers of Chinese and foreign audiences.

Games in China can be variously categorized as dice play, board games with dice, card games, and board games without dice. These categories are not absolute. Card games, for instance, probably developed from dice play. Nor is the following survey comprehensive. The material evidence for even quite recent games has often proved too ephemeral to survive. Also, the vastness of China precludes completeness. For example, forms of *mancala*—a strategy of counting predominantly associated with games in Africa—have been documented in southwest China only during the last few decades.

DICE

Cube dice inscribed with the Chinese numerals one to six have appeared in tombs dated as early as the Qin empire (221–206 BCE). By the ninth century, dice faces were bored with their familiar patterns of dots. Chinese dice differ from dice in the West in that the dots on the two faces for one and four are colored red. Dice were often rattled in lidded porcelain shakers. The noisy allure of these implements is recreated vividly during a disastrous gambling scene in Zhang Yimou's film *Huozhe* (*To Live*, 1994). Four is often the highest throw.

Dice, most recently called *touzi* (or *shaizi*), have long been imagined as devices through which supernatural powers intercede in human affairs. Wu Youru, for instance, illustrated a newspaper report of how spirits had communicated to an impoverished young man and the master of a female servant that the former young man could take the woman as his wife if he could cast "six reds" (i.e., six fours) in one throw—a feat that he apparently managed. Such gossip was typical of affairs decided by dice.

Six dice featured also in games at which players collect tallies, made of ivory or high-quality bone, with values corresponding to several prescribed dice scores. This game, borrowing its symbolic structure from the state examination system, was called "tallies for first on the list" (*zhuangyuan chou*). "First on the list" refers to the single tally worth thirty-two points, which any player can gain by throwing five "reds" (fours). A number of lesser combinations earns the player other tallies within the full set of sixty four. Throwing six fours permits the player to possess all tallies and to win the game outright.

Other forms of the game use the same scoring and are still named "first on the list," but they substitute other names and images on the tallies, in one case adopting the names of the leading characters in Cao Xueqin's novel *Honglou meng* (*Dream of Red Mansions*), first published in 1792. This dice game, in all its forms, became popular in a period that witnessed also the rise of huge lotteries, which accepted bets on the triennial examination results reported from Beijing.

Perhaps related to play with six-sided dice yet formally different was another group of throwing games dominated by the cleaned ankle joints ("knucklebones") of sheep or goats. Most commonly called *guaizi* in north China, these objects were often imitated in more expensive materials. Play involved casting these dice onto one of its four sides or two ends and scoring accordingly. This game was reported in Beijing during the late Ming (1368–1644) and was still a common pursuit in the early twentieth century. Particularly interesting is the fact that the same implements used for similar games are found in several ancient cultures. For instance, the tomb of the Egyptian pharaoh Tutankhamun (fourteenth century BCE) contained ivory imitations.

The most basic form of dice play, ubiquitous in recent gambling history in China, was covered dice (*baozi*), though, strictly speaking, these are not dice. Yet, like dice, they materialize chance—now reduced to two possible results—in the form of blocks with dark and light halves to determine betting outcomes. The entire equipment consists of a four-sided metal chamber riveted to a square plate. The banker, unobserved, places the die inside the chamber and covers it with a lid. This combination is then placed at the center of a table and spun repeatedly until it rests with its edges squarely facing the four quarters of the table. When the chamber is opened, the winner(s) will have correctly declared which out of four directions one or the other half of the die faces. Such simple devices were easily adapted, with small interior springs and plates that turn 90 degrees, to defraud the unwary.

BOARD GAMES WITH DICE

Dice are also used in board games to determine a player's moves. One of the most famous boards from the nineteenth century is the promotions chart (*shengguan tu*), which dates from the Ming period or earlier. This game has the distinction of being one of the earliest Chinese games reported to a Western readership, by the Oxford scholar Thomas Hyde in 1694. Players throw dice and, according to their score, promote or demote their board pieces across an intricate chart of the bureaucracy that ascends from village student to the winning position of chancellor.

Promotions inspired numerous other board and dice games. These were often based on religious lore and popular characters from nearly all the most famous Ming and Qing dramas and novels, including once more *Dream of Red Mansions*. Another notable counterpart, eventually more popular in Japan, is the promotions chart of accumulated *karma* (*shōka zōshin no zu*), a Buddhist-inspired game played up and down an elaborate scale of rebirths and karmic retributions leading up to the final goal of enlightenment.

Several other race-to-the-finish games have been imported into China. Notable are the board games Parcheesi (Ludo in Britain) and Snakes and Ladders, both derived from older games in India. The former is played in China under the name "flying chess" (*feixing qi*), since provision is made for pieces to fly over extra squares. Snakes and Ladders has frequently been adapted to carry visual messages that promote public awareness of leading national, political, and social issues.

Editions of Monopoly appeared in China before 1949, but property deals were low-status economic activities during the Maoist era, and so the game was politically tainted, even if not officially banned. During the 1990s the game was reinvented and marketed under the name "champion's chess" (*qiangshou qi*), but this soon changed to "Shanghai millionaire big shots" (*Shanghai baiwan daheng*), a particularly apt title for the period. Reintroduced Monopoly shows some radical divergences from the Western game. For example, a player, having reached a square marked "Industrial Spy," is permitted to move a special piece once around the board and to enjoy certain privileges, such as exemptions from taxes, jails sentences, and rent. The Chinese game also represents the starker realities of economic survival in China from the 1990s on. The notion of social security, albeit only faintly represented in Monopoly's Community Chest, has been dropped in favor of cards called "Fate."

DOMINOES AND CARDS

Undoubtedly the most popular category of games during the last few centuries comprises dominoes and cards. Chinese dominoes—known as "bone tiles" (*gupai*), to distinguish them from paper cards, also called *pai*—are rectangular tiles. Each tile combines two dice faces. A complete set of Chinese dominoes uses thirty-two tiles, comprising a series of combinations, of which eleven are duplicated to form the pairs. A famous domino game is making nine (*paijiu*), in which each of four players draws four tiles from the stack and then redraws and discards in order to combine his tiles into a winning hand of two pairs. Onlookers can also bet. Dominoes are common in fortune-telling, and paper dominoes are often burned as funeral offerings.

Mah-jongg (*majiang*), perhaps the most popular game in China, is barely two centuries old, even though folklore claims an origin in high antiquity. The game also engendered a brief yet intense playing craze in the American and European middle classes between the two world wars. Although based on tiles, mah-jongg in fact fits better in the category of card games, for the strategic object of

Men playing Chinese chess, Badaling, China, May 18, 2006. *Board games such as* xiangqi, *known in English as Chinese chess, have been enjoyed for many centuries.* Xiangqi *continues to be a popular activity in China and South Asia into the twenty-first century, with organized leagues and regular competitions held throughout the region.* © FRANK LUKASSECK/CORBIS

mah-jongg and card games is indistinguishable. Four players compete in a game using 136 tiles, first stacked in four walls two tiles deep. Each player draws 13 tiles, and then redraws and discards back to the table to collect the highest-scoring combinations. A winning hand consists of any four sets of tiles and a pair, but there are many variations in different regions of China. Experienced mah-jongg players usually pride themselves on playing "blind" (instead of reading a tile, merely rubbing the tile's marked surface with the thumb to register whether to keep the tile or discard it). Some players observe an even greater challenge by discarding tiles into a basket suspended above the table, which forces each player to remember rather than to see what values have emerged during the game.

Paper card games in China were frequently named literally "games with leaves" (*yezi xi*), a term later superseded by *pai*. Cards had made their appearance by the Tang dynasty (618–907), but little is known concerning their appearance until much later. Sets of characteristically elongated cards use either three or four identical suits consisting of nine, ten, or eleven values. Many card games have been developed from domino games, and some borrow the values of Chinese chess pieces, if not the tactics of that board game.

Drinking contests were once regulated by cards of similar suits and values, which dictated subjects for lyrical composition and forfeits for inferior performances. By the late nineteenth century, cards themselves had become collectible. For instance, a famous production of forty drawings for a set of drinking cards, based on characters from the novel *Shuihu zhuan* (*Water Margin*), was executed by the influential late Ming painter Chen Hongshou (1598–1652). Soon after Chen's lifetime, surviving cards were even reprinted as illustrations to new editions of the novel, and some sets were bound and preserved as books that still survive.

BOARD GAMES

Pure board games include most famously Chinese chess (*xiangqi*) and "surrounding chess" (*weiqi*), often known by its shortened Japanese name *go*. The rules of these games are available in numerous publications and online resources. Over many centuries a lot has been published concerning development in play, but the materials and social histories of both games have attracted less attention. For example, remaining to be explored are remarkable publications that promoted technical expertise and historical knowledge of both games from the eighteenth century on. And although old Chinese-chess pieces, especially bronze specimens, are sometimes collected by coin-collectors, since they comprise a category of circular token, this activity has stimulated little deep research.

Legend says that the mythical sage king Yao (c. 2300 BCE) invented go. This is certainly not the case, but the myth reflects the intellectual preeminence that go players assume is theirs above all other games. This preeminence from early on is indicated by the game's massive literature, some of which has survived for fifteen hundred years. Visual media and comments throughout the last two centuries certainly reinforce the prejudice that go is the most refined board game. Chinese chess features more frequently as an object of satire in the visual culture of the same period. Images show disputatious contestants throwing game pieces and furniture at each others' heads. Nevertheless, in the early twenty-first century, only these two games have acquired the status of national symbols, regularly celebrated on special postage stamps and in other forms of public celebration. Both games have provincial and national levels of competition. International matches between China and other East Asian countries absorb significant media attention and seldom escape intense diplomatic pressure.

BIBLIOGRAPHY

Bell, R. C. *Board and Table Games from Many Civilizations*. 2nd ed. London: Oxford University Press, 1969. First published, 1960.

Culin, Stewart. *Korean Games, with Notes on the Corresponding Games of China and Japan*. New York: Brooklyn Museum, 1991. First published, 1895.

Ge Chunyuan. *Dubo shi* [A history of gambling]. Shanghai: Shanghai Wenyi Chubanshe, 1995.

Li Jiaofa. *Zhidu shijian* [Lessons from the history of the regulation of gambling]. Changsha: Yuelu Shushe, 1997.

Ma Guojun and Ma Shuyun. *Zhonghua chuantong youxi daquan* [An encyclopedia of traditional chinese games]. Beijing: Nongcun Duwu Chubanshe, 1990.

Prunner, Gernot. *Ostasiatische Spielkarten*. Bielefeld, Germany: Deutsches Spielkarten Museum, 1969.

Yang Yinshen. *Zhongguo gudai youyi huodong* [Recreational activities in traditional china]. Taibei: Guowen Tiandi Zazhishe, 1989. First published, 1946.

Oliver Moore

GANSU

Gansu Province stretches like an elongated amoeba from southeast to northwest between the Qinghai-Tibetan Plateau and Inner Mongolia. With the Silk Route coursing its length, it connects China's heartland with Inner Asia and has long been of strategic and economic importance. In 2009, its population of approximately twenty-six million was dominated by Han Chinese (some 92 percent), but included a large number of Hui (Sino-Muslims) and Tibetans, as well as Dongxiang, Tu, Manchu, Uygur, Yugur, Bonan, Mongolian, Salar, and Kazaks. This is a border world of complex loyalties, where ethnic tensions, natural disasters, famine, and war have historically taken their toll.

GANSU

Capital city: Lanzhou
Largest cities (population): Lanzhou (3,140,000 [2006])
Area: 454,000 sq. km. (175,000 sq. mi.)
Population: 26,060,000 (2006)
Demographics: Han, 91%; Hui, 5%; Dongxiang, 2%; Tibetan, 2%
GDP: CNY 227.7 billion (2006)
Famous sites: The Jiayuguan Pass of the Great Wall, the Mogao Caves of Dunhuang, Bingling Temple, Labrang Monastery

THE MUSLIM UPRISINGS

In the 1860s, the region of present-day Gansu Province was administered by the governor general of Shaan-Gan, who was based at Lanzhou—still today the seat of provincial government. In the late Qing dynasty (1644–1912), however, the "Gan" region included present-day Ningxia, Gansu, and parts of northeastern Qinghai and eastern Xinjiang. The history of Gansu in the late nineteenth century is therefore inseparable from what has become known as the "Great Muslim Rebellion" (1862–1877) of the northwest.

The cause of this rebellion, or rather uprisings, is generally linked to the revivalist Sufi teachings that took root in the region in the eighteenth century and vied for adherents, not only among themselves but also with the established Muslim communities, the *gedimu*, based around local mosques. The impact of the Jahrīya Sufi teaching introduced to Gansu by Ma Mingxin (c. 1719–1781) on his return from Yemen in the 1760s, was considerable, not merely because of conflicts with the more established Khafīya order but because it tended to attract adherents who were opposed to Qing rule. By the late eighteenth century, intercommunal tensions had boiled

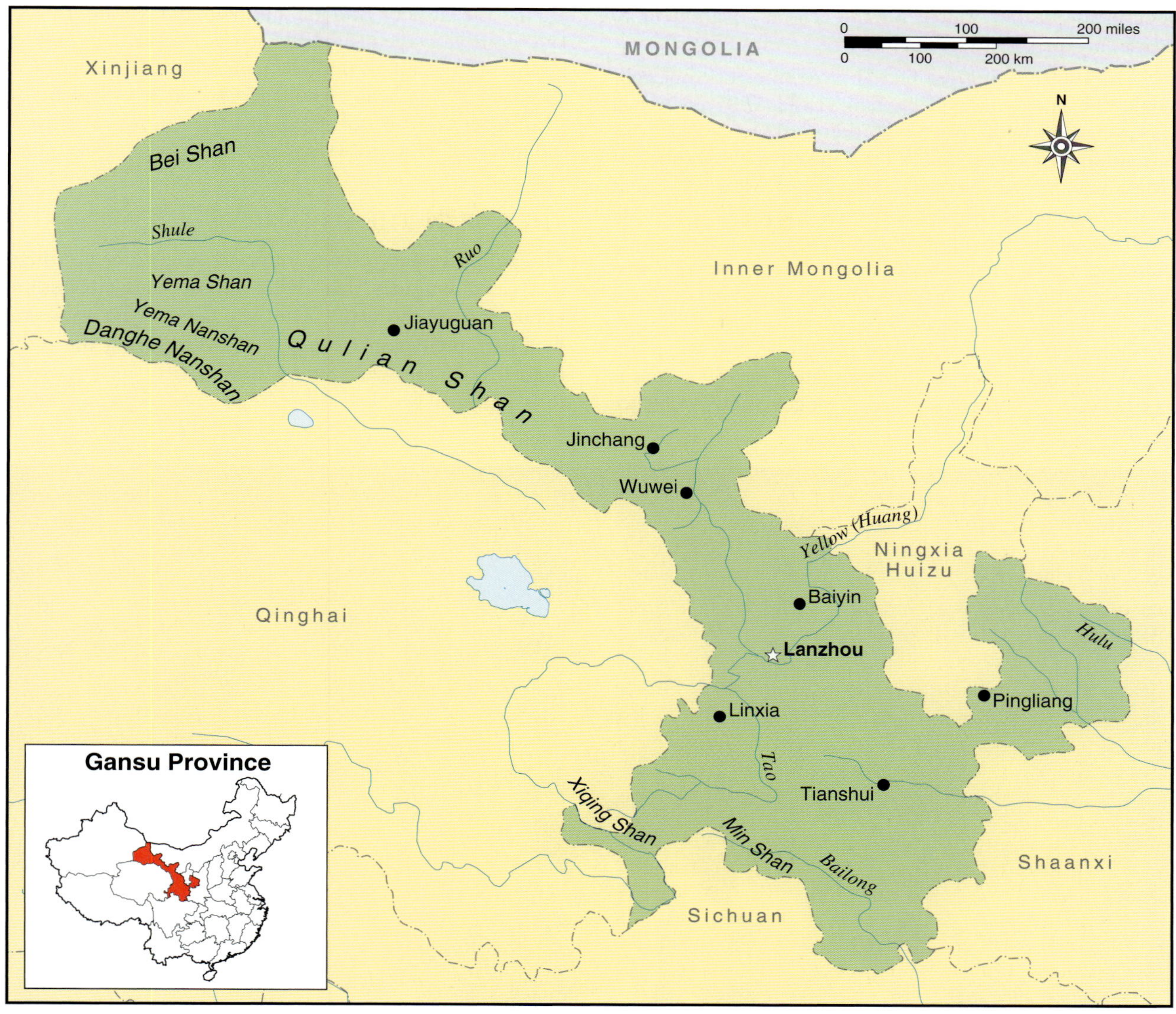

over, notably among the Salars (Turkic Muslims). As the violence escalated, Qing troops took action to repress what they loosely termed the "New Teachings." Yet as scholars such as Jonathan Lipman (1998) have shown, just as the violence was not simply a matter of Muslim pitted against Muslim, or of Muslims against the state, the cause of the violence was frequently secular, deep-rooted, and localized. Acute poverty, official corruption and embezzlement, legal discrimination against Muslims, the increasing militarization of society, and the rise of charismatic religious leaders all contributed to an atmosphere in which violence was easily sparked.

The disturbances of the eighteenth century were swiftly suppressed, but the combination of secular and religious grievances persisted, and more than fifty years later, uprisings born of the same potent mix shook the northwest from Shaanxi to Xinjiang. By this time, however, the Qing military hold on the region was significantly weaker.

In 1862 a wave of unrest spread from Shaanxi to eastern Gansu, fueled by several thousand rioting Shaanxi Muslims who spilled over into Gansu and formed the so-called Eighteen Great Battalions. Brawls became battles and, as tension and fear mounted, entire villages were massacred. One after another, cities across the south from Pingliang to Hezhou fell to the Muslims. The Qing troops, many on reduced rations and with salaries unpaid, were sorely overstretched. Large numbers deserted. Pillaging and raping as they fled, they added to the maelstrom of devastation. Without the resources or leadership to regain control of the region, over the next six years regional officials vacillated between acts of violent suppression and policies of reconciliation toward "good

Muslims," as they waited for the central government to send an expeditionary force.

In 1869, having pacified Shaanxi, the governor general of Shaan-Gan, Zuo Zongtang (1812–1885), who had been charged with "pacifying" the northwest, turned his attention to Gansu. In 1871 he forced the surrender of Ma Hualong, the spiritual descendent of Ma Mingxin, at his stronghold in Jinjibao (in present-day Ningxia). Ma and his family were put to death and thousands of his adherents were massacred. Zuo's troops then moved across Gansu to Xining and finally northward through the Gansu Corridor, where they overpowered resistance at Suzhou. Zuo had reestablished Qing rule, but the problems persisted. Twenty-five years later, in 1895, southwestern Gansu saw a resurgence of antigovernment violence around the cities of Xunhua, Hezhou, and Xining. By the end of the year, the rising had been suppressed, but only at great cost to life. This time the repression was harsher than that inflicted by Zuo, who had favored resettlement of Muslim captives in isolated parts of the province: tens of thousands of Muslims were massacred.

THE RISE OF THE MA FAMILY

The political legacy of these nineteenth-century uprisings is a clear reminder that there was no unified Muslim opposition to the state. The Ma family who came to dominate politics in China's northwest during the early twentieth century were Sino-Muslims (frequently referred to as Tungans) who had assisted Zuo Zongtang in subduing

A camel caravan following the Silk Road in the Mingsha Shan desert, Dunhuang, Gansu. *The ancient Silk Road stretches throughout Gansu, a long, narrow province extending through northwest China. While the majority of the province is Han Chinese, other ethnic groups, such as Hui and Tibetans, comprise a significant portion of the population, a legacy of generations of exchange between different cultures along the famous trade route.* © REDLINK/CORBIS

the region after the revolts of 1866 to 1872. With the total collapse of the central authority, they gradually asserted their authority.

After the warlord Feng Yuxiang's (1882–1948) Guominjun (National People's Army) seized power in 1925, the brothers Ma Qi (1869–1931) and Ma Lin (1876–1945) ruled the Gansu Corridor and Qinghai, nominally under Feng's authority. Then, in the early 1930s, Ma Qi's sons, Ma Bufang (1903–1975) and Ma Buqing (1898–1977), took control of the region. Meanwhile, the seventeen-year-old Ma Zhongying (c.1910–1936), from another branch of Ma Qi's family, pitted himself against the Guominjun in the south. But as the Ma militarists switched their loyalties back and forth, it was Ma Fuxiang (1876–1932), whose family dominated Ningxia, who did the most to bring the region into the Nationalist fold. Finally breaking with Feng Yuxiang in 1929, Ma Fuxiang allied himself with Chiang Kai-shek (Jiang Jieshi) under the Nationalist banner. In 1933 Chiang Kai-shek moved to secure his hold on Gansu. Clashing with local troops on the Shaan-Gan border, he founded a Nationalist base in southern Gansu, but simultaneously the Communist Party had established a presence in Lanzhou and was penetrating local communities. By 1937, the Shaan-Gan-Ning border-region government was working actively to promote rural reform and anti-Japanese resistance.

INDUSTRIALIZATION AND DEVELOPMENT

When in 1949 the CCP took over Gansu (now separated from the Qinghai and Ningxia regions), with its population of nine million, the party inherited a region wracked by banditry, ethnic hatred, poverty, military extortions, opium addiction, and the effects of the devastating earthquakes of 1920 and 1932. Yet within twenty years, the province was experiencing rapid industrialization, with Lanzhou set to become the second-largest industrial center of the northwest. Rich in iron ore and coal, Gansu became a major steel-making center, while other mineral resources—nickel, copper, lead, and zinc—supported a variety of heavy industries. Nevertheless, with over 65 percent of the population living in rural areas, grain production in the 1980s remained no better than in the 1950s, and in the 1990s Gansu still had the lowest rural per capita income of any province in China. The enduring poverty reflected not only the low start point, but a hostile natural environment, intensified by severe soil-erosion problems and an expanding population.

Assisted by poverty-relief funds from the central government, however, developments in the reform era, and particularly since the 1990s, have brought significant changes. Most importantly, there has been a gradual shift from heavy industry to labor-intensive nonagricultural activities, and even to tourism at sites such as the Buddhist caves of Dunhuang and the Lamaist monastery at Labrang. The removal of many of the restrictions on labor mobility has brought new expertise to the province and also allowed movement from the countryside into the cities. Farming has been stimulated by huge investment in the development of water conservancy and hydroelectric projects. Meanwhile, with the easing of economic hardship, primary school attendance has improved, as has life expectancy. The Great Western Development Scheme (1999) has brought a massive investment in infrastructure development, and most significantly perhaps, the scheme's slogan, "stability through development," appears to be holding strong; notwithstanding the Cultural Revolution (1966–1969), for over sixty years the region has seen no major outbreaks of violence.

SEE ALSO *Islam; Muslim Uprisings; Ningxia; Zuo Zongtang.*

BIBLIOGRAPHY

Fields, Lanny. *Tso Tsung-t'ang and the Muslims: Statecraft in Northwest China 1868–1880.* Kingston, ON: Limestone Press, 1978.

Lipman, Jonathan. *Familiar Strangers: A History of Muslims in Northwest China.* Seattle: University of Washington Press, 1998.

Zhu Wenzhang (Chu Wen-djang). *The Moslem Rebellion in Northwest China, 1862–1878: A Study of Government Minority Policy.* The Hague, Netherlands: Mouton, 1966.

L. J. Newby

GAO XINGJIAN
1940–

Translator, painter, novelist, playwright, and the 2000 Nobel Laureate in literature, Gao Xingjian was born in 1940 in Ganzhou, Jiangxi Province. When interviewed by the Taiwan United Press, Gao attributed his worldly success to his mother's upbringing, honoring her as the source of his artistic talents. He recalled to his friend Chen Jun that his mother, who was an actress at one time, had influenced his literary career the most, introducing him to Western myths and fairy tales when he was only five. It was also on his mother's advice that he chose to attend Beijing Foreign Studies University (instead of the Central Academy of Fine Arts) in 1957. With a college degree in French literature from Beijing Foreign Studies University, he was assigned to work in Zhongguo Guoji Shudian (China International Bookstore) in 1962, and in 1975 he began working as a translator for the magazine *China Reconstructs*. When China began opening up to the outside world (1978), he was able to visit France, and soon after his return to China he joined the Beijing Renmin Yishu Juyuan (Beijing People's Art Theater) as a screenwriter and playwright.

THE SMALL PERSON'S STRUGGLE FOR AUTHENTICITY

Gao's rank among modern Chinese literary writers has to do with the overall social and cultural transformation of which he is not only a product but also a forerunner. Sick and embarrassed by the stale language of socialist realism, the mode of literary writing endorsed and privileged by the state, Gao and other writers, artists, and playwrights known as China's modernists desperately sought from the West new modes of perception and new forms of artistic expression. Among them, Gao is perhaps one of the most active and informed, experimenting and adopting aesthetics then considered avant-garde. In 1981 he published *Xiandai xiaoshuo jiqiao chutan* (A Preliminary Examination of Modern Fictional Techniques) in which he discusses the writing styles of many Western modernist novelists, as well as of Chinese writers from the May Fourth era (1919–1925) on. A pioneer of the theater of the absurd in China, Gao also produced several plays, including *Juedui xinhao* (Absolute Signal, 1982) and *Chezhan* (Bus Stop, 1983; noticeably modeled on Samuel Beckett's *Waiting for Godot*), and *Bi'an* (1986; "The Other Shore"). These plays, in their essence, express human desire for authentic experience, free from ideological control, but with his reputation as an avant-garde artist, Gao risked being seen as openly subversive and critical of the state.

Lingshan (1989; *Soul Mountain*), the fictional work for which he won the 2000 Nobel Prize in Literature, is the capstone of his modernist writing. Based on his own misdiagnosis of lung cancer, the loosely autobiographical work is the story of a man seeking his primitive origins in Soul Mountain, a nonexistent place in the wild, to avoid modern industrial civilization, where modern man arrives at only a fragment of himself. This quest for wholeness of self in opposition to one's culture follows the threads of several characters referred to as "I," "him," or "you" and representing the split personae of the author, characters painfully conscious that the rules of language do not allow them to articulate their authentic existence. Almost an exercise in deconstruction, the work is marked by its textual self-awareness in that the narrative, consisting of fragmented thoughts, intellectual reflections, interviews, and recollections, constantly undermines its own authority to tell a story with plot and meaning. Yet, as this monumental work lengthens to eighty-one chapters, Gao manages to create many mini-dialogues between and among his fictional characters that represent many intellectual discourses: official history, the language of Marxism and Maoism, local legends, Confucian classics and Buddhist beliefs, popular songs, and famous poems. What emerges from his craftsmanship as a fiction writer, and what is truly meaningful, is an inward psychological journey toward identity and selfhood, undertaken by each and every character. Gao thus brings to the fore the existential anguish that only an enlightened person at war with culture can relate to and appreciate. The problems of meaning and life are thus rendered experiential through the difficulties of fiction writing itself. Such is the psychological meaning of the futile journey to find Soul Mountain. The narrative marks the advent of a new literary Self on a par with its Western counterpart, one that is stubbornly self-referential, like Shakespeare's Hamlet.

This prize-winning work, though not the monumental product of genius, grows naturally from the literary thoughts of Gao Xingjian, who believes in intellectual self-reflection, or what he calls "cold literature" (*leng wenxue*), literature that is basically for the writing subject himself and totally detached from social or historical reality as defined by those in power. Novels such as *Soul Mountain* and *Yige ren de shengjing* (1998; *One Man's Bible*) exemplify this cold literature with their freedom from the moral burdens compelling previous generations of Chinese writers to take it upon themselves to save China through fiction, to serve as a voice of the Chinese people, or to be their conscience. Gao's short fiction is far less ambitious and presumptuous. His aesthetics are that of the private lives of small individuals, who are by no means legitimate subjects of Chinese history or society. The focus on these marginalized lives gives his fiction an authenticity and originality not seen in political or historical novels that "represent" reality. His fictional characters, sometimes even nameless, offer moments of true reflection, awakening, and enlightenment free from ideological thinking. Little wonder that he tried to free himself from what he viewed as a repressive political culture by a self-imposed exile in France as a necessary condition for his own creative writing and self-expression.

GAO'S PROBLEMATIC PLACE IN MODERN CHINESE LITERATURE

Ironically, nothing marks Gao's unique and problematic place in modern Chinese literature more than the Nobel Prize in Literature awarded to him in 2000, which in no small way calls into question the criteria conventionally held dear by the state-sanctioned Zhongguo Zuojia Xiehui (China Writers Association), which ranked Gao's work as "very average." From its perspective, great fiction writers in twentieth-century China are those—such as Lu Xun, Ba Jin, and Mao Dun—whose realistic works are overwhelmingly valued and canonized mainly for their reflections or representations of social transformation, often despite the novelist's strong desire to be free from the context of social history. Gao's award comes from a different aesthetic authority, one that honors and recognizes its seeming indifference to social ideology and politics.

Then there is Gao's French connection. Gao admitted that studying French enabled him to read Western literary texts in the original during a time when many translations of the works by Western authors were banned in China. This connection makes the concept of national literature in China problematic. His French citizenship and his subsequent literary publications in French do not help this situation, although they seem to be characteristic of an age in which a writer or writing itself no longer has a specific home or country.

BIBLIOGRAPHY

Gao Xingjian. *Buying a Fishing Rod for my Grandfather.* Trans. Mabel Lee. London: Flamingo, 2004.

Gao Xingjian. *One Man's Bible.* Trans. Mabel Lee. New York: HarperCollins, 2002.

Gao Xingjian. *Soul Mountain.* Trans. Mabel Lee. London: Flamingo, 2001.

Gao Xingjian. *The Other Shore.* Trans. Gilbert C. F. Fong. Hong Kong: The Chinese University Press, 1999.

Soong, Stephen C., and John Minford, eds. *Trees on the Mountain: an Anthology of New Chinese Writing.* Hong Kong: The Chinese University Press, 1984.

Rujie Wang

GAOXIONG

SEE *Kaohsiung (Gaoxiong).*

GARDENS AND PARKS

According to the oldest extant comprehensive dictionary of Chinese characters, Xu Shen's *Explanation of Simple and Compound Graphs*, the Chinese word for "garden," *yuan*, refers etymologically to an enclosure with fruit and trees. The Chinese counterpart for the English word "park," *gong yuan* or "public garden," was not in its modern use as such until the nineteenth century. That same dictionary has defined the word *gong* as "equal shares" or "equal division." The right of the general public was not unknown in ancient China: For instance, Confucius was cited, in the chapter "Evolution of Rites" in the *Book of Rites*, as having said, "When the Great Tao has its way, all under heaven is shared equally." Throughout much of China's long history, however, gardens primarily served the private use of the selected few. Most remained closed to the public until the beginning of the nineteenth century.

Until 1800 the numerous gardens in China could be roughly classified into three major types: (1) Imperial gardens for the exclusive use of the Manchu Qing emperors and their family, such as the Imperial Western Garden (also know as the Three Seas—the Central, the Northern, and the Southern Sea); the Yuan Ming Yuan, or Garden of Perfect Brightness (a Summer Palace for the imperial house), in Beijing; and the Mountain Hamlet to Escape the Summer Heat, in Chengde. (2) Private gardens owned by nobilities, senior government officials (often after their retirement), and, less frequently, rich merchants, mostly in the lower reaches of the Yangzi River, especially in the cities of Yangzhou and Suzhou. (3) Gardens attached to Buddhist or Daoist temples, such as Lion Grove and West Garden, both part of Buddhist temples in Suzhou, and shrines of celebrated historical figures, such as the Shrine of Zhuge Liang and Du Fu's Thatched Cottage, both in Chengdu, Sichuan.

In addition, some famous scenic spots in the country, such as West Lake in Hangzhou, Slender West Lake in Yangzhou, Daming Lake in Ji'nan, and Tiger Hill in Suzhou, were enriched through artificial vegetation and structures such as bridges, embankments, pavilions, and pagodas, and were open to the general public as popular tourist attractions. (Other scenic areas, such as the Five Sacred Mountains and the Yellow Mountains, remained entirely natural.) These scenic spots preceded the national parks that emerged in China in the late twentieth century.

THE EVOLUTION OF GARDENS

Gardening, which dates to ancient China, reached a stage of sophistication during the late Ming dynasty (1368–1644) when, around the turn of the seventeenth century, Ji Cheng's *The Craft of Gardens* appeared. Based on the widespread practice of garden construction, this book was possibly the first general manual on garden design in the Chinese tradition. To various degrees most gardens in the nineteenth century followed the principles discussed and delineated in the book. As the Qing dynasty (1644–1912) declined in power during the nineteenth century, China suffered from foreign invasions and the rioting of the Taiping Uprising (1851–1864). Many of the gardens mentioned above were either deserted or destroyed. The Yuan Ming Yuan, built in 1709 with the help of the Italian artist and missionary Giuseppe Castiglione (1688–1766) and known as the "Garden of Gardens," was burned down by the allied Anglo-French forces when they invaded Beijing in 1860 at the end of the Second Opium War (1856–1860). The ruins of the garden, northwest of the Forbidden City in China's capital, still provide a glimpse of its former beauty and splendor. Toward the end of the century, there was a revival in the construction of gardens, both imperial and private. The Yi He Yuan or Garden of Sustenance in Peace (Summer Palace) was rebuilt to celebrate the birthday of Empress Dowager Cixi, and a number of private gardens, many renovated on the basis of former gardens, were built in the cities of Yangzhou and Suzhou. One such private garden, the He Yuan (He's Garden) in Yangzhou, was built by a retired senior official who became disillusioned after his experience of working

West Lake Garden's Moon Gate, Hangzhou. *Traditional Chinese gardens generally aim to create a heightened, yet relaxing experience with the outdoors. Wood and stone elements appear frequently in Chinese gardens, often designed to imitate nature, such as the moon shape of the gate shown above.* © JOCHEN SCHLENKER/ROBERT HARDING WORLD IMAGERY/CORBIS

under the British superintendent of customs, and chose to seek refuge and shelter in the privacy of his family garden.

The park, a tract of land set aside for public use that may include enclosures or open areas like gardens, woods, and pastures, came late to China. However, the first urban park in China was built not much later than its Western equivalent, Peel Park in Salford, England, established in 1846. After the first Opium War (1839–1842), Shanghai, formerly a fishing village by the Yangzi, became an international trading port and quickly developed into a modern city; much of its land within the concessions was under the rule of Western powers. The Shanghai Municipal Council, the governing body that administered the combined British and American concessions, commissioned the construction of a *gong hua yuan* (public flower garden), a triangular stretch of green, along the western bank of the Huangpu River at the northern end of the Bund. In 1868 this garden, now known as Huangpu Park, became the first park in China. Designed by a Scottish gardener in European style, it included a pavilion and tennis court and served as a place of rest and entertainment for the growing number of Westerners living in the city; however, it remained closed to the Chinese public until 1928. According to a popular story used as Communist propaganda during the Mao era, at one time there was a sign at the park's gate that read, "No dogs or Chinese allowed." This sign has remained in the mind of the Chinese public as a symbol of past humiliation by the Western powers.

FROM PRIVATE TO PUBLIC

With the downfall of the Qing dynasty, imperial and private gardens gradually became available for public use. As early as 1914, only two years after the founding of the Republic of China, a former imperial garden located in the center of Beijing was turned into a sixty-acre complex known as Central Park. Once the site of the Altar of Land and Grain, where the emperor made sacrificial offerings to the gods of earth and agriculture, the garden was renamed Zhongshan Park in 1928, in honor of Sun Zhongshan (Sun Yat-sen), the first president of the Republic of China. The Northern Sea, formerly a part of the Imperial Western Garden, became Beihai Park in 1925. However, further development of parks in China was severely impeded by warfare (the Northern Expedition in 1927, the Anti-Japanese War [1937–1945], and the civil war [1946–1949]). During World War II Huangpu Park in Shanghai was used as a military camp, first by the Japanese and then by U.S. troops.

After the founding of the People's Republic of China in 1949, former owners of private gardens felt obliged to give up their private property, and almost all private gardens, such as the He Yuan, were turned over to public use. Over the years more urban parks were built around the country. By the end of 1990 the total number of parks in small and large cities on the Chinese continent was 1,900 (Yao Yongzheng 1993, p. 156). Shanghai, China's most cosmopolitan metropolis, is a good example of such growth. Prior to 1949 there were only about a dozen parks in the city, but over time the construction, renovation, and preservation of parks were placed on the agenda of urban planning. For instance, in 1953, by the order of the municipal government, a Jewish cemetery in the western part of the city was renovated and turned into the Jing'an Park. By 2001 the number of parks within the city had reached more than fifty. Public squares, notably Beijing's Tiananmen Square and Shanghai's People's Square (formerly the racecourse of the Shanghai International Settlement), serve different purposes from those of urban parks. Official ceremonies often take place in the squares, which, on occasion, have also been scenes of public unrest, as was the case in Tiananmen Square in 1989.

As high-rise buildings have proliferated since the late twentieth century, the number of small street-corner parks, known as the *lü di* (green lots), has grown. Most parks in the city now offer free admission to all; the few that still charge a fee offer free admission to children and seniors. As in all other Chinese cities, people use these parks and green lots from dawn to dusk for physical exercise, artistic endeavors, musical gatherings, dating, and even practicing English conversational skills. The British prime minister William Pitt (1759–1806) once called parks "the lungs of London," and the same metaphor may also apply to Shanghai's parks.

Between 1982 and 2005 the Chinese State Council, perhaps following the example of the United States' national park system, issued six executive orders declaring 187 official scenic places (literally, Zhongguo guojiaji fengjing mingsheng qu, "regions of scenic landscape spots of national class in China"). Given the official English name National Parks of China, the list includes almost all the famous scenic places around the country.

SEE ALSO *Architecture, History of: Architecture to 1949; Architecture, History of: Architecture, 1949–1979; Imperial Household Department; Shanghai; Suzhou; Urban China: Organizing Principles of Cities; Urban China: Urban Planning since 1978; Yangzhou.*

BIBLIOGRAPHY

Chen Lifang and Yu Sianglin. *The Garden Art of China*. Portland, OR: Timber Press, 1996.

Du Hai. *He Yuan* [He's garden]. Nanjing: Nanjing University Press, 2002.

Ji Cheng. *The Craft of Gardens*. Trans. Alison Hardie. New Haven, CT: Yale University Press, 1988.

Kutcher, Norman. China's Palace of Memory. *Wilson Quarterly* 27 (Winter 2003): 30–39.

Major Attractions and Cities in China, National Park of China. http://www.gjgy.com.

Morris, Edwin T. *The Gardens of China: History, Art, and Meanings*. New York: Scribners, 1983.

Wu Shenyuan. *Shanghai zuizaode zhongzhong* [A miscellany of the earliest in Shanghai]. Shanghai: East China Normal University Press, 1989.

Xu Jianrong. *Yuanlin fudi* [Gardens and mansions]. Shanghai: People's Fine Arts Press, 1996.

Yao Dongmei. *Yuehui gongyuan* [Appointments in the parks]. Shanghai: People's Publishing House, 2001.

Yao Yongzheng. *Zhongguo yuanlin jingguan* [Landscape in Chinese gardens]. Beijing: Chinese Forestry Press, 1993.

Yang Ye

GE GONGZHEN

1890–1935

An innovative journalist and a scholar of journalism, Ge Gongzhen tirelessly strove to professionalize Chinese journalism. This is manifest in his contributions to photojournalism and reportage (*tongxun*) and also in his efforts to establish professional organizations in Shanghai, at lobbying for equal rights for Chinese journalists at international conferences, and in raising Chinese journalism to the international standard.

Born in Dongtai (Nantong, Jiangsu) into a literati-official family, he joined the *Dongtai ribao* (Dongtai Daily) as a graphics editor in 1912 after graduating from the local secondary school. He quickly proceeded to Shanghai, where his talents were recognized by Di Chuqing, who gave him employment first in Youzheng Shuju (Youzheng Publishing House) and then in the daily *Shibao* (The Eastern Times), where he remained from 1914 to 1927. During these years he studied English and Japanese (later also Russian), helped found the first professional organization for journalists in Shanghai in 1925 (Shanghai Baoxue She), and served as a professor of journalism studies. Ge's *Zhongguo baoxue shi* (History of Chinese journalism), the single most influential study on the subject until very recently, was first published in 1926. In 1927 he traveled to Japan, America, and Europe to investigate journalistic practices in foreign countries and to participate in the International Journalism Conference held in Geneva that year. In 1929, after his return to China, he joined the staff of Shi Liangcai's *Shenbao*, Shanghai's most prestigious daily, in a leading position, and became a sought-after lecturer in the mushrooming journalism departments at colleges and universities. Believing in the power and informative value of images and committed to photojournalism, in 1920 he started *Shibao*'s first pictorial supplement, and in 1930 he launched *Shenbao*'s weekly pictorial. While at *Shenbao*, he set up a modern reference library to professionalize routine work.

His international experiences qualified him to join the Lytton Commission in 1932 as an official Chinese delegate, with credentials issued by the Nationalist government. This experience, including a brief detention by the Japanese, marked a turning point in his career toward a decidedly political, rather than simply professional, commitment. After his return to China, his reportage on the situation in Manchuria was published in *Shenbao*. He was subsequently sent by the Nationalist government to participate in the League of Nations meeting in Geneva, where the "Manchurian question" was discussed. From there he reported as the European correspondent of the Central News Agency (Zhongyang Tongxun She). He was soon disillusioned, however, with the work of the League of Nations, calling it a "paper tiger." One year later, after the reestablishment of diplomatic relations between the Soviet Union and China in 1933, he took the opportunity to join a diplomatic mission to the Soviet Union, traveled widely in the country, and reported from there, not only for the Shanghai press, but also for the Tianjin *Dagongbao*. He returned to Shanghai in the summer of 1935 to join Zou Taofen in publishing *Shenghuo zhoubao* (Life Weekly) and support the anti-Japanese resistance, but died soon after his arrival at Shanghai after an operation for enteritis.

As a professional journalist, Ge struggled to improve working conditions and maintained high ethical standards rather than leaning toward any political power. He gained historical fame only in the 1990s, when society could accept that one could be a true patriot without being a political partisan. This was preceded by the insight of the 1980s that had he not died so untimely, he, like Zou Taofen, would have made the transition "from a bourgeois democrat to a proletarian news soldier" (Xinwenjie Renwu Bianweihui 1983). His chronological biography (*nianpu*) was published in 1990, and a television series about his life was produced and aired in 1994. Ge was married briefly and had a son, who was raised by his sister.

SEE ALSO *Newspapers.*

BIBLIOGRAPHY

Ge Gongzhen. *Zhongguo baoxue shi* [The history of Chinese journalism]. Beijing: Sanlian Shudian, 1955.

Ge Gongzhen. *Cong Dongbei dao Shulian* [From the Northeast to the Soviet Union]. Ed. by Zou Taofen. Shanghai: Shenghuo Shudian, 1935. 3rd ed., 1936.

Xinwenjie Renwu Bianweihui, ed. Ge Gongzhen. In *Xinwenjie renwu*, vol. 1, 146–175. Beijing: Xinhua Chubanshe, 1983.

Andrea Janku

GENDER IMBALANCE, GOVERNMENT POLICY

SEE *Sex Ratio.*

GENDER RELATIONS

Confucian ideals prescribed that women were subordinate to men: They were to follow the "three obediences" (obedience to their fathers in youth, to their husbands when married, and to their sons upon the death of their husbands) and the "four virtues" (proper virtue, speech, countenance, and merit). By the Qing dynasty (1644–1911) they were also to aspire to the cult of chastity (a pledge not to remarry after the death of their husbands), and conform to the ideal of being still (*jing*) by confining themselves to the domestic realm. In spite of these ideals, gender roles and relations were questioned, challenged, and changed throughout Chinese history. And as was always the case, there was a dichotomy between state-prescribed gender roles and social practice, and social practice varied by region, class, and ethnicity. Yet beginning late in the Qing, gender contestations were articulated in a new set of contexts: foreign imperialism, nationalism, industrialization, and modernity.

Throughout the Qing, women behaved in ways that defied conventional gender norms. In urbanized and commercialized Jiangnan, elite women formed poetry clubs, while the "teachers of the inner chambers" wrote, published, and traveled. Many nonelite women formed associations that gathered to study Buddhist sutras. In many parts of rural China, poor women engaged in field work in spite of the ideal that unmarried women should not be in "public" space. By the late Qing, conflicts about ideal gender roles were particularly evident in the foreign-controlled treaty ports of Shanghai, Tianjin, and Hankou. The appearance of women actresses in Beijing opera (which had previously excluded women performers) provoked public controversy precisely because it challenged the division between the inner and outer spheres of women and men, respectively.

Challenges to conventional ideals about gendered norms and space became even more acute in the context of the anti-Manchu nationalist movement. In the context of increasing imperialist aggression, Chinese intellectuals such as Kang Youwei and Liang Qichao portrayed foot-bound women as victims and as both a symbol and cause of China's backwardness vis-à-vis the West. The ideal of women as virtuous mothers was transformed into the ideal of women as mothers of citizens. Women not only fought, and in some cases died, for the Nationalist revolution, but staged attacks on the offices of the newly established Republican government—appearing with weapons, breaking windows, and fighting with guards—when it refused to grant them the right to vote.

THE AFFECT OF INDUSTRIALIZATION ON WOMEN

Industrialization in the late nineteenth and early twentieth centuries highlights the complex intersection of shifting gender norms and class. Women's entry into factory work was neither the cause nor result of increased gender equality. In many cases, such as Shanghai's textile industry, women were employed to perform jobs previously done by men, as a result of male labor activism (and the belief that women workers would be more docile) and the increasing cost of male labor. The resulting new definitions of women's work were linked to beliefs about skill: work deemed appropriate for women was defined as unskilled, while men continued to dominate the jobs defined as skilled (which received higher remuneration). Meanwhile, the changing gendered division of labor did not treat all women workers equally as an undifferentiated category. In Shanghai, at least, women's factory jobs largely reflected divisions based on native place of origin. In some areas, poverty forced women to leave home to work in factories, while in other areas, wealthier women stayed home and did embroidery.

Industrialization did cause changes in gender relations, enabling some women to use their earnings to purchase more fashionable clothes or even to rent a room away from their families. In at least one area of Guangzhou (Canton), earnings from work in the silk industry was a significant factor in the emergence of marriage-resistance "sisterhoods"—groups of women who pledged never to marry and instead lived in Buddhist vegetarian halls. Other women in the same area engaged in "delayed-transfer marriages," remaining with their natal families, who benefited from their daughters' earnings.

It was not until the New Culture and May Fourth movements of the 1910s that conventional marriage practices, women's status, and broader gender roles were more explicitly and widely challenged. May Fourth radicals advocated for free-choice marriages based on love (as opposed to arranged marriages), while attacking the authority of the family patriarch. Their writings to a greater degree represented women as symbols of China's weakness, often focusing on prostitutes as the epitome of women's victimization. Modern women, they proposed, would be educated, employed, independent, and committed to building a modern nation.

COMMUNIST TREATMENT OF WOMEN

Most of these views informed the cry for women's liberation by the Chinese Communist Party when it was established in 1921. The early Communist Party's promulgation of gender equality attracted many women to its revolutionary cause, and a number of women rose to prominence as leaders. Their positions were invariably subordinate to those of male leaders, however, and many held positions because of their relationships with men prominent in the Communist Party. They also found that whenever the cause of gender equality threatened broader revolutionary goals, it was subordinated or postponed. This problem was particularly acute in rural areas (where the Communist Party was based from the late 1920s until it took power in 1949), for there the promotion of free-choice marriage and women's right to divorce met with opposition from male peasants as well as older women (who did not want to lose the household services of a daughter-in-law). In the Communist base areas, peasant women were mobilized to aid the war effort by spinning yarn, weaving cloth, and sewing shoes, while men were recruited to join the army.

Nevertheless, when the Communist Party established the People's Republic of China in 1949, some if its first acts reflected its belief that gender equality was key to building a strong, modern, revolutionary state. The Marriage Law of 1950, for example, promulgated free-choice marriage, granted women the right to initiate divorce, banned the sale of girls, and prohibited concubinage. Slogans such as "Women hold up half the sky" encouraged women to contribute to the revolution and men to recognize and honor women's contributions. Believing in Engles's theory of "liberation through labor," the Communist Party mobilized women to work outside the home. For relatively poor urban women, working outside the home was not new; what changed was that Communist Party mobilization helped remove the stigma formerly attached to their work outside the domestic sphere. Similarly for many peasant women, government mobilization of rural women to work in agricultural production rendered honorable the field work that poor peasant women had done in the past. Meanwhile, throughout the 1950s and early 1960s, the desirability of women's working in the outside sphere was contingent on economic fluctuations. During times of economic growth and labor shortages, women's roles as factory and farm workers was emphasized; during times of labor surplus, women's role as "socialist" and "scientific" housewives was emphasized. And even when women's role as

Male family members enjoying tea, 1941. *In traditional Chinese culture, male members of a family received higher status than female members. Additionally, a son remained in his father's home after marriage, creating multigenerational households under one male family name.* CARL MYDANS/TIME LIFE PICTURES/GETTY IMAGES

workers was emphasized, their responsibility for managing housework and child rearing was never questioned.

During the decade of the Cultural Revolution (1966–1976), gender as a category of analysis was rejected by the state. The media propagated Mao Zedong's slogan "The times have changed, men and women are the same," and celebrated Iron Girls—strong, robust, muscular women who boldly performed physically demanding jobs traditionally done by men. Jiang Qing, Mao Zedong's wife, appeared in military attire, symbolizing to her audiences a presumably gender-neutral style, which was emulated by teenage-girl Red Guards who cut their hair short, donned army clothes, and marched barefoot through city streets. To be revolutionary, in other words, was to appear male. Yet in spite of state propaganda, gender roles were continually contested. While the media valorized examples of women who joined oil-drilling teams, assumed jobs as tractor, truck, and diesel locomotive drivers, or learned to repair high-voltage electric wires, managers of textile factories at least sometimes explained their continued preference for women workers by emphasizing their manual dexterity and patience. Many young urban women sent to live in the countryside challenged local officials who assigned jobs based on beliefs about physiological differences between men and women, yet some married local peasant men to avoid physically taxing jobs. While the media glorified women's public roles as proletarian fighters, their domestic roles and responsibilities were left unquestioned. Foreign observers applauded the plain-colored, loosely-fitting clothes worn by men and women alike to prevent the sexual objectification of women that they so abhorred in their own countries. Yet countless young women sent to live in the Chinese countryside were the objects of sexual abuse by local male officials, while young adolescent girls who remained in the cities were often the objects of sexual exploits by young male neighborhood gangs.

THE TREATMENT OF WOMEN IN THE REFORM ERA

Even if gender roles and relations during the decade of the Cultural Revolution were more complex than state ideology suggested, the period of economic reform (beginning in the late 1970s) has been marked by a heightened emphasis on gender difference. During the rejection of Maoism, the Iron Girls became objects of popular satire, and the traditional Confucian ideal of virtuous wife and good mother, attacked during the Cultural Revolution, was revived. Decreased government control over economic planning, the replacement of state and collective ownership by private enterprise, the rapid development of consumer culture, and the increased role of global capital in China's economy has resulted in a renewed emphasis on women's roles as housewives and mothers, on feminine fashion, and on women's sexual appeal to men. When confronted with labor surpluses, employers in many cities have sent women back to the home (or "back to the wok," as Tamara Jacka puts it), while owners and managers of labor intensive, low-wage clothing, shoe, electronics, and toy-manufacturing factories in special economic zones have relied on young unmarried women migrant workers (working sisters). Meanwhile, for many working sisters, migration from their rural homes to cities is seen as critical to becoming a modern woman. In the face of migration by men and young women, agricultural production has become the domain of older married women.

Perhaps more than at any time since the late Qing, the quest for modernity (along with industrialization and integration into the global economy) is an important context for negotiating the meanings attached to being male and female. And more than ever before, gender roles and relations vary and are inflected by region, class, and ethnicity.

SEE ALSO *Family: One-Child Policy; Life Cycle: Marriage; Love and Friendship; Women in Politics; Women in the Visual Arts; Women, Employment of; Women, Status of.*

BIBLIOGRAPHY

Brownell, Susan and Jeffrey Wasserstrom, eds. *Chinese Femininities, Chinese Masculinities: A Reader.* Berkeley: University of California Press, 2002.

Gilmartin, Christina, Gail Hershatter, Lisa Rofel, and Tyrene White, eds. *Engendering China: Women, Culture, and the State.* Cambridge, MA: Harvard University Press, 1995.

Goodman, Bryna and Wendy Larson, eds. *Gender in Motion: Divisions of Labor and Cultural Change in Late Imperial and Modern China.* Lanham, MD: Rowman and Littlefield, 2005.

Honig, Emily. *Sisters and Strangers: Women in the Shanghai Cotton Mills, 1919-1949.* Stanford, CA: Stanford University Press, 1986.

Hershatter, Gail. *Women in China's Long Twentieth Century.* Berkeley: University of California Press, 2007.

Jacka, Tamara. Back to the Wok: Women and Employment in Chinese Industry in the 1980s. *Australian Journal of Chinese Affairs* 24 (1990): 1–23.

Ko, Dorothy. *Teachers of the Inner Chambers: Women and Culture in Seventeenth-Century China.* Stanford, CA: Stanford University Press, 1994.

Emily Honig

GEOGRAPHICAL REGIONS, NATURAL AND HUMAN

In 1800 the Qing dynasty (1644–1912) was at the height of its power. The Qianlong emperor (r. 1736–1796) secured Chinese control over Xinjiang, Tibet, Mongolia, Taiwan, and much of eastern Siberia. After the early nineteenth century, some portions of Qing territory were lost to military defeats, while others gradually loosened their ties to the central government. Hong Kong, a small, barren island strategically located at the mouth of the Pearl River (Zhujiang) Delta, was ceded to Britain at the end of the Opium War in 1842. In 1849 Macau, a small peninsula and two islands 64 kilometers west of Hong Kong, which had been administered by Portugal since the sixteenth century in return for payment of annual tribute, was declared a free port, and in 1887 it was ceded to Portugal. From 1858 to 1860, China lost much of the Maritime Provinces of Siberia to Russia, followed in 1881 by parts of the Yili (Ili) region through the Treaty of Saint Petersburg. The Sino-Japanese War (1894–1895) resulted in the transfer to Japan of Taiwan and the Pescadores Islands. In 1904 an armed British mission forced its way into Tibet and demanded that the Tibetan government sign a trade agreement. By 1910 the Qing administration reasserted military control over Tibet, shortly before its own demise. The Russo-Japanese War (1904–1905) resulted in Japanese victory and the transfer of Russia's rights over most of the South Manchuria Railway and the southern tip of Liaoning Province to Japan.

When the Republic of China was established in 1912, it claimed sovereignty over all Qing territories, but was unable to enforce its authority as political and military control within China devolved to regional warlords. In 1911 Mongolia declared independence and in 1924 established the Mongolian People's Republic with support from the Soviet Union. Xinjiang experienced several Uygur uprisings, but remained under the control of autonomous Chinese governors for most of the Republican period. Tibet had no official Chinese presence from 1913 until 1933, and effectively functioned independently until the arrival of Chinese troops in 1950. In the early twentieth century, Japan steadily increased its military, civilian, and commercial presence in the Northeast, and in 1931 ejected the local Chinese forces and created the puppet state of Manzhouguo (Manchukuo) in 1932.

In 1949 the Communist armies under Mao Zedong restored Chinese control over most of the area ruled by the Qing. The main exceptions were Mongolia, eastern Siberia, Taiwan, Hong Kong, and Macau. Hong Kong was returned to China by the United Kingdom in 1997, under the condition that it would retain its own political and economic system for a period of fifty years. In 1999 Portugal returned Macau to Chinese sovereignty under similar terms as Hong Kong. China regained Taiwan at the end of World War II, but when Chiang Kai-shek's (Jiang Jieshi's) Nationalist forces fled to the island in 1949, they maintained an ambiguous separate political status into the twenty-first century. The United States protected Taiwan against the People's Republic, but after the Shanghai Communiqué of 1972, did not officially regard it as a separate country. In the second half of the twentieth century, Taiwan developed one of Asia's most technologically advanced economies, and with the opening of the People's Republic to outside trade, Taiwanese businesses became major investors in mainland industry. In the early twenty-first century, tourism, trade, and investment across the Taiwan Strait grew rapidly, despite sporadic military tensions.

MACROREGIONS

All of China's major rivers flow east from the Tibetan Plateau, providing natural transportation, but also creating natural barriers to north-south movement. Consequently, the densely inhabited agricultural regions of China's traditional core areas were effectively isolated from each other for most of China's history. Sociologist and anthropologist G. William Skinner identified eight integrated regional marketing networks, labeled *macroregions*, that historically formed the basis of the economic, political, and social lives of the vast majority of Chinese people. In the twentieth century, the introduction of railway transportation gave rise to a ninth macroregion in the Northeast.

North China The North China macroregion is formed by the North China Plain, which extends from the Huai River (Huaihe) in the south to the range of hills, capped by the Great Wall, that rises just north of Beijing. The region encompasses most of the provinces of Hebei, Henan, and Shandong, and the northern portions of Anhui and Jiangsu. The plain consists mainly of the fertile yellow, loess soil that gives the Yellow River (Huanghe) its name. The Yellow River is the region's major waterway and provides water for irrigation, but only limited transportation because of the silt that it deposits annually in its lower reaches. Silting raises the river bottom, and in some years of heavy rainfall the Yellow River has overflowed its banks, flooding wide reaches of farmland and causing extensive destruction. Chinese governments from ancient times have constructed elaborate dikes along the river's route. The area is also vulnerable to drought, since its rainfall is carried by the annual southeast monsoon winds, which drop most of their moisture on the southern coastal areas. North of the Yellow River, five rivers flow eastward across the plain, joining at Tianjin to form the Hai River (Haihe). The Grand Canal was begun during the Sui dynasty (581–618) and extended under the Mongols (Yuan, 1279–1368) to transport rice from the Yangzi region north to Tianjin, then west to Beijing. The canal fell into disuse in the late nineteenth century due to competition from steam shipping by sea.

Historically, the North China Plain has supported a dense agrarian population. For most of the modern era, it has also been China's political center, as the location of the capital, Beijing. Beijing was an important terminus for trade routes from the west and northwest, and in the twentieth century it became a major center for industry. North China is an important producer of coal, and in the late twentieth century, of oil. Beijing's link with the sea is the port city of Tianjin, also an important industrial area, located about 100 kilometers to the east, on the Hai River, some 45 kilometers from its mouth at the Gulf of Bo Hai. Other large cities in the area include Shijiazhuang, Baoding, Jinan, Luoyang, Kaifeng, and Zhengzhou, all of which experienced strong growth of industry and population in the late twentieth century.

In 1843 the population of the North China macroregion was around 112 million, nearly one-quarter of China's total; in 2005 the region had a population of around 255 million, around 20 percent of the national total.

Northwest China The Northwest China macroregion, located upstream along the Yellow River from the North China Plain, is a loess plateau encompassing most of the provinces of Shanxi, Shaanxi, and Gansu. It is separated from the Yangzi River (Changjiang) watershed by the Qinling Mountains; on the north it is bounded by the stony Ordos Desert that lies within the great bend of the Yellow River. The panhandle of arable land that extends west from the city of Lanzhou, just south of the Gobi Desert, is the Gansu Corridor. The main agricultural regions are the watersheds of the Wei River in Shaanxi Province, the Fen River in Shanxi Province, and the stretch of the Yellow River valley between these two tributaries. This is a more mountainous and arid region than the North China Plain, and much of the agriculture requires terracing of steep hillsides. Chinese culture first emerged here, and it was the location of imperial China's earliest capital, now the site of the industrial city of Xi'an. Traditionally, the region has produced grain, cotton, and livestock. It also contains more than half of China's coal reserves, and in the later part of the twentieth century the region became a major mining center.

The population in 1843 was an estimated twenty-nine million; in 2005 the population was around ninety-six million.

Lower Yangzi Three macroregions lie along China's greatest waterway, the Yangzi River, which stretches some 6,300 kilometers from its source in the Tibetan Plateau. The Yangzi has over 3,600 tributaries, and its drainage comprises a navigable network of over 70,000 kilometers.

The Lower Yangzi macroregion includes the Yangzi Delta, much of the provinces of Anhui, Jiangsu, and Zhejiang, as well as the major cities of Nanjing and Shanghai, along with other urban centers. As the point where China's greatest inland transportation network meets the sea, as well as a major silk- and rice-producing region and the southern terminus of the Grand Canal, this has been China's most densely populated and heavily urbanized area throughout the modern period. Following the Opium War (1839–1842), one of the first five cities opened as a "treaty port" was Shanghai, which became the commercial capital of China. This status was diminished during the centrally planned period of the People's Republic (1949–1978), but it was largely regained in the market-reform period since 1978.

The Lower Yangzi is China's most intensively farmed region and a major producer of rice, wheat, silk, and tea. It is also an important industrial region, and with the construction of the Pudong open economic development zone, across the Huangpu River from central Shanghai, an increasingly important center of finance and commerce. It has a well-developed transportation network of highways, waterways, and railways, and two major airports.

The population of the Lower Yangzi macroregion in 1843 was sixty-seven million; by 2005 it reached approximately 136 million.

Middle Yangzi The Middle Yangzi region is defined by the numerous lakes and tributaries of the Yangzi River in the south-central provinces of Hubei, Hunan, and Jiangxi. These bodies of water form the largest network of natural transportation routes in China. They include one of China's largest lakes, Dongtinghu, and the Yangzi's largest tributary, the Han River, which flows from Shaanxi Province in the northwest through Hubei to the Yangzi at the city of Hankou. Other major rivers in the region include the Yuanjiang, the Cushui, and the Xiangjiang, which all flow north through Hunan into Dongting Lake.

The region's traditional commercial focus was the three cities that lie at the confluence of the Yangzi and the Han, collectively called Wuhan. The broad plains and warm climate of Hunan and Hubei made this region a major grain source, and the waterways provided the transportation for a thriving interregional grain trade linked to North China and ultimately to the international market. Economic growth and immigration from provinces to the east led to land reclamation projects around Dongting Lake that reduced its capacity to absorb rising river water and increased the frequency of devastating floods in the modern period. In the twentieth century, Wuhan became an important industrial area, as well as the administrative, commercial, and cultural hub of the region.

In 1843 the population of the Middle Yangzi macroregion was estimated to be eighty-four million; by 2005 it reached 163 million.

Upper Yangzi: Sichuan The core of the Upper Yangzi macroregion is the Sichuan ("four rivers") Basin, a rich agricultural area, isolated by surrounding mountains. The western third of Sichuan Province lies on the rugged ridges that run off the Tibetan Plateau, an arid region inhabited mainly by Tibetan herders. The basin is watered by several major tributaries of the Yangzi River and the climate is mild, producing good crops of rice, wheat, oilseeds, silk, citrus, sugarcane, and tea. The area possesses large deposits of coal. Traditionally, access to the markets of central and eastern China depended on the Yangzi River, but the link was always perilous because of the gorges where the river cuts through the Wu Mountains. One of the goals of the massive Three Gorges Dam project, mostly completed in 2008, was to make Chongqing accessible to seagoing ships. In the twentieth century, railways were constructed to North China through Shaanxi and to southeast China through Guizhou, and Chengdu and Chongqing, Sichuan's two major cities, became important industrial centers.

In 1843 the Upper Yangzi macroregion had a population of approximately forty-seven million; in 2005 the population was 110 million. In 1997 the city of Chongqing and the surrounding countryside became the province-level municipality of Chongqing, with a 2005 population of twenty-eight million, leaving Sichuan Province with eighty-two million people. The population of the basin of Sichuan is almost entirely Han. The western and southern mountainous regions have around one million Tibetans, 2.5 million Yi, and 200,000 Qiang.

Southeast Coast The Southeast Coast macroregion includes the province of Fujian, the southern section of Zhejiang, and the eastern tip of Guangdong. The region is mountainous, with economic and social activity defined by the drainages of the many small rivers that flow east out of the Wuyi Mountains. Agriculture occurs mainly in the river valleys and narrow coastal plains. The climate is subtropical, with abundant rainfall and high average temperatures making this China's largest tea-producing region. The other major crop is rice. The coastline has many good natural harbors and ports, including the major cities of Fuzhou and Xiamen (Amoy) and a strong seafaring and fishing tradition. Many inhabitants of Taiwan came from this region, and it received a large share of investment from Taiwan in the reform era after 1978.

In 1843 the Southeast Coast macroregion's population was twenty-six million; in 2005 it was about thirty-five million.

Lingnan The Lingnan macroregion consists of the Guangxi Zhuang Autonomous Region and most of Guangdong Province. It is formed by the drainages of the Xijiang (West River), the Beijiang (North River), and the Dongjiang (East River), which meet at the Canton Delta, also known as the Pearl River Delta. The delta is a rich alluvial plain, crossed by channels and canals that provide both irrigation and transportation. The commercial and administrative center is the city of Guangzhou (Canton). Outside the delta the terrain is hilly, with the Nanling Mountains to the north and the Yunnan-Guizhou Plateau to the west. To the southwest, the region is bordered by Vietnam, and to the direct south, by the South China Sea and the Gulf of Tonkin. The region includes Hainan Island, China's southernmost territory. Near the northern tip of Guangxi is the city of Guilin, famous for its spectacular karst limestone formations. Guangxi is one of the most ethnically diverse parts of China, with the Zhuang people the largest minority group, constituting nearly a third of the total population. Other groups include the Yao, Miao, Dong, and on Hainan Island, the Li.

The region is an important producer of rice, with the warm climate allowing two crops a year, and three on Hainan. It is also a major producer of silk and subtropical fruits and vegetables, including sugarcane, oranges, and pineapples. Since 1978, the Pearl River Delta has industrialized rapidly due to its proximity to Hong Kong. Shenzhen, located directly north of Hong Kong, was designated China's first special economic zone in 1979 and has grown to become one of China's most modern cities, with a population of twelve million in 2005 and one of the nation's two stock exchanges. Guangzhou City has also become a major manufacturing center, drawing in a steady flow of migrant workers from inland areas.

The population of the region in 1843 was twenty-nine million; by 2005 the combined population of Guangxi and Guangdong came to 139 million.

Yunnan-Guizhou Plateau The provinces of Yunnan and Guizhou occupy a plateau in the eastern Tibetan highlands. It is crossed from north to south by the turbulent headwaters of several of the major rivers of Asia—the Red, Black, and Mekong of Vietnam, the Salween of Myanmar (Burma), and the Yangzi—which cut deep gorges through the plateau. Its average elevation ranges from 2,000 meters in Yunnan to around 700 meters in Guizhou. To the south is the mountainous borderland with Vietnam, Laos, and Myanmar, an area of few roads, populated by minority peoples. Yunnan has more minority groups than any other province in China, with over twenty-five, including the Yi, Bai, Hani, Tai, Dai, Lisu, Tibetan, Mongolian, Shui, and Miao. Guizhou also has a large minority population, including the Miao, Yi, Qiang, Dong, Zhuang, Buyi, Bai, Tujia, Gelao, and Shui peoples, with autonomous regions constituting over half of the province's area.

Agriculture is practiced on the upland plains, in the river valleys, and on elaborately terraced hillsides. Where irrigation is possible, rice is the main crop; other areas grow corn, barley, wheat, and millet. Forestry is a major industry, although it is constrained by transportation difficulties. Significant mineral resources include tin, copper, and coal. In the early twenty-first century, this was among the poorest regions in China, and it received substantial assistance to improve roads, water conservation, electricity supply, and forest conservation. Its main industries included tobacco, mining, biology, and tourism.

The Chinese state controlled the area as early as the third century BCE, but it was not colonized by Han settlers until the fourteenth century. By the early years of the People's Republic, about 70 percent of the population was Han, with the minority peoples inhabiting mainly the mountainous border regions. In 1843 the population was around eleven million; by 2005 the combined populations of Yunnan and Guizhou had grown to eighty-two million, including twenty-one million members of minorities.

Guangxi and Yunnan, along with Tibet, Xinjiang, and Inner Mongolia, are among the regions referred to under the People's Republic as *bianqu*, or "border regions," which along with the "old revolutionary base areas" (*lao geming diqu*) and the national minority areas (*shaoshu minzu diqu*), are generally remote, mountainous or desert or both, and very poor. From the earliest days of the People's Republic, these regions were accorded special attention by the party and the government due to their strategic importance as buffer zones between China and its continental neighbors, and their sensitive ethnic mixes.

The Northeast China's three northeastern provinces, Liaoning, Jilin, and Heilongjiang, are known in Chinese as *Dongbei*, the Northeast, widely referred to in English as Manchuria, the Manchu homeland. The region is geographically linked by the Northeast Plain, which runs from northern Heilongjiang down the middle of Jilin and Liaoning to the Gulf of Bo Hai. The Northeast is bounded on the east by the Changbaishan range along the border with North Korea, and by the Wanda Mountains, which separate the region from the Russian Far East. To the north lie the Lesser Xing'an (Khingan) mountain range and the Heilongjiang (Amur River), the border with Russia. To the west is the Greater Xing'an range and the Mongolian Plateau. At the southwest tip of the plain, a narrow coastal corridor extends to Hebei Province, through Shanhaiguan, "mountain sea gate," the point where the Great Wall meets the sea.

The Northeast Plain is the largest arable plain in China, and although it has a shorter growing season than the North China Plain, it is very fertile and receives adequate rainfall for cultivation of grains and beans. Historically, it was a major producer of soybeans. The region possesses extensive forests, and some of China's most important deposits of coal and iron. It is also the site of China's largest oil field, Daqing, in Heilongjiang.

In 1800 the Northeast was lightly populated due to an official ban on immigration, and to inadequate natural transportation routes. The population included Mongol tribes in the western steppes, hunting and gathering groups in the north, Koreans on the eastern slopes of the Changbaishan range, and Han and Manchu farmers in the south. The ban on immigration was finally lifted late in the nineteenth century, as Russia and Japan encroached on the region. Following its defeat in the Sino-Japanese War (1894–1895), the Chinese government allowed Russia to build two railways through the Northeast: the Chinese Eastern, from west to east across Heilongjiang, and the South Manchuria Railway, from Harbin south to the Liaodong Peninsula. Japan took over the South Manchuria Railway after winning the Russo-Japanese War (1904–1905). The region was rapidly industrialized through the late 1930s by Japanese, Russian, and Chinese interests. Immigration from North China swelled in this period.

After 1949 the Northeast was the focus of intensive development efforts by the People's Republic. It was a major source of grain, coal, oil, iron, and steel, and other heavy industrial products. The cities of Shenyang, Anshan, Benxi, Jilin, Changchun, and Harbin were national leaders in heavy industry.

In 1800 the population of the Northeast may have been around six million. By 1900 it was around seventeen million, and in 2005 it was 107 million, including around three million Mongols, Manchus, Koreans, and other minorities.

OTHER REGIONS

Inner Mongolia and Mongolia The modern independent country of Mongolia (Outer Mongolia) is a vast region of steppe and desert north of central China and west of the three northeastern provinces. With a population of only 2.9 million in 2008, it has the lightest population density of any country in the world. Although it was subjugated by the early Qing emperors and was included in the Qing empire of 1800, it was never settled by Han Chinese in any numbers and fell away from Chinese control after 1911.

Inner Mongolia lies between the Great Wall and the southern border of Mongolia. It encompasses expanses of steppe and the Gobi Desert along the southern lip of the Mongolian Plateau, the forested mountains of the Greater Xing'an range to the east, the gravel Ordos Desert to the south, and irrigated lowlands along the great northern bend of the Yellow River. Mongol tribes have inhabited the area since the thirteenth century, and under the People's Republic it was designated the Inner Mongolia Autonomous Region. Its boundaries have often changed; by the 1980s it included much of the area that historically fell within the western parts of the Northeast.

The river valleys in the south produce wheat and other grains. The extensive grasslands support the largest numbers of sheep and goats in China, as well as a substantial dairy industry. Inner Mongolia is a major source of coal, accounting for around 10 percent of the national total. It also produces substantial amounts of iron, steel, and a variety of chemical products. Since the advent of railways in the early twentieth century, large numbers of Han Chinese immigrated, a trend that increased after 1949. In 2005 Inner Mongolia's population of twenty-four million people was nearly half urban, and included around five million Mongols.

Xinjiang Xinjiang ("new frontier") is China's westernmost region, its largest province-level unit, and one of the least densely populated. To the south lie the Kunlun Mountains and the Tibetan Plateau, to the southwest the Karakoram range and the Pamirs, and to the west the Tianshan range and the borders of the Central Asian states of Tajikistan, Kyrgyzstan, and Kazakhstan. To the northeast Xinjiang is separated from Mongolia by the Altai Mountains.

Most of the area of Xinjiang is contained in two great depressions separated by the main range of the Tianshan, the Dzungarian Basin in the north, and the huge Tarim Basin in the south. Both basins are ringed by mountains and receive water primarily from streams that flow down from snow fields and glaciers. The Dzungarian Basin receives enough rainfall to support broad grasslands where nomadic herding peoples, including Kazakhs and Mongols, have historically raised sheep, goats, cattle, camels, and horses. Runoff from the north slopes of the Tianshan range provides water for a major irrigation project cultivating wheat, cotton, and other crops.

The Tarim Basin receives negligible rain and much of its area consists of the Taklamakan Desert, an uninhabitable expanse of sand. Around the rim of the desert are oases, watered by streams running down out of the mountains through irrigation channels constructed by generations of Uygur farmers to supply orchards, vineyards, and fields of grain, vegetables, and cotton. The ancient Silk Road took two routes from the trading city of Kashgar at the western end of the basin, one running along the south rim of the Taklamakan, the other following the north rim, before rejoining on the east side of the desert. The first railway to Xinjiang was constructed from Gansu in the 1950s; it was extended to the border of Kazakhstan in the late 1980s, and was entirely double-tracked by 2006.

Xinjiang's most important industrial resources are oil and natural gas, which exist in large reserves under the Taklamakan Desert, and in smaller amounts in the Dzungarian Basin. Development of these fields was hindered by their distance from China's major population centers and by the difficulties of working in the Taklamakan. By 2006, with improvements to railways and highways, and completion of a 4,000 kilometer gas pipeline to Shanghai in 2004, Xinjiang was the third-largest oil producer among China's provinces and the second-largest source of natural gas. A vigorous petrochemical industry developed in the area around the capital Ürümqi, and generated around 60 percent of the provincial gross domestic product. Since the 1980s, substantial cross-border trade has developed, most significantly with Kazakhstan.

In 1953 Xinjiang's population was 4.9 million, of whom 75 percent were Uygurs and 6 percent were Han Chinese. The following decades saw large influxes of Han Chinese, mainly to the urban industrial centers of the southern Dzungarian Basin. The 2005 population of Xinjiang was twenty million, including 8.2 million Han Chinese, 8.4 million Uygurs, 1.3 million Kazakhs, and 2.1 million Khirgiz, Mongols, Hui, and Russians.

Tibet (Xizang) Tibet, officially the Tibet Autonomous Region, is the highest landmass in the world and the least habitable area in China. It is delineated and isolated by its altitude, bounded on the south by the high Himalaya range, to the west by the Karakoram range, and to the north by the Kunlun and Altun ranges. Significant cultivation of crops occurs only in the southern valleys formed by the headwaters of the Indus and Brahmaputra rivers. Here the elevation falls below 3,750 meters, and this is the location of most of the population and the only cities. North of these valleys lies the Chang Tang Plateau, a vast high, arid region that averages nearly 4,500 meters in altitude and is rimmed by higher mountains. It supports only scattered herding of yaks, sheep, and goats, and is mostly uninhabited. To the east, long ridges and plateaus slope down between the valleys of great rivers toward eastern China. This area historically was known as Amdo and was populated by nomadic Tibetan herders. Under the People's Republic, the southern part of Amdo, known as Kham, was added to Sichuan Province, while the northern part became the province of Qinghai. The populations of both areas remained mainly Tibetan into the twenty-first century.

The Tibetan economy was traditionally based on cultivation of barley, buckwheat, rye, and peas in the lower elevations of the southern valleys, on herding of yaks, sheep, camels, and horses on the high plateaus, and on overland caravan trade. In the 1950s the Chinese government constructed the first highways into Tibet from Qinghai, Sichuan, Xinjiang, and Nepal. In 1956 an airport was opened at Lhasa and additional airports were opened in Qamdo in 1995, and at Nyingchi, near the borders of India and Myanmar, in 2006. Also in 2006, China completed construction of the first railway into Tibet, from Qinghai, a major engineering achievement. The new transportation modes have opened Tibet to modern economic activities, most prominently tourism. Modern hotels have opened in Lhasa and other cities. Economic growth has drawn in Han Chinese workers, while ethnic tensions have resulted in the garrisoning of Chinese troops and police in the region.

In 2005 the population of Tibet was 2.8 million, with just over a quarter living in cities. The non-Tibetan population was reported to be 180,000, consisting mostly of Han Chinese workers who lived mainly in urban areas. By 2008 the population of Lhasa was reportedly over half Han Chinese, while rural areas remained almost entirely Tibetan. An additional one million Tibetans live in Sichuan, 900,000 live in Qinghai, and 367,000 live in Gansu.

BIBLIOGRAPHY

Bell, Lynda S. *One Industry, Two Chinas: Silk Filatures and Peasant-Family Production in Wuxi County, 1865–1937.* Stanford, CA: Stanford University Press, 1999.

Brandt, Loren. *Commercialization and Agricultural Development: Central and Eastern China, 1870–1937.* New York: Cambridge University Press, 1989.

Donald, Stephanie Hemelryk, and Robert Benewick. *The State of China Atlas: Mapping the World's Fastest Growing Economy.* 2nd ed. Berkeley: University of California Press, 2005.

Eastman, Lloyd E. *Family, Fields, and Ancestors: Constancy and Change in China's Social and Economic History, 1550–1949.* Oxford: Oxford University Press, 1988.

Elvin, Mark, and G. William Skinner, eds. *The Chinese City Between Two Worlds.* Stanford, CA: Stanford University Press, 1974.

Goldstein, Melvyn C. *The Snow Lion and the Dragon: China, Tibet, and the Dalai Lama.* Berkeley: University of California Press, 1997.

Gottschang, Thomas R., and Diana Lary. *Swallows and Settlers: The Great Migration from North China to Manchuria.* Ann Arbor: University of Michigan, Center for Chinese Studies, 2000.

Huang Zongzhi (Philip C. C. Huang). *The Peasant Family and Rural Development in the Yangzi Delta, 1350–1988.* Stanford, CA: Stanford University Press, 1990.

Kuhn, Philip A. *Rebellion and Its Enemies in Late Imperial China: Militarization and Social Structure, 1796–1864.* Cambridge, MA: Harvard University Press, 1970.

Lattimore, Owen. *Inner Asian Frontiers of China.* 1940. Boston: Beacon Press, 1967.

National Bureau of Statistics of China. *China Statistical Yearbook 2006.* Beijing: China Statistics Press, 2006.

Pomeranz, Kenneth. *The Making of a Hinterland: State, Society, and Economy in Inland North China, 1853–1937.* Berkeley: University of California Press, 1993.

Perdue, Peter C. *China Marches West: The Qing Conquest of Central Eurasia.* Cambridge, MA: Harvard University Press, 2005.

Rawski, Thomas G. *Economic Growth in Prewar China.* Berkeley: University of California Press, 1989.

Rawski, Thomas G., and Lillian M. Li, eds. *Chinese History in Economic Perspective.* Berkeley: University of California Press, 1992.

Rowe, William T. *Hankow: Commerce and Society in a Chinese City, 1796–1889.* Stanford, CA: Stanford University Press, 1984.

Shabad, Theodore. *China's Changing Map: National and Regional Development, 1949–71.* Rev. ed. New York: Praeger, 1972.

Skinner, G. William. Marketing and Social Structure in Rural China. *Journal of Asian Studies* (Pt. 1) 24, 1 (1964): 3–43; (Pt. 2) 24, 2 (1965): 195–228; and (Pt. 3) 24, 3 (1965): 363–399.

Skinner, G. William. Regional Urbanization in Nineteenth-Century China. In *The City in Late Imperial China*, ed. G. William Skinner, 211–249. Stanford, CA: Stanford University, 1977.

Spence, Jonathan D. *The Search for Modern China.* New York: Norton, 1990.

U.S. Central Intelligence Agency. *People's Republic of China Atlas.* Washington, DC: U.S. Government Printing Office, 1971.

Wiens, Herold J. *Han Chinese Expansion in South China.* Hamden, CT: Shoe String Press, 1967.

Xu Zhongyue (Immanuel C. Y. Hsü). *The Rise of Modern China.* 6th ed. New York: Oxford University Press, 2000.

Zhao Songqiao. *Geography of China: Environment, Resources, Population, and Development.* New York: Wiley, 1994.

Thomas R. Gottschang

GERMANY, RELATIONS WITH

In 1949 a new chapter was opened in Sino-German relations with the founding of new Chinese and German states. In the beginning, the relationship was dominated by the larger political constellation of the Cold War. China and Germany both represented the front lines in that battle: There were two Chinese states and two German, each competing with its opposite for international recognition. The reunification of Germany in 1990 was another turning point. With ideological factors receding, economy, trade, and cooperation in a broad range of sectors from the environment to law quickly gained importance.

RELATIONS WITH EAST GERMANY

The People's Republic of China (PRC) and East Germany declared mutual diplomatic recognition on October 27, 1949, and Beijing maintained close relations with East Berlin, particularly until 1959. High-level diplomacy entailed not only the exchange of ambassadors but also regular official visits by heads of state. Prime Minister Zhou Enlai visited East Berlin in 1954. The two countries signed a treaty of friendship in 1955, and developed a close and cooperative economic and cultural relationship. Otto Grotewohl (1894–1964), the East German prime minister, visited China in 1955 and 1959. In 1956 the secretary general of the German Communist Party, Walter Ulbricht (1893–1973), met with Mao Zedong in Beijing.

In 1960 the growing conflict between the Soviet Union and China began to affect relations between China and East Germany. Bilateral relations worsened, and, with the start of the Cultural Revolution in 1966, diplomacy and economic cooperation practically came to an end. East Germany responded with irritation when, in 1972, China made moves to establish official relations with West Germany as part of its new foreign policy of cooperation with the West. Relations between Beijing and East Berlin were normalized in the 1980s, but that process ended with the unification of Germany in 1990.

RELATIONS WITH WEST GERMANY

During the Cold War, West Germany maintained official ties with the Republic of China on Taiwan as the sole representative of China, but the scope of their relations was limited. The Federal Republic of Germany and the PRC established diplomatic relations in 1972. Like the United States and its European partners, West Germany agreed to adopt a one-China policy and withdrew its ambassador from Taibei (Taipei). In the following years, Germany concluded a large number of bilateral treaties with the PRC that created the basis for increasingly close cooperation in many sectors, reaching from trade and law to education and culture. Frequent mutual official visits by heads of state sent clear signals as to the importance both sides attached to bilateral relations. Cooperation also entailed a law dialogue (Rechtsdialog), which started in November 1999 when the two countries agreed to maintain a comprehensive exchange on rule-of-law issues. In addition, several programs encompass joint projects in a wide range of legal areas, as well as a bilateral dialogue on human rights.

Scientific and technological cooperation became another important sector. In October 1978, West Germany and the

German trade balance with China (in million euros)

	Export	Import	Balance of trade
1980	1.063	750	313
1990	2.157	4.136	−1.979
2000	9.459	18.553	−9.094
2007	29.923	54.649	−24.726

SOURCE: Statistisches Bundesamt Deutschland, 2008.

Table 1

PRC signed an intergovernmental agreement on scientific and technological cooperation. Initially, in the late 1970s and early 1980s, cooperation focused on contacts and visits by individual scientists. This was followed by a second phase of more project-oriented cooperation. Institutional cooperation has also been initiated, with joint research institutes being set up in 2004 and 2005. In addition, Germany has sought to expand development cooperation with China, with a focus on environmental policy, the protection and sustainable use of natural resources, and sustainable economic development. Bilateral cultural relations between Germany and the PRC began in 1979 with a cultural agreement (Kulturabkommen), leading to the opening in 1988 of a Goethe Institute and a Beijing field office of the German Academic Exchange Service in 1994.

ECONOMIC RELATIONS

Trade between the two countries surged after the beginning of the opening and reform period in China. China became Germany's most important economic partner in Asia, and Germany became China's leading trading partner in Europe. In 2007 German enterprises exported $29 billion U.S. dollars worth of goods to China. In the same year, Germany imported goods worth approximately $49 billion. Since 2002, China has been Germany's second-largest export market outside of Europe, after the United States, even ahead of Japan. Germany is by far China's largest European trading partner, ranking sixth among China's trading partners overall (fourth, excluding Hong Kong and Taiwan). Since 1998, German exports to China (without Hong Kong) have been growing by double-digit percentage figures (16 percent in 2004). German imports from China also continue to record high rates of growth (22.8 percent in 2006).

Like other countries in the West, Germany imports far more goods from China than China does from Germany, resulting in a growing German trade deficit. The deficit ranged between 5 billion euros and 9 billion euros for several years, but since 2004 it has risen significantly, reaching more than 24 billion euros in 2007. The principal commodities sold to China by German companies are machinery and equipment, as well as electronic goods, special devices, and motor vehicles. The main Chinese exports to Germany are electronic products, textiles, clothing, machinery, and equipment.

Since 1999, Germany has been China's largest European investor in terms of annual new investments, although it lies far behind Hong Kong, the United States, and Taiwan. By the end of 2006, German companies had made direct investments totaling some $14 billion in China. In addition to the chemical industry (the investments of BASF and Bayer are worth billions), German investments have mainly been made in the traditional automobile sector (Volkswagen, BMW, and Daimler) and in machinery and plant construction.

TENSIONS AND PROBLEMS

Despite the overall positive developments in bilateral relations, tensions have occasionally surfaced. The German government responded to the violent suppression of the democracy movement by the Chinese government in 1989 by imposing sanctions on China. The human rights situation in China has been a subject of repeated critical discussion. The situation in Tibet and its status have also caused frictions, including that surrounding German chancellor Angela Merkel's decision to receive the Dalai Lama in Berlin in September 2007. China retaliated by cancelling events and limiting diplomatic contacts.

Problems also exist in bilateral trade. Germany asserts that issues relating to the trade deficit are not actively dealt with by China. The German side also argues that China needs to improve basic conditions for foreign investors and to create more transparent and reliable conditions, especially for small and medium-sized companies. Effective protection of intellectual property (i.e., genuine efforts to combat product piracy and illicit technology transfer), more reliability in law, freedom of contract, and the same access to public tenders as Chinese companies have are other areas of concern. China has frequently countered such criticism by complaining about German attempts to intervene in internal affairs.

SEE ALSO *European Union, Relations with.*

BIBLIOGRAPHY

Leutner, Mechthild, and Tim Trampedach. *Bundesrepublik Deutschland und China 1949 bis 1995: Politik, Wirtschaft, Kultur, eine Quellensammlung.* Berlin: Akademie Verlag, 1995.

Meissner, Werner, and Anja Feege. *Die DDR und China 1949 bis 1990: Politik, Wirtschaft, Kultur: Eine Quellensammlung.* Berlin: Akademie Verlag, 1995.

Schüller, Margot. Chinas wirtschaftlicher Aufstieg: Implikationen für die deutsche Wirtschaft. In *Statistische Berichte Niedersachsen.* Niedersächsisches Landesamt für Statistik, Sonderausgabe, Tagung der NLS am 12. März 2007. Der Aufstieg Chinas: Konsequenzen für Niedersachen. Datenlage und Datenbedarf, pp. 30–35.

Statistisches Bundesamt Deutschland. Aussenhandel mit der Volksrepublik China: Technisch hochwertige Waren Gefragt. *Destatis* 14 (July 2008): 1–4.

Klaus Mühlhahn

GIQUEL, PROSPER
1835–1886

Prosper Marie Giquel, a French naval officer born in Lorient, built the first modern Chinese navy yard in Fuzhou and promoted scientific and industrial education of Chinese in Europe. The son of a low-ranking tax collector with seamen among his kin, he got a scholarship to attend high school and naval preparatory classes in Cherbourg, and entered the Naval School in 1852.

After serving in the Crimean War (1854–1856), Giquel volunteered for the Chinese campaign in 1857. As assistant (in charge of police) to the French commissioner in occupied Guangzhou (Canton) during the Second Opium War (1858–1860), Giquel enhanced his English-language skills by learning Chinese well. The French navy granted him leave in September 1861 to enter Chinese service as maritime customs commissioner at Ningbo. When the Taiping forces took the city two months later, he moved to Shanghai and served as an interpreter and fighter in the joint Sino-foreign defense against the rebels.

Back to Ningbo in May 1862, he organized the Ever-Triumphant Army, a French-led unit with foreign arms that eventually grew to three thousand Chinese mercenaries. This corps suppressed the rebels in eastern Zhejiang, a region that supplied the French silk industry, in conjunction with the operations of the Anglo-French corps in Jiangsu and those of Zuo Zongtang, then governor-general of Zhejiang and Fujian. On the disbandment of the corps in September 1864, Zuo, who had come to value the technical ability of its surviving commanders, Giquel and Paul-Alexandre Neveue d'Aiguebelle (1831–1875), asked them to submit plans for a dockyard. The project was delayed while Giquel returned to the customs in Ningbo, then Shanghai, and later Hankou, where he set up another Sino-French corps of 1,500 men to protect the city from Nian rebels.

The program for a navy yard to be built in Fuzhou received imperial approval in July 1866, with Giquel's appointment as director and funding secured from local customs receipts. The contract with Giquel and d'Aiguebelle, spelling out an ambitious plan that combined infrastructure, production, and education, was registered at the French consulate in Shanghai in October. When Zuo was called to suppress Muslim rebellions in the northwest, Shen Baozhen, a most able official, replaced him as high commissioner of the navy yard. In spite of obstructive tactics from French diplomats in China, enraged by Giquel's high salary and Chinese loyalty, Giquel enlisted support from the French navy and Emperor Napoleon III (1808–1873) to obtain supplies and expertise from the best French contractors. Shen Baozhen smoothed over the many difficulties that arose from discord among foreign staff and from their poor business skills by dismissing d'Aiguebelle and keeping economic management in Chinese hands with adequate funding. Through Shen's wisdom and Giquel's empathy, relations with the Chinese were good. By late 1873, at the end of the contract, achievements surpassed objectives.

The large navy yard at Mawei, downstream from Fuzhou city, was a first-rate naval service with four ship-building slips and fully mechanized metalworks that used local iron and Taiwanese coal. It had built fifteen steam vessels of over 15,000 tons in total between 1869 and 1875. A thousand workers had been trained to use modern machinery. In addition, 496 personnel had received scientific and practical education, including 50 English-taught naval officers. The others, taught in French, included 20 engineers, draftsmen, foremen, and highly skilled workers who eventually became the core of China's workforce for railway building and industrial development. In addition to generous money rewards to the staff, Giquel was awarded the Yellow Riding Jacket, an imperial distinction that he and Charles Gordon were the only foreigners ever to receive.

When Shen Baozhen secured permission to send Fuzhou students to Europe for advanced training, Giquel took five of them with him in 1875. The rest of the educational mission he headed in 1877 included thirty-two students. He sent twelve to England; the others remained in France in top engineering schools, at shipyards and in the school for political science.. They returned to China in 1880. Another ten went abroad in 1882, with Giquel again acting as director of the mission. By that time, he was serving as private adviser to the Chinese minister to France. He helped the minister succeed in his negotiations in Saint Petersburg over the Ili question in 1881, and he played an active but fruitless part in trying to find a peaceful solution to the Sino-French conflict over Tongking (Tonkin) in northern Vietnam. He died before the arrival to France of a third educational mission of Fuzhou students he was supposed to head.

SEE ALSO *Industrialization, 1860-1949; Taiping Uprising.*

BIBLIOGRAPHY

Giquel, Prosper. *A Journal of the Chinese Civil War, 1864.* Ed. Steven A. Leibo. Trans. Steven A. Leibo and Debbie Weston. Honolulu: University of Hawai'i Press, 1985.

Giquel, Prosper. *L'Arsenal de Fou-tcheou, ses résultats.* [The Foochow Arsenal and its results]. Trans. H. Lang. Shanghai: Shanghai Evening Courier, 1874.

Pong, David. *Shen Pao-chen and China's Modernization in the Nineteenth Century.* Cambridge, U.K.: Cambridge University Press, 1994.

Marianne Bastid-Bruguière

GONG ZIZHEN

1792–1841

Gong Zizhen (also known as Gong Gongzuo, assumed name Ding'an) was a scholar, poet, social critic, and historical thinker. He was born and raised in a mandarin family in Hangzhou, a major city in the Lower Yangzi region. Both his father and grandfather were ranking officials in the Qing government, and his mother, a poet in her own right, was the daughter of Duan Yucai (1735–1815), a renowned evidential (*kaozheng*) scholar.

EDUCATION AND CAREER

Gong received his early education from Duan and his parents. In his early years, Gong showed superb literary talent and a strong interest in academic study. Having succeeded in the first two levels of the civil service examination, he traveled to Beijing, then the capital, at age twenty-six to enter government service, where he befriended a number of important officials and worked with several distinguished scholars. His subsequent effort to become a *jinshi*, one who has passed the highest level of the examination, however, was met with frustrations. It did not occur until 1829, when he was already thirty-seven years old. Though he was delighted with this belated success, Gong was also unhappy that his examination essay, which discussed the need of shoring up the dynastic frontier, was not received well among his examiners.

Gong remained in Beijing for another decade, working mostly in the Department of Rites. He repeatedly presented memorials to the government, arguing for the need for reform, a belief he had developed since his youth. His outspokenness and political insight turned him into an influential social critic and thinker, though his radicalness also irked some others. In 1839, for an unknown reason, he resigned from the government and left Beijing. Two years later, Gong died, suddenly and somewhat mysteriously, in Danyang, near Nanjing, where he had held a teaching position.

SCHOLARSHIP AND POETRY

Gong was a man of contradictions and controversies. Thanks to the influence of Duan Yucai and the tradition of evidential learning in general, he received solid training in textual and historical criticism, using the methods of philology and epigraphy. He retained this interest and pursued evidential study intermittently throughout his life. But his real passion was for poetry and statecraft scholarship. Although he was a talented and prolific poet, Gong did not hold poetry in high regard; rather, he tried several times to quit poetry writing because he considered it trivial and inconsequential. He was passionate about statecraft scholarship, which was the reason he eventually turned away from evidential learning. He believed that scholars should not bury themselves in ancient texts, but should seek a way to render their study useful to society. But from midlife on, out of career frustration, Gong turned to Buddhism and at times expressed in his poems the desire to forsake his political ideals and other worldly interests by entering a Buddhist monastery.

Gong was well respected for his astute political mind, his genuine concern for social problems, and his strong commitment to social and government reform. As revealed in his poems, he often failed to live up to the ideals and morals he himself advocated, and he indulged himself instead in brothels and alcoholism. In light of Gong's character and influence, Liang Qichao (1873–1929), the late Qing reformist thinker and historian, compared him to the French philosopher Jean-Jacques Rousseau (1712–1778).

Like Rousseau, whose ideas presaged the French Revolution, Gong predicted the historical changes of his age. Indeed, Gong was more keenly aware than most of his peers of the early decline of the Qing dynasty. The reign of the Qianlong Emperor (r. 1736–1796), a prosperous era in Qing history into which Gong was born, left a legacy marred by rampant corruption and budget deficits. In subsequent reigns, as the English pressed their demand for the opium trade, the dynasty was also challenged by a number of rebellions, one of which occurred in the northwest region bordering Russia. In his writings, Gong discussed perceptively the potential harm of these events and explained the need for reform in order for the dynasty to strengthen its borders and government. He was sharply critical of the complacency among Qing officials and urged the regime to open more channels for recruiting new talent.

Gong's scholarly interest mirrored his political stance. Having worked with Liu Fenglu (1776–1829) and befriended Song Xiangfeng (1779–1860), noted New Text Confucian scholars, Gong became convinced that a new hermeneutic strategy, exemplified in New Text scholarship, was needed to interpret the Confucian classics so that Confucian teaching could be better applied to solving the problems of his time. Though he remained impressed by the exegetical works of Wang Niansun (1744–1832) and Wang Yinzhi (1766–1834), leading evidential scholars with whom Gong studied and acquainted respectively, he gradually turned his back on evidential learning and became dissatisfied with its overemphasis on textual criticism of ancient texts and reliance on philological methods. He believed that though exacting philological research was a necessary step for the study of the classics, its importance should not be overstated.

Regarding his interest in statecraft scholarship, Gong maintained that a more important task was to develop a holistic understanding of Confucian teaching—as attempted by New Text scholars—rather than become obsessed with exegetical details, as did the evidential scholars. He was particularly attracted to the "three-age theory," a major discovery by New Text scholars in their hermeneutic reading of the Confucian classics, because it propounded the idea of epochal change of time and history; Gong wanted to convey the same message to his contemporaries for their support of his reformist ideas. Like other New Text scholars, such as Wei Yuan (1794–1857), Gong deemed historical study an integral component in the study of Confucianism because the essence of Confucian teaching was expounded by historical examples. Indebted to Zhang Xuecheng (1738–1801), he also argued that all Confucian texts were historical in nature, and hence required a historicist understanding.

Gong was an innovative poet and accomplished essayist, whose literary success helped disseminate his precocious ideas. Distinct from most poets of his time who were either formalists or classicists, Gong was a realist; in his poetry, he extended his passion for political reform and his commitment to statecraft scholarship. Meanwhile, he wrote a number of love poems, for his wife and his lovers and female friends. His poetry style was as versatile as the topics he covered; Gong was at once criticized and commended for his bold experiment, such as using colloquial phrases and Buddhist terminology. These innovations found their imprints in poetry of later times.

Gong is remembered mostly for his sharp perception and for being an incisive harbinger of historical change. He died in the midst of the Opium War (1839–1842), which ushered in a new era for the Qing dynasty, along with the dangers and detriments Gong foresaw. Though his calls for reform went unheeded in his time, as the need for change became more and more apparent, his writings, especially his New Text understanding of Confucianism, became an important source of inspiration for such reformers as Kang Youwei (1858–1927) in their advocacy of political reform in the late nineteenth century. Meanwhile, Gong's belief in epochal change in history also intrigued revolutionaries because it overtly justified their cause as well.

SEE ALSO *Classical Scholarship and Intellectual Debates: 1800–1864; Kang Youwei; Liang Qichao; Poetry: Classical Poetry.*

BIBLIOGRAPHY

Chen Ming. *Gong Zizhen pingzhuan* [A biography of Gong Zizhen]. Nanjing, China: Nanjing Daxue Chubanshe, 1998.

Fan Kezheng. *Gong Zizhen nianpu kaolue* [Annotations on the chronological biography of Gong Zizhen]. Beijing: Shangwu Yinshuguan, 2004.

Gong Zizhen. *Gong Zizhen quanji* [Complete works of Gong Zizhen], ed. Wang Peizheng. Beijing: Zhonghua Shuju, 1959.

Mai Ruopeng. *Gong Zizhen zhuanlun* [Biography and discussions of Gong Zizhen]. Hefei, China: Anhui Daxue Chubanshe, 2005.

Wong, Shirleen S. *Kung Tzu-chen*. Boston: Twayne, 1975.

Zhang Shou'an. *Gong Zizhen xueshu sixiang yanjiu* [A study of Gong Zizhen's ideas and scholarship]. Taibei, Taiwan: Wenshizhe Chubanshe, 1996.

Qingjia Edward Wang

GORDON, CHARLES

1833–1885

Charles George Gordon is a key figure in the mythology of the Victorian age. A restless military man of high purpose, he looked for action where he could find it, going from the Crimean War (1855–1857) and the Second Opium War (1860) to serving (1863–1864) as a Chinese brigadier general under Li Hongzhang in the civil war against the Taipings led by Hong Xiuquan, whom his followers regarded as god's second son. Gordon later rose to governor-general in the Sudan under Ottoman rule (1874–1879). After an interlude as advisor to Li Hongzhang during the Yili crisis with Russia in 1880, he returned to Sudan and died in Khartoum in battle during the millennial Muslim "Mahdi" rebellion against Egyptian rule. While lionized as "Chinese Gordon" and "Gordon Pascha," the English-language press was also often critical. He inspired biographies, paintings, novels, films, and public statues, as well as school and street names. His male entourage and disinterest in women have fed speculations about his sexual orientation.

Gordon joined a pool of westerners hired by independent rulers (China, the Ottoman Empire) or colonial governments to help run the customs, train the military, put down rebellions, or translate Western works and newspapers. Their capital was their familiarity with the West, that is, modernity. While some of them were mercenaries, Gordon was as disinterested in money as some westerners fighting for the Taiping side. He joined a mixed band of some three thousand Chinese and foreign mercenaries hired to clear a perimeter around Shanghai of Taipings. When Li Hongzhang, who led the Chinese court's campaign against the Taipings fell out with the commander Burgevine, an American who had become a Chinese subject, Gordon was put in charge in 1863 of what was officially dubbed the "Ever-Victorious Army" and was henceforth in official Chinese service. Gordon quickly matched Taiping familiarity with the terrain, and offset his unit's lack of military organization by using artillery and armed ships. Eventually, he played an important and often exaggerated role in helping the government troops against the Taipings. While Li Hongzhang learned to appreciate Gordon's valor, he kept this unit under tight control. The slaying of Taiping leaders for whose safety Gordon had vouched was followed by a public outcry in Britain and a reimposition of the ban for British citizens to serve in foreign armies. Gordon had by then dissolved his contingent and proudly returned to Beijing a huge money gift sent to assuage him.

When Gordon returned to China upon the requests of Robert Hart and Li Hongzhang in 1880, he was advocating a thorough reform of Chinese institutions, and argued against a military confrontation with Russia. Given the isolation of the court from the people, and the exposed geographic position of Beijing, China could only give in to Russian demands. In case of war, however, he was willing to forfeit his British citizenship and fight for the Chinese side. His proposals were dismissed as abrasive and out of tune with the times.

Gordon's letters from China show a marked empathy with the sufferings of the people. His religion increasingly followed the "social gospel" orientation that succeeded the high tide of the Second Great Awakening, which had brought so many missionaries to China during the first half of the century. When he returned to England in 1865, he became involved in Lord Shaftsbury's (1801–1885) ragged school movement, which initiated the move to general popular education. Gordon donated large parts of his salary to new charitable organizations such as the YMCA, the Salvation Army, and the Mendicant Society. It is ironic that this man of a strong religious commitment to charity and a willingness to support national causes should have been pitted against opponents who themselves had strong religious—and in the Taiping case even Christian-inspired—motives, as well as a strong commitment to secure independence from "foreign" (Manchu or Ottoman) rulers. His triumphal statue at Victoria Embankment in London stands on a broken canon, holds a Bible, and has emblems of charity, fortitude, justice, and faith on the pedestal. Lytton Strachey elevated him to one of the emblematic figures of the Victorian age.

SEE ALSO *Li Hongzhang; Taiping Uprising.*

BIBLIOGRAPHY

Boulger, Demetrius. *The Life of Gordon*. London: Unwin, 1896.

Gordon, Charles. *General Gordon's Private Diary of His Exploits in China*. Ed. Samuel Mossmann. London: Low, Marston, Searle, and Rivington, 1885.

Hake, Egmont. *The Story of Chinese Gordon*. London: Remington, 1884

Heasman, Kathleen. *Evangelicals in Action: An Appraisal of Their Social Work in the Victorian Era*. London: Bles, 1962.

Hsü, Immanuel C. Y. (Xu Zhongyue). Gordon in China, 1880. *Pacific Historical Review* 33, 2 (1964): 147–166.

Smith, Richard J. *Mercenaries and Mandarins. The Ever-Victorious Army in Nineteenth Century China*. Millwood, NY: KTO Press, 1978.

Strachey, Lytton. The End of General Gordon. In *Eminent Victorians*. London: Chatto & Windus, 1918.

Rudolf G. Wagner

GOVERNMENT ADMINISTRATION, 1800–1912

The Qing government's civil administration was organized at three principal levels: (1) center; (2) middle (province, circuit, and prefecture); and (3) local (county, town, and village). Four important structural principles underlay the operation of the Qing government: (1) centrality, with verticality proceeding from that; (2) checks and balances; (3) concurrent (overlapping) posts; and (4) during the second half of the nineteenth century, a growing willingness to adopt new elements from foreign governments.

The final Qing century (1800–1912) followed the dynasty's three greatest seventeenth- and eighteenth-century reigns (1661–1795), a period generally regarded as the dynasty's height. In accordance with Chinese beliefs in historical cycles, the nineteenth century came to be viewed as the cycle's decline phase, depicted as a period in which China slept, unable to muster the administrative modernization required to respond to large-scale rebellions, the Western intrusion, and the problem of child emperors. Yet in spite of assumptions of decline, the century displays much administrative resourcefulness, especially at the central-government level.

THE CENTRAL GOVERNMENT

The emperor was the head of all government, dealing with civil, military, cultural, social, and religious matters. Below the monarch, the center consisted of two large rival bureaucracies inherited from earlier dynasties: a large "Outer Court" (*Waichao*) and a smaller "Inner Court" (*Neiting*), the latter expanded by eighteenth-century autocrats to increase their personal control. Each court had its own administrative regulations and practices, communications system, and official publications. All through the Qing, elements of these frameworks changed to meet the major challenges of the times. For instance, by the end of the eighteenth century, major shifts had taken place in the central-government balance of power between the Outer and Inner Courts, with the old Outer-Court system still functioning but a revived Inner Court supporting the activism of mid-Qing monarchs and officials.

The Outer Court Until changes largely initiated during the reform years beginning in 1898 to 1900, the Outer Court housed traditional agencies that discharged executive and judicial functions. At the helm was the old Outer-Court executive council inherited from the Ming (1368–1644), the "Grand Secretariat" (*Neige*), staffed by high-ranking "grand secretaries" (*daxueshi*). Other Outer-Court organizations included the Six Ministries (*Liubu*), which oversaw Civil Appointments (*Libu*), Finance (*Hubu*), Rites (*Libu*), the Military (*Bingbu*), the Judiciary (*Xingbu*), and Public Works (*Gongbu*). Three High Courts of Judicature and Revision (*Sanfasi*), consisting of the Censorate (*Duchayuan*), the Ministry of Justice (*Xingbu*), and the Court of Judicature and Revision (*Dalisi*), oversaw judicial matters. The Censorate was the government's monitoring branch, with "investigating censors" who reported on official behavior and monitored the activities of officials in their assigned circuits (*dao*). Censors in the Six Offices of Scrutiny (*Liuke*) attached to the Six Ministries monitored Outer-Court communications, counting and copying memorials, thereby creating "Historical Records" (*Shishu*) to ensure that each recorded document would be available for the official works of history. In these censors' responsibilities to monitor official behavior and productivity we see one kind of checks and balances so important in the Qing governing system, with ministry officials and clerks discharging duties that others then reviewed.

The Inner Court Two agencies dominated the Inner-Court officials, clerks, eunuchs, and servants closest to the emperor and the imperial family. One, the "Imperial Household" (*Neiwufu*), was staffed by both eunuchs and Manchu "bondservants" of the three top military echelons, the Internal Banners (*Neiqi*). Imperial Household agencies reached into many aspects of government administrative and financial affairs, including managing the imperial family's personal wealth and possessions; maintaining imperial gardens, hunting parks, libraries, and the printing office (*wuyingdian*); and collecting certain customs duties (both foreign and internal).

In the eighteenth century, the Inner Court had been enlarged to accommodate the new Grand Council and its staff. Until it was dissolved four months before the dynasty's collapse in 1911, the Grand Council discharged responsibilities ranging from advising the emperor on policy and drafting most imperial edicts to carrying out mundane clerical functions, such as tracking, copying, and filing documents. Every day the councilors read all but the most confidential reports (both Inner- and some Outer-Court) addressed to the emperor and discussed possible replies with him, then drafting many of the responses (although later the Council clerks drafted many edicts). With this enhanced apparatus, the early and mid-Qing monarchs achieved strong staff support for effective autocratic rule.

Communications: Reporting, Consultation, and Decision Making Throughout much of China's history, central-government policy making had been conducted in two major ways, orally and in writing. In the first, the emperor held large public Outer-Court audiences ("hearing about government at the imperial gate," *yumen tingzheng*) nearly every day, receiving reports orally (some read aloud), consulting officials waiting nearby, and announcing his decisions. Although these occasions were conducted almost entirely through conversations and spoken announcements, officials stood by the imperial throne to make a written record, an ancient form known in English as the "[Court] Diaries" (*Qijuzhu*) or "Records [of the Emperor's] Acts and Speech." The Diaries became one of the major sources used to compose official histories.

This public audience system continued through the Qing, but was strenuously modified by the Yongzheng emperor's (r. 1723–1735) quest for greater confidentiality, stressing small-group consultations and reports, recommendations, and responses in writing. By the beginning of the nineteenth century, the daily formal audiences that had been a mainstay of court decision making in the early Qing were being held only every ten days. At the same time, the Diaries, deprived of their spoken evidence, came to include written copies of other Outer-Court decision-making material.

The Outer-Court "Routine" System The Qing government was unusual in that it had two communication systems, the "Routine System" (so-called in English but not in Chinese) inherited from the Ming and the "Palace Memorial System" introduced in the seventeenth century. The Outer-Court Grand Secretariat staff ran the Routine System (*Tiben, Geben*). Reports (in English called "memorials") from the Outer-Court agencies and field officials were delivered to the Grand Secretariat, where bureaucrats prepared "draft rescripts" (*piaoqian, piaoni*). The suggested responses then went to the emperor, who either authorized the one draft submitted to him, or chose between two or more drafts (when he had been given alternatives). On very unusual occasions, he intervened and wrote his own reply. Many rescripts were laconic, four-character notices for action (checking and filing, for instance), with simple instructions such as "Let the appropriate board be informed" (*Gaibu zhidao*). Some routings assigned responsibility for deliberation, as in "Let the appropriate board discuss and report back" (*Gaibu yizou*). Once a deliberation had taken place and a recommendation was prepared, the process would begin all over again, with submission of the new recommendation in the form of a new memorial, preparation of its draft rescript or rescripts, and imperial authorization of a response.

Some contemporaries thought the Outer-Court system was too large and open, and incapable of preserving a state secret because its documents passed through dozens of hands, were likely candidates for publication in the court circular, the *Peking Gazette* (*Tangbao, Jingbao*), and might even later be chosen for the dynastic history. (Nonetheless, the Routine System did have rarely used provisions for secrecy.) Others viewed the system's transparency as a safeguard against malfeasance. Nonetheless, the Inner-Court Palace Memorial System eventually overshadowed the entire Routine System, which lapsed in 1901.

Inner-Court Communications By the mid-eighteenth century, the newly established Grand Council was managing a new system for correspondence and record keeping, the Palace Memorial (*Zouzhe*) System. This consisted of a reporting system, possibilities for consultation, and new types of imperial responses that supported the direct personal rule sought by the early- and mid-Qing monarchs. The key difference between the Outer-Court communication system and the Inner-Court palace memorials was that the latter allowed the emperors and their Inner-Court staff to be more interventionist. Where the palace memorials were concerned, the emperors used the special imperial color, vermilion, to write their replies (*zhupi*) directly on the memorials, thus inaugurating a personal correspondence between monarch and field official. Some imperial comments ran to considerable length, flattering the distant official with his monarch's concern not only about policy but also about his health and favorite foods.

As in the old system, varieties of consultation were available in the new system, because the imperial reader had several groups he might order to research and deliberate. The Grand Council was frequently used, but other groups, such as one of the Outer-Court Six Boards or a larger group known as the "Nine Ministers," might be designated, the resulting recommendations being known as "deliberation memorials" (*yifu zouzhe*).

At the third phase of the court's treatment of a Palace Memorial was a variety of court responses, including the emperor's personal vermilion rescripts on memorials and the imperial orders to deliberate. In addition, once the Guangxu emperor (r. 1875–1908) attained maturity, the empress dowager was said to influence his decisions by whispering from behind a curtain (*chuilian tingzheng*). Several forms of written edicts were also possible parts of this phase. Many of the openly disseminated (*mingfa*) Grand Secretariat edicts (*Neige feng Shangyu*) came to be drafted in the Grand Council, a result of grand secretaries being concurrently appointed grand councillors. Edicts of the court-letter form (*jixin, tingji*, or *ziji*) introduced in the eighteenth century might also be drafted by the Council or its staff, presumably after discussion with the monarch. Beginning in 1884, the telegraph was used to transmit some of the court letters (*dianji*). Occasionally the emperor would dictate part of an edict. He might also correct edict drafts by "going over [them] with vermilion" (*guozhu*); some of these, displaying the monarch's own revisions, are still held in the archives.

In the late nineteenth century, this system could be bent to allow high officials to manage the government in spite of the series of three infant monarchs. Vague edict formulations, such as "The grand councillors have received the imperial decree . . .", masked the exact source of the decree and allowed the Council to create appropriate directives when the child-emperors were too young to contribute to what was being done in their names. Nineteenth-century adjustments strengthened the Grand Council and probably enabled the dynasty to endure and cope with its numerous nineteenth-century challenges for several generations. It may well be that inevitable decline is not the appropriate narrative for the Qing final century.

Official Record Keeping and Publications Both the Outer and the Inner Courts had strong publication programs, important as part of the dynasty's effort to convince the literate public of its worth. One quasi-government publication enterprise was the *Peking Gazette*, a court circular primarily for officials. This was prepared in the palace offices but then usually offered to private local companies that sent representatives to the palace to select and copy documents of interest to their particular constituencies. Accordingly, not all copies of a single day's issue would be the same. (A selected document, however, had to be copied in full.) The *Gazette* had an avid roster of readers, not only officials but also diplomatic and missionary foreigners scattered all across the empire, for it was a good medium for keeping up with government news. The *North China Herald* translated and published excerpts, and near the end of the Qing there were reprints in Chinese journals.

The *Peking Gazettes* provided information the court deemed important for its official-literati readership. During most of the dynasty, the court also allowed a reverse flow of opinion from the official-literati group, known as the "avenue of words" (*yanlu*). In 1885, at the time of the Sino-French War (1884–1885), the empress dowager summarily intervened against tradition and closed this avenue, after receiving perhaps more views than she wanted to hear.

The court also published its documents in a more permanent form than the ephemeral gazettes allowed: Vast numbers of original documents and summaries were published in court-sponsored compilations. The most important was each dynasty's massive official history (*zhengshi*) of its predecessor. These voluminous histories usually had four parts: Imperial Annals, Monographs, Tables, and Biographies, often (but not always) based on archival documents. The official Qing history ran to several hefty tomes and was based on the aforementioned Diaries and Historical Records, as well as on the "Veritable Records" (*Shilu*), which were annals for each reign, consisting of a daily chronological record of major documents and imperial activities.

THE BUREAUCRACY

The Qing bureaucracy was large by the standards of a premodern empire, but small in comparison with present-day governments. During the nineteenth century, there were probably about twenty thousand posts, both in the capital and across the empire, for men with the two highest degrees (*jinshi*, *juren*). Another twenty thousand lower-level positions were occupied by lower-degree holders. But there were not enough posts for all who wanted them, and to make matters worse, the financially pressed central government had increased the sale of offices, intensifying the competition for places.

Ranks and Income Qing civil-official posts were arranged in nine ranks, with a higher ("A") and a lower ("B") step in each rank, for a total of eighteen grades. An official's rank determined his official salary, but a rank's salary was only a small part of his income. Additional government funds came in the form of grants of rice and money for firewood, vegetables, candles, and stationery. The payments and supplements were woefully inadequate: A popular saying asserted that three years of a magistracy could ruin a family. In the early eighteenth century, the government acknowledged that its meager payments were inviting questionable methods of realizing sufficient income and introduced "nourish-honesty" (*yanglian*) emoluments of considerable size, determined by rank and the burdens of the post.

Even this concession was not sufficient, and an official could reap far more than the government payments by charging extra fees for various services, demanding percentages of taxes collected, investing, and receiving gifts from other officials (although these incurred return-gift obligations). Chung-li Chang (Zhang Zhongli), who in the 1950s made a detailed study of Qing official incomes, concluded that in spite of an officeholder's many expenses, in the traditional China of the 1880s, government service in any one of the nine ranks would yield the best income of all possible careers.

Appointments The emperor made higher-level appointments, both civil and military, often on the basis of lists of appropriate candidates prepared in the Grand Council or a related ministry. Many considerations determined appointments. Although appointments were usually for three years, they could be extended or cut short if need be; by the late Qing, one or two years was the general rule. Within central-government agencies, appointments were determined by the checks-and-balances stratagem of dyarchy between numbers of Manchus-Mongols and Han Chinese. For instance, a ministry generally had two presidents and four vice presidents, split equally between Manchus and Chinese. For much of the dynasty, the large numbers of Manchu imperial princes were not appointed to official posts, except to the interim regency councils at the beginnings of new reigns (*zongli shiwu wang dachen*). In addition to the checks and balances imposed by dyarchy, there were many overlaps in responsibilities. For instance, a provincial governor might find himself checked by his governor-general. Lines of authority were rarely drawn with absolute clarity, with a resulting tension that was expected to produce superior decisions.

Over the years, exceptions to standard appointment procedures developed, creating yet another form of checks and balances. The Grand Council, for instance, was allowed to present its own "noted names" (*jiming*) lists for appointments, by which its own preferred appointees were considered ahead of those put forward by other bodies. Eventually, the Council was able to dominate so much of the appointment process that some of the checks-and-balances aspects of the appointment process were effectively ignored, a fact that was vigorously protested by agencies whose candidates were being passed over. Cases of reconsideration that gave some "dismissed officials" (*feiyuan*) a second chance also gradually increased. The late-Qing surge of interest in government appointments left many without posts. Some of these, however, had the prestige of being listed as "expectant" (*houbu*) officials and did eventually win posts.

LATE QING CHANGE AND REFORM

During the first half of the dynasty's final century, China's several military failures in the face of both internal rebellions and external invasion led to a debate about possible changes. One early reform (1861) consisted of a new office to oversee foreign affairs, literally "Office in Charge of the Affairs of Various Nations" (*Zongli Geguo Shiwu Yamen*), sometimes known, even in English, as the Zongli Yamen. (In 1901 its cumbersome name was shortened to "Ministry of Foreign Affairs," *Waiwubu*.) Thus began the series of many changes in public administration during the last half of the Qing's final century. Moreover, by this time, the Grand Council had expanded its influence over nearly all government activities, and the old distinction between the Outer and Inner Courts was gradually disappearing. In some quarters, a growing admiration for the West's (and later, Japan's) governments inspired the desire to know more on which to base reforms. Accordingly, in the 1870s and 1880s, the government sponsored groups of students who were sent to study science and technology in the United States, France, and Germany.

With the turn of the century, the pace of change picked up notably. The Boxer Rebellion and the incarceration of foreign legation members and their families (1900), which brought on the foreign invasion known in the West as the "Eight-Nation Victorious Army," gave further impetus to reforms as the Chinese people were jolted by the humiliation of this defeat and the ensuing tough international agreements. Japan's victory over Russia in 1905 reverberated across China, where this was regarded as a victory for constitutionalism and reform in contrast with Russia's autocracy and subservience to the past. In 1901 a new Bureau of Government Affairs (*Zhengwuchu*) was set up to consider the many proposals for reforms now being submitted. Education was an early focus: Peking University (Beijing Daxue or "Beida") was founded in 1898, and a new Ministry of Education (*Xuebu*), partly replacing some Board of Rites responsibilities, grew out of organizations created at the same time. At first women were not permitted to participate in the new education establishments, but this was soon altered. The new century brought the end of the sale of offices (*juanna*), abolition of footbinding, abolition of the examination system, and creation of new provincial legislatures.

In 1905 to 1906, a study of foreign governments was carried out by missions to Japan, the United States, Britain, France, Germany, Italy, Russia, and other countries, resulting in recommendations for a constitutional government. A wave of enthusiasm for new political institutions led to several new central-government agencies in the dynasty's final decade. Some of the most important were a new Ministry of the Interior (or Police) (*Xunjingbu*), a renovated judiciary, a Board of Customs Control (*Shuiwuchu*), a new Ministry of Agriculture, Industry, and Commerce (*Nong-Gong-Shangbu*), and a new Ministry of Posts and Communications (*Youchuanbu*).

Late Qing changes in the kinds of ministries were accompanied by a reorganization of their tables of organization. During the last decade, the old system of six dyarchically divided officers at the top of each board was abandoned in favor of fewer top officials and a weakened dyarchical balance. In addition, the board superintendents (*zongli*), who in the eighteenth century could be either Chinese or Manchu, were now all from the Manchu side. All through the government, the former evenhanded dyarchy was being replaced by a growing preponderance of Manchus. Even princes received high-level appointments in spite of a long-standing dynastic policy against this.

A Guangxu edict (1908) had promised a national legislature ("Parliament," *Yiyuan*, sometimes *Guohui*) by 1917, but widespread demand forced a revising edict that set the earlier date of 1913. In 1909 small numbers of qualified voters (mostly male degree and property holders and other gentry) elected assemblies in all the provinces, but the top provincial officials could easily thwart these bodies' acts. These were followed in 1910 by a National Assembly (*Zizhengyuan*), with half its delegates elected by the provincial assemblies and half appointed by the imperial court. But like its provincial counterparts, this body was not given true legislative powers, with the result that it is sometimes termed merely an "advisory council": The emperor retained control, being permitted both to convene or dissolve it at any time and to appoint its president who, in case of a tie, was empowered to cast the deciding vote. In addition, the demand for a cabinet form of government responsible to the national legislature failed when the weak and frightened Manchu government refused to sponsor it. These efforts may have been better than nothing, but at the outset the constitutional movement produced legislatures in name only.

Less than half a year before the beginning of the revolution, both the Grand Secretariat and the Grand Council were abolished (May 8, 1911) and replaced with new bodies. The Grand Council's successor, known as the "Cabinet" (*Zeren Neige*), proved largely a change in name: Most of the Council's top officials moved into the new body, and its records continued to be maintained in the Council's form. The president of the new Cabinet (*Neige zongli dachen*) acted as a chief executive immediately subordinate to the emperor. The Grand Secretariat was not directly replaced, but instead a Privy Council (*Bideyuan*) came into being, charged with advising the monarch on constitutional matters and questions relating to the imperial family. At the same time, several other central-government high councils and committees were brought into being, subordinate to these two directorates, but the Manchus retained control of key military agencies.

THE FIELD ADMINISTRATION

The field administration that operated beyond the capital city consisted of two principal levels of regular bureaucrats (*zhengguan*): (1) a middle level of provincial leaders, circuit intendants (*daotai*), and prefects (*zhifu*); and (2) the county level of district magistrates (*zhixian*). The latter was significantly supplemented by three other important groups: (1) the gentry-literati living in the countryside; (2) the expectant officials or candidates-in-waiting (*houbuguan*); and (3) quasi-official staff and other members of the sub-bureaucracy (including private secretaries and local organizations that administered police and taxation). In addition, there were special arrangements for treaty ports and for territories that had not been organized into provincial structures. The following description relates only to the eighteen provinces that constituted the main part of the empire, generally referring to the situation up to 1906 when numerous reforms began to be introduced.

Provinces For most of the nineteenth century, China had eighteen provinces, a figure that was augmented late in the century by the creation of the provinces of Xinjiang (1884), Taiwan (1887 to 1895, when it was handed over to Japan), and Manchuria (created in 1907 out of territory earlier known as the "Northeast," Dongbei). The new Northeast consisted of three provinces: Fengtian, Jilin, and Heilongjiang. By the end of the dynasty, China had twenty-two provinces. These provincial divisions constituted the great mass of the empire known as "China proper." Other territories existed, sometimes overseen by a military governor (*jiangjun*) until being elevated to provincial status.

Most provinces were governed by four top officials. The governors-general, in English sometimes known as "viceroys" (*zongdu*), headed the hierarchy. They usually oversaw groups of two provinces, but there were some exceptions: for instance, two provinces had only a governor-general and no governor. Next came the governors (*xunfu*), most of whom governed in tandem with the governors-general but three of whom were not thus supervised and presided alone over their jurisdictions. Two other high provincial officials were the provincial treasurer (*buzhengshi*) and the judicial commissioner (*anchashi*). These four possessed the cachet of being direct imperial appointees, but generally only the two top ranks submitted palace memorials to the emperor. Another official with province-wide responsibilities was the provincial director of education (*xuezheng*). He supervised education and examinations, conferring the lowest degree (*xiucai*) on those successful in the province's examinations.

Some appointees outside the capital controlled territorial configurations that did not conform to provincial boundaries and yet ranked equivalently with the top provincial officers. One example was the directors-general of the Conservation of the Yellow River and the Grand Canal (*Hedong hedao zongdu*), who oversaw these waterways as they traversed several provinces.

These were the traditional configurations, but in contrast with the extensive reforms introduced among capital agencies, late Qing reforms were largely absent from the provincial scene. The chief exception was the approximately five thousand councils that had come into being at the local level by 1911. Provincial assemblies (*ziyiju*), which had to work in tandem with the National Assembly, were decreed for the provincial level in 1907 and elected in 1909. The earliest of these were hardly legislatures, although they were expected to develop eventually into lawmaking bodies.

Many considerations applied to provincial appointments. As with capital appointments, dyarchy was generally practiced. The two top provincial officials were usually divided between Manchus and Han Chinese: If the governor-general was a Manchu, the governors, or at least one of the governors under him, were likely to be Han, and vice versa. The assignment of official responsibilities to these two top officials offered a variety of methods of control, as duties overlapped and all individuals held more than one post concurrently, creating a kind of checks-and-balances system in the provinces. No one was permitted to serve in his native province, nor in that part of a neighboring province close to his own home residence. A Rule of Avoidance (*Huibi*) imposed the further restriction that one could not serve in the same area as a relative. These restrictions meant that newly appointed officials often faced unfamiliar dialects and local customs. Given the short average length for holding one office (usually less than three years), there was hardly time to learn the local dialect; few made the attempt. These practices made it difficult for the appointee when he found himself ministering to an area with an unfamiliar dialect and customs. The situation frequently led a new local official to depend on a poorly paid local staff of assistants, private secretaries, clerks, and runners who have often been castigated in the literature as taking advantage of both the local populace as well as the innocent outsider official.

Circuit Intendants and Prefects. Below the top province-wide officials were two main classes of officials, sometimes called "mid-provincial" or "secondary": circuit intendants (*daotai*) and prefects (*zhifu*). In the hierarchy, they were located between the top provincial authorities whose responsibilities covered entire provinces and the county governments of the bottom echelon. By the end of the Qing, there were about one hundred circuits in the empire, and the circuit intendants were usually in charge of two, three, or four prefectures, over which they had supervisory responsibilities but no direct governing duties (another example of checks and balances). At the same time, the number of prefects in the eighteen provinces came to slightly more than two hundred.

Counties, Villages, and the Subadministration Counties (*xian*) and villages (*cun*) made up the bulk of what was known as the "local" (*difang*) or rural part of China. In late Qing times, probably 80 to 85 percent of the population resided in the countryside, most in farming families. The local level was presided over by the district or county magistrate, his official title being "district magistrate" or literally "knows the county" (*zhixian*). But he had another sobriquet: "father-and-mother official" (*fumuguan*), suggesting the extraordinary variety of tasks and micromanagement required. His office was located in the "county seat," in the county office (*yamen*), usually a walled town. The district magistrate was expected to defray his governing expenses out of his own pocket, for there was no distinction between his private concerns and what might be regarded as public interests. Even his residence was in the county yamen, and to attend to business he simply walked from his living area to the formal halls of government. The empire's twelve hundred or more district magistrates were responsible for overseeing the government's reach into the largest part of China's population and territory. Counties and indeed all middle and lower provincial posts were rated according to four kinds of difficulty that a local official might expect to face: "centrally located [and therefore pressed with much business]" (*chong*), "burdensome" (*fan*), "wearisome tax problems" (*pi*), and "difficult" (*nan*).

One notable feature of the two millennia of county government was that in spite of population increases and territorial expansion, the number of counties in the empire remained about the same, vacillating between 1,200 and 1,500 units from ancient times down to the end of the imperial era. If new districts had to be added on the frontiers, old ones in the interior would be consolidated, part of a continuous process. This was indubitably deliberate, as the overwhelming number of 8,500 counties required to match the population increase from the Han dynasty (206 BCE–220 CE) to the mid-nineteenth century would have created an unwieldy governing apparatus far beyond a premodern central government's capacity. As a result, whereas in the ancient Han period the average population of an individual county stood at about 50,000, the figure by the middle of the nineteenth century had reached approximately 250,000 (possibly more by other reckonings), leading to a deterioration in government supervision and services. Although a magistrate had some staff (an assistant magistrate, a registrar, and a jail warden), the situation was dealt with through several subcounty remedies.

Unofficial Extensions of Government in Rural Areas. It is often said that even as late as the nineteenth century, the imperial government did not reach beyond the county seat, leaving China's nearly ten thousand villages beyond the immediate control of the central government. To deal with the rural communities, an official residing in the county seat was forced into dependence on several kinds of local assistance: gentry-literati families living in the area, expectant officials, a secretarial staff of specialists, police and taxation networks, and clerks and yamen runners. The astonishing point about all this assistance is its size: It may have totaled thousands or even tens of thousands of low-paid or unpaid volunteers helping to carry out the central government's will all across China's vast rural areas. Moreover, many in this kind of service were ideologically trained or at least nurtured in a Confucian environment, thus fulfilling another aspect of the central government's methods of keeping order in the countryside.

The Gentry-Literati Role in Rural Administration. Probably the most effective unofficial group in the countryside was the gentry-literati (*shenshi*, *shenjin*). These were not the exact equivalent of the group of appointed officials, although the officials would have been part of the gentry-literati, for by no means all gentry held official posts. But this small group, especially the educated males, had an influence far beyond its size.

Chung-li Chang makes clear the gentry's important leadership roles in China's rural scene. Being resident in the countryside, they were in a position to know their own area's special characteristics, and accordingly were often called on to advise the appointed officials who, being deputed to serve short terms in unfamiliar localities, were likely to need guidance. Being the best educated of all on the local scene, some gentry set up local schools and occasionally also served as teachers. In addition, they were responsible for local temples and shrines. Another responsibility was that twice a month they read the Sacred Edict, consisting of Confucian ideological maxims, to assembled villagers.

Beyond cultural matters, the gentry often took responsibility for local transportation and water conservancy. They led local efforts to build and maintain roads and bridges, often contributing the necessary funds out of their own pockets. On occasion, they oversaw agriculture, waterways, dams, dredging, and irrigation projects. They were often active in natural disasters, leading efforts to deal with floods or droughts. On occasion, they might organize local self-defense forces. In this way, with minimal legal sanction and acting on a voluntary basis for the benefit of the common good, gentry members discharged crucial tasks of rural government in their own habitats.

Private Secretaries. Another local gentry group were men who, following success at the lowest examination stage, took appointments as staff (or "tent friends," *muyou* or *mufu*) to a local official. Officials at all provincial ranks, but especially the county magistrates, needed technical advice that these educated men supplied. Some went to the trouble of boning up on needed specialties: the law, taxation and finance, military technology, Western weaponry, water transport of grain taxes, official correspondence, or whatever was required in the jurisdiction. On average, each county yamen had thirty such specialists, making a total of approximately 45,000 such persons serving across the empire.

One of the chief advantages of these posts was that, in contrast with the expectant officials, these men were highly paid. Indeed, those well versed in the law, a subject rarely studied by examination candidates, enjoyed the highest emolument of all. Some who emerged impoverished from their examination studies deliberately preferred to serve a provincial official rather than hoping for an official appointment that might never materialize. During the late Qing, when China faced massive internal rebellions and foreign intrusions, the private secretaries system expanded as another way of dealing with the new challenges. Magistrates might recommend their particularly successful secretaries, who then could receive official appointments. Thus these posts could be both well paid and a stepping-stone to bright future.

Local Administration of Police and Taxation. The Qing inherited two important groups of local administrators organized out of local residents to oversee taxation and local police functions. These were not usually configured according to village boundaries but instead consisted of fixed numbers of households rather than the number living in any one village or part of a village, an arrangement probably expected to discourage the formation of village-level activist groups. Police functions were carried out by a well-organized security (*baojia*) system, with ten households organized in the smaller unit (*pai*), ten such units making up the next level (*jia*), and one hundred units constituting the largest grouping (*bao*). The magistrate appointed a head at each of the upper levels, so one should not seek evidence of popular elections of local leaders or democracy in these arrangements.

The taxation and labor-service system (*lijia*) was organized in much the same way, with the magistrate appointing the heads of the units, who were often from the wealthiest households in their part of the district. These were responsible for tax collections and the labor service that some rendered in place of or in addition to taxes. (Many labor-service taxes were ended during the eighteenth century, but there were holdouts where the corvée lasted into the early nineteenth century.) The magistrate's job performance was evaluated in part on the completeness of his tax collections, and it was well known that the perfection that the government demanded in this area was almost impossible to achieve, with the hapless official and indeed sometimes his supervising officials being denied both salary and promotion for falling short. As a result, in some cases the magistrate had to resort to various subterfuges, such as paying what was needed himself or persuading the local wealthy to help in order to produce the desired accounts. In contrast, the government did acknowledge that natural disasters and poor harvests left the magistrate and his people in an impossible position and as a result the emperor often issued compassionate tax remissions for hard-hit counties.

In theory, these organizations were in place and ran uniformly and smoothly all across the empire. But the reality may have been different, especially once the numerous problems of local violence erupted in the nineteenth century. In the end the taxation system was largely taken over by the police system and neither functioned optimally in the late nineteenth century.

Clerks and Yamen Runners. The bottom level of a county magistrate's group of assistants consisted of clerks and runners. The clerks assisted the county magistrate. They were closely involved in the minutiae of legal cases, including on-the-spot investigation of circumstances described in the plaints and the taking down of testimony in the magistrate's court.

Runners operated almost entirely out in the county. At times, they collected taxes for the yamen, made arrests, helped with public works, and supervised the keeping of village records. Some runners served as granary watchmen, made sure that roads were available for official travelers, and inflicted corporal punishment on miscreants when the magistrate so ordered. The influx of foreigners was responsible for much new work, as foreigners had to be escorted and were not permitted to roam at will without a yamen representative at their side.

THE MILITARY ADMINISTRATION

China's nineteenth-century military innovations were the by-product of the deteriorated and decayed Chinese Green Standard (*Luying*) and Manchu Eight Banner (*Baqi*) systems inherited from the early Qing and still stationed in garrison enclaves all across the country. But by the time of the White Lotus Rebellion (1796–1805), the empire's traditional military forces were clearly in decline and could no longer deal with guerrilla-style forces fleeing back and forth in the mountainous terrain and across the provincial boundaries that constituted the limits of the official pursuit jurisdictions. The Qianlong emperor (r. 1736–1796) grasped his military's demoralization when he scathingly chastised a general's field report of yet another failure with his plaintive vermilion exclamation: "Surely we are not operating on the principle of waiting for the rebels to commit suicide!" Increasingly desperate challenges called for innovations, and during the nineteenth century they arrived in the shape of new types of military organization on both local and national levels.

The White Lotus Rebellion was the first to summon forth a new response. Local residents, threatened by disaffected people who had escaped beyond the settled countryside, organized militia (*tuanlian*) forces at several levels: village, leagues of villages, and extended leagues, with considerable variation across China. The extended leagues were often grounded in lineages or market towns, some organized by gentry and some by influential and respected commoners. Financing came from a variety of sources, but the new "likin" (*lijin*) tax (1853) supplied important funding.

Other military innovations in the dynasty's waning years included a special group set up in 1862 within the banners and, drawing on them, twenty thousand armed troops in the "Peking Field Force" (*Shenjiying*). By contrast, during the nineteenth century, China's naval forces were not organized on the national level in the pattern of the traditional land contingents (Green Standard and Banner armies). Instead, the few naval efforts were province-based.

SEE ALSO *Constitutionalism; Examination System, 1800–1905; History: Overview, 1800–1860; History: Overview, 1860–1912; Newspapers; White Lotus.*

BIBLIOGRAPHY

Bartlett, Beatrice S. *Monarchs and Ministers: The Grand Council in Mid-Ch'ing China, 1723–1820*. Berkeley: University of California Press, 1991.

Britton, Roswell S. *The Chinese Periodical Press, 1800–1912*. Shanghai: Kelly & Walsh, 1933. Reprint, Taibei: Ch'eng-wen, 1976.

Elliott, Mark C. The Manchu-Language Archives of the Qing Dynasty and the Origins of the Palace Memorial System. *Late Imperial China* 22, 1 (June 2001): 1–70.

Elman, Benjamin A. Naval Warfare and the Refraction of China's Self-strengthening Reforms into Scientific and Technological Failure, 1865–1895. In *Warfare in China since 1600*, ed. Kenneth Swope, 145–188. Burlington, VT: Ashgate, 2005.

Fincher, John H. *Chinese Democracy: The Self-Government Movement in Local, Provincial, and National Politics, 1905–1914*. Canberra: Australian University Press, 1981.

Folsom, Kenneth E. *Friends, Guests, and Colleagues: The Mu-fu System in the Late Ch'ing Period*. Berkeley: University of California Press, 1968.

Gongzhongdang Guangxu chao zouzhe [Palace memorials of the Guangxu reign]. 26 vols. Taibei: Palace Museum, 1973.

Ichiko Chuzo. Political and Institutional Reform. In *The Cambridge History of China*, Vol. 11: *Late Ch'ing 1800–1911*, ed. John F. Fairbank and Liu Guangjing (Liu Kwang-Ching), Pt. 2, chap. 11, 375–415. New York: Cambridge University Press, 1980.

Kuhn, Philip A. *Rebellion and Its Enemies in Late Imperial China: Militarization and Social Structure, 1796–1864*. Cambridge, MA: Harvard University Press, 1970.

Leung, Edwin Pak-wah. China's Decision to Send Students to the West: The Making of a "Revolutionary" Policy. *Asian Profile* 16, 5 (1988): 391–400.

Leung, Philip Yuen-sang. Crisis Management and Institutional Reform: The Expectant Officials in the Late Qing. In *Dragons, Tigers, and Dogs: Qing Crisis Management and the Boundaries of State Power in Late Imperial China*, ed. Robert J. Antony and Jane Kate Leonard, 61–77. Ithaca, NY: Cornell University East Asia Program, 2002.

Leung, Yuen-sang. *The Shanghai Taotai: Linkage Man in a Changing Society, 1843–90*. Honolulu: University of Hawai'i Press, 1990.

Min Tu-gi (Min Tu-ki). The Late Ch'ing Provincial Assembly. In *National Polity and Local Power: The Transformation of Late Imperial China*, ed. Philip A. Kuhn and Timothy Brook, 137–179. Cambridge, MA: Harvard University Council on East Asian Studies, 1989.

Pong, David. *Shen Pao-chen and China's Modernization in the Nineteenth Century*. New York: Cambridge University Press, 1994.

Qu Tongzu (Ch'ü T'ung-tsu). *Local Government in China under the Ch'ing*. Cambridge, MA: Harvard University Press, 1962.

Rankin, Mary Backus. Alarming Crises/Enticing Possibilities: Political and Cultural Changes in Late Nineteenth-Century China. *Late Imperial China* 29, 1 (Suppl.: *Towards the Nineteenth Century: A Special Issue in Honor of William T. Rowe*) (2008): 40–63.

Rawlinson, John L. *China's Struggle for Naval Development, 1839–1895*. Cambridge, MA: Harvard East Asian Research Center, 1967.

Reed, Bradly. *Talons and Teeth: County Clerks and Runners in the Qing Dynasty*. Stanford, CA: Stanford University Press, 2000.

Rudolph, Jennifer. *Negotiated Power in Late Imperial China: The Zongli Yamen and the Politics of Reform*. Ithaca, NY: Cornell University Press, 2008.

Skinner, G. William. Introduction: Urban Development in Imperial China. In *The City in Late Imperial China*, ed. G. William Skinner, 3–31. Stanford, CA: Stanford University Press, 1977.

Thompson, Roger R. *China's Local Councils in the Age of Constitutional Reform, 1898–1911*. Cambridge, MA: Harvard University Press, Harvard Council on East Asian Studies, 1995.

Wei, Betty Peh-T'i. *Ruan Yuan, 1764–1849: The Life and Work of a Major Scholar-Official in Nineteenth-Century China before the Opium War*. Hong Kong: Hong Kong University Press, 2006.

Wright, Mary C., ed. *China in Revolution: The First Phase, 1900–1913*. New Haven, CT: Yale University Press, 1968.

Xiao Gongquan (Hsiao Kung-ch'üan). *Rural China: Imperial Control in the Nineteenth Century*. Seattle: University of Washington Press, 1960.

Zhang Zhongli (Chung-li Chang). *The Income of the Chinese Gentry*. Seattle: University of Washington Press, 1962.

Beatrice S. Bartlett

GOVERNMENT ADMINISTRATION, 1912–1949

Government administration in Republican-era China (1912–1949) is framed by a decreed abdication in the name of the young Manchu emperor Puyi (1906–1967) in Beijing's Forbidden City (Zijin cheng) and a public celebration orchestrated by the Chinese Communist Party (CCP) at the Gate of Heavenly Peace (Tiananmen), through which visitors now gain access to the areas once restricted to emperors and their families. Between the February 1912 Qing abdication and the October 1949 founding of the People's Republic of China, the center of Republican administration shifted to Nanjing in 1927, to Chongqing in late 1937, and back to Nanjing in 1945. The last Qing emperor and a few of his advisers traveled to Manchuria in China's northeast in 1932 and took on imperial titles bestowed by the Japanese occupiers of the Manchu's ancestral homeland. It was a complicated, confusing, and pivotal era.

YUAN SHIKAI'S PRESIDENCY, 1912–1916

For most of these momentous thirty-seven years China was at war, either internally or externally. The revolution of 1911 that ended Qing rule in its 268th year threatened widespread civil war and anarchy, conditions that would have excused further imperialist encroachments on Chinese territory and sovereignty. Neither the revolutionary leader Sun Yat-sen nor the Qing official and military strongman Yuan Shikai wanted to provide foreigners with such an opportunity. With their compromises—Yuan assuming the presidency Sun held provisionally, Sun focusing on electoral politics, and relocating the national capital to Nanjing—the era of the Republic of China began.

Yuan Shikai's military connections—he had long championed the modernization of China's military and had numerous protégés in the new-style Beiyang Army in north China—and his national reputation as a civilian reformer made it easy for him to renege on his promise to move the capital to Nanjing. Sun Yat-sen, who had little military backing and who had spent most of his adult life outside China, had no recourse but to focus his energies and that of the newly formed National People's Party on the upcoming parliamentary elections.

Yuan Shikai, meanwhile, was faced with the daunting task of reintegrating China after the revolutionary tumult of 1911 to 1912. Although Sun Yat-sen's Revolutionary Alliance had provided the anti-Manchu nationalistic rhetoric that finally doomed China's long-lived imperial system, the conflict between Beijing and the provinces over issues of autonomy, initiative, and resources also contributed to the provincial declarations of independence telegraphed across the country in fall and winter 1911 to 1912. It was not unusual for Sun's youthful followers to force respected Qing officials or scholars to front their revolutionary regimes in the provinces. These were men who could, and did, work with Yuan Shikai as he fashioned the Qing bureaucracy into a Republican bureaucracy. Yuan's efforts to reestablish central control of the provinces would not be apparent until 1913 to 1914, but he had immediate power and influence over Beijing's bureaucracy.

In another of the important continuities across the 1911 to 1912 divide, Qing bureaucrats manned the new Republican bureaucracy in Beijing. Yuan Shikai had been a powerful voice for change in the late Qing, and his "Tianjin model" of reforms had brought him a national reform reputation in the post-Boxer era. He championed the careers of young men who had returned to China after having studied in Japan. The Western-style cabinet structure of central administration that had been established in the reorganization of 1906, with ministries of education, interior, and foreign affairs, to name a few, was familiar and welcome under President Yuan Shikai.

As governor of Hebei Province Yuan had sponsored the prototypical Tianjin County Council, which was elected in the summer of 1907, but he had shared with his fellow Qing officials a preference for changing China sequentially, privileging administrative reforms before the so-called self-government reforms. Even as President Yuan attempted to recentralize powers that had been either devolved to or seized by the provinces during late-Qing administrative reforms or revolutionary opportunity, he had to immediately face the consequences wrought by the Qing-era decision to "advance" the establishment of a national parliament from 1916 to 1913. Elections were held in late 1912 and early 1913, and to Yuan's irritation Sun Yat-sen's National People's Party was the clear victor. This culmination of the Qing-era idea of establishing a hierarchy of elected assemblies—local, provincial, national—a reform program that Governor Yuan first championed as a provincial official in Tianjin—only distracted President Yuan from his administrative priority: recentralizing power in Beijing.

Whereas some might have seen electoral politics in China's age of constitutional reform as the modern way to integrate the nation, Yuan preferred a more familiar and time-honored approach: competitive civil service examinations. The imperial examinations, which had been abolished in September 1905, had yet to be replaced by a viable modern system. Yuan sought to complete this unfinished business, and his Republican administration drafted regulations in 1915 that were implemented in 1916. He was attempting to accomplish for all of China what he had accomplished as a Qing official, making sure his young, well-trained returned students in Hebei received the credentials they needed for the positions he wanted them to fill. Yuan wanted nothing less than a new selection system that would bring new-style "men of talent" into the government. This revised process, informed by centuries of experience, would usher China into a new century in which technocratic expertise was desperately needed in the bureaucracy.

Yuan's top-down, bureaucratic, centralizing approach to creating a modern nation-state provided a template for succeeding Republican regimes. But the promise and progress of Yuan's early efforts foundered, a victim of two specters that would also bedevil his successors: Hubris and imperialism unraveled the accomplishments of Yuan's short presidency.

The hubris is understandable. People with executive power tend to want more, and Yuan was no exception. The annoyance he felt with Sun's National People's Party culminated in late 1913 with his outlawing the party and turning the national parliament into a travesty. Thus tarnished, electoral politics down to the local level came under fire, and by 1914 Yuan had abolished all elected assemblies. With no mechanism by which to allow a sovereign people to voice their will, Yuan returned to the antiquated imperial ideas abandoned in February 1912. In 1915 he attempted to orchestrate the establishment of a new dynasty that he would head as constitutional monarch. Opposition on many fronts doomed the effort, which Yuan finally abandoned in March 1916.

More menacing, however, was the specter of imperialism. To understand government administration in Republican China one must recognize the role played by foreigners in China. Again, Yuan inherited a Qing legacy. Western influence had steadily grown since the Treaty of Nanjing in 1842. In the treaty ports that numbered from initially five to about fifty at dynasty's end, Westerners and Japanese were an urban presence with extraterritorial powers across China. They were also instrumental in government. The Chinese Imperial Maritime Customs, led by a foreign officer corps, had provided steady and dependable revenue stream for the Qing since the 1860s, and now the customs agency did the same for the Republic of China. The success of this model encouraged a similar Sino-foreign fiscal agency responsible for the salt tax: the Sino-Foreign Salt Inspectorate (Yanwu jihe zongsuo). This second agency, established in 1913, became a fixture in Republican China and furnished significant revenue to cash-starved central administrations.

The privileges and influence that had been enjoyed by Westerners for decades were highlighted by the Japanese in May 1915, when Yuan Shikai was forced to recognize their economic interests in Manchuria, Shandong and the Yangzi region and to accede to their wishes to influence government decision making. In their Twenty-one Demands the Japanese were making explicit what often had been left implicit by other foreigners. The result was even more humiliating for Yuan and the Chinese.

THE WARLORD PERIOD, 1916–1927

Humiliated by the Japanese, whose modernizing model of administrative reform he had tried to emulate, and by the Chinese people, who were not willing to renounce their Republican citizenship, Yuan died a broken man in June 1916. In a sense, China, too, was broken in 1916. But not as broken as the label *warlord China* suggests. Nor were things as different in the post-Yuan era as the label also suggests. Beijing and its Republican constitutional legitimacy were seldom questioned. The dance between civilian and military power holders continued at the local, provincial, and national levels. Even warlords sought the mantle of civilian constitutional legitimacy. No warlord ever presumed to declare a new republic or found a new country. These men accepted Beijing's legitimacy, they just were not inclined to share provincial resources, and Beijing was not able to force the provincial hand. That capability had ended with Yuan's death. Yuan's military protégés were powerful men, and some held Beijing, but none was able to unify China.

Government administration in the warlord era, then, is difficult to assess. Beijing relied on taxes under its control—customs and salt—and those prerogatives made the rump Republican government in Beijing a prize worth fighting for among revenue-hungry warlords; modern armies are expensive. But warlords tended to accept the legitimacy of these taxes and Beijing's right to collect them. They certainly did not want to take over any of the debt obligations for foreign loans and indemnities still being serviced by Beijing.

Paradoxically, the central government in Beijing had more respect and standing among foreigners than its own people. This respect resulted in part because of reasons of self-interest—the banker must be paid; trade must flourish—but also because of the technocratic expertise and effectiveness of the bureaucrats and diplomats of China's Ministry of Foreign Affairs. From 1912 until 1949, when the Communists replaced the Republican diplomats, China was able to hold on to virtually all of its Qing legacy (only Outer Mongolia was lost). Given China's extraordinarily weak international position in these years, this was a signal accomplishment.

In these aspects of Republican administration—finance and diplomacy—both subbureaucracies provided a career open to talent that was protected from the corrupting influences of family and money. The Chinese government could work. But more often it did not.

Government administration also includes provinces and localities. Yuan Shikai's efforts to recentralize power, and privilege the civilian over the military, would not be realized until the People's Republic of China was established in 1949. This reintegration, however, was made possible by a continuing integration at the provincial level. Because warlords numbered in the hundreds, this integration was not absolute, but some of China's provinces were well administered in the warlord era. Perhaps the best example was Shanxi, the landlocked, coal-rich province in North China ruled over almost continuously from 1912 to 1949 by Yan Xishan (1883–1960). Yan, a Shanxi native from a declining merchant family who bet on the military as a career for the ambitious, had trained in Japan, joined Sun Yat-sen's Revolutionary Alliance, fought against the Qing in 1911, became sole ruler of the province in 1917, and was quite troubled by the ascendancy of Sun's political heir Chiang Kai-shek in 1925 to 1926. Although Yan challenged Chiang in 1930 and lost, his reputation as a reformer and modernizer never dimmed. By dint of will, location, and luck he was able to maintain significant provincial autonomy. Yan's reform programs, which included economic and industrial aspects, also included an attempt to make Shanxi's villages more responsive to the provincial government. His social and education programs sought to reach the local level through a reformed village administration inaugurated in 1917. The Shanxi model was championed by Chiang Kai-shek in September 1928 in the national government's County Organization Law (Xian zuzhi fa).

THE ROAD TO NANJING, 1925–1927

Yan Xishan's relationship with Chiang Kai-shek is instructive. Although conventional histories mark the end of the warlord era with Chiang Kai-shek's rise to power in 1927 to 1928 and the establishment of a new Republican capital in Nanjing in 1927, it is well to consider that this was at the outset simply another regional regime headed by a military man. Focusing on government administration helps one to better understand this important transition, which began in 1925, the year of Sun Yat-sen's death.

Chiang Kai-shek was not content to ignore Beijing; he wanted to reunify China. From his base in Sun's home province of Guangdong Chiang Kai-shek trained thousands of military officers at the Whampoa Military Academy (Huangpu junxiao) outside Guangzhou. In addition to the relatively technical curriculum that had been studied by his adversaries in the north, many of whom had been trained by Yuan Shikai's patron Li Hongzhang in his Tianjin Military Academy (Wubei xuetang; founded 1885) or, like Chiang himself, in one of the the military schools established by Yuan Shikai in the old provincial capital of Baoding in the post-Boxer era, Chiang followed the advice of his Communist International advisers and indoctrinated his students with a strongly political and nationalistic rhetoric. He was training the National Revolutionary Army. Informed by Sun Yat-sen's Three Principles of the People—nationalism, democracy, and the people's livelihood—Chiang Kai-shek was trying to "partify" (*danghua*) the army. If he succeeded in fulfilling Sun's dream for a northern expedition that would defeat Beijing and unify China, he could then "partify" the government. Especially at the upper reaches of party, army, and state, one person wearing three hats would be able to bring unity, and party directives, to government administration.

Chiang Kai-shek's antiwarlord and anti-imperialist stance defined his enemies: most of China. But he had an important set of allies in the members of the CCP who had agreed in 1923 to make common cause with Sun's Nationalist Party. Sun's part of this Comintern-brokered deal was to reorganize the Nationalist Party, which he did in 1924, in accord with Leninist principles. Like Sun's Nationalists, the CCP was influenced by a Leninist model of a tightly organized party characterized by "democratic centralism" in decision making. The "partifying" of army and state was a Communist goal as well. Indeed, the CCP member Zhou Enlai was the head of the political bureau at the Whampoa Military Academy, and skills he learned in Guangdong would be useful later for the CCP.

The other element of the "party-army-state" that was being developed in the mid-1920s, an element that helps one better understand the outreach functions of government administration in the Republican period, had to do with propaganda. The two revolutionary parties—Nationalist and Communist—experimented throughout this period with mechanisms to reach and mobilize the people. From training schools for activists to boycotts, publications, strikes, and canvassing, the parties tried to reach the people. Although this was not unusual in China—one thinks of the moralistic and prescriptive maxims of the Sacred Edict (Sheng yu; 1670) that were to be read aloud in every village and town in imperial times—the parties also were trying to persuade the people and embolden them to act.

With a trained officer corps, arms supplies, and propaganda Chiang was ready in 1926 to launch Sun's long-awaited Northern Expedition. Shanghai fell in April 1927, and the campaign reached Beijing, with Yan Xishan taking over the city at Chiang's request, in June 1928. By that time Chiang had turned on his Communist allies, declared the social revolution over, and turned to the hard work of governing.

CHIANG KAI-SHEK'S NANJING DECADE, 1927–1937

Seventeen years after the 1911 revolution had broken out in Wuhan a new phase of the Republican area was celebrated with fanfare and a formal ceremony on October 10, 1928, in Nanjing. Eighteen months after Nanjing was first declared the national capital, Chiang now controlled the party, the government, and the military. He presided over a Sun-style central administration, with two Chinese-style functions—examination and control (government supervision)—added to the Western-style executive, legislative, and judicial branches. Beginning with his control of Jiangsu, Anhui, and his native Zhejiang at the outset, Chiang patiently extended his span of control. Most of the warlords had signed on to the new regime, but they also were waiting to see just how much power Chiang had. The northern governors Yan Xishan and Feng Yuxiang (1882–1928) challenged Chiang in 1930, and lost a short civil war in which casualties on both sides numbered 250,000. Others fell or capitulated as Chiang strengthened his grip. But it was an administrative grip that did not encompass all of China's provinces or villages. In the early years of his rule Chiang could not get his hands on the land tax, and had to rely instead on the customs and salt taxes (in the 1930s the latter provided 20–25% of the total income) as well as his dominance of Shanghai's banking community, which floated the loans he needed to finance government operations.

Two events in 1931 compromised Chiang's gains. In Manchuria the Japanese took over these three resource-rich provinces and, in the following year, installed the last Qing emperor as head of the puppet state of Manchukuo. The energetic and effective work of Chiang's diplomatic corps contributed to the international community's nonrecognition of this puppet state at its inception, but nonrecognition could not assuage the devastating economic blow caused by Japan's cutting off the strong interregional trade between Manchuria and the rest of China, especially the lower Yangzi provinces. The loss of Manchuria joined the virtual loss of Tibet, Xinjiang, and Outer Mongolia that dated to 1911 to 1912. The second loss of 1931 occurred in November, when the national leaders of the Communist insurgency in Jiangxi Province, just up the Yangzi River from Nanjing, declared the county seat of Ruijin, in southern Jiangxi, the national capital of the Chinese Soviet Republic (Zhonghua suwei'ai gongheguo).

COMMUNIST COUNTERPOINT: THE JIANGXI SOVIET, 1931–1934

Chiang's capitulation in Manchuria was influenced in part by his calculation that the Communist insurgency in Jiangxi was a more important and immediate threat. Chiang spent much time in Jiangxi managing these anti-Communist campaigns, the first of which had begun in 1930. After encirclement-and-blockade tactics suggested by German military advisers were implemented, Chiang's Communist foes finally fled in October 1934 in a retreat to the west that ended in the northwestern province of Shaanxi.

Like Chiang Kai-shek, the CCP was experimenting with different approaches to government administration. At its height, the Jiangxi Soviet administered a population of about three million. Like Chiang in Guangdong in 1925, the CCP had realized after their defeats in Jiangxi in 1927 that the party needed an army. That army was formed during fighting in Nanchang, Jiangxi's capital, in 1927, and it continued to grow in the years that followed. Unlike their Nationalist foes, the Communists had continued the social revolution in Jiangxi, often engaging in radical land-reform policies. The CCP's version of the party-army-state would reappear in barren north Shaanxi in late 1935.

CONTENDING PARTY-ARMY-STATES IN REPUBLICAN CHINA, 1945–1949

Both the Communists and the Nationalists sought to co-opt autonomous social groups into quasi-state structures. Students, merchants, women, workers—all were subject to organizational frameworks defined by the state (and by extension, the party). These organizations usually were urban in their focus; China's peasants, as always, were depended upon for food production. Although Chiang's Nationalist regime did not try to wrest control of the land tax from local and provincial authorities, they were concerned, as were the Communists, about rural populations and the agrarian economy. Whereas the CCP worked on economic and social policies in Jiangxi in 1931 to 1934 that could persuade young men to leave their families and villages to fight in the Red Army, Chiang Kai-shek's initial efforts to solve China's agrarian crisis in the late 1920s and early 1930s were required in order to alleviate the economic conditions that had pushed young men into warlord armies as a matter of survival at worst, or of social mobility at best. He sought to eliminate one of the preconditions of warlordism. But by 1937, when Japan and China were at war again, Chiang needed hundreds of thousands of recruits from rural China. Quotas were established for all provinces under Chiang's control, though most recruits came from a handful of provinces: Henan, Hunan, Jiangxi, Guangxi, Shaanxi, and Sichuan. A second United Front established with the CCP in 1937 meant that Chiang, at least nominally, was the wartime national leader of all China not occupied by the Japanese (who added to Manchuria much of North China and the eastern seaboard provinces after 1937).

As in other nations around the world during the 1930s and 1940s, total war mobilization required vast bureaucracies; even liberal democracies were forced to adopt "planned-economy" bureaucratic solutions to resource-allocation questions usually answered by the market. China was no exception, marked by a "hyperexpansion" of its bureaucracy centered in the wartime capital of Chongqing in Sichuan Province beginning in late 1937. Yuan Shikai's efforts in 1915 to 1916 to establish a modern-style examination system for government personnel had come to naught, and the quality of China's bureaucrats was uneven. Many were young, inexperienced, and not up to the challenges of a war mobilization under extraordinarily adverse conditions.

The rival party-army-states that emerged from wartime China after Japan's surrender in August 1945 now faced each other for the final battle. The demands for a constitution and elections that finally would bring the citizens' voice to bear on a government administration essentially co-opted by a party subservient to one man, Chiang Kai-shek, led to the 1946 constitution and elections in 1947 and 1948. But Chiang's bureaucracy, which returned to Nanjing in 1945, was unable to handle the economic challenges of the postwar years. China was not alone in facing this plight, but the deteriorating political and military situation as the country headed back to civil war meant there would be no Marshall Plan for China, even if there was a futile mediating Marshall mission in 1946. Moreover, the Soviet Union was doing all it could to help its Communist ally establish a foothold in Manchuria after Japan's surrender. For its part, the United States was doing all it could to help Chiang return to North China and the eastern seaboard. And in Shanxi Province the "model governor" Yan Xishan was relying on surrendered Japanese troops to defend the capital city of Taiyuan from Communist attacks.

As these examples suggest, government administration from the beginning to the end of the Republican period must always be seen though the lens of internationalization. Moreover, this overview of government administration in Republican China suggests continuities across both the divides of 1912 and 1949. Qing legacies were bequeathed to Yuan Shikai, some of which were still intact in 1949. Likewise, the revolutionary crucible of the 1920s, in which both the Nationalists and the Communists were strongly influenced by the Leninist model of organizing party, army, and state, helps one to discern legacies that cross boundaries that Cold War perspectives would otherwise mark as impenetrable. Underlying all of this was an emerging Chinese nationalism that had brought to power, as surely as it might someday transcend them, the main contenders in Republican China.

SEE ALSO *Chiang Kai-shek (Jiang Jieshi); Propaganda; Salt, 1800–1949; Shaanxi; Shanxi; Treaty Ports; Warlord Era (1916–1928); Yuan Shikai.*

BIBLIOGRAPHY

Fitzgerald, John. *Awakening China: Politics, Culture, and Class in the Nationalist Revolution.* Stanford, CA: Stanford University Press, 1996.

Kirby, William C. The Internationalization of China: Foreign Relations at Home and Abroad in the Republican Era. *China Quarterly* 150 (1997): 433–458.

Qian Duansheng (Ch'ien Tuan-sheng). *The Government and Politics of China, 1912–1949.* Cambridge, MA: Harvard University Press, 1950.

Sheridan, James E. *China in Disintegration: The Republican Era in Chinese History, 1912–1949.* New York: Free Press, 1975.

Strauss, Julia C. The Evolution of Republican Government. *China Quarterly* 150 (1997): 329–351.

Thompson, Roger R. *China's Local Councils in the Age of Constitutional Reform, 1898–1911.* Cambridge, MA: Council on East Asian Studies, Harvard University, 1995.

Thompson, Roger R. The Lessons of Defeat: Transforming the Qing State after the Boxer War. *Modern Asian Studies* 37 (2003): 769–773.

Twitchett, Denis, and John K. Fairbank, eds. *The Cambridge History of China.* Vols. 11–13. Cambridge, U.K.: Cambridge University Press, 1980–1986.

Van de Ven, Hans J. The Military in the Republic. *China Quarterly* 150 (1997): 352–374.

Van de Ven, Hans J. *War and Nationalism in China, 1925–1945.* London and New York: RoutledgeCurzon, 2003.

Roger R. Thompson

GOVERNMENT HISTORICAL PUBLICATIONS

SEE *Archives, Public: Historical Preservation and Government Historical Publications.*

GOVERNMENT-ORGANIZED NONGOVERNMENTAL ORGANIZATION

A government-organized nongovernmental organization (GONGO) seems at first glance to be an oxymoron. How can an organization that defines itself as being nongovernmental be organized by government? Yet being founded by the government does not necessarily mean that the organization is completely subordinate to it, especially if the organization raises an increasing amount of its operating funds from private sources. Nor does it imply that the organization does not carve out increasing autonomy for itself in the course of its development. Conversely, if a self-declared nongovernmental organization was established by private persons but draws significant resources from government, as has been the case with several Scandinavian developmental nongovernmental organizations, is it not in fact a GONGO? The point here is to emphasize the need for care in ascribing fixed features too readily to organizations and the importance of empirical analysis.

After the liberation of China in 1949 and up until the early 1980s, the spaces for autonomous organizing in China were severely limited. The Chinese Communist Party established Leninist-style intermediary organizations that served as transmission belts between the party and different social groups according to the principles of democratic socialism. These mass organizations included the All-China Federation of Trade Unions, the All-China Women's Federation, the Communist Youth League, the China Association for Science and Technology, and the All-China Federation of Returned Overseas Chinese.

These relayed party policy down to the various social groups and transmitted the views of, for example, women, workers, and returned overseas Chinese back up to central party leaders. Mass organizations were an essential part of the socialist architecture binding the party to society. The Communist Party paid the salaries of cadres working in these mass organizations and provided offices and buildings. The GONGOs were key channels through which the party-state mobilized people and through which people participated in public life.

After Deng Xiaoping and his allies rose to power in the late 1970s, the Communist Party embarked upon a gradual process of market reforms. The decollectivization of agriculture, the collapse of the commune system, the diversification of ownership, the relaxation of controls over rural to urban movement, and greater opening up to the global economy all combined to fundamentally change the socioeconomic landscape of China. The pluralization and diversification of socioeconomic interests created new challenges for China's GONGOs. First, the GONGOs began to adapt, though to varying degrees, to the changing needs of their respective client groups. The All-China Federation of Trades Unions, for example, had to address the needs of millions of migrant workers who had poured into the coastal urban cities to work in foreign-invested, export-oriented factories. It also had to deal with the new phenomenon of mass layoffs, which left state workers, once the aristocracy of the working class in China, without hope for stable future employment. Similarly, the All-China Women's Federation could no longer assume that women could be neatly divided into simple categories such as rural women versus urban women or working-class women versus intellectual women. Mass organizations had to adapt their structures, activities, and images.

A second major challenge for GONGOs was the emergence since the mid-1980s of more autonomous types of organizing initiated from below and supported through voluntary activity or by foreign donor agencies. Many of these were business associations (such as the China Entrepreneurs' Association), trades associations, learned societies, professional associations (such as the China Lawyers' Association), and from the mid-1990s onward, social welfare, health, and women's organizations. The development of these more autonomous organizations reached a peak during the prodemocracy movement of 1989, when independent trades unions and students' organizations mushroomed across China. The government clampdown on these organizations in the aftermath of June 4, 1989, put a hold on their further growth. However, as the political situation eased in the early 1990s and especially after the Communist Party agreed to host the U.N. Fourth World Conference on Women, the development of more independent forms of association took off once more. The preparations for this conference spurred the growth of more independent women's organizations. The All-China Women's Federation responded variously to these developments. As leading cadres of the All-China Women's Federation traveled and learned more about women's groups in other countries, they became exposed to different ways of thinking about gender issues and of working with women. In some instances, cadres saw independent women's groups as potential threats; on other occasions, they sought to draw such groups into their activities. By the late 1990s, mass organizations such as the All-China Women's Federation were alternately labeling themselves as mass organizations and as nongovernmental organizations.

In the reform period the Communist Party encouraged government departments to set up nongovernmental organizations for various reasons. First, nongovernmental organizations have enabled the party-state to devolve certain functions to associations and thereby reduce its role in micromanaging the market economy. By encouraging the formation of national industrial associations, for example, the party-state can pass the tasks of regulating and coordinating certain sectoral activities to those associations. Second, provincial governments have sometimes set up nongovernmental organizations as a way of downsizing government departments and providing alternative employment to surplus government personnel. Some government officials are keen to take up such positions because they gain the space to experiment and innovate with fewer restraints. Third, nongovernmental organizations can attract foreign funds for developmental purposes. Finally, nongovernmental organizations can serve as an alternate route for conducting diplomacy (as in the case of China-Taiwan relations) or for promoting bilateral relations (as with the various friendship associations).

GONGOs will continue to be a salient feature of China's associational landscape. As China opens up further to global economic, social, and political influences, the Communist Party is likely to cede further space for people to associate more independently. While the party encourages the development of social-welfare-type nongovernmental organizations providing services, it remains reluctant to allow workers to organize independently or any political groups to form that might threaten its political rule. It is also pushing mass organizations to seek more of their funding for activities from society and business.

SEE ALSO *All-China Women's Federation; Labor: Trade Unions; Three-Self Patriotic Movement.*

BIBLIOGRAPHY

Brook, Timothy, and Michael B. Frolic, eds. *Civil Society in China*. Armonk, NY: M. E. Sharpe, 1997.

Harper, Paul. The Party and the Unions in Communist China. *China Quarterly* 37 (January–March 1969): 84–119.

Howell, Jude. Organizing around Women and Labor in China: Uneasy Shadows, Uncomfortable Alliances. *Communist and Post-Communist Studies* 33 (2000): 355–377.

Howell, Jude. New Directions in Civil Society: Organizing around Marginalized Interests. In *Governance in China*, ed. Jude Howell, pp. 143–171. Lanham, MD: Rowman and Littlefield Publishers, 2004.

Saich, Tony. Negotiating the State: The Development of Social Organizations in China. *China Quarterly* 161 (March 2000): 124–141.

White, Gordon, Jude Howell, and Shang Xiaoyuan. *In Search of Civil Society: Market Reform and Social Change in Contemporary China*. Oxford: Clarendon Press, 1996.

Jude Howell

GRAMOPHONE AND GRAMOPHONE RECORDS

Until the arrival of the "talking machine" in the last decade of the nineteenth century, the only way for the Chinese to hear music was to attend a live performance. The invention of the phonograph (playing wax cylinders) by Thomas Edison (1847–1931) in 1877 and the gramophone (playing flat discs) by Emile Berliner (1851–1929) in 1888 changed this scenario. Edison's National Phonograph Company in West Orange, New Jersey, produced their first phonograph recordings of Cantonese opera as early as 1903. The targeted customers were Chinese immigrants from Guangdong Province who were working as laborers in North America.

That same year, Frederick Gaisberg (1873–1951), a young acoustic engineer representing England's Gramophone Company, traveled to Shanghai and subsequently Hong Kong as part of a two-year "Far East" tour to acquire recordings of the music of India, Japan, China, Malaya, Thailand, and Burma. In a small Shanghai hotel, assisted by a local agency, Moutrie & Company, Gaisberg recorded about three hundred Beijing opera songs, as well as some pieces of *Kunqu* (an operatic form characterized by its elegant and refined style, favored mainly by the educated elite). While in Hong Kong, Gaisberg recorded more than two hundred songs of Cantonese opera. The master recordings of this "native music" were sent back to the pressing plant in Europe (and later India) for processing. The recordings were sold to buyers in the regions where the music was recorded, together with "talking machines" manufactured by the company. In other words, by that era, China had already become incorporated into the global commercial network of the international gramophone enterprises, and modern technology and economic colonialism had changed the musical experiences of the Chinese people, bringing them a new listening culture.

When comparing the gramophone business of China and Japan, Gaisberg remarked that "outside the Treaty Ports, the gramophone never achieved in China the vogue it enjoyed in Japan. Among the Chinese America, the Malay States and Australia, however, there was a large sale of records, proving that it was largely a question of affluence and accessibility" (Gaisberg 1943, p. 52). In its early stage, the consumption of gramophone music was concentrated in China's urban centers—for instance, Shanghai, Tianjin, Xiamen, and Hong Kong. In the same decade, the Gramophone Company of England was joined by Pathé-Frères of France, Beka-Record G.m.b.H of Germany, and the Victor Talking Machine and Columbia Phonograph companies of the United States, which all set up branches in those comparatively Westernized cities, actively exploiting the markets of China's upper and upper-middle class. Heinrich Bumb of the Beka Company noted the rapid expansion of the gramophone business in Hong Kong in the early 1900s: "The Columbia Graphophone Company had just finished its latest recordings—said to be of 1000 titles, for which fees of 5000 dollars had been paid. 'Victor', 'Grammophon' as well as 'Zonophon-Records' and 'Odeon' were represented in the colony" (Bumb 1976, p. 731).

Between the 1910s and the 1920s, Shanghai established its status as the center of the Chinese gramophone industry. Major transnational gramophone companies established their central branches or pressing factories in the metropolis, and successfully promoted the "talking machine" as a leisure commodity for domestic entertainment. When shopping in a modern department store such as Sincere, Wing On, or Sun Sun, a Shanghai citizen would find no difficulty in accessing local operas or Western music played by imported gramophones represented by eye-catching trademarks.

The development of electrical recording and the portable gramophone further popularized the consumption of gramophone records. Through stylish advertisements in pictorials (e.g., the *Young Companion*) and popular magazines, gramophones were positioned as modern equipment that could bring musical performance from the theaters into an individual's home for private consumption, enabling gramophone users to enjoy different styles of Chinese opera without stepping out of their sitting rooms. In the public arena, gramophone music was played along main streets and outside markets, shops, and even brothels in order to attract patrons, constructing unprecedented and distinctive soundscapes in Chinese cities.

In 1931 the Gramophone Company and the Columbia Graphophone Company, which had acquired the French company Pathé-Frères in 1929, merged to form

Members of a female orchestra with traditional Chinese instruments, c. 1920. *In the early twentieth century, residents of Western-influenced urban areas enjoyed the introduction of the gramophone, purchasing substantial quantities of the invention. Consequently, European music companies capitalized on these new listeners, recording Chinese music for distribution not only in the local market, but also for Chinese immigrants overseas.* HULTON ARCHIVE/GETTY IMAGES

Electric and Musical Industries (EMI), after which the EMI brand Pathé-Orient (known in China as Dongfang Baidai) became one of the most influential Chinese record producers. The table of contents of a songbook, *Baidai changci* (Pathé lyrics), published in the mid-1930s, captured the genres and repertoire of gramophone music produced by the company. A majority of its recordings consisted of excerpts of regional opera songs, instrumental music, and musical narratives from a wide range of provinces and counties. These "traditional" musical types contrast with another "modern" category: songs of movie stars and vocal artists. Because of the high royalties demanded by Beijing opera stars, as well as the popularity of the film industry in Shanghai, gramophone companies turned to Chinese movie stars, including Li Minghui, Hu Die, and Xu Lai, to record songs from films. This body of screen music merged with music originally performed by Chinese song-and-dance troupes, bringing about the emergence of a new category of popular song, later known as modern Chinese pop (*shidai qu*).

SEE ALSO *Music, Popular.*

BIBLIOGRAPHY

Bumb, Heinrich. The Great Beka "Expedition," 1905–1906. *Talking Machine Review* 41 (August 1976): 729–733.

Gaisberg, Frederick William. *Music on Record.* London: Hale, 1943.

Gronow, Pekka. The Record Industry Comes to the Orient. *Ethnomusicology* 25, 2 (1981): 251–284.

Jones, Andrew F. *Yellow Music: Media Culture and Colonial Modernity in the Chinese Jazz Age.* Durham, NC: Duke University Press, 2001.

Rong Shicheng (Yung Sai-shing). *Yueyunliusheng: Changpian gongye yu Guangdong quyi* (1903–1953) [Cantonese opera from the gramophone: a cultural history, 1903–1953]. Hong Kong: Institute for the Research of Humanities, Chinese University of Hong Kong, Cosmos Press, 2006.

Steen, Andreas. *Zwischen Unterhaltung und Revolution: Grammophone, Schallplatten und die Anfaenge der Musikindustrie in Shanghai, 1878–1937* [Between entertainment and revolution: Gramophones, records, and the beginning of the music industry in Shanghai, 1878–1937]. Wiesbaden, Germany: Harrassowitz, 2006.

Wong, Isabel K. F. The Incantation of Shanghai: Singing a City into Existence. In *Global Goes Local: Popular Culture in Asia*, ed. Timothy Craig and Richard King, 246–264. Vancouver: University of British Columbia Press, 2002.

Yung Sai-shing (Rong Shicheng)

GRAND CANAL

The Grand Canal served as the Qing dynasty's strategic north-south route for the transport of grain supplies from the grain districts of the lower and middle Yangzi valley to the imperial capital at Beijing. The canal extended from Hangzhou in the southern province of Zhejiang to the capital, a distance of approximately 1,800 kilometer, and its operation depended on state construction and maintenance of large-scale hydraulic engineering works.

Begun during the Sui dynasty (581–618), the Grand Canal under the Qing dynasty followed the general route of the canal during the Yuan dynasty (1279–1368): northward from Huaiyin across the Shandong Massif to the capital near modern Beijing. Throughout the imperial age, the most difficult obstacles to canal transport lay in the North China Plain, which was subject to high levels of flooding silting, and erratic shifts in the lower course of the Yellow River, which caused the river to exit to the sea either north or south of the Shandong Massif. During the Ming and Qing dynasties to 1855, the Yellow River flowed south of the massif, usurping the bed of the Huai River, filling the lake reservoirs (Lakes Hongze, Baima, Baoying, Gaoyou, and Shaobo), and often seeping into the Yangzi via the Grand Canal and into a maze of canals that laced the agricultural lands between the Grand Canal and the East China Sea. Control of floods, silting, and river meanders in the corridor between the Yellow and Yangzi Rivers in northern Jiangsu posed daunting challenges for late imperial canal managers.

THE GRAND CANAL IN THE LATE EMPIRE, 1368–1911

Ming engineers constructed an extensive narrow-diking system along the Yellow River to intensify current velocity to scour silt from the riverbed, and they also built dikes along the eastern perimeter of the lake reservoirs to protect the canal, the main part of which was the stone-faced Gaojia Dike measuring approximately 68 kilometers in length and 9 meters in height. The dikes were linked to the canal head on the south side of the Yellow River by an intricate network of diversion channels that controlled the release of lake water through the canal head to float the grain fleets into the Yellow River and simultaneously scour silt from the canal head.

In the Kangxi (1662–1722) and Yongzheng (1723–1735), the Qing dynasty invested heavily in the Grand Canal system, streamlining its management and linking it to empire-wide grain-storage and distribution networks. The Qing emperors carefully monitored both canal and grain transport operations and centered their management in two bureaucratic agencies: the Grand Canal and the Grain Transport Directorates, each of which had military-labor organizations (*hebiao, caobiao*) to perform canal-transport-related work in the eight-province canal zone.

THE GRAND CANAL CRISIS IN THE NINETEENTH CENTURY

By the early nineteenth century, silt penetration of the entire canal-riverine network in northern Jiangsu seriously undermined the continued operation of the Grand Canal, slowing the yearly grain-shipment cycle and leaving little time or resources for crucial reconstruction tasks. In late 1824, these issues came to a head when floods burst the Gaoyan Dike on Hongze Lake, buried the hydraulic facilities at the junction under a blanket of mud, and brought grain transport to a halt in 1825.

Believing that the accumulated damage to the canal was irreversible, the Daoguang Emperor (1821–1850) and his inner court advisers, led by Yinghe (1771–1839), began an empire-wide debate on canal reconstruction and alternative methods of grain transport. The debate raged from March to early September 1825, when the Daoguang Emperor ordered the trial use of sea transport in 1826 and placed Qishan (d. 1854), governor-general of Liangjiang, in charge of efforts to reconfigure the southern canal head at the entrance to the Yellow River. These decisions led to two important innovations: First, the construction of a pound lock on the southern canal head to "impound" inflows of silted water from the Yellow River in order to cross the government grain fleets (a change designed to replace the Hongze strategy that had been used since the late Ming period); and second, the introduction of sea transport as an alternative to canal transport during periods of canal dysfunction.

Reconstruction of the Grand Canal in 1825–1826 brought a measure of stability to canal operations until the Yellow River changed course in the early 1850s, destroying the canal and bringing grain transport on the canal to an end. Although the canal was not rebuilt during the troubled years of the late nineteenth century, government grain transport was not abandoned. The

Qing leadership crafted a three-way collaboration with Chinese and foreign merchant shippers to transport government tax grain to Tianjin by sail and steam, guided by the precedents established in the 1826 sea transport plan. The China Merchants' Steam Navigation Company, which played a prominent role in these grain shipments, represents a continuation of the pattern of state-private collaboration in grain transport, as well as an initial step in the development of modern Chinese business organizations.

CANAL RESTORATION IN THE TWENTIETH CENTURY

After years of political upheaval in the first half of the twentieth century, the newly established People's Republic of China initiated the construction of large, multipurpose hydraulic-engineering projects on the rivers that flowed through the canal zone, such as the Huai, Yellow, Yangzi, Qiantang, and Yongding Rivers. An integral part of the First Five-Year Plan (1953–1957), these projects centered on flood control, irrigation, local shipping, and

SEA TRANSPORT EXPERIMENT, 1826

The sea transport plan was a state-private collaboration in which private Shanghai merchant shippers successfully transported 1.6 million *shi* (4.7 million U.S. bushels) of tax grain collected from the Jiangnan grain districts of Susongchangzhentai (Suzhou, Songjiang, Changzhou, Zhenjiang, Taicang) from Shanghai to Tianjin. Qishan, the Manchu governor-general of Liangjiang, supervised the implementation of the plan, and Tao Zhu and He Changling, the governor and treasurer of Jiangsu Province respectively, negotiated the "recruitment" (*zhaoshang*) agreement with the Shanghai Merchant Shipping Guild (Shangchuan Huiguan), an agreement that resulted in the hire of 1,500 sand junks to carry the grain in two shipments during the spring and summer of 1826. This was the first use of sea transport during the Qing dynasty (1644–1912), and the first time that a private, nongovernmental organization was enlisted to ship strategic grain to the capital. It represents a significant expansion of the Qing use of state-private collaborations that had been used to manage trade and port cities in the four southeastern coastal provinces.

BIBLIOGRAPHY

Leonard, Jane Kate. Negotiating across the Boundaries of State Power: Organizing the 1826 Sea Transport Experiment. In *Dragons, Tigers, and Dogs. Qing Crisis Management and the Bonds of Civil Community, 1644–1911*, ed. Robert J. Antony and Jane Kate Leonard, 183–211. Ithaca NY: East Asia Program, Cornell University, 2002.

Leonard, Jane Kate. Coastal Merchant Allies in the 1826 Sea Transport Experiment. In *Maritime China in Transition, 1750–1850*, ed. Wang Gungwu and Ngu Chin-keong, 271–286. Wiesbaden, Germany: Harrassowitz Verlag, 2004.

Li Wenzhi. Qing Daoguanghou gaige caozhiyi (Late Qing Daoguang reforms in the grain system). *Zhongguo jingjishi yanjiu* 1 (1989): 29–44.

Jane Kate Leonard

hydroelectric power generation and sought to restore the hydraulic infrastructure necessary for economic development. These projects led to the revival of agriculture and local transport in the canal zone near the Huai and Yellow Rivers and the corridor.

Because of the political turmoil associated with the Great Leap Forward and the Cultural Revolution from 1958 to the early 1980s, these projects languished, as did plans to restore navigation along the entire length of the Grand Canal and use it as an artery for the north-south transfer of Yangzi River water to North China. Since 1984 navigation on the canal has been restored between Jining, located south of the Yellow River in Shandong Province, to Hangzhou, the southern terminus of the canal in Zhejiang Province. In this region the canal provides a vital transportation link for commerce and tourism. The northern part of the canal in Hebei Province, however, remains dried up because of acute water shortages caused by industrial and residential overuse of scarce water resources.

SEE ALSO *China Merchants' Steam Navigation Company; Irrigation and Management of Water Resources; River Systems: Yellow River.*

BIBLIOGRAPHY

Chan, Wellington K. K. Government, Merchants, and Industry to 1911. In *The Cambridge History of China*, vol. 10, pt. 2: *1800–1911*, ed. John K. Fairbank and Kwang-ching Liu, 416–462. Cambridge: Cambridge University Press, 1968.

Economy, Elizabeth C. *The River Runs Black: The Environmental Challenge to China's Future*. Ithaca, NY: Cornell University Press, 2004.

Hummel, Arthur W., ed. *Eminent Chinese of the Ch'ing Period, 1644–1912*. 2 vols. Washington, DC: U.S. Government Printing Office, 1943–1944.

Lai Chi-kong. The Qing State and Merchant Enterprise: The China Merchants' Company, 1872–1902. In *To Achieve Security and Wealth: The Qing Imperial State and Economy, 1644–1911*, ed. Jane Kate Leonard and John R. Watt. Ithaca, NY: East Asia Program, Cornell University, 1992.

Leonard, Jane Kate. *Controlling from Afar: The Daoguang Emperor's Management of the Grand Canal Crisis, 1824–1826*. Ann Arbor: Center for Chinese Studies, University of Michigan, 1996.

Leonard, Jane Kate. Coastal Merchant Allies in the 1826 Sea Transport Experiment. In *Maritime China in Transition, 1750–1850*, ed. Wang Gungwu and Ngu Chin-keong, 271–286. Wiesbaden, Germany: Harrassowitz Verlag, 2004.

Leonard, Jane Kate. Negotiating across the Boundaries of State Power: Organizing the 1826 Sea Transport Experiment. In *Dragons, Tigers, and Dogs: Qing Crisis Management and the Bonds of Civil Community, 1644–1911*, ed. Robert J. Antony and Jane Kate Leonard. Ithaca, NY: East Asia Program, Cornell University, 2002.

Li Wenzhi and Jiang Taixin. *Qingdai caoyun* [Tax-grain transport in the Qing period]. Beijing: Zhonghua, 1995.

Nickum, James E. *Water Management Organization in the People's Republic of China*. Armonk, NY: M. E. Sharpe, 1981.

Jane Kate Leonard

GREAT DEPRESSION

China, like many other countries in the world, suffered from the Great Depression starting in October 1929, even if its index of industrial production did not fall as sharply as in the industrialized countries. As the financial crisis spread to many parts of the world after changes in monetary regimes, China could not be immune to its impact. However, because China was virtually the only country on the silver standard in an international monetary system dominated by the gold standard, the external shock to the Chinese economy and China's reactions differed from other countries'. Changes in international silver prices had an impact on China's monetary system and affected both its urban and rural financial markets.

Exchanges between gold-standard countries were based on a fixed par of exchange, which was the ratio of the gold content of the two currencies concerned. In contrast, in exchanges between China and gold-standard countries, there was no fixed par of exchange. Given the price of silver in, for example, London (in terms of shillings per ounce), one would calculate the value of silver per unit of Shanghai silver currency, either tael or yuan, in terms of London gold currency (in terms of shillings per tael or yuan). This was taken as the parity for that particular silver price, and as the price of silver in London varied, the parity varied, but always proportionately. If the exchange rate in Shanghai was quoted above parity drawn from the price of bullion, then the value of silver was higher in Shanghai, encouraging the purchase of silver in London and its sale in Shanghai. If the opposite was true, if the rate was below parity, it was advantageous to purchase silver in Shanghai and sell it in London.

DEPRESSION YEARS, 1929–1935

The world economy fell into an unprecedented slump in October 1929, and most countries suffered from severe depression. China avoided the dire effects of the first two years of the crisis because silver depreciated considerably against gold and other commodities. Because the value of silver was higher in China than in other parts of the world, large amounts of silver flooded into China. The urban economy, particularly the Shanghai financial market, flourished, but the rural areas could not escape the downturn in agricultural prices caused by the worldwide slump of the market.

Beginning in September 1931, many governments abandoned the gold standard and devalued their currencies in an attempt to inflate their economies. When Great Britain first left the gold standard, the price of silver in terms of the British pound sterling rose, and the Chinese exchange rate began to improve. In Shanghai, the exchange rates for countries in the sterling bloc rose in accordance with the depreciation of the pound sterling. One country after another—India, the Straits Settlements and the Malay States, Japan, and so on—depreciated their currencies. In March 1933 the United States terminated its gold standard monetary system.

The appreciation of China's silver currency had a profound impact on the country's economy in terms of import and export prices and the current of international trade. Deprived of the benefits of a low exchange rate, Chinese textile industries faced keener competition from their foreign counterparts. The Chinese silk-reeling industry, one of the nation's most important exporters, competed with Japan's silk in the world market, particularly in the United States. Facing severe price cuts, in 1933 China's exports decreased by 45 percent, which was 88 percent less than in 1930 in terms of value and 71 percent less in terms of volume, whereas Japan increased its exports to both Europe and the United States during the same period. Overall, although the value of imports also decreased, the shrinkage in exports was out of proportion to it: The ratio of the value of exports to imports dropped from 63.4 percent in 1931 to 47 percent in 1932, and to 45.5 percent in 1933 (Shiroyama 2008, p. 149).

China's trade deficit was not unusual, but until 1931, the invisible trade in investments from abroad and remittances from Chinese living overseas had countered the trade deficit. In a world depression with an appreciating currency, though, the amount of invisible trade was clearly diminishing. In order to make up for deficiencies in its international trade balance, China was forced to export silver. For the first time since 1918, China recorded net exports of silver, valued at 7,346,000 yuan in 1932. Following the slump in import and export prices and reflecting the deflationary consequences of the appreciating silver exchange rate, Chinese wholesale prices seriously declined at the end of 1931. The average annual percentage change in wholesale prices for the six principal cities in China was about –5 percent in 1932; Shanghai saw a drop of –11.3 percent (Shiroyama 2008, p. 150).

The United States' suspension of the gold standard in March 1933 had a decisive impact on China's exchange rate for dollars. China's trade deficit was at its largest ever, 733,739,000 yuan, and the Chinese economy continued to worsen. The movement of treasure resulted in a net export of $189.4 million in gold and $14.2 million in silver. Wholesale prices continued to fall—9.4 percent, on average, in the six largest cities, and 7.7 percent in Shanghai (Shiroyama 2008, p. 150).

It was the U.S. Silver Purchase Act, approved in June 1934, that fatally destabilized the Chinese silver-standard monetary system. The United States was one of the world's major producers of silver, and as the price of silver declined considerably after 1930, the American Silver

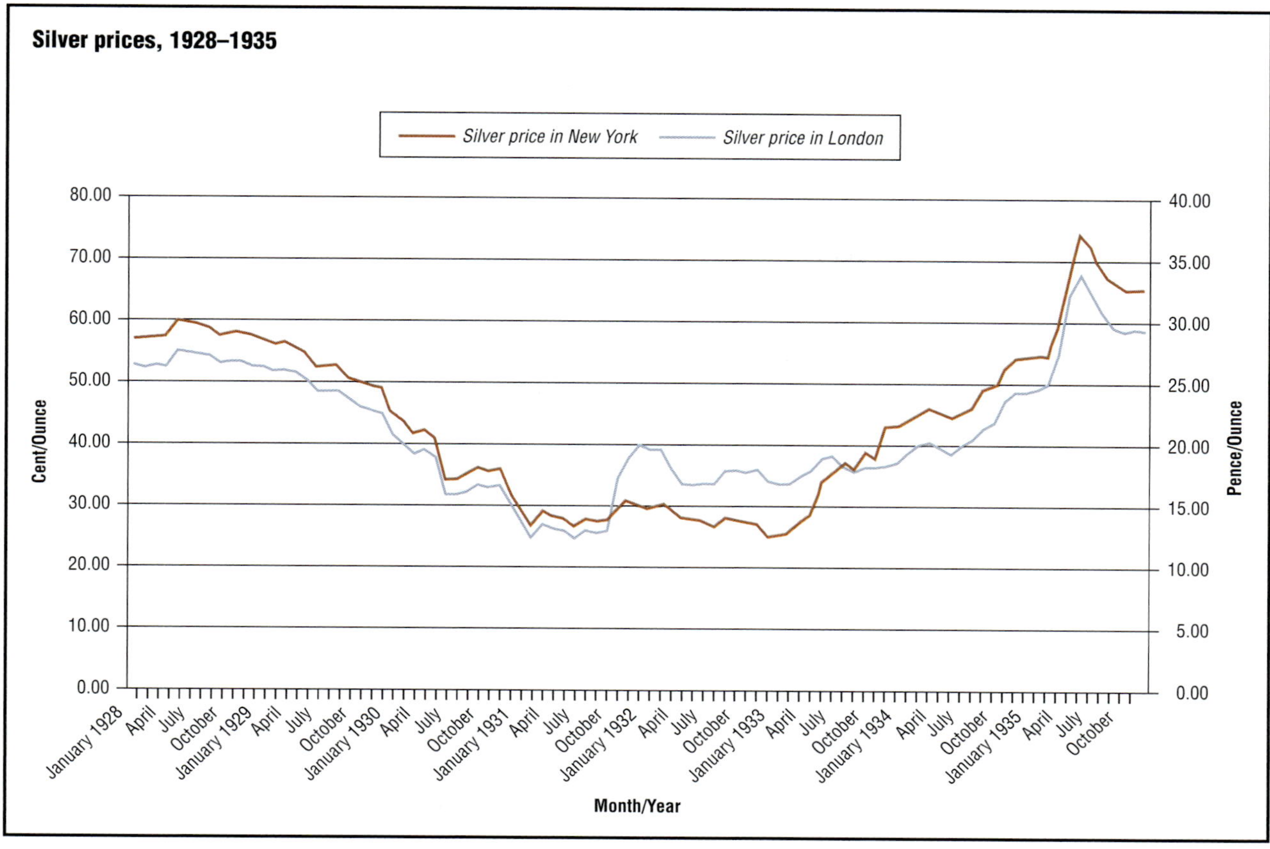

Figure 1

Producers' Association and senators from silver-producing states looked to the government for subsidies. Under the Silver Purchase Act, the United States increased its stock of silver, aiming to make it one-quarter of its total monetary stocks. No silver was to be purchased at a price greater the monetary value, $1.29 per ounce, nor was any domestic silver to be purchased at over 50 cents per ounce.

Although the U.S. Silver Purchase Act was not meant to target China, the sudden and massive rise in the international price of silver caused by the U.S. purchases upset the silver-standard Chinese economy. In the first half of 1934 Chinese silver imports and exports had been minimal, but in June, 12,936 yuan worth of silver was exported (compared to 14,122 yuan in the whole of 1933). The outward movement of silver became even more conspicuous thereafter, rising to 24,308 yuan in July 1934, 79,094 yuan in August, and 48,140 yuan in September (Shiroyama 2008, pp. 156–157).

Although they were alarmed by the massive outflow of silver, the Nationalist government could not take immediate and effective action against it. Large exports increased fears that the government would have to depreciate the Chinese currency and further increase silver exports before it was too late. Finally, on October 14, 1934, the minister of finance, Kong Xiangxi (1881–1967), announced a silver export duty of 10 percent (less 2.25% in the case of silver dollars and minted bars, which already had paid the amount in seigniorage) together with an equalization charge. Soon after the announcement of the equalization charge, the exchange rate fell by more than 10 percent in a few days. Thereafter, it fluctuated around 19 percent below parity with New York silver prices. The imposition of duty and equalization charges caused official silver exports to fall off sharply, from 57 million yuan in October to around 12 million yuan per month in November and December (Shiroyama 2008, p. 159). Beginning in 1935, official silver exports practically ceased, but the amount of silver smuggled out of China was estimated to be as great as the amount legally exported in 1934. As long as the price of silver in China was significantly higher than the price of silver abroad, it remained profitable to export silver.

The silver drain ushered in a struggle for liquidity. Falling prices further curtailed credit, which in turn put more pressure on business enterprises. Under this deflationary cycle, Shanghai wholesale prices gradually declined from February to September 1935, when they were 6.4 percent below the level of the previous September. However, the downward movement suddenly reversed in October. Uncertainty about the future of the Chinese economy, particularly the recurrent rumors that the government would devalue the yuan, spurred people to change their cash into foreign exchange or commodities. At the end of October 1935 the Chinese currency was overwhelmed by market fears.

CURRENCY REFORM AND RECOVERY

In order to shield the economy from the negative effects of fluctuations in the international price of silver, on November 4, 1935, the Nationalist government implemented currency reform, declaring that only notes issued by the three government banks were legal tender. At the same time, the Chinese yuan ceased to be backed by silver; instead, it could be changed into British pounds and U.S. dollars at fixed rates. Silver, which for centuries had been the country's basis of currency, had to be surrendered, and the multicurrency system was relinquished. With the Chinese yuan no longer pegged to silver, and devalued in relation to foreign currencies, Chinese trade revived and the trend of commodity prices reversed upward.

SEE ALSO *Financial Regulation; Money and Monetary Policy, 1800–1927.*

BIBLIOGRAPHY

Shiroyama, Tomoko. *China during the Great Depression: Market, State, and the World Economy, 1929–1937.* Cambridge, MA: Harvard University Asia Center, 2008.

Wright, Tim. Coping with the World Depression: The Nationalist Government's Relations with Chinese Industry and Commerce, 1932–1936. *Modern Asian Studies* 25, 4 (October 1991): 649–674.

Wright, Tim. Distant Thunder: The Regional Economies of Southwest China and the Impact of the Great Depression. *Modern Asian Studies* 34, 3 (July 2000): 697–738.

Tomoko Shiroyama

GU HUA
1942–

Gu Hua (formerly known as Luo Hongyu) was born in the county of Jiahe in southern Hunan. He began his literary career in the early 1960s, when he was working as a trained technician in the countryside. Almost all of his writings are about rural life in the mountainous area of southern Hunan, with which he is familiar. In 1981 he received national recognition for his short story "Pa man qingteng de muwu" (The ivy-covered wooden hut). Earlier in the same year he published his best-known novel *Furong zhen* (*A Small Town Called Hibiscus*), for which he was awarded the inaugural Mao Dun Literary Prize in 1982. His work also includes a number of novels, novellas, short stories, and essays. In 1988 he emigrated to Canada and has since kept a low profile on the literary scene in China.

Upon its publication in the leading journal *Dangdai* (Contemporary times) in 1981, *Furong zhen* was appreciated, both in the literary field and by the reading public, for its incisive and humanistic representation of the Cultural Revolution era (1966–1976). It was regarded as an outstanding example of the then popular "reflection literature" (*fansi wenxue*), whose critical thrust was to expose and reflect on the devastating consequences of the highly politicized life of the preceding decades. Reflection literature, together with the protesting "literature of the wounded" (*shanghen wenxue*) from roughly the same period, served the historical function of calling for and legitimating social and economic reforms in the wake of the Cultural Revolution.

What Gu Hua presents in *Furong zhen* is a deeply sympathetic and melodramatic historical narrative about life in a small town from 1963 to 1979, a period dominated by intense political mobilizations and reversals in government policies, which in turn translate into personal sufferings and tragedies. Each of the four chapters focuses on a select historical moment, and each of the seven sections within a chapter follows one of the central characters.

At the center of this allegorical novel is Hu Yuyin, the attractive owner of a food stall that sells rice-based tofu, a local specialty and delicacy. The novel opens with an extended ethnographical account of the mountainous landscape in southern Hunan, its people, and their time-honored customs, reminiscent of narratives by Shen Congwen. Hu Yuyin is introduced as a married woman in her mid-twenties and a reasonably prosperous small business owner. Yet during the course of the novel, her husband commits suicide under political pressure, while she is denounced for being a capitalist entrepreneur, loses all her property, falls in love with and secretly marries a similarly disgraced intellectual, and sees her second husband arrested and imprisoned. Yet she persists against all odds and eventually welcomes her husband back when the Cultural Revolution is finally repudiated. The ending is a happy one, as the underlying message of the novel is an endorsement of the new order, which is naturalized as a return of things to their former state.

Even though she may be a protagonist, Hu Yuyin does not function as the central consciousness or even determining perspective of the novel. Each of the characters around the young woman represents a social type or agency and is vested with rich sociopolitical references. For example, Qin Shutian, Hu Yuyin's second husband, embodies wisdom and knowledge, and their union brings together the local and the cosmopolitan, nature and culture, vitality and faith. Gu Yanshan, a father figure to the heroine and witness to the love between her and Qin Shutian, represents the Communist Party as a liberating force compromised by the aberrations of the Cultural Revolution. Equally deliberate is the creation of Li Guoxiang, a spinster who zealously persecutes Hu Yuyin and Qin Shutian and whose politics are explicitly attributed to her sexual frustrations.

The broad appeal of *Furong zhen* as a tragicomedy owes much to its adroit weaving of political arguments and historical experiences into a moral melodrama and libidinal economy. Its readability also comes from a narrative voice evocative of traditional fiction, a regional sensibility, and entrenched value judgments.

In 1986 the director Xie Jin adapted the novel into a widely successful film with the same title, starring Liu Xiaoqing and Jiang Wen.

BIBLIOGRAPHY

Gu Hua. *Furong zhen* [A small town called Hibiscus]. Beijing: Renmin Wenxue Chubanshe, 1981.

Gu Hua. *A Small Town Called Hibiscus*. Trans. Gladys Yang. Beijing: Chinese Literature Press, 1983.

Hunan Renmin Chubanshe, ed. *"Furong zhen" pinglun xuanji* [Selected reviews of *A Small Town Called Hibiscus*]. Changsha: Hunan Renmin Chubanshe, 1984.

Xiaobing Tang

GU WENDA

1955–

One of the seminal figures in the development of experimental art in China in the 1980s, Gu Wenda has committed his artistic career to challenging cultural conventions in pursuit of a utopian vision of cross-border communication and understanding. Born in 1955, Gu graduated from the Shanghai College of Arts and Crafts in 1976 and later attended the Zhejiang Academy of Fine Arts (ZAFA), now called the China National Art Academy, where he received a master's degree in 1981 and continued to teach until 1987. At ZAFA, Gu studied traditional Chinese landscape painting under the renowned ink painter Lu Yanshao (1909–1990).

Gu's training in traditional ink and brush technique continues to resonate in his work. However, rather than emulate his teacher's signature works with their zigzagging compositions and agitated brushwork, Gu's early landscape painting reveals an affinity for the rolling hills, sinuous contours, and patches of saturated ink that typified the late work of the seventeenth-century individualist artist Shitao. But Gu's artistic practice did not stay traditional-looking for long. Taking full and energetic advantage of the relatively liberal atmosphere at ZAFA, which in the 1980s had an unusually well-stocked and growing library of books about Western art and theory, Gu read voraciously, from Sigmund Freud (1856–1939) and Ludwig Wittgenstein (1889–1951) to books on Chan Buddhism, and began to experiment boldly. Unlike his colleagues who rejected traditional media in favor of imported Western modes of expression, Gu has remained determinedly independent and waged his revolution, at least initially, in ink and brush on paper. Challenging ancient conventions as inviolate as calligraphy and the written word, Gu created in the mid-1980s a powerful series of enigmatic compositions that combined, by turns, cryptic phrases, invented characters, and erotic elements that were often crossed out or distorted. Typical of these inventions is the centerpiece of a loosely organized multi-part series, called Contemplation of the World, in which a pseudo character hovers mysteriously in a gloomy sky over a rock-strewn riverbed.

Gu's groundbreaking work continued during his association with the Institute Art Tapestry Varbanov (IATV). With resources provided by IATV, which was founded by the Bulgarian tapestry artist Maryn Varbanov (1932–1989) as a joint venture between ZAFA and a local carpet factory, Gu embarked on experiments in textile design, complex installation formats, and performance. These experiments culminated in the production of a massive multimedia triptych called *Inspiration Comes from Tranquility*. One of the most sophisticated and certainly ambitious experimental artworks created in the 1980s, this piece met wide acclaim and was exhibited in 1987 at the thirteenth Lausanne Tapestry Biennale.

In 1987 Gu moved to the United States, eventually settling in New York, where he continues to test the limits of cultural norms. And just as his experiments elicited criticism and acclaim inside China, his use of alternative media, including bodily substances such as menstrual blood, powdered placenta, and human hair, has provoked wide debate and even censure. Particularly sensitive was an early realization of his multiyear United Nations project in 1992 in Łódź, Poland, which was quickly closed down when his use of human hair evoked harrowing memories of the Holocaust among local residents. Testifying to the importance of cultural and institutional context, however, is the varied response to Gu's series called the *Enigma of Blood*. Raising religious and feminist hackles in 1990 when it was shown in San Francisco under the name of *2000 Unnatural Deaths*, this site-specific installation of a series of used tampons placed delicately on rows of plump white pillows barely raised eyebrows in Hong Kong in 1993 where it was overshadowed by the enthusiastic media response to colorful oil paintings in a style that has become known as political pop.

As a global artist with studios in Shanghai and Beijing, in addition to New York, Gu has made a historic contribution to the development of contemporary art in China through his innovative engagement with the millennium-old tradition of ink painting. In more recent years, Gu has continued to pursue his utopian goal of cultural synthesis and exchange, producing challenging large-scale works of which the long-term multilocation United Nations and Forest of Stone Steles projects are notable examples.

SEE ALSO *Calligraphy; New Wave Movement, '85; Political Pop and Cynical Realism; Textiles.*

BIBLIOGRAPHY

Bessire, Mark H. C., ed. *Wenda Gu: Art from Middle Kingdom to Biological Millennium.* Cambridge, MA: MIT Press, 2003.

Erickson, Britta. Wenda Gu's Silent Selves and Pseudo-Characters. *Art Asia Pacific* 26 (2000): 78–83.

Jaivin, Linda. Gu Wenda Goes West: Tao and the Art of Aesthetic Line Maintenance. *Art and Asia Pacific* 1, 2 (1994): 42–47.

Lutfy, Carol. Brush with the Past. *ARTnews* 99, 8 (2000): 140–143.

Refound Oedipus Complex: Wenda Gu (catalog). Milan: Enrico Gariboldi Arte Contemporanea, 1992.

Wenda Gu: The Mythos of Lost Dynasties, 1984–1997 (catalog). Hong Kong: Hanart TZ Gallery, 1997.

Wu Hung. Monumentality and Anti-monumentality in Gu Wenda's Forest of Stone Steles: A Retranslation and Rewriting of Tang Poetry. *Yishu: Journal of Chinese Contemporary Art* 4, 4 (2005): 51–58.

Jane DeBevoise

GUANGDONG

Guangdong, bordering on the South China Sea, is, except for Hainan, China's southernmost province. It is bounded on the north by the Nanling (the "southern range"), which separates the vast Yangzi (Chang) River Valley of central China from the West (Xi) River Basin of South China. Another set of mountains athwart the West River divides Guangdong from its upstream neighbor, Guangxi Province.

Within the province, the West River and its tributaries are the most significant topographical features. Beginning in the Yunnan-Guizhou Plateau and entering Guangdong below Wuzhou, the West River flows eastward to Sanshui, where it meets the North (Bei) River, descending from the Nanling, and together they flow out to the South China Sea through the large and intricate Pearl (Zhu) River Delta. The East (Dong) River, coming down in a southwesterly direction from Jiangxi Province, reaches the sea though the same delta.

Until recently, Guangdong occupied about 220,000 square kilometers (85,000 square miles) of territory. However, in 1965 the coastal lowlands next to Vietnam were assigned to Guangxi to give the latter province direct access to the sea, and in 1988 Hainan Island was detached and made a separate province. In addition, when the two foreign colonies previously carved out from the province, Portuguese Macau and British Hong Kong, were in the late 1990s returned to Chinese sovereignty, they were not placed under Guangdong's jurisdiction; each became instead a "special administrative region." As a result, the province has been reduced in size to about 178,000 square kilometers (69,000 square miles).

The core of this region is the Pearl River Delta and the adjacent West and East River areas. This is the largest expanse of level land and is economically the most developed part of Guangdong; its major urban center is Guangzhou (Canton). Surrounding this core within the province are three peripheral subregions, of which the most important is Eastern Guangdong, as defined by the Han River and its upstream tributary, the Mei River, and whose most important city is Shantou (Swatow) at the mouth of the Han River. The other two peripheral subregions in the province are Northern Guangdong, which is drained by the North River, and Southwestern Guangdong, which consists of the Leizhou Peninsula and the coastal lowlands to the east and west of the peninsula. The major urban centers of these two subregions are, respectively,

GUANGDONG

Capital city: Guangzhou
Largest cities (population): Guangzhou (7,610,000 [2006]), Shenzhen (1,970,000 [2006])
Area: 178,000 sq. km. (69,000 sq. mi.)
Population: 93,040,000 (2006)
Demographics: Han, 98%; Zhuang, Yao, Miao, and others, 2%
GDP: CNY 2,620 billion (2006)
Famous sites: Yuexiu Hill and Shamian Island in Guangzhou, Star Lake and the Seven Star Crags, Dinghu Mountain, the "diaolou" towers of Kaiping County

Shaoguan on the North River and Zhanjiang at the base of the Leizhou Peninsula.

THE PEOPLES

The population of Guangdong at the end of 2006 was about ninety-three million, three times what it was in mid-Qing, two centuries earlier. Ninety-eight percent or more of the population of the province are of the Han nationality; the remaining 2 percent belong to minority nationalities in the mountains of southern Hainan Island; the Zhuang, near the Guangxi border; and the Yao and the Miao, in Northern Guangdong. The Han majority are themselves divided among three distinct speech groups or subethnicities: the Cantonese, the Teochiu (Chaozhou), and the Hakka. Each of the groups speaks a language (often misleadingly called a dialect) that is unintelligible to the others, as it is to speakers of Mandarin (*putonghua*), the official national language. The Cantonese, the largest by far of the three speech groups, are concentrated in the Pearl River Delta of Central Guangdong, but they are found as well throughout the province, particularly in urban centers. The Teochiu live mostly in the coastal area of Eastern Guangdong, adjacent to southern Fujian, whose native language resembles Teochiu. The Hakka live mostly along the Mei River and the East River in Eastern and Central Guangdong, respectively.

Relations among these subethnicities of the Han have often been strained. Those between the Cantonese and the Hakka were particularly contentious. The Taiping Uprising (1851–1864) spawned a thirteen-year communal war (1854–1867) between the Cantonese and the Hakka on the edge of the Pearl River Delta; the war only ended when a separate Hakka subprefecture (*ting*), Chixi, was carved out of Xinning (now Taishan), a predominantly Cantonese county. The rivalry between the Hakka and the Teochiu was no less intense, especially for dominance in their native Eastern Guangdong. For example, Hakkas played a leading role in the Republican revolutionary movement in the region, but when the revolution succeeded in 1911 and the triumphant

Hakkas tried to impose their authority over Shantou, Teochiu merchants strenuously resisted.

Due to Guangdong's location on China's southeast coast, the province was, along with neighboring Fujian, the ancestral home to most of the Chinese who went abroad in the nineteenth and early twentieth century. As many as two-thirds of all "overseas Chinese" (*huaqiao*) were natives of Guangdong. Subject to the push of poverty at home and the pull of labor demands abroad, the emigrants came from all three of Guangdong's major subethnic groups, with members of each group tending to go to different parts of the world. Thus, the Cantonese were apt to go to North and South America, Hawaii, and Australia; the Teochiu to Thailand and Singapore; and the Hakka to Java. As most emigrants went abroad not as permanent settlers but as temporary sojourners, they maintained close ties to their home communities. Typically men went without their wives or children and intended to return when they had earned enough to improve their family's economic well-being. The remittances they sent home were a significant source of income for their families and their villages, and they themselves, when they came home, were important agents of social and cultural change.

In more recent times, particularly since the adoption by the Communists in 1978 of the policy of "reform and opening out" (*gaige kaifang*), Guangdong, in addition to being a source of out-migration, has also become a magnet for in-migration. With travel and residency restrictions eased throughout China in the post-Mao era, millions of Chinese from poor inland provinces have flocked to Guangdong, particularly to the Pearl River Delta, to meet the labor needs of burgeoning factories and construction sites. As a result, migrants from other provinces now make up more than 15 percent of Guangdong's total population. In many places in Central Guangdong, including Shenzhen, Dongguan, and Foshan, migrants outnumber natives, and Mandarin has replaced Cantonese as the most commonly spoken language.

THE ECONOMY

Up until the 1980s, Guangdong was predominantly an agricultural economy. Much of the province is either mountainous or hilly, and only about 20 percent of the land is cultivable. Nevertheless, the region is blessed with plentiful rainfall and a subtropical climate, where double-cropping is common and, in some places, triple-cropping is possible. The principal grain crop is rice, grown in flooded paddy fields. Cash crops include sugar, fruit, and vegetables. Along the rivers and the coast and in inland ponds, fishing is economically important, as was sericulture—the breeding of silk worms and the production of silk—in the nineteenth century, though no longer. Other traditional handicrafts include ceramics, with Shiwan (Shek Wan) ware, produced near Foshan, particularly in demand throughout South China.

Already in the nineteenth century, the economy of Guangdong was highly commercialized. Before the First Opium War (1839–1842), Guangzhou was the only port in China that was open to maritime trade with the West. However, Guangdong lost its economic prominence when, following the Opium War, other ports were opened to foreign trade and residence, and Guangzhou was eclipsed by Shanghai as China's most cosmopolitan center. Even so, the province was home to several of the "treaty ports" where, in addition to Guangzhou, foreigners were allowed to live and trade—specifically, Shantou in the east and Beihai and Haikou in the southwest—as well as, of course, Hong Kong, which was ceded to Britain in 1842.

Economically, Guangdong fared poorly during the first three decades of Communist rule. Maoist ideology, on the one hand, condemned commerce and consumption, at which the province had excelled, and, on the other hand, favored the development of heavy industry, which Guangdong singularly lacked.

With the change of policies following the death of Mao Zedong and the ascension of Deng Xiaoping in the late 1970s, Guangdong once again came to the forefront of China's economic development. Under the policy of reform and opening out, the province has served as a laboratory where various economic reforms were tried out before they were extended to other places. In 1979 three locales in the province—Shantou in the east and Shenzhen and Zhuhai in the center—were designated "special economic zones," where foreigners and Chinese businesspeople in Hong Kong and Taiwan were enticed by low taxes and cheap wages to establish factories to manufacture low-cost consumer goods like toys and shoes that were destined primarily for export. As a result, much of the Pearl River Delta, as well as the Shantou area in Eastern Guangdong, have become highly industrialized and urbanized. When doubts about the policy arose in the late 1980s, Deng personally made an investigatory visit to Shenzhen in 1992 and expressed satisfaction with the results. Following Deng's southern tour (*nanxun*), what has been called "market socialism" took hold in the rest of the country.

POLITICS

Owing to its distance from the centers of political power (Beijing and Nanjing), as well as its direct exposure to the outside world, Guangdong was, at least in the late nineteenth and early twentieth centuries, the breeding ground of radicals and revolutionaries. It was at his academy, the Wanmu Caotang, in Guangzhou that Kang Youwei in the early 1890s developed and propagated his radical interpretation of Confucianism that formed the ideological basis of the Hundred Days of Reform in 1898. And it was mostly in Guangdong that Sun Yat-sen (Sun Zhongshan), beginning in 1895, organized a series of

Sampans crowding the Pearl River, Guangzhou, Guangdong province, c. 1900. *The coastal capital of Guangdong province, Guangzhou remains a center of commerce in China. As the only port open to foreign merchants before the Opium Wars, Guangzhou became a heavily commercialized city in the early nineteenth century, a characteristic that reemerged during China's conversion to a market-based economy in the late twentieth century.* © CORBIS

revolutionary uprisings that led eventually, in 1911 to 1912, to the overthrow of the Qing emperor and the establishment of a republic. And it was again in Guangdong that Sun Yat-sen in the early 1920s, following the failure of the Republican revolution, attempted, with the support of the Soviet Union and the fledgling Chinese Communist Party, to organize yet another revolution, this time to take China back from the warlords and the imperialists.

The province, however, ceased to be politically important when, after Sun's death in 1925, his non-Cantonese successor, Chiang Kai-shek (Jiang Jieshi), established his

Guangxi

Tourists visiting a rock formation known as "The Elephant's Trunk" in Guilin, Guangxi Zhuang Autonomous Region, January 17, 1996. *Situated in southern China, Guangxi features a subtropical climate amid a mountainous landscape, making the region a favorite for tourists.* AP IMAGES

Guangxi has been much affected by connections across the land border to Vietnam. Armies have passed through many times, most recently in the Sino-Vietnamese War (1979). A flood of ethnic Chinese refugees came across to Guangxi after the end of the Vietnam War (1957–1975).

THE REFORM ERA IN GUANGXI

Despite poverty in Guangxi, rendered even more obvious by booming economic activity in neighboring Guangdong, the economic reforms after liberalization started in 1978 were slow to take hold. The region was opened to foreign trade and investment in 1984. Since then,

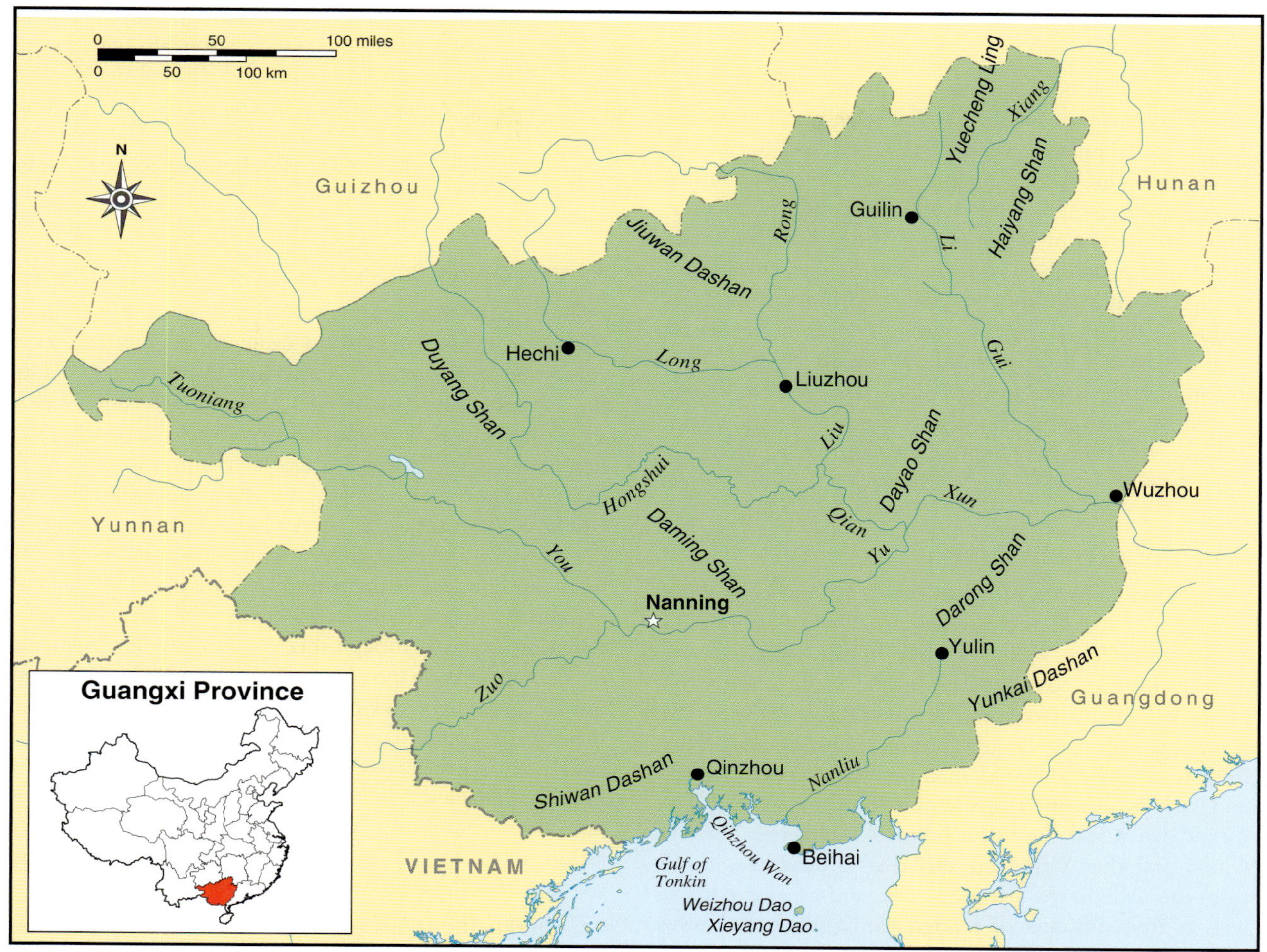

tourism, especially in the Guilin area, and cross-border trade with Vietnam have flourished. In 2006, a Beibu Gulf Economic Zone was established for commercial, manufacturing, and infrastructural development.

SEE ALSO *Provincial and Subprovincial Government Structure since 1949: Autonomous Regions.*

BIBLIOGRAPHY

Kaup, Katherine P. *Creating the Zhuang: Ethnic Politics in China.* Boulder, CO: Lynne Rienner, 2000.

Lary, Diana. *Region and Nation: The Kwangsi Clique in Chinese Politics, 1925–1937.* Cambridge, U.K.: Cambridge University Press, 1975.

Levich, Eugene. *The Kwangsi Way in Kuomintang China, 1931–1939.* Armonk, NY: Sharpe, 1993.

Diana Lary

GUANGZHOU (CANTON)

Guangzhou, or Canton in Western literature, is located at latitude 22°26'–33'N and longitude 112°57'–114°3'E and lies at the confluence of two navigable rivers of the Pearl River (Zhujiang) system. With a population of 7.6 million and total area of 7,434 square kilometers, Guangzhou is one of the most populous cities in China. As the capital of Guangdong Province, it has long been the most important political, economic, and cultural center in South China, as well as the center of Cantonese language and culture. Its geographical setting and natural endowments, in conjunction with the practicality, flexibility, and initiative of Cantonese people, contributed to a flourishing cultural exchange between China and the West, and the development of Guangzhou as the dominant city of South China. The present municipality of Guangzhou comprises ten administrative districts in the city proper (Baiyun, Dongshan, Fangcun, Haizhu, Huangpu, Liwan, Tianhe,

Yuexiu, Huadu, and Panyu), and two rural cities (Zengcheng, and Conghua).

Guangzhou has a subtropical climate with an average annual temperature of 22°C. The lowest temperature is normally in January, averaging 18.3°C, and the highest temperature in July, averaging 32.6°C. Average annual precipitation ranges from 1,600 to 2,600 millimeters, about 80 percent of which occurs in the monsoon season of April to September, with the highest concentration in spring. Thanks to the wetland environment and the basin-like terrain of the city, humidity is high year round, with an average relative humidity of 80 percent. Most uncomfortable is the spring "plum rain" season, characterized by continuous rain, rising temperatures, low wind velocity, and extremely high relative humidity (Weng and Yang 2004).

HISTORY AND CULTURE

Guangzhou's history of urban development spans 2,000 years (Xu 1990). It originated as a small village about 300 BCE. Its first city wall was built in the third century, during the Han dynasty. From the sixth century on, Guangzhou benefited from the growth in maritime trade, becoming China's largest seaport. During the Qing dynasty it was designated an international port of trade, and in 1757 became the sole port for foreign trade. This meant that it was the major point of interaction between China and the West, and also that it benefited hugely from the trade in tea, porcelain, silk, and other exports, as well as from imports of foreign cloth, silver, and other goods. Efforts by the imperial government to stem the opium trade were the proximate cause of the Opium War (1839–1842), which led to Guangzhou's designation as one of the first five treaty ports by virtue of the Treaty of Nanjing (1842). In 1856 clashes at Canton again led to a war, sometimes known as the Second Opium War.

Guangzhou's economic, political, and strategic importance during this period are reflected in the careers of major historical figures of the nineteenth century, including Ruan Yuan, Wei Yuan, and Lin Zexu. The Taiping leader Hong Xiuquan was first exposed to Christianity here. Kang Youwei was a native son, and Liang Qichao, also from Guangdong province, was a student at its famous academy, the Xuehaitang. The first Western medical clinic in China was opened there in 1835, and provided medical training for Chinese students, including Sun Yat-sen, for a brief period. A Christian college founded in Guangzhou in 1883 evolved into Lingnan University, one of the city's two major centers of higher education in the early twentieth century; the other is Sun Yat-sen University, founded in 1923 by Sun himself.

Guangzhou played an important part in the political history of the Republican era, serving as the power base for Sun Yat-sen and the National Revolution in the 1920s. Although it was increasingly overshadowed by Shanghai as a port of foreign trade, its close relationship with Hong Kong helped sustain its economic and cultural significance through to the period of the Japanese occupation. Among its great cultural products of this era was the Lingnan school of painting, epitomized by the brothers Gao Jianfu (1879–1951) and Gao Qifeng (1889–1933).

TRANSFORMATIONS SINCE 1949

Following the establishment of the People's Republic of China in 1949, Guangzhou came to be regarded as a "decaying" capitalist city, dominated by merchants before the Communists took it over (Lo, Pannell, and Welch 1977). Industrial developments were typically small-scale, household types, largely because of political instability. A main goal in the early 1950s, therefore, was to convert the city from a consuming city to a producing city. To contain the growth of the inner city, most of the new developments were concentrated in the suburbs, as organized clusters for accommodating industries, warehouses, or external transportation facilities, though there were a few developments on the outskirts of the old city core (Xu 1985). Huangpu was designated the out port of the city. In the late 1950s there was significant growth in industrial and associated land uses. Factories were built in the selected areas of Haizhu, Fangcun, and Huangpu Districts. Housing developments spread out in Tianhe District, where higher education, research, and medical units blossomed, and a new research and cultural cluster was emerging.

During the 1960s and 1970s urban development was sluggish due to the political instability of the Cultural Revolution (1966–1969) and its aftermath. New factories were restricted to Haizhu District, and production and port facilities were expanded on the northeast riverbank of Fangcun District. The city's port function started to shift largely to Huangpu District, where heavy chemical and power industries also had been initiated. During the 1960s and 1970s Guangzhou was sanctioned as the only foreign trade center in prereform China (Lo, Pannell, and Welch 1977). This designation warranted some significant landmarks, and they were built on the northern fringe of the old city. Among them were the luxury Dongfang Hotel, Liuhua Hotel, and Chinese Export Commodities Fair Center. In addition, the city's major railway terminus was developed immediately adjacent to the old city core. These developments promoted the city's northern and northwestern expansion.

With the end of the Vietnam conflict and the rise in prosperity of Southeast Asia, the advantages of the city's location became evident (Xu 1985). In the early 1980s city planners set forth an overall development objective for the city—to become a multifunctional economic center of South China with five areas of emphasis: foreign trade, light industry, transportation, commerce, and tourism (Guangzhou Bureau of City Planning 1989). Foreign trade was emphasized in order to take advantage of the city's location near the coast of the South China Sea, its proximity to Hong Kong, and the high productivity in manufactures in the Pearl River Delta. The 1980s were a golden age for Guangzhou's urban development. A triangular Guangzhou Economic and Technological Development Zone was established to attract foreign investment in industries. A specialized industrial zone was set up to house heavily polluting industries. The Huangpu New Port finished building eight 20,000-tonnage deepwater berths for ships. These projects, in conjunction with other port facilities, residential and office buildings, hotels, schools, and recreational facilities, shaped the modern Huangpu District. Baiyun International Airport was reconstructed and expanded, and new bridges were constructed to link the old city core with the island of Ho Nam (*Henan*), laying the foundation for future southern expansion. The most striking achievement during the period, however, was the completion of the Tianhe Sports Complex, making it possible for the city to host the sixth National Sport Games.

Rapid economic development and urban growth in the 1980s and 1990s greatly reshaped the city's landscape (Weng, Qiao, Yang, and Guo 2003). A new master plan was therefore called for and implemented in 1996. It determined that Guangzhou should be developed into a "central city in South China and a modern international metropolis," emphasizing the development in seven areas: high-tech manufacturing, financial and insurance, transportation, trade, tourism, real estate, and information technology. Although the new plan confirmed that the major direction of development in the short term would continue to be eastward, the city planners decided that the long-term direction of development should be northeastward. Urban development in the 1990s proceeded even more rapidly than in the 1980s, primarily because of the development of commercial housing and redevelopment. A modern business and residential zone, Zhujiang New Town, was developed along the northern waterfronts of the Pearl River. In addition, there were substantial developments in Tianhe High-Tech Industrial Park, and heavy industries continued to build up in Huangpu District. By the end of the 1990s the urban sprawl had made Baiyun Hill a green island surrounded by a sea of high-rise buildings.

Key construction projects initiated in the 2000s in the north of the city include a new international airport, a railway hub, and a national tourism center. The completion of several highways and the construction of the Beijing-Guangzhou expressway, as well as the northern extension of the Guangzhou subway, provide the essential infrastructure to support the intended northeastward expansion. It is anticipated that northward development will strengthen Guangzhou's economic connections with surrounding cities and provinces along the Yangzi River, promising competition with Shanghai, the nation's most important economic center in the Yangzi valley.

Economically, Guangzhou is now one of the top ten cities in the nation. In 2000 its gross domestic production (GDP) reached 238 billion yuan (RMB), with per capita GDP of 34,500 yuan. Although tertiary and secondary production accounted for 52.35 percent and 43.69 percent respectively, primary production accounted for less than 4 percent. The top three industries, electronics and information technology, construction and real estate, and automobiles, contributed more than 20 percent to its GDP.

SEE ALSO *Cantonese; Guangdong; Urban China: Cities and Urbanization, 1800–1949; Urban China: Organizing Principles of Cities; Urban China: Urban Planning since 1978.*

BIBLIOGRAPHY

Guangzhou Bureau of City Planning. *Guangzhou Shi Shiqu Guihua Baogaoshu* [Report on the planning of the city area of Guangzhou]. Guangzhou, China: Author, 1989.

Lo, Chor-Pang. Economic Reforms and Socialist City Structure: A Case Study of Guangzhou, China. *Urban Geography* 15, 2 (1994): 128–149.

Lo, Chor-Pang, Clifton W. Pannell, and Roy Welch. Land Use Changes and City Planning in Shenyang and Canton. *Geographical Review* 67, 3 (July 1977): 268–283.

Miles, Steven. *The Sea of Learning: Mobility and Identity in Nineteenth-Century Guangzhou.* Cambridge, MA: Harvard University Asia Center, 2006.

Tsin, Michael. *Nation, Governance, and Modernity in China: Canton, 1900–1927.* Stanford, CA: Stanford University Press, 1999.

Weng, Qihao, Lijia Qiao, Shihong Yang, and Hengliang Guo. Guangzhou's Growth and Urban Planning, 1960–1997: An Analysis through Remote Sensing. *Asian Geographer* 22, 1–2 (2003): 77–92.

Weng, Qihao, and Shihong Yang. Managing the Adverse Thermal Effects of Urban Development in a Densely Populated Chinese City. *Journal of Environmental Management* 70, 2 (2004): 145–156.

Xu, Junming. *Lingnan Lishi Dili Lunji* [A collection of essays on lingnan historical geography]. Guangzhou, China: Zhongshan University Press, 1990.

Xu, Xueqiang. Guangzhou: China's Southern Gateway. In *Chinese Cities: The Growth of the Metropolis since 1949*, ed. Victor F. S. Sit, 167–187. Hong Kong: Oxford University Press, 1985.

Qihao Weng

GUANXI

SEE *Nepotism and Guanxi.*

GUIZHOU

Located in southwest China, adjoining Hunan to the east, Sichuan to the north, Yunnan to the west and Guangxi to the south, the province of Guizhou has an area of 176,100 square kilometers, with its capital, Guiyang (a population of 3.55 million in 2006), roughly in the center. In this mountainous and high-lying province, the great Yunnan-Guizhou Plateau slopes downward toward the east.

Owing to karst limestone, the soil is thin, and little land is agriculturally productive. Yet Guizhou is rich in mineral deposits, coal, and forests. Because of the Sichuan Basin to the north and the Guangxi Basin to the south, rivers flow north, east, and south. The climate is mainly mild, and rainfall is plentiful, with wet summers but dry winters.

GUIZHOU

Capital city: Guiyang
Largest cities (Population): Guiyang (3,550,000 [2006]), Zunyi, Kaili
Area: 176,100 sq. km. (68,000 sq. mi.)
Population: 37,570,000 (2006)
Demographics: Han, 62%; Miao, 12%; Buyi, 8%; Dong, 5%; Tujia, 4%; Yi, 2%; Gelao, 2%; Shui, 1%; other, 2%
GDP: CNY 228.2 billion
Famous sites: Maotai Distillery; Dong Nationality Villages; Huangguoshu Waterfalls near Anshun City

HISTORY

Not until early in 1413, during the Ming dynasty, did Guizhou become a Chinese province. Control of minorities was left to local chieftains and leaders but gradually moved toward central-government appointment. In the eighteenth century, in response to disaffection and rebellion, Guizhou's ethnic areas were incorporated into normal provincial administration. Worse rebellions followed sporadically until the mid-twentieth century. The most serious were those of the Miao, led by Zhang Xiumei, and the Kam, led by Jiang Yingfang, both connected with the Taipings and affecting especially Guizhou, but also the neighboring provinces of Hunan and Yunnan. These rebellions, which dominated the period from 1854 to 1873, were savagely suppressed.

The collapse of the Qing dynasty in 1911 ushered in a period when warlords competed in Guizhou, Sichuan, and Yunnan, often not respecting provincial boundaries. Guizhou's General Yang Zisen, of Han ethnicity, despised ethnic minorities and applied a policy of assimilation that included intermarriage with members of the Han majority and Han dress for the Miao.

Zunyi, north of Guiyang, hosted a major Communist Party meeting in January 1935, at which Mao Zedong became chairman of the politburo. Since Guizhou was near the national capital of Chongqing and outside Japanese occupation, the Anti-Japanese War played out to the advantage of Guizhou. Some businesspeople and others fled Japanese control to Guizhou, and educational institutions and students rose in number. After the war, Guizhou slipped backward, being in a sorry state by the time the Communists gained control over Guiyang in November 1949.

In 1956 the government established two autonomous prefectures, with a third following in 1982, these three autonomous prefectures constituting the province's southern half. Owing largely to tourism, minority culture has become a saleable commodity under China's economic reforms, with the effect of increasing the government's political control over the minorities. This has provoked a reaction and could result in "a new role for ethnic minority groups, as keepers of a non-commercialized lifestyle and traditional morality" (Oakes in Hendrischke and Feng 1999, p. 58). Yet the People's Republic has probably integrated Guizhou into China better than any previous government.

POPULATION, ETHNICITY

Eastern Guizhou and western Hunan belong to the original Miao heartland; records from before the common era attest to Miao ancestors living there. Ethnic minorities still constituted the majority in the mid-seventeenth century. Han migration gathered momentum from the late eighteenth century, extending government control over the area. Generally, the Han occupied any fertile land, driving the ethnic minorities into the mountains.

Table 1 shows figures for Guizhou from the five Communist censuses and for two years prior to Communist control. The sharp rise in the minority proportion of the population between 1940 and 1953 is because the People's Republic included more people as minorities than the previous Republican government. The big differences between 1982 and 1990, and to some extent between 1990 and 2000, are due to two factors. First, many Han re-registered as minorities, because of affirmative-action policies toward minorities. For instance, the Tujia, who are not too different from the Han, rose from 1,600 in 1982 to 1 million in 1990 because of re-registration. Second, although ethnic minorities were encouraged to practice

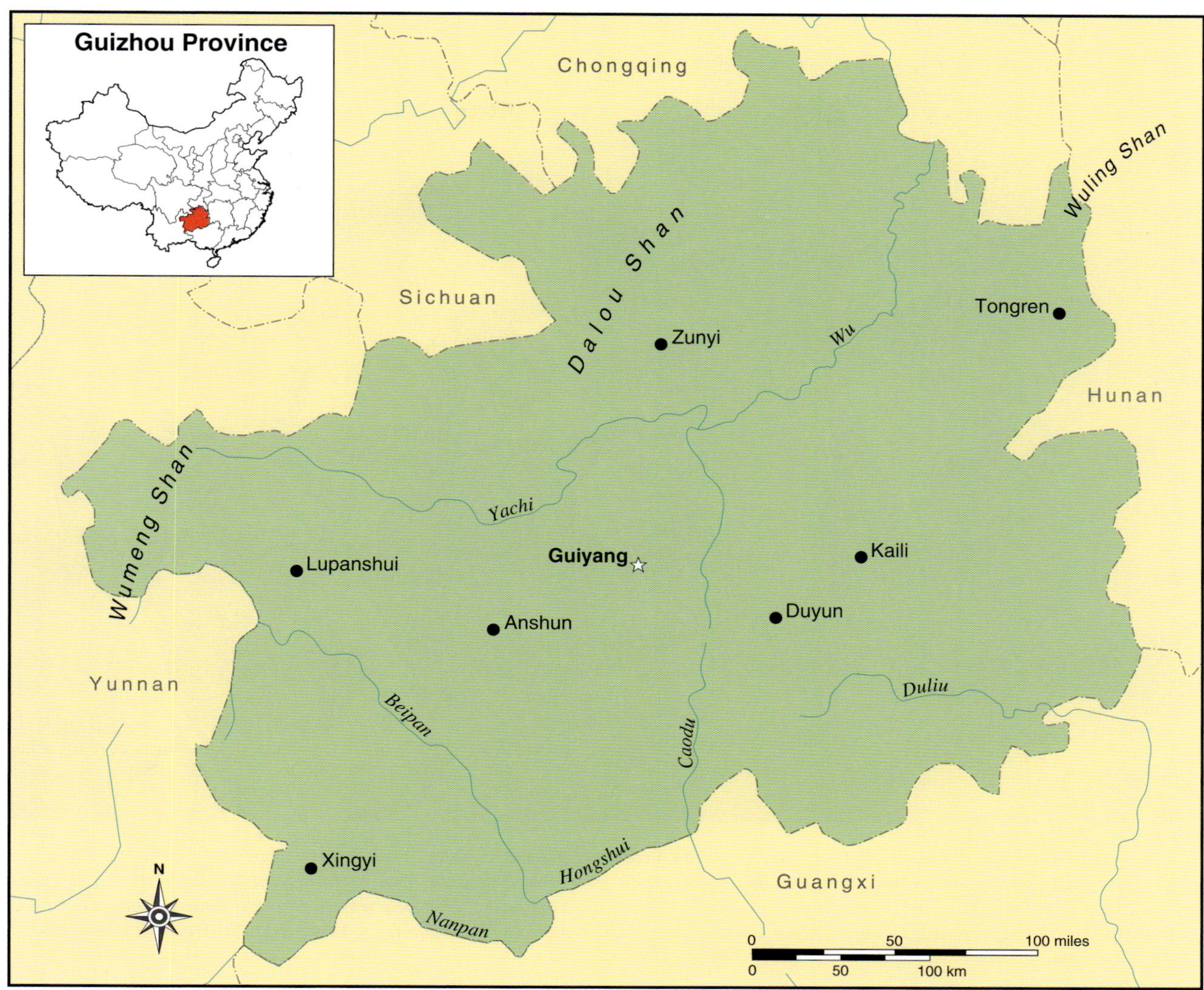

Census data for Guizhou, 1936–2000

Year	Total population (millions)	Minority population (millions)	Minority percentage of total
1936	9.92	0.91	9.2%
1940	10.21	1.06	10.4%
1953	15.04	3.99	26.5%
1964	17.14	4.0	23.3%
1982	28.55	7.4	25.9%
1990	32.39	11.24	34.7%
2000	35.25	13.4	38%

Table 1

birth control, the one-child policy was applied more flexibly to them.

By far the most widespread and populous of Guizhou's ethnic minorities has always been the Miao, whom the 2000 census put at 12 percent of the province's population, the main concentrations being in eastern Guizhou. Other significant Guizhou ethnic groups include the Bouyei, concentrated mainly in southwest and south-central Guizhou, and the Kam (Chinese: Dong), who inhabit a region along Guizhou's borders with Hunan and Guangxi. Any political importance that Guizhou has is due to its minorities, especially the Miao.

Two periods of population decline stand out. Rebellion reduced the 1854 population of about 5.44 million so drastically that this figure was again attained only after 1900. Group banditry became a feature of Guizhou life. Because of the famine following the 1958 Great Leap Forward, the 1959 population of 17.44 million declined to 16.23 million in 1961. Official figures put Guizhou's population at 37.57 million in 2006. In 2000 life expectancy was 65.96 at birth, lower than the national average of 71.4.

Women in traditional Miao dress, Guiyang, Guizhou province, May 11, 2008. *While part of China since the early 1400s, the province of Guizhou has seen periodic rebellions by regional ethnic groups, including the Miao and the Kam peoples. With the expansion of the tourism industry in China at the turn of the twenty-first century, however, these once repressed peoples have become major attractions for visitors interested in experiencing cultures outside the dominant Han majority.*

ECONOMY

There is irony in the fact that the Precious Prefecture (the literal meaning of *Guizhou*) has a traditional reputation as the poorest and most backward province in China. The German geographer and geologist Baron Ferdinand von Richthofen (1833–1895) regarded it as "the least productive, the least populous, and the least important" of China's provinces (quoted in Goodman 1986, p. 37). For much of the nineteenth and twentieth centuries, up to two-thirds of arable land was used for opium cultivation. Warlord regimes encouraged opium, which by 1935 accounted for 65 percent of the province's income.

Under Mao Zedong, the government made serious attempts to industrialize Guizhou, partly on account of perceived defense needs to send industry inland to areas safe from foreign enemies. This involved major improvement of infrastructure, such as roads. Mining of coal, iron ore, and minerals expanded greatly. The Cultural Revolution (1966–1969) and its aftermath did the economy no good. There were drops in crucial sectors, and official figures have 1965 and 1975 consumption at the same levels.

Economically, Guizhou has always been at or near the bottom of China's provinces. Economic development has accelerated under China's economic reforms, especially in mining. Tourism has brought in wealth and helped modernize the minorities. However, important measures still place Guizhou as the poorest province in China. In 2006 the total per capita annual income of urban households in Guizhou was CNY 9,439, the lowest in the country, the national average being CNY 12,719. Total per capita annual income for rural households was CNY 1,985, also China's lowest, the national average being CNY 3,587.

SEE ALSO *Provincial and Subprovincial Government Structure since 1949: Autonomous Regions.*

BIBLIOGRAPHY

Geary, D. Norman, Ruth B. Geary, Ou Chaoquan, et al. *The Kam People of China: Turning Nineteen*. London: Routledge Curzon, 2003.

Goodman, David S. G. *Centre and Province in the People's Republic of China, Sichuan, and Guizhou, 1955–1965.* Cambridge, U.K.: Cambridge University Press, 1986.

Hendrischke, Hans, and Feng Chongyi, eds. *The Political Economy of China's Provinces: Comparative and Competitive Advantage.* London: Routledge, 1999.

Jenks, Robert D. *Insurgency and Social Disorder in Guizhou: The "Miao" Rebellion, 1854–1873.* Honolulu: University of Hawaii Press, 1994.

Oakes, Tim. *Tourism and Modernity in China.* London: Routledge, 1998.

Schein, Louisa. *Minority Rules: The Miao and the Feminine in China's Cultural Politics.* Durham, NC: Duke University Press, 2000.

Colin Mackerras

GUO MORUO
1892–1978

Born Guo Kaizhen on November 16, 1892, Guo Moruo came from a merchant family in Leshan, Sichuan Province. In March 1912 he obeyed his parents and married Zhang Qionghua, whom he had never met. Five days after the wedding, however, he left home and went to Chengdu. He never formally divorced Zhang and apparently never lived with her.

Following his elder brother's footsteps, Guo Moruo left China in December 1913 and arrived in Japan in January 1914. After a year of preparatory study in Tokyo, he enrolled in the Sixth High School in Okayama. In 1918 he entered the Medical School of Kyushu Imperial University in Fukuoka. There he fell in love with and married a Japanese woman named Satō Tomiko (whom he referred to as Anna in his writing). Guo became interested in foreign languages and literature, especially Johann Wolfgang Von Goethe, William Shakespeare, Walt Whitman, and the Bengali poet and Nobel laureate Rabindranath Tagore (1862–1941). In addition to translations, he started writing poetry and fiction. His epistolary discussions of poetry with Tian Han (1898–1968) and Zong Baihua (1897–1986) were collected in a volume titled *San ye ji* (Three leaves) in 1920. In June 1921 he and several fellow students in Japan, including Cheng Fangwu (1897–1984), Tian Han, Yu Dafu (1895–1945), and Zhang Ziping (1893–1959), founded the Creation Society (Chuangzao She), which embraced Romanticism and promoted modern vernacular literature. In August of the same year, his first book of poems, titled *Nüshen* (Goddesses), was published. In 1922 he returned to China and edited *Chuangzao zhoubao* (Creation weekly).

Nüshen was hailed as the true beginning of modern Chinese poetry, as it managed to shake off the constraints of traditional poetry in diction and rhythm. Guo used plain speech frequently accented with foreign words and exclamation marks (the latter a recent borrowing from the West). More important, his poetry champions individualism and celebrates self-expression. His signature pieces—"Tiangou" (Heavenly dog), "Diqiu, wo de muqin" (Earth, my mother), and "Fenghuang niepan" (Nirvana of the phoenix)—equate the individual with the cosmos and with a dynamic metropolis. These three share the same energy and move to the same beat.

In 1927 Guo joined the Communist Party and took part in the Nanchang Uprising against the Guomindang (Nationalist Party) on August 1. After the abortive uprising he became a fugitive and fled to Japan in February 1928. During his ten-year exile, he devoted himself to paleography, researching oracle bones and bronze inscriptions. His first monograph, *Zhongguo gudai shehui yanjiu* (A study of ancient Chinese society), in which he used Marxist theory to analyze the class structure of Chinese antiquity, was published in 1930. In the 1930s he went on to develop a methodology for dating bronze inscriptions and produced several seminal works, including *Liang Zhou jinwenci daxi tulu kaoshi* (An illustrated and annotated compendium of bronze inscriptions from the two Zhou dynasties, 1935), which argued that ancient China was a slave society. Although some of his work is controversial and open to debate, he is generally considered one of the most original and influential scholars of Chinese antiquity in the twentieth century.

After the War of Resistance against Japan broke out in 1937, Guo Moruo returned to China, leaving behind his wife and children. During the war, he was a key figure on the literary scene. With the forming of a united front between the Guomindang and the Communist Party, Guo was put in charge of propaganda and, later, cultural affairs in the Nationalist government, first in Wuhan, then in Chongqing, the wartime capital. At the same time, he continued prolifically producing creative and scholarly writing. His creative work consists mainly of six historical plays. Among them, *Qu Yuan*, with its portrayal of the eponymous protagonist as a patriot and national hero, premiered in Chongqing in 1942 to wide acclaim. In 1939 Guo married Yu Liqun (1916–1979), although he maintained contact with Satō Tomiko and their children, who had come to live in China after the war.

After the founding of the People's Republic, Guo occupied many prominent positions in the political and cultural sectors, among them: member of the Central Government Commissary, vice chair of the Standing Committee of the National People's Congress, first president of the Chinese Academy of Science (1949–1978), vice premier of the Government Administrative Council, director of the Culture and Education Committee, and founding president of China Science and Technology

University. He was arguably the most famous and powerful cultural figure in the New China.

Guo did not escape criticism, however. During the Cultural Revolution (1966–1969) he was singled out. Although he survived the turmoil and even managed to regain political power in the early 1970s, he suffered tragic losses. His fourth son, Minying (1943–1967), committed suicide in 1967 for unknown reasons. His second son, Shiying (1942–1968), founded the X Poetry Society in 1963, for which he was labeled "reactionary" and sent to a labor camp in Henan Province. In spring 1968 he was abducted and tortured for days by the Red Guard. Whether he jumped out of a third-floor window or was thrown out remains a mystery. What is certain is that he died before his father could intervene.

Guo Moruo achieved distinction as a poet, dramatist, translator, scholar, revolutionary, and politician. His political career, especially during the Mao era, was controversial, but his accomplishments in creative writing and his scholarship in paleography have established him beyond doubt as a leading figure in twentieth-century China. Guo passed away in Beijing on June 12, 1978.

SEE ALSO *League of Left-Wing Writers; Literary Societies; Yu Dafu.*

BIBLIOGRAPHY

Chen, Rose Jui-chang. *Human Hero and Exiled God: Chinese Thought in Kuo Mo-jo's "Chu Yuan."* Ann Arbor: University of Michigan Press, 1985.

Doleželová-Velingerová, Milena. Kuo Mo-jo's Autobiographical Works. In *Studien zur modernen chinesischen Literatur*, ed. Jaroslav Průšek, 45–75. Berlin: Akademie-Verlag, 1964.

Roy, David Tod. *Kuo Mo-jo: The Early Years.* Cambridge, MA: Harvard University Press, 1971.

Yuan, Emily Woo. *Kuo Mo-jo: The Literary Profile of a Modern Revolutionary, 1924 to 1949.* Ann Arbor: University of Michigan, 1985.

Michelle Yeh

GUOMINDANG

SEE *Nationalist Party.*

H

HAINAN

Hainan province, historically called Qiongzhou, meaning "beautiful jade sub-prefecture," is an island located in the South China Sea. High mountains rise and stretch along the middle and western part of the island. The three main rivers of Hainan can all be traced to their origin here. Hainan's climate is tropical, and the year-round high temperature and abundant rainfall are conducive to the cultivation of rice, betel nut, tropical fruits, rubber trees, and in recent years, coffee. The province is separated from the Leizhou Peninsula to the north by a shallow, narrow strait. Hainan's capital is Haikou City, located in northern part of the island, and serving as the political, economic, cultural, and transportation center of the whole province. The city of Sanya is famous for its tropical beach landscapes.

Hainan is a multi-ethnic region. The total population of 8 million includes 1,200,000 Li people, Miao people, and Muslims. Most of the Li, Miao, and Hui minorities inhabit middle and south Hainan.

Hainan Island was incorporated into China in early times for three reasons: pearl fishing beginning in the Han dynasty (206 BCE–220 CE), the Arab trade beginning in the Tang dynasty (618–907), and the incense trade beginning in the Song dynasty (960–1279). Aside from trade, Hainan served as way station for attacks on Vietnam during the Yuan dynasty (1279–1368), for which reason an army was massed on the island. Only during the Yuan period was an effective county government gradually set up on the island, taking over authority from local ethnic Li chieftains.

In the Ming (1368–1644) and the early Qing (1644–1912) periods, Hainan Island produced numerous high-ranking officials, including the famous scholar Qiu Chun (1421–1495). The presence of such men at that time, and their absence from the second half of the Qing dynasty, suggests that Hainan had established a scholarly tradition early among its elite. Its academic and administrative prominence probably reflects its economic importance in earlier centuries. The impression that it became an academic backwater during the Qing is an indication that as Guangdong Province moved ahead economically, Hainan was left behind. Only after the Treaty of Tianjin in 1858, which opened Haikou as a treaty port, did the Hainan economy once again advance.

Imperial Maritime Customs reports suggest that Hainan was culturally and administratively peripheral to the Guangzhou heartland. Its ports traded primarily with Hong Kong, Shantou, and such Guangdong ports as Jiangmen (in Xinhui County). Economic development was hampered by a lack of roads; Hainan's own coastal ports were connected by junks. Through the 1880s and 1890s, Haikou rapidly grew into a supplier of pigs for Hong Kong. Pigs were its largest export, followed by betel nuts, herbal medicines, seafood, and sugar. Owing to its climate, Hainan appeared promising for rubber and coffee plantations. Plantations, mostly for rubber, were developed primarily in the twentieth century. From 1916 to 1949, more than twenty plantation companies were operating along Wanquan River in Hainan.

From the sixteenth century, Han and Li interactions were characterized by war. In the nineteenth century, the Li people were known to be rebellious. As their rebellions were put down in the second half of the nineteenth century, the Li became more and more confined to the Wuzhi Mountain area, while on the plains, agricultural

HAINAN

Capital city: Haikou
Largest cities (population): Haikou (1,770,000 [2006]), Sanya, Danzhou
Area: 35,400 sq. km. (13,668 sq. mi.)
Population: 8,360,000 (2006)
Demographics: Han, 82.8%; Minority (including Li, Miao, Zhuang, and Hui), 17.2% (2004)
GDP: CNY 105.3 billion (2006)
Famous sites: The Five Officials' Temple, Hai Rui Tomb, Shishan Volcanic Cluster National Geopark, Dongbo Academy in Danzhou City

land was gradually taken over by the Han or by indigenous Li populations that adopted Han ways.

In 1912 an administrative office was set up on Hainan by the new Republican government. After 1913 various warlords controlled the island in succession. In 1926 Nationalists eradicated the warlords' remaining forces and set up an administrative commission. Its rival, the Chinese Communist Party, also established a branch in Haikou in the same year. After 1927 the armed conflict between the Nationalists and the Chinese Communist Party intensified. Both parties were quelled by the Japanese occupation from 1939 to 1945. The Japanese considered Hainan as a base for expansion into Southeast Asia. To achieve their military goals, the Japanese exploited the island's natural resources and developed its communication and transport infrastructure. Nationalists regained control after the war, and in 1948 made Hainan a special administrative region,

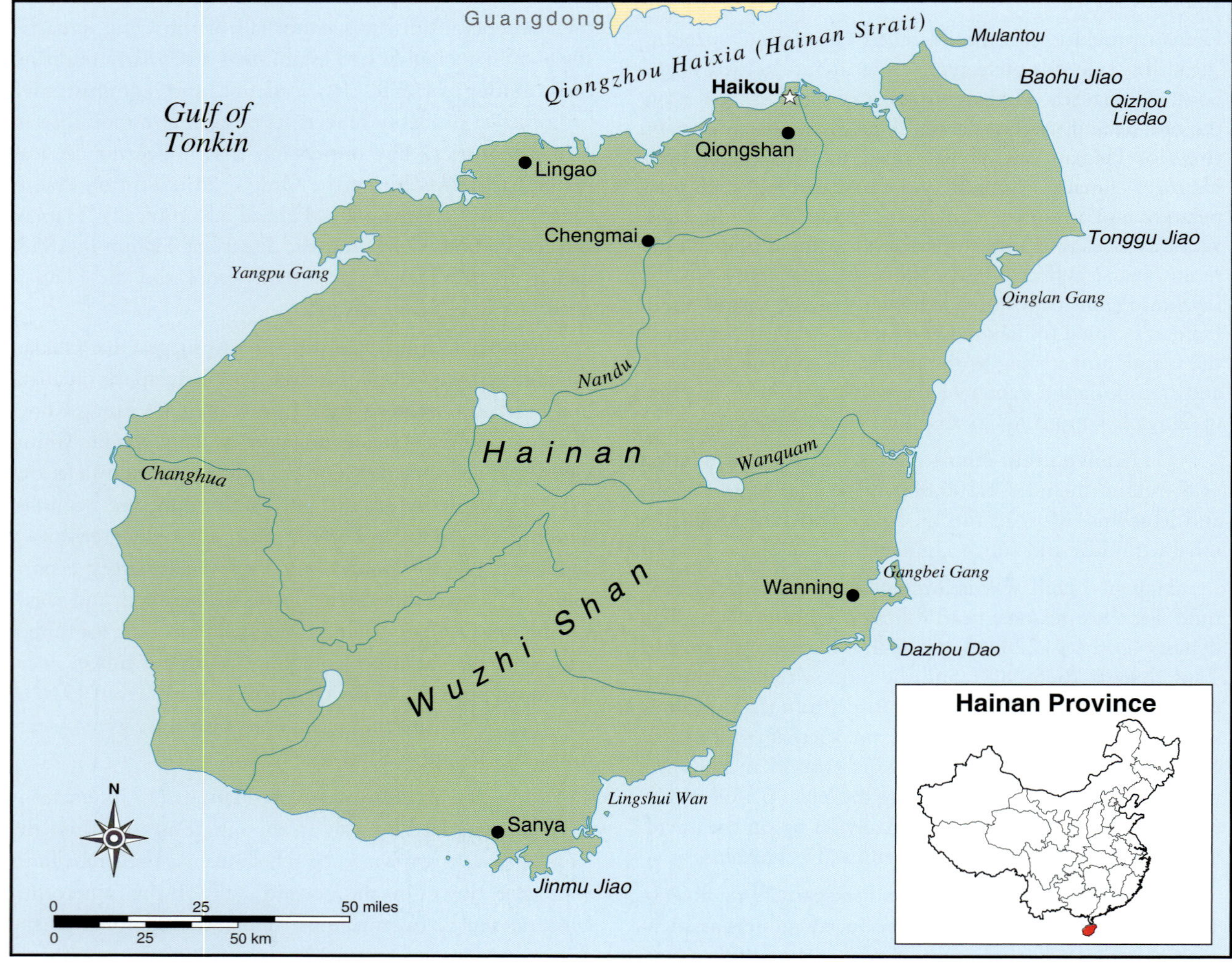

answering directly to the Executive Yuan, in preparation for its incorporation as an independent province. By 1950 Nationalist forces on the island were overpowered by People's Liberation Army operations launched from Zhanjiang.

In the 1950s the government of the People's Republic of China set up state farms on Hainan to cultivate tropical produce, such as rubber, coffee, and pepper. Hainan experienced land reform and the Cultural Revolution as did the rest of China. In the 1980s Hainan played an important role in China's rapid economic development, with special tax privileges being given to the island to encourage investment. The policy of rapid development for Hainan was called into question in 1985 when it was discovered that massive numbers of automobiles were being smuggled via Hainan into mainland China. In 1988 Hainan was set up as an independent province, and declared China's largest special economic zone. In recent years, tourism has become an important source of income for Hainan.

Owing to its position in regional trade, Hainan's ethnic composition is complex. The increasing numbers of Han settlers include Chaozhou (Teochiu)-speaking migrants from Shantou; Cantonese speakers from the western parts of Guangdong, who imported Hainan's most prominent deity, Madam Xian; a small community of Cham speakers connected with the Arab community in the south; Miao natives who arrived with the military during the Qing dynasty; and northerners who moved to Hainan from the 1950s through the 1980s. Beginning in the nineteenth century, Hainan has also sent many emigrants abroad to Indonesia, Vietnam, and Malaysia, some of whom returned to work in the plantations in the 1950s.

SEE ALSO *Guangdong; Special Economic Zones.*

BIBLIOGRAPHY

Daoguang Qiongzhoufu zhi [The gazetteer of Qiongzhou Prefecture, Daoguang reign]. Taibei: Chengwen Chubanshe, 1967.

Decennial Reports on the Trade, Navigation, Industries, etc., of the Ports Open to Foreign Commerce in China and Corea, and on the Condition and Development of the Treaty Port Provinces. Shanghai: Statistical Department of the Inspectorate General of Customs, 1882–1891.

Wanli Qiongzhoufu zhi [The gazetteer of Qiongzhou Prefecture, Wanli reign]. Beijing: Shumu Wenxian Chubanshe, 1990.

Wei Zheng. *Sui shu* [The history of the Sui dynasty]. Beijing: Zhonghua Shuju, 1973.

He Xi

HAIRSTYLES

Hairstyles say a lot about a nation, its people, and its sociopolitical situation. Nowhere is this more so than in China, where great symbolic importance has historically been attached to hairstyle. Management of one's hair according to custom, fashion, or law constitutes a clear statement of allegiance, preference, and subservience. The specific details of how hair is worn in China have differed over time and across geographical locations. These variations can shed light on the relationship between hairstyles and sociopolitical change. Broadly speaking, China's hairstyles in the modern era have been shaped by four major events: the 1911 revolution, the Nationalist revolution, the Cultural Revolution (1966–1969), and the reform era after Mao Zedong's death in 1976.

THE QUEUE

Most men in nineteenth-century China wore their hair in the way imposed by the Manchus when they took over China in the seventeenth century. Men were made to partially shave their foreheads and grow their hair to maximum length at the back, braiding it into a queue as the Manchus themselves did. After initial resistance, Han Chinese people adopted the queue as part of their culture, and wore it proudly until the Xinhai revolution in 1911, when the queue became unpopular due to its strong association with a fallen government. Europeans saw it both as a humorous example of the backwardness of the Chinese, and as a more sinister sign of oriental despotism and repression.

The link between hair and social change can be seen through such events as the Taiping Uprising (1851–1864) and the 1911 revolution. The Taiping rebels were known as the long-haired rebels, a reference to their refusal to shave their hair off at the front and to tie it into a queue at the back. Rejection of the Manchu hairstyle subsequently became a symbol of resistance and the movement for rebellion and change in China. In the late nineteenth century, however, opposition to the queue had both political and fashionable origins. Many nineteenth-century emigrants cut their hair to fit in with the customs of the countries where they resided. This created problems if they returned to China, when they would no longer be recognized as Chinese. In cutting off their queues to conform to the social norms of the host society, they had abandoned the social norms of their place of origin (Firth 1973). Chinese students, who were beginning to travel abroad to further their studies, faced a similar predicament. They quickly became aware of how the queue influenced foreigners' views of them, but cutting off their queues would mean problems on their return.

China's embarrassing defeat in the Sino-Japanese War (1894–1895) was the catalyst for anti-Manchu and hence anti-queue sentiments. Reformers such as Chen Qiu (1851–1903) and Kang Youwei (1858–1927) argued that a hairstyle that once suited the cavalry was dangerous and no longer proper in the machine age. For revolutionaries such as Sun Yat-sen (Sun Yixian) and Zou Rong (1885–1905),

Hairstyle of a Chinese woman, c. 1871. *While unmarried girls generally collected their hair into one long pony tail to symbolize their status, married women during the late Qing dynasty pinned their hair to the head, adorning the arrangement with fresh flowers and large decorative pins.*

the removal of the queue was an important symbol of China's struggle to throw off Manchu rule and emerge as a modern republican nation. Many others followed suit, with Zhang Binglin (1868–1936) cutting his queue in 1900 (Finnane 2007, p. 78).

Awareness campaigns began, reminding Chinese about the subjection that the queue signified and the injustices and incompetence of the Qing rulers. Queue-cutting societies operated more and more openly, especially in Shanghai, and with the 1911 revolution, queue cutting became mandatory. Hair from millions of discarded queues was sold for Western wigs to finance the revolution. The revolutionaries also argued that the initial imposition of the queue was a bloody affair, due to some spectacular cases of resistance to its adoption combined with the Manchus "wear it or die" policy. Therefore its demise represented more than just a fashion being phased out; it represented the downfall of a foreign ruler, the dismantling of a political system that had been in place for millennia, and the beginning of a new, modern nation-state. Westerners were bemused all over again by the ritual removal of Manchu hairstyles, but as the "pigtails" came off and the Republic was established, it must have seemed that China was belatedly making its way into the modern world.

Following the revolution in 1911, the army and police implemented an order to remove by force all queues still attached to heads. Short haircuts and shaved heads became the popular style following the revolution, although the queue continued to be in evidence for about twenty years afterward in rural areas and even in a few urban centers. Lu Xun (1881–1936) captured the importance of hair as a symbol in early twentieth-century China in "The Story of Hair," in which he argued that the changing hairstyles of the Republican era were not accompanied by any real changes in society. More famously, in "The True Story of Ah Q," he portrayed the simple-minded protagonist, Ah Q, as coiling his queue on the back of his head so as to pass for a revolutionary. In this way, the queue was made to represent the Chinese people's bond to tradition (Lu Hsü 1941).

WOMEN'S HAIRSTYLES

Women in China traditionally wore their hair long, which was seen as a sign of beauty, youth, romance, and femininity. Unmarried girls would wear their hair long and braided, usually in a single plait like a queue, with a fringe of hair over the forehead. Married women wore their hair long and tied into a knot at the nape of the neck. Numerous different styles of hair-knot went in and out of vogue. Around the time of the 1911 revolution, an extremely popular hairstyle was the "butterfly do," a hair-roll that represented freedom for women and could therefore be interpreted as "signaling sexual availability" (Finnane 2007, p. 99).

The abandonment of long hair by women in modern China offers an insight into how hairstyles were associated with social and political change. For Chinese women, the mid-1920s to 1930s saw a change from long hairstyles to very short styles, such as the bob, which were initially associated with liberation for women. The bob was influenced by European fashions and American films, and was made familiar through the circulation of images in newspapers, magazines, and posters. Domestic political issues also influenced the move toward short hair. Young women who joined the Nationalist revolution in the 1920s cut their hair short, sometimes shaving it off altogether to be like their male counterparts. Japan's invasion of China in 1937 prompted the adoption of a similarly militarized hairdo. Such changes were met with different degrees of resistance in society. In the 1920s, girls with bobs were attacked by antirevolutionary forces, while in the 1930s, permed hair was banned in some parts of China as part of a conservative reaction against decadent foreign ways.

HAIR AND HAIRSTYLES IN MAO'S CHINA AND AFTERWARD

The fashion for elaborate hairstyles among women ended in 1949 with the establishment of the People's Republic of China, when long hair came to be regarded as frivolous. Mao's influence and the regime of 1949 led to a widespread abandonment of long hairstyles, particularly in urban areas. This trend was strengthened during the decade of the Cultural Revolution when fashions were essentially military uniforms, with little difference between the sexes. Short hair now represented a revolutionary ethos, as during the Nationalist revolution, and also an egalitarian one. For practical purposes, short hair made working in the fields or factories easier, and made hair care simpler.

A dearth of shampoo and other hair-care products meant that fashion was often dictated by practicality. Ideologically, short hair represented a shunning of Western ideas of beauty, a rejection of decadence, and the promotion of a sense of classless proletarian unity. In the arts, however, the Maoist era is best represented by a figure with long hair: *The White-Haired Girl.* The story in this model opera, one of a handful approved for public showing during the Cultural Revolution, centers on a peasant girl with long black hair. Her suffering under evil feudal forces turns her hair white, but when she is rescued by the Communist forces, her hair regains its initial healthy black sheen. Her restored black hair means all that is good and right with the world, and has particular resonances in a place where the common people are referred to as "the black-haired people."

POST-MAO TRENDS

When China opened up to the world in the post-Mao era, people had more freedom to try out new hairstyles and embrace new trends. By 1977, perms for women were being advertised. During the 1980s, television series, particularly those from Japan, popularized new hairstyles. Under Western influence, long hair for women came back into fashion, with long braided styles becoming popular. Just as in Western countries, hair styles and alterations such as hair extensions have also became fashionable, illustrating the revived desire among young women for long hair. Boys, too, began wearing their hair longer, provoking their parents to the sort of reaction evident in the West in the 1960s.

These changes were not uniform throughout China. There are stark contrasts between the hairstyles of rural

years Luo supplied a detailed history of the routes of migration taken by the Hakkas from the center of China.

The sense of Hakka identity and common history as formulated in the 1920s and 1930s took hold not only in China but also among overseas Chinese communities. Every few years beginning in the 1970s, meetings have been held through international conferences under the aegis of Hakka associations in Hong Kong, Taipei, San Francisco, Bangkok, and, since 2000, cities with substantial Hakka populations in the People's Republic of China. The early years of these efforts coincided with the Taiwan government's promotion of the tracking of common genealogical descent as part of a revival of Chinese culture in its efforts to maintain connections with overseas Chinese communities. In Taiwan, where the Hakka population formed a noticeable minority of just under 20 percent, the introduction of electoral politics in the 1990s led to further efforts at identity building. In the People's Republic the revival of overseas investment beginning in the 1980s and increasing cultural tourism in the decades that followed heightened connections between the homeland and communities beyond, including Hong Kong, Taiwan, and elsewhere, and also led to an increase of activities, in the form of international meetings, publications, and cultural festivals, highlighting the common Hakka history. Ironically, this heightened interest has run parallel to an academic skepticism of the Hakka origin myth of the southern migration. The dualism in the telling of Hakka history is thus likely to continue.

SEE ALSO *Minority Nationalities.*

BIBLIOGRAPHY

Cheng, Meibao. *Di yu wen hua yu guo jia ren tong: Wan Qing yilai "Guangdogn wen hua" guan de xing cheng.* Beijing: Sanlian, 2006.

Constable, Nicole, ed. *Guest People: Hakka Identity in China and Abroad.* Seattle: University of Washington Press, 1996.

Fang, Xuejia. *Kejia yuan liu tan'ao.* Guangzhou: Guangdong Gaodeng Jiaoyu Chubanshe, 1994.

Leong, Sow-Theng. *Migration and Ethnicity in Chinese History: Hakkas, Pengmin, and Their Neighbors.* Ed. Tim Wright. Stanford, CA: Stanford University Press, 1997.

David Faure

HANDICRAFTS

Before the introduction of modern machinery in the late nineteenth century, China's entire industrial output was produced manually. Contrary to the common assumption that China's craft industries collapsed under the onslaught of foreign goods after the Opium War (1839–1842), foreign economic penetration led to the decline of some handicraft industries but stimulated growth in others. As late as 1952, handicraft industries accounted for 42 percent of industrial output in then-current prices (weighted in favor of heavy industry) and for 68 percent in more realistic prewar prices. Handicraft industries contracted rapidly in the 1950s and 1960s, due to the replacement of handmade by machine products, the merger of urban artisanal workshops into collective and state-owned factories, and the absorption of rural artisans into agricultural collectives. By 1962, employment in the "second light industry" sector (which included most handicrafts) had dropped to 5.5 million, down from an estimated 20 million in the early 1950s, and anecdotal evidence suggests that common products such as baskets and straw mats were often in short supply.

The post-Mao reform period saw a recovery of rural and urban crafts, as small-scale production in private homes and workshops became legal and rising living standards boosted demand. It also saw a flood of cheap, mass-produced goods that soon replaced many handmade items. Paradoxically, these changes led to a positive reevaluation of handicrafts. For most of the twentieth century, Chinese consumers had purchased handmade items mainly because they were cheap and readily available, not because they were seen as inherently desirable. Now that handmade products are often more difficult to obtain than factory products, urban consumers have begun to appreciate them for their aesthetic value and their perceived connection to a romanticized past.

HANDICRAFTS BEFORE MODERN INDUSTRIALIZATION

Chinese handicrafts before modern industrialization can be divided into three main types: (1) urban or rural industries catering to nearby customers; (2) export-oriented protoindustries; and (3) dispersed, small-scale rural sidelines. Each urban center, from the metropolises of Beijing and Shanghai down to the smallest market, was served by a large number of sedentary and itinerant artisans. The "360 trades" (*sanbailiushi hang*) of Beijing, for example, included large metal- and woodworking workshops but also small itinerant repairmen who mended broken bowls or repaired copper kettles.

Specialized production for nearby customers can be contrasted to the production of standardized goods for distant markets. As in early modern Europe, such "protoindustries" were typically based in the countryside to take advantage of low labor costs; the semiprocessed goods were then packaged in urban workshops and shipped to their final markets. This type of manufacture was typically coordinated by merchants who sold raw materials and lent money to primary producers. Some of the largest industries in Qing China—cotton and silk production in the Yangzi Delta, tea and sugar along the southeast coast, porcelain in Jingdezhen—belonged to this type.

A worker in a silk embroidery workshop near Hangzhou, May 1, 2007. *As the Communist government looked to modernize China through industrialization, many citizens began to regard handmade items as inferior to mass produced ones. However, by the turn of the twenty-first century, the production of handicrafts had become respected again, with artisans using traditional fabrication methods to create goods for a growing domestic market.* © ADRIAN BRADSHAW/EPA/CORBIS

A third and numerically very important type was the dispersed production of handmade goods by semi-specialized households, for home use or for direct sale in nearby markets. The best example here is cotton textiles (by far the most important good in terms of output value), which were produced in almost every part of China. In terms of organization, the household unit was predominant. The imperial government maintained large workshops in the palace and the provinces, which produced silk, porcelain, weapons, and other goods for the court, and capitalist workshops employing large numbers of wageworkers existed in the larger cities, but most products originated in household workshops using domestic labor.

IMPACT OF INDUSTRIALIZATION AND FOREIGN IMPORTS

The impact of treaty-port industrialization and of the opening of Chinese markets to foreign imports is complex and contradictory. Factory-made cotton yarn—initially from India and Japan, later from Chinese factories—made rapid inroads into Chinese markets, growing from zero to more than 50 percent between the 1870s and the early twentieth century. However, hand spinning never disappeared, as handloom weavers combined machine-spun warp (used for tensile strength) with handspun woof (used for durability and warmth). Moreover, as cheap machine-spun yarn became available, handloom weaving boomed and new weaving districts emerged in the north and west of China, in areas that had previously imported their cloth readymade from the cotton-growing districts. While machine-made cloth found ready markets in the cities, most people in the countryside continued to wear handloom cloth until the 1960s.

In other sectors, the picture is similarly complex: For each industry that was severely hit by foreign imports (vegetable lamp oil was replaced by kerosene; silk weaving declined in consequence of Japanese competition and the advent of rayon), it is possible to name others in which new and old products coexisted (imported paper supplied new needs in the modern sector but did not supersede traditional usages) or one in which foreign examples stimulated the growth of new industries (such as workshops for cigarettes, matches, Western-style hats, etc.).

Another result of the Western presence was the conceptualization of handicrafts (*shougongye*) as an early and less-advanced version of "real" industry (*gongye*), bound to be superseded, and a conceptual split of handicrafts into two parts, one concerned with the making of humble objects for everyday use, the other with "arts and crafts products" (*meishu gongyipin*) that represented "genuine" and "authentic" folk traditions. From the 1920s on, folklorists began to study handicraft traditions, often with the intention to distill from them a new aesthetic that was both modern and Chinese. Outside the small circle of folklorists, the perception of handicrafts remained negative: There was a strong feeling that only modern industry could save China in its struggle for national survival, and the widespread existence of handicraft industries until the middle of the twentieth century served as a reminder of how much China had fallen behind the industrial nations of the West and Japan.

STANCE OF THE COMMUNIST PARTY TOWARD HANDICRAFTS

These views also informed the stance of the Chinese Communist Party (CCP), which defined handicraft as a "technically outmoded method of production," indicative of the nation's economic backwardness and destined to be phased out in the course of socialist development. While still based in Yan'an, the CCP promoted handloom weaving and other small-scale crafts; after 1949, by contrast, it embarked on a course of rapid industrialization, financed by surplus extraction from agriculture and handicraft. Party leaders in the early 1950s envisaged the same course for handicraft and agriculture: gradual collectivization, capital accumulation through self-reliance and hard work, followed by mechanization and transition to full public ownership.

Statistics from this time differentiate between three types of handicrafts. (1) *Capitalist handicraft workshops*, employing four to ten workers, were scheduled for mechanization and public ownership. This category encompassed fewer than one million workers. (2) *Independent handicraft producers*, that is, household workshops with three or fewer workers, employed about eight million workers overall, evenly divided between city and countryside. Urban workshops of this type were scheduled for collectivization; rural workshops were to be concentrated in market towns or phased out. (3) *Peasants engaged in part-time handicraft commodity production*, estimated to number over ten million, were not officially recognized as part of handicraft. With few exceptions, they were scheduled to join the general agricultural workforce, though they were permitted to engage in sideline handicraft production.

The Great Leap Forward saw a short-lived upgrading of many workshops into public ownership, followed by their downgrading after the catastrophic failure of the Leap and by the return of their workers and remaining assets to collective ownership. The period following the Leap saw a very sharp contraction in employment (from nine million in 1954 to five million in 1963), as urban workshops were reduced in size and rural workshops that did not "serve agriculture" were almost universally closed down. Rural handicraft production for urban markets, which had historically provided income and employment for millions of households, remained banned throughout the entire collective period and revived only under the post-Mao reform policies of the 1980s.

The early 1980s saw a rapid recovery of handicrafts, as craftspeople rediscovered half-forgotten skills and consumer spending for nonessential items grew. In many industries, however, expansion was soon followed by contraction, as factory products (considered more "modern" and desirable by most consumers) became available in growing numbers. By the late 1990s, handmade goods had been replaced in most areas of life: vinyl floor coverings were more durable than straw mats; ready-made apparel more attractive than hand-tailored (let alone handwoven) clothes; mass-produced kitchenware cheaper than handmade pots and pans, and so on. In rural areas, handmade items of daily use may still be seen as the more "basic" option, but in the city, the appeal of handmade goods now comes increasingly from their cachet as unique items that serve to express the lifestyle and personality of the buyer. This is especially true in the case of tourist handicrafts, a category that has expanded from the traditional brushes, ink sticks, cloisonné, and Yixing tea ware to a plethora of traditional and new products. This is particularly true in areas with large non-Han Chinese populations, such as Guizhou and Yunnan, which now produce "ethnic" handicraft products (lacquerwares, embroideries, tie-dyed textiles, etc.) for the domestic and international market.

SEE ALSO *Folk Art; Silk since 1800.*

BIBLIOGRAPHY

Feuerwerker, Albert. Economic Trends in the Late Qing Empire, 1970–1911. In *The Cambridge History of China*, Vol. 11, eds. John K. Fairbank and Denis Twitchett, 1–69. Cambridge, U.K.: Cambridge University Press, 1980.

Feuerwerker, Albert. Economic Trends, 1912–1949. In *The Cambridge History of China*, Vol. 12, ed. John K. Fairbank, 28–127. Cambridge, U.K.: Cambridge University Press, 1983.

Feuerwerker, Albert. *Studies in the Economic History of Late Imperial China: Handicraft, Modern Industry, and the State.* Ann Arbor, MI: Center for Chinese Studies, 1995.

Schran, Peter. Handicrafts in Communist China. *China Quarterly* 17 (1964): 151–173.

Jacob Eyferth

HANGZHOU

Hangzhou, the capital of Zhejiang Province, is located south of the Yangzi Delta, with access to the East China Sea through Qiantang River and Hangzhou Bay. With an area of 16,596 square kilometers, Hangzhou has eight urban districts, two counties, and three county-level municipalities. Its total population was 6,663,100 in 2006. Situated in the north of the province, it borders Anhui Province in the west. Rivaling the most spectacular tidal bores of the Amazon River in Brazil and the Bay of Fundy in Nova Scotia in Canada, the Qiantang bore witnesses the amazing confluence of lunar and solar gravity and a sandy river bottom, creating tidal waves of 3.5 to 8 meters high around the eighteenth day of the eighth lunar month of the Chinese lunar calendar. Qiandaohu (the "lake of a thousand islands"), located south of Hangzhou, is more than one hundred times as large as West Lake in central Hangzhou, and features numerous islets crosscutting blue waters and green forests.

ANCIENT NATIONAL CAPITAL

The name *Hangzhou* can be traced back more than 1,400 years to 589 CE. One of China's seven ancient capital cities, Hangzhou (then named Lin'an) served as the capital of the Southern Song dynasty (1127–1279) from 1138 until 1276, when it fell to the Mongols.

Historically known, along with Suzhou, as a paradise on earth, Hangzhou is one of the most attractive cities in China. West Lake in the center of urban Hangzhou, covering an area of 6.5 square kilometers, has long been a popular tourist destination. It boasts a large number of famous scenic spots with such poetic names as *Su di chun xiao* (spring dawn at Su Causeway) and *Lei feng xi zhao* (sunset glow at Leifeng Pagoda), together with historical monuments, including the tombs of the renowned patriots Yue Fei (1103–1142) and Qiu Jin (d. 1907). Longjing tea (a green tea), one of the most popular teas in China, is produced in the vicinity of West Lake. It has long been known for its taste, fragrance, and therapeutic effects.

As the capital of a wealthy, cultured province, the southern terminus of the Grand Canal, and the site of an imperial silk manufactory, Hangzhou had a natural prominence in the eyes of the Qing emperors. The Kangxi emperor (r. 1661–1722) visited the city on each of his six southern tours, and his grandson, the Qianlong emperor (r. 1735–1795), did the same. In the nineteenth century, Hangzhou was overshadowed by the treaty ports of Ningbo and, increasingly, Shanghai, and suffered extensive loss of life and property during the Taiping Uprising (1851–1864). In 1895, following the first Sino-Japanese War (1894–1895), Hangzhou was declared a treaty port, and a Japanese concession area was established around Gongchen Bridge (located in the city's north). In 1897 Hangzhou built its first modern textiles factory.

In the early twentieth century, Hangzhou stood on the periphery of major political developments that led to regime change, but its historical significance as the organizing center of a talent-producing province remained evident. Students from other parts of Zhejiang flocked to the city, making it one of the liveliest provincial centers of literary activity during the May Fourth movement. The Marxist Study Society in Shanghai, which contributed to the formation of the Chinese Communist Party, was largely made up of Hangzhou natives. The city's status as provincial capital meant that it was also the site of significant modernization projects during the Republican era, including the completion in 1937 of the 1,453-meter Qiantang River Bridge, China's first modern double-layered bridge.

HANGZHOU SINCE 1949

Tan Zhenlin (1902–1983), the first deputy political commissar of the Third Field Army of the People's Liberation Army, took Hangzhou on May 3, 1949, and became concurrently the first mayor of Hangzhou and first governor of Zhejiang in the People's Republic of China. Chairman Mao Zedong visited Hangzhou forty times. He drafted China's first constitution there in 1953 and 1954, wrote a number of poems, and finished several famous works, including an article on the sources of correct ideas ("Where Do Correct Ideas Come From?"). At the Hangzhou Conference, held January 2 to 4, 1958, Mao famously criticized Zhou Enlai's "opposition to rash advance" in the context of the Great Leap Forward, which subsequently led to economic disaster in China. Later, Mao chaired two conferences in Hangzhou in March and April 1966 in preparation for launching the Great Proletarian Cultural Revolution, yet another political disaster for China.

HANGZHOU UNDER REFORM

Hangzhou's economy grew rapidly in the era of reform and opening. Its gross domestic product (GDP) increased from 2.84 billion yuan in 1978 to 138.26 billion yuan in 2000 and further to 344.15 billion yuan in 2006.

Hangzhou began to accept foreign direct investment (FDI) in 1980, with a total contract for $1.28 million (U.S. dollars) for the year. The contracted FDI increased to $1,219.5 million in 1993 and $5,379.9 million in 2006. The main investors in 2006 were from Hong Kong, the British Virgin Islands, the United States, Taiwan, and Singapore. Hangzhou's foreign trade also expanded rapidly, from $84 million in 1989 to $10.5 billion in 2000 and $38.9 billion in 2006. Its trade surplus in 2006 was $13.6 billion. Hangzhou's major export destinations are the United States, Japan, Germany, Hong Kong, the United Kingdom, and South Korea.

RIVALRY BETWEEN HANGZHOU AND NINGBO

Hangzhou and Ningbo, two of the most important ports in China since the Tang dynasty (618–907), have been rivals throughout history. Hangzhou, however, was not opened as a treaty port until 1895, forty-two years after Ningbo became so designated, giving the latter a huge advantage in connecting its economy to international trade. Nearly a century later, in the era of reform, the State Council opened Ningbo's port to foreign investment and trade on June 1, 1979, and made Ningbo one of fourteen open coastal cities in April 1984. Hangzhou did not enjoy such status until 1988. But Hangzhou was selected earlier, in September 1984, as the site for an experiment in comprehensive economic reform. As such, it enjoys the status of subprovincial city, with its own economic plan separate from that of its parent province, Zhejiang. Ningbo was also made a single planning municipality (*jihua danlie shi*) in February 1987. Hangzhou still ranks first in Zhejiang in terms of population, GDP, and revenue, but Ningbo is first in terms of foreign trade, utilized foreign investment, and total investment in fixed assets.

SEE ALSO *Urban China: Cities and Urbanization, 1800–1949; Urban China: Organizing Principles of Cities; Urban China: Urban Planning since 1978; Zhejiang.*

BIBLIOGRAPHY

Chen Mingzhao. *Hangzhou*. Beijing: Foreign Language Press, 2002.

Hangzhou nianjian 2007 [Hangzhou yearbook 2007]. Beijing: Fangzhi Chubanshe, 2007.

Hangzhou shi [Hangzhou city]. Beijing: Zhonggong Chengshi Chubanshe, 1994.

Hangzhou tongji nianjian 2007 [Hangzhou statistical yearbook 2007]. Beijing: Zhongguo Tongji Chubanshe, 2007.

Ningbo shi [Ningbo city]. Beijing: Zhonggong Chengshi Chubanshe, 1995.

van Dijk, Monique. *The Lake of a Thousand Islands*. Beijing: Atomic Energy Press, 2005.

van Dijk, Monique, and Alexandra Moss. *Hangzhou: China Through the Looking Glass*. Beijing: Atomic Energy Press, 2006.

Zhejiang tongji nianjian 2007 [Zhejiang statistical yearbook 2007]. Beijing: Zhonggong Tongji Chubanshe, 2007.

Zhiyue Bo

HARBIN

Harbin is the capital of Heilongjiang Province in China's Northeast. As of 2006 it had a population of 4.64 million in its municipal area. It is located on the south bank of the Songhua River, but some urbanization has also spread along the northern bank. The city is known mainly for its long, icy-cold winters and for its many beautiful buildings of Western, particularly Russian, design—a testimony to Harbin's complicated past.

ORIGINS

Harbin was originally no more than a concentration of fishing villages. In 1896 a railway agreement between the Qing dynasty and Tsarist Russia allowed Russia to build and operate a railway across Manchuria and work on a bridge across the Songhua River for the new Chinese Eastern Railway, started at Harbin in 1898. During construction of the Chinese Eastern Railway from 1898 to 1903, the fishing villages grew rapidly into a small city. Many Russian workers and soldiers were sent to Harbin, and job opportunities generated by the Chinese Eastern Railway attracted thousands of Chinese laborers, servants, and merchants. At the time of the first census in Harbin, in 1903, 15,579 Russians were counted, along with 28,338 Chinese. It was a wild boomtown, with many brothels and a high crime rate. During the Boxer uprising of 1900, the city was the site of battles between Russian and Chinese government troops. During the first few years, the city was run directly by the Russian company for the Chinese Eastern Railway, but after Russia's defeat in the 1904–1905 war with Japan, Harbin became an "open city" in 1907, attracting settlers from many countries, among them many Jews. The Russians remained dominant, but the Russian Revolution of 1917 split Russian influence in the area into Red and White forces. Having received a large influx of refugees from the Russian Revolution, Harbin remained a White Russian stronghold for most of the 1920s, but gradually White Russian influence was eclipsed by that of the Soviet Union, which gained control of the Chinese Eastern Railway in 1924. During this period, Chinese began to play a larger role in the city's economic and political life, and a powerful nationalist and anti-imperialist movement swept through the Chinese sections of the population, always a majority in Harbin despite the conspicuous presence of large numbers of non-Chinese.

JAPANESE OCCUPATION

Harbin, which at this time had about 400,000 inhabitants, was captured by the Japanese army in early 1932 and incorporated in the puppet state of Manchukuo (Manzhouguo). Japan gained control of the Chinese Eastern Railway in 1935, and the number of Westerners in Harbin started to decline as the number of new Japanese arrivals grew. By the end of 1939 these two main groups of non-Chinese in Harbin each numbered around 40,000. During the Sino-Japanese War (1937–1945), Japanese industrial investment in the Harbin area attracted more Chinese laborers, and the Chinese population grew to around 700,000 in the early

Tourists scaling an illuminated ice palace during a winter festival, Harbin, Heilongjiang province, December 31, 2007. *The growth of the modern city of Harbin began in the late nineteenth century after the Russians built a railway through a collection of small fishing villages. Refugees from Russia and other European nations commanded a strong influence over the growing city until Communist victory in the Chinese Civil War prompted their migration to other countries.* TEH ENG KOON/AFP/GETTY IMAGES

1940s. But Japanese rule was ruthless toward the Chinese, and Harbin was no exception. At a location some 12 miles (20 kilometers) to the south of the city center, the Japanese established the infamous Unit 731, Japan's main research facility for biological warfare for the duration of the war. According to Chinese estimates, more than 3,000 Chinese prisoners died at the facility as victims of atrocious Japanese experiments.

SOVIET INFLUENCE

Soviet forces took Harbin in 1945 and allowed the Chinese Communist Party to establish a secure base in the city. During the civil war of 1946–1949, Harbin was the only northeastern metropolis to remain consistently under Communist control, and it became crucial to the Communist war effort as a transportation hub and industrial base. At the time of the establishment of the People's Republic in 1949, there were still some 25,000 Russians left in Harbin, but most of them left the city during the 1950s. After half a century of foreign domination, Harbin thus became a fully Chinese city, but one with its semicolonial past etched on its face. The Communist Party recast the city as a center of anti-imperialist struggles and of Chinese economic dynamism during the first half of the twentieth century.

AFTER LIBERATION

After 1949 Harbin quickly developed into one of China's ten most important industrial centers. The city's proximity to the Soviet Union gave it a natural advantage for heavy-industrial development during the heyday of the Sino-Soviet alliance in the 1950s. Harbin became a center of the machine-building industry, as well as of the chemical and construction-material industries, while continuing its role as the center of the soybean industry. By 1960 the population had passed the 2 million mark. During the late Maoist period, Harbin earned some fame in the Cultural Revolution as the place for China's first revolutionary committee in 1967; such committees were subsequently established all over China to take over leadership from defunct government structures. With the start of the Reform and Opening Up in 1978, Harbin entered a new course of development as the tertiary sector (services) became important as the engine of economic growth. But owing to the reduced flow of state funds for heavy-industrial investments in Harbin as compared with the period of the planned economy, the city has not entirely escaped becoming a part of what is often referred to as the rust belt of the northeastern provinces, with its many large and unprofitable heavy-industrial state enterprises. Yet Harbin has also been able to benefit from its proximity to Russia, Japan, and Korea to attract a considerable amount of foreign investment and trade. The city has thus retained its place among China's ten top industrial cities, and the international aspect of the city's life has revived.

The annual Harbin International Ice and Snow Festival, among the largest in the world, was initiated in 1985. Throughout the month of January, ice sculptors from around the world compete with Chinese artists at the exhibition, which attracts many tourists.

Harbin gained the attention of Chinese and foreign media in 2005 when a toxic leak at a benzene factory upstream from Harbin endangered the city's water supply. Adding to the frustrations of the citizens was the fact that the city's leadership initially hesitated fully to disclose the menace to the public; after a few hours, however, circumstances forced the mayor to admit to the "well-intended lie." A reorganization of Harbin's administrative structure took place in 2006. As a result, Harbin governs eight city districts as well as seven counties and three prefectural cities, encompassing a municipal area of 2,700 square miles (7,000 square kilometers) and a total area of 20,000 square miles (53,000 square kilometers).

SEE ALSO *Heilongjiang; Manchuria; Urban China: Cities and Urbanization, 1800-1949; Urban China: Organizing Principles of Cities; Urban China: Urban Planning since 1978.*

BIBLIOGRAPHY

Carter, James H. *Creating a Chinese Harbin: Nationalism in an International City, 1916–1932.* Ithaca, NY: Cornell University Press, 2002.

Clausen, Søren, and Stig Thøgersen. *The Making of a Chinese City: History and Historiography in Harbin.* Armonk, NY: Sharpe, 1995.

Lahusen, Thomas, ed. Harbin and Manchuria: Place, Space, and Identity. Special issue, *South Atlantic Quarterly* 99, 1 (2001).

Wolff, David. *To the Harbin Station: The Liberal Alternative in Russian Manchuria, 1898–1914.* Stanford, CA: Stanford University Press, 1999.

Søren Clausen

HARMONIOUS SOCIETY

The concept of "harmonious society" (*hexie shehui*) is meant to generate new foundations for stability. It was first presented at the fourth plenary session of the Sixteenth Central Committee of the Chinese Communist Party (CCP) in September 2004 and was exemplified by Premier Wen Jiabao in his address to the National People's Congress in February 2005. He described a "harmonious society" as being characterized by democracy, rule of law, justice, principles (as opposed to corruption), and social compensation. In June 2005, party chief Hu Jintao presented the following attributes as additional factors: development of ideology and morality, proper treatment of contradictions among the people, development in ecology and the environment, good governance, and social stability.

In principle, the concept of harmonious society involves how societal conflicts can be resolved while eradicating the roots of these conflicts and achieving social stability. This is to be accomplished by creating a solid economic foundation and new ethics, and producing economic and social justice, a functional legal system, and steadily rising educational standards. Part of this concept, as sociologist Hang Lin has emphasized, is to expand the middle class, lower the numbers of people in low-income groups, and fight corruption. In the process, the ideal of this society is supposed to replace the abstract goal of "communism" (Wang and Zhu). The party's newspaper, *Renmin Ribao,* describes the harmonious society as a—no longer distant—societal ideal, in which everyone has a piece of the pie. And while social conflict will continue to exist, it will be resolved peacefully.

The concept of harmonious society brings to mind the Confucian ideal of "great harmony" (*datong*), a society without social injustice or insecurity, characterized by social and political harmony. In addition, such a society would distinguish itself from the Western model of a neoliberal market society, shaped by maximization of profit, wealth, and consumerism.

The concept of harmonious society also brings to mind the Western notion of "good society." In the latter, however, the implementation of such an ideal by the state is rejected, because it would imply restraints imposed from above. Instead, the process would have to be set into motion by consciously acting citizens. In contemporary China too, the situation is no longer one of edicts being passed down from above. Rather, the party-state is making efforts to motivate the people to take part in the conscious implementation of harmonious society. Therefore, the two concepts are really not far apart. The broader framework does vary, however, so that the term *authoritarian communitarianism* is an apt description of the Chinese situation. The essential difference is the emphasis placed on individual autonomy by Western states, while China tends to highlight social stability and order as the ultimate pragmatic goals of political and "harmonious" decision making.

SEE ALSO *Hu Jintao.*

BIBLIOGRAPHY

Jiang Xunqing and Ding Yuanzhu. *Goujian chengxin youai de hexie shehui* [Build-up a candid and fraternal harmonious society]. Beijing: Zhongguo Jingji Chubanshe, 2005.

Wang Weiping and Zhu Lin. *China Economic Review: China Aims at Harmonious Society*. 2004. http://news.xinhuanet.com/english/2004-12/17/content_2348778.htm

Wu Junjie and Zhang Hong, eds. *Zhongguo goujian hexie shehui wenti baogao* [Report on the construction of a harmonious society in China]. Beijing: Zhongguo Fazhan Chubanshe, 2005.

Thomas Heberer

HART, ROBERT
1835–1911

Robert Hart, inspector-general of the Chinese Imperial Maritime Customs Service for more than forty years, was unquestionably the most powerful westerner in China during most of that period. Yet he came from humble origins. Born in a small town in northern Ireland, Hart was the eldest child in a poor but deeply religious Protestant family. Bright, studious, and highly motivated, Hart attended a Methodist school as a young boy and won a scholarship to Belfast University. After graduation, on the urging of his favorite teacher, he decided to join the British consular service in China.

Hart arrived in Hong Kong in the spring of 1854 and was soon posted to Ningbo, where he studied the Chinese language assiduously and began keeping detailed personal journals. In his three and a half years at Ningbo, he served as a supernumerary interpreter for the British consulate, and in 1858 he was transferred to the British consulate in Guangzhou (Canton), where he began to learn the ins and outs of Chinese customs administration. At about this time, Hart acquired a Chinese mistress named Ayaou, with whom he had three children.

There are two large gaps in Hart's journals up to 1908: from August 1855 to February of 1858 and from January 1859 to May of 1863. In both cases it is clear that Hart destroyed this material because of its sensitivity; much later Hart expressed the wish that he had destroyed all seventy-seven volumes. The period from 1858 to 1863 was particularly sensitive, not only because of his relationship with Ayaou, but also because it was a time when Hart replaced the arrogant and intractable Horatio Nelson Lay (1832–1898) as the inspector-general of the Chinese Customs Service.

As the new inspector-general, headquartered in Beijing, Hart conferred regularly with high-ranking bureaucrats such as Prince Gong (Yixin, 1833–1898), Wenxiang (1818–1876), and Dong Xun (1807–1892). He also cultivated personal relationships with powerful provincial leaders, Li Hongzhang (1823–1901) in particular.

Recent scholarship shows Hart to be a man who was honest, hardworking, politically astute, culturally sensitive, and a master at building and sustaining personal relationships. He also appears to have been secretive, suspicious, autocratic, and supremely self-interested. Torn between his loyalty to China as a Qing bureaucratic and his commitment to Western-inspired notions of what China could and should be, Hart played the role of a constantly frustrated reformer, occillating wildly between optimism and pessimism, now praising and now condemning both his employers and the foreign powers with which he and they had to deal.

Despite his frustrations, Hart achieved much. By virtue of his connections in both China and the West, Hart facilitated arms purchases, gave the Chinese a wealth of technical advice, and performed a variety of diplomatic functions. In the 1867–1869 period, for example, he assisted in the negotiations for the Alcock Convention; in 1876 he helped to prevent war between China and Great Britain over the so-called Margary affair (1875). He also helped to arrange a peace between China and France during the Sino-French War (1884–1885), and he enabled the Chinese government to obtain desperately needed loans after the disastrous Sino-Japanese War (1894–1895). In 1901 Hart helped to negotiate the Boxer Protocol.

In 1906 the Qing dynasty made its first moves to take the Customs Service away from foreign control, and within two years Hart had left China (although technically he remained inspector-general until the day he died). He passed away on September 10, 1911, three weeks before the dynasty he had worked so hard to strengthen fell to Republican revolution.

SEE ALSO *Chinese Maritime Customs Service.*

BIBLIOGRAPHY

Bickers, Robert. Purloined Letters: History and the Chinese Maritime Customs Service. *Modern Asian Studies* 40, 3 (2006): 691–723.

Bredon, Juliet. *Sir Robert Hart: The Romance of a Great Career.* New York: Dutton, 1909.

Bruner, Katherine, John K. Fairbank, and Richard J. Smith, eds. *Entering China's Service: Robert Hart's Journals, 1854–1863.* Cambridge, MA: Council on East Asian Studies, Harvard University, 1986.

Brunero, Donna. *Britain's Imperial Cornerstone in China: The Chinese Maritime Customs Service, 1854–1949.* London and New York: Routledge, 2006.

Chen Shiqi. *Zhongguo jindai haiguan shi wenti chushen* [A preliminary investigation into questions about the history of China's recent martime customs]. Beijing: Zhongguo Zhanwang Chubanshe, 1987.

Chen Xiafei and Han Rongfang, eds. *Archives of China's Imperial Maritime Customs: Confidential Correspondence between Robert Hart and James Duncan Campbell, 1874–1907.* 4 vols. Beijing: Foreign Languages Press, 1990–1994.

Eberhard-Bréard, Andrea. Robert Hart and China's Statistical Revolution. *Modern Asian Studies* 40, 3 (2006): 605–629.

Fairbank, John K., Katherine Bruner, and Elizabeth Matheson, eds. *The I.G. in Peking: Letters of Robert Hart, Chinese Maritime Customs, 1868–1907.* 2 vols. Cambridge, MA: Harvard University Press, 1975.

Haiguan congshu yanjiu shi, ed. *Diguo zhuyi yu Zhongguo haiguan* [Imperialism and the Chinese maritime customs]. Beijing: Kexue Chubanshe, 1957–1959.

Horowitz, Richard S. Politics, Power, and the Chinese Maritime Customs: The Qing Restoration and the Ascent of Robert Hart. *Modern Asian Studies* 40, 3 (2006): 549–581.

Hu Sheng. *Diguo zhuyi yu Zhongguo zhengzhi* [Imperialism and Chinese politics]. 1948. Beijing: Renmin Chubanshe, 1998.

King, Frank H. H. Sealing the Mouth of Outrage: Notes on the Meaning and Intent of Hart's *These from the Land of Sinim. Modern Asian Studies* 40, 3 (2006): 725–736.

Lu Hanchao. *Hede zhuan* [Biography of Hart]. Shanghai: Renmin Chubanshe, 1986.

Qiu Ke. *Junei pangguan zhe: Yingren Hede yu Zhongguo jindai waijiao* [An outside observer on the inside: The Englishman (Robert) Hart and China's modern foreign relations.] Shaanxi, PRC: Renmin Chubanshe, 1990.

Smith, Richard J., John K. Fairbank, and Katherine Bruner, eds. *Robert Hart and China's Early Modernization: His Journals, 1863–1866.* Cambridge, MA: Council on East Asian Studies, Harvard University, 1991.

Spence, Jonathan. *To Change China: Western Advisers in China, 1620–1960.* Boston: Little, Brown, 1969. See especially chap. 4 on Horatio Nelson Lay and Robert Hart.

van de Ven, Hans. Robert Hart and the Chinese Maritime Customs Service: Preface. *Modern Asian Studies* 40, 3 (2006): 545–548.

Richard J. Smith

HEALTH CARE, 1800–1949

The history of health care from 1800 to 1949 was marked by the intersection as well as interaction of several strands of development, namely, the decline of the Qing (1644–1912) state's involvement in public health care, the work of Western medical missionaries, the activities of foreign philanthropic organizations, and the nationalist government's effort to build a modern health care system after 1928.

LATE QING HEALTH CARE

It may be misleading to speak of a state "system" of health care in nineteenth-century China. In fact, late in the Ming (1368–1644) and Qing dynasties, the state became less active in public health care. Increasingly, government-supported infirmaries and dispensaries were replaced by those of private, charitable, or religious organizations. Moreover, the system of government medical bureaus at various levels of local administration had disintegrated. By the second half of the century, Christian medical missionaries were also providing health care primarily to foreigners, their constituencies, and a small segment of the population.

During the Qing dynasty, the palace system of medical care consisted of a number of imperial physicians, as well as physicians of lower ranks, serving the imperial family and high officials. At local levels, "official" physicians employed by the authorities had, by late Qing, often fallen into a state of disrepute. Members of the upper strata of society could seek help from networks of elite learned physicians, whose knowledge, based on medical classics and contemporary local knowledge and innovations, had gained higher prestige and respect since Song times (960–1279). In addition to an increasing diversity of healing concepts, there was also growing specialization among these physicians. In times of need, ordinary patients would also appeal to religious healers, including Daoist or Buddhist priests, as well as mediums and shamans. Ordinary people also relied on physicians in local medicine shops and lower-class healers, including herbalists and itinerant practitioners. State supervision of medical practice was often lacking, although the government did intervene in time of crisis, such as during epidemics.

With the relative decline in state medical activism, private initiatives and efforts played increasingly greater roles in public health care. Religious charities had a long tradition of providing medical care. In addition, local elites (including officials, gentry, scholars, and wealthy merchants) organized charitable dispensaries and infirmaries, as well as societies, to distribute free prescriptions or provide medical relief for the needy. Such private philanthropic efforts gradually became institutionalized and often received government approval and financial support. To some extent, the rise of these institutions represented the assertion of social and moral leadership by local elites in an area where the state had abdicated its authority, as well as an assertion of local and regional identities. Government attempts to centralize control over health matters did not take place until 1906, when a Sanitary Bureau was established in the Ministry of Civil Affairs. The epidemic of pneumonic plague that ravaged Manchuria in 1910–1911 did lead to some government attempts to adopt modern measures of disease control under the direction of Dr. Wu Liande (Wu Lien-teh), a Cambridge University graduate. However, the outbreak of the 1911 Revolution meant that the development of modern health care would have to wait until after the founding of the new republic.

MISSIONARY MEDICINE

The opening of a clinic in Guangzhou (Canton) in 1835 by Peter Parker marked the beginning of attempts by Western missionaries to use medicine for Christian proselytization. Other medical missionaries entered the country after China's defeat in the Opium War (1839–1842) and, with their dispensaries and hospitals, became the chief transmitters of Western medical knowledge and practices to China. By 1889 there were 61 mission hospitals, and shortly after the founding of the Republic, Protestant missions ran 265 hospitals, with approximately 420 foreign doctors. In Hong Kong, a British colony after 1842, the London Missionary Society constructed a hospital and put Benjamin Hobson, a medical missionary, in charge. Mission hospitals were usually small—with an average of fifty beds per hospital—and, as late as the 1910s, generally understaffed and ill equipped. Moreover, except for isolated dispensaries in the countryside, most of the hospitals were in urban locations near mission centers, and their impact on the health care of the vast majority of the population in rural areas was rather limited. Yet even by the 1910s and 1920s, mission hospitals provided the majority of hospital beds in China. The experience of medical missions in Hong Kong proved to be more positive as a result of encouragement from the colonial government, local voluntarism on the part of Chinese and foreign elites, and a growing demand for Western medicine in the colony.

Medical missionaries focused mostly on cures in their hospitals and clinics, not only because the dramatic and visible results—as in the case of surgery—could be particularly useful in attracting favorable attention, but also because public-health work, which tended to be long-term in nature, proved to be difficult to develop and sustain without substantial financial and manpower support from the Chinese government. Notwithstanding, there was a limited but notable effort on the part of Dr. W. W. Peter, an American medical missionary, who, with the cooperation of the Young Men's Christian Association (YMCA) and Western-trained Chinese doctors, organized the Joint Council of Public Health in 1916 to promote public-health education.

Initial efforts on the part of medical missionaries to recruit native helpers gradually became institutionalized into training in mission medical schools. Individual missions established schools, and in addition, cooperative efforts among mission groups resulted in the founding of such schools as the Union Medical College in Beijing in 1906. Missionaries were pioneers in the education of Chinese women in medicine. For example, Dr. Mary Fulton, an American Presbyterian missionary, organized the Hackett Medical College in Guangzhou in 1899. Before that, two young Chinese mission-school graduates with Westernized names, Ida Kahn and Mary Stone, were brought to the United States by an American missionary in 1892. Four years later, after earning their medical degrees at the University of Michigan, they returned to open their practices in China. In Hong Kong, the efforts of Chinese and Western elites led to the founding in 1887 of the Hong Kong College of Medicine for Chinese, whose famous alumni included Dr. Sun Yat-sen (Sun Zhongshan).

The relatively small number of medical missionaries, the urban location of most hospitals, and the focus on cures accounted for the limited impact of missionary health care. Moreover, the missionaries' linkage of medicine to Christianity and their insistence on conversion alienated some Chinese, who, while finding Western medicine attractive, opted instead for a secular approach to attaining physical

A medical worker examining a patient's foot in Beijing, 1874. *Throughout the nineteenth century, private charities provided much of the health care services in China. In the late 1920s, the newly formed Nationalist government attempted to improve access to modern medical care, though their efforts eventually suffered from under funding and invading Japanese troops in the 1930s.* SPENCER ARNOLD/HULTON ARCHIVE/GETTY IMAGES

health. By the turn of the nineteenth century, many Chinese intellectuals began to embrace science and biomedical knowledge as the means to bring modern health care to the Chinese people.

BIOMEDICINE AND THE ROCKEFELLER FOUNDATION

The concern for China's salvation at the turn of the century prompted many Chinese to link physical health with strengthening the nation, and they exalted modern medical science, which seemed to promise both physical betterment and social renewal. By the early Republican period (1912–1949), this approach was promoted by a newly emerged medical elite of modern-trained professions and by intellectuals, groups that considered the healing modalities of indigenous medicine and medical missionaries inadequate and outdated. For them, advances in biomedicine in the West, especially the revolution in medicine brought about by the germ theory of disease, meant that China's health-care system should be based on the Western biomedical model of health. In the development of biomedicine in China, the Rockefeller Foundation played a critical role.

In 1915 the foundation took over Union Medical College, renamed it Peking Union Medical College, and developed it into the premier medical institution in China. This college promoted a health-care model that combined clinical practices with sophisticated techniques and specialized laboratory research. The foundation also provided funding for endowments and research fellowships for Chinese to further their studies abroad, as well as grants to upgrade science education in Chinese universities, including mission institutions. In 1920 it opened the School of Nursing at Peking Union Medical College, which helped to establish nursing as a career for Chinese women. The Department of Public Health at the college, in an agreement with the Beijing municipal government, maintained in a city ward a demonstration health station where public health practices and improvements were introduced. The model of biomedicine at Peking Union Medical College was urban-centered and to a significant extent elitist, yet the school's graduates constituted a corps of highly trained specialists in medicine and public health, many of whom would staff the new health bureaucracies and organizations after the institution of the Nationalist regime in 1928. Through their positions in government agencies and institutions of higher learning in the pre-1949 period, they exerted far-reaching influence in shaping the development of health care.

HEALTH CARE DURING THE NATIONALIST PERIOD

Political instability and the lack of a strong central government early in the Republican period meant that no nationwide health-care programs were introduced, and that programs developed by individual regions or municipalities were not coordinated. Except for those who had access to modern health care, provided by missionary institutions or by the few modern-trained physicians and medical facilities, the overwhelming majority of the population continued to rely on Chinese medicine, as before.

In its quest to modernize the country, the new Nationalist government decided to adopt biomedicine as the basis of the national health-care programs that it intended to develop. As in other areas of state building, the Nationalist government adopted a proactive approach in the planning, organization, and supervision of health-care developments. In addition to the Ministry of Health, the government established modern health agencies and organizations, including the National Quarantine Service, the Central Field Health Station, and the National Midwifery Board. It founded national and provincial medical schools and introduced a system of physician licensing. The laws regulating the registration of physicians, pharmacists, nurses, and midwives in the late 1920s and early 1930s were all based on biomedical knowledge and standards, thereby effectively excluding practitioners of Chinese medicine from the state health-care system. Yet the latter continued to provide relief for the majority of the population, especially in the countryside; even in the cities, scholar-physicians still enjoyed much support. To strengthen their position, these physicians identified indigenous medicine as "national medicine" and called for the standardization and scientific study of Chinese medical practice and Chinese drugs. The passage in 1935 of regulations governing the practice of Chinese medicine essentially allowed practitioners of Chinese medicine to bypass the criteria for modern-trained physicians. The health-care system was thus a combination of traditional health care provided by practitioners of Chinese medicine and a veneer of biomedical physicians, facilities, and medical agencies.

The Nationalist government also tried to develop modern health care at local levels. At first it established several demonstration centers that carried out organized campaigns of mass vaccination, environmental sanitation, communicable-disease control, maternal and child health care, school health care, and health education. As for the structure of rural health care, it eventually adopted as the basis of state medicine the three-tier system first introduced in 1929 by James Yen and Dr. Chen Zhiqian (C. C. Chen) in the Mass Education Movement at Dingxian. To facilitate access to basic health care, even at the lowest level, provision of health care was divided into three levels: the rural district's health substation, with village health workers; the subdistrict health station, with a doctor or nurse; and the county, with its hospital, laboratory, and curative and preventive facilities. Since the Nationalists did not have complete control over the entire country, such a structure was established only in a number of counties in areas under Nationalist control. Moreover, inadequate financial and human resources, as well as political constraints, conspired against the government's attempt to expand such programs nationwide. Finally, the outbreak of war against Japan seriously disrupted the Nationalists' process in constructing a modern state health-care system.

After the government relocated to Chongqing in the interior, it tried to continue developing a hierarchy of health services in provinces relatively bereft of modern health care. Moreover, it had the pressing task of quickly developing modern and efficient military medical services. Not surprisingly, priority was given to the demands of the military system, and as funding, material, equipment, and manpower were diverted to meet the exigencies of war, the quality and quantity of civilian health care suffered. Most people suffered under poor health conditions, as malnutrition, epidemics, and drug shortages aggravated the woes and hardship caused by the massive social and economic dislocations. The end of the war brought neither the stability nor a long enough interval for the normal development of a modern health-care system before the civil war intervened. After 1949 the People's Republic of China, building on the foundation of prewar efforts, would try to develop a health-care system in accordance with its ideological, political, social, and economic beliefs and commitments.

SEE ALSO *Medicine, Traditional; Medicine, Western, since 1949; Medicine, Western, 1800–1949; Missionaries.*

BIBLIOGRAPHY

Chen, Bangxian. *Zhongguo yixue shi* [A history of medicine in China]. Rev. ed. Taipei: Shangwu Yinshuguan, 1981. Originally published in 1937.

Chen, C. C. *Medicine in Rural China: A Personal Account.* Berkeley: University of California Press, 1989.

Rogaski, Ruth. *Hygienic Modernity: Meanings of Health and Disease in Treaty-Port China*. Berkeley: University of California Press, 2004.

Scheid, Volker. *Currents of Tradition in Chinese Medicine, 1626–2006.* Seattle, WA: Eastland Press, 2007.

Unschuld, Paul V. *Medicine in China: A History of Ideas*. Berkeley: University of California Press, 1985.

Wong, K. Chimin, and Wu Lien-teh. *History of Chinese Medicine*. 2nd ed. Shanghai: National Quarantine Service, 1936.

Yip, Ka-che. *Health and National Reconstruction in Nationalist China: The Development of Modern Health Services, 1928–1937*. Ann Arbor, MI: Association for Asian Studies, 1995.

Yip, Ka-che. Health, National Resistance, and National Reconstruction: The Organization of Health Services in China during the Sino-Japanese War, 1937–1945. In *Resisting Japan: Mobilizing for War in Modern China, 1935–1945*, ed. David Pong, pp. 105–126. Norwalk, CT: Eastbridge, 2008.

Ka-che Yip

HEAVY INDUSTRY

When the Communists took power in 1949, the Chinese leadership chose to adopt the Soviet development model, giving absolute priority to heavy industry. Their aim was for the nation to achieve basic industrial development within ten to fifteen years with the help of the Soviet Union and a transfer of wealth from agricultural regions to the cities. The Chinese remained financially modest when they signed a mutual-assistance treaty with the Soviets in February 1950: The forecasted investments totaled only two billion in U.S. dollars, a portion of which was long-term bank loans. The Soviet assistance, however, helped the Chinese to import new technologies and to train Chinese engineers in Moscow. The Soviets also sent some ten thousand technicians to China to pass on managerial and organizational know-how.

THE DOMINANCE OF THE NORTHEAST

The Northeast, which had been occupied by the Japanese, was the most industrialized region in China when the Communist Party took power. The Northeast contributed as much as 52 percent of national industrial production in 1952, when the region regained its prewar level of production. The Northeast was also more oriented toward heavy industry than China's other major industrial centers, such as Shanghai and Wuhan. That is why the new regime chose to concentrate its new investment there. Soon, thanks in part to the Japanese legacy and Soviet assistance, the Northeast would become the vanguard of socialism in China. It was designated a laboratory of Soviet-style development in China, and aimed to be the showcase for the whole country. Some sixty industrial sites with important production capacities were either expanded or set up. For example, the seventeen coal mines in the Northeast produced 32 million tons of the total national annual capacity of 41 millions tons of coal in 1952.

The strategic importance of the region's mineral resources and the existence of an industrial base can only partly explain the strong Soviet influence there. The Northeast lies near the Soviet Union geographically, and the existence of a railway network and a port (in Lüshun, or Port Arthur), inherited from the period of Russian occupation in Manchuria, gave this region better access to Soviet assistance. The special role of the Northeast during the early years of the China's Communist regime can be further explained by the influence of Gao Gang, governor of Manchuria in the 1950s. As governor of the richest region of China, Gao was responsible for the new regime's economic plan for the entire country, and he became the privileged interlocutor of the Soviet Union. Gao probably hoped to use the redevelopment of the Northeast as a political instrument to serve his personal ambitions. He visited Moscow in 1948, even before Mao did so, to negotiate economic assistance. When Gao stepped down in the mid-1950s, the attempt to "Sovietize" the Northeast ended, marking the prelude to the establishment of socialism with Chinese characteristics.

During the period covered by the First Five-Year Plan (1953–1957), some eighty-seven projects were located in other parts of China. Coal mines were developed in Fengfeng (Hebei) and Datong (Shanxi), petrochemicals and power generation in Taiyuan (Shanxi) and Lanzhou (Gansu), steel in Baotou (Inner Mongolia), electrical equipment in Xi'an (Shaanxi), metallurgy in Luoyang (Henan), and shipbuilding in Henan and Shanxi. Forty-three military and armaments projects were also established in Shanxi and Shaanxi. All these projects were located away from the coast and the former industrial cities of Shanghai and Tianjin.

Production in millions of tons

2001	154.55
2002	182.37
2003	222.34
2004	250.6
2005	349.36
2006	418.78
2007	490

SOURCE: Years 2001, 2002: Gao Lu and Zhang Xinsong. "China steel production world number one for seven consecutive years." Journal of Economic Information, July, 2003, http://funds.money.hexun.com/413140.shtml. Year 2003: Heavy Industry Yearbook 2004, baidu.com, http://tjsj.baidu.com/pages/jxyd/28/91/929257a9c65c76018ed4c280a7890ea0_0.html. Year 2005: Northern Future.com, http://www.bfh.com/news_show.php?id=161063. Years 2006, 2007: sina.com.cn, http://finance.sina.com.cn/money/future/20080131/10294477408.shtml.

Table 1

The increase in industrial production contributed greatly to the high rate of growth in the gross domestic product (GDP) of the 1950s: Average GDP growth from 1952 to 1957 was 9.2 percent. In 1952, overall industrial output accounted only for 17.6 percent of GDP, and heavy industry accounted only 35.5 percent of the total industrial output. But by the late 1950s, industrial output accounted 33.2 percent of GDP, and heavy industry contributed 55 percent of the total industrial output. China's huge investment in heavy industry was a major cause of budgetary deficits in the 1950s. In 1956 as much as 48 percent of the public budget was pooled into industrial projects, with a total amount of 14,735 million renminbi, representing an increase of 70 percent from 1955, far above the total investment made in 1953 to 1954.

FROM THE GREAT LEAP FORWARD TO THE CULTURAL REVOLUTION

Although the Sino-Soviet split did not take place until 1960, economically the pertinence of the Soviet development model was already at issue in the 1950s as it became apparent that it did not suit China due to the importance of China's rural population and the very low level of industrialization. Indeed, the slow increase in agricultural production during the First Five-Year Plan, despite collectivization, exemplified the fact that industrialization could not rely on the transfer of wealth from agriculture alone.

The Great Leap Forward could be analyzed as an attempt to better balance the rate of development between cities and the countryside by taking advantage of the huge pool of rural labor. The Great Leap Forward also marked an evolution in China's industrialization strategy, giving less importance to heavy industry. The new industrial projects developed during this period were not capital-intensive and were designed to meet local needs. The policy, which aimed to promote smaller, relatively autonomous industrial units, played an important role in making provinces into economically autarchic units. The Great Leap Forward significantly increased the autonomy of provinces and municipalities in terms of budgetary control and economic-development planning. As a result, 80 percent of companies controlled by the central government in 1957 came under the control of provincial and municipal governments in 1958. The benefits of these enterprises strengthened the financial position of local governments that made investments in local projects. These funds, called *extrabudgetary* because they did not appear on the central government budget, were invested in variety of new projects whose only commonality was that they aimed to increase production capacities by all possible means. Thus, within a few months, the number of collective enterprises and subsidiaries of large enterprises had increased. Most of the new workers were peasants hired on a temporary basis.

Nevertheless, the break with the Soviet Union had serious economic consequences for China. Trade contracted sharply, and the party was unable to sustain the rapid development of heavy industry without Soviet technical assistance. During the 1960s, some automobile and petrochemical equipment was imported from France and Great Britain. But beginning in 1964, instead of building new factories, China launched a massive relocation of heavy-industry plants to remote regions in western China. This "third-front project," however, was initiated mainly for military reasons.

During the Cultural Revolution (1966–1969), the party made no major changes to its industrial policy. However, technology transfers from abroad were stopped, and production suffered from the growing importance of mass movements and from the ideological opinions of factory workers. As with the Great Leap Forward, the Cultural Revolution was characterized by a decentralization of industrial management that began spontaneously but became formalized by 1969. This decentralization process weakened the coherence of China's modernization efforts, but led to the development of many small enterprises under the responsibility of local authorities. In Shenyang, for example, fertilizer, construction materials, and agricultural-tool plants were created in order to improve agricultural production. In the end, these disorganized attempts at industrialization left vestiges that, in some cases, were available for enhancement and development after the launching of reforms in 1978.

Workers at a steel manufacturing facility, Chengde, Heibei province, October 11, 2007. *Many of the early Communist efforts to transform China's agrarian economy into one based on heavy industry failed, as the country lacked the financial resources and technical knowledge to make the conversion. With market-based reforms in the late 1970s, however, heavy industries became more profitable, fueling China's economic growth at century's end.* FENG LI/GETTY IMAGES

THE REFORM ERA

The reforms ushered in by Deng Xiaoping in 1978 marked a significant shift in China's economic policy. The state tried to promote light industries that were less capital intensive and more capable of creating jobs. State actors (state-owned enterprises [SOEs] but also administrative bodies) were given incentives to develop new activities. The reforms permitted the development of a private sector and foreign investment, leading to a slow process of privatization that is not yet fully complete. Even so, the Communist regime did not drop its heavy industries, because their development remains important to the progress of modernization. Throughout the reform period, SOEs have garnered a significant portion of bank loans, and the authorities have made many attempts to restructure SOEs. Since the end of the 1970s, SOEs have been encouraged to import new technologies from Japan and Western countries.

However, the ideological debates around privatization, as well as the maintenance of lifetime employment, have slowed the restructuring of these enterprises. By deferring these difficult decisions, SOEs were looted from the inside, sometimes in order to develop new "private" income-generating activities. These multiple straddling practices led to the carving up of many enterprises (Kernen 2004). By the time of the Ninth National People's Congress in 1998, it was too late to imagine a restructuring of the entire sector. The Chinese government therefore decided to focus its efforts on two thousand of the best SOEs, merging enterprises in some cases, a policy summarized by the slogan "grasp the big, let go the small." Most of the selected enterprises are involved in energy, steel, petrochemicals, and automobiles.

The speeding up of SOE reforms was accompanied by a reinforcement of "budget constraints" and the granting of greater leeway in personnel management. The costs of raw materials, energy, and labor, which had already damaged the profitability of firms, have been increasing sharply. As a result, SOEs have regularly eliminated portions of the workforce through preretirement schemes and *xiagang*. *Xiagang* are workers who have been furloughed from SOEs with little chance of recall. *Xiagang* first began to appear in the middle 1990s, when party-state officials permitted managers to start shrinking their workforce at SOEs. The Chinese government does not consider these workers to be unemployed (at least till 2002), because SOEs are responsible for issuing stipends to their *xiagang*. It was intended that this process would be accompanied by the implementation of a new urban social safety net, but this has not occurred as planned in many places. The *xiagang* workers, the unemployed, and the preretired receive their salaries or pensions on only a very irregular basis, if they get paid at all, a situation that has led to the multiplication of workers' protests in a context characterized by the loss of social benefits won under socialism. In addition, the government has faced difficulties in setting up a new social-welfare system in a climate of widespread corruption (Kernen and Rocca 2000).

With the reforms, the engine of socialist industrialization also had to confront changes in the rules of modernization with regard to the environment. From 1957 to 1978, China's energy consumption multiplied sixfold to reach 571.44 million tons. During the same period, energy efficiency decreased sharply: GDP per ton of energy produced dropped from 942 to 527 renminbi, or 44 percent. In 2007 China's energy efficiency stood at the same level as that of Western countries twenty years earlier. Due to their low energy efficiency, Chinese SOEs have a major environmental impact.

MAJOR HEAVY INDUSTRIES

During the first decade of the twenty-first century, with the transformation of China's heavy industries not yet complete and the social costs of the reforms to state enterprises still apparent, new major industrial groups emerged. In the steel industry, China reached a steel-production capacity of approximately 100 million tons in 1996 and became the largest producer of the world. But the strongest growth in steel production occurred after 2001, one year after China entered the World Trade Organization (WTO), with annual increases reaching 18 percent in 2001, 20.3 percent in 2002, and 21.9 percent in 2003. Steel production climbed to 222.34 million tons in 2003. Approximately one-third of the world's steel is produced in China. The sector is characterized by a high dependence on imported iron ore from Latin America and Australia. Inside China, the large number of small producers increases competition.

China's largest steel producer is Baosteel, located in Shanghai, Jiangsu, and Zhejiang. Baosteel acquired Shanghai Steel and Meishan Steel in 1998 and BaYi Steel Xinjiang in 2006. In late 2001, Baosteel became the first SOE to experiment with a system in which at least half the board of directors are external members, similar to a joint-stock corporation. Even so, Baosteel took advantage of government protectionist measures, particularly between 2002 and 2005, when foreign imports were prohibited. By 2007, Baosteel had become the third-largest steel producer in the world, with a capacity of 23.8 millions tons. Internationally, Baosteel was negotiating with the Brazilian producer Vale to build a factory in Brazil.

The automobile sector has also been booming in China, with the passenger-vehicle segment registering the most impressive growth. In 1979 the proportion of passenger vehicles accounted for only 1.6 percent of China's total auto production. By 2007 the proportion had reached 54 percent. At a time when world auto production is declining due to weak demand, China is experiencing healthy growth. In 2006 China has surpassed Japan in total sales to become the second-largest consumer market for cars, behind the United States.

The auto industry in China is highly concentrated, with the top ten producers representing more than two-thirds of market share. Joint ventures account for about 1 percent of GDP. The country's largest auto producer is China FAW-Volkswagen group, composed by a Volkswagen venture with China First Automation Group and Shanghai Automation Group. This producer had an 18 percent market share in passenger vehicles in 2008. The second-largest group is Shanghai General Motors (with 7 percent market share in 2008). Their dominant position is largely due to their early entry into the Chinese market at the beginning of the 1990s. Among the top ten, the first fully Chinese producer is Chery, which was ranked number five as of 2009. Chery was created by the merger of five small SOEs, all based in Anhui Province.

All the players in the truck segment are Chinese, including Dongfeng, which had a 21 percent market share in 2008. China's top four truck manufacturers accounted for 70 percent of market share. Despite rapid increases in production, the entire auto industry operates in a highly competitive environment. Price cuts have been very important since 2002. The largest producer, China FAW-Volkswagen, has managed to make a small profit only since 2006, after twenty years of operations.

The petrochemical industry represents roughly 10 percent of GDP, making it an important mainstay of the national economy. There are more than 21,000 chemical factories throughout the country. Many new capacities have been added since the European Union imposed much-tighter norms on chemical industries and pushed many major European firms to relocate part of their production to Asia, in particular in Vietnam and China. In 2004, after an explosion at Sinopec's Jilin factory caused a large quantity of benzene to flow into the Songhua River, the central government released new regulations to better address environmental problems.

SEE ALSO *Industrial Policy since 1949; State-Owned Enterprises.*

BIBLIOGRAPHY

Domenach, Jean-Luc. *The Origins of the Great Leap Forward: The Case of One Chinese Province*. Trans. A. M. Berrett. Boulder, CO: Westview, 1995.

Kernen, Antoine. *La Chine vers l'économie de marché: Les privatisations à Shenyang* [China toward market economy: The privatization in Shenyang]. Paris: Karthala, 2004.

Kernen, Antoine, and Jean-Louis Rocca. The Social Responses to Unemployment and the "New Urban Poor." *China Perspectives* 27 (January–February 2000): 35–51.

Naughton, Barry. The Third Front: Defense Industrialization in the Chinese Interior. *China Quarterly* 115 (1988): 351–386.

Naughton, Barry. The Pattern and Legacy of Economic Growth in the Mao Era. In *Perspectives on Modern China: Four Anniversaries*, ed. Joyce Kallgren, Kenneth Lieberthal, Roderick MacFarquhar, and Frederic Wakeman, 226–254. Armonk, NY: Sharpe, 1991.

Rawski, Thomas. *Economic Growth and Employment in China*. New York: Oxford University Press, 1979.

Rawski, Thomas. *China's Transition to Industrialism: Producer Goods and Economic Development in the Twentieth Century*. Ann Arbor: University of Michigan Press, 1980.

Solinger, Dorothy. *Chinese Business under Socialism: The Politics of Domestic Commerce, 1949–1980*. Berkeley: University of California Press, 1984.

Solinger, Dorothy. *From Lathes to Looms: China's Industrial Policy in Comparative Perspective, 1979–1982*. Stanford, CA: Stanford University Press, 1991.

Antoine Kernen

HEBEI

Hebei Province occupies a special position within China's political geography. It encircles Beijing and Tianjin municipalities and together with them forms the Jing-Jin-Ji (Beijing-Tianjin-Hebei) Economic Zone. The topography of Hebei is characterized by mountainous areas in the west (Taihang Mountains) and northeast (Yanshan Mountains) and fertile plains in the south and east that are part of the North China Plain. The name *Hebei*, which means "north of the river," is due to the province's location north of the Yellow River (Huang He). Today, however, the river no longer constitutes the provincial boundary. Hebei shares borders with Henan in the south, Shanxi in the west, Inner Mongolia in the northwest, Liaoning in the northeast, and Shandong in the southeast. The coastal line of Hebei along the Bohai Sea is roughly 300 miles long.

Hebei has a temperate continental monsoon climate with annual precipitation ranging from 13 to 30 inches. Monthly average temperatures in the provincial capital Shijiazhuang rise from 30°F in January to 81°F in June with clear seasonal changes. Annual precipitation peaks during the hot and humid summers; winters are cold and dry. Hebei is administratively divided into eleven prefecture-level cities and 172 counties (including county-level cities and districts). With a total land area of about 72,465 square miles Hebei ranks twelfth among China's provinces. In 2006 the population was 68.98 million. Population density varies greatly between the mountainous areas in the north and west and the agricultural settlement areas on the North China Plain. In 2006 nearly two-thirds (62%) of the provincial population were classified as rural. Members of the acknowledged fifty-five ethnic minorities account for roughly 4 percent of Hebei's populace. Most of them (2.1 million according to the 2000 census) are Manchus and live in Chengde Prefecture

HEBEI

Capital city: Shijiazhuang
Largest cities (population): Shijiazhuang (9,400,000 [2006]), Tangshan, Baoding
Area: 187,700 sq. km. (72,500 sq. mi.)
Population: 68,980,000 (2006)
Demographics: Han, 96%; Manchu, 3%; Hui, 0.8%; Mongol, 0.2%
GDP: CNY 1,166 billion
Famous sites: East end of the Ming Great Wall at Shanhaiguan, Beidaihe, East and West Qing Dynasty Tombs, Zhaozhou (Anji) Bridge, Xumi Pagoda

in the northeast, followed by Hui (540,000) and Mongols (170,000).

During the Qing dynasty (1644–1912) the greater part of present-day Hebei was included in Zhili Province, indicating that it was "directly ruled." In 1928 the province received its present name through the newly established Nanjing Nationalist government. The provincial capital was first located in Beiping but was moved to Tianjin in 1930 and finally to Baoding in 1935. The discovery of the remains of the Peking man (Sinanthropus pekinensis) in the 1920s at Zhoukoudian (today Beijing Municipality) established a link to prehistory.

During the years of the Chinese Republic (1912–1949), Hebei became the stage on which both domestic and international competitors fought bloody wars that resulted in turning the agriculturally fertile region into a "land of famine." Especially the so-called Zhili clique around Feng Guozhang (1859–1919), Cao Kun (1862–1938), and Wu Peifu (1874–1949) fought with contending alliances and warlords before being defeated by the Guomindang troops during Chiang Kai-shek's Northern Expedition in 1928. After the Marco Polo Bridge incident in 1937, the province was seized by Japanese troops and continued to be under foreign dominion until 1945. Chinese Communist forces, however, managed to establish a number of base areas in Hebei that became part of the so-called Jin-Cha-Ji border area, crossing the provincial boundaries of Shanxi, Chahar, and Hebei. Another important *lieu de mémoire* of the Chinese Revolution is Xibaipo village, located some 55 miles northwest of Shijiazhuang in Pingshan County, from where the Chinese Communist Party (CCP) Central Committee and the People's Liberation Army headquarters directed the military campaigns during the final stages of the civil war.

Administrative reorganization during the early years of the People's Republic led to an extension of Hebei's territory beyond the reaches of the Great Wall. The most notable changes were the addition of the Zhangjiakou region in the northwest and the imperial summer residence Chengde (designated a UNESCO World Heritage Site in 1994) in the northeast, along with Shanhaiguan city, which marks the eastern end of the Great Wall at the Bohai Bay. Between 1958 and 1966 Tianjin was temporarily integrated into Hebei Province and came to serve as its capital. In February 1968 the provincial capital was finally moved to Shijiazhuang, a city that at the turn of the twentieth century had been only a small village. Owing to its strategic location, Shijiazhuang developed into one of China's most important railway hubs. There the north-south line connecting Beijing with Guangzhou intersects with east-west lines between Dezhou (Shandong) and Taiyuan (Shanxi). The number of inhabitants in the city district increased twentyfold in sixty years (1947: 120,000; 2007: 2.37 million).

The provincial transportation infrastructure is among the best developed in China. Besides the extensive railway network (2,994 miles), 89,340 miles of highways (including 1,447 miles of expressways) have been constructed, especially since the 1990s. Incredible devastation—in terms of both human cost and infrastructure damage—was wrought on northern Hebei by the major earthquake that hit Tangshan city in the early morning hours of July 27, 1976. With a magnitude of 7.8 on the Richter scale, the earthquake destroyed the whole city district and resulted in at least 240,000 deaths. Today Tangshan has been rebuilt and again has become the industrial center of northern Hebei. It also has a seaport, but it is less significant than Qinhuangdao port at the border of Liaoning Province. In 2006 about 205 million tons of freight were handled in Qinhuangdao, ranking it sixth in China, surpassing neighboring Dalian.

Although agricultural products dominated Hebei's economy for most of the late imperial and Republican eras, the rapid industrialization instigated by the CCP since the 1950s made light and heavy industry increasingly important. Today, Hebei's iron and steel production ranks first in China. Other important sectors include the construction industry, petrochemicals and pharmaceuticals, equipment manufacturing, and textiles. In 2006 the secondary sector accounted for 52.4 percent of Hebei's gross regional product which was RMB 1.166 trillion (agriculture: 13.8%; service sector: 33.8%). International exchange and cooperation is frequent. By 2006, 3,819 foreign-funded firms had registered in Hebei and total exports and imports reached US $23.5 billion. In addition, new business sectors such as tourism have become important.

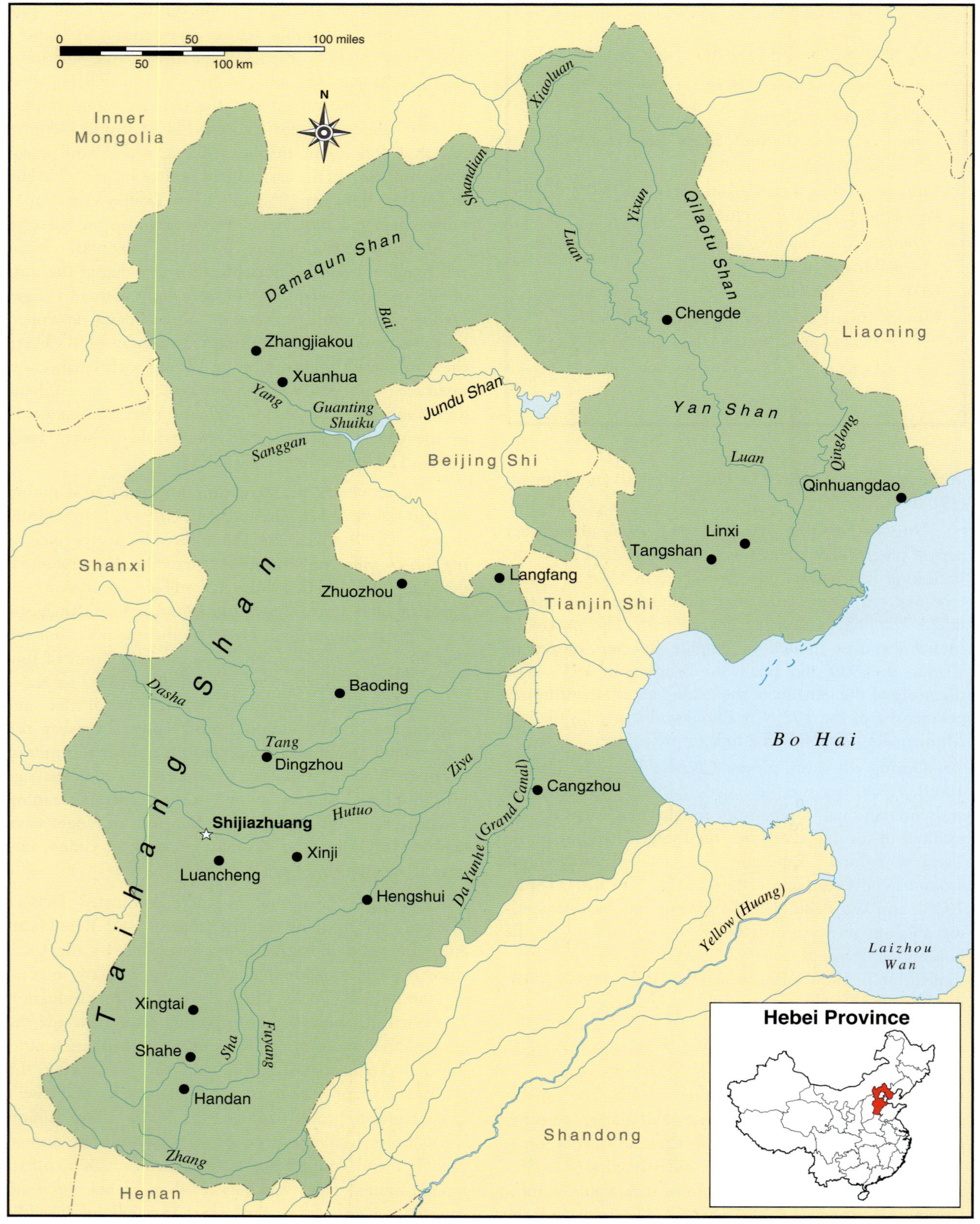

0 50 100 miles
0 50 100 km
N
Inner Mongolia
Damaqun Shan
Shandian
Xiaoluan
Yixun
Luan
Qilaotu Shan
Chengde
Liaoning
Bai
Zhangjiakou
Xuanhua
Yang
Guanting Shuiku
Jundu Shan
Yan Shan
Sanggan
Beijing Shi
Luan
Qinglong
Qinhuangdao
Linxi
Tangshan
Shanxi
Taihang Shan
Zhuozhou
Langfang
Tianjin Shi
Dasha
Baoding
Tang
Dingzhou
Ziya
Cangzhou
Bo Hai
Hutuo
Shijiazhuang
Xinji
Luancheng
Da Yunhe (Grand Canal)
Hengshui
Yellow (Huang)
Laizhou Wan
Xingtai
Sha
Fuyang
Shahe
Handan
Zhang
Shandong
Henan
Hebei Province

Worker cleaning at a dairy farm, Yangjiazhai village, near Yuanshi, Hebei province, September 20, 2008. *With a large, fertile plain in the southern and eastern portions of the province, Hebei has traditionally been an agriculturally productive province of China. After the 1950s, the province became home to large amounts of industry, taking advantage of the area's abundant natural resources, including coal, petroleum, and natural gas.* AP IMAGES

Hebei is rich in natural and mineral resources, so the energy sector is of great significance. Besides confirmed coal reserves of about 17 billion tons, Hebei also is endowed with natural gas (42 billion cubic meters) and petroleum (1.7 billion tons). Other mineral resources include gold, limestone, and quartzite. Agriculture and animal husbandry still play an important economic role, especially in the southeast and northwest. Hebei currently has 17 million acres (6.88 million hectares) of cultivated land, about 5.3 percent of the national total. Main agricultural products are grain, cotton, vegetables, fruit, and oil.

During the period of declining imperial rule and political infighting of the Chinese Republic, Hebei's proximity to Beijing as the political and cultural center of China turned out to be highly disadvantageous, but more recently the province has profited from its geographic location. Since the advent of the reform era in 1978, Hebei has experienced continuous economic growth, even above the national average. Living standards and net incomes have likewise increased. Per capita income reached 16,962 yuan in 2006, but great differences between rural and urban areas remain. Prospects are good, though, particularly because of Hebei's inclusion in the Jing-Jin-Ji Economic Zone, which has a consumer group of about 120 million that accounts for an important share in China's overall market capacity and offers attractive conditions for foreign investment.

SEE ALSO *Beijing.*

BIBLIOGRAPHY

Dangdai Zhongguo bianjibu. *Dangdai Zhongguo de Hebei.* 2 vols. Beijing: Zhongguo Shehui Kexue Chubanshe, 1990.

Li, Lillian M. *Fighting Famine in North China: State, Market, and Environmental Decline, 1690s–1990s.* Stanford, CA: Stanford University Press, 2007.

National Bureau of Statistics of China. *China Statistical Yearbook 2007.* Beijing: Author, 2007.

Daniel Leese

HEILONGJIANG

After 1949, the challenge facing the People's Republic of China in governing Heilongjiang Province and its sister provinces of Jilin and Liaoning lay in fully integrating them into China. The new government referred to the region as Dongbei (Northeast) to supersede its identity as Manchuria, homeland of the Manchu dynasty (1644–1912). Both Russia and Japan had tried to take over Manchuria in the early twentieth century. The Japanese created the puppet state of Manchukuo (Manzhouguo) in 1932, and Joseph Stalin (1879–1953) at the end of World War II (1937–1945) dreamed of regaining control of Manchuria's railways and warm-water ports.

Although the people of the Northeast had welcomed the Soviet armies in 1945 as liberators, Beijing arranged for the Russian troops to depart quickly in 1946. In the early 1950s, Soviet aid and loans built factories, schools, and other projects in the Northeast. Still, friendship with Soviet Russia did not mean China would ever allow a permanent Soviet Russian presence in the Northeast.

Following the cease-fire in the Korean War (1950–1953), Chinese authorities shored up defenses along the 2,700-mile (4,350-kilometer) border between Heilongjiang and the Soviet Union. Borrowing an ancient Chinese defense stratagem, the People's Liberation Army settled demobilized troops and their families in border villages. They served as a useful defensive network when Sino-Soviet relations soured after 1956.

Heilongjiang holds China's largest timber reserves in the Greater Xing'an and Lesser Xing'an Mountains. The broad grasslands of the Nen (Nonni) and Songhua (Sungari) river basins lie between and south of these two ranges. Heilongjiang's grasslands have a short 120-day growing season that still permits production of huge amounts of grain and soybeans.

In the late 1950s, geological explorations confirmed a major oil field in the Songhua Basin. China brought the field into production after 1960 as Daqing (Great Celebration) oil field. Daqing remains China's largest oil field and gave China petroleum independence until the mid-1990s, when domestic production could no longer keep up with burgeoning domestic demand. The Daqing oil field has proven a mighty resource, providing two-thirds of Heilongjiang's provincial government revenues.

In the 1960s, Daqing became a national model of self-reliance. All China was encouraged to emulate the sacrifices of oil-field workers and their families. During these years of hardship, the considerable industrial base that China's Northeast inherited from Japanese imperialism or built with Soviet loans began to deteriorate.

In 1969 tensions between the Soviet Union and the People's Republic of China produced armed clashes along the Heilongjiang border. Major incidents occurred at an island the Russians call Damanski and the Chinese called Zhenbao (Treasure) Island, about 200 kilometers (125 miles) south of Khabarovsk. Today, it is generally accepted that the Chinese initiated these clashes as a test of Soviet intentions. Sino-Russian border issues in Heilongjiang were finally settled in 2005.

The provincial capital of Harbin became a center of the Cultural Revolution (1966–1969). Mao's nephew, Mao Yuanxin, was a student at Harbin's Military Institute of Engineering in 1964. He emerged as a radical leader in the Northeast. Mao Yuanxin's star rose and fell with the Cultural Revolution. He was imprisoned with the fall of the Gang of Four in 1976.

Heilongjiang's leaders greeted Deng Xiaoping's reforms with caution during the 1980s and 1990s. This led to economic stagnation, and the Northeast became known as China's "rust belt." In 2004 Premier Wen Jiabao announced a massive plan to revitalize the Northeast's economy. By 2008 the results included technologically updated factories, new superhighways, all-weather commercial airports, and massive urban housing and commercial construction in Harbin and other Heilongjiang cities. Heilongjiang's population in the 2000 census was 36.8 million, and by 2007 had increased modestly to 38,240,000.

As elsewhere in China, corruption has followed in the wake of Heilongjiang's economic prosperity. A well-publicized case concerned Tian Fengshan, former minister of land and resources and a member of the Central Committee of the Chinese Communist Party. Tian was

HEILONGJIANG

Capital city: Harbin

Largest cities (population): Harbin (9,870,000 [2007]), Qiqihar (1,438,000 [2007]), Daqing (1,309,200 [2007])

Area: 460,000 sq. km. (180,000 sq. mi.)

Population: 38,240,000 (2007)

Demographics: Han, 95%; Manchu, 3%; Korean, 1%; Mongol, 0.4%; Hui, 0.3%

GDP: CNY 618.9 billion (2006)

Famous sites: Daoli/Pristan (Wharf) District of Harbin, Harbin Ice Festival (January), Jingbo (Mirror) Lake and Diaoshuilou Falls, Zhalong Nature Reserve, Yabuli Ski Resort, Wudalianchi Nature Reserve, Japanese Germ Warfare 731 Unit

convicted of taking more than $500,000 in bribes, most while he was governor of Heilongjiang from 1994 to 2000. In 2005 Tian forfeited all his property and received a sentence of life imprisonment.

Heilongjiang has suffered from serious ecological problems directly traceable to human activity. In 1987 manmade fires burned large swaths in the forests of the Xing'an Mountains, and in 2005 a chemical-factory spill in Jilin Province left the Songhua River burning at Harbin. Nevertheless, Heilongjiang's rivers, forests, and natural resources remain national treasures.

SEE ALSO *Harbin; Heavy Industry; Manchuria.*

BIBLIOGRAPHY

Chen Jian. *Mao's China and the Cold War*. Chapel Hill: University of North Carolina Press, 2001.

Christoffersen, Gaye. The Political Implications of Heilongjiang's Industrial Structure. In *Rethinking China's Provinces*, ed. John Fitzgerald, 221–246. London: Routledge, 2002.

Lieberthal, Kenneth, and Michel Oksenberg. *Policy Making in China: Leaders, Structures, and Processes*, 169–218. Princeton, NJ: Princeton University Press, 1988.

Worthing, Peter. *A Military History of Modern China: From the Manchu Conquest to Tian'anmen Square*, Chap. 12. Westport, CT: Praeger, 2007.

David D. Buck

HENAN

Henan is China's most populous province. It has long played a strategic role in Chinese history, and in more recent decades has played a prominent part in the country's politics. The province is rich in natural resources, and for this reason served as a granary for the empire. But Henan is also the site of frequent natural disasters. According to Chinese annals, Henan has seen 1,982 large-scale disasters over the past 2,100 years. Today, no year passes without drought in one part of the province or serious flooding in another. The frequency of natural disasters is connected to the geographical and climatic conditions: A period of heavy cloudbursts in June and July is followed by a rainless period of eight months.

Further, the region's fertile loess soil requires regular maintenance using a sophisticated irrigation system. Even then, irrigation cannot always compensate for the fickle meandering of the Yellow River, often called "China's sorrow," which has changed course many times along its lower reaches threading through Henan. Floods and droughts have often resulted in famine, with disastrous consequences for the people of the province. But nature cannot be blamed in every instance. Frequently, the opening of dikes was used as a military measure, as occurred in 1938 when Chiang Kai-shek (Jiang Jieshi) ordered a dike blown up to stop the Japanese advance. The resulting torrents destroyed eleven cities and four thousand villages, leaving twelve million people homeless and ruining the harvest in three provinces. Approximately 890,000 people died as a direct result of this futile attempt to halt the Japanese.

The prosaic name the province bears today (*Henan* means, literally, "south of the river") derives from the province's location south of the Yellow River. But two thousand years ago, Henan was known as Zhongzhou ("central prefecture"), or the prefecture at the center of the nine prefectures that made up China at that time (then known as Zhongguo, or Middle Kingdom, a term later applied to all of China). Henan's topography afforded its inhabitants strategically favorable conditions. Several mountain ranges and rivers form a natural boundary to the south, west, and northwest, while the plain in the east could be employed to produce two or three grain harvests a year. These conditions help explain why Henan was chosen as the site for imperial capitals for no less than nineteen dynasties in China's history. The three cities of Anyang, Luoyang, and Kaifeng account for more than half of China's imperial capitals, indeed for almost all of them until the medieval period.

HENAN

Capital city: Zhengzhou
Largest cities (population): Zhengzhou (6,920,000 [2006])
Area: 167,000 sq. km. (64,000 sq. mi.)
Population: 93,920,000 (2006)
Demographics: Han, 98.8%; Hui, 1%
GDP: CNY 1249 billion
Famous sites: Three of the Seven Ancient Capitals of China (Anyang, Kaifeng, Luoyang); Gaocheng Astronomical Observatory; Mount Song; Shaolin Temple; Longmen Grottoes; Songyue Temple Pagoda; Yinxu archaeological site; Youguo Temple Iron Pagoda; White Horse Temple

HISTORICAL AND CULTURAL DIMENSIONS

Henan natives make a number of strong claims about the centrality of their province in Chinese history. Henan is said to be the cradle of Chinese culture and civilization: specifically, the home of the Chinese script, the source of Chinese family names, and the birthplace of the major martial arts traditions. Henanese claim to be descendants of the Yellow Emperor (Huangdi), the fictive founder of the Chinese genealogical line. In fact, many emperors and historical personalities hailed from the province, including figures still revered today, such as the philosophers Laozi (sixth to seventh century BCE) and Zhuangzi (369–286), the patriotic military leader Yue Fei (1103–1141), and the poet Du Fu (712–770).

The religious traditions with the greatest impact on Henan's modern history have been the many streams of heretical folk religion that surfaced as popular chiliastic movements in the late imperial period, and that continue to invite suspicion in Beijing to this day. These movements have tended to emerge in times of flood, drought, and war, of which Henan has had more than its share.

This was a major reason why the province, which is rich in natural resources, also has been home to bandits, protest movements, and underground societies with a religious orientation. Religious sects that promised relief from want or that held out hope for a better future have always flourished in Henan. In the nineteenth and early twentieth centuries, Henan was a rallying site for the White Lotus sect (Bailianhui), the Nian movement, the Heavenly Bamboo movement (Tianzhujiao), the Society of Elder Brothers (Gelaohui), the Green and Red Gangs (Qinghongbang), the Persistent Way (Yiguandao), and the Big Sword Society (Dadaohui), to name a few. These groups tended to emerge in times of crisis, when membership expanded through recruitment of impoverished and uprooted peasant farmers or demobilized soldiers.

DEVELOPMENTS AFTER THE FOUNDING OF THE PEOPLE'S REPUBLIC OF CHINA (PRC)

The Communist government in the early 1950s moved the provincial capital from Kaifeng to Zhengzhou, which soon developed from a railroad juncture and a small city to a major industrial hub. By establishing Zhengzhou as the capital of the province in 1954, the leadership emphasized its objectives for the province. They chose a new,

Beizhuang performers in Songxian county, Henan province, February 11, 2006. *The residents of Zhenxidian Village, located in China's Henan province, participate in traditional Beizhuang folk art performances. Members of the community sing, dance, and share stories, all the while balancing small children, dressed in bright colors, over their heads.* AP IMAGES

socialist city, dominated by the modern industrial sector to undermine the orientation to the old historio-cultural centers and embody the spirit of the new age. As a result of the construction of colleges, universities, and research institutes in the new provincial capital, Kaifeng lost its old position as the cultural center of the province, though Henan University remained there. Luoyang and Anyang also were patterned after the Communist notion of development and built up as industrial production bases. This development, however, did not lead to a comprehensive modernization, but produced great intraprovincial socioeconomic disparities, which still exist.

After the founding of the PRC, in each of the collectivization and political movements of the Mao era, Henan was more or less a revolutionary model. For example, after Mao openly approved of the establishment of people's communes combining industry, agriculture, trade, education, and defense functions, Henan was the first province to begin establishing such communes on a province-wide basis in August 1958. At the same time, an egalitarian remuneration for all commune members was introduced. During the subsequent Great Leap Forward (1958–1960), Henan paid a price: Its position as a revolutionary model led to the highest starvation rate in the country.

The Cultural Revolution (1966–1969) was initiated with the first big-character poster campaign at Peking University and at Zhengzhou University and other universities in Henan in June 1966. As in earlier campaigns, the Cultural Revolution and its different campaigns were carried out relatively violently in Henan. Mao had many times commended the province and said in October 1966: "Only Henan has the character 'boldness' in mind;

the majority have the character 'fear' in mind." Some of the most active critics of the "top party leaders in authority" came from Henan. Their criticism resulted, for example, in the arrest and probably also the subsequent death of Liu Shaoqi in prison in Kaifeng.

After the Cultural Revolution, the purge of supporters of the Gang of Four and the implementation of the centrally agreed-upon reform policy was very difficult in Henan. Because Henan was one of the most heavily disputed provinces during the Cultural Revolution and a revolutionary stronghold, it took time to implement reform policies there.

In 1999 a new campaign was waged under the title, "Have deep love for Henan, add splendor to the Central Plains." The aim was to integrate Henan's people by strengthening their sense of provincial identity and focusing their efforts on provincial development. The core of this campaign, placing Henan first, means that the province has to develop regional policies suited to its particular characteristics, even if these policies differ from those put forward by the center.

Henan's top industries include electronics, chemicals, foodstuff, textiles, and building materials. Henan is also a major transportation hub. The provincial capital is at the juncture of two important rail lines, Beijing-to-Guangzhou and Shanghai-to-Ürümqi. Zhengzhou is also the largest relay station for both passengers and freight for the eastern part of the European-Asian transcontinental line. In contrast, rural areas in Henan that are not linked to the transportation network remain poor.

SEE ALSO *River Systems: Yellow River.*

BIBLIOGRAPHY

Domenach, Jean-Luc. *The Origins of the Great Leap Forward: The Case of One Chinese Province*. Trans. A. M. Berrett. Boulder, CO: Westview, 1995.

Heberer, Thomas, and Sabine Jakobi. Henan as a Model: From Hegemonism to Fragmentism. In *Rethinking China's Provinces*, ed. John Fitzgerald, 89–124. London and New York: Routledge, 2002.

Wou, Odoric Y. K. *Mobilizing the Masses: Building Revolution in Henan*. Stanford, CA: Stanford University Press 1994.

Thomas Heberer

HERITAGE PROTECTION

The history of heritage protection in China is long and uneven, and has been shaped by competing scholarly, economic, and political interests. Cultural heritage, as defined by the World Heritage Committee of the United Nations Educational, Scientific, and Cultural Organization (UNESCO), includes both tangible cultural heritage (such as monuments, architectural works, archaeological sites, and artifacts) and intangible cultural heritage (including poems, stories, legends, folk performing arts [e.g., music, dance, drama, puppet shows], rituals, festivals, and handicrafts). While modern concepts of heritage protection did not begin in China until the 1930s, two millennia of traditional historiography provided a fertile foundation for the collection and scholarly study of antiquities. During the twentieth century, the evolution of museums in China and the development of scientific archaeology reflected growing concerns about how best to protect the past and brought to light new data for understanding China's heritage. Since the 1980s heritage protection statutes and policies have been increasingly clarified and refined, often incorporating international standards, in order to protect China's rich cultural heritage from an onslaught of new threats brought on by rapid economic development, vastly increased tourism, and archaeological looting.

THE RISE OF COLLECTIONS AND MUSEUMS

China has a long tradition of imperial and scholarly collecting of art and antiquities. During the heyday of traditional antiquarianism in the eleventh century in the late Northern Song period, scholars published sophisticated studies of their collections of ancient bronzes and inscriptions on stone in an effort to understand the origins of various rituals and to correct errors and fill gaps in the rich surviving corpus of historical texts. It is possible that at least some of these efforts represented a growing desire to define a Chinese cultural identity in the face of political and military crises brought on by aggressive non-Chinese neighbors to the north.

With the decline of the Qing dynasty in the late nineteenth and early twentieth centuries, the vast imperial collections of art and artifacts built up during the previous centuries were increasingly threatened by dispersal among imperial sites, loss through palace corruption, and destruction during warfare (e.g., the burning of Yuanming Yuan [Old Summer Palace] by the Anglo-French Expedition in 1860 and the destruction of Yihe Yuan [Summer Palace] during the 1900–1901 occupation of the Forbidden City by the Allied Expeditionary Forces). By 1912 there were increasing calls to protect and organize these collections, and the newly formed Republican government responded. By 1914 some 120,000 royal treasures had been shipped from various locales to Beijing to be housed in China's first public museum, the Guwu Chenliesuo (Gallery of Antiquities, sometimes called the Government Museum), in the Forbidden City. In 1925 some 1.17 million additional imperial objects were brought together under the new Palace Museum (Gugong Bowuyuan). Facing the growing threat of Japanese military expansionism in China in the 1930s, these collections were transferred from Beiping (as Beijing was then known) to Shanghai, then evacuated to Nanjing, and then moved to the relative safety of southwest China. In 1949, with the imminent collapse of the Republican government to the Communists, many of the finest objects were transferred to Taiwan, eventually to be housed in the National Palace Museum in Taibei.

After the establishment of the People's Republic in 1949, the government developed a nationwide network of national, provincial, and local museums for archaeology, art, and history, now numbering more than 2,200. While many of these museums during their early years functioned as an educational tool to provide the public with material evidence to support the Marxist paradigm for social evolution, many of China's museums today are truly world-class in terms of their collections, design, and programming.

THE DEVELOPMENT OF ARCHAEOLOGY

Archaeology as a scientific discipline in China evolved from traditional historiography and antiquarianism. Fieldwork by both Western and Chinese archaeologists, beginning in the early 1920s, provided a new and major source of data for understanding China's ancient past. The rise of scientific archaeology was fostered by growing efforts to stem the largely unregulated collecting expeditions on behalf of Western art museums during the 1920s. To curb the flood of exports of antiquities, China in 1930 passed its first regulations banning the excavation or sale of antiquities to foreigners. Rules concerning archaeological and historical sites and materials were considerably expanded in 1950. These rules proclaimed that all buried or excavated ancient relics belong to the state, and mandated protection during construction and regulation of excavation.

During the early 1950s, a network of national and provincial archaeological institutes was established under the Ministry of Culture to oversee archaeological research. Formal training programs in archaeology, conservation, and museology were established at key universities. Cultural sites, about 300,000 to date, and historic cities were inventoried across China to assess their historical, scientific, and artistic significance, and to prioritize protection, conservation, and restoration projects. Since the 1970s China has enacted numerous statutes relating to the excavation, sale, and export of cultural property, and to the management of heritage sites, the most significant being the 1982 Cultural Relics Protection Law (and its amendment in 1991 and major revision in 2002), China's 1989 approval of UNESCO's 1970 Convention on the Means of Prohibiting and Preventing the Illicit Import, Export, and Transfer of Ownership of Cultural Property, and the 1989 Regulations on the Protection and Administration of Underwater Cultural Relics. Since the early 1990s, China's regulations have allowed foreign scholars to participate in approved collaborative archaeological and conservation projects in China, and dozens of such projects have been undertaken. Within these evolving guidelines administered by the State Bureau of Cultural Relics (now the State Administration of Cultural Heritage), archaeology in China has flourished during the past forty years, and this activity has resulted in an enormous body of scholarly publications, as well as an expansion of archaeological exhibitions both in China and abroad.

HERITAGE PROTECTION IN THE TWENTY-FIRST CENTURY

China's commitment to cultural heritage continues to expand. The recognition of the inherent social and historical value of cultural heritage sites, as well as of the potential for economic rewards through increased tourism (both domestic and foreign), provides strong incentive for the further protection and development of heritage sites. Since ratifying the UNESCO 1972 Convention Concerning the Protection of the World Cultural and Natural Heritage in 1985, China has had 37 cultural and natural heritage sites included on the World Heritage List, which brings with it financial and technical aid, as well as increased international awareness. The State Administration of Cultural Heritage, working with the Chinese and Australian offices of the International Council on Monuments and Sites and the Getty Conservation Institute, in 2002 established Principles for the Conservation of Heritage Sites in China, drawing on international practices and experience to provide an authoritative guide for heritage management in China.

Despite these many advances, the challenges remain enormous. The booming international trade in antiquities continues to spur disastrous looting of China's archaeological sites, a situation increasingly exacerbated by growing domestic demand for antiquities among China's nouveau riche. The situation is worsened by the difficulties of policing remote sites and enforcing existing laws, as well as certain levels of corruption and collusion within China and confusion about ambiguities in certain relevant statutes. In an effort to stem this looting, the Chinese government in 2004 submitted a petition to the U.S. State Department, via the U.S. Cultural Property Advisory Committee, to enact a ban on the import into the United States of most categories of Chinese cultural objects created before 1911. Following much discussion and debate in the United States, on January 14, 2009, the United States and China signed a memorandum of

Buddhist statues from the Yungang Grottoes, near Dataong, Shanxi province, June, 2004. *China's economic growth at the turn of the twenty-first century has unwittingly threatened many sites of historical importance. As citizens become increasingly prosperous, more tourists visit sites sensitive to large crowds, compromising the attractions for future generations.* © DEMETRIO CARRASCO/ JAI/CORBIS

understanding that imposed U.S. import restrictions on a broad and inclusive range of Chinese archaeological materials from the Paleolithic period through the Tang dynasty (618–907), as well as monumental sculpture and wall art more than 250 years old, unless documentation can prove that it left China legally. The memorandum also undertakes to establish closer collaboration in the promotion of international cultural and scientific exchanges utilizing archaeological materials, and to facilitate long-term loans of Chinese archaeological objects to American museums.

China's burgeoning economy and resulting construction threatens thousands of historical and archaeological sites, particularly in its cities. Beijing stands as but one example. Destruction wrought in the early 1950s by efforts to modernize the city resulted in the razing of Beijing's ancient city walls and gates, vast neighborhoods of traditional *hutong* residential streets and alleys, *siheyuan* courtyard houses, Ming- and Qing-dynasty princely mansions, and some 2,000 temples. With increased market pressures on urban real estate, including the multibillion dollar construction projects related to the 2008 Summer Olympics, this wave of demolition has expanded in recent years. Other major projects, such as the Three Gorges Dam on the Yangzi River, have also had an enormous impact on local historical and cultural sites. The challenge for China is to find a way to balance its economic and developmental needs with its growing recognition of the national and international importance of protecting its cultural heritage for the future.

SEE ALSO *Archaeology, History of; Archaeology, Politics of; Architecture; Art Museums; Folk Art; Handicrafts; Museums.*

BIBLIOGRAPHY

Agnew, Neville, and Martha Demas. *Principles for the Conservation of Heritage Sites in China.* Los Angeles: Getty Conservation Institute, 2002.

Balachandran, Sanchita. Object Lessons: The Politics of Preservation and Museum Building in Western China in the

Early Twentieth Century. *International Journal of Cultural Property* 14 (2007): 1–32.

Murphy, J. David. An Annotated Chronological Index of People's Republic of China Statutory and Other Materials Relating to Cultural Property. *International Journal of Cultural Property* 3, 1 (1994): 159–167.

Murphy, J. David. *Plunder and Preservation: Cultural Property Law and Practice in the People's Republic of China.* Hong Kong: Oxford University Press, 1995.

Ruan, Yisan. The Conservation of Chinese Historic Cities. *Antiquity* 67 (1993): 850–856.

Zhuang, Min. The Administration of China's Archaeological Heritage. In *Archaeological Heritage Management in the Modern World*, ed. Henry Cleere, 102–108. London: Unwin Hyman, 1989.

Robert E. Murowchick

HIGH TECHNOLOGY

High technology is, loosely speaking, technology for which success depends largely on the ability to keep up with rapid innovations in products, production processes, or both. Microelectronics, biotechnology, new materials, telecommunications, civilian aviation, robotics and machine tools, and computer hardware and software are considered high technology because they are crucial in global competition. Nanotechnology is the most recent addition to the high-tech family.While engaged in the Cultural Revolution and its aftermath between 1966 and 1976, China missed the new technology revolution with high technology as the core. After China reopened its door in the late 1970s, catching up with the world in science and technology became essential. In 1986 four senior scientists who had contributed to China's strategic-weapons program suggested to Deng Xiaoping, then China's paramount leader, to follow global high-tech trends and develop China's own high-tech industry. The State High Technology Research and Development Program (or the 863 Program, so called because it was initiated in March of 1986) was thus implemented, and two years later the Torch Program was launched to carry out high-tech industrialization. Aimed at enhancing China's international competitiveness and improving China's overall research-and-development capability in high technology, the 863 Program initially covered seven priority areas: biotechnology, space, information, lasers, automation, energy, and advanced materials (marine technology was added in 1996). The civilian-oriented technology projects of the 863 Program have been managed by the State Science and Technology Commission and its successor, the Ministry of Science and Technology. Research in space and laser technology fall under the jurisdiction of the Commission of Science, Technology, and Industry for National Defense, which merged into the Ministry of Industry and Information Technology in the 2008 government reorganization.

In the mid-1980s, China also started to reform its science-and-technology management system with the rationale of better linking research and the economy. In particular, the Chinese Academy of Sciences (CAS) implemented a "one academy, two systems" experiment, keeping a small number of its research personnel in basic research while leaving the rest to seek outside support for applied research-and-development work that directly benefits the economy and meets market needs. Inspired by what had been occurring in California's Silicon Valley and along Route 128 in Massachusetts in the United States, Chinese scientists turned their technological findings toward the development of marketable products. Zhongguancun in Beijing—home to Peking University, Tsinghua University, some sixty institutions of higher education, and more than two hundred research institutes affiliated with the CAS, government ministries, and the Beijing municipality—stood out as China's hub of entrepreneurship. Zhongguancun-based enterprises, including what is now known as Lenovo, a spin-off from the CAS Institute of Computing Technology, focused on meeting market needs and integrating technological development, industry, and commerce. Operating on the principle of "self-chosen partnership, self-financing, self-operation, and self-responsibility for gains and losses" (the "four-self principle," sizi yuanze), the enterprises promoted technology transfer from universities and research institutes and created a series of products with market potential and competitive edge.While designated by the State Council in 1988 as a high-tech zone, Zhongguancun was not called a science park until 1999. The Zhongguancun Science Park now has a total area of more than 200 square kilometers, with its industrial structure centering on information technology, integrated optical-mechanical-electronic technology, biotechnology, pharmaceuticals, new materials, and energy-saving and environment-friendly technologies. Companies spun-off from research institutes and universities, high-tech firms set up by domestic entrepreneurs, and students and scholars returned from overseas, and multinational corporations have been competing with each other in the Zhongguancun Science Park.

More important, Zhongguancun has shown a spillover effect in promoting high-tech development throughout China. As a whole, fifty-three national high-tech parks have been established across the country, including those in Guangzhou and Shenzhen in Guangdong Province, Hefei in Anhui Province, Shanghai municipality, Wuhan in Hubei Province, and Xi'an in Shaanxi Province (see Table 1). Only Qinghai, Ningxia, and Tibet do not have national high-tech parks.

Entering the twenty-first century, China's technology policy has focused on building an indigenous technological capability in industry, which has led to new policies affecting intellectual property rights and venture capital. The most recent initiatives include allowing research-and-development

China's national high-tech zones (2008)

Region	Municipality/ province	Name of high-tech zone (year established)
East	Beijing	Zhongguancun (1988)
	Tianjin	Tianjin (1991)
	Shanghai	Shanghai (1991)
	Liaoning	Shenyang, Dalian (1991), Anshan (1993)
	Hebei	Shijiazhuang (1991), Baoding (1993)
	Shandong	Jinan, Weihai (1991), Qingdao, Weifang, Zibo (1993)
	Jiangsu	Nanjing (1991), Suzhou, Wuxi, Changzhou (1993)
	Zhejiang	Hangzhou (1991)
	Guangdong	Guangzhou, Zhongshan, Shenzhen (1991), Foshan, Huizhou, Zhuhai (1993)
	Fujian	Fuzhou, Xiamen (1991)
	Guanxi	Guilin (1991), Nanning (1993)
	Hainan	Hainan (1991)
Middle	Heilongjiang	Harbin (1991), Daqing (1993)
	Jilin	Changchun (1991), Jilin (1993)
	Neimenggu	Baotou (1993)
	Shanxi	Taiyuan (1993)
	Henan	Zhengzhou (1991), Luoyang (1993)
	Hubei	Wuhan Donghu, Xiangfan (1993)
	Hunan	Changsha (1991), Zhuzhou (1993)
	Anhui	Hefei (1991)
	Jiangxi	Nanchang (1993)
West	Shaanxi	Xi'an (1991), Baoji (1993), Yangling (1997)
	Gansu	Lanzhou (1993)
	Xinjiang	Urumuqi (1993)
	Chongqing	Chongqing (1991)
	Sichuan	Chengdu (1991), Mianyang (1993)
	Yunnan	Kunming (1993)
	Guizhou	Guiyang (1993)

Table 1

expenditures to be written off as costs, implementing a technology standard and patent-focused strategy in innovation endeavors and supporting Chinese technology in government procurements. China's most technology-intensive companies have taken the innovation issue seriously by increasing investment in research and development and reinforcing their innovation activities. As a whole, enterprises now account for more than two-thirds of China's research-and-development expenditures, reaching the level of developed countries, at least at face value.

China's telecommunications equipment manufacturing sector was among the first opened to global competition, as well as the sector in which domestic players have attained a critical mass. China started its massive telecommunications equipment manufacturing in the early 1980s. Initially, technology transfer through direct imports and Sino-foreign joint ventures played an important role. By absorbing and assimilating foreign technology and, most important, through indigenous research-and-development efforts, some Chinese firms—especially Julong, Datang, Zhongxing, and Huawei (together known as JuDaZhongHua, according to the first characters of each firms' Chinese name)—have gradually acquired the advanced technology necessary to develop their own products. These firms employ a high percentage of scientists and engineers with master's and doctoral degrees, and invest 10 percent or more of their sales revenue on research and development. They may still lack critical technology, such as application-specific integrated circuits, but could acquire them by participating in the international division of labor and outsourcing those aspects of projects to foreign firms. As of 2008, Chinese technology firms were not in the same league with the world's major players in size, technology, quality, or performance of the equipment because most Chinese manufacturers are technology followers rather than innovators. By the time they reverse-engineer imported products and develop the manufacturing capability to imitate them, their international competitors have introduced a new generation of products. Nevertheless, because of the presence of these Chinese firms, foreign firms have had to relinquish the low-end product market or reduce prices for similar products sold in China.

Because China is moving toward the 3G (third generation) mobile communications technology along with other countries, it offers a domestically proposed standard approved by the International Telecommunications Union—TD-SCDMA, jointly developed by China's Datang and Germany's Siemens—to compete with standards set by the United States mobile-network developer Qualcomm (CDMA) as well as by the European (WCDMA). China will likely request that one of its telecom operators adopt this 3G mobile telecommunications standard, which will boost research-and-development activities among China's leading high-tech firms. Although the Chinese standard may not be as advanced as the CDMA and WCDMA standards, the case itself suggests that China's technical community has realized the importance of indigenous intellectual property rights and has devoted its innovative capability to developing the most advanced technology.

One of the consequences of China's open-door policy is the flow of a very large volume of investment into the country. First came those companies run by businesspeople from Hong Kong, Macau, and Taiwan, as well as businesspeople of Chinese origin from other areas. These companies primarily focused on labor-intensive manufacturing in toys, fashions, and other low-end products. With the steady improvement and normalization of the Chinese investment environment, especially after Deng Xiaoping's tour to southern China in 1992, multinational corporations have gradually moved their higher value-added operations to China. This became particularly true after China became a member of the World Trade Organization (WTO) in late 2001. Not only has penetrating the huge Chinese market of increasingly affluent consumers become a high priority, but so too has been the

Workers assembling cellular telephones, Ningbo, China, April 27, 2007. *Years of isolation under Mao Zedong kept China's technology industry at a disadvantage. During the 1970s, Deng Xiaoping hoped to see China become economically competitive, pushing the country to invest heavily in education, research, and development to become a global leader in high-tech manufacturing.* © **MICHAEL REYNOLDS/EPA/CORBIS**

opportunity to take advantage of the high-quality but low-cost labor force.

Since the late 1990s, foreign-based companies have expanded their research-and-development presence in China by setting up independent research-and-development centers, some of which also actively collaborate with Chinese researchers or research organizations. According to some estimates, there were over one thousand foreign corporate research-and-development centers in China at the end of 2007. There is little doubt that the establishment of such research-and-development labs by foreign-invested corporations is part of the global development strategy of the parent companies—becoming closer to their Chinese operations and localizing technology developed in the "home base." Many of these centers take advantage of the preferential policies that the Chinese government has offered to entice foreign research-and-development activities. And there is a high likelihood that these centers are tapping the domestic pool of high-quality researchers from across China's local enterprises, research institutes, and universities. But centers set up by well-known multinational corporations such as IBM, Microsoft, Intel, GE, and others have gone beyond these reasons and have become an important node in the global research-and-development network. Having experienced a steady increase, high-tech exports seem to be an important growth engine of the Chinese economy. China's computer and telecommunications technology has risen to international competitiveness, enjoying a trade surplus over several years. The country's export-oriented strategy has shown results; processing and assembling with supplied materials from abroad for export purposes accounts for a significant portion of China's high-tech exports. China's export-led high-tech industry has been based on low labor costs and imported foreign technologies or even components. China has become, in effect, a massive assembly linefor products made of high-tech parts from abroad plus low-tech domestic components. And in areas where China is enjoying a certain level of competitiveness, most of it has come from foreign-invested enterprises, with wholly owned foreign enterprises having seen their portion increasing while state-owned enterprises have been declining. To become a high-tech power, China has to move beyond its comparative advantage in labor to gain a competitive edge in a cluster of technologies so as to climb the technology value chain.

SEE ALSO *Research in Engineering; Research in the Sciences.*

BIBLIOGRAPHY

Lu Qiwen. *China's Leap into the Information Age: Innovation and Organization in the Computer Industry.* Oxford, U.K.: Oxford University Press, 2000.

Segal, Adam. *Digital Dragon: High-Technology Enterprises in China.* Ithaca, NY: Cornell University Press, 2002.

Sun, Yifei, Max von Zedtwitz, and Denis Fred Simon, eds. *Global R&D in China.* London: Routledge, 2008.

Zhou Yu. *The Inside Story of China's High-Tech Industry: Making Silicon Valley in Beijing.* Lanham, MD: Rowman and Littlefield, 2008.

Cong Cao

HISTORY

This entry contains the following:

OVERVIEW, 1800–1860

From 1800 to 1860, the Qing empire faced new and daunting economic, political, and security challenges that initially sparked a burst of imperial, official, and literati activism which sought the reform and renewal of the Qing government; but these efforts were overwhelmed by the Taiping Uprising (1851–1864) and the Western and Russian assaults on the maritime and northern borders respectively from 1839 to 1860.

IMPERIAL LEADERSHIP

The period began inauspiciously after the punishment of Heshen (1750–1799), a favorite of the aging Qianlong emperor (r. 1735–1796), whose twenty-four-year trail of corruption and extortion had undermined the operation of the two most important agencies of the imperial government: the Board of Civil Office that administered the merit-based system of bureaucratic appointments, and the Board of Revenue that husbanded the empire's fiscal resources. The Jiaqing emperor (r. 1796–1820) began his reign fully cognizant that most of the empire's serving bureaucrats were tainted by the Heshen scandal, and he worked assiduously to reverse the decline in bureaucratic morale that threatened to undermine his administration. His successor, the Daoguang emperor (r. 1821–1850), showed a willingness to undertake incremental administrative change in response to governing problems, and he pursued fiscal reform and retrenchment with modest success. The efforts of both emperors centered on problems that lay within the state's governing mandate, which narrowly defined the state's strategic functions and prerogatives under the "six boards" of the central government. However, the emperors did not tackle the systemic weaknesses in the thinly spread layer of local county government, nor did they extend the vertical reach of the imperial government to the subcounty community to address socioeconomic issues related to the "people's livelihood" (*minsheng*) at the local level.

CHALLENGES OF THE EARLY NINETEENTH CENTURY

Many of the problems of the early nineteenth century were long-term evolutionary consequences of the successes of 150 years of conscientious and imaginative Qing imperial leadership that had led to peace and prosperity throughout interior China and the northern and western borderland dependencies. Qing stewardship of both agriculture and commerce had raised the standard of living and also brought about momentous socioeconomic changes that affected the everyday lives of ordinary Chinese, drawing them into a flourishing commodity economy connected to urban life in coastal and riverine markets, and sparking the rise of powerful commercial organizations whose members often served as extra-bureaucratic personnel in government work requiring entrepreneurial, capital, and shipping resources. None of these changes was more profound in terms of its impact on governance and political stability than the dramatic growth of the population: growing from 100 million to 150 million in 1660 to 300 million in 1800, then 356 million in 1821, and 430 million by 1850. Population growth heightened competition for economic resources and created tensions and conflicts at the subcounty level that China's thinly spread governing apparatus was unable to mediate or resolve because of a dearth of bureaucratic and fiscal resources.

Long-term ecological degradation also contributed to soil erosion, siltation, and flooding in China's major river valleys, which undermined large-scale hydraulic facilities designed to harness, contain, and divert floodwaters in order to protect and irrigate agricultural land.

Catastrophic floods in the Yellow-Huai river basin in 1824 in northern Jiangsu destroyed the Grand Canal and brought government grain transport on the canal to a halt in 1825 and 1826. Natural disasters of this kind placed heavy burdens on the imperial government that had traditionally borne responsibility for the repair and maintenance of large-scale hydraulic works, such the Yangzi Great Dikes at the confluence of the Han and Yangze rivers and the retaining walls on the Hongze Lake reservoir in northern Jiangsu.

Paralleling these long-term problems was the emergence of troubling signs of monetary instability related to silver shortages, caused by a decline in international silver supplies, increased domestic demand for silver coins (Mexican dollars), and deflationary trends in rice prices that made it difficult for peasants to pay taxes. More dangerous still were increasing incidents of collective violence and rebellion, many of which reflected simmering tensions between religious, ethnic, and secret societal groups. These included the White Lotus Rebellion (1796–1805) and the Eight Trigrams Rebellion (1813) in North China; Yao, Miao, and Zhuang unrest in central and south China; nearly seventy documented cases of disturbances involving non-Han and Chinese Muslims (Hui) in Yunnan between 1796 and 1856; and savage rebellions in Altishahr in southern Xinjiang in the 1820s.

QING ACTIVISM AND REFORM

These cascading problems sparked intense concern among the Qing leadership, from emperor to officials and literati. Inspired by the Qing tradition of imperial direction of the decisional process, the periodic revision of the administrative codes, and the use of temporary governing tools to manage problems and crises, they mobilized local groups to quell rebellion; they reconfigured the hydraulic facilities at the critical Hongze Lake–Grand Canal junction with the Yellow River (1825–1827); they experimented with a new administrative framework for sea transport of government tax grain (1826); they recruited grain merchants to assist in the supply and transport of grain supplies for the military, popular sustenance, and famine relief; they reformed the Lianghuai salt monopoly (1830–1850); and in southern Xinjiang, they began a thoroughgoing review and adjustment of the pattern of Qing military occupation with its dependence on native headmen (*begs*) for local governance. In addition, innovative hydraulic engineers developed new approaches to dike construction that succeeded in controlling Yellow River flooding from 1844 to 1855 when the river finally succumbed to centuries of silt buildup and changed to a northward course to the sea. All of these initiatives involved a careful review and adjustment of existing administrative practice. The approach was pragmatic and incremental, reflecting the limited prerogatives of the state's ruling mandate, but within that mandate, the Qing leadership worked with commitment and imagination.

The spirit and nature of the Qing renewal was captured in the important 1826 "statecraft" collection: *Essays on Qing Imperial Statecraft* (*Huangchao jingshi wenbian*), compiled and edited by He Changling (1785–1848) and Wei Yuan (1794–1857). While six introductory chapters briefly spell out the Confucian principles that informed the compilers' approach to governance, the work centers on the administrative mission of the "six boards" and the actual problems they faced in this discrete period, and it also offers practical solutions to looming concrete problems. It is primarily a work of advocacy that reflects the experience and inspiration of leading Chinese officials and literati serving in the lower Yangzi provinces in the early nineteenth century, such as Tao Zhu, Lin Zexu, and Bao Shichen. They were prepared, in a sense, to tinker with the machinery of imperial government and to devise small-scale innovative improvements to make the government work more efficiently.

It is difficult to determine whether or not this approach to political problem-solving might have worked to solve the problems facing the Qing in this period, given the fragility of the Qing government at the local level and the scale of socioeconomic problems that it faced, but these efforts were overwhelmed in the 1840s and 1850s by domestic rebellion and foreign invasion.

THE FOREIGN ASSAULT

From the Opium War (1839–1842) to the sack of Beijing in 1860, the Western maritime powers, led by Great Britain, forced the Qing dynasty to accept a series of treaties that fundamentally altered the Qing system for controlling its trade, ports, and maritime customs along the entire China coast from Guangdong to Zhili provinces reaching as well to the middle Yangzi ports. The treaty system gave foreigners the rights to diplomatic representation in the imperial capital, residence in the newly designated treaty ports, travel in the interior, and to propagate Christianity. The treaty also provided for the legalization of opium, exemption of foreigners from Chinese law (extraterritoriality), and a fixed low tariff on foreign goods, plus forcing China to pay indemnity for foreign war costs. These treaties set the pattern for future Western demands for treaty rights that compromised China's sovereignty into the next century.

The British assault on the maritime border encouraged imperial Russia to do the same on the northern borders. The treaties of Ili (1851), Aigun (1858), and the Supplementary Treaty of Peking (1860) enabled Russia to plant trading bases and consulates in northern Xinjiang and to gain territorial concessions north of the Amur and Sungari rivers and east of the Ussuri River to

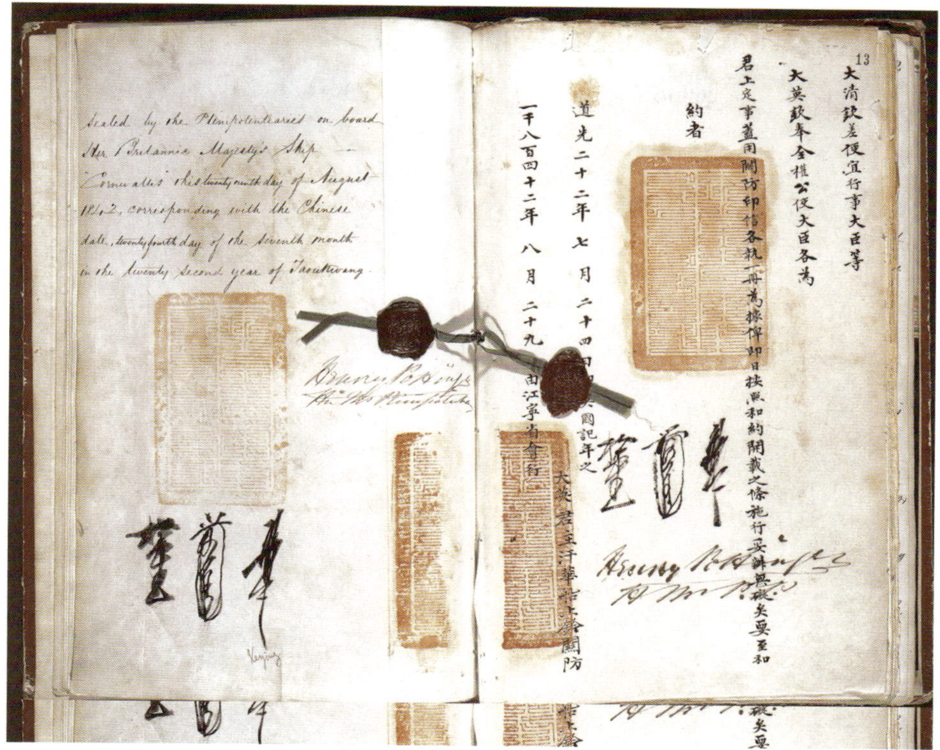

Photo of the Nanking Treaty, ending the First Opium War between China and Britain, August 29, 1842. *Prior to the First Opium War, Chinese Imperial officials allowed Britain access to Chinese markets only through the port city of Guangzhou. After achieving victory, the British forced the Chinese to sign the Nanking Treaty, giving Westerners new access to port cities along China's coast as well as the ability to exempt those areas from local authority.* © PUBLIC RECORD OFFICE / HIP / THE IMAGE WORKS

the sea—concessions that enabled the Russians to penetrate the Manchu homeland.

THE TAIPING UPRISING (1851–1864)

Far more important at midcentury than foreign pressures on the borders was the Taiping Uprising. Born of ethnic conflict between the Han, Hakka, Yao, and Miao and economic hardship in Guangdong and Guangzi in the wake of the Opium War (1839–1842), the Taiping Revolutionary organization was galvanized by a hybrid ideology of Christian and Chinese heterodox elements and by the leadership of an aspiring but unstable Hakka degree candidate, Hong Xiuquan (1814–1864). The Taipings burst out of Guangxi Province in 1852, swept north, taking Changsha in September and Wuchang on the Yangzi River in January 1853. They then moved down the river to Nanjing, where they set up their capital for the next eleven years. The rebellion raged over sixteen provinces and constituted a major threat to the Qing dynasty as well as to Chinese Confucian social norms. At the same time, the Nian Uprising (1851–1868) erupted in the Huaipei region of north-central China along the Anhui-Henan-Jiangsu border; the Muslim Panthay Rebellion (1855–1873) reignited simmering ethnic-religious conflict in Yunnan Province; and finally, in 1862, the Muslim Rebellion in the northwest spread from Shaanxi to Gansu Province and threatened strategic communications between Beijing and Xinjiang.

The foreign assault on the Qing frontiers and the savage rebellions that raged across China overwhelmed the Qing government during the last years of the Daoguang reign and the Xianfeng reign (1851–1861). With perhaps the exception of the Xianfeng emperor, the Qing leadership—emperors, officials, and literati—had worked diligently to craft small-scale innovations in administrative practice to improve the operation of Qing government, and they did, indeed, manage successfully many pressing problems and crises. The spiraling effects of socioeconomic transformations and exploding population growth caused conflict and upheaval in the subcounty community, and this placed unbearable pressure on the fragile structures of government at the county level. More attuned to its core strategic governing tasks, Qing leadership was slow to address the systemic weaknesses of local government or recognize its crucial role in managing socioeconomic conflicts at the local level. Already reeling from these internal problems, the Qing regime was unable to counter the threat of rebellion and foreign invasion.

SEE ALSO *Population Policy: Demographic Trends since 1800; Opium Wars; Taiping Uprising.*

BIBLIOGRAPHY

Antony, Robert J. *Like Froth Floating on the Sea: The World of Pirates and Seafarers in Late Imperial South China*. Berkeley: Institute of East Asian Studies, University of California, 2003.

Antony, Robert J., and Jane Kate Leonard, eds. *Dragons, Tigers, and Dogs: Qing Crisis Management and the Boundaries of State Power in Late Imperial China*. Ithaca, NY: East Asia Program, Cornell University, 2002.

Atwill, David. Trading Places: Resistance, Ethnicity, and Governance in Nineteenth-Century Yunnan. In *Dragons, Tigers, and Dogs: Qing Crisis Management and the Boundaries of State Power in Late Imperial China*, ed. Robert J. Antony and Jane Kate Leonard, 245–271. Ithaca, NY: East Asia Program, Cornell University, 2002.

Borei, Dorothy V. Ethnic Conflict and Qing Land Policy in Southern Xinjiang, 1760–1840. In *Dragons, Tigers, and Dogs: Qing Crisis Management and the Boundaries of State Power in Late Imperial China*, ed. Robert J. Antony and Jane Kate Leonard, 273–301. Ithaca, NY: East Asia Program, Cornell University, 2002.

Dodgen, Randall A. *Controlling the Dragon: Confucian Engineers and the Yellow River in Late Imperial China (1835–1850).* Honolulu: University of Hawaii Press, 2001.

Elvin, Mark, and Liu Cuirong (Ts'ui-jung Liu), eds. *Sediments of Time: Environment and Society in Chinese History*. Cambridge, U.K.: Cambridge University Press, 1998.

He Bingdi (He Ping-ti). *Studies on the Population of China, 1368–1953.* Cambridge, MA: Harvard University Press, 1959.

He Changling and Wei Yuan. *Huangchao jingshi wenbian* [Essays on Qing statecraft]: 120 *juan*. N.p., [1826] 1965. Reprint. Taibei: Shijie.

Huang Pei. *Autocracy at Work: A Study of the Yung-cheng Period, 1723–1735.* Bloomington: Indiana University Press, 1974.

Kuhn, Philip A. *Rebellion and Its Enemies in Late Imperial China: Militarization and Social Structure, 1796–1864.* Cambridge, MA: Harvard University Press, 1970.

Leonard, Jane Kate. *Controlling from Afar: The Daoguang Emperor's Management of the Grand Canal Crisis, 1824–1826.* Ann Arbor: Center for Chinese Studies, University of Michigan, 1996.

Metzger, Thomas. The Organizational Capacity of the Qing State in the Field of Commerce: The Liang-Huai Salt Monopoly, 1740–1840. In *Economic Organization in Chinese Society*, ed. W. E. Willmott, 9–45. Stanford, CA: Stanford University Press, 1972.

Metzger, Thomas. *The Internal Organization of Ch'ing Bureaucracy: Legal, Normative, and Communication Aspects*. Cambridge, MA: Harvard University Press, 1973.

Millward, James. *Beyond the Pass: Economy, Ethnicity, and Empire in Qing Central Asia*. Stanford, CA: Stanford University Press, 1998.

Murray, Dian. *Pirates of the South China Coast, 1790–1810.* Stanford, CA: Stanford University Press, 1987.

Naquin, Susan. *Millenarian Rebellion in China: The Eight Trigrams of 1813.* New Haven, CT: Yale University Press, 1976.

Perdue, Peter C. *China Marches West: The Qing Conquest of Central Asia*. Cambridge, MA: Belknap Press, 2005.

Skinner, G. William, ed. *The City in Late Imperial China*. Stanford, CA: Stanford University Press, 1977.

Vogel, Hans Ulrich. Chinese Central Monetary Policy, 1644–1800. *Late Imperial China* 8, 2 (1987): 1–52.

von Glahn, Richard. *Fountain of Fortune: Money and Monetary Policy in China, 1000–1700.* Berkeley: University of California Press, 1996.

Wang Yejian (Wang Yeh-chien). The Secular Trend of Prices during the Ch'ing Period. *Journal of the Institute of Chinese Studies of the Chinese University of Hong Kong* 5, 2 (1972): 347–371.

Wang Yejian (Wang Yeh-chien). *Land Taxation in Imperial China, 1750–1911.* Cambridge, MA: Harvard University Press, 1973.

Will, Pierre-Étienne. State Intervention in the Administration of a Hydraulic Infrastructure: The Example of Hubei Province in Premodern Times. In *The Scope of State Power in China*, ed. Stuart Schram, 295–352. New York: St. Martin's Press, 1985.

Will, Pierre-Étienne, and R. Bin Wong. *Nourish the People: The State Civilian Granary System in China, 1650–1850.* Ann Arbor: Center for Chinese Studies, University of Michigan, 1991.

Xu Zhongyue (Immanuel C. Y. Hsu). *The Rise of Modern China.* 6th ed. New York: Oxford University Press, 2000.

Jane Kate Leonard

OVERVIEW, 1860–1912

It is perhaps one of the greatest paradoxes of the late Qing that the forces that came to its aid during the wave of peasant rebellions that swept across the Chinese countryside in the middle of the nineteenth century would, by the first decade of the twentieth century, eventually bring about its fall in the revolution of 1911. At midcentury, the Qing dynasty faced its greatest threat to date—the Taiping rebels, who had since 1850 sought to overthrow the Qing and establish their own dynasty. With its traditional military forces fallen into a state of decrepitude, the Qing turned first to the Confucian gentry and later to the intervention of the Western powers for aid in putting down the rebellion. The Qing survived the Taiping challenge, but at the fatal cost of accelerating the forces of regionalism already underway and establishing a precedent for Western intervention in China's internal affairs. Over the course of the next half century, this devolution of power from the center to the periphery, combined with the spread of Western influence, paved the way for the fall of the Qing in 1912.

SELF-STRENGTHENING (1860–1895)

In 1860 China was still very much steeped in the traditions of Confucianism, and the Confucian gentry that had for the last millennium supported the imperial state remained, for the most part, committed to the Qing dynasty. When the imperial forces proved incapable of quelling the Taiping Uprising, the Qing state turned to the gentry, granting top-ranking officials such as Zeng Guofan and Li Hongzhang virtual autonomy to mobilize and lead provincial armies (Kuhn 1970). As long as

SELF-STRENGTHENING

"Self-strengthening" (*ziqiang*), a Confucian concept, is both a process and a goal for personal edification, moral cultivation, self-discipline, and introspection, so that one can become strong as a person, worthy of oneself and one's family, and therefore fit to serve one's parents, be benevolent and nurturing to one's children, and thus equipped to serve the ruler. There is nothing inherently radical about "self-strengthening"; even conservatives used the term to mean character-building along Confucian lines.

There is, however, another dimension to "self-strengthening," one implying a collective effort. During the Southern Song period (1127–1279), when the country was threatened by nomadic invaders, the minister Dong Huai insisted that the best strategy was "self-strengthening." By this he included strengthening of both the civil administration and defense. Leading officials in the post-1860 era—Zeng Guofan, Zuo Zongtang, Shen Baozhen, and Ding Richang—used "self-strengthening" to mean just this: reform or revitalization of the civil administration, and strengthening of the military, including the use of Western weaponry, armament production, and training. To these they also added modern business and industrial enterprises, to generate the funds to support their undertakings. The paths of "self-strengthening" and "restoration" were thus joined. Still, many officials, like Li Hongzhang, thought of "self-strengthening" largely in military and economic terms, and this meaning is adopted by most modern historians, overlooking the other dimensions of "self-strengthening." The result is the frequent confusion between "self-strengthening" and *yangwu* (foreign affairs), which, despite similarities, are different.

The 1861–1895 period is often labeled the "Self-strengthening era." It began with a call for "self-strengthening" by Prince Gong, Guiliang (1785–1862), Uprising such as and Wenxiang, leading members of the newly created Zongli Yamen. It ended with China's defeat by Japan, which ushered in reforms of a different character. Historians speak of a "Self-strengthening movement," a term not used by those active in it; it was a twentieth-century invention. The Qing prohibited overt political associations among officials, but officials did exchange ideas by correspondence, read memorials published in the *Jingbao* (Peking gazette), and often supported like-minded officials in their endeavors. To this extent, then, one can speak of a movement, but it is one without leadership, membership, or organizational form. The term *Self-strengthening movement* is not used in the People's Republic of China, whose scholars prefer "Westernization movement" (*yangwu yundong*). Its promoters, the ruling elites, are said to have adopted western methods and technology merely to protect their interests, not for strengthening the country.

BIBLIOGRAPHY

Kuo Ting-yee (Guo Tingyi) and Liu Kwang-ching (Liu Guangjing). Self-strengthening: The Pursuit of Western Technology. In *The Cambridge History of China*, Vol. 10, *Late Ch'ing, 1800–1911*, ed. John K. Fairbank, Pt. 1, 491–542. Cambridge, U.K.: Cambridge University Press, 1978.

Liu Kwang-ching (Liu Guangjing). The Beginnings of China's Modernization. In *Li Hung-chang and China's Early Modernization*, ed. Samuel C. Chu and Liu Kwang-ching, 3–16. Armonk, NY: Sharpe, 1994.

Pong, David. The Vocabulary of Change: Reformist Ideas of the 1860s and 1870s. In *Ideal and Reality: Social and Political Change in Modern China, 1860–1949*, ed. David Pong and Edmund S. K. Fung, 25–61. Lanham, MD: University Press of America, 1985.

Wu Anjia. Zhongguo dalu lishi xuezhe dui yangwu yundong de pingjia [The appraisal of the Western Affairs movement by mainland Chinese historians]. In *Qingji ziqiang yundong yantaohui lunwenji* [Papers from the Conference on the Self-strengthening Movement in the Late Qing], ed. Zhongyang Yanjiuyuan Jindaishi Yanjiusuo [Institute of Modern History, Academia Sinica], Vol. 1, 43–64. Taibei: Academia Sinica, 1988. See also comments and discussion, 65–71.

David Pong

the commanders of these regionally based armies remained loyal to the Qing state—and they would until the end of the century—the Manchu rulers had little cause to be concerned over the decentralization of military control.

The Confucian gentry further demonstrated their support of the dynasty by their leading role in the self-strengthening movement. An implicit assumption of theirs was that culture and technology could be compartmentalized, as suggested by Zhang Zhidong's famous formula to strengthen the (Chinese) base (*ti*) with (Western) utility (*yong*). It was thought that the goals of self-strengthening—creating institutions and procedures for handling foreign affairs and acquiring Western technology to build up the military and industrial bases of the country—would not affect the fundamental nature or character of Chinese culture. In short, China needed to learn from the West the tools to defeat the West and preserve Chinese culture.

Beginning with the Tongzhi restoration in 1861, the Qing court initiated a program to modernize the military and create new institutions to deal directly with foreign powers, the most notable of which was the Zongli Yamen (Office for the Management of Foreign Affairs). In later years, the self-strengthening movement broadened to include modernization programs in transportation, communications, mining, and light industry. Schools were established to train Chinese in foreign languages, and the best and brightest were sent abroad to study the sources behind Western power.

Taking the lead in the self-strengthening movement were men such as Li Hongzhang, whose entrepreneurial projects and educational initiatives attest to the diverse interests and activities of the Confucian gentry. Realizing the vital role industry and commerce would play in China's economic development, Li set aside the Confucian disdain for trade and established the China Merchant Steamship Navigation Company in 1872 in an attempt to wrest control of coastal shipping from foreign hands. Recognizing the shortcomings of the exclusively Confucian curriculum, Li recommended the establishment of schools that would teach foreign languages and Western mathematics and sciences; he also gained imperial approval for an educational mission to the United States.

In the treaty ports, a new intellectual elite was adding its voice to the calls for reform. The scholar and journalist Wang Tao (1828–1897) exemplifies this Westernized intelligentsia. His connections with missionaries and with the press, as well as his experiences in Europe, gave him a different perspective as he proposed institutional changes in government administration and education.

In the end, the self-strengthening movement proved too limited in both its impact and scope. On the one hand, the Qing state was completely dependent on regional power holders to implement the policies and changes proposed. On the other hand, ultraconservatives in the imperial court who saw in the reforms the unraveling of Chinese civilization stymied the efforts from the top. When China lost yet another war in 1895, this time to Japan, the self-strengtheners also had to acknowledge defeat; after more than thirty years of self-strengthening, China was not any better capable of defending itself against foreign encroachment.

THE REFORM MOVEMENT OF 1898

As the nineteenth century ended, a new generation of leaders emerged who would offer more radical solutions to China's problems. Influenced by ideas from abroad but still committed to Confucianism and the Qing dynasty, men such as Kang Youwei and Liang Qichao lobbied for reforms that would transform the imperial state into a constitutional monarchy modeled after the West. To reconcile these sweeping institutional changes with the Confucian tradition, Kang offered a reinterpretation of Confucianism that portrayed Confucius as a progressive reformer. Kang apparently made a persuasive argument, for during the Hundred Days' Reform in the summer of 1898, Kang and his followers persuaded the young Guangxu emperor (1871–1908) to implement a series of reforms aimed at streamlining and modernizing China's political, military, and educational systems.

For the ultraconservatives in the imperial court who had earlier opposed the self-strengtheners, the reforms not only betrayed China's Confucian heritage but also attacked their basis of power; the reforms would create a new system in which they would be cast out as relics of the past. Rallying behind the Empress Dowager Cixi, they brought the reform movement to an abrupt and violent end. The empress dowager had the young emperor confined to the palace—effectively dethroning him—and persecuted the reformers. A segment of the Confucian gentry was growing increasingly frustrated and dangerously hostile to the Manchu rulers.

THE BOXER MOVEMENT

That same year, another drama was unfolding in the countryside outside Beijing that would bring the Qing one step closer to extinction. Referred to collectively as the Boxers United in Righteousness (*Yihequan*), a motley crew of peasants, laborers, and drifters launched a movement in 1898 that came to be known as the Boxer Uprising. From their origins in northwestern Shandong, the Boxers spread across the North China Plain, extending as far as Manchuria and Inner Mongolia.

A combination of deteriorating conditions in the countryside and increasing Chinese resentment of the missionary presence in Shandong fueled the Boxer movement. The Boxers' physical assault on missionaries and Chinese Christians as well their destruction of railroad and telegraph lines—hated symbols of the Western presence in China—defined the Boxer Uprising as an antiforeign, anti-Christian, and antimissionary movement. However, the Boxers were not anti-Qing—after all, their slogan was "Revive the Qing; destroy the foreigner." Despite later representations portraying the Boxers as rebels, the Qing court did support the Boxers and declared war on the foreign powers in mid-1900. This brought about yet another defeat at the hands of the foreigners, who captured Beijing and drove the emperor and the empress dowager into temporary exile. The Qing emerged from the Boxer Uprising severely weakened, if not fatally crippled, and could barely hold on to the reins of power during the next decade.

THE NEW POLICIES (1901–1911)

That China managed to retain its territorial sovereignty was the only bright note as the twentieth century opened. In the aftermath of the Boxer debacle, the empress dowager abruptly reversed her position on reform. The changes that were implemented, collectively referred to as the New Policies,

LATE IMPERIAL CHINA

Chinese historians are agreed that "imperial China" began with the foundation of the Qin dynasty in the third century BCE and continued until the collapse of the Qing dynasty in 1912 and its replacement by a republic, and they have periodized these two millennia in various ways. A schema employed by some historians (e.g., Ichisada Miyazaki, Jacques Gernet, Conrad Schirokauer, and Miranda Brown), following the leading hypothesis of Naitō Torajirō (1866–1934), perceives a major break in the tenth-century transition from the late Tang dynasty to the Northern Song, when a government dominated and administered by an aristocratic elite—the pattern since ancient times—was replaced by a predominantly meritocratic, Confucian-educated, scholar-official class recruited into civil service through a system of rigorous written examinations maintained more or less continuously until 1905. Naitō's hypothesis even went so far as to claim that the Song's meritocratic emphasis plus its commercial dynamism, urbanization, and advances in science, technology, and maritime trade, made it the world's first "modern" society, well ahead of Europe.

More recently, many scholars have tended to view the Ming dynasty's institutional reorganization of its post-Mongol empire as a more fitting starting point for a "late imperial" phase. Although based on Tang and Song precedents, the Ming version of the imperial system was maintained by the Manchus with relatively little variation throughout the Qing period. Numerous textbook surveys of late imperial China (e.g., Frederic Wakeman's *The Fall of Imperial China*) and of modern China (e.g., Immanue Hsu's *The Rise of Modern China*, and Jonathan Spence's *The Search for Modern China*) thus begin with the late Ming period.

BIBLIOGRAPHY

Fogel, Joshua A. *Politics and Sinology: The Case of Naitō Kōnan, 1866–1934*. Cambridge, MA: Harvard University Asia Center, 1984.

Gernet, Jacques. *A History of Chinese Civilization*. 2nd ed. Cambridge, U.K.: Cambridge University Press, 1996.

Hsu, Immanuel C. Y. *The Rise of Modern China*. 6th ed. New York: Oxford University Press, 2000.

Miyakawa, Hisayuki. "An Outline of the Naitō Hypothesis and Its Effects on Japanese Studies of China." *Far Eastern Quarterly* 14, 4 (August 1955): 533–552.

Miyazaki, Ichisada. *China's Examination Hell: The Civil Service Examinations of Imperial China*. New Haven, CT: Yale University Press, 1981.

Schirokauer, Conrad, and Miranda Brown. *A Brief History of Chinese Civilization*. 2nd ed. Belmont, CA: Thomson/Wadsworth, 2006.

Spence, Jonathan. *The Search for Modern China*. 2nd ed. New York: W.W. Norton, 1999.

Wakeman, Frederic, Jr. *The Fall of Imperial China*. New York: Free Press, 1975.

Roland L. Higgins

reflected many of the same ideas proposed during the Hundred Days' Reform in 1898.

Indeed, the New Policies went even further by creating the foundation for a more representative government. A timetable was worked out for the election of popular assemblies at the district, provincial, and national levels. In 1905 the civil service examination system, which had indoctrinated China's leaders in Confucianism for more than a millennium, was abolished. One scholar describes this as "the most revolutionary act of the twentieth century" (Schoppa 2000, p. 52). In an ironic twist of events, the Qing court in one fell swoop had dismantled an institution that had defined the Chinese imperial system and produced its most loyal supporters—the Confucian gentry.

EMERGENT NATIONALISM

Even before the formal abolition of the civil service examination system, however, the loyalty of the gentry to the Qing could no longer be taken for granted, and Confucianism no longer held a monopoly on all learning. The changes of the nineteenth century had created a new elite, one that was younger and eager for change. Many of its members had traveled abroad and been impressed by the material evidence of Western power; they returned home inspired to rejuvenate an enfeebled China. In contrast to the Confucian gentry reformers and the first generation of Westernized intelligentsia that had emerged in the treaty ports in the middle of the nineteenth century, this new elite no longer saw saving China as synonymous with saving the Qing.

Representative of this new group were Liang Qichao and Sun Yat-sen (Sun Yixian or Sun Zhongshan), whose collective writings document the birth of Chinese nationalism. Liang played a vital role in the development of a political press in China, spearheading numerous journals and newspapers that offered a public forum for the discussion of national issues. Sun, revered as the father of modern China, put forward a set of revolutionary

Imperial officials fleeing Tientsin during the Chinese Revolution, 1911. *During the last decades of the nineteenth century, rebellions erupted throughout China against the imperial order. While late Qing leaders initially held these uprisings in check through increased reliance on regional military forces, by 1911, the imperial system collapsed in the rising tide of nationalism sweeping the country.* HULTON ARCHIVE/GETTY IMAGES

principles (published as *Three Principles of the People* in 1924), which would become one of the founding documents of the Republic of China. Both Liang and Sun drew extensively from Western political philosophy in their discussion of rights, sovereignty, and democracy. The future they painted reserved no place for the Manchu rulers.

THE REVOLUTION OF 1911

In the last few years of their rule, the Manchus demonstrated again their lack of commitment to genuine reform. Revolutionary societies expanded their underground networks and formed alliances in preparation for wresting power from the Manchus. Yet the revolution that broke out in 1911 was remarkable for its lack of planning, direction, leadership, and ideology. An accidental explosion at the office of a revolutionary society sparked a spontaneous revolt in the city of Wuchang on October 10. In cities across China, regional players—some revolutionary-minded, others merely power hungry—followed suit and wrestled with the Qing military forces for control.

The Republic of China, officially proclaimed on January 1, 1912, would inherit the problems that had plagued the Qing. The past century of imperialist incursions had resulted in China being "carved up like a melon." The treaty ports with their foreign concessions served as a physical reminder to the Chinese of their subordinate status in their own country. Yet imperialist interests had also helped to finance the construction of a modern infrastructure in China. And despite Chinese resentment of the missionary presence—which often exploded into open violence—many Chinese benefited from the greater educational opportunities offered by missionary schools and from access to better health care in hospitals run by missionaries.

Despite its revolutionary break from the late imperial past, the Republic was built upon foundations established in the late Qing. The idea of a representative system of government had its origins in late nineteenth-century public discussions. Legal reform in the late Qing reveals the influence of the language of rights and the idea of the rule of law. Social activists focused on raising women's status by campaigning against the practice of footbinding and by promoting women's education. Although the Republic struggled with many of the same problems that had brought about the fall of the Qing, it also sought to bring to fruition many of the developments begun in the twilight years of China's last dynasty.

SEE ALSO *Boxer Uprising; Hundred Days' Reform; Nationalism; Revolution of 1911.*

BIBLIOGRAPHY

Cohen, Paul A. *Discovering History in China: American Historical Writing on the Recent Chinese Past.* New York: Columbia University Press, 1984.

De Bary, William Theodore, and Richard Lufrano, comps. *Sources of Chinese Tradition: From 1600 through the Twentieth Century.* 2nd ed. New York: Columbia University Press, 2000.

Huang, Philip C. C. *The Peasant Economy and Social Change in North China.* Stanford, CA: Stanford University Press, 1985.

Hunt, Michael H. The Forgotten Occupation: Peking, 1900–1901. *Pacific Historical Review* 48, 4 (1979): 501–529.

Kuhn, Philip A. *Rebellion and Its Enemies in Late Imperial China: Militarization and Social Structure, 1796–1864.* Cambridge, MA: Harvard University Press, 1970.

Ning Lao Taitai (Ning Lao T'ai-t'ai) and Ida Pruitt. *A Daughter of Han: The Autobiography of a Chinese Working Woman.* 1945. Stanford, CA: Stanford University Press, 1967.

Schoppa, R. Keith. *The Columbia Guide to Modern Chinese History.* New York: Columbia University Press, 2000.

Lisa Tran

OVERVIEW, 1912–1949

Revolution in 1911 created the Republic of China, and revolution in 1949 would expel the Republic from the mainland. Formally established on January 1, 1912, the Republic signaled the end of the imperial system and symbolized China's birth—and some would argue, failure—as a modern nation-state. Certainly, political rivalry, internecine warfare, foreign invasion, and widespread poverty crippled the already fragile Republic; but these years were also marked by significant cultural, social, legal, and economic achievements.

THE MAY FOURTH MOVEMENT

The May Fourth movement (1915–1925), also referred to as the New Culture movement, reflected these two sides of the Republic. On the one hand, it highlighted China's weakness in the face of Japanese imperialism. On the other hand, the events associated with the May Fourth movement gave voice and direction to a nascent nationalism and sparked a cultural rejuvenation that reveals a more hopeful China. As in many other countries faced with similar threats to their sovereignty, nationalism in China was synonymous with anti-imperialism and was accompanied by a rejection of those traditions perceived as holding the country back. As activists attacked China's foreign enemies, they also targeted the internal threats weakening the population, namely Confucianism and the system it sustained.

In what has been described as China's "Enlightenment," May Fourth ideologues embraced the ideas of anarchism, socialism, and other foreign ideologies and accepted as universal principles such concepts as equality, monogamy, and individualism (Schwarcz 1986; Wang Zheng 1999). It was in the midst of this cultural ferment that the Chinese Communist Party (CCP) was founded in 1921, a development that would eventually bring about the fall of the Republic.

Many of the ideas introduced during this formative period paved the way for the dramatic restructuring of family and gender relations. The "small family" ideal, made up of a wife and husband and their children, emerged as an alternative to, if not a replacement for, the Confucian model of the extended family, which privileged age over youth and men over women (Glosser 2003). In the May Fourth discourse, marriage was increasingly seen as a union between individuals and not families, and the happiness of the conjugal unit took precedence over the interests of the clan. Alongside the "small family" ideal was the image of the "new woman," characterized by her independent spirit, well-rounded education, and urban sophistication. For many, the "new woman" featured on the covers of magazines and portrayed in fiction epitomized modernity. In the political arena, women activists lobbied for laws that would protect women's interests and joined political parties (Gilmartin 1995). To be sure, the social reality did not always reflect May Fourth ideals, particularly in the countryside, where Confucian ideas persisted. But these ideals would inspire changes that would pave the way for their realization later in the century.

THE WARLORD ERA

Meanwhile, in the political realm, the rise to power of the military general Yuan Shikai threatened the very existence of the Republic within months of its founding. His role in securing the abdication of the Qing emperor, combined with his military leadership, much needed during this period of disorder and instability, earned him the presidency. Yuan's obdurate resistance to constitutional reform and his plans to establish his own dynasty soon made him an enemy to the revolutionaries, now organized as a political party called the Guomindang (GMD) under the leadership of Sun Yat-sen (Sun Yixian or Sun Zhongshan), who had earlier relinquished the presidency to Yuan. Yuan's control of the military enabled him to crush the revolutionaries, who were driven into exile, not to return to China until after Yuan's death in 1916.

Sun and his followers returned to a fragmented China controlled by warlords. In 1923 Sun accepted the invitation of the Communist International (Comintern) to form a united front with the fledgling CCP to eliminate the warlords and reunite the country. Although ideological enemies, the GMD and the CCP were willing to unite their forces now, and again in 1937, against a common foe.

Sun's death in 1925 created a power vacuum. Chiang Kai-shek (Jiang Jieshi), the leader of the Northern Expedition to eliminate warlordism, used his control of the military to assume leadership of the GMD. Driven by practical expediency, Chiang defeated those warlords he could and co-opted those he could not. In 1927 he declared the Northern Expedition a success and, suspicious of a Communist conspiracy, turned against the CCP, unleashing a wave of terror aimed at wiping it out.

Sun Yat-sen presiding over the Republic of China's parliament, 1912. *After the fall of the Qing dynasty, revolutionaries established the Republic of China in 1912, naming the head of the Guomindang (GMD), Sun Yat-sen, as provisional president.* © BETTMANN/ CORBIS

THE GMD AND THE CCP

Although the GMD now officially represented the government of the Republic, it held effective jurisdiction over only the eastern portions of China, centered around the Yangzi Delta; the rest was either still under the control of residual warlords or the influence of the CCP, which had recovered from Chiang's attack and had by 1931 established a rival soviet government in the southern province of Jiangxi. During this short period of relative peace and stability, both the GMD and the CCP implemented policies aimed at consolidating their power.

The Nanjing Decade (1927–1937) The GMD, now under Chiang's leadership, established Nanjing as the new capital of the Republic and initiated a program of state-building and economic reconstruction that, coupled with local initiatives from a new entrepreneurial elite that had grown in power and influence in the absence of a strong central government, would characterize the "Nanjing decade." A five-branch government was established following the model proposed by Sun Yat-sen. The executive, legislature, and judiciary mirrored the American political system, but the control and examination branches represented updated versions of the traditional censorate and civil service examinations. Urban centers such as Shanghai held the largest concentration of factories producing consumer items and already showed signs of the shift to an industrial economy, with double-digit annual growth rates in some years (Fairbank and Goldman 2006, p. 270). By 1935 a central bank and a state mint were established, and a national currency adopted. In the legal realm, a criminal code was promulgated in 1928 and revised in 1935, and China's first civil code was promulgated in 1929.

These years also witnessed the growing influence of a new class of entrepreneurs, often described as the "Chinese bourgeoisie" or "Confucian modernizers" (Fairbank and

Goldman 2006, p. 272). Often in cooperation with the traditional gentry elite, these entrepreneurs founded chambers of commerce, formed joint-stock companies, and funded Western-style schools. Certainly, their activism in community affairs and the autonomy they enjoyed attest to a growing public sphere. Yet this new elite lacked political representation. China may now have a constitution, but power remained in the hands of the state. People spoke about the rights of citizens, but the vast majority still held to the mentality of the duties of subjects. Much like Japan and Germany at this time, China represented a state-centered political model.

Despite appearances, the process of state-building was limited and the progress of economic development stunted, ironically, by the GMD itself. Chiang's premature conclusion of the Northern Expedition had left intact pockets of warlordism, which continued to challenge GMD political control. In addition, the GMD's decision to not impose a national land tax deprived the financially pressed government of an important source of revenue. In addition, the GMD supported fiscal policies that strengthened the government's monopoly of banking and industry at the expense of the economic growth favored by the new entrepreneurial elite. In the cultural sphere, the GMD launched the New Life movement in 1934 in an effort to reinvigorate the population through appeals to traditional Confucian values such as filial piety and through a new emphasis, inspired by discourses on social Darwinism and fascism imported from the West, on physical fitness, personal hygiene, and military discipline. With the New Life movement, Chiang hoped to fuse Confucian values with modern ideas.

The Jiangxi Soviet (1931–1934) Meanwhile, the CCP established a soviet government in the southeastern province of Jiangxi in an effort to mobilize the peasantry for a revolution against the GMD. Under Mao Zedong's leadership, it gained the active cooperation and enthusiastic support of the most exploited and downtrodden of the peasantry. Peasants rallied behind the CCP not so much because of the appeal of Communism, but because of the success of the party's socioeconomic policies in alleviating their poverty, and giving them something they would have to fight to keep—land.

While the GMD succeeded in driving out the CCP from Jiangxi in 1934, sending into flight those who managed to escape Chiang's encirclement campaign on the famed Long March, the GMD was less able to deal with the Japanese threat. In 1931 Japan invaded Manchuria in northeastern China and, by the next year, established a puppet regime that the Japanese referred to as Manchukuo. In 1937 Chiang reluctantly agreed to unite forces with his most bitter enemy, the CCP, in order to check Japanese expansionism in China.

THE WAR OF RESISTANCE AGAINST JAPAN

In the summer of 1937, war officially broke out between China and Japan. By the end of that year, Nanjing had fallen in an event known as the Rape of Nanjing. The GMD split, with one faction under Wang Jingwei collaborating with the Japanese beginning in 1940 and the group under Chiang fleeing to Chongqing where, with American aid, the GMD fought a defensive war.

Meanwhile, the CCP, now based in Yan'an in northwestern China, took advantage of the situation to build a popular base of support in the countryside and to draw former supporters of the GMD into the CCP fold. The CCP's steadfast resistance to Japan, in contrast to the GMD's appeasement of Japanese aggression in the early 1930s, attracted intellectuals, students, and the middle class, who had grown increasingly disillusioned and frustrated with what they saw as GMD ineptitude. Combined with a coherent ideology, unified leadership, skillful organization, and socioeconomic policies designed to satisfy the immediate material needs of the peasantry, the CCP's unwavering stance against Japan earned the party the trust and support of the vast majority of the Chinese population.

Japan's surrender in 1945 left a power vacuum that both the GMD and the CCP rushed to fill. The failure of the Marshall mission, headed by the American general George C. Marshall (1880–1959), to form a coalition government led to open civil war in 1947. The odds were heavily in favor of the GMD, with its larger and better equipped army, control of the more industrialized regions of China, and continued American military and financial support. Yet it would be the CCP that would emerge victorious in 1949.

WHY THE CCP WON

Explanations for CCP success either emphasize the superior strategy of the CCP or blame GMD incompetence. Certainly, both contributed to the CCP's victory despite the overwhelming odds stacked against it. A power struggle among the GMD top leadership, combined with dictatorial tactics, rampant corruption, brutal conscription, and fiscal irresponsibility, contributed to mass desertions, spiraling inflation, a demoralized public, and ultimately the collapse of the government, all of which offset the technological and financial advantages the GMD enjoyed (Eastman 1990). The CCP exploited the mistakes of the GMD, both on and off the battlefield. Building upon earlier successes acquired during the war against Japan, the CCP continued to expand its popular base of support. By 1948 the GMD began moving its base of operations to Taiwan, where the government of the Republic of China is located today. On October 1, 1949, Mao formally proclaimed the birth of the People's Republic of China (PRC).

If viewed as an interregnum between the Qing and the PRC, the Republic appears to be an incomplete revolution or a prelude to the rise of the CCP. But the Republican years also tell the story of China's transition from an empire to a nation, of the emergence of the political party and a new entrepreneurial elite, of the development of an industrial economy and a modern infrastructure, and of changing relationships between state and society. Rather than viewing the Republic as a failed experiment, one should see these years as crucial stepping-stones in China's development as a modern nation-state.

SEE ALSO *May Fourth Movement; Nanjing Massacre; Warlord Era (1916–1928).*

BIBLIOGRAPHY

Eastman, Lloyd E. *The Abortive Revolution: China under Nationalist Rule, 1927–1937.* 1974. Cambridge, MA: Harvard University Press, 1990.

Fairbank, John King, and Merle Goldman. *China: A New History.* 2nd enlarged ed. Cambridge, MA: Belknap Press, 2006.

Gilmartin, Christina K. *Engendering the Chinese Revolution: Radical Women, Communist Politics, and Mass Movements.* Berkeley: University of California Press, 1995.

Glosser, Susan L. *Chinese Visions of Family and State, 1915–1953.* Berkeley: University of California Press, 2003.

Hinton, William. *Fanshen: A Documentary of Revolution in a Chinese Village.* 1966. Berkeley: University of California Press, 1997.

Mao Zedong. *Selected Readings from the Works of Mao Tse-tung.* Honolulu, HI: University Press of the Pacific, 2001.

Schwarcz, Vera. *The Chinese Enlightenment: Intellectuals and the Legacy of the May Fourth Movement of 1919.* Berkeley: University of California Press, 1986.

Wang Zheng. *Women in the Chinese Enlightenment: Oral and Textual Histories.* Berkeley: University of California Press, 1999.

Lisa Tran

OVERVIEW, SINCE 1949

On October 1, 1949, the People's Republic of China was formally established, with its national capital at Beijing. Announcing the creation of a "people's democratic dictatorship," Mao Zedong declared, "The Chinese people have stood up!" The people were defined as a coalition of four social classes: the workers, peasants, petite bourgeoisie, and national capitalists (industrialists and business people). The four classes were to be led by the Chinese Communist Party, as the vanguard of the working class. At the time, the party claimed a membership of 4.5 million, of which members of peasant origin accounted for nearly 90 percent. The party was chaired by Mao Zedong, and the government was headed by Zhou Enlai as premier of the State Administrative Council (the predecessor of the State Council).

The Soviet Union recognized the People's Republic on October 2, 1949. Earlier in the year, Mao had proclaimed his policy of "leaning to one side" as a commitment to the socialist bloc. In February 1950, after months of hard bargaining in Moscow, Mao and Joseph Stalin signed the Treaty of Friendship, Alliance, and Mutual Assistance, valid until 1980. This treaty provided not only for security protection but also for a program of loans and assistance, in the context of which China proceeded to adopt a rapid industrialization program modeled after that of the Soviet Union. This was the first time that the country was at peace in more than two decades of civil war and foreign invasion. Beijing proceeded to lay claim to all of China's traditional territory, excepting only Outer Mongolia (a Soviet client state), Taiwan (where the defeated Nationalist regime took refuge), and the small colonies Hong Kong and Macau. Peace was short-lived, however. As a corollary of the Sino-Soviet alliance, Beijing opted to intervene in the Korean War (1950–1953), thereby facilitating closer relations with P'yŏngyang and Moscow but at the cost of at least 400,000 Chinese casualties.

The history of the People's Republic after liberation in 1949 may be divided into three periods: economic reconstruction and political consolidation (1949–1957), a struggle to realize an economically developed revolutionary utopia (1958–1977), and reform and opening to the outside world (1978–present).

CONSTRUCTION AND CONSOLIDATION

Despite the Korean diversion, during the first period the new regime promptly launched several campaigns designed to consolidate the new regime and effect revolutionary social change. The first piece of legislation was the Land Reform Law, which destroyed the landlord class. This was followed by a new marriage law to eliminate the power of the clan and emancipate women. These were enforced not by the party-state apparatus but by "mobilizing the masses" to carry out the law "voluntarily." Thus popular support was enlisted for the new order of things.

Campaigns were also launched against popular films and art works found to have a pernicious ideological impact. In the cities the Three-Anti's and Five-Anti's Campaigns were launched to purge holdover (and hence ideologically suspect) public officials and civil servants, to suppress distrusted private entrepreneurs ("bureaucratic capitalists" dependent on the former Guomindang regime and "big bourgeoisie" dependent on foreign investment), and to eliminate or remold people of other social categories suspected of harboring anticommunist proclivities (e.g., Western-educated intellectuals). Party-state control over the media and all institutions of learning was implemented, work units (*danwei*) were set up, and personnel dossiers (*dang'an*) were instituted. In 1954 a National People's Congress was established and its delegates were indirectly elected (though all nominees were appointed from the party *nomenklatura*, or list of approved candidates). The leadership seemed to maintain internal cohesion throughout (except for the purge of two leading officials, Gao Gang and Rao Shushi, in 1954–1955).

The new regime was very popular in its early years, for several reasons. First, the previous Guomindang regime was so corrupt, and had bequeathed an economic situation so hopeless, that it had utterly lost credibility in the eyes of the people. Second, the new regime carried out a land reform exactly as it had promised during the civil war, with every peasant receiving an equal plot of land. Naturally, the new regime was wholeheartedly supported by the peasants. Third, the new regime promised urban workers and the middle classes that under the centralized control of the party-state, a strong industrial state would be built, and that in the next several decades China could catch up and surpass the most powerful countries in the world, and it showed every early sign of doing so. Finally, the new government was extremely upright because of the revolutionary spirit then prevailing among the cadres. Indeed, anyone of rank who took a bribe of more than RMB 2,000 received immediate capital punishment.

In 1956 China launched a policy of "rapid industrialization" based on "self-reliance" in the face of capitalist hostility—a policy consistent not only with the Stalinist precedent but also with import-substitution policies then popular in the third world. To achieve this rapid industrialization, all private firms, factories, banks, and so forth, were taken over by the state. There was very little private ownership in the economy, the market was destroyed, and in its stead came a series of five-year plans (the first for 1953–1957), in which prices were set administratively. Everyone from the chief of state to the youngest workers received roughly the same salary, and party members worked even longer hours than non-party-members. In the countryside, peasants were organized along military lines into brigades and teams and finally communes, their land pooled in "rural socialism." Thus by the end the first decade of socialist construction, despite a choppy business cycle and several sharp setbacks, China had established command of a centralized, hierarchical, and highly disciplined political system based on collective ownership and centralized planning, and it built a complete industrial infrastructure from scratch. Yet these accomplishments resulted not in a prolongation of the successful model but in the inauguration of nearly two decades of sociopolitical experimentation, in which all previous gains were gambled in a bold bid to realize a communist utopia.

STRIVING FOR UTOPIA

The leadership strove for a communist utopia from 1958 to 1976 for two reasons. The first is that completion of the basic socialist transformation raised the question, What next? Further perfection of socialist institutions resulted only in suffocating conformity. Why not break through to the final stage? The second reason is that the Communist Party leadership had run off the rails of its Stalinist model. Though China had already encountered some difficulties in applying the model, the primal blow was the secret speech Nikita Khrushchev delivered to the Twentieth Congress of the Communist Party of the Soviet Union in 1956. This speech subjected Stalin to rigorous and comprehensive criticism for serious deviations from the correct political line.

Contrary to subsequent reports, this speech made a deep and uncontroversial impact on the Chinese Communist Party (CCP) leadership, as reflected in the decisions and policies implemented in the Eighth Party Congress held later that year. Yet Mao came to feel that the CCP had overreacted. The Central Committee's repudiation of a personality cult and its critique of "rash advance" (policies he had favored) may have inclined Mao to encourage intellectuals to criticize the leadership in the campaign to "let a hundred flowers bloom, let a hundred schools of thought contend," launched early in 1957. The official pretext of this experiment with liberalism was Mao's theoretical discovery that socialist society contained nonantagonistic contradictions, as well as antagonistic contradictions, and that the former could be resolved through peaceful discussion and debate. Thus intellectuals might be permitted to think innovatively without concern that they might deviate ideologically. But the criticisms and suggestions voiced at this time exceeded the regime's bounds for tolerance and precipitated the anti-rightist campaign, which subjected some 550,000 dissidents to protracted rectification. This first call for post-Stalinist innovation thus resulted only in the discovery that the intellectual community was ideologically unreliable.

The following year Mao and the Communist Party leadership launched the Great Leap Forward and the people's commune movement on the assumption that a higher scale of socialist organization and various populist technical innovations would lead to an upsurge of productivity, causing massive increases in gross domestic product and facilitating rural industrialization. When Soviet advisers questioned some of these innovations, their interventions were rebuffed, and so Moscow withdrew them, also suspending other programs for civilian and military assistance. When Marshal Peng Dehuai raised questions at the Lushan Conference (8th Plenum of the 8th Central Committee) in July–August 1959 Mao exploded, Peng and his followers were purged, and the policies reaffirmed. Even when the Great Leap proved to be an economic disaster of historic proportions, resulting in a

Chinese Red Guards attending a May Day celebration, Tiananmen Square, Beijing, May 1, 1969. *Beginning in 1966, thousands of Red Guard members followed Mao Zedong's command to purge China of citizens thought to hold traditional attitudes counter to those of the Communist government. The ensuing Cultural Revolution resulted in the deaths of thousands, the imprisonment of millions, and the disintegration of China's educational system.* AFP/GETTY IMAGES

famine incurring an estimated 20 million to 40 million deaths, it did not entirely derail this era of radical social experimentation. One reason was that the magnitude of the setback was not publicly revealed at the time, because comprehensive media controls suppressed the information until after Mao's death.

But more basic is that the disaster exposed a split in the elite over its causes. On the one side, Liu Shaoqi, Deng Xiaoping, and most other leaders, though erstwhile staunch supporters of the purge of Peng Dehuai in support of the Great Leap now agreed that the policy was flawed and required a fundamental shift of line. Mao's argument to the contrary was that the program was right but that the people had been inadequately prepared to implement it, and that a "cultural revolution" was thus required to transform people's "hearts." This split, never publicly acknowledged at the time, was incorporated into an elite division of labor in which the "first front" of the leadership, led by Liu and Deng, assumed responsibility for practical, routine decisions and the "second front," consisting of Mao and some of his radical supporters, assumed leadership of more theoretical, strategic issues (including continuing rhetorical support for the Leap). This division functioned reasonably well, allowing the first front to introduce pragmatic adjustments under radical rhetorical cover, until 1966 (albeit with occasional interruptions when Mao interceded with radical proposals for policy changes in education, medical care, and above all culture). In 1966, however, leadership differences over the resulting discrepancy between theory and practice culminated in the Great Proletarian Cultural Revolution (1966–1969), in which Mao encouraged youthful Red Guards to criticize the leadership, which he now believed had been infiltrated by "revisionists," "capitalist-roaders," and representatives of a "bourgeois reactionary line." The Cultural Revolution led to a sweeping purge and demotion (*xiafang*) of the leadership to labor reform, experimentation with "revolutionary committees" and other organizational innovations, a decline in economic production, and ultimately a return to the bureaucratic status quo, underwritten by the People's Liberation Army.

After three decades of "socialist construction," most Chinese were still peasants living at a basic subsistence level, industrial policy was nearing exhaustion as the policy of self-reliance cut China off capital markets and technical innovation, and the revolutionary spirit had been lost despite pervasive ideological socialization. These setbacks came despite respectable economic performance and international political gains: a cumulative growth rate in the gross domestic product of some 6 percent per annum and construction of a complete industrial infrastructure on the one front and China's divorce from the Soviet Union and its initiation of détente with the United States, the leading bourgeois superpower, on the other front.

REFORM AND OPENING

After Mao's death in September 1976, there ensued a split between his radical and moderate successors (i.e., between the Gang of Four and Hua Guofeng (1921–2008), and their respective supporters). Ironically, at the Third Plenum of the Eleventh Central Committee in December 1978, the leadership was recaptured by Deng Xiaoping, one of the chief previous victims of the Cultural Revolution, who promptly rehabilitated many of those purged with him and instituted a new policy of reform and opening to the outside world. Essentially a revival (and extension) of many of the policies introduced in the wake of the failed Great Leap Forward in the early 1960s, the new line ended radical sociopolitical experiments in favor of "stability and unity" (*anding tuanjie*), while at the same time permitting gradual but relatively uninhibited economic innovation whenever it could be shown to promote economic growth.

To support this new policy, the leadership gradually stripped foreign policy of its ideological bearings and sought to improve relations in all directions. This included normalizing relations with the United States, opening up to foreign direct investment (1979), and negotiating a reconciliation with the Soviet Union in 1989 (since reaffirmed with Russia and the other fourteen post-Soviet republics).

The first domestic success was in rural reform beginning in the early 1980s. The regime approved a "household responsibility" system in which peasants redivided land according to the size of households and assumed responsibility for running family farms. Thus the communes were disbanded and the family became the basic unit of production. Each family got a thirty-year lease, which it could transfer or inherit. The switch to private enterprise resulted in an early boom of agricultural production and of auxiliary rural industry (township and village enterprises). This provided the inspiration (and capital) for urban reform, as the responsibility system implied devolution of control of industry to local authorities, who assumed responsibility for sources of material supply and for sale of products. China thus gradually created a market system in both agriculture and industry, and the focus on heavy industry gave way to a more balanced emphasis allowing greater ambit for light industry and consumer choice.

As growth accelerated into a boom of historically unprecedented proportions, per capita incomes rose as well. By the end of the 1980s, controversy had arisen concerning political reform, the general premise being that an economic transformation of such magnitude must be accompanied by political and ideological changes. This assumption inspired a series of spontaneous popular demonstrations beginning in 1986 and culminating in the spring 1989 Prodemocracy Movement at Tiananmen

New building construction in Beijing, December 15, 2006. *After Communist leaders looked to bring greater prosperity to the nation by easing restrictions on the economy in the late 1970s, many areas of China saw increased levels of growth, particularly in coastal regions. Many large urban areas, such as Beijing and Shanghai, subsequently embarked on major building campaigns, both to create office space for growing companies and housing for workers earning larger incomes.* © ADRIAN BRADSHAW/EPA/CORBIS

demanding liberalization, press freedom, and political democratization. But on the morning of June 4 the movement was ruthlessly suppressed by the leadership, with the help of the People's Liberation Army, decisively underscoring the regime's continuing commitment to socialist political institutions.

Despite the military crackdown and ideological revival, the success of China's economic reforms gave them a certain immunity to reversal, and following Deng Xiaoping's "southern tour" (*nanxun*) in early 1992, reform made a vigorous resurgence. Price reform resumed despite an upsurge of inflation, in response to which the leadership centralized control of the financial and fiscal system in 1994. Further opening stanched the flight of foreign investment in the aftermath of Tiananmen, and China soon became a leading magnet for foreign direct investment. The harnessing of investment to technology transfer and to China's booming export sector allayed Marxist fears of neoimperialism.

By the turn of the millennium, two additional changes registered their economic impact: China's entry into the World Trade Organization guaranteed China's integration into international markets, and the ideological taboo on privatization (euphemistically referred to as "ownership reform") began to disintegrate in the face of foreign investment, the corporatization of domestic industry, and constitutional recognition of private property. Except for a few episodes of nationalist assertion (e.g., the 1995–1996 Taiwan Strait crisis and several spontaneous anti-American or anti-Japanese demonstrations), Chinese foreign policy, wary of prematurely provoking guardians of the international status quo, remained low-key. Meanwhile, despite such ideological adjustments as Jiang Zemin's "Three Represents" theory of the party and Hu Jintao's replacement of "class struggle" with "socialist harmony," Tiananmen gave the regime a pretext to eschew further experiments with political reform, and fiscal reform has had no discernible impact on the market logic of growing inequality, which has led to increasing local protest.

SEE ALSO *Economic Development; Political Control since 1949; Prodemocracy Movement (1989).*

BIBLIOGRAPHY

Baum, Richard. *Burying Mao: Chinese Politics in the Age of Deng Xiaoping*. Princeton, NJ: Princeton University Press, 1994.

Bernstein, Thomas. *Up to the Mountains and Down to the Villages.* New Haven, CT: Yale University Press, 1977.

Dittmer, Lowell. *China under Reform.* Boulder, CO: Westview Press, 1994.

Fewsmith, Joseph. *China since Tiananmen.* New York: Cambridge University Press, 2001.

Lieberthal, Kenneth, and Michel Oksenberg. *Policy Making in China.* Princeton, NJ: Princeton University Press, 1988.

MacFarquhar, Roderick, and Michael Schoenhals. *Mao's Last Revolution.* Cambridge, MA: Harvard University Press, 2006.

Martin, Helmut. *Cult and Canon: The Origins and Development of State Maoism.* Armonk, NY: M. E. Sharpe, 1982.

Nathan, Andrew. *Chinese Democracy.* Berkeley: University of California Press, 1986.

Schurmann, Franz. *Ideology and Organization in Communist China.* 2nd ed., enlarged. Berkeley: University of California Press, 1968.

Schwartz, Benjamin. *Communism and China: Ideology in Flux.* Cambridge, MA: Harvard University Press, 1968.

Shue, Vivienne. *The Reach of the State: Sketches of the Chinese Body Politic.* Stanford, CA: Stanford University Press, 1988.

Yan Jiaqi and Gao Gao. *Turbulent Decade: A History of the Cultural Revolution.* Trans. D. W. Y. Kwok. Honolulu: University of Hawaii Press, 1996.

Lowell Dittmer

INTERPRETING MODERN AND CONTEMPORARY CHINA

The remembering, understanding, and writing of China's past have undergone several notable changes from the early nineteenth century to the present. These changes reflected the modern transformation of Chinese society and, at the same time, also left notable imprints on the course of modern Chinese history.

NEW TEXT CONFUCIANISM AND CHANGES IN HISTORIOGRAPHY

Prior to the nineteenth century, evidential learning (*kaozheng xue*), the main intellectual trend in classical study, helped reorient the ideas of history and improve its methodology in the eighteenth century. Yet in the nineteenth century, this tradition experienced a marked decline and gave way to the revival of New Text, or New Script, Confucianism (*jinwen jingxue*). This Confucian school first emerged in the Han period (206 BCE–220 CE) and, over the subsequent centuries, developed a hermeneutic strategy for plumbing and revealing the deep meanings of Confucian teaching by closely examining the language of the classics. Gong Zizhen (1792–1841) and Wei Yuan (1794–1857), two leading intellectuals of the age, were both New Text scholars. They emphasized the importance of studying history to understand and solve problems of the present, of which the most imminent and threatening was the British encroachment in the south, and the Russian encroachment in the north, on the territorial borders of the reigning Qing dynasty (1644–1912).

Having witnessed the Qing's defeat by the British in the Opium War (1839–1842), Wei put his ideas into practice by authoring several historical texts, hoping to extract useful lessons from the past to help cope with new challenges. One such text attributed to Wei, *Haiguo tuzhi* (An illustrated treatise on the sea kingdoms), was an early attempt by a mandarin to broaden the Chinese worldview by describing, perhaps for the first time favorably, the rise of the Western world. What prompted Wei and like-minded historians at the time was the belief that the best way to deal with military challenges from the West was to "learn from the barbarians to rein them in" (*shiyi zhiyi*).

This process of learning was also aided by the writings of Wang Tao (1828–1897), who, having made a short visit to Britain, was arguably the most cosmopolitan Chinese of the time. Bridging history and journalism, Wang's works covered recent events in European history, which were entirely new in the Chinese historiographical tradition. Huang Zunxian (1848–1905), who authored *Riben guozhi* (A treatise of the Japanese nation, 1887), also wrote in this vein. Wang, Wei, and Huang incorporated more narrative into their writings, their styles thus departing from the annals-biographic form prevalent in dynastic historiography, the official genre in history writing during the imperial period.

This stylistic change mirrored changes in historical thinking. The annals-biographic form prioritized the need to uphold an idealized moral and sociopolitical order, censoring and condemning those, including emperors, whose behavior deviated from it. In contrast, by describing the history of the Western world in "treatises" (*zhi*)—as Wang, Wei, and Huang did—these historians indicated that the annals-biographic form and the moralistic concern had become inadequate and outdated as historians pursued and presented an enlarged worldview in writing history.

Yet by no means had these writers completely forsaken the entrenched Sinocentric conception of the world, the notion of China being the "Middle Kingdom" under heaven. Instead, most historians and historical thinkers of the late nineteenth and early twentieth centuries strove to accommodate and domesticate new ideas from the West by offering ingenious and creative readings of Confucian teaching, reflecting the persistent influence of New Text Confucianism. For example, to propagate social Darwinism, Kang Youwei (1858–1927) reworked the three-age doctrine (*sanshi shuo*)—a thesis developed by New Text Confucians that the idea of and for historical change (from the age of chaos to that of rising peace and eventually to that of universal harmony) had been encoded by Confucius in such classics as *Chunqiu* (Spring and autumn annals). Drawing on the Spencerian idea of survival of the fittest, Kang and his disciple Liang Qichao (1873–1929) argued for the need for political reform in the Qing government. They became the chief advocates and prime movers of the short-lived 1898 reforms.

THE RISE OF NATIONALIST HISTORIOGRAPHY

Though the reforms ended in a bloody coup d'état, they bred a radical cultural iconoclasm that occasioned a seismic change in Chinese historical thinking and writing. In his exile in Japan after the reform, Liang Qichao acquainted himself with the history, philosophy, and politics of the West via Japanese translations. He was particularly attracted to the genre of nationalist history prevalent in the West, and also gaining popularity in Japan. In 1902 his serialized seminal text *Xin shixue* (New historiography) called for a "historiographical revolution." Liang hoped to launch a thorough reform of history writing in China so that it could be rendered useful for nation building. Considering nationalist history as the new norm for writing history and evolutionism as its main interpretive framework, he announced that the Confucian tradition of writing history in imperial China had become outdated and irrelevant. Though imperial historians had produced an immense body of historical literature, in each age it was all about only one person, the monarch, and so the entire tradition of history writing in imperial China failed to assist in promoting Chinese nationalism and hence was pure dross.

At the time, this iconoclastic sentiment was in vogue among those who, like Liang, had studied and sojourned in Japan. Some of them edited and contributed to *Guocui xuebao* (National essence journal), which published experimental writing in nationalist history. Begun in 1905, this publication, like Liang Qichao's *Xin shixue*, registered a certain amount of Japanese influence, for the term *national essence* had been coined earlier in Japan. Indeed, if in the late nineteenth century, works of Wei Yuan and Wang Tao had inspired their Japanese counterparts to gain knowledge of the New World and seek new ways of writing history, in the early twentieth century Japan in turn helped reform- and revolution-minded Chinese to conceive a new historical outlook on their country's past, as well as on East Asia and the world in general.

Fukuzawa Yukichi (1835–1901) and Taguchi Ukichi (1855–1905), two leading intellectual figures in Meiji Japan (1868–1912), successfully propagated the notion of the history of civilization (*bunmeishi*). In addition, Japanese sinologists produced textbooks on Chinese history from the nationalist perspective and, in presenting its course of evolution, shifted attention from the monarch to the people and civilization. These textbooks were widely adopted in Chinese schools, inspiring Liang to sound a call for a historiographical revolution and Chinese writers to produce their own such texts. One example was Xia Zengyou's (1863–1921) *Zuixin zhongxue Zhongguo lishi jiaokeshu* (The newest middle school textbook of Chinese history, 1905). Though incomplete, it featured an evolutionist perspective and a narrative structure, both regarded as novel at the time, and was hailed as an exemplar of historiography.

Yet official history writing, dynastic historiography, was by no means coming to an end in the period, nor, to some extent, in later years. Despite the political upheavals that caused the Qing dynasty to collapse in 1912, the History Office (Guoshi Guan) in the Qing government was able to operate more or less continuously, preserving archives and producing historical texts about the dynasty.

Not only did the tradition of official historiography continue, there were also new attempts to improve it. Several official Qing historians carried on the evidential research of the eighteenth century. Because the earlier *Yuan shi* (Yuan history), a product of the History Office of the Ming period (1368–1644), had been deemed inadequate in its use of sources and inferior in quality to its peers, they worked on revising and eventually rewriting the dynastic history of the Mongol Yuan dynasty (1279–1368). This project of improving the history of the Yuan dynasty went on well after the end of the Qing dynasty and resulted in several important publications, of which Ke Shaomin's (1850–1933) *Xin Yuan shi* (New Yuan history, 1922) was the most comprehensive and best received.

While Ke was working on Yuan history, he also became a chief editor of the History Office in the Republican government, where he was responsible for compiling an official history of the Qing dynasty, *Qing shi gao* (Manuscript history of the Qing), in 536 traditionally bound volumes. Through the Republican era, this interest in Qing history continuously grew and generated more studies, in part because, as the immediate bygone era, the rise and fall of the Qing remained of help for understanding the challenges facing China at the time. Of the Qing historians during this period, Meng Sen (1868–1937), Jin Zhaofeng (1870–1933), and Xiao Yishan (1902–1978) commanded considerable respect. Meng was a Japan-trained historian known for his expertise on Qing-court politics. Jin offered a complete and concise survey of Qing history. Yet Xiao's *Qingdai tongshi* (A general history of the Qing period) was most notable, owing to his zealous Han nationalist stance and his unrivaled mastery of a great variety of sources (Western sources excepted). When he began publishing this multivolume history, Xiao was still in his twenties.

During the 1960s, in light of the political turmoil of the previous decades in China, Qing history again aroused interest among scholars in Taiwan. Works by Meng Sen, Jin Zhaofeng, and Xiao Yishan were all reprinted and, in the case of Xiao, also revised, and all became benchmarks in the field. There also emerged new works on the Qing (general histories and monographs alike) by a younger generation of scholars, most of whom had received their education on the mainland. In addition, efforts were made to reprint and revise *Qing shi gao* (Manuscript history of the Qing) and, by renaming it *Qing shi* (Qing history), have it accepted as an official history of the dynasty. But this project, having spawned many concerns and criticisms, was not well received in the field of history. Historians in Taiwan have continued to plow the field of Qing history and have produced a host of valuable works focusing on Taiwan's colonization and development during the Qing dynasty and the effect of Qing policy toward the island. Last but not least, in the 1990s and early 2000s, the Chinese government on the mainland assembled a large group of historians to work collectively on compiling multivolume histories of the Qing dynasty and the Republican era (1912–1949). All this suggests that the tradition of dynastic historiography and official sponsorship of history writing remains alive in contemporary China.

THE SCIENTIFIC TURN AND THE PROFESSIONALIZATION OF THE FIELD

During the 1920s, while the tradition of official history writing persisted, one also saw more drastic changes in history writing and thinking, owing to the iconoclastic zeitgeist of the May Fourth or New Culture era (1915–1925). Indeed, the historical work of May Fourth intellectuals—represented by Hu Shi (1891–1962), a young professor at Peking University with a doctoral degree from the United States, and Gu Jiegang (1893–1980), Hu's protégé—injected a scientific turn into the research and writing of history. This scientific turn coincided with the professionalization of history in China. Not only was history now taught and researched by college professors, but research institutions were also set up, for example, the Lishi Yuyan Yanjiusuo (Institute of History and Philology), founded in 1928 by Fu Sinian (1896–1950), another protégé of Hu's. Here a host of scientific methods, ranging from archaeology and anthropology to epigraphy and philology, were introduced to the field of history, particularly in the study of ancient China.

This scientific turn changed the idea of history among modern Chinese. If Liang Qichao, Xia Zengyou, and others of the previous generation had established that history ought to be understood and presented from an evolutionary perspective, Hu Shi and his disciples followed up with attempts to scientifically legitimize the study of history. Hu argued that evolutionism is not only an outlook on history but also a new approach to historical study. He hoped to trace, reconstruct, and verify the historical process of how things become as they are. While Hu's own research focused on ascertaining and authenticating the authorship of several popular novels of the late imperial period, his approach inspired many, particularly Gu Jiegang. In tracing the origins of Chinese antiquity, Gu discovered that many previous claims and beliefs about ancient China had drawn on unreliable or even forged sources from a much later period, and he disputed their validity. By launching "discussion of ancient [Chinese] history" (*gushibian*), Gu and Hu succeeded in propagating the importance of scientific research in history, of basing historical narratives on verified sources using scientific methods, even though few scholars, including their friend Fu Sinian, agreed with their doubts on and challenge to the accepted history of ancient China. By conducting archaeological excavations in an ancient historical site, the Institute of History and Philology was able to prove with hard scientific evidence that there was a high level of civilization in ancient, pre-Confucian China.

As scientific history advanced in the 1920s, it modified and improved people's understanding of China's past. In his advocacy of scientific research in history, Hu Shi maintained that while modern scientific research did not arise in China, scientific reasoning and method were not foreign to the Chinese mind. In fact, Hu contended, in their textual and historical criticism, evidential scholars of the Qing period had used the same regime of scientific procedure and, in their exegetical work, applied it with the same rigor as Western scientists did in studying the natural world.

By promoting scientific history, Hu Shi and his followers partially and selectively revived the tradition of Chinese historical scholarship. Liang Qichao's writings in this period were particularly telling, for in contrast to his early assault on imperial historiography, Liang now worked on rehabilitating the tradition and reevaluating it as a worthy cultural heritage. His *Zhongguo lishi yanjiu fa* (Methods for the study of Chinese history), which appeared in the early 1920s, is a case in point.

MARXIST HISTORIOGRAPHY

The iconoclasm of the May Fourth era also prepared the ground for a Marxist view of history. During the 1930s, as China faced Japan's military aggression, which threatened its national existence, Marxist historiography became increasingly attractive to young students as they searched for new ways to render history more useful to the cause of national salvation. In the "social-history controversy," which began in 1928 but continued well into the early 1930s, Marxist historians debated among themselves about the nature of Chinese society in their analyses of the evolution of Chinese history in the context of Marxist theory of social development. They hoped that by resolving such greater issues as whether China in the past had followed the Marxist course of historical development, and whether it was now ready to launch a socialist revolution, which to them was a means for saving China from its woes at the time, historical study could become more valuable and have a more direct social impact.

Marxist historians, some of whom were also working in academic settings, criticized the empirical approach advocated by Hu Shi and other academic historians. To them, as well as to other nationalist historians known for their cultural conservatism, historians such as Qian Mu (1895–1990) and Liu Yizheng (1879–1956), the scientific history promoted by Hu and his followers, with its evidential interest in source collection and examination, was of little help in rallying the Chinese people behind the nationalist cause. Though unfair to Hu Shi and his group, who were by no means apathetic to nationalist needs, this observation reflected the urgent need for Chinese historians to refute claims made by Japanese historians to justify Japan's invasion and occupation of China.

Indeed, no sooner had modern historical scholarship been established in Japan than it became subjugated to nationalist goals for turning the country into an empire, defined and designed by the conservative forces of Shintoism and militarism. The study of Asian history (*Tōyō shi*), which emerged as an academic subject, was quickly transformed into an imperialist scheme to find Japan's "Orient" in the hope of making Japan the new leader and justifying its aggression in Asia. During the Second Sino-Japanese War (1937–1945), Japanese historians stepped up their effort to champion the government project of establishing the Greater East Asia Co-prosperity Sphere, which was a brazen attempt to subdue the Chinese and support Japanese militarism.

In response, both Qian Mu and Liu Yizheng, along with their Marxist counterparts Fan Wenlan (1893–1969) and Lü Zhenyu (1900–1980), hoping to boost the national esteem in wartime, published popular general histories that exalted the evolution of the Chinese nation, even though their historical interpretations were distinctly different. To help raise the morale of his compatriots in fighting the Japanese, Guo Moruo (1892–1978), another famous Marxist historian, known for his study of slavery in ancient China, wrote several plays depicting courageous historical figures.

In 1949 the Communists took over power in China and turned Marxist historiography into orthodoxy on the mainland, a situation that remains intact more or less to the present (2009). Despite the help of Soviet historians, whose works in the early days of the People's Republic were extolled as the exemplars of Marxist historiography, Chinese Marxists still struggled with the apparent incongruence between Marxist theory and the Chinese historical experience. They heatedly debated such questions as the transition from slavery to feudalism in the early imperial period and the possibility that China developed capitalism on its own in the late imperial era. These debates were pertinent to the problems inherent in using Marxism, a product of European culture and history, to interpret the course of Chinese history.

Notwithstanding this incompatibility, Marxist historiography advanced in the People's Republic in certain areas. The study of peasant rebellions in imperial China became a booming field, commanding the interest of historians. Such new areas of study effectively shifted the attention of the historian from the ruler to the ruled and paved the way for the rise of sociocultural history. In the post-Mao years, sociocultural history has emerged as a major historiographic trend in the People's Republic, even though the study of peasant rebellions itself has declined.

SINOLOGY IN THE WEST

Chinese peasants, and Chinese social history generally, was also one of the main focuses of Euro-American study of China in the years after World War II. Indeed, this period witnessed the transformation of China studies in the West. In the late nineteenth century, when sinology first emerged as a legitimate academic pursuit, it remained heavily influenced by the practical need to help diplomats and missionaries obtain knowledge and understanding of Chinese language and culture. Sinologists concentrated on translating, annotating, and interpreting Chinese classical texts; less emphasis was placed on studying social and political changes in modern times. Indeed, most sinologists, or Orientalists, perceived and portrayed China as a changeless society. Though apparently fond of Chinese culture, they presented China as an ill-fated foil to the ever changing and jubilant West.

The important role that China played in World War II and the success of the Communist movement in the postwar years gave rise to a new trend in China studies, led most notably by John K. Fairbank (1907–1991) and his disciples in the United States. Having lived and worked in China before and during the war, Fairbank witnessed firsthand the regime changes in the country and developed an interest, which coincided with that of the U.S. government, in offering explanations for China's modern transformation. Assisted by his colleagues in the United States, most of whom shared his experience, and some leading Chinese historians, such as Jiang Tingfu (1895–1965), a Columbia Ph.D. who had mentored Fairbank while in China, Fairbank developed an influential thesis known as challenge-response to interpret modern Chinese history. He attributed key changes in modern China, those that helped make modern Chinese history fundamentally different from its imperial past, to the Western challenge to China from the mid-nineteenth century, to which it had to respond.

The challenge-response thesis bore the imprint of modernization theory. The latter, which held considerable sway in postwar studies in the social sciences and history, emphasized the dichotomy between tradition and modernity in explaining sociopolitical change around the globe, and considered modernization, along the Western model, an ineluctable trend in modern history (a view that retains residues of the Orientalist view of non-Western cultures as unfortunate, negative contrasts with the triumphant modern West). The radicalism of the 1960s, however, gave rise to criticism of the modernization theory and Eurocentric views in historical study. China scholars in the United States, including Fairbank in his later years, began to see more traditional and indigenous factors shaping the course of modern Chinese history. In analyzing the rise of the Communist movement, for example, historians sought similarities in peasant uprisings in the past.

In 1984 Paul A. Cohen, a student of Fairbank, published the widely noted *Discovering History in China: American Historical Writing on the Recent Chinese Past*, which gives a full summary of the effort by postwar historians to go beyond the tradition-modernity divide and analyze the rise of modern China as a historical continuity, rather than as an abrupt transition supposedly brought about by modernity. More important, departing from the emphasis of Fairbank's challenge-response thesis, Cohen and like-minded historians refused to see imperial China as stagnated and ageless, unable to generate epochal changes on its own. They instead strove to demonstrate intrinsic and internal dynamics for change in China's past and present.

Since the 1990s, owing to postmodern and postcolonial critiques of modern historiography, new attempts have been made by Western scholars of China seeking alternative ways to interpret Chinese history and challenge the readily accepted teleologies characterizing the work of postwar modernist scholars. As feminist scholars problematize the ingrained image of Chinese women as submissive, illiterate, and homebound, sociopolitical historians question the deep-rooted notions of the Qing empire as quaint, incapable, and moribund. Cultural historians too have developed new outlooks on such imperial institutions as the civil service examination system, have analyzed the ebb and flow of the Confucian influence at the imperial level and in Chinese schools, and have documented the growth and impact of print and book culture in southeastern China. In describing the forces shaping the rise of modern China, more attention has been drawn to the complex yet palpable ties of these forces with past traditions, including those underpinning the May Fourth iconoclasm of the 1910s and the 1920s.

ALTERNATIVE METHODOLOGIES OF THE POST-MAO ERA

As a result of the Cold War, China was isolated from the outside world, especially the West, for three decades after 1949. When the isolation finally came to an end in the late 1970s, new efforts were made by mainland historians to explore other ways of studying history than the Marxist historiography imposed by the government. In the so-called culture-fever (*wenhua re*) movement of the 1980s, for example, historians explored and exchanged ideas about finding alternative methodologies in historical study and enthusiastically followed new developments in Western historiography. During this period sociocultural history began to attract more attention, and it has since become a major trend of historical research. This trend has merged with similar interests that emerged in the China field overseas during the postwar years, and since the mid-1990s it has absorbed elements of the postmodernist criticism of modern historiography. Like their foreign counterparts, Chinese sociocultural historians cast doubt on the teleological outlook in nationalist historiography and borrow methods from anthropology, ethnography, semiotics, and literary theory to engage in studies often considered marginal and inconsequential by nationalist historians.

From the 1990s there have also been efforts to revive the Qing-era tradition of evidential learning. These efforts extend the experiments with scientific history advanced by Hu Shi and Fu Sinian in the Republican period, in which in-depth knowledge and careful examination of source materials are identified as necessary for a successful career in history. Despite their anti-Communist stance, Hu and Fu are now rehabilitated and revered as "master historians." Chen Yinke (1890–1969) and Chen Yuan (1880–1971), two of their peers famous for their unmatched erudition and masterful techniques in source criticism, have also been placed on pedestals as exemplars in historical scholarship. All this can be viewed as part of a general undertaking by mainland historians to mitigate the dominating influence of Marxist ideology in historiography.

Despite these efforts, ideology retains its tight grip, especially on historical education, which exerts a decisive influence on the minds of Chinese youth. The writing of history textbooks remains under government control. The avowed aim is to glorify traditional China as an advanced world civilization and to teach students about how China was bullied and exploited since the Opium War by such foreign imperial powers as England and Japan. Historical museums across the country, which are usually organized around such themes, as well as the remains of the Old Summer Palace (Yuanming Yuan), looted and burned by foreign forces in 1860 and again in 1900, are used as sites for nationalist education and are visited regularly by students of all levels.

This nationalist thinking is also reflected in the study of world history. Since its establishment in the early years of the People's Republic, world history has focused on the rise of Western powers in the modern world, aiming to deliver the message that by advancing modernization, China will catch up with these advanced countries and become a new world power. As a result of China's explosive economic expansion since the 1980s, nationalism has replaced Marxism, in practice if not in rhetoric, to become the ruling ideology in today's China. Nationalist ideology is promoted by the government and embraced by the general populace and, to some extent, by some members of the intellectual community. Hence, it is reasonable to predict that nationalist ideology will continue to shape how history is remembered and interpreted in China in the near future. As such, it will remain as a major force in the study and understanding of Chinese history.

SEE ALSO *Chinese Marxism; Confucianism; Guo Moruo; Hu Shi; Liang Qichao; May Fourth Movement; Sinology.*

BIBLIOGRAPHY

Cohen, Paul A. *Discovering History in China: American Historical Writing on the Recent Chinese Past.* New York: Columbia University Press, 1984.

Cohen, Paul A. *China Unbound: Evolving Perspectives on the Chinese Past.* London: RoutledgeCurzon, 2003.

Dirlik, Arif. *Revolution and History: The Origins of Marxist Historiography in China, 1919–1937.* Berkeley: University of California Press, 1978.

Duara, Prasenjit. *Rescuing History from the Nation: Questioning Narratives of Modern China.* Chicago: University of Chicago Press, 1995.

Evans, Paul M. *John Fairbank and the American Understanding of Modern China.* New York: Blackwell, 1988.

Fairbank, John K. *Chinabound: A Fifty-Year Memoir.* New York: Harper and Row, 1982.

Hon, Tze-ki, and Robert J. Culp, eds. *The Politics of Historical Production in Late Qing and Republican China.* Leiden, Netherlands: Brill, 2007.

Hu Fengxiang and Zhang Wenjian. *Zhongguo jindai shixue sichao yu liupai* [Ideas and schools in modern Chinese historiography]. Shanghai: Huadong Shifan Daxue Chubanshe, 1991.

Hu Shih. *The Chinese Renaissance: The Haskell Lectures, 1933.* Chicago: University of Chicago Press, 1934.

Ku Chieh-kang. *The Autobiography of a Chinese Historian.* Trans. and ed. Arthur Hummel. Leiden, Netherlands: Brill, 1931.

Leutner, Mechthild. *Geschichtsschreibung zwischen Politik und Wissenschaft: Zur Herausbildung der chinesischen marxistischen Geschichtswissenschaft in den 30er und 40er Jahren* [History writing between politics and science: The development of Chinese Marxist historiography during the 1930s and 1940s]. Wiesbaden, Germany: Harrassowitz, 1982.

Liang Ch'i-ch'ao. *Intellectual Trends in the Ch'ing Period.* Trans. Immanuel C. Y. Hsü. Cambridge, MA: Harvard University Press, 1959.

Unger, Jonathan, ed. *Using the Past to Serve the Present: Historiography and Politics in Contemporary China.* Armonk, NY: Sharpe, 1993.

Wang, Q. Edward. *Inventing China through History: The May Fourth Approach to Historiography.* Albany: State University of New York Press, 2001.

Wasserstrom, Jeffrey, ed. *Twentieth Century China: New Approaches.* London: Routledge, 2002.

Xu Guansan. *Xin shixue jiushi nian* [New historiography over the past ninety years]. 2 vols. Hong Kong: Zhongwen Daxue Chubanshe, 1986–1988.

Q. Edward Wang

HIV/AIDS

China's first reported case of AIDS (acquired immunodeficiency syndrome) occurred in Beijing in 1985. The spread of the epidemic has since accelerated year by year, and HIV (human immunodeficiency virus) and AIDS are now recognized as a major problem facing China. AIDS deaths outnumbered those from any other infectious disease. In 2007, according to an estimation produced jointly by the Chinese Ministry of Health, the Joint United Nations Program on Aids (UNAIDS), and the World Health Organization (WHO), there were 700,000 PLHIV, "people living with HIV," in China, including 85,000 AIDS patients. These figures imply a low prevalence, considering China's population is around 1.3 billion. However, all HIV/AIDS statistics for China must be viewed with caution, because stigma and ignorance make data difficult to collect. Moreover, pockets of high infection among specific subpopulations have created a danger that the epidemic could spread further into the general population.

Early official attitudes toward HIV/AIDS were characterized by denial. Public health authorities claimed that HIV/AIDS would not become established in China because the main causes were "drug addiction and abnormal sex." The Chinese word for AIDS, *aizibing*, which sounds like "loving capitalism disease," reinforced a tendency to link it to contact with the West. The first official actions taken to counter AIDS were limited and sometimes illogical; for example, compulsory AIDS testing was introduced for foreign students registering at Chinese universities beginning in 1986, but testing was not required for other foreign visitors such as businesspeople, a group more likely to be at risk through engaging in commercial sex transactions.

A sharp increase in AIDS cases in the 1990s led to a thorough reappraisal. Real efforts were made to identify the main channels for infection, and programs have been developed to raise awareness, reduce infection among at-risk groups, and treat PLHIV.

GEOGRAPHIC DISTRIBUTION AND DEMOGRAPHIC CHARACTERISTICS OF HIV/AIDS CASES

Although cases of HIV/AIDS are found in all of China's thirty-one provinces, certain provinces have heavy concentrations of cases (see map).

Of the total population of PLHIV reported in China to October 2007, 80.5 percent were in six provinces: Yunnan,

Henan, Guangxi, Xinjiang, Guangdong, and Sichuan. AIDS-related deaths have also been concentrated in certain provinces, with 80.5 percent in Yunnan, Henan, Guangxi, Hubei, Anhui, Guangdong, and Sichuan. In addition, there are regional subepidemics. In Yunnan, thought to have been a major entry point for the disease in the 1980s, most cases are found among urban intravenous drug users, whose infection rate has been estimated at 80 percent. Intravenous drug users also account for most infections in Guangxi and Guangdong. In Sichuan, where the epidemic developed initially among intravenous drug users on drug-trafficking routes, HIV/AIDS is now moving into the general population. Nearly 10 percent of all China's HIV/AIDS cases are in Xinjiang, mainly among intravenous drug users. Here the male-to-female ratio is unusually high at 6 to 1. In Henan and Anhui, there are serious clusters of cases due to dangerous blood-collection practices in the 1990s. In Hunan, a sharp rise in HIV prevalence from the early 2000s was attributed to heterosexual transmission.

Although ethnic minorities account for only 8 percent of China's total population, over a third of PLHIV belong to these groups. Of the cumulative total of PLHIV by the end of October 2007, 71.3 percent were male and 28.7 percent female. Of cumulative AIDS cases, 64.7 percent were male and 35.3 percent female. Of cumulative HIV infections, people in the twenty-to-thirty age group accounted for 70 percent of the total, while 69.9 percent of AIDS-related deaths were in the twenty-to-forty-nine age group.

TRANSMISSION CHANNELS

Over time, there have been shifts in the relative importance of the various transmission channels (see Table 1). Drug use has gradually given way to unsafe sex as the

HIV modes of infection in China

Mode of transmission	Cumulative PLHIV to October 2007	HIV cases reported from January–October 2007	Estimation of HIV-positive people living in China in 2000 (7,000,000)
Intravenous drug use	38.5%	29.4%	38.1%
Blood and plasma collection	19.3%	6.1%	9.3% (blood and plasma collection and transfusion combined)
Blood transfusion and blood products	4.3%	4.2%	—
Heterosexual transmission	17.8%	37.9%	40.6%
Homosexual transmission	1.0%	3.3%	11.0%
Mother-to-child transmission	1.2%	1.6%	1%
Unknown	17.9%	17.5%	

SOURCE: State Council AIDS Working Committee Office and UN Theme Group on AIDS in China. *A Joint Assessment of HIV/AIDS Prevention, Treatment, and Care in China*, 2007, p. 3.

Table 1

major channel, while infection associated with the collection and transfusion of blood is becoming less important.

Intravenous drug use, reported to be responsible for around two-thirds of all infections in China in the early 2000s, now accounts for less than two-fifths. These cases are primarily located in Yunnan, Guangxi, and Xinjiang, where drug use is a serious problem. The incidence of HIV infection from intravenous drug use is thought to be spreading. China has almost one million *registered* intravenous drug users, but the real total may be three or four million. Needle sharing is common, and many drug users are HIV positive.

Unsafe sex is now the dominant mode of transmission in China. Most heterosexual transmission is the result of unprotected sex between sex workers and their clients, although clients may then infect regular partners. The commercial sex industry reappeared in the coastal cities in the mid-1980s and spread rapidly inland. The Public Security Bureau estimated the number of sex workers at four to ten million. Their rate of HIV infection is much higher than that of the general population. Commercial sex provides a bridge that carries HIV from users to the population at large. Many female intravenous drug users are sex workers, and male intravenous drug users are more likely than nonusers to frequent prostitutes. Transmission through heterosexual sex is comparatively evenly spread geographically. Migrant workers are a particular at-risk group that faces barriers in accessing information and health care. If they contract HIV when working away from home, they may carry it back to regular partners in the villages.

Homosexuality, only removed from the Chinese Psychiatric Association's list of mental disorders in 2001, is still stigmatized in China. The WHO takes the position that homosexual transmission as a result of unprotected anal sex has probably therefore been underestimated. Beijing's two AIDS hospitals report that one-third of their patients contacted HIV through male-to-male sex. Homosexual transmission appears to be mainly focused in cities and in areas with large migrant populations. Stigma and secrecy impede information drives on safer sex practices. Gay men experience heavy family and social pressure to hide their sexual orientation. It is thought that at least 50 percent marry, thus providing a bridge for infection between the homosexual and heterosexual population. Nonetheless international health professionals regard China as a model for other countries in that homosexual activity is not criminalized.

The subepidemic associated with blood donation is a particular tragedy in China. A significant number of HIV victims were infected through unsafe commercial collection in the 1990s. In the worst cases, untested blood was pooled, plasma was extracted, and the remaining blood was returned to the donors to "speed their recovery." Infected blood could thus spread HIV not only to those receiving transfusions, but also to donors and to the spouses of both groups. Unsafe blood collection is now admitted to have been widespread in China. The worst affected province is Henan, where local government officials organized large-scale blood-collection drives to raise funds, illegal blood-collection enterprises flourished, and impoverished peasants queued up to give blood for money. HIV prevalence among commercial donors in rural eastern China has been estimated at 12.5 percent. There are villages where more than half the population has tested positive, treatment became available late, and there have been many deaths.

Mother-to-infant transmission appears to be very low at only 1 to 2 percent of the total. It may be seriously underestimated, however, because prevalence surveys have been limited to high-risk areas and diagnostic facilities are inadequate.

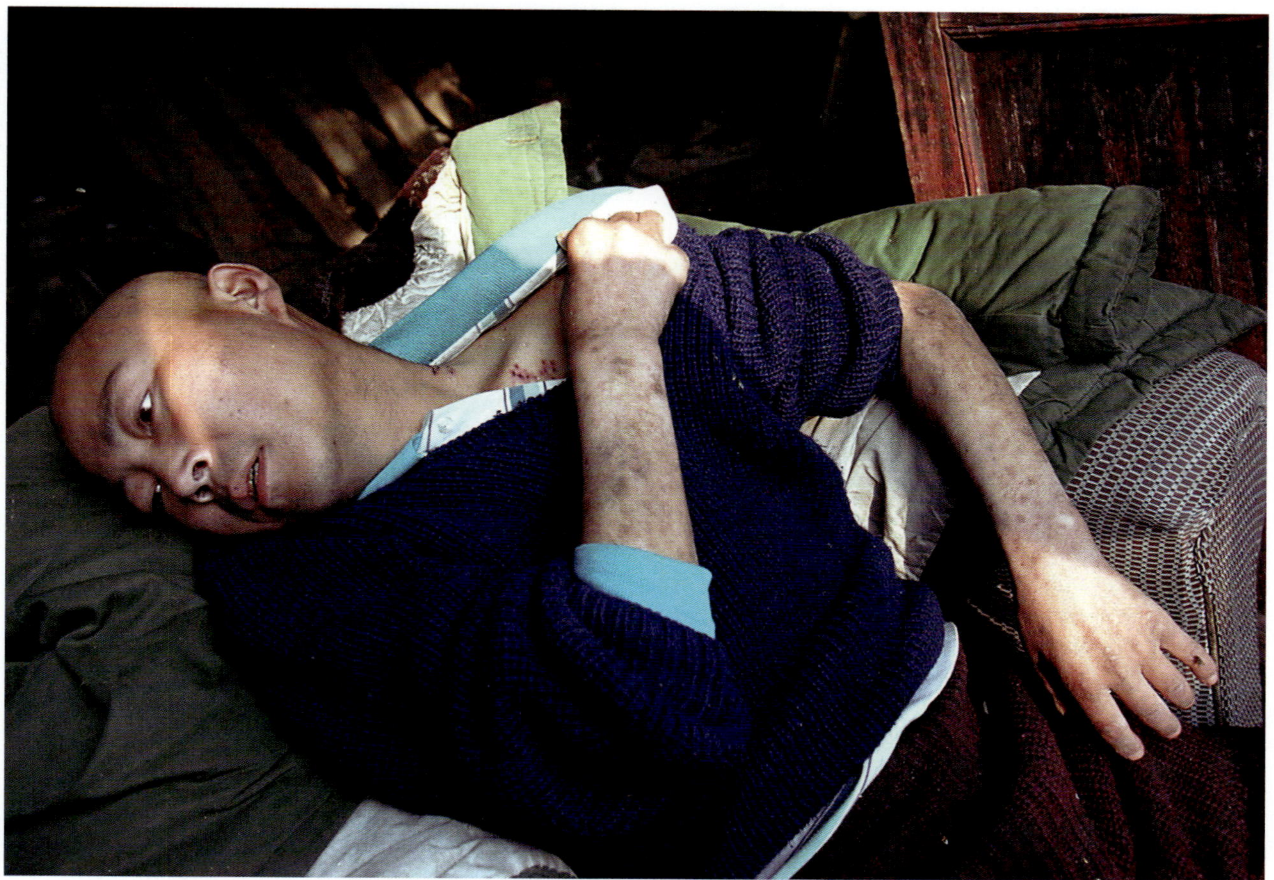

AIDS patient at home in Henan province, January 28, 2002. *While the majority of China's AIDS patients are thought to be intravenous drug users, some sufferers have contracted the disease in other ways. In both the provinces of Henan and Anhui, many poor residents, such as the man pictured above, became infected after selling blood to institutions practicing improper blood-collecting techniques.* AFP/GETTY IMAGES

AIDS ACTIVISTS

A number of nongovernmental organizations in China do AIDS-related work. In some cases, the state treats them as partners, but in many cases, nongovernmental organizations and activists doing AIDS-related work have faced harassment and repression. A noted example is the case of Gao Yaojie, a gynecologist who received national and international awards for her AIDS prevention and treatment work in Henan. When she exposed the connection between HIV infection and blood collection in 1996, she was harassed by local officials. She was briefly put under house arrest in February 2007 to prevent her from traveling to the United States to receive an award. The ban was subsequently lifted.

In another case, a former public-health official, Wan Yanhai, was fired when he set up an HIV/AIDS information hotline in 1994. As director of the Beijing-based AIDS Institute of Health Education, Wan has been detained for his activism on several occasions. In some cases, local officials, angry or frightened at the exposure of corruption, neglect, or inefficiency in their areas, were responsible for the repression. However, the detention of some prominent AIDS activists has clearly received high-level approval. These are activists who have criticized government policy or linked their AIDS work to human or gay rights. There remains an enduring government determination that individuals should not reveal China's problems to the outside world, and an inability to appreciate the considerable contribution that nongovernmental organizations can make to HIV/AIDS education and prevention.

POLICY AND PROGRAMS SINCE THE LATE 1990s

From the late 1990s, the central government has become markedly more proactive in its response to HIV/AIDS. China's HIV/AIDS action plans have been praised by international bodies, including UNAIDS and WHO. Campaigns have been developed to educate the general public about

AIDS and to reduce stigma. President Hu Jintao and Premier Wen Jiabao have been shown on television shaking hands with AIDS patients. Programs have also targeted high-risk groups. It became legal to advertise condoms in 2002. Now free-condom programs focus on sex workers, young people, migrants, and men who have sex with men. Formerly called pregnancy-prevention sheaths, they have been renamed safety sheaths to emphasize their role in safe sex. Blood-collection and transfusion practices have also been brought under tighter control. In addition, hundreds of methadone clinics and needle-exchange centers have been established.

From 2004, China CARES (Comprehensive AIDS Response), a Chinese government program with UN funding began work in specified provinces. Under this program, antiretroviral treatment is to be free to rural people and poor urban residents. Testing and counseling is also free. Care and economic assistance is to be offered to people with HIV/AIDS, while children orphaned by AIDS receive free schooling.

There are still many problems. Much ignorance remains to be overcome. It will take resources, effort, and conviction to translate the rhetoric of China's excellent programs into action at the regional and local level. International nongovernmental organizations have expressed concern over certain coercive tendencies—for example, the compulsory testing of sex workers in some provinces. But progress has been considerable. Official unwillingness to discuss even the existence in China of drug users, sex workers, and men who have sex with men has been replaced by a recognition that these are key groups to work with if the epidemic is to be brought under control.

SEE ALSO *Drugs and Narcotics; Epidemics; Prostitution.*

BIBLIOGRAPHY

Hyde, Sandra Teresa. *Eating Spring Rice: The Cultural Politics of AIDS in Southwest China.* Berkeley: University of California Press, 2007.

State Council AIDS Working Committee Office and UN Theme Group on AIDS in China. *A Joint Assessment of HIV/AIDS Prevention, Treatment, and Care in China (2007).* Beijing: United Nations Development Program, 2007. http://www.undp.org.cn/downloads/otherlocal/HIV/20080104.pdf

Xia Goumei. *HIV/AIDS in China.* Beijing: Foreign Languages Press, 2004.

Zaccagnini, Marta. *HIV and AIDS in China.* AVERT (an international AIDS charity). 2008. http://www.avert.org/aidschina.htm

Delia Davin

HOKKIEN (MIN)

The Min dialects of China are located in the southeastern coastal province of Fujian with incursions into Guangdong. They represent a diverse group of languages that tend not to be mutually comprehensible among their major subdivisions, with Min speakers comprising about 4 percent to 5 percent of China's population. Outside of China, the languages belonging in particular to the subgroup of Southern Min are better known as Hokkien.

SOCIOCULTURAL ORIGINS

Min is one of the most conservative branches of the Sinitic or Chinese languages. Its ancestor probably split off from Archaic Chinese early in the first millennium CE, that is, during the Han dynasty (206 BCE–220 CE). This would account for many of the archaic words preserved in Min dialects that are no longer used in standard Mandarin with the same sense—including lexical items such as *tia*^{n3} 鼎 originally pertaining to a "three-legged cooking vessel," but now the common name for any cooking pot, *bak*^{8}*-chiu*^{1} 目珠 "eye" (with respect to just the first character in this instance), and *bin*^{7} 面 "face"—whereas Mandarin has replaced these terms respectively by *guo*^{1} 鍋 "wok," *yan*^{3}*jing*^{1} 眼睛 "eye," and *lian*^{3} 臉 "face." A striking contrast between literary and colloquial pronunciations is an equally well-known phenomenon for Min, known as *wen bai yi du* in standard Chinese. For example, the character 共 has *kā* as its colloquial pronunciation but *kiōng* as its literary or reading pronunciation in Taiwanese Hokkien (Lian Jinfa 2001).

Regarding the history of the Min dialects, Fujian Province appears to have been settled, and sinicized, at a much later period than other parts of southern China due to its remoteness and inaccessibility. The first major migration occurred during the third century CE, from (modern-day) Jiangxi in the west and Zhejiang in the north, while the second major migration occurred during the seventh century, moving down the coast from the same starting points (Bielenstein 1959). The main formation period for Min thus took place during the Tang dynasty (618–907), with it emerging as an identifiable dialect group by the time of the Northern Song dynasty (960–1127).

During the Song dynasty, the Min continued to spread southward along the coast to Chaozhou (Teochiu) and Shantou (Swatow) areas in northeastern Guangdong, even settling as far south as the Leizhou Peninsula in this province. Beginning in the early Qing dynasty (1644–1912), Min speakers began to migrate to Hainan Island and to Taiwan from southern Fujian, in other words, from the seventeenth century onward. More specifically, the variety of Southern Min, or Hokkien, spoken in Taiwan evolved from a fusion and neutralization of the Zhangzhou and Quanzhou dialects of Fujian Province.

The basic division for Min languages is between Inland (or Western) Min and Coastal (or Eastern) Min (see Norman 1988, 1991). This classification supersedes an earlier one with a simpler division into Northern and Southern Min.

Inland Min

- Northwestern: Jian dialects
- Far Western: Shaowu, Jingle
- Central: Yong'an

Coastal Min

- Northeastern: Fuzhou, Fu'an
- Puxian: Putian
- Southern: Xiamen (Amoy), Zhangzhou, Quanzhou, Taiwanese, Chaozhou (Teochiu), Shantou, Hainanese

Examples of Hokkien use Taiwanese Southern Min as the representative variety, with examples transcribed using the revised Church romanization system.

TERRITORIAL EXTENSION TO TAIWAN AND SOUTHEAST ASIA

Apart from the use of Hokkien as a major language in Taiwan, it is spoken in many overseas Chinese communities in Southeast Asia. For example, Thailand, Burma (Myanmar), Laos, Malaysia, Singapore, Indonesia, and the Philippines all have sizeable communities of Southern Min speakers, including principally the dialect of Chaozhou (Teochiu). The Hokkien dialects are far less common, however, in the Americas, Europe, Australia, and New Zealand, where the Cantonese dialects predominate among the established Chinese communities (Wurm and Li Rong 1988, maps B16a and 16b).

While the Min dialect group is one of the smallest for continental China, comprising only 4 to 5 percent of speakers of Sinitic languages, it is the mother tongue for 72 percent of the population in Taiwan (approximately sixteen million out of twenty-two million people). In total, there are claimed to be 52.5 million speakers for all the Min dialects in China and Taiwan (Wurm and Li Rong 1988, map B-12), and over sixty-two million if we include speakers in Southeast Asia. With respect to just the Southern Min dialects, Benjamin T'sou (1988) estimates there are twenty million speakers in Fujian and Guangdong provinces, compared with an estimated sixteen million in Taiwan and another nine million in the Indo-Pacific Basin, including second-language speakers in the latter case.

CHARACTERISTICS WITH REFERENCE TO OTHER MAJOR CHINESE LANGUAGES

Southern Min shows the basic word order of subject–verb–(object), as do most Chinese languages. Several markers for aspect (perfective and imperfective types) precede, rather than follow, the verb in Hokkien, the latter being generally the case for most other Chinese languages that use suffixes. Passive, causative, and dative functions are typically coded by either the marker *khit*^{4} 乞 or the marker *hō*^{7} 與, depending on the dialect area, and thus not by either *bèi* 被 or *gĕi* 給, as in Mandarin. Gender is distinguished for a subset of animate nouns (in particular, domestic animals, including poultry) by means of the suffix *–kang*^{1} 公 for the male of the species and the suffix *–bu*^{2} 母 for a reproductive female of the species—for example, *ti*^{1}*–kang*^{1} 猪公 "boar" and *ti*^{1}*–bu*^{2} 猪母 "a sow that has produced a litter." Note that this feature is shared with Hakka and Cantonese, while Mandarin makes use of prefixes in this function.

Number can be explicitly coded by means of plural classifiers (CLF), such as *kua*^{2} in *chit*^{8} *kua*^{2} *lang*^{5}一寡 儂 (one-CLF-people) "some people" or by plural adverbs such as *long*^{2} 攏 "all." The plural pronouns all end in the suffix *–n*, which may represent a trace of *lang*^{5} 儂"person, people." Note, however, that this does not occur elsewhere in the lexicon as a plural marker, unlike Mandarin *–men* 們, which is used for certain animate nouns. There is also an inclusive-exclusive distinction for first-person plural. Compare the singular and plural forms of the Southern Min pronominal paradigm:

> *gua*^{2} 我 '1SG', *li*^{2} 你 '2SG', and *yi*^{1} 伊 '3SG'
>
> *guan*^{2} 阮 '$1PL_{exc}$', *lan*^{2}咱 '$1PL_{inc}$', *lin*^{2} 恁 '2PL' and, *yin*^{1} 亻因 '3PL'

MANIFESTATION IN LITERARY, MUSICAL, AND CULTURAL FORMS

Southern Min is more fortunate than other nonstandard Chinese languages, such as Cantonese and Hakka, in having preserved a much longer history of written works. Documents written in Min go back to the sixteenth century and include plays, *nanyin* (opera), and liturgical material. Most of these reflect Southern Min dialects, and include versions of the popular Ming dynasty (1368–1644) play, *Li jing ji* (Romance of the litchi mirror, 1566), written in a mixture of the Quanzhou and Chaozhou dialects of Southern Min. Other pedagogical and religious materials from the same period have been traced to the Philippines. These include a translation into Southern Min of the *Doctrina Christiana* (Christian Doctrine, 1597–1605), two Southern Min–Spanish dictionaries, *Dictionarium Sino-Hispanicum* (Chinese-Spanish Dictionary, c. 1604) and *Bocabulario de lengua sangleya* (Lexicon of the Sangley Language, c. 1617), and an early grammar of a Southern Min dialect, *Arte de la lengua chiō-chiu* (Grammar of the Chiō Chiu Language, 1620), written by Spanish missionaries in collaboration with native speakers in Manila and Cebu. Chinese communities in these locations were set up in the wake of established trade routes between southern Fujian and the Philippines.

The writing system used for Southern Min is based on the same set of characters used for Mandarin, the language of education and most official domains. However, typical of this genre is the use of homophonous characters from the standard written language to represent native colloquial words that are unique to Southern Min and for which no ready-made forms are available. For example, 卜 *beh*^{4} "want" is represented by a character that means "to practice divination" in standard forms of Chinese. Southern Min was not committed to alphabetic writing until the introduction in the nineteenth century of the church romanization system, mainly used in Christian religious circles.

HOKKIEN AS A SOLIDARITY MARKER IN TAIWAN

The demotic characters mentioned above were not widely used, except among the semiliterate authors of folk ballads, before an upsurge of interest in Hokkien arose following the change of the political situation in Taiwan in the late 1980s (Huang Shuanfan 1993). Prior to the lifting of martial law in July 1987, Hokkien had in fact been heavily restricted in official domains such as those of education and the media from the mid-1950s onward.

Hence, a movement to standardize the writing system in Taiwan is underway, given that Southern Min has been revived as an officially sanctioned medium of communication in certain areas, including parliament, health care, and some sectors of the education system. Since 2001, for example, it has become possible in certain regions of Taiwan to take a local language as an elective subject, particularly at the primary school level (Klöter 2005). For many Taiwanese for whom it is their mother tongue, the use of Hokkien increasingly serves as a marker of solidarity, tantamount to a badge of identity as a Taiwanese. In addition to the graphic representation in Chinese characters, there are two major competing romanization systems: (1) *peh*^{8}*-oe*^{7}*-ji*^{7} "vernacular writing," based on the church romanization system; and (2) *Taiwan minnanyu yinbiao xitong* (Taiwanese Southern Min Spelling System). No consensus has been reached yet as to which system is to be adopted for the education system and in official domains. In mainland China, dialect writing has no status, given that *putonghua*, or standard Mandarin, is being promoted as the common form of both spoken and written communication.

SEE ALSO *Fujian; Taiwan, Republic of China.*

BIBLIOGRAPHY

Bielenstein, Hans. The Chinese Colonization of Fukien until the End of the T'ang. In *Studia Serica Bernhard Karlgren Dedicata: Sinological Studies Dedicated to Bernhard Karlgren on his Seventieth Birthday*, ed. Søren Egerod and Else Glahn, 98–122. Copenhagen: Ejnar Munksgaard, 1959.

Chappell, Hilary. Synchrony and Diachrony of Sinitic Languages: A Brief History of Chinese Dialects. In *Sinitic Grammar: Synchronic and Diachronic Perspectives*, ed. Hilary Chappell, 3–28. Oxford: Oxford University Press, 2001.

Huang Shuanfan. *Yuyan, Shehui, yu Zuquan Yishi* (Language, society, and ethnic identity). Taibei: Crane, 1993.

Klöter, Henning. *Written Taiwanese.* Studia Formosiana 2. Wiesbaden: Harrassowitz, 2001.

Lian Jinfa (Lien Chinfa). Competing Morphological Changes in Taiwanese Southern Min. In *Sinitic Grammar: Synchronic and Diachronic Perspectives*, ed. Hilary Chappell, 309–339. Oxford: Oxford University Press, 2001.

Norman, Jerry. *Chinese.* Cambridge, U.K.: Cambridge University Press, 1988.

Norman, Jerry. The Min Dialects in Historical Perspective. In *Languages and Dialects of China*, ed. Wang Shiyuan (William S.-Y. Wang), 325–360. Berkeley: Project on Linguistic Analysis, University of California, 1991.

Wurm, Stephen, and Li Rong, eds. *Language Atlas of China.* Hong Kong: Longman, 1988.

Zou Jiayan (Benjamin K. T'sou). Chinese Dialects Overseas: Indo-Pacific and Other Parts of the World. In *Language Atlas of China*, ed. Stephen Wurm and Li Rong, text for maps B16a and B16b. Hong Kong: Longman, 1988.

Hilary Chappell

HOMOSEXUALITY

Homosexuality has always been a permissible and open practice in traditional Chinese culture. Although homosexual interests are seen by many Chinese to be peculiar or unnatural, China has never had laws to specify that homosexuality is a crime, and traditional Chinese medicine has never considered homosexuality to be a disease. A number of factual and fictional accounts of male homosexual love affairs were published in the late Qing dynasty (1644–1912), and it is known that there were "beauty contests" for male homosexual prostitutes. Well-known lesbian groups included the Mojing Dang (Rubbing-Mirrors Party) of Shanghai and the Jinlanhui (Golden Orchid Association) and the Zi-shu (Self-combed) women's groups in southern China. These women vowed to remain unmarried and to live an independent life together under one roof. They were well respected by their kin (Lau and Ng 1989).

With the influence of Christian puritanism, homosexuality in China came under stronger social sanctions, and in the early decades of the twentieth century progressively became a secretive and unmentionable practice, although occasional scholarly reports confirmed its continued existence (Zhang Jingsheng [1926] 1967; Pan 1947). This secretiveness extended into the early period of Communist China, and homosexuality came to be viewed with puzzlement and apprehension. The official stance was to deny its existence and downplay its prevalence or significance. This negative attitude reached its peak during the decade of the Cultural Revolution (1966–1976), when authorities suggested that homosexuality was a danger to social morality and physical and mental health, damaging to the development of youth, and a form of "spiritual pollution" from the West that should be declared a crime. Since there were no ready-made laws to criminalize homosexuality specifically, it was incorporated into the ill-defined crime of "hooliganism" (rude misbehavior), and some homosexuals were reportedly jailed for up to five years for this "crime"

The first version of the *Chinese Classification of Mental Disorders*, published after the Cultural Revolution in 1981, included homosexuality as a mental disorder. However, with better sex education and more open discussion about sex under the open-door policy of the reform era, mainland Chinese gradually returned to their previous accommodating and pragmatic attitudes toward sex (Ng 2006). The onset of AIDS in this period had the positive effect of stimulating more understanding and rational attitudes toward and treatment of homosexuals, to the extent that in 1993 many of the staff running the AIDS hotline of the China Health Education Research Institute and broadcast in CCTV were homosexuals (Fang 1995).

Hence, homosexuality came to be better tolerated by the public as well as the government. It ceased to be considered a disease or a crime in itself and was removed from the third version of the *Chinese Classification of Mental Disorders* (Chen Yanfang 2003). In a survey of college students in ten major cities in China in 1989, 7.5 percent of respondents reported experiences of erotic hugging with the same sex, and only 6 percent of the male students and 9 percent of the female students considered homosexuality to be criminal or unethical (Ng and Haeberle 1997).

The situation has been different in Taiwan and Hong Kong. Hong Kong, for most of its years under British rule, had to follow Victorian British law, which treated male homosexuality as a crime. But while the British were able to decriminalize homosexuality in 1967, conservatives in Hong Kong succeeded in delaying a similar decriminalization until 1991. A series of sexuality surveys in Hong Kong since the late 1980s have shown that Hong Kong's youth have been progressively more accepting of homosexuality (Family Planning Association of Hong Kong 1989, 2001, 2006). However, due to strong antihomosexual voices, mainly from a minority of influential Christians, there have been no other significant changes in the law to make the rights of homosexuals more equal to those of heterosexuals.

In Taiwan, negative attitudes toward homosexuality never reached the extremes evident in mainland China during the Cultural Revolution. The practice remained tolerated, although not discussed openly, until the mid-1980s when, stimulated by Western ideas and the impact of AIDS, gay movements arose. These led to extensive discussions on homosexual rights, resulting in better understanding and social acceptance of homosexuality. Homosexual couples have repeatedly challenged discriminatory laws by publicly holding marriage ceremonies and adopting children, though legislation to recognize such family formations was still pending as of 2008.

In general, Chinese governments have never been keen to make laws specifically addressing homosexuality, either to prosecute it or to protect homosexuals' rights. Hence, social discrimination has been left unchecked, allowed to wax and wane, occasionally to extreme degrees, depending on the ethos of the time. Nowadays, in many major Chinese cities, such as Beijing, Shenzhen, Taibei (Taipei), and Hong Kong, there are public places that are known to be or tolerated as gathering spots for homosexuals. These range from public parks, bars, and nightclubs to street corners and public baths and toilets (Fang 1995). There are also about a dozen active gay/lesbian groups in Taiwan (e.g., the Tong-Kwang Light House Presbyterian Church) and Hong Kong (e.g., the Ten Percent Club and the Women's Coalition of Hong Kong), as well as a few less bold groups in mainland China (such as the Rainbow Club in Sun Yat-Sen University and Midnight Blue in Shenzhen), all of which voice and work for the rights and welfare of homosexuals. These organizations are allowed to operate within the limits of the law. Public displays of affection between homosexual couples are tolerated to the same degree that they are for heterosexual couples.

Antihomosexual violence or homicides rarely occur in Chinese communities. However, opinion surveys and interviews with homosexuals at different times in China show that many feel they have consistently lived in circumstances of oppression, discrimination, fear, and mistreatment of varying degrees of severity. They also do not feel hopeful of achieving full equality with heterosexuals at any time in the near future.

SEE ALSO *Gender Relations; Human Rights since 1949; Sexuality.*

BIBLIOGRAPHY

Chen Yanfang, ed. *Chinese Classification of Mental Disorders* (CCMD3). 3rd ed. Beijing: Chinese Society of Psychiatry, 2003.

Family Planning Association of Hong Kong. *Adolescent Sexuality Study 1986*. Hong Kong: Author, 1989.

Family Planning Association of Hong Kong. *Youth Sexuality Study*. Hong Kong: Author, 2001, 2006.

Fang G. [Homosexuality in China]. Hong Kong: Cosmos, 1995.

Lau M. P. and Ng M. L. Homosexuality in Chinese Culture. *Culture, Medicine, and Psychiatry* 13, 4 (1989): 465–488.

Ng M. L. The Transformation of a Sexual Culture: The Chinese Paradigm. *Sexual and Relationship Therapy* 21, 2 (2006): 137–141.

Ng M. L. and Erwin J. Haeberle. *Sexual Behavior in Modern China: A Report of the Nationwide Sex-Civilization Survey on 20,000 Subjects in China*. New York: Continuum, 1997.

Pan K. T. Cases of Homosexuality in Chinese Documents and Literature. 1947. In *Psychology of Sex*, ed. Havelock Ellis, trans. and adapted by Pan K. T. Taibei: Cactus Publishing, 1970.

Zhang Jingsheng (Chang Ching-Sheng). *Sex Histories: China's First Modern Treatise on Sex Education*. 1926. Trans. Howard S. Levy. Yokohama, Japan: Bai Yuan, 1967.

Ng M. L.

HONG KONG

This entry contains the following:

HONG KONG

Area: 1,104 sq. km. (426 sq. mi.)
Population: 6,963,100 (2007)
Demographics: Chinese, 95%; Filipino, 1.96%; Indonesian, 1.89%; other, 3.83%
GDP: US$292.2 billion (2007); per capita, US$42,000 (2007)
Famous sites: Hong Kong Island: Victoria Peak, Repulse Bay, Victoria Harbour, Aberdeen Harbour, Lan Kwai Fong, Soho; Kowloon: Hong Kong Art Museum, Avenue of Stars, Chungking Mansions, Nathan Road, Ocean Terminal, Star Ferry, Wong Tai Sin Temple; New Territories: Che Kung Temple, Cheung Chau Island, Ping Shan, Tai O Village, Tian Tan Buddha, Ting Kau Bridge, Tsing Ma Bridge, Tung Chung Fort

OVERVIEW

Hong Kong's role in modern China is unique and paradoxical. For most of the last two centuries, the development of this territory in Southern China stood at odds with the politicoeconomic circumstances in mainland China. Hong Kong was once a British colony, a center for political dissidents, the only gateway of China to the West, a capitalist economy untouched by the communist revolution, and subsequently a model for economic growth and experimental ground for self-government. Even after China resumed sovereign rule over Hong Kong in 1997, the territory's social and political systems stand in sharp contrast with those of mainland China in many ways. Yet it is precisely such incongruities that have allowed Hong Kong to play a vital role in modern Chinese history.

Hong Kong's unique position owes much to its strategic location. It possesses a natural deep-water harbor and enjoys easy access from both inland China and the open sea. Hong Kong Island and its adjacent peninsula formed part of the larger Canton delta region in southern China. This region had been a center of transnational trade between China, Southeast Asia, and the West in the eighteenth century.

BRITISH CONTROL

The strategically located territory soon became the focus of Sino-British contention when European trade with China expanded in the nineteenth century. Britain suffered an increasing trade deficit as Chinese tea and silk were exported to Britain in exchange for silver. To balance the trade, the British exported to China opium produced in India. Alarmed by the increasing number of addicts in China, the Qing authorities banned the drug trade and in 1839 confiscated and destroyed the opium stocks of British traders. This led to a series of armed conflicts between Britain and China in the First Opium War (1840–1842). During the war, British forces took control of Hong Kong Island in 1841 and threatened to attack other Chinese cities. The Qing government yielded and in 1842 signed the Treaty of Nanjing, which ceded Hong Kong Island permanently to Britain. Before long, Britain and France attacked a number of ports and cities, including Beijing, during the Second Opium War (1856–1860), forcing the Qing court to sign the 1860 Convention of Peking (Beijing), which ceded the Kowloon Peninsula and nearby Stonecutters Island to Britain. In 1898 Britain gained possession of the area north of the Kowloon Peninsula on a ninety-nine-year lease from the Qing authorities, which expired on June 30, 1997. The area was renamed the New Territories. Together with Hong Kong Island and the Kowloon Peninsula, these areas became the British colony of Hong Kong.

From the outset, Britain took control of Hong Kong not for settlement, acquisition of natural resources, or religious missions, but for trade in the Far East. The first hundred years of colonial rule in Hong Kong was

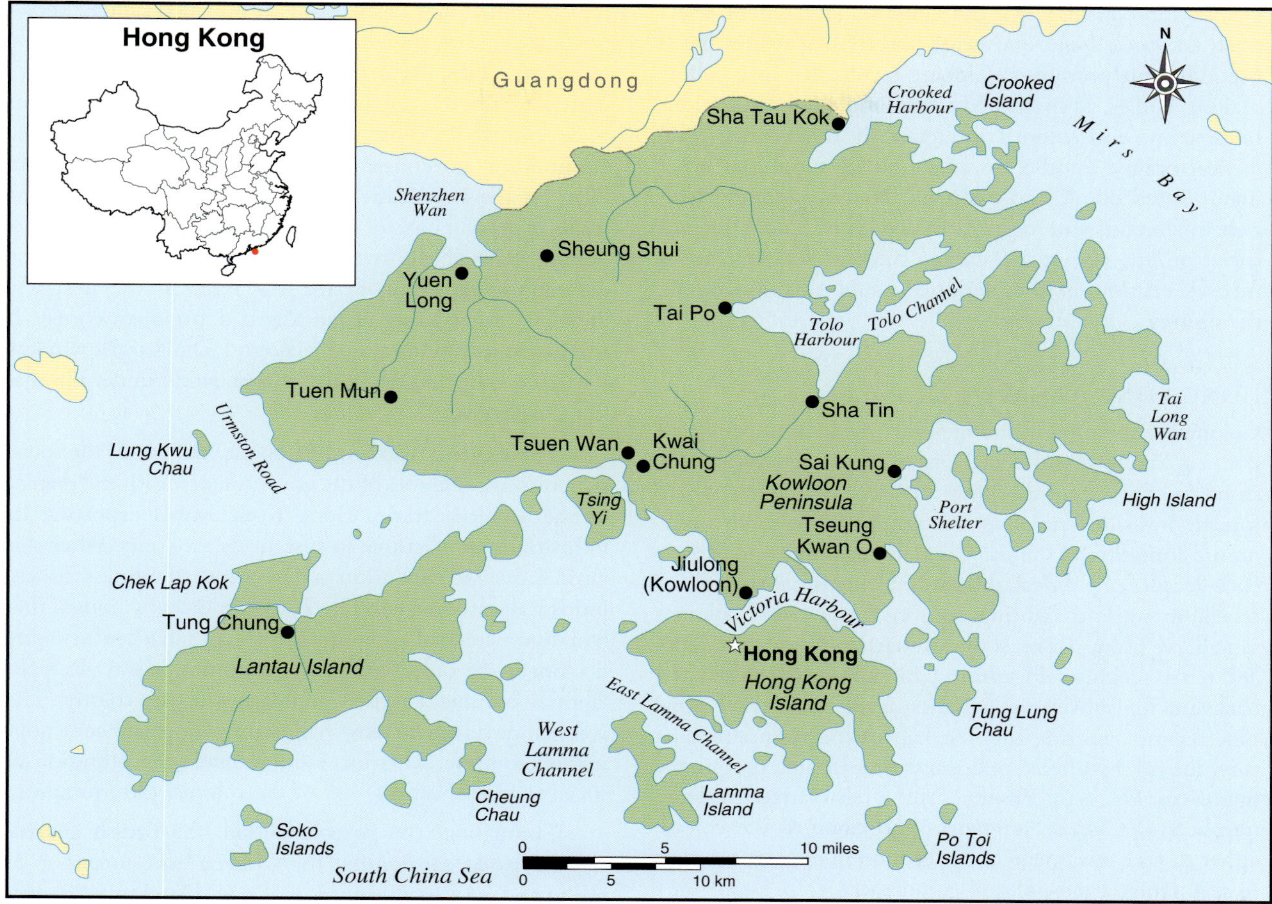

essentially shaped by such trade imperatives. Britain declared Hong Kong a free port, with the intention of turning the place into a Far Eastern trading post. The entire colonial administration was designed and set up to facilitate trade. Taking advantage of its strategic position and the extensive Chinese trading networks in East and Southeast Asia, Hong Kong became the regional trade center for British manufactures and Chinese traditional products such as silk, tea, and porcelain. In the early years, the colony also played a key role in the opium and coolie trade. Some Chinese merchants in the colony obtained their first ingot of gold from their involvement in the highly exploitative coolie trade, under which tens of thousands of poor peasants were shipped to Southeast Asia and North America as contracted labor.

In due course, the Chinese population developed intricate relations both with its colonial ruler and the Chinese government. From the outset, the founding of the colony faced both cooperation and resistance from its Chinese inhabitants. On the one hand, Britain's acquisition of Hong Kong depended not only on military strength but also on the indispensable help of Chinese contractors, compradors, and other merchants in providing essential supplies during the Opium War. After the occupation, British businesses relied on preexisting Chinese trading networks to penetrate other Asian markets. In exchange for their collaboration, British authorities rewarded some native Chinese in Hong Kong with social and economic privileges, with the result that these collaborators became the first generation of the Chinese bourgeoisie in the colony.

On the other hand, colonial rule also met with resistance from Hong Kong's indigenous inhabitants, especially those from the New Territories. Such resistance resulted in harsh military suppression from the colonial authorities. As soon as order was secured, the colonial government implemented measures to pacify potential anticolonial hostilities. The landownership system in rural areas was reformed to limit the power of the pro-China landholding elite. A criminal-justice system was established not only to secure law and order, but also to police Chinese inhabitants and secure easy convictions of potential troublemakers among the populace.

In subsequent years, the colonial government selectively co-opted the business elite (mostly British merchants but also some prominent Chinese merchants) into policymaking bodies. It sponsored urban and rural associations to preempt anti-colonial influence. It backed one local faction against another to create social support. And it manipulated ethnic and dialectal differences among Chinese inhabitants and migrants to divide and rule. Different social groups also made use of colonial state power to mediate relations of domination and subordination among themselves.

HONG KONG AS HAVEN

Colonial occupation in Hong Kong provided unparalleled political stability and social order to the territory. This stood in stark contrast with the rest of China, where foreign invasions seriously undermined the politicoeconomic condition of China. China then went on to experience decades of political upheavals during the anti-imperial rebellion, warlord fighting, and civil war. As a colonial sanctuary, Hong Kong soon attracted political dissidents and rebels seeking refuge from China. It was also used as a backyard for subversive activities against successive Chinese regimes. During the first half of the twentieth century, the colony offered political shelter to such prominent figures as Dr. Sun Yat-sen. Yet it also attracted large numbers of Chinese migrants, who came to the colony either to take advantage of the economic opportunities or to seek refuge from political turbulence.

Such political instability in China led the colonial authorities to take a pessimistic view of the long-term prospects of the colony. During the first hundred years of British rule, there was little attempt to invest in the colony, because of this lack of confidence over Hong Kong's future. Economic planning and industrial investment in a borrowed place living on borrowed time were considered politically undesirable. When local industries sprouted in the 1930s, the colonial government looked upon these industries with great skepticism and refused to offer any protection or commitment to promote industrialization. The Communist takeover of China in 1949 and the Communist government's refusal to recognize the three unequal treaties reinforced Britain's belief that minimal investment in the colony was the right policy.

AFTER LIBERATION

The rapid economic development of Hong Kong after World War II was an unintended consequence of a confluence of circumstances. The most important events were the Communist takeover of mainland China in 1949 and the outbreak of the Korean War in 1950. These events sparked a chain reaction in Hong Kong. The civil war and Communist takeover led to a huge influx of refugees and refugee capital into Hong Kong. It provided capital, know-how, and cheap labor for the expansion of manufacturing industries. This occurred at a time when Hong Kong's entrepôt trade was brought to a halt by the United Nations trade embargo against China, instituted because of the Communist government's involvement in the Korean War. At the same time, the Korean War underlined the strategic importance of this British colony. Hong Kong became part of the overall U.S. project of constraining communist expansion in the Far East. In the next few decades, Hong Kong again played a paradoxical role. It was a base for Western intelligence on China and a window for China to get access to the outside world under international isolation.

These events also brought about changes in the social structure and the role of the government. With the demise of the entrepôt trade, Hong Kong began exporting its industrial manufactures to sustain its economy. After this rapid industrial expansion, a new group of ethnic Chinese industrialists emerged. The British merchant houses that had dominated the economy for more than a century were no longer the only significant economic players. Refugee laborers became a settled population in the colony. The colonial government now had a growing permanent population to serve. This increasingly made the provision of social services a central task of the colonial government.

Throughout the postwar period, the British government avoided confronting the Chinese government so as not to endanger its rule of Hong Kong. Decolonization was deemed inappropriate for Hong Kong for fear of arousing strong and immediate reaction from China. An authoritarian government structure was maintained because any attempt to introduce popular elections might raise suspicion in Beijing, not to mention the opposition of the British merchant houses. The delicate balance was successfully maintained, except during a short period in 1967. During the high tide of the Cultural Revolution in China, pro-Beijing labor unions and underground Communist Party agents staged anticolonial riots throughout the territory in an attempt to undermine the colonial authorities. The colonial authorities eventually suppressed the riots with an iron fist, with the support of the Hong Kong public at large. For its part, the Beijing government instructed its agents in Hong Kong not to ruin the strategic value of the territory as China's only window to the West and as the main source of foreign exchange flowing into China.

In the aftermath of the riots, the colonial government expanded its social-service provisions in an attempt to enhance social support. High-rise housing was built to provide cheap accommodation for the working class. Nine-year compulsory education, free medical service, and a social-security system were implemented in the 1970s. These measures not only raised the quality of the labor force, but also

Celebration of Queen Victoria's Jubilee, Hong Kong, January 1888. *Taking over Hong Kong Island during the First Opium War, Britain retained control of the colony until 1997. An important center of trade in the region, Hong Kong became a unique territory as British nationals blended Western culture with the traditions of the Chinese natives.* HULTON ARCHIVE/GETTY IMAGES

nurtured the rise of a middle class and subsequently a new generation of locally born Hong Kongers who saw the territory as their home rather than as a transient refugee center.

THE HANDOVER

The status quo was called into question in the early 1980s when the British government was obliged to negotiate with the Chinese government over the future of Hong Kong because the lease of the New Territories would expire on June 30, 1997. China, which had consistently rejected the unequal treaties, refused any extension of what it considered an invalid lease and insisted that it should again exercise de facto sovereignty over the whole territory. After a few years of painful negotiations, a pragmatic compromise was reached and the Sino-British

Soldiers from the People's Liberation Army entering Hong Kong, July 1, 1997. *On June 30, 1997, the ninety-year-old treaty leasing the colony of Hong Kong to the British expired, returning the outpost to mainland China. Though now under Chinese control, Hong Kong retained a large degree of autonomy under an agreement which preserves the territory's existing political and economic systems for a fifty-year period.* PAUL LAKATOS/AFP/GETTY IMAGES

Joint Declaration was signed in 1985. Under the Joint Declaration, Hong Kong would become a Special Administrative Region under Chinese sovereignty on July 1, 1997. Hong Kong was allowed to keep in place its existing capitalist economy and social lifestyle for fifty years under the "one country, two systems" policy. Hong Kong would exercise self-government by "Hong Kong people ruling Hong Kong" under a "high degree of autonomy."

The Joint Declaration only set down gross principles for the post–1997 government. Details about precise governmental, legal, and social structures were to be filled in by a Basic Law, a miniconstitution for the Hong Kong Special Administrative Region. The drafting of this blueprint unleashed unprecedented political contention in the territory. Different social groups strove to ensure that their interests were registered in the future government. The political system became the main focus of contention. Disagreements over the speed of political reform and the implementation of universal suffrage dominated the public debate in the countdown to 1997.

Amid the debate, the Hong Kong populace was shocked by the crackdown of the Tiananmen student movement in 1989. Over a million marched the streets of Hong Kong to demonstrate against the June 4 suppression. The fragile confidence of the Hong Kong people over its future after 1997 was completely shaken by the crackdown. The event also led to an irreconcilable rift in relations between Hong Kong and Beijing. Many Hong Kong people lost faith in the Communist regime because of its brutality. Yet Beijing was anxious that Hong Kong could be turned into a subversive base against China's existing regime, a role that Hong Kong played in the past. Despite such tensions, Hong Kong played an indispensable role in securing foreign investments, management know-how, and global information for China's market reforms. It assumed the role of a strategic middleman between the domestic Chinese market and the global economy.

Such intricate relations continued after the handover. Beijing has repeatedly refused to speed up political reform in Hong Kong for fear that it would return an anti-Beijing administration if popular elections were introduced. This has led to more political discontent and frustration in Hong Kong and perpetuates the mutual distrust between Hong Kong and Beijing.

BIBLIOGRAPHY

Ngo, Tak-Wing, ed. *Hong Kong's History: State and Society under Colonial Rule*. London: Routledge, 1999.

Pepper, Suzanne. *Keeping Democracy at Bay: Hong Kong and the Challenge of Chinese Political Reform*. Lanham, MD: Rowman and Littlefield, 2008.

Tsai, Jung-fang. *Hong Kong in Chinese History: Community and Social Unrest in the British Colony, 1842–1913*. New York: Columbia University Press, 1993.

Tak-Wing Ngo

EDUCATION IN HONG KONG SINCE 1842

Hong Kong was a British colony until July 1, 1997. It therefore has an education system similar to that of Britain. A new academic structure, known as "3+3+4," for senior secondary and higher education was to be fully adopted by 2012. Thereafter, undergraduate programs at Hong Kong's universities were to be four-year programs, preceded by six years of secondary education.

THE EARLY COLONIAL PERIOD

Modern Hong Kong's education system was developed by Protestant and Catholic missionaries. Prior to British colonization, there were a few traditional Chinese schools on the island serving local Chinese children. In 1842 the trustees of the Morrison Education society received a grant of land from Hong Kong's British governor, Henry Pottinger (1789–1856), for the purpose of establishing a school. After being transferred from Macau, the first Western-style school in Hong Kong opened in temporary premises in November 1842 (Sweeting 1990, p. 143). Thereafter, more religious organizations, including the London Missionary Society and various Roman Catholic groups, also built schools to promote evangelization in Hong Kong (Endacott 1973, pp. 133–135). Mission schools were the primary form of educational institution in Hong Kong until the establishment of the first government school, the Central School, in 1862 (Endacott 1973, p. 140). Despite the emergence of government schools, aided schools, which are government-funded but are managed by non-government organizations, remained an essential part of Hong Kong's education system in the following decades.

In 1873 the government introduced the Grant-in-Aid scheme to provide financial assistance to mission schools (Sweeting 1990, p. 140). The scheme had a significant impact on the long-term development of the education system in Hong Kong. More aided schools were established, especially by Roman Catholics. By 1881 the number of students enrolled in aided schools exceeded the number of students in government schools (Sweeting 1990, p. 293).

The post–World War II period witnessed the reconstruction and expansion of education in Hong Kong. Extreme population pressure caused by the influx of refugees led to a rapid expansion, mainly at the primary-school level, in the 1950s. The Seven Year Plan of 1954 (effective from 1955 to 1961) emerged from this background. Its goal was to create 26,000 to 33,000 additional school places each year (Sweeting 2004, pp. 211–221). The plan was seen as a milestone in the territory's educational development because it marked the beginning of a new policy, with planning based on demographic estimates and rational predictions of the demand for schooling, although there was a sacrifice in quality in terms of classroom space and class size (Sweeting 1993, pp. 108–116). As a consequence, the number of primary and secondary students increased from 16,041 and 80,998 in 1947 to 160,810 and 628,479 in 1964, respectively (Sweeting 2004, pp. 209).

Though the government was willing to increase its investment in education, non-profit-making bodies such as churches and welfare organizations still played an important role in establishing schools during the reconstruction period. This was due to the political consideration that Christian-subsidized schools would provide a bulwark against the encroachment of communism in education. Indeed, "the provision of schools in the new resettlement areas was almost entirely through subsidized schools sponsored by Maryknoll Fathers and Sisters, the Rotary Club, and various district welfare associations" (Sweeting 1993, pp. 163–164). However, there was growth in the educational bureaucracy, which was reflected by a conflict between the Anglican Grant Schools and Hong Kong's Education Department over the arrangements of the Grant Code and the use of *tong fai* (additional tuition charged by schools to build their contingency funds) during the period (Sweeting 2004, p. 144). Generally speaking, although government expenditures on education increased continuously after the mid-1950s, the religious and private sectors remained important providers and sponsors of education. Nevertheless, the government sought control over education through various forms of intervention, including fees, scholarships, assistance, and examinations (Sweeting 1993). Such bureaucratization planted the seeds of struggle between the sponsoring bodies of religious schools and the government.

REFORMS SINCE THE 1960s

By the mid-1960s, Hong Kong's education system had come a long way toward mass access, given the considerable economic growth during the time. Free and compulsory primary education was introduced in 1971 and was extended to the junior secondary level in 1978. These developments led to a tremendous growth in the numbers of schools, as well as an increase in the numbers and types of school-sponsoring bodies. A variety of nongovernmental organizations, including religious groups, volunteer agencies, welfare organizations, and trade associations, began to participate in Hong Kong's education-delivery system during this period. The pluralistic landscape of the aided-school sector drew government concerns about quality. The public-sector reform, begun in 1989, also raised the government's awareness of the need for autonomy, stakeholder participation, flexibility, and accountability in public-subsidized schools.

In 1991 the government of Hong Kong launched the School Management Initiative to induce a school-based management governance framework. The Education Commission Report No. 7 (1997) and the School-based Management Consultative Document (2000) indicated the government's intention to further develop school-based management in Hong Kong. The enactment of the Education (Amendment) Ordinance 2004 represents the full implementation of school-based management. The ordinance requires all aided schools to establish an incorporated management committee by 2009. Yet, some of the sponsoring bodies, especially the Christian groups, remain concerned about losing their autonomy in school governance and thus refused to form incorporated-management committees in their schools (Leung 2001). Negotiations between the government and Christian groups were underway in 2008.

The Direct Subsidy Scheme (DSS), introduced in 1988, was another important development in the governance of Hong Kong's schools. In its early stages, the scheme was offered as a means of survival for schools marginalized by the Secondary School Place Allocation Scheme. These included leftist schools and schools formerly operating under the Bought Place Scheme, an ad hoc and supplementary financial arrangement to guarantee sufficient school places for the implementation of compulsory universal education.

The DSS was reinvigorated in the 1990s to diversify Hong Kong's school sector. In 1999 the government launched a revised DSS, under which DSS schools are free to design their own curriculum, choose their language of instruction, and determine their own entrance requirements without being bound by the centralized Secondary School Place Allocation Scheme. DSS schools can also choose whether or not to establish an incorporated-management committee. In addition, DSS schools are allowed to impose tuition fees and accept social donations for their endowment funds, while the government continues to subsidize these schools on a per capita basis and in inverse proportion to the fees charged. Although the DSS category is often considered to be quasi-private because of its preservation of government subsidies, the revised DSS successfully attracted popular "elite schools" to join the system by responding to the government's call for "a strong private sector" in education (Dong 2000).

In addition to changes in school governance, the adoption of mother-tongue (Cantonese) teaching is another important reform initiative of the post-1997 era. Starting in 1998, most (307) government and aided secondary schools were required to adopt mother-tongue teaching, while 114 schools were allowed to continue with English-medium instruction after establishing their ability to do so effectively (Tsui et al. 1999, p. 196). Although denied by the government, some people link this policy to the change of sovereignty in 1997. No matter what the rationale, the decision has been controversial. Some teachers, parents, and students worry that mother-tongue teaching will cause a decline in students' overall English proficiency, but the government defended its decision by claiming that "educational research worldwide and in Hong Kong has shown that students learn better through their mother tongue" (Hong Kong Department of Education 1997, p. 1). Nevertheless, the government decided to adjust the mother-tongue teaching policy to provide flexibility for schools to enhance student's exposure to English (Education Bureau 2008).

HIGHER EDUCATION

The University of Hong Kong, founded in 1910 (the university evolved from the Hong Kong College of Medicine for Chinese, founded in 1887), was the only university in the territory until the establishment of the Chinese University of Hong Kong in 1963. Hong Kong's higher education remained elitist until the 1990s. A preliminary round of tertiary-education expansion had began under Governor Edward Youde (1924–1986) in the early 1980s in response to a policy of the Margaret Thatcher government. In 1989 Governor David Wilson decided to raise the higher-education enrollment rate to 18 percent by the 1994–1995 academic year. He hoped this move would help Hong Kong maintain political legitimacy and social stability during the last years of British colonial rule (Lee and Gopinathan 2005, p. 62).

Thereafter, institutions of higher education that were funded by the University Grants Committee, a funding body allocating government funding to the university sector, increased from two to eight through the establishment of a new university (the Hong Kong University of Science and Technology) and the upgrading in 1995 of several of Hong Kong's postsecondary schools, including two existing polytechnic schools, to university status.

The government of the Hong Kong Special Administrative Region continued to expand higher education after 1997. In 2000 Chief Executive Dong Jianhua (Tung Chee-hwa) announced a plan to increase the participation rate of tertiary education to 60 percent by encouraging the nongovernmental sector's participation in the provision of subdegree tertiary education (Dong 2000). The number of full-time, accredited, self-financing associate-degree and higher-diploma programs then rapidly increased from thirty-eight in the 2001–2002 academic year to 261 in the 2006–2007 academic year (Education Bureau 2007). Nevertheless, after this rapid expansion, many expressed concerns about recognition of associate-degree qualifications, the quality of the programs, and an oversupply in the market.

BIBLIOGRAPHY

Dong Jianhua (Tung Chee Hwa). *The 2000 Policy Address: Quality Education, Policy Objective for Education and Manpower Bureau.* Hong Kong: Government Printer, 2000.

Education and Manpower Branch, Education Department. *The School Management Initiative: Setting the Framework for Quality in Hong Kong Schools.* Hong Kong: Government Printer, 1991.

Education Bureau, Government of the Hong Kong Special Administration Region. Statistical Information: Statistics for Full-time Accredited Self-financing Post-secondary Programmes. 2007. http://www.edb.gov.hk/.

Education Bureau, Government of the Hong Kong Special Administration Region. *Further Discussions on the Way Forward for Medium of Instruction Policy.* 2008. http://www.edb.gov.hk/.

Education Commission. *Education Commission Report No. 7: Quality School Education.* Hong Kong: Author, 1997.

Endacott, G. B. *A History of Hong Kong.* Rev. edition. Hong Kong and London: Oxford University Press, 1973.

Hong Kong Department of Education. *Medium of Instruction Guidance for Secondary Schools.* Hong Kong: Government Printer, 1997.

Lee, Michael H. H., and S. Gopinathan. Reforming University Education in Hong Kong and Singapore. In *Globalization and Higher Education in East Asia,* ed. Mok Ka Ho and Richard James, 56–98. Singapore: Marshall Cavendish, 2005.

Leung, Joan Y. H. The Politics of Decentralization: A Case Study of School Management Reform in Hong Kong. *Education and Society* 19 (2001): 17–36.

Sweeting, Anthony. *Education in Hong Kong Pre-1841 to 1941: Fact and Opinion.* Hong Kong: Hong Kong University Press, 1990.

Sweeting, Anthony. *A Phoenix Transformed: The Reconstruction of Education in Post-War Hong Kong.* Hong Kong: Oxford University Press, 1993.

Sweeting, Anthony. *Education in Hong Kong, 1941–2001: Visions and Revisions.* Hong Kong: Hong Kong University Press, 2004.

Tsui, Amy B. M., Mark S. K. Shum, Wong Chi Kin, et al. Which Agenda? Medium of Instruction: Policy in Post-1997 Hong Kong. *Language, Culture, and Curriculum* 12, 3 (1999): 196–214.

David K. K. Chan

NATIONALITY ISSUES SINCE 1983

A state is free to determine the criteria and conditions for entry and residence and for its citizenship, but valid citizenship under international law requires a genuine connection between the state and the individual. The issue of Hong Kong nationality was settled through a series of British and Chinese legislative acts and the 1984 Sino-British Joint Declaration in preparation for the return of Hong Kong to Chinese sovereignty on July 1, 1997. Unlike British law, Chinese law does not recognize dual nationality. Under Chinese law, Chinese nationality may not be divested except with the permission of the state.

BEFORE JULY 1, 1997

Under the British Nationality Act 1981, three categories of British nationality were created, effective January 1, 1983: British citizen, British Dependent Territories citizen, and British Overseas citizen. Persons born in Hong Kong became British Dependent Territories citizens.

To conform to the requirements of the Joint Declaration, the category of British National (Overseas) was created by the Hong Kong Act 1985. The status of British National (Overseas) was granted upon application by Hong Kong British Dependent Territories citizens and was not automatic. It confers a limited right of entry to the United Kingdom—and not the right of abode or the right to work without permission—with a renewable British passport and visa-free entry to 120 countries and territories (as at May 2008). British Nationals (Overseas) must enter the United Kingdom and European countries as non-European citizens and, until December 2006, had to obtain an entry visa for most European countries. Persons born before July 1, 1997, must apply before December 31, 1997, for the status. To retain the confidence of highly skilled persons in Hong Kong, China has agreed to allow its nationals in Hong Kong to use British "travel documents" as of July 1, 1997, for travel purposes. British Nationals (Overseas) are not entitled to British diplomatic or consular protection in China, Hong Kong, or Macau, which returned to Chinese sovereignty in 1999.

In light of the quashing of the prodemocracy movement in 1989, in order to dissuade mass emigration of highly skilled persons in Hong Kong, the United Kingdom enacted the British Nationality (Hong Kong) Act 1990, whereby up to 50,000 Hong Kong British Dependent Territories citizens, together with their spouses and minor children, may apply to the Governor of Hong Kong for recommendation for British citizenship. China does not recognize British citizenship so acquired, although such British citizenship, which carries the right of abode in the United Kingdom, precludes the holder from standing for high office in Hong Kong as of July 1, 1997, unless he or she renounces it.

Any woman whose husband (alive or deceased) defended Hong Kong in war and who has been assured a right to settle in the United Kingdom may apply to be registered as a British citizen under the Hong Kong (War Wives and Widows) Act

1996, provided that she is resident in Hong Kong and has not remarried.

Chinese law does not automatically consider non-Chinese persons, even if born and/or permanently resident in Hong Kong, to be Chinese nationals. To avoid rendering such persons stateless when Hong Kong returned to Chinese sovereignty, the United Kingdom enacted the British Nationality (Hong Kong) Act 1997, whereby Hong Kong British Dependent Territories citizens and British Nationals (Overseas) who would otherwise become stateless as of July 1, 1997, may apply to be registered as British citizens.

AS OF JULY 1, 1997

Under the Basic Law of Hong Kong (a domestic law of China implementing the Joint Declaration), Hong Kong permanent residents (as opposed to residents) with the right of abode in Hong Kong include:

1. Chinese persons born in Hong Kong at any time
2. Chinese persons born outside Hong Kong who have resided in Hong Kong for seven years continuously
3. Chinese persons born outside Hong Kong to categories (1) or (2)
4. Non-Chinese persons who have entered Hong Kong with valid travel documents, who have resided in Hong Kong for seven years continuously, and who have taken Hong Kong as their place of permanent residence
5. Their children born in Hong Kong and under 21
6. Any other persons who, before July 1, 1997, had the right of abode in Hong Kong only

Chinese citizens without the right of abode in Hong Kong must enter Hong Kong with an Exit-entry Permit (to visit) or a One-way Permit (to settle) issued by the mainland authorities. In 1999, the Hong Kong Court of Final Appeal ruled that Chinese persons born in China to Hong Kong permanent residents possessed the right of abode in Hong Kong by reason of either of their parents' permanent residency even if born before the parent attained the status. The Hong Kong government refused to implement the ruling and brought the matter before the Standing Committee of the National People's Congress, which has the power to interpret the Basic Law when an issue involves the relationship between the Central Government and Hong Kong. The Committee decided that these persons did not possess the right of abode in Hong Kong.

All Chinese citizens who are Hong Kong permanent residents may apply for a Hong Kong Special Administrative Region passport issued by the Hong Kong Immigration Department, which entitles the holder to enter more than 130 countries and territories without a visa or with a visa granted upon arrival (as at May 2008) and to seek Chinese diplomatic protection in foreign countries (including the United Kingdom). To enter mainland China, a Hong Kong Chinese national must possess a Mainland Travel Permit for Hong Kong and macau Residents issued by the mainland authorities, and to enter Macau, a Hong Kong Identity Card, Hong Kong Permanent Identity Card or Hong Kong Reentry Permit or a British National (Overseas) or foreign, but not Hong Kong Special Administrative Region, passport.

Unlike British National (Overseas) passport holders, persons holding Hong Kong Special Administrative Region passports may enter most European countries without a visa since April 2001. Interestingly, most permanent residents of Macau retain Portuguese nationality and may enter and settle in the United Kingdom as European citizens.

BIBLIOGRAPHY

Chan, Phil C. W. Hong Kong's Political Autonomy and Its Continuing Struggle for Universal Suffrage. *Singapore Journal of Legal Studies* (2006): 285–311.

Ghai, Yash. Nationality and the Right of Abode. *Hong Kong Law Journal* 26 (1996): 155–161.

Ghai, Yash. Citizenship and Politics in the HKSAR: The Constitutional Framework. *Citizenship Studies* 5 (2001): 143–164.

Mushkat, Roda. Hong Kong as an International Legal Person. *Emory International Law Journal* 6 (1992): 105–170.

White, Robin M. Hong Kong: Nationality, Immigration, and the Agreement with China. *International and Comparative Law Quarterly* 36 (1987): 483–503.

White, Robin M. Nationality Aspects of the Hong Kong Settlement. *Case Western Reserve Journal of International Law* 20 (1988): 225–251.

Phil C. W. Chan

POLITICAL PARTIES AND SOCIOPOLITICAL CONSTITUENCIES

Political parties in post–1997 Hong Kong are essentially political brokers. They have very little membership, control few resources, and possess limited mobilization power. Their main goal is to secure as many seats as possible in the legislature, rather than to take over governmental power. They secure electoral support by pledging to protect the interests of narrow constituencies and by demonstrating their ability to broker the conflicting demands of Beijing, the wider public, and particular interests. The main issue of contention in party and electoral politics has been the pace and forms of democratic reform—or more precisely, when and how the chief executive and the Legislative Council should be directly elected by universal suffrage. In other words, political parties battle over the rules of the game that determine which political brokers can share the limited legislative power.

THE GENESIS OF BROKER POLITICS

Such broker politics had its origin in the colonial period. During a century and a half of British rule, Hong Kong was not allowed to develop popular forms of political representation. Until the final transition to Chinese rule, there were no political parties, no universal franchise, and no elected assemblies in the colony, except the Urban Council, which was a partially elected assembly with very limited responsibility, the most important functions of which were the licensing of liquor sales, urban waste disposals, and management of recreational facilities such as football fields. Interest mediation was achieved by a system of co-optation. Under such a system, a handful of peak associations were recognized—by fiat and by the licensing power of the colonial state—as representing the interests of specific social and economic sectors. Their leaders were appointed to various advisory committees, the Legislative Council, and the Executive Council to "advise," and in fact to share in making decisions. These privileged associations included most notably the Hong Kong General Chamber of Commerce, the Federation of Hong Kong Industries, and the Hong Kong Association of Banks. These committees and councils covered all major policy areas. Among them was Heung Yee Kuk, a statutory assembly responsible for advising the government on rural affairs. The assembly was unique in that its members were elected from rural committees comprised of indigenous inhabitants of the New Territories. Over the years the assembly has played an assertive role in protecting land rights and social customs of the indigenous population, which became increasingly marginalized in Hong Kong's emigrant society.

In such an oligarchical system, political representation was based on sectional interests. The only territory-wide civic groups existing before the 1980s were the Reform Club and the Civic Association. Both had few members, formulated no clear policy platforms, and enjoyed little popularity. They took part mostly in the Urban Council elections and had little access to the Legislative Council and Executive Council.

THE DEVELOPMENT OF POLITICAL GROUPS

It was not until the 1980s that new political groups began to emerge. In preparation for the handover of Hong Kong to China, the colonial government introduced universal franchise for the first time in the 1982 District Board election. Although the district board had no real power other than consultative functions, its creation met with initial enthusiasm. As a response to the possibility of having more future elections, new groups sprang up. These included Meeting Point (1983), Hong Kong Affairs Society (1984), Progressive Hong Kong Society (1984), and the Association for Democracy and People's Livelihood (1986). Except for the last one, all ceased to exist after a few years.

Further development of political parties was thwarted by the colonial government's efforts to strengthen the century-old form of broker politics. In 1984 the government introduced functional-constituency election to the legislature. Functional constituencies consisted of important economic sectors such as industry, commerce, and banking. Representation was again based on state licensing. Certain associations were given the privilege of electing representatives to the Legislative Council. As a result, sectoral economic interests were institutionalized as political groups. These associations subsequently opposed any change to the system, which accrued political privileges in their favor.

Ironically, the colonial political arrangement was endorsed by the Chinese government. In an attempt to enlist the support of business interests, Beijing allowed an expansion of the sectoral arrangement for the post–1997 Hong Kong political system. Major sectors such as tourism, real estate, finance, import and export, and wholesale and retail were added. In the post–1997 legislature, half of the seats are elected from functional constituencies. Many of the functional constituencies consist of only a few hundred eligible electors. Elections are essentially competitions among business associations. Many candidates have been returned uncontested. There is hardly any necessity for mass electoral mobilization, and hence little room for party activities.

THE RISE OF POLITICAL PARTIES

The most important event stimulating the formation of political parties was the crackdown on the Tiananmen student movement in 1989. Fearing similar high-handed policy after the handover, prodemocratic reform groups coalesced in 1990 to form a united political party, the United Democrats of Hong Kong. The party won a landslide victory in the 1991 partially direct election to the Legislative Council. In response, pro-Beijing forces in Hong Kong formed the Democratic Alliance for the Betterment of Hong Kong, which became the main rival of the democrats. In 1994 the Liberal Party was established as the first political group calling itself a party. The party was formed by businessmen and professionals and had strong backing from big business. In the same year, the United Democrats merged with Meeting Point to form the Democratic Party. Since leaders of the Democratic Party continued to denounce the June 4 crackdown, Beijing still refuses to recognize the party and bans its leaders from entering mainland China.

After the handover, political contention in the Hong Kong Special Administrative Region has been staged among three major parties: the probusiness Liberal Party, which strives to maintain the status quo; the Democratic Alliance, which brokers the Beijing government's stand and traditional grass-roots interests; and the pro-reform parties (including the Democratic Party, Frontier, and the Civic Party), which identify with middle-class interests and embrace the Western ideal of a democratic government. In addition, there are numerous functional constituencies representing sectoral interests.

The post–1997 political system was deliberately designed to prevent the emergence of a ruling party. The chief executive and principal officials are not allowed to have party affiliations. As a result, the public has no way of evaluating the performance of individual political parties. And since there is no genuine connection between government policies and party platforms, competition during legislative elections is seldom based on policy differences. In the functional-constituency elections, electoral success depends on the ability of a candidate to convince voters that he will be the best broker for the sector's interests. In district direct elections, political parties manipulate popular trust or distrust toward Beijing and present themselves either as middlemen between Hong Kong and Beijing or as defenders of Hong Kong's local interests against Beijing. In addition, most candidates offer special services to local communities in exchange for votes. Such practices reinforce the role of broker politics in Hong Kong's political development.

BIBLIOGRAPHY

Lam, Wai-man. *Understanding the Political Culture of Hong Kong: The Paradox of Activism and Depoliticization*. New York: Sharpe, 2004.

Ma, Ngok. *Political Development in Hong Kong: State, Political Society, and Civil Society*. Hong Kong: Hong Kong University Press, 2007.

Tak-Wing Ngo

GOVERNMENT AND POLITICS SINCE 1997

The post–1997 political system in Hong Kong manifests a high degree of continuity with the colonial structure. Similar to the colonial situation, the ultimate political authority lies not in the Hong Kong Special Administrative Region but in the central government in Beijing. The Hong Kong government enjoys limited autonomy in political and constitutional matters. Public participation is restricted to the legislature, with an electoral system deliberately designed to limit universal franchise and with procedures aiming at restraining popular influence. The whole political system is dominated by big-business interests that have strong connections with Beijing.

The Basic Law (Jiben Fa) guarantees in a number of ways that business interests will dominate in post-1997 politics. First, the chief executive (*xingzheng zhangguan*) is elected by an Election Committee (Xuanju Weiyuanhui) that consists of the business sector (25%); professionals (25%); labor, social services, and religion (25%); and the so-called political sector (25%). This last sector comprises members who are appointed or indirectly elected, again with a majority coming from the business sector. It is therefore not surprising that a business tycoon, the shipping magnate Tung Chee-hwa (Dong Jianhua), was chosen as the first chief executive. The Basic Law also stipulates that half of the seats in the Legislative Council (Lifa Hui) have to be returned by functional-constituency elections. Functional constituencies consist of major business sectors and business-related professional sectors, such as accounting, insurance, and surveying. In many constituencies, votes are cast by groups, corporations, or associations, rather than by individuals.

Business leaders closely follow the intentions of the Beijing government and support the latter's policies toward Hong Kong. This explains why Tung Chee-hwa was reelected uncontested in 2002 for a second term as chief executive, even though he was extremely unpopular among the general public. The business-dominated Election Committee returned him to office because Tung was handpicked and supported by the Beijing government. In the absence of any backing from a ruling party, the chief executive and his principal officials often have to rely on the authority of Beijing to secure majority support in the Legislative Council. This is achieved not only by winning the support of the functional constituencies, but also by enlisting the loyalist votes from legislators of pro-Beijing political parties. The political agenda of the Special Administrative Region is thus set and controlled by an intricate alliance forged among the Hong Kong government, the Beijing authorities, business interests, and the loyalist political parties.

Ironically, the Basic Law stipulates that the ultimate goal is universal suffrage and direct election of the chief executive and the Legislative Council. This has created heated debates since the handover about when and how such elections should be implemented. Despite strong popular support for universal suffrage, little progress has been made because of strong opposition from Beijing and big business. Beijing's stand is that any radical departure from the status quo should not take place until at least 2017.

The most significant development during the first ten years of postreversion politics was the reform of the civil-service system. The change came in 2002 with the introduction of the political appointment of principal officials.

TUNG CHEE-HWA (DONG JIANHUA)

Tung Chee-hwa (Dong Jianhua), born in 1937, was the first chief executive of the Hong Kong Special Administrative Region. He resigned after eight years in office under mounting criticism of his incompetence.

Tung came from a rich business family with close connections to the Chinese government. His father was a shipping magnate and founder of the Oriental Overseas Container Line (OOCL). Tung was born in 1937 in Shanghai and moved to Hong Kong when he was ten years old. He took over OOCL in 1982 after the death of his father. He kept a low political profile before he was appointed in 1993 by the last British governor, Chris Patten, to become a member of the inner cabinet, the Executive Council. Despite his limited political experience and public service record, Tung turned out to be a strong candidate for the post-1997 chief executive because he was deemed acceptable to both the British and Chinese governments as well as to the business community in Hong Kong. With the blessing of Beijing, Tung won a landslide victory in his run for the post of Hong Kong's first chief executive. This came with a price, since the overwhelming majority of the four hundred voters of the Election Committee who (s)elected Tung were either pro-Beijing business tycoons or their representatives. In his subsequent years of governing, Tung had to look after the interests of this constituency.

Tung was eager to reform the colonial system and its long-standing laissez-faire policy toward economic planning. He launched an ambitious housing program, established a compulsory provident fund, emphasized civic education and innovative teaching, introduced political appointments in the civil service system, and earmarked a number of industrial sectors for strategic development. However, the Asian financial crisis seriously disrupted his housing plan. Many people blamed Tung's plan for the property-market collapse. His economic projects were criticized for creating privileges for his supporters. Despite his unpopularity, Tung was elected uncontested for a second term in 2002, but his competence was further challenged by the SARS (severe acute respiratory syndrome) epidemic that filled the entire population with panic and brought the territory to a standstill in early 2003. The outburst of public anger came on July 1, 2003, when a mass demonstration (with an estimated 500,000 people) was staged to protest Tung's attempt to push for the passage of Article 23 of the Hong Kong Basic Law. The article aimed to prohibit acts of sedition and subversion against the central government, but would severely compromise civil liberty in Hong Kong. Eventually, the progovernment Liberal Party withdrew its support, forcing the Tung administration to drop the bill.

After this event, it became clear that Tung was incapable of brokering the interests between Beijing and Hong Kong. He resigned in 2005 for "health" reasons after the press reported that he had been criticized by Beijing leaders as indecisive and weak. He was immediately elected vice chairman of the Chinese People's Consultative Conference, and was later awarded a Grand Bauhinia Medal and two honorary doctorate degrees for his contributions to Hong Kong.

Tak-Wing Ngo

It changed the long-standing system under which the heads of all government departments were civil servants on permanent contracts. After the reform, the chief secretary, the financial secretary, the secretary for justice, and the secretaries of eleven government bureaus have been staffed by political appointees. They are nominated by the chief executive and appointed by the central government for a five-year term concurrent with that of the chief executive. The post of secretary resembles that of a cabinet minister. Accountable for their policies, ministerial secretaries are assisted by permanent secretaries, who are civil servants of the rank of administrative officer. In 2007 Donald Tsang (Zeng Yinquan) proposed a further change after he was reelected chief executive: the introduction of the new positions of deputy secretaries and political assistants. Both are political appointments.

The reform was meant to enhance the executive authority of the chief executive, improve the coherence of government policies, enlarge the ruling elite, protect the neutrality of the civil service, and increase the accountability of policy makers. In practice, governance seems marginally affected, if not more compromised. Since the chief executive does not have the support of a ruling political party, he can fill these posts only with personal contacts. It is therefore no surprise that the overwhelming majority of the ministerial secretaries still consist of former civil servants. The handful

DONALD TSANG

Donald Tsang (Zeng Yinquan), born in 1944, became the chief executive of the Hong Kong Special Administrative Region in 2005. He succeeded Tung Chee-hwa (Dong Jianhua), who resigned during his second term in office.

Tsang came from a family of civil servants. His father was a policeman and his younger brother was the police commissioner of Hong Kong. Born and educated in Hong Kong, Tsang joined the civil service in 1967. During his decades-long service in the government, Tsang held positions in various departments, and was once in charge of the widely criticized British Nationality Selection Scheme. He became the financial secretary of the colonial government in 1995, a position he continued to hold after the handover of Hong Kong in 1997. He was praised for his competence in steering the Hong Kong economy through the Asian financial crisis in the late 1990s. He succeeded Anson Chan (Chenfang Ansheng) as the chief secretary when the latter resigned in 2001 because of her clash with Chief Executive Tung Chee-hwa. Tsang then became the acting chief executive when Tung himself resigned in 2005. Subsequently, Tsang was formally elected uncontested by an 800-member Election Committee as the chief executive for the remaining period of Tung's incomplete term. He was elected for a "second" term in 2007.

Tsang's assumption of power signified a return of the strong influence of the civil servants in running the government. During his second term in office, he appointed mostly his former civil service colleagues to be the principal officials. In contrast to Tung Chee-hwa, Tsang has not launched ambitious social and economic programs or attempted to change the conventional mode of planning. Having served in the colonial government for decades, Tsang internalized the bureaucratic ethos of minimum government and incrementalism.

Unlike his predecessor, Tsang does not have a close relationship with the Beijing authorities. He also has no strong backing from business interests. His appointment was once seen as providing a chance for rapprochement between the government and the pro-reform parties and groups. This has proved to be unattainable as the logic of the game compels Tsang to increasingly rely on pro-Beijing loyalists and business interests in order to secure support for his policies as well as those policies imposed from Beijing.

Tak-Wing Ngo

of new officials coming from the business sector have either run into conflicts with the bureaucratic ethos or excessively relied on their civil-service subordinates to deal with public inquests and policy debates. Worse still, bureaucratic sectionalism has increased rather than diminished, as witnessed during the epidemic of SARS (severe acute respiratory syndrome), when ministerial secretaries valued their personal political careers more than the collective responsibility of the administration as a whole.

BIBLIOGRAPHY

Ma, Ngok. *Political Development in Hong Kong: State, Political Society, and Civil Society*. Hong Kong: Hong Kong University Press, 2007.

Poon, Kit. *The Political Future of Hong Kong: Democracy within Communist China*. London: Routledge, 2008.

Tak-Wing Ngo

HOUSEHOLD REGISTRATION

The household registration (*hukou*) system covers all residents in China. It is a major component of the Chinese socio-political structure and a key feature of Chinese social and cultural life. The *hukou* system performs crucial functions affecting China's political stability, governance, economic growth, social stratification and equality, demography, internal migration, and interregional relations.

Earlier versions of the *hukou* system can be traced to the fifth century BCE during the Warring States period. It was institutionalized and adopted with different names such as *baojia* and varying degrees of effectiveness and extensiveness as an important part of the Chinese imperial political system from the Qin dynasty (third century BCE) to the Qing dynasty (1644–1911). The Republic of China (ROC, since 1911) and the People's Republic of China (PRC, since 1949) both established a national *hukou* system. However, the *hukou* system achieved an unprecedented level of uniformity, extensiveness, effectiveness, and rigidity only in the PRC, especially after the promulgation on January 9, 1958, of the Regulation on *Hukou* Registration of the People's Republic of China. Twenty-seven years later, on September 6, 1985, Beijing adopted its Regulation on Resident's Personal Identification Card in the People's Republic of China (amended to the Law on Resident's Personal Identification Card in the People's Republic of China on June 29, 2003). These two regulations and their implementation procedures are the main legal basis for the *hukou* system. Every Chinese citizen knows the *hukou* system, yet it remains an administrative system and is not even mentioned in the PRC constitution.

The PRC State Council and its ministries have issued numerous regulations, provisional regulations, directives, decrees, and documents that have substantiated and fine-tuned the *hukou* system. The majority of these, estimated to number over six hundred from 1958 to 2005, have been the ever-changing criteria and mechanisms for the control of internal migration, especially *qianyi* (permanent migration with *hukou* relocation). The Ministry of Public Security and the local public security bureaus and police stations are the administrators of the *hukou* system. Specialized *hukou* police officers are assigned to be in charge in each *hukou* zone: a neighborhood, street, *danwei* (work unit), or township. With the authorization of the central government, provincial and municipal governments can make and have made marginal changes and experimental modifications of the *hukou* system in their jurisdictions.

The *hukou* system requires every Chinese citizen to be officially and constantly registered with the *hukou* authority (the *hukou* police) from birth. This registration is the legal basis for the personal identification of every Chinese citizen. The categories of nonagricultural (urban) or agricultural (rural), legal address and location, affiliation (employment), and a host of other personal and family information, including religious belief and physical features, are documented and verified to become the person's permanent *hukou* record. A person's *hukou* location and categorization are determined by his or her mother's (or father's after 1998) *hukou* location and type, rather than his or her birthplace.

One cannot acquire legal permanent residence and the numerous community-based rights, opportunities, benefits, and privileges in places other than where one's *hukou* is. Only through proper authorization of the government can one permanently change one's *hukou* location and especially one's *hukou* categorization. Travelers, visitors, and temporary migrants must be registered with the *hukou* police for extended stays (longer than three days) in a locality (often through local innkeepers). For stays of longer than one month and especially when seeking local employment, a person must apply and be approved for a temporary residential permit. Violators are subject to fines, detention, forced repatriation, and criminal prosecution. *Hukou* files are now computerized and routinely used by the police for investigation, social control, and crime-fighting purposes.

Largely operating in secrecy, the PRC *hukou* system performs three central functions. First, it is the basis for resource allocation and subsidization for selected groups of the population (mainly the residents of major urban centers). This function has shaped much of Chinese economic development since the mid-twentieth century by politically affecting the movement of capital and human resources. Second, the *hukou* system allows the government to control and regulate internal migration. The basic principles of PRC migration control have been to restrict rural-to-urban and small-city-to-large-city migration but encourage migration in the reverse direction. The scale of China's urbanization, as a consequence, is relatively small and its pace is slow compared to China's economic development level. China's urban slums are also smaller and less serious than those in many other developing nations, such as Brazil or India. Third, the *hukou* system has the less well-known but powerful role of managing the so-called targeted people (*zhongdian renkou*). Based on the *hukou* files, the police maintain a confidential list of selected segments of the population in each community to be specially monitored and controlled. This has contributed significantly to the political stability of China's one-party authoritarian regime.

The *hukou* system has also contributed to China's rapid industrialization and economic growth, which features sectoral and regional unevenness without serious problems of sociopolitical instability and urban poverty. However, the system has many negative implications. A major consequence of the *hukou* system has been China's strikingly rigid and clear-cut rural-urban division. For most of PRC history, the majority of the Chinese population—the rural residents—have been excluded and openly discriminated against under the *hukou* system. There are only a few limited ways (such as entering a state-run college or becoming a state employee or a military officer) for a rural resident to become a privileged urban *hukou* holder. The much smaller urban population (only 14 to 26 percent of the total population) has had qualitatively much better access to economic and social opportunities and benefits, and has also dominated PRC politics. To a lesser extent, urban residents in smaller cities and remote regions have also been excluded from the life of major urban centers or regions more favored by the government in terms of investment, subsidies, or policy flexibility. Outsiders and temporary residents are treated differently and often openly discriminated against in just about every aspect of their lives. Enormous regional disparities and gaps are therefore created and maintained.

During the reform era that started in 1978, the *hukou* system demonstrated both significant changes and remarkable continuities. Its basic structure and leading functions largely remained intact thirty years later. The system continues to register and identify the 1.3 billion Chinese by their administratively determined location and categories. People with different *hukou* locations and types continue to be treated differently and to have different social status and economic opportunities. However, the administration of the *hukou* system has become more localized and relaxed. The enforcement of the system has become less intrusive and also less effective. Forced repatriation and the associated abuses of *hukou*-less unregistered migrants (*mangliu*), for example, have slowed or even stopped since 2004. Internal migration, still regulated by the *hukou* system, has developed considerably as the rich and the talented and skilled have acquired substantial nationwide mobility. Rural residents with appropriate income and housing that meet the locally set "entry conditions" can now easily become urban residents in small cities and towns. Temporary residential permits have allowed more than one hundred million rural residents to work and live in the cities for extended periods. *Hukou*-based biased resource allocation is still important, but many of the old exclusive subsidies for urban consumers have shrunk or even disappeared, replaced by market-based resource allocation. Other reform efforts have further obscured, both cosmetically and substantively, the divisiveness and the offensiveness of the *hukou* system.

Despite an increase in criticism based on ethics concerns, and despite the continuing reform efforts needed by the new market economy, China's *hukou* system is likely to remain omnipresent and powerful, albeit with adaptation and adjustment, for the foreseeable future. It will continue to be a key aspect of statecraft for the Chinese government and an important factor in China's sociopolitical organization, population control, economic development, and social and spatial stratification.

SEE ALSO *Corruption; Labor: Market; Migrant Workers; Political Control since 1949; Social Welfare; Unit* (danwei).

BIBLIOGRAPHY

Wang Feiling (Fei-Ling Wang). *Organization through Division and Exclusion: China's Hukou System.* Stanford, CA: Stanford University Press, 2005.

Whyte, Martin K., ed. *One Country, Two Societies: China's Rural-Urban Gap in Contemporary China.* Cambridge, MA: Harvard University Press, 2008.

Fei-Ling Wang

HOUSEHOLD RESPONSIBILITY SYSTEM (*BAOGAN DAOHU*)

The term *household responsibility system* refers to an agricultural-management system in which individual households in rural China take responsibility for agricultural production while maintaining the system of collective ownership of land and other major means of farm production.

ORIGINS

Some areas experimented with the household responsibility system in the 1950s and 1960s, especially in southern provinces such as Zhejiang and Anhui. In the more permissive atmosphere of the late 1970s, this system was revived in Anhui and later spread to the rest of the country.

The household responsibility system is one form of the responsibility system in agriculture that emerged in the late 1970s in China. Other forms of the responsibility system include the work-group responsibility system (where production responsibility is devolved from the production team to the work group) and the individual-farmer responsibility system (where output quotas are fixed for an individual farmworker).

TWO VARIANTS

The household responsibility system has two variants. The first is *baochan daohu*, that is, assignment of responsibility for production to the household. Under this system, agricultural production was contracted to individual households and the output was shared among the state, the collective, and the household. Feixi County in Anhui, which implemented this system in 1978, was the first county to do so. With the support of the provincial party secretary, Wan Li, this system soon spread to other poor counties in Anhui. By June 1981, 19.9 percent of production teams in rural China had adopted this system.

The second variant of the household responsibility system is *baogan daohu* (or *da baogan*), that is, assumption of total responsibility by the household. The eighteen households in the Xiaogang Production Team in Liyuan Commune in Fengyang County in Anhui Province were the first in the post-Mao period to adopt such a system, which they did in the spring of 1978 in secrecy, in fear of political reprisals. Under this system, the household rents land from the production team and retains all its produce after paying taxes and selling its grain to the state under a system of unified purchase and after handing over to the team its share of collective accumulation and welfare funds, as well as other levies.

By the end of 1982, 89.7 percent of all production teams in China had adopted one of the variants of the household responsibility system. Because of its simplicity, *baogan daohu* became the dominant form in later years. Initially, the household was allowed to rent the land for a period of fifteen years. But according to the Land Contract Law in Rural Areas of the People's Republic of China, which was approved by the National People's Congress on August 29, 2002, and went into effect on March 1, 2003, the term of contract for arable land was revised to thirty years, from thirty to fifty years for grassland, and from thirty to seventy years (or longer in some cases) for forestland.

VILLAGE COMMITTEES

Production teams, along with people's communes, were disbanded in the 1980s and were replaced by popularly elected village committees. The village committee is responsible for coordinating rural economic activities based on households and for limited social-welfare functions, such as distributing minimum livelihood subsidies.

SEE ALSO *Rural Cooperative Medical Systems.*

BIBLIOGRAPHY

Fewsmith, Joseph. *Dilemmas of Reform in China: Political Conflict and Economic Debate.* Armonk, NY: Sharpe, 1994.

Shue, Vivienne. The Fate of the Commune. *Modern China* 10, 3 (1984): 259–283.

Zou Dang (Tsou Tang). *The Cultural Revolution and Post-Mao Reforms: A Historical Perspective.* Chicago: University of Chicago Press, 1986.

Zhiyue Bo

HOUSING

This entry contains the following:

OVERVIEW

Forms of residential architecture remained essentially unchanged in most parts of China from ancient times through the mid-twentieth century. Traditional features included walled enclosure, symmetry along a central axis, north-south orientation, and a central courtyard. Minor climatic variations notwithstanding, the internal spatial arrangements within traditional homes were remarkably similar: Rooms faced inward to the central courtyard and were distributed to family members according to their status within the family. The traditional Chinese home was a highly symbolic architectural space, providing physical manifestation for the hierarchical social relationships implicit within Confucian moral philosophy. Socioeconomic differences were reflected in size and quality rather than architectural form: The poor lived in shacks constructed of mud-brick and thatch, while the wealthy had homes built of fired brick and ceramic tile.

New forms of housing began to appear in Chinese cities from the late nineteenth century, a result of the increasing pace of urbanization and industrialization, and growing foreign influence. To accommodate the rapidly expanding urban workforce, property developers pioneered terrace-style residential estates. Typically two or three stories, this new form of housing enabled more efficient construction processes and higher-density living, while retaining some traditional features, such as internal courtyards and walled enclosures. Wealthier urban clients, particularly in cities such as Shanghai, could choose from a selection of Western-style apartments and garden villas.

Urban housing development in Maoist-era China (1949–1976) was characterized by three key features: centralization of design, industrialization of construction, and workplace (or *danwei*) control of housing distribution. Following Soviet models, two forms of accommodation epitomized housing in this era: dormitory style, consisting of individual rooms opening off long corridors with shared facilities; and apartment style, with two or more rooms forming a rudimentary independent residence. Residential buildings were generally four to six stories high, constructed primarily of brick and concrete, and arranged in clusters adjacent to the residents' workplace. In most cases, the workplace also provided a range of collective services such as catering, child care, and health care. Years of underinvestment, however, ensured that by the end of the Maoist era, housing shortages were endemic: between the 1950s and 1970s, urban per capita residential space actually declined.

Economic reforms implemented since 1978 saw dramatic changes in housing provision. Increasing rural incomes allowed many farmers to build larger and better-quality homes; breaking with traditional designs, new rural homes divide domestic space into private and public realms, reflecting changes in cultural attitudes associated with the privatization of everyday life. In urban China, housing privatization, the emergence of property markets, and substantial investment in new construction has seen per capita residential space increase five- or sixfold. As a result, most urban families have moved into new, larger, and better-quality apartments. Since the early 1980s, commercial residential development has taken the form of integrated "small districts," or *xiaoqu*, designed as enclosed, planned neighborhoods where housing is combined with communal facilities and infrastructure under the control of professional property managers. In marked contrast, a massive influx of itinerant and low-paid laborers from rural China has seen the emergence of a new urban underclass whose housing options are confined to construction sites, slum rentals, or shantytowns on the urban margins. China's economic rise over recent years has been accompanied by an increasing disparity in housing conditions.

SEE ALSO *Urban China.*

BIBLIOGRAPHY

Bray, David. *Social Space and Governance in Urban China: The Danwei System from Origins to Reform.* Stanford, CA: Stanford University Press, 2005.

Knapp, Ronald. *The Chinese House: Craft, Symbol, and the Folk Tradition.* Hong Kong: Oxford University Press, 1990.

Lü Junhua, Peter G. Rowe, and Zhang Jie, eds. *Modern Urban Housing in China, 1840–2000.* Munich, Germany: Prestel, 2001.

Yan Yunxiang. *Private Life under Socialism: Love, Intimacy, and Family Change in a Chinese Village, 1949–1999.* Stanford, CA: Stanford University Press, 2003.

David Bray

1800–1949

Traditional housing in nineteenth-century China, congenial to the peoples of an agricultural society, was made compatible with the requirements of a modernizing state and urban industrial life by 1949. Despite the political, administrative, juridical, economic, and social changes set in motion by reformers and revolutionaries and the factors that shaped domestic and international events, transformation of the built environment was conditioned by an enduring vernacular architecture that reflected the diverse cultural and geographic peculiarities of China's long history.

TRADITIONAL HOUSING

Although Chinese traditional housing generally shares certain fundamental elements—the use of local building materials, orientation to the cardinal directions, siting according to geomantic principles that included natural features such as water supply, rudimentary sanitary provisions (night soil was collected for use as fertilizer), and gender-defined interiors—the diversity of housing designs can be grouped roughly into three major geographic regions: north of the Yangzi River, south of the Yangzi River, and the west and border regions, which exhibit cultural styles of indigenous (non-Han) peoples and hybrid forms due to Han settlement.

In the north the most distinctive housing form was the *siheyuan*, or courtyard house, a four-sided enclosed space with living quarters (which included an ancestral hall or area), storage spaces, and a kitchen ranged against the walls and usually oriented to the south to maximize sun exposure. The open courtyard area was used for various domestic and food-processing activities, and may have included a garden to provide ventilation because the rooms opened only to the interior space, providing security against intruders. Materials used were brick or wattle and daub, timber beams and rafters (handy for keeping food, household goods, and even babies suspended from the dampness of the pounded-earth floors, or from insect and rodent infestations), and ceramic tiles for the sloping roofs. There was a *kang*, or sleeping platform, that could be heated from below, where the family gathered during the cold winters. The *siheyuan* were built in cities such as Beijing, divided by narrow lanes, and in the countryside to provide for extended families and lineages. A rural variation was the *sanheyuan* (three-sided or u-shaped) housing compound, which had more open space at the front for agricultural activities.

In the fertile south, which had a greater concentration of people, buildings were more substantial, with thick walls for insulation and windows placed high to encourage air circulation. Often, dwellings were two stories tall and had sky wells for ventilation. The overhanging tiled roof eaves provided protection from the sun. In the cities, houses abutted and had wall extensions jutting out from the sides of the top stories to form firewalls. Sliding poled gates across the main doors allowed air to circulate and prevented access to outsiders. Whereas the rectangle was the most common house design for both humble farmers and wealthy city merchants, ethnic minorities in remote regions built fortified villages, and in the southwest the Hakka (*kejia* or "guest people") built contiguous multistoried domiciles (*yuanlou*) arranged in large circles (as well as oval, square, octagonal, and rectangular configurations) around open areas for security against rival clans. During the unsettled warlord era in the 1920s unique watchtower structures (*diaolou*) combining Chinese and Western architectural features were built in Guangdong for surveillance and refuge during hostilities.

In the west and in the loess plateau, an area with few building material resources, subterranean pit and cliff-side cave dwellings were dug into the yellow earth and limestone hills. Cool in summer and warm in winter, these houses retained the general features of Chinese housing with a southern orientation, and pit dwellings were configured around a courtyard. In the 1930s Yan'an's cliff-side dwellings provided shelter for the Red Army and Communist leadership after their retreat (the Long March) to the interior. In the great plains of Mongolia, pastoralists used circular portable houses (yurts or *zhanzhang*) constructed with poles, sided with felt made from compressed animal fibers, with a smoke hole in the center. Interior spaces were defined by the use of carpets, and the entrances faced south.

MODERN HOUSING

Changes in housing design and structure occurred first in the treaty port settlements opened to foreign trade and residence at the conclusion of the Opium Wars. Western notions of planning, urban governance, infrastructure (sanitation, sewerage, piped water supplies, indoor plumbing, lighting, scavenging, transportation, and policing), architectural styles, and new building techniques and housing requirements were emplaced over areas where Westerners could exert control. Alongside traditional Chinese urban housing, detached and semidetached homes, grand suburban villas, and multistoried apartment blocks began to rise, changing the horizontal lines of the traditional city. By the turn of the twentieth century foreign and Chinese entrepreneurs provided dormitory housing for factory workers (male and female) in the newly established industrial sectors.

These ideas and practices were adopted and adapted before and after the 1911 revolution by Chinese reformers who were faced with the rapid growth (and rising real estate values) of their own administered areas contiguous with the foreign-controlled areas. During the Republican period, Chinese modernizers devised grand schemes and master plans for cities that fully incorporated Western infrastructure and building techniques such as reinforced concrete, steel frames, lifts, and fireproofing, which in turn required building codes and zoning provisions, all of which had an impact on housing design and construction. In Shanghai, for example, Sino-foreign real estate companies adopted London row or terraced three-story house design and adapted it to Chinese spatial and aesthetic form. The *shikumen* (stone-gate houses) were built along both sides of the *lilong* (neighborhood lanes) running off the main streets and enclosed by stone gates. They had access to piped water and privies (indoor plumbing in the more substantial *shikumen*), and they housed the majority of the urban population. However, population pressure and lack of affordable housing encouraged the interior subdivision of living spaces in the lane houses, and with the rapid influx of population from the unsettled countryside, shanty towns and mat-shed houses without sanitary provisions materialized in the peripheral areas, posing public health problems.

To address these imbalances, public housing figured in the program of reconstruction by the Nationalist government. Model working-class homes with subsidized rents and equipped with basic amenities were built by municipal authorities, but with the Japanese invasion and occupation of China's major cities, the devastation in the rural areas during World War II, and the subsequent outbreak of civil war with the Communists, housing stocks deteriorated, affecting peasants and urbanites alike. The establishment of the People's Republic of China in 1949 heralded a new era in housing provision, ownership, distribution, and supply, in line with the socialist and modern industrial goals of society. Some traditional and early twentieth-century housing has survived, but after the reforms of 1978 to 1979 and unprecedented economic growth fueling a modernization agenda, these structures face the wrecking ball or conservation as historical artifacts.

SEE ALSO *Nanjing (Nanking); Shanghai; Urban China.*

BIBLIOGRAPHY

Golanyi, Gideon S. *Chinese Earth-sheltered Dwellings*. Honolulu: University of Hawaii Press, 1992.

Knapp, Ronald G. *China's Old Dwellings*. Honolulu: University of Hawaii Press, 2000.

Lao fangzi [Old houses]. Nanjing, China: Jiangsu Meishu Chubanshe, 1993–.

Liu Dunzhen. *Zhongguo zhu zhai gai shuo* [Chinese vernacular architecture]. Beijing: Jianzhu Gongcheng Chubanshe, 1957.

Lu Hanchao. *Beyond the Neon Lights: Everyday Shanghai in the Early Twentieth Century.* Berkeley: University of California Press, 1999.

Kerrie L. MacPherson

1949–1980

Living conditions in China were poor before 1949. On the eve of the foundation of the People's Republic of China, owing to population growth and years of warfare, the housing shortage had been an acute problem for a long time. For instance, in Shanghai the average living space was 36 square feet per person. At the same time, very little public housing was available for rent to low-income households. After the foundation of the People's Republic, the government demolished unsafe houses and built new houses to meet the housing shortage. In Shanghai in the first three years, more than 3.875 million square feet of public housing was built.

In 1956 and 1958, the party released two reports—"Report on Urban Private Housing Property and Suggestions for a Socialist Transformation" and "Report on the Transformation of Urban Private Housing"—suggesting a socialist transformation. The state began to purchase privately owned property. In 1956, 95 percent of urban land was under state ownership. The state thus took on responsibility for providing, allocating, maintaining, and managing urban housing. Housing, formerly a commodity, became a component of state welfare.

To guarantee that citizens would be accommodated, the state issued a series of low-rent policies. By the end of the 1950s, the ratio of rent to household income decreased to the international average or lower, and it kept decreasing. In the 1980s, the ratio was about only 1 percent in the largest cities and even less in smaller cities.

Yet housing was still a severe problem. In cities, the urban working class lived in overcrowded or substandard conditions. It was not rare for three generations to live in a single room. In the case of single-story houses, several households shared one small courtyard. Such houses were old, and conditions were poor. Residents had no proper sewerage, lacked private bathrooms inside the home, and had to share one water spigot with all other households facing the courtyard. Winter was the hardest time because there were no heating facilities. People burned coal briquettes to keep the room warm.

Density of habitation in three Chinese cities, 1949–1978

Qingdao (Shandong province)		Changde (Hunan province)		Haikou (Hannan province)	
Year	Density of habitation People/km^2	Year	Density of habitation People/km^2	Year	Density of habitation People/km^2
1949	6,306	1953	174.06	1949	501.09
1957	8,937	1964	197.71	1952	562.95
1966	9,875	1982	275.9	1964	731.74
1978	10,499	—	—	1982	1,299

SOURCE: Official government web sites of Qingdao, Changde, and Haikou.

Table 1

Density of habitation in China, 1949–1975

Year	Density of habitation People/m^2	Year	Density of habitation People/m^2	Year	Density of habitation People/m^2
1949	57	1958	69	1967	80
1950	58	1959	70	1968	82
1951	59	1960	69	1969	84
1952	60	1961	69	1970	87
1953	61	1962	70	1971	89
1954	63	1963	72	1972	91
1955	64	1964	74	1973	93
1956	66	1965	76	1974	95
1957	68	1966	78	1975	97

SOURCE: National Bureau of Statistics of China. *2006 China Statistics Yearbook*. Beijing: China Statistics Press, 2006.

Table 2

Since the 1950s, low-rise buildings have been built to replace single-story houses in cities. The government allocated these new apartments to urban citizens through the work-unit (*danwei*) system. Most public housing was funded, built, owned, and managed by work units. Work units allocated their housing units to workers according to certain criteria. People were evaluated and received an appropriate living space. Under the welfare housing system, people lived in apartments rent-free and paid only a nominal fee for utilities. With these advantages came disadvantages. People could not choose the location, area, and style of their houses and could not move freely. Living conditions in such apartments were better than in single-story houses. But many households still had to share a common cooking area and public toilets. Few families had showers in their apartments.

Because the welfare housing policy was applied only to urban citizens and there was no free market for housing, rural peasants could not migrate into cities. In rural areas in the 1950s, the second land reform compelled individual farmers to join collectives. Land ownership was transferred from individuals to collectives. However, residential-housing land (*zhaijidi*) was land distributed to peasants for their use. They then could build houses on this land. Peasants could also apply for more land if they needed more housing area. In the 1960s, several policies sought to protect peasants' right to use residential-housing land and attached assets.

While there were improvements from the founding of the People's Republic to the 1950s, housing construction slowed in the 1960s and 1970s (see table 1). During the decade of the Cultural Revolution (1966–1976), living conditions grew even worse than before (see table 2). In Shanghai, for example, newly built housing amounted to only 2.368 million square feet in 1970. This was even less than in 1950. Due to the failure of governmental control, the provision of accommodation was in a state of disorder. Many houses were rebuilt regardless of their original construction and function. During this period, structures and facilities were badly damaged. Some living places were occupied for industrial use. Many persecuted families lost their houses.

SEE ALSO *Urban China.*

BIBLIOGRAPHY

Wang, Yaping, and Alan Murie. *Housing Policy and Practice in China*. New York: St. Martin's Press, 1999.

Zhang, Xingquan. Chinese Housing Policy, 1949–1978: The Development of a Welfare System. *Planning Perspectives* 12 (1997): 433–455.

Yiran Zheng

HOUSING SINCE 1980

In the 1950s the Communist government nationalized most landlord-owned rental properties in cities. Since then government-owned enterprises and work units built and distributed public housing to their employees as part of the socialist welfare system. In the early 1980s, 82 percent of urban housing was owned by the state, with 54 percent directly managed by various public-sector work units and 28 percent by municipal governments. This socialist public-dominated urban-housing system had many problems, including severe shortage, underinvestment, unequal and corrupt distribution, inefficient management, and poor maintenance. To address these problems, a series of housing-reform schemes were piloted at various locations throughout the 1980s. In 1988 these experiments resulted in a national plan for comprehensive reform of the urban housing system. This plan sought to commercialize housing according to the principles of a socialist-planned market economy. Specific policies included rent increases and the sale of public housing. This reform momentum was briefly interrupted by the political turmoil of the Tiananmen Square protests in 1989.

The second resolution on housing reform was issued in 1991 to reinforce the policies of 1988. This resolution led to the large-scale sale of public housing to their residing tenants usually at very low prices. Housing-reform policies were revised in 1994 to develop a dual housing system with a socialist housing supply of comfortable yet affordable housing for low- and middle-income households and a commercial housing supply for high-income families. The policies also sought to establish systems for public- and private-housing savings, finance, market exchange, insurance, repair, and management.

These policies were gradually implemented in all cities and towns. By 2002 over 80 percent of public housing was privatized. To help families save for housing, a housing savings system was introduced requiring employer and employee to make contributions to the employee's housing savings account each month. This savings could be used only to purchase housing or to supplement a pension when the employee reached retirement age. Rents in the public sector increased gradually, but did not reach the planned target of 15 percent of income, owing to high unemployment caused by the restructuring of state-owned enterprises.

Housing reform in the 1980s and the early 1990s did not fundamentally alter the relationship between the state, the work unit, and the employee in the public sector. Housing was still the responsibility of the employer, though individual employees contributed more. Housing entitlement and distribution was calculated not on the basis of household need or affordability, but on the basis of the employee's political and work status. To speed up the commercialization of urban housing, the central government made a major decision in 1998. Henceforth, public-sector work units would no longer distribute public housing to urban employees. Public-sector employers were allowed to issue housing cash subsidies to their employees, but not to be involved in housing construction, distribution, and management.

Urban housing reform has brought many changes to the housing system in Chinese cities. Commercial developers have become the main provider for new housing in the urban market. And there have been obvious improvements in general living conditions in Chinese cities. At the beginning of the reform (1978), the urban population had an average of 3 square meters of residential floor space per person. By 2007 this had increased nine-fold to 27 square meters. Most urban residents enjoy much better housing now than at any other time in their lives. There has also been diversification of housing investment, with more and more housing costs being met by urban residents themselves. This has increased the total volume of investment for housing. Government statistics show that by 2001 about 82 percent of urban residents (excluding migrant workers) owned their homes.

Urban housing reform has had no impact on rural communities where private family ownership and building one's own house still dominate. Housing reform, as an adjustment to the old welfare system, has also had little impact on the large numbers of rural migrants living in cities. The people most affected by housing reform have been those employed by public-sector work units and state-owned enterprises. Leaders and professionals, who already enjoyed better housing under the old system, have benefited most from the privatization policy, receiving large sums as housing subsidies. People working in ailing state-owned enterprises are more likely to live in poorer-quality housing. Inequalities in new housing resulting from privatization are further aggravated by the increased gap between the rich and poor since the 1990s. The ever increasing demand by the rich for bigger and better housing in good locations in major cities has resulted in high inflation in housing prices since 2000. New commercial housing is well beyond the reach of low-income, ordinary urban residents. As a result, Chinese cities are highly segregated, with the new rich and middle class living in select housing estates and gated communities and the urban poor and migrants overcrowded in poor quarters or peripheral rural villages around the cities.

SEE ALSO *Urban China: Urban Housing.*

BIBLIOGRAPHY

Wang, Ya Ping. Housing Reform and Its Impacts on the Urban Poor. *Housing Studies* 15, 6 (2000): 845–864.

Wang, Ya Ping. Urban Housing Reform and Finance in China: A Case Study of Beijing. *Urban Affairs Review* 36, 5 (May 2001): 620–645.

Wang, Ya Ping. *Urban Poverty, Housing and Social Change in China.* London and New York: Routledge, 2004.

Wang, Ya Ping. From Socialist Welfare to Support Home Ownership, the Experience of China. In *Housing and the New Welfare State*, ed. Richard Groves, Alan Murie, and Christopher Watson, 127–154. Aldershot, U.K.: Ashgate, 2007.

Wang, Ya Ping, and Alan Murie. The Process of Commercialisation of Urban Housing in China. *Urban Studies* 33, 6 (1996): 971–989.

Wang, Ya Ping, and Alan Murie. Commercial Housing Development in Urban China. *Urban Studies* 36, 9 (1999): 1475–1494.

Wang, Ya Ping, and Alan Murie. *Housing Policy and Practice in China.* London: Macmillan; New York: St. Martin's Press, 1999.

Wang, Ya Ping, and Alan Murie. Social and Spatial Implications of Housing Reform in China. *International Journal of Urban and Regional Research* 24, 2 (2000): 397–417.

Ya Ping Wang

HU DIE
1908–1989

The actress Hu Die began acting in the silent era, pioneered China's early talkies, and sustained a four-decade career in cinema. Born in Shanghai of Cantonese parents, the young Hu Ruihua was raised mainly in northern China and Guangzhou (Canton). As a sixteen-year old in 1924, she took the stage name Hu Die (butterfly) and entered, in the first cohort, Shanghai's Zhonghua Dianying Xuexiao (China Film School), studying under Zheng Zhengqiu and Hong Shen, leading figures of the new drama and film.

Her numerous early silent roles at Da Zhonghua Baihe, Youlian, and Tianyi film studios ranged from characters in period dramas, such as *Tieshan gongzhu* (Princess Iron Fan, 1927), to modern women, including female lawyers, movie stars, and detectives. She moved to Mingxing Film Studio in 1928, appearing in the eighteen-episode martial-arts blockbuster *Huoshao Honglian Si* (Burning of Red Lotus Temple, 1928–1931) and the six-part serial *Tixiao yinyuan* (Fate in Tears and Laughter, 1932), based on the novel by the popular fiction writer Zhang Henshui. Butterfly Woo, as Hu Die was also known, soon shared the spotlight with China's reigning star of silent cinema, Ruan Lingyu, and worked with the nation's best directors. A versatile actress, her characters extended from working women to middle-class housewives and elegant matrons. Her star persona was, by turns, defiant and lighthearted, illuminated by a signature dimpled smile.

When Mingxing produced China's first sound-on-disk feature film *Genü Hongmudan* (Singsong Girl Red Peony, 1931), Hu Die was cast in the lead role. During the transition to standard-Mandarin sound films, Hu Die, unlike Ruan, who spoke only Cantonese, had the advantage of having learned Mandarin from her father's northern concubine. In *Zhifen shichang* (Rouge and Powder Market, 1933), she played a young woman who needs to support her ailing mother and defies conventional biases against women being employed by taking a job in a department store, only to encounter exploitative discrimination from her supervisor and coworkers. In 1933 she was voted China's "movie queen" by film fans. For the all-talking film *Zimei hua* (Twin Sisters, 1933–1934), Hu Die played twin sisters separated as infants, raised in different settings, and later reunited as adults. The contrast between the siblings' behavior—a sympathetic, plain country girl alongside her vain, privileged city sister—foregrounded the actress's distinctive range. In 1935 Hu Die, along with Peking Opera star Mei Lanfang, participated in a Chinese film delegation to the Soviet Union and Europe, and during the Moscow International Film Festival they screened eight recent Chinese feature films dramatizing contemporary social issues.

When war broke out with Japan in 1937, Hu Die made fewer films as she moved with her family to Hong Kong and then to Chongqing. In 1945 she made a brief return to postwar Shanghai before settling in Hong Kong and Taiwan, where she starred in both Cantonese and Mandarin films, including the Shaw Brothers melodrama *Houmen* (Rear Entrance, 1959–1960), which garnered prizes at the Seventh Asian Film Festival of 1960. After retiring from filmmaking in 1967, Hu Die settled overseas in Vancouver and published her memoirs in 1986. Three years later, approaching death, she reportedly remarked, "Butterfly will soon flutter away."

SEE ALSO *Film Industry; Film Industry: Hong Kong; Ruan Lingyu.*

BIBLIOGRAPHY

Hu Die and Liu Huiqin. *Hu Die huiyilu* [Memoirs of Hu Die]. Beijing: Xinhua Chubanshe, 1987.

Kristine M. Harris

HU FENG
1902–1985

A literary critic, poet, editor, and translator whose views of literature contrasted with those promoted by the Chinese Communist Party, Hu Feng's stance ultimately led to his purge in a 1955 campaign.

LIFE AND CULTURAL POLITICS

Hu Feng, originally named Zhang Guangren, was born in Qichun County, Hubei Province, third-eldest son of a peasant-turned-entrepreneur. He attended traditional local schools before gaining a Western-style education, first in Wuhan, the provincial capital, then in Nanjing, and finally in Beijing. In Beijing he attended the prestigious preparatory school affiliated with Beijing University, where he audited Lu Xun's course on the history of Chinese fiction, and then Yanjing (Yenching) University, where he studied English literature. In 1926 he returned to Qichun to participate in the Northern Expedition, working principally in women's and cultural affairs. In 1929 he continued his studies in Japan, where he intensified an interest in literature and joined radical literary circles. Hu Feng was arrested in 1932 for his political activities and eventually deported back to China; he was welcomed in the leftist cultural world as something of a hero. He quickly joined the League of Left-Wing Writers and was given high-ranking administrative positions that allowed him to work closely with Lu Xun, the League's titular head.

During his time in the League, Hu Feng began to have conflicts with the Communist Party cultural bureaucracy, which promoted a more doctrinaire and dogmatic Marxist view of literature than he preferred. He argued against Zhou Yang's view that a Marxist worldview was necessary for the creation of a realist literature. Hu Feng clashed with Zhou Yang again in the 1936 Two Slogans debate, which centered on the issue of finding an appropriate slogan for anti-Japanese resistance literature. With the dissolution of the League in March 1936, Hu Feng became an independent literary figure, though one with a clear affiliation with, if not continuing ties to, the left. One of his most important contributions in this regard was the editing and publishing of small literary journals, most notably *Qiyue* (July, 1937–1941) and *Xiwang* (Hope, 1945–1946), which published the varied work of young and largely unknown writers that Hu Feng himself nurtured. Throughout the war period, which he spent in Wuhan, Chongqing, Hong Kong, and Guilin, Hu Feng's journals and book series asserted a politically and socially engaged position in the literary field unbeholden to the Communist Party and its ideology, in contrast to the situation in Yan'an.

The Communist Party cultural bureaucracy launched an assault on Hu Feng and his literary thought in 1944–1945 when the Rectification Campaign first launched in 1943 in Yan'an made its way to the Nationalist capital of Chongqing. The focus of the attack was "subjectivism" (*zhuguanzhuyi*)—the notion that true realist literature could only be written with the active and creative infusion of the writer's personality—a notion that might seem rather commonsensical in other contexts but that marked, at least to Hu Feng's detractors, a threat to the objectivism of Marxist materialist ideology and smacked of Western bourgeois individualism. In view of this background of conflict with the party cultural bureaucracy and his promotion of May Fourth notions of intellectual autonomy, it is not surprising that after the establishment of the People's Republic in 1949, Hu Feng was attacked first in a short campaign in 1952, then in the major campaign of 1955. In May 1955 Hu Feng and scores of his followers were arrested as members of an "antiparty, counterrevolutionary" clique. For the next twenty years or so, he suffered various forms of incarceration. Only in the liberal climate of the 1980s were Hu Feng and his literary thought rehabilitated.

LITERARY CRITICISM

There are two central concepts in Hu Feng's literary thought: realism and subjectivism. In the Chinese literary field of the 1920s and 1930s, *realism* was a much contested term. Hu Feng tended to look at realism as a literary mode that sought to expose the darkness of society, a mode that Lu Xun's fiction and essays embodied. When Hu Feng first emerged in the literary field, this May Fourth notion of realism was attacked on the left as no longer relevant to the new revolutionary epoch. In its stead young radicals promoted "revolutionary literature" (eventually referred to as "socialist realism"), which should embody the interests of the oppressed classes and promote their liberation. Only armed with a proper worldview could the writer create such a literature; without it, the writer was doomed to express the interests of his own class (it should be noted that most Chinese writers of the time were not from either proletarian or peasant backgrounds). By holding to and arguing forcefully for critical realism, Hu Feng was bucking the revolutionary tide.

The key to Hu Feng's realism—what gave it its vitality and enabled it to reflect social truth—was subjectivism, what he sometimes called the "subjective fighting spirit" (*zhuguan zhandou jingshen*). True realism could emerge in a work of literature only through the writer's dynamic subjectivity as shaped by his experiences in the real world. Suppressing the personality of the writer, he argued, would lead to a superficial photographic representation of reality that could never get at the essence of life and society.

Another important characteristic of Hu Feng's critical writings is his abiding admiration for Lu Xun, whom he fashioned into an emblematic figure of May Fourth enlightenment and its ideals of intellectual autonomy and literary integrity. As an admirer of Lu Xun and a promoter of May Fourth radical iconoclasm, Hu Feng was ardently opposed to the "national forms" (*minzu xingshi*) promoted on the left during the Anti-Japanese War (1937–1945) and in Yan'an. For writers to use traditional forms was, Hu Feng felt, an abrogation of the May Fourth ideal. He believed that writers instead should embrace internationalism and use the modern forms developed by the world's great realist writers (Honoré de Balzac, Fyodor Dostoyevsky, Nikolai Gogol).

Though he never opposed the Communist Party, Hu Feng promoted a spirit of literary independence from it both in his theoretical writings and in his practice in the literary field. This is most evident in his "Ten Thousand Word Memorial" to the Central Committee, in which, among other things, he highlighted the "five knives" that threatened writers in the post-Liberation climate: literature as the handmaiden of politics; literature as advancing the interests of workers, peasants, and soldiers; the hegemony of the communist worldview; thought reform; and national forms. His report also proposed the radical idea that small journals should be independent of the state and that editors, not party cadres, should run them unimpeded.

POETRY

Though less well known for his poetry than for his literary criticism, Hu Feng wrote several volumes of poetry and ardently promoted poetry in his literary criticism. His poetry is usually narrative and free-verse in style, though he also wrote long poems in classical style, especially during his years of incarceration. Contrary to what might be expected for someone who is sometimes portrayed as an opponent of the party, some of his poetry consists of rather sycophantic eulogies to Mao Zedong and the new Communist regime. Hu Feng's relationship with the party was highly ambivalent.

SEE ALSO *League of Left-Wing Writers; Lu Xun; Northern Expedition; Poetry.*

BIBLIOGRAPHY

Dai Guangzhong. *Hu Feng zhuan* [Biography of Hu Feng]. Yinchuan, China: Ningxia Renmin Chubanshe, 1994.

Denton, Kirk A. *The Problematic of Self in Modern Chinese Literature: Hu Feng and Lu Ling*. Stanford, CA: Stanford University Press, 1998.

Denton, Kirk A. The Hu Feng Group: Genealogy of a Literary School. In *Literary Societies in Republican China*, ed. Kirk A. Denton and Michel Hockx, 413–473. Lanham, MD: Lexington Books, 2008.

Hu Feng. *Hu Feng zizhuan* [Autobiography of Hu Feng]. Nanjing: Jiangsu Wenyi Chubanshe, 1996.

Hu Feng. *Hu Feng quanji* [Complete works of Hu Feng]. 10 vols. Wuhan: Hubei Renmin Chubanshe, 1999.

Huters, Theodore. Hu Feng and the Critical Legacy of Lu Xun. In *Lu Xun and His Legacy*, ed. Leo Ou-fan Lee, 129–152. Berkeley: University of California Press, 1985.

Mei Zhi. *Hu Feng zhuan* [A biography of Hu Feng]. Beijing: Shiyue Wenyi Chubanshe, 1998.

Peng, Xiaolian, and S. Louisa Wei, directors. *Storm under the Sun*. Hong Kong: Blue Queen Cultural Communications, 2007. Documentary film.

Shu, Yunzhong. *Buglers on the Home Front: The Wartime Practice of the Qiyue School*. Albany: State University of New York Press, 2000.

Wang Lili. *Zai wenyi yu yishi xingtai zhi jian: Hu Feng yanjiu* [Between literature and ideology: Studies on Hu Feng]. Beijing: Zhongguo Renmin Daxue Chubanshe, 2003.

Wen Zhenting and Fan Jiyan, eds. *Hu Feng lun ji* [A collection of essays on Hu Feng]. Beijing: Zhongguo Shehui Kexue Chubanshe, 1991.

Xu Wenyu. *Hu Feng lun* [Discussions on Hu Feng]. Wuhan, China: Hubei Renmin Chubanshe, 2005.

Zuojia Chubanshe. *Hu Feng wenyi sixiang pipan lunwen huiji* [A compilation of essays on Hu Feng's literary thought and criticism]. 6 vols. Beijing: Zuojia Chubanshe, 1955.

Kirk A. Denton

HU JINTAO

1942–

When the sphinxlike Hu Jintao became general secretary of the Chinese Communist Party (CCP) in November 2002, most Chinese, let alone foreign observers, had difficulty answering the "Who's Hu?" question. There were expectations that the then fifty-nine-year-old leader—whose principal patrons have included liberal party leader Hu Yaobang (no relation) and "chief architect of reform" Deng Xiaoping—might morph into a "Chinese Gorbachev" or a "Chinese Yeltsin." Certainly, Hu, like his immediate predecessor, former president Jiang Zemin, has persevered with market-oriented reforms begun by Deng in 1978. Yet in areas ranging from domestic politics to foreign affairs, the policies of the former chief of the Communist Youth League (CYL)—often deemed a hothouse of progressive opinion among the staid *nomenklatura*—bear a remarkable resemblance to conservative figures ranging from Chairman Mao Zedong to Hu's early mentor, hard-line ideologue and former Politburo Standing Committee member Song Ping.

Part of the mystery behind Hu's statecraft lies in his upbringing. Born into a relatively well-off family in Anhui Province in 1942, Hu went to top-notch Tsinghua University in the early 1960s, when the nation's intelligentsia was bewitched by Maoist and Stalinist norms. The young man's role models were the larger-than-life, all-for-the-revolution heroes in Ukrainian novelist Nikolai Ostrovsky's (1904–1936) propaganda masterpiece, *How the Steel Was Tempered* (1932–1934). After graduating with a degree in hydraulic engineering in 1965, Hu stayed on at Tsinghua to work as a political commissar. Unlike third-generation leaders such as Jiang or former premier Zhu Rongji, Hu had no exposure to either American ideas or the unorthodox socialist views popular in Hungary and Yugoslavia in the 1950s and 1960s.

HU'S RISE TO POWER

Hu worked in hydraulic engineering and infrastructure in the poor, remote northwestern province of Gansu from 1968 to 1982, when he became a party functionary as head of the CYL Gansu Branch. Hu's big break came in early 1983 when he was sent to CYL headquarters in Beijing for training. The earnest apparatchik caught the eye of then party general secretary (and former CYL first secretary) Hu Yaobang, who recommended that he stay on in the capital. In 1984 Hu Jintao became CYL first secretary—a ministerial-level position—at forty-two years of age. The elder Hu liked him so much that he made his protégé party secretary of Guizhou Province in 1985; administrative experience in the regions has always been a prerequisite for promotion to the top.

In January 1987, Hu's career suffered a blow when his mentor Hu Yaobang was sacked by Deng for failing to contain "bourgeois liberalization," which manifested itself in late 1986 in a wave of student demonstrations. A year later, Hu Jintao was transferred—or exiled—to Tibet as party secretary. At first, the erstwhile rising star was dispirited: He developed altitude sickness upon arriving in Lhasa; more significantly, pro-independence protests, in many cases led by monks loyal to the exiled Dalai Lama, began to take place with alarming frequency. Yet these adversities turned out to be blessings in disguise. When the most severe anti-Beijing riots since 1959 flared up on March 5, 1989, Hu demonstrated his mettle by proclaiming martial law in Lhasa and ordering the soldiers and the People's Armed Police to put down the disturbances. An estimated sixty Tibetans were killed. But Deng, who had nursed a guilty conscience for dumping Hu Yaobang, was impressed by this Hu protégé, who proved to be as loyal to the party as he was ruthless toward its enemies. At the Fourteenth CCP Congress in 1992, three years after the Tiananmen Square crackdown—which was partially modeled on Hu's successful suppression of Tibetan "antirevolutionaries"—Deng inducted Hu into the Politburo Standing Committee.

From 1992 to 2002, Hu served as a humble aide to the "core" of the third-generation leadership, Jiang Zemin. The two had an uneasy relationship. A former party boss of Shanghai, Jiang would have preferred as successor a member of the Shanghai Faction—had it not been for Deng's earlier anointment of Hu. While Hu was not given a major portfolio, he bided his time—and concentrated on grooming promising young men in his own CYL clique, which could eventually emerge as the CCP's largest faction.

THE GENESIS OF "THE SCIENTIFIC OUTLOOK ON DEVELOPMENT"

Not long after taking over power at the Sixteenth CCP Congress of 2002, Hu (who became state president in March 2003) and his close ally, Premier Wen Jiabao, revived with gusto Chairman Mao's "serve the people" credo by vowing to "put the people first" in all major policies. This was in reaction to the widespread perception that disadvantaged sectors such as peasants, migrant laborers, and blue-collar urbanites had not been able to adequately share the fruits of the nation's high-speed economic growth since the early 1990s. A series of memorable slogans, including Hu's "new Three Principles of the People"—"power must be used for the sake of the people; profits must be sought for the people; and [cadres'] feelings must be tied to those of the people"—underscored the fourth-generation leadership's commitment to *xinzheng*, or a "new deal" for the masses. Hu and Wen successfully used television and the Internet to project themselves as twenty-first-century CCP populists, visiting poverty-stricken villagers on Chinese New Year, and even shaking hands with HIV patients.

In both theory and practice, Hu's most important contribution to the CCP and the country could be the controversial *kexue fazhan guan* ("scientific outlook on development"). This is an attempt to rectify the perceived shortcomings of more than two decades of Deng Xiaoping–style reform, which was anchored upon no-holds-barred development of the coastal region. By contrast, the Hu-Wen administration is putting at least as much emphasis on gross domestic product expansion perse as a more equitable distribution of wealth among different social sectors and geographical regions. *Kexue fazhan* presupposes a growth model that strikes a better balance between rich and poor, coast and hinterland, industrialization and ecological well-being. It also means that Beijing will devote as many resources to the software of modernization—which includes education, public health, the environment, rule of law, social equality, and spiritual values—as to hardware such as infrastructure, factories, skyscrapers, and high-tech zones.

The *kexue fazhan guan* was enshrined in the CCP constitution at the Seventeenth CCP Congress in late 2007. At least during the Hu-Wen administration's first five-year term, however, Beijing had a checkered record in promoting "scientific development." On the positive side, the lot of the peasants as well as the estimated 150 million rural workers was improved. The agriculture tax was abolished and the take-home income of farmers increased by around 8 percent a year. For the first time, the social security net—including education subsidies, unemployment benefits, and pensions—was extended from the cities to the countryside. Yet the rich-poor, coast-hinterland gap kept yawning wider. The average city dweller's income was 3.28 times that of a rural resident's in 2006, up from 3.23 times in 2003. In 2007, more than 318 million Chinese languished below the poverty line.

Yet it is doubtful whether the goals of the fourth-generation leadership can be achieved in the absence of political reform, which the president has essentially frozen. Take, for example, grassroots polls first introduced by Deng in 1979 to enable peasants to elect village administrators. In the last few years of the Jiang era, experiments were undertaken in provinces ranging from Sichuan to Guangdong to elevate the elections from the level of villages to that of towns and rural townships. Such innovations petered out after 2002. There were no worker or farmer representatives within the CCP Central Committee endorsed at the Seventeenth CCP Congress. Instead, the Hu-Wen team is empowering the fast-expanding "new class" of businesspeople from both the state and private sectors. A few dozen former entrepreneurs have been appointed to party and government posts at the level of vice minister or above. Large-scale corruption, which often involves collusion between cadres and their business cronies, has remained unchecked. These developments have fed criticisms that senior cadres are fattening themselves via an "unholy alliance" with "red capitalists," while the disadvantaged sectors only qualify for handouts and other dispensation from on high in the noblesse oblige tradition.

Chinese president Hu Jintao (center), Beijing, March 13, 2005. *A former hydraulic engineer in northwest China, Hu Jintao earned attention as Communist Party secretary of Tibet in 1988, where he instituted martial law in response to anti-government protests by Tibetan monks. Hu eventually advanced to the national stage, becoming Communist Party chair, president of the People's Republic of China, and chair of the military, a three-fold position confirming his status as paramount leader of the country.* © CLARO CORTES IV/REUTERS/CORBIS

HU'S LASTING LEGACY: DIPLOMATIC ACHIEVEMENTS

It is perhaps in diplomacy that the achievements of President and Commander in Chief Hu are less in dispute. Apart from party affairs, Hu's portfolio in the Politburo Standing Committee has been foreign and military policies. He is, of course, also the head of the CCP Leading Group on Foreign Affairs as well as chairman of the Central Military Commission. Going much further than his predecessor Jiang, Hu has made significant revisions to Deng's early 1990s dictum on diplomacy: "Keep a low profile and never take the lead." Under President Hu's watch, Beijing's profile has been enhanced in regions as far away as Africa and Latin America. More significantly, the CCP leadership has taken a leap forward in its "policy of good neighborliness," that is, that China can best meet its ambitious economic targets in an environment of peace—particularly in the Asia-Pacific region. Relations with Russia, India, Japan, the Koreas, as well as the Association of Southeast Asian Nations, have been improved.

The rapid modernization of the People's Liberation Army's arsenal, however, has stoked fears about the "China threat." The United States, together with Japan, Australia, India, and Vietnam, has expressed anxieties about the fact that Chinese hard-power projection has gone far beyond the need for self-defense—or even the imperative of thwarting Taiwanese independence. The Hu leadership evidently believes that feats such as building China's own aircraft carriers and putting a Chinese astronaut on the moon before 2020 would promote national pride and cohesiveness. Yet to reassure China's neighbors—and defuse any "anti-China containment policy"—Hu and his Standing Committee colleagues must convince the world that the emerging quasi superpower is willing to abide by global norms ranging from democratic institutions to military transparency.

SEE ALSO *Taiwan, Republic of China: Politics since 1945.*

BIBLIOGRAPHY

Communiqué of the Sixth Plenum of the 16th CCP Central Committee, October 12, 2006. http://english.peopledaily.com.cn/200610/12/eng20061012_310923.html

Davis, Daniel K. *Hu Jintao.* New York: Chelsea House, 2007.

Fewsmith, Joseph. *China since Tiananmen: From Deng Xiaoping to Hu Jintao.* New York: Cambridge University Press, 2008.

Forney, Matthew, and Susan Jakes. Requiem for Reform? *Time,* January 23, 2005. http://www.time.com/time/magazine

Hu Jintao. Political Report to the Seventeenth CCP Congress, October, 2007. http://news.xinhuanet.com/english/2007-10/24/content_6938749.htm

Lam, Willy Wo-Lap. *Chinese Politics in the Hu Jintao Era: New Leaders, New Challenges.* Armonk, NY: Sharpe, 2006.

Willy Wo-Lap Lam

HU SHI

1891–1962

Hu Shi (Hu Shih) was twentieth-century China's most celebrated New Culture movement leader, and a public intellectual, scholar, educator, ambassador to the United States (1938–1942), president of the National Peking University (1946–1949), and president of Academia Sinica in Taiwan (1957–1962).

A new Hu Shi biography is long overdue. Since the mid-1990s a wealth of material on Hu Shi has been published, the most important of which are two sets of manuscripts and correspondence from the Hu Shi archives deposited at the Institute of Modern History, Chinese Academy of the Social Sciences, in Beijing: the forty-two-volume set published in 1994 and the forty-four-volume set published in 2003. This autobiographical archive assembled by Hu Shi is testimony to his lifelong effort to set the parameters for how his life would be constructed and appreciated, providing a master narrative for his future biographers.

Hu Shi was born in Shanghai in 1891. From 1895 to 1904 he received a traditional education in the family school in his native village in Jixi County, Anhui Province. In spring 1904 he went to Shanghai to seek a modern education. He was enrolled in three schools consecutively without receiving a diploma from any one of them. In June 1910 he went to Beijing to sit for the examination for the Boxer Indemnity scholarships to study in the United States. He was one of the seventy successful candidates who sailed that August. After a year at the College of Agriculture at Cornell University, Hu transferred to become a philosophy major at the university's College of Arts and Sciences. He was elected to Phi Beta Kappa in 1913 and received his B.A. degree the following year. Although he was accepted to Cornell's Ph.D. program in 1914, the university discontinued his fellowship a year later, so Hu applied and was admitted to Columbia University in fall 1915. It was at Columbia under the American philosopher John Dewey (1859–1952) that Hu completed his Ph.D. dissertation, "The Development of the Logical Method in Ancient China," in 1917.

Returning to China for a professorship at Peking University, Hu quickly became a celebrated cultural leader. His campaign to use the vernacular (*baihua*) rather than classical Chinese, which he had started to champion during the last years of his sojourn in the United States, was wildly successful. What he had reckoned to be a twenty-year, arduous campaign was accomplished by 1922 when the Ministry of Education decreed that all primary-school texts had to be written in the vernacular. In demonstrating that the vernacular had been the "living tongue" in China for one thousand years, Hu pioneered the use of modern methodology in the study of China's vernacular literature. Similarly, the first volume of his *Zhongguo zhexueshi dagang* (Outline of the history of Chinese philosophy), published in 1919 and based on his Ph.D. dissertation, revolutionized the study of Chinese philosophy. As he proceeded to work on the second volume of the work (which was never completed), Hu set in motion a new historicist approach to the study of Chan/Zen Buddhism.

Much has been said about John Dewey's influence on Hu Shi, who has been labeled a pragmatist and a liberal by both scholars and the reading public. It is all but forgotten that it was Hu himself who promoted these images about himself. Hu declared that it was Dewey who taught him how to think, and he asserted that Dewey's pragmatism was not only the guiding principle for his history of Chinese philosophy, but also manifested in his ideas for the literary revolution, as evidenced by the title of his vernacular poems, *Changshi ji* (A collection of experiments). Although a systematic analysis of the trajectory of Hu's lifelong intellectual endeavors is yet to be undertaken, new scholarship has shed light on how his history of Chinese philosophy is anything but a pragmatist study. Far from being informed by Dewey's pragmatist philosophy, his history of the Chinese philosophy was instead a product of his syncretic appropriations of positivistic approaches to history and of objective idealism, both of which he acquired while studying philosophy at Cornell University. Whereas Dewey acknowledged that there was a "permanent Hegelian deposit" in his thinking, Hu was silent on how idealism was a way station in his intellectual journey. It may have been that he came to rebel against this idealist phase of his education. In contradistinction to Dewey's "Hegelian deposit," what Hu had was a "permanent positivist deposit." A case can be made that while Hu claimed to have been converted to pragmatism, positivism constituted the core of his philosophical conviction throughout his life. Thus, even though pragmatism became his language, positivism remained the spirit of his philosophy.

Hu Shi had already achieved a measure of celebrity while he was a student in the United States. He was the winner of two essay contests: the Corson Browning Prize at Cornell University for his 1914 essay "A Defense of [Robert] Browning's Optimism," and the 1916 competition "Is There a Substitute for Force in International Relations?" sponsored by the American Association for International Conciliation. Contrary to the conventional characterization of Hu as chary of political activism, he was in fact a student activist in the United States. At Cornell he was president of the Cosmopolitan Club from 1913 to 1914. At the 1915 annual convention in Columbus, Ohio, not only did he craft his address at the plenary session as a critique of the faction that viewed pacifism as a political move to be shunned by the Cosmopolitan Clubs, but also he discharged his duty as the chair of the Committee on Resolutions by defeating the opposition and passing all the resolutions introduced by pacifists, whom he termed *progressives*. By the time he wrote his second award-winning essay, he had evolved from a "zealous pacifist" renouncing the use of force under any circumstance, to an advocate of an international organization to maintain peace through law, arbitration, and force. This belief in a mechanism for the maintenance of peace, with recourse to the use of force, remained the cornerstone of his political philosophy.

When Hu visited the United States again in 1927 he returned as a true celebrity; at every stop of his visit, he was hailed as the spokesperson and savant of new China. On the East Coast, Harvard and Columbia competed to host him as a speaker. Hu's stature in the United States peaked with his ambassadorship from 1938 to 1942. Although Hu's tenure as China's ambassador to the United States has yet to receive scholarly attention, the success with which he discharged his duties can be gleaned from the overwhelmingly favorable media reports and personal testimonies. After his ambassadorship, Hu moved to live in New York. In addition to conducting research and making plans to write sequels to his first volume of *Zhongguo zhexueshi dagang*, he lectured widely, including at Cornell, Harvard, and Columbia universities. In 1946 he returned to China to assume the presidency of the national Peking University. Two years later, as the civil war worsened, he was flown out of Peking by a plane sent in by Chiang Kaishek (Jiang Jieshi) on December 16, 1948. After a few months in Nanjing and Shanghai, he left China for the United States again.

Hu Shi's last sojourn in the United States lasted for ten years, until 1958, when he went to Taiwan to take up the presidency of the Academia Sinica. His twilight years in Taiwan paled in comparison with his earlier, heroic years, such as when in 1929 he took the rising Nationalist government to task for its illiberal doctrine and practice. It is in contrast to this fearless action of Hu's in the face of real threats of persecution that he has been criticized for his failure to stand up to Taiwan's Nationalist government when it closed down the *Free China* (*Ziyou zhongguo*) semimonthly in 1960 and arrested its publisher, Lei Zhen (1897–1979), on trumped-up charges. On February 24, 1962, during a reception for the newly elected academicians at the Academia Sinica, Hu suffered a heart attack and died.

SEE ALSO *Academia Sinica (Zhongyang Yanjiuyuan); Classical Scholarship and Intellectual Debates: Debates, 1900–1949; Liberalism; May Fourth Movement.*

BIBLIOGRAPHY

PRIMARY WORKS

Zhongguo zhexueshi dagang [Outline of the history of Chinese philosophy]. Shanghai: Shangwu Yinshuguan, 1919.

Changshi ji [A collection of experiments]. Shanghai: Yadong Tushuguan, 1920.

SECONDARY WORKS

Grieder, Jerome. *Hu Shih and the Chinese Renaissance: Liberalism in the Chinese Revolution, 1917–1937*. Cambridge, MA: Harvard University Press, 1970.

Yung-chen Chiang. Performing Masculinity and the Self: Love, Body, and Privacy in Hu Shi. *Journal for Asian Studies* 63, 2 (May 2004): 305–332.

Yung-chen Chiang

HU YAOBANG
1915–1989

Hu Yaobang was a leading Communist who emerged to national and international prominence as chairman and general secretary of the Communist Party in the 1980s. In his youth, he took part in the struggles against the Guomindang (GMD) and Japan and he organized for the Communist Youth League. After the establishment of the People's Republic of China in 1949, he occupied a number of important posts in the Communist Party before becoming chairman and then general secretary. Hu collaborated closely with China's intellectuals, but his liberal and reformist ideas led the old-guard leadership to purge him in 1987. His death in April 1989 was a catalyst for the student demonstrations that ended in repression in June.

REVOLUTIONARY YEARS

Hu Yaobang was born in Liuyang County in Hunan on November 20, 1915, to a peasant family with limited economic resources. His education was broken off during his second year of junior middle school when the school closed due to the instability caused by the confrontations between the Communists and the Nationalist Party. In 1927 Hu took part in the Autumn Harvest Uprising led by Mao Zedong. After its failure, Mao and his followers moved to the Jinggang Mountains in Jiangxi Province, where they set up the first Communist military base. In 1931 Hu also went to Jinggang, where he joined the Communist Youth League; at age eighteen he was admitted as a member of the Chinese Communist Party (CCP).

Hu later participated in the Long March, surviving serious injury and capture by the forces of Qinghai warlord Ma Bufang (1903–1975) to reach Yan'an in 1935. There he served as director of the Organization Department of the Chinese Communist Youth Central Bureau till its abolition after the formation of the Second United Front between the CCP and GMD in 1937.

In the spring of 1937, Mao Zedong established the Kangda, or Resistance University, in Yan'an. Hu Yaobang was in the first group of students. In early 1938, Hu was promoted to the position of assistant director of the Kangda political department. In this capacity, he was responsible for young intellectuals, and he succeeded in persuading a large number of students to join the CCP.

In 1941 Hu was sent to join the Eighteenth Army Corps, which was operating in the Taihang Mountains in northwestern China, where Deng Xiaoping occupied an important position. From then on, Deng and Hu worked together and forged a close friendship.

Following Japan's defeat in 1945, conflict between the GMD and the CCP resumed, and Hu was transferred to the north of China. In mid-1949, Hu was one of ten representatives of the China New Democratic Youth League who went to Beijing to participate in the first session of the Chinese People's Political Consultative Conference. Hu was present at the founding ceremony of the People's Republic of China on October 1, 1949.

BETWEEN MAO AND DENG

In 1949 Hu Yaobang was once again under the orders of Deng Xiaoping in the establishment of CCP authority in Sichuan and the southwest. When Deng was transferred to Beijing in 1952, he took Hu with him. In September of that year, Hu became first secretary of the New Democratic Youth League, for which he recruited new members, including Hu Qili, who were later to form the group of intellectuals who supported his proposals for political reform. Publications such as *Zhongguo qingnian* (China Youth) served to transmit views against ineffectual bureaucratic practices and the abuse of power.

In 1957 the New Democratic Youth League became the Chinese Youth League, and Hu Yaobang was designated its first secretary. He lent his support to the Hundred Flowers movement, disseminating Mao's policies as outlined in the speech "On the Correct Handling of Contradictions among the People." However, Hu resisted the subsequent Anti-Rightist campaign against those critical of the party. When the campaign was launched, Hu was in Moscow taking part in a meeting of youth organizations. He resisted criticizing his colleagues and tried to defend them as far as possible against punishments imposed by the CCP.

During the Cultural Revolution (1966–1969), Hu Yaobang was removed from his post in the Youth League. Between 1967 and 1972, he was subjected to humiliating treatment: for a time he was held in a "cow shed" and was afterward sent to the May 7 Cadre School. Toward the end of 1971 he fell ill and was allowed to return to Beijing. In 1972 and 1973, several party cadres were rehabilitated at the initiative of Zhou Enlai, among them Deng and Hu. By 1975 Hu was once more working alongside Deng. Hu was also appointed vice president of the Chinese Academy of Science, in which post he worked to restore the confidence of intellectuals and appointed specialists to positions of leadership in various departments. He placed emphasis on work and research rather than politics, and stressed the importance of acquiring technical equipment and know-how from developed countries.

REFORMER

The group of radicals headed by Jiang Qing criticized the work of Deng Xiaoping and Hu Yaobang. When Zhou Enlai died in January 1976, Deng and Hu once again became victims of political purges, though both were rehabilitated in May 1977. At the Eleventh Communist Party Congress of 1977, Hu was elected to the Central Committee and made deputy chairman of the Central Committee's Higher Party School. Deng and Hu launched a campaign against the "whatever" faction, consisting of Mao's successor, Hua Guofeng, and his supporters. Deng prevailed by late 1978, as he emphasized the need to "search for truth in facts" (*shishi qiushi*).

Hu Yaobang found support in his network of intellectuals, a group made up of Marxist theorists who had worked with him in the Youth League, those who suffered the ravages of the Cultural Revolution, and those involved in politics who demanded reforms to the Chinese political system. Among these were Yu Guangyuan, Wang Ruoshui, and Hu Qili, who drew up documents upholding the need to liberalize political life. Hu Yaobang coined the slogan "emancipation of thought" (*sixiang jiefang*) and played an important role in the rehabilitation of the victims of Maoist movements. At the Fifth Plenum of the Eleventh Party Congress in February 1980, Hu was promoted to a position on the Politburo Standing Committee.

Hu argued for review of policies regarding Tibet. In May 1980, he traveled to Lhasa, where he observed the severity of Tibet's poverty. Hu suggested the replacement of the party cadres in that region, along with major changes in policies toward minorities. Talks with the Dalai Lama were initiated after this visit.

SCAPEGOAT

After Hu was appointed general secretary of the CCP at the Twelfth Congress in 1982, he promoted economic and political reform. He always maintained that old cadres should make way for younger generations, and he advocated the institutionalization of clear rules so as to avoid the arbitrary use of political power. When student protests that began in Hefei in 1986 spread to other cities, the Politburo and Deng Xiaoping responded by condemning intellectuals who were inciting the students to mobilize. Hu Yaobang expressed greater tolerance toward the students, which led to his being forced to resign his post as general secretary of the CCP in January 1987. Upon his death on April 15, 1989, Tiananmen Square became the stage for new protests by students demanding an opening of the political arena. The protests reached unprecedented levels in terms of both their magnitude and the repression they elicited.

SEE ALSO *Hundred Flowers Campaign; Prodemocracy Movement (1989).*

BIBLIOGRAPHY

Goldman, Merle. Hu Yaobang's Intellectual Network and the Theory Conference of 1979. *China Quarterly* 126 (1991): 219–242.

Schoenhals, Michael. The 1978 Truth Criterion Controversy. *China Quarterly* 126 (1991): 243–268.

Wang Shushi. Hu Yaobang: New Chairman of the Chinese Communist Party. *Asian Survey* 9 (1982): 801–822.

Yang Zhongmei. *Hu Yao Bang: A Chinese Biography*. Ed. Timothy Cheek. Trans. William A. Wycoff. Armonk, NY: Sharpe, 1988.

Marisela Connelly

HUA GUOFENG
1921–2008

One of six Chinese Communists to hold the formal position of leader of the People's Republic of China (PRC) as of 2009, and (with Mao Zedong, Deng Xiaoping, Jiang Zemin, and Hu Jintao) one of five to actually exercise decisive authority, Hua Guofeng has been largely ignored in official histories and Western scholarship. This is a consequence of his limited time at the top: four and three-quarter years as formal leader (October 1976–July 1981) and about two and a quarter years when as party chairman he was the most authoritative figure (October 1976–December 1978). As such, Hua was a transitional figure between Mao Zedong, the founder of the PRC who bequeathed a badly damaged system at his death in September 1976, and Deng Xiaoping, who presided over the reform program that assumed coherent shape in the 1980s. But the nature of Hua's transitional leadership has been distorted by the traditional Communist approach of denigrating "failed" leaders, making Hua a quasi nonperson and overlooking his vital leadership role at a true turning point in the history of modern China. Unfortunately, Western accounts have by and large accepted the official narrative.

JUNIOR REVOLUTIONARY, 1938–1965

A native of Shanxi in north China, Hua joined the anti-Japanese resistance and then the Chinese Communist Party (CCP) in 1938. Thus he was a junior member of the party compared to those who joined before the Long March during the southern phase of the revolution. As a "1938 cadre," Hua was one of many new recruits who played their part in advancing the revolutionary cause, but with virtually no opportunity for heroic contributions and the accompanying prestige. Hua's junior status was appropriate for his subsequent march up the ranks of the party apparatus to a provincial-level post before the Cultural Revolution, but it was the fundamental political weakness that explains his demise at the very top of the CCP four decades later.

After joining the party, Hua served in various county-level posts in Shanxi, rising to a county party secretary by the late 1940s. In early 1949 he joined others of his status as "southbound cadres" who followed the victorious Communist armies and established CCP rule in the vast areas that were opened up. In Hua's case, his posting was in Hunan, Mao's native province. Hua advanced rapidly from county to prefecture level, and in 1956 to the province level, becoming by 1964 Hunan's de facto governor. In his rise Hua demonstrated a broad range of competencies and showed himself to be adept at leading Maoist movements, and he came to Mao's attention during agricultural cooperativization in 1955. Subsequently, presumably because of Hua's support when the Great Leap Forward came under attack, Mao personally nominated Hua as a provincial secretary in 1959. Mao's backing was also critical to later promotions, but it is important to note that although Hua faithfully implemented Mao's campaigns, he was pragmatic and avoided the worst excesses of those efforts.

RISE DURING THE DECADE OF THE CULTURAL REVOLUTION, 1966–1976

When Mao unleashed the Cultural Revolution in mid-1966, Hua came under rebel attack as part of the "red capitalist class" that ruled Hunan. Soon, however, he received Mao's endorsement as a "leftist who could not be knocked down" and assumed a leading role in the new provincial power structure, becoming top leader in 1970. Shortly thereafter, Hua was brought to Beijing by Mao and assigned key administrative roles in the State Council under Zhou Enlai, as well as crucial political tasks such as handling the aftermath of the Lin Biao affair. In 1973 he was elected to the Politburo. In January 1975, when a new State Council was organized with Deng Xiaoping as de facto premier given Zhou's terminal illness, Hua became one of three vice premiers responsible for daily work. In this role he fully supported Deng's consolidation program to rectify damage caused by the Cultural Revolution, earning the support of Deng and Zhou as a possible successor who could combat the radical Gang of Four in the future. Hua's significance was further indicated by his appointment as minister of public security in the 1975 State Council reorganization, although it is unclear how active he was in this role. By fall 1975, however, Mao began to criticize Deng, removing all of his power by the end of the year. When Zhou died in January 1976, to everyone's surprise Mao selected Hua as acting premier, and following the April Tiananmen incident, further promoted him to full premier and the unprecedented post of first CCP vice chairman, thus removing any doubt that Hua was the designated successor.

Although Mao presumably saw Hua as a balancing force between the radicals and party moderates and someone who ultimately would be loyal to the Cultural Revolution of which he was a beneficiary, Hua's instincts were pragmatic, reflected the ethos of the party establishment that had been badly damaged in 1966 to 1976, valued stability and economic growth, and respected party seniority. Until Mao's death Hua steered a course that, while fully affirming the sanctity of Mao's "line," prevented serious radical inroads despite ongoing criticism of Deng. After Mao died, Hua moved immediately to deal with the Gang of Four. Despite efforts in both Chinese and Western literature to paint Hua as an indecisive leader dependent on Marshal Ye Jianying (1897–1986) for backbone, Hua was the initiator, driving force, and decisive decision maker at all points in the process that culminated in the arrest of the Gang in early October 1976. Ye later observed that he could not "dare to even think of [such a plan]," whereas the 1981 historical resolution that shamelessly distorted Hua's leadership tacitly acknowledged his preeminent role by listing him first among those praised for "smashing the Gang of Four."

THE NEW HISTORICAL ERA, 1977–1978

Given Mao's designation and broad elite admiration for Hua's decisiveness in dealing with the Gang of Four, Hua received widespread support as the new party chairman. In the period from the arrest of the Gang to the Third Plenum at the end of 1978, Hua fully exercised the position's authority, albeit in a deliberately consultative manner and in circumstances where Deng Xiaoping played an important and dynamic role. This period has been widely misunderstood due to subsequent events and the official rewriting of history to glorify Deng and denigrate Hua. With Hua eased from power, the historical resolution depicted the two-plus years of his leadership as persisting in "leftist" errors that led China into a dead end, in contrast to the great progress under Deng since the Third Plenum. Subsequently, the Third Plenum has been regarded universally as the start of "reform and opening," even though that formulation was not used officially until 1985. In addition to this broad characterization, Hua has been depicted as a neo-Maoist supporting "whatever" policies the late chairman advocated, and as in conflict with Deng throughout the period, first attempting to prevent his return to work and then battling him on a variety of issues until finally losing out at the Third Plenum. In all respects these claims are misleading.

The basic problem facing Hua in fall 1976 was to link his and the party's leadership to the dead Mao, the only reliable source of regime legitimacy, while steadily moving away from Mao's Cultural Revolution policies. This led to dissonance between official rhetoric and actual policies, a dissonance increasingly apparent and controversial as the period continued. But the clear orientation of Hua's program for this "new historical era" was not "whateverist," but restoration of the methods and policies of the pre-1966 period. Tellingly, the first reference point was Deng's 1975 consolidation program, now implemented more widely and systematically. The key elements were restoring public order, creating "stability and unity" within the party by rooting out radicalism, and giving clear priority to economic development. In none of this was there any divergence from Deng. Indeed, on the central issue of economic development, Hua and Deng both pushed for excessive growth using Western technology—the so-called Western Great Leap in 1978—with Deng advocating even more reckless targets, but Hua was blamed at the time of his fall.

Although the period before the Third Plenum can be viewed as a more successful version of Deng's 1975 effort to get things back to normal, the depth of problems facing the CCP led to differing views on what went wrong and proposals for new approaches. Hua created a tolerant atmosphere in which such ideas could be raised, and at times he was the first Politburo leader to authorize innovative policies, such as special economic zones and experiments with household responsibility systems in agriculture. Though particularly cautious in the ideological sphere, Hua supported Hu Yaobang's effort to develop liberal ideas at the Central Party School, and he did not attempt to

Hua Guofeng, Chinese Premier and Chair of the Chinese Communist Party, Beijing, November 4, 1976. *Hua Guofeng assumed a leadership role in China during the period separating two of China's most significant leaders in the twentieth century, Mao Zedong and Deng Xiaoping. Recent scholars have begun to reexamine his previously underestimated role in stabilizing China after the death of Mao and the excesses of the Cultural Revolution.* © BETTMANN/CORBIS

obstruct the 1978 debate concerning "practice is the sole criterion of truth" (as he was alleged to have done); instead, he deliberately avoided stating his position so as not to curb the discussion. On this issue Hua was somewhat more circumspect than Deng, but differences in their approaches to handling the matter were relatively limited before the central work conference preceding the Third Plenum.

Although there was little to distinguish between Hua and Deng in policy outlook, there were profound differences in temperament and revolutionary status. On all evidence, Hua lacked a lust for power, whereas in Ye Jianying's observation, Deng loved to "monopolize power" (Xiong Lei 2008). Whether this inevitably led to Hua's demise is speculative, but his position was vulnerable due to the inversion of proper party status resulting from the Cultural Revolution that placed a "1938 cadre" above a true hero of the revolution. This disparity in revolutionary prestige could not be overcome by the artificial personality cult built to support Hua's public position, a cult producing skepticism and even derision within the elite. But this was perceived as necessary under the circumstances and was not primarily Hua's doing. Ye Jianying coined the phrase "wise leader" (*yingming lingxiu*), and even when Hua was under attack within the leadership in 1981 it was only claimed that he enjoyed the cult, not that he created it.

In any case, Hua did not attempt to obstruct Deng's return to work, and the two men seemingly worked cooperatively, albeit distantly, thereafter. Yet, though the elite as a whole accepted Hua as chairman, it looked to Deng as the leader with the experience to see the party through the post-Mao transition. When there was dissatisfaction, senior cadres tended to focus on Hua and other junior leaders, not Deng. Ironically, the most potent dissatisfaction concerned the "reversal of verdicts" on Cultural Revolution victims, a slow and complex process in which Hua achieved considerable results whereas Deng, a victim himself, made little contribution. This became a major issue at the critical pre–Third Plenum work conference, one of several issues that threw the meeting off stride. The result was that Hua's authority was damaged as the participants increasingly looked to Deng for leadership, and another old revolutionary of enormous prestige, Chen Yun, was elected to the Politburo Standing Committee. Deng was as much taken by surprise by these developments as Hua, but he seized on them to enhance his power.

DECLINE AND FALL, 1979–1981

The Third Plenum did not mark a sudden turning point to reform. Measures later treated as major reform policies began to emerge under Hua's leadership, and nothing like a systematic reform concept was advanced at the plenum. But Hua's position had been diminished, though there was no alteration of his duties and for at least the next half year he spoke authoritatively on various issues. In a process that remains unclear, power increasingly flowed to Deng and secondarily to Chen Yun as the rule of revolutionary seniority over formal party position took hold. By summer 1979 Deng had begun to clearly if indirectly criticize Hua, and by the start of 1980 Hua had authority in name only. By the end of 1980 he was forced to relinquish all power, with his replacement as chairman by Hu Yaobang formalized in mid-1981 at the same time the historical resolution passed a grossly unfair verdict on his leadership. Hua did not suffer the disgrace of fallen leaders in the Maoist era; he continued to receive respect from sections of the public and held Central Committee membership until 2002, yet officially he was ignored. Upon his death in 2008, however, the verdict on Hua was finally reversed, although as unobtrusively as possible in order to protect Deng's image. The official funeral notice not only acknowledged formally Hua's role as the decisive leader in "smashing the Gang of Four," but also praised Hua for restoring social order, reviving inner-party life, starting to reverse unjust verdicts, achieving relatively rapid economic recovery and development, and placing science, education, and culture on the correct path *before* the Third Plenum.

SEE ALSO *Deng Xiaoping; Lin Biao.*

BIBLIOGRAPHY

Baum, Richard. *Burying Mao: Chinese Politics in the Age of Deng Xiaoping.* Princeton, NJ: Princeton University Press, 1994.

Gardner, John. *Chinese Politics and the Succession to Mao.* London: Macmillan, 1982.

Garside, Roger. *Coming Alive! China after Mao.* New York: McGraw-Hill, 1981.

MacFarquhar, Roderick. The Succession to Mao and the End of Maoism, 1969–82. In *The Politics of China: The Eras of Mao and Deng*, 2nd ed., ed. Roderick MacFarquhar, 248–321. New York: Cambridge University Press, 1997.

Oksenberg, Michel, and Sai-cheung Yeung. Hua Kuo-feng's Pre–Cultural Revolution Hunan Years: The Making of a Political Generalist. *China Quarterly* 69 (March 1977): 3–53.

Teiwes, Frederick C. *Leadership, Legitimacy, and Conflict in China: From a Charismatic Mao to the Politics of Succession.* Armonk, NY: Sharpe, 1984.

Teiwes, Frederick C., and Warren Sun. *The End of the Maoist Era: Chinese Politics during the Twilight of the Cultural Revolution, 1972–1976.* Armonk, NY: Sharpe, 2007.

Ting Wang. *Chairman Hua: Leader of the Chinese Communists.* London: C. Hurst and Company, 1980.

Xiong Lei. September 10, 2008. Hua Guofeng he Ye Jianying. http://2newcenturynet.blogspot.com/2008/09/blog-post_2304.html.

Frederick C. Teiwes

HUANG BINHONG

1865–1955

Huang Binhong is recognized as one of the greatest Chinese landscape painters of the twentieth century. He was also an important art historian, editor, and connoisseur. His ancestral home was in Shexian, situated close to Huangshan (Yellow Mountain) in Anhui. This locale and the Xin'an school of artists whose paintings were inspired by Huangshan exerted a lifelong influence on Huang's art and scholarship.

Born into a family of merchants, scholar-officials, and artists, Huang Binhong began life as Huang Maozhi in Jinhua, eastern Zhejiang. From a young age he learned calligraphy and painting from his father Huang Dinghua (1829–1894), and later from Cheng Chongguang (1839–1896) and Zheng Shan (1809–1897). He spent his early years studying for the civil service examinations, and in 1886 he gained a Tribute Student degree and government stipend. That year he changed his name to Huang Zhi and married Hong Siguo (1868–1936). He adopted the style name (*zi*) *Pucun* and artist name (*hao*) *Binhong*. Over the course of his lifetime he used many other names, including Binhongsanren, Yuxiang, Honglu, and Hongsou.

Following the abolition of the examination system in 1905, Huang taught Chinese at the newly established Xin'an Secondary School. Like many of his contemporaries he became involved in anti-Manchu activities and was a founding member of the Huang Society (1906) and Southern Society (1909).

In 1909 Huang moved to Shanghai, where he lived for thirty years and married his second wife, Song Ruoying (1903–1970). In Shanghai he was a member of many art and literary societies, participated in exhibitions, and played an important role in the nascent publishing industry. Huang wrote for influential journals and newspapers including the *Journal of the National Essence* (*Guocui xuebao*), *True Record* (*Zhenxiang huabao*), and *Chinese Painting Monthly* (*Guohua yuekan*), and was a regular contributor to newspapers such as *The Eastern Times* (*Shibao*) and *Shenzhou Daily*. He worked at the Commercial Press (*Shangwu yinshuguan*) and edited and appraised art works for inclusion in early art magazines including *National Glories of Cathay* (*Shenzhou guoguang ji*), *Famous Chinese Paintings* (*Zhongguo minghua ji*), and *Art View* (*Yiguan*). Together with Deng Shi (1877–1951) he edited *A Collectanea of the Arts* (*Meishu congshu*), first published in 1911, and taught Chinese art history and theory at Ji'nan University, Changming Art College, Xinhua Art College, and Shanghai Art College.

During the period 1928 to 1935 Huang travelled to Guangxi, Guangdong, Hong Kong, and Sichuan to teach. During these years he made many sketches, and the experience of travel exerted an important influence on the development of his art. In 1935 Huang was invited by the Capital District Court (*Shoudu difang fayuan*) to examine the authenticity of paintings in the collection of the Palace Museum. The study of ancient works of art provided an important stimulus to his creative practice. At an invitation from Beiping National Art College (*Beiping Guoli yishu zhuanke xuexiao*) he moved to Beiping (Beijing) where he lived for close to ten years (1937–1948), much of it under Japanese occupation. Huang Binhong's first solo exhibition was held in Shanghai in 1943 to mark his eightieth birthday and was organized by Fou Lei (1908–1966), translator, man of letters, art critic, and friend.

In 1948 Huang moved to Hangzhou to take up a position as professor at the National Art Academy (*Guoli yishu zhuanke xuexiao*). Huang's art had strong links to the scholar-gentry tradition of painting, and after 1949 it was considered out of step with contemporary society. After a number of difficult years, he was invited to attend the Third Meeting of the First National Committee of the People's Political Consultative Conference in Beijing in 1951. In 1953, at the age of ninety *sui* (the traditional Chinese system of counting age; ninety *sui* is equivalent to eighty-eight Western years), he was named Outstanding Artist of the Chinese people and appointed to honorary positions including inaugural director of the Chinese Painting Research Center (*Zhongguo huihua yanjiusuo*). That year he underwent a cataract operation and in the final years of his life he created some of his most remarkable and acclaimed paintings, works characterized by their freedom and spontaneity.

In 1954 a large exhibition of Huang's art was organized by the East China Artists' Association. Huang Binhong died in Hangzhou on March 25, 1955 at the age of ninety-two *sui*. After his death Huang's paintings, archive,

Camellia, Narcissus, and Plum Blossoms ***by Huang Binhong, 1951.*** *In addition to his works featuring plants and flowers, Huang Binhong remains recognized as one of the most accomplished landscape painters of twentieth-century China. While much of his work fell out of favor during the Cultural Revolution, critics at the beginning of the twenty-first century have started to reassess his work, leading to a renewed appreciation of his contributions to Chinese art.* ARTHUR M. SACKLER GALLERY, SMITHSONIAN INSTITUTION, WASHINGTON, D.C.: GIFT OF ARTHUR M. SACKLER, S1987.243

and collection of historic works totalling more than 10,000 items were bequeathed to the state. This collection is housed in the Zhejiang Provincial Museum, Hangzhou. Huang Binhong's former residence at 32 Qixialing, near the West Lake is a memorial museum and open to the public.

Huang Binhong was a fine colorist and painter of flowers and plants, but he is best known for his landscape paintings using the accumulated ink technique (*ji mo fa*) in which repeated layers of ink create a feeling of solidity and substantiality. Many of his landscape paintings are consequently very dark. During the Cultural Revolution Huang's paintings were criticized as "black mountains and black water" and his grave was desecrated. In 2005 and 2006 the Zhejiang Provincial Museum mounted a series of exhibitions for the fiftieth anniversary of the artist's death, marking a reassessment of his art.

SEE ALSO *Art, National Essence Movement in; Chinese Painting* (guohua).

BIBLIOGRAPHY

PRIMARY WORKS

Huang Binhong. *Huang Binhong wenji* [The Collected writings of Huang Binhong]. 6 vols. Shanghai: Shanghai Shuhua Chubanshe, 1999.

Huang Binhong. *Huang Binhong quanji* [Complete works of Huang Binhong]. 10 vols. Jinan, China: Shandong Meishu Chubanshe; Hangzhou, China: Zhejiang Renmin Meishu Chubanshe, 2006.

SECONDARY WORKS

Chu, Christina, ed. *Homage to Tradition: Huang Binhong, 1865–1955.* Hong Kong: Urban Council of Hong Kong, 1995.

Kuo, Jason C. *Transforming Traditions in Modern Chinese Painting: Huang Binhong's Late Work.* New York: Peter Lang, 2004.

Wang Zhongxiu. *Huang Binhong nianpu* [Chronology of Huang Binhong]. Shanghai: Shanghai Shuhua Chubanshe, 2005.

Claire Roberts

HUIZHOU

The region of Huizhou, now known as Huangshan ("yellow mountain"), has an extraordinary history and a special place in China's long-term development. It is located in southern Anhui Province, some 360 kilometers from Shanghai. Huizhou borders Chizhou to the northwest, Xuancheng to the northeast, and the provinces of Jiangxi and Zhejiang to the southwest and southeast, respectively. The urban area of Huangshan was originally the city of Tunxi, which is now the name of one of Huangshan's seven county-level divisions. The Huangshan range, which consists of seventy-two peaks, forms the backdrop of this mountainous locale, celebrated for its panoramic scenery and great beauty. The well-known poet Li Bai (701–762) described Huangshan as a "series of high towers blooming like golden lotus flowers amidst red crags and rock columns." Nowadays, the Huangshan region is a major center of tourism.

Huizhou was first populated in the seventh century when migrants fleeing rebellions and disturbances elsewhere sought shelter in the area's myriad narrow valleys. Although land for growing grain or other foodstuffs was limited, the topography and soil conditions were ideal for tea production and forestry. The local economy thrived on the sale of tea, timber, and timber products (tung oil, ink, lacquer, paper), and by the Song dynasty (960–1279), Huizhou had achieved a reputation as a center of commercial agriculture. Local traders and merchants exported these goods along the abundant river ways that linked the prefecture to Hangzhou on the coast, and inland commercial centers such as the well-known porcelain-making center Jingdezhen (Jiangxi). These merchants relied on their families and lineages for capital, which they invested in enterprises all over the empire. By the Ming era (1368–1644), the most successful Huizhou merchants began to dominate the highly profitable salt trade. They also established pawnshops in many cities and forged commercial alliances as far away as southwest to northeast China.

Huizhou merchants were known to sojourn long distances, but they always considered Huizhou their home region, and returned there for New Year festivities and other important ritual celebrations, which reinforced kinship bonds. The large number of extant lineage ancestral halls is testimony of the centrality of family and lineage in the life of local people. Successful Huizhou merchants were also generous patrons of local educational institutions, endowing Confucian schools and academies. Many merchants themselves had the benefit of years of Confucian education behind them before turning to trade. No doubt Huizhou's reputation for the great numbers of its men with academic degrees may be attributed to the high regard local people had for learning.

The heyday of Huizhou traders was the eighteenth century when they became the unchallenged merchant princes of China. Living in towns in Jiangnan, or in the center of the salt trade in Yangzhou, or in the developing commercial region of Hankou (Hankow), the richest among them engaged in a lifestyle of connoisseurship, not unlike that of wealthy literati with whom they mingled easily. In these locations, they erected and maintained fine homes and gardens, collected art, rare books, and antiques, and entertained scholars and even members of the imperial family on a lavish scale. Huizhou merchants' extravagance also extended to establishing vast libraries and to the passionate pursuit of the arts. The fame of such painters as Hongren (1610–1664) or Shitao

(1630–1707) may be traced to the patronage these merchants first lent them.

By the early nineteenth century, the fortunes of many of these well-to-do families was reversed. Although it is tempting to attribute their demise to overindulgence, Huizhou merchants and their gentry relatives were just as much affected by the general administrative decay, economic deflation, and ecological crises of that ensuing age as other groups. By then, Huizhou was suffering the consequences of a sizeable population increase, which had decreased the land-man ratio significantly and which had caused extensive deforestation that exacerbated depleting timber and fuel stocks. The Qing government's inability to revitalize in the first decades of the nineteenth century sent rice prices soaring, and entire Huizhou families faced destitution. The local economy languished as Huizhou tea now competed with Fujian brands that relied on the burgeoning Guangzhou (Canton) trade network. Lineages were now less effective in organizing their assets, and by mid-century, Huizhou had settled into abject poverty.

An important legacy of Huizhou's more prosperous age is its architecture. Many of the massive whitewashed multistoried houses that the former status-conscious affluent inhabitants had once commissioned remain standing. These edifices also incorporated a whole range of local crafts from the hand-carved wood-latticed doors and windows to the colored-brick ornamentation. A number of these buildings are now marked for conservation and form part of a series of local heritage sites in Huangshan, including several villages in Yi county, that attract several million visitors every year. Interest in Huangshan was further bolstered recently when the Peabody Essex Museum in Salem, Massachusetts, imported and had re-erected a late Qing dynasty merchant's home, Yin Yu Tang, within its quarters.

SEE ALSO *Commercial Elite, 1800–1949; Tourism.*

BIBLIOGRAPHY

Berliner, Nancy. *Yin Yu Tang: The Architecture and Daily Life of a Chinese House.* Boston: Tuttle, 2003.

Finnane, Antonia. *Speaking of Yangzhou: A Chinese City, 1550–1850.* Cambridge, MA: Harvard University Asia Center, 2004.

Zurndorfer, Harriet T. *Change and Continuity in Chinese Local History: The Development of Hui-chou Prefecture, 800–1800.* Leiden, Netherlands: Brill, 1989.

Harriet Zurndorfer

HUMAN DEVELOPMENT REPORT ON CHINA

SEE *Economic Development: UNDP Human Development Report on China, 2005.*

HUMAN RIGHTS SINCE 1949

From 1949, human rights were regarded by the new Chinese leadership as a bourgeois idea having no place in China's development toward a socialist society. The constitutions the leadership adopted did not refer to human rights, though they all included protection for such substantive rights as equality before the law, the right to vote and stand for election, freedom of speech, religion, and assembly, and socioeconomic rights like the rights to work, social security, and education. Despite constitutional guarantees, no legal framework was created to protect these rights and freedoms. The country was ruled by the Communist Party mainly through ad hoc documents. Party control was achieved and maintained by political campaigns, where targets and methods shifted over time. Citizens were unable to predict what constituted a crime; nor did they have formal channels to claim their rights. Thus, law was used as a political tool following the model set up by the Soviet Union.

HUMAN RIGHTS UNDER THE CHINESE COMMUNIST PARTY

During the 1950s, the land reform and subsequent collectivization of agriculture abolished private farming, the Three-Antis and Five-Antis campaigns paved the way for nationalization of industry, and the Anti-Rightist movement silenced opposition from intellectuals. Forced collectivization during the Great Leap Forward from 1958 to 1961 caused a famine, which killed an estimated thirty million people. All these campaigns were backed by state-supported violence, as was the Cultural Revolution and its aftermath, which for a decade (1966–1976) partly broke down the party-state administration. The methods used in these campaigns included public humiliation and struggle meetings, exposing landlords, intellectuals, or party cadres to severe physical and psychological pain, execution without a trial, exile into remote border areas, placement in labor camps, or torture committed by fellow citizens. The perpetrators of the crimes were never brought to trial, except for nine people receiving long prison sentences in a public, but unfair, trial after the end of the Cultural Revolution.

Concerning protection of economic and social rights, citizens were effectively guaranteed work, health care, and education at a very low level, except during periods where political campaigns disrupted production and social relations. Urban citizens would be assigned a job in a work unit, and farmers were born into a production team. The work unit and the team were responsible for the social protection of their members. Freedom of choice concerning occupation and residence was abolished, and freedom of movement was restricted through a household-registration system, which made it virtually impossible to move around in the country.

Human rights advocate Harry Wu led by Chinese police, Beijing, 1995. *Since its founding, the People's Republic of China has earned international condemnation for the government's treatment of dissidents. Human rights activist Harry Wu has worked to expose China's treatment of political prisoners in state prisons, alleging the government allows torture, starvation, and the harvesting of organs from executed citizens.* AP IMAGES

PARTICIPATION IN THE INTERNATIONAL HUMAN RIGHTS SYSTEM

China became a member of the United Nations in 1971, and with this followed adherence to the United Nations Bill of Rights, including the human rights agenda. But only after adoption of the open-door policy in 1978 did China begin to participate in the international human rights system. The government ratified five of the six core human rights conventions, including the Convention on the Elimination of All Forms of Discrimination against Women in 1980, the Convention on the Elimination of All Forms of Racial Discrimination in 1981, the Convention against Torture and Other Cruel, Inhuman, or Degrading Treatment or Punishment in 1988, the Convention on the Rights of the Child in 1992, and the International Covenant on Economic, Social, and Cultural Rights in 2001. China signed the International Covenant on Civil and Political Rights in 1998 but had not ratified it as of 2008.

China has played an increasingly active role in the international human rights system and other international forums. Human rights became an accepted topic in academic debates, human rights centers were established at universities, and a substantial body of scholarly literature was published. An article promising that the state will respect and protect human rights was added to the constitution in 2004, helping Chinese scholars and activists in their advocacy work toward improving human rights protection. The constitutional rights and freedoms were codified in criminal, civil, and administrative law, as well as in specific laws protecting women and children, the elderly, inheritance rights, property, labor relations, and other areas. Thus, China has gradually been moving in the direction of a society ruled by law within the framework of a one-party autocracy.

INTERNATIONAL CRITICISM AFTER THE 1989 TIANANMEN INCIDENT

A turning point in China's image in the international human rights community came in 1989 with the crackdown on student demonstrations in Beijing. China's human rights record did not attract much international attention before that incident, but thereafter China became subject to harsh criticism by foreign governments

The wife and daughter (center) of civil rights activist Hu Jia after learning of his prison sentence, Beijing, April 3, 2008. *China's human rights record came under scrutiny upon the announcement that the International Olympic Committee selected Beijing as the host city for the 2008 Summer Olympics. Some activists accused the Chinese government of secluding certain citizens, such as the wife of imprisoned civil rights advocate Hu Jia, from inquisitive foreign journalists.* AP IMAGES

and human rights organizations. The criticism prompted publication of an ongoing series of official Chinese white papers defending the country's human rights situation. The papers support the universality of all human rights, but at the same time stress that protection of human rights is linked to historical conditions. The papers also prioritize economic and social rights over civil and political rights by stressing the rights to subsistence and development. Furthermore, in international relations, China insists on noninterference in internal affairs. The Chinese government signed the 1993 Bangkok Declaration, which was the result of an Asian preparatory meeting to the World Conference on Human Rights in Vienna that year. The Bangkok Declaration stresses the importance of national particularities.

The international criticism of China has been focused on several issues pertaining to civil and political rights. Journalists and alleged dissidents are receiving harsh prison sentences for exercising their rights to freedom of speech or assembly. Critics of the government have been charged under articles in the Penal Code on so-called crimes of counterrevolution, and after 1997 under articles on crimes endangering national security or disturbing public order. The use of the death penalty has reached excessive proportions, though the exact number of executions each year is not known. Capital punishment is mainly given for violent crimes, corruption, and drug dealing. Torture is reported to be widespread in pretrial detention, reeducation-through-labor camps, and police stations (UN Economic and Social Council 2006). In addition, the guarantees to a fair trail are weak because China's courts are still not independent; judges are in many places undereducated, and they are hired and paid by the local government, through which the party can exert its influence. The police can sentence people to up to four years in a labor camp under a system of administrative detention known as reform-through-education. The enjoyment of religious freedom, especially for minorities like Tibetans and Uygurs, is restricted, and claims for self-rule for Tibet and Xinjiang are violently suppressed by the central government. Migrants are subject to dangerous working conditions and delayed payment, and they do not enjoy the same rights as urban citizens. Furthermore, the rights of assembly, demonstration, and association are not well protected.

Less international attention has been given to other potential violations related to economic and social rights, such as the breakdown of public health-care and education services. Both health and education have to a large extent been commercialized, and other social services like pensions, unemployment benefits, and occupational-injury insurance have also not been sufficiently guaranteed.

Measures have been taken by the government to solve some of the problems described above, or at least to accommodate critics. Institutional reform has bestowed the country's Supreme Court with the mandate to review all death sentences passed in the High Courts, a measure that should bring down the number of executions. On torture, the Criminal Procedure Law was under revision to strengthen protection of detainees; proposed reforms included the role of defense council, the admission of evidence, and conditions for bail. On social security, the government has allocated funds for the establishment of a minimum living standard, though this protection is far from sufficient. The central government has also issued circulars and directives ordering localities to protect the rights of migrant workers.

Since 1979, civil and political rights in China have improved gradually, though they still do not live up to state obligations under the various human rights treaties. Economic and social rights are also under pressure as a consequence of marketization and the breakdown of the work unit and commune system.

SEE ALSO *Communist Party; Cultural Revolution, 1966–1969; Dissidents; Education through Labor, Reform through Labor; Hundred Flowers Campaign; Individual and the State, 1800–1949; Law since 1949.*

BIBLIOGRAPHY

Angle, Stephen C. *Human Rights and Chinese Thought: A Cross-Cultural Inquiry.* Cambridge, U.K.: Cambridge University Press, 2002.

Becker, Jasper. *Hungry Ghosts: China's Secret Famine.* London: Murray, 1996.

Chen Jianfu. *Chinese Law: Context and Transformation.* Leiden, Netherlands: Martinus Nijhoff, 2008.

Jacobsen, Michael, and Ole Bruun. *Human Rights and Asian Values: Contesting National Identities and Cultural Representations in Asia.* Richmond, U.K.: Curzon, 2000.

Kent, Ann. *Beyond Compliance: China, International Organizations, and Global Security.* Stanford, CA: Stanford University Press, 2007.

Svensson, Marina. *The Chinese Conception of Human Rights: The Debate on Human Rights in China, 1898–1949.* Lund, Sweden: Lund University, 1996.

Thelle, Hatla. *Better to Rely on Ourselves: Changing Social Rights in Urban China Since 1979.* Copenhagen: NIAS Press, 2004.

United Nations Economic and Social Council: Commission on Human Rights. *Civil and Political Rights, including the Question of Torture and Detention: Report of Special Rapporteur on Torture and other Cruel, Inhuman, and Degrading Treatment or Punishment, Manfred Nowak, Mission to China.* 2006.

Hatla Thelle

HUNAN AND HUBEI

Hunan and Hubei (also Hupei, Hupeh) are neighboring inland provinces in central south China. They are major economic and political entities; each has a land area and a population comparable to that of a medium-sized European country.

Hubei and Hunan have a close interrelationship. They were part of the common cultural area of ancient Chinese civilization, and from the Tang dynasty (618–907) their prosperous agricultures supplied the capital with food grain and more specialized products. Under the Ming dynasty (1368–1644) Hubei and Hunan formed the single province of Huguang with the major commercial city of Hankou (today part of Wuhan) as the capital. Even under the Qing dynasty (1644–1912) the provinces were ruled by a single governor general. Wuhan remains the major commercial city of the whole region.

Much of Hunan's trade moves from its own river system via Dongting Lake onto the Yangzi, and is transshipped for further distribution at Wuhan. The provinces are united by a common need for water and flood control. Dongting hu, the lake from which Hunan and Hubei take their names, lies in the north of Hunan near the border with Hubei. Several great rivers, the Xiang, Zi, Yuan, and Li, flow into the lake and are linked by it to the Yangzi River (Chang Jiang). Rich alluvial plains surround these rivers, but four-fifths of Hunan's land area is mountainous. Its area is 210,500 square kilometers (81,250 square miles). The province has a temperate subtropical climate with considerable precipitation. January temperatures average 4°C to 8°C; July temperatures average 27°C to 30°C. Average annual rainfall is 1,200 to 1,700 millimeters. Changsha, the provincial capital, is in the northeast of the province.

The Yangzi River flows from west to east through Hubei. The famous Three Gorges Dam Project is on the Yangzi in Hubei Province, upstream from Yichang City. Most of the province is a great, low-lying plain, broken up by many lakes. In west Hubei there are thickly forested mountains. The area of Hubei is 187,500 square kilometers (72,380 square miles). It has a subtropical monsoon climate with a humid and hot summer and a dry winter and strong sunlight in autumn. Average

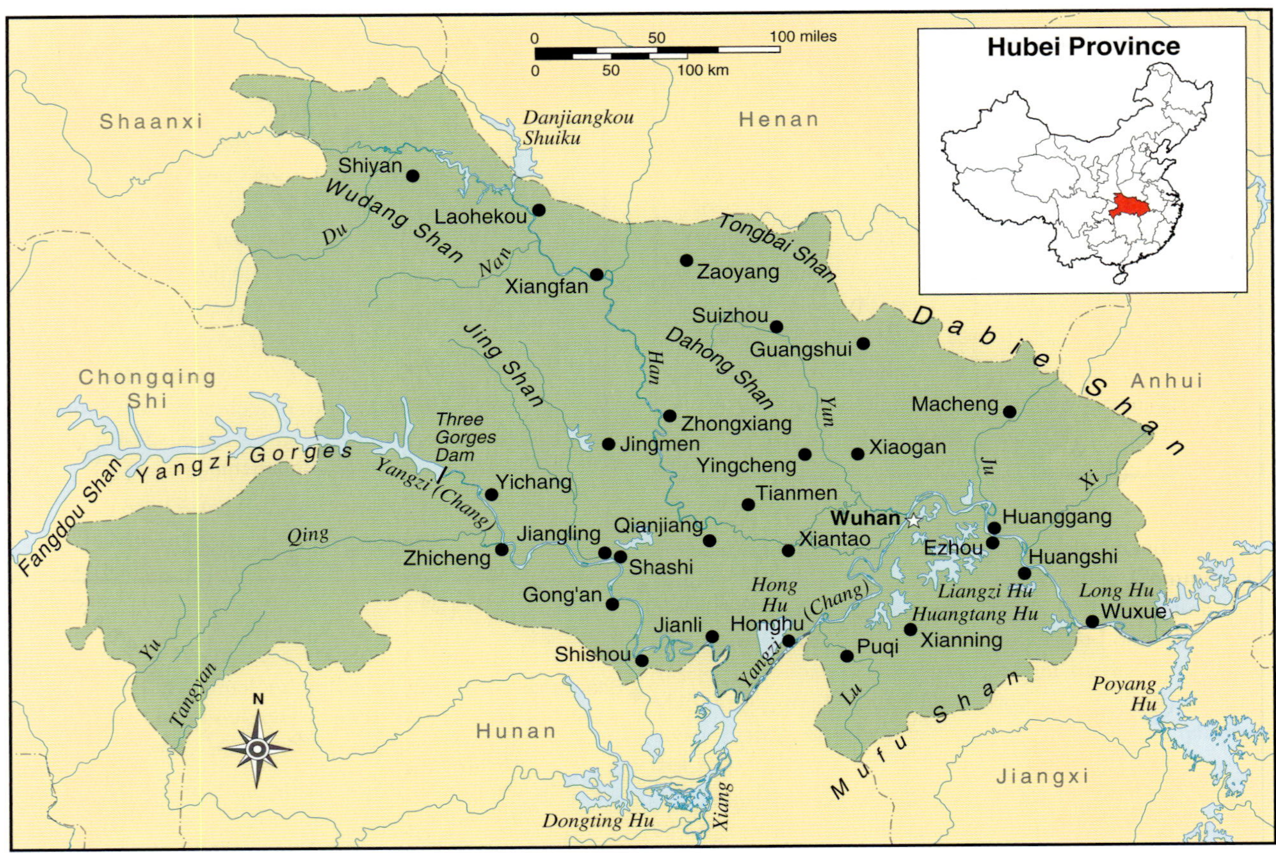

Hubei's warm climate, rich soils, and good rainfall have long made it a productive agricultural area. However, as it is comparatively industrialized, the primary sector provided only 15.5 percent of GDP in 2000 and 48 percent of total employment. Less than half the arable area is sown with cereals, including rice, wheat, corn, and potatoes. Oil-bearing crops, primarily rape and sesame, are important. Other major crops include soybeans, vegetables, sugar, cotton, tobacco, and tea. Silk cocoons, lotus roots, silver fungus, and various fruits are also produced. Forestry products include tung oil, tea oil, and medicinal plants. Hubei is a major producer of livestock and honey. Its rivers and lakes provide fish and shellfish—mostly now farmed—and cultivated pearls are a valuable source of income.

Hubei's industrialization is clearly reflected in economic statistics. In 2000 the industrial sector contributed almost half of GDP but only 18.3 percent of employment. Important manufactures are motor vehicles and chemicals. Trade and transport through Hubei have been stimulated by the improvement of its road, rail, and waterway networks, by the construction of three bridges across the Yangzi in 1957, 1995, and 2000, and by air links with the rest of China. The Three Gorges Dam at Sandouping on the Yangzi in Hubei is the largest water conservation project in the world. If all goes to plan, it will greatly boost Hubei's output of electricity and will help to control the flooding that has plagued the province on many occasions in the past. The construction of the dam, which involved the permanent evacuation of two million people from their homes and the flooding of a historic area of great beauty, was met with opposition from traditionalists and environmentalists. There are still fears that a breach of the dam would result in disastrous flooding.

When economic indicators are considered, Hunan and Hubei occupy a middle place among Chinese provinces. Neither province has matched the extraordinary growth in prosperity of the coastal regions since the beginning of the economic reforms. Neither has attracted high rates of foreign direct investment, although Hubei has received considerable state investment. Although less wealthy than the coastal provinces, by the standards of western and central provinces they are well off on most counts. For example, for per capita gross domestic product, Hunan ranks lower middle among provinces, and Hubei upper middle. Both are ranked as "upper middle" on the human development index, and both score better than the national average for average life

Young girls watching the taping of a television show in Changsha, Hunan province, June 21, 2006. *Economic growth in the provinces of Hunan and Hubei has enjoyed steady progress at the turn of the twenty-first century, with Hebei housing a large industrial sector complementing Hunan's primarily agricultural output.* GUANG NIU/GETTY IMAGES

expectancy. Both have below average birth rates. Hunan's literacy rate is slightly better than the national average and Hubei's slightly worse. Hubei has a particularly noteworthy number of good universities and research institutes, and both provinces have excellent rates of higher education participation, which may be expected to stimulate future economic growth.

SEE ALSO *Changsha; Taiping Uprising; Wuhan; Zeng Guofan.*

BIBLIOGRAPHY

Bowland-Crewe, Tara, and David Lea, eds. *The Territories of the People's Republic of China.* London: Europa Publications, 2002.

Esherick, Joseph W. *Reform and Revolution in China: The 1911 Revolution in Hunan and Hubei, 1897–1913.* Berkeley: University of California Press, 1976.

State Statistical Bureau of China. China Statistical Yearbooks. Beijing: State Statistical Publishing House, 2001–2005.

United Nations Development Programme and the China and China Development Research Foundation. *China Human Development Report, 2005: Development with Equity.* Beijing: China Translation and Publishing, 2005.

Delia Davin

HUNDRED DAYS' REFORM

The term *Hundred Days' Reform* refers to the events that occurred between June 11 and September 21, 1898, when the Guangxu emperor (1871–1908) implemented policies to revitalize the Qing Empire's administrative, cultural, economic, and military institutions. Ever since China's defeat in the Sino-Japanese War (1894–1895), especially after the onset of the foreign powers' scramble for concessions in late 1897, Guangxu had been trying to address the country's weaknesses through reform. Plans were afoot in early 1898, for instance, to revamp educational practices by establishing an imperial college in Beijing and schools in the provinces, to test military-degree candidates on their skills with modern weapons rather than their memorization of the military classics, and to recruit government officials through special examinations of practical studies (*jingji teke*). Now, as the June 11 edict explained, a centrally orchestrated effort would replace the isolated projects to promote nationwide change.

In the several months that followed, Guangxu announced an impressive array of corrective and innovative measures, such as those to substitute the long-criticized, formulaic "eight-legged essay" in the civil service examinations with the free-style treatise; to facilitate long-term economic development with a new Ministry of Agriculture, Industry, and Commerce; to drill and outfit troops by Western methods; to improve administrative efficiency by streamlining the court bureaucracy and simplifying government regulations; to build a fleet of thirty-four warships over a four-year period with earmarked contributions from the provinces; and to inaugurate, at long last, the Imperial College (Jingshi Daxuetang). These measures were consistent not only with the throne's post-1895 stance on reform, but also with the still earlier Qing elite discourse of change since the 1860s. Highly suggestive of the continuity was Guangxu's decisions during the Hundred Days to have Feng Guifen's *Jiaobinlu kangyi* (Straightforward discussion from the Jiaobin Studio) and Zhang Zhidong's *Quanxue pian* (Exhortation to study) reprinted and distributed to government officials for discussion. Both authors argued, in the 1860s and 1890s, respectively, for the adoption of Western-inspired reforms without prejudice to the sages' moral teachings—a bicultural strategy known in late-Qing parlance as "self-strengthening" (*ziqiang*) or "foreign matters" (*yangwu*). As such, the 1898 reforms were conceptually familiar and moderate.

It was, therefore, not so much the radicalism of Guangxu's policies that alienated support as his draconian style in pursuing change. On various occasions, he revised the wording of edict drafts to convey his uncompromising resolve. In pointed language, he rebuked prominent officials like governors-general Liu Kunyi (1830–1902) and Tan Zhonglin (1822–1905) for their evasive attitude to the court's reform directives. His decision to eliminate about five thousand low-level court positions was promulgated without plans for reassignment, leaving those affected by it disgruntled. Enraged by the Board of Rites' attempt to block a subordinate's memorial from reaching him, Guangxu had all six of its ministers cashiered, peremptorily crippling this branch of the court administration. Personal imprints like these hardly endeared Guangxu's reform projects to officials, high and low, whose loyalty and cooperation he needed for success.

To augment the sources of reform input, Guangxu allowed low-ranking officials and commoners, hitherto denied the privilege, to memorialize him. He seemed favorably disposed toward the proposals submitted by the scholar-official Kang Youwei, who, along with his students like Liang Qichao and their associates at court, organized the most energetic attempt to influence Guangxu's deliberations. Memorials drafted by Kang's group and submitted by others under their own names were among the background factors that inspired the June 11 edict. Kang's activism has since given rise to the view that he masterminded the 1898 reforms. As much as Guangxu valued Kang's intellectual and literary abilities and formulated some of his policies on Kang's recommendations, he never relied on Kang alone; nor did he ever appoint him to any important position. The Kang-centered perspective on the Hundred Days (e.g., Tang Zhijun 1984) thus seeks, ill-advisedly, to interpret high-court politics and policies in terms of the aspirations and intrigues, not to mention propaganda, of peripheral figures in the imperial structure.

Kang's efforts to overcome his political constraints, on the other hand, generated scandals that gave Guangxu's critics pretext for action. Subsequently, the censor Yang Chongyi appealed directly to the empress-dowager Cixi for her intervention. Cixi's so-called coup, which ended the Hundred Days, led to the September 21 proclamation that Guangxu had requested her tutelage in government. Guangxu survived this turn of events in both his imperial role and private life under Cixi's scrutiny. Five court officials and Kang's brother, Guangren (1867–1898), were summarily executed for collusion with Kang, while Kang and Liang managed to elude their captors and fled overseas. Many of Guangxu's earlier policies were now suspended or cancelled, but they surfaced again when the Qing court embraced reform as dynastic policy after the Boxer trouble (1900).

SEE ALSO *Cixi, Empress Dowager; Emperors, 1800–1912; Kang Youwei; Liang Qichao; Zhang Zhidong.*

BIBLIOGRAPHY

Kwong, Luke S. K. (Kuang Zhaojiang). *A Mosaic of the Hundred Days: Personalities, Politics, and Ideas of 1898.* Cambridge, MA: Council on East Asian Studies, Harvard University, 1984.

Mao Haijian. *Wuxu bianfa shishi kao* [Research on the 1898 reform]. Beijing: Sanlian Shudian, 2005.

Tang Zhijun. *Wuxu bianfa shi* [History of the 1898 reform]. Beijing: Renmin Chubanshe, 1984.

Luke S. K. Kwong (Kuang Zhaojiang)

HUNDRED FLOWERS CAMPAIGN

The Hundred Flowers campaign (1956–1957) was an intellectual movement for political, ideological, and cultural freedom in China. It was initiated by the Chinese Communist Party (CCP) and derived its name from the CCP slogans "Let a hundred flowers bloom together" and "Let a hundred schools of thought contend." Taking advice from his secretary Chen Boda (1904–1989), Mao Zedong first used these slogans to summarize party policy on intellectual life in a speech delivered at a Politburo meeting on April 28, 1956.

The task of elaborating the policy was left to Lu Dingyi (1906–1996), director of the Propaganda Department of the CCP Central Committee. According to Lu, the Hundred Flowers policy meant "freedom of independent thinking, of debate, freedom of creative work; freedom to criticize and freedom to express, maintain and reserve one's opinions on questions of art, literature or scientific research" (Lu 1956).

FACTORS CONTRIBUTING TO THE POLICY

The year 1956 marked the victory of the three-year programs of "socialist transformation," and there was an urgent need to mobilize expertise for economic and cultural development. Whereas the Marxist ideal of socialism stipulated a complete subordination of the state to society, the CCP, like its counterparts in the Soviet Union and elsewhere, took socialism to mean state domination over society, including state control over the means of production. By 1956 the CCP leadership believed that the remaining task for the party-state was rapid socioeconomic development. The rationale behind and the measures to be used to mobilize the intelligentsia were articulated by Zhou Enlai (1898–1976) at a conference organized by the Central Committee in January 1956 to deal with the issue. Zhou announced that "the overwhelming majority of intellectuals have become government workers in the cause of socialism and are already part of the working class," a status never before accorded by the party (Zhou 1984, p.162).

The Hundred Flowers policy indicated the confidence of Mao and the CCP leadership. In their assessment of the situation, the Communist regime had been fully consolidated, and all people, including intellectuals, had been organized "as a force in the service of socialism." In addition, developments in international communism in 1956, notably Nikita Khrushchev's (1894–1971) denunciation of Joseph Stalin (1879–1953) and uprisings in Poland and Hungary, prompted the CCP leadership to improve the relationship of the party and the people. The policy also reflected Mao's personal ambition to become the supreme leader of the international communist movement. The Hundred Flowers policy was part of Mao's experiment in finding a better way to build socialism. It was, in particular, seen as the solution to "contradictions among the people" that arose under socialism.

RELUCTANCE OF THE INTELLECTUALS

In response, China's scholars seized the opportunity to broaden the scope of their research. Most intellectuals initially remained silent on political issues, however. Their reluctance was understandable, given that the brutal political and ideological campaigns that arose for six years after 1949 had led to the deaths, imprisonment, and humiliation of millions. To reassure them, Mao delivered a speech on February 27, 1957, that confirmed the nonantagonistic nature of contradictions among the people—between intellectuals and the party in particular. In Mao's assessment, large-scale class struggle had concluded, and the main task facing the party was to consolidate the system by adjusting imbalances and easing tensions in the economy and society

Another measure was to involve non-Communist politicians and intellectuals in a CCP "open-door rectification" campaign. The campaign was launched on April 27, with the objective of combating the "three evils" of subjectivism, bureaucratism, and sectarianism. On May 4, the Central Committee issued a directive drafted by Mao inviting non-Communist personnel in all walks of life to participate in the rectification. The committee organized a series of forums for the leaders of "democratic parties" and other nonparty people to voice their concerns, with their speeches published in major newspapers. CCP committees at other levels, those at universities in particular, organized similar forums. These forums led to a genuine "blooming and contending" that was shared by students through campus speeches and posters.

BLOOMING AND CONTENDING

Following the instructions of Mao and the CCP leadership, the "blooming and contending" focused on subjectivism (including doctrinarism or dogmatism), bureaucratism, and sectarianism, three pronounced evils of the party and its cadres. Critiques on subjectivism were directed at the behavior of party officials in setting unrealistic economic development targets, in copying the Soviet Union in a doctrinaire manner, and in making decisions based on outdated dogmas rather than professional expertise or practical knowledge. Examples of bureaucratism included excessive bureaucratic control on literature, art, education, and academic research; abuses of power by party organs and members; the privileges of the Communist bureaucracy at work and in life; and substitution of the party for the government (*yi dang dai zheng*). The attacks on sectarianism pointed mainly to the fact that, due to the domination of the CCP as a whole and the CCP committee at each work unit, posts held by non-Communist personnel were merely nominal and the "democratic parties" were unable to function as political parties; a "wall" had been created between the CCP and the rest of the population, including the democratic parties.

A few critics went a step further to trace the root causes of the problems and propose remedies. For them, the problems' source was the monopoly of political power by the CCP, which had turned China into a "country belonging to the party" (*dang tianxia*), as suggested by Chu Anping, editor in chief of *Guangming Daily*. These critics saw checks and balances on power, as well as the rule of law, as the solution. Echoing calls by many colleagues for the strengthening of the rule of law and an end to punishment in retaliation for criticism, Luo Longji, vice president of the Democratic League, proposed a "rehabilitation committee" composed of both CCP members and non-Communists to deal with past wrongs and future grievances.

THE ANTI-RIGHTIST MOVEMENT

Unfortunately, the "blooming and contending" were allowed to continue for only one month, and the solicited criticisms were met with severe punishment. On June 8, 1957, Mao and the party launched the anti-rightist movement. The movement lasted until 1959 and claimed about 550,000 "rightists" who were accused of antisocialism and of being antiparty, with work units allocated quotas for purges. Leaders of the "democratic parties" and other non-Communist intellectuals were the primary targets, but outspoken CCP officials were also purged. The rightists were denounced at public meetings and in newspapers, exiled to remote areas for reform through labor, demoted, dismissed, or imprisoned.

Mao himself made the decision to implement the policy U-turn. His May 15, 1957, article "Things Are Just Beginning to Change" designated "bourgeois rightists" for counterattack, and indicated that Mao had realized that the campaign had not served the purpose of strengthening either his or the party's power. On May 16 the Central Committee issued a directive drafted by Mao to make arrangements for "enemies to fully expose themselves," thus creating a trap for further "blooming and contending."

REVERSAL OF THE VERDICTS

The rightists were neither guilty of being antiparty nor of antisocialism as alleged by the party. Instead of opposing socialism, the rightists criticized the party for deviating from its socialist ideal of a free, democratic, and equal society and turning the Communist cadres into a highly privileged ruling class. Even when the most outspoken critics expressed their objection to the party's monopoly on power, they were always careful to point out that they accepted the general leadership of the party. Their criticism of the party and its cadres was actually much milder than the Maoist discourse on degeneration of the Communist bureaucracy. The key to the confrontation between the rightists and the party was the rightists' humanistic and liberal values and their interest in individual freedom and democratic rights. The anti-rightist movement carried out under the administrative direction of the then Party's General Secretary Deng Xiaoping (1904–1997) was nothing but the function of a totalitarian regime that would not tolerate political or cultural pluralism.

Some rightists were rehabilitated during the early 1960s, but most of them remained outcasts until the end of the 1970s, when more than 99 percent were granted a "reversal of the verdict" (*pingfan*). Some rehabilitated rightists, including Premier Zhu Rongji and Minister of Culture Wang Meng, were promoted to important posts in the 1980s and 1990s. However, in order to prove that the anti-rightist movement was correct and necessary at the time and the only mistake was to "broaden the scope," the verdicts on six well-known rightists—Zhang Bojun, Luo Longji, Chu Anping, Peng Wenying, Chen Bingren, and Lin Xiling—were allowed to stand.

Since the 1980s, some former rightists and their supporters, who believe the movement was a national disaster, have attempted to commemorate the anti-rightist movement. In 1986 senior rightists tried to organize a symposium in Beijing commemorating the thirtieth anniversary of the movement, but their effort was blocked by the party-state. In June 2007 former rightists and their supporters organized international conferences in Los Angeles and Princeton. Those unable to make the trip to the United States gathered in Beijing, Chengdu, Hong Kong, and elsewhere for the anniversary.

SEE ALSO *Chinese Marxism: Mass Movements; Classical Scholarship and Intellectual Debates: Debates since 1949; Mao Zedong.*

BIBLIOGRAPHY

Das, Naranarayan. *China's Hundred Weeds: A Study of the Anti-Rightist Campaign in China.* Calcutta: Bagchi, 1979.

Lu Dingyi. Baihua qifang, baijia zhengming [Let a hundred flowers bloom together, let a hundred schools of thought contend]. *People's Daily*, 13 June 1956, p. 2.

MacFarquhar, Roderick. *The Origins of Cultural Revolution.* Vol. 1: *Contradictions among the People, 1956–1967.* London: Oxford University Press, 1974.

Teiwes, Frederick. *Politics and Purges in China: Rectification and the Decline of Party Norms, 1950–1965.* 2nd ed. Armonk, NY: Sharpe, 1993.

Zhou Enlai. *Zhou Enlai xuanji* [Selections of Zhou Enlai]. Beijing: People's Press, 1984.

Zhu Zheng. *1957 Nian de xiaji: Cong baijia zhengming dao liangjia zhengming* (Summer 1957: From the contending among a hundred schools to the contending between two schools). Zhengzhou: Henan People's Press, 1998.

Feng Chongyi

HUTONG

A *hutong* is a narrow street that represented the "soul" of residential life in Beijing from the Yuan dynasty (1279–1368) until the mid-1990s. Most sources suggest that the word was derived from the Mongolian for "water well." Later it came to represent the community that lived near the well. When Kublai Khan (1215–1294) built his new

A snow-covered hutong in Beijing, February 24, 2005. *In the 1990s, Beijing government officials began dismantling many traditional hutongs, small residential streets housing much of the city's population. While many Chinese have enjoyed improved living conditions in the new apartments that replaced the overcrowded hutongs, some citizens have recognized the historic loss of the neighborhoods and pressed for their conservation.* MARKUS EICHENBERGER/GETTY IMAGES

imperial capital city (1272), *hutong* was the term used for the smallest road unit—measuring six horse's steps (about nine meters) in width. The layout was a "chessboard" pattern running east to west. This directional orientation was favored so that *siheyuan* (residential "quadrangles" containing interior courtyards) could be built facing south to receive the winter sun. Residents were forbidden to obstruct passage to the wells, and the term *hutong* came to include very narrow lanes between homes. Some *hutongs* remaining today are less than one meter wide.

Throughout the Yuan, Ming (1368–1644), and Qing (1644–1912) dynasties, a *hutong* way of life developed, focusing on extended families living in a single *siheyuan.* Many *hutongs* had colorful names—examples include Huoyaoju (Ammunition Bureau) Hutong and Nanqian-chuan (South Coin Rope) Hutong—reminders of the city's rich cultural history. Life in feudal Beijing revolved around the imperial family, however, and vernacular features such as *hutong* and *siheyuan* were not considered important. This continued into the socialist era. After being nationalized, until the late 1980s, housing was treated as a welfare good, controlled by work units that let rooms to employees for a very nominal rent. The overcrowded conditions that developed meant residence in the *hutongs* represented poverty, while residence in a new apartment represented progress.

The 1990s witnessed the greatest changes to Beijing's layout since Kublai Khan's time. The passage of the Old and Dilapidated Housing Program by the city government, along with other legislation, created a real-estate market. Local government officials acted in concert with quasi-public-sector real estate development companies to construct large commercial and apartment complexes. Many *hutong* neighborhoods were entirely demolished. Hundreds of thousands of residents were relocated. Yet the severity of overcrowding was such that this draconian solution raised little civil unrest among the broader public.

Proponents of conservation were initially greatly outnumbered, though the city government did engage in housing experiments during the 1980s as a way to keep alive the spirit of *hutong* neighborhoods. In the early 1990s, *hutong* tourism became an instant hit with international tourists. The activity featured a pedicab ride through the *hutongs*, particularly in Shichahai district, and included a visit to a resident's home. This attention from foreigners did not go unnoticed and helped elevate *hutongs'* heritage value in the eyes of many. As demolition continued and rarity increased, buying and renovating a siheyuan in a *hutong* neighborhood became chic and prices soared.

In 2002 Beijing passed a law establishing twenty-five conservation zones throughout the city; this has since been increased to thirty-three zones. Many *hutong* neighborhoods were included. The period of demolition is ending for the "Old City." The *hutong* spirit of feudal and socialist China is being replaced by a new way of life in the remaining neighborhoods. Yet overcrowding and substandard conditions continue to be the norm for tens of thousands of residents. The *hutong* way of life ironically now has both a poor and a rich lifestyle interpretation. This situation is likely to remain for some time.

SEE ALSO *Urban China.*

BIBLIOGRAPHY

Abramson, Daniel B. The Aesthetics of City-Scale Preservation Policy in Beijing. *Planning Perspectives* 22, 2 (2007): 129–166.

Yang Yin, ed. *Find the Old Beijing*. Beijing: China Nationality Art Photograph Publishing House, 2005.

Charles S. Johnston

I

IDENTIFICATION AND BELONGING

Like elsewhere in the world, the transition from empire to nation-state in modern China dramatically reshaped the sociopolitical processes of identification and belonging. Yet, unlike in Europe, nation and state building occurred alongside one another in China, ensuring that the cacophony of new social categories (gender, class, place, ethnicity, etc.) that emanated from China's nascent civil society and public sphere were immediately mobilized by the state and its agents in the name of a shared national imaginary. In short, these new modes of modern belonging came to be configured within an increasingly bounded system of globally competing, territorial nation-states.

FOREIGN IMPERIALISM AND BIRTH OF THE NATION

Placing themselves at the center of the Confucian ecumene (*tianxia*), the Manchu rulers of China's last imperial regime, the Qing dynasty (1644–1912), constructed an elastic multiethnic empire that incorporated five distinct ethnic constituencies (Manchu, Mongol, Han, Tibetan, and Sino-Muslim). In exchange for their loyalty toward the court, each polity was largely free to govern themselves in accordance with local tradition and free of daily oversight. Yet, as the empire unraveled under internal pressures (rising population, corruption, millenarian revolts) and external encroachment, the Chinese state sought to expand its capacities to demarcate, govern, and patrol its sovereignty, as reflected by the ballooning of 20,000 Mandarin officials in 1800 into over forty million state and party cadres today.

The rise of state-centered nationalism and the steady enclosure of the Chinese geo-body was a direct reaction to foreign imperialism. What began in 1839 as a distant nuisance in Guangzhou (Canton) escalated into a major crisis when the British navy outmaneuvered, attacked, and easily defeated Qing forces during a series of skirmishes that became known as the Opium War. The humiliating terms of the Treaty of Nanjing (1842) marked the opening salvo of the "century of humiliation" (*bainian guochi*) that helped to fuel the rise of Chinese nationalism. The British were granted the barren island of Hong Kong in perpetuity, and other "unequal treaties" (*bupingdeng tiaoyue*) soon followed that provided most Western trading nations with access to Chinese ports, legal extraterritoriality, and major trade concessions.

The so-called carving of the Chinese melon was not limited to European and American powers; after defeating the Qing navy and army in 1895, Meiji Japan joined the scramble for concessions by obtaining the island of Taiwan. By the time the Qing dynasty collapsed in 1912, the imperialist powers had even made inroads into the empire's vast nomadic frontier of Tibet (Xizang), Xinjiang, Mongolia (Menggu), and Manchuria (Dongbei), resulting in a dramatic increase in the discussion of "national sovereignty" (*guojia zhuquan*) and the unwanted image of China as the "sickman of the Far East" (*yuandong bingfu*) among late Qing and Republican elites.

MIGRATION AND EMERGENT CHINESENESS

The forced opening of China sparked an unprecedented wave of migration, as over twenty million Chinese were pushed and pulled onto the gold fields of California and Victoria, Australia, the agricultural plantations of Hawaii and Sumatra, and the urban centers of San Francisco and São Paulo; millions more flooded into the treaty port cities of Shanghai, Guangzhou, and Tianjin. Native-place associations (*tongxiang huiguan*) and sworn brotherhoods (*jiebai xiongdi*) facilitated this mass migration by providing a familiar sense of belonging and identity in these new, more cosmopolitan surroundings, but the increased intermingling of people outside of their village environs also opened up spaces (parks, restaurants, cinemas, and bathhouses) for the emergence of a new collective identity: a burgeoning yet fluid sense of "Chineseness" that was defined in opposition to both the alien Other of the foreign concessions and countries and the familiar Other of the nomadic frontier. There was no single articulation of this communal identity—some spoke of the common blood and descent ties of the *hanzu* (Han race), others of the shared cultural traditions of the *huaren* (Chinese), and yet others of the political rights of all *zhongguoren* (Chinese), and their possible extension to the *huaqiao* (Chinese sojourners) living overseas. Rather, this shared identity was rooted in the widespread recognition that the former subjects of the Qing empire shared a common past of subjugation and a future route of liberation.

In sum, the shift from empire to nation-state in China accompanied an epistemic rupture in space and time, as a fixed notion of territoriality replaced the fluid space of empire and a notion of linear, progressive time supplanted the cyclical dynastic cycle. Within this new framework, hierarchical and overlapping subjectivities were reimagined as bounded and equal citizens, as the state sought to bring identity space into line with decision-making space, and replace particularistic loyalties with a collective, territorial sovereignty. Yet, the dynamic and multiple nature of identity formation ensured that this new national identity continued to compete and interact with a whole series of local and transnational ties.

THE NATION AND ITS ETHNIC FRAGMENTS

The establishment of the Republic of China in 1912 formally ushered in this new community of citizens on the Chinese mainland, as a series of civic rituals (national day parades and military reviews) and symbols (national flags and anthems) replaced the imperial rites and regalia of old. When Liang Qichao spoke of the "new citizen" (*xinmin*) and Sun Yat-sen (Sun Yixian) of a "single race" (*tongzhong*), they both envisioned a new national collective that would, in their words, "smelt together in single furnace" (*rong er ru yu yilu*) the disparate subjects of the Qing empire into a new unified body politic. Throughout the twentieth century, Chinese state elites sought to transform what Sun Yat-sen saw as a "loose sheet of sand" (*yipian sansha*) into the "coagulate core" (*ningju hexin*) that leading sociologist Fei Xiaotong spoke of as central to Chinese identity today.

Yet, the lack of a single strong state during the Republican period (1912–1949) ensured that local, provincial, and transnational ties remained salient, while regional militarists facilitated the opening of China's inland frontiers by pushing Chinese institutions and Han settlers deep into the interior. There the non-Han minorities were first colonized and then nationalized, as their formerly imprecise borderlands were bordered and garrisoned. Both the Republican state and the People's Republic of China (PRC, 1949–) envisioned the nation-state as a multiethnic mosaic. On the one hand, they formally recognized the independent existence of first five and then fifty-six *minzus* (peoples, races, or nationalities), while on the other hand, they actively encouraged their nonviolent fusion (*ronghe*) into a single national whole—what was termed the *zhonghua minzu* (Chinese race/nation).

The colonial context of the Chinese nation's birth ensured that territorial sovereignty became a central focus of the Chinese state and its elites. Successive state leaders such as Sun Yat-sen, Chiang Kai-shek (Jiang Jieshi), Mao Zedong, and Deng Xiaoping each spoke of the need to fight foreign imperialism, recover lost territories, and guard against regional splittism. The PRC has maintained a firm grip over the frontier regions of Tibet and Xinjiang, whereas the recent return of Hong Kong (1997) and Macau (1999) to Chinese sovereignty has only intensified the problem of Taiwan in domestic and international affairs. At the same time, the dramatic economic rise of the PRC since the death of Mao in 1976 has caused many overseas Chinese to redirect their attention and investment dollars back to the motherland.

Belying these radical changes in identity and belonging is the continued tension between the transnational flows of modernity and the enclosure of political sovereignty that is fundamental to the nation-state system. The result for modern China has been the continual mediation of new forms of social identity by an overarching sense of national collectivity, no matter how ambiguously defined.

SEE ALSO *Chinese Overseas: Diaspora and Homeland; Hong Kong; Macau; Nationalism; Taiwan, Republic of China.*

BIBLIOGRAPHY

Crossley, Pamela Kyle. *A Translucent Mirror: History and Identity in Qing Imperial Ideology*. Berkeley: University of California Press, 1999.

Duara, Prasenjit. *Rescuing History from the Nation: Questioning Narratives of Modern China*. Chicago: University of Chicago Press, 1995.

Fei Xiaotong. *Zhongguo minzu duoyuan yiti geju* [The plurality and organic unity of the Zhonghua minzu]. Beijing: Zhongyang Renmin Xueyuan Chubanshe, 1989.

Fitzgerald, John. *Awakening China: Politics, Culture, and Class in the Nationalist Revolution*. Stanford, CA: Stanford University Press, 1996.

Goodman, Bryna. *Native Place, City, and Nation: Regional Networks and Identities in Shanghai, 1853–1937*. Berkeley: University of California Press, 1995.

Harrison, Henrietta. *The Making of the Republican Citizen: Political Ceremonies and Symbols in China, 1911–1929*. Oxford, U.K.: Oxford University Press, 2000.

Leibold, James. *Reconfiguring Chinese Nationalism: How the Qing Frontier and Its Indigenes Became Chinese*. New York: Palgrave Macmillan, 2007.

McKeown, Adam. Conceptualizing Chinese Diasporas: 1842–1949. *Journal of Asian Studies* 58 (1999): 306–337.

Zarrow, Peter. *China in War and Revolution, 1895–1949*. London: Routledge, 2005.

James Leibold

IDENTITY, CHINESE

The status of Overseas Chinese in relation to both China and their countries of residence has remained a persistent issue throughout Chinese history. In 1955, Zhou Enlai addressed this issue in a speech at the Bandung Conference, during which a treaty was signed specifying that overseas Chinese could no longer claim dual nationality (Poston and Yu 1990, p. 482).

Currently, diverse forms of cultural, racial, and political identification characterize the ways that Chinese people in the mainland and abroad conceive of Chinese identity. Modern Chinese notions of Chineseness, both folk and official, were formed around discourses of race, culture, and nation that crystallized as part of nation-building efforts at the beginning of the twentieth century. This occurred alongside the collapse of the imperial order, as China struggled to find its place as a nation among nations (Duara 1993; Townsend 1992).

Contemporary government discourses define Chineseness in terms of citizenship, race, and culture. But these conceptions of "Chinese" citizenship neglect both transnational forms of identity and the diversity of identities that exist within the borders of mainland China and abroad. The various terms used to describe Chinese identity in China and overseas (*zhongguoren, zhonghua minzu, huaren, huaqiao*) carry a range of connotations and were formed under specific political and historical circumstances (Wu 1991). Furthermore, it has become increasingly evident that it is possible for one to identify culturally, but not politically, with mainland China. Taiwan and Singapore also lay claims on Chinese culture, and overseas Chinese identities are marked by complex variation. Overseas Chinese identities are constructed in relation to economic, political, and identity politics in the country of residence, by mainland Chinese claims to the identities of the overseas Chinese, and by transnational flows that both link Chinese people in new ways and allow for the production of new forms of Chinese subjectivity.

Chinese identity thus must be understood as both emerging from complex histories and also as fluid, negotiated, and conceptualized in relation to power and place. Chinese identities can be conceptualized on multiple levels, from native-place, regional, and ethnic forms to broader forms including race, nation, and diaspora. These forms are not necessarily mutually exclusive, and a given individual or community can possess identities as Chinese on a number of levels and in varying ways.

CHINESENESS AS RACIAL IDENTITY

Notions of Han Chinese racial identity, in which Han Chinese are seen as descending from a common mythical ancestor, are central to demarcating Han Chinese from non-Chinese identities. What came to be known as Han civilization is thought to have originated five thousand years ago in the Yellow River basin. According to the origin myth, the emperor Huangdi defeated Yandi, and the two tribes combined to form the Hua Xia. From the Hua Xia evolved the Xia state, marking the beginning of Chinese civilization. These Han people spread throughout China, creating the Chinese empire.

Frank Dikotter (1994) documents the development of racial discourses in China from the fifteenth century to the present. Racial discourses, he argues, were a product of intellectual and political ideologies that served to bolster conceptions of Chinese national identity largely in contrast to the foreign "other." An emphasis on race over culture helped smooth over the question of cultural diversity and ethnic conflicts within China.

MINORITY AND REGIONAL IDENTITIES

According to contemporary official Chinese government discourses, China is a nation composed primarily of Han peoples, along with fifty-five minority nationalities. But the modern Chinese nation and its borders are a construction rooted in a prenational polity. Throughout much of early Chinese history, the geographical area that now comprises modern China has been home to numerous culturally diverse peoples who together did not easily or willingly conform to a cohesive identity uniting them within a nation or empire. Han identities both within China and abroad are characterized by great internal differentiation at various levels. Reevaluations of ethnicity in China, inspired in part by symbolic and poststructuralist social theories of ethnicity and identity, have involved a reexamination of center/periphery negotiations and of the existence of ethnic differences in China (Crossley 1990). Marked variations in culture, language, and customs persist among people calling themselves Chinese today.

Anthropologist James Watson argues that in the context of late imperial China, being Chinese was more a question of following accepted rites (such as death and marriage rituals) than a process of conversion to a standard set of cultural beliefs. This emphasis on "orthopraxy" over "orthodoxy" left room for the maintenance of differences of ethnicity and region, while at the same time producing a sense of identity connected to a larger Chinese society through adherence to shared rites. While Chinese national identity was a construction imposed from above, Watson asserts that Chinese cultural identity, as defined through participation in a unified system of rites, was practiced by "ordinary people" (Watson 1993). Some scholars have taken issue with Watson's argument, questioning the effectiveness of government efforts at the "standardization" of rituals and cultural integration, and instead focusing on the ways in which late imperial Chinese culture was "flexible and mobile" (Sutton 2007, p. 16).

A number of scholars have combined anthropological and historical data to try to understand contemporary variations in Chinese regional practices and beliefs, which some may call "ethnicities" (Honig 1992; Crossley 1990; Gladney 1991). Current variation in Chinese cultural traits has been attributed to the influence of aboriginal cultures and local variations resulting from semi-enclosed patterns of interaction in marketing communities (Cohen 1991, p. 120).

The ethnic politics of the People's Republic of China (PRC) attempted to integrate the Chinese nation through the identification of officially recognized minority nations that were defined in relation to a Han Chinese core. Dru Gladney (1991) demonstrates how Hui national identity coalesced as a result of PRC policy toward minorities. In practice, the group is spread throughout China, and those claiming this identity vary greatly in their cultural practices and degree of similarity to Han culture. Prior to their definition as a distinct minority by the state, the Hui shared no common identity, and Hui ethnicity has less to do with common practices of Islam than ideas of descent from a common Muslim ancestor. Gladney's work demonstrates the ways that ethnicity is dynamic and politicized, negotiated in relation to state power.

The Bai of Yunan Province are a classic example of the constructed nature of minority statuses and of the fluidity of identities. When anthropologist Francis L. K. Hsu (1909–1999) studied the group, he viewed them as representative of a traditional Han society. However, David Y. H. Wu later studied the group after they had been redefined by the state as a Bai minority (*shaoshu minzu*), and found that though the "Bai" reinterpreted their cultural practices as distinct from Han culture, in actuality these "Bai" features were no more distinct than other patterns of local variation of Han culture (Wu 1991; Cohen 1991). As demonstrated in the cases of the Hui and the Bai, the cultural markers defining a group as Han or non-Han are to some extent arbitrary, and are only made socially and culturally significant within the context of state power and politics. Prasenjit Duara (1993) describes the process through which "soft boundaries" that are potential points of division and definition of groups are crystallized and made salient through the "hardening of boundaries."

Regional and ethnic identities continue to exist among Han Chinese, as native-place identities take on ethnic meanings within a Han population that is itself constructed by state discourses as an ethnic group (Honig 1992). In early- to mid-twentieth-century Shanghai, identities based on the Subei region as a place of ancestral origin emerged as an "other" to a Shanghai identity, and as metaphor for low-class status. Native-place identities were socially constructed, "malleable constructions" that became significant forms of identity as people migrated within China (Honig 1992, p. 7). Modern Chinese national identity, which builds on native-place and regional identities, has also been shown to be a contested concept, with regional identities threatening to disrupt the idea of a unified Chinese nation-state (Friedman 1994; Lary 1996).

CHINESE IDENTITIES ABROAD

Tu Wei Ming's (1991) concept of "cultural China" portrays Chinese culture as an essential form of historically rooted Chinese identity that has expanded beyond the nation-state and is no longer dependent on mainland China as the center. This expansive form of Chinese identity is at once unifying, in the sense that Chinese people from multiple places share it, but it is also subject to local variation and marked by shifts in the center and periphery of the Chinese cultural universe. The possibility that Chinese diaspora populations can hold varied forms of Chinese identity and relationships with China as a center opens up the potential for the expansion of what it means to be "Chinese." At the same time, others have questioned the limits of the diaspora paradigm and of shared Chinese identity as a unifying factor among diaspora Chinese (Ang 2001).

Along these lines, many scholars have argued that racial or cultural markers defining Chineseness cannot be understood apart from the attempts of various state regimes to shape notions of Chinese culture and identity in the process of creating ideas of inclusive or exclusive cultural or political citizenship. As Aihwa Ong and Donald Nonini observe, concepts such as "'Chinese culture,'

A bride and groom in traditional Han dress on their wedding day, Xi'an, Shaanxi province, October 3, 2007. *The second largest country on the Asian continent, China remains home to a wide variety of peoples, cultures, and languages. With over ninety percent of the population describing themselves as Han, this ethnic group has perhaps the largest influence on defining Chinese identity.* CHINA PHOTOS/GETTY IMAGES

Chinese family values, *guanxi*, and 'Confucian Capitalism'" should be viewed as "discursive tropes" that "do not merely explain Chinese identity, networks, and economic activity; rather, such discourses and their connections to power in large part *constitute* Chinese identities and transnational practices, and are therefore in need of deconstruction and study" (Ong and Nonini 1997, p. 9).

Many studies have examined overseas Chinese communities and practices and the formation of "new Chinese subjects" within a framework of globalization and transnational migration, in the context of late capitalism. Aihwa Ong's work (1999) on Chinese transnational subjects places overseas Chinese practices within the context of global capitalism, asserting that these conditions have created new, flexible citizens, such as Chinese "astronauts" (*taikongren*) from Hong Kong who employ the flexibility of global capital and exercise strategic forms of citizenship to maximize their economic and cultural capital. In response to migration theories that viewed migration and assimilation as one-way processes, historical studies (Hsu 2000; McKeown 2001) have recast early twentieth-century Chinese migration within a transnational framework, focusing on the deeply rooted and complex ties and social networks that these populations maintained with the Chinese homeland and with other diaspora Chinese.

In the context of the open policy and economic reform (*gaige kaifang*), overseas Chinese participation in the social, political, and economic affairs of their motherland has been framed by the mainland Chinese government as a patriotic act, emerging from love for the motherland. This has been referred to as the "politics of native roots" (Siu 1993). However, the actual sentiments of Chinese diaspora populations toward China are highly varied, reflecting differences in immigrant generation, social class, circumstances of emigration, and country of residence. While some Chinese abroad may identify strongly with their Chinese "hometowns" (*zuji, xiangxia*) and maintain or reinitiate connections with them (Ke 2000), others may only identify with

China in an abstract, apolitical, and romanticized sense. The notions of overseas Chinese nationalism espoused in official government policy, which assume a correlation between racial, cultural, and national identification with China, do not necessarily correspond with the actual sentiments of Chinese populations abroad, particularly those born outside of China (Louie 2004).

For many overseas Chinese, ties to China carry little emotional or practical importance, and personal identity may only partly involve identification as Chinese (Siu 1993, p. 33). Wang Gungwu observes that *huayi* (descendants of overseas Chinese) are "able to distinguish between Chinese culture and the Chinese state and may identify with the culture and not the Chinese regime" (Wang 1991, p. 154). Though people of Chinese descent born outside of China may look toward China as a source of roots or heritage, their perceptions of China and their relationship to China as a "homeland" can only be understood when framed in relation to processes of subject-making and citizenship of both their country of residence and mainland China itself. For example, American-born Chinese Americans may identify in complex ways with mainland China. Removed from mainland China by time and cultural distance, they may hold abstract and essentialized views of "China" and "Chinese culture" that have been shaped through indirect experiences with China—through media images, popular culture, transnational flows of media, and discourses of cultural citizenship framing the status of Chinese populations in the United States—as well as by the specifics of their family history. Though the PRC may reach out to them through cultural-heritage programs that cast them as "descendants of the dragon" and patriotic sons and daughters returning to build the Chinese nation, their conceptions of what it means to be Chinese and to visit China do not necessarily involve political commitments to China as a homeland. In the case of Chinese Americans, conceptions of Chinese identity might be influenced more directly by Asian American identity politics, transnational popular culture and media flows, and U.S. racial and multicultural politics that have defined Asian Americans more broadly in the context of U.S. history (Louie 2004).

Newer studies of Chinese diaspora populations point to similar processes of negotiation between "the role of the state, the contending forces of cultural nationalisms, and the power of geopolitics" (Siu 2005, p. 10). Chinese of mixed racial descent, Chinese adoptees, and other Chinese diaspora populations from around the world—groups that are marked by variations in language and in cultural, political, and racial identifications, and influenced by multilayered and complex policies—constitute increasingly varied and vocal forms of Chinese identity.

SEE ALSO *Chinese Overseas; Minority Nationalities; Nationalism.*

BIBLIOGRAPHY

Ang, Ien. *On Not Speaking Chinese: Living between Asia and the West.* New York: Routledge, 2001.

Cohen, Myron. Being Chinese: The Peripheralization of Traditional Identity. *Daedalus* 120, 2 (1991): 113–134.

Crossley, Pamela Kyle. Thinking about Ethnicity in Early Modern China. *Late Imperial China* 11, 1 (1990): 1–34.

Dikotter, Frank. Racial Identities in China: Context and Meaning. *China Quarterly* 138 (June 1994): 404–413.

Du, Weiming (Tu Wei Ming). Cultural China: The Periphery as Center. *Daedalus* 120, 2 (1991): 1–32.

Duara, Prasenjit. De-Constructing the Chinese Nation. *Australian Journal of Chinese Affairs* 30 (1993): 1–26.

Fitzgerald, Stephen. *China and the Overseas Chinese: A Study of Peking's Changing Policy, 1949–1970.* Cambridge, U.K.: Cambridge University Press, 1972.

Friedman, Edward. Reconstructing China's National Identity: A Southern Alternative to Mao-Era Anti-Imperialist Nationalism. *Journal of Asian Studies* 53, 1 (1994): 67–91.

Gladney, Dru. *Muslim Chinese: Ethnic Nationalism in the People's Republic.* Cambridge, MA: Harvard Council on East Asian Studies, 1991.

Goodman, Bryna. *Native Place, City, and Nation: Regional Networks and Identities in Shanghai, 1853–1937.* Berkeley: University of California Press, 1995.

Honig, Emily. *Creating Chinese Ethnicity: Subei People in Shanghai, 1850–1980.* New Haven, CT: Yale University Press, 1992.

Hsu, Madeline Yuan-yin. *Dreaming of Gold, Dreaming of Home: Transnationalism and Migration between the United States and South China, 1882–1943.* Stanford, CA: Stanford University Press, 2000.

Ke, Qunying (Kuah, Khun Eng). *Rebuilding the Ancestral Village: Singaporeans in China.* Aldershot, U.K.: Ashgate, 2000.

Lary, Diana. The Tomb of the King of Nanyue—The Contemporary Agenda of History: Scholarship and Identity. *Modern China* 22, 1 (1996): 3–27.

Louie, Andrea. Chineseness across Borders: Re-negotiating Chinese Identities in China and the United States. Durham, NC: Duke University Press, 2004.

McKeown, Adam. *Chinese Migrant Networks and Cultural Change: Peru, Chicago, Hawaii, 1900–1936.* Chicago: University of Chicago Press, 2001.

Ong, Aihwa. *Flexible Citizenship: The Cultural Logics of Transnationality.* Durham: Duke University Press, 1999.

Ong, Aihwa, and Donald Nonini. *Ungrounded Empires: The Cultural Politics of Modern Chinese Transnationalism.* New York: Routledge, 1997.

Poston, Dudley L., Jr. and Mei-Yu Yu. The Distribution of the Overseas Chinese in the Contemporary World. *International Migration Review* 24, 3 (Autumn 1990): 480–508.

Siu, Helen. Cultural Identity and the Politics of Difference in South China. *Daedalus* 122, 2 (1993): 19–44.

Siu, Lok C. D. *Memories of a Future Home: Diasporic Citizenship of Chinese in Panama.* Stanford, CA: Stanford University Press, 2005.

Sutton, Donald. Ritual, Cultural Standardization, and Orthopraxy in China: Reconsidering James Watson's Ideas. *Modern China* 33, 1 (2007): 3–27.

Townsend, James. Chinese Nationalism. *Australian Journal of Chinese Affairs* 27 (1992): 97–130.

Wang, Gungwu. Among Non-Chinese. Daedalus: Boston. Spring 1991. Vol. 120. Issue 2. p. 135–157.

Watson, James. Rites or Beliefs? The Construction of a Unified Culture in Late Imperial China. In *China's Quest for National Identity*, eds. Lowell Dittmer and Samuel S. Kim. Ithaca, NY: Cornell University Press, 1993: 80–113.

Wu, David Yen Ho. The Construction of Chinese and Non-Chinese Identities. *Daedalus* 120, 2 (1991): 159–180.

Andrea Louie

ILLITERACY

During the nineteenth century, an estimated 30 to 45 percent of males and 2 to 10 percent of females in China possessed some ability to read and write. The modern Chinese struggle to eliminate the scourge of illiteracy began around 1900 in conjunction with the Nationalist effort to create a cohesive, disciplined, and economically productive citizenry. From its inception down to the present, China's anti-illiteracy movement has focused on three broad areas: the creation and expansion of a nationwide system of compulsory education for school-age children, the development of multiple forms of nonformal education for adult illiterates, and language reform. Before 1949, progress on all three fronts was slow, sporadic, and primarily local.

Following the establishment of the People's Republic of China in 1949, the government mounted a vigorous nationwide movement to eliminate illiteracy. More than eighty million adult illiterates participated in literacy classes at the height of the movement from 1956 to 1960. Since the 1980s, adult literacy efforts have constituted a relatively small and declining focus of local education bureaus in most parts of the country. This has been made possible not only by the success of previous adult-literacy campaigns but also, to a greater extent, by the massive expansion of the formal school system and its penetration into rural areas. In 1949 only 35 percent of school-age children across China attended primary school, but by 1981 the national figure was 93 percent, and by 2001 it was officially 99 percent. More difficult to assess has been the impact of the language reforms implemented since 1949. Between 1955 and 1960, a series of sweeping changes to the linguistic environment were enacted, including formal establishment of Mandarin (Putonghua) as the country's common speech and medium of instruction, introduction of a romanization scheme known as hanyu pinyin, to facilitate character recognition and correct Mandarin pronunciation, and the promulgation of 515 simplified characters (later increased to more than 2,000 in 1964). To expedite the use of phonetic writing, the traditional vertical style of writing was also abandoned in favor of horizontal writing.

The government's record in eradicating illiteracy is reflected in official statistics (which, for a variety of reasons, should be regarded as signifying general trends rather than precise measurements). During the 1950s, when adult literacy campaigns were at their peak, the illiteracy rate fell from 80 percent to 43 percent. By 1981 it was 34.5 percent. And by 2000 China's official illiteracy rate was less than 10 percent. (Literacy among the rural population has been defined since 1956 as knowledge of at least 1,500 characters plus the ability to read and write simple notes and perform simple calculations; for urbanites and workers, the minimum standard is 2,000 characters.) Despite these remarkable achievements, illiteracy continues to vary significantly according to gender, ethnicity, region, and urban versus rural residence. In 2007 the greatest concentrations of illiterates in China were in the western and impoverished rural regions and among women and members of the country's fifty-five officially recognized national minorities. According to the 2000 national census, three-quarters of China's nearly 87 million adult illiterates were to be found in rural areas, and more than 71.4 percent of all illiterates were female. In addition, seven provinces and autonomous regions—all with significant minority populations—had illiteracy rates substantially higher than the national average. They were Tibet, Yunnan, Guizhou, Gansu, Qinghai, Ningxia, and Inner Mongolia, with Tibet recording the highest illiteracy rate (38 percent). Illiteracy rates among national minorities were on average 25 percent higher than that of the Han ethnic population. Even in urban areas, new educational disparities have appeared in recent years. Members of China's "floating population" (up to 200 million by some estimates), because they reside illegally in cities, are unable to access public education unless they qualify for a temporary urban-residence permit or are willing and able to pay.

Funding has been one of the greatest obstacles in the struggle to eradicate illiteracy. During the period of collective agriculture (1956–1982), local collectives assumed responsibility for anti-illiteracy work and basic education in rural areas. Under this system, the unpaid labor of production-team members served as the main source of the commune's social-welfare fund, out of which the costs of basic education and other social-welfare services were provided. The dismantling of the commune system in the early 1980s undermined the fiscal foundation of rural primary education, precipitating a crisis in rural-education funding and the passage of a compulsory-education law in 1986 (reissued in 1995).

In 1985 the government began a major restructuring of the education system, under which funding for rural basic education has become increasingly decentralized and diversified. County, township, and village governments now hold primary responsibility for providing basic education, but increasingly emphasis is also placed on the development of multiple channels of financing, including tuition fees; miscellaneous fees for the use of school desks, winter heating, and other operating costs; donations; and the rapidly increasing use of private schooling. The current emphasis on multiple channels of funding for rural basic education will quite likely continue for the foreseeable future until China implements an effective system of local taxation or intergovernmental transfers, similar to that found in many developed countries, to fund basic education.

SEE ALSO *Education.*

BIBLIOGRAPHY

Lam, Agnes S. *Language Education in China: Policy and Experience from 1949.* Hong Kong: Hong Kong University Press, 2005.

Peterson, Glen. *The Power of Words: Literacy and Revolution in South China, 1949–95.* Vancouver: University of British Columbia Press, 1997.

Tsang, Mun C. Financial Reform of Basic Education in China. *Economics of Education Review* 15, 4 (1996): 423–444.

Zhou, Minglang, ed. *Language Policy in the People's Republic of China: Theory and Practice since 1949.* Boston: Kluwer Academic Publishers, 2004.

Glen Peterson

IMPERIAL HOUSEHOLD DEPARTMENT

During the Qing dynasty (1644–1912), operations of the whole imperial-palace establishment, including eunuchs, were controlled by a large and important agency called the Imperial Household Department, or Neiwufu. This was an aggregation of more than fifty service agencies, many of which in turn supervised their own subordinate agencies. Early Qing emperors often used the Imperial Household Department to perform diplomatic and fiscal tasks that exceeded its primary responsibility of managing the emperor's household affairs. More than any previous dynasty, the Qing succeeded in controlling their palace servants and in mobilizing the Imperial Household Department to serve the throne.

ORIGINS

The Imperial Household Department operative in the last century of imperial rule had evolved during the seventeenth century, apparently from arrangements for the personal household administration of Nurgaci. The department was in charge of the wardrobes, food, residences, and daily activities of the emperor and his family. It exercised jurisdiction over palace construction, security, rituals, and palace staff. Staff members of the Imperial Household Department came principally from bondservants, or *booi* in Manchu. *Booi* were a hereditarily servile people registered in the banners. The status of *booi* was similar to that of slaves, who were called *aha* in Manchu or *booi aha*. Both *aha* and *booi* were legally defined servile groups during the Qing. Most were descended from Chinese and other northeastern residents who had been taken captive during the conquest period and divided among the banner nobles, like other booty. Whereas *aha* worked in the fields, *booi* were in domestic service. Some bore arms and fought in battle alongside their masters during the conquest period. By 1636 they were enrolled in the developing banners as separate units. After the upper three banners—the Bordered Yellow, Plain Yellow, and Plain White—were taken over by the emperor, *booi* in these banners became the emperor's household servants. With the Manchu conquest of China, their activities were "elevated from a family level to a state level of operations." The Imperial Household Department was an ingenious new solution devised by the Qing to the problem of insubordinate eunuchs. By introducing a new element, the bondservant, into the palace administration, Qing rulers expanded the system of checks and balances within the palace (Rawski 1998, pp. 166–167, 179).

The Imperial Household Department ceased to exist for a short time early in the dynasty. It was abolished in 1653 by the Shunzhi emperor, who replaced it with a new department called the Thirteen Bureaus (Shisan Yamen). This new department divided imperial household affairs into thirteen administrations, each in the charge of a senior eunuch. The change implied a revival of the system of the previous Ming dynasty (1368–1644), but was not of long duration. After the death of the Shunzhi emperor in 1661, the Qing court under the Kangxi emperor abolished the Thirteen Bureaus and revived the old Manchu system of the Imperial Household Department.

ORGANIZATION

The Imperial Household Department had its own bureaucratic regulations, which were compiled and revised at intervals throughout the dynasty. Its highest officials, the ministers of the Imperial Household Department (Zongguan Neiwufu Dachen), eventually held the third rank in the eighteen-rank hierarchy of the civil service, but these officials were not Han Chinese degree holders. There was no limit on the number of persons who could hold this title at any one time. These ministerial posts were instead held by Manchu princes with prior experience in the Imperial Guard (Shiwei), especially in the position of grand minister of the Imperial Household Department concurrently controlling the Imperial Guard (Ling Shiwei Neidachen) and by bondservants who had climbed up through service in the Imperial Household Department itself. These ministers had overall responsibility for the functioning of the Imperial Household Department. Individual ministers were appointed on a rotating basis for one-year terms to supervise subsidiary units deemed especially sensitive, such as the Department of the Privy Purse (Guangchu Si), which was in charge of imperial revenues and expenditures; the Six Storehouses (the Silver Vault, Fur Storehouse, Porcelain Storehouse, Silk Storehouse, Clothing Storehouse, and Tea Storehouse); the Department of Works, in charge of palace maintenance and repair; and the Office of Eunuch Affairs (Jingshi Fang), the unit in charge of the recruitment, appointment, and punishment of eunuchs. Ministers were also appointed to manage the imperial villas and were assigned to ritually important sites, such as the imperial cemeteries (Rawski 1998, pp. 180–181).

DEVELOPMENT

The Imperial Household Department was extensively expanded during the eighteenth and nineteenth centuries. The number of its officials, which stood at over 402 in 1662, had increased to 939 by 1722 and to 1,623 by 1796. Eventually, in the late nineteenth century, the department oversaw the operations of over fifty-six subagencies.

With its organizational expansion, the activities of Imperial Household Department extended far beyond the Forbidden City and the imperial villas. The department became a major publisher, producing outstanding examples of printed works under imperial commission. It also held monopoly rights over the profitable jade and ginseng trades. In Hangzhou, Suzhou, and Jiangning, it ran textile factories that produced textiles for the court. Using the taxing powers of the state, it gathered precious objects such as furs from parts of Mongolia and the Northeast through the annual tribute system, reserving a portion for imperial use and disposing of the rest through the customhouses. The Imperial Household Department issued permits for the salt trade and the jade trade from Central Asia, and it licensed state merchants to import copper for coinage during the early Qing. It issued loans at interest, acquired pawnshops, and derived revenues from its many rentals in the imperial city (Rawski 1998, p. 179).

The activities of the Imperial Household Department blurred the boundary between state affairs and the emperors' personal affairs from the start. For example, the private funds of the emperors, which were managed by the Department of the Privy Purse, were taken from taxes collected by the Board of Revenue. From the early eighteenth century, the Privy Purse received quota surpluses (*yingyu*) at the customhouses, which taxed trade in Beijing, Jiujiang, Hangzhou, Hushu, and Guangzhou. Moreover, when officials' estates were confiscated, they frequently ended up in the hands of the Imperial Household Department (Rawski 1998, pp. 179–180). Despite a blurring of the boundary between state affairs and the emperors' personal affairs, the Qing emperors, compared to the Ming emperors, increased their private funds enormously but legitimately.

BIBLIOGRAPHY

Hucker, Charles O. *A Dictionary of Official Titles in Imperial China.* Stanford, CA: Stanford University Press, 1985.

Rawski, Evelyn S. *The Last Emperors: A Social History of Qing Imperial Institutions.* Berkeley: University of California Press, 1998. This entry draws extensively on this work.

Torbert, Preston M. *The Ch'ing Imperial Household Department: A Study of Its Organization and Principal Functions, 1662–1796.* Cambridge, MA: Council on East Asian Studies, Harvard University, 1977.

Sui-wai Cheung

IMPERIAL PALACES

Throughout the course of China's two-millennium imperial history, the emperor's palace has been the ultimate symbol of imperial China. It has also been considered an unsurpassed achievement in Chinese imperial-city planning. The place where the emperor held court and entertained, the site of many imperial ceremonies, and the residence of the emperor, the palace is more intimately associated with Chinese imperialism than any other building. The plan for an ideal Chinese imperial palace was first described late in the first millennium BCE in the *Zhou li* (Rites of Zhou). The layout of subsequent imperial palaces of every major Chinese dynasty, including the Forbidden City (Zijincheng) in Beijing, exhibited aspects of this textual prescription from China's classical age.

THE FORBIDDEN CITY

In modern times the Forbidden City was the site of China's most important palatial architecture. From 1406 in the Yongle reign until the fall of the Qing dynasty in 1912, it was the primary residence of twenty-four Ming and Qing emperors who ruled from Beijing. Positioned on the ruins of imperial palaces of the non-Chinese Liao (947–1125) and Jin (1115–1234) dynasties, and on the site of the Mongol imperial city from the 1260s to 1360s, the main palaces of the Forbidden City were on the same north-south line as Kublai Khan's hall of audience and residence, and the area of Beijing known as the Lake District were bodies of water that had been dug by the Jin and used by the Mongols. New construction, serious renovation, and expansion of the Forbidden City occurred during the reigns of the emperors Yongle (r. 1403–1424), Jiajing (r. 1522–1566), Kangxi (r. 1661–1722), and Qianlong (r. 1736–1796). The years following the Qianlong emperor's abdication in 1795 were a period of limited building and eventual decline in the Forbidden City. This was also true at the Three Hills and Five Gardens (Sanshan Wuyuan), including Yuanming Yuan, which spread northwest of the Forbidden City; at the summer palace in Chengde; and at the early Manchu imperial city in Shenyang. Only at the Beijing Summer Palace, Yihe Yuan, did construction continue in the nineteenth century, particularly under the Empress Dowager Cixi (1835–1908).

The design of the Chinese imperial palace was intended to emphasize the emperor's central position in a universe bordered by imperial monuments. In the year 1800, the approach to the emperor in the Beijing imperial city began at the Gate of Eternal Settlement (Yongding Men), the central entry to the southern enclosed portion of Beijing known as the outer city, which was walled in 1553 during the Jiajing reign. The avenue north from the gate bisected the outer city and was flanked by the Temple of Heaven (Tian Tan) on the east and Altar of Agriculture (Xiannong Tan) on the west. In those sacred spaces, enclosed by walls that combined the shape of a circle, representing heaven, and of a square, representing the earthly human world, only the emperor was allowed to perform ceremonies. The next gate, known as the Due South Gate (Zhengyang Men), marked the central position in the next walled area of Beijing, known as the inner city, a name chosen to contrast with the outer city and indicate closer proximity to the emperor. Next straight northward was the Great Qing Gate (Da Qing Men), followed by the Gate of Heavenly Peace (Tianan Men). The T-shaped approach to the Gate of Heavenly Peace was announced by passage across five marble bridges, marking entry inside the next city wall, which enclosed the area known as the imperial city. The Gate of Uprightness (Duan Men) and the Meridian Gate (Wu Men) followed, flanked on their outer sides by the Temple of the Emperor's Ancestors (Zong Miao) on the east and the twin Altars of Soil and Grain (Sheji Tan) on the west. Behind the Meridian Gate one again crossed one of five marble bridges. Only then was one inside the Forbidden City after crossing six gates, two sets of bridges, and four walls. From there on, arrival at the throne required ascent and descent as well as passage through. The first ascent was toward the Three Great Halls—the Great Harmony, Central Harmony, and Preserving Harmony Halls (Taihe Dian, Zhonghe Dian, Baohe Dian)—and their front gate. Elevated together on a three-level marble platform, the emperor celebrated the New Year, winter solstice, and his birthday in the first hall; prepared for those celebrations in the small second hall; and honored successful scholars of the highest rank, made certain official appointments, and entertained foreign ambassadors in the third. Behind the Three Great Halls were another gate and the Three Back Halls, all four elevated on a one-tier platform of marble. Entered by the Gate of Heavenly Purity (Qianqing Men) and exited through the Gate of Earthly Repose (Kunning Men), the second group of halls were more private space: first, the Palace of Heavenly Purity (Qianqing Gong), for the emperor; last, the Palace of Earthly Repose (Kunning Gong), for the empress; and equidistant between the two was the small Hall of Mutual Ease (Jiaotai Dian), a reference to the interface between the male and female rulers. One more gate designated the terminus of the Forbidden City, followed by the artificial small peak known as Coal Hill (Meishan) and a gate at the center of the north imperial-city wall. Farther north on the same axial line was a bell tower, followed by a drum tower, the ringing of the bell and beating of the drum marking the beginning and end of each day.

Also inside the Forbidden City were residences for members of the imperial family and those who most directly supported the imperial household. East and west of the Three Back Halls were two sets of six residential palaces for the imperial household, primarily women. The two main additional residential palace compounds in the nineteenth century were Cultivating the Mind Hall (Yangxin Dian), sometimes used by Empress Dowager Cixi, and the Palace of Repose and Longevity (Ningshou Gong), which is larger, south of the six western residential palaces, and east of the eastern residences.

Palatial-style architecture used by the Chinese emperor spread beyond the outer walls and across Beijing. Architectural details and sometimes entire buildings of altar complexes to the sun and moon, silkworms, and the planet Jupiter and at tombs of emperors were often indistinguishable from structures of the Forbidden City. In the nineteenth and twentieth centuries, tombs of the Qing emperors and their wives and concubines were constructed east and west of the capital in northern Hebei Province, in Zunhua and Yixian, respectively. Other sites in and around Beijing with the same kind of imperial architecture at times functioned as palaces, or places where the emperor spent leisure hours, often staying for long periods and sometimes making imperial decisions or holding court. Officially, these spots were known as gardens (*yuan*).

IMPERIAL SUMMER PALACES

The handy name of the imperial pleasure palaces and parklands west of the Beijing imperial city was Three Hills and Five Gardens. The hills were Fragrance Hill (Xiang Shan), Jade Spring Hill (Yuquan Shan), and Longevity Hill (Wanshou Shan), associated, respectively, with Jingyi, Jingming, and Qingyi Gardens, which were constructed on or around them. The other two gardens were Yuanming Yuan and Changchun Yuan. All five had been built in the first century of the Qing dynasty and repaired or expanded before the end of the eighteenth century during the Qianlong reign. Two were of particular importance in the nineteenth century.

Yuanming Yuan (Perfect Bright Garden) was begun in 1707, expanded in 1725, and expanded again in the

Snowfall at the Forbidden City, Beijing, February 6, 2006. *Built in the early 1400s, the Forbidden City served as a residence for the emperor of China as well as a center of government. Perhaps the most recognizable structure in the compound, the Hall of Supreme Harmony was once used by emperors for holding court, impressing visitors with its size and opulence.* © JASON LEE/REUTERS/ CORBIS

middle of the eighteenth century, when the Qialong emperor asked Giuseppe Castiglione and Michel Benoist, Jesuit priests resident in Beijing, to design some of the buildings. Housing Tibetan- and Mongolian-style structures, traditional Chinese palaces, and parkland, Yuanming Yuan was several times larger than the Forbidden City. In October 1860, during the Second Opium War, Yuanming Yuan was attacked and destroyed by Franco-British forces. Most of the Chinese buildings were burned to the ground, but because the Jesuit-designed palaces were made of stone, pieces of them survive today in ruins. Another attack by Western troops during the Boxer Uprising destroyed the few wooden structures that had survived or been rebuilt.

The Qingyi (Clear Ripples) Garden, begun in 1750, was also destroyed by European forces in 1860. In the 1880s Empress Dowager Cixi rebuilt it on a much grander scale, renaming it the Yihe Yuan (Nurtured Harmony Garden) in 1888. Destroyed again, like Yuanming Yuan, during the Boxer Uprising in 1900, Cixi again rebuilt it. Her expenditures on a personal imperial retreat at times when China was facing severe national economic and international political pressure have been criticized ever since. Today it is usually known as the Summer Palace. One of the guiding principles in its original and later constructions was the "borrowed view," a configuration of natural scenery from elsewhere in China into the imperial garden landscape in the north. The artificial Lake Kunming, for example, was intended to be a re-creation of West Lake in the beautiful southern city Hangzhou.

The Summer Palace is divided into four parts. In the southeast, east of Longevity Hill, which dominates the view of the Summer Palace from a distance, Cixi held court, resided, and received officials. Bliss and Longevity Hall (Renshou Dian) and nearby buildings are arranged in axial lines and around courtyards, like the halls of the Forbidden City. Two large pavilions, Buddha Fragrance (Foxiang) and Precious Cloud (Paiyun), and Prolonging Life Monastery (Yanshou Si) on Longevity Hill opposite Lake Kunming form the second part. Less-developed land behind Longevity Hill comprises the third part, and the rest, south and west of Lake Kunming, includes the famous Seventeen Arch, and Jade Belt Bridges (Shiqikong Qiao, Yudai Qiao).

The most extraordinary pleasure palace built by Qing emperors for summer enjoyment, the Mountain Resort for Escaping the Heat (Bishu Shanzhuang), is about 155 miles northeast of Beijing in Chengde, Hebei Province. In earlier times the location was known as Rehe (Jehol). The majority of construction occurred under the Kangxi and Qianlong emperors, who designated seventy-two scenic spots, some of them borrowed views. Divided into four sections, the Chengde resort served important political, as well as recreational, purposes.

Like all Qing pleasure retreats, the Mountain Resort for Escaping the Heat included palatial halls, in the first section, where the emperor would hold court. The four building complexes of the palace area were constructed in the early part of the eighteenth century, decorated with furnishings that could have been found in the Forbidden City of Beijing, but with unpainted exterior columns and grey roofs, a mode more in line with a rustic retreat than the Three Great Halls. The second part of the Mountain Resort focuses on the lake. Much of the landscape architecture was based on garden designs of South China. The third area, the plain, is where eighteenth-century emperors relaxed in tents during their time in Chengde. It also included Buddhist temples and pagodas, fields used as testing ground for horses and for archery, and Literary Ford Pavilion (Wenjin Ge), built in 1774 as a near copy of a famous pavilion in Ningbo, Zhejiang. These two pavilions and one in Yuanming Yuan housed three of the four copies made before 1781 of one of the most extensive literary compilations of Chinese history, *Siku quanshu* (Complete writings of the Four Treasuries). Last were the hills, occupying 80 percent of the entire resort. North of the Mountain Resort were the Eight Outer Temples, eleven different religious complexes designed in Chinese, Manchu, Mongolian, and Tibetan styles to symbolize the political and ethnic unity of the Qing empire.

No new buildings rose after the year 1800, but emperors came to the mountainous resort through the nineteenth century. The Jiaqing emperor died there in 1820. The Xianfeng emperor suffered a similar fate there in 1861, having taken refuge there as the Franco-British forces captured Beijing and destroyed Yuanming Yuan.

THE MANCHU IMPERIAL CITY

Another Qing palace outside Beijing was the first built. It stands in Shenyang, capital of Liaoning Province. Shenyang traces its history as a walled city probably to the Liao dynasty (907–1125). The Manchus moved their capital to Shenyang, known in Manchu as Mukden, in 1625, remaining there until their move to Beijing in 1644. The Manchu palaces at Shenyang are sometimes considered a miniature Forbidden City. The approximately seventy buildings divide into three parallel north-south sets. At the center are the Great Qing Gate and three halls—Eminent Administration (Chongzheng Dian), Phoenix Tower (Fenghuang Lou), and Pure Tranquility (Qingning Gong)—the first and last also the names of buildings in the Forbidden City in Beijing. Their functions followed a principle employed in Beijing: administrative halls in front of more private chambers. To the east is an octagonal Great Administration Hall (Dazheng Dian), with six pairs of small halls in front on each side. The western sector of the Shenyang imperial city was constructed during the reign of the Qianlong emperor. Its focus is the multistory Imperial Library (Wensu Ge).

THE TEMPLE OF CONFUCIUS AND THE POTALA PALACE

Two more building groups should be mentioned in discussion of Chinese imperial-palace architecture. In Qufu, Shandong Province, imperial-palace-style buildings are arranged along nine courtyards in a north-south line. The number nine is a symbol of the Chinese emperor. The Great Achievement Hall (Dacheng Dian), which honors Confucius, is in front of the hall to honor his wife, just as the emperor's residence precedes the empress's residence in the Forbidden City in Beijing, and the Qufu halls are elevated together on a three-layer, I-shaped marble platform, also following the form at the core of the Beijing Forbidden City. As with the forbidden cities, most of the construction occurred before the end of the nineteenth century. Finally, although different in style, the Potala Palace, an equivalent of an imperial palace, was built for the Dalai Lama in Lhasa in the seventeenth century, with additions as recently as the twentieth century. Also similar to Chinese imperial practice, a summer palace with gardens known as Norbulingka was built outside the city in the mid-eighteenth century, with additions as recent as 1956.

LEGACY

By the beginning of the twentieth century, only the Forbidden City and Summer Palace in Beijing were actively used by the imperial family. Electricity and modern plumbing entered the walled enclosure, but in 1912 the 491-year history of the Beijing Forbidden City ended. One of the first acts of the Republican government was to establish an exhibition hall for antiquities in 1914. In October 1925, shortly after the departure of the last emperor Puyi, the Palace Museum was established. Major changes south of Tianan Men to make space for government offices had occurred before the end of the nineteenth century. In the decades following 1949, after the People's Republic was formally announced from Tianan Men, the area to the south was dramatically transformed. In Tiananmen Square, which can hold nearly half-a-million people for a rally, the Great Hall of the People, the Monument to the People's Heroes, Chairman Mao's Mausoleum, and the Museums of Chinese Revolutions and Chinese History stand where walls and gates rose in imperial times.

SEE ALSO *Architecture, History of: Architecture to 1949; Architecture, History of: Architecture, 1949–1979; Gardens and Parks; Heritage Protection.*

BIBLIOGRAPHY

Beijing Summer Palace Administration Office and Department of Architecture of Qinghua University. *Summer Palace.* Beijing: Zhaohua, 1981.

Hedin, Sven. *Jehol, City of Emperors.* Trans. E. G. Nash. New York: Dutton, 1933.

Jianzhu Lishi Yanjiu Suo [Architectural History Research Institute]. *Beijing gujianzhu* [Premodern architecture in Beijing]. Beijing: Wenwu Chubanshe, 1986.

Liu Junwen. *Beijing: China's Ancient and Modern Capital.* Beijing: Foreign Languages Press, 1982.

Siren, Osvald. *The Imperial Palaces of Peking.* Paris: G. van Oest, 1926.

State Cultural Relics Bureau and Beijing Jingxin Cultural Development Co. *The Mountain Resort and Outlying Temples.* Beijing: China Pictorial Publishing House, 1999.

Sun Dazheng. *Zhongguo gudai jianzhu shi* [History of premodern Chinese architecture]. Vol. 5: *Qingdai jianzhu* [Qing architecture]. Beijing: Zhongguo Jianzhu Gongye Chubanshe, 2002.

Weng, Wan-go, and Yang Boda. *The Palace Museum, Peking.* New York: Abrams, 1982.

Wong, Young-tsu. *A Paradise Lost: The Imperial Garden Yuanming Yuan.* Honolulu: University of Hawai'i Press, 2001.

Yan Chongnian, ed. *Zhongguo lidai ducheng gongyuan* [Chinese imperial cities and palaces through the ages]. Beijing: Zijincheng Chubanshe, 1987.

Yu Zhuoyun, ed. *Palaces of the Forbidden City.* New York: Viking, 1982.

Yu Zhuoyun, ed. *Zhongguo gongdian jianzhu lunwen ji* [Collected essays on Chinese palace architecture]. Beijing: Zijincheng Chubanshe, 2001.

Nancy Steinhardt

IMPERIALISM

Perhaps more than any other term, the meaning of *imperialism* in China depends on the historical context. Up until the early nineteenth century, imperialism in East Asia existed in the form of the Chinese tribute system, which affirmed China's image of itself as the "Middle Kingdom" and symbolized its role as the overlord of the Asia-Pacific region. For the rest of that century, however, as China was "carved up like a melon" by the European, American, and Japanese powers, imperialism came to be perceived as a threat, and the struggle against foreign imperialism became the basis of Chinese nationalism. China's emergence as a regional power and its aspirations to great-power status have revived the country's dream of "Greater China," an imagined, but for the Chinese no less real, cultural universe that transcends the political borders of modern nation-states.

CHINESE IMPERIALISM AND THE TRIBUTE SYSTEM

At its height, the Chinese empire under the Qing (1644–1912) stretched across most of Eurasia. Furthermore, through the tribute system, China expanded its influence and power beyond its territorial boundaries, bringing much of the Asia-Pacific region within its sphere of influence. Through an elaborate set of rituals in which envoys from participating tribute states were required to pay homage to the Chinese emperor and acknowledge China's superiority, the tribute system cloaked what was, at heart, trade relations. On condition of the envoys' satisfactory completion of the nine-kowtow prostration, the emperor allowed their merchants to trade in a designated area for a fixed period of time. Built upon the assumptions that China possessed unique goods the world wanted—indeed, Chinese tea, silk, and porcelain were in high demand around the globe—and that China was self-sufficient, the tribute system was portrayed not as a free exchange of goods between equals but rather as a manifestation of the Chinese emperor's benevolence toward countries that affirmed China's view of itself as the center of the world.

For the Chinese state, the tribute system was less about consolidating China's status as an economic superpower than about promoting China's political and cultural superiority. For in addition to the goods exchanged, the tribute system offered an effective way to promote China's view of itself as the "Middle Kingdom" and to spread the cultural products of Chinese civilization, namely Confucianism and the political, cultural, and social system it sustained. Korea, Vietnam, and Japan also adopted the Chinese calendar and incorporated the use of Chinese characters in their written languages. As the Chinese surveyed the world, it certainly seemed to reflect their view of China as the center of civilization.

THE WESTERN PRESENCE IN ASIA

Beginning in the early nineteenth century, however, the Chinese empire began to crumble, due in large part to the demands of the Western "barbarians," the epithet the Chinese used to refer to anyone who had not adopted Chinese culture. Beginning with the Portuguese, who arrived on the coast of China in the early sixteenth century, other European countries soon established their presence in the Asia-Pacific region. The decision of the Ming imperial court (1368–1644), the dynasty immediately preceding the Qing, to withdraw from its self-appointed role as the protector of the Indian Ocean in order to more effectively deal with the real threat from the Mongols on China's northern border in the 1430s meant that when the first Portuguese ships sailed into the Indian Ocean at the end of that century, the Europeans encountered no significant naval challenge. Yet Chinese imperial power remained great enough that, at least for the time being, the Europeans who wished to trade had to follow China's rules.

From the Canton System to the Treaty Port System In the mid-eighteenth century, a bungled attempt by a British merchant to improve conditions for European traders resulted in the Canton system, which, among other restrictions, confined foreign merchants to a small area in the port of Canton (Guangzhou) in the southeast, limited the trading season to a few months a year, and required foreigners to deal exclusively with a select group of Chinese merchants belonging to the merchant guild called the Cohong. Not surprisingly, the European merchants found the Canton system oppressive and sought to replace it with their version of free and equal trade. The British took the lead, first using diplomacy, and, when that failed, resorting to war.

In many respects, the first Opium War that broke out in 1839 represented a crucial turning point in the Chinese understanding of imperialism. After China's defeat in 1842, imperialism came to mean the diminution, and no longer the spread, of Chinese power and influence. Defeat in war and the unequal treaty system that resulted cost the Qing not only imperial prestige and territorial loss, but also reduced China to a semicolonial status. The Qing remained the nominal representative of the Chinese state, but real power rested in the hands of the foreign powers, which included Britain, France, Russia, and, by the late nineteenth century, Germany, Japan, and the United States. As a condition of the treaties, China was required to open up to foreign trade increasingly more ports; these "treaty ports" became the centers of the spheres of influence controlled by the foreign powers. At the turn of the century, the United States advocated an "open-door" policy in China, which prevented the spheres of influence from becoming minicolonies controlled by different foreign powers.

Although the Qing retained nominal control of China, it had surrendered many of the rights of a sovereign nation to the imperialist powers whose spheres of influence dotted the Chinese landscape. Among the concessions the imperialist powers wrested from the Qing state that undermined Chinese sovereignty was the right of extraterritoriality, which exempted foreigners from Chinese law. Through the most-favored-nation clause, which all treaty powers insisted on incorporating into their agreements with China, the Qing state had to extend to each country all the rights and privileges granted to all other treaty powers; the clause also guaranteed the automatic extension of any future concessions China would make in treaties with other countries.

The Many Faces of Imperialism On the one hand, the treaty ports served as a physical reminder to the Chinese of their second-class status in their own country. On the other hand, they were the source for many of the ideas and innovations that shaped China's development. Chinese translations of Western texts proliferated. Western political models inspired Chinese reformers. Scientific studies and technical handbooks helped the Chinese to build a modern infrastructure for industry. And legal treatises influenced the late Qing and Republican architects of China's modern legal system and law codes.

Missionary activities in China also represent a mixed blessing. In the Treaty of Tianjin (1858), Western missionaries acquired the right to proselytize in China, but their activities were not limited to religious conversion.

Nineteenth-century print depicting Western powers plus Russia and Japan dividing China into spheres of influence. *Previously a leading force in East Asia, China found its influence waning at the beginning of the nineteenth century. Western powers took advantage of China's military decline, laying claims to the country's resources and eventually inspiring a resurgence in Chinese nationalism.* © LEONARD DE SELVA/CORBIS

Alongside the churches built by missionaries stood schools and hospitals, providing Chinese converts access to education and health care they would otherwise not have been able to obtain in their own communities. Missionaries also sought to raise women's status by campaigning against the practice of footbinding, by educating young girls, and by providing women with new opportunities for work and travel. Many Chinese, however, viewed the missionary presence in their country with hostile suspicion and regarded Chinese converts as traitors.

The Zongli Yamen As a sign of the dramatic shift in the balance of power in China's relations with foreign countries, a new institution was created to formally manage foreign relations, yet another concession to Western imperialism. The Qing state preferred the tribute system through which China had conducted its foreign policy; in that system, the Lifan Yuan (variously translated as Court of Colonial Affairs or Office of Border Affairs) had supervised relations with peoples outside China. However, China's military weakness in the face of foreign imperialism made it impossible to maintain the traditional model of tribute relations with its assumption of Chinese supremacy and Western barbarity. In 1861 the Qing reluctantly agreed to the establishment of the Zongli Yamen (Office of General Management) to direct foreign affairs. Overall, the Zongli Yamen functioned as an effective institution for dealing with the West until its replacement by the Ministry of Foreign Affairs, yet another concession to the foreign powers in the Boxer Protocol of 1901.

THE GROWTH OF CHINESE NATIONALISM

In the eyes of a growing number of Chinese, nationalism came to be defined in ethnic terms, pitting the Han population against the Manchu rulers. Some, like Zhang Binglin (1868–1936) and Sun Yat-sen (Sun Yixian or Sun Zhongshan), turned against the Qing when it became clear to them that the Manchu rulers were not genuinely committed to reform. Others, like Zou Rong (1885–1905), blamed the Manchus for failing to strengthen China and resist foreign invasion.

Many Chinese expressed their nationalism through hatred of all things foreign. Latent hostility toward foreigners erupted into open violence with the Boxer Uprising (1898–1901), a peasant-based movement that spread through much of the North China Plain. In 1905 another antiforeign movement began in response to the American government's mistreatment of Chinese entering and residing in the United States. In reaction to what they considered a national insult, Chinese merchants in a number of cities boycotted all American goods. The boycott lasted three months, and signaled the growing maturity of Chinese nationalism.

A decade later, it would be Chinese students who would lead a movement that would become synonymous with Chinese nationalism. Having absorbed into its empire regions formerly within the Chinese sphere of influence, Japan sought through the infamous Twenty-one Demands in 1915 to make China into a Japanese protectorate. Although unsuccessful, Japan's aggressive stance sparked a nationwide protest against Japanese imperialism and a boycott of Japanese products that surpassed previous mass movements against European and American imperialism. On May 4, 1919, Chinese students marched through the streets of Beijing to protest the Allied decision reached at the Versailles peace talks to transfer to Japan control over the Shandong Peninsula, an area that had—in Chinese eyes—been illegally seized by Germany in 1898. Expecting the return of the Shandong territory after Germany's defeat in World War I (1914–1918), the Chinese felt betrayed by the Versailles settlement and alarmed by the growing Japanese presence in China. As the threat of Japanese imperialism grew in the next few decades, Chinese nationalism would become inseparable from anti-imperialist sentiment directed toward Japan.

The Role of the Comintern Under the influence of the Communist International (Comintern), established by Russian Bolsheviks in 1919 for the explicit goal of fomenting proletarian revolution on a worldwide scale, the nationalist basis of Chinese hostility toward imperialism would be elevated to a global struggle against capitalism. The Comintern helped to found the Chinese Communist Party (CCP) in 1921 in preparation for a worldwide communist movement, but the Comintern recognized that conditions in China were not yet ripe for a proletarian revolution. For the moment, the CCP was to unite forces with the Guomindang (GMD), the official representative of the government of the Republic of China, to rid the country of the imperialism and warlordism that threatened the existence of the young Chinese republic.

Ironically, given the Comintern's diatribe against imperialism, the leading role Comintern advisers assumed in directing China's affairs bespeaks of an alternative form of imperialism. Comintern advisers guided policy with the interests of the Soviet Union—not China—in mind. While ostensibly there to help the Chinese, the Comintern presence was to ensure that China remained within the Soviet sphere of influence.

Peasant Nationalism In the face of the resurgence of Japanese expansionist activities in the 1930s, the CCP's staunch opposition to imperialism inspired what has been described as "peasant nationalism" (Johnson 1962). The CCP's consistent policy of resistance drew into the CCP fold many students, intellectuals, and members of the middle class who had formerly supported the GMD. While the GMD's appeasement of Japanese imperialism cost it popular support, the CCP effectively directed widespread feelings of anti-imperialism into a nationalist movement that helped the CCP to defeat Japan in 1945 and the GMD in 1949.

With the establishment of the People's Republic of China (PRC) in 1949, the imperialism that had threatened Chinese sovereignty for well over a century finally came to an end. However, the legacy of imperialism persisted: in historical narratives that portrayed China as a victim of foreign imperialism; in the urban landscape of areas that had once been international concessions; in the political rhetoric that categorically labeled all things foreign as evil; and in the underdevelopment of vast sectors of the Chinese economy. Certainly, more than a century of battling imperialism had left scars, both physical and psychological, on China and its people. But in the post-1949 era, as the CCP matured and emerged from the shadow of the Comintern, a new chapter began in China's relationship with imperialism.

FROM COLD WAR TO "GREATER CHINA"

In a world dominated by the Cold War, history and geopolitics indicated that China would align with the Soviet Union against the United States in the ideological conflict between communism and capitalism. The "lean to one side" stance that would characterize China's foreign policy until the mid-1950s, however, was not inevitable. Shortly after its founding, the PRC had hoped to establish diplomatic relations with the United States. However, the latter's military presence in the Taiwan Strait following the outbreak of the Korean War in 1950 and the conclusion of a mutual defense treaty between the United States and Taiwan in 1954 hardened the PRC's attitude toward the United States. Differences of opinion on the Taiwan issue also contributed to increasing tensions between China and the Soviet Union.

As relations with the Soviet Union began to cool, China's foreign policy in the mid-1950s signaled a new emphasis on improving relations and forging alliances with the nonaligned countries in Africa and Asia. The Bandung Conference in 1955 came to symbolize the spirit of mutual cooperation, commitment to peaceful coexistence, and opposition to imperialism that informed China's foreign policy. A modest foreign-aid program and a failed attempt to convene a conference of third-world countries in Algiers in 1965 attest to China's ambition to lead the developing world.

The late 1960s witnessed escalating tensions between China and the Soviet Union over border skirmishes. Chinese leaders interpreted the Brezhnev doctrine, proclaimed in 1968 to justify the Soviet invasion of Czechoslovakia, as a thinly disguised rationale for Soviet interference in the domestic affairs of countries in the communist world. In the hopes of gaining a powerful ally in the face of what appeared to be Soviet imperialism, China made overtures to the United States that would eventually lead to the normalization of relations between the two countries in 1979.

In many respects, the 1970s signaled an important shift in Chinese perceptions of the world and China's place within it. In 1971 China gained membership in the United Nations, with a permanent seat on the Security Council. Despite its rhetorical commitment to developing countries and communism, China aligned itself with the developed countries and the institutions of global capitalism, joining the World Bank, the International Monetary Fund, and the World Trade Organization. When the collapse of the Soviet Union left the United States the sole superpower, China improved or established relations with countries in the Middle East, Central Asia, and Latin America, forming alliances to check American hegemony. Some of China's neighbors, however, interpreted China's actions as expansionist and took steps to protect themselves. Indonesia, for instance, set aside its long-standing differences with Australia and signed a mutual defense treaty in 1995.

As a result of the reforms launched under the leadership of Deng Xiaoping beginning in 1978, China has become an economic powerhouse in the Asia-Pacific region. Whether or not China will recapture its place of supremacy during its golden age of empire remains uncertain, particularly within today's global system of sovereign nation-states. At the very least, the recovery of Taiwan and other areas considered to be part of China remains a top priority. Whatever the future holds, all signs indicate that the twenty-first century will be the Pacific century, with China playing a dominant if not central role.

SEE ALSO *Extraterritoriality; Foreign Concessions, Settlements, and Leased Territories; Harbin; Scramble for Concessions; Shanghai Mixed Court.*

BIBLIOGRAPHY

Cohen, Paul A. *Discovering History in China: American Historical Writing on the Recent Chinese Past.* New York: Columbia University Press, 1984.

Fairbank, John King, and Deng Siyu (Ssu-Yu Teng), eds. *China's Response to the West: A Documentary Survey, 1839–1923.* Cambridge, MA: Harvard University Press, 1954.

Hark Tsui, dir. *Once Upon a Time in China.* 1991.

Hu Sheng. *Imperialism and Chinese Politics.* Beijing: Foreign Language Press, 1955.

Johnson, Chalmers A. *Peasant Nationalism and Communist Power: The Emergence of Revolutionary China.* Stanford, CA: Stanford University Press, 1962.

Metzger, Thomas A., and Ramon H. Myers, eds. *Greater China and U.S. Foreign Policy: The Choice between Confrontation and Mutual Respect*. Stanford, CA: Hoover Institution Press, 1996.

Sheng, Michael M. *Battling Western Imperialism: Mao, Stalin, and the United States*. Princeton, NJ: Princeton University Press, 1997.

Spence, Jonathan D. *The Search for Modern China*. 2nd ed. New York: Norton, 1999.

Waley, Arthur. *The Opium War through Chinese Eyes*. Stanford, CA: Stanford University Press, 1958.

Lisa Tran

INCOME

A most desired effect of economic growth is the increase of personal or household income for all groups and individuals in a society. In this regard, economic growth during the Maoist period of the People's Republic of China (PRC) did not produce sizeable effects on income, which stagnated for two decades for the majority of the population. After economic reforms had been launched in 1978, economic growth produced a steep increase in income per capita for all groups in society, eventually lifting an estimated 200 million people out of absolute poverty. Yet, the Chinese miracle is not a success without flaws, because almost all observers agree that income disparities have grown very quickly. This matches a relatively robust regularity of economic growth, the Kuznets curve, which states that in the course of economic development, income disparities follow an inverted 'U', beginning with a relatively equal distribution, moving through a state of rapidly increasing inequality, and returning to a more equal distribution in the final stage. The driving force of this pattern is the shift of labor from the agricultural to the industrial sector, concomitant with large-scale rural-urban migration. In China, the special pattern of rural-urban migration imposed by the household registration system played an important role in shaping the dynamics of income distribution. Furthermore, China is a large country in which geography has a great effect on income distribution, which is bolstered by regional economic policies, especially the policies that favored the coastal provinces in opening up the nation to the global economy between 1978 and 2001, the year of China's entry into the World Trade Organization.

MEASUREMENT ISSUES

The measurement of personal income in China is fraught with many difficulties, both conceptual and operational.

In the first two decades of economic reforms the urban population enjoyed many kinds of open and disguised subsidies, including participation in collective consumption of work units, for example, the free provision of services such as health care and even the free distribution of consumer goods. An objective assessment of household income would have to monetize all these benefits. With the almost complete privatization of urban housing at the end of the 1990s, it became necessary to calculate imputed income from private housing. Comparable difficulties arise, for example, with the transition of urban health care from a publicly funded system to a partly marketized one.

By comparison, the rural population never did enjoy large-scale subsidies. Instead, its large share of in-kind consumption would require the calculation of imputed income from both agricultural production and housing, which raises difficult questions regarding the selection of appropriate prices. Furthermore, sources of rural income changed considerably in the course of reforms; for example, nonagricultural wage income and entrepreneurial profits from family business increased rapidly during that time.

All comparisons over time require the calculation of real values by means of appropriate deflators. However, there are substantial interregional and rural-urban differences in price levels and in the pertinent consumption baskets, inducing large margins of error in comparisons across households, if deflators only apply for larger spatial units such as provinces, or if they cannot accurately reflect the rapidly changing basket of consumption goods since the 1980s.

On an operational level, the assessment of income is much more difficult than the assessment of GDP per capita, which can be based directly on national accounts. Personal income requires the inclusion of all possible sources of income on the individual level, such as imputed income, and this is only possible by means of household survey data. In China different longitudinal surveys have been conducted by several institutions. The official national data are compiled by the National Bureau of Statistics, but they do not fully include imputed incomes and do not include statistics on migrants. Also there is a basic distinction between rural and urban surveys that relates to the long-standing organizational separation between statistical organizations, such as the special rural surveys of the Ministry of Agriculture. This fragmentation is overcome by independent national surveys, the most important of which is conducted regularly by Chinese and international researchers for the Chinese Academy of Social Sciences. Another important survey is undertaken by the Chinese Center for Disease Control and Prevention with other Chinese and international partners. Until most recently, this institutional fragmentation implied that important aspects of income distribution were depicted differently, depending on the survey and its methodology. As a result, even some fundamental issues remain open to debate, such as the fate of the poorest segments in society.

EVOLUTION OF INCOME DISTRIBUTION SINCE 1978

According to the official data, between 1978 and 2007 both rural and urban incomes grew tremendously: The index of 2007, with its basis in 1978, was 752.3 for urban incomes and 734.4 for rural incomes. Starting out from a lower basis, this results in 4140.4 RMB per capita annual net income for rural households and 13785.8 RMB per capita disposable income for urban households. Over time, after an early stage that saw a relative improvement of the rural position, the ratio deteriorated in a wavelike pattern (see figure 1). This was the result of a number of complex developments, especially the growing economic power of the coastal provinces that spurred rapid urbanization, turning a growing number of the most affluent rural residents into urbanites. Thus urbanization increases rural-urban inequality without producing a commensurate welfare loss for the rural population, because there is a continuous outflow of the most affluent rural households into the urban group. The wave-like pattern also shows a relatively strong impact of determinants with medium-term reach, such as the role of prices for agricultural products.

The growth of the standard indicator for national income inequality, the Gini coefficient, probably obscures more than it reveals, because it is a composite of the respective rural and urban developments, which do not manifest the same dynamics. This implies that the urban-rural gap was a major determinant of the growth of the Gini in the 1990s. Recently it also has been driven by increasing urban inequality: One major determinant is growing urban unemployment, both open and hidden. For example, workers who keep the employment relation but are simply sent home on hold, are cut off from bonus payments and other wage supplements. At the other end of the income scale, skilled and educated employees benefit from the inflow of foreign direct investment, which drives up wages with its high demand for these labor groups. In the 2010s, the fate of urban pensioners will strongly determine income disparities.

All these data can be seriously distorted by the different costs of living across China, which are lower in the poorer areas. This applies to both the rural-urban distinction and the interregional distinction. Therefore, the overall income disparity in China might be overestimated to a substantial degree by official data.

Highly aggregate measures of inequality in a country of the size of China blur the fact that total inequality is

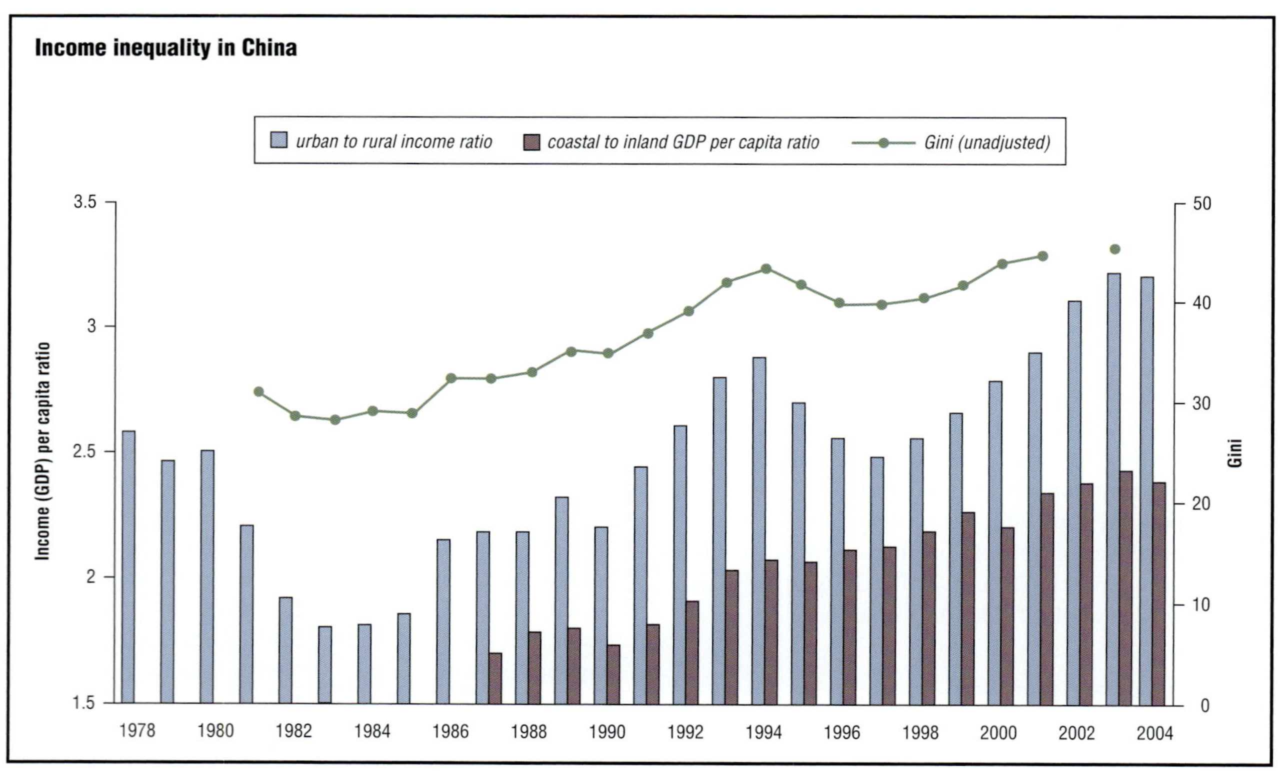

Figure 1

most strongly influenced by inequality within the smaller units of measurement. For example, intrarural income inequality is determined less by interregional inequality than by inequality within villages. This reflects the strong impact of the very unequal distribution of opportunities on the grassroots level. In particular, variations in educational attainments and networking opportunities beyond the locality strongly determine entrepreneurial success.

The larger patterns of disparities, in particular the gap between the western part of China and the coastal areas, are driven also by the fact that inequalities such as rural-urban inequalities are more pronounced in the western part. This implies that redistributive policies need to be focused more on particular groups and determinants of inequality and less on the large units, such as the division of China into the so-called three belts of the coastal, the central, and the western provinces.

In sum, increasing inequality of income is a phenomenon that goes hand in hand with rapid economic growth and structural change in a very large country. In China, it is still an expression of the exceptionally strong income growth of the most advanced segments and regions in the economy, which is accompanied by an income growth in other segments that still meets reasonable expectations. Whether income inequality becomes a serious policy issue will depend crucially on whether there is a hardening of structural determinants of unequal opportunities, such as the unequal quality of primary- and middle-school education across China, and whether the costs of structural adaptation are partly shouldered by social policies for the most vulnerable.

BIBLIOGRAPHY

Benjamin, Dwayne, Loren Brandt, and John Giles. The Evolution of Income Inequality in Rural China. *Economic Development and Cultural Change* 53, no. 4 (2005): 769–824.

Khan, Azizur Rhaman, and Carl Riskin. China's Household Income and Its Distribution, 1995 and 2002. *China Quarterly* 182 (2005): 356–384.

Wan Guanghua, ed. *Inequality and Growth in Modern China.* Oxford, U.K.: Oxford University Press, 2008.

Carsten Herrmann-Pillath

INDIA, RELATIONS WITH

With more than one billion people, India is the world's second most populous country after China. The two Asian giants also share a long history of intellectual, cultural, and religious exchanges dating back two thousand years. As India gained independence from British colonial rule in August 1947, the Nationalist government of China was struggling to hold on to power in the face of a determined Communist onslaught, culminating in the founding of the People's Republic of China in October 1949. Facing enormous challenges, Asia's great new republics embarked on different paths to political, social, and economic development. While Communist China, under the leadership of Mao Zedong and Zhou Enlai, chose a highly centralized system of government and economic management, the newly independent India, under a British-educated Jawaharlal Nehru (1889–1964), opted for a democratic form of government and a mixed economy, combining private and public enterprise. These differences in ideology and political and economic systems were, however, relatively easily surmounted as, in January 1950, India became one of the first few countries outside the Soviet bloc to recognize the new Chinese government. The two countries forged a close friendship in the early 1950s, characterized by the slogan *Hindi-Chini bhai bhai* (Indians and Chinese are brothers). There was also much talk of Asian unity and cooperation following the 1954 Panchsheel Agreement unveiled by Zhou and Nehru.

However, this initial optimism and mutual respect gave way to suspicion and derision as differences over boundary and Tibet began to occupy the minds of leaders and the general public on both sides. The two governments found it difficult to reconcile their respective positions on the border, a situation that was further complicated by India's decision in 1959 to grant the Fourteenth Dalai Lama political asylum in India as he escaped from Tibet following a failed uprising there. This led to the two countries fighting a brief border war in the autumn of 1962. The origins and causes of this war are still hotly debated, and scholarly opinion remains divided. Over the years, a number of studies have been published on this conflict, but most rely almost exclusively on interviews and data collected from Indian sources (see, for example, Maxwell 1970 and Hoffmann 1990). A comprehensive study using both Indian and Chinese sources is yet to be written, mainly because of the difficulty of getting free access to documents and decision makers in China. Nevertheless, the bitter legacy of this war left deep scars on the psyche of people and leaders in both countries, especially in India, which came off second best. It is believed that Nehru, who had invested so much in the Sino-Indian relationship, never recovered from the shock of this war and died a broken man in 1964.

Following the 1962 war, the relations between the two great Asian powers went into deep freeze. Diplomatic relations were downgraded and ambassadors withdrawn. India adopted a more sympathetic attitude toward Tibetan refugees and began strengthening its defense preparedness, leading to its first nuclear test in May 1974. China, on its part, intensified its efforts to bolster Pakistan by providing it with political, diplomatic, and material support in its rivalry with India—a strategy that continues to cause anger and resentment in India despite improvements in

of population." The next stage is to agree on a framework for the delineation of the line of actual control between the two countries. This task is proving to be much harder.

The final settlement of the boundary dispute would require political will and courage on both sides. While the Chinese government does not have to deal with parliamentary opposition, in democratic India, political consensus will be needed before any settlement is accepted. However, as one prominent Indian analyst said, "the very mention of a final settlement of the boundary question with China sends a shiver down the spine of the Indian political establishment" (Raja Mohan 2003, p. 166). Nevertheless, a fair, reasonable, and mutually acceptable settlement of the boundary dispute will remove the biggest hurdle to a full normalization of relations between the two Asian neighbors. This would undoubtedly be good for the two countries, but it would also enhance the security of the whole region.

SEE ALSO *Influences Abroad: Influence of Chinese Art on India's Nationalist Movement; Pakistan, Relations with.*

BIBLIOGRAPHY

Athwal, Amardeep. *China-India Relations: Contemporary Dynamics*. New York: Routledge, 2007.

Garver, John W. *Protracted Contest: Sino-Indian Rivalry in the Twentieth Century*. New Delhi: Oxford University Press, 2001.

Hoffmann, Steven A. *India and the China Crisis*. Berkeley: University of California Press, 1990.

Liu Xuecheng. *The Sino-Indian Border Dispute and Sino-Indian Relations*. Lanham, MD: University Press of America, 1994.

Maxwell, Neville. *India's China War*. London: Cape, 1970.

Raja Mohan, C. *Crossing the Rubicon: The Shaping of India's New Foreign Policy*. New Delhi: Penguin, 2003.

Pradeep Taneja

INDIVIDUAL AND THE STATE, 1800–1949

The notion of "society" as made up of free, individual citizens, like the notion of the state as distinct from the ruler, is a relatively modern one even in the West, where it originated. China had little preparation for such radical ideas. In 1800, at the summit of the Qing dynasty, individuals in most facets of their existence were regarded as vehicles, the carriers of the identities and values of groups—clans, guilds, social strata like the scholar gentry, the merchants, and the imperial bureaucracy. Institutions of imperial governance cultivated collective norms of behavior, such as the repressive *baojia* system, under which groups of households were held collectively responsible for the actions of their members.

Despite this heritage, a series of dramatic events had popularized a key notion, that of popular sovereignty (*minquan*): the late Qing Hundred Days' Reform (Wuxu, 1898), the Republican revolution of 1911, opposition to Yuan Shikai's attempted restoration of the empire, the May Fourth movement (1919), and the Northern Expedition (1926–1928). As the other side of the *minquan* coin, *renquan* (human rights) was debated just as eagerly through these times. Under the modernizing drive of the Republican era, a great deal of this debate was translated into statute and daily life. In probably the greatest period of openness in Chinese history, freedom of the press reached unsurpassed levels, thanks to a thriving print culture and despite many repressive measures and limited circulation to the remote countryside.

By 1949 a body of civil law had been formally enacted, defining the rights of citizens as individuals. Control of one's person and one's property was deemed to reside rightfully in the individual (or private) realm. Talk of citizen rights (as formal contractual relations to the state) as well as human rights (deemed noncontractual and implicit in natural law) had come into wide circulation and practical application. This was true in many places but particularly in booming coastal cities such as Shanghai.

To dismiss the notion of individual rights as incompatible with Chinese tradition thus means ignoring a crucial passage of history. After 1949 the incoming Communist regime would rely more on doctrines copied from Vladimir Ilyich Lenin and Joseph Stalin, which labeled talk of rights as "bourgeois" or a figleaf for the archaic, oppressive order. Paradoxically this allowed the imperial *baojia* system of collective surveillance to be reinvented in modern form. When human rights and related ideas emerged at the end of the decade of the Cultural Revolution (1966–1976), they were not without some local traditions to build on but had to contend with a repressive legacy.

Cultural issues in the development of individual rights remained in play, however. These issues related less to the absence of anything like human rights in traditional thought than to a plethora of institutions that closely resembled rights without quite coinciding with them in detail. Thus Confucianism spoke less of rights than of obligations: Social superiors were, like fathers, obliged to listen to and provide for their dependents. As expressed in the work of Mencius, the monarch's obligation to provide for the subsistence of his people was almost equivalent to a right on their part—something to which individual subjects could, in extremity, lay claim. Qing laws provided the functional equivalent of rights of various kinds, including the right to protest. To gain favorable settlements, litigants often cited a rule that court judgments be voluntarily accepted. Despite the official desire to keep litigation to a minimum, it was quite frequent, speaking of a certain confidence among the populace that their appeals had to be listened to.

In practice, however, Confucian obligations, including the obligation to hear complaints, could often be satisfied by outward shows with little substance behind them. Modernist reformers opposed to Confucianism such as Liang Qichao (1873–1929) forcefully argued that a modern state required its citizens to be capable of far more than mute acquiescence in such arrangements. Critical thinkers such as Yan Fu (1853–1921) found a deeper problem in Chinese culture: a blurring of the boundary between two realms, that of the group (or public) and that of the individual (or private). Much, though by no means all, of China's traditional culture venerated self-sacrifice, a tendency strengthened by Buddhist notions of selflessness as a life ideal. Even where individual rights were in question, they needed to be expressed in public as other than individual and as other than rights. Hence human rights in the modern sense had developed, but in dwarf form.

Modern notions of rights, especially as enshrined in civil law, assume that individual (or "selfish") motives exist, and indeed, given correct institutional designs, are of value to society. The formerly blurred boundaries between self and group must, at the very least, be clearly defined, so that the rules applying to the self and to the group become distinct in turn. The arc of social and intellectual development from 1800 to 1949 followed this trend. It remains a work in progress.

SEE ALSO *Baojia System; Liang Qichao; Rights Defense Movement; Yan Fu.*

BIBLIOGRAPHY

Dikötter, Frank. *The Age of Openness: China before Mao*. Berkeley: University of California Press, 2008.

Karl, Rebecca E., and Peter Zarrow, eds. *Rethinking the 1898 Reform Period: Political and Cultural Change in Late Qing China*. Cambridge, MA: Harvard University Press, 2002.

Kirby, William C., ed. *Realms of Freedom in Modern China*. Stanford, CA: Stanford University Press, 2004.

David Kelly

INDUSTRIAL DEVELOPMENT SINCE 1949

Industrial development has been the main target of economic policies adopted by the Chinese Communist Party since 1949, however different the policies were in scope and content. Until the late 1990s, agricultural and rural development were not the central concern of the Chinese modernization effort, which was driven by the belief that China needed to adopt the newest and most advanced technologies in order to achieve prosperity and resume its proper place in the concert of powerful nations. Since the mid-nineteenth century, following the model of Western industrializing nations, East Asian reformers perceived a close relation between industrial development and geostrategic power. This perception engendered a strong competitive stance toward industrial development, which in China was fused with Marxist ideology in its Maoist shape, resulting in divergent development in the East Asian region, in spite of a shared motivation.

INDUSTRIALIZATION STRATEGY AND HISTORICAL BACKGROUND

Chinese industrialization was shaped by the Marxist theory of accumulation, which emphasizes the conflict between accumulation and consumption. This view implies interference with the economic process in order to maximize investment. Particular expressions of this conceptual framework in the Chinese setting include the use of distorted administrative prices benefitting industrial sectors (i.e., keeping the relative prices of agricultural inputs, energy, and basic commodities low), a low-wage policy, and a directive plan for investment. Under Maoist rule, this approach was ideologically supported by austere social control of individual lifestyles and the political mobilization of workers. This accumulation-oriented growth pattern represents a strong continuity between the Maoist era and the reform era, with indirect levers substituting for the command-economy levers such as credit allocations and interest rates, state-led investment planning, or sectoral industrial policies.

In 1949 China was an agricultural country, with modern manufacturing playing only a minuscule role in the economy. The northeast (Manchuria), Shanghai, and Wuhan formed the nuclei of China's industrialization. All had suffered destruction during the civil war and, in the case of the northeast, dismantling by Soviet forces in the aftermath of the war. Thus, these regions lacked physical infrastructure for modern industry when the socialist modernization drive set in. In 1952, after recovering from the war, industrial gross value-added was about 15 percent of that of the Soviet Union and 3 percent of the U.S. level, whereas already 5.3 percent of total employment was in manufacturing, compared with 18.3 for the Soviet Union and 25.4 for the United States. These data reveal China's low labor productivity at the onset of industrialization.

At the same time, however, there was a knowledge base from earlier industrial activity that was, in part, socially and regionally concentrated, such as with the Shanghai industrialists. This knowledge base was jeopardized when anti-capitalist movements caused a brain drain out of China, especially to Hong Kong, where Shanghai industrialists contributed to the industrial take-off in the 1950s. In addition, by the 1940s the Nationalist government had already nationalized almost all modern industry, which was taken over by the Communist government. Together with the confiscation of Japanese assets in China, this state of affairs implied that even before the introduction of Soviet central planning in the First Five-Year Plan, modern industry in the People's Republic of China (PRC) was mainly state-owned. The only private industry was in labor-intensive manufacturing, which was closer to traditional handicrafts than to industry.

In spite of these many obstacles, industrialization in China sprang from the county's historical legacy, with important steelworks emerging at Wuhan, where ironworks had already been established during the nineteenth-century self-strengthening movement, as well as at Anshan, which built on the Japanese Showa steelworks.

STAGES OF INDUSTRIALIZATION

Chinese industrial development after 1949 can be divided into six stages, which differ in terms of policy priorities and the resulting structural changes. Interestingly, only three stages can be discerned in the history of China's labor productivity: one in the 1950s, manifesting instability; the second from the 1960s to the mid-1980s, when a jump in labor productivity following the restructuring of the Great Leap Forward led to a plateau effect without further changes; and finally the reform era, with accelerating growth in labor productivity (see Figure 1). The growth in gross value-added even suggests a division into two stages: a stage with incipient growth and instability from 1950 to 1970, and a stage of continuous growth after 1970. Each stage left a particular legacy for the subsequent stages.

Soviet-style Industrialization, 1949–1958 Whereas in the first years after the founding of the PRC, the "New Democracy" initially envisaged a symbiotic relation between private enterprise and state-led industrialization, by the mid-1950s the industrialization effort mainly concentrated on 156 key projects that were realized in cooperation with the Soviet Union. This was accompanied by the establishment of a Soviet-style system of central planning and by a complete transfer of Soviet technologies and standards to China. This

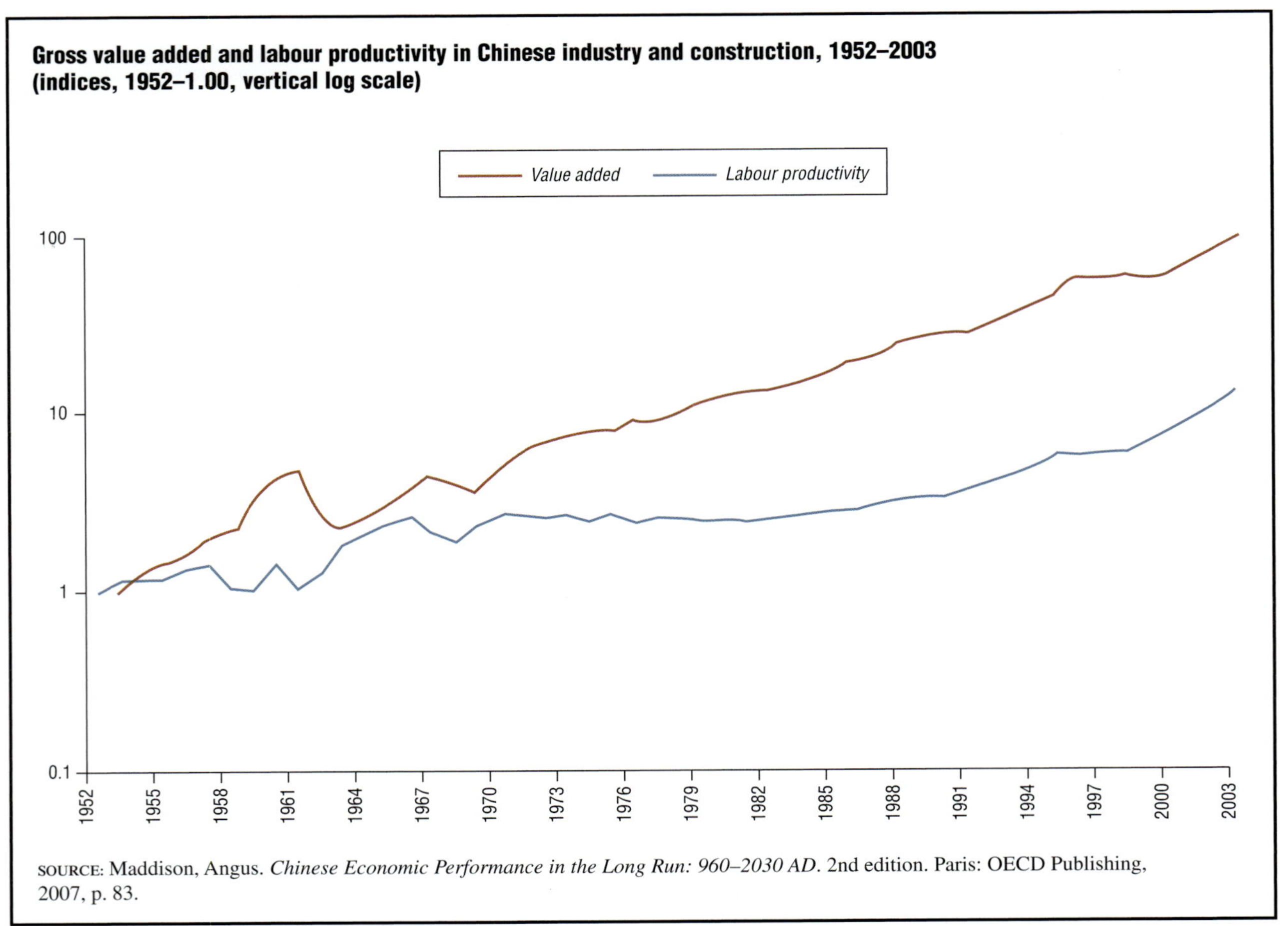

Figure 1

Steel factory in Anshan, Liaoning province, April 5, 2007. *In the 1950s, Chinese government planners concentrated on building a strong industrial economy, similar in design to the Soviet Union. While the Chinese absorbed factories already established by foreign countries, such as the Japanese-built steel factories in Anshan, not until the late 1970s did China begin to realize large advancements in heavy industry.* AP IMAGES

industrialization effort also introduced a lasting structural bias toward heavy industries and upstream industries, which were seen as the crucial bottlenecks in the economy. The resulting growth process was capital-intensive, thus contributing to an increasing imbalance in the labor market, which was suppressed by setting up tighter controls on rural-urban migration. Soviet-style industrialization was therefore also an important determinant of social change in China, engendering the rise of a worker elite in the Chinese cities, with claims to lifelong employment and cradle-to-grave social security, especially in the large state-owned enterprises (SOEs).

Great Leap Forward and Restructuring, 1958–1966 The Great Leap Forward set the scene for a radical departure from the Soviet model. It lasted only briefly, but left two important legacies. One is that the need for labor-intensive industrialization strategies was recognized, at least in principle. The second is that China became decoupled from international technology transfers after the Sino-Soviet rift. The Great Leap Forward mainly affected agriculture and brought a disastrous expansion of quasi-industrial activities to the countryside (such as the infamous backyard furnaces) but resulted in a sharp cyclical downturn in industry.

Cultural Revolution and Its Aftermath, 1966–1976 The Cultural Revolution affected industrial development much less than the Great Leap Forward. Industrial policy was dominated by strategic considerations, which resulted in a capital-intensive relocation and establishment of industries in the interior provinces. The organizational and institutional features of SOEs were politically enforced by PLA interference to restore civil order. After 1968, the gradual political normalization in China's relations with Western countries led to a slow improvement in conditions for accessing technological knowledge. The heavy industrialization strategy continued, while the policy of "walking on two legs" was intended to mitigate negative effects on rural development. In the mid-1970s, rural industrialization began with the expansion of commune enterprises, such as cement and textile production, that catered to the pressing needs of the rural economy.

Rural Industrialization, 1977–1991 Chinese economic reform started in agriculture, with industrial reforms being launched in 1984. However, from the beginning, a shift in industrial policy priorities took place, with a heightened emphasis on so-called light industries—that is, labor-intensive downstream industries, in particular consumption goods. Beyond the economic rationale, this policy aimed at rapidly improving the living conditions of the population after the "lost decade." However, because reforms in the SOE sector proceeded slowly, the opportunities offered by liberalization were mainly seized by rural township-and-village enterprises (TVEs). TVEs emerged as a peculiar institutional form of Chinese industry; they operated outside the formal industrial-planning system, thus reinforcing an industrial dualism in China.

Corporatization and Modernization, 1991–2001 As a result of austerity policies in the aftermath of the 1989 Tiananmen incident, credit allocations to TVEs were curtailed, triggering a shakeout that during the 1990s ended in a cold privatization of many TVEs. Meanwhile, SOE reforms, aimed at establishing a "modern enterprise system," were speeded up. Apart from a gradual improvement of corporate governance and management, a major effect was the shedding of surplus labor in the state sector, and a rapid privatization of small and medium-scale SOEs, especially on the local level.

Globalization, 2001 to the Present China's entry into the World Trade Organization (WTO) in 2001 marked a new stage in the country's industrial development by rapidly intensifying the global competitive pressure on Chinese companies. The Chinese government concluded a move from capital-intensive industrial policies to technology-driven policies. Since the mid-1990s, the foreign-invested sector emerged as a major factor in Chinese industrialization, especially in the export-oriented sectors. The increasing competition on the domestic market triggered responses by Chinese industry, from which the first global players emerged. This development was actively supported by industrial policies, which identified key branches of industry, such as car manufacturing.

PATTERNS AND RESULTS OF INDUSTRIALIZATION

Behind these politically and institutionally diverse stages, a remarkable continuity of the growth process can be observed after 1970 (see Figure 1). This continuity results from the fact that until today, China pursued a capital-intensive industrialization strategy, with a transition from central planning to efficiency-enhancing market institutions only after 1991. This is clearly recognizable in data of total factor productivity (TFP): Between 1978 and 1993, technological progress contributed 3 percent of total growth, whereas between 1993 and 2004, growth of TFP amounted to 6 percent of the total.

Share of value-added and employment across economic sectors, 1978–2004

	Agriculture	Industry	Services
		Value-added (percent of total)	
1978	28	48	24
1993	17	51	33
2004	9	58	33
		Employment (percent of total)	
1978	71	17	12
1993	56	22	21
2004	47	23	31

SOURCE: Bosworth, Barry, and Susan M.Collins. Accounting for Growth: Comparing China and India. *Journal of Economic Perspectives* 22, 1 (2008): 57.

Table 1

The crucial point in China's industrial development was the onset of reforms in 1978. In 1978 China manifested sharp structural distortions, with the industrial sector producing almost 50 percent of value-added but accounting for only 17 percent of employment, whereas the share of agriculture was 28 and 71 percent respectively (Table 1). That is, China was far more industrialized than other countries on the same level of development, yet at the same time China had the employment structure of a low-income country. This distortion provided the starting ground for rural industrialization, which brought employment to huge masses of underemployed farmers. Again, this is different from other less-developed countries, where the pressure of unemployment is normally released to the growth of the service sector, both formal and informal. This situation is an expression of China's peculiar institutional setting, in which regional and local authorities adopt partly autonomous capital-intensive strategies for industrial development. In the 1980s, this practice was strongly supported by the prevailing price discrimination against agricultural products ("price scissor"), highlighting the legacy of the Maoist era.

As a result, Chinese industrialization had achieved a level in 1978 that has not been surpassed during three decades of reforms, in spite of high growth rates. This is also true for the average employment share. Industry was always the main contributor to growth, with services only catching up after WTO entry. For almost all Chinese provinces, secondary industry (i.e., industry plus construction) accounts for more than 40 percent of the gross domestic product (GDP) (only Tibet and Hainan fall significantly below that line). At the same time, however, there is much more variation in employment shares across the provinces. In the Lower Yangzi Delta provinces, industrial employment shares already surpass the 40 percent mark, whereas in less-developed provinces, the structural distortions remain sharp. For example, Yunnan and Guizhou have a secondary industry share in GDP of more that 40 percent, while the employment share is only about 10 percent. Remarkably, the old centers of industrialization in the northeast hover around the 20 percent mark, which indicates a landslide change toward the south in the regional structure of Chinese industry.

Since entering the WTO, China's industrial development exhibits the marks of transition to a market-oriented and competitive environment. This is reflected by the slow growth of industrial employment while productivity increases, with a rapid adoption of modern technologies. Chinese industry manifests the coexistence of old industrial regions suffering from the legacy of socialist planning, and highly dynamic emerging industries, such as biotechnology, special chemicals, and information-technology manufacturing. As a result, the importance of traditional light industries is declining, whereas more differentiated manufacturing has become dominant. This triggers the stronger growth of heavy industries related to resource extraction, chemistry, and machinery. A major force driving these changes is the deepening integration of Chinese industry into global production chains, which are so far dominated by corporate actors from the developed industrial countries. This situation frames the rapid dissemination of global benchmarks in manufacturing, logistics, and technological innovation.

SEE ALSO *Economic Development; Rural Development, 1949–1978; Rural Development since 1978.*

BIBLIOGRAPHY

Bosworth, Barry, and Susan M. Collins. Accounting for Growth: Comparing China and India. *Journal of Economic Perspectives* 22, 1 (2008): 45–66.

Garnaut, Ross, and Yiping Huang, eds. *Growth without Miracles: Readings on the Chinese Economy in the Era of Reform.* New York: Oxford University Press, 2001.

MacFarquhar, Roderick, and John K. Fairbank, eds. *The Cambridge History of China.* Vol. 14, Pt. 1: *The Emergence of Revolutionary China, 1949–1965.* Chaps. 3 and 8. Cambridge, U.K.: Cambridge University Press, 1978–.

Maddison, Angus. *Chinese Economic Performance in the Long Run.* 2nd ed., rev. and updated, 960–2030 A.D. Paris: OECD Development Centre, 2007.

Carsten Herrmann-Pillath

INDUSTRIAL POLICY SINCE 1949

The concept of industrial policy refers to all kinds of government intervention that shape the sectoral structure and the organization of industry, both statically and dynamically. In the latter case, the boundaries to technology policy are fluid. The notion of industry organization includes both aspects of market structure and partly the internal organization of enterprises, insofar as the impact of property rights regimes on governance structures is considered. There is no predestined authority for designing and implementing industrial policies (as compared to, for example, monetary policy); that is, the degree of decentralization and the assignment of competences in particular countries and historical episodes are subject to complex determinants, mainly political in nature.

These general remarks are useful to define the proper perspective on Chinese industrial policies after 1949. Firstly, Chinese industrial policies were part and parcel of a strategy for industrial development, that is, inherently dynamic. This means that after 2000, the shift from industrial policy to technology policy stays in a certain continuity with the past. Secondly, industrial policy was always deeply enmeshed with general policies of systems design, especially the establishment of socialist planning in the 1950s and economic reforms after 1978. Thirdly, it was precisely the establishment of socialist planning that caused the emergence of a very complex governmental structure underlying specific industrial policies across branches and regions, which defies any notion of an integrated national policy. As a result, national industrial policy was directed not only at industrial enterprises and branches, but also, simultaneously, at the actions of government units in a political system that since the beginning of economic reforms in 1978, is best described as "fragmented authoritarianism."

CHANGE AND CONTINUITY OF INDUSTRIAL POLICY FROM MAOISM TO REFORMS

In the 1950s Chinese industrial policy was deeply influenced by the Soviet model of central planning. The core concern was the buildup of 156 enterprises under central control which were regarded to be the technological vanguard in the catch-up of the Chinese economy. These projects were concentrated mostly in the upstream industries in order to provide the basis for extending industrialization across all sectors. In the course of the decade, this policy was supported by the eventual suppression of privately owned industrial enterprises, especially by means of creating an urban collective industry. Collectivization introduced similar principles of internal organization and external coordination, as in state-owned enterprises across all branches of industry, albeit with highly diverse levels of capital endowments and social benefits to the employees.

This Soviet-style approach implied a trajectory of technological change that was dependent on technology transfers from the Soviet Union. Once the Sino-Soviet rift widened, Chinese industrial policy turned to indigenous development of technology as the default option. The inflow of technological knowledge was revived only after the renormalization of external relations in the mid-1970s. Technology transfer has been a major element in all measures of Chinese industrial policy since then. In particular, external economic policies after 1978 explicitly fostered technology transfer, both directly and indirectly. Especially after 1992, China pursued an active strategy of integrating its economy into global production networks, through which a continuous flow of knowledge could be maintained, via a variety of channels, such as the diffusion of industrial standards, training of the workforce, or imitation of benchmark competitors. Thus, external economic policies have been always partly subordinated to industrial policy.

Direct measures began with provisions for technology transfer in the approval process for Sino-foreign joint ventures. China's entry into the World Trade Organization

DAQING

The Daqing oil field, situated between Harbin and Qiqihar in Heilongjiang Province, was made a national model in 1964 when Mao Zedong issued the call, "In industry, learn from Daqing." Daqing was the first major oil field to be opened up in China. To prove that China could do without the support of Soviet or other foreign technicians and assistance and to counter (mostly American) claims that the country would never be self-sufficient in oil, major exploration activities were started in the Daqing area in early 1960. By May of that year, over forty thousand workers and staff from more than thirty factories and mining institutes had started the "massive battle" of opening up Daqing, using 70,000 tons of equipment. One of the exemplary workers involved in this "battle" was Wang Jinxi (1923–1970), who earned the nickname "Iron Man" for braving fatigue, injuries, and difficulties. By the end of 1963, Daqing was operating at full speed, producing 4.4 million tons of oil. In the following years, it became the ultimate model of self-sufficiency and sacrifice that all industrial sectors had to emulate.

Daqing has more than paid back the original investments made. Exploiting the more than 2 billion tons of underground oil reserves, it has been the major oil-production facility in China, despite the fact that the oil, paraffin-based and low in sulfur, is difficult and expensive to extract and refine. By the end of the 1990s, the country was faced with an increased demand for oil and was forced to look for other prospects, both within the nation and worldwide, even though 2.2 billion tons of reserves could be pumped up with existing technologies and equipment. In the meantime, parts of the company that managed China's former premier oil field have been privatized, and many oil workers have been laid off. In 2001 this led to massive demonstrations of disgruntled workers demanding benefits they had been promised under the "iron rice bowl" system.

BIBLIOGRAPHY

Jiang Shanhao. *Impressions of Taching Oilfield.* Beijing: Foreign Languages Press, 1978.

Li Kwok-sing, ed., and Mary Lok, trans. *A Glossary of Political Terms of the People's Republic of China.* Hong Kong: Chinese University Press, 1995.

Taching: Red Banner in China's Industrial Front. Beijing: Foreign Languages Press, 1972.

Stefan R. Landsberger

(WTO) prompted a synthesis of industrial, technological, and external economic policies in which all cooperative economic relationships receive strong support if they contribute to the upgrading of China's technology-intensive manufacturing and high technology. Indirect measures also relate to the intended and unintended effects of the weak protection of patents and intellectual property rights, which has contributed to the rapid emergence of imitators in the Chinese industrial structure. This includes the highly dynamic role of township and village enterprises, epitomized in the industrial revolution of Zhejiang and Jiangsu provinces, in particular.

A fundamental feature of industrial policy in China lies in the close interaction between spontaneous forces of structural change and the resulting need to define a balance between targeted intervention (planning in the past) and soft guidance. This is especially true for the coordination of rural industrialization and the mainstream industrial sector in the shape of urban state-owned enterprises. Rural industrialization was firstly triggered and aborted with the Great Leap Forward. This gave rise to another peculiarly Chinese expression of industrial policy, the fusion of macroeconomic stabilization and structural adjustments. Between 1962 and 1965, this aimed at the restabilization of the core of the central planning system. Later periods saw the shift to light industries and rural reforms after the launch of economic reforms in 1978, the shakeout of rural industries in the early 1990s by means of credit tightening, and the use of environmental regulations to rectify the rural industrial structure in the second half of the 1990s.

The great regional diversity of China defies any attempts at unifying goals and levers of industrial policy. In contemporary China, major aspects of industrial policy merge with regional policies. Important examples include the need to modernize old industrial bases in northeastern China that suffer from technological backwardness, underemployment, and the legacy of state ownership, and the Western development strategy, which simultaneously has to restructure state-owned enterprises (SOEs) and overcome the obstacles to rural industrialization. In comparison, industrial policy in the Lower Yangzi Delta provinces focuses on technology policy and the streamlining of supplier networks in Jiangsu Province, and the upgrading of private small and medium enterprises (SMEs) in Zhejiang Province.

The fundamental nature of Chinese industrial policies has shifted from the dominance of military objectives in the 1960s and 1970s to the dominance of efficiency considerations and development goals in the 1980s and 1990s, and eventually to an emphasis on advanced technology in the new millennium. These shifts define the benchmark for assessing the success of industrial policy. In particular, evaluations of the Maoist era need to take into consideration the tense geostrategic situation: During that period, industrial policies took up the pre-1949 tradition of warfare, and at the same time, first-rate technological capabilities were created in the field of aerospace and nuclear technology. In contemporary China, industrial policy should be evaluated less in terms of efficiency than in terms of the dynamic knowledge economy. Correspondingly, topics such as university-industry collaboration have become more prominent. Today, one of the principal aims of Chinese industrial policy is to foster the emergence of "national champions" with global impact, with measures ranging from creating international public companies under government control to supporting emerging private companies with the promise of global reach.

INDUSTRIAL POLICY UNDER FRAGMENTED AUTHORITARIANISM

A crucial and permanent feature of industrial policy in China has been the existence of multiple decision-making bodies at different levels of government, reflecting the fragmented nature of government authority in China. Following the *tiao kuai* (lines and blocks) approach, authority in industrial policy is divided along the lines of administrative authority in the regions and professional guidance across levels of government. This implies that there are many agents of industrial policy, even down to the level of the county. In principle, all levels of government in China may pursue strategic goals in industrial development and implement industrial policies in the sense mentioned in this entry's introduction. This even includes systemic aspects such as property rights regimes. For example, when in 1996 the central government announced the motto "release the small and grasp the big ones," it left to local governments' discretion in how to deal with the local SOEs.

This complexity of industrial policy is a reflection of the regional property rights system that emerged under socialist planning in China. For example, even in the context of today's market system, a large share of stocks in corporatized SOEs belong to government units being managed by the State-owned Assets Supervision and Administration Commission of the State Council on different regional levels. The establishment of these units interrupted the close fusion of interest between regional governments and regional enterprises that had been a major issue in Chinese industrial policy until recently. Regional governments subordinated industrial policy to other goals, in particular regional employment and regional fiscal income. The result was the phenomenon of regional protectionism, which was rampant in the 1980s and 1990s. Regional industrial policy was directed mainly at supporting the regional economy by many means, such as preferential credits, legal and informal tax reliefs, and privileged access to industrial sites. This produced widespread parallel investments in many industrial sectors, maintaining or even expanding the highly decentralized and fragmented industrial structure. This did not exploit regional advantage, but instead left industries with many regionally dispersed enterprises operating without substantial economies of scale. Similar phenomena emerged in the 1990s and in the early 2000s in the area of technology parks or creative industry precincts.

Given this background, national industrial policy frequently has been an intragovernmental policy rather than a policy directed at the enterprise sector. A typical example was the attempts at industrial restructuring that highlighted the conceptions of "trusts," "conglomerates," and "industrial holdings" in different initiatives. In many of these cases, lead SOEs were assigned the task of developing cross-regional enterprise networks that eventually would impose efficient patterns of specialization in supplier relations. This presupposed an alignment of interests between responsible government units. Today, industrial policy often falls to the newly established regulatory bodies, which balance industry and government interests in maintaining control of the commanding heights of the economy. Shifting balances of power emerge, from government influence from increasingly powerful business interests to state-capitalist dynamics.

A positive side of this multiplicity of agents of industrial policy is competition among government units, which is secured mainly by imposing tight budget constraints on local governments. These were implemented after the fiscal centralization of 1994 and the parallel restructuring of the Central Bank (People's Bank of China) according to larger regional units. Tight budget constraints enforced industrial restructuring, symbolized on the national level in the austere personality of Zhu Rongji (b. 1928). Since the mid-1990s industrial policy has been shaped increasingly by modern conceptions such as the notions of "industrial clusters" and "competitive advantage," which appear even in official political documents. At the same time, old-style policies are more constrained by the WTO agreement. Indeed, the perceived distortions caused by industrial policies are the main reason why important trade partners refuse to recognize China's status as a market economy. This refusal has produced a gradual change in industrial policy in China, for example, by encouraging the use of technological standards in order to foster national competitiveness, as in the mobile communications industry.

SEE ALSO *Central Planning; Heavy Industry; Township and Village Enterprises.*

BIBLIOGRAPHY

Blecher, Marc, and Vivienne Shue. Into Leather: State-Led Development and the Private Sector in Xinji. *China Quarterly* 166 (2001): 368–393.

Harwit, Eric. Building China's Telecommunications Network: Industrial Policy and the Role of Chinese State-Owned, Foreign, and Private Domestic Enterprises. *China Quarterly* 190 (2007): 311–332.

Naughton, Barry. *The Chinese Economy: Transitions and Growth.* Cambridge: Massachusetts Institute of Technology Press, 2007.

Pearson, Margaret M. Governing the Chinese Economy: Regulatory Reform in the Service of the State. *Public Administration Review* 67, 4 (2007): 718–730.

Carsten Herrmann-Pillath

INDUSTRIALIZATION, 1860–1949

Late imperial China had some of the world's most advanced industries—for example, in textiles and iron production—but the nineteenth century saw China fall far behind many European countries. Growth of modern industry was rapid in China in the first half of the twentieth century, but it started from a very low base, and it was the 1990s before China's workforce ceased being predominantly agricultural.

Statistics for industrial production are entirely absent before 1912 and severely lacking up to 1949. The most complete survey was conducted by Liu Dajun in 1933, and these figures have formed the basis for most studies of the structure of the Republican economy. For trends through time, researchers are still mainly reliant on the pioneering index of the output of fifteen industrial commodities compiled in the 1960s by John Key Chang, although this was biased toward mining and notably did not include the important food-processing industries. Ongoing work by Kubo Tōru, working with the Asian Historical Statistics Project at Hitotsubashi University, is broadening the coverage and improving the accuracy of the index, while other revisions have been suggested by Tim Wright. Figure 1 shows trends in industrial output (seventeen commodities) between 1912 and 1949 according to Chang's figures, with some additions and adjustments.

Despite this growth, industry and particularly modern industry played no more than a marginal role in the Chinese economy during the pre-1949 period. Table 1 shows that, even including mining and utilities, modern industry contributed only 3.4 percent to net domestic product, and less than 1 percent to employment.

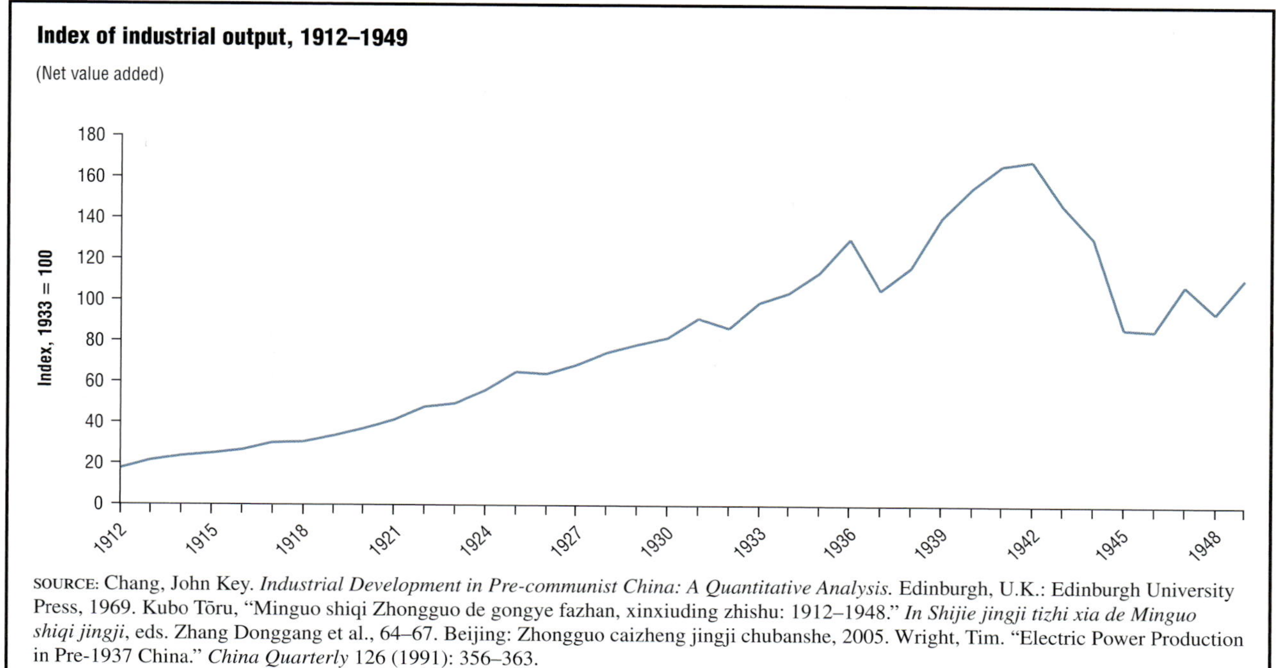

SOURCE: Chang, John Key. *Industrial Development in Pre-communist China: A Quantitative Analysis.* Edinburgh, U.K.: Edinburgh University Press, 1969. Kubo Tōru, "Minguo shiqi Zhongguo de gongye fazhan, xinxiuding zhishu: 1912–1948." *In Shijie jingji tizhi xia de Minguo shiqi jingji*, eds. Zhang Donggang et al., 64–67. Beijing: Zhongguo caizheng jingji chubanshe, 2005. Wright, Tim. "Electric Power Production in Pre-1937 China." *China Quarterly* 126 (1991): 356–363.

Figure 1

STAGES OF INDUSTRIAL DEVELOPMENT

Modern industry appeared only on the margins of the economy in the late nineteenth century. The most important enterprises were the arsenals established by late Qing officials such as Li Hongzhang, and the shipping, mining, and other enterprises that were established to support them. While there were some smaller predecessors, the main arsenals were opened in the mid-1860s: The Jiangnan Arsenal at Shanghai was producing muskets and howitzers by the late 1860s. The first Chinese steamship company was established in 1872, and the first coal mine was opened in 1878, the first match mill in 1894, the first bean-pressing mill in 1895, and the first flour mill in 1896.

Foreign companies were prohibited by treaties from establishing industrial enterprises in China for most of the nineteenth century. Most of the eighty-eight foreign companies in China up to 1894 were engaged in shipbuilding and ship repair in the treaty ports, processing of exports and imports, or other light manufacturing. There were a few unsuccessful attempts to establish textile or soybean-processing plants.

In most cases, the introduction of modern technology met with problems and resistance, and in this early period there were few unambiguous successes. Problems included a supposed incompatibility between China's Confucian culture and modern technological and business operations, widespread opposition by vested interests in China (for example, by boatmen on the Grand Canal opposing the use of railways or steamships), the unreliable quality of locally sourced inputs, and the inappropriateness of some Western technology for China's factor proportions.

The major change came when the Treaty of Shimonoseki in 1895 gave foreigners the right to establish industrial

Structure of the Chinese economy by output and employment (1933)

	Net domestic product		Employment	
Sector	**Billion Ch$**	**%**	**Million**	**%**
Agriculture	18.76	65.0	204.91	79.1
Factories, mining, utilities	0.98	3.4	1.94	0.7
Handicrafts	2.04	7.1	15.74	6.1
Trade and transport	4.34	15.0	26.18	10.1
Other	2.74	9.5	10.44	4.0
Total	**28.86**		**259.21**	

SOURCE: Liu Dazhong and Ye Gongjia. *The Economy of the Chinese Mainland: National Income and Economic Development, 1933–1959.* Princeton, NJ: Princeton University Press, 1965, pp. 66, 69.

Table 1

enterprises in China (at least in the treaty ports). This led to a rapid expansion of foreign investment in industrial and mining ventures and, at least as importantly, to the emergence of Chinese enterprises in competition with them. For the first decade, and to a considerable period beyond, Chinese enterprises were set up by people in or with links to the bureaucracy, as part of late Qing or warlord modernization programs, or as means for the state at various levels to extract resources from society or for individuals to take advantage of rent-seeking opportunities in profitable sectors.

World War I (1914–1918) saw further growth in the infant Chinese industrial sector, though the estimates offered in Figure 1 belie the proposition that this was a particularly rapid period of growth. Growth was due to two main factors, the relative importance of which is not clear: (1) the coming into operation of China's major railway lines; and (2) import substitution as well as more buoyant export markets because of the withdrawal of European goods from the market during the war.

In the 1921–1922 period, as was the case in most countries, a postwar depression affected industrial profits and prices, but total output growth only slowed down. After that, growth resumed, and continued through years of warlord disruption and chaos during the 1920s, except for a small decline in 1926. While many products and markets were badly affected by the civil wars, Shanghai was able to continue to develop relatively free of warlord interference, enjoying the "golden age" of Chinese capitalism. Japanese power in Manchuria also limited disruption there. Growth temporarily halted in 1932, when output fell slightly owing to the Japanese attack on Shanghai, but it resumed thereafter. Between 1933 and 1935 the impact of the global depression was severe for some industries, particularly silk, but overall was manifested in below-trend growth rates, rather than any decline in production. Indeed, for the prewar period as a whole, Figure 1 suggests a relatively stable pattern of growth of around 7 to 8 percent.

World War II (1937–1945) disrupted industrial production to a much greater extent than any previous disturbances. Nationally, output fell sharply following the Japanese invasion, but later recovered. Production in Shanghai, by far China's largest consumer-goods center, boomed between 1937 and 1940 as foreign protection made the city a "solitary island" of economic prosperity while surrounding areas were devastated by war. At the same time, war-related heavy industrial production increased in North China. Meanwhile, as the Japanese advanced, much of the equipment of China's military industries, and of 639 private factories, was relocated, often by hand, first to Wuhan and then to new locations in western China; this amounted to only a small part of China's total industrial plant, however.

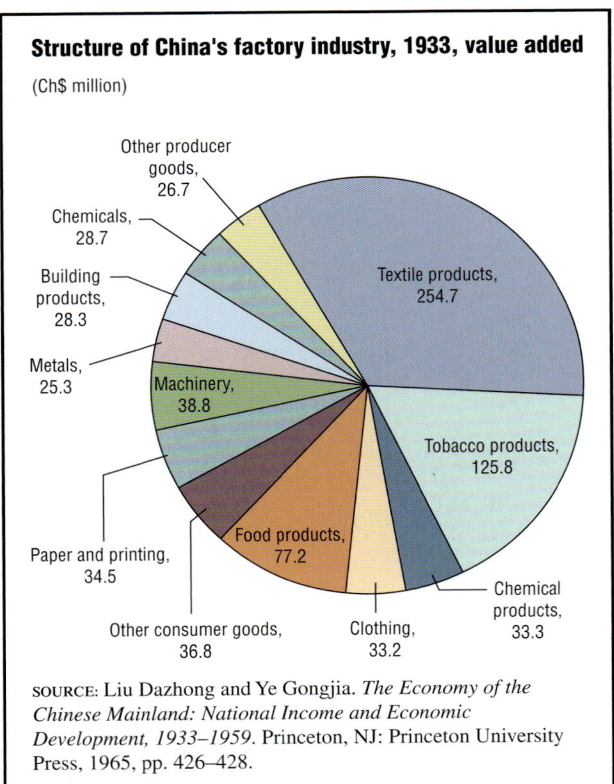

SOURCE: Liu Dazhong and Ye Gongjia. *The Economy of the Chinese Mainland: National Income and Economic Development, 1933–1959*. Princeton, NJ: Princeton University Press, 1965, pp. 426–428.

Figure 2

As Figure 1 shows, China's national industrial output grew to a wartime peak in 1942 (different estimates, based on different mixes of industries, put the wartime peak in 1939). After 1942, output collapsed to a level that by 1945 was slightly over half that of 1942. There was some recovery in the late 1940s, though it did not reach the prewar peak.

STRUCTURE OF CHINESE INDUSTRY

The structure of the manufacturing sector reflected China's early stage of industrialization, with most production concentrated in the consumer-goods industries. The largest industries included cotton yarn and textiles, tobacco and cigarettes, and silk yarn and cloth. Chinese scholars have tended to perceive this in negative terms, as reflecting an "unbalanced" pattern of development aimed at serving foreign interests. However, most successful examples of industrial development have started with consumer-goods industries, while those that have followed the Stalinist model, concentrating on heavy industry, have had to bear massive costs and inefficiencies.

As shown in Figure 2, textiles comprised over one-third of modern factory production. Cotton textiles accounted for most of that and constituted the most prominent part

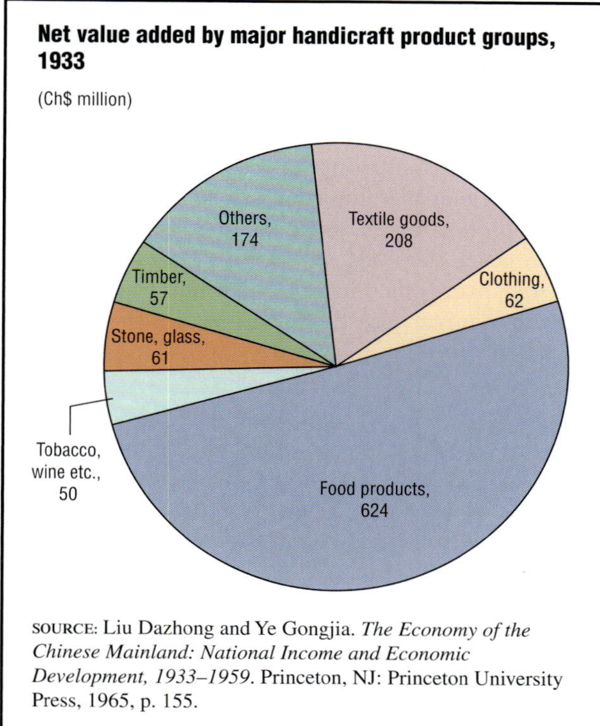

SOURCE: Liu Dazhong and Ye Gongjia. *The Economy of the Chinese Mainland: National Income and Economic Development, 1933–1959*. Princeton, NJ: Princeton University Press, 1965, p. 155.

Figure 3

of the modern industrial sector, especially in Shanghai and the Lower Yangzi. There was also a large handicraft-cotton textile sector, which was profoundly affected by the availability of factory-produced yarn and iron-gear looms. The silk industry, one of the few in China to be based predominantly on production for export, provided substantial employment and incomes in both urban and rural areas in Guangdong and the Lower Yangzi and to a lesser extent in Sichuan. Both production and incomes declined sharply in the context of the global depression.

The second largest of the consumer-goods industries was tobacco, which accounted for around 17 percent of industrial production. Growth of output and employment was rapid, at around 20 percent per year: From fewer than one thousand workers in the late 1910s, employment expanded to more than forty thousand workers in the 1930s. For most of the period, the tobacco industry was dominated by foreign capital in the form mainly of the British American Tobacco Company. Smaller Chinese companies, of which the Nanyang Brothers Tobacco Company was the most prominent, were, however, able to use their greater flexibility and nationalist appeal to compete with some success.

Not surprisingly in a predominantly agricultural country, the processing of food products was another important consumer-goods sector. While much of this sector remained within the bounds of traditional production in the villages, two major products—wheat flour and soybean cakes and oil—originated mainly in modern industry. Modern flour mills were found in many regions in central, northern, and northeastern China, and wheat flour was the third-largest factory sector in terms of gross value of output, though it had a low rate of value added.

Soybean processing was most widespread in Manchuria, and indeed the whole economy of the region in the 1910s and 1920s has been described as a "soybean economy." Production was heavily oriented toward the export sector, and in the 1920s soybean products were China's major export. Exports of bean oil and bean cake (excluding unprocessed beans) amounted to around Ch $100 million at their peak in 1926, some 11.6 percent of total exports, about the same as reeled silk. The oil was used, often in Europe, as a lubricant or to produce margarine and other food products; the residual bean cake was widely used as fertilizer in Japan and South China. The industry was seriously affected by the global depression—as with silk, it faced both a cyclical downturn in demand and longer-term substitution threats, in this case the rise of chemical fertilizer.

China reflected the general pattern of economic development in having only a limited producer-goods sector. Many of its large producer-goods enterprises, such as the Hanyeping Company, failed. Nevertheless, Chinese enterprises were very successful in small-scale machine building. Many started out as repair shops, repairing imported machinery. They developed to the manufacture of parts, and on the eve of the war began to make their own machinery. By the 1920s and 1930s they were providing machinery not only for handicrafts but also for a wide range of food-processing industries and even, to a limited extent, agriculture.

Modern industrial technology was not limited to manufacturing industries, narrowly defined. Utilities, and particularly electricity generation, were central to the modernization of China's cities. By far the largest enterprise was the foreign-owned Shanghai Power Company, which in the mid-1930s converted half a million tons of coal annually into 750 million kilowatt-hours, three-quarters of which was sold to cotton mills. Smaller plants could be found across the country, and electric utilities contributed about Ch$100 million to the gross domestic product. A comparison with Figure 2 shows that this sector outranked all others except textiles and tobacco in terms of value added. It was, however, capital intensive, so its share of employment was lower.

Railway workshops constituted another major locus of modern industrial technology. Chinese national railways ran major workshops at Changxindian near Beijing,

Jiang'an north of Hankou, and Tangshan. Such workshops could be of considerable size: The shop run by the Japanese-owned South Manchurian Railway Company at Shahekou near Dalian employed around three thousand workers in 1930.

GEOGRAPHICAL DISTRIBUTION OF INDUSTRY

Geographically, industry was heavily concentrated in two locations, with Shanghai alone accounting for almost 40 percent of manufacturing output in 1933, and Manchuria adding another 14 percent. Shanghai was the main focus for consumer-goods industries, particularly textiles, while Manchuria under the Japanese dominated the heavy industrial sector. Other smaller centers, such as Tianjin, Qingdao, and Guangzhou, were also mainly located in the coastal provinces. Chinese nationalists tended to attribute this distribution to the impact of imperialism, but it is likely that the economics of location played a more important part, as is perhaps indicated by the reemergence of similar patterns during the post-Mao reform period.

While industry was heavily concentrated in large urban areas, there was another model, that of much smaller rural industrial districts. Several such districts emerged in North China on the basis of textile production using iron-gear looms in the first half of the twentieth century. The best-known was Gaoyang, 130 kilometers south of Beijing. There, the industry developed on the basis of supplies of Japanese machinery and yarn, reaching a peak in the mid-1930s.

RURAL INDUSTRY AND HANDICRAFTS

Throughout the first half of the twentieth century, the rural handicraft sector remained larger than the modern industrial sector. Ta-Chung Liu and Kung-Chia Yeh's (Liu Dazhong and Ye Kongjia 1965) estimates for 1933 suggested that handicrafts contributed Ch$2.04 billion to the gross domestic product, while modern factories contributed only Ch$640 million. Handicraft production was spread over a vast number of products, as shown in Figure 3. Processing of foodstuffs was by far the most important, followed by textiles, but there were many others: Lumber, transportation equipment, stone, clay and glass products, tobacco, wine and liquor, and paper all contributed over Ch$30 million in net value added.

While much of the production was for local consumption, some handicraft sectors developed substantial national or even export markets. For example, carpets and strawbraid from North China were substantial contributors to China's total exports. The 1930s saw difficult times for many handicraft lines of trade, with sales reduced by the global depression and by the loss of the Manchurian market following the region's occupation by the Japanese. Nevertheless handicrafts and rural industries remained important in China until the socialization of industry in the 1950s concentrated industry in the urban areas.

In most cases, handicraft producers used traditional technology. But modern inputs began early to transform handicraft production in many ways. The best-known example is the iron-gear and jacquard looms that underlay the resurgence of handicraft weaving of cotton cloth, but there were many other lines of production where partially modernized inputs played a role.

Handicraft production played an important role in peasant income in many areas. In handicraft centers such as Nantong, handicrafts contributed the largest proportion of peasant household income. This has been interpreted by some as indicating the "involution" of the peasant economy, but others see it as one of a range of strategies adopted by peasant households to increase household income and improve living standards.

While the orthodoxy has long been that modern production, especially but not only in textiles, spelled the end for peasant handicrafts, that was far from the case. Some industries did decline—vegetable oil for lighting was replaced by kerosene—but, more broadly, different locations and different preexisting industrial structures could lead to a wide range of outcomes for peasant handicrafts. Even in the 1930s, over half of cotton-cloth production in terms of square yards came from handicraft producers.

CHINESE-OWNED AND FOREIGN-OWNED INDUSTRY

A key distinction throughout the period, especially up to the Sino-Japanese War in 1937, was, in the eyes of Chinese observers, that between Chinese-owned and foreign-owned enterprises. A great deal of the discourse in China, both before and after the 1949 revolution, has focused on the "oppression" of infant modern Chinese enterprises, which were unable to overcome unfair competition either from imported goods or from the products of foreign-owned factories in China. The advantages of foreign companies were both economic, such as generally better access to capital, and a higher level of technology, leading to the ability to undercut Chinese competitors, and political, involving protection by the governments of the foreign companies, often using the provisions of extraterritoriality. Britain and, later, Japan were particularly active in supporting their economic interests by political and, if necessary, military means.

It is difficult to prove or disprove the "oppression" hypothesis, but in 1933 foreign companies accounted for only 27 percent of total industrial production. Moreover, a Chinese study in the late 1980s by Wang Yuru of Nankai University concluded that Chinese enterprises grew more rapidly than foreign enterprises: Between 1920 and 1936, output of Chinese enterprises grew at 9.0 percent per year, and that of foreign enterprises by 3.9 percent. While foreign companies enjoyed some of the advantages outlined above, Chinese companies had other strengths, such as better networks linking them to suppliers, and the ability to play the nationalist card in competition in the domestic market.

TECHNOLOGY AND INDUSTRIAL MANAGEMENT

China's industry has often been held to be technologically backward in relation to that in the West, and Chinese owned and operated enterprises to have lagged behind their foreign counterparts in China. How far this stereotype reflected reality, however, might be questioned, and Thomas Rawski finds little evidence that foreign companies in China enjoyed major productivity or profit advantages over their Chinese competitors in the key industries of cotton textiles and cigarettes. Moreover, low labor costs often made unmechanized and "backward" technologies economically rational.

Particularly in the earlier period, perceived technological backwardness has been attributed to a shortage of trained technicians and the limited technical capacities of bureaucratic managers. In fact, however, many skilled Chinese engineers were trained, often in the nineteenth century by working in foreign-owned shipyards along the coast. Building on technological transfer from foreign firms and from study abroad, Chinese companies in the first half of the twentieth century gradually developed technological skills, moving from repairing and servicing imported machinery to a situation where some firms in the 1930s were, in Rawski's view, over the threshold where they had the capacity to produce a wide range of industrial equipment.

Both the Communist and the modernization-theory narratives of China's history portrayed Chinese industrial management as backward and inadequate and focused on the failures and shortcomings of Chinese enterprises. Common charges included nepotism, lack of proper cost accounting, an aversion to technology, and excessively bureaucratic styles of operation. They were compared unfavorably with ideal Western forms of management. Nevertheless, prewar China showed considerable interest in Western ideas such as Taylorism, which was introduced through translations by Mu Ouchu (1876–1943), a pioneering textile industrialist who used the ideas in his cotton mills. Both government and nongovernment organizations actively promoted ideas of "scientific management," particularly in the 1930s. Human-resource issues were of particular interest, though even in the most modern firms there was a tension between meritocratic ideas and traditional practices of nepotism.

Moreover, as China began to embark on a more capitalist form of modernization in the 1980s, Chinese scholars began to cite the capitalists of the 1930s as models worthy of study by contemporary entrepreneurs, especially in areas such as customer service. Finally, it is increasingly being acknowledged that many of the so-called backward Chinese practices can be widely found in the early histories of Western industrial countries as well, and that some of them, such as nepotism, could play a positive function in the institutional situation in which Chinese industrialists operated.

SEE ALSO *Li Hongzhang; Mines and Metallurgy, 1800–1949; Qing Restoration; Rong Zongjing; Zeng Guofan; Zhang Jian; Zuo Zongtang.*

BIBLIOGRAPHY

Asian Historical Statistics Project. Institute of Economic Research, Hitotsubashi University. http://www.ier.hit-u.ac.jp/COE/English/index.html

Bergère, Marie-Claire. *The Golden Age of the Chinese Bourgeoisie, 1911–1937.* Trans. Janet Lloyd. Cambridge, U.K.: Cambridge University Press, 1989.

Chang, John Key. *Industrial Development in Pre-Communist China: A Quantitative Analysis.* Edinburgh, U.K.: Edinburgh University Press, 1969.

Coble, Parks M. *Chinese Capitalists in Japan's New Order: The Occupied Lower Yangzi, 1937–1945.* Berkeley: University of California Press, 2003.

Cochran, Sherman. *Big Business in China: Sino-foreign Rivalry in the Cigarette Industry, 1890–1930.* Cambridge, MA: Harvard University Press, 1980.

Feuerwerker, Albert. *China's Early Industrialization: Sheng Hsuan-huai (1844–1916) and Mandarin Enterprise.* Cambridge, MA: Harvard University Press, 1958.

Feuerwerker, Albert. *The Chinese Economy, 1870–1949.* Ann Arbor: Center for Chinese Studies, University of Michigan, 1995.

Grove, Linda. *A Chinese Economic Revolution: Rural Entrepreneurship in the Twentieth Century.* Lanham, MD: Rowman & Littlefield, 2006.

Hou Jiming (Hou Chi-ming). *Foreign Investment and Economic Development in China, 1840–1937.* Cambridge, MA: Harvard University Press, 1965.

Kennedy, Thomas L. *The Arms of Kiangnan: Modernization in the Chinese Ordnance Industry, 1860–1895.* Boulder, CO: Westview, 1978.

Kobu, Tōru. Minguo shiqi Zhongguo de gongye fazhan, xinxiuding zhishu: 1912–1948 [China's industrial development in the Republican Period: A revised index,1912–1948]. In *Shijie jingji tizhi xia de Minguo shiqi jingji* [The Chinese economy within the global economic framework], eds. Zhang Donggang et al., 64–67. Beijing: Zhongguo Caizheng Jinji Chubanshe, 2005.

Liu Dajun. *Zhongguo Gongye Diaocha Baogao* [Report of a survey of Chinese industries], 3 vols. Nanjing: Zhongguo Jingji Tongji Yanjiu Suo, 1937.

Liu Dazhong (Liu Ta-chung) and Ye Kongjia (Yeh Kung-chia). *The Economy of the Chinese Mainland: National Income and Economic Development, 1933–1959.* Princeton, NJ: Princeton University Press, 1965.

Perkins, Dwight H., ed. *China's Modern Economy in Historical Perspective.* Stanford, CA: Stanford University Press, 1975.

Rawski, Thomas G. *Economic Growth in Prewar China.* Berkeley: University of California Press, 1989.

Wang Yuru. Economic Development in China between the Two World Wars, 1920–1936. In *The Chinese Economy in the Early Twentieth Century: Recent Chinese Studies,* ed. Tim Wright, 558–577. Basingstoke, U.K.: Macmillan, 1992.

Wright, Tim. Electric Power Production in Pre-1937 China. *China Quarterly* 126 (1991): 356–363.

Wright, Tim, ed. *The Chinese Economy in the Early Twentieth Century: Recent Chinese Studies.* Basingstoke, U.K.: Macmillan, 1992.

Tim Wright

INFLUENCES ABROAD

This entry contains the following:

NINETEENTH-CENTURY CHINOISERIE AND CHINESE EXPORT

The term *chinoiserie* refers to non-Chinese products or decorations that evoke China or are based (often loosely) on Chinese themes. Chinoiserie encompasses furniture, ceramics, textiles, painting, architecture, literature, music, and drama. It usually involves fantasy, suggesting "Cathay" or a largely imaginary China based on travelers' tales and distorted images.

The fashion for chinoiserie reached a peak in the middle years of the eighteenth century, when little distinction was made between imported Chinese objects and European-made imitations; both were combined in "the Chinese style." Often this meant elaborate and whimsical rococo design. As the British author Oliver Goldsmith (1730–1774) observed in 1759, "we have seen gardens laid out in the eastern manner; houses ornamented in front by zig-zag lines; and rooms stuck round with Chinese vases and Indian pagods" (Goldsmith 1966, p. 170).

Garden chinoiserie, in the form of pavilions, pagodas, bridges, and railings, had its origin in the early landscaped gardens of England of the 1730s; from these emerged the *jardins anglo-chinois* (Anglo-Chinese gardens) that appeared throughout Europe in the late eighteenth and early nineteenth centuries. Some of the grander exotic structures had royal associations. From King Louis XIV (1638–1715) onward, several members of the royal families of Europe commissioned "Chinese" palaces, pavilions, and teahouses, sometimes to accommodate their collections of Chinese porcelain.

By the early nineteenth century, European artists, notably William Alexander (1767–1816), had brought back detailed pictures of China, and China could no longer be regarded as a mysterious land of the imagination. Yet the tradition of royal chinoiserie was maintained in the early years of the nineteenth century: King Ferdinand of Naples (1751–1825), while exiled to Sicily, built a "palazzo Cinese" outside Palermo, known as La Favorita, which survives, as does the spectacular Royal Pavilion at Brighton, England, erected in an exotic style for King George IV (1762–1830) from 1818 to 1822. As finally built, the Royal Pavilion was largely Mogul on the outside and largely Chinese within—combining Chinese "export" artifacts and paintings with chinoiserie decorations made in England and France. In his last years, the king spent his summers at a "Chinese fishing temple" built for him on the banks of Virginia Water. In the late 1840s, Queen Victoria (1819–1901) abandoned the Royal Pavilion at Brighton, but transferred its "Chinese" contents to Buckingham Palace in London, where many of them remain.

Chinoiserie was generally out of favor in Europe in the middle years of the nineteenth century, as neoclassical and gothic revival styles became dominant. The appeal of China was moreover diminished by anti-Chinese propaganda associated with the Opium Wars of 1839 to 1842 and 1856 to 1860. Nevertheless, China-themed artifacts continued to be produced, notably porcelain: the most famous and long-lasting chinoiserie theme is the willow pattern, which since the 1790s has been produced in Europe, North America, and Japan.

In more recent times, the term *chinoiserie* has been employed (within wider debates concerning "orientalism") to refer to Western stereotypes of Chinese culture. In France, the phrase *chinoiseries administratives* is used to mean "pointless bureaucracy" or "red tape."

CHINESE EXPORT ART

The notion of Chinese "export art" is relatively recent. The phrase was not used in the eighteenth or nineteenth centuries, the era in which the trade in such art was at its height. The expression was given currency in 1950 by the pioneering book *Chinese Export Art in the Eighteenth Century* by

Aquatint of the Chinese Gallery, from John Nash's* Views of the Royal Pavilion, Brighton, *1826. *Chinese-themed objects remained highly fashionable throughout early nineteenth century Europe, regardless if the sought-after object was an authentic item from China. Known as chinoiserie, this art form promoted an image of China based largely on Western imagination, as contact with the nation was limited until the latter part of the 1800s.* THE CHINESE GALLERY, FROM *VIEWS OF THE ROYAL PAVILION, BRIGHTON* BY JOHN NASH (1752–1835). PRIVATE COLLECTION, THE BRIDGEMAN ART LIBRARY INTERNATIONAL

Margaret Jourdain (d. 1951) and R. Soame Jenyns (1904–1976). Since then, "Chinese export art" has come to refer to objects produced in China specifically for external rather than Chinese markets. Such objects have been modified in form, style, or pattern to meet the requirements of a foreign consumer. Thus "export art" is not the same as "exported art." It includes "export porcelain," "export furniture," "export silver," and "export painting"—all in some way tailored to suit foreign tastes.

Export Porcelain Of all the forms of export art, porcelain was brought back from China in the greatest quantities. In the sixteenth century, wares with armorial designs were made for Portuguese clients, and other Western nations followed, commissioning porcelain with a wide variety of patterns; these patterns, often elaborate European subjects sent out to China in the form of engravings, were copied with scrupulous precision by the Chinese craftsmen. Most of the production took place in Jingdezhen in Jiangxi Province, and the finished articles were exported (from the turn of the seventeenth century) through the port of Guangzhou (Canton). By the early years of the nineteenth century, the export of porcelain to Europe was in decline, partly as a result of tariffs imposed to protect Europe's own porcelain manufacturers. Exports to North America flourished for a little longer, as did exports to India and Persia, but were further diminished when the kilns of Jingdezhen were destroyed by the Taipings in 1853.

Export Painting Chinese export painting developed in the later eighteenth century, and most examples date from the nineteenth. At this time, Chinese painting in the traditional manner was little admired or understood by Western visitors. Export paintings, however, adopted Western ideas of composition and perspective: They might be shaped in a typically Western format; they might show subjects or attitudes that would be unacceptable within China; and they might even be painted in the characteristically Western medium of oil paint, sometimes with the addition of a Western-style frame. Typical subjects included topographical views, trades and occupations, natural history, portraits, landscapes, and the stages in the production of tea, silk, rice, cotton, and porcelain. Most "export artists" remained anonymous; the best-documented individual was known as Lamqua (1801–1860).

"Reverse-glass pictures" were a particular specialty of the Cantonese export studios. These were paintings, generally in oil, applied to the backs of sheets of glass that had themselves been imported from Europe. In addition to framed pictures, rolls of painted paper, often depicting trees and birds or landscapes peopled with active figures, were exported to the West for use as wallpaper. From about 1820, small vivid paintings were also executed on pith paper—the spongy stem tissue of the plant *Tetrapanax papyrifera*—and exported in large quantities, often in silk-covered albums.

SEE ALSO *Art Market, 1800–1949; Foreign Trade, 1800–1950; Gardens and Parks.*

BIBLIOGRAPHY

Clunas, Craig. *Chinese Export Watercolours*. London: Victoria and Albert Museum, 1984.

Conner, Patrick. *Oriental Architecture in the West*. London: Thames and Hudson, 1979.

Conner, Patrick. Lamqua, Western and Chinese Painter. *Arts of Asia* 29, 2 (1999): 46–64.

Crossman, Carl L. *The Decorative Arts of the China Trade: Paintings, Furnishings, and Exotic Curiosities*. Woodbridge, U.K.: Antique Collectors' Club, 1991.

Goldsmith, Oliver. Review of Arthur Murphy's *Orphan of China*. In *Collected Works of Oliver Goldsmith*, edited by Arthur Friedman. Oxford, U.K.: Clarendon Press, 1966.

Honour, Hugh. *Chinoiserie*. London: John Murray, 1961.

Howard, David, ed. *A Tale of Three Cities: Canton, Shanghai, and Hong Kong*. London: Sotheby's, 1997.

Howard, David S., and John Ayers. *China for the West: The Mottahedeh Collection*. 2 vols. London: Philip Wilson, 1978.

Jacobson, Dawn. *Chinoiserie*. London: Phaidon, 1993.

Jourdain, Margaret, and R. Soame Jenyns. *Chinese Export Art*. London: Country Life, 1950.

Kjellberg, Sven T. *Svenska Ostindiska Compagnierna, 1731–1813* [The Swedish East India Company]. Malmö, Sweden: Allhems Förlag, 1975.

Wappenschmidt, Friederike. *Chinesische Tapeten für Europa* [Chinese wallpaper for Europe]. Berlin: Deutscher Verlag für Kunstwissenschaft, 1989.

Patrick Conner

NINETEENTH- AND TWENTIETH-CENTURY JAPANESE *BUNJINGA* (LITERATI) PAINTING

To refer to literati painting, the Japanese have employed two terms. One is *bunjinga*, which literally means "literati painting." The other is *nanga*, which literally means "southern painting." The term *nanga* is derived from "Southern School of Painting" or *nanshūga* (*nanzonghua* in Chinese), coined by Dong Qichang (1555–1636) and his associates, to refer to the tradition of literati painting in China. Yet *nanga* is best translated into English as "literati painting," rather than "Southern School of Painting," because *nanga* developed separately from Dong Qichang's theory. In Japan, *bunjinga* and *nanga* are used interchangeably, and both mean "literati painting." It was inspired by Chinese literati painting, which upheld the scholars' ideal that art should express their inner feelings.

Literati painting and Chinese language calligraphy epitomized the Sinophile culture of Japan during the Edo period (1603–1867). These arts were thought by many to have declined after the opening of Japan in the mid-nineteenth century, as Japanese artists increasingly turned to European and American art for models. Yet the opening of Japan also led to frequent artistic interchanges between China and Japan and a rapid increase in Japanese holdings of Chinese objets d'art. These interactions triggered in Japan a new style of calligraphy known as the Six Dynasties school (*rikuchō ha*) and a nationwide movement of new literati painting (*shin nanga*).

LITERATI PAINTING IN THE NINETEENTH CENTURY

Literati painting first became popular in Japan in the eighteenth century, when the shogunate's isolationist policy permitted contact with China only through the port of Nagasaki. Japanese artists studied woodblock-printed painting manuals and paintings brought from China, and studied with Chinese who traveled to Nagasaki. The Japanese soon developed their own version of literati painting, characterized by individual expression, eclectic styles, and expressionistic brushwork. When Japan ended its isolation, literati painting was widespread, with major centers in the Kyoto-Osaka region, Nagasaki, and Edo (present-day Tokyo).

In the third quarter of the nineteenth century, Japan's contact with China gradually increased. Fleeing from the aftermath of the Taiping Uprising (1851–1864), more Chinese went to Nagasaki, generating in the city a community of Chinese and Japanese literati painters, including Wang Kesan (1822–1872?), Xu Yuting (1824–1867?), Tetsuō Somon (1791–1871), Kinoshita Itsuun (1802–1866), and Okada Kōsho (1819–1903). By the 1880s,

Chinese literati such as Luo Xuegu (d. after 1877), Jin Bin (Binhuai, d. after 1872), Wang Yin (Yemei, 1828?–after 1892), and Hu Zhang (Tiemei, 1848–1899) had visited various parts of the main island of Honshu. Japanese also traveled to China to pursue literati arts. From the late 1860s Yasuda Rōzan (1830–1883), Nagai Unpei (1833–1899), and Murata Kōkoku (1831–1912), among others, studied in Shanghai with such painters as Hu Gongshou (1823–1866) and Zhang Zixiang (Xiong, 1803–1886).

A harsh attack on literati painting came in 1883 from Ernest F. Fenollosa (1853–1908), an American art critic active in Japan. Okakura Tenshin (1862–1913), an art historian instrumental in shaping the field of art, also projected a negative view toward literati painting. Others in the late nineteenth century frequently dismissed literati painting as "potato landscapes" (*tsukune-imo sansui*)—the phrase referring to rough execution and predictable compositions. Yet at the same time Tanomura Chokunyū (1814–1907) and Okuhara Seiko (1837–1913) produced works in the vein of orthodox Qing landscapes, displaying consummate skill and fine brushwork. Many literati painters had powerful patrons, including members of the imperial family and high-ranking statesmen—a backing that shows the deep roots of Sinophile art in Japan.

CALLIGRAPHY OF THE SIX-DYNASTIES SCHOOL

The calligraphy and seal carving of Qing epigraphers were known to Japanese at the beginning of the Meiji period (1868–1912). However, the actual ancient writings that the Chinese epigraphers studied were rarely seen in Japan at that time. In 1880 Yang Shoujing (1839–1915) brought to Japan a large number of rubbings, inspiring Iwaya Ichiroku (1834–1905) and Kusakabe Meikaku (1838–1922) to develop the style of calligraphy known as the Six Dynasties school. These artists, like those of the stele school in China, drew on inscriptions on stelae from the Han (206 BCE–220 CE), Wei (220–265), and Six Dynasties (304–439) periods and on metal and other objects from preceding periods. In the late nineteenth century, Nakabayashi Gochiku (1827–1913), Yamamoto Kyōzan (1863–1934), Mizuno Sobai (1864–1921), and Miyajima Eishi (1867–1943) went to China, studying with Pan Cun (1818–1892?), Yang Shoujing, Zhang Yuzhao (1823–1894), and Wu Changshi (1844–1927). Kawai Senro (1871–1945) and Nagao Uzan (1864–1942) became the first Japanese members of the Xiling Seal Society (Xiling Yinshe, est. 1904), under Wu's leadership. Nakamura Fusetsu (1866–1943), who was well known for his oil paintings, and was also a Six-Dynasties school calligrapher, amassed an extensive collection of objects from China, including bronzes, oracle bones, and various rubbings, and established the Shodō Hakubutsukan (Calligraphy Museum) in Tokyo in 1936.

LITERATI PAINTING IN THE TWENTIETH CENTURY

Japan during the Taishō period (1912–1926) witnessed the rapid spread of literati painting, which grew into a nationwide art movement known as new literati painting (*shin nanga*). In the early twentieth century, the collections of the imperial family and scholar-officials in China were dispersed, and many Chinese paintings found their way to Japan. At the same time, modernist European art, such as postimpressionism and expressionism, reached Japan. The collision of arts from China and Europe led Japanese artists and art historians to rediscover the subjectivism inherit in literati painting.

Tomioka Tessai (1836–1924) spearheaded this trend, closely associating with the Qing loyalist Luo Zhenyu (1866–1940), the sinologist Naitō Konan (1866–1934), and the scholar-artist Nagao Uzan. New literati painting encompassed landscapes by artists whose works primarily used traditional Japanese media and techniques (*nihonga*), such as Imamura Shikō (1880–1916) and Murakami Kagaku (1888–1939). It also included ink paintings by artists who primarily produced oil paintings inspired by Western art (*yōga*), such as Kishida Ryūsei (1891–1929) and Yorozu Tetsugorō (1885–1927). In 1921 the Nihon Nanga-in (Japan Literati Painting Academy) held the first annual exhibition; its members included Komuro Suiun (1874–1945), Yamaguchi Hachikushi (1890–1933), and Yano Kyōson (1890–1965).

In the 1920s and early 1930s, as hundreds of Chinese artists visited Japan and Japanese continued to travel to Shanghai and elsewhere, literati painting came in vogue in the Sino-Japanese art world. The close contact between the two countries led, for example, to a Chinese translation of Ōmura Seigai's *Bunjinga no fukkō* (The revival of literati painting), published in 1921, only a year after its initial publication in Japan. Joint associations of Chinese and Japanese artists proliferated. The Chū-Nichi Bijutsu Kyōkai (Zhong-Ri Meishu Xiehui, Association of Sino-Japanese Art, est. 1920) organized a series of exhibitions in the two countries between 1921 and 1929. The major players in these associations included ardent promoters of literati painting: from China, Wang Yiting (1867–1938), Zheng Wuchang (1894–1952), Huang Binhong (1865–1955), Qian Shoutie (1897–1967), and Liu Haisu (1896–1994); and from Japan, Kosugi Hōan (1881–1964), Hashimoto Kansetsu (1883–1945), Morita Tsunetomo (1881–1933), and Dōmoto Inshō (1891–1975), to name only a few.

As Japan intensified its military aggression in China, Sino-Japanese exchanges significantly waned in the 1930s until the normalization of diplomatic ties between the two countries in 1972. Japanese interest in Chinese art nonetheless persisted. The Six Dynasties school remains a vibrant calligraphy movement, and the Japan Literati Painting Academy continues to hold annual exhibitions.

SEE ALSO *Chinese Painting (guohua); Huang Binhong; Literati Painting (wenrenhua); Liu Haisu; Wang Zhen (Wang Yiting); Wu Changshi (Wu Junqing).*

BIBLIOGRAPHY

Fogel, Joshua. Lust for Still Life: Chinese Painters in Japan and Japanese Painters in China in the 1860s and 1870s. In *Acquisition: Art and Ownership in Edo-Period Japan*, ed. Elizabeth Lillehoj. Warren, CT: Floating World Editions, 2007.

Kawakita Michiaki and Horie Tomohiko. *Bunjinga* [Literati painting]. Vol. 12 of *Genshoku gendai Nihon no bijutsu* [Modern Japanese art, illustrated in color]. Tokyo: Shōgakkan, 1979.

Shimonaka Yasaburō, ed. *Nihon: Meiji, Taishō* [Japan: The Meiji and Taishō eras]. Vol. 25 of *Shodō zenshū* [Comprehensive volumes on calligraphy]. Tokyo: Heibonsha, 1957.

Tomita Noboru. *Ruten Shinchō hihō* [The circulation of hidden treasures of the Qing dynasty]. Tokyo: Nihon Hōsō Shuppan Kyōkai, 2002.

Wong, Aida Yuen. *Parting the Mists: Discovering Japan and the Rise of National-Style Painting in Modern China*. Honolulu: University of Hawaii Press, 2006.

Tamaki Maeda

INFLUENCE OF CHINESE ART ON INDIA'S NATIONALIST MOVEMENT

India's nationalist movement that sought independence from British rule through cultural regeneration and nonviolent means centered around three major figures: Mohandas Karamchand Gandhi (1869–1948), the poet laureate and visionary educator Rabindranath Tagore (1861–1941), and the artist Nandalal Bose (1882–1966). Gandhi and Tagore saw in Bose's work the icons of a new, strong nation, with images depicting the equality and dignity of all its citizens, imbued with a spirituality rooted in tradition and synthesizing techniques and styles from the best that the world's cultures had to offer. Early in his career Bose drew significant inspiration from Japanese sources; however, as Japanese aggressions in China escalated, Bose and his circle looked more to China as a partner against imperialism and as a source of inspiration in art and ideologies.

Nandalal Bose related to Chinese art on a deeply spiritual level. He recognized a parallel between the Daoist concept of *qi*, the life force that runs through all nature, and the Hindu notion of the divine creator whose life rhythm pervades all creation. Chinese landscape paintings inspired Bose's depictions of the Himalayan mountain passes through which he traveled on pilgrimage to the ashram of Swami Vivekananda (1863–1902), who spearheaded the anticolonial Hindu spiritual revival movement of the late nineteenth century. Bose made frequent use of calligraphic line derived from Chinese sources because he felt that a strong sense of line imbues the subjects of a painting with life rhythm.

Bose was exposed to Chinese art on his visit to Shanghai with Tagore in 1924 and thereafter with the arrival of Chinese scholars, artists, and students to Visva-Bharati University at Santiniketan in rural West Bengal, where he served as director of the art school from 1920 until 1951. Gao Jianfu (1879–1951), founder of the Chinese nationalist Lingnan school of painting, traveled throughout South Asia for one year beginning in October 1930. Like Bose, Gao was interested in absorbing into his own work elements from a variety of traditions, including most notably Nihonga and Indian Buddhist art, in order to achieve the ideal of a world art, characterized by a universal syncretism where modern nationalist art draws elements from different cultures worldwide. In 1939 Xu Beihong, who had deeply impressed Tagore and Gandhi by patriotically using his art to aid Chinese refugees in Southeast Asia, arrived at Santiniketan to work for two years and exhibit his eclectic paintings that often drew from both ancient Chinese classics and Western styles while making biting political commentary.

SEE ALSO *India, Relations with; Lingnan School of Painting; Xu Beihong.*

BIBLIOGRAPHY

Croizier, Ralph. *Art and Revolution in Modern China: The Lingnan (Cantonese) School of Painting*. Berkeley and Los Angeles: University of California Press, 1988.

Das Gupta, Uma. *Rabindranath Tagore: A Biography*. New Delhi: Oxford University Press, 2004.

Quintanilla, Sonya Rhie. *Rhythms of India: The Art of Nandalal Bose*. San Diego, CA: San Diego Museum of Art, 2008.

Tan, Chung. *In the Footsteps of Xuanzang: Tan Yun-shan and India*. New Delhi: Indira Gandhi National Centre for the Arts, 1999.

Wong, Aida Yuen. *Parting the Mists: Discovering Japan and the Rise of National-Style Painting in Modern China*. Honolulu: University of Hawaii Press, 2006.

Sonya Quintanilla

MAOISM AND ART

The most striking thing about the influence of Maoist art is that it has had a greater impact on the international art market than it did on radical political movements. This is perhaps a logical consequence of the Chinese Communist Party's turn from global revolution to globalization in the decades after Mao's death in 1976, but it is still astonishing to see world-class prices paid for iconic works and images from the Cultural Revolution years (1966–1969), and ironic pastiches of Maoist art produced by the internationalized younger generation of Chinese artists.

It was different during Mao's lifetime, when there was no art market in China and no Chinese participation in the international art market. All art was supposed to serve the state, and the art disseminated abroad through foreign-language publications and mass-produced posters portrayed the progress of the "new China" and, especially after the Sino-Soviet split, called for worldwide revolution following the Maoist model.

It is not clear how much of specifically Chinese styles revolutionary movements abroad incorporated into their own art. Works from the high tide of Maoist influence, mostly in the 1960s and 1970s, show more affinity for the revolutionary message than for the specific techniques of Chinese art. Whether one looks at the Black Panther posters of Emory Douglas (b. 1945) or political art of the African National Congress in South Africa, Maoist influence is there, but it is subordinated to native styles and images. This was consistent with Maoist cultural policy that, in contesting too much Soviet influence in Chinese art, had already established the principle of "national in form, socialist in content."

But there are two more reasons why the art of revolutionaries sympathetic to China did not look more Chinese. One was competing Soviet influence, with the USSR able to provide much more material aid to revolutionary governments and movements in places such as Ethiopia and Angola, and even Vietnam. The other was the appeal of more modern styles in poster art, notably those produced by the Soviet's model third-world client state, Cuba. The stronger blocks of color, dramatically simplified compositions, and elements of photomontage generally had more direct impact on third-world revolutionary art from Nicaragua to South Africa.

This does not mean that Maoist visual propaganda was insignificant. In the heartlands of world capitalism it spread the message of uncompromising revolutionary struggle to disaffected youth of the 1960s. During the Paris demonstrations of 1968 Simone de Beauvoir (1908–1986) addressed a crowd with a large woodcut image of Mao directly behind her. In the third-world, it made a visible impact on the art produced by the most Maoist and most violent of South America's revolutionary movements, the Shining Path (Sendero Luminoso) in Peru. Its leader, Abimael Guzmán (Presidente Gonzalo, b. 1934), visited China several times and closely copied Mao's peasant-based revolutionary strategy. It was therefore natural that poster images of Peru's "Great Leader" showed him towering over the revolutionary masses, at times even dressed in a Mao suit with a little book of his own writings in hand. The Shining Path is still active, though on a much reduced scale since the capture of its leader in 1992. Mao-type revolution has few followers left in either the less developed or industrialized countries. No longer a threat to globalized capitalism, the styles and tropes of its art has had great success in international art markets, mostly since the Tiananmen Incident of 1989.

A visitor examining American artist Andy Warhol's set of prints featuring Mao Zedong, Hong Kong, May 26, 2008. *As a significant figure in the twentieth century, Mao Zedong influenced both fine art, as seen in this 1972 work by Andy Warhol, and propaganda art, such as in posters created by Peru's Shining Path revolutionary group.* © VICTOR FRAILE/REUTERS/CORBIS

Wind farm in Inner Mongolia, China, August 8, 2006. *Inner Mongolia remains for China a rich source of natural resources, with large coal reserves providing fuel to operate power plants. As China attempts to curb air pollution by relying on greener sources of energy, wind farms have taken hold on Inner Mongolia's wind-swept plateau.* © RYAN PYLE/CORBIS

resolved to reduce IMAR's size. The eastern banners were reassigned to the Manchurian provinces Heilongjiang, Jilin, and Liaoning, while some of the western banners were swallowed by the neighboring Gansu and Ningxia. As a result, Inner Mongolia was reduced to only one-third its former size. This measure was reversed in 1979.

Traditionally a pastoral economy, though with substantial land cultivation, Inner Mongolia came to play an important role in the industrialization of China because of its rich coal deposits. The annual output of coal in IMAR increased from 460,000 tons in 1949 to 9 million tons in 1959; in 2000 it exceeded 72 million tons. Mining of rare earth elements in Inner Mongolia has reached astounding proportions—the world's largest deposit is found at Bayan-Obo mine (near Baotou). Inner Mongolia has seen a surge in electricity output, from 13 million kilowatt hours in 1949 to almost 44 billion in 2000. The Inner Mongolian cashmere industry also has been a driving force in the regional economy. IMAR has seen its share of the Chinese economic boom: gross domestic product increased from about 4 billion yuan in 1970 to over 500 billion yuan in 2000, with most of this growth occurring in the 1990s.

SEE ALSO *Manchukuo (Manzhouguo); Mongolia, People's Republic of, Relations with.*

BIBLIOGRAPHY

1949–2000 China Statistical Data Compilation. Beijing: All China Marketing Research, 2001.

Kotkin, Stephen, and Bruce A. Elleman. *Mongolia in the Twentieth Century: Landlocked Cosmopolitan*. Armonk, NY: Sharpe, 1999.

Sneath, David. *Changing Inner Mongolia: Pastoral Mongolian Society and the Chinese State*. Oxford, U.K.: Oxford University Press, 2000.

Williams, Dee Mack. *Beyond Great Walls: Environment, Identity, and Development on the Chinese Grasslands of Inner Mongolia*. Stanford, CA: Stanford University Press, 2002.

Woody, W. *The Cultural Revolution in Inner Mongolia: Extracts from an Unpublished History*. Ed. and trans. Michael Schoenhals. Stockholm, Sweden: Center for Pacific Asia Studies at Stockholm University, 1993.

Sergey Radchenko

INSPECTION AND AUDIT

Although inspection or administrative control has always been part of the Chinese Communist Party (CCP) and People's Republic of China (PRC) institutional landscape, from the early 1950s until Mao Zedong's death in 1976 these activities were both very secretive and often run by ad hoc rather than formal organs. Since the beginning of the reforms in 1978, CCP as well as state inspection organizations have been restored and gradually strengthened to better control corruption. Simultaneously, for the first time since 1949, auditing work has been introduced. However, the growth of inspection organs is no guarantee of their efficacy.

Modeled on the Bolshevik Party, the CCP always has been equipped with internal inspection bodies, but after Mao took control of the party in 1935, he preferred to rely on "rectification movements" (*zhengfeng*) to verify party members' probity, and more importantly, political conformism. Movements such as the one that occurred in 1942 to 1944 gave considerable power to the secret police, which was headed by Kang Sheng (1898–1975) in the 1940s and again in the 1960s, and to ad hoc inspection teams or "organs in charge of special affairs" (*zhuan'an jigou*), especially during the Cultural Revolution (1966–1969). After the establishment of the PRC, some kind of Soviet normality prevailed for a while with the establishment of a CCP Central Control Commission chaired by Dong Biwu (1886–1975), an illustrious but rather powerless leader, and a Ministry of Control under the central government but directly led by the CCP Central Control Commission. In 1959 this ministry was abolished because all the leading cadres were already party members, and hence had been inspected by the CCP control commission of the immediate higher level. After the outbreak of the Cultural Revolution in 1966, these commissions ceased to operate.

In 1977 they were restored as "discipline inspection commissions" (DICs), and at the end of 1978 a Central Discipline Inspection Commission (*zhongyang jilü jiancha weiyuanhui*, CDIC) was created. Its secretary was Chen Yun (1905–1995). Simultaneously, the ad hoc special affair organs were formally dismantled at all levels. After a new state constitution was enacted in December 1982, in March 1983 a ministry-level National Auditing Administration (*shenjishu*) was established for the first time. This was a breakthrough, although the hopes of some constitutionalists for a more independent organ, directly responsible before the National People's Congress or Parliament, did not materialize. In 1986 a Ministry of Supervision (*jiancha bu*) in charge of controlling state and in particular nonparty administrative cadres was established.

Today, the CDIC remains the most powerful of these three control institutions. Its secretary sits in the CCP Politburo Standing Committee (*He Guoqiang* since 2007) and, since 1993, one of its deputy-secretaries has always headed the Ministry of Supervision, after the DICs and the state supervision organs merged their activities. It underscores the fact that the large majority of cadres—or public servants—are still party members and therefore subject to "double rules" (*shuanggui*) inspection procedures in case of corruption or breach of discipline. In such a system, the DIC of the higher-level party committee plays a decisive role in determining the need for an investigation, with assistance, if it wishes, from the public security or judicial organs. However, party members are prosecuted only if the CCP endorses it. In other words, they are submitted to a particular justice that is sometimes privileged or lenient, and sometimes harsher and without legal guarantees. Their misconduct may be tolerated as long as they are politically useful or obedient, or conversely, they can be de facto detained in party facilities indefinitely and without the assistance of a lawyer if the leadership has decided to purge them.

Since the early 2000s the CCP has tried to centralize the DICs apparatus, but DICs have remained under the leadership of both the party committee to which they belong and the higher DIC. In order to circumvent this limitation, the CDIC has increasingly relied on centrally dispatched large inspection teams when it wants to crack important corruption cases.

The Auditing Administration has managed to gradually enhance its competence and professionalism, thanks to the active support of the Ministry of Finance. However, it still holds limited disciplinary power and has remained unable to investigate sensitive cases without the support of the CDIC.

SEE ALSO *Corruption.*

BIBLIOGRAPHY

I-huai Chang. An Analysis of the CPP's Role in Mainland China's State Supervisory Systems. *Issues and Studies* 36, 1 (January 1998): 38–78.

Manion, Melanie. *Corruption by Design: Building Clean Government in Mainland China and Hong Kong*. Cambridge, MA: Harvard University Press, 2004.

Organisation for Economic Co-operation and Development. *Governance in China: China in the Global Economy*. Paris: Author, 2005.

Yasheng Huang. Managing Chinese Bureaucrats: An Institutional Economics Perspective. *Political Studies* 50, 1 (March 2002): 61–79.

Jean-Pierre Cabestan

INTERNAL MIGRATION AND INTERNAL COLONIZATION SINCE 1800

As China entered the nineteenth century, the population was more than twice as large as it had been at the time of the Manchu conquest and growing steadily; by 1850 the population had nearly tripled to approximately 430 million. High population densities provided a powerful incentive for migration from the rural areas of China's traditional core regions. One outlet was the southwestern region that included Sichuan Province, as well as Jiangxi, Hubei, and Hunan, which had been partially depopulated by the destructive military campaigns at the end of the Ming dynasty (1368–1644) and the War of the Three Feudatories (1673–1681) in the early Qing (1644–1912). Smaller numbers of migrants went to the rugged southwestern border areas of Yunnan, Guizhou, and Guangxi, continuing a centuries-long movement of Han population, culture, and political control into southern lands once controlled by non-Chinese peoples whose descendants now form minority groups located mainly in the mountainous and hilly regions. Another migration focus in the mid-Qing was from the Middle Yangzi region, northwest to Gansu Province. Smaller numbers of migrants, most from Fujian and some from Guangzhou, settled in Taiwan, taking advantage of increasing political integration of the island into the Chinese state in the nineteenth century, reaching province status in 1885.

In the late nineteenth century, as the west and southwest became densely populated, migratory flows turned toward Inner Mongolia and China's three northeastern provinces, Liaoning, Jilin, and Heilongjiang, known collectively in Chinese as *Dongbei*—the Northeast—and widely known in English as Manchuria, the homeland of the Manchu people who founded the Qing dynasty. The Northeast was well suited to settlement, but, except for southern Liaodong, which was cordoned off by a line of willow trees (the Willow Palisade), the region was protected by the Qing government for most of its reign as a sanctuary for the traditional Manchu way of life. Migration flows also developed in the mid to late nineteenth century due to the devastation wreaked by the great rebellions, the Taiping (1851–1864) and the Nian (1851–1868). During the Taiping Uprising, thousands of desperate people fled the Lower Yangzi region to seek work and safety in the area of Wuhan. After the defeat of the rebels, battle, starvation, and disease left virtual wastelands in parts of the Lower Yangzi, near the Taiping capital at Nanjing, and in the Nian area of operations in the western part of the North China Plain, drawing in settlers from land-poor regions.

NATIVE-PLACE ORGANIZATIONS AND MIGRATION

Migrants gained key information and crucial assistance from family members, neighbors, or people from the same village or region. Many were informal contacts, but some involved organized groups from the same area who provided assistance for their members. Much of the social organization in Qing-dynasty Shanghai involved native-place organizations and guilds. These groups were most numerous and active for people from Guangdong, Ningpo, and Jiangsu.

Migrants who went to the Northeast in the early twentieth century were often recruited by labor contractors from their region. Some contractors simply served as arrangers, planning travel and finding jobs. Others retained control over their workers, housed them, fed them, and kept their pay. In many cases, a relative or neighbor would take young workers to the Northeast, help them find jobs and housing, and help them return home, often for Spring Festival (the lunar New Year). In other instances, a young worker would go and live with the family of a relative in the Northeast.

MIGRATION IN THE FIRST HALF OF THE TWENTIETH CENTURY

In the early twentieth century, by far the largest population movement was to the Northeast, from the North China provinces of Shandong and Hebei, as new railways provided market access for the region's resources and as industry grew, much of it funded by the encroaching Japanese empire. The Northeast was the only large arable area contiguous to China's traditional core areas that was not densely populated by the nineteenth century. While the Qing prohibition on immigration beyond the Willow Palisade was not entirely successful, it did leave the Northeast with a much smaller population relative to its size than any other major agricultural region. Equally important was a scarcity of transportation routes linking the northern half of the area with the markets of North China. While the Liao River allowed boat traffic to the Gulf of Bo Hai for the southern part of the region, the northern half was traversed by the Songhua (Sungari) River, which flows north to the Heilongjiang (Amur River), on the border with Russia. Even in periods of strong governments before the Qing, Chinese settlement had rarely extended beyond the Liao River drainage.

The situation changed drastically at the end of the nineteenth century, when, with Chinese permission, Russia built the Chinese Eastern Railway from the western border of Heilongjiang, through Harbin, to Vladivostok on the Pacific Ocean, quickly followed by the Southern Manchuria Railway, from Harbin south to Dalian. The two railways provided efficient, economic transportation that linked all areas of the Northeast to markets in China and the wider world and prompted the flood of migration that finally completed the region's settlement. Between the late 1890s and the late 1930s, hundreds of thousands of workers from the poor, crowded provinces of Shandong and Hebei traveled to the Northeast each year by sea, by rail, or on foot. The total number of migrants came to roughly twenty-five million. About two-thirds of the migrants eventually returned to their home villages with their earnings, leaving approximately eight million who settled in the Northeast permanently. The surge in migration began with a demand for workers to build the railways. Once the railways were in place, they stimulated the export market for the Northeast's traditional cash crop, the soybean. In addition, development efforts by the Russians, by their successors the Japanese, and by Chinese government and business leaders added coal, iron, and other industrial goods to the area's products and further increased the need for labor.

The early years of the twentieth century also saw a significant influx of migrants from northern China into the arable areas of Inner Mongolia, particularly the irrigated region near Hetao, at the northernmost point of the Great Bend of the Yellow (Huang) River. This movement was accelerated by the construction of the Beijing-Baotou Railway, which was begun in 1905. Other substantial settlements of Chinese migrants developed near Chahar, Ordos, and Tumed. From this time forward, the population of Inner Mongolia became increasingly dominated by Han Chinese.

The other major population movement in this period was from the countryside to the rapidly industrializing cities all over China. The growth of commerce and industry required a steady influx of labor into cities like Beijing, Tianjin, Shanghai, Wuhan, Chongqing, Shenyang, and Guangdong (Canton). In most cases, workers—many of them young women—were drawn from nearby rural areas and stayed for only a few years. Cities in less heavily populated regions, such as Wuhan and Shenyang, attracted migrants from more distant provinces. Data from Wuhan indicate that in the mid-nineteenth century a substantial majority of the population and labor force came from other localities. Many factories in Shenyang and other cities in the Northeast were staffed at least partially by labor gangs from Shandong, supplied and supervised by labor contractors.

World War II, known in China as the War of Resistance against Japan (1937–1945), actually increased migration into the Northeast, which at the time was called Manzhouguo (Manchukuo), a puppet state established under Japanese control. As the war expanded, Japan accelerated industrial development in the Northeast, requiring even larger flows of Chinese workers than in earlier years. The other major migration of the war years was the movement of hundreds of thousands of Chinese people to join the wartime bases of the Nationalist and Communist forces in Chongqing, Sichuan, and in Yan'an, Shaanxi, respectively.

The civil war between Mao Zedong's Communist forces and the Nationalist armies of Chiang Kai-shek (Jiang Jieshi), which began in 1946, not long after Japan's surrender, and ended in 1949, caused the movement to Taiwan of the remnants of the Nationalist forces, accompanied by many government officials and civilian supporters, a total of around half a million people. Flight from the new Communist regime also sent thousands to Hong Kong in the 1950s.

MIGRATION IN THE CENTRALLY PLANNED PERIOD (1949–1978)

In the initial years of the People's Republic, many rural workers moved into cities to find jobs. At the same time, the government moved large numbers of intellectuals, officials, and specialized workers to Beijing, Shanghai, and other major cities to develop the agencies and infrastructure of the new state. Analysis of census data finds that between 1950 and 1954 nearly 7.5 percent of all people moving between provinces in China went to Beijing, while over 8 percent were destined for Shanghai. Between 1950 and 1960, migration made a net addition to the Beijing population of over four million people. Over the same decade, Shanghai's population more than doubled, implying immigration of nearly five million. Similarly, in the southern province of Guangdong, the city of Guangzhou grew by 70 percent in the decade of the 1950s, indicating net immigration of over 600,000 people. Large-scale government-sponsored migration also took place in the 1950s to the three Northeast provinces, to rebuild war-damaged industry and infrastructure, to exploit the still lightly populated plains, to tap the forest and mineral resources of northern Heilongjiang, and, toward the end of the decade, to firm up the northern border against possible military actions by the Soviet Union. In the 1950s, nearly a quarter of all interprovincial migrants went to the Northeast, and net migration for the decade came to nearly 3.6 million. For similar reasons, migration to Inner Mongolia was also promoted in the 1950s.

The residence-registration (*hukou*) system, which was put in place in 1958, required urban residents to be registered in order to receive ration coupons for grain, oil, and other necessities. From this point on, voluntary movement from the countryside to the cities was severely restricted. Nonetheless, a substantial amount of migration continued, much of it organized for official policy purposes. Disagreements between China and the Soviet Union caused rising border tensions in the early 1960s, prompting additional migration to the northern and western border areas, including Heilongjiang Province, Inner Mongolia, and Xinjiang.

In the first half of the 1960s, Heilongjiang received 13 percent of all people moving between provinces, while Xinjiang received 8.6 percent and Inner Mongolia nearly 6.5 percent. In the late 1960s and early 1970s, the Cultural Revolution policy of sending down (*xiafang*) urban students to the countryside resulted in another wave of migrants to remote locations, particularly Heilongjiang, which accounted for over 10 percent of all interprovincial migrants in these years. The *xiafang* policy may have also accounted for a burst of migration to Henan Province, which accounted for over 10 percent of all migrants in the early 1970s.

Migration to Hong Kong has been strictly regulated since the founding of the People's Republic, but a strong flow has existed throughout the period since 1949, providing a steady supply of new labor. The main incentives have been the high wages and living standards of Hong Kong, supplemented at times of turmoil in China by fears of chaos or persecution, causing exceptional waves of immigration in periods such as the Great Leap Forward famine of the late 1950s, and the Cultural Revolution of the late 1960s. Between 1961 and 1981, Hong Kong's reported population grew from 3.13 million to 5.11 million, primarily as a result of immigration from the mainland.

MIGRATION IN THE REFORM ERA (1978–)

The introduction of market-based economic reforms beginning in 1978 resulted in the revival of large-scale migration from rural areas to cities. Once the necessities of daily life became available in open urban markets, the urban registration system no longer deterred rural workers from moving to cities. The numbers of migrants have been largest in the eastern coastal cities that have modernized most rapidly. Some of the migrants stay permanently, while others return to their home villages after a few years. In the 1990s, official estimates placed the national "floating population" of migrant workers at around 100 million; the number reached nearly 150 million in the early years of the twenty-first century. One of the major destinations of migrant workers is the vast area of factories linked to Hong Kong and the Shenzhen Special Economic Zone in Guangdong Province, which is believed to account for nearly a third of the national total.

In the 1980s, one effect of the reform policies was a reverse migratory flow of former urban students who had been sent down to rural villages during the Cultural Revolution. This trend is believed to account for a decline in migration to Inner Mongolia, Jilin, and Heilongjiang, and is credited for some of the increase in migration to Beijing and Shanghai in these years. A second reverse migration consisted of former migrants returning from the Northeast, particularly Heilongjiang, to their home villages in Shandong, in order to claim the right to contract farmland under the new contract responsibility system.

A policy trend that has continued in the reform era is government encouragement of Han Chinese migration into strategically important minority areas, particularly Inner Mongolia, Xinjiang, Tibet, and southern Yunnan. As of 2005, Mongols constituted only 21 percent of the population of Inner Mongolia, Uygurs were 60 percent of the population of Xinjiang, the nine major minorities in Yunnan made up 54 percent of the province's autonomous regions, and Tibetans accounted for 93 percent of Tibet's population. Many Han immigrants have become shopkeepers, merchants, and officials and their presence has occasionally sparked hostility from the minority groups, most notably the Uygurs of Xinjiang and the Tibetans. Members of minorities have also migrated, mainly to cities in search of economic opportunities. In Beijing, small enclaves or "villages" of Uygurs, Tibetans, and other minorities have developed.

Throughout the reform period the flow of Chinese immigrants into Hong Kong has continued at a rate of around 45,000 per year, offsetting an exceptionally low fertility rate of only 0.95 children per woman in the Hong Kong population, and causing the population to grow at around 0.5 percent per year.

SEE ALSO *Chinese Overseas; Labor: Outmigration.*

BIBLIOGRAPHY

Day, Lincoln, and Xia Ma, eds. *Migration and Urbanization in China*. Armonk, NY: Sharpe, 1994.

Duara, Prasanjit. *Culture, Power, and the State: Rural North China, 1900–1942*. Stanford, CA: Stanford University Press, 1988.

Eastman, Lloyd E. *Family, Fields, and Ancestors: Constancy and Change in China's Social and Economic History, 1550–1949*. Oxford, U.K.: Oxford University Press, 1988.

Gottschang, Thomas R., and Diana Lary. *Swallows and Settlers: The Great Migration from North China to Manchuria*. Ann Arbor: University of Michigan, Center for Chinese Studies, 2000.

He Bingdi (Ho Ping-ti). *Studies on the Population of China, 1368–1953*. Cambridge, MA: Harvard University Press, 1959.

He Lian (Franklin L. Ho). *Population Movement to the North Eastern Frontier in China*. Shanghai: China Institute of Pacific Relations, 1931.

Hershatter, Gail. *The Workers of Tianjin, 1900–1949*. Stanford, CA: Stanford University Press, 1986.

Honig, Emily. *Sisters and Strangers: Women in the Shanghai Cotton Mills, 1919–1949*. Stanford, CA: Stanford University Press, 1986.

Huang Zongzhi (Philip C. C. Huang). *The Peasant Economy and Social Change in North China*. Stanford, CA: Stanford University Press, 1983.

Liang Zai and Michael J. White. Internal Migration in China, 1950–1988. *Demography* 33, 3 (1996): 375–384.

National Bureau of Statistics of China. *China Statistical Yearbook 2006*. Beijing: China Statistics Press, 2006.

Reardon-Anderson, James. *Reluctant Pioneers: China's Expansion Northward, 1644–1937*. Stanford, CA: Stanford University Press, 2005.

Riskin, Carl. *China's Political Economy: The Quest for Development since 1949*. Oxford, U.K.: Oxford University Press, 1987.

Rowe, William T. *Hankow: Commerce and Society in a Chinese City, 1796–1889*. Stanford, CA: Stanford University Press, 1984.

Shen Jianfa. Population and Migration Trends in Hong Kong. *Geography* 82, 3 (1997): 269–271.

Spence, Jonathan D. *The Search for Modern China*. New York: Norton, 1990.

Vogel, Ezra. *Canton under Communism: Programs and Politics in a Provincial Capital, 1949–1968*. Cambridge, MA: Harvard University Press, 1969.

Wiens, Herold J. *Han Chinese Expansion in South China*. Hamden, CT: Shoe String Press, 1967.

Xu Zhongyue (Immanuel C. Y. Hsü). *The Rise of Modern China*. 6th ed. New York: Oxford University Press, 2000.

Thomas R. Gottschang

INTERNATIONAL DEVELOPMENT AID

Chinese sources date the beginning of China's aid program to 1950, the year after the establishment of the People's Republic. Although the first aid transfers went to North Korea, North Vietnam, and other socialist countries in China's immediate neighborhood, China's aid program quickly expanded beyond the socialist bloc into South Asia, the Middle East, and Africa. In 2006 China had ongoing aid projects in 86 developing countries and counted nearly 120 countries and territories as current or former recipients of Chinese aid.

THE FORMAT OF AID

For many decades Chinese aid was delivered almost exclusively as zero-interest loans that funded turnkey projects in agriculture, industry, and infrastructure. China also funded some of the costs of scholarships and rotating medical teams, costs usually shared with recipient governments. A major policy shift in 1995 created a new instrument, concessional or low-interest loans, and increased the proportion of grants. Although a single project might combine a grant, zero-interest loan, and concessional loan (as in the Pakistani Gwadar Port project), selective targeting is more typical. Grants are targeted to nonproductive social-sector construction projects (e.g., rural water supply, clinics, and schools), as well as training and medical teams. Zero-interest loans generally pay for infrastructure projects (stadiums, government office buildings, roads, and bridges). And concessional loans finance larger projects with concrete possibilities of repayment, in the fields of telecommunications, electric power, manufacturing, and natural-resource extraction.

THE ORGANIZATION OF AID

China's aid is coordinated at the highest level by the Ministry of Foreign Affairs, the Ministry of Finance, and the Ministry of Commerce, under the guidance of the State Council. Decisions on aid commitments are primarily political and may be made by China's top leaders, though the relevant ministries still follow procedures and exercise due diligence. The Ministry of Commerce's Department of Aid to Foreign Countries formulates aid policies and organizes aid implementation. This involves drafting regulations governing aid, coordinating the aid activities of other government ministries and departments, and compiling annual aid budgets to send to the Ministry of Finance. The Ministry of Commerce's International Economic Cooperation Bureau oversees procurement, monitoring and evaluation, selection of experts, capacity building for Chinese aid offices, and other concrete tasks involved in the implementation of projects funded by grants and zero-interest loans. It also organizes seminars and training programs for officials from developing countries. The Chinese make much use of cross-ministerial networks and committees to coordinate debt relief, humanitarian aid, and the evaluation of aid (Huang 2007).

Since 1995 China's Export Import Bank (Eximbank) has been the only source of official foreign-aid concessional loans. The principal for Eximbank loans comes from funds raised on domestic and international capital markets, but the Ministry of Finance provides the Eximbank with a subsidy that makes up the difference between its cost for funds (say 6 percent) and the concessional interest rate that it charges borrowers (generally 2 percent). This subsidy is included in the government's annual budget for foreign-aid expenditures. The Eximbank does its own appraisals of projects submitted for concessional financing, but it coordinates with the Ministry of Commerce on financing decisions, the selection of the company that will implement the project, and onsite monitoring.

THE SCALE OF AID

According to government officials, China's aid more than doubled between 1996 and 2006, and is set to double again by 2009. However, Beijing rarely releases any figures on official aid, even at the country level. In 2006 a top-ranking Chinese leader commented that by the end of 2005, Africa (including North Africa) had received a cumulative total of RMB 44.4 billion (approximately US$5.7 billion) in aid from China for more than 800 projects (Qi 2007). Approximately 44 percent of China's aid goes to Africa, which would make China's cumulative worldwide total aid close to RMB 100 billion, distributed among some 2,000 projects.

China's annual budget for aid includes the face value of the Ministry of Commerce's grants and zero-interest loans, and the government's interest subsidy (but not the

China's government expenditure for external assistance, 1998–2007

Year	Chinese RMB (million)	Exchange rate RMB/$*	Total $US (million)
1998	3,720	8.28	449
1999	3,920	8.279	474
2000	4,588	8.28	554
2001	4,711	8.277	569
2002	5,003	8.277	604
2003	5,223	8.277	631
2004	6,069	8.27	734
2005	7,470	8.07	926
2006	8,200	7.8	1,050
2007	10,800**	7.6	1,421**

*Exchange rates are end of period averages 1998–2006. The exchange rate for 2007 is that current in July.
**Estimates.

SOURCE: *China Statistical Yearbook* (Beijing, various years); Qi Guoqiang. China's Foreign Aid: Policies, Structure, Practice, and Trend. Paper presented at the Conference on New Directions in Foreign Aid, Oxford University, June 2007, and Qi personal communication. International Monetary Fund, *International Financial Statistics* (2007).

Table 1

face value) of the concessional loans made by the China Eximbank. In contrast, other donor nations generally report the entire face value of concessional loans as "official development assistance," equivalent to grants. China's official budget for foreign aid has expanded over the past ten years from around US$450 million per year in 1998 to an estimated US$1.4 billion in 2007 (Table 1). If concessional loans were included at their face value, the total would be considerably higher.

In contrast, Taibei (Taipei) does count the face value of concessional loans in reporting its aid. Net official development assistance from Taiwan totaled US$421 million in 2004, US$483 million in 2005, and US$513 million in 2006 (OECD/DAC 2007).

MULTILATERAL INITIATIVES

In 2007 China pledged for the first time to donate to the World Bank's International Development Association, the soft-loan window that offers concessional loans to the lowest-income countries. China also became a contributor to the United Nation's World Food Program after many years as a recipient of food aid. China supports the South-South Cooperation Program of the Food and Agriculture Organization in Rome. Between 2003 and 2007, China sent more than 20 experts and 500 agricultural technicians to Nigeria under the Food and Agriculture Organization program, an initiative cofinanced by the Nigerians. China is also a member of several regional development banks, including the African Development Bank and the Asian Development Bank. In 2005 China established a US$20 million Poverty Alleviation Fund for Asia (the funds were channeled through the Asian Development Bank). China regularly offers humanitarian aid in kind and in cash during crisis situations. In 2005 the government pledged US$60 million for relief and reconstruction after the Asian tsunami and after a large earthquake in the mountains of Pakistan. Some of these funds were channeled through the United Nations Children's Fund (UNICEF). The country has recently begun to contribute small contingents of peace-keeping forces (including engineers) to assist in United Nations peace and reconstruction efforts.

AID AND CHINESE GEOPOLITICAL AND SECURITY INTERESTS

China's aid program enables the country to build business, cement political ties, and enhance its image at home and abroad as a rising but "responsible" power. During the 1960s and 1970s, aid assisted its quest for political recognition and support from other developing countries for Beijing's claim to the United Nations Security Council seat, held by Taibei from 1949 to 1971. Since China's market-oriented reforms began in late 1978, aid tied to trade has boosted Chinese exports and foreign-exchange earnings, and aid agreements have prompted profitable construction and management contracts for state-owned companies. Aid still figures as a tool in the dollar diplomacy of both Mainland China and Taiwan. Some small countries in the Caribbean, the South Pacific, and sub-Saharan Africa have switched diplomatic recognition back and forth several times between Taibei and Beijing according to the size of the inducements offered by each. In Africa, for example, ten countries that had recognized Beijing switched back to Taibei between 1989 and 2005. Many of these were later persuaded to return to Beijing's fold. As of 2008 only four African countries recognized Taibei: Burkina Faso, Swaziland, Saõ Tomé and Príncipe, and the Gambia.

Since 1995, concessional loans have increasingly been used to fund large projects with important geopolitical and security benefits, for example, development of Pakistan's deep harbor Gwadar, which, along with the Karakoram Highway, provides a sea outlet for southwest China. Although some media reports have linked Chinese aid primarily to natural-resource extraction, the available evidence suggests that aid continues to be used primarily for infrastructure (energy, roads, and telecommunication). While grants are targeted to lower-income countries and zero-interest loans are spread widely, countries with greater repayment prospects receive larger concessional loans. Those that can repay are often natural-resource-exporting countries, such as Botswana or Sudan, but not always. Mauritius (an upper-middle-income country) and Pakistan are two examples of countries with relatively large concessional loans from China but little in the way of natural resources for export.

SEE ALSO *International Development Programs in China.*

BIBLIOGRAPHY

Brautigam, Deborah. *Chinese Aid and African Development: Exporting Green Revolution*. Houndmills, Basingstoke, U.K.: Palgrave Macmillan, 1998.

Brautigam, Deborah. China's Foreign Aid in Africa: What Do We Know? In *China in Africa: Geopolitical and Geoeconomic Considerations*, ed. Robert Rotberg. Washington, DC: Brookings Institution Press, 2008.

Huang Meibo. Zhongguo duiwai yuanzhu jizhi: Xianzhuang he qushi [The mechanism of China's foreign aid system: Characteristics and trends]. *Guoji jingji hezuo* 258 (July 2007).

Organization for Economic Cooperation and Development, Development Assistance Committee (OECD/DAC). Net Official Development Assistance. 2007. http://www.oecd.org/dataoecd/52/10/1893151.xls [accessed April 7, 2008].

Qi Guoqiang. China's Foreign Aid: Policies, Structure, Practice, and Trend. Paper presented at the Conference on New Directions in Foreign Aid, Oxford University, June 2007.

Deborah Brautigam

INTERNATIONAL DEVELOPMENT PROGRAMS IN CHINA

This entry contains the following:

OVERVIEW

International development assistance to China dates back to the late 1970s, following China's resumption of its United Nations (UN) seat in 1971. Prior to this, China had limited engagement in international development processes. It participated in early UN conferences such as the 1972 Stockholm environment conference and the 1975 Nairobi women's conference. From the late 1970s, the number of international development organizations operating in China increased dramatically, and China soon became one of the largest recipients of development loans. The 1980s saw the international financial institutions (IFIs) and a range of other multilateral and bilateral donors and international nongovernmental organizations (NGOs) becoming involved in China.

DEVELOPMENT ORGANIZATIONS IN CHINA

In 2008 twenty-one UN organizations were represented in China, including the Bretton Woods institutions—the World Bank (WB), the International Finance Corporation (IFC), and the International Monetary Fund (IMF). Other key UN organizations include the Food and Agriculture Organization (FAO), the International Labor Organization (ILO), the Joint UN Program on AIDS (UNAIDS), the UN Development Programme (UNDP), the UN Educational, Scientific, and Cultural Organization (UNESCO), the UN Children's Fund (UNICEF), the UN Development Fund for Women (UNIFEM), the World Health Organization (WHO), and the UN Population Fund UNFPA). UN organizations work together in China as part of the UN Resident Coordinator system to support China in its development through the United Nations Development Assistance Framework (UNDAF).

Between 1979 and 1981 China signed bilateral agreements on development cooperation with a large number of countries, including Japan, Australia, Canada, Germany, and the European Union. The list was rapidly extended over subsequent years to include most major donor countries. The exception was the United States: Due to China's family planning policies the U.S. Agency for International Development did not establish a presence in China, but since 2001 has provided assistance to the Tibetan community as well as support for projects on law, governance and the environment.

China has been slower to accept international NGOs, though there have been prominent exceptions: Voluntary Service Overseas (VSO) and the Ford Foundation, for example, have had a presence since the 1980s. During the 1990s more NGOs have been able to operate in China, including the World Wildlife Fund, Oxfam, Save the Children, World Vision, Action Aid, and a number of foundations. Recent changes in the regulations governing domestic and international NGOs have paved the way for more organizations to register, but the procedures are cumbersome.

International development organizations operate in China through an official counterpart agency. For most UN and bilateral agencies, this is the China International Center for Economic and Technical Exchanges (CICETE) in the Ministry of Commerce of the People's Republic of China (MOFCOM). The international financial institutions such as the WB, IMF, and the Asian Development Bank (ADB) have as their counterpart the Ministry of Finance. Officially, NGO registration is with the Ministry of Civil Affairs, but the lack of clear regulations has led many to register as nonprofit enterprises with the Industrial and Commercial Bureau. Most multilateral and bilateral donors operate within an agreed framework set out in a country strategy lasting three to five years and linked to China's strategic development priorities.

DEVELOPMENT GOALS

Reflecting China's rapid economic growth, development priorities and areas of donor engagement have evolved over time. Early support focused on technical assistance and funding for areas such as education, science and technology, infrastructure, rural development, and economic reform. From the late 1980s a stronger focus was placed on poverty reduction as a core development objective, demonstrated particularly in the programs of the multilateral agencies. Bilateral donors often have their own national strategic priorities: Scandinavian agencies have a strong focus on rule of law and civil society programs, as does the Canadian International Development Agency (CIDA). Governance and policy reform has been the hallmark of many programs, including those supported by the European Union, the Australian Agency for International Development (AusAID), and UNDP. Since the 1990s the Department for International Development (DFID) has focused on its core goal of poverty reduction, most recently linked to the achievement of the Millennium Development Goals (MDGs).

In the first decade of the 2000s many donors strengthened their work on sustainable development and environmental management, reflecting global concerns about climate change and the severe environmental problems accompanying China's growth. Other current areas for assistance aligned with the priorities of China's Eleventh Five-Year Plan (2006–2010) include reducing inequality and narrowing income gaps; reducing poverty in poor regions and among disadvantaged groups; improving natural resource management and efficiency; and supporting China's efforts to combat HIV/AIDS and other communicable diseases (one of the MDGs). An emerging arena of engagement for a number of donors, including UNDP and DFID, concerns China's changing global role—as an increasingly influential development actor and investor in Africa; as a key partner in South-South Cooperation initiatives; and as a more influential player in global institutions of governance of, for example, trade, climate change, and security.

The modalities for development assistance also have changed over time, reflecting both China's changing development priorities and capacities and donors' need to maximize the impact of limited (in relation to China's size) financial resources. Most donors now place a premium on using program funding to influence policy through demonstration effects, piloting innovations, the transfer of skills, and capacity building. Achieving influence through knowledge and ideas transfer, rather than through financing for specific projects, has become the central tenet of many donor programs.

China's rising wealth, particularly following its accession to World Trade Organization (WTO) and its classification as a middle-income country, has led a number of countries to reduce official development assistance (ODA) to China. In 1999 China graduated from eligibility for concessionary (IDA) grants and loans from the World Bank. Canada, the United Kingdom, and Japan are among the donors phasing out some forms of development assistance or scaling back their programs, and others are expected to follow suit. Japan, for example, began to offer ODA to China in 1979, and for a long time it was China's largest donor. Its ODA comprised grants, loans, and technical cooperation through the Japan International Cooperation Agency (JICA), Japan Bank for International Cooperation (JBIC), and the embassy. Between 1981 and June 2006 the Ministry of Commerce received grants of US$1.26 billion for 139 projects in areas of health, education, agriculture, poverty alleviation, and environmental protection. In 2000 the Japanese government ended preferential loans to China, and since then it has been reducing the amounts of its grants and loans.

Most European donors have provided a mixture of grant funds and technical assistance, and many are similarly scaling back their assistance. Swedish development aid (coordinated through the Swedish International Development Cooperation Agency, or SIDA) started in 1979 and has included grants and technical assistance focusing on structural reform, environmental protection, healthcare, and human resources. In 1997 Sweden formulated its first country strategy program, and by the end of 2004, thirty-four projects had been completed, amounting to US$160 million. Sweden is currently committed to an annual development grant of US$8 million a year to assist China's Eleventh Five-Year Plan.

The United Kingdom's DFID provides development assistance to China entirely on grant terms, with an overarching focus on poverty reduction. The current five-year development assistance plan (2006–2010) focuses on programs relevant to China's fulfilment of the MDGs—basic education, HIV/AIDS prevention, tuberculosis prevention, and water and sanitation. The budget for development assistance is being scaled down from £40 million in 2006 to 2007 to £30 million in 2008 to 2009, with no major new programs approved. Activities in their current form will conclude by 2013. Instead, U.K. development assistance to China is increasingly focused on China's role as a development actor, on South-South collaboration, and on China's impact on African development.

Australia's AusAID is another key donor. It has operated in China since 1981, and by 2006 Australia had completed 126 joint projects with China, with development grants totalling US$300 million. Projects have focused on agriculture, forestry, energy, transportation, education, and environmental protection. Australian aid to China is likely to decrease gradually, though the Australian government has committed to maintain its program, which focuses on governance, environment and water resources management, and HIV/AIDS and communicable diseases. As with other countries, Australia's aid policy to China has shifted to focus on experience and policy exchange rather than funding and hardware assistance.

CHINA IN THE UN SYSTEM

As a member of the UN system China has participated in most major UN conferences since the 1970s. It hosted the Beijing Women's Conference in 1995. It is a signatory to conventions arising from UN conferences, including the Convention on the Elimination of All Forms of Discrimination against Women and the Convention on the Rights of the Child. Reinforced by the work of relevant UN agencies and other international organizations, participation in these conferences has produced ideas and approaches that have influenced China's domestic policies on issues such as population and birth-planning policies, gender, and the environment.

China is also a key partner in the Millennium Declaration agreed at the 2000 Millennium Summit, which commits the global community to halving global poverty by 2015. Given its size, China's achievements are essential for meeting global targets, and China's own progress is generally impressive, though on a number of goals (such as combating HIV/AIDS and other communicable diseases, and environmental sustainability) it may struggle to meet the targets.

China's role in the international development community is changing rapidly as the country's growing wealth and demand for commodities spurs overseas investment and trade, and as it becomes a significant donor. Its activities in Africa and Southeast Asia in particular reflect approaches to development aid linked closely to strategic and trade interests, and these present challenges to current development assistance practices.

SEE ALSO *International Development Aid.*

BIBLIOGRAPHY

Australian Agency for International Development Web site. http://www.ausaid.gov.au.

Ministry of Commerce. *Jie shou guo ji wu chang yuan zhu zi liao hui bian* [Collections of materials on international assistance (grant) to China]. Beijing: Author, 2006. http://big5.hzc.hunancom.gov.cn/Upload/doc/EditorPic/200742162147829.doc.

UK/China: Partners in International Development. Department for International Development Web site. http://www.dfid.gov.uk/countries/asia/China/partners.asp.

United Nations Country Team in China. *Millennium Development Goals: China's Progress.* Beijing: Office of the United Nations Resident Coordinator in China, 2004.

Sarah Cook
Wing Lam

ASIAN DEVELOPMENT BANK

China's reliance on major international financial institutions has been one of the pillars of the successful modernization strategy in the post-Mao era. Following the fruitful developments of its partnership relations with the World Bank (since 1980), China in 1986 joined the Asian Development Bank (ADB), which had been operating in the region since 1966 as an influential intergovernmental financial organization that aims to secure its members' sustainable economic growth, reduce poverty, and promote regional economic integration. ADB's investment strategy has been focused primarily on stimulating social, environmental, and institutional factors of development by providing loans and grants, technical assistance, and advice, and by knowledge sharing.

Despite the fact that ADB's annual lending to the People's Republic of China (PRC) has been less than 0.15 percent of the total fixed assets investment of more than $1 trillion in the country (by 2008), Beijing's stable partnership with ADB has helped China elaborate a balanced strategy of economic development and wealth accumulation, aimed at maintaining a high growth rate and raising the living standards of the population. By the end of 2007 the PRC had received from ADB $19.17 billion in sovereign and nonsovereign loans as cumulative lending (to finance 139 projects), and in 2008 China remained the second largest borrower and the second largest client for private sector financing. In addition, by the end of 2007 China had received technical assistance grants totalling more than $290 million, to finance more than 550 projects in the areas of governance and institutional strengthening, finance and banking, natural resource and environmental management, energy and infrastructure, and poverty reduction.

In pursuance of its investment strategy, ADB has been responsive to the changing international and domestic conditions of China's economic development. ADB formulates and updates the "country strategy," which considers China's development trends and challenges, emphasizes portfolio management issues and performance, and monitors ongoing operations. At the first stage of Beijing's structural economic reforms in the 1980s, ADB prioritized environmental and infrastructure projects in China's coastal areas. In the 1990s China received the majority of loans and technical assistance grants to support energy conservation projects, resource management and environmental protection, institutional strengthening in the spheres of government and finance, and innovative reforms of state-owned enterprises and the social security system.

In 2001 China adopted a new poverty reduction strategy, as ADB made a dramatic shift toward pro-poor development and new social policies. In the Agreement on a Poverty Reduction Partnership (2003) ADB and China focused on supporting pro-poor sustainable economic growth through infrastructure and environmental improvement projects, by promoting a vibrant private sector to create the necessary jobs, and undertaking policy studies related to poverty. Since the early 2000s, ADB has been considering the challenges resulted from China's rapid economic growth as its high priority. The new Country Strategy and Program (CSP) for 2007 to 2011

Cumulative Asian Development Bank (ADB) lending to the People's Republic of China (1986–2007)

ADB loan projects in the PRC	Amount mln US$
Agriculture and natural resources	1,142.60
Energy	2,680.70
Finance/Industry/Trade	1,125.52
Multisector	1,435.12
Transport and communications	1,435.12
Water supply, sanitation, and waste management	11,172.50
Others	1,617.66
Total (as of December 31, 2007)*	**19,174.10**

*The total amount of loans differs from the 2008 Fact Sheet data at the ADB Web Site: in the section on ADB's relationship with China, the sum of $19.25 billion was mentioned.

SOURCE: Asian Development Bank and People's Republic of China: A Fact Sheet, 2008. Manila: Asian Development Bank, March, 2008, p.2.

Table 1

Summary of ADB technical assistance projects in China (1986–2007)

	Number of projects (by category)						
Year	Infrastructure/ transport	Energy/ Industrial modernization	Environment/ Natural resources	Rural reconstruction/ Poverty reduction	Finance/ Banking	Governance/ Institutional strengthening	Total mln US$
1986	—	1	—	—	—	—	0.075
1987	—	3	—	—	2	—	1.402
1988	2	3	1	—	1	3	3.359
1989	2	—	2	1	1	—	3.585
1990	—	—	1	1	1	1	1.777
1991	7	4	6	2	6	5	14.426
1992	9	4	10	1	4	4	13.767
1993	8	8	4	7	7	3	16.298
1994	9	8	10	1	7	6	17.437
1995	8	9	14	1	8	5	18.409
1996	5	6	7	—	5	2	13.094
1997	6	10	9	2	3	4	19.382
1998	4	9	8	1	6	5	23.510
1999	5	2	10	3	4	4	19.930
2000	4	2	9	1	3	6	16.715
2001	3	1	7	2	2	5	12.448
2002	5	3	8	1	5	4	13.197
2003	4	2	7	5	1	6	12.960
2004	6	4	8	3	4	7	16.704
2005	9	3	9	4	4	5	18.335
2006	9	4	5	3	1	5	13.580
2007	6	9	9	2	1	6	19.822
Total	**111**	**95**	**144**	**41**	**76**	**86**	**290.212**

SOURCE: Asian Development Bank.

Table 2

shifts ADB's operational activity from a growth-oriented strategy toward more sophisticated policies to tackle the problems of increasing income inequality, environmental pollution, low energy efficiency, and weaknesses in the financial system.

In 2005 China began to contribute to the Asian Development Fund with a $30 million contribution, and was the first of the ADB developing countries to devote funds ($20 million) to set up the Regional Cooperation and Poverty Reduction Fund.

In 2008 ADB's strategy in China emphasized a balanced approach toward opportunity-based inclusive growth and developmental and social issues. China cooperates with ADB in coordinating rural and urban development, improving the "development-poverty nexus," securing energy conservation measures, and emphasizing the efficiency of governmental agencies. High priority is accorded to regional cooperation and balanced development among regions. ADB increased its assistance to the PRC energy sector in clean energy projects (the Asia Pacific Carbon Fund), food safety, and small and medium enterprise development in poor regions. China is coordinating ADB strategies and its own policy of stimulating rural development, increasing farmers' incomes, promoting science and education, and building a resource-conserving and environmentally friendly society. Institutional reforms and good governance, along with strengthening regional integration, remain the pillars of Beijing's fruitful cooperation with ADB.

SEE ALSO *Economic Development: Overview; International Development Aid.*

BIBLIOGRAPHY

ADB and PRC—Partners in Development. Manila, Philippines: Asian Development Bank, 2005.

Asian Development Bank and People's Republic of China: A Fact Sheet, 2008. Manila, Philippines: Asian Development Bank, 2008. Available from http://www.adb.org/Documents/Fact_Sheets/PRC.pdf.

Asian Development Bank Annual Report 2007. Vol. 1. Manila, Philippines: Asian Development Bank, 2008.

Country Strategy and Program: People's Republic of China (2004–2006). Manila, Philippines: Asian Development Bank, 2003.

Effectiveness of ADB Approaches and Assistance to Poverty Reduction. Manila, Philippines: Asian Development Bank, 2000.

Fighting Poverty in Asia and the Pacific: The Poverty Reduction Strategy. Manila, Philippines: Asian Development Bank, 1999.

List of Approved Technical Assistance (TA) by Year, 1986–2006. Asian Development Bank. http://www.adb.org/PRC/documents/loans-end-2006-year.pdf.

Roland-Holst, David W. *Overview of PRC's Emergence and East Asian Trade Patterns to 2020.* Tokyo: Asian Development Bank Institute, 2002.

Toward a New Asian Development Bank in a New Asia: Report of the Eminent Persons Group to the President of the Asian Development Bank. Manila, Philippines: Asian Development Bank, 2007.

Wang Gungwu and John Wong, eds. *Interpreting China's Development.* Singapore and Hackensack, NJ: World Scientific, 2007.

Vitaly Kozyrev

FOOD AND AGRICULTURE ORGANIZATION

After the People's Republic of China took over the China seat in the United Nations (UN) in 1971, it assumed membership in the UN Food and Agriculture Organization (FAO) in April 1973. In September 1974, China participated in the Twelfth FAO Regional Conference for Asia and the Pacific in Tokyo, the first time China had taken part in this conference. In the meeting, the Ministry of Agriculture invited FAO to send missions to China, opening the way for China to receive FAO technical assistance. Three months later, in November 1974, China attended the first World Food Conference in Rome, marking the start of China's engagement with FAO and the international community on food-security issues.

In September 1975, FAO sent its first mission to China, concentrating on agricultural production and the study of the people's communes. A second mission to China was sent in April 1976 to study China's aquaculture development, paving the way for a series of FAO technical-assistance projects on fisheries and aquaculture starting from 1978. In January 1983, FAO opened a representative office in Beijing. China hosted the FAO Regional Conference for Asia and the Pacific in Beijing in 1990 and 2004, and actively participated in the World Food Summit in 1996. In April 1998, former president Jiang Zemin was awarded the Agricola Medal, the FAO's highest distinction, in recognition of his successful efforts to develop agriculture in China.

FAO assistance is coordinated by the Ministry of Agriculture. Nearly all FAO projects are implemented by Chinese institutions (government ministries, academic institutions, and nongovernmental organizations) to support the FAO mandate in the promotion of agricultural development and food security. FAO also collaborates with other UN agencies, such as the World Health Organization, the World Food Program, and the United Nations Development Programme to fund projects in China, with FAO playing the key role in providing technical expertise and support in agriculture and food security. FAO does not have an annual budget for individual member countries. All project assistance is demand-driven. Funding is mobilized from the FAO's regular program funding and trust funds through contributions from UN agencies, international financing institutions, government donors, the private sector, and the general public.

From 1978 to 2005 FAO provided over $60 million to support more than two hundred programs and projects in crop and livestock production, fisheries, forestry, agricultural extension, agricultural trade and marketing, emergency response, natural-disaster management, and other areas. At the end of 2008, forty-three FAO projects were operationally active, with total assistance valued at $35 million, of which about 10 percent is mobilized from regular FAO program funding through the Technical Cooperation Program.

As a member of the UN China Country Team, FAO is committed to the United Nations Development Assistance Framework 2006–2010 and has agreed to focus its activities in areas that promote key national priorities set forth in the Eleventh Five-Year Plan (2006–2010). FAO set a resource mobilization target of $7 million in three prioritized project areas: promoting equitable and sustainable development of the agricultural and industrial sectors, enhancing the capacity for analysis and evaluation of food security and food safety, and promoting China's participation in international cooperation in food security and rural-development monitoring.

FAO technical assistance to China is widely recognized as a positive catalyst to China's agricultural and economic development in the reform years, especially in bridging China's knowledge gap. The close working relationship between the Chinese government and FAO also strengthens China's information exchange with the rest of the world. FAO funded four projects and provided technical assistance (a sum of $16.4 million) between 1987 and 1996 in support of China's preparation for its First National Agricultural Census. More cooperation in agricultural-statistics collection and database management followed.

FAO has enthusiastically promoted China's successful experience in agricultural development to other developing countries. China is an active member of South-South Cooperation (SSC) initiatives within the framework of FAO's Special Program for Food Security. The SSC initiatives entail tripartite cooperation between China, FAO, and a host developing country. Between 1996 and mid-2007, China signed ten SSC agreements with ten developing countries, including Bangladesh, Ethiopia, Ghana, Mali, Mauritania, Nigeria, and Gabon—nearly one-fourth of all SSC agreements signed in the period. Thousands of Chinese technicians and experts worked directly with farmers in these developing countries, sharing their knowledge and skills for the enhancement of food security.

SEE ALSO *Agricultural Production.*

BIBLIOGRAPHY

Food and Agriculture Organization. http://www.fao.org.

National Bureau of Statistics of China. Technical Cooperation in the Context of Food and Agriculture Statistics in China: The FAO Experience. 2001. http://www.stats.gov.cn/english/specialtopics/nbsimf/t20020331_15735.htm.

Permanent Mission of the PRC to the UN Office at Geneva. China and Food and Agriculture Organization (FAO). 2004. http://www.china-un.ch/eng/zmjg/jgjblc/t85559.htm.

United Nations China Country Team. United Nations Development Assistant Framework for the People's Republic of China 2006–2010. 2005. http://www.un.org.cn/cms/p/resources/30/309/content.html.

Zhu Pirong. Lián hé guó liáng nóng zǔ zhī yǔ zhōng guó de hé zuò xiàng mù (FAO-China Cooperation Projects). *World Agriculture* 11 (2001): 45–48.

Wing Lam

INTERNATIONAL MONETARY FUND

Headquartered in Washington, D.C., the International Monetary Fund (IMF) was established in 1944 as part of the postwar institutional architecture laid down by the Bretton Woods agreement. Although nominally affiliated with the United Nations, the IMF has a separate budget denominated in special drawing rights (SDR) that are based on a currency basket (SDR1 = approx US$1.6), and it employs its own diplomatic staff.

The founding members of the IMF were made up of the former Allied powers. Still weighted toward the West and Japan, the IMF apparatus nevertheless has absorbed into its ranks over the last three decades staff from a number of nonaligned and former Communist countries, including the People's Republic of China (PRC, joined 1980) and the Russian Federation (joined 1992). In 2008, of the twenty-four executive directors on the IMF board, one was directly appointed by the PRC government.

The fund was initially entrusted with the rehabilitation of international monetary settlements after World War II. Nowadays, its terms of reference range from securing financial stability and facilitating international trade to fostering economic growth, poverty reduction, and the provision of monetary expertise to member states. The latter inform the IMF's involvement with China in particular.

At times of global financial turmoil, the IMF is seen as an arbiter of assistance to vulnerable countries. It provides short-term loans to governments experiencing a run on their national currencies, lender foreclosures, or liquidity crises. These loans are designed to help governments in developing countries stabilize exchange rates, rebuild their foreign reserves, and, ultimately, restore their creditworthiness. Unlike the World Bank, the IMF does not bankroll specific development projects; instead, it advises member states on what Washington sees as sound monetary policy—for example, foreign-currency exchange deregulation, trade liberalization, and market reform.

With backing from the Roosevelt administration, and as one of the Allied powers, the Republic of China (ROC) became a member of the IMF and World Bank in 1945. In fact, the ROC's share of voting rights on the executive board was at first five times larger than France's. The PRC took over the China seat from the ROC in Taiwan (with the support of influential figures in the West) and joined the UN in 1971, paving the way for its IMF and World Bank membership a decade later.

The PRC was and remains openly critical of the IMF's voting right quota system, which it sees as overstating the significance of developed nations, and running contrary to China's professed foreign-policy principle of the equality of all countries. PRC pressure yielded considerably more voting rights by 1983 (commensurate with its preliminary SDR2.39 billion stake in the fund), and the appointment of a Chinese director. By 2001 the PRC controlled nearly 3 percent of voting rights, and its percentage has increased steadily since then. Yet the PRC was not able to wrest control of the ROC's original stake in the fund—about US $500 million in gold bars. These were handed back to Taiwan upon the PRC's entry.

Differences over voting rights notwithstanding, IMF membership continues to play a significant role in integrating China's economy with the global economy. The most serious conflict between the PRC government and the fund broke out in December 1995 when Hong Yang, a People's Bank of China official posted to the IMF, was arrested by the Chinese authorities on corruption charges during a visit to Beijing. Hong was sentenced to ten years in prison for offenses allegedly committed before he joined the fund. The IMF initially protested the incident because its staff are meant to enjoy a form of diplomatic immunity, but it relented after the sentence was reduced to five years.

In 1981 the PRC borrowed its first credit tranche, SDR750 billion, which was needed for capital investment to stimulate economic reform. In 1986 China borrowed a further SDR597 million. Those two loans were fully repaid in line with the Chinese reform rationale of avoiding foreign debt as much as possible. The fact that China has not borrowed from the IMF since then partly explains why it was able to withstand IMF pressure and carry on fixing the RMB exchange rate.

Chinese monetary policy was vindicated during the Asian financial crisis of 1997, when speculation against the Thai currency sparked a financial panic that fanned rapidly across the region's bourses, and later spread as far as Brazil and Russia. Contrary to IMF prescriptions, China was still enforcing severe restrictions on offshore financial investment; the RMB was strictly regulated, and listed equity was capped. Experts agree, by and large, that these factors spared the PRC economy the currency devaluation, bank asset write-offs, insolvency, and negative growth rates that hit the rest of the region. At the height of the crisis the PRC even lent as much as US$1 billion to Thailand and US$200 million to Indonesia to restore faith in their economies.

China's successful record in dealing with the Asian financial crisis was often cited by IMF critics as proof for free-market dogmatism on its part, in other words, neoliberal espousal of deregulation irrespective of regional circumstances. More recently, following the 2008 sub-prime mortgage crisis in the United States, which rapidly degenerated into the most serious global financial meltdown since 1929, and was widely seen as a result of under-regulation of multinational financial institutions, criticism of the IMF has intensified. Calls for the reform of the global financial architecture are growing, with China supporting more stringent regulation of equity markets, currency exchange, and tax havens.

Additionally, PRC policy makers have themselves realized that China's economy shares many of the structural weaknesses that buffeted other Asian countries during the 1997 crisis (e.g., poor corporate governance, speculative overtrading, export-led growth), and that greater integration with world markets would inevitably eliminate the policy buffers that shielded China's economy in the past.

China has therefore strengthened its collaboration with the IMF and the World Bank in the areas of accountancy standards, corporate transparency, and reform of state-owned enterprises. Though the PRC no longer borrows from the IMF on call, it is by far the largest recipient of technical assistance, which accounts for one-fifth of the fund's budget. China consults fund experts on issues ranging from its balance of payments to fiscal reform. The IMF's Statistics Department trains officials from the People's Bank of China, the Ministry of Finance, the National Bureau of Statistics, the State Administration of Foreign Exchange, and the Customs General Administration in the development and reform of China's system of macroeconomic statistics.

IMF training courses are offered at its Washington, D.C., headquarters and in seven centers around the world, including Beijing, where the fund set up an office in 1991. Two other regional offices were opened later, in Dalian (2000) and Hong Kong (2001). These offices underpin policy dialogue with Chinese authorities and help coordinate the monitoring of the local economies.

SEE ALSO *Financial Regulation.*

BIBLIOGRAPHY

Eichengreen, Barry, and Raul Razo-Garcia. The International Monetary System in the Last (and Next) Twenty Years. *Economic Policy* 21, 47 (2006): 393–416, 420–439.

Hooke, A. W., ed. *The Fund and China in the International Monetary System*. Washington, DC: International Monetary Fund, 1983.

International Monetary Fund. *2007 Annual Report*. Washington, DC: Author, 2007.

Kent, Ann. *Beyond Compliance: China, International Organizations, and Global Security*. Stanford, CA: Stanford University Press, 2007.

Yang Xueyu. *Guoji huobi jijin zuzhi daodu* [An introduction to the IMF]. Beijing: Zhongguo Jinrong Chubanshe, 2003.

Niv Horesh

UNITED NATIONS DEVELOPMENT PROGRAMME (UNDP)

The People's Republic of China resumed state membership in the United Nations (UN) in 1971. In June 1979 a Basic Agreement on Cooperation with the UN Development Programme (UNDP) was signed, marking the start of a new phase in China's international cooperation and opening the way for China to receive development assistance. Projects were initiated under a temporary arrangement with funding of US $15 million from the UNDP's new member reserve fund. In June 1982 the UNDP signed its first framework agreement with China.

The UNDP provides funding and technical assistance to the Chinese government with priorities set over five-year program cycles, supporting China's overall economic and social development priorities as expressed in its national Five-Year Plans. UNDP assistance is coordinated by the China International Center for Economic and Technical Exchanges (CICETE) of the Ministry of Commerce. Over 85 percent of UNDP projects are implemented by Chinese institutions (government ministries, nongovernmental organizations, and the private sector), contributing to the UNDP goal of strengthening national capacities for human development. Funding is mobilized from many sources including UNDP core funding, the Chinese government, donors, the private sector, and global trust funds.

From 1979 to 2006 UNDP provided over $873 million to support more than 600 projects in fields including agriculture, industry, energy, public health, education, and governance, with approximately one-third of its projects focusing on poverty alleviation. The UNDP's first China Country Programs (CCP) ran from 1982 to 1986, followed by a second set from 1986 to 1990 that had a budget of US $122 million and focused on fields of human resource development, industrial transformation and technology, and improving living standards. The third CCP (1991–1995) shifted to a stronger focus on agriculture, basic industries, and infrastructure, and strengthened education, science, and technology, with an allocation of US$190 million.

Renamed Country Cooperation Frameworks (CCFs), UNDP activities have evolved in line with China's changing priorities, with an enhanced focus on poverty alleviation, human development, and the environment. From 2001 to 2005 CCF mobilized over $250 million, prioritizing democratic governance, poverty reduction, fighting HIV/AIDS, and sustainable development. The 2006–2010 CCF focuses on key national priorities closely aligned to the government's vision of achieving a well-off (*xiaokang*) and harmonious society. Core program areas are aimed at achieving the Millennium Development Goals (MDGs) and reducing human poverty; protecting the environment and providing energy for sustainable human development; and responding to HIV/AIDS and other communicable diseases. In 2007 the UNDP had about seventy ongoing projects with activities in almost all provinces and regions of China.

Illustrating the interplay between the goals of the international community and the UN system, in 2005 the UNDP launched its flagship Xiaokang program, which entails broad-based consultations for achieving the MDGs as complementary to China's *xiaokang* vision. This reflected a shift in the country program from project support to flagship programs that inform and support policy making, and use knowledge-based approaches to promote more balanced human development outcomes. In 2006 UNDP delivered assistance to China totaling US $53.5 million, with close to half of these resources (47.1%) for projects to support the MDGs, poverty reduction, and HIV/AIDS programs. The second-largest part (44.8%) contributed to results in the areas of environmental protection and energy.

Among its contributions to China's development, the UNDP has appropriated over $50 million for thirty reform and governance projects involving government restructuring and reform of economic, financial, and legal institutions and the social security system. Complementing China's national poverty alleviation programs, the UNDP has supported more than forty pilot projects in poor counties, and was instrumental in efforts to expand microfinance programs in China. In recognition of its work it was awarded the Prize of International Cooperation for Poverty Reduction in China in 2006 by the Chinese Foundation for Poverty Reduction. On the environment, the UNDP has implemented thirty-six projects in collaboration with the State Environmental Protection Administration (SEPA) and other key institutions, contributing to efforts in sustainable energy use, China's entry into the global carbon market, and biodiversity conservation. The UNDP also has supported the publication of five China Human Development Reports, including "Growth with Equity" and "Making Green Development a Choice," which have proven effective at drawing the attention of policy makers and the public to pressing development challenges and innovative solutions. The UNDP also supports development partnerships with the private sector to promote corporate social responsibility for sustainable development and poverty reduction, and regional and South-South cooperation, for example, through the China-Africa Business Council.

The UNDP resident representative also acts as the UN resident coordinator, representing the UN secretary general and leading UN system operational activities at the country level. Since 2007 UNDP day-to-day operations are led by a country director. The UNDP Country Programme represents the UNDP contribution to achieving the outcomes of the UN Development Assistance Framework. The UNDP participates in UN activities, including theme groups on issues such as AIDS, gender equality, and poverty reduction, and contributes to UN joint programs. It is in a unique position to use its cross-cutting role and corporate mandate to contribute substantively to priority areas of the government of China, while assisting in the coordination of aid as a mechanism for accessing global lessons and international experience.

SEE ALSO *Poverty.*

BIBLIOGRAPHY

China International Center for Economic and Technical Exchanges. *21 Years: An Overview of UNDP-China Cooperation 1970–2001.* Beijing: Author. http://www.cicete.org/english/achievement.htm.

United Nations Development Programme. *UNDP Country Programme for the People's Republic of China (2006–2010).* Beijing: Author, 2005. Available from http://www.undp.org.cn/downloads/keydocs/cpd2006.pdf.

United Nations Development Programme. *United Nations Development Programme at Work in China: Annual Report 2007.* Beijing: Author, 2007.

United Nations Development Programme. *Annual Report 2007/2008—UNDP China.* Beijing: Author, 2008. Available from http://www.undp.org.cn.

Sarah Cook
Wing Lam

WORLD BANK

The People's Republic of China resumed representation in the World Bank Group in May 1980, and lending commenced the following year. The World Bank Resident Mission in China opened on July 1, 1985, with China quickly becoming the bank's largest borrower. The World Bank (or International Bank for Reconstruction and Development, IBRD) comprises a number of institutions that provide various forms of financial and technical assistance. These include grants and concessional loans (IDA), nonconcessional loans to government initiated projects, and loans and equity finance for business ventures through the International Finance Corporation. Through Analytical and Advisory Activities the bank also provides research and advisory inputs to support program development.

The World Bank operates in China under a framework agreement with the Ministry of Finance, which initiates and approves programs and oversees lending. The National Development and Reform Commission plays a key role in program formulation and approval, particularly in relation to infrastructure, whereas project implementation is undertaken by relevant government agencies. Priorities for assistance are agreed in line with China's national development priorities. The first Country Assistance Strategy (CAS) ran from 1995 to 1998, overlapping substantially with China's Ninth Five-Year Plan. A second CAS covered the period 2003 to 2006, and the third covers the period of the Eleventh Five-Year Plan (2006–2010).

China's relationship with the World Bank has evolved rapidly as its economy has grown. Lending was suspended in 1989 following the suppression of the student movement in Tiananmen Square but resumed in 1991, at which point China became the largest recipient of World Bank funding. In 1999 China attained middle-income status, thus graduating from eligibility for concessional funding. By that time China had received a total of US$9.95 billion in IDA grants and loans, with total borrowing exceeding $40 billion for more than 280 investment projects. China continues to borrow on nonconcessional terms. In 2007 ten new loans were made totalling US$1.6 billion; amounts were expected to remain stable at this level.

The changing portfolio of World Bank activities reflects China's changing needs. Early programs focused on strengthening higher education and research, especially in the fields of science and engineering; during the 1980s projects included support for infrastructure, agriculture, health, and education, particularly in the poorest regions of north- and southwest China. These projects played a critical role in illuminating the nature of poverty in China's western regions, leading to a landmark report, "China: Strategies for Reducing Poverty in the 1990s," and the development of a strong partnership with the Chinese government for alleviating poverty. Since the launch of the first poverty alleviation project in 1995, approximately US $680 million has been spent in 119 counties in eight provinces or regions, benefiting over 10 million poor people. Current program priorities reflect the government's concern with the environment, with approximately 60 percent of World Bank projects now focused on sustainable development.

The World Bank's role in China has evolved from its early position as a key government adviser to one of many, and the significance of its funding has declined relative to China's economic size. This has required a shift to a greater emphasis on knowledge, policy ideas, and innovative reform mechanisms. The bank undertakes core diagnostic work (such as country economic memoranda, public expenditure reviews, and poverty assessments) together with in-depth analytic work and sector studies, both of which are needed to maintain a knowledge base to deliver quality services and respond to the government's policy needs. Despite the reduced significance of its funding, World Bank projects remain important as a mechanism for piloting reforms and ensuring the relevance of services.

Several notable contributions of the World Bank during almost thirty years of engagement with China include its partnership for reducing poverty, which was highlighted in a 2004 Global Learning Event in Shanghai. In financial sector reform, the bank has supported high-level technical dialogues and analytic work leading to significant governmental reforms (of interest rates and bankruptcy law, for example). In the social sectors, there has been long-term engagement for piloting rural health system reforms that are entering mainstream policy. In the field of pensions, the bank has contributed international experience and introduced necessary tools such as building actuarial capacity.

As in other countries where it operates, the World Bank attracts controversy for some of its work in China. In a publicized case over a new Western China Poverty Alleviation Program in 1999, international protest about resettlement in traditionally Tibetan areas led the Chinese government to withdraw its request for funding. Other criticisms focus on the extent to which issues of gender equity, ethnicity, and public participation are integrated into World Bank programs, and on the balance between market-based solutions and the role of government in areas such as pension and health reform.

China's relationship with the World Bank continues to change rapidly as China becomes a more confident development partner and donor. The appointment in 2008 of a Chinese national, Justin Yifu Lin (b. 1952), as the World Bank's first chief economist and senior vice president from a developing country is a sign of a new phase in China's status within the world Bank and a recognition of the growing role and influence of China as a global development actor.

SEE ALSO *Banking.*

BIBLIOGRAPHY

World Bank. *China: Strategies for Reducing Poverty in the 1990s.* Beijing: Author, 1992.

World Bank. *China: Country Partnership Strategy, 2006–2010.* Washington, DC, and Beijing: Author, 2006.

World Bank China Web site. http://www.worldbank.org.cn.

World Bank Group. *China and the World Bank: A Partnership for Innovation.* Beijing: Author, 2007.

Sarah Cook
Wing Lam

INTERNATIONAL ORGANIZATIONS, RELATIONS WITH, 1900–1949

Imperial China's unhappy relationship with foreign powers was a product not only of its military and economic weakness vis-à-vis the West, but also of its inward-looking political culture and legal system. George Morrison early on pointed out, "In China, the laws, whether the fundamental ones in the imperial code, or the subsidiary rules, or the provincial and local orders of government, are all more or less hostile to a free and amicable intercourse with foreigners" (cited in MacNair 1923, p. 14). China's preferred solution for handling Western powers within its territory was to invoke its traditional custom of fending off "barbarians" by allowing them peripheral participation in Chinese society and cooperating with them in joint enterprises. Thus, the Sino-Western institutional arrangements of the Shanghai International Settlement, the Shanghai Mixed Court, and the Chinese Imperial Maritime Customs Service have been viewed as "in effect types of international organization" on Chinese soil (Cohen and Chiu 1974, p. 1286).

EARLY PARTICIPATION

Despite its early attitude, by the late nineteenth and early twentieth centuries, imperial China accepted the need to establish diplomatic relations with foreign powers, and began to participate formally in intergovernmental organizations. It was invited to participate in the Association for the Reform and Codification of the Law of Nations in 1878; it joined the Universal Postal Union in 1897; and it sent delegations to the 1899 and 1907 Hague Conferences. It also established relations with international nongovernmental organizations like the International Red Cross, and set up Red Cross activities in China in 1894. By the time of the establishment of the Republic of China in 1912, China's leaders were adopting a far more positive view of the outside world. In the manifesto "To Our Foreign Friends," published on November 17, 1911, the Provisional Government Minister of Foreign Affairs Wu Tingfang stated, "We are fighting to be men in the world.... We must not be judged by the past; we are trying to bring China into her own; to elevate her to the standard that the people of the Occident have been urging her to attain" (cited in MacNair 1923, p. 716).

Wu's sentiments were hardly reciprocated by the foreign powers. Rather than accepting China as an equal in the family of nations, the European state system, for the most part, maintained China on the periphery (Zhang Yongjin 1991, p. 188). For most of the twentieth century, the history of China's participation in international organizations was governed either by its attempts to resist dismemberment at the hands of the imperialist powers or, after 1949, by a struggle between the Republic of China and the People's Republic to assert their competing claims to represent the official government of China, and thereby to avoid the two-Chinas solution in the United Nations and other international organizations.

THE AFTERMATH OF WORLD WAR I

World War I brought China into increasing engagement with the outside world. The Republic of China refused to sign the Treaty of Versailles because it transferred legal control of Shandong from Germany to Japan, prior to its eventual return to China. However, by signing the Treaty of St. Germain, which also contained the League of Nations Covenant, with Austria on September 10, 1919, China automatically joined the league (Elleman 2002, p. 130). Fifty-five nations, including Japan, accepted the obligations of the covenant. China, unlike Japan, also accepted the jurisdiction of the Permanent Court of International Justice (Chih Meng 1932, p. 154). In 1919 the Republic of China also became a founding member of the International Labour Organization. Yet at the inaugural conference of this organization, in 1919, delegates from countries enjoying extraterritoriality in China requested that the Republic of China be classed as one of the "special countries" to which resolutions adopted at the conference, such as that on the eight-hour day, did not apply (Chesneaux 1968, pp. 474–475, n. 96). China also joined international nongovernmental organizations, such as the International Olympics Committee in 1924, and established branches of the Young Men's Christian Association and the first Chinese branch of International PEN (the writers' association).

China's experience of the League of Nations was a painful one (Shi Yuanhua 1989, pp. 390–393). In 1930, for instance, it failed in its bid to become a nonpermanent member of the League Council because of its disunity and inability to pay its dues. More important, the league's failure to confront Japan over its expansion into Manchuria weakened not only China but also the league itself (Craft 2004, pp. 98–100). This was despite the fact that, in the words of Lord Robert Cecil in 1932, "throughout this matter, China has throughout acted in accordance with what she believed to be the wishes of the League [and] has acted as a loyal and honourable member" (cited in Chih Meng 1932, p. xiv). It led Chiang Kai-shek (Jiang Jieshi) to observe, "The eventual failure of the League of Nations was due mainly to the ignoring of this principle [of self-determination and equality among nations]" (Chiang Kai-shek 1947, p. 234).

REPUBLICAN REPRESENTATION

World War II elevated China's international standing. Because of its significant role in the war, the Republic of China was heavily involved in the establishment of the United Nations. It was one of the original signatories of the Declaration by United Nations, signed by twenty-six allied nations on January 1, 1942. It was a member of the second phase of the Dumbarton Oaks Conversations, which, from September 29 to October 7, 1944, drafted the Dumbarton Oaks Proposals for establishing a general international organization. It agreed to join the United States, United Kingdom, and Soviet Union in sponsoring invitations to a conference in San Francisco to prepare a charter for the proposed organization. And at San Francisco it served as a member of the Executive Committee of the Preparatory Commission (United Nations 1946–1947, pp. 4–50).

The Republic of China duly became a founding member of the United Nations and one of the four original Permanent Members of the United Nations Security Council (not yet including France). It signed and ratified the United Nations Charter on June 26 and September 28, 1945, respectively, and continued to represent China in the United Nations until October 25, 1971. Its claim to do so, despite the establishment of the People's Republic of China in October 1949, was partly based on Article 23, Section 1, of the United Nations Charter, which specifically listed the Republic of China as a permanent member of the Security Council (Chou Keng-sheng [1961] 1974, p. 273). By virtue of this permanent-member status, the Republic of China became a member of the Atomic Energy Commission, the Commission for Conventional Armaments, and the Military Staff Committee. It also became a member of the Economic and Social Council and the Trusteeship Council. By July 1947 it had become a member of all the existing specialized agencies of the United Nations: the International Labour Organization; the United Nations Educational, Scientific, and Cultural Organization; the Food and Agricultural Organization; the International Civil Aviation Organization; the International Monetary Fund; the World Bank; the Interim Commission of the World Health Organization; and the Preparatory Commission of the International Refugee Organization (United Nations 1946–1947, pp. 453–454, 865–866). As of December 31, 1949, it was a member of twelve out of fourteen specialized agencies (with the exception of the World Meteorological Organization and the Preparatory Committee for the Inter-governmental Maritime Consultative Organization)

(United Nations 1948–1949, p. 1120). However, because the People's Republic subsequently contested its claim to represent China, the Republic of China, unlike the other permanent members of the Security Council, was excluded from the Economic and Social Council from 1961 to 1971 (Kim 1979, p. 297). Although a member of the United Nations Industrial Development Organization, it was also the only permanent member of the Security Council to be excluded from its principal policy organ, the Industrial Development Board (Kim 1979, p. 308).

THE QUESTION OF REPRESENTATION

After the People's Republic of China was established in October 1949, membership in international organizations became a focal point of its struggle for legitimacy vis-à-vis the Republic of China, which, in 1949, retreated to the island of Taiwan. The alteration in its material circumstances initially weakened the power of the Republic of China within the United Nations. It was one of the contracting parties to the General Agreement on Tariffs and Trade in 1947, but in May 1950 it gave notice of withdrawal. The Republic of China subsequently had observer status at the General Agreement on Tariffs and Trade. Its membership in other bodies was also discontinued. Thus, it gave notice of withdrawal from the World Health Organization on May 7, 1950, from the International Civil Aviation Organization on May 31, 1950, and from the Food and Agricultural Organization in 1951 (effective July 21, 1952) (Kim 1979, p. 366; United Nations 1950, p. 982), in part because it could not meet its financial obligations.

Initially, the United Nations was inclined not to support the Republic of China in its complaints to the United Nations about the People's Republic, and as of the first half of 1950, the latter might well have succeeded in its bid to replace the Republic of China as the official representative of China in the United Nations (Cordier and Foote 1969, pp. 17–20, 165). However, the Soviet Union's high-handed yet ambiguous attempts to support the People's Republic in its bid, the outbreak of the Korean War on June 25, 1950, China's entry into the war in mid-October, and the adoption of Security Council Resolution 498 (V) charging the People's Republic with aggression in Korea virtually put an end to the hopes of the People's Republic until 1971 (Kent 2007, pp. 36–46; Levi 1953, pp. 273–276).

BIBLIOGRAPHY

China Institute of International Affairs Study Group. *China and the United Nations: Report of a Study Group Set up by the China Institute of International Affairs*. New York: Manhattan, 1959.

Chesneaux, Jean. *The Chinese Labor Movement, 1919–1927*. Stanford, CA: Stanford University Press, 1968.

Chiang Kai-shek, with notes by Philip Jaffe. *China's Destiny and Chinese Economic Theory*. London: Dennis Dobson, 1947.

Chih Meng. *China Speaks: On the Conflict between China and Japan*. London: Macmillan, 1932.

China Handbook Editorial Board. *China Handbook*. Taiwan, Taipei: China Publishing Company, vols. 1937–1955.

Chou Keng-sheng. China's Legitimate Rights in the United Nations Must Be Restored. In *People's China and International Law: A Documentary Study*, ed. Jerome Alan Cohen and Hungdah Chiu, vol. 1, p. 273. Princeton, NJ: Princeton University Press, 1974. First published, *Renmin Ribao*, December 5, 1961, p. 5.

Cohen, Jerome Alan, and Hungdah Chiu, eds. *People's China and International Law: A Documentary Study*. 2 vols. Princeton, NJ: Princeton University Press, 1974.

Cordier, Andrew W., and Wilder Foote, eds. *Public Papers of the Secretaries-General of the United Nations: Trygve Lie, 1946–1953*. New York: Columbia University Press, 1969.

Craft, Stephen. G. *V. K. Wellington Koo and the Emergence of Modern China*. Lexington: University Press of Kentucky, 2004.

Elleman, Bruce A. *Wilson and China: A Revised History of the Shandong Question*. Armonk, NY: Sharpe, 2002.

Kent, Ann. *Beyond Compliance: China, International Organizations, and Global Security*. Stanford, CA: Stanford University Press, 2007.

Kim, Samuel S. *China, the United Nations, and World Order*. Princeton, NJ: Princeton University Press, 1979.

Levi, Werner. *Modern China's Foreign Policy*. Minneapolis: University of Minnesota Press, 1953.

MacNair, Harley Farnsworth. *Modern Chinese History: Selected Readings*. Shanghai: Commercial Press, 1923.

Shi Yuanhua, ed. *Zhong-wai guanxi sanbai ti* [Three hundred topics in Sino-foreign relations]. Shanghai: Shanghai Guji Chubanshe, 1989.

United Nations. *Yearbook of the United Nations*. New York: Columbia University and United Nations, 1946–1971 (annual).

Wang Xingfang, ed. *Zhongguo yu Lianheguo: Jinian Lianheguo chengli wushi zhounian* [China and the United Nations: Commemorating the fiftieth anniversary of the founding of the United Nations]. Beijing: Shijie Zhishi Chubanshe, 1995.

Zhang Yongjin. *China in the International System, 1918–20: The Middle Kingdom at the Periphery*. Basingstoke, U.K.: Macmillan, in association with St. Antony's College, Oxford, 1991.

Ann Kent

INTERNATIONAL ORGANIZATIONS, RELATIONS WITH, SINCE 1949

Well before the establishment of the People's Republic of China (PRC) in 1949, its leaders supported China's entry into the world of international organizations. Thus, in

1945, Mao Zedong articulated his party's policy on the proposed United Nations: "The Chinese Communist Party fully agrees with the proposals of the Dumbarton Oaks conference on the establishment of an organization to safeguard international peace and security after the war. It . . . welcomes the United Nations Conference on International Organization in San Francisco. It has appointed its own representative on China's delegation to this conference" (quoted in Cohen and Chiu 1974, p. 1290). Accordingly, party members Dong Biwu (1886–1975) and Qiao Guanhua (1913–1983) joined the Republic of China (ROC) delegation at the San Francisco Conference and signed the UN Charter.

INTERNATIONAL RECOGNITION OF THE PRC AND ROC

Following the establishment of the PRC, China's new foreign minister, Zhou Enlai, sent numerous letters to the UN secretary-general requesting the expulsion of the ROC and its replacement by the PRC as the official representative of "China" in the United Nations. A favorable UN decision would not only legitimize PRC sovereignty over China's mainland and help promote diplomatic recognition of the PRC; it would also delegitimize the ROC's claims and ensure against the possibility of a "two Chinas" solution. Disappointed by repeated UN rebuffs, PRC leaders became more and more critical of the organization and its domination by a "hegemonic power" to the point where, in 1965, Premier Zhou Enlai called for the United Nations to be replaced by another organization. China's belief that multilateral organizations had become the tools of great powers to dominate the less powerful and, in particular, to weaken the PRC led it to prefer to resolve its international problems through bilateral means.

Thus, until the replacement of the ROC as the official representative of "China" in the United Nations, the PRC enjoyed only limited opportunities for multilateral interaction. It briefly participated in the Universal Postal Union in 1950 to 1951, and took part in the Geneva Conference of 1954, the 1955 Bandung Conference, and the 1961–1962 International Conference for the Peaceful Settlement of the Laotian Question. It also joined or sent observers to various Communist intergovernmental organizations. By 1960 the PRC had only succeeded in joining a small number of intergovernmental organizations (IGOs) and international nongovernmental organizations (INGOs). Between 1949 and 1967, the PRC concluded some two thousand international agreements, of which only forty-nine were multilateral agreements with four or more parties.

By contrast, the ROC sought to bolster its hitherto successful claims to represent "China" in international organizations by increasing its membership therein. Thus, in 1952 it rejoined the International Civil Aviation Organization (ICAO) and in 1953 the World Health Organization (WHO). The ROC also began to take a more active role in the United Nations by applying for UN technical assistance from October 1951. For more than twenty years, and particularly within the United Nations, the ROC emphasized questions relating to its own claims to represent China. The ROC also spent much energy opposing Soviet policies in the United Nations and Soviet "aggression on China through the instrumentality of the Chinese communists," and expressed support for human rights—in particular, opposition to forced labor.

GRADUAL INTERNATIONAL INTEGRATION OF PRC

It was not until the United Nations voted in 1971 to recognize the People's Republic as the organization's official representative of "China" that the PRC officially became part of the multilateral system. Within six months of its entry into the United Nations, the PRC was recognized as the only official representative of China by, among others, ICAO, WHO, the International Labor Organization (ILO), the International Atomic Energy Agency (IAEA), and the General Agreement on Tariffs and Trade (GATT). By contrast, the International Monetary Fund (IMF), World Bank, International Development Agency, and International Finance Corporation failed to instigate action, leaving the initiative to the PRC.

Rather than pursuing all the openings that immediately became available, China assessed its priorities on the basis of its still limited capabilities and expertise. Until 1979, when the United States finally established formal diplomatic ties with the PRC, it also had to contend with the obstacles posed by strong U.S. influence and opposition, particularly in UN specialized agencies. Nevertheless, the PRC remained single-minded in its purpose and scrutinized its UN commitments in line with the requirements of Article 55 of its first interim constitution, the Common Program of 1949, which had provided that "the Central People's Government of the People's Republic of China shall examine all treaties and agreements concluded between the Guomindang and foreign Governments and recognize, abrogate, revise, or renew them according to their respective contents."

China's integration into international organizations was a gradual process that was linked to its increase in status and power (Rao 2001). The first phase was influenced by the political values and inhibitions of the ongoing Cultural Revolution, although it was also marked by a degree of idealism. In this period, China was primarily interested in IGOs, both because they conferred legitimacy and because, contrary to PRC policy, many INGOs were apolitical and ready to maintain "two Chinas" as members. The PRC chose to join, or participate in, technical, scientific, and

The People's Republic of China's first delegation representing China at the United Nations, November 16, 1971. *Prior to its victory in the Chinese Civil War, the People's Republic of China (PRC) supported the establishment of the United Nations, sending a representative to the body's founding in 1945. However, not until 1971 did the international organization recognize the PRC as the sole representative of China, expelling the Republic of China in both the General Assembly and the Security Council.* © JP LAFFONT/SYGMA/CORBIS

educational IGOs, as well as certain basic IGOs. On the other hand, it did not initially respond to overtures from the ILO, IAEA, and GATT. China's behavior in these bodies demonstrated a general unwillingness to be heavily involved in politics or in the organizations' secretariats; its presence was more symbolic than substantive and, as in the United Nations proper, it placed an emphasis on learning. During this period, China also became a member of several regional IGOs.

1977 THROUGH 1980s

By 1977 the PRC's membership in IGOs had increased to twenty-one, from only one in 1966. The second phase, from 1977 to the early 1980s, saw a further increase in membership in INGOs, from seventy-one to 307 (Chan 1989, p. 17), including such organizations as the International Olympic Committee and the International Committee of the Red Cross.

Only after the launching of China's new opening up and modernization policies, and only after the United States and China had finally established formal diplomatic relations in 1979, did China move into the third phase of its organizational participation. The climax of this period was the announcement by Premier Zhao Ziyang in 1984 concerning support for the work of the United Nations. By the end of 1986, China was involved in almost all important areas of intergovernmental diplomacy. It had joined nearly 400 international organizations and ratified and acceded to more than 130 international conventions. China's greater self-confidence and the loosening of ideological constraints allowed it to seek entry into the more politically sensitive and strategically important international organizations, such as the World Bank and the IMF, as well as the UN Conference on Disarmament and UN human rights bodies. In 1983 China also began to participate more fully in the ILO.

China's entry into such organizations had a legitimizing effect on its international role and its domestic rule, as well as on the international organizations themselves. In all phases of its integration, national self-interest and considerations of sovereignty in ousting Taiwan from these bodies were determining factors. The PRC's obligations, as opposed to its rights, as a member of international organizations were not uppermost in its consideration. Even general norms were not a priority. The process of its involvement therefore saw spirited interaction between China and the executives and state parties of international organizations. This, through a combination of jawboning, procedural pressures, and norm communication, resulted over time in China's acceptance of the majority of its procedural and substantive responsibilities, and its compliance with most of its obligations under the international treaties to which it was a party, although its cooperation was less apparent in international environmental and human rights organizations. Where once China was a revolutionary state operating outside the international system, it was now an economically developing country operating within the system to preserve stability.

China's increasing compliance with international rules was also the product of its own reassessment of the advantages and disadvantages of multilateral activity. Apart from legitimizing its rule and increasing its stability, such activity also enhanced China's opportunities for economic development and technical innovation, provided unlimited opportunities for improving interstate relations, and increased its international status and influence. More immediately, multilateral activity became a means of compensating for the downturn in China's bilateral relations resulting from its crackdown on the democracy movement in June 1989. Although international organizations, in particular the World Bank and the ILO, imposed sanctions on China for its attack on its own citizens, they provided a public stage on which China could exhibit a responsible internationalism, offsetting fears aroused by its often maladroit and misconceived bilateral diplomacy.

1990s AND AFTER

In the late 1990s, this intensified multilateralism was also reflected in a heightened regional multilateralism via participation in the new security, trade, and financial institutions of the Association of Southeast Asian Nations (ASEAN). In June 2001, China even cosponsored its first regional multilateral organization—the Shanghai Cooperation Organization, a formalization of the "Shanghai Five" forum established in 1996.

By the beginning of the twenty-first century, China had moved into a fourth phase of multilateralism, bespeaking a new flexibility, confidence, and maturity in a globalized environment in which it sought to boost its role as a key international player. By this time, China had become a party to 273 multilateral treaties, of which 239 had become applicable to China only after 1979 when it adopted an open policy. Its new confidence followed the September 11, 2001, terrorist attack on the United States, which, for the first time since World War II (1939–1945), united the United States and China against a common enemy: international terrorism.

From this period, China's participation in the UN Security Council became more meaningful and positive, both in terms of its role in facilitating solutions to international problems and in its readiness to make more practical concessions on issues of sovereignty. Thus, despite its preference for negotiated solutions, China voted for three Security Council resolutions allowing noncoercive sanctions to be imposed on Iran, with the explicit understanding that "sanctions are not the end but a means to urge Iran to return to negotiations." China was the principal power negotiating and underwriting a solution to the nuclear standoff with North Korea, and China helped persuade that state to shut down its Yongbyon nuclear reactor. It also began to take a more active role in UN peacekeeping. Between 1990 and 2008, the PRC sent nearly six thousand military personnel to participate in sixteen UN peacekeeping operations. China also claimed to have been instrumental in the diplomatic breakthrough after June 2007 when Sudan accepted the stationing of a combined peacekeeping force, and it offered 275 military engineers as part of the forces in Darfur.

At the same time, the costs of China's participation in international organizations became more apparent, with its entry into the World Trade Organization (WTO) in 2001 and, with the onset of SARS (severe acute respiratory syndrome) in China in 2002, revelations of its failure to abide by its obligations as a member of the WHO. By 2007 mounting complaints from the United States and European Union against record trade deficits with China suggested that China's compliance and its cooperation with WTO rules were likely to be tested more rigorously in the future. By the end of July 2007, the United States had initiated two cases against China to be considered by the WTO's Dispute Settlement Body, together with two other cases that had not yet reached the panel stage.

This development, however, provided the ultimate example of the importance of the role of international organizations in engaging China, in this case by facilitating the peaceful resolution of disputes with a fast-rising and once unbiddable power. This engagement was now far-reaching. By the end of 2006, China had become a member of 208 IGOs and 4,493 INGOs. On November 9, 2006, a further milestone in the history of China's participation in international organizations was reached with the appointment of Margaret Chan as WHO director-general.

She became the first PRC national to head an international organization.

SEE ALSO *Avian Influenza; Epidemics; International Development Programs in China; International Organizations, Relations with, 1900–1949; International Relations; Severe Acute Respiratory Syndrome.*

BIBLIOGRAPHY

An Wei and Li Dongyan, eds. *Shizi lukou'r shang di shijie: Zhongguo zhuming xuezhe tantao 21 shiji di guoji jiaodian* [World at the crossroads: China's leading scholars explore central international issues of the twenty-first century]. Beijing: Zhongguo Renmin Daxue Chubanshe, 2000.

Chan, Gerald. *China and International Organisations: Participation in Non-Governmental Organisations since 1971*. Hong Kong: Oxford University Press, 1989.

Cohen, Jerome Alan, and Chiu Hungdah. *People's China and International Law: A Documentary Study*. Princeton, NJ: Princeton University Press, 1974.

Deng Yong and Wang Feiling (Fei-ling Wang), eds. *In the Eyes of the Dragon: China Views the World*. Lanham, MD: Rowman and Littlefield, 1999.

Economy, Elizabeth, and Michel Oksenberg, eds. *China Joins the World: Progress and Prospects*. New York: Council on Foreign Relations Press, 1999.

Goldstein, Avery. The Diplomatic Face of China's Grand Strategy: A Rising Power's Emerging Choice. *China Quarterly* 168 (2001): 835–864.

Han Nianlong, ed. *Diplomacy of Contemporary China*. Hong Kong: New Horizon, 1990.

Hu Weixing, Gerald Chan, and Zha Daojiong, eds. *China's International Relations in the 21st Century Dynamics of Paradigm Shifts*. Lanham, MD: University Press of America, 2000.

Information Office of the State Council of the People's Republic of China. *China's National Defence in 2006*. Beijing: Author, 2006.

Kent, Ann. *Beyond Compliance: China, International Organizations, and Global Security*. Stanford CA: Stanford University Press, 2007.

Kim, Samuel S. *China, the United Nations, and World Order*. Princeton, NJ: Princeton University Press, 1979.

Lanteigne, Marc. *China and International Institutions: Alternate Paths to Global Power*. London: Routledge, 2005.

Mason, Edward S., and Robert E. Asher. *The World Bank since Bretton Woods: The Origins, Policies, Operations, and Impact of the International Bank for Reconstruction and Development and the Other Members of the World Bank Group*. Washington, DC: Brookings Institution, 1973.

Medeiros, Evan S., and M. Taylor Fravel. China's New Diplomacy. *Foreign Affairs* 82, 6 (2003): 22–35.

Meng Yan. China Opposes US Measure. *China Daily* 14 (2003).

Rao Geping. *Guoji zuzhi gailun* [An introduction to international organizations]. Beijing: Zhongguo Renmin Daxue Chubanshe, 2001.

Union of International Associations. *Yearbook of International Organizations: Guide to Global Civil Society Networks, 2007–2008*. Edition 44, Vol. 5. Munich: K. G. Saur, 2008.

United Nations. *Yearbook of the United Nations*. New York: Columbia University Press and United Nations, 1948–1971.

Wang Taiping, ed. *Xin Zhongguo waijiao wushi nian* [Fifty years of new China's foreign policy]. Vol. 2. Beijing: Beijing Chubanshe Chuban, 1999.

Wang Xingfang, ed. *Zhongguo yu Lianheguo: Jinian Lianheguo chengli wushi zhounian* [China and the United Nations: Commemorating the fiftieth anniversary of the establishment of the United Nations]. Beijing: Shijie Zhishi Chubanshe, 1995.

Xue Hanqin. China's Open Policy and International Law. *Chinese Journal of International Law* 4, 1 (2005): 133–139.

Ann Kent

INTERNATIONAL RELATIONS

This entry contains the following:

1800–1949

The history of China's international relations between 1800 and 1949 was shaped by wars and revolutions, domestic and international. It was accompanied by the transformation of China from an empire to a nation-state, and by China's gradual integration into an emerging global system of sovereign states.

ENCOUNTERS WITH THE EXPANDING EUROPEAN INTERNATIONAL SYSTEM

At the turn of the nineteenth century, imperial China's relations with neighboring countries and the outside world continued to be governed by the rules, norms, and institutions of the tribute system, which the Qing rulers had inherited from the Ming and previous dynasties. Emperor Qianlong's (r. 1736–1796) rejection in 1793 of demands made by the first British embassy to China, led by Lord George Macartney (1737–1806), to open China to trade with Great Britain, along with the failure of William Pitt Amherst's (1773–1857) mission in 1816, reaffirmed the prevalence of the traditional Chinese world order in imperial China's conception and practice of international relations.

The Opium War and the military clashes between imperial China and Great Britain from 1839 to 1842 were but the first of a succession of violent encounters between the traditional Chinese world order and the expanding European international system. Imperial China's defeat in the Opium War led to the signing of the Treaty of Nanjing on August 29, 1842. By virtue of the treaty, five ports were opened for trade—namely, Guangzhou (Canton), Xiamen, Fuzhou, Ningbo, and Shanghai—and Hong Kong was ceded "in perpetuity" to Great Britain. The Qing government made three additional concessions: It agreed to include a most-favored-nation clause in the treaty; it consented to the demand for fixed tariffs on trade in the treaty ports; and it accepted the introduction of extraterritoriality in the treaty ports. The Treaty of Nanjing was followed by the Treaty of the Bogue in 1843, again with the British, the Treaty of Wangxia with the United States, and the Treaty of Whampoa with France, both in 1844. By virtue of the most-favored-nation clauses unilaterally imposed upon China, the United States and France were also granted the same privileges and rights. A "treaty system" was emerging, which came to dominate China's international relations and heralded what the Chinese regard as "a century of humiliations."

It was the Second Opium War (1856–1860) that further consolidated the establishment of the treaty system in China's international relations. The Treaty of Tianjin (1858) and the Convention of Beijing (1860) opened ten ports along the Yangzi River for foreign trade and extended a wide range of rights and privileges to foreigners in China, including, in particular, freedom of movement in all China for Christian and Catholic missionaries to preach. The treaties further confirmed such arrangements as consular jurisdiction and extraterritoriality in China for the signatory powers. Most importantly, Great Britain secured its right to send a permanent resident diplomatic mission to the Qing court in Beijing.

As a signatory to both the Treaty of Tianjin and the Convention of Beijing, Russia firmly established itself as a treaty power in China. With the Supplementary Treaty of Beijing in 1860, Russia further secured new territorial concessions east of the Ussuri River and legalized its earlier acquisitions under the Treaty of Aigun (1858), which the Qing government had previously refused to sign. By 1861, when the Treaty of Tianjin between Prussia and China was signed, the treaty system was firmly entrenched, replacing the tribute system in China's international relations with the West. Imperial China's relations with its neighbors and traditional vassal states in Asia, however, continued to be dominated by the tribute system.

THE COLLAPSE OF THE CHINESE WORLD ORDER

The entrenchment of the treaty system was accompanied by unprecedented changes in Chinese worldviews and traditional institutions. In an edict sanctioning the Treaty of Tianjin in 1861, Emperor Xianfeng (r. 1851–1861) grudgingly conceded the equal status of Great Britain as an independent sovereign state, compromising the presumption of China as the center of the world, a core institutional foundation for constructing the hierarchy of the Chinese world order. Resident diplomacy in the capital, a key institution in European diplomatic practice, was forcibly accepted, though it was widely regarded as incompatible with the traditional system and institutions (*tizhi*) of imperial China. The first British minister took up residence in Beijing in 1862. In 1873 the *kowtow* was formally abolished in Sino-foreign relations.

The most significant institutional change was, however, the establishment of the Zongli Yamen (Office of General Management) as a central government office in 1861 to handle all aspects of relations with Western treaty powers. Prince Gong (1833–1898) was appointed its first minister. The Zongli Yamen centralized the administration and management of China's relations with the West, a task hitherto in the hands of imperial commissioners and governors-general. It sent China's first diplomatic mission to the United States and Europe—the Anson Burlingame (1820–1870) mission—in 1868 and conducted treaty-revision negotiations with Great Britain in 1868 to 1869. The Zongli Yamen was also responsible for introducing international law into imperial China's diplomatic practice.

Although the establishment of the Zongli Yamen signaled imperial China's practical acceptance of the principles of international relations as defined by European powers, many Qing officials continued to view the Zongli Yamen as an adaptation of the traditional tribute system. The diplomacy of imperial China continued to be dominated by traditional statecraft, in particular, "playing one barbarian against another."

It was during the period of dynastic revival known as the Tongzhi restoration that imperial China established its first permanent diplomatic legation abroad, in London (1877), sixteen years after the British set up its legation in Beijing. Guo Songtao was appointed the first Chinese minister to Great Britain. This was followed by the establishment of Chinese legations in Germany, also in 1877, in the United States and France in 1878, in Russia and Spain in 1879, and in Peru in 1880.

Taken together, these institutional changes, often made under duress, indicated that imperial China was taking tentative steps to accommodate in its foreign relations the foundational institutions of the Westphalian international system, such as sovereignty, territoriality, equality, resident diplomacy, and international law.

Members of the Zongli Yamen, c. 1901. *Forced to cooperate with foreign governments after losses in both Opium Wars, the Imperial Qing government established the Zongli Yamen, a department devoted to engaging China diplomatically with the West.* © CORBIS

What further precipitated the crumbling of the Chinese world order was European, and later Japanese, imperialist expansion into East Asia. The subjection of China through the treaty system is an integral part of this expansion. From the 1870s onward, the British, French, Japanese, and Russian expansion progressively took away tributary states and frontier areas along the peripheries of imperial China and physically dismantled its tribute system. Russia occupied Yili (Ili) in 1871. Liuqiu was formally annexed by Japan in 1879. After a short and disastrous military encounter with France, Annam, a traditional tributary state, was lost to France. Great Britain took Burma after the Third Anglo-Burmese War in 1885 and made it a province of British India in 1886. Laos became a French protectorate in 1893. The loss of Korea to Japan after imperial China's military defeat in the Sino-Japanese War in 1895 reduced the Chinese tribute system to an empty shell. In addition, Taiwan was ceded to Japan by the Treaty of Shimonoseki (1895). It was only as a consequence of the Triple Intervention that the Liaodong Peninsula, ceded to Japan in the Treaty of Shimonoseki, was returned to China.

After the Sino-Japanese War, Japan replaced China as the dominant power in East Asia. This position was further consolidated with the Anglo-Japanese Alliance Treaty in 1902 and the Japanese military victory over Russia in the Russo-Japanese War in 1904 to 1905. The emergence of Japan as an imperialist power had profound implications for international relations in East Asia and for Sino-Japanese relations in the twentieth century.

In the wake of China's defeat in 1895, the imperialist powers—Great Britain, France, Russia, Germany, and Japan in particular—engaged in a "scramble for concessions," carving up China into spheres of influence. The Western

CANTON SYSTEM

The Canton System was a unique form of trade that emerged in Guangzhou (Canton) in the early eighteenth century and lasted until the opening of the treaty ports in 1842. The system was regulated by Beijing and administered conjointly by the Guangzhou customs superintendent and the governor general of Guangdong and Guangxi provinces. Four groups of licensed professionals controlled and serviced the trade: pilots, compradors, linguists, and merchants (the last collectively known as *gonghang* or *cohong*). Their numbers were limited to a small pool of individuals, but competition was maintained within each group to ensure that prices fluctuated according to supply and demand, that services were efficient, and that fees were fair.

By the early eighteenth century, Guangzhou emerged as the port where both foreigners and Chinese officials preferred to conduct the China trade. In 1757 its position as the center of trade became official when foreigners were barred from other Chinese ports. Foreign ships were required to anchor twelve miles downriver at Huangpu (Whampoa), and foreign trading officers (factors) had to reside in designated buildings called factories outside the city walls. After the ships left, foreigners who remained in China were required to move to Macau. Every ship hired a Chinese pilot to guide it up- and downriver, which is how the customs superintendents controlled their comings and goings. Foreigners contracted with compradors to supply provisions and laborers, and compradors guaranteed prices and wages at the lowest market rate. A linguist was appointed to every ship to mediate trade, procure necessary permits, and collect duties and fees. In the early eighteenth century, foreign companies usually chose one merchant to handle most of their trade, a circumstance (called the security-merchant system) that was later made compulsory.

Incentives were built into fees and duties to encourage growth. *Cohong* merchants paid large entry fees for their positions, were responsible for each other's debts, and had to make periodic "contributions" to officials, which introduced high risk to their occupations. The merchants depended heavily on foreign loans and advances to expand trade, which led many of them into bankruptcy. The debts they left behind were distributed to the remaining merchants for repayment.

Chinese officials paid special attention to the settling of large companies' debts so they would not be discouraged from returning to China. Private traders had less leverage, but could sell Chinese debts to the companies for collection. Because of this high level of protection, foreign capital continued to flow into China in increasingly larger quantities. The Canton system depended heavily on foreign capital to finance growth, but at the expense of many *cohong* merchants falling in debt to patrons.

All four licensed groups were responsible for the actions of foreigners during their stay in China and were subject to civil punishments if problems emerged. When major disputes arose, the customs superintendent would forbid Chinese from contact with the foreigners to pressure them into submission, but he had to be careful not to discourage them from returning. All duties had to be paid and accounts settled before a ship was granted an exit permit (called a grand chop).

BIBLIOGRAPHY

Ch'en, Kuo-tung Anthony. *The Insolvency of the Chinese Hong Merchants, 1760–1843.* 2 vols. Taibei: Academia Sinica, 1990.

Van Dyke, Paul A. *The Canton Trade: Life and Enterprise on the China Coast, 1700–1845.* Hong Kong: Hong Kong University Press, 2005.

Paul A. Van Dyke

domination of the Chinese economy was palpable, as seen in the foreign control of the banking and shipping industries and in the expansive foreign interests and concessions in railway construction and operation and in mining and manufacturing. With the inexorable dynastic decline in the final years of the Qing dynasty, this deepening imperialist encroachment, together with the fiasco of the Boxer Uprising (1900), exacerbated an acute sense of national crisis in China. National salvation became a rallying call for reformers and revolutionaries. Not surprisingly, Chinese politics and foreign policy in the twentieth century were characterized by reforms and revolutions.

THE RISE OF CHINESE NATIONALISM

Nationalism was a new ideology and a powerful driving force that shaped Chinese politics and international relations in the twentieth century. Incipient Chinese nationalism could be traced back to nationalistic resistance to imperialist encroachment on Chinese sovereignty, as in the diplomacy conducted by the Zongli Yamen and in the exertion of mercantile nationalism during the Self-Strengthening movement. Chinese nationalism was also apparent in the anti-Christian riots and attacks after 1860, such as the Tianjin massacre in 1870, and in the Boxer Uprising and the anti-American boycott in 1905.

The influx of Western ideas toward the end of the nineteenth century inspired the emergence of modern nationalism in China, the intellectual origins and ideological foundations of which are found in the ideals of the French and the American revolutions. There were two main thrusts of Chinese nationalism in the first decade of the twentieth century. The first was revolutionary, that is, to overthrow Manchu rule and establish a republic, making China a nation-state in the family of nations. This was nominally accomplished by the 1911 revolution and the establishment of the Republic of China. However, building a centralized modern nation-state capable of advancing China's aspirations in political, social, economic, and cultural life in the international environment of the twentieth century proved more challenging.

The second thrust was anti-imperialistic. Its short-term goal was to roll back imperialist encroachment through asserting China's sovereign rights. Its long-term objective was to erase the stigma of unequal treaties dominant in China's international relations, making China a full independent sovereign state of equal status with other members of the international community. The Chinese quest for the recovery of sovereign rights claimed partial victory in 1905, when the Hankou-Guangzhou Railway was successfully reclaimed by the Chinese from the American China Development Company. Also championed in the rights-recovery movement was the recovery of administrative power over the foreign-controlled Chinese Maritime Customs Administration, as well as the abrogation of the extraterritoriality enjoyed by foreigners in China. These rights were only recovered under the Nationalist government of Chiang Kai-shek (Jiang Jieshi), although the Postal Service was turned over to the Chinese in 1911.

It was China's entry into World War I (1914–1918) in 1917 and its subsequent participation in the Paris Peace Conference in 1919 that brought Chinese nationalism into full play. China's assertive diplomacy in Paris was significant. Inspired by the idea of national self-determination championed by both President Woodrow Wilson (1856–1924) and the Russian Revolution (1917), the Chinese delegates, Wellington Koo (Gu Weijun, 1887–1985) in particular, effectively used the peace conference as a forum to present to the international community China's aspirations to become a fully independent sovereign state. At home, popular nationalism as manifested during the May Fourth period gave the intellectual revolution of the New Culture movement a new dimension.

China eventually refused to sign the Versailles Treaty. However, by signing separate treaties with the defeated powers—the Saint-Germain Treaty with Austria in Paris and the Sino-German Peace Treaty—China revoked the extraterritoriality rights once granted to nationals of these nations. China also secured its membership in the League of Nations.

At the Washington Conference of 1921 to 1922, China secured the Western powers' commitment to respecting its territorial integrity and administrative independence. The Nine-Power Treaty further committed all signatories to the principles of the open-door policy advocated by the United States. The Shandong question, unsettled at the Paris Peace Conference, was also resolved. The powers made grudging concessions to China's demand for tariff autonomy, but insisted on keeping extraterritorial rights and other privileges.

China's nationalistic aspirations received a much more sympathetic response from the Soviet regime in the 1920s. In May 1924, the Sino-Soviet Agreements were signed, confirming the annulment of all conventions, treaties, agreements, contracts, and protocols concluded between the czarist government and China.

CHINA AND POWER POLITICS IN EAST ASIA

By the early 1920s, power politics in East Asia were undergoing fundamental changes. The end of the Great War saw the beginning of the end of European preeminence in global politics. The rise of Japan and the outreach of the United States to East Asia intensified great-power rivalries. The Soviet Union, as a revolutionary power, arrived in East Asian power politics in its own fashion. China's relationship with each great power was pivotal to the evolution of East Asian power politics and the international order in East Asia in the coming decades. Within China, two major political events unfolding in the 1920s, the rise of the Chinese Communist Party established in 1921 and the formation of the Nationalist government led by Chiang Kai-shek in Nanjing in 1927, came to shape the course of China's contemporary history and to redefine its relations with the great powers in world politics.

No sooner did the Nationalist government gain recognition by the Western powers than it started to negotiate for tariff autonomy and for the total abrogation of extraterritoriality for foreign powers in China. Tariff autonomy was achieved in 1930 after the Nationalist government concluded separate treaties with twelve countries, the last with Japan on May 16, 1930. A number of foreign concessions—the British in Hankou and Jiujiang and the Belgians in Tianjin, for example—were also recovered by the Nationalist government between 1927 and 1931. The total abrogation of extraterritoriality in China had to wait, however, until 1943.

The decade of 1927 to 1937 witnessed the ravages of civil war between the Nationalists and the Communists. In September 1931, the Japanese military launched a series of aggressive actions in northeast China (Manchuria). By early 1932, the Japanese military occupation of northeast China was complete. China appealed to the League of Nations, which was, however, toothless in its response to the Japanese aggression. All-out war between China and Japan broke out on July 7, 1937. By then, a national anti-Japanese United Front had been formed by the Nationalists and Communists in the wake of the Xi'an Incident in December 1936. In August 1937, the Sino-Soviet Nonaggression Pact was signed. Considerable Soviet aid was sent to China between 1937 and 1940.

The outbreak of the Pacific War in December 1941 and the American declaration of war against Japan changed the perception of the Anti-Japanese War, which was incorporated into the Allied grand strategy. The Allied powers established the China-Burma-India theater of war, with Chiang Kai-shek as the supreme commander of the China theater, in January 1942. Through the Lend-Lease program, substantial American aid flowed into China to sustain its war efforts.

One important landmark of China's wartime-alliance diplomacy was Chiang Kai-shek's participation in the Cairo Conference in 1943, together with U.S. president Franklin Roosevelt (1882–1945) and British prime minister Winston Churchill (1874–1965). The Cairo Declaration of December 1, 1943, committed the Allies to the complete restoration of all Chinese territories lost to Japan.

Franklin D. Roosevelt (center), seated with Chiang Kai-shek (left), and Winston Churchill during the Cairo Conference, November 22-26, 1943. *During the late nineteenth century, Western nations as well as Japan gained control of many countries in eastern Asia, limiting China's sphere of influence. Looking to diminish these losses, Nationalist leader Chiang Kai-shek sided with the Allied powers, hoping to reestablish dominance in the region.* © CORBIS

BANDUNG CONFERENCE, 1955

The Asian-African Conference of April 18 to 24, 1955, or the Bandung Conference, was China's second major international conference (since the Geneva Conference in 1954). It signaled a new emphasis in China's foreign policy that laid the foundation for its relations with Afro-Asian countries and elevated its status among third-world countries.

Twenty-nine Asian and African countries attended the conference at Bandung, Indonesia, which expressed the aspirations and anti-imperialist, anticolonial sentiments of third-world nations. The Chinese, sharing these sentiments, saw in the conference an opportunity to play an international role. The organizers of the conference (Burma, Ceylon [Sri Lanka], India, Indonesia, and Pakistan), however, gave priority to inviting United Nations (UN) members and disagreed on whether or not to invite China, which was not a UN member and also had close ties with the Soviet Union. Chinese records show that whereas India and Burma supported inviting China, Pakistan and Ceylon were opposed. Indonesia supported China's participation, but, as the host country, wanted to take into account each organizer's viewpoints. The Chinese therefore had to campaign hard for an invitation, assuring the organizers of China's peaceful intentions. After receiving a formal invitation in January 1955, they worked at a strategy for success, building it around the Five Principles of Peaceful Coexistence (*heping gongchu wuxiang yuanze*) that Zhou Enlai had formulated in 1953.

At Bandung, the Chinese were handicapped by perceived religious and political differences and border disputes with several Asian nations. They also had to combat fears of Chinese expansionism and aid to Communist insurgents in countries with overseas Chinese communities. Zhou, however, focused on "seeking common ground while reserving differences" and used his diplomatic dexterity, conciliatory nature, and persuasiveness to emphasize the neutralist nature of the conference and promote a foreign policy based on peaceful coexistence. Zhou's declaration that overseas Chinese should owe their allegiance primarily to their home countries also helped allay fears of Chinese expansionism. Key elements of his Five Principles of Peaceful Coexistence were incorporated into the conference's Declaration on the Promotion of World Peace and Cooperation; given disagreement over the meaning of "peaceful coexistence," however, Zhou suggested the declaration use "live together in peace with one another," a phrase from the UN Charter.

China's stature among Afro-Asian nations rose, creating opportunities for it to establish and improve relations with them. Nearly all the diplomatic relations the Chinese established in the mid-1950s were with Asian and African countries, including Nepal, Egypt, Syria, Yemen, and Sri Lanka.

The Bandung Conference was a seminal event in the annals of Chinese foreign policy; its influence is still visible in China. Despite a more confrontational third-world policy in the late 1950s and the end of the "Bandung era" by the 1980s, Chinese leaders continue to attach great significance to the conference. During the fiftieth anniversary celebrations in Bandung, Hu Jintao advocated a "new strategic partnership" among Afro-Asian nations, emphasizing south-south cooperation based on "mutual respect, equality, trust, and dialogue."

BIBLIOGRAPHY

Asia-Africa Speaks from Bandung. Jakarta: Ministry of Foreign Affairs, Republic of Indonesia, 1955.

China and the Asian-African Conference: Documents. Beijing: Foreign Languages Press, 1955.

Mackie, Jamie. *Bandung 1955: Non-alignment and Afro-Asian Solidarity*. Singapore: Éditions Didier Millet, 2005.

Ministry of Foreign Affairs of the People's Republic of China. *Zhonghua renmin gonghe guo waijiao dangan xuanbian (di er ji): Zhongguo daibiaotuan chuxi 1955 nian Yafei huiyi* [Selections from the archives of the ministry of foreign affairs of the People's Republic of China (volume 2): The Chinese delegation's participation in the Asian-African Conference of 1955]. Beijing: Shijie Zhishi Chubanshe, 2007.

Zhang, Shu Guang. Constructing "Peaceful Coexistence": China's Diplomacy toward the Geneva and Bandung Conferences, 1954–55. *Cold War History* 7, 4 (November 2007): 509–528.

Myra Pong

brief border skirmish in 1969. This split, along with the establishment of the Association of Southeast Asian Nations (ASEAN) in 1967 and the announcement of the Nixon Doctrine in Guam in 1969 (in which the South Vietnamese would do the main fighting in the Vietnam War, allowing U.S. troops to withdraw), led China to reappraise its foreign and security policies, as it then perceived the United States as less of a threat to China's security interests in the region.

United States President Richard Nixon (center) seated with Chinese Premier Zhou Enlai (left) and Communist Party leader Zhang Chunqiao, Shanghai, February 27, 1972. *While initially an ally of the Soviet Union, China broke ties with most foreign nations during the Cultural Revolution. However, by the early 1970s, the country lessened its isolationist position, replacing Taiwan as China's representative at the United Nations, hosting a visit with U.S. President Richard Nixon, and eventually joining global economic entities, including the World Bank.* © BETTMANN/CORBIS

THE NIXON VISIT

The year 1971 marked a watershed in China's relations with the outside world. First came Henry Kissinger's "secret" visit to Beijing in July. In October, the PRC was admitted to the United Nations, replacing Taiwan. Since then, China has gained entry to a large number of international organizations and signed many multilateral treaties, especially since 1979. China's admission to the United Nations marked a shift in its policy toward the world body from one of resentment and rejection in the previous decades to one of participation and support thereafter.

In February 1972, U.S. president Richard Nixon (1913–1994) made a surprise visit to Beijing, starting a process of rapprochement between China and the United States and forcing a major shift in the triangular relationship between China, the United States, and the Soviet Union. China began then to lean more toward the United States. The so-called Nixon shock goaded Japan and most countries in the Western world to take the initiative to establish diplomatic relations with China in late 1972. China normalized its relationship with the United States by establishing diplomatic relations in 1979.

In the wake of Nixon's visit, many countries in the West switched their diplomatic relations from Taiwan to China. China upheld its credentials of antihegemonism and third-world solidarity, with Deng Xiaoping enunciating Mao's Three Worlds theory at the United Nations in 1974. However, Zhou Enlai's announcement in 1975 of the Four Modernizations (of industry, agriculture, science and technology, and defense), Mao's death in the following year, and the subsequent overthrow of the Gang of Four (led by Mao's wife) allowed moderate voices to shape Chinese foreign policy. Deng, in particular, opted for a policy that favored economic development and the improvement of relations with the West, as well as with Japan. Such a policy was meant to contribute to the creation of a more peaceful external environment for China's domestic economic development.

REFORM AND OPENING UP

The adoption of the reform and opening-up policy in the late 1970s heralded a new era in China's international relations. The country began to integrate itself increasingly into the world. The perception of an external threat, however, never disappeared in Beijing. In February 1979, China launched a seventeen-day punitive attack on northern Vietnam for its invasion of Cambodia. This campaign resulted in considerable economic and human costs, revealing the weakness of the People's Liberation Army (PLA), and it raised fears of China in the Asian region.

Moscow's invasion of Afghanistan in December 1979 drove Beijing to abrogate its 1950 treaty with the Soviet Union. The Soviet Union remained China's primary enemy, even though in March 1982 Soviet leader Leonid Brezhnev (1906–1982) offered to discuss with Beijing the obstacles to Sino-Soviet relations. In late 1981 China enunciated an "independent" and equidistant foreign policy with respect to the two superpowers. In the later half of the 1980s, the Soviet Union took a number of actions that led to the normalization of Sino-Soviet relations. These included the support of the withdrawal of Vietnamese forces from Cambodia, the Paris peace talks to resolve the conflict in Indochina, and the removal of Soviet troops from the Sino-Soviet border and from Afghanistan. A thaw in mutual relations culminated in a historic visit by Mikhail Gorbachev to China in May 1989.

The Tiananmen Square massacre two weeks later, in which protesting students and civilians were shot by the PLA, set back temporarily China's relations with the West. Western isolation of China was lifted only gradually. The fall of communist regimes in Eastern Europe and eventually in the Soviet Union had little long-term impact on China. Russia became its strategic partner in the mid-1990s.

The Gulf War in 1991, in which the United States demonstrated its arsenal of lethal weapons with pinpoint accuracy, stimulated the modernization of the PLA. The bombing in 1999 of the Chinese Embassy in Belgrade, Yugoslavia, by U.S.-led NATO (North Atlantic Treaty Organization) forces, and the midair collision between an American spy plane and a Chinese jet fighter off the coast of southern China in April 2001, resulting in the loss of the Chinese pilot, plunged bilateral relations to new lows. Relations were largely resurrected when the United States rallied the world to fight terrorism after the terrorist attacks on the United States in September 2001, and China's successful hosting of the annual Asia-Pacific Economic Cooperation (APEC) meeting in Shanghai in October 2001. Two months later, China joined the World Trade Organization, marking a significant step in China's integration into the global economic system. China had joined the World Bank and the International Monetary Fund in 1980.

The war on terror mounted by the United States has strengthened the Shanghai Cooperation Organization, formed by China, Russia, and four post-Soviet Central Asian nations (Kazakhstan, Kyrgyzstan, Tajikistan, and Uzbekistan) to fight Islamic militancy and to promote security and trade cooperation. It replaces the so-called Shanghai Five, formed in June 2001. The Shanghai Cooperation Organization criticized U.S. plans for a missile defense system as damaging to global security. The organization also serves as a counterweight to the United States' increasing influence in and around Central Asia as a result of its campaign against terrorism in Afghanistan.

Hong Kong was returned to China in 1997, followed by Macau two years later. The return of both territories marked the end of a long period of colonial rule under Britain and Portugal. However, the reunification of Taiwan with the mainland remains a distant goal, not only because of Taiwan's links with the United States but also because of its accelerating pace of democratization. Taiwan held its first presidential election by universal suffrage in March 1996. Pro-independence presidents were elected thereafter, until March 2008, when the Nationalist Party's chairman, Ma Ying-jeou (Ma Yingjiu), won the presidential election. For its part, China has vowed to take Taiwan by force if necessary.

China's increasingly active role in world affairs has earned praise as well as criticism. Its participation in organizing the six-party talks to halt North Korea's nuclear-weapons program has been singled out for appreciation. So has China's increasing involvement in UN peacekeeping operations in various parts of the world, as well as its effort to reduce tension between Iran and the West over Iran's nuclear program. However, China's relentless search for oil and other natural resources around the world, especially in Africa and the Middle East, with little regard for human rights, has been severely criticized by Western governments and nongovernmental groups. In their defense, the Chinese argue that they are always guided by the principle of noninterference in the internal affairs of another nation. In addition, competition from China's cheap exports and the low standard of its product safety have raised fears among workers and consumers in many parts of the industrialized world.

CONCLUSION

Since China's adoption of its reform and opening-up policy, the country has experienced phenomenal economic growth, averaging about 9 to 10 percent per annum. In 2008, China was the fourth-largest trading nation in the world, and it had accumulated $1.5 trillion in reserves by the end of 2007, part of which could be used to make overseas investments, with the ability to have a significant impact on the world's financial market. China is a member of nearly all major international organizations, and it has signed or ratified most of the important international treaties. By all accounts, China has become a significant player in the world of international relations, and its relationship with the United States is arguably one of the most important bilateral relationships in the world.

China is rising in power, but at the same time it is facing myriad domestic problems, including calls for political reform, an uneven distribution of wealth, social unrest, environmental degradation, and rampant corruption. The rise of China inevitably poses a challenge, if not a threat, to others. To counter the China-threat theory, in late 2003 the PRC began to espouse a theory of China's peaceful rise in an era of economic globalization. This peaceful-rise theory aims partly to allay the fears of Southeast Asian countries, with whom China wants to maintain a good relationship and to boost bilateral trade. In 2005 Chinese leaders started to emphasize the construction of a harmonious society as a socioeconomic goal, both domestically and internationally. The United States, being the sole superpower, is concerned about China's challenge to its supremacy in global affairs and China's potential threat to its national security. Other lesser powers and neighboring countries are also feeling the pressure.

China's economic growth has raised its international profile. Its soft power is being felt, with the establishment of some two hundred Confucius Institutes around the world to promote Chinese language and culture. China's foray into Africa in search of raw materials and political friendships has raised alarm in the West, as China offers an alternative model of development to African countries that will lessen the influence and interests of the West. China wants to be seen as a responsible member of the international community, but outside perception may give a different picture. The Olympic Games in August 2008 in Beijing not only showcased China's economic achievements, but also marked a stage in its global reach. How China evolves in the future—whether or not it will conform to the existing norms of international society and to what extent—will pose a serious challenge to the world. It is difficult to accurately predict China's future role in world affairs, but China is likely to remain a huge developing country for some time to come, with its own unique characteristics and promising potentials.

SEE ALSO *ASEAN, Relations with; Four Modernizations; Hong Kong; Macau; People's Liberation Army; Russia, Relations with; Sino-Soviet Schism; Taiwan, Republic of China; United States, Relations with; Vietnam, Relations with.*

BIBLIOGRAPHY

Deng Yong. *China's Struggle for Status: The Realignment of International Relations*. Cambridge, U.K.: Cambridge University Press, 2008.

Economy, Elizabeth, and Michel Oksenberg, eds. *China Joins the World: Progress and Prospects*. New York: Council on Foreign Relations Press, 1999.

Gill, Bates. *Rising Star: China's New Security Diplomacy*. Washington, DC: Brookings Institution Press, 2007.

Johnston, Alastair Iain. *Social States: China in International Institutions, 1980–2000*. Princeton, NJ: Princeton University Press, 2008.

Johnston, Alastair Iain, and Robert S. Ross, eds. *New Directions in the Study of China's Foreign Policy*. Stanford, CA: Stanford University Press, 2006.

Kent, Ann E. *Beyond Compliance: China, International Organizations, and Global Security*. Stanford, CA: Stanford University Press, 2007.

Kim, Samuel S. *China, the United Nations, and World Order*. Princeton, NJ: Princeton University Press, 1979.

Kim, Samuel S., ed. *China and the World: Chinese Foreign Policy Faces the New Millennium*. 4th ed. Boulder, CO: Westview, 1998.

Lampton, David M., ed. *The Making of Chinese Foreign and Security Policy in the Era of Reform, 1978–2000*. Stanford, CA: Stanford University Press, 2001.

Sutter, Robert G. *Chinese Foreign Relations: Power and Policy since the Cold War*. Lanham, MD: Rowman & Littlefield, 2008.

Zhao Suisheng, ed. *Chinese Foreign Policy: Pragmatism and Strategic Behavior*. Armonk, NY: Sharpe, 2004.

Gerald Chan

TREATIES, 1800–1949

The first international treaty that China entered into with a European country was the Sino-Russian Treaty of Nerchinsk of 1689. It was not until the mid-nineteenth century, however, that international treaties became a defining feature in East Asian international relations, as the European international society expanded into the region.

The Sino-British Treaty of Nanking, signed in 1842, occupies a unique place in modern Chinese history. Followed by a series of unequal treaties between China and imperialist powers, it initiated a treaty system that came to regulate China's relations with the Western powers in place of the traditional tributary system in the second half of the nineteenth century. By the 1860s the treaty system was firmly entrenched in governing Chinese international relations, which culminated in the Sino-Japanese Treaty of Shimonoseki in 1895 and the Boxer Protocol of 1901. It is through the treaty system that China eventually was incorporated into the Westphalian international system, gradually accepting prevailing principles, rules, and norms such as sovereignty, territorial integrity, residence diplomacy, and international law in conducting its international relations. This constitutes an important part of China's transformation from an empire to a nation-state at the turn of the twentieth century.

The treaty system in China began to crumble after the end of World War I. The Sino-Bolivia Treaty of Friendship, signed on December 3, 1919, marked a new beginning in China's foreign relations because it was China's first bilateral treaty with an independent sovereign state that was based upon the principles of sovereign

UNEQUAL TREATIES

In Chinese history, the term *unequal treaties* refers to international treaties that China was forced to sign with foreign imperialist powers during the nineteenth and early twentieth centuries. The origin of the term remains a matter of controversy. These treaties compromised Chinese sovereignty and conceded many of China's territorial and sovereign rights. The rights of extraterritoriality gained under these treaties, for example, afforded foreigners in China independent legal, judicial, police, and taxation systems within the treaty ports.

The unequal treaties were initiated by the Opium War (1839–1842) between China and Great Britain. The Treaty of Nanjing (Nanking), concluded in 1842, ceded Hong Kong to Britain in perpetuity and opened five Chinese ports to foreign trade—namely, Shanghai, Guangzhou (Canton), Xiamen (Amoy), Fuzhou (Foochow), and Ningbo (Ningpo). Through the treaty, the Qing government also agreed to the principle of fixed tariffs for foreign trade and accepted the practice of extraterritoriality in the treaty ports.

By virtue of the most-favored-nation clause in the Treaty of Nanjing, these rights and privileges were extended to other treaty powers: to the United States through the Treaty of Wangxia (Wanghsia) in 1844; to France through the Treaty of Whampoa (Huangpu), also in 1844; and to Russia through the Treaty of Aigun in 1858, for example. It is through the Treaty of Tianjin (Tientsin) in 1858, following the first part of the so-called Second Opium War (1856–1860), that the Qing government conceded to the demands by foreign powers for further rights and privileges, the most important of which were resident missions at the Chinese capital and freedom for foreigners to travel and to preach outside the treaty ports. An additional eleven treaty ports were also opened. The unequal treaties and the treaty system became an important instrument through which the Qing government managed its turbulent relationships with Western powers.

Following China's defeat in the Sino-Japanese War (1894–1895), the Treaty of Shimonoseki, signed between China and Japan in 1895, ceded Taiwan to Japan and recognized the independence of Korea. The Boxer Protocol, signed in 1901 in the wake of the suppression of the Boxer Uprising and the occupation of Beijing by the Allied forces, provided for the stationing of foreign troops at key strategic points between Beijing and the sea.

Unequal treaties were a dominant feature in China's international relations between 1840 and 1949. It was only after World War I (1914–1918) that China started to negotiate treaties with other sovereign nations according to the principles of sovereign equality and reciprocity as stipulated in international law. The Sino-Bolivian Treaty of 1919 is the first such treaty. Although after the Russian Revolution in 1917, the Soviet government terminated unilaterally in 1924 most of the privileges gained by czarist Russia under unequal treaties, extraterritorial privileges were not formally relinquished by Great Britain and the United States until 1943 and by France until 1946.

BIBLIOGRAPHY

Wang Dong. *China's Unequal Treaties: Narrating National History.* Lanham, MD: Lexington, 2005.

Yongjin Zhang

equality and reciprocity. Through the 1919 St. Germane Treaty with Austria and the Sino-German Treaty in 1921, China was able to put its relationship with the "vanquished powers" on an equal footing. Equally important, in the Sino-Soviet Agreements of May 1924, the Soviet government declared its readiness to nullify voluntarily all treaty privileges in China established by the czarist government.

At the Washington Conference of 1921 to 1922 China became party to the Nine-Power Treaty, actively involving itself in multilateral diplomacy outside the framework of the League of Nations.

The Nationalist government established in Nanjing began to negotiate actively with treaty powers in 1927 to recover China's tariff autonomy. By the end of 1928 it had succeeded in concluding new bilateral treaties with the United States, Germany, Norway, Belgium, Italy, Denmark, Portugal, the Netherlands, Britain, Sweden, France, and Spain, granting China full autonomy in tariff matters. In May 1930 China and Japan signed a bilateral treaty to the same effect. Between 1926 and 1930 China negotiated a number of other international agreements that restored Chinese control over maritime customs, postal communications, and salt monopoly revenues.

International treaties played a significant role in shaping China's alignment and alliance relationships with other powers during the 1930s and the 1940s. Among the most important are the Sino-Soviet Non-aggression Treaty of 1937, the Sino-American Treaty for the Relinquishment of Extraterritorial Rights in China and the Regulation of Related Matters (January 11, 1943), and the Sino-British Treaty Relating to the Abrogation of Extraterritoriality in China (also January 11, 1943).

On October 9, 1944 the United States, Great Britain, the Soviet Union, and China promulgated the draft for the charter of the United Nations (UN). On June 26, 1945, at the United Nations Conference on International Organization in San Francisco, sponsored by the United States, Great Britain, the Soviet Union, and China, China was among the first signatories of the UN Charter. When the UN officially came into existence on October 25, 1945, China became one of five permanent members of the UN Security Council, acquiring great symbolic power within the UN system.

The Sino-Soviet Treaty of Friendship and Alliance of August 1945 arguably was concluded in extremis; the Nationalist government not only quietly acknowledged the legitimacy of Mongolia's independence, but also made concessions to Soviet demands for special privileges and rights in northeast China. Those Soviet demands were in fact part and parcel of the postwar arrangements for East Asia secretly agreed at Yalta in February 1945 by the Big Three—Franklin Roosevelt, Winston Churchill, and Joseph Stalin.

In the period from 1946 to 1949, the most important international treaty concluded by the Nationalist government was the five-year Treaty of Friendship, Commerce, and Navigation between China and the United States, signed on November 4, 1946. Besides that treaty, raging civil war between the Nationalists and Communists dominated the domestic and international agenda of the Nationalist government. When Mao Zedong declared the establishment of the People's Republic of China on October 1, 1949, the Chinese Communists had already decided to repudiate all international treaties concluded by the Nationalist government and renegotiate China's international relations with a clean slate.

SEE ALSO *Extraterritoriality; Foreign Concessions, Settlements, and Leased Territories; Most-Favored-Nation Treatment; Opium Wars; Sino-Japanese War, 1894–1895; Treaty Ports.*

BIBLIOGRAPHY

Hsü, Immanuel C. Y. (Xu Zhongyue). *The Rise of Modern China.* 6th ed. Oxford, U.K.: Oxford University Press, 2000.

Kirby, William C. The Internationalization of China: Foreign Relations at Home and Abroad in the Republican Era. *China Quarterly* 150 (January 1997): 433–458.

Zhang, Yongjin. *China in the International System, 1918–1920: The Middle Kingdom at the Periphery.* Basingstoke, U.K.: Macmillan, 1991.

Yongjin Zhang

TREATIES SINCE 1949

International treaties since 1949 have been a key means of developing of China's foreign relations. Treaties of the People's Republic of China (PRC), both bilateral and multilateral, are regarded as the most important international documents, formalizing relationships between states and requiring maximum binding force from the signatories. The Chinese government specifies a series of international documents of different nature and scope (both politically and judicially) that may be perceived broadly as "treaties." Treaties are classified as comprehensive bilateral treaties (of friendship, alliance, cooperation), diplomacy and administration treaties/agreements, boundary treaties (agreements), economic/trade treaties (agreements), and transportation/navigation treaties (agreements). China considers important political declarations and statements (despite their nonbinding character) also to be international treaties.

Throughout the PRC's history, Beijing's treaty policy has reflected China's evolving worldview and its changing perception of national goals and interests. In pursuance of its "lean to one side" policy of 1949 to 1959, China concentrated primarily on its independence, sovereignty, territorial integrity, and regional and global position. As China-Soviet relations deteriorated in the early 1960s, Beijing's foreign relations focus shifted to the developing countries in Asia and Africa. Between 1959 and 1969 China signed about 150 international treaties/agreements, predominantly with socialist and developing countries. They included fourteen friendship treaties with Afro-Asian states, five boundary treaties/agreements with neighboring countries, fewer than twenty transportation and navigation agreements, and multiple trade and economic cooperation agreements with more than thirty countries.

China's international activities in 1969 to 1979 were influenced by Sino-Soviet tensions, amelioration of China's relations with developed capitalist countries (the United States in particular), and Beijing's balancing role in U.S.-Soviet confrontation. On October 25, 1971, the PRC gained membership in the United Nations (replacing the Republic of China on Taiwan), and the Three Worlds theory was formulated by Chinese leaders. On the domestic scene, the rise of the Deng Xiaoping's "second generation" of Chinese leaders, and the Four Modernizations strategy were determinate factors in Beijing's international behavior. China's foreign activity resulted in more than

560 treaties and agreements, about 80 percent of which were diplomatic and administrative and trade/economic cooperation documents.

China's foreign treaties in the 1980s reflected a dramatic shift in Beijing's foreign policy toward a more pragmatic, less ideologically determined foreign policy, with the emphasis on economic reforms, technical cooperation with advanced nations, and the promotion of a peaceful international environment. The majority of the more than 1,300 treaties/agreements signed in the 1980s dealt with issues of economic/technical cooperation, trade and financial aid, foreign investment protection, and fiscal and loan policies.

In the 1990s China was preoccupied with its role in shaping regional security and reassessing its relations with the world's sole superpower—the United States. Beijing's 1,422 international treaties of the 1990s were bilateral and multilateral agreements aimed at establishing a new, multipolar order and a favorable international security environment. The new security concept formulated by Jiang Zemin and Qian Qichen (b. 1928) from 1997 to 1999 predetermined China's cooperative approach in the international arena. Hu Jintao's rise to power in 2002 brought about the "peaceful rise" concept, which aimed to form a "peaceful democratic civilized nation" in China by means of active participation in international affairs.

SEE ALSO *Four Modernizations; Russia, Relations with; Taiwan, Republic of China: Foreign Relations since 1949; United States, Relations with.*

BIBLIOGRAPHY

China International Laws and Treaties with Foreign Countries Handbook. Washington, DC: International Business Publications, 2008.

Chiu, Hungdah. *Agreements of the People's Republic of China: A Calendar of Events, 1966–1980.* New York: Praeger, 1981.

Falkenheim, Victor C. *Chinese Politics from Mao to Deng*. St. Paul, MN: Paragon House, 1989.

Ministry of Foreign Affairs, People's Republic of China. http://www.fmprc.gov.cn/eng/default.htm.

Ministry of Foreign Affairs, Republic of China (Taiwan). http://www.mofa.gov.tw.

Nuclear Threat Initiative. http://www.nti.org.

Online Collection of the Treaties of the People's Republic of China. Beijing University. (北大法宝—外国与国际法律库) http://www.fsou.com/Html/mulu/eag/2.html.

Rhode, Grant F., and Reid E. Whitlock. *Treaties of the People's Republic of China, 1949–1978: An Annotated Compilation*. Boulder, CO: Westview Press, 1980.

Roy, Denny. *China's Foreign Relations*. Lanham, MD: Rowman & Littlefield, 1998.

Wan, Ming. Human Rights Lawmaking in China: Domestic Politics, International Law, and International Politics. *Human Rights Quarterly* 29 (2007): 727–753.

United Nations Office of High Commissioner for Human Rights. http://www.ohchr.org.

United States Department of State. Bureau of Public Affairs. http://www.state.gov/r/pa/ei/bgn/index.htm.

Vitaly Kozyrev

INTERNATIONAL STUDENTS

Evidence points to a few rare instances of international students in China in early periods of history, and during the nineteenth and early twentieth centuries hundreds of missionaries undertook formal language training in China, almost invariably at missionary institutions. Regular admission of international students into Chinese educational institutions commenced only after the establishment of the People's Republic of China in 1949. In the Mao Zedong years, China received students mainly from other socialist countries as well as from African countries under government scholarship programs (Gillespie 2001). After China opened up to the world in 1978, study in China entered a new era. Two phases can be identified: The first phase was from 1979 to 1989; the second phase began in 1990.

From 1978, as part of the open-door policy, the Chinese government began to allow Chinese universities to receive self-paying international students. About 26,000 international students, mainly from developed countries, studied in China between 1979 and 1989 (Hu Zhiping 2000). Although the universities were permitted to admit self-paying international students, recruitment was controlled. The central government allocated a quota to each university and directly approved individual applications.

The second phase was inaugurated in 1990. As a gesture to show it would continue its open-door policy after the June Fourth movement, China's central government devolved the authority for approving universities' right to recruit international students to provincial governments. In 1993, as part of the experiment with a socialist market economy, the document titled *Guidelines for China's Education Reform and Development* gave the approved universities more autonomy in international student recruitment. Rapid development was reported every year, and self-paying students became the dominant component of the international student body in China.

Between 1979 and 2007, a total of about 1,229,540 international students studied in China. The trajectory of change coincides with the economic development and opening up of society. In 1978 about 1,200 international students studied in China. In 1991 the number first surpassed 10,000, and by 2000 the number reached

52,000. A dramatic increase followed until the number reached 195,503 in 2007 (Ministry of Education 2008a). The increase in self-paying students is remarkable: There were only about 300 self-paying international students in 1979, but the number had reached 154,211 by 2006, accounting for 94.8 percent of the total.

Statistics since the late 1990s suggest that more than 70 percent of international students in China come from other Asian countries. Apart from Chinese-background students, this category includes large numbers of Koreans and Japanese. Europe is the second-largest source (10–14%), followed by America (including North and South America, 9–11%), Africa (2–3%), and Oceania (1–2%). A decrease in the percentage of students from Asian countries can be observed since 2004.

Another trend is the increasing percentage of international students in long-term programs (six months or longer) and degree programs. In 2000, 68.4 percent of students were in long-term programs, and the number increased to 73.6 percent in 2006. Similarly, the percentage of students pursuing degrees over the same period increased from 26.3 percent to 33.7 percent.

A diversification of student distribution among disciplinary areas can also be observed over time. In order to reflect the reality of an increasing number of international students in disciplines other than the Chinese language and culture yet within the humanities and social sciences (*wenke*), the *China Education Statistics Yearbook* recategorized this broad area into Chinese language, arts, history, philosophy, economics, management, law, and education. In 2007 nearly 70.6 percent of all international students were enrolled in Chinese-language studies, 12.5 percent in medicine, 4.5 percent in economics, 3.7 percent in management, 3.6 percent in engineering, 2.3 percent in law, and 4.2 percent in other disciplines.

The Chinese government has provided scholarships to international students since 1950. The policy originally reflected China's commitment to solidarity with other socialist countries and with the third world. In the reform era, scholarships have also become a way to enhance exchange and cooperation with countries around the world. The provision of scholarships has kept increasing. In 2007 about 10,151 international students from 150 countries received Chinese government scholarships. Other scholarships include the Great Wall Scholarship (provided through UNESCO), the Excellent student Scholarship, the Foreign Chinese Teacher-training Scholarship, the HSK Winner Scholarship, and the Scholarship for Research on Chinese Culture.

The range of tuition fees for study in China is prescribed by the Ministry of Education. In 2007, the tuition for degree and refresher programs ranged from 14,000 to 68,000 renminbi per year (about $2,000 to $9,700 U.S. dollars), depending on the university, the level, and the field of study. Higher-level study requires higher tuition; natural science and engineering, medicine, arts, and sports programs require higher fees than do humanities and social science programs.

Behind the striking increase in the number of international students lies a whole new system. At the national level, the Service Center for Scholarly Exchange was restructured in 1989, and the China Scholarship Council was established in 1996 to manage programs for study abroad and in China, as well as educational exchanges and research cooperation. Confucius Institutes, sponsored by the Office of Chinese Language Council International, are offered in a franchise-type arrangement to universities around world, and have developed rapidly since 2004. There were more than 170 such institutes at the end of 2007 (Ministry of Education 2008b). At the institutional level, some Chinese universities set up International Student Offices under their International Exchange and Cooperation Office, and others founded Schools of International Education. Chinese universities began to extend their programs abroad and establish branch schools outside China in the end of the 1990s. (The data above do not include international students studying in Taiwan, Hong Kong, and Macau, or branch schools of Chinese universities outside of China; data without citation are from the *China Education Statistics Yearbook.*)

SEE ALSO *African States, Relations with; Central Asian States, Relations with; Education; European Union, Relations with; International Relations: Since 1949; Southeast Asian States, Relations with; United States, Relations with.*

BIBLIOGRAPHY

China Education Statistics Yearbook. Beijing: People's Education Publishing House, 1979–2007.

Gillespie, Sandra. *South-South Transfer: A Study of Sino-African Exchanges*. New York: Routledge, 2001.

Hu Zhiping. Dali fazhan laihua liuxuesheng jiaoyu, tigao woguo gaoxiao guoji jiaoliu shuiping [Prompt international student education, improve the level of communication between Chinese and foreign universities]. *China Higher Education Research* 3 (2000): 32–35.

Ministry of Education of the PRC. *2007 nian laihua liuxue sheng renshu tupo 19 wan* [2007 international students number surpassed 190,000 in China]. 2008a. http://www.moe.gov.cn/edoas/website18/info1205393837304296.htm

Ministry of Education of the PRC. *2010 nian qian zhongguo jiangjian 500 suo kongzixueyuan* [China plans to establish 500 Confucius institutes by 2010]. 2008b. http://www.moe.gov.cn/edoas/website18/info35060.htm

Liu Ji'an

INTERNET

The development of the Internet in China mirrors all the contradictions of the Chinese Communist regime: Seen as a necessity of modernity, information technologies are praised and embraced; seen as a potential threat to the party-state monopoly on power, the information highways are being groomed in a "golden cage," therefore submitted to very tight and comprehensive means of regulatory and political control. The paradox is thus that China ranks number one in the world by the number of its Internet users, while at the same time, to quote Reporters without Borders (2007), China stands as "the largest prison in the world for cyber-dissidents." The tyranny of the figures—huge numbers, as usual with China—and the belief that every new technology is being used to the best of its potential have proven to be misleading when one analyzes the development of the Internet in China since it became commercial in 1995.

There were, as of February 2008, 220 million Internet users in China, against 15,000 in 1995, and the number has been growing by an average of 5 million per month. China also boasts 3 million domain names and close to 800,000 Web sites. Chinese Internet users are young (72 percent are below thirty), live in cities, are educated (50 percent have some kind of tertiary education), and connect from home mainly via broadband access. Their primary activities are reading the news, browsing search engines, chatting via instant messaging networks (the largest one, QQ, has more than 100 million active users), posting on forums and bulletin board systems (BBS), and exchanging e-mail.

Online commerce is also developing fast, despite the limitations imposed by an outdated credit-card system. Major Chinese portals and search engines—Sohu, Sina, Baidu, Alibaba, and so forth—are the movers and shakers of e-commerce, with revenues estimated at close to 60 billion yuan in 2007. Online advertisement has even overtaken printed ads, and its turnover reached 10 billion yuan in 2007.

The Internet in China has thus opened new channels to obtain information, to communicate, to socialize, and to consume. Even when it comes to more sensitive subjects, no one can deny the Internet's impact: blogs and BBS provide fast dissemination of news, reports, pictures, and even videos of events not reported in the official press. For example, in March 2003, the beating death of a college graduate from Hubei, Sun Zhigang, while in administrative custody for failing to produce a temporary-resident permit in Guangzhou attracted widespread attention in blogs, chat-rooms, and online news sites, including those run by the state media. The activism of Internet users, along with articles published in the newspaper *Nanfang Dushi bao* (Southern Metropolitan Daily), spurred an investigation that resulted in the eventual conviction of the officials responsible for Sun's death, and led to the abolishment in June 2003 of the custody and repatriation system. In 2007, coverage of the "nail house" incident—a David and Goliath-like battle between a tenacious couple and a real-estate developer in Chongqing—by a blogger known as Zuola (or Zola, in reference to Emile Zola) attracted the attention of thousands, until the Web site was shut down in China proper.

The Internet has helped people facing injustice acquire momentum and organize protests with palpable results—as long as the protests remained local and amounted to "not-in-my-backyard" demonstrations. Such was the case in June 2007 when residents in Dongshan County (close to Xiamen) used online activism to mobilize protests and halt construction of a petrochemical plant over health concerns. In Shanghai, residents took to the streets in January 2008 to protest the extension of the Maglev train in their neighborhood—again over health concerns—and managed to have the plan temporarily suspended.

However, the development of the Internet in China has been closely monitored and tightly controlled by the government from the start. Authorities have espoused a "panoptic" approach to controlling electronic communications by resorting to preventive, selective, and punitive measures. Filtering, blocking, and cleansing of both international and domestic Web sites, e-mails, and blogs are the most widely documented methods. Such efforts have been enabled by "filtering" technologies sold to public security officials by foreign firms. In parallel, regulations restrict certain content, and ultimately Internet users can be condemned for so-called crimes to "subvert the state" or "topple the Chinese Communist Party."

The OpenNet Initiative study titled *Internet Filtering in China in 2004–2005* concluded that "China operates the most extensive, technologically sophisticated, and broad-reaching system of Internet filtering in the world. The implications of this distorted on-line information environment for China's users are profound, and disturbing." Reporters without Borders (2007) offers a firsthand account of censorship in China written by a Chinese technician working for an Internet company hosting blogs and Web sites, and confirms the largely successful attempt at "total control." The party-state is also extremely proactive in flooding the Internet with propaganda-like material, so that quantity becomes the enemy of quality.

The enforcement of strict censorship, often openly acknowledged by the authorities in the name of decency and social stability, along with the workings of online posting activities that are mostly striving for recognition and distinction, have encouraged self-censorship. What is the use of maintaining a blog if a posting gets immediately

Internet user, Beijing, September 22, 2007. *As the Internet gains users in China and becomes an increasingly important method of communication, the central government struggles to control access to information available on the medium. Government officials filter out material deemed subversive to national interests and regularly shut down Web sites that run counter to Communist Party principles.* TEH ENGKOON/AFP/GETTY IMAGES

erased and can land the blogger behind bars? The deletion of postings and the wiping out of archives also pose a threat to the constitution of "memory." Far too often attention is devoted to the circulation of information and not to its accumulation or preservation.

The Internet is tolerated in China as long as it encourages further segmentation of the society and acts as a cathartic sounding board for the desires and "sufferings" of the privileged urban middle class that the regime wants to keep "content" if not entirely loyal. But the Internet is relentlessly censored and constrained when it is used to build collective movements, be they cultural, religious, social, or more blatantly political.

SEE ALSO *Social Rituals.*

BIBLIOGRAPHY

Hughes, Christopher R., and Gudrun Wacker, eds. *China and the Internet: Politics of the Digital Leap Forward*. New York: Routledge, 2003.

OpenNet Initiative. *Internet Filtering in China in 2004–2005: A Country Study*. 2005. http://www.opennetinitiative.net/studies/china/

Reporters without Borders; Chinese Human Rights Defenders. *China: Journey to the Heart of Internet Censorship*. 2007. http://www.rsf.org

Zheng Yongnian. *Technological Empowerment: The Internet, State, and Society in China*. Stanford, CA: Stanford University Press, 2007.

Eric Sautedé

INTERPRETERS OF THINGS CHINESE TO THE WEST

In the centuries following the Industrial Revolution in Europe, Westerners went to China and interpreted China's responses to change in ways that reflected their own predispositions as much as China's situation, framing China variously as a unique world, a model, a menace, or, most often, a follower of the West.

THE GREAT REVERSAL AND THE SEARCH FOR FRAMEWORKS

In earlier centuries Europeans marveled at Marco Polo's tales of China's exotic prosperity and the Jesuit's learned disquisitions on China's benevolent Confucian emperors and peaceful kingdom. In 1793 Lord George Macartney's embassy started a tradition of diplomats supplying the public with comprehensive accounts that combined personal observation, the sinology of the Jesuits, and their own learning. Sir John Francis Davis (1795–1890), a pillar of the East India Company, admired Chinese aesthetics but wrote *The Chinese* (1836) to show that China needed Western science and British trade. The common but misleading picture of an unchanging, isolated empire with rulers opposed to progress reflected the British mercantile view of the Qing government, which controlled trade and denied access to the inland markets.

After the Opium Wars dramatized European military progress and rapacity, Westerners debated, as did some Chinese, whether Asian countries, in order to modernize, had to revitalize their classical traditions or destroy them. Western diplomats urged a break with tradition to import technology, but *The Middle Kingdom* (1848; rev. ed. 1882) by the American missionary S. Wells Williams presented a vast historical catalogue to show that what China needed was Christianity, not Western institutions. The Scotsman James Legge translated Confucian classics with accuracy and respect. The American missionary Arthur Smith was among the first to live in a Chinese village. Later handbooks extrapolated from Smith's *Chinese Characteristics* (1894) to explain China not in terms of historical circumstance but by unchanging "character," often a synonym for "race."

British writers dominated political reporting. Thomas Taylor Meadows, in *The Chinese and Their Rebellions* (1856), historically analyzed the midcentury upheavals. J. O. P. Bland and Sir Edmund Backhouse, in *China under the Empress Dowager* (1912), partly based on a forged diary, chronicled exotic affairs at the court. The Australian George Morrison reported insider news for the *Times of London*, without, however, feeling the need to learn Chinese. Arthur Waley in 1917 launched a series of elegant literary translations, without feeling the need to visit China. These interpreters presented either a China in need of Western tutelage or an eternal China outside the realm of modern industrial society, rarely a China in charge of its own modernization.

COMING TO GRIPS WITH NATIONALISM AND REVOLUTION, 1911–1949

After 1911, Western interpreters debated nationalism and revolution in China. While University of Wisconsin agronomist F. H. King's *Farmers of Forty Centuries* (1911) vaunted Asian agricultural efficiency as being superior to Western wastefulness, and John Dewey's *Letters from China and Japan* (1922) applauded the nationalist May Fourth movement, Rodney Gilbert's *What's Wrong with China* (1926) presented the British treaty-port view that the Chinese race was incapable of forming a modern nation.

André Malraux's novel *La Condition Humaine* (1933) caught the romance in revolutionary violence, while Alice Tisdale Hobart's *Oil for the Lamps of China* (1933) portrayed the corrosion of Confucian social values by the Standard Oil Company and nationalist revolution. Carl Crow's genial *400 Million Customers* (1937) urged American businesses to accept China, not try to change it. Pearl S. Buck in *The Good Earth* (1931) portrayed a competent but beleaguered farmer who needed neither Communist revolution nor Western models, while British Fabian socialist R. H. Tawney's *Land and Labor in China* (1931) portrayed a failing economy in the feudal stage and ready for revolution. Lin Yutang countered by elegantly presenting an eternally wise China in *My Country and My People* (1935).

After 1937, the Japanese invasion again changed the question. Edgar Snow's *Red Star over China* (1938), Theodore White and Annalee Jacoby's *Thunder Out of China* (1946), and Jack Belden's *China Shakes the World* (1949) all reported that the Communists were organized and ruthless but that their social revolution could produce a strong nation.

INTERPRETING MAO'S REVOLUTION

Westerners, especially Americans, saw "New China" as a Soviet satellite and Mao Zedong as an unlikely combination of peasant, emperor, and Joseph Stalin (1879–1953). By the 1960s, many in the West looked hopefully on Mao's revolutionary economic model and anti-imperialism as an alternative to dehumanized modern society and American Cold War hegemony. Edgar Snow's *On the Other Side of the River* (1962) extolled the success of Mao's communes, but denied the famines in which tens of millions starved. Felix Greene, an Englishman living in San Francisco, reported in *A Curtain of Ignorance* (1964) on the very achievements in bourgeois comfort that the Cultural Revolution (1966–1969) would soon denounce, while William Hinton's *Fanshen* (1965), a "documentary of revolution," showed how Mao's populist strategies had transformed a village in the 1940s. The Committee of Concerned Asian Scholars reported on their 1971 whirlwind tour in *China! Inside the People's Republic* (1972).

The era of opening and reform changed the framework once again. Chinese food and fashions became popular, and Westerners explored traditional Chinese medicine, feng shui, and acupuncture, but journalists soon found the People's Republic to be authoritarian, insular, and backward. Roger Garside in *Coming Alive* (1981), Fox Butterfield in *China: Alive in the Bitter Sea* (1982), and Richard Bernstein in *From the Center of the Earth* (1982) reported initial hope, frustration, and disillusionment in the years after Mao's death in 1976.

Western students and teachers could live in China once again. Starting with *In the People's Republic* (1977), Orville Schell's books trace the evolution of reform in China. Mark Salzman's *Iron and Silk* (1986) and Rosemary Mahoney's *The Early Arrival of Dreams* (1990) chose to avoid politics—a politically significant thing to do—and evoked the daily life of English teachers in China. Vikram Seth, later a distinguished novelist, studied economics in Beijing, then chronicled his trip home to India in *From Heaven Lake* (1983). Steven W. Mosher became the first American to do anthropological field research in China since 1949; his *Broken Earth* (1983) sensationally documented oppression and failure in the countryside.

A new genre, the Red Guard memoir, was invented by those who left China to write in English for Western audiences. Among the first were Liang Heng and Judith Shapiro's *Son of the Revolution* (1981) and Gao Yuan's *Born Red* (1987, with Judith Polumbaum). Chang Jung's (Zhang Rong's) memoir, *Wild Swans* (1991), chronicles her bound-foot grandmother, her revolutionary mother, and her own Red Guard generation; the book sold more than five million copies worldwide. These memoirs echoed Cold War themes: initial belief in Mao; realization of political repression of freedom and individualism; then liberation by escape to the West.

Interpretation of the Tiananmen incident of 1989 as a democracy movement was reinforced by televised images, especially the "tank man," the iconic individual facing down mechanized authority. Nicholas D. Kristof and Sheryl WuDunn's *China Wakes* (1994) was one of the eyewitness accounts to also convey a China trying to reconcile economic growth and political control.

Ironically, while China then became more prosperous, stable, unified, and proud than at any time since 1793, Western perceptions became more demanding and negative. John Pomfret's *Chinese Lessons* (2006) and Peter Hessler's *Oracle Bones* (2006) sympathetically but critically present stories of their classmates and students who juggled cultural freedom against political control.

SEE ALSO *China Hands; Chinese Overseas.*

BIBLIOGRAPHY

Bickers, Robert. China in Britain, and in the British Imagination. In *Britain in China: Community, Culture, and Colonialism, 1900–1949*, 22–66. Manchester, U.K.: Manchester University Press, 1999.

Spence, Jonathan D. *The Chan's Great Continent: China in Western Minds*. New York: Norton, 1998.

Charles W. Hayford

IRRIGATION AND MANAGEMENT OF WATER RESOURCES

The ancient Chinese believed that initially the world was in chaos because of a great flood. Water, the yin force, complemented the yang force of the sun. Water, along with wood, metal, fire, and earth (the five phases, *wuxing*), defined the processes of nature. Grass and trees flourished, and animals ran wild, but humans had no grain to eat. The legendary sage king Yu dredged the major rivers and channeled them to the sea to control the floods. Such human control of water, that is, irrigation and flood control, allowed agriculture and thus created civilization.

Ever since, Chinese officials and writers have discussed water conservancy (*shuili*) as both a technical and philosophical subject. They wanted first of all to direct the flow of rivers and lakes so as to protect the population from floods and make agriculture productive. One tradition, the Legalist, stressed active manipulation of water through heavy investments in dikes and dredging. An opposing tradition, the Daoist, argued for letting water flow naturally, while adjusting human settlements to its course. Strong dynasties built and repaired major dikes and canals, either through official projects or by encouraging the people. Many dynasties, when they neglected water conservancy, collapsed because floods and droughts upset the agrarian order that was the base of their rule. No dynasty, however, completely controlled water, and no uniform practice of irrigation applied to all of China.

REGIONAL DIFFERENCES

The watersheds of China's major rivers defined its main macroregions. Each region had a particular climate and form of water supply. North and Northwest China, along the Yellow (Huang) River, generally did not use river water for irrigation, but instead relied heavily on wells and rainfall. The three basins of the Yangzi (Chang) River—Sichuan, the middle Yangzi, and the lower Yangzi—all relied heavily on the huge river system and its tributaries to irrigate rice paddies in the plains and fields for other crops in the hills. Guangdong and Guangxi in the South relied equally on the Pearl River. The one macroregion without a single major watershed, Yunnan and Guizhou, was fragmented by mountains into many river basins. Beyond the heartland of sedentary agriculture, southern Manchuria was centered on the Liao River, Mongolia was mainly grassland and desert, and Xinjiang used melted snow led through underground channels from the mountains to irrigate large oasis fields.

In the North China plain, the most heavily settled part of China until after the eighth century, rainfall was sporadic, there were few rivers, and dry-field agriculture depended heavily on wells. Peasants put most of their effort into digging for water and praying for relief from drought. In most of the North, irrigation was an activity of millions of individual households. The state did not control their water supply. The imperial state took responsibility for maintaining the Yellow River, but when state capacities declined, millions suffered. Periodically, the great river burst its banks, flooding vast regions and spreading its silt over abandoned fields.

South China, whose intensive cultivation began only after the eighth century, had abundant supplies of water and an extended growing season. The early settlement of the region resulted from major migrations from the North, and depended on large-scale investments of labor directed by monasteries and large manors. After intensive settlement cleared the marshes, peasant households carefully maintained the small channels that fed their fields. Controlling the multiple rivers and irrigation channels supported high-yield agriculture and a dense population. Some villages banded together to create larger-scale irrigation organizations. State involvement was limited, and larger-scale water conservancy difficult.

Rice-paddy agriculture demanded a great investment of labor, but its yields were more secure than those of crops in the arid regions of the North. Southern Chinese learned how to cultivate many crops together, such as fish ponds, mulberry trees, silkworms, and rice fields, recycling the waste products of each for consumption in another cycle.

A third wave of migration brought settlers in South China up from the lowlands to the hillsides, where they planted crops like sweet potatoes and maize, which could flourish without the intensive labor needed for rice. These plots were not intensively irrigated, but they affected water flows downstream. By clearing the forests and directing streams toward hillside plots, the settlers caused more silt to flow into downstream rivers, blocking their flows and leading to floods. The eighteenth-century population boom of China arose from this hill settlement and settlement around lowland lakes. These trends combined to make China's agricultural environment more fragile than ever before.

In the nineteenth century China suffered from unceasing attacks of drought and flood. Water supplies throughout the empire seemed to be beyond human control. Heavy floods on the Yangzi River threatened major cities. The Yellow River burst its banks in 1855 and shifted its course from south to north of the Shandong Peninsula. In 1887 a great flood killed over 1 million peasants. The weakened Qing state, trying to suppress major rebellions, relieve famine, and fend off attack by foreign imperialists, had few resources to invest in the infrastructure for water conservancy. Disruption of water sources was one of the causes of the domestic uprisings, local conflicts, and mass migrations that besieged the empire until its collapse in 1912. In 1931 the Nationalist government deliberately broke the banks of the Yellow River to stop the Japanese invasion.

THE TWENTIETH CENTURY

In the twentieth century, modern engineering technology offered new hope for controlling China's turbulent water supplies. From 1960 to 2001, the People's Republic built twelve hydroelectric power stations on the Yellow River. In the early twentieth century Sun Yat-sen had dreamed of a large dam on the Yangzi River that would permanently eliminate the major floods, provide safe navigation, and irrigate the fields of the region. The Nationalist government, despite many plans, never realized his vision, but the People's Republic finally achieved it, building the Gezhouba Dam from 1970 to 1988 and the Three Gorges Dam from 1994 to 2011. These dams not only controlled flooding but also generated hydropower, supporting rapid industrialization.

Yet floods and droughts have not gone away. In North China, the Yellow River often never makes it to the sea, because its water is diverted to residential, industrial, and agricultural use. Drought has afflicted farmers there for decades. The Three Gorges Dam has prevented floods on the Yangzi itself, but many tributaries can overflow. Earthquakes have caused new lakes to form, which threaten further flooding. New stresses on China's water supplies affect both urban and rural people. Heavy pollution of water supplies allows toxic chemicals to get into the food, causing mental damage and disease. Conservation of water has not yet become an effective policy. Although the government has recently raised the price of urban water usage, rapid industrial growth deprives farmers of the water they need.

On a smaller scale, the national government began to invest heavily in electric water-pumping stations in the 1970s. Electric pumps replaced the foot-operated water wheels that farmers had used for centuries, and they increased yields on crops in paddies and on hills. Believers in strict Maoist principles objected that China's large population had plenty of labor to work the fields, and they feared that mechanization would uproot farmers from the land. But the more stable water supplies allowed intensive multicropping, and the time saved in working treadle pumps gave farmers opportunities to work in rural industries. By 2007, mechanically irrigated fields had risen to 117 million acres, or 36 percent of China's total cultivated land. But the more intensive use of water lowered the water table in North China, caused more lakes to dry up, and threatened to cause salination in arid areas. The spread of mechanical irrigation to the very arid regions of China's far west made possible extensive and profitable cotton cultivation, attracting rural migrants from densely populated Sichuan. Xinjiang, which produces 30 percent of China's cotton, mechanically irrigates 55 percent of its land. Yet such intensive use of water has threatened the water table and severely strained water resources. In addition, global warming has reduced the size of glaciers on China's high mountains, which provided snowmelt to the oases of Xinjiang. Water is the crucial component of raising China's agricultural output, but it is becoming increasingly scarce.

New great plans, like moving surplus water from the South to the North, still cannot change the fact that China's water supplies are extremely scarce, badly contaminated, and precarious. Getting enough water to the soil to produce sufficient healthy food to support over 1 billion people is still a constant challenge. The Yus of the future have their work cut out for them.

SEE ALSO *Natural Resources; River Systems.*

BIBLIOGRAPHY

Chi Ch'ao-ting. *Key Economic Areas in Chinese History.* London: Allen and Unwin, 1936.

Dodgen, Randall A. *Controlling the Dragon: Confucian Engineers and the Yellow River in Late Imperial China.* Honolulu: University of Hawai'i Press, 2001.

Economy, Elizabeth C. *The River Runs Black: The Environmental Challenge to China's Future.* Ithaca, NY: Cornell University Press, 2004.

Lewis, Mark Edward. *The Flood Myths of Early China.* Albany: State University of New York Press, 2006.

Needham, Joseph. *Science and Civilisation in China.* Vol. 4, pt. 3, *Civil Engineering and Nautics.* Cambridge, U.K.: Cambridge University Press, 1971.

Perdue, Peter C. *Exhausting the Earth: State and Peasant in Hunan, 1500–1850.* Cambridge, MA: Council on East Asian Studies, Harvard University Press, 1987.

Schoppa, Keith. *Song Full of Tears: Nine Centuries of Chinese Life around Xiang Lake.* New York: Perseus, 2002.

Smil, Vaclav. *China's Environmental Crisis: An Inquiry into the Limits of National Development.* Armonk, NY: Sharpe, 1993.

Peter C. Perdue

ISLAM

In 2000 there were approximately twenty million Muslims in China, almost all Sunni. Provinces with Muslim concentrations include Xinjiang, Ningxia, Gansu, Henan, Qinghai, and Yunnan, but Muslims are found in most of China. The People's Republic tolerates Islam as long as it poses no threat to political stability. Early twenty-first-century figures put the number of mosques in China at about 30,000, some two-thirds in Xinjiang, and the Islamic clergy at about 40,000. Halal restaurants are numerous in areas with Muslim populations. Sufism, which became significant early in the Qing dynasty (1644–1911), still retains some following.

ISLAM AND ETHNICITY

The government recognizes fifty-six ethnic groups: the Han majority, which the 2000 census showed at 91.59 percent of China's total population, and fifty-five minorities, the remaining 8.41 percent. Muslims in China are officially allocated to one of ten ethnic minorities: the Hui, Uygurs, Kazaks, Kirgiz, Uzbeks, Tatars, Salars, Bonans, Dongxiang, and Tajiks. To be Han is to be non-Muslim.

The most populous and widely dispersed of the Muslim ethnic groups is the Hui (numbering 9,816,805 in the 2000 census). Members of the Hui ethnic minority are Chinese speakers and, other than in matters relating to Islam, are Han by culture. Over the centuries they have contributed to Chinese literature, to scholarship, and to quintessentially Chinese art forms like Peking opera.

The Uygurs (numbering 8,399,393 in the 2000 census), Kazaks (1,250,458), Kirgiz (160,823), Uzbeks (12,370), and Tatars (4,890) are all Turkic linguistically and culturally, almost all living in Xinjiang. Uygurs and Uzbeks are mainly sedentary farmers and similar culturally, while Kazaks and Kirgiz, most of whom live near China's border with Kazakhstan and Kyrgyzstan respectively, are mostly pastoral herders of goats and sheep, the Kazaks being especially renowned for their horsemanship. Tajiks (41,028) live in the area of Xinjiang bordering Tajikistan. Among China's ethnic groups, they are unique in speaking an Iranian language. Most of China's few Shiite Muslims are Tajik.

The other three Islamic ethnic groups live in the Gansu-Qinghai border region in or near Linxia, southern Gansu. The Dongxiang (513,805) are farmers who speak a Mongolic language. The Turkic-speaking Salars (104,503) are herders with an unusually strong dedication to Islam. Their ancestors were fourteenth-century migrants from the Samarkand region. In the mid-nineteenth century the ancestors of the Bonans (Baoan, 16,505) moved to their present location from the Tibetan region of Tongren, Qinghai, owing to religious friction with Tibetan Buddhist neighbors.

HISTORY

Islam was introduced to China shortly after Muhammad's death in 632. The earliest conversion of a Turkic people to Islam was in Kashi, currently in southwestern Xinjiang, through the Karakhanid ruler Satuk Bughra Khan (d. c. 955). By 1759 a process of conquest by the Manchu Qing dynasty had brought Xinjiang, by then firmly Muslim, under Manchu/Chinese rule.

The Qing practiced a policy of even-handedness toward Muslims. However, this policy began to break down in the 1770s, largely owing to prejudice by local officials against a religion whose beliefs and customs differed profoundly from Confucianism. The deterioration in relations between Muslims and the state resulted in a series of bloody rebellions.

The nationalist leader Sun Yat-sen (Sun Zhongshan, 1866–1925) divided China's people into five ethnicities: the Han, Manchus, Tibetans, Mongolians, and Muslims. Though Chiang Kai-shek (Jiang Jieshi, 1887–1975) accepted Sun's categorization, his 1943 book *Zhongguo zhi mingyun* (China's Destiny) insisted that all people of China were of Chinese blood, so the distinction between Muslim and Han was religious only, not ethnic.

The early decades of the twentieth century were a period of reform and growth in Chinese Islam. There were increased interchanges with Islam farther west, burgeoning Islamic journals, and intellectual ferment, one major issue being the extent to which Islam should be Sinicized and Muslims should support Chinese nationalism. A major representative Muslim was Ma Wanfu (1853–1934), a member of the Dongxiang minority from near Linxia. He founded a fundamentalist movement based on venerating the scriptures and opposing Sufism or any external influence on Islam. He refused to learn to read or write Chinese, though he could speak it, or to let his children learn Chinese. However, influenced by other Muslim thinkers and by events in China, especially Japan's encroachments, he later became a strong supporter of Chinese nationalism.

Such trends contrasted with Turkic Islam in Xinjiang. Underlying a series of anti-Chinese Muslim or Muslim-influenced rebellions was a complex web of changing alliances involving the Soviet Union, Hui and Turkic Muslims, dictators of Xinjiang, especially the mostly pro-Soviet Sheng Shicai (r. 1933–1944), and the central Chinese Republican government.

The People's Republic declared religion to be a free matter of conscience, and Islam continued to be openly practiced. In Xinjiang during the 1950s, the Sufi orders "experienced an explosion of popularity" (Starr 2004, p. 89). At the same time, government land reform and universal replacement of Islamic law by secular law had the effect of reducing the clergy's political and social influence. By the late 1950s, government policy was becoming more radical, and during the Cultural Revolution (1966–1969) and its aftermath, there was unrelentingly fierce persecution of Islam and other religions.

The period since the 1980s has seen a major revival of Islam and of ethnic identity. Almost all Muslims, especially among the Hui, have adapted well to the increasingly prevalent consumerism of Chinese society. Islam retains influence with the government. This is evident from a series of Muslim demonstrations in 1989 protesting against the book *Xing fengsu* (Sexual Customs), which Muslims found insulting to their religion. The state intervened on the side of the Muslims, punishing the book's authors and putting its publisher out of business.

In 1990 a mainly Uygur rebellion in Baren Township, in southwest Xinjiang, led to a series of mostly separatist disturbances against the Chinese state. The Chinese authorities blamed the unrest on the Muslim theory of war against the infidel and suppressed the disturbances, but as a result, relations between the Han and Uygurs deteriorated.

After the attacks of September 11, 2001, on the United States, Chinese authorities intensified suppression of activities threatening the state and increased its denunciations against Islamic terrorism. The economy has improved, and separatism has declined, with fewer serious incidents since 2000 than in the preceding decade.

DIVERSITY OF ADHERENCE

Chinese official accounts regard anybody belonging to one of the ten Islamic ethnic minorities as being Muslim. This belief usually reflects reality, with members of Islamic ethnic groups generally taking their Muslim identity seriously. However, the intensity of the belief in and practice of Islam varies among and within ethnic groups and individual communities. In 2000 Xinjiang had 400,388 Communist Party members from ethnic minorities. Since almost all of Xinjiang's ethnic minorities are Islamic and the official ideology of the party is atheist, probably most of Xinjiang's minority party members are Muslim only in the sense that they take part in Islamic social events and practices. Gladney reports interviewing people outside Quanzhou, in Fujian Province, who claimed to be and were officially recognized as Hui, but who ate pork and, though cognizant of their Islamic heritage, had "not practiced Islam nor attended the mosque for generations" (1991, p. 262).

ISLAM IN FOREIGN RELATIONS SINCE 1990

The fall of the Soviet Union in 1991 made Islam a factor in China's relations with its Western neighbors. In 1996 the presidents of China, Russia, Kazakhstan, Kyrgyzstan, and Tajikistan began annual meetings to discuss mutual problems. Their 1998 Almaty Declaration denounced "any form of national splittism, ethnic exclusion and

Chinese Muslims at prayer, Beijing, August 4, 2008. *While followers of Islam may be found throughout China, the greatest concentrations of Muslims inhabit the western province of Xinjiang. Persecuted during the Cultural Revolution, Chinese Muslims of the early twenty-first century enjoy a significant measure of religious liberty.* TEH ENG KOON/AFP/GETTY IMAGES

religious extremism," referring mainly to Islamic extremism. In June 2001 the five states added Uzbekistan and set up the Shanghai Cooperation Organization. Despite some problems and individual government changes, these countries have remained friendly, opposition to Islamism serving to buttress their good relations.

The September 11 attacks had the effect of improving Sino-American relations, because China supported U.S. President George W. Bush's "war on terror." Twenty-two Uygurs were imprisoned as Islamist fighters in Guantánamo Bay after capture along the Afghanistan-Pakistan border. In 2002 the Bush Administration and the United Nations labeled as a terrorist organization the East Turkestan Islamic Movement, which the Chinese had accused of trying to use Islam to split Xinjiang from China. However, from its beginning in 2003, China's leadership opposed the American-led Iraq War. Chinese Muslims were vehement in their denunciation of the war, regarding it not only as an infringement of Iraq's sovereignty but as anti-Islamic.

ASSESSMENT

The literature on China's Muslims, especially on the Hui, draws different conclusions concerning their success in accommodating themselves to Confucian-based Chinese culture and Marxist-Leninist ideology. On the basis of the "demand of Islam that Muslims should live under Islamic rule" (2002, p. 1), Raphael Israeli sees enduring and deep-seated hostility between the Han and the Hui. Taking a more positive approach, Jonathan Lipman sees the Hui as "normal and familiar" in China and argues "that violence is no more natural to the Muslims of northwest China than it is to other people" (1997, pp. 226, 220). Dru Gladney (1991) emphasizes the revival of ethnic consciousness among the Hui, while Xiaowei Zang finds no contradiction for an individual Hui to be "well integrated into mainstream society" but simultaneously have "a very high level of ethnic consciousness" (2007, p. 149). Most studies of Han-Uygur relations in Xinjiang (e.g., Starr 2004) show them as tenser than other Han-Muslim relations, with the Uygurs still much less loyal to the Chinese state than other Muslim ethnic groups, notably the Hui.

Modernization and globalization are bringing the Islamic groups closer to the rest of China and the world, with the result that the cultures of China's Islamic ethnic groups could weaken over the next decades. However, because of Islam's profound differences from Han culture in beliefs and practices it will continue to face problems integrating. With about 20 million adherents in 2000, Islam will likely remain a strong force in society indefinitely.

SEE ALSO *Muslim Uprisings.*

BIBLIOGRAPHY

MAINLY CONTEMPORARY ISLAM

Gladney, Dru C. *Muslim Chinese Ethnic Nationalism in the People's Republic*. Cambridge, MA: Harvard University Press, 1991.

Starr, S. Frederick, ed. *Xinjiang China's Muslim Borderland*. Armonk, NY: Sharpe, 2004.

Zang, Xiaowei. *Ethnicity and Urban Life in China: A Comparative Study of Hui Muslims and Han Chinese*. London: Routledge, 2007.

MAINLY HISTORICAL ISLAM

Dillon, Michael. *China's Muslim Hui Community, Migration, Settlement, and Sects*. Richmond, Surrey, U.K.: Curzon, 1999.

Israeli, Raphael. *Islam in China: Religion, Ethnicity, Culture, and Politics*. Lanham, MD: Lexington Books, 2002.

Lipman, Jonathan N. *Familiar Strangers: A History of Muslims in Northwest China*. Seattle: University of Washington Press, 1997.

Colin Mackerras

J

JAPAN, RELATIONS WITH

China's relations with Japan were suspended in the immediate aftermath of World War II (1937–1945) as China engaged in civil war and the Allied occupation forces took control in Japan. The resumption of diplomatic relations with Japan did not take place until 1972, Japan having recognized the Republic of China on Taiwan in 1952. This is not to say, however, that the People's Republic of China (PRC) and Japan did not enjoy some measure of interaction in the intervening years, but it took place through private channels and was constrained by U.S. pressure on Japan to limit its contacts with China for strategic reasons. Nonetheless, three trade agreements were concluded and cultural exchange took place in the prenormalization period under the rubric of China's "people's diplomacy" and Japan's "separation of politics from economics" (*seikei bunri*). The relationship was, however, vulnerable to the changing domestic and international environments of the time. This invariably led to ruptures in the relationship, particularly during times of radicalization in Chinese domestic politics, such as the Great Leap Forward. There were signs of improvement in 1960 with the beginning of "friendly trade" (in which China would trade only with Japanese companies deemed friendly to China), but relations suffered once again in the mid-1960s with the onset of the Cultural Revolution (1966–1969).

THE JOINT COMMUNIQUÉ

Sino-American détente in the early 1970s provided the impetus for Japan and China to sign the Joint Communiqué (September 1972), which marked the resumption of diplomatic relations between the two countries and in which the PRC waived demands for reparations and Japan expressed deep reproach for the damage caused to the Chinese people through war. Echoing Chiang Kai-shek's (Jiang Jieshi's) "magnanimous policy" toward Japan on the reparations issue, the decision to renounce reparations was made by Mao Zedong and Zhou Enlai, ostensibly to avoid inflicting the costs of compensation on the Japanese people, who, in the eyes of the Chinese leadership, were not to be held responsible for Japanese militarism. However, more strategic reasons, such as the desire to gain leverage over Japan on issues relating to Taiwan and the Soviet Union, may also explain the decision.

In the Joint Communiqué, Japan recognized the PRC as the sole legal government of China, and expressed understanding and respect for the PRC's position on Taiwan as an "inalienable part of [its] territory." Tokyo's recognition of China inevitably meant the abrogation of the 1952 Treaty of Peace between Japan and the Republic of China, but it did not lead to a complete dislocation of ties between Japan and Taiwan. Trade and exchange continued, albeit through nongovernmental channels. Japan's relatively friendly relations with Taiwan, boosted in the 1990s by high volumes of trade and investment and the popularity of Japanese pop culture among Taiwanese youth, have been carefully monitored by the PRC, which has tended to be highly critical of any signs of closer political or security arrangements between the two countries.

THE TEXTBOOK ISSUE AND OTHER PROBLEMS

The Treaty of Peace and Friendship was signed between China and Japan in 1978 along with a series of trade agreements that facilitated a boom period in China-Japan relations in the 1970s and early 1980s. Problems emerged, however, in both the economic and diplomatic spheres. Friction developed, for example, in the area of technology transfer, leading to China's unilateral cancellation in 1979 of a series of contracts signed with Japanese businesses. This led to some disillusionment on the part of Japanese industry and a reluctance to invest in what was perceived as an unstable business environment. Diplomatically, the relationship was shaken in 1982 with the so-called textbook issue in which the Chinese (and also the South Korean) government lodged an official protest about the content of Japanese high school history textbooks, which were thought to be downplaying Japan's aggression in Asia during World War II. The textbook issue was resolved, temporarily, by an agreement on the part of the Japanese government to amend the textbooks and revise Japan's textbook authorization criteria to ensure that they reflected the spirit of the 1972 Joint Communiqué.

The textbook issue marked the beginning of a recurring problem that has continued into the twenty-first century. Since 1982 there have been a number of diplomatic disputes not only relating to the content of Japanese history textbooks, but other aspects of the history problem, such as the visits of high-ranking Japanese politicians, including prime ministers and cabinet ministers, to the Yasukuni Shrine in Tokyo (where the souls of Japan's war dead are enshrined, including Class A war criminals), gaffes made by Japanese politicians about Japan's war of aggression, and the perceived failure on the part of the Japanese government to apologize fully for Japan's actions in China during the war. In addition, since the 1990s, Chinese (and Asian) citizens who were victims of human experimentation, indiscriminate bombings, military sexual slavery ("comfort women"), and forced labor have been seeking compensation and official apologies through the Japanese courts for their suffering. At times, popular anti-Japanese sentiment in China has developed to the extent that demonstrations have taken place. In 1985, for example, demonstrators in Beijing protested Prime Minister Nakasone Yasuhiro's official visit to the Yasukuni Shrine and the influx of Japanese goods into China. And in 2005 protests were staged in major cities across China about the reauthorization of a right-wing Japanese textbook and Japan's quest to gain a permanent seat on the United Nations Security Council, among other issues. The period between 2001 and 2006, when Prime Minister Koizumi Junichirō angered the Chinese government by making regular visits to the Yasukuni Shrine, is considered to be a particularly low period in postwar Sino-Japanese relations.

The history problem can be partly explained by the inability of the two countries, for various political and strategic reasons, to effect full reconciliation in the immediate aftermath of the war. The war crimes trials in the 1940s and 1950s and the signing of the Joint Communiqué in 1972 satisfied the immediate need for legal and political settlements but did not fully address issues that, by the 1980s and 1990s, were deemed to be of greater importance to the reconciliation process (for example, an unambiguous apology) or that had only begun to emerge (for example, through the discovery of new documentary and oral evidence about the military sexual-slavery system). In addition, the disparities between Japanese and Chinese narratives of the war (which had been developed in isolation from one another during the aftermath of the war and the onset of the Cold War) and the ongoing internal debates in Japan about war responsibility further exacerbated the problem.

"HOT ECONOMICS, COOL POLITICS"

From 2006, China's relations with Japan took a more positive turn. In the joint statement issued during Prime Minister Abe Shinzō's visit to China in October of that year, both sides agreed to cooperate in various areas such as energy, the environment, finance, information and communications technology in order to build a "mutually beneficial relationship based on common strategic interests" (Japan-China Joint Press Statement 2006). On the basis of the joint statement, the two governments established a joint history project and agreed to "face history squarely." This more future-oriented approach continued under Abe's successors, Fukuda Yasuo and Aso Tarō.

Despite the recurrence of the history problem, the commercial and financial aspects of the Sino-Japanese relationship have been gaining strength since the 1980s, giving rise to the phrase "hot economics, cool politics." China surpassed the United States as Japan's top trading partner in 2004, and Japan is China's third-largest trading partner. Two-way trade reached a record high in 2008 of $266.4 billion. Japan also ranks in the top four of China's foreign direct investors, although this amounts to a relatively small percentage of Japan's outward investment. In 2007, for example, Japan's outward investment to China was $6.2 billion (approximately 8.5 percent of total outward investment). Japan's aid to China has also been an important element of China's economic growth and modernization. Official development assistance began in 1979 under Prime Minister Ohira Masayoshi (1910–1980), and Japan was China's top aid donor for many years, contributing to some of China's major infrastructural developments. Cultural exchange between the two countries has received much official support since normalization, with both governments implementing regular cultural, sports, and student exchange programs in order to facilitate friendship between the two countries. Japan is the top Asian destination for Chinese students, who represented nearly 60 percent of the total number of overseas students in Japan in 2008.

China's rapid economic growth and reentry onto the international political stage have given rise to a view that China and Japan have become rivals for power in East

Chinese Premier Wen Jiabao (left center), before the Diet, Tokyo, Japan, April 12, 2007. *Diplomatic relations between the People's Republic of China and Japan suffered during the twentieth century, due in part to punitive Chinese reparations after the Sino Japanese Wars, Japanese atrocities committed during World War II, and Japan's initial recognition of the Republic of China after the Chinese Revolution. However, as China reentered the world stage at century's end, ties between the two countries improved, including Chinese heads of state addressing Japanese government bodies.* © EVERETT KENNEDY BROWN/EPA/CORBIS

Asia, with each seeking a regional leadership role. Other areas of friction include mutual threat perceptions, territorial disputes, and energy security. Japan's security relationship with the United States, which began with the signing of the Security Treaty in 1951, forms the mainstay of Japan's defense policy and was viewed for many years by the PRC as a welcome means of preventing a resurgence of Japanese militarism. However, since the mid-1990s, the U.S.-Japan security relationship has been strengthened (for example, with the revision of the U.S.-Japan Defense Guidelines in 1997 and the agreement to engage in joint research on theater missile defense); this was considered to be an attempt to contain China (as well as North Korea). China's rapid military modernization, lack of transparency in relation to military expenditure, and naval activities in the seas around Japan have become the focus of some concern in the Japanese military establishment since the early 2000s. The dispute over the Diaoyu (Senkaku) Islands (to which China, Taiwan, and Japan lay claim) was famously shelved by Deng Xiaoping in the 1970s, but the dispute has flared up occasionally, most notably in 1996. The governments of China and Japan have tended to take a pragmatic approach to the dispute, but the islands have become central to the more complex, and ongoing, negotiations over geographic boundaries and the potential gas and oil reserves in the East China Sea in the first decade of the 2000s.

China-Japan relations have long been described in terms of the dualities of mutual admiration versus suspicion, and complementarity versus competition. In the twenty-first century, such dualities remain: China and Japan continue to view each other with some caution in areas such as security and energy policy, but they enjoy strong economic ties and greater levels of cooperation at both bilateral and multilateral levels.

SEE ALSO *Anti-Japanese War, 1937–1945; ASEAN, Relations with; Nanjing Massacre; Sino-Japanese War, 1894–1895; Tourism: Foreign; United States, Relations with.*

DIAOYUTAI, SOVEREIGNTY OVER

The Diaoyu or Senkaku Islands (*Diaoyutai* in Chinese, *Senkaku* in Japanese) are a group of uninhabited islands 200 kilometers northeast of Taiwan and 300 kilometers southwest of Okinawa. The islands are claimed by Japan, China, and Taiwan. The first Chinese mention of the islands dates from the early fifteenth century; this historical claim is used to argue that the islands belong to China. Japan incorporated the islands into its territory in 1895, and after World War II (1937–1945), the islands came under American jurisdiction. A United Nations report in 1968 revealed the presence of oil in the area; Beijing and Taibei (Taipei) thereafter began to express interest in the islands' sovereignty. In 1971 a major protest calling for the reversion of the islands to China took place in Hong Kong and among the Chinese diaspora, but in 1972 the islands reverted to Japanese control, along with Okinawa.

In July 1996 the Japan Youth Federation, a right-wing group, constructed a lighthouse on one of the islands, and by mid-September massive protests against Japan erupted in Hong Kong and Taibei. Flotillas of demonstrators sailed from Hong Kong and Taiwan, vowing to plant the Chinese flag on the islands. On September 26, protest leader David Chan was drowned while trying to swim to the islands; on October 7, another flotilla succeeded in briefly hoisting Chinese and Taiwanese flags. In the years since, activists have set forth in flotillas several times, but there have been no large-scale protests in Hong Kong or elsewhere. The 1996 protests were arguably linked to fears over the reversion of Hong Kong to China. The islands continue to be a point of contention between China and Japan in their competing nationalisms and jockeying for regional dominance; for the time being, the conflict is dormant, but it could erupt at any time.

Gordon Mathews

BIBLIOGRAPHY

Drifte, Reinhard. *Japan's Security Relations with China since 1989: From Balancing to Bandwagoning?* New York and London: RoutledgeCurzon, 2003.

Japan-China Joint Press Statement. October 18, 2006. http://www.cn.emb-japan.go.jp/bilateral_e/jc-pressstatement_e.htm.

Mendl, Wolf. *Issues in Japan's China Policy*. London: Macmillan, 1978.

Whiting, Allen S. *China Eyes Japan*. Berkeley: University of California Press, 1989.

Caroline Rose

JEWISH COMMUNITIES AND REFUGEES

The history of Jewish communities in China between 1842 and 1949 has attracted wide-ranging interest from the scholarly world. That said, a comprehensive picture of the Jewish presence within a *longue-durée* framework still needs to be pieced together. Within this context, one should mention that a Jewish settlement took shape in Kaifeng during the Northern Song dynasty (960–1127) and that it maintained its distinct identity for centuries. However, by the time Baghdadi Jews reached China, Kaifeng Jews had already been largely assimilated into Han and Hui communities, and any effort to try to revive their interest in Judaism proved unsuccessful.

BAGHDADI JEWS IN HONG KONG AND SHANGHAI

Baghdadi Jews based in Bombay (Mumbai) and Calcutta (Kolkata) extended their commercial interests to the treaty port of Shanghai and the British colony of Hong Kong in the aftermath of the Opium War (1839–1842). The Sassoons, Baghdad's most eminent Jewish family, and their two firms played a pivotal role in attracting young Baghdadi Jewish men to settle with their families in these two cities, where they either enjoyed the lifelong security of a job with the Sassoon concerns or founded their own businesses as brokers and general importers and exporters of commodities. By the first decades of the twentieth century, as many as one thousand Baghdadi Jews resided in Hong Kong and Shanghai. Both cities had developed into major nodes of the Baghdadi trade diaspora, a network of trading posts that stretched from its major bases in Bombay and Calcutta to England and Japan.

Many quick fortunes were made through the trade of Indian opium, which was legal between 1860 and 1917, and which was largely controlled by the Sassoons and other Baghdadi traders after the 1860s. Opium money was often invested in the booming real-estate markets of Hong Kong and of Shanghai's foreign settlements, an investment strategy that proved winning in both cities. In Shanghai's International Settlement, where votes to elect councilors were allotted on the basis of a property franchise, Baghdadi Jews asserted themselves as the main

VICTOR SASSOON

Sir (Ellice) Victor Sassoon (third baronet) (1881–1961) a colorful entrepreneur, bon vivant, and art collector, was the main inheritor of E. D. Sassoon & Co. and its related commercial and industrial assets. The family firm had been established by his grandfather Elias David (1820–1880), who had broken away from the main family business after the death of his father, David (1792–1864), the scion of Baghdad's most eminent Jewish family. The latter had established an international commercial house in Bombay, with leading branches in Hong Kong and Shanghai.

Sir Victor was educated in Britain and was trained to take over the family business both in Bombay and Shanghai. During War World I he volunteered for the Royal Naval Air Service but was crippled for life by an accident. After the end of the war, he worked for the family business in Bombay, but, in the late 1920s made the bold decision to move to Shanghai, where he transferred a large share of his assets with a view to taking advantage of the city's prolonged business boom. In the footsteps of his forefathers, he heavily invested in the local real-estate market and built some of Shanghai's most luxurious property developments, as well as Cathay Hotel, an imposing art-deco building at the corner of Nanjing Road and the Bund. Eighty years after its erection, the building, now known as Peace Hotel, remains one of the main landmarks of the city.

Sir Victor is widely remembered for the generous financial help he gave to European Jewish refugees who fled to Shanghai from Nazi persecution. After the foundation of the People's Republic of China in 1949, his immovable assets were seized by the Communist government, but he still managed to re-establish his business empire in the Bahamas. Late in life he married his American nurse.

BIBLIOGRAPHY

Jackson, Stanley. *The Sassoons*. London: E. P. Dutton, 1968.

Chiara Betta

allies of the local British oligarchy. The latter controlled the affairs of the settlement, a gray zone that was not formally ruled by a Western power. The highest echelons of Baghdadi Jews sought acceptance within Shanghai's British society, and social relations with Chinese were usually confined to dealing with servants.

RUSSIAN JEWS

Toward the beginning of the twentieth century, the establishment of a Russian Jewish community in the northeastern city of Harbin, the main center of the Russian-built Chinese Eastern Railway, opened a new phase of Jewish presence in China. In Harbin and in other stations of the Chinese Eastern Railway, which were all under Russian control, Jews enjoyed better rights than in Russia, thus making residence in remote places such as Manzhouli, Hengdaohezi, and Qiqihar attractive. The Jewish population of Harbin increased further due to the presence of demobilized soldiers from the Russo-Japanese War (1904–1905), and by refugees from brutal pogroms that took place between 1905 and 1907. The arrival of Jews fleeing the Bolshevik Revolution of 1917 brought a new wave of destitute refugees. The Manchurian city of Mukden (Shenyang) also hosted a community of Russian Jews; smaller groups resided in Port Arthur (Lüshun) and Dairen (Dalian). At its peak, the Russian Jewish population of Harbin was around 13,000, but numbers decreased dramatically after the Japanese occupation of Manchuria in 1931.

From Harbin, Russian Jews headed south to the treaty ports of Tianjin and Shanghai. As many as five hundred to six hundred Russian families resided in Tianjin at the beginning of the 1920s, while about two thousand Jews joined the newly founded Shanghai Ashkenazi Association in Shanghai in 1932.

Russian Jewish communities in China enjoyed a vibrant cultural and social life characterized by the publishing of newspapers and the establishment of clubs and Zionist groups. One should not generalize the economic status of Russian Jews in China. A handful were wealthy entrepreneurs in Harbin; many more had small businesses or were employed in offices in various positions. A large share of the population was extremely poor and had difficulties making ends meet. Most important, Russian Jews had to endure the brand of anti-Semitism that was brought to China by White Russians, though the Chinese did not show any form of prejudice toward them. In Shanghai, relations with Baghdadi Jews were marred by misunderstandings because the two communities spoke different languages, occupied different economic positions, and held distinct cultural traditions.

WORLD WAR II

The final chapter of Jewish migration to China started in 1938 when central and eastern European Jews flocked to the open port of Shanghai trying to escape Nazi persecution. In the following four years, fifteen to eighteen thousand

SILAS AARON HARDOON

Silas Aaron Hardoon (1851–1931) reputedly the wealthiest foreigner in East Asia, was typical of Jews who immigrated to Bombay in the mid-nineteenth century in search of commercial opportunities. He was an employee of Sassoon enterprises in Hong Kong (1870–1874) and in the International Settlement of Shanghai. Although he had no formal education, his exceptional business acumen enabled him to become a partner and manager of E. D. Sassoon & Company (1890–1911).

Hardoon branched out independently into various commercial ventures and became "respected for his uncanny foresight, his grasp of the fundamentals of the property business, and his intimate knowledge of China" (*Israel's Messenger*, July 3, 1931). When he died, his estate, which included most of the prestigious sites in the foreign concession of Shanghai, was worth about US $150 million.

The *Shanghai Evening Post and Mercury* described Hardoon as an individualist and "a symbol of the white man's position in the Far East—a blend of all faiths and hopes, a talented man who lived his life in an exotic setting as he thought best" (June 23, 1931). In sharp contrast to his Baghdadi peers, he was the only prominent foreign businessman to have close ties with Chinese society and politicians, enjoying "the complete confidence of the men who hold China's reins of government" (*Israel's Messenger*, February 4, 1927).

Hardoon married Luo Jialing (Liza Roos, 1864–1941), a Eurasian disciple of Huang Zongyang, the celebrated Buddhist monk. They had no children, but adopted eleven of European extraction, whom they brought up as Jews, and five Chinese. They lived in a large pagoda home, and their forty-acre Aili Gardens housed a Buddhist monastery and a college attended by Chinese intellectuals. He financed the publication of over 8,000 volumes of the Buddhist Tripitaka Canon for distribution to universities worldwide.

Hardoon's friendships included influential members of various factions in the warlord politics of the 1920s. He regarded China as his home and contributed large sums to preserve its cultural heritage for the benefit of the Chinese people. He was awarded twelve decorations, including the highest honor that the Chinese government ever bestowed upon a foreigner.

Hardoon sat on the councils of both the French Concession (1892–1901) and the International Settlement (1900–1903). Nonetheless, the Shanghai Municipal Police were suspicious of his involvement with Chinese political figures and regarded Mrs. Hardoon as a great intriguer, noting that they both expressed anti-British views. Such views notwithstanding, Hardoon generously supplied food and accommodation to the first units of the British Defence Forces in 1927 and housed the British Military Hospital in his garden.

The Hardoons maintained links with the Jewish community and supported Jewish organizations. In 1927 they donated the funds to construct the monumental Beth Aharon Synagogue, built at the "entire expense of Mrs. S. A. Hardoon of US $300,000" (*Israel's Messenger*, July 17, 1927). In a little over a decade, it was used to house some 250 students of the Mir Yeshiva who escaped from German-occupied Poland.

Hardoon was buried in his garden. His funeral, which appeared to be more Chinese than Jewish, was attended by about 2,000 mourners, including Daoist and Buddhist monks, Chinese intellectuals, and Jewish officials, each group engaging in their own funeral rites. Hardoon left his entire fortune to his wife. His relatives disputed the will in a sensational legal battle in Her Britannic Majesty's Supreme Court for China. In February 1933 the judge decided that his wife should inherit his whole fortune.

BIBLIOGRAPHY

Betta, Chiara. Myth and Memory: Chinese Portrayal of Silas Aaron Hardoon, Luo Jialing, and the Aili Garden between 1924 and 1995. In *Jews in China: From Kaifeng to Shanghai*, ed. Roman Malek, 275–400. Nettetal, Germany: Steyler Verlag, 2000.

Betta, Chiara. Silas Aaron Hardoon and Cross-Cultural Adaptation in Shanghai. In *The Jews of China*, vol. 2: *Sourcebook and Research Guide*, ed. Jonathan Goldstein, 216–230. Armonk, NY: Sharpe, 1998.

Israel's Messenger. Shanghai: Shanghai Zionist Association. A journal of Baghdadi Jews in Shanghai, published between 22 April, 1904, and 17 October, 1941.

Meyer, Maisie J. *From the Rivers of Babylon to the Whangpoo: A Century of Sephardi Jewish Life in Shanghai*. Lanham, MD: *University Press of America*, 2003. See especially pp. 98–110.

Maisie J. Meyer

Jewish refugees examining postings of concentration camp survivors, Shanghai, 1946. *After the British victories in the Opium Wars, Jewish merchant families from Baghdad established a commercial presence in the port cities of Shanghai and Hong Kong. During World War II, persecuted Russian and European Jews joined this community, with most departing for other countries after the founding of the People's Republic of China.* © ARTHUR ROTHSTEIN/CORBIS

Jews managed to reach the city, mainly by sea, though a minority took the overland route via the Soviet Union. During their stay in Shanghai, refugees were helped by the existing Sephardi and Ashkenazi communities and by an umbrella of Jewish associations that provided them with much-needed financial and logistical assistance. Daily survival strongly depended on the degree of inventiveness of individual refugees and their families as much as on the support they could secure from coreligionists.

In December 1941 the Japanese occupation of Shanghai's International Settlement changed dramatically the lives of many Jews residing in the city. Baghdadi Jews who held British passports were forced to live in enemy alien detention camps together with other British passport holders. Two years later, European Jewish refugees were virtually interned by the Japanese in the Hongkou district, where they endured extremely harsh living conditions alongside destitute Chinese. Notwithstanding the difficulties, most managed to survive until the end of the war. Russian Jews, who were either stateless or held Soviet passports, remained free.

JEWS IN THE PEOPLE'S REPUBLIC

Following the foundation of the People's Republic of China in 1949, the great majority of Jews residing in China found a new life in a number of countries; a tiny number of Russian Jews stayed behind in Shanghai and Harbin. Only the Jewish community of Hong Kong remained active. Hong Kong is still a thriving center of Jewish life in East Asia, and new communities have recently taken shape in mainland China. Most significantly, former Jewish sites are routinely visited by tourists, thus keeping alive the memory of Jewish presence in the country over the centuries.

SEE ALSO *Harbin; Shanghai.*

BIBLIOGRAPHY

Betta, Chiara. The Baghdadi Jewish Diaspora in Shanghai: Community, Commerce, and Identities. In *Sino-Judaica: Occasional Papers of the Sino-Judaic Institute*, Vol. 4, 81–104. Menlo Park, CA: Sino-Judaic Institute, 2003.

Betta, Chiara. From Orientals to Imagined Britons: Baghdadi Jews in Shanghai. *Modern Asian Studies* 37, 4 (2003): 999–1024.

Finnane, Antonia. *Far from Where? Jewish Journeys from Shanghai to Australia.* Carleton, Victoria, Australia: Melbourne University Press, 1999.

Heppner, Ernest. *Shanghai Refuge: A Memoir of the World War II Jewish Ghetto.* Lincoln: University of Nebraska Press, 1993.

Kranzler, David. *Japanese, Nazis, and Jews: The Jewish Refugee Community of Shanghai,* 1938–1945. New York: Yeshiva University Press, 1976.

Leslie, Donald Daniel. *The Survival of the Chinese Jews: The Jewish Community of K'aifeng.* Leiden, Netherlands: Brill, 1972.

Meyer, Maisie J. *From the Rivers of Babylon to the Whangpoo: A Century of Sephardi Jewish Life in Shanghai.* Lanham, MD: University Press of America, 2003.

Ristaino, Reynders Marcia. *Port of Last Resort: The Diaspora Communities of Shanghai.* Stanford, CA: *Stanford University Press*, 2001.

Chiara Betta

JIA PINGWA
1952–

A resident of Xi'an, the capital city of Shaanxi Province in Northwest China, Jia Pingwa is a prolific producer of novels, novellas, short stories, essays, and an occasional poem. By 2008 he had published eleven novels; dozens of collections of short stories, novellas, and essays; and one book of poetry. The eleven novels are *Shangzhou* (1984), *Fuzao* (1988; translated as *Turbulence*), *Renshen* (Pregnancy, 1989), *Feidu* (The abandoned capital, also known as Defunct capital; 1993), *Baiye* (White nights, 1995), *Tumen* (Earth gate, 1996), *Gaolaozhuang* (Old Gao village, 1998), *Huainian lang* (Remembering wolves, 2000), *Bingxiang baogao* (Health reports, 2002), *Qinqiang* (Shaanxi opera, also known as Local accent, 2005), and *Gaoxing* (Happiness, 2007). Jia Pingwa commands such an enormous readership in the Chinese-speaking world that many of his publications have numerous editions in China, Taiwan, and Hong Kong. His works have been translated into many languages, especially French and Japanese. However, to date, only his second novel *Turbulence* and earlier short stories are available in English.

Jia Pingwa was born and grew up in a village called Dihua in the prefecture of Shangzhou less than 130 miles from Xi'an to the southeast. At the age of nineteen he went to university in Xi'an and has been living there since. He regards both Shangzhou and Xi'an as his native places and accords them a central role in his writings, not only as settings for his narratives but also as the focus of narratives. His ethnographic depiction of native place reveals his conviction that through his literary descriptions of Shaanxi he is creating a more "authentic China."

Signaling the arrival of root-searching literature with his novella *Shangzhou sanlu* (Three records of Shangzhou) in the early 1980s, Jia Pingwa is regarded as one of the pioneers of this literary trend. Throughout his literary career, he has devoted great efforts to reviving Chinese narrative traditions, focusing on the structure of narrative flows and on the use of local language. He distances himself from China's major metropolitan centers, remaining deeply rooted in his local communities. From the mid-1990s, his novels have tended to expose the degeneration of local cultural traditions as a result of China's rapid urbanization and industrialization at the expense of rural communities. His 2005 novel *Qinqiang*, which features the performance, reception, and decline of Shaanxi opera, in 2006 won the inaugural *Dream of the Red Chamber* prize, the most prestigious literary prize in the Chinese-speaking world, administered in Hong Kong.

To date, Jia Pingwa's best known and most popular novel is *Feidu*. It sold half a million copies within six months of its publication, but the heated national debates that it generated about its subject matter of intellectual disillusionment and its explicit sexual descriptions led to a government ban on the novel. With no grand historical moments or heart-breaking tragedy, *Feidu* details the daily life and love affairs of a writer named Zhuang Zhidie, whose sex life and involvement in a literary lawsuit provide the only plot complications. Short, ordinary-looking, and middle-aged, Zhuang, who is more of a literatus than a contemporary writer, finds life meaningless in the fictional city of Xijing, which is recognizably Xi'an. Despite the ban, pirated copies of the book are still readily available in China.

SEE ALSO *Root-Searching Literature.*

BIBLIOGRAPHY

Hu Heqing. *Lingdi de mianxiang* [Affectionate thoughts in the land of the spirits]. Beijing: Xuelin, 1994.

Lai Daren. *Hungui hechu: Jia Pingwa lun* [Where can the soul settle? On Jia Pingwa]. Beijing: Huaxia, 2000.

Lu, Sheldon H. *China, Transnational Visuality, Global Postmodernity.* Stanford, CA: Stanford University Press, 2001. See especially pp. 239–259.

MCLC Resource Center. http://mclc.osu.edu/rc/secbib2.htm#J Bibliographic information.

Rojas, Carlos. Flies' Eyes, Mural Remnants, and Jia Pingwa's Perverse Nostalgia. *Positions: East Asia Cultures Critique* 14, 3 (Winter 2006): 749–773.

Wang, Yiyan. *Narrating China: Jia Pingwa and His Fictional World.* London: Routledge, 2006.

Yiyan Wang

JIANG JIESHI

SEE *Chiang Kai-shek (Jiang Jieshi).*

JIANG ZEMIN

1926–

Jiang Zemin, general secretary of the Chinese Communist Party (1989–2002) and president of China (1993–2003), entered China's top leadership as neither a founder of the country nor a military hero. When he became general secretary of the party in the wake of the 1989 Tiananmen incident, China was in crisis: Political divisions, economic stagnation, and international isolation all posed severe challenges. In the following decade and beyond, Jiang presided over a period of unprecedented rapid growth. People's living standards improved, and China's international status rose. Yet political reforms were very limited, and corruption remained rampant. Jiang's endorsement of China's entry into the World Trade Organization in 2001 ensured China's embrace of economic globalization, and market reforms no longer encountered severe ideological and political resistance.

EARLY POLITICAL ORIENTATION

Jiang Zemin was born in Yangzhou on August 17, 1926. The Jiang family was respectable, even honored, in Yangzhou, a prosperous city at the junction of the Grand Canal and the Yangzi River. Jiang described his youth as follows:

> The time I was studying in middle school and in university was precisely the time when the Communist Party was leading the Chinese people toward the climax of the national democratic revolution. I accepted Marxism at that time, joined the Party, and took part in the struggle led by the Party to oppose the aggression of Japanese fascists and the Kuomintang reactionary rule. I take pride in and feel happy about the political faith and the road of life I have chosen. (Kuhn 2004, p. 559)

It has been suggested that Jiang's value system, developed gradually throughout his entire career, has four levels: at the foundation, Chinese pride and patriotism, as well as Chinese values and culture; at the next level, economic development or China's modernization; at the third level, Communist Party leadership, that is, Leninism and the rejection of democracy; and at the fourth level, socialism and communism, including Jiang's "Three Represents" ideas (Kuhn 2004, p. 559).

Jiang traveled abroad for the first time when he was twenty-eight, after completing his education of electrical engineering at Shanghai Jiaotong University. The radical Maoist movements in the 1950s brought Jiang hardship but not persecution (in contrast to Zhu Rongji). During the anti-rightist campaign of the 1950s, Jiang imposed sanctions rather than suffering from them. During the Cultural Revolution of the 1960s, he was basically sidelined.

Jiang's technocrat background made him a beneficiary of China's economic reforms and the country's opening to the outside world beginning in late 1978. He moved from the Ministry of First Machine-Building to become vice chairman and party secretary of two new commissions in the State Council in charge of import-export and foreign investment. In these positions, Jiang became heavily involved in the establishment of the special economic zones. He then was promoted to the position of first vice minister and party secretary of the Ministry of Electronics Industry, where he concluded one of China's first joint ventures, with the American computer company Hewlett-Packard.

POLITICAL PATRONS

When the term of office for Shanghai mayor Wang Daohan (1915–2005), Jiang's patron, was due to expire in 1985, Jiang was strongly recommended by Wang to succeed him. Jiang had also won Premier Zhao Ziyang's support after Jiang impressed Zhao with his ideas concerning the American futurist Alvin Toffler and the "Third Wave" of industrial development centered on computers. As mayor and party secretary of Shanghai, Jiang was able to attract the attention of the central leadership, which accorded top priority to economic development; Jiang's credentials as an economic reformer were firmly established.

According to many sources, Li Xiannian (1909–1992) and Bo Yibo (1908–2007), two of the party elders in the late 1980s, were instrumental in Deng Xiaoping's decision to appoint Jiang Zemin to replace Zhao Ziyang as general secretary of the party at the end of May 1989 in the midst of the pro-democracy demonstrations. Chen Yun (1905–1995) also accepted the proposal. This appointment paved the way for Jiang to stamp his mark on China and Chinese history. The Jiang era, however, did not truly begin until 1995, when Deng Xiaoping's health had deteriorated to the point that he could no longer rein Jiang in.

Former president Jiang Zemin appearing before the 17th National Congress of the Communist Party of China, Beijing, October 15, 2007. *As president at the turn of the twenty-first century, Jiang Zemin continued Deng Xiaoping's modernization of China's economic, political, and legal systems. The central government led by Jiang encouraged entrepreneurs, began allowing limited debate within the Communist Party, and promoted a coherent body of laws to guide the country.* © MICHAEL REYNOLDS/EPA/CORBIS

"THREE REPRESENTS"

The theory of "Three Represents" was a bold attempt by the Chinese Communist Party (CCP) to ensure the political organization's relevance in the twenty-first century. Collectively put together in the late 1990s by party leaders and theorists, including President Jiang Zemin and former Fudan University professor Wang Huning, the "Three Represents" says that the party of more than seventy-two million members must "always represent the requirements of the development of China's advanced productive forces, the orientation of the development of China's advanced culture, and the fundamental interests of the overwhelming majority of the people in China." The theory was enshrined in the CCP Charter at the Sixteenth Congress in November 2002.

While both Chinese and foreigners have fretted that the clumsily worded "Three Represents" theory is little more than Communist orthodoxy with Chinese characteristics, the much-cited mantra has practical significance. It provides the theoretical justification for the CCP to open its doors to members of the "new classes," including private businessmen, who were demonized as exploiters by Karl Marx (1818–1883) and Friedrich Engels (1820–1895). As Jiang put it in a landmark speech commemorating the eightieth birthday of the CCP in 2001, it is necessary to "accept those outstanding elements from other sectors of society who have subscribed to the party's program and constitution." From the Sixteenth Congress onward, approximately two dozen cadres with experience in state-controlled enterprises—including those listed on the Chinese stock market—have been inducted into the CCP Central Committee or appointed to ministerial-level positions. More owners of private companies have been inducted into the Chinese People's Political Consultative Conference; a sizeable number of these "red capitalists" have also become top administrators in villages, towns, and townships.

"Three Represents" also marks the CCP's formal goodbye to class struggle as it metamorphoses into a *quanmindang* or "party for all the people," and not just the proletariat "elite." The theory has in effect relegated peasants and workers—the CCP's traditional pillars of support—to the sidelines. Therefore, the "Three Represents" has been bitterly attacked by remnant Maoists and traditionalist cadres.

The "scientific theory of development" as well as the "Harmonious Society"—key slogans of Jiang's successors Hu Jintao and Wen Jiabao—could be seen, therefore, as an effort to reassure peasants, migrant workers, and other disadvantaged sectors that they would not be left behind in an increasingly polarized society. The future of China—especially the CCP's ability to maintain the proverbial mandate of heaven—could hinge on how well Beijing can resolve growing contradictions among the classes.

BIBLIOGRAPHY

Bao Tong. Three Represents: Marking the End of an Era. *Far Eastern Economic Review*, September 5, 2002.

Fewsmith, Joseph. Studying the Three Represents. *China Leadership Monitor* 8 (Fall 2003): 1–11. http://media.hoover.org/documents/clm8_jf.pdf

Lam, Willy Wo-Lap. *Chinese Politics in the Hu Jintao Era: New Leaders, New Challenges*. Armonk, NY: Sharpe, 2006.

Willy Wo-Lap Lam

Most China watchers agree that Jiang was generally successful in building bridges to both the left and the right. Given his neoconservative political views, he could enlist the support of leftists. At the same time, Jiang tried to repair ties with the followers of Hu Yaobang, including the so-called Communist Youth League Faction. In 1992 Jiang visited Hu's grave in Jiangxi Province.

Jiang owed his rise to the Shanghai Faction, a solid group of loyal, pragmatic operators with cosmopolitan exposure. Among the elders, Jiang's most important adviser was Wang Daohan. Among the younger generation, Zeng Qinghong, Wu Bangguo, Huang Ju, Zeng Peiyan, and Xu Kuangdi were the more prominent. The first three all became members of the Standing Committee of the Politburo in 2002.

To fill the ideological vacuum in his era, Jiang exploited nationalism, patriotism and even Confucianism, and he tried to revive traditional Marxist values. The sixth plenum of the Central Committee of October 1996 passed the "Resolution on the Construction of Socialist Spiritual Civilization." The spiritual civilization document appealed to the idea of "developing the tradition of the motherland and its cultural quintessence" (Lam 1999, pp. 51–52). In a speech marking the one-hundredth birthdays of the great Beijing opera stars Mei Lanfang (1894–1961) and Zhou Xinfang (1895–1975), Jiang boasted that "the Chinese race is one that has a five-thousand-year tradition of splendid history and culture as well as tremendous life force and creativity." Although cadres and ordinary Chinese went through the motions, it became clear that the spiritual civilization campaign was not sustainable.

POLITICAL AND ECONOMIC PROGRAMS

By early 1997, Jiang had made a new commitment to reforming the political structure, although given his political conservatism, he had no intention of compromising the party's monopoly of political power. He was more interested in establishing a separation between government and business, and, at the initial stage, converting the economic ministries to state corporations. Later, he tried to promote the ideal of "running the country according to law," and the National People's Congress was given more authority to draft laws.

In the economic arena, Jiang argued that while public ownership should remain the dominant sector of the economy, it could manifest itself in many forms. Joint-stock or shareholding companies were recognized as falling within the domain of public ownership, and the shareholding system was perceived as the key to solving the problems of state-owned enterprises.

Jiang was never an ideologue, though he was very concerned with his historical status as a Chinese Communist leader. He attempted to integrate Communist objectives, free-market methods, and traditional Chinese values in a way that worked for China's modernization and the maintenance of one-party rule in China. His "Three Represents" theory made the party more inclusive and classless by reaching out to innovators in science and business. Jiang considered that entrepreneurs and business executives were an important part of the most advanced productive forces in China at this stage of development; and they had to be involved in the expansion of the CCP's base of support. He retained communism's unifying name and its ultimate goal, but modernized its economic structures and social rules. He was willing to promote intraparty democracy though, with more checks-and-balances mechanisms.

In foreign policy, Jiang pursued security and stability and promoted national interest after the Tiananmen incident. He resisted American pressure and yet accorded good relations with the United States a high priority so that China could concentrate on modernization. He also managed to redefine China's Taiwan policy from one of confrontation in the mid-1990s to economic integration by 2004.

Jiang Zemin guided China through a significant transformation: from the turmoil and crackdown in Tiananmen Square to a primary engine of global economic growth. He made governance in China more normal. But, unfortunately, he was not a much admired and respected leader; his pomp and showmanship did not endear him to the intellectuals; his administration was in a period when appeal of the party and its official ideology had been in decline; and he had to absorb the blame for the spread of corruption and the widening of the gap between the rich and poor. History might perhaps be kinder to him.

SEE ALSO *Chinese Marxism: Postrevolutionary Marxism other than Mao Zedong Thought; Communist Party; Deng Xiaoping; Foreign Policy Frameworks and Theories: Overview.*

BIBLIOGRAPHY

Gilley, Bruce. *Tiger on the Brink: Jiang Zemin and China's New Elite*. Berkeley: University of California Press, 1998.

Kuhn, Robert Lawrence. *The Man Who Changed China: The Life and Legacy of Jiang Zemin*. New York: Crown, 2004.

Lin Heli (Willy Wo-Lap Lam). *The Era of Jiang Zemin*. Singapore and New York: Prentice Hall, 1999.

Weng Jieming, et al., eds. *Yu zongshuji tanxin* [A heart-to-heart talk with the general secretary]. Beijing: China Social Sciences Press, 1996.

Zheng Yushuo (Joseph Y. S. Cheng), ed. *China in the Post-Deng Era*. Hong Kong: Chinese University Press, 1998.

Joseph Y. S. Cheng (Zheng Yushuo)

JIANGSU

Jiangsu, one of China's smaller provinces in area, is also more densely populated, productive, and wealthy than most others. Formed by the alluvial deposits of China's longest river, the Yangzi, and the Huai River to the north, most of Jiangsu is exceedingly flat and less than 50 meters above sea level. South of the Huai, annual rainfall averages about 1,140 millimeters (45 inches) and the growing season is about nine months long, making the major part of Jiangsu especially well suited for rice agriculture. By contrast, north of the Huai—at Jiangsu's northern border with Shandong Province—annual rainfall averages about 910 millimeters (36 inches) and the growing season lasts eight months. This area at the southern edge of the North China Plain, part of a larger region described by Pearl Buck in *The Good Earth,* is better suited for dryland crops such as wheat and *gaoliang* (sorghum). Administrative boundaries during the Qing dynasty (1644–1912) reflected these differences: The region north of the Yangzi, sometimes called Subei or "northern Jiangsu," was administered from Nanjing. In addition to the poor area north of the Huai, this region can be further subdivided into the area of coastal salt pans, an inland region with saline soils suited for cotton production, and a well-irrigated western region where rice is grown. The region south of the Yangzi, part of a broader region called Jiangnan

JIANGSU

Capital city: Nanjing
Largest cities (population): Nanjing (6,070,000 [2006]), Suzhou, Wuxi
Area: 102,600 sq. km. (39,600 sq. mi.)
Population: 75,500,000 (2006)
Demographics: Han, 99.6%; Hui, 0.2%
GDP: 2.56 trillion yuan (2007)
Famous sites: Mount Zijin (Purple Mountain), Sun Yat-sen Mausoleum, Ming Xiaoling Mausoleum, Lake Xuanwu, Jiming Temple, Nanjing Massacre Memorial, Nanjing Confucius Temple, Classical Gardens of Suzhou, Hanshan Temple (Cold Mountain Temple), Huqiu Tower, Grand Buddha at Ling Shan (world's tallest Buddha statue), Chaotian Palace, Tianning Temple Pagoda

(literally, "south of the river"), was administered from Suzhou, a city located between Nanjing and Shanghai in the Yangzi Delta. In its imperial heyday, Suzhou was a city of superlatives: largest, richest, most influential, most advanced. While Shanghai and Nanjing now contend for these accolades, the Jiangnan region as a whole is one of contemporary China's most important.

ECONOMY AND GOVERNMENT

Jiangsu's preeminence results from twenty-first century policies and opportunities that build on centuries of agricultural, commercial, and industrial development. By the sixth century CE, Jiangsu's peasants had made it the most productive grain-producing area in China, especially in rice production. In this "land of water," rice paddies were irrigated, and a network of towns and villages was connected by inexpensive water transport. Lyman P. Van Slyke has written of the Jiangnan region: "It is a rich, low-lying alluvial plain with many lakes and a few low hills, almost as much water as land. Virtually all cities and towns are connected by a dense network of streams and canals; from Shanghai one can go in any inland direction for at least a hundred miles by water" (1988, p. 24).

Commercial factors, however, contributed to the transformation of this region in late imperial times into a major cotton-producing and textile-manufacturing region. In 1860 almost half of China's peasant households wove cotton for themselves (and most of these households raised their own cotton), but Jiangsu's peasants produced for national and international markets. Much of this raw cotton, grown throughout Jiangnan, but especially in the areas near Shanghai, was spun into yarn and woven into cloth by Jiangsu's peasant women and children. With soil and climatic conditions perfectly suited for these tasks, Jiangsu's labor force could be productive through the year. Able to buy rice shipped to Jiangsu from Middle Yangzi provinces such as Hunan, this crucial household handicraft industry kept individual households economically viable even with scare land resources, and, in the aggregate, made Jiangsu very wealthy.

A measure of this economic importance can be seen in imperial land-tax figures. In 1908 Jiangsu contributed about 15 percent of the value of the total land tax collected; 75 percent of this provincial tax was collected from southern Jiangsu. In addition to this disproportionate burden, Jiangsu was one of eight provinces responsible for the "tribute grain" system that kept Beijing's elite fed. Again, this special tax burden fell heavily on the peasants of Jiangsu, especially those in the region near Shanghai, which was responsible for about 33 percent of the total national quota. In the 1850s, this region of rice and cotton-production in southeastern Jiangsu, with an area of about 10,000 square kilometers (about 4,000 square miles), had a population of ten million persons (nearly 2 percent of China's population).

This tribute grain was transported from Jiangsu to Beijing along the Grand Canal until the mid-nineteenth century, when the course of the Yellow River, whose waters were important for the functioning of the Grand Canal, shifted from its intersection with the Grand Canal just north of Jiangsu to a course some 400 kilometers to the north. The southern half of the Grand Canal, however, continued to function and provided an important north-south communication artery that passed through Yangzhou, just north of the Yangzi River, and Suzhou, just south, before continuing on to its terminus at Hangzhou in Zhejiang Province.

The Qing government delegated most regional responsibilities to provincial officials, but there were three crucial functions whose transprovincial nature required direct metropolitan-level management. Each of these functions involved Jiangsu: tribute grain, the Yellow River Conservancy, and the salt monopoly. The last of these, salt, intersects with Jiangsu's history in significant ways. There are three main sources of salt in China, and the eastern seaboard of Jiangsu, perfectly suited for salt production, was the most important. The Qing dynasty administered its salt monopoly, which generated significant revenues, through a licensing and sublicensing system that depended on merchant initiative and leadership. The center of this lucrative trade for the Yangzi provinces

was Yangzhou, whose salt merchants became famous for their wealth and lavish lifestyles in the eighteenth century.

Another example of Jiangsu's importance to imperial Beijing and to China can be found in the silk industry, which was centered in the southern Jiangsu districts near Lake Tai (Taihu). As with cotton, this household handicraft industry helped make it possible for Jiangsu to support a population in excess of what the land itself could feed. Peasant households collected mulberry leaves, fed and raised silkworms, and reeled silk, which was then shipped to Suzhou for weaving. The imperial court stationed a high-level official in Suzhou to supervise its silk orders, but like Jiangxi's porcelain, most silk was produced for the market. Suzhou City became China's most important silk-weaving and cotton-processing center by the early nineteenth century, when its population may have reached as high as one million persons.

The industry of Jiangsu's peasants was matched by the renown of its scholars, whose accomplishments were extraordinary. After every imperial administration of the triennial civil service examination for the *jinshi* degree in Beijing, the top-ranked scholar was named. Of these celebrated men, 18 percent came from one of the three counties administered from Suzhou. Men who held the degree, a prerequisite for high-level government service, came disproportionately from Jiangsu. Of the approximately 25,000 men who won this coveted degree in the Qing, about 4,000 came from Jiangsu and nearby Anhui. Six hundred *jinshi* degrees, or

Traditional houses along a canal in Suzhou, Jiangsu province. *A coastal province on the Yellow Sea, Jiangsu features a large network of waterways which have fostered economic wealth for centuries. Used for trade as well as agriculture, Jiangsu's system of canals transverse many cities in the southern portion of the province, such as the ancient city of Suzhou, pictured in the above photo.* © TONY WALTHAM/ROBERT HARDING WORLD IMAGERY/CORBIS

2.4 percent of the national total, were awarded to Suzhou men alone. There were entire provinces that did not fare as well as the men from Suzhou. (The lifestyles of the most successful of these men can be imagined today as one tours the nine scholarly gardens in Suzhou that have been designated since 1996 as UNESCO World Heritage sites.)

IMPACT OF THE WEST

It is not surprising, then, that Western commercial interests sought to establish a presence in the Lower Yangzi region as early as the eighteenth century. But it was not until British warships threatened Nanjing itself that China agreed to open this region to Western merchants. The Treaty of Nanjing (1842) established the small administrative and trading center of Shanghai as one of China's first five "treaty ports." In 1852 Shanghai's population was estimated at 500,000; by 1910 the population had increased to 1,000,000. (The devastation in Suzhou wrought by the mid-nineteenth-century Taiping Uprising had reduced its population drastically; by 1895 Suzhou's population was estimated to have recovered to about 500,000 persons.) Attracting Westerners from around the world, and Chinese from many parts of China, especially Guangdong, nearby Zhejiang, and other parts of Jiangsu, especially the Subei region, this city of immigrants surpassed both Suzhou and the old imperial capital of Nanjing in importance. The presence of Westerners in Shanghai contributed to the successful defense of the city from Taiping forces that had conquered both Nanjing in 1853 and Suzhou in 1860. Western-style factory-based machine manufacturing was established in Shanghai, and Jiangsu's economy moved into a new phase. By 1894 modern-style silk and cotton textile manufacturing, along with shipbuilding and chemical production, to name a few of the products produced, employed more than 36,000 factory workers in Shanghai or almost half of the number of factory workers in all of China. This industrialization continued in the twentieth century as peasants from other parts of China, and especially the Subei region of Jiangsu, became factory workers in the textile industries. While many Subei women filled these low-skilled, low-paying jobs, Subei men dominated the ranks of Shanghai's rickshaw pullers and dockworkers in the 1930s.

TRADE

It was in trade, however, that Shanghai made its greatest contribution to China's economy. With the only practical harbor near the mouth of the Yangzi, Shanghai is the gateway to and from the Yangzi River valley and its population, about a third of China's total population. By the 1920s, Shanghai's international trade statistics dominated its competitors in China and made it the eighth-largest port in the world in 1929. By 1949, when Shanghai's population topped five million persons, 60 percent of China's modern-style factories were located in the city. In the post-1949 period, Shanghai's light and heavy industries produced textiles, ships, iron and steel, tires, and pharmaceuticals, among other products. In 2004 Shanghai's factories processed crude oil and produced iron, steel, cement, synthetic fibers, fertilizers, motor vehicles, and cigarettes. It would not be until after 1949 that Nanjing began its own industrialization. Nanjing's industrial base, which is less diversified, produces cement, fertilizer, chemicals, and electronics. Given that Jiangsu is resource-poor (although it does possess iron and coal deposits), most of the raw materials for these products must be imported.

TRANSPORTATION

The "land of water," which connected Shanghai to an estimated 40,000 kilometers (about 25,000 miles) of waterways throughout the southern part of the Yangzi River Delta in imperial times and which in 1941 was part of a transportation system in Jiangsu, Zhejiang, and Anhui that involved 118,292 native boats and 459,178 men (in 2004 there were 26,832 kilometers [16,662 miles] of navigable waterways in Jiangsu, more than doubled from 1952), is now also home to the most modern forms of transportation, including a maglev high-speed train in Shanghai, high-speed rail links between Shanghai and Nanjing, and much improved north-south road and rail links. Jiangsu's highways have increased in length from 4,178 kilometers (2,595 miles) in 1952 to 86,067 kilometers (53,448 miles) in 2004, an increase that has been proportional between Shanghai (7,805 kilometers [4,847 miles] in 2004) and the rest of the province since 1978. In 1961 there were 6,500 enterprise-owned vehicles (mostly passenger vehicles and trucks) in Jiangsu. In 2004, when these totals also included vehicles owned by individuals, there were 3,640,400, of which 2,028,500 were in Shanghai. These totals included, in 2002, 1,246,000 enterprise and private vehicles, a figure that grew to 2,210,000 in 2004, of which 1,428,000 were in Shanghai.

The Yangzi was first bridged at Nanjing in 1969, and three new bridge complexes built downriver from Nanjing, opened since 1999, will help integrate Jiangsu. The Jiangyin Suspension Bridge (1999; 1,385 meters [1,510 yards]) was joined by the Runyang Suspension Bridge (2005; 1,490 meters [1,624 yards]) to the west at Yangzhou and the Sutong Bridge (2008; 1,088 meters [1,186 yards]) to the east at Nantong. The Jiangyin and Runyang bridges are among the longest suspension bridges in the world.

Jiangsu, a province with two distinct personalities defined by history and geography, is best known for its three famous cities south of the Yangzi and for Yangzhou to the north. It should not be surprising, given its administrative, fiscal, and economic importance, that Jiangsu should be viewed only for its cities or the important episodes or series of events in national history that took place there—the final stages of the Opium War, the Taiping Uprising, the constitutional and revolutionary agitations of the late Qing, the founding of the Chinese Communist Party in Shanghai, Chiang Kai-shek's Nationalist "Nanjing decade," Wang Jingwei's collaborationist government in Nanjing, the beginning of the Cultural Revolution, and the remarkable urban development of Shanghai in the twenty-first century. What is often overlooked is the centuries-old centrality of Jiangsu in China's national history, as well as the extraordinary contributions of Jiangsu's peasants, whose efforts transformed the landscape and whose productivity supported, and continues to support (in 2004 Jiangsu's rural workers—6 percent of the national total—produced 6 percent of China's grain and 8 percent of its cotton along with seed oil, sugar, fruit, and aquatic products) the nation.

SEE ALSO *Examination System, 1800–1905; Foreign Trade, 1800–1950; Foreign Trade since 1950; Handicrafts; Nanjing (Nanking); Opium Wars; Salt, 1800–1949; Shanghai; Silk since 1800; Suzhou; Textiles; Yangzhou.*

BIBLIOGRAPHY

Bergère, Marie-Claire. *The Golden Age of the Chinese Bourgeoisie, 1911–1937.* Trans. Janet Lloyd. Cambridge, U.K., and New York: Cambridge University Press, 1989.

Carroll, Peter J. *Between Heaven and Modernity: Reconstructing Suzhou, 1895–1937.* Stanford, CA: Stanford University Press, 2006.

Chen Yung-fa (Chen Yongfa). *Making Revolution: The Communist Movement in Eastern and Central China, 1937–1945.* Berkeley: University of California Press, 1986.

Cressey, George Babcock. *China's Geographic Foundations: A Survey of the Land and Its People.* New York and London: McGraw-Hill, 1934.

Elman, Benjamin A. *A Cultural History of Civil Examinations in Late Imperial China.* Berkeley: University of California Press, 2000.

Finnane, Antonia. *Speaking of Yangzhou: A Chinese City, 1550–1850.* Cambridge, MA: Harvard University Asia Center, 2004.

Goodman, Bryna. *Native Place, City, and Nation: Regional Networks and Identities in Shanghai, 1853–1937.* Berkeley: University of California Press, 1995.

Guojia Tongjiju Guomin Jingji Zonghe Tongjisi [Department of Comprehensive Statistics of the National Bureau of Statistics], comp. *Xin Zhongguo wushiwunian tongji ziliao huibian* [China compendium of statistics, 1949–2004]. Beijing: Zhongguo Tongji Chubanshe, 2005.

Honig, Emily. *Sisters and Strangers: Women in the Shanghai Cotton Mills, 1919–1949.* Stanford, CA: Stanford University Press, 1986.

Huang, Philip C. C. (Huang Zongzhi). *The Peasant Family and Rural Development in the Yangzi Delta, 1350–1988.* Stanford, CA: Stanford University Press, 1990.

Lipkin, Zwia. *Useless to the State: "Social Problems" and Social Engineering in Nationalist Nanjing, 1927–1937.* Cambridge, MA: Harvard University Asia Center, 2006.

Perry, Elizabeth J. *Shanghai on Strike: The Politics of Chinese Labor.* Stanford, CA: Stanford University Press, 1993.

Shao, Qin. *Culturing Modernity: The Nantong Model, 1890–1930.* Stanford, CA: Stanford University Press, 2004.

Twitchett, Denis, and John K. Fairbank, eds. *The Cambridge History of China.* Vols. 10–12. Cambridge, U.K.: Cambridge University Press, 1978–1983.

Van Slyke, Lyman P. *Yangtze: Nature, History, and the River.* Stanford, CA: Stanford Alumni Association, 1988.

Wang Yeh-chien (Wang Yejian). *Land Taxation in Imperial China, 1750–1911.* Cambridge, MA: Harvard University Press, 1973.

Roger R. Thompson

JIANGXI

Flowing from south Jiangxi north to China's largest lake, Poyang, which empties into China's longest river, the Yangzi (Chang), the Gan River and its tributaries define the geographical reach of the strategically important south China province of Jiangxi. Once these waterways were connected in the early seventh century to North China via the Grand Canal, Jiangxi was at the crossroads of empire. People, goods, and information traversed Jiangxi on the way to Guangzhou (Canton) in the south, and they skirted the part of Jiangxi's northern boundary defined by the Yangzi River on east-west riverine trips along that great waterway. Jiangxi was at the center of thousands of miles of waterways ramifying throughout the Chinese empire. Jiangxi's Gan River tributaries reached every corner of the province.

Although the province is rimmed by mountain ranges on its western border with Hunan, its southern border with Guangdong, and its eastern border with Fujian, passes traversed these geographical obstacles and made it both possible and feasible for short land routes, sometimes paved with granite slabs, to connect Jiangxi's waterways with its neighbors' rivers, including Anhui and Zhejiang to Jiangxi's northeast.

JIANGXI IN HISTORY

This geographical situation, modified by human endeavor, is one reason why Jiangxi has played a significant role in history. The Taiping Rebellion, which ravaged parts of strategically located Jiangxi, was suppressed in part because Jiangxi's rich fiscal resources were diverted with Beijing's permission to Qing commanders in the field. In 1906 one of the most widespread rebellions against the Qing involved Jiangxi's peasants, workers, and miners. A large-scale workers' strike at the Anyuan coal mines in western Jiangxi in 1922 was an iconic moment in the history of the Chinese Communist Party (CCP). Jiangxi also figured in the some of the fiercest fighting of the Northern Expedition in fall 1926 as control of Nanchang, the provincial capital, and Jiujiang, its Yangzi River treaty port, was wrested from warlords. The collaboration of Mao Zedong and Zhu De in the west Jiangxi mountain fastness of Jinggangshan in 1928 presaged the pivotal role played by Jiangxi in the CCP's rural turn in the early 1930s. During the Jiangxi Soviet Period (1931–1934) the outlawed CCP, which at one point controlled thirty counties and three million persons, fought an increasingly desperate battle with Chiang Kai-shek, who developed his strategies from Nanchang, where Zeng Guofan also had been headquartered for a time as he battled the Taiping rebels in mid-nineteenth-century Jiangxi.

MODERN TRANSPORTATION

The demands and needs of modern war gave a special urgency to Chiang's effort to modernize Jiangxi's transportation grid—specifically, to create a road system that would allow men and materiel to be moved quickly and efficiently. By March 1934 almost 1,500 miles of paved roads had been built in Jiangxi; one highway bisected the Jiangxi Soviet, with its capital in the southeastern county seat of Ruijin, and others approached or skirted its boundaries. Chiang and his 800,000 troops encircled and economically strangled the Jiangxi Soviet in 1933 to 1934.

JIANGXI

Capital city: Nanchang
Largest cities (population): Nanchang (4,840,000 [2006]), Jiujiang, Ji'an
Area: 166,900 sq. km. (64,400 sq. mi.)
Population: 43,390,000 (2006)
Demographics: Han, 99.7%; She, 0.2%
GDP: CNY 547 billion (2006)
Famous sites: Mount Lushan, Lushan National Park, Donglin Temple, Mount Longhushan, Longhushan National Park

In addition to Jiangxi's waterways and modern road network, railroads were built that followed traditional trade routes. By 1949 Jiangxi's fledgling rail network included an east-west line in north Jiangxi connecting Nanchang with Zhejiang and Hunan Provinces, and the beginning of a north-south line that first connected Nanchang with the Yangzi port of Jiujiang. After 1949 this route reached Guangdong Province via Ganzhou, the major city in south Jiangxi. A route from Nanchang to Fujian was completed after 1949.

JIANGXI'S AGRARIAN ECONOMIES

Interconnected with its geography and history is Jiangxi's rich tradition of agriculture, industry, and commerce. Its subtropical climate allows a growing season that is year-round in the South and about 320 days in the North; it is has plentiful rainfall. In imperial times Jiangxi's peasants fed grain-deficient provinces, and its tribute rice could be conveyed to Beijing along the Grand Canal. About 35 percent of Jiangxi's 64,438 square miles is under cultivation, a figure that has almost doubled since 1949; by yield, grain crops predominate, with annual production figures as high as 16 to 17 million tons (*Xin Zhongguo wushi nian de Jiangxi,* pp. 42–45, "Table of Main Social and Economic Indicators for Jiangxi, 1949–1998").

Although rice is grown throughout Jiangxi, much of the production is focused in the central Jiangxi plain at the southern boundary of Lake Poyang and the lower valleys of the Gan River. Nanchang, Jiangxi's capital, is located in this alluvial plain. The rest of Jiangxi is characterized by hill country of 200 meters to 1,000 meters (656 feet to 3,281 feet) that lacks the level irrigated land needed for rice-paddy agriculture. Whereas 40 to 60 percent of land in alluvial Jiangxi can be devoted to paddy agriculture, only 5 to 20 percent of the total land surface in the highlands is suitable for rice agriculture. In northwestern Jiangxi, where the important Yangzi port of Jiujiang is located, the rugged uplands produce more wheat than rice. Northeastern Jiangxi, contiguous with Anhui and Zhejiang provinces, is hilly and mountainous, but its lowlands are densely populated and rice is the major crop. The porcelain center of Jingdezhen, located at a river crossing intersecting with trade routes to Zhejiang, Anhui, and Fujian, is its most famous city. Tea is grown in the uplands of this region, one of the most important in China for this commodity. (Tea is also cultivated in northwestern Jiangxi.) The middle reaches of the Gan River Valley in western Jiangxi that bisects Jiangxi on a north-south axis, with Ji'an its major city, is another rice-growing region. Rice is also grown in the other major region of Jiangxi, the hilly region in the Southeast, where Ganzhou is the regional center and most land is above 500 meters (1,640 feet). This region is also noted for its timber resources, including pine, cedar, and camphor, and wood products. Pitch, resin, and turpentine are produced here. In imperial times, and continuing into the twentieth century, small rafts of pine and cedar, which began journeys along the tributaries of the Gan River, eventually became parts of huge floating rafts, some almost as long as a football field, that ultimately reached the Yangzi.

In addition to rice, Jiangxi's farmers raise winter wheat in most regions; sweet potatoes are another important crop, as are other cereal crops such as millet, buckwheat, and sorghum (*gaoliang*). Important commercial crops and products in Jiangxi are cotton, oil-bearing crops including peanuts, rapeseeds, and sesame, sugarcane, jute and hemp, ramie, tobacco, fruits, meats, hogs, and aquatic products.

JIANGXI'S INDUSTRIES

Jiangxi's most famous industrial product is porcelain, produced in the northeastern Jiangxi town of Jingdezhen. With origins dating to at least the eleventh century, Jiangxi's "chinaware" was distributed throughout China, Asia, the Middle East, and Europe. The scale of production in late-imperial times, involving hundreds of thousands of workers, hundreds of kilns, and millions of pieces of porcelain ranging in quality from everyday to imperial, has prompted economic historians to characterize Jingdezhen's enterprises as one of the few large-scale handicraft industries in traditional China. Although Jingdezhen's industry was given prestige by virtue of its Ming and Qing dynasty-era contracts to supply the imperial househould, the demand for high-quality porcelain was not limited to the imperial court. Moreover, porcelain for everyday use was produced in huge quantities. At the height of production in the pre-1800 period, estimates of annual production range as high as 50 to 60 million pieces, less than 1 percent of which was produced for the court. Although severely affected by the Taiping rebels, who sacked Jingdezhen (which was located at a strategic communication nexus) and destroyed its imperial kilns, the porcelain industry quickly recovered in the post-Taiping era, beginning in 1866. The fall of its imperial patron in Beijing in 1912 did not end this industry, which survived during the Republican era and was revived further in the post-1949 period. State ownership made possible the capital-intensive modernization of the industry, which can now draw on advice from a research institute in Jingdezhen. Moreover, since 1983 the secrets of craftsmanship that were closely guarded within familial or village groups of artisans that survived into the 1950s are being passed on once again in a traditional master-apprentice relationship within the confines of modern state-owned enterprises. Provincial production figures have ranged as high as 600 million pieces annually in the post-1949 period. (*Xin Zhongguo wushi nian de Jiangxi*, 1999, p. 60.)

Before the early 1950s the range of other industrial products produced in Jiangxi was limited: yarn, cloth, paper,

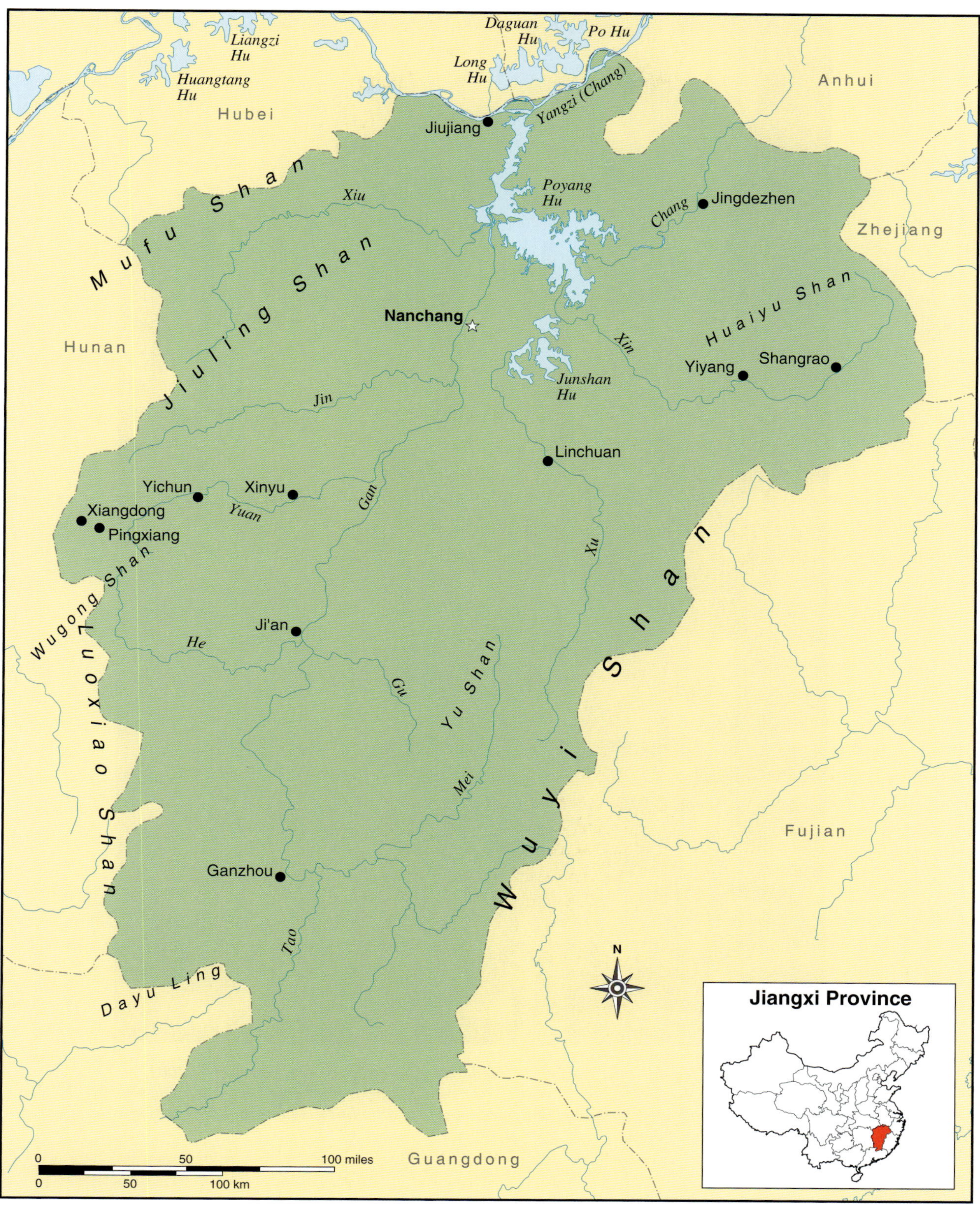
Jiangxi Province
Liangzi Hu
Huangtang Hu
Daguan Hu
Po Hu
Long Hu
Hubei
Anhui
Jiujiang
Yangzi (Chang)
Mufu Shan
Xiu
Poyang Hu
Chang
Jingdezhen
Zhejiang
Jiuling Shan
Nanchang
Huaiyu Shan
Hunan
Xin
Yiyang
Shangrao
Junshan Hu
Jin
Linchuan
Yichun
Xinyu
Gan
Yuan
Xiangdong
Pingxiang
Xu
Wugong Shan
Ji'an
He
Luoxiao Shan
Gu
Yu Shan
Wuyi Shan
Mei
Fujian
Ganzhou
Tao
Dayu Ling
N
Guangdong
0
50
100 miles
0
50
100 km

Local porcelain for sale at a market in Jingdezhen, Jiangxi province, January 7, 2001. *Considered one of the most notable cities in the province of Jiangxi, Jingdezhen is known throughout China for the manufacture of high quality porcelain objects, a tradition begun over 1,000 years ago.* © FRITZ HOFFMANN/CORBIS

matchsticks, sugar, cigarettes, alcoholic beverages, pig iron, coal, electricity, and timber products, often in small amounts. Since then the list has grown in scope and scale to include chemical fibers, watches, synthetic detergents, steel, rolled-steel final products, crude-oil processing, sulfuric acid, caustic soda, chemical fertilizer, chemical pesticides, chemical raw medicines, metal-cutting machines, motor vehicles, TVs, cameras, and cement. (*Xin Zhongguo wushi nian de Jiangxi*, 1999, pp. 60–63: "Table of Output of Major Industrial Products, 1949–1998.")

Jiangxi boasts significant coal deposits, including a major seam of coal 60 miles long that is west of the Gan River. A spur off this main seam at Anyuan was developed in the early twentieth century to supply the iron works at Wuhan in Hubei. Jiangxi's first railroad was constructed to transport this coal to the nearby Xiang River in Hunan for transshipment to Wuhan. In 1922, 13,000 miners and 1,000 railway workers at Anyuan engaged in a massive nonviolent strike, led in part by young members of the fledgling CCP, founded the previous year. Future leaders of the party, including Mao Zedong, Liu Shaoqi, and Li Lisan (1899–1867), saw in Anyuan's miners the industrial proletariat needed for the revolution.

JIANGXI UNDER THE PRC

Jiangxi's revolutionary heritage continued to influence national politics in post-1949 China. One of Mao Zedong's CCP allies in 1930s Jiangxi was the Sichuanese leader Deng Xiaoping, whose Hakka background provided affinities with this important subgroup of the overwhelming Han majority in Jiangxi (99% of the population). Young Deng was given administrative responsibilities for three counties at the southern edge of the Jiangxi Soviet, in the heart of Hakka-dominated territory. One of these counties was Xunwu, where Mao had investigated local conditions in May 1930 with a special emphasis on commerce and the economy.

Although the Communists were forced out of Jiangxi in 1934, these formative revolutionary experiences were not forgotten in the post-1949 period. During the Great Leap Forward a Nanchang-based Jiangxi Communist Labor University was established in 1958 and praised by Mao in 1961 for its work-study orientation. The Nanchang university and its branches, located in every prefecture and county in Jiangxi, combined study and production, with students, teachers, and staff working part-time in fields and factories affiliated with the university and its branches. By the end of the academic year 1979 to 1980, when it was reorganized as an agricultural college, the university had graduated more than 200,000 students.

The ethos of the university was a lived experience for Deng Xiaoping after he and some of his family were "evacuated" from Beijing to Jiangxi in October 1969 on the order of Lin Biao. Deng worked half days as a fitter in a tractor factory in central Jiangxi as he plotted his strategy to return to Beijing and power. Deng did not forget Jiangxi as he brought out from the archives and published in 1982, for the first time, Mao's *Report from Xunwu* (*Xunwu diaocha*). Using Mao's 1930 text as a way to underscore the importance of social investigation (one of the tasks required of the Labor University's faculty) and "seeking truth from facts," Deng used the young Mao to argue against the discredited older Mao of the 1960s and 1970s. Once again, Jiangxi played a critical role in China's national history. At the beginning of the twenty-first century, almost seventy years after the demise of the Jiangxi Soviet, state officials began promoting "red tourism" to revolutionary sites in an attempt, like Deng's, to legitimate the state, and to bring scarce resources to this still-poor area in southeastern Jiangxi.

Other, more conventional tourist destinations in Jiangxi include Lushan National Park, located in a mountainous area near Jiujiang, which was designated a UNESCO World Heritage Site in 1996. Located in this park is the Guling summer resort, which was a favorite mountain retreat of Westerners in pre-1949 China and also was used by Chiang Kai-shek and other high-ranking Nationalist leaders in 1928 to 1938.

SEE ALSO *Taiping Uprising.*

BIBLIOGRAPHY

Averill, Stephen C. Party, Society, and Local Elite in the Jiangxi Communist Movement. *Journal of Asian Studies* 46 (1987): 279–303.

Averill, Stephen C. *Revolution in the Highlands: China's Jinggangshan Base Area.* Preface and intro. by Joseph W. Esherick and Elizabeth J. Perry. Lanham, MD: Rowman and Littlefield, 2006.

Dillon, Michael. Transport and Marketing in the Development of the Jingdezhen Porcelain Industry during the Ming and Qing Dynasties. *Journal of the Economic and Social History of the Orient* 35 (1992): 278–290.

Mao Zedong. *Report from Xunwu.* Trans. and intro. by Roger R. Thompson. Stanford, CA: Stanford University Press, 1990.

Moll-Murata, Christine. Guilds and Apprenticeship in China and Europe: The Ceramics Industries of Jingdezhen and Delft. Paper presented at Technology and Human Capital Formation in the East and West, S. R. Epstein Memorial Conference, June 18–21, 2008. http://www.lse.ac.uk/collections/economicHistory/Epstein%20Memorial%20Conference/PAPER-MollMurata.pdf

Perry, Elizabeth J. Reclaiming the Chinese Revolution. *Journal of Asian Studies* 67 (2008): 1147–1164.

Polachek, James M. The Moral Economy of the Kiangsi Soviet (1928–1934). *Journal of Asian Studies* 42 (1983): 805–829.

Pong, David. The Income and Military Expenditure of Kiangsi Province in the Last Years (1860–1864) of the Taiping Rebellion. *Journal of Asian Studies* 26 (1966): 49–65.

Twitchett, Denis, and John K. Fairbank, eds. *The Cambridge History of China.* Vols. 10–15. Cambridge, U.K.: Cambridge University Press, 1978–1991.

Wei, William. *Counterrevolution in China: The Nationalists in Jiangxi during the Soviet Period.* Ann Arbor: University of Michigan Press, 1985.

Wright, Stanley. *Kiangsi Native Trade and Its Taxation.* [1920]. New York and London: Garland, 1980.

Xin Zhongguo wushi nian de Jiangxi [Fifty years of new China: Jiangxi]. Beijing: Zhongguo Tongji Chubanshe, 1999.

Roger R. Thompson

JILIN

Beginning in 1949 the new Communist government worked to fully integrate the former three provinces of Manchuria, including Jilin, as an inviolable part of China. The Japanese residents and military quickly were repatriated or taken off to the Siberian gulag. What remained of Manchukuo was the Japanese-built infrastructure, especially the mines, railroad, factories, and buildings of the modernist capital city called Xinjing (New Capital; Japanese: Shinkyō) erected at Changchun. Changchun regained its old name and the Japanese buildings were converted to hospitals, schools, and Chinese government offices.

In the first flush of their temporary occupation of Jilin in 1945, Soviet armies began dismantling and shipping back to the Soviet Union a great deal of Japanese modern industrial equipment. This included huge electric turbines from the Fengman Dam outside the city of Jilin.

The Communist Party plan for China's cities in the early 1950s was to transform them into centers of industrial production. Jilin's two major cities are Changchun and Jilin. Jilin already had considerable chemical industry started by the Japanese, so its transformation was fairly easy. Changchun presented a bigger challenge, with its Manchukuo national ministry buildings, broad avenues, and an extensive section of modern apartment houses and detached homes.

In 1951 Changchun was selected as the site for a major Soviet loan project in the form of the First Automobile Works (FAW). This replica of a Moscow truck factory became China's first trucks and automobiles producer. The plant produced 30,000 trucks annually when vehicles first came off the assembly lines in 1956. Its principal production were the 2- and 4-ton Jiefang (Liberation) trucks. Later in the 1950s Dongfeng (East Wind) sedans and Hongqi (Red Flag) limousines came into production for the Communist elite. These vehicles were used everywhere in China and remained in production until the mid-1980s. Changchun came to boast a number of other factories, including one for railway passenger cars and another for tractors, as well as many plants supplying parts to FAW. Beginning in 1988 FAW began joint ventures with Volkswagen and Audi, and by 2007 FAW boasted a huge new truck plant as well as a state-of-the-art joint-venture automobile plant with Volkswagen. New factories were under construction in Changchun and elsewhere in North China. FAW is one of the ten-largest corporations in China.

JILIN

Capital city: Changchun
Largest cities (population): Changchun (3,200,000 [2000]), Jilin City (4,300,000 [2000]), Liaoyuan
Area: 187,400 sq. km. (72,400 sq. mi.)
Population: 27,280,000 (2000)
Demographics: Han, 91%; Korean, 4%; Manchu, 4%; Mongol, 0.6%; Hui, 0.5%
GDP: CNY 427.5 billion (2006)
Famous sites: Goguryeo Tombs at Jian, Changbaishan (Ever White Mountain; Korean: Baekdusan), Lake Tianchi (Heavenly Lake), Balhae Tombs at Longtou Mountain

Another major industrial firm is the Jilin Petro-Chemical Corporation, now a part of Petro China, which produces chemical fertilizers and polyethylene. Its facilities in Jilin City began construction in 1954 and started production in 1957. Like FAW, it has undergone major reorganization and modernization since 2005.

Jilin Province shares a long border with Korea. Because of the mountainous terrain along the border, the railroad linking Jilin to the northern Korean city of Chongjin was never as important as the road and rail links between Shenyang and P'yŏngyang. In 2005 around two million ethnic Koreans lived in Jilin Province, mostly in the Yanbian Korean Autonomous Prefecture adjacent to the border. Since the North Korean food crisis of 1995 to 2003, many North Koreans have crossed illegally into China.

Jilin Province produces large amounts of maize, wheat, and soybeans on its central and western plains; the eastern mountains contains extensive timber reserves. Cattle and sheep are raised on the western grasslands, where some Mongols still reside. As elsewhere in China, rural residents are flocking to Jilin's cities; the 2010 census is expected to reveal the extent of the population shift.

Like its neighbors Heilongjiang and Liaoning provinces, Jilin experienced all the national campaigns since 1949, and all three fell behind coastal China during the

post-1978 reform movement. Reform in Jilin, under less energetic leadership, took a leisurely pace, particularly in large state-owned industrial and commercial concerns. Nevertheless, by 2005 FAW was reorganized and modernized as part of the Eleventh Five-Year Plan (2006–2010). The Jilin Petro-Chemical Corporation underwent a similar transformation. Other of Jilin's older production facilities are undertaking major technological improvements and building new plants financed by central government funding earmarked for the northeast region.

Changchun was home to Li Hongzhi (b. 1951), the founder of the Falun Gong movement. In 1999 Chinese authorities outlawed and suppressed all Falun Gong activities. Li Hongchi moved to the United States in 1998 and now lives there in seclusion.

Jilin's estimated population in the 2000 census was 27.28 million; later figures suggest little or no growth. In 2000 Changchun had an urban population of 3.2 million, and it has added large new sections in the subsequent years; Jilin City claimed a total population in its combined urban and rural districts of 4.3 million at the end of 2007.

SEE ALSO *Automobile Industry; Heavy Industry; Korean Community in China.*

BIBLIOGRAPHY

Buck, David D. Railway City and National Capital: Two Faces of the Modern in Changchun. In *Remaking the Chinese City: Modernity and National Identity, 1900–1950*, ed. Joseph Esherick, 65–89. Honolulu: University of Hawai'i Press, 2000.

Chang, Yoonk, Stephen Haggard, and Marcus Noland. Migration Experiences of North Korean Refugees: Survey Evidence from China. Peterson Institute for International Economics Working Paper, no. 4. Washington, DC, 2008.

Marton, Andrew, Terry McGee, and Donald G. Paterson. Northeast Asian Economic Cooperation and the Tumen River Area Development Project. *Pacific Affairs* 68, 3 (Autumn 1995): 9–33.

Ownby, David. *Falungong and the Future of China.* New York: Oxford University Press, 2008.

People's Daily (China) Tumen River Area Development Program Makes Fruitful Achievement in Ten Years. September 5, 2005.

A young girl helping with the corn harvest, Gongzhuling, Jilin province, October 9, 2005. *While occupying Manchuria in the 1930s, the Japanese established manufacturing facilities in the region, with a large chemical industry centered in the province of Jilin. In rural areas of the province, farmers take advantage of a flat interior, adequate amounts of rainfall, and cooler temperatures to concentrate on grain production, particularly corn and wheat.* CHINA PHOTOS/GETTY IMAGES

Pleskacheuskaya, Inesa. New Life for the Old Industrial Bases. *China Today* 54, 10 (October 2005): 31–32.

Thun, Eric. *Changing Lanes in China*. New York: Cambridge University Press, 2006.

David D. Buck

JINAN

Jinan (Tsinan), the capital of Shandong Province, lies on the North China alluvial plain just south of the Yellow River. The city's streets extend into the first hills of the central Shandong limestone massif. Administratively defined as a subprovincial city, Jinan controls a territory of over 8,000 square kilometers with a total population of 5,900,000. The population of its six urban districts was three million in 2004.

In addition to its administrative importance, Jinan is a transportation hub. It lies at the heart of the province's railway and highway networks. The modern Yaoqiang airport is located 40 kilometers northwest of the city center. Jinan has heavy industrial production including trucks and steel, growing information-technology and medical-research sectors, and numerous institutions of higher learning. It also boasts flourishing commercial and residential sections. Since the mid-1990s, both Shandong Province and Jinan have had extraordinary growth rates, up to 14 percent per annum, matching those of Guangdong Province and the Shanghai region. Jinan now features shopping malls with international retailers such as Wal-Mart, new high-rise offices and apartment buildings, and expressways filled with trucks and private automobiles. In 2006 Shandong's total gross domestic product reached 218.5 billion renminbi, or US $4,750 in per capita terms.

Jinan's climate is the same as most of Shandong's, with hot, humid, and rainy summers and cold, dry winters. Spring and fall are distinct seasons and provide the city's best weather.

The city itself lies in a slight basin south of the present channel of the Yellow River. Qianfoshan (Thousand Buddha Hill) overlooks the city, but the view is usually marred by smog. The Yellow River no longer floods, but heavy rains brought serious flooding to lower parts of the city in July 2007. The Jinan depression contains many natural springs created by underground runoff from the nearby limestone karst mountains. The most famous is Baotu (Leaping) Springs. This source also feeds Jinan's scenic Daming Lake and the canals in Quancheng Park. To the city's east lies the fertile alluvial plain north of the Shandong massif; to the south and west there are more alluvial plains. The mountains and valleys of the Shandong central massif, southeast of the city, were less densely populated and inconvenient to traverse.

The Jinan area has a long history of human occupation dating back to at least the first millennium BCE. It has served as the seat of provincial government since the late fourteenth century CE. From the fifteenth through the early nineteenth century, Jinan's economic importance was overshadowed by such cities as Jining, Linqing, and Dezhou along the Grand Canal. Still, Jinan's central location made it the natural center of administration and commerce.

NINETEENTH-CENTURY STASIS

Jinan's status as the seat of provincial administration and its role in Shandong intraprovincial commerce changed during the nineteenth century. Jinan slowly became more important because of overall population growth in Shandong and the Grand Canal's decline. Yellow River floods, rather than the Taiping or Nian rebel armies, became the main threat to the city after the 1850s. The Yellow River emptied south of the Shandong Peninsula into the Yellow Sea until 1853 to 1855, when the main course shifted northward, passing Jinan on its way to the Bohai Gulf. This course change brought serious flooding to the Jinan region. Extensive dikes were raised to protect the city itself, but major floods disrupted life in surrounding towns and villages into the mid-twentieth century. In the late nineteenth century, however, Jinan managed to escape the worst depredations of the great North China famines.

EARLY TWENTIETH-CENTURY DEVELOPMENT

German imperialism brought change to Jinan after 1898 through the new German colony at Qingdao. A German-built Qingdao-to-Jinan railway opened in 1905. In 1910 this rail line connected with the Beijing-to-Shanghai line. To handle the anticipated economic boom, the Qing authorities created a special commercial zone immediately west of Jinan's walled city. Jinan and its new extension remained under Qing administration, rather than being controlled by foreigners, as China's treaty ports were. Under Chinese leadership, Jinan quickly installed electric lights, telephones, and paved streets. Foreign-style shops, banks, and hotels operated both by Chinese and foreigners also appeared. In addition, Jinan became a center for modern Qing military detachments, police, and schools. Even today, Jinan is the seat of a major Chinese military command.

After 1911 a series of warlords ruled Shandong from Jinan. The most notorious was Zhang Zongchang (1881–1932) who served as governor from 1925 to 1928. The Japanese occupied Jinan after driving out the last warlord, Han Fuju (1890–1938), in 1937. They retained control through puppet Chinese administrators until 1945. Chiang Kai-shek's (Jiang Jieshi's) forces took Jinan quickly after the Japanese surrender, but lost the city to Chinese Communist armies in 1948.

THE MAOIST ERA

The maxim for all Chinese cities after 1949 was to become centers of production. This led to new industrial plants, including steel, automobile, and heavy machinery works in Jinan. These needed worker housing, health care, and schools, but investment in these ancillary facilities was limited. Factories, schools, and government offices all experienced repeated waves of political campaigns, and production suffered. By the time of Mao Zedong's death in 1976, Jinan had become a dull, colorless place with temples and churches converted to other uses.

THE REFORM PERIOD

The completion of a highway suspension bridge across the Yellow River at Jinan in 1980 heralded the new era. Even though a railway bridge across the Yellow River had been in place since 1910, all vehicular traffic before 1980 in Shandong Province had to be ferried across the Yellow River. The 1980s also saw the construction of new factories and office buildings, the expansion of university facilities, and the rehabilitation of temples and churches. However, beginning in the mid-1990s, a great burst of urban development took place in Jinan. Massive new housing projects, modern factories, large stores with a greatly expanded array of consumer goods, and dramatically improved highways are the hallmarks of these years in Jinan, as elsewhere in urban China.

Jinan has not escaped urban China's familiar problems. Air and water pollution are serious, and the spread of the automobile has changed the rhythm of life in both old and new neighborhoods. Cases of government and business corruption in Jinan have attracted national attention. Still, bustling universities, flourishing biomedical research centers, new parks, and improved public services give Jinan a pleasant, purposeful air, even as many features of the pre-1900 city have disappeared under the sweep of new construction. Continuing economic growth and more rural-to-urban migration will further transform Jinan.

SEE ALSO *Northern Expedition; Shandong; Urban China: Cities and Urbanization, 1800–1949; Urban China: Organizing Principles of Cities; Urban China: Urban Planning since 1978.*

BIBLIOGRAPHY

Buck, David D. *Urban Change in China: Politics and Development of Tsinan, Shantung, 1890–1949*. Madison: University of Wisconsin Press, 1978.

Lary, Diane. Treachery, Disgrace, and Death: Han Fuju and China's Resistance to Japan. *War in History* 13, 1 (2000): 65–90.

Min Li. Ji'nan in the First Millennium B.C.: Archeology and History. *Journal of the Economic and Social History of the Orient* 46, 1 (2003): 88–126.

Zhao Yingshun and Steven C. Bourassa. China's Urban Housing Reform: Recent Achievements and New Inequities. *Housing Studies* 18, 5 (2003): 721–744.

David D. Buck

JOURNALISM

The profession of journalism was part of a Western modernization package introduced to China in the late nineteenth century. At this time, the claim implicit in newspaper publishing that private citizens should have a public voice in national affairs was far from well established. Officials and gentry in earlier times, as people "with judgment" (*lunzhe*), did have some standing to discuss national affairs, and their opinions might well be quoted in dynastic histories and private writings, but the culture of journalism was essentially alien.

BEGINNINGS OF COMMERCIAL JOURNALISM IN CHINA

The first Chinese newspapers and journals were cultivated by foreign missionaries and businessmen. Often bilingual, they published works in Chinese or foreign languages in Southeast Asia or in the treaty ports outside the Qing court's control. Official gazettes such as *Jingbao* (Peking gazette) and *Yuanchao* (Yamen courier), produced by the court and local magistrates, carried official documents, without news or editorial matter. Illustrated "leaflets about things heard recently" (*xinwenzhi*), privately printed, partly filled the void.

Pivotal in establishing the profession of Chinese-language journalism was *Shenbao* (Shanghai daily, 1872–1949), which was founded in Shanghai and managed until 1889 by an Englishman, Ernest Major (1842–1908). In Hong Kong, Wang Tao (1828–1897), sometimes hailed as the "father of (ethnic) Chinese journalism," set up a counterpart with *Xunhuan ribao* (Universal daily, 1874–1947), modeled on *The Times* of London. Chinese-language papers were eager to prove their legitimacy as enlightened newspapers. *Shenbao* stressed "Western" journalistic ideals of independence from Chinese and foreign authorities, incorruptibility, the search for truth in facts, and disdain for Chinese or Western religious propaganda while professing its critical commitment to China's best interests.

Journalists came from the pool of educated people who, often frustrated in their hopes for an official career by the widespread sale of offices, found a market for their modern knowledge on the private staffs of leading Han-Chinese officials and in the booming treaty ports—above all Shanghai. With their Western knowledge and foreign-language skills, acquired in missionary schools or while working with missionaries on translations, they formed the beginnings of a new national class of urban intellectuals, identified by their profession rather than by their ancestral place. *Shenbao*'s success prompted missionary journalists Young Allan (1836–1907) and Timothy Richard (1845–1919), both of the China Inland Mission, to emphasize modern news rather than religious advocacy in their *Wanguo gongbao* (Review of the times, 1874–1907), published in Shanghai.

The blossoming of urban life in the treaty ports also encouraged the emergence of entertainment journalism. Pioneered by Li Boyuan's (1867–1906) *Youxi bao* (Entertainment, 1897–1902), papers of this sort combined news about courtesans and opera stars with serialized novels of social criticism.

THE ADVANCE OF POLITICAL-ADVOCACY JOURNALISM

Political-advocacy journalism came to the fore in Liang Qichao's (1873–1929) Chinese-managed reform newspapers after China's defeat in the Sino-Japanese War in 1895. Liang's easy-to-read journalistic style and reform arguments drew heavily on Japanese newspapers. His willingness to transform his advocacy paper, *Shiwu bao* (Chinese progress), into a government gazette set a precedent for such mergers. By 1900, Chinese-language journalists were writing for "big" commercial papers, "small" entertainment papers (with authors often contributing to both genres), political-advocacy papers, and, in inland China, government gazettes. In the early twentieth century, Chinese investors bought many of the foreign-owned Chinese-language papers, but they kept their foreign links and the associated legal protection. The notion of an independent commercial press with a staff committed to high journalistic standards thus retained its foreign tinge.

Journalistic work was closely integrated into the growing transnational and translingual circuit of news and opinion operating in China through Japanese wire services, foreign correspondents, and foreign journalists writing for foreign-language papers in China with their mostly Chinese audiences. Professionalization advanced. Some Chinese journalists underwent training at the Missouri School of Journalism in the United States. In Beijing, a journalism department was established by the foreign-run Yenching University. Professional associations were also formed: one for foreign journalists in 1903, another for Chinese journalists in 1910. In addition, histories of the Chinese-language press appeared. The master narrative to this day is Ge Gongzhen's (1890–1935) 1928 China-centered history of the Chinese press. Ge regarded Liang Qichao's advocacy papers as the true beginning of Chinese journalism. He dismissed earlier papers as products of cultural imperialism and disregarded the contemporary foreign-language press and foreign journalists in China altogether.

Government gazettes and press restrictions, especially on Chinese papers, provided an official response to claims by journalists to a right to comment on matters of state. Only factual commercial and technical news was considered legitimate for coverage in privately owned papers. Strict controls on press freedoms were established by the 1903 press law, but successive governments lacked the power to enforce such controls nationwide, and the fragmentation of political power in the late Qing and early Republican eras eventually created an open if risky environment for journalists. Between the Versailles Treaty in 1919 and the Japanese southward advance in 1937, the politicization of both Chinese and foreign journalists increased. However, commercial Chinese papers—such as *Shenbao*, now under Shi Liangcai (1880–1934), and later *Shijie ribao* (World daily, 1925–1949), under Cheng Shewo (1898–1991)—managed among themselves to establish a credible, free commercial press.

Worldwide, however, these years saw the professionalization of propaganda by governments and political groups together with the spread of advertising by commercial interests. The Chinese Communist Party, founded in 1921, followed the Communist International's emphasis on propaganda, with most party leaders, including Mao Zedong, active in this field. Reorganizing along Leninist lines, the Guomindang (GMD) leadership also professionalized its propaganda work. After gaining state power in 1928, the GMD used its government gazette, *Zhongyang ribao* (Central Daily News) for propaganda purposes, and in 1930 passed a new and restrictive press law.

Most Chinese journalists were becoming politically aligned. Fan Changjiang (1909–1970) is an example. In 1936 he pioneered a journalistic style for *Dagong bao* (L'Impartial) in Tianjin, reporting in rich language on the sorrows of simple folk, but he joined the Communists in 1939 to produce "paper bullets" against Japan. Foreign journalists in China also tended to be aligned politically. The U.S. propaganda arm, the Committee on Public Information, had a China branch with journalists aligned against Japan, including Carl Crow (1883–1945), Thomas F. F. Millard (1868–1942), and William Henry Donald (1875–1946). George Bronson Rea (1869–1936) of the *Far Eastern Review* was aligned with Japan, and Edgar Snow (1905–1972) and Agnes Smedley (1892–1950) with the Communist International. There was a public suspicion that every newspaper in China was somehow aligned with one or another foreign power.

Xinhua News Agency journalists at work in Beijing, August 6, 2008. *After the Communists outlawed independent journalism in 1949, members of the Chinese media acted in cooperation with the government to promote party propaganda. Restrictions on the media eased, however, in the late-twentieth century, giving journalists greater freedom of the press, so long as they avoided writing about topics political in nature.* JEWEL SAMAD/AFP/ GETTY IMAGES

THE PRESS UNDER THE PROPAGANDA DEPARTMENT OF THE COMMUNIST PARTY

With the 1949 victory of the Chinese Communist Party (CCP), the independent journalist was outlawed altogether. No protests are recorded. Even the English-language *Millard's Review* (published 1917–1953 under changing Western names) had passed into the hands of foreign communists and recast itself as the PRC propaganda paper *China Reconstructs*. This figure of the independent objective journalist had not been able to shed its alien associations. V. I. Lenin's image of the newspaper reporter as a "cog and screw in the revolutionary machinery," quoted by Mao Zedong in his 1942 *Talks at the Yan'an Forum*, became the norm for journalists in the People's Republic of China

(PRC). They worked under a unified propaganda system managed by the CCP's Propaganda Department (Zhonggong Zhongyang Xuanchuanbu), which encompassed all media. Mao's secretary, Hu Qiaomu (1912–1992), was instrumental in framing the accepted attitude and language of early PRC journalists. Journalism education was offered only at the new People's University in Beijing, an institution constructed for cadre training along Soviet lines. International news and news about the leadership were reserved for the official Xinhua News Agency.

In the "thaw" after Joseph Stalin's death in 1953, the Soviet journalists Ilja Ehrenburg (1891–1967) and Valentin Ovechkin (1904–1968) became alternative role models for some PRC journalists, such as Liu Binyan (1925–2005). These journalists employed a form of literary reportage in which socialist ideals informed their critique of Stalinist *nomenklatura*. The journalist in this context was envisaged as the "scout" or the "eye and ear" of the top leadership and a mouthpiece for the "people." Since March 1957, the official New China news agency also published *Cankao Xiaoxi* (Reference News), a unique daily paper with translations of excerpts from the world press. *Cankao Xiaoxi* had more subscribers than the party paper *People's Daily* and greatly enhanced familiarity with world affairs. The liberal trend was joined by independent editors such as Chu Anping (1909–1966) of *Guangming ribao* (Enlightenment daily), and even Party journalists such as Deng Tuo (1912–1966) of the *People's Daily*. Over the next two decades, they suffered terribly for this "mistake," with many going to their deaths. During the Cultural Revolution (1966–1969), centralized control of the press by the CCP Propaganda Department collapsed. However, the heightened political temperature created by the cult of the "Great Helmsman" was enough to keep the papers produced by thousands of unlicensed Red Guard propagandists in line.

From the 1980s, the party relaxed controls on the economy. While maintaining a tight grip on journalists and the media, the CCP opened a sector of consumption-related news that could operate in relative freedom, as long as it steered clear of politics. In the long run, the mainstream of Chinese journalism had come to be defined by the propagandist in the government press rather than by the independent journalist. The development of a diverse and free press in Taiwan after the end of martial law in 1987, emblematized by the bold writing of Long Yingtai (Lung Ying-tai), has shown, however, that the notion of the independent-minded Chinese journalist is not incompatible with Chinese political culture.

SEE ALSO *Chu Anping; Fan Changjiang; Ge Gongzhen; Liu Binyan; Newspapers; Snow, Edgar; Xiao Qian (Xiao Bingqian).*

BIBLIOGRAPHY

Britton, Roswell. *The Chinese Periodical Press, 1800–1912*. Shanghai: Kelly and Walsh, 1933.

Chao, Thomas Ming-heng. *The Foreign Press in China*. Shanghai: China Institute of Pacific Relations, 1931.

Cheek, Timothy. *Propaganda and Culture in Mao's China: Deng Tuo and the Intelligentsia*. Oxford: Clarendon Press, 1997.

Ge Gongzhen. *Zhongguo baoxue shi* [History of the Chinese press]. Shanghai: Commercial Press, 1928.

Gentz (Vittinghoff), Natascha. Useful Knowledge and Appropriate Communication: The Field of Journalistic Production in Late Nineteenth Century China. In *Joining the Global Public: Word, Image, and City in Early Chinese Newspapers, 1870–1910*, ed. Rudolf Wagner, 47–104. Albany: State University of New York Press, 2007.

Goodman, Bryna, ed. Transnational Dimensions of the Chinese Press. Spec. issue. *China Review* 4, 1 (2004).

Harrison, Henrietta. Newspapers and Nationalism in Rural China, 1890–1929. *Past and Present* 166 (2000): 181–204.

Hu Qiaomu. *Tantan baozhi gongzuo* [Talks on newspaper work]. Jiaoxue cankao ziliao 1. Beijing: 1978.

Janku, Andrea. *Nur leere Reden: Politischer Diskurs und die Shanghaier Presse im China des späten 19. Jahrhunderts*. Wiesbaden, Germany: Harrassowitz, 2003.

Lin Yutang (Lin Yü-t'ang). *A History of the Press and Public Opinion in China*. Chicago: University of Chicago Press, 1936.

Liu Hoh-hsüan and Chang Ching-ming. Education in Journalism at Yenching University. *Collectanea Commissionis Synodalis* 14, 2 (1941): 347–359.

Long Yingtai (Lung Ying-tai). *Yehuo ji* [Wild fire, a collection]. Taibei: Yuanshen Press, 1987.

Mittler, Barbara. *A Newspaper for China? Power, Identity, and Change in Shanghai's News Media, 1872–1912*. Cambridge, MA: Harvard University Asia Center, 2004.

Powell, John Benjamin. *My Twenty-five Years in China*. New York: Macmillan, 1945.

Selle, Earl Albert. *Donald of China*. New York: Harper, 1948.

Vittinghoff, Natascha. *Die Anfänge des Journalismus in China (1860–1911)*. Wiesbaden, Germany: Harrassowitz, 2002.

Volland, Nicolai. The Control of the Media in the People's Republic of China. Ph.D. diss., University of Heidelberg, 2003.

Wagner, Rudolf G. *Inside a Service Trade: Studies in Contemporary Chinese Prose*. Cambridge, MA: Harvard University Press, 1992.

Wagner, Rudolf G. The Role of the Foreign Community in the Chinese Public Sphere. *China Quarterly* 142 (June 1995): 423–443.

Wagner, Rudolf G. The Early Chinese Newspapers and the Chinese Public Sphere. *European Journal of East Asian Studies* 1, 1 (2001): 1–34.

Wagner, Rudolf G., ed. *Joining the Global Public: Word, Image, and City in Early Chinese Newspapers, 1870–1910*. Albany: State University of New York Press, 2007.

Yeh, Catherine. Shanghai Leisure, Print Entertainment, and the Tabloids, *xiaobao*. In *Joining the Global Public: Word, Image, and City in Early Chinese Newspapers, 1870–1910*, ed. Rudolf Wagner, 201–234. Albany: State University of New York Press, 2007.

Yu Junsheng. *Zou Taofen zhuan* [Zou Taofen, a biography]. Tianjin, PRC: Tianjin Jiaoyu Chubanshe, 1994.

Zhao Yuezhi. *Media, Market, and Democracy in China: Between the Party Line and the Bottom Line*. Urbana: University of Illinois Press, 1998.

Rudolf G. Wagner

K

KANG YOUWEI
1858–1927

Kang Youwei (Zuyi, Guangxia, Changsu) was a controversial scholar and political activist. Kang was born into a scholar-official family in Nanhai, Guangdong, in 1858. With his status as "tribute student by virtue of distinguished ancestral service" awarded him in 1877 when his grandfather died, Kang sat for the civil service examinations and obtained his provincial and metropolitan degrees in 1893 and 1895, respectively. He had by then gathered a loyal following of students, such as Liang Qichao (1873–1929), from his Changxing Academy in Guangzhou (Canton) and begun to advocate reform as the key to dynastic survival. His involvement in the Hundred Days' Reform (1898) forced him to seek refuge abroad. In exile, he competed with revolutionaries like Sun Yat-sen (Sun Zhongshan or Sun Yixian) for overseas Chinese support. Fighting old battles still in the Republic, Kang continued to oppose Sun and took part in the abortive 1917 restoration of the monarchy under the deposed Qing emperor Xuantong (Pu-Yi, 1906–1967). Deemed by many a reactionary, Kang died in 1927 at sixty-nine.

INTELLECTUAL PROFILE

Kang's fame rested on his dual role as intellectual and political leader. His early schooling under his grandfather and other teachers had provided him with a solid, generalist grounding in traditional learning. His embrace of the "new text" polemics was therefore a shift in his classicist's orientation, marked by the 1891 publication of his *Xinxue weijing kao* (Inquiry into the forged classics of the Xin period). Inspired by the work of a contemporary, Liao Ping (1852–1932), Kang argued that the so-called Han discovery of authentic Confucian canons, written in an archaic script (ancient text), was a fabrication by the scholar Liu Xin (c. 53 BCE–23 CE). Since the earlier Qin order of burning books to control thought had not, in fact, applied to government collections, copies of the Confucian classics, inscribed in a more or less contemporary script (new text), had survived into the Han. Kang's erudite argument was not entirely new, but he went further than most new text partisans in refuting all of the ancient text canons as apocryphal, forged by Liu Xin to legitimize the usurper Wang Mang (d. 23 CE).

Criticisms of Kang's radical conclusions reached the throne in 1894, causing his work to be banned. Undeterred, in 1897, he published *Kongzi gaizhi kao* (Confucius as institutional innovator), in which he portrayed Confucius, like other major Eastern Zhou (770–256 BCE) thinkers, as a reformer concerned with sociopolitical reconstruction. Masking his utopianism as ideals once attained by the legendary sage-rulers Yao and Shun, Confucius authored the Six Canons to convey his vision of a better world. Of these, the *Chunqiu* (Spring and autumn annals), interpreted according to the *Gongyang Commentary*, was the most important, since it contained Confucius's "hidden but vital meaning," including his charting of humankind's historical passage through the Three Ages of Chaos, Approaching Peace, and Universal Peace. Kang revered Confucius not only as the new text "uncrowned king" but also as founder of China's unique religio-cultural order, not unlike Jesus, Muhammad, and Gautama of the world religions.

Kang's new text exegesis, which he carried on in exile, had been enriched by his reading of translated materials on world history and on Western theories of progress, evolution, and Social Darwinism. Indicative of this influence was his view in the late 1890s that China could readily revitalize itself by learning from the modernizing experiences of Petrine Russia and Meiji Japan. His global awareness, first aroused after his visits to British Hong Kong and the treaty port Shanghai, was reinforced after 1898 when he circumnavigated the world three times, visiting thirty-one countries in four continents. His blueprints for the future, free from human suffering and informed by Confucius's notion of great harmony and by the Christian and Buddhist teachings of equality and universal love, were explained in his *Datong shu* (Book of great harmony), which, though unfinished, began to appear in installments in 1913.

POLITICAL PROFILE

Never an armchair academician, Kang sought action in the public arena. His first political venture came in 1888, when, during a visit to Beijing, he petitioned the throne on good government. Without a court sponsor, the project fell through but set a decade-long pattern of his activities, which aimed to secure imperial attention for his views amid a dynastic crisis, whether in 1888 when the Guangxu emperor (1871–1908) was about to assume full power, or in 1895 when China had lost the Sino-Japanese War, or in 1898 when the foreign powers had started their scramble for concessions. His subject was invariably reform, its scope expanding from traditional issues like the careful selection of the emperor's personal staff to postwar reconstruction and to an institutional overhaul of the central government with twelve new bureaus to promote comprehensive change.

Recognizing the political potential of group action and print power, Kang formed study societies and published periodicals. By early 1898, he had gained the patronage of powerful ministers like Weng Tonghe (1830–1904) and Zhang Yinhuan (1837–1900). Some of the court's censors (*yanguan,* lit. "speaking officials") also agreed to submit to the throne, as their own memorials, drafts prepared by Kang and his students. With these connections, Kang organized aggressive forays into court politics. Two memorials drafted by his group and submitted by Xu Zhijing (1826–1900) and by Yang Shenxiu (1849–1898) helped inaugurate what came to be known as the Hundred Days' Reform. In mid-June 1898, Kang had an audience with the Guangxu emperor, who, though favorably impressed, assigned him only to politically inconsequential duties, like those of a secretary of Zongli Yamen (Office for the General Management of Foreign Affairs) and later of converting *Shiwu bao* (Chinese progress), a Shanghai periodical, into a government organ. Though some of Kang's own memorials and those by his group forwarded by others had inspired reform measures, his career prospects remained uncertain, prompting him to contemplate military maneuvers against identified obstructionists like the empress-dowager Cixi. By late summer, his illicit collaboration with the censors had given those opposing Guangxu's reforms an easy target. They urged Cixi to check Guangxu's misrule, and her intervention ended the Hundred Days.

After fleeing the country, Kang canvassed the support of overseas Chinese and founded the China Reform Association (Baohuang hui) to call for the restoration of Guangxu and China's adoption of a constitutional monarchy. His multinational organization had by 1903 set up branches in 170 cities in the Americas alone, outperforming Sun Yat-sen's revolutionary group in fund-raising and membership numbers. The success of the 1911 revolution proved a setback to Kang, but did not dissuade him from believing in what he termed "titular monarchical republic" (*xujun gonghe*) as the ideal polity for China. To his death, he considered this combination of the monarchy's symbolic role and parliament's real power, like the British, China's best safeguard against political fragmentation.

SEE ALSO *Gong Zizhen; Hundred Days' Reform; Liang Qichao.*

BIBLIOGRAPHY

Kwong, Luke S. K. (Kuang Zhaojiang). Chinese Politics at the Crossroads: Reflections on the Hundred Days Reform of 1898. *Modern Asian Studies* 34, 3 (2000): 663–695.

Luo Rongbang (Lo Jung-pang) ed. *K'ang Yu-wei: A Biography and a Symposium.* Tucson: University of Arizona Press, 1967.

Xiao Gongquan (Hsiao Kung-chuan). *A Modern China and a New World: K'ang Yu-wei, Reformer and Utopian, 1858–1927.* Seattle: University of Washington Press, 1975.

Luke S. K. Kwong (Kuang Zhaojiang)

KAOHSIUNG (GAOXIONG)

Kaohsiung (Gaoxiong) sits on the southwestern coast of Taiwan. It is the second-largest city in Taiwan, with a population of around 1.51 million in 2007. Situated south of the Tropic of Cancer, Kaohsiung has a tropical climate with average temperatures ranging between 19 and 29 degrees Celsius. It is one of the driest cities in Taiwan (on average it rains ninety days per year), and the weather is often bright and sunny. However, the combination of humidity (averaging between 60 and 81%), heat, pollution, and the density of the city can make Kaoshiung sweltering in summer.

There are three harbors in Kaohsiung: Zuoying Military Harbor, which is a large navy base; Kaohsiung Harbor,

Taiwan's major port for importing oil; and the No. 2 Harbor, formerly the export port for bananas, wood, and steel but now a sightseeing spot known as Kaohsiung Fisherman's Wharf. The capacity of Kaohsiung Harbor, ranking fourth largest in the world in its heyday but eighth in 2007, makes Kaohsiung a city of heavy industry. Oil, steel, sugar, fertilizer, shipping, textiles, chemical products, and assembly-line factories all contribute to its prosperity. However, since manufacturing industries began to leave Taiwan in the late 1980s and the early 1990s in search of cheaper labor cost, Kaohsiung's economy has suffered.

The city's close association with harbors has gained Kaohsiung a nickname embraced warmly by locals—Gangdu (Harbor City). A famous Taiwanese folk song, "Gangdu Yeyu" (A rainy night in the Harbor City, 1953), is often mistaken today for an unofficial theme song of Kaohsiung; it was originally written about the fishing port of Keelung (Jilong) in the north of Taiwan.

TOURIST ATTRACTIONS

As the Harbor City of Taiwan, Kaohsiung has many tourist attractions that are related to water. For example, the Love River flows into Kaohsiung Harbor through the Old City. After a massive cleanup in the late 1990s and early 2000s, the Love River is now a popular tourist site, with boats taking sightseers up and down the river. Cultural events including concerts, dragon-boat races, and Chinese New Year activities regularly take place here.

Siziwan, a harbor inlet flanking Wanshou Mountain and National Sun Yat-sen University, is popular with local people, who often go there for a stroll or to sit by the harbor to watch ships and wait for the sunset. Indeed, the sunset at Siziwan is regarded as one of the eight most scenic views in Taiwan. A former British consulate established in the Qing dynasty (1644–1912) stands nearby.

Next to Siziwan is a ferry station with frequent service to and from Cijin (Qijin) Island, which is otherwise linked to Kaohsiung City by road. Cijin was the first Chinese settlement in the Kaohsiung area and has retained strong traditional cultural characteristics. Cijin is essentially a long, thin sandbar, 11 kilometers long and a mere 200 meters wide. After links to the main city were opened, Cijin took off as a favorite destination for city residents looking for beachside relaxation close at hand.

Other popular attractions include Chengqing Lake, where the Kaohsiung Grand Hotel and one of Chiang Kai-shek's (Jiang Jieshi's) villas are situated; Liuhe Night Market, a bustling pedestrianized area where street vendors, food stalls, restaurants, and shops are open until the small hours; the Urban Spotlight Arcade; the Tuntex Sky Tower; Lotus Lake; the Kaohsiung Museum of Fine Arts; Chai Mountain; Foguangshan Monastery; and Holy Rosary Cathedral.

POLITICS

Kaohsiung is one of the two central municipalities under the administration of the Republic of China. The mayor of Kaohsiung, directly elected by its citizens, is deemed a prestigious position.

Observers often view Kaohsiung as the political mirror image of Taibei (Taipei). While Taibei usually leans toward the Pan Blue coalition, Kaohsiung often leans toward Pan Green. This is not surprising in light of the modern history of Kaohsiung, especially the *Meilidao* Incident of 1979. Also known as the Formosa Incident, the *Formosa Magazine* Incident, or simply the Kaohsiung Incident, this event marked a turning point in Taiwan's political history.

The *Meilidao* (*Formosa Magazine*) was launched at a time when Taiwan was still ruled by the Guomindang government under martial law, but when citizens were becoming eager for a more democratic society. The popularity of *Meilidao*, a more radical magazine than had yet appeared in Taiwan, at first astonished and then frightened the government, which had allowed the magazine to circulate. The crunch came when the activists behind the magazine began to organize political meetings throughout Taiwan that attracted thousands in attendance. A series of rallies and demonstrations ended in Kaohsiung on December 10, 1979, to coincide with Human Rights Day. The police were called to prevent the public from congregating because permission to meet had been denied. A riot finally ensued after *Meilidao* was seized and demonstrators were beaten by the police.

Many activists were arrested and their trials received intense media attention in Taiwan and abroad. Although the government managed to win the legal battles and sent the accused to prison, the authorities failed to win a moral-political victory. The political dissidents of the *Meilidao* Incident were seen as martyrs by the public, and the *Meilidao* Incident became a turning point for the prodemocracy movement in Taiwan. Almost all leading members of the present-day Democratic Progressive Party (DPP) had a role in the event either as defendants or as defense lawyers. The DPP finally ended the Guomindang's political domination in the 2000 presidential election.

SEE ALSO *Taiwan, Republic of China; Urban China: Cities and Urbanization, 1800–1949; Urban China: Organizing Principles of Cities.*

BIBLIOGRAPHY

Government Information Office of the ROC. *The Taiwan Yearbook 2006.* Taibei: Author, 2007. http://www.gio.gov.tw/taiwan-website/5-gp/yearbook/

Rawnsley, Gary, and Ming-Yeh Rawnsley, eds. *Critical Security, Democratisation, and Television in Taiwan.* London: Ashgate, 2001.

Taiwan External Trade Development Council. *Doing Business with Taiwan, 2005–2006.* Taibei: Author, 2005.

Ming-Yeh T. Rawnsley (Cai Mingyeh)

KOREA, RELATIONS WITH (NORTH AND SOUTH)

Due to their geographical proximity, China and Korea have interacted extensively over a long history that has spanned at least two millennia. Sino-Korean relations became institutionalized, especially since the Ming dynasty (1368–1644), within the framework of tributary relations—the traditional Sinocentric mode of international affairs in Asia. Korea sought to maintain autonomy over its internal affairs while fulfilling largely symbolic tributary obligations to the dynasties that ruled the Middle Kingdom.

After the Qing dynasty (1644–1912) was defeated by Japan in 1895, China's suzerainty over Korea was formally severed. With the civil war in China and the division of the Korean Peninsula during the 1940s, Sino-Korean relations bifurcated into two pairs of alignments: the People's Republic of China with the northern Democratic People's Republic of Korea (North Korea), and Taiwan with the southern Republic of Korea (South Korea). Mainly for ideological and strategic reasons, during much of the Cold War era China maintained close relations—often dubbed as a "friendship sealed in blood" cultivated through fighting the Korean War (1950–1953) together—with North Korea.

Despite some fluctuations, especially during the Cultural Revolution (1966–1969), China's overall relations with North Korea remained friendly thanks to the Cold War atmosphere. Even in the face of the Sino-Soviet schism, North Korea was savvy enough not to take sides, thereby maximizing protection and assistance from both China and the Soviet Union. Emotionally, however, Pyongyang was always closer to Beijing than to Moscow. Hence, China had no incentives or intentions to improve relations with South Korea, North Korea's archrival. While Seoul made some overtures toward Beijing in the early 1970s after U.S. president Richard Nixon's (1913–1994) surprise visit to China, they were quietly turned down by Beijing.

The global and regional strategic environments began to change drastically during the 1970s, however. With its eye set on reform and opening from the late 1970s, China sought to minimize ideological and structural constraints on its external relations. China gradually moved from an ideology-driven foreign policy to a pragmatic one based on "separating economics from politics" in order to expand foreign trade, solicit foreign investment, and maintain stable environments for its reforms. In 1980 such leaders as Hu Yaobang and Zhao Ziyang even mentioned that South Korea's developmental experiences could provide a useful model for China to emulate.

This new position meant that China would establish and expand economic relations with South Korea while maintaining its political affinity toward North Korea. While Beijing's perennial concern for Pyongyang worked as a key obstacle to expediting Sino–South Korean rapprochement, the fruits of bilateral economic relations—both trade and foreign direct investment—were so sweet that China became increasingly more active in expanding its cooperative relationship with South Korea, even at the expense of infuriating North Korea.

Expanded economic contacts generated an acute need for governmental institutional mechanisms, which led to the exchange of trade offices in January 1991 and, eventually, to the normalization of diplomatic relations in August 1992. Since then, bilateral trade grew at an exponential rate, from $6.4 billion in 1992 to $118 billion in 2006, making China South Korea's top trading partner and South Korea China's third. By 2004 China had already replaced the United States as the number one outbound destination for South Korea's foreign investment. The largest number of foreign students in China also comes from South Korea.

Sino–South Korean relations—currently termed officially as a "comprehensive cooperative partnership for the twenty-first century"—have faced some unpleasant problems as well. With the rise of China's economic might, concerned voices were heard about the prospect of South Korea losing out in the international market. As hedging has become a popular mode of responding to the rising China, South Korea has often been placed in a strategic dilemma of having to weigh the gains from economic cooperation with China against the gains from security alignment with the United States. Additionally, more traditional sources of conflict—history and territorial controversies—are also lurking behind the extensive cooperative relationship between China and South Korea.

With China's normalization of relations with South Korea, Sino–North Korean relations went through a transformational phase. Particularly after Kim Il Sung's death in 1994, along with the drastic generational changes in the Chinese leadership, the conventional channels of bilateral communication were constricted and the frequency of top leadership exchanges between the two countries reduced. The "friendship sealed in blood" began to phase out, giving way to "traditionally amicable ties."

Having both of its former allies—China and the Soviet Union—normalize relations with South Korea,

South Korean protestor outside the Chinese Embassy, Seoul, South Korea, September 7, 2006. *After the Korean War, China gave preference to the Communist North, providing political and economic support for the new regime. During policy shifts in the 1970s, however, China looked to take advantage of South Korea's prosperity by restoring historic ties to the region, leading some citizens to fear China would again dominate the peninsula.* AP IMAGES

North Korea was placed in a serious security dilemma. Kim Jong Il's strategic choice for his way out was to develop nuclear weapons to cancel out all the odds against his regime. During the first nuclear crisis of 1993 to 1994, China mostly sat on the fence, letting Pyongyang and Washington resolve the issue through the Agreed Framework produced in Geneva.

China's position became rather different when the second nuclear crisis erupted in 2002. Beijing was directly involved in hosting the three- and six-party talks in efforts to prevent Pyongyang from going nuclear. When North Korea carried out its first nuclear test in October 2006, China went so far as to brand it as a "brazen act." Due mainly to its strategic calculus of North Korea as a key buffer state, China has always been careful to minimize the sense of betrayal that Pyongyang might feel toward Beijing. Yet, one may wonder if China has already begun to think of North Korea as just one of its neighboring countries, not so different from others.

China's relations with both Koreas will face significant new challenges down the road. The prospect of U.S.-China relations, as well as North Korea's growing contact with the United States, along with South Korea's evolving complex relations with China, will all contribute to the delineation of a future direction where China's relations with the two Koreas will be heading.

SEE ALSO *Korean Community in China; Korean War, 1950–1953.*

BIBLIOGRAPHY

Chung Jae Ho. *Between Ally and Partner: Korea-China Relations and the United States.* New York: Columbia University Press, 2007.

Koh Byung Chul. *Foreign Policy Systems of North and South Korea.* Berkeley: University of California Press, 1984.

Lee Chae-jin. *China and Korea: Dynamic Relations.* Stanford, CA: Hoover Institution Press, 1996.

Shambaugh, David, ed. *Power Shift: China and Asia's New Dynamics.* Berkeley: University of California Press, 2005.

Jae Ho Chung

KOREAN COMMUNITY IN CHINA

Korean Chinese (Chinese, Chaoxianzu; Korean, Chosŏnjok) constitute the thirteenth-largest ethnic minority in China. The community has a population of 2 million and is located mostly in the three northeastern provinces of Jilin, Liaoning, and Heilongjiang. About 44 percent of Korean Chinese live in the Yanbian Autonomous Prefecture in Jilin.

INCEPTION AND EXPANSION

Developing through four stages—inception, rapid expansion, resettlement, and reorganization—the modern Korean community in China has a 150-year history marked by struggles against harsh natural and political environments. The community started in the 1860s in south Manchuria, or the Yanbian area currently, when destitute farmers crossed the border from neighboring famine-ridden northeastern Korean villages. Japan's annexation of Korea in 1910 greatly increased migration. The number of Koreans in China was about 77,000 in 1870, but increased to 220,000 in 1910; 459,000 in 1920; 607,000 in 1930; 1,450,000 in 1940; and 1,659,000 in 1944—a growth of 7.5-fold in the 35 years of Japanese colonialism. Migration trends were largely determined by Japan's expansionist policies in Korea and China. Japan's annexation of Korea ignited a large-scale diasporic exodus to China. Migration to China subsided after the Korean Independence Movement in 1919 because Japan subsequently clamped down on Koreans in Manchuria and restricted Koreans' movement into China. Japan's invasion of China and plan to develop Manchuria as a food-supply base brought about a large-scale collective migration of Korean farmers to remote areas in Manchuria in the 1930s.

RESETTLEMENT AND REORGANIZATION

After Japan's defeat and the resultant liberation of Korea in 1945, a large number of Koreans in Japan and China returned to Korea. About 700,000 Koreans are estimated to have returned from China. According to Chinese census figures, the Korean minority numbered 1,120,000 in 1953, increased to 1,765,000 in 1982 and 1,923,000 in 1990, and showed no growth in the 1990s. At the beginning of the twenty-first century, this community's population began to decline, and a rapid decrease in population is projected for the coming years.

After the establishment of the People's Republic of China, Koreans were officially recognized as an ethnic minority and given Chinese citizenship. They survived such tumultuous events as the Korean War (1950–1953) and the Cultural Revolution (1966–1969), and succeeded in setting down their roots in their adopted homeland. They even became known as a model ethnic minority for their achievements in education, business, politics, and population control. Thanks to government policies on ethnic minorities, they retained their language and cultural traditions and developed a sense of Korean ethnic identity. Unfortunately, their traditions and ethnic identity have isolated the Korean Chinese community from mainstream Chinese culture and society.

RECENT DEVELOPMENTS

The political and economic environment surrounding Korean Chinese has changed drastically since the late 1980s. Then, most Korean Chinese lived in rural villages, engaged in rice farming, and valued family ties and community solidarity. But their world and lifestyles began to change rapidly with China's market-oriented reforms and the normalization of Sino-Korean relations. Korean labor migration has been closely tied to Korean policies on ethnic Koreans overseas and the penetration of Korean industries into China. Most Korean laborers in rural villages headed for big cities or Korea, and schoolchildren went to school in nearby towns, leaving only the elderly in rural villages and making interregional/international family dispersion an ordinary affair. In their destinations—Beijing, Qingdao, and Korea—Korean Chinese have built new communities. These social and demographic changes have aroused great anxiety among Korean Chinese intellectuals about the loss of Korean Chinese identity and the virtual disappearance of the Korean Chinese community. Yet many believe that Korean Chinese will survive this challenge as they have survived others in the past.

SEE ALSO *Korea, Relations with (North and South); Minority Nationalities: Cultural Images of National Minorities; Minority Nationalities: Large National Minorities.*

BIBLIOGRAPHY

Chang Taehan, ed. The Korean Diaspora in China: Ethnicity, Identity and Change. *Korean and Korean American Studies Bulletin* 12, 1 (2001).

Chaoxianzu jianshi [A brief history of Korean Chinese]. Yanji, China: Yanbian Renmin Chubanshe, 1986.

Han Sang-Bok and Kwon Tai-Hwan. *Chungguk yŏnbyŏnŭi Chosŏnjok* [Korean Chinese in Yanbian, China]. Seoul: Seoul National University Press, 1993.

Kwon Tai-Hwan, ed. *Chungguk Chosŏnjok sahoeŭi byŏnwha* [Changes in China's Chosŏnjok society]. Seoul: Seoul National University Press, 2005.

Lee Kwang-Gyu. *Chaejung Hanin* [Koreans in China]. Seoul: Iljogak, 1994.

Kwon Tai-Hwan

KOREAN WAR, 1950–1953

When World War II ended in 1945, the Allied powers divided Korea along the 38th parallel. In 1948 the Soviet Union helped the Korean Communist Party (or the Korean Workers' Party) establish the Democratic People's Republic of Korea (DPRK) in the north with Kim Il Sung (1912–1994) as its president. With the support of the United States, the south held an election and created the Republic of Korea (ROK) with Syngman Rhee (1875–1965) as its president. Both regimes claimed themselves to be the sole and legal government for the country.

THE WAR

On June 25, 1950, ninety thousand northern Communist troops crossed the 38th parallel and invaded the south. Two days later, President Harry Truman (1884–1972) authorized U.S. armed forces to provide air and naval support to the ROK. On July 7, the United Nations (UN) adopted a resolution to use all possible means to aid the ROK and established the UN Forces (UNF) under the command of General Douglas MacArthur (1880–1964) for the war. The United States composed 90 percent of the UNF, and sixteen other nations sent ground forces to serve under the UN command.

On September 15, the U.S. troops staged the Inchon landing, and in two weeks crossed the 38th parallel into North Korea. Kim asked Soviet leader Joseph Stalin (1879–1953) for help and told Stalin to ask China to send troops. Upon receiving urgent telegrams from Moscow, Mao Zedong, chairman of the Chinese Communist Party (CCP), called Politburo meetings and decided on October 5 to send troops to aid North Korea, even though Stalin had retracted his promise of air support. On October 25, the Chinese government announced that it was sending "volunteers" to Korea in the name of "resisting U.S. aggression, aiding Korea, and defending the homeland." In fact, the first wave of the Chinese People's Volunteer Force (CPVF), about 300,000 regular troops, crossed the Yalu River and entered Korea on October 19. Thereafter, the Korean War became a war between China and the United States.

From November 1950 to May 1951, the CPVF, under the command of Marshal Peng Dehuai, launched five offensive campaigns and pushed the UNF back to the south, taking Pyongyang and Seoul. Such quick deployment apparently was unexpected by the UNF. The CPVF's superiority in manpower enabled the Chinese to overcome their inferiority in equipment and technology. The CPVF concentrated a large force and attacked with a human wave. It seemed rational to the Chinese generals that a large army should serve as a decisive factor for their victory. By mid-April, Chinese forces in Korea had increased to 950,000 men. After he replaced MacArthur, General Matthew Ridgway (1895–1993) stopped the last CPVF offense. Lacking the firepower to break through the UN lines and suffering heavy casualties, the Chinese fell back to the north.

TRUCE NEGOTIATIONS AND ARMISTICE

In the summer of 1951, the war reached a stalemate. On July 10, truce negotiations began between the Chinese–North Korean and UN-U.S. delegations. In an effort to achieve a favorable position at the negotiating table, by October China increased its troop level to 1.15 million men. In early 1952, Peng shifted his focus from eliminating enemy units in mobile warfare to securing lines in trench warfare. They infiltrated the UN trenches, using small arms fire and killing as many UN soldiers as possible, then slipped away only to repeat the attack a few nights later. Other major attacks, such as Old Baldy, Bunker Hill, and Pork Chop Hill, occurred against the UN outposts scattered across the front. By March 1953, the Chinese forces had reached a record high, about 1.35 million men. In a limited war, it was difficult for either side to overpower its opponent completely. The Chinese leaders changed their goal of driving the UNF out of Korea to a more modest one of defending China's security and ending the war with a truce agreement.

After Stalin died in March 1953, there were some positive signs in favor of an armistice. The big break came on March 28, when the Communist negotiators suddenly agreed to a previous proposal for an exchange of the sick and wounded prisoners of war (POWs). Two days later, Zhou Enlai, China's premier, issued a statement that promised a breakthrough on the POW issue. He suggested that all POWs who did not wish to be repatriated should be turned over to a neutral state. On July 27, China, North Korea, the United Nations, and the United States signed the Korean Armistice Agreement at Panmunjom.

CONSEQUENCES OF THE WAR

More than three million Chinese troops participated in the Korean War, with more than one million casualties, including 152,000 dead, 383,000 wounded, 450,000 hospitalized, 21,300 POWs, and 4,000 missing in action. China spent ten billion yuan in renminbi (equal to $3.3 billion according to the exchange rate at that time) on the war. An estimate of the military deaths of North Korean forces was over 120,000. A total of 36,914 American soldiers lost their lives in the war. In addition, 3,960 non-Americans in the UNF died. South Korean military deaths were 300,000, and nearly one million civilians were killed.

The Korean War enhanced the Chinese government's political consolidation in its early years. Mao used the challenge and the threat brought about by the war to cement Communist authority over China's state and society. In late 1950, the CCP announced "national emergency" and martial law in some regions to label all the anti-communist activities as anti-government crime. In 1951, it launched a nationwide campaign to suppress "counterrevolutionaries," eradicate any resistance against CCP control, and disarm the local masses of weapons that had once been used during the long years of World War II and civil wars. Then, the party began its "three-anti" and "five-anti" campaigns to regulate China's industry and commerce by following the Soviet model in order to supply the war. As a result, China's implementation of the Soviet model was one way to emphasize the revolutionary and Communist nature of the new state.

Soviet technology and fiscal support aided China's reconstruction and economic growth. In 1955, with Soviet help, China started its first nuclear weapons program and also launched a military reform to modernize the People's Liberation Army. This marked the period of closest collaboration between Beijing and Moscow, and China became a "frontline soldier" fighting against the U.S. imperialists in the Cold War and isolated itself from most of the industrial countries. The American government viewed China's military intervention and social radicalization as an acute and imminent threat, which provoked a deep antagonism to China in the 1960s and 1970s. After the Sino-American rapprochement, the Korean War was seriously studied in China in the 1980s. The most important lesson that China learned from its involvement is to prevent such a war in the future. A largely neutral unified Korea and a less militarily oriented Korea-U.S. alliance are in the interest of China.

SEE ALSO *Korea, Relations with (North and South); Mao Zedong; Peng Dehuai; People's Liberation Army; Russia, Relations with; Sino-Soviet Schism; United States, Relations with; Wars since 1800.*

BIBLIOGRAPHY

Chen Jian. *Mao's China and the Cold War.* Chapel Hill: University of North Carolina Press, 2001.

Li Xiaobing (Xiao-bing Li), Allan Millett, and Bin Yu. *Mao's Generals Remember Korea.* Lawrence: University Press of Kansas, 2001.

Millett, Allan. *The War for Korea.* 3 vols. Lawrence: University Press of Kansas, 2005–2008.

Stueck, William. *Korean War in World History.* Lexington: University Press of Kentucky, 2004.

Li Xiaobing (Xiao-bing Li)

KUOMINTANG

SEE *Nationalist Party.*

L

LABOR

This entry contains the following:

OVERVIEW

China's transition from an agrarian to an industrial society is characterized by three distinct phases: (1) the emergence of industrial labor before 1949; (2) the transformation of a nascent working class into a socialist workforce; and (3) its diversification after the beginning of economic and social reforms in the 1980s. Today, China has the largest labor force in the world, accounting for 26.8 percent of the total figure.

THE EMERGENCE OF INDUSTRIAL LABOR

In 1919 the new working class accounted for only 1.5 million people and formed a tiny minority of 0.5 percent of China's vast population. Even in major cities, the vast majority of workers were self-employed or worked in family-run stores and workshops. There was no significant industrialization in China before 1949. A main feature of economic development was the dominant position of the Great Powers. A national Chinese industry only mushroomed once imperial rule ended. After a short period of rapid development in the 1920s, modern industrial enterprises still accounted for only 2.2 percent of the net social product in 1933. Precapitalist economic relations not only predominated in the countryside but also in the towns.

THE RISE OF A SOCIALIST WORKFORCE

When the Communists took power in 1949, the Chinese labor force, according to postreform statistics, numbered 181 million, its structure similar to that of other underdeveloped countries: 91.5 percent were rural laborers, 4.5 percent (or 8 million) were urban staff and workers (mostly employed in small private workshops), and 4 percent were urban self-employed. Within only eight years, handicraftsmen were organized into cooperatives, private workshops were transferred to collective and state-owned work units (*danwei*), and China's manufacturing economy was transformed into large-scale "modern" enterprises—accompanied by an unprecedented industrial expansion, especially in heavy industry.

Employment in the industrial sector had risen to twenty-one million by 1957, while collectivization of agriculture and the introduction of the household-registration system (*hukou zhidu*) effectively restricted rural-to-urban migration and erected an "invisible Great Wall" between the cities and the countryside. With the exception of the Great Leap Forward, which briefly swelled the ranks of the industrial workforce, industrial employment remained constant at around 8.6 percent of the working population, only growing from the natural increase of the urban population. Strict controls on labor mobility created a stable pattern of rural-urban dualism in employment with sectoral inequalities that affect labor-market segmentation to this day.

REFORM AND DIVERSIFICATION

It was only in the 1970s that industrial employment began to rise again. Rural collectives were allowed to channel savings into small-scale industries creating alternatives to farm employment. With the dissolution of the collectives and the relaxation of the *hukou* system, peasants could choose to move to the cities.

The 1980s saw a massive return to self-employment—introduced to absorb the youth returning from the countryside where they had been sent during the Cultural Revolution (*xiaxiang qingnian*), along with a rise of foreign investments after the opening of China and the reemergence of private enterprises. The development of new forms of ownership was accompanied by the restructuring of collective and state-owned enterprises and the dismantling of comprehensive welfare provisions. Many small and medium-sized state-owned enterprises were privatized.

Between 1978 and 2006, the Chinese labor force rose from 401.5 million people to 764 million. The Chinese employment structure is profoundly influenced by China's urbanization patterns. According to official statistics, the ratio of urban-to-rural employment only changed from 23.7 percent urban/76.3 percent rural at the beginning of the reforms in 1978 to 37.1 percent urban/62.9 percent rural in 2006. This figure does not include rural-to-urban migrants, however, 24.2 percent of whom were employed in industry, 21.1 percent in construction, and approximately 50 percent in trade and services. In dangerous industries such as mining, chemical engineering, or firework production, more than half of the employees are rural residents.

Labor reforms helped China to undergo a structural change from a predominantly agrarian to a modern industrial and service economy, as well as a systemic change from a planned to a market economy. The share of jobs in agriculture decreased from 70.5 percent (1978) to 42.6 percent (2006), whereas the shares of jobs in industry and the service sector increased from 17.3 percent to 25.2 percent and 12.2 percent to 32.2 percent respectively. In the same period, the share of jobs in state-owned and collectively owned enterprises decreased from 99.8 percent to 25.4 percent as a result of rising employment in foreign-owned and privately owned firms and, especially, increased self-employment (39.8% as a cumulative figure). The changes in employment patterns were made even more obvious by the growing number of rural migrants that filled the workers' ranks.

NEW LABOR RELATIONS

Labor planning guaranteed full employment and low wages. Abiding by this idea, unemployed young people were euphemistically referred to as "waiting for jobs" (*daiyezhe*)—for many years. Only later did the Chinese labor authorities acknowledge that the restructuring of the urban economy and the downsizing of the labor surplus in state-owned enterprises might lead to unemployment.

Employment growth during the 1990–2002 period is entirely accounted for by the growth of urban employment, and this is wholly attributable to the rapid growth of irregular employment (of migrant workers and laid-off urban workers). Informal work in China includes all productive, commercial, and professional activities in rural and urban areas that are not subject to labor legislation and administrative rules. It increased dramatically in the second half of the 1990s when Chinese labor policy used informal employment as a way out of urban unemployment.

As Chinese statistics state, rural migrants comprise the biggest share of those in informal (or irregular) employment. Official figures—not including rural residents—show a share of 11.6 percent for nonclassified laborers in urban areas in 1995, rising to 40 percent in 2006. The increasing use of informal and atypical labor in urban areas displays enterprises' endeavors to cope with reforms and economic globalization, but these have actually led to employment conditions deteriorating (with extremes like slavery-type work and child labor) and income inequality increasing.

The massive expansion of China's manufacturing industry has spawned thousands of "sweatshops" that often violate labor and safety rules. Especially small coal mines—meeting high energy demands of the booming industry and protected by greedy local officials—have become notorious for deadly accidents. Growingly aware of their rights, workers resort to different modes of collective action. In order to ease tension in labor relations and to further institutionalization the Chinese government began its biggest modernization project in labor legislation so far in 2007.

The "invisible Great Wall" between the countryside and cities has become more permeable. The growing private employment sector has opened up an unexpected degree of job mobility and regional migration. Rural migrants, however, remain second-class citizens and face discriminatory treatment in a number of ways. Estimations that urban labor will become scarce around 2015 have raised awareness about the necessity of a unified labor market and an unrestrained inflow of workers from the countryside.

SEE ALSO *Labor: Unemployment; Migrant Workers; Peasantry, 1800–1900; Urban Employment and Unemployment since 1949; Women, Employment of.*

BIBLIOGRAPHY

Brooks, Ray, and Ran Tao. China's Labor Market Performance and Challenges. IMF Working Paper: WP/03/210. International Monetary Fund, 2003. http://www.imf.org/external/pubs/ft/wp/2003/wp03210.pdf

Chesneaux, Jean. *The Chinese Labor Movement, 1919–1927*. Trans. H. M. Wright. Stanford, CA: Stanford University Press, 1968.

Hebel, Jutta, and Günter Schucher, eds. *Der chinesische Arbeitsmarkt: Strukturen, Probleme, Perspektiven* [The Chinese labor market: Structures, problems, perspectives]. Hamburg, Germany: Institut für Asienkunde, 2004.

State Council of the People's Republic of China, Information Office. White Paper: China's Employment Situation and Policies. 2004. http://www.china.org.cn/e-white/20040426/index.htm

Walder, Andrew G. *Communist Neo-traditionalism: Work and Authority in Chinese Industry*. Berkeley: University of California Press, 1986.

Wang Feiling (Fei-Ling Wang). *From Family to Market: Labor Allocation in Contemporary China*. Lanham, MD: Rowman and Littlefield, 1998.

Günther Schucher

CHINA AND THE INTERNATIONAL LABOUR ORGANIZATION

China has been a member of the International Labour Organization (ILO) since its inception in 1919. The Republic of China on Taiwan retained the membership when the People's Republic of China was proclaimed in 1949. In 1971 the ILO recognized the People's Republic as the legitimate representative of China, but China was not an active ILO member until 1983, when a Chinese delegation was sent to the International Labour Conference.

China's membership in the ILO has been marked by controversy. China has persistently refrained from endorsing the fundamental rights and principles of the ILO, particularly the right to freedom of association. Moreover, China has not ratified core ILO conventions, including convention 87, concerning freedom of association, and convention 98, concerning collective bargaining. China insists that all union activity on Chinese territory must be authorized "according to law" and fall within the purview of the All-China Federation of Trade Unions, but the Committee on Freedom of Association of the ILO Governing Body has argued since 1951 that the All-China Federation of Trade Unions obstructs independent unionizing. Meanwhile, the ILO and China have gradually agreed to the terms of a framework for procedural cooperation.

The 1971–1989 period was characterized by specific exemptions and entitlements in favor of China. In 1983 the ILO canceled China's accrued debt and a member of the All-China Federation of Trade Unions gained a worker seat in the ILO Governing Body. The following year China abrogated twenty-three conventions ratified by the Republic of China, but welcomed technical assistance, and an ILO branch office was opened in Beijing in 1985. China's shift from a low-key player to an assertive one culminated in March 1989, when Guan Jinghe, China's ILO symposium delegate, stated that it was "not possible [for China] to meet with the requirement of extensive application of ILO conventions and recommendations."

International reaction to the Chinese government's crackdown on the 1989 Prodemocracy Movement set the stage for an adversarial period from 1989 to 1994. Seeing that trade-union activists had suffered from the crackdown, the ILO suspended all plans for technical assistance and held China responsible for breach of constitutional ILO principles. On the basis of complaints by the International Confederation of Free Trade Unions, the Committee on Freedom of Association instituted the famous Case No. 1,500, charging China with violations of the right to freedom of association. A test of strength ensued after China's initial response that the actions of the committee were "blatant intervention in the internal affairs of China." By the time the case concluded in 1992, China had withdrawn its claim that the ILO should not interfere and provided the information required for the case. Three other cases followed, with similar outcomes. In 1990 the All-China Federation of Trade Unions lost the worker seat in the ILO Governing Body, and in 1994 China failed to obtain the chairmanship of the body.

From 1994 to the present (2008), China has lobbied across the ILO tripartite structure of government, employers, and workers for acknowledgement from such influential Worker's Group members as the International Confederation of Free Trade Unions. In 1998 China voted in favor of the ILO Declaration on Fundamental Principles and Rights at Work, which highlights freedom of association. China has repeatedly expressed great willingness to strengthen its cooperation with the ILO, and the Ministry of Labor and Social Security and the All-China Federation of Trade Unions have signed several memoranda of understanding to that effect. In 2001 the National Tripartite Consultative Committee was set up, and the All-China Federation of Trade Unions pursues an ongoing strategy of attaining and keeping a worker seat on the ILO governing body. By April 2008 China had ratified 25 of 188 conventions.

SEE ALSO *International Organizations, Relations with, 1900–1949; International Organizations, Relations with, since 1949.*

BIBLIOGRAPHY

Kent, Ann. China, International Organizations and Regimes: The ILO as a Case Study in Organizational Learning. *Pacific Affairs* 70, 4 (Winter 1997–1998): 517–532.

Mads Holst Jensen

LABOR AND PERSONNEL ADMINISTRATIONS

Prior to the launch of economic reforms in 1978, the Chinese Communist government adopted a bureaucratic system for administering wages and allocating labor. It was this system, rather than market wages, that governed labor supply and demand. Job assignments were normally made without reference to the wishes of either the employer or the employee. Although workers received promotions in wage grades, these rarely involved reassignments to different jobs. Nor were transfers from one employing unit to another common: Without official consent—rarely granted—such transfers were practically impossible. There was little or no private sector to which workers could move from their official assignments. The spatial mobility of labor was severely controlled and restricted by means of the residential-registration (*hukou*) system.

THE CADRE/WORKER DISTINCTION

Under this system, Chinese employees were identified as belonging to one of two major categories—cadre (*ganbu*) and worker (*gongren*). *Ganbu* indicated a broader range of occupations, including administrative staff in government departments and in institutions and schools; managerial staff in enterprises; and all types of professionals, including medical and legal professionals, engineers, teachers, scientists, artists, journalists, and those in other occupations for university graduates. The majority of workers (*gongren*) were without university or college education. Some cadres might have worker status but were employed in *shiye danwei* (similar to the public sector in the Western sense) as junior managerial or administrative staff, and could eventually be transferred into *ganbu* status. Their status was referred to as "replacement of gongren with ganbu status." This system stopped functioning after 1985, when permanent jobs were not granted to newcomers without tertiary-education qualifications.

Generally speaking, the administration of manual workers was undertaken by the Ministry of Labor, while the Ministry of Personnel administered cadres. The two ministries had official branches in all levels of local government and in most organizations in the state sector, and they maintained tight control of labor and personnel affairs. Historically, there have been periodic mergers and separations of these ministries in response to political needs or changes in socioeconomic circumstances. However, their main roles—one in charge of employees at the lower end (manual or blue-collar workers) and the other of employees at the higher end (political elites and those with tertiary-level education)—remained distinct. The Ministry of Labor (known since 1989 as the Ministry of Labor and Social Security) was put in charge of employment management and job training for both rural and urban labor forces. It also administered social security programs, including pensions, medical care, unemployment benefits, injury insurance, and maternity leave, mostly designed for the urban labor force. The Ministry of Personnel was primarily involved in the arena of general planning at the macro level—designing policies on organization restructuring, wages, and quota allocation within government departments and the wider public sector.

Promotions, appointments, and transfers between work units for cadres would usually be administered by the Ministry of Personnel. For high-ranking cadres, other government departments would make final decisions, which were then documented by the Ministry of Personnel. For workers, a job transfer between work units or between localities prior to the reform period was nearly impossible. The residential-registration system was the main obstacle. Before the economic reform, many married couples who worked in different localities could only enjoy a reunion once a year during their restricted annual leaves.

CADRES

Before 1984, cadres' salaries were determined by their ranks and were administered by the Ministry of Personnel. After 1984, dual components were considered in setting cadres' salaries: (1) the basic payment was fixed and equalized for all ranks of cadres; and (2) a cadre's salary was linked to his or her job responsibility. Those in ranks one through thirteen were designated *gaoji ganbu,* simplified as *gaogan* (superior-ranked cadres). *Gaogan* were directly appointed by the State Council or central level of the Chinese Communist Party according to a regulation issued by the State Council in September 1957. *Gaogan* were the most important administrators in charge of the country. Cadres ranked between fourteen and eighteen were intermediate-level cadres who usually worked in administrative positions as "section leaders" (*chuzhang*) or "division leaders" (*kezhang*). Those below rank nineteen, extending to twenty-one (then to twenty-four in the 1980s), were office clerks. *Gaogan* before the economic reform were those who joined the "revolution" (i.e., became party members) before a certain period. The lines separated the Red Army period (1921–1937), the Anti-Japanese War period (1937–1945), and the anti-Nationalist period (1946–1949).

All new cadres since 1950, including such professionals as doctors, engineers, accountants, teachers, and departmental administrative staff, were expected to be university or college graduates or were promoted through some specific educational scheme. Once one was on the payroll for *ganbu*, one's social status and occupational duties would be higher than those of workers. Most important, there would be the possibility of promotion into higher ranks. Most of these new cadres were, in fact, professionals in the Western sense rather than real cadres. Categorizing them as "cadres" was probably the easiest way to manage their salaries or to differentiate them from workers who had lower qualifications and hence were paid less. Within all professions, salary level was linked to education, skills, and seniority, and the Ministry of Personnel oversaw detailed assessment of professionals. Even after the implementation of economic reforms, the *ganbu* ranking system remains firmly in use in the state sector and government departments. Administrative ranks such as minister (*buzhang*), bureau leader (*juzhang*), section leader (*chuzhang*), and division leader (*kezhang*) are still very important in China. Wages and welfare payments—while employed and after retirement—remain closely related to these ranks.

WORKERS

The wages of manual laborers were divided into eight grades, with slight regional (cost of living) and industrial variations. Workers were categorized into broad occupations, and each occupation spanned a number of grades. The pay specified for an occupation varied according to the size and importance of the employing organization. More important, interenterprise differences could arise on account of piece rates, bonuses, and subsidies, depending on the profits or resources of each employer. Within the employing unit, training and educational qualifications were relevant, but seniority—one's length of employment—was the dominant criterion. Wages were more attached to individuals than to the precise jobs they performed. Grades three to eight designated higher-skilled workers, whose qualification for promotion was based on job-skill assessment. The wage gap between the lowest and the highest was narrow—about ten times more at the highest level. Seniority also decided workers' welfare entitlements. For example, housing allowances and pension scales were calculated on the basis of seniority. With the reduction of state-owned enterprises and the emergence of nonstate sectors, workers have lost many of their past entitlements.

SEE ALSO *Cadre System; Unit (danwei).*

BIBLIOGRAPHY

Howe, Christopher. *Wage Patterns and Wage Policy in Modern China, 1919–1972.* Cambridge, U.K.: Cambridge University Press, 1973.

Knight, John, and Lina Song. *Towards a Labour Market in China.* Oxford, U.K., and New York: Oxford University Press, 2005.

Li Weiyi. *Zhougguode gongzi zhidu* [China's wage system]. China Labour Publishing House, 1992.

Lina Song

TRADE UNIONS

Following the nation's advance toward market socialism, new hybrid patterns of industrial relations in the workplace signify convergence with those of capitalist economies. Yet mindful of its socialist heritage, the state seeks to reinstate a low-profile soft regime of political control at the basic work-unit level.

CHINESE TRADE UNIONS AND THE ALL-CHINA FEDERATION OF TRADE UNIONS

The Trade Union Law of 1950 enshrined the All-China Federation of Trade Unions (ACFTU) as an integral part of the politico-ideological system of "democratic centralism," but its grass-roots workplace unions were docile and accommodating toward management. The ACFTU was suspended in 1967 during the Cultural Revolution (1966–1969) and revived later in 1978 at its Ninth National Congress. Yet the 1982 Constitution did not reinstate workers' right to strike, underscoring the state's anxiety to contain the power of unions. In 2007, the ACFTU comprised ten industrial unions at the national level and thirty-one trade-union federations at the regional level, with a total membership of 150 million workers.

Since the early 1980s, the ACFTU has pledged to promote and support the state's economic reforms. This mission to act as an agency of the state in its drive toward modernization is consistent with its role as a conduit for transmitting party policy, as endorsed by the 1992 Trade Union Law and its 2001 amendments. To prevent widespread labor agitation arising from enterprise reforms, the ACFTU has been entrusted with retraining and providing reemployment assistance to laid-off workers—a mission that it has pursued with rigor and efficacy. Vis-à-vis the increasingly contractual nature of employment which emphasizes individualism bred by competitive performance and rewards, Chinese unions serve as an appropriate agent for the state for arresting and containing such an anomic drift, which could undermine the collectivistic tradition of Chinese industrial relations.

In an increasingly commercialized labor market, unions within the ACFTU began to defend the employment and occupational interests of vulnerable workers, especially in foreign-funded firms where deplorable working conditions exist. They developed a less state-controlled, more worker-oriented agenda that addresses hitherto politically sensitive issues of labor-management disputes, industrial conflicts, strikes, and collective bargaining. Such a strategy is also preemptive. By genuinely representing workers, mainstream Chinese unions can compete more effectively with the underground labor movement. Where the workplace is already organized, the Trade Union Law of 2001 enshrines as the bargaining agent the single-shop union invariably belonging to the ACFTU.

To address the explosion of labor unrest as the gulf between labor and management widens in post-reform China, labor unions within the ACFTU have been tasked with formalizing a new pattern of collective labor relations with enterprises. The 1994 Labor Law was drawn up in part to facilitate the process in two specific ways. First, it prescribes that unions are to engage in collective contract bargaining, enabling the state to use these negotiated contracts to bring employment practices into conformity with the labor law. Second, state, enterprise, and labor are mandated to jointly resolve labor disputes. To this end the state has created a nationwide hierarchical network of tripartite commissions to adjudicate wage and labor disputes at the provincial, municipal, and district levels. These commissions are empowered to intervene in workplace disputes. Although collective contracts are heavily biased toward accommodation, union recognition has been limited within the foreign-funded sector, notwithstanding the 2001 Trade Union Law that obliges employers to recognize workplace unions within the ACFTU. In contrast, state-owned enterprises are more prone to recognize the unions and negotiate collective contracts.

The state remains ambivalent about the legality of strikes. An earlier provision in the Constitution safeguarding workers' right to strike, rescinded in the 1960s, is not likely to be reinstated. This is because the state, apprehensive about escalating levels of labor disputes, fears a possible increase in industrial unrest stimulated by enshrining the right to strike.

WORKPLACE DEMOCRACY

According to government, democratic management of the workplace has always been a key concern of industrial relations in state-owned enterprises. Workers' congresses, designated for the practice of workplace democracy, were designed to help regulate the interests of the state, enterprises, and workers by monitoring and resolving contradictions in enterprises.

In the 1980s workers' congresses were at their zenith in prerogatives and status with workers made responsible for key positions in plant administration and even election of directors and managers (Provisional Regulations Concerning Congresses of Workers and Staff Members in State-Owned Industrial Enterprises, 1981, Article 3). Although the euphoria attached to the workers' congresses appears to have ebbed around the turn of the twenty-first century, recent initiatives herald a state-sponsored movement to mandate workers' congresses to recollectivize labor relations and to practice industrial democracy, for example, the implementation of a new Labor Contract Law in January 2008. The law urges companies to vest workers' congresses with the power of vetting managerial decisions affecting employment and endorsing the labor contracts of personnel. The new model of workers' congresses appears to be inspired by the European system of works councils and is consistent with the consultative management style that the state encourages, yet this blueprint falls short of wholesale convergence with Western practices in capitalist societies, inasmuch as the workplace trade-union branch still serves as the congress's administrative arm when it is in recess. By such a design the state can still hold each in check and prevent either from aggrandizing power.

BIBLIOGRAPHY

Chan, Anita. Chinese Trade Unions and Workplace Relations in State-Owned and Joint-Venture Enterprises. In *Changing Workplace Relations in the Chinese Economy*, ed. Malcolm Warner. London: Macmillan, 2000.

Chen, F. Between the State and Labor: The Conflict of Chinese Trade Unions Double Identity in Market Reform. *China Quarterly* 176 (2003): 1006–1028.

Child, John. *Management in China during the Age of Reform*. Cambridge, U.K.: Cambridge University Press, 1994.

Clarke, S. Post-socialist Trade Unions: China and Russia. *Industrial Relations Journal* 36, 1 (January 2005): 2–18.

Ng, Sek Hong. One Brand of Democracy: The Workers Congress in the Chinese Enterprise. *Journal of Industrial Relations* 25, 2 (1984): 56–75.

Ng, Sek Hong, and Olivia Ip. Unemployment in China and the All-China Federation of Trade Unions. In *Unemployment in China*, ed. Malcolm Warner and Grace Lee, 65–86. London: Routledge, 2007.

Ng, Sek Hong, and Malcolm Warner. *China's Trade Unions and Management*. London: Macmillan, 1998.

Sek Hong Ng
Olivia Ip

MARKET

From the beginning, Chinese labor reforms have aimed at eliminating everything that fetters the development of labor's productive forces—an ambitious goal given that China previously had the most rigid labor system in the socialist world. It strictly separated rural from urban labor by means of household registration (*hukou*), concentrated almost all urban staff and workers (*zhigong renyuan*) in public enterprises, governed labor supply and demand by labor planning, and controlled mobility tightly. Wages were determined administratively without any regard to productivity, their levels low and egalitarian. But employees enjoyed lifelong job tenure and social security from the cradle to the grave provided by their work unit (*danwei*). Enterprises lacking the ability to adapt to changing production requirements relied on labor hoarding and produced a huge surplus of workers.

LABOR REFORMS

Reforms were aimed at raising labor efficiency in order to support the economic modernization project. Driven by the desire to enhance public living conditions, China's leadership permitted competition among state firms and with the nonstate sector, and it initiated changes in enterprise management. Priority, however, was given to rural reforms: Restraints on off-farm activities were relaxed, leading to the remarkable growth of cooperative "township and village enterprises" (TVEs) and private firms. With the abandonment of food rationing and the loosening of *hukou* controls, urban migration became a second alternative to farming.

The first national work conference on urban labor in 1980 adopted a more flexible employment strategy: Urban job seekers were allowed to find work themselves to ease pressure resulting from young people "waiting for jobs" (*daiye qingnian*), and enterprises were granted more autonomy in choosing their workforce according to their own needs and in deviating from preset wage scales. The state gradually retreated from its responsibility for matching supply and demand, finally exposing even high-school graduates to market forces.

Labor reforms were a highly sensitive issue. Under Maoist ideology, labor had been considered a general right. Low but egalitarian wages and high employment were part of the legitimization of Communist rule. Reforms thus prompted a reevaluation of labor and were accompanied by controversial theoretical debates that finally led to the acknowledgment of labor as a "production factor."

The most significant reform was the implementation of a "contract labor system" in 1986. Four new labor regulations concerned the introduction of fixed contracts for all newly employed workers; the selection, engagement, and dismissal of new employees; and provisions for unemployment benefits. Although limited to state-owned enterprises and the newly employed—a restriction that was conducive to social stability but reduced its effectiveness—the regulations marked the beginning of the gradual dismantling of the "iron rice bowl," the permanent-employment system for state employees.

The adoption of a new labor law in 1994 (effective from 1995) marked the transition from the planned labor system to a labor market. For the first time, a labor law addressed all kinds of workers in institutions with all types of ownership and set in place a uniform legal framework. The legislation recognized the disparity of interests between workers and management and shifted the financial burden of welfare away from the state-funded *danwei* and onto the employers and workers themselves by stipulating a contribution-based social security system.

Finally focusing reforms on the formerly privileged group of state workers in the second half of the 1990s, the program of layoffs (*xiagang*) enabled the still overstaffed state-owned enterprises to remove surplus labor. With the complete termination of state-planned labor, labor had finally become a commodity. By 2006, the socialist forms of labor organization had been remarkably reduced. Former privileged workers and staff in state-owned and collectively owned working units accounted for less than 10 percent of China's total workforce. Forty percent of the urban laborers worked in units with private (domestic and foreign) ownership or were self-employed. In the countryside, the same share of laborers (41%) worked in township and village enterprises, in private firms, or on a self-employed basis. This dramatic transformation of the socialist labor system has had far-reaching implications for the institutional setting of the Chinese labor regime in general, especially in the realms of industrial relations, social control, social security, and welfare.

THE CONSEQUENCES OF COMPRESSED DEVELOPMENT

Due to the accelerated pace of late industrialization and the accompanying transformation from a planned to a market economy, China is a case of compressed development that has not always been staged or sequential, thus old and new institutions exist simultaneously. One consequence of this is the parallel occurrence of industrialization and deindustrialization, that is, the rapid rise of a service sector, another one of the opposite trends of flexibilization of labor conditions in public sectors and standardization in private sectors. While some workers still enjoy full employment on the basis of an unlimited labor contract, evidence suggests that irregular and informal work is not a transitory phenomenon but rather a persisting one.

Although the productive characteristics of workers are increasingly being rewarded, labor reforms nevertheless lag behind. The present labor market is still influenced by its socialist past, having inherited a considerable inequality between different segments of labor. Market participants lack job-specific information that attaches importance to social networks. The voluntary mobility rate is still especially low, while the involuntary rate has increased since the implementation of the retrenchment program in the state sector. In the Chinese "three-tier" labor market, non-retrenched urban workers enjoy higher wages than retrenched and reemployed workers or migrants. The most competitive market is that for rural-urban migrants.

Flexibility and security have become the central parameters of modern labor markets. Both are highly significant in China, which has ruled out its former socialist welfare system. Therefore, new social protection systems have to be erected that reconcile the need for flexible labor with that of employment and income security.

Only recently has labor legislation taken a new turn. In 2007 legislators adopted the Labor Contract Law, the Employment Promotion Law, and the Labor Dispute Law—the biggest-ever modernization of labor laws in China, which sets a clear framework for future labor-market development. The Chinese government is taking an inclusive approach to non-regular and private employment, and enforces labor contracts in order to limit arbitrary dismissals and hiring under unsuitable conditions. Thus, recent labor policy in China intends to tame the market forces.

SEE ALSO *Socialist Market Economy; Unit (danwei).*

BIBLIOGRAPHY

Baur, Michaela, et al., eds. *Labour Mobility in Urban China: An Integrated Labour Market in the Making?* Berlin: LIT Verlag, 2006.

Cai Fang, et al. *Zhongguo laodongli shichang zhuanxing yu fayu* [How close is China to a labor market?]. Beijing: Shangwu Yinshuguan, 2005.

Hebel, Jutta, and Günter Schucher. *Zwischen Arbeitsplan und Arbeitsmarkt: Strukturen des Arbeitssystems in der VR China* [From labor plan to labor market: Structures of the PRC labor system]. Hamburg, Germany: Institut für Asienkunde, 1992.

Hebel, Jutta, and Günter Schucher, eds. *Der chinesische Arbeitsmarkt: Strukturen, Probleme, Perspektiven* [The Chinese labor market: Structures, problems, perspectives]. Hamburg, Germany: Institut für Asienkunde, 2004.

Knight, John, and Song Lina. *Towards a Labour Market in China.* New York: Oxford University Press, 2005.

Günter Schucher

MOBILITY

Before the establishment of the socialist planned economy, China was an exceptionally mobile society. Many groups in Chinese society made their living moving around, including petty traders in the rural market system and merchants who ran long-distance trade among regional cities. Furthermore, large-scale migration was a permanent feature of Chinese society, as exemplified by the colonization of Sichuan in late Qing times. The main cause of such migration was population pressure on scarce land, recurrently aggravated by war and such civil unrest as the Taiping Uprising (1851–1864). This mobility was embedded into enabling social structures, which also supported the outflow of Chinese migrants to other regions of the world, such as Southeast Asia. "Sojourning" was a leitmotif of Chinese life both on the mainland and globally.

In contrast, one of the striking features of the Chinese socialist economy was its tight constraint on labor mobility. Such constraint stood in stark contrast to the Soviet model of forced industrialization, which supported urbanization by destroying and depopulating rural society. The shadows of this peculiar institutional arrangement continue to have an impact on China's economic development, in particular on the competitiveness of the Chinese export sector, the social-structural evolution of the urban economy, and regional development and imbalances. This mainly refers to interregional mobility, the focus of this entry. Intersectoral mobility was also tightly constrained in the pre-reform economy, even down to the enterprise level. This constraint was partly related to the general suppression of spatial mobility, such as the constraints on people's efforts to move up in the hierarchy of the Chinese urban system.

Further constraints on mobility resulted from the closed nature of the Chinese work unit, which operated as a cradle-to-grave system. In the urban economy, these constraints on mobility within the urban economy began rapidly disintegrating, especially after the launch of serious reform of the state-owned enterprise sector in the mid-1990s. This development stands in contrast to the lasting repercussions of institutional constraints on interregional mobility. According to the 2000 census, the rate of interprovincial migration in China was much lower than in other large developed economies, the public image of crowded main stations at spring festival notwithstanding.

After the upsurge of rural-to-urban migration in the mid-1950s, China instituted a unique system of migration control that effectively tied Chinese farmers to their native area, even constricting short-term mobility by means of travel permits. In addition, the urban system of food rationing made it almost impossible to survive in cities as an illegal migrant. This situation resulted in a dualistic economic and social system, with few contacts between the urban and the rural sectors, outside of those resulting from the production quotas imposed on the rural economy. The only migration flows that played a visible economic role were the policy-induced relocations of workers and personnel to the western provinces, which accompanied the so-called third-line investment surge of the mid-1960s.

In the mid-1980s, this system was slightly liberalized for the first time when temporary residence certificates for rural migrant workers were introduced. Despite possession of such certificates, migrant workers could be sent back to their rural homes on short notice, a measure that was taken, for example, during the post-Tiananmen recession.

After the resurgence of the urban economy, the number of migrant workers exploded, resulting in what was perceived by the Chinese public as a "blind wave" and was classified statistically as the "floating population" (*liudong renkou*). With urban resentment growing, the Chinese government switched to a more positive propaganda. Migrant workers now contribute crucially to the urban construction boom and to the competitiveness of the Chinese export sector. To this group must be added the increasing number of people who change their *hukou*; this occurs mainly on the lower level of the urban hierarchy and in provinces with rapid urbanization, such as Zhejiang.

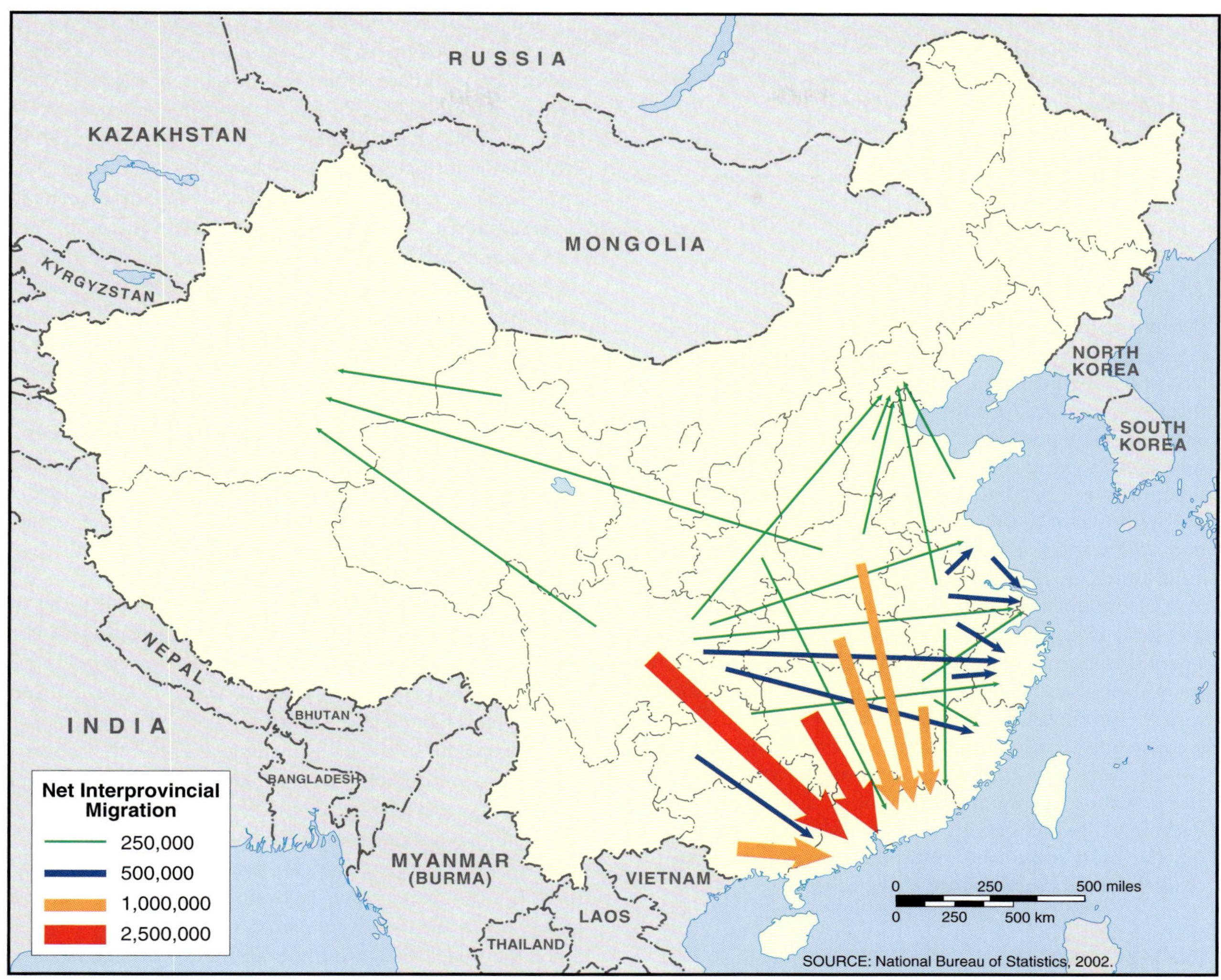

Interregional mobility in China is structured along a regional hierarchy. The primary contributors to overall mobility are people who move between urban areas and adjacent rural areas. This fact is important for assessing the statistical data about migration, because such intercounty migration was not included in earlier censuses, thus leading to probable overestimation of the growth in volume of migration flows. Interprovincial flows of labor manifest a distinct pattern. The largest flows move from the southwestern and western provinces to Guangdong, thus feeding the export economy with cheap labor. In the 2000 census, Guangdong was the province with the highest in-migration rate, as well as the lowest out-migration rate. By comparison, flows toward the northern provinces are minuscule. The only noncoastal province with a net inflow was Xinjiang, reflecting the attraction of its resource-rich economy.

Labor mobility is a major cause of structural change in China's modernizing society. The almost complete repression of mobility in the Maoist system resulted in closed rural communities and a stratified urban society with distinct privileges attached to different kinds of workplaces. Today, mobility triggers economic and social changes. For example, many migrant workers return to their native places to set up independent businesses based on the skills and knowledge they accumulated as sojourners. Intraprovincial migration is the driving force of rapid urbanization, especially on the level of the prefectural center. Historical patterns that were disrupted by the socialist planned economy are finally unfolding—in particular, the Han colonization of the far west, especially Tibet, which is mainly caused by economic factors.

SEE ALSO *Internal Migration and Internal Colonization since 1800; Migrant Workers.*

BIBLIOGRAPHY

Fan, C. Cindy. Interprovincial Migration, Population Redistribution, and Regional Development in China: 1990 and 2000 Census Comparisons. *Professional Geographer* 57, 2 (2005): 295–311.

Knight, John, and Lina Song. *Towards a Labour Market in China.* Oxford, U.K., and New York: Oxford University Press, 2005.

Pieke, Frank N., and Hein Mallee, eds. *Internal and International Migration: Chinese Perspectives.* Richmond, U.K.: Curzon, 1999.

Carsten Herrmann-Pillath

UNEMPLOYMENT

Because of the demographic composition of its population, China has a large working-age population and a high rate of labor-force participation. Until 2008, the vast majority of this workforce faced a labor market that was largely unregulated, with few provisions for the unemployed and few legal constraints to keep companies from laying off workers. This situation was exacerbated by the comprehensive reform of the public sector of the urban economy that started after the mid-1990s and was only gradually complemented by the build-up of an urban social security system. Thus, at the turn of the millennium, Chinese socialism featured one of the most deregulated labor markets in the world. After a period of incremental experiments in decentralized reform, re-regulation was finally launched in a comprehensive fashion with the promulgation of the Labor Law in 2008. This law increases job security for all kinds of employment contracts. Nevertheless, labor-market forecasts suggest that China will face a serious unemployment problem until at least 2015. Because China still manifests an underdeveloped service sector, the most important contribution toward meeting this challenge is structural change of the economy.

INSTITUTIONAL DETERMINANTS OF UNEMPLOYMENT

Under the pre-reform system, unemployment was regarded as nonexisting by definition, because rational economic planning was expected to suppress the cyclical and structural causes of unemployment. As a consequence of the post-1978 transition to a market economy, unemployment emerged as a major policy issue. This is the central paradox of the "Chinese miracle": China has achieved a unique growth performance, but it has been accompanied by rising unemployment.

However, this perception is misleading once one takes into consideration the distinction between underemployment and unemployment, which is mainly determined by institutional factors. Under the Maoist command economy, unemployment was hidden because of the employment guarantee in the urban state-owned sector and because of the *hukou* (household registration) system, which blocked the flow of the rural unemployed into the cities. The rural sector was repeatedly used as a safety valve for the urban economy, such as when large numbers of urban youths were "sent down" to the countryside in the aftermath of the Cultural Revolution.

This immense hidden unemployment surfaced in the very low productivity of the Chinese economy. For example, econometric estimates of the productivity of Chinese state-owned enterprises (SOEs) in the early 1990s revealed surplus labor of more than 20 percent of the workforce. These institutional factors continue to shape the issue today. The main result is that the measurement of unemployment in China continues to be divided into rural and urban regions. The status of migrant workers in cities lingers in between, as they can be sent back to their rural homes, thus opening a safety valve for the urban labor market. As a result, the true rate of unemployment in China can only be approximated for the registered urban population. According to official statistics, the unemployment rate in Chinese provinces varies around 4 percent in the first decade of the new millennium. Most experts estimate the true rate to be up to 10 percent in the same period.

RURAL UNEMPLOYMENT

The severity of the Chinese unemployment problem can be indirectly observed in the country's rapidly increasing income inequality, as well as in the gap between the average per capita incomes of rural and urban workers, which reflects the scarcity of skilled labor and the oversupply of nonskilled labor in the countryside. In the past, unemployment in the countryside was assumed away, because every rural citizen was entitled to access to a minimum level of agricultural land. In this sense, all rural workers could be at least self-employed. Therefore, the common procedure for measuring rural unemployment is to estimate surplus labor under the assumption that thelevel of productivity approximates the technology frontier. Since the mid-1980s, a number of these econometric exercises have resulted in staggering numbers of "superfluous" workers (more than 100 million). This surplus was identified as the source of large-scale migration to the cities, as these workers targeted job opportunities generated by high industrial growth and, in particular, the construction boom.

This hidden unemployment has increasingly turned into open unemployment because reallocation of agricultural land to nonagricultural uses takes place mainly at the fringes of the cities. Although farmers are compensated for abandoning their land-use rights, they lose their implicit social security and turn into landless rural workers. Because this process is often enforced by local authorities, the growing anguish among farmers feeds collective action against the perceived injustice. Thus, social unrest in the Chinese countryside is mainly driven by creeping fears of permanent unemployment without any income support. There is an increasing number of rural youths who receive no training in agriculture and therefore perceive themselves as unemployed workers when they are laid off. The true unemployment rate in the Chinese countryside is thus difficult to estimate, but a safe bet would arrive at double the urban rate.

Laid-off workers looking for jobs, Shenyang, Liaoning province, October 10, 2006. *With little work available in rural areas and restrictions on travel relaxed in the late twentieth century, many Chinese migrated to larger cities, taking advantage of new factories established during the country's transition to a market economy. However, few social security benefits exist for these migrant workers, leaving many without resources if they become unemployed.* © SUN HAI/EPA/CORBIS

URBAN UNEMPLOYMENT

On the occasion of its Sixteenth Party Congress in 2002, the Chinese Communist Party for the first time identified the creation of employment as a central task of government policies. This shift in emphasis was part and parcel of the propagation of the "harmonious society" under the Hu

Jintao and Wen Jiabao leadership. The sense of urgency resulted from the fact that the increasing open unemployment in rural areas met with a parallel trend in the cities. Again, the best indicator of the seriousness of the issue is the swelling ranks of the urban poor, which are almost identical with permanently unemployed people.

The true rate of urban unemployment over time is almost impossible to evaluate, because the statistics changed together with institutional changes. In the early stages of reform, the ranks of the unemployed were composed partly of laid-off workers who remained affiliated with their company (the so-called *xia gang* workers) and partly of those in special statistical categories, such as "waiting for employment." Today, urban unemployment is mainly fed by the following sources: (1) laid-off workers, (2) college graduates without jobs, (3) unemployed temporary migrant workers, and (4) the self-employed with failed businesses.

A major factor determining urban unemployment is the restructuring of the public-owned sector. This includes mainly the state-owned sector, but may also include enterprises with mixed ownership regimes, such as township and village enterprises (TVEs), in the more developed and urbanized regions of the Chinese countryside. In all these cases, companies face competitive pressure to upgrade their products and their process management in order to cope with international competition. Very often, this implies the adoption of more capital-intensive production techniques, which triggers the shedding of low-skilled labor. This effect stands in continuity with the fact that China after 1949 pursued a capital-intensive industrialization strategy, which was accompanied by the aforementioned institutional containment of hidden unemployment in the rural sector. Thus, the rapid modernization of the Chinese urban economy is a driving force of unemployment.

SOCIAL SECURITY AND UNEMPLOYMENT

The Labor Law of 2008 strengthens the institutional barriers for shedding labor. This normally reduces incentives for hiring workers at all, and further unemployment will certainly result. The employment prospects of university graduates continue to worsen, particularly for women. At the same time, the unemployed in China enjoy only fragmented and incomplete social security. In the rural areas, policies dealing with the unemployed are designed and implemented by local governments. Up to the mid-1990s, local governments operated as "employers of last resort," which contributed to the strong growth in public employment. Subsequent to tax reforms and the tightening of fiscal constraints on local governments, this option has been closed, and organizational alternatives are being tested, with great regional variety.

In cities, a nationwide system of unemployment insurance was gradually established to support SOE restructuring. This followed systematic institution-building measures. In 1998 a Ministry of Labor and Social Security was created, which launched the nationwide establishment of reemployment centers. These centers take over the workers' affiliation and provide support for retraining and job searches. They also pay a wage-substitute funded by contributions from companies and employees. This approach is less effective in less-developed urban regions. In particular, the financial support given to laid-off workers can be minuscule or even absent, leading to widespread discontent and unrest in some regions of China, such as the industrialized northeast, where the legacy of the planned economy looms large and industrial restructuring is still under way.

SEE ALSO *Social Policy Programs; Social Welfare; Socialist Market Economy.*

BIBLIOGRAPHY

Knight, John, and Song Lina. *Towards a Labour Market in China.* Oxford, U.K., and New York: Oxford University Press, 2005.

Lee, Grace O. M., and Malcolm Warner, eds. *Unemployment in China: Economy, Human Resources, and Labour Markets.* London and New York: Routledge, 2007.

Li Shi and Sato Hiroshi, eds. *Unemployment, Inequality, and Poverty in Urban China.* London and New York: Routledge, 2006.

Carsten Herrmann-Pillath

OUTMIGRATION

Reform in China and changes in the world economy have led to a significant increase in labor outmigration from China. At the end of 2004, 600,000 Chinese were working overseas on contracts that were longer than one year, more than ten times the 1990 figure of 58,000 (CHINCA 2004; Ministry of Commerce 2005; Center for International Exchanges 2005). However, with 25 percent of the world labor force, China contributes only 1 percent of international labor migrants. A mere 0.06 percent of the Chinese labor force works overseas, compared to the world average of 1 percent and more than 10 percent for the Philippines. The Chinese case illustrates the deeply asymmetrical nature of the process of globalization (the free flow of capital and goods in contrast to captive labor) and challenges various conventional wisdoms about labor migration.

HISTORICAL LEGACY: STATE-MANAGED, PROJECT-TIED MIGRATION

International labor migration from the People's Republic of China (PRC) started with foreign-aid projects in the 1950s, when the government sent personnel to more than fifty developing countries in Africa, Asia, Eastern Europe, and

Latin America (He Xiankai 1994, pp. 150–162). For example, 10,000 Chinese were dispatched every year to Mongolia in the second half of the 1950s, and 50,000 went to Tanzania and Zambia to build the TaZara railway from the 1960s to the 1980s (Sautman 2006, p. 8, note 38). Most of them returned, but some stayed on (see Bei Jianzhang 1994, p. 87; Hsu 2007).

Foreign-aid projects were managed by the Foreign Economic Liaison Ministry, which had branches in every province, with branch offices in prefectures. After the ministry finalized plans for aid projects, it required the provincial bureaus and their prefectural branches to organize workers to be dispatched overseas. This chain of command laid the foundation for the current commercialized labor-migration system. Agents at the higher level—normally former state-owned companies located in large cities—pass on foreign employers' orders to agents in countryside towns for labor, thus forming "agent chains."

In the late 1970s, the Chinese government introduced "self-financing aid projects" and charged aid-receiving countries fees (though at rates lower than the market price), thus starting the commercialization of overseas projects. The State Council set up four companies in 1982 specifically for carrying out international projects on a commercial basis. The number of labor migrants from the PRC increased from 22,000 in 1979 to 50,000 in 1984, almost all working through the few state companies (Yin Hao 2002).

Project-tied migrants were recruited from state-owned or collective enterprises, were paid salaries in China and a minimum foreign allowance, lived in exclusive camps with supporting staff from China, and resumed their previous positions upon their return.

NONGOVERNMENTAL CHANNELS

In 1988 the government of Fujian Province coined the term "nongovernmental channels" (*minjian qudao*) in reference to labor migration, which meant that a company sent workers as independent individuals to work for others, rather than as state employees for its own projects. A source estimated that nongovernmental channels accounted for 90 percent of all labor outmigration in the early 1990s (Long Guoqiang 1995, p. 180). In 1992 the State Council assigned the Ministry of Labor (later the Ministry of Labor and Social Security) to manage individual overseas employment, and tasked the Ministry of Foreign Technology and Economy Cooperation (later the Ministry of Commerce) to manage project-tied labor deployment. But, in reality, most labor outmigration of either type fell under the purview of the Ministry of Commerce.

In 2002 the Ministry of Labor and Social Security issued Decree Number 15 and started promoting labor outmigration as a means of alleviating domestic unemployment. The ministry licensed more than 300, mostly private, labor migration agents by 2007. The Ministry of Commerce, which had licensed about 1,600 state-owned companies for labor deployment, changed its policy in 2005 and opened the business to non-state-owned companies. Labor migration thus became further "privatized" and commercialized.

Instead of charging fees from employers, agents now rely on migrants for profits. Despite the government regulation that agents' fees should not exceed 12.5 percent of the worker's total income over the contract period that the agent guarantees, agents in 2007 charged 180,000 renminbi for a job in the United States, 140,000 for the United Kingdom, and 120,000 for Australia, far exceeding the ceiling given the workers' low wages overseas. Agent fees for jobs in Japan, South Korea, and Singapore increased from zero in the early 1990s to 40,000 renminbi in the late 2000s. In many cases, it is more expensive to migrate legally than illegally. At the same time, migrant wages remained stagnant and even decreased, in some cases dropping by more than half, over the 1990s. Labor outmigration is to a great extent engineered by agents for their own profit.

GLOBALIZATION AT THE MARGIN

In 2004 about 40 percent of Chinese migrants worked in manufacturing industries (especially textiles and food processing), with 26 percent in construction and 14 percent in agriculture, forestry, and fishing industries (CHINCA 2004, pp. 10–11). Geographically, more than 70 percent were in Asia (CHINCA 2004, p. 11), with 16 percent in Africa, 5 percent in Europe, 3 percent in Australia and New Zealand, and 2 percent in North America. The three largest destination countries were Japan (with 100,000 registered Chinese workers in November 2004), Singapore (80,000), and South Korea (47,000) (CHINCA 2004, pp. 16–17, 40–48). This is clearly at odds with the global pattern, for which North America and Australia are the major destinations. Furthermore, within the destination countries, most Chinese work in remote areas instead of major cities.

Large numbers of Chinese also migrate to other, seemingly unlikely, destinations. For example, there are about 10,000 Chinese workers in Saipan (Central Statistics Division CNMI 2008, p. 46, Table 41) and 15,000 to 20,000 in Mauritius (Mauritius Ministry of Labor, cited in Lincoln 2006, p. 76, e.n. 9) in the early 2000s. These two islands had been exempted from major countries' textile-import limits and had thus attracted foreign factories, including many invested in by Chinese from Hong Kong and Taiwan. When the enforcement of the international Agreement on Textiles and Clothing in 2004 deprived Mauritius and Saipan of special advantages, some factories relocated to such countries as Vietnam and Cambodia, and brought Chinese managers and technicians over. Jordan hosted 7,000 Chinese workers in 2003 (Xu Guolei 2003, p. 25). In order to make Jordan a "democratic" role model for the Middle East, the United States set up the first Qualified Industrial Zone in

HUMAN TRAFFICKING

Policy discussion and public media often conflate illegal migration, human smuggling, and human trafficking. Research shows that an increasing proportion of unauthorized Chinese migrants enter their destination country legally and subsequently overstay their visas. For Chinese who migrate without the approval of the authorities, the majority are smuggled—that is, they willingly paid smugglers to help them cross borders. The price ranges from $50,000 to enter the United States to $30,000 to enter western Europe and $10,000 to reach Japan (figures are based on the author's field data in 2007, corroborated with other sources). Smuggling networks operate transnationally but are not always well organized (Chin 1999; Skeldon 2003, p. 13), and migrants often face harsh working conditions but are not necessarily forced.

The conflation between human smuggling and human trafficking is partly due to technical difficulties. The United Nations (2000) defines *trafficking* as the transportation of persons by force or deception for the purpose of exploitation. *Smuggling* implies a voluntary choice on the part of the migrant. However, the United Nations defines *force* broadly and is of the view that persons subjected to power cannot consent to being exploited. In 2005 the U.S. State Department proposed the notion of *labor trafficking*—migrating to work in highly exploitative conditions. Such broad definitions could classify a large proportion of labor migrants from China, both legal and illegal, as trafficked.

The conflation is also intrinsically related to the larger world politics after the Cold War. The notion of human trafficking captured the political imagination in western Europe in the early 1990s (Wong 2005). It was feared that the social turmoil and new freedom to exit that followed the collapse of communism would bring an unstoppable human flood to the West. At the same time, with the socialism-versus-capitalism ideological debate being replaced by a civilization-against-barbarianism divide, moralist discourses such as human rights dominate the global political consciousness. The moral anxiety about migrant sex workers reinforces the discourse of human trafficking. The curious marriage between genuine concerns about human rights and the desire to contain migration is constitutive to the current global order. The human trafficking discourse calls attention to the dark side of global migration, but also bears the danger of criminalizing irregular migration that is, for many, one of the few feasible means of pursuing a better life.

BIBLIOGRAPHY

Chin Ko-Lin. *Smuggled Chinese: Clandestine Immigration to the United States*. Philadelphia: Temple University Press, 1999.

Skeldon, Ronald. *Myths and Realities of Chinese Irregular Migration*. Geneva, Switzerland: International Organization for Migration, 2003.

United Nations. *United Nations Protocol to Prevent, Suppress, and Punish Trafficking in Persons*. December 2000.

Wong, Diana. The Rumor of Trafficking: Border Controls, Illegal Migration, and the Sovereignty of the Nation-State. In *Illicit Flows and Criminal Things: States, Borders, and the Other Side of Globalization*, eds. Willem van Schendel and Itty Abraham, 69–100. Bloomington: Indiana University Press, 2005.

Xiang Biao

1998, in addition to other investments. Jordan needed cheap and organized labor, and began importing Chinese workers in 1999. Labor outmigration from China is thus part of "globalization at the margin," that is, the intensification of connections among selected peripheral places in low value-added sectors of the world economy.

While low-skilled legal migrants are confined to the margin, undocumented migrants enter the "centers" of the word economy, especially the United States and western Europe. The U.S. government estimated that between 25,000 and 50,000 Chinese arrived annually by illegal means in the 1990s (Chin Ko-Lin 1999, p. 6), and that 230,000 unauthorized Chinese lived in the United States in 2005 (Hoefer et al. 2006, p. 7, table 3). A report commissioned by the International Labor Organization estimates the number of unauthorized Chinese migrants in France to be 50,000 (Gao and Poisson 2005).

"TRANSPLANTING" LABOR

In contrast to the image that ever-expanding migrant networks make Chinese migration self-perpetuating and thus unstoppable and impervious to state intervention, labor migration in eastern Asia and to countries such as Mauritius, accounting for at least 70 percent of all labor outmigration from China, is tightly regulated. Governments of migrant-receiving countries hold employers and recruiting agents responsible for migrants' violation of rules, particularly for going underground. South Korea and Japan evaluate labor-sending countries and companies (agents) annually, blacklist those whose workers appeared to have a high tendency of absconding, and deduct their quotas or simply ban them from sending more migrants.

Under these pressures, agents in China try to control migrants by collecting security bonds (about 20,000 renminbi for Japan and 30,000 for South Korea in 2006) and housing property certificates, which will be confiscated if the migrant violates rules. It is also compulsory for a migrant to have a minimum of one civil servant (normally a relative or family friend) as a guarantor who would be fined by the agent for the migrant's wrongdoings overseas. In the receiving country, migrants are put under strict surveillance and are repatriated once the work permit terminates. In Singapore, employers and recruiting agents often work with private "security companies" to enforce deportation. Thus, Chinese migrant workers are "transplanted" from their hometowns to overseas workplaces, then back to China.

SEE ALSO *Chinese Overseas.*

BIBLIOGRAPHY

Bei Jianzhang, ed. *Zhonghuarenmingongheguo waijiaoshi: 1949–1956* [A history of the diplomacy of the People's Republic of China]. Beijing: World Knowledge, 1994.

Center for International Exchanges, Ministry of Labor and Social Security of the People's Republic of China. Jingwai jieye tongji gongzuo jiben qingkuang yu fenxi [Basic facts and analyses of the survey on overseas employment of 2004]. Unpublished report. 2005.

Central Statistics Division of the Department of Commerce, Commonwealth of the Northern Mariana Islands (CNMI), USA. *Report on the 2005 CNMI Household, Income, and Expenditures Survey.* April 1, 2008.

Chin Ko-Lin. *Smuggled Chinese: Clandestine Immigration to the United States.* Philadelphia: Temple University Press, 1999.

China International Contractors Association (CHINCA). *Zhongguo duiwai laowu hezuo niandu baobao 2004* [Annual report on China's international labor collaboration]. Beijing: China's International Contractors' Association, 2004.

Gao Yun and Véronique Poisson: *Le trafic et l'exploitation des immigrants chinois en France: Programme d'action spécial pour combattre le travail forcé* [The trafficking and exploitation of Chinese immigrants in France: Special action program to combat forced labor]. Geneva, Switzerland: International Labor Organization, 2005.

He Xiankai, ed. *Guoji laowu hezuo shiwu* [Practice of international labor cooperation]. Beijing: Industrial University Press, 1994.

Hoefer, Michael, Nancy Rytina, and Christopher Campbell. *Estimates of the Unauthorized Immigrant Population Residing in the United States: January 2005.* Washington, DC: U.S. Department of Homeland Security, 2006.

Hsu, Elisabeth. Zanzibar and Its Chinese Communities. Spec. Issue. *Populations, Space, and Place* 13 (2007): 113–124.

Lincoln, David. Beyond the Plantation: Mauritius in the Global Division of Labour. *Journal of Modern African Studies* 44, 1 (2006): 59–78.

Long Guoqiang. *Zhongguo duiwai wufu maoyi* [Trade in service from China]. Beijing: CITIC Press 1995.

Ministry of Commerce of the People's Republic of China. *Zhongguo duiwai jingji tongji nainjian* [Chinese annual statistics for overseas economy]. Beijing: Ministry of Commerce, 2005.

Sautman, Barry. Friends and Interests: China's Distinctive Links with Africa. Center on China's Transnational Relations Working Paper No. 12. Hong Kong: Hong Kong University of Science and Technology, 2006.

Xu Guolei. Zhong yue laowu hezuo xianzhuang ji qianjing. [The current situation and prospects for Sino-Jordan labor cooperation]. In *Guoji gongcheng yu laowu* [International project contracting and labor service] 12 (2003): 24–26.

Yin Hao. Gaige kaifang yilai Zhongguo duiwai laowu shuchu fazhan zongshu [A summary of the development of international labor dispatch since the reform]. *Renkou Xuekan* [Population journal] 6, 136) (2002): 12–17.

Xiang Biao

LAND TENURE SINCE 1800

The Qing Code (*Da Qing lüli*) established the basic legal framework for how magistrates adjudicated property disputes in the Qing dynasty (1644–1912). The code was, however, a criminal code that specified crimes and punishments and provided no framework for making civil adjudications. Provisions were organized in six sections patterned after the six ministries of the Qing government. Property provisions are found mostly in the "Land and House" (*tianzhai*) chapter of the "Board of Households" (*hubu*) section of the code. In keeping with the ideological framing of the code—the assertion in principle of the ruler's total power—those provisions did not recognize rights. The code treated all contract violations as criminal acts, stipulating punishment for specific violations.

Because the Qing state had an interest in nurturing agriculture, minimizing social conflict, and collecting the land tax, the Qing Code included criminal provisions against property-related crimes such as fraudulent sales, trespassing, theft, and rent arrears, as well as violations of obligations such as registering property sales with the state and payment of land taxes. Litigants drew on the legal system to protect against violations of these laws and to protect their claims to property.

The absence of a genuine civil code meant that for the great majority of people, everyday property transactions and claims were handled through custom, a set of informal norms developed and imposed by communities. Individuals within communities took on the tasks of enforcement, acting as facilitators, witnesses, guarantors, and mediators. On occasion these same individuals were also tasked by the state with reporting crimes and registering land for taxation. But those responsibilities were distinct from their informal roles as facilitators and mediators of contracts. The state was unwilling to grant notary or litigation functions to any person outside the bureaucracy.

LAND OWNERSHIP AND TENURE IN QING CUSTOM

China's tremendous geographic diversity made for different forms of customary ownership, land exchange, and land tenure practices, with varying degrees and levels of rights and claims. Some of these practices such as the conditional sale or topsoil rights were referenced in the Qing Code because these customs tended to breed legal and social conflict.

Vacant land in theory belonged to the emperor, but it could be settled and ownership could be acquired as long as it was registered for the land tax. The early Qing emperors encouraged resettlement of land vacated because of war, often providing tax holidays of three years or so. However, colonial policy varied by region. In the Qing homeland in the northeast, the state forbade Han Chinese colonization. On Taiwan and in the southwest, Han were initially prohibited from permanent settlement, and later prohibited from settling on aboriginal land for fear of conflict between Han and aboriginals. In the case of newly settled land (as well as purchased land), completing registration for the land tax secured the state's recognition of ownership. In theory, only land deeds that carried the state's mark for the land tax demonstrated land ownership, though in disputes local magistrates would recognize deeds without the mark, requiring registration after passing judgment.

Land ownership was transferred by inheritance or purchase. Land transferred by inheritance was divided in equal shares of similar quality among all sons when the household was divided (*fenjia*). Eldest sons might receive a larger share to facilitate the preservation of the patriline and support the obligatory rites associated with ancestral worship. If the household was divided when a parent was alive, one son typically received an extra share of "land for nurturing the old" (*yanglao di*) to care for the parents. The division of a household was done privately and in the presence of sons and father or a paternal uncle. No official registration was demanded other than notifying the state of changes to the land tax obligations. Daughters received land from their parents only in the absence of sons and paternal nephews. The Qing Code followed these customs, providing punishment for any violation of customary succession rules.

In addition to enforcing the rights of fathers, grandfathers, and sons to family land, custom and law recognized corporate ownership by lineages or clans. In parts of China, corporately owned ancestral land could amount to half or more of cultivated land. Lineage members inherited shares, but the land itself was held in indivisible trusts. Lineage land was seldom sold, and could be transferred only by agreement of the trustees, usually elected from lineage elders. The Qing supported ancestral property, granting it tax-exempt status and prohibiting its sale by individual lineage members. There existed other forms of cooperate property, such as temple and school lands that were similarly tax exempt. The proceeds from corporate lands supported the activities and interests of the corporate body.

Land was sold in two ways. It was sold outright (*juemai*), in which case the seller in principle severed all claims to the land. Most sellers sold their land conditionally (*dian*), however, meaning they could later redeem (*huishu*) the land at the original sale price. The buyer could farm the land, rent it out, and even sub-*dian* to a third party. If the seller did not redeem the land, the buyer could purchase the land outright by paying the *zhaotie*, the difference between the original price and the current value. The conditional sale benefited sellers. When land values rose, sellers could redeem the land at the preinflated price. This led to disputes and litigation. In 1730 the Qing state mandated that *dian* contracts stipulate the period of time in which the land was redeemable. In 1753 the state limited land redemption at thirty years. Even so, in the nineteenth and early twentieth centuries some peasants still expected that land was redeemable for indefinite periods.

The notion that claims to land could be asserted many years after the sale was apparent in other ways. Sellers often demanded a second and even a third *zhaotie* payment. In 1730 the state sought to limit this practice of supplementary payments, prohibiting any seller from demanding more than one. There is evidence that the law had some effect. Nevertheless, the *zhaojia*, a similar practice of demanding and receiving supplementary payments, was very common in the early twentieth century. Finally, there was the practice of *diya*, a loan secured by land. The lender held a lien over the land while the borrower retained use rights but could not sell without the lien holder's permission. If the borrower defaulted on the loan, the land passed into the possession of the lien holder. Interest on the loan was generally calculated as a percentage of the yearly harvest.

A similar range of claims and control of land can be seen in China's tenure systems. Tenants in Qing China generally held strong rights to the land they rented, particularly in the southern and more commercialized regions. The clearest example of strong tenant claims was the separation of "topsoil" rights from "subsoil" rights, a practice that began in the Song and spread during the Yuan and Ming dynasties. This split in rights was captured in the phrase "one field, two owners" (*yi tian, liang zhu*). Permanent topsoil rights were granted to peasants for opening waste land or for significant investments of labor and capital, or they were acquired with the payment of a deposit (*yazu*). By custom, topsoil owners could sell their rights conditionally or outright, pledge them as security on a loan, pass them on by inheritance, or lease them to another party. The owner of these rights could not be removed from the land except for failure to pay rent, and sometimes not even then. Typically, landlords could not raise rents on topsoil owners. In regions where peasants turned from one to two harvests per year during the Ming and Qing dynasties, landlords were unable to demand a rent on the second harvest.

Qing lawmakers had two main concerns when it came to tenancy. First, they monopolized legal authority over tenants. The code required landlords to bring rent-arrears tenants to court and prohibited landlords from "tying up and beating" tenants. Second, lawmakers supported the landlords' right to collect rent because landlords paid the land tax from their rental income. This was the extent of the provisions regarding tenancy in the code. However, in some provinces provincial regulations (*shengli*) did forbid the practice of receiving "topsoil" rights. Provincial administrators feared that topsoil rights made it difficult for landlords to collect their rent, leaving them unable to pay the land tax. These regulations had no demonstrable effect, and the practice of acquiring topsoil ownership continued into the twentieth century.

PROPERTY AND THE REPUBLICAN CIVIL CODE

To establish a stable tax base for the new state, landowners—including those who had not registered under the Qing—were required to register their property. The new government issued land deeds that demonstrated ownership. Vacant property could be colonized as long as it was registered.

Civil legal procedures were introduced and a civil code drafted in the late Qing, but the first civil code was not introduced until 1929 to 1930. A major concern of lawmakers in these years was the clarification and codification of land rights, balancing social equity and the needs of a capitalist economy, and introducing modern legal norms. The 1930 Land Law (which was never implemented) and the Republican Code reflected these concerns as well as ideological tensions between the left and right wings of the Guomindang. Men such as Hu Hanmin (1879–1936), the first president of the Legislative Yuan, close associate of Sun Yatsen, and subscriber to Sun's *Three Principles of the People*, pushed for greater social equity in law. Sun had called for "equalizing landownership, restraining capital" (*pingjun diquan jiezhi ziben*), having developed his ideas from Henry George's study *Progress and Poverty*, published in 1879. Sun called for the redistribution through taxation of gains made by landlords from the rising land value that came from general "social improvements." Land reform was never carried out under the Guomindang, and the 1930 Land Law did not address the question directly, though it did contain elements that reflected Sun's general concern for the "People's Livelihood" (*Minsheng*), the third of his *Three Principles of the People*. Thus, the Land Law rents were capped at 37.5 percent of the harvest, and tenants could purchase land from absentee landlords if they had cultivated the land for ten years or longer.

A national survey of customary practices was commissioned in 1907. Work continued into the Republican era, and the survey was published in 1930 as "Abstract reports on investigations of civil and commercial customs" (*Minshang shi xiguan diaocha baogao lu*). The survey framed the thinking of Republican lawmakers in their efforts to bring Chinese property law into line with Western legal norms. Conditional sales, the associated practice of *zhaojia*, and topsoil rights posed particular problems because "ownership" under these practices was not clearly defined.

Though early drafts of the Land Law had sought to end the *dian*, the final version recognized the *dian* and upheld the right of the seller to redeem the property within thirty years. Ultimately, lawmakers and politicians such as Hu Hanmin were unwilling to meddle with the conditional sale because, they maintained, it provided protections to the seller, who was understood to be the disadvantaged party. Greater restrictions were placed on topsoil owners, however. Though still allowed to sell their topsoil outright or conditionally, pass it on to heirs, or use it as security, topsoil owners could no longer freely sublease their rights. For the first time, the law made all of these rights contingent upon the payment of rent: Landlords could evict a topsoil owner who owed two years' rent. The Land Law also gave daughters and widows the right to inherit land, rejecting the Qing legal and customary practice of patrilineal succession. In the end, though, the Land Law was never implemented. The Guomindang was unwilling by the 1930s to harm the interests of landlords, its political base in the countryside, and failed to implement even the moderate rent-reduction provisions.

THE COMMUNIST AGRARIAN LAND REFORM LAW

In 1950 the Chinese Communist Party simultaneously repaid its debt to the peasantry and established an administrative foothold in every Chinese village through land reform. The means was the Agrarian Land Reform Law (ALRL), passed in June 1950. After a period of radical land-to-the tiller reforms and perceived political excesses during the civil war, the new law was more modest. Land was redistributed to poor peasants and tenants from landlords, who made up about 4 percent of the rural population and owned 30 percent of the farmland, as well as from religious bodies, schools, and clans. Landlords received shares of land equal to those of poor peasants. However, the ALRL protected most of the lands of rich peasants, who constituted about 6 percent of the rural population and controlled about 20 percent of the farmland. Rich peasants were permitted to continue to rent land to others and to hire labor. Only leased land in excess of what the rich peasants and their hired laborers worked themselves was redistributed.

Middle peasants, who by definition had just enough land to support their family and constituted 20 percent of the rural population, were untouched.

Completed in 1952, land reform redistributed 44 percent of farmland to 60 percent of the rural population, greatly expanding the middle peasantry. In 1954 middle peasants constituted 62 percent and poor peasants 29 percent of the rural population. Women's rights to land under the ALRL were equal to those of men. Moreover, the 1950 Marriage Law guaranteed unmarried, divorced, and widowed women the right to hold land. However, patrilocal practices and unwillingness of village leaders to enforce these rights combined to deny many women control over land. The ALRL was soon superseded by policy. In 1955 Mao's speech "The Question of Agricultural Cooperation" launched China on a Maoist developmental path. In 1956 private ownership of land ended as peasant lands, capital, and labor were pooled first into cooperatives, and by 1958 into 24,000 communes that remained the mainstay of agricultural production until 1980.

MARKET REFORMS AND THE HOUSEHOLD RESPONSIBILITY SYSTEM

In 1980 the party sanctioned the Household Responsibility System (HRS) and formally dismantled the communes. Under the HRS, households contracted from the village peasants' collective to farm privately in return for meeting their part of the collective's grain quota. Tools and animals were divided among farming households. Voluntary at first, the HRS soon became policy. By 1983, 98 percent of rural households were contracting land. Initially, rules limited contracts to five years. This was extended to fifteen years in 1984, and an additional thirty years on top of the original contract period was added in 1993. In 1998 the revised Land Management Law stipulated a maximum lease of thirty years. Despite mandated periods, contracts were subject to readjustments by the collective before the contracts expired. Perhaps 80 percent of all contracts were readjusted in the 1980s and 1990s to ensure that land is adjusted to household demographic structure. In principle, all land is owned by the "peasant collective," though the legal definition of this body remains unclear.

Soon after the HRS was implemented, contractors of land started to transfer rights to third parties. This practice was permitted under the 1986 Land Management Law, but only to members of the collective. After 1998 the law was changed to allow noncollective members to subcontract land, a practice that was already fairly common. Local rules vary tremendously: In some villages, the only requirement is that the state grain quota continues to be fulfilled; in other villages all land transfers must be agreed by the village collective. In Jiangsu Province, subcontracting is possible as long as it does not affect ownership or land use, or extend beyond the term of the original contract. Nationally, however, the government has sought to ensure that contracting does not remove too much land from agricultural production. The 1998 law specifies that 80 percent of farmland in every province is designated for agricultural use only.

In 2004 the Land Administration Law was revised again to clarify legal rights. Article 8 confirms that rural land is owned by the "peasants collective," though in practice the administrative village is more likely to lease the land to contracting households. It is on this legal basis that the state claims the economy remains "socialist" in character. Article 14 limits contract duration to thirty years. The 2004 law has two ends. First, it consolidates the market reforms in a period of transition by enshrining a land market in law. This clarifies land rights, but it also promotes individual over collective farming, in line with the pro-market policies of the economic reforms. Second, it clarifies individual and group rights during a time of rampant official abuse. Illegal land seizures and occupations, and fraudulent transfers of land by local officials and even collectives to commercial interests, have stirred public protest and central government concern. Nevertheless, problems with implementing the law remain at the local level.

SEE ALSO *Land Use, History of; Rural Development, 1949–1978: Overview; Rural Development since 1978.*

BIBLIOGRAPHY

Bernhardt, Kathryn. *Women and Property in China, 960–1949.* Stanford, CA: Stanford University Press. 1999.

Buoye, Thomas. *Manslaughter, Markets, and Moral Economy.* Cambridge, U.K.: Cambridge University Press, 2000.

Ho, Peter. Who Owns China's Land? Policies, Property Rights, and Deliberate Institutional Ambiguity. *China Quarterly* 166 (2001): 394–421.

Ho, Samuel P. S., and George C. S. Lin. Emerging Land Markets in Rural and Urban China: Policies and Practices. *China Quarterly* 175 (2003): 681–707.

Huang, Philip C. C. *Civil Justice in China: Representation and Practice in the Qing.* Stanford, CA: Stanford University Press, 1996.

Huang, Philip C. C. *Code, Custom, and Legal Practice in China.* Stanford, CA: Stanford University Press, 2001.

Isett, Christopher Mills. *State, Peasant, and Merchant in Qing Manchuria, 1644–1862.* Stanford, CA: Stanford University Press, 2007.

Jing Junjian. Legislation Related to the Civil Economy in the Qing Dynasty. In *Civil Law in Qing and Republican China,* ed. Kathryn Bernhardt and Philip C. C. Huang, 42–84. Stanford, CA: Stanford University Press, 1994.

Jones, William C. *The Great Qing Code.* Oxford, U.K.: Clarendon Press, 1994.

Land Administrative Law of the People's Republic of China (2004 revision).

Lippit, Victor. *Land Reform and Economic Development in China: A Study of Institutional Change and Development Finance.* White Plains, NY: International Arts and Sciences Press, 1974.

Perdue, Peter C. *Exhausting the Earth: State and Peasant in Hunan, 1500–1850.* Cambridge, MA: Harvard University Press, 1987.

Shepherd, John R. Rethinking Tenancy: Explaining Spatial and Temporal Variation in Late Imperial and Republican China. *Comparative Studies in Society and History* 30, 3 (1988): 403–431.

Stacy, Judith. *Patriarchy and Socialist Revolution.* Berkeley: University of California Press, 1984.

Staunton, John. *Ta Tsing Leu Lee* [The great Qing Code]. London: T. Cadell and W. Davies, 1810.

Wakefield, David. *Fenjia: Household Division and Inheritance in Qing and Republican China.* Honolulu: University of Hawai'i Press, 1998.

Wong, John. *Land Reform in the People's Republic of China: Institutional Transformation in Agriculture.* New York: Praeger, 1973.

Yang Guozhen. *Ming-Qing tudi qiyue wenshu yanjiu* [Research on Ming and Qing land contracts and documents]. Beijing: Renmin Chubanshe, 1988.

Zelin, Madeleine, Jonathan Ocko, and Robert Gardella. *Contract Property in Early Modern China.* Stanford, CA: Stanford University Press, 2004.

Zhang Jinfan. *Qingdai minfa zonglun* [General account of civil law in the Qing]. Beijing: Zhongguo Zhengfa Daxue Chubanshe, 1998.

Zhou Yuankang and Xie Zhaohua. *Qingdai zudianzhi yanjiu* [Research into the Qing system of tenancy]. Shenyang, China: Liaoning Renmin Chubanshe, 1986.

Christopher M. Isett

LAND USE, HISTORY OF

The conformation of land use in China was a gradual but inexorable process of subordinating the natural environment to the dictates of agriculture relative to population growth. Two millennia before the nineteenth century, the reciprocity between physical conditions and the shaping of Chinese social, political, and economic institutions flexible enough to respond to changing conditions set the pattern for land use. That pattern began to shift by the end of the century due to urbanization, modern commercial and industrial development attendant on China's opening to foreign trade and residence, and relations to the international capitalist economy at the conclusion of the opium wars. For the past two hundred years, successive regimes, despite their ideological differences, have struggled to find a balanced path to development by an optimal and productive use of land, urban and rural, that can support a large population as well as generate resources for industrial, manufacturing, and commercial activities.

LAND USE IN THE NINETEENTH CENTURY

Prior to the mid-1800s, land under cultivation based on extant technologies reached a historic maximum—297,956 square miles out of a total of 1.3 million square miles in what was called "China proper" (Buck 1937). Population rose to an estimated 295.5 million concentrated in central-east-south China, and the urban population declined to a historical nadir of only 6.9 percent of the total population. Population growth relative to arable land was explainable by changes in productivity. Increased irrigation, land reclamation, fertilization, the introduction of new food crops and higher-yield and pest-resistant strains of various grains, and double cropping helped to expand the amount of land brought under cultivation and the intensity of land use. Champa rice, an early maturing, high-yield, and drought-resistant strain had revolutionized rice production in the Jiangnan region, increasing food output and absorbing surplus labor. New World crops such as corn, sweet potatoes and Irish potatoes, and peanuts allowed marginal lands to be cultivated. But intensive farming and land reclaimed for cultivation depleted the soil and changed the natural watersheds, and diverted rivers and deforestation increased soil erosion.

Land use was predicated on land ownership, land-use rights, and taxation policies. The separation of land ownership and land use by the Qing was codified in the tax system. Land could be freely bought, sold, or rented. Although there were no standardized measurements in the Qing period, land was divided according to topographical and land-use characteristics—irrigated or paddy land, dry land, hilly land or marshland to determine tax liabilities. Cadastral records (fish-scale registers) were regularly kept to verify ownership. Arable land was traditionally viewed as an imperishable, safe, and preferable investment by farmers and merchants alike, but limited supply and population increase encouraged diversification of ownership. Owners accounted for about half of the fiscal acreage, part-owners for 25 percent, and tenants (with lifetime tenure or specified contractual periods) for the remainder. Tenancy was more prevalent in the more intensively cultivated south (the rice-growing region), where plot sizes were smaller than in the north (the wheat growing region), but overall, the trend shows an increase in the number of small to medium landholdings, whose owners had to augment their grain output by renting land either in the form of crop-sharing or cash tenancy. Land fragmentation, partially the result of the inheritance system, whereby land was divided equally among the male heirs, contributed to the increase of scattered, small, and uneconomical parcels of land, encouraging farmers to rent land adjacent to their holdings.

By the end of the century and despite natural checks on population growth (e.g., epidemics, drought, and floods), and war and rebellions (the Taiping Uprising was estimated to have caused well over 20 million deaths and massive destruction of property), the population continued to grow, adding over one million people to the total, while the amount of arable land did not. One important demographic shift was the gradual rise of urban population as a proportion of the total. The establishment of modern commerce and industry

erroneous estimation that higher agricultural yields were possible on a reduced arable land supply. The communes abolished the private sector (and therefore material incentives). Rural iron and steel production diverted labor from farming, and several bad harvests attributed to climatic conditions and the need to supply the cities (which had absorbed surplus labor) with grain caused widespread famine with 20 million to 43 million estimated deaths. In 1961 the Great Leap policies were reversed. The communes continued to exist, but were scaled down in size and given more control over land use and production. Private plots (and rental of property from the communes) were restored to provide work incentives to increase production. The state's imposition of high procurement quotas on grain (at low procurement prices) forced regional and local governments to plow up pastures, replace industrial crops with grain, and encourage more multiple cropping over the following decade; these moves had serious environmental consequences. Another impact of these policies was the doubling of the rate of increase of the urban population, from 6.43 percent of the total population between 1950 and 1956 to 12.2 percent between 1957 and 1960 (Chen 1984). Cities were allowed to annex surrounding rural areas for industrial and residential use, and some of these areas achieved the size of small cities.

THE ERA OF REFORM: 1978 AND BEYOND

One of the most important reforms introduced in 1978 to the socialist economic system that profoundly changed the structure of land use was the allocation of resources not through centralized planning but by markets, prices, and consumer demand. The collectives that had dampened rural economic growth were to be dismantled and government policies supported, raising rural incomes and consumption. This was possible partly because of the "opening to the outside world" and access to foreign agricultural products and investment. Rural economic development was predicated on rural industries and services, a reduction in land devoted to grain production, and an increase in land use favoring livestock, forestry, and fisheries. Rural township and village-run enterprises, particularly in the eastern coastal regions, helped to absorb excess rural labor, as did the loosening of restrictions on mobility, but rising incomes also favored population growth, which was addressed through population control measures. With the establishment of special economic zones, transportation infrastructure, and urbanization, arable land contracted by about 25.5 million acres between 1991 to 1997. To control the loss of farmland, a new policy was announced to freeze the conversion of arable land to non-agricultural uses. What was particularly worrying was that the loss of arable land occurred in the southeast, the most fertile and productive agricultural region, causing soil degradation, deforestation, and water pollution due to uncontrolled industrialization and residential construction. A state-level investigation into land misuse was initiated on an annual basis using satellite technology and in 1997 the first agricultural census was conducted adopting United Nations Food and Agriculture Organization definitions and standards that helped to correct erroneous official statistics.

The economic boom since the reforms has also increased the value of land for development, and illegal seizures of rural property (owned by the village collectives) by local officials without reasonable compensation to the holders of land-use rights have increased exponentially. In 2004 an estimated 160,000 illegal land deals were identified, and the central government admonished local officials; nevertheless, in 2006 there were 130,000 cases—an increase of 17.3 percent over the previous year. In 2006, 106,250 acres of collectively owned land was seized, escalating conflicts and violence at the local level by farmers protesting these "forced" transactions by local officials The central government promulgated a landmark property law in 2007 to raise compensation to those who lost their land-use rights, but farmers continue to demand ownership rights over collectively owned land as the only curb to these seizures. At the Third Plenary Session of the Seventeenth Central Committee, rural reform and development were at the top of the agenda and markets for the lease of contracted farmland are to be established and the transfer of land-use rights (subcontracting, leasing, exchanging or swapping of land) by farmers was sanctioned, a recognition that their citizenship rights compared to urban residents were circumscribed. Granting individual ownership to farmers for their contracted land, their houses, and the land on which the houses are built, however, was not addressed.

The future security of China's 1.3 billion people will depend on finding a way to balance rural and urban land use, conserve natural resources, and protect the environment. Sustainable development of land use tied to economic viability will depend also on evolving political, social, and economic responses to those needs.

SEE ALSO *Agricultural Production; Energy; International Development Programs in China: Food and Agriculture Organization; Land Tenure since 1800; River Systems; Rural Development, 1949–1978; Rural Development since 1978; Special Economic Zones; Urban China: Real Estate Management.*

BIBLIOGRAPHY

Ash, Robert, ed. *Agricultural Development in China, 1949–1989: The Collected Papers of Kenneth R. Walker (1931–1989).* Oxford, U.K.: Oxford University Press, 1998.

Ash, Robert, and Richard Edmonds. China's Land Resources, Environment, and Agricultural Production. *China Quarterly* 156 (December 1998): 836–879.

Buck, John Lossing. *Land Utilization in China: A Study of 16,786 Farms in 168 Localities, and 32,256 Farm Families in Twenty-*

two Provinces in China, 1929–1933. Shanghai: Commercial Press, 1937.

Chao, Kang. *Man and Land in Chinese History: An Economic Analysis*. Stanford, CA: Stanford University Press, 1986.

Chen, Cheng-siang. *China: Essays on Geography*. Hong Kong: Joint, 1984.

Ho, Samuel P. S., and George C. S. Lin. Emerging Land Markets in Rural and Urban China: Polices and Practices. *China Quarterly* 175 (2003): 681–707.

Kueh, Y. Y. *Agricultural Instability in China, 1931–1991*. Oxford, U.K.: Clarendon Press, 1995.

Myers, Ramon, ed. *The Modern Chinese Economy*. New York: Garland, 1980.

Perkins, Dwight H. *Agricultural Development in China, 1368–1968*. Chicago: Aldine, 1969.

Smil, Vaclav. China's Agricultural Land. *China Quarterly* 158 (June 1999): 414–429.

Kerrie L. MacPherson

LANGUAGE AND LANGUAGE POLICY

The number of languages in China extends well beyond the number of recognized nationalities or ethnic groups, since many of them have several languages or dialects. China recognizes fifty-six ethnic nationalities, including the majority Han population that speaks Sinitic languages or dialects. These Sinitic or Han languages—what are commonly called Chinese—are dominated by Mandarin, the term early Christian missionaries gave it in the seventeenth century, referring to Manchu (Qing dynasty) officials. Mandarin is a form of northern speech, now standardized in textbooks, that started to take its modern form in the fifteenth century and was adopted as a *koiné* (lingua franca) among officials to conduct legal and administrative work throughout the empire, hence the Chinese term *guanhua* (language of officials). Mandarin spread through many other occupations as a second language, and writers developed a written form, most famously in fiction. However, Mandarin did not displace the numerous dialects or local languages of the Han people, and Classical or Literary Chinese, learned through the ancient texts of older languages, remained the writing style of education, official business, and high culture until the twentieth century. The local languages (*fangyan*) of Han Chinese are most frequently referred to as dialects, in deference to their distant historical affinities, much as Spanish, French, Italian, and Romanian are all Romance languages. Yet, like these Romance languages, the local languages of China are mutually unintelligible. Linguistically they are grouped into seven types: Mandarin, Wu, Min, Yue (Cantonese), Xiang, Hakka, and Gan. Geographically, varieties of Mandarin extend throughout northern and southwestern China; the other six groups each occur in distinct regions of the south, where they are believed to be modern forms of the earlier languages of populations migrating from the north during different historical periods. It is important to note that varieties of Mandarin also may be quite distinct and not mutually intelligible. The same may be said for varieties of the other language groups. For example, within the Min group, the Eastern Min of the capital city of Fujian Province, Fuzhou, is entirely unintelligible to speakers of Southern Min in the Fujian port city of Xiamen, which is in turn unintelligible to speakers of another form of Southern Min in the port of Chaozhou in Guangdong. Both forms of Southern Min are, as well, distinct from those of the Fujian cities of Zhangzhou and Quanzhou, from which the dominant forms of Southern Min spoken on the island of Taiwan derive.

CREATING A STANDARD LANGUAGE FOR MASS EDUCATION

After 1900 Qing dynasty scholars and officials concerned with educational reforms were persuaded by the example of Japan to create a standard national language (*guoyu*; from Japanese: *kokugo*) by introducing *guanhua* Mandarin into mass education. In 1911 the National Assembly adopted this proposal, together with a set of phonetic symbols using character strokes, derived from Japanese *kana* script, to standardize pronunciation of Chinese characters and teach the standard to both Han and non-Han Chinese subjects of the empire. The subsequent Republican government in 1913 affirmed the proposal for a unified, standard language and a set of phonetic symbols (*zhuyin zimu*; later redesignated *zhuyin fuhao* in 1930). Given that standard Mandarin uses approximately 7,000 characters, of which 2,500 account for 99 percent of those used to form words, some scholars held that Chinese characters are too cumbersome a vehicle for promoting literacy, and as early as 1918 proposed that a romanized alphabet should replace them. In 1928 the Ministry of Education adopted the national language romanization system Gwoyeu Romatzyh, created by the distinguished linguist Y. R. Chao (Zhao Yuanren; 1892–1982), but only as a supplement, along with *zhuyin fuhao*, to guide in pronunciation, not a writing system independent of characters. In 1936 the ministry abandoned a plan to simplify Chinese characters themselves by reducing the number of strokes in each character. Meanwhile, a group of scholars led by the Chinese Communist Party official Qu Qiubai (1899–1935), inspired by script reforms of Chinese writing introduced in the Soviet Union for ethnic Chinese living there, introduced a script known as Latinxua or Sin Wenz (Xin wenzi; "new characters") in 1930. Latinxua was designed to replace writing in Chinese characters, and the Communist Party supported some publications and literacy initiatives using it. However, the War of Resistance to Japan (1937–1945) and the subsequent civil war limited the further development of most language reforms until the 1950s.

Chinese citizens gathering in a park to practice English, defying the posted government ban, Beijing, December 26, 1989. *In the early 1950s, the People's Republic of China (PRC) standardized the Chinese language, allowing for easier communication across the country. As the PRC emerged from isolation at century's end, party leaders increased their efforts to control how the language should be spoken, countering the influences of Chinese speakers from Hong Kong and Taiwan.* AP IMAGES

On the mainland the new government of the People's Republic of China (PRC) proceeded through the 1950s with promoting a standard language, simplifying Chinese characters, and reinventing a phonetic writing system. In addition, the PRC made new, more extensive provisions for non-Han languages of ethnic minorities. In 1956 the State Council acted on the proposals of scholarly committees to begin reducing the number of strokes used to write Chinese characters in order to create simplified characters (*jianhuazi*; *jiantizi*), established a common language (*putonghua*) based on the pronunciation of Beijing Mandarin, and received the proposal for a new Scheme for the Phonetic Spelling of [Putonghua] Chinese (*Hanyu pinyin fang'an*), known commonly as pinyin. The scheme for simplified characters largely followed practices already in use for centuries in handwritten, cursive (*xingshu*) calligraphy but not previously common in block print or formal documents. Simplified characters were introduced gradually; the bulk of them (2,236) were adopted by 1964, with an additional list proposed in 1977, then modified in 1986. The 1956 proposal to adopt pinyin as the phonetic writing for *putonghua* Mandarin went into effect in 1958. However, it was not until the end of 1978 that Xinhua News Agency and other organs of the state making use of romanization announced their adoption of pinyin, commencing in 1979.

LANGUAGE POLICIES SINCE THE 1950s

Although the State Council plan for the common language, *putonghua* Mandarin, in the 1950s prescribed Beijing pronunciation, it also set to work a committee to grant recognition for variant pronunciations, and acknowledged that vocabulary and grammar would follow not Beijing local language but rather forms prescribed in style manuals commissioned by the party and in literature. A number of important writers such as Lao She and Ye Shengtao (1894–1988) revised their fictional works to reduce the occurrence of local language expressions.

The education system promoted *putonghua* with substantial success, yet education itself was retarded by the onset of the Cultural Revolution in 1966. Following the Cultural Revolution, the growing response to vocabulary and pronunciation accents coming into the media from Hong Kong and Taiwan prompted a renewed initiative by the State Language Commission to promote a standard vocabulary and Beijing-based pronunciation, culminating in the National Proficiency Grading System for Putonghua that defined more rigorous standards for broadcasters, educators, and administrators, and the Language Law of 2001 (Law of the People's Republic of China on the National Commonly Used Language and Script).

Han Chinese communities outside Beijing's administration have adopted various language policies. Although Singapore did adopt policies quite similar to those of the mainland, Chinese residents of Hong Kong as a British crown colony in the 1970s engaged in a successful movement to make their dominant form of Cantonese an official language. On Taiwan, the Nationalist Party administration carried out a vigorous policy of promoting Guoyu Mandarin, employing *zhuyin fuhao* for a supplementary phonetic system. After democratic liberalization the new administration promoted recognition of local languages, particularly Taiwanese Southern Min; consequently, in 2001 the Ministry of Education prescribed at least one course in a local language, in addition to Mandarin, for all students, and in 2002 the central government adopted a new romanized phonetic system, Tongyong pinyin. It is not surprising, then, that various communities on the mainland also have sought to maintain their local languages, even while acknowledging the dominance of *putonghua* and its benefits as a common language.

Although the Language Law of 2001 attempted to limit the use of nonstandard, local Han Chinese languages, the situation for the bilingual ethnic minority nationalities has remained more complex and ambiguous. On the one hand, since 1949 the state has demonstrated a deference to the languages of minority nationalities that it never accorded Han local languages, assuring minorities that it recognized their rights to use their languages. On the other hand, out of concern for national cohesion, the state also promoted using *putonghua* Mandarin. Since the 1950s the state has worked with minority communities to identify a standard language for each, and to adopt or invent writing systems to be used in education, the media, legal proceedings, and official administration. The constitutions of 1954 and 1982, together with all laws since 1982, have most fully articulated the policy of recognizing linguistic diversity and equality. However, in the 1960s and 1970s, the priorities placed on conforming to Maoist socialism and introducing *putonghua* Mandarin were powerful forces for cultural assimilation that led to reduced minority language rights for a time, notably in the constitutions of 1975 and 1977. Even before socialism, as well as since the Maoist era, minority communities have varied greatly in their degree of internal cohesion and diversity, as well as their assimilation and common language use.

BIBLIOGRAPHY

De Francis, John. *Nationalism and Language Reform in China.* Princeton, NJ: Princeton University Press, 1950.

Gottlieb, Nanette, and Ping Chen, eds. *Language Planning and Language Policy: East Asian Perspectives.* Richmond, U.K.: Curzon, 2001.

Seybolt, Peter J., and Gregory Kuei-ke Chiang, eds. *Language Reform in China.* White Plains, NY: Sharpe, 1978.

Zhou, Minglang, ed. *Language Policy in the People's Republic of China: Theory and Practice since 1949.* Boston: Kluwer, 2004.

Edward Mansfield Gunn Jr.

LAO SHE
1899–1966

Lao She, the pen name of Shu Qingchun, was a prolific novelist and dramatist celebrated for his creativity in use of the Beijing dialect. Born into a humble Manchu bannerman family in Beijing, he managed on meager means to complete his secondary education at a teacher's college, thereafter assuming teaching and educational-administration positions in Tianjin and Beijing schools while taking evening classes in English. In 1924 he went to London, where he taught Chinese language at the University of London until 1929, also helping Clement Egerton translate the classic novel *Jin Ping Mei* (*Golden Lotus*). During this time he began writing novels for publication in China.

After returning to China to teach Chinese and foreign literature at Qilu University in Jinan, Shandong, he married the painter Hu Jieqing in 1931 and moved to a position at Shandong University in Qingdao in 1934. In 1936 he resigned to write full time, but with the outbreak of the War of Resistance against Japan in 1937, moved to Chongqing via Wuhan, where in March 1938 he was elected president of the All-China Resistance Association of Writers and Artists and editor of the important journal *Kangzhan wenyi* (Literature of National Defense). After the war, from 1946 to 1949, he visited the United States as the guest of the U.S. State Department, continuing to write and to provide consultation on English translations of his fiction, until he returned to China in late 1949, shortly after the founding of the People's Republic of China. There he was appointed vice chairman of the China Writers Association and of the Federation of Literary and Art Circles of China. He also served as a delegate to the National People's Congress and a member of the Standing Committee of the Chinese People's Political Consultative Conference. In August 1966 Red Guards detained Lao She and a number of other writers for interrogation and criticism, and it was after a session of this treatment that Lao She died, reportedly by suicide.

EARLY FICTION OVERSEAS

In his early period as a writer, Lao She was inspired in England by Charles Dickens's fiction first to write novels drawing on his teaching experience in North China. *Lao Zhang de zhexue* (The philosophy of Lao Zhang, 1926) presents an entrepreneurial schoolteacher bent on raising his social status and taking the sister of one of his high-school pupils as a concubine. *Zhao Ziyue* (1926) narrates the transformation of a university student's good qualities into self-defeating and irresponsible activism and corruption in search of official position. The novels appealed to readers' sense of humor because Lao She presented the careers of his major characters as farcical antics, with minor characters representing individual moral integrity. Thus did Lao She establish a reputation as a humorist. His third novel written in England, *Er ma* (1929, translated as *The Two Ma's* and as *Ma and Son*), offers a relentless exploration of racial tensions between Chinese and whites in London and resulting conflicts among Chinese living there.

CREATIVE PEAK IN FICTION

After returning to China, Lao She entered his most productive and critically successful period, from 1931 to 1937. His first novel, *Mao cheng ji* (Cat country, 1932), about an astronaut's visit among cats populating Mars, written in the wake of the conflict with the Japanese in the Shanghai Incident of 1932, satirized what Lao She continued to see as the disastrous consequences of the lack of individual integrity among his countrymen. Returning to realism, Lao She wrote *Lihun* (Divorce, 1933; translated as *The Quest for Love of Lao Li*), which satirizes the opportunism among student activists in the name of the Marxist revolution and the compromising attitude of petty bureaucrats even in their search for love in favor of security. Also among the most memorable works of this period are the novel *Niu Tianci zhuan* (Biography of Niu Tianzi, 1934; translated as *Heavensent*), the novellas *Yueyar* ("Crescent Moon," 1935) on a prostitute's life, and *Wo zheyi beizi* (In my lifetime, 1937) on the career of a Beijing policeman.

During this time Lao She, absorbing the advice of academic colleagues, increased his use of colloquial language, emphasized more the role of environment as a determining factor in morality, and considered the futility of individual effort and the possibility of collective social action. These concerns culminated in Lao She's most famous novel, *Luotuo xiangzi* (1936, translated as *Rickshaw: The Novel L'o-t'o Hsiang Tzu*). An episodic account of a Beijing rickshaw puller's downward spiral from a conscientious worker to an impoverished, amoral drifter, the novel struggles with how Chinese sought to understand their society at that time. The novel asserts that the protagonist is a victim of his social environment, but never fully relinquishes a vision of individual capacity for moral responsibility or offers an unambiguously strong affirmation of the potential for collective action.

PLAYWRIGHT AND NOVELIST DURING THE WAR OF RESISTANCE

The outbreak of the War of Resistance against Japan interrupted the serial publication of the novel *Luotuo xiangzi* in 1937 and also opened the third period of Lao She's career. During this period he joined a patriotic movement among writers to offer affirmation of the culture of his countrymen and support the war effort. To these ends, Lao She first joined in formulating and carrying out a collective policy of promoting patriotism through popular oral- and performing-art forms. He collaborated with several popular folk artists and published a selection of the results in the volume *San si yi* (Three, Four, One, 1939), which contained three drum songs, four Chinese operas, and a novel in traditional form. As Chongqing developed into the center of modern theater in the interior of China, Lao She turned to spoken drama, writing or coauthoring some ten plays between 1939 and 1943, many commissioned for specific occasions, all on patriotic themes, such as *Zhang Zizhong* (1941), commemorating the famous general killed in action, and *Taoli chunfeng* (Peaches and plums in the spring, 1943), on a model teacher's dedication in the face of repeated misfortunes, written with Zhao Qingge to celebrate Teachers' Day. Among the best known of these plays are *Canwu* (Lingering fog, 1939), which introduces a comely agent for the Japanese who manipulates and destroys a venal Chongqing official; *Guojia zhishang* (The nation above all, 1940), which presents Chinese Muslims struggling against being used by the Japanese; *Mianzi wenti* (A problem of face, 1941), which satirizes the self-obsessed values of an ageing official; and *Guiqulai xi* (Returning, 1942), which depicts the collapse and remorse of a scheming profiteer, reintroducing Lao She's previous work in folk literature through the use of boatmen's songs.

In 1942 Lao She's wife, Hu Jieqing, who had remained in Beiping (Beijing) under Japanese occupation, rejoined him in Chongqing, and Lao She in 1944 began a monumental trilogy of life in wartime Beiping, assisted by Hu's information. Under the overall title *Sishi tongtang* (Four generations under one roof), the first two volumes, titled *Huanggan* (Bewilderment, 1944) and *Tousheng* (Ignominy, 1946), were completed by the time he went to the United States, where he continued work on the third volume, *Jihuang* (Famine), and where an abridged translation appeared under the title *The Yellow Storm* (1951). Focused on how members of two families living in a Beijing lane resisted occupation, were victimized, or turned to opportunistic collaboration with the Japanese, the novel criticizes traditional values placing career success, family, education, and security above obligations to the nation as fundamental causes of national failure in the war and offers the hope that the resistance will purge China of such a socially debilitating mentality. After revisions, the full novel was published in 1959.

PLAYWRIGHT AFTER LIBERATION

In New York, Lao She completed a novel on performers of oral folk literature during the war that appeared in English as *The Drum Singers* (1951), and after returning to China, he reworked some of the material into a play on the Liberation of 1949, *Fang Zhenzhu* (1950). This also signaled his return to playwriting and the start of the fourth period of his creativity. The play *Longxu Gou* (Dragon Beard Ditch, 1951), celebrating in local language how Liberation both cleaned up the sewer system and eliminated local thugs in a humble Beijing neighborhood, won Lao She public and official approval. While writing several more plays celebrating the new society in the lives of ordinary Beijing residents, Lao She also returned to satire of the bureaucracy in the play *Xi wang Chang'an* (Looking toward Chang'an, 1956) and in revising the popular Peking opera *Shiwu guan* (Fifteen strings of cash, 1956). His most successful play was *Chaguan* (Teahouse, 1957), in three acts, each depicting progressively deteriorating conditions of life within a teahouse and among its patrons from the late Qing dynasty (1644–1912) up to the eve of Liberation. Characters and customs were presented with special attention to Lao She's own Beijing Manchu ethnicity, a theme toward which he turned increasingly at the end of his career. In 1960 he completed the play *Shenquan* (Invincible fist), a sympathetic portrait of ordinary people drawn in desperation to rebel in the 1900 Boxer Uprising, during which his father had been killed in action as an Imperial Palace guard. He also began a historical novel on life among Manchus in Beijing titled *Zhenghong qi xia* (Under the plain red banner), which he left behind uncompleted upon his death.

SEE ALSO *Plays (huaju).*

BIBLIOGRAPHY

Hung, Chang-t'ai. New Wine in Old Bottles. In his *War and Popular Culture: Resistance in Modern China, 1937–1945.* Berkeley: University of California Press, 1994.

Slupski, Zbigniew. *The Evolution of a Modern Chinese Writer: An Analysis of Lao She's Fiction, with Biographical and Bibliographical Appendices.* Prague: Czechoslovak Academy of Sciences, 1966.

Vohra, Ranbir. *Lao She and the Chinese Revolution.* Cambridge: Harvard University Press, 1974.

Wang, David Der-wei. *Fictional Realism in Twentieth-Century China: Mao Dun, Lao She, Shen Congwen.* New York: Columbia University Press, 1992.

Edward Mansfield Gunn Jr.

LATIN AMERICAN STATES, RELATIONS WITH

From the Chinese perspective, Latin America consists of all countries and territories in Central America, South America, and the Caribbean. Prior to the Cuban Revolution in 1959, Beijing had neither the opportunity nor incentive for involvement in Latin America. For China, Latin America was too remote geographically, and the new regime in Beijing was preoccupied with domestic issues. In 1960 Cuba became the first Latin American country to recognize the People's Republic of China (PRC). In 1970 Chile and Mexico shifted diplomatic recognition to Beijing before the PRC's entry into the United Nations in 1971.

Throughout much of the 1960s, political, economic, and cultural exchanges between China and Latin American nations (except Cuba) were virtually nonexistent, but they rose dramatically after Deng Xiaoping launched market-oriented reform in 1978. Since then, from the Chinese perspective, Sino–Latin American ties entered their best period in history, and by the 2000s, China was a major economic partner in the region. Many Latin American presidents, including Brazil's Lula da Silva, Argentina's Néstor Kirchner, and Venezuela's Hugo Chávez, have spent more time in Beijing than in Washington, D.C. Chinese leaders eye Latin American markets as a new expansion destination for trade and investment. Politically, China needs Latin America's support and cooperation in playing a pivotal role in the international arena.

TRADE AGREEMENTS

China has increased its participation in regional international organizations in Latin America and the Caribbean. China signed, for example, a free trade agreement with Chile, and has formal relations with Mercosur. In 2004 China was accepted as a permanent observer to the Organization of American States (OAS), and it joined the Inter-American Development Bank (IDB) in October 2008. In addition to its close relations with Cuba, Beijing has established strategic partnerships with Argentina, Brazil, Mexico, and Venezuela. To promote further bilateral interaction, an increasing number of Latin American countries have been designated as "tourist destinations," a status that allows Chinese tour groups to travel to these countries with few travel restrictions.

China's trade with Latin America has increased exponentially. In 2000 China's trade volume with Latin America was $12.6 billion; in 2007 it skyrocketed to $100 billion, an all-time high. Chinese 2007 import volume accounted for $51 billion, a 49.4 percent increase over the previous year, and export volume climbed to $51.5 billion, a rise of 43.1 percent over 2006. But its impressive trade relations with the area have not affected all countries in the same way. South American countries have benefited from the rise in Chinese demand for the commodities they produce, especially soybeans, iron ore, and copper. China's exports to those countries are dominated by machinery and electrical products, especially those with high value added such as automobiles, tractors, motorcycles, televisions, and computers. The increased trade relations are therefore complementary.

However, Mexico and Central American nations have suffered from a growing trade deficit with China. China imports less than 1 percent of Mexico's total exports, but it is the second supplier for its imports. In global manufacturing markets, China is a direct competitor of many Latin American manufacturers. The Central American nations and Mexico also have been severely hurt by Chinese competition in the U.S. market, despite their greater proximity. In fact, Mexico sees China as a threat because of its ability to lure investment away from the low-cost manufacturing plants just south of the U.S. border and trade frictions.

DIRECT INVESTMENT

Since the late 1990s China has become one of the most intrepid investors in the Western Hemisphere, with Chinese foreign direct investment (FDI) in Latin America and the Caribbean reaching $11.5 billion in 2005—more than half of the country's total investments abroad that year. A high percentage of Chinese FDI is located in offshore banking centers such as the Cayman Islands and the British Virgin Islands; the next four-largest host countries were Mexico ($141 million), Peru ($129 million), Brazil ($81 million), and Venezuela ($43 million). Chinese direct investments in Latin America are concentrated in energy and mining sectors. The expectation of a huge Chinese investment initially cheered many, but with the significant exceptions of the Cayman Islands and the British Virgin Islands, China's investment in Latin America and the Caribbean remains small.

There is a small but fast-growing overseas Chinese community in Latin America, and these ethnic Chinese play a key role in bridging the business interests of both sides and in supporting China's unification with Taiwan.

RELATIONS WITH BRAZIL

As Latin America's largest country, Brazil has attracted special attention from China. It is China's largest trade partner in Latin America, and China is Brazil's second-largest trading partner in the world, surpassed only by the United States. China has benefited greatly by importing huge quantities of petroleum, iron ore, and soybeans. However, China is replacing Brazil as a supplier of manufactured goods to other countries in South America, and Brazil has had a trade deficit with China since 2007. Since 1988 the two nations have jointly developed an earth resources satellite program. Politically, both China and Brazil are leaders in the G-20 group of developing nations and work together for greater "south-south" cooperation. In addition, Brazil gained Beijing's support for its ambitions to become a permanent member of the United Nations Security Council. While both China and Brazil favor a multipolar international system without the dominance of the United States, neither nation has an interest in directly challenging the United States.

RELATIONS WITH CUBA

With the end of the Cold War and breakup of the Soviet Union, Sino-Cuban relations improved significantly. China supports Cuba's right to determine its own political system as well as its protests against U.S. sanctions. In return, Havana firmly endorses Beijing's positions on human rights, Tibet, and Taiwan issues. China is now Cuba's second most important trade partner, and Cuba's exports to China have risen from less than 6 percent of total Cuban exports in 1998 to more than 18 percent of the Cuban exports in 2006. China also agreed to invest in the nickel-mining sector and an oil field in Cuba. Sino-Cuban relations are not strategically significant for China, but do represent vital support for Cuba.

POLITICAL AFFAIRS

Since the late 1970s China has largely abandoned the export of revolutionary ideology and replaced it with the economically successful model of market socialism; yet, it has not deserted its policy of support for antihegemony. China's economic development model, the Beijing Consensus, refutes Western notions of political liberalization or market reforms as indispensable for long-term, sustained development. For Latin America, the Beijing Consensus is an attractive alternative to the Washington Consensus largely because Beijing respects the sovereignty of Latin American nations, not meddling in their affairs and certainly not dictating their policies, as in the famous structural adjustment of neoliberalism. As Chinese leaders see it, their country could be both a partner and a model for the developing world—a model of state-directed market economy without liberal democracy. Indeed, Fidel Castro and several other Latin American officials expressed their admiration for China's economic model.

IMPLICATION FOR THE UNITED STATES

The burgeoning Chinese involvement in Latin America is a cause for concern and even alarm in some quarters of the U. S. political and military establishment. Beijing's evolving ties with countries directly opposed to the policies of the United States, such as Cuba and Venezuela, put Beijing itself at odds with Washington. China is viewed as a

Venezuelan President Hugo Chavez in prayer at the mountain of Taishan, Shandong province, August 27, 2006. *Chinese interests in Latin America have increased since 2000, as the country looks for new trade opportunities, diplomatic ties, and sources of natural resources. Leftist leaders, such as Venezuela's Hugo Chavez, look to engage China's support to counter dominance by the United States in the region.* © JUAN CARLOS SOLORZANO/EPA/CORBIS

potential threat to the long-standing pillar of U.S. policy in the hemisphere, the Monroe Doctrine. Compared with U.S. trade with Latin America ($561 billion in 2007), China's $100 billion trade with the region seems insignificant. Similarly, Chinese direct investment represents a fraction of the total direct investment from the United States to Latin America. In absolute terms, U.S. economic and political relations in the region are still preeminent, but the Chinese have been catching up rapidly since the turn of the twenty-first century. At present, China's role in Latin America is based primarily on trade.

COMPETITION WITH TAIWAN

Reunifying Taiwan with the mainland is a key tenet of China's Latin American strategy. Fearing that Taiwan's push for international recognition will lead to its declaration of independence, Beijing is determined to contain Taiwan in every corner of the world, especially in Central America and the Caribbean, the stronghold of Taiwanese foreign relations. Currently, Taiwan maintains formal diplomatic relations with 24 countries, half of which are located in Latin America and the Caribbean. The Chinese strategy in the region is pragmatic. Panama's diplomatic relations with Taiwan has proved no barrier to Chinese investment pouring into the Panama Canal. In 2004 China decided to deploy 125 riot police to Haiti, a country with which the PRC has no diplomatic relations. While Ma Ying-jeou, Taiwan's president, pledges to improve relations with China, the competition between Taibei (Taipei) and Beijing in the region is likely to continue.

In spite of trade frictions, many in the region view the engagement with China as a welcome opportunity to promote economic growth and diversification—and to reduce their dependence on the United States. With its remarkable economic growth and increasing appetite for minerals and agricultural products, China's involvement in Latin America is likely to deepen and intensify in the years to come.

BIBLIOGRAPHY

Devlin, Robert, Antoni Estevadeordal, and Andres Rodriguez, eds. *The Emergence of China: Opportunities and Challenges for Latin America and the Caribbean*. Cambridge, MA: Harvard University Press, 2006.

Domínguez, Jorge. China's Relations with Latin America: Shared Gains, Asymmetric Hopes. Inter-American Dialogue Working Paper. Harvard University, 2006.

Li, He. *Sino-Latin American Economic Relations*. New York: Praeger, 1991.

Roett, Riordan, and Guadalupe Paz, eds. *China's Expansion into the Western Hemisphere: Implications for Latin America and the United States*. Washington, DC: Brookings Institution Press, 2008.

He Li

LAW COURTS, 1800–1949

The court system of the Qing dynasty (1644–1912) provided for the maintenance of justice and of law and order, and embodied the supremacy of imperial order, but it did not entail judicial autonomy nor the protection of individual rights. The emperor, as the ultimate legal authority for legislation and adjudication, carried out his judicial duty with the professional support of the Ministry of Justice (*xingbu*), the Censorate (*duchayuan*), and the Court of Judicial Review (*dalisi*) at the central judiciary. At the bottom of the administrative apparatus, Qing local governance was enforced through approximately two thousand counties headed by magistrates. These civil officials managed all matters of governance under their jurisdictions, including the adjudication of civil disputes and the administration of criminal justice. They played a combined role of investigator, prosecutor, and adjudicator at trials, with little legal training. Between the county and the central judiciary, judicial functions of imperial rule were implemented by a territorial bureaucracy consisting of the governor-generals of the provinces and their subordinate regional officials. Unless specially appointed to particular duties, these regular heads of local governments all had, among other administrative responsibilities, judicial power and presided at court, regardless of whether or not they had legal backgrounds.

Beginning in the 1840s, the number of foreigners traveling to China greatly increased, as did reports of unjust legal practices, such as defendants being tortured until they made a false confession during trial, resulting in a miscarriage of justice. One notorious case involving a man named Yang Naiwu was prominently reported in the Shanghai newspaper *Shen Bao* in the 1870s. As in many other reported cases, Yang was tortured into confession along with a married woman whose husband had been poisoned. The case was only quashed by a special court of appeal in the central judiciary after a lengthy appellate hearing where evidence of the earlier trial was found unsustainable.

As an increasing number of foreigners were involved in and subject to the Qing legal system, Western powers also increased their demand for deferential treatment to their subjects in China. The perception that the Qing law fell short of Western standards of justice eventually gave rise to extraterritoriality treaty agreements with Western powers that the Qing government was forced into signing.

Beginning in the 1890s, the Qing government initiated legal reforms to regain the nation's judicial integrity, issuing new codes, proposals for reform, and a new draft constitution before the 1911 revolution. These reforms were modeled on the new codes of Meiji Japan, the common law, and the civil law, among others. The Shanghai Mixed Court provided a platform for Chinese legal practitioners to understand Western laws in action. However, in the absence of a Chinese legal profession supported by a legal academia, these reforms were at best incipient imitations of Western laws of various jurisdictions with inadequate coherence. For instance, a company code introduced in 1904 largely represented a rough mixture of common law and civil law in this branch. The result was so unsatisfactory that it was replaced in 1914 with a company ordinance by the newly established republican government in Beijing.

Further legal reforms in the Republican era embraced the ideals of protection of individual rights, due process, and the separation of powers. These reforms resulted in the emergence of a new set of criminal and civil procedure laws, a prospering legal profession, and an expanding legal-education sector. In 1928 the Nanjing regime consolidated reforms made since the 1900s and reaffirmed the commitment to separation of powers by separating the executive yuan (council), the legislative yuan, and the judicial yuan. The judicial yuan administered courts at all levels. However, under the Guomindang's grand strategy of tutelage of governance (*xunzheng*), the party continued to control all judicial personnel.

Consolidating the judiciary inherited from the warlord regimes, the Nanjing government in 1932 reorganized the court system into three tiers: regional courts at the county and municipal levels, high courts at provincial capitals, and a supreme court in the national capital. The regional courts handled the first trials of ordinary civil and criminal cases, and the high courts handled the first trials for specified criminal cases, as well as cases on appeal against judgments of the regional courts. The supreme court heard appeals against decisions of the high courts, as

Two peasants testifying before a judge in a land dispute, May, 1947. *As Western countries became increasingly powerful in China, the legal system began to take on reforms during the Qing dynasty to more closely resemble Western legal standards. These reforms continued into the twentieth century, as the Republican government restructured the courts, placing an emphasis on recognizing the rights of the individual.* MARK KAUFFMAN/TIME & LIFE PICTURES/GETTY IMAGES

well as the first and final trials of specified types of cases. The supreme court was the highest authority for judicial interpretation, in both civil and criminal issues. Procuratorate offices with operational autonomy were set up in the corresponding courts. The 1946 constitution further installed the grand justices and their joint council as the highest authority for judicial interpretation of the constitution and other national laws.

From 1917 to 1947, China managed to abolish the extraterritoriality agreements, partly due to its progress in legal reform. The high courts and regional courts surged in number from 302 in 1937 to 748 in 1948, though more than half the counties nationwide remained without a law court.

SEE ALSO *Codified Law, 1800–1949; Customary Law, 1800–1949; Legal Training and the Legal Profession,*

1800–1949; Penal Systems, 1800–1949; Shanghai Mixed Court.

BIBLIOGRAPHY

Alford, William P. Of Arsenic and Old Laws: Looking Anew at Criminal Justice in Late Imperial China. *California Law Review* 72, 6 (1984): 1180–1256.

Allee, Mark A. *Law and Local Society in Late Imperial China: Northern Taiwan in the Nineteenth Century.* Stanford, CA: Stanford University Press, 1994.

Bernhardt, Kathryn, and Philip C. C. Huang, eds. *Civil Law in Qing and Republican China.* Stanford, CA: Stanford University Press, 1994.

Bodde, Derk, and Clarence Morris. *Law in Imperial China: Exemplified by 190 Ch'ing Dynasty Cases.* Cambridge, MA: Harvard University Press, 1967.

Cohen, Jerome Alan, R. Randle Edwards, and Fu-mei Chang Chen, eds. *Essays on China's Legal Tradition.* Princeton, NJ: Princeton University Press, 1980.

Huang, Philip C. C. *Code, Custom, and Legal Practice in China: The Qing and the Republic Compared.* Stanford, CA: Stanford University Press, 2001.

Ma Hanbao (Herbert Han-pao Ma). *Law and Traditions in Contemporary Chinese Society.* Taibei: National Taiwan University, 1999.

Meijer, Marinus Johan. *The Introduction of Modern Criminal Law in China.* 1950. Arlington, VA: University Publications of America, 1976.

Ch'ü T'ung-tsu. *Law and Society in Traditional China.* Paris: Mouton, 1961.

Ch'ü T'ung-tsu. *Local Government in China under the Ch'ing.* Cambridge, MA: Harvard University Press, 1962.

Billy K. L. So (Su Jilang* 蘇基朗*)

LAW ON THE PROTECTION OF WOMEN AND CHILDREN

Almost immediately after its foundation in 1949, the People's Republic of China (PRC) established the All-China Women's Federation with the aim of consolidating and promoting women's welfare, equality, and participation in economic and social development. Since then, the federation has been working for women's rights in China and has been engaged in international multilateral exchanges. Until the post-Mao period, the federation's achievements were modest, but the situation improved after China's opening up. In 1995, with the support of the federation, the United Nations Fourth World Conference on Women and the nongovernmental Forum on Women were held in Beijing, during which the Beijing Declaration and the Platform for Action (on women's rights) were adopted.

MAINLAND CHINA

The core laws for the protection of children and women in China are the Laws on the Protection of Women's Rights, Children's Rights, and Preadults Rights. The laws on women's rights ensure that women have equal rights relative to men in political representation, employment, wages, social welfare, and personal safety. Additionally, women are ensured rights to special care during menstruation, pregnancy, and prenatal and postnatal periods. The laws also prohibit prostitution; the abandonment of female babies; discrimination against infertile women; and the torture, abduction, and trafficking of women and children.

The laws protecting preadults and children on mainland China are largely similar to those of Hong Kong. A major difference is that the legal age of consent for sex is lower in China, fourteen instead of sixteen, and publications for both children and adults on the mainland are less explicit and erotic than publications in Hong Kong. Another difference is China's one-child policy, which, through financial and social rewards and punishments, encourages each couple to have only one child. The nation sees the policy as essential for protecting the rights and quality of life of the younger generations under the pressures of overpopulation and limited resources. Local governments are allowed a certain degree of flexibility in carrying out the policy, and as China moves out of poverty, the one-child policy is being reviewed for possible relaxation or removal.

HONG KONG

The laws in Hong Kong define "children" variously as below the age of twenty-one, eighteen, or sixteen, depending on the context. To guard them against inappropriate sexual stimulation, the Control of Obscene and Indecent Articles Ordinance and the Film Censorship Ordinance monitor the types of public materials that are available to children, and Hong Kong's criminal laws provide heavy penalties for sexual incitement, erotic interest (including possession of child pornography), and sexual activities with children below the age of sixteen, irrespective of consent. Anal sex with people younger than twenty-one is also a crime.

For the general physical and mental health of children in Hong Kong, the Domestic Violence Ordinance provides for the separation of abused children from the parent exercising violence, the Protection of Children and Juveniles Ordinance provides refuge for abused children, and the Child Abduction and Custody Ordinance and the Widows and Orphans Pension (Increase) Ordinance ensure that all children have proper care by proper caregivers. It is illegal in Hong Kong to leave young children unattended at home or to fail to send school-age children to school. Corporal punishment is also prohibited in Hong Kong. The government provides nine years of free education to children (six years of primary and three years secondary schooling) and is considering extending free schooling to twelve years. The Toys and Children's Products Safety Ordinance ensures the safety of toys and gadgets for children. The promotion and selling of alcohol to persons below eighteen is forbidden by the Dutiable Commodities Ordinance, and tobacco products and tattoo services are likewise prohibited by the Smoking (Public Health) Ordinance and the Tattooing of Young Persons Ordinance.

Hong Kong's criminal laws protect women by providing heavy penalties for sexual assault, rape, and spousal battery. The Sex Discrimination Ordinance prohibits discrimination on the basis of sex and family status in the job market, workplace, media, services, welfare, and daily activities. A subsection of the ordinance deals with sexual harassment, that is, sexual victimization by means of unwelcome sexual advances, requests, or conduct that is offensive, humiliating, or intimidating. Within the limits of the heterosexual monogamous marital system, women are free to plan their marriages, pregnancies, and families, and to make divorce petitions to the law court for fair arrangement of child custody and alimony. Termination of pregnancy is legal if it is confirmed to be necessary by two doctors for the physical or mental health of the woman. The Human Reproductive Technology Ordinance forbids gender selection in the process of medically assisted reproduction.

TAIWAN

The legal protection of women in Taiwan is exercised in its civil and criminal laws. Women's personal safety is protected by laws on social order, sexual assault, victim protection, the prohibition of prostitution, and the abduction and trafficking of women. The family rights of women are protected by laws concerning marriage, adoption, guardianship, adultery, family violence, divorce, alimony, and inheritance. The main milestones are the Sexual Assault Prevention Act and the Domestic Violence Prevention Act (Chung 2001). There are also special nighttime waiting zones for unaccompanied women in subway stations, which are constantly monitored by surveillance. Women's work and social opportunities are protected by the Gender Equality Labor Law. Taiwan's laws for the protection of children cover child abduction, adoption, guardianship, child abuse and prostitution, and the welfare of children and young people.

AID SERVICES AND INTERNATIONAL RANKINGS

The governments of the PRC, Taiwan, and Hong Kong all promote their protective laws and services to children and women regularly, through school education, public talks, posters and other media, and awards and festivals. These efforts are assisted by nongovernmental organizations, which provide hotlines and aid services on different aspects of children's and women's rights and laws. Permanent governmental boards, committees, and commissions have been established to oversee, implement, and review most of the laws. For some services, such as those for battered spouses, rape victims, and abused children, the government and nongovernmental organizations join forces to form multidisciplinary teams composed of different professionals, including police, medical and social workers, and legal experts, to assist in investigation and management.

Hong Kong has the highest level of public awareness of women's and children's rights and services, followed by Taiwan and mainland China. According to the 2007–2008 United Nations Human Development Report (UNDP 2008), which reviewed 177 countries and regions, Hong Kong ranked twenty-first (between Italy and Germany) and China ranked seventy-second on the gender-development index. Hong Kong ranked twenty-first and China fifty-seventh on the gender-empowerment measure. Taiwan was not included in the UNDP report, but has been reported to rank among the top twenty-five in both indexes (*China Post* 2007) and stands among the best in its ratio of female representatives relative to men among public officials, national and local legislators, and management in private corporations.

SEE ALSO *All-China Women's Federation; Family; Life Cycle: Infancy and Childhood; Marriage Laws; Sex Ratio; Women, Status of.*

BIBLIOGRAPHY

All-China Women's Federation. http://www.women.org.cn/english/index.htm.

China Post. Taiwan Improving Women's Rights: U.N. November 23, 2007. http://www.chinapost.com.tw/taiwan/2007/11/23/132053/Taiwan-improving.htm.

Chung, Oscar. Liberating Women. Government Information Office, Republic of Taiwan. 2001. http://www.gio.gov.tw/taiwan-website/5-gp/rights/tr_06.htm.

Department of Justice. Government of the Hong Kong Special Administrative Region. Bilingual Laws Information System. http://www.legislation.gov.hk/eng/home.htm.

Legislative Affairs Office of the State Council of the People's Republic of China. *Marriage Laws and Regulations of the PRC.* Beijing: Legal Publishing House, 2006.

United Nations. Department of Economic and Social Affairs. Division for the Advancement of Women. Fourth World Conference on Women, 1995. Department of Public Information brochure: *Conference to Set Women's Agenda into Next Century*. http://www.un.org/womenwatch/daw/beijing/dpibrochure.html.

United Nations Development Program (UNDP). Human Development Reports: 2007/2008 Gender Empowerment Measure. 2008. http://hdrstats.undp.org/indicators/279.html.

Xinhuanet.com. http://big5.xinhuanet.com/gate/big5/news.xinhuanet.com/ziliao/2003-09/10/content_1073241.htm.

Yam Women Web site. http://taiwan.yam.org.tw/womenweb/law.htm.

M. L. Ng

LAW SINCE 1949

China's program of legal reform has been closely linked with its policies on economic development. Driven by the need to increase its legitimacy and by the perception that legal reform will further economic growth and development, the party leadership reached a fragile consensus on a law reform program, articulated in broad terms at the Third Plenum of the Eleventh Central Committee in November and December 1978. The first decade of legal reform saw significant albeit qualified achievements in legislation and institution building (Dicks 1989), yet the suppression of the Tiananmen Prodemocracy Movement in 1989 revealed the extent to which the ideals of legal reform remained subject to supreme Communist Party power. Deng Xiaoping's 1992 inspection tour of South China reinvigorated the reforms that had been held dormant after Tiananmen, and by the end of 1999, law making and institution building had reached impressive levels. In addition, China's accession to the World Trade Organization in 2001 signaled the government's willingness to comply with international standards for trade liberalization (Ostry et al. 2002, Cass et al. 2003). Also, the rapid pace of China's economic growth has given rise to major challenges in the areas of social control. Throughout these changes, the government has consistently insisted on maintaining the party's monopoly on political power.

LAW AND ECONOMIC DEVELOPMENT

Contracts and property represent key legal relationships for China's economic development. Legislation in these two areas began early on in the post-Mao reform period since 1978 and has continued with the Unified Contract Law (1999) and the Property Rights Law (2007).

Contracts Legislation on contracts in China seeks to balance the imperatives of state control with the need to promote transactional autonomy. The Economic Contract Law (1981) recognized limited autonomy for contracting parties while entrenching the state's approval authority. The Foreign Economic Contract Law (1985) provided broader contract autonomy for foreign business transactions, albeit still subject to the restraints of state approvals and policy guidance. The General Principles of Civil Law (1986) characterized contracts as civil law obligations, thus suggesting even greater autonomy for contracting parties and their transactions. Revisions to the Economic Contract Law in 1993 reduced the influence of state planning on contract relations, but still made contracts subject to state policies and retained general restrictions against contracts deemed contrary to state and public interests.

The drafting of the Unified Contract Law (1999) began nearly simultaneously with the enactment of the 1993 revisions to the Economic Contract Law and reflected an ongoing effort to harmonize the norms for contract autonomy with the requirements of the state-managed economy. China's general orientation toward autonomy is evident in the new law's provision that lawfully concluded contracts are effective upon conclusion and are not delayed until after approval and registration. Contract autonomy is limited, however. Aside from the general illegality provisions of the law, contracts are invalid when detrimental to state interests, where malicious collusion damages state or collective interests, where legal means are used to conceal illegal purposes, and when harmful to public welfare (Unified Contract Law, Art. 52).

Property Law The 1982 Constitution extended legal protection to "lawful property," the definition of which remained the exclusive province of the state (Constitution, Art. 13). The Constitution requires that the exercise of citizens' rights, including property rights, must not conflict with the state's or society's interests (Constitution, Art. 51). The state is the sole authority for interpreting those interests and thus can determine the extent to which private-property rights are recognized and enforced. The dependency of property rights on state control is evident in many areas, but the examples of land, intellectual property, and corporate property are particularly instructive.

Since China's Constitution reserves land ownership to the state in urban areas and to the collective in the countryside, private rights generally concern only the use of land. The Land Administration Law (1986, rev. 1998) permitted land-use rights to be conveyed to private entities. In 1990 China enacted regulations permitting businesses to acquire long-term interests in land for the purpose of subdivision and development. Local governments, such as the Shanghai Municipality, began enacting implementing regulations for their own real-property markets. The Law on Urban Real Estate Administration (1994, rev. 2007) expanded the possibilities for private acquisition and management of land-use rights, but also tightened state control over perceived abuses.

Rights to intellectual property are property rights in expressions of knowledge. China has promulgated an impressive array of laws and regulations on intellectual property, including the Trademark Law (1982; rev. 1993, 2001), Patent Law (1984; rev. 1992, 2000), Copyright Law (1991, 2001), and Law against Unfair Competition (1993), which protects trade secrets (Asian Law and Practice 1998). China's accession to the World Trade Organization brought with it obligations under the Agreement on Trade-Related Aspects of Intellectual Property Rights (TRIPs Agreement 1999). Yet enforcement remains problematic. Industry estimates suggest that piracy rates in China are at 85 to 93 percent of all products across all sectors; Internet and end-user piracy of business software, books, and journals continue.

Property rights are also important in connection with the formation and operation of corporations. From the late 1980s and increasingly after the establishment of securities exchanges at Shanghai and Shenzhen, early efforts to regulate corporate property revealed policy conflicts over the goals of regulation (Potter 1992). With the enactment of uniform standards for the issue and trading of stock aimed at strengthening central control over local securities markets, securities regulation in China gradually extended to the national level in 1992–1993. These standards were formalized yet further in the Company Law (1994, rev. 2006) and Securities Law (1998, rev. 2005). In response to increased international market and regulatory linkages and ever-growing investor interest, China's regulatory apparatus for securities reflects an ongoing commitment to maintaining state control over corporate property (Zhu 2000).

Enabled in part by the 2004 Constitutional revisions enshrining a right to own private property, the Property Rights Law was enacted in 2007 after lengthy debate and delay. The law clarifies the rights and obligations attendant on a wide range of property relationships involving real property, movable property, and intangibles. The law's provisions on property transfers require specific administrative action by officials, which may then be subject to judicial review under the principles of administrative law.

ADMINISTRATIVE LAW

Administrative agencies under the State Council have long dominated governance in China. Attempts to formalize rule-making processes, such as the Tentative Regulations on the Procedure for Enacting Administrative Laws and Regulations (1987) and the Legislation Law (2000), purport to establish limits on the rule-making authority of administrative offices and departments based on their relative ranking in the bureaucratic hierarchy. The Administrative Supervision Law (1997) and Administrative Procedure Law (1998) also specify processes for administrative rule making and enforcement. The State Council's influence on rule making is evident through its increasingly active use of white papers to formalize government policy.

The Administrative Litigation Law (1989) gave the people's courts the authority to review administrative agencies' decisions imposing fines, restricting or infringing on property rights, intervening in business operations, denying licenses, and a number of other matters (Potter 1991b). These provisions for judicial review are augmented by those of the State Compensation Law (1994), which permits awards of compensation to individuals and organizations harmed by unlawful bureaucratic action. Yet as a limit on party and state power, these laws remain relatively weak. The State Compensation Law does not apply to officials acting outside the scope of their duties, while the Administrative Litigation Law does not permit review of discretionary decisions or party actions. Augmenting the formal administrative processes of these two laws, the "Letters and Visits System" affords citizens opportunities to petition the government for redress (most often over practical matters such as unpaid wages and benefits) (Thireau and Hua 2005).

DISPUTE RESOLUTION

While China has traditionally emphasized informal dispute resolution, with the expansion of economic reform, and particularly the expansion of market-oriented policies in the 1990s, the courts began to play a stronger role in private commercial litigation. The revised Civil Procedure Law (1991), building on the earlier 1982 draft, signaled an effort to give the courts greater authority to resolve an increasingly large and complex array of private disputes. Initially subdivided into specialized criminal, economic, and civil trial divisions (*shenpanting*), the people's courts were expanded with new divisions for foreign economic relations, intellectual property, and administrative law. Further revisions in late 2007 sought to improve enforcement of judgments (Ye and Liu 2008). The people's courts also took responsibility for recognizing and enforcing foreign arbitral awards under the New York Convention on the Recognition and Enforcement of Foreign Arbitral Awards; China's accession was effective in 1987. The Rules on Certain Issues Relating to Jurisdiction over Proceedings of Foreign-Related Civil and Commercial Cases (2001), issued by the Supreme People's Court, clarifies court responsibilities for enforcing foreign arbitral and judicial awards (Huang and Du 2008). Increased attention has also been paid to training judges, first in the Supreme People's Court Senior Judges Training Centre and later at its Judicial Institute. In an effort to improve quality, the Judges Law (1995) imposes education and testing requirements for judges.

Arbitration of disputes has emerged as a compromise between the informal procedures of traditional mediation and the formality of the judicial system (Cohen et al. 2004, Chua and Sanger 2005). The Arbitration Law (1994) provides general rules for arbitration institutions and procedures. Arbitration of disputes involving foreigners are most often handled by the China International Economic and Trade Arbitration Commission, although local government arbitration bodies such as the Shanghai Arbitration Commission also have jurisdiction to handle these types of cases. Maritime disputes are subject to the China Maritime Arbitration Commission.

Unfortunately, Chinese institutions for dispute resolution have been hampered by their generally low level of political status and authority. This impedes their capacity to compel production of evidence and enforce awards. Ingrained traditions of local protectionism and personal interference in judicial outcomes have made it difficult for these outside tribunals to enforce judicial and arbitral

Pirated computer software and movies for sale in Beijing, April 19, 2006. *Since the 1980s, the Chinese government has instituted a host of new laws respecting intellectual property rights in hopes of gaining more trade with foreign countries. However, many international companies complain of lax enforcement of these laws, leading to the widespread availability of pirated goods throughout China.* © CLARO CORTES IV/REUTERS/CORBIS

awards. Processes of internal and informal fact finding and decision making often leave disputants vulnerable to abuses of power. Also, the party continues to play a dominant role through the adjudication committees attached to each court. These committees in effect review and approve judicial decisions, notwithstanding official directives to the contrary. Finally, judicial corruption remains a serious problem.

Despite these concerns, the early 2000s have seen expanded use of legal mechanisms by citizens to achieve redress in such areas as labor relations, the environment, and government abuse. There have been workers seeking payment of wages, villagers seeking compensation for illnesses resulting from pollution and harms resulting from environmental degradation, military veterans seeking payment of pensions, urban-neighborhood residents seeking redress for allegedly unlawful relocation and expropriation of housing—all of which suggests the extent to which law has become part of the public domain (Diamant et al. 2005). An important element in this process has been the expansion of Chinese law schools and the training of a new cohort of legal specialists, many of whom are able and willing to help citizens challenge government decision making. The government has aggressively tried to suppress the use of law to protect rights of which it does not approve. Building on a set of regulatory pronouncements aimed at curbing legal representation for collective disputes and protesters (Human Rights Watch 2006), the new Lawyers Law (2008) does little to reverse government efforts to restrict the use of law to challenge policies and practices of the party and state. Nonetheless, the movement to defend rights has expanded steadily. Despite government pressures on lawyers to conform to state orthodoxy (Human Rights Watch 2008), the growing trend of public citizens using the law to enforce their rights against government abuse suggests a new and important phase in China's legal development.

SOCIAL CONTROL AND CRIMINAL LAW

China strongly emphasizes the need for stability as a fundamental requirement for development, which takes precedence over civil and political rights. In a series of human-rights white papers from 1991 to 2004, the government has articulated a position that supports giving primacy to economic growth by stressing that the right to subsistence is a primary right from which all other rights derive (Text of Human Rights White Paper 1991, State Council Information Office 2005). These perspectives are reiterated in a white paper on the rule of law, which asserts that China's fundamental stand on human rights is "placing top priority on people's rights to subsistence and development" (State Council Information Office 2008).

The right to development imposes requirements for social control. Driven to reassert a monopoly on the legitimate use of force after the excesses of the Cultural Revolution (1966–1969) and its aftermath, and mindful of its need to build legitimacy through law, the post-Mao regime in 1980 enacted the Criminal Law Code and the Code of Criminal Procedure soon after passing, in 1979, Regulations on Arrest and Detention, which replaced measures enacted in 1954 (Clarke and Feinerman 1995). Under the Regulations on Security Administration and Punishment (1957; rev. 1986, 1994), administrative detention was commonly applied to individuals who committed minor criminal acts. As part of a broad effort to reform the criminal-justice system in response to international criticisms and domestic pressures, administrative detention was restricted under the revisions to the Criminal Procedure Law in 1996 and the subsequent amendment of the Criminal Law in 1997 (Hecht 1996). In 1994 legislation articulating ideals about the treatment of prisoners and aimed at reforming the prison system was enacted as part of an effort to regularize the administration of prisons and labor camps. The Administrative Punishment Law (1996) was instituted to unify the procedures for administrative organs imposing penalties ranging from fines to detention in response to legal and regulatory violations.

ASSESSMENT

The steady expansion of China's use of law as an instrument of policy enforcement has led to a steady increase in the number of laws and regulations enacted and a concomitant expansion in the numbers of legal officials and specialists. China's legal regime performs only as well as these interpretive agents do in carrying out the work of interpreting and applying the law in light of local normative and organizational conditions. While China's legal regime has changed significantly since the founding of the People's Republic, the content of laws and the performance of legal organizations remain subject to the imperatives of party leadership and state control.

SEE ALSO *Codified Law, 1800–1949; Customary Law, 1800–1949.*

BIBLIOGRAPHY

Asia Law and Practice, ed. *Intellectual Property Protection in China: The Law.* 2nd ed. Hong Kong: Asia Law and Practice, 1998.

Balme, Stephanie. The Judicialisation of Politics and the Politicisation of the Judiciary in China (1978–2005). *Global Jurist Frontiers* 5, 1 (2005): 1–41.

Cass, Deborah Z., Brett G. Williams, and George Barker, ed. *China and the World Trading System: Entering the New Millennium.* Cambridge, U.K.: Cambridge University Press, 2003.

Chua, Eu Jin, and Katherine Sanger. Arbitration in the PRC. *China Law and Practice* 19, 4 (May 2005): 19–21.

Clarke, Donald C., and James V. Feinerman. Antagonistic Contradictions: Criminal Law and Human Rights. *China Quarterly*, no. 141 (1995): 135–154.

Cohen, Jerome A., Neil Caplan, and Peter Malanczuk, eds. *Practical Guide to Arbitration in China.* Vol. 2. Hong Kong: Sweet and Maxwell, 2004.

Diamant, Neil J., Stanley B. Lubman, and Kevin J. O'Brien. *Engaging the Law in China: State, Society, and Possibilities for Justice.* Stanford, CA: Stanford University Press, 2005.

Dicks, Anthony. The Chinese Legal System: Reforms in the Balance. *China Quarterly* 119 (1989): 540–576.

Hecht, Jonathan. *Opening to Reform? An Analysis of China's Revised Criminal Procedure Law.* New York: Lawyers Committee for Human Rights, 1996.

Huang Jin and Du Huanfang. China's Judicial Practice in Private International Law: 2003. *Chinese Journal of International Law* 7, 1 (2008): 227–256.

Human Rights Watch. China: Curbs on Lawyers Could Intensify Social Unrest. 2006. http://www.hrw.org/english/docs/2006/12/12/china14791.htm

Human Rights Watch. "Walking on Thin Ice": Control, Intimidation, and Harassment of Lawyers in China. 2008. http://hrw.org/reports/2008/china0408/china0408webwcover.pdf

Lawyers Committee for Human Rights, ed. *Opening to Reform? An Analysis of China's Revised Criminal Procedure Law.* 1997. http://www.ciaonet.org/book/lch08/index.html

Ostry, Sylvia, Alan S. Alexandroff, and Raphael Gomez, eds. *China and the Long March to Global Trade: The Accession of China to the World Trade Organization.* London: Routledge, 2002.

Potter, Pitman B., ed. The Administrative Litigation Law of the PRC. Spec. issue, *Chinese Law and Government*, Fall 1991b.

Potter, Pitman B. The Legal Framework for Securities Markets in China: The Challenge of Maintaining State Control and Inducing Investor Confidence. *China Law Reporter* 7, 2 (1992): 61–94.

State Council Information Office. China's Progress in Human Rights in 2004. April 2005. http://english.gov.cn/official/2005-07/28/content_18115.htm

State Council Information Office. China's Efforts and Achievements in Promoting the Rule of Law. February 28, 2008. http://english.gov.cn/2008-02/28/content_904901.htm

Text of Human Rights White Paper. *FBIS Daily Report: China*, suppl., Nov. 21, 1991.

Thireau, Isabelle, and Hua Liushan. Mobilizing the Labor Law in Arbitration Committees and in Letters and Visits Offices. In *Engaging the Law in China: State, Society, and Possibilities for Justice*, ed. Neil J. Diamant, Stanley B. Lubman, and Kevin J. O'Brien, 84–107. Stanford, CA: Stanford University Press, 2005.

TRIPS Agreement. In *The Legal Texts: The Results of the Uruguay Round of Multilateral Trade Negotiations*, ed. World Trade

Organization, 321–353. Cambridge, U.K.: Cambridge University Press, 1999.

Ye, Ariel, and Liu Xiangwen. PRC Civil Procedure Law Revised. *China Law and Practice* 22, 2 (March 2008): 19–21.

Zhu Sanzhu. *Securities Regulation in China*. Ardsley, NY: Transnational Publishers, 2000.

Pitman B. Potter

LEAGUE OF LEFT-WING WRITERS

The League of Left-Wing Writers (Zuoyi Zuojia Lianmeng, 1930–1936) was a leftist cultural institution formed by the Chinese Communist Party in the aftermath of the May Fourth movement, when a rise of leftist radicalism occurred in China. This shift away from the May Fourth legacy was captured in the phrase "From a Literary Revolution to a Revolutionary Literature," the title of a 1928 essay by Cheng Fangwu. Intellectuals on the left could not, however, present a unified cultural front. Instead, they squabbled on a variety of issues. Writers like Lu Xun and Mao Dun, associated with the May Fourth movement, were attacked as dinosaurs of a bygone era no longer relevant to the age of revolution. Qian Xingcun wrote that the new era needed a writer very different from the moody and pessimistic Lu Xun: "This violent, stormy age can only be represented by a writer with a violent and stormy revolutionary spirit" (Denton 1996, p. 287). Members of the two leading leftist literary societies—the Creation Society and the Sun Society—quarreled bitterly over who first raised the mantle of revolutionary literature and what precisely the nature of that literature should be. After the 1927 Nationalist coup against the Communists, the Communist Party was forced out of the cities and sought refuge in the remote countryside of Jiangxi. A reflection of its relative impotence in the political sphere, the party began at precisely this time to place increasing importance on the cultural sphere.

THE LEAGUE AND ITS FORMATION

The Communist Party initiated the League as a way of bringing an end to literary squabbles, presenting a united front in the leftist cultural field, and exerting a positive political influence. Although the League made important contributions in a variety of areas, these specific goals would prove elusive.

The League was formally established on March 2, 1930, following a series of meetings between Communist Party cultural figures and Lu Xun. Throughout its six-year existence it was officially banned by the ruling Nationalists and forced to become an underground organization. Participating in League activities was dangerous. Indeed, early in 1931, five members of the League were caught and executed by the Nationalists. To circumvent what the left was calling the "white terror" of repression, the League adopted a cell structure similar to that of the Communist Party itself.

The League's agenda was to end sectarianism, encourage writers to adopt a "scientific method" (i.e., Marxist theory), and to promote the use of literature for revolutionary purposes. In short, the League promoted an explicitly political role for literature in the revolutionary movement, a viewpoint summed up in a League document thus: "Our art has to devote itself to the bloody 'victory or death' struggle. Our art is anti-feudal, anti-bourgeois, and against the trend of those of the petit bourgeoisie who 'have lost their social standing.' "

Lawrence (Wang-chi) Wong suggests that membership in the League was around 400, the bulk of whom were young and some of whose literary qualifications were not always clear. The League had a collective leadership organized into executive and standing committees, with secretariats doing most of the day-to-day administrative work. According to Wong (1991, pp. 72–74), the following six committees functioned at one time or another:

- Committee for Creation and Criticism
- Committee of Mass Literature and Art
- International Liaison Committee
- Committee for the Study of Theories
- Committee for the Study of Fiction
- Committee of the Culture of Workers, Peasants, and Soldiers

A Party Group served as liaison between the Communist Party and the League. Although League members also participated in events of a purely political nature—mass demonstrations, commemorations, issuing manifestos, putting up posters—they also published numerous literary journals, engaged in literary debates, and promoted the popularization of literature. In his writings, Qu Qiubai, former Communist Party general secretary and now de facto leader of the League, criticized the elitism of the Western-style literature favored during the May Fourth movement and drew attention to the need for language and forms (literary and nonliterary) that could appeal to readers and spectators in a country that was still predominantly illiterate. In terms of the production of actual revolutionary or mass literature, the results were meager. In some camps, the works of such League members as Mao Dun and Zhang Tianyi are hailed as exemplary; in other camps, these same works are denounced as tendentious and of poor literary quality.

DEBATES AND DEMISE OF THE LEAGUE

Although in its first two years of existence the League was relatively harmonious, this began to change in 1932 with what would be called the "free man" (*ziyou ren*) and "third category" (*disan zhong ren*) debates. Both debates concerned the issue of whether a writer can or should be independent of politics and class affiliation. The former debate began when a certain Hu Qiuyuan quit the League and wrote essays criticizing the League's promotion of literature as a "political gramophone"; he declared himself a "free man" (also translatable as "liberal") whose only cause was creative freedom for writers. Su Wen, who edited an independent literary journal called *Xiandai* (*Les contemporaines*), wrote in support of Hu Qiuyuan's polemic and declared himself to be a writer of the "third category," neither proletarian nor bourgeois. These appeals for literature and the writer to be autonomous from politics did not go unchallenged. Qu Qiubai accused the two apostates of glorifying literature as some lofty realm of transcendent truths, which of course did not mesh with the League's "scientific method," namely, historical materialism.

The conflict that spelled the end for the League was the "two slogans" debate. As Japanese encroachment in China continued and Chinese popular opposition to it rose, it became increasingly apparent in the mid-1930s that war with Japan was imminent. League intellectuals began to think about the question of what literature's role should be in a period of war. A slogan, they thought, would be just the ticket to rally writers around the cause of anti-Japanese resistance. Zhou Yang, one of the most prominent party voices in the League, reaffirmed his support for the slogan "national-defense literature" (*guofang wenxue*), which he had proposed back in 1934, and which seemed to capture the new united-front policy being promoted at party headquarters in Yan'an, a policy that the Communist Party inherited from the Comintern. From Lu Xun's point of view, this slogan seemed to abandon the class orientation that the League had worked so hard to promote. In conjunction with Lu Xun, Hu Feng proposed "mass literature of national revolutionary struggle" as a slogan that maintained this element of class struggle.

This debate, which partly reflected a growing factional dispute between Lu Xun and his supporters (especially Hu Feng and Feng Xuefeng) and Zhou Yang and his supporters, led to the disbandment of the League in early 1936. Under the new united-front policy, which sought political unity between the Communists and the Nationalists for the larger cause of resistance against Japan, these factional squabbles appeared petty and reflected poorly on the Communist Party.

LEGACY

Until recently in the People's Republic, the League was always portrayed as a key chapter in the narrative of the development of modern Chinese literature from the May Fourth movement to Yan'an. Since the liberalization of the post-Mao era, the League has been viewed more perniciously as an institution that sought ideological uniformity and stifled literary creativity. As such, it was a precursor to the Chinese Writers Association established in the 1950s as a national union for all literary workers. That said, the League helped raise important issues about language and literary form, audience, the relationship of the writer to class and politics, and the role of literature in a period of national crisis.

SEE ALSO *Communist Party; Hu Feng; Lu Xun; Mao Dun; Yu Dafu; Zhou Yang.*

BIBLIOGRAPHY

Chugoku gendai bungakushi shiryo [Materials on modern Chinese literary history]. Tokyo: Daian, 1969.

Denton, Kirk A., ed. *Modern Chinese Literary Thought: Writings on Literature, 1893–1945*. Stanford, CA: Stanford University Press, 1996.

Su Wen, ed. *Wenyi ziyou lunbian ji* [A collection of essays debating literary freedom]. Shanghai: Shanghai Shudian, 1933.

Tagore, Amintendranath. *Literary Debates in Modern China, 1918–1937*. Tokyo: Centre for East Asian Cultural Studies, 1967.

Wong, Wang-chi. *Politics and Literature in Shanghai: The Chinese League of Left-Wing Writers, 1930–1936*. Manchester, U.K.: Manchester University Press, 1991.

Wong, Wang-chi. A Literary Organization with a Clear Political Agenda: The Chinese League of Leftwing Writers, 1930–1936. In *Literary Societies of Republican China*, ed. Kirk A. Denton and Michel Hockx, 313–338. Lanham, MD: Lexington Books, 2008.

Zhongguo Shehui Kexue Yuan Wenxue Yanjiusuo, ed. *Zuolian huiyi lu* [Recollections on the Left League]. 2 vols. Beijing: Zhongguo Shehui Kexue Chubanshe, 1982.

Kirk A. Denton

LEE, ANG
1954–

The internationally acclaimed film director Ang Lee (Li An), born in Taiwan in 1954, is one of the world's most talented, versatile, and multicultural directors. Lee's parents were Han Chinese mainlanders who crossed over to Taiwan with the Nationalist Party after the end of the Chinese civil war (1946–1949). After finishing college, Lee went to the United States, where he studied theater at the University of Illinois at Urbana-Champaign and then enrolled in a master's program in film production at New York University. Currently residing in the United States,

Scene from* Crouching Tiger, Hidden Dragon, *2000. *Born in Taiwan, Ang Lee studied film at universities in the United States before beginning his directing career. In 2000, Lee earned widespread international acclaim for the Academy Award-winning* Crouching Tiger, Hidden Dragon, *introducing the heroic martial arts genre known as* wuxia *to a new audience.* **CHAN KAM CHUEN/ AFP/GETTY IMAGES**

Lee has produced more than ten films and has garnered numerous awards worldwide. His films include:

- 1992: *Pushing Hands* (*Tuishou* 推手)
- 1993: *Wedding Banquet* (*Xiyan* 喜宴)
- 1994: *Eat Drink Man Woman* (*Yinshinannu* 饮食男女)
- 1995: *Sense and Sensibility* (*Lixing yu ganxing* 理性与感性)
- 2000: *Crouching Tiger, Hidden Dragon* (*Wohucanglong* 卧虎藏龙)
- 2003: *Hulk* (*Lujuren haoke* 绿巨人浩克)
- 2005: *Brokeback Mountain* (*Duanbi shan* 断臂山)
- 2007: *Lust, Caution* (*Se, jie* 色，戒)

Lee's films often deal with cross-cultural, cross-generational, and diasporic interactions, which he uses to explore conflicts between modernity and tradition and between paternal collectivism and individual freedom. The best examples of these themes can be seen in the early family-drama trilogy *Pushing Hands, Wedding Banquet*, and *Eat Drink Man Woman*. Lee has also directed several films that were adapted from novels, including *Sense and Sensibility, Crouching Tiger, Hidden Dragon, Brokeback Mountain*, and his more recent Japanese-resistance film *Lust, Caution*. The nondubbed Chinese-language film *Crouching Tiger, Hidden Dragon* remains the most successful foreign film, in terms of box-office draw, ever to have been screened in the United States and is arguably the most famous of his many well-known films. Its exploitation of the martial-arts (*wuxia*) genre ensured the film a high level of critical attention.

CROUCHING TIGER, HIDDEN DRAGON

Set in the Qing dynasty (1644–1912), *Crouching Tiger, Hidden Dragon* is based on Wang Dulu's romantic and martial-arts novel written from 1938 to 1942. The plot tells the story of the young aristocrat woman Jen, who has stolen Li Mubai's precious sword Green Destiny. Jen is about to marry into a high-ranking official family yet aspires to the carefree lifestyle of a knight-errant, represented by Li Mubai and Yu Shulian. After her lover Dark Cloud attempts to intercept her on her wedding day, Jen runs away from home and becomes a roaming swordfighter. Eventually she leaps from a mountain into an abyss after Mubai's death in an ambush plotted by her master Jade Fox.

While clearly a Chinese film, *Crouching Tiger* has a transnational character arising from its international funding and audience. Christina Klein concludes that the film has "emerged not out of any neatly bounded national or cultural space . . . , but from the boundary-crossing processes of war, migration, capitalist exchange, aesthetic appropriations, and memory" (2004, p. 21). At the same time, this decentering boundary crossing in the era of globalization raises anxiety and ambivalence in the quest for a Chinese identity. The culturally diverse, inclusionist portrayal of China, effected by the use of a multiethnic cast of characters and settings in far-flung locations, from the capital Beijing, to the Gobi Desert, to the bamboo forests of Jiangnan, are all seen from an ethnically Han-centered viewpoint. The Turkic Dark Cloud and the Manchurian Jen can been seen as the ethnic antithesis of the Han couple Li Mubai and Yu Shulian, though they are in the end Sinicized when they accept the values of Wudang Daoism, which, for Lee, serves as a symbol of indigenous Chinese culture even though Daoism is mingled with a Buddhist sensibility, particularly that of Chan (Zen) Buddhism.

The centrality of the female protagonists constitutes another layer of ambivalence. These powerful female sword-fighters from three different generations are carriers of Chinese culture, variously accepting, challenging, and negotiating with the Confucian patriarchy, represented by Li Mubai. At the same time, they are at the center of a cinematic spectacle susceptible to an Orientalist perception (Chan 2004; Kim 2006). The scriptwriter James Schamus (2004), however, claims that this film is not a superficial kung fu movie but is about "inner strength and centeredness," as symbolized in the choreography of the fighting scene in the bamboo forest. Jen's "suicidal" leap into the abyss from a mountain after the death of Li Mubai and reunion with Dark Cloud imbues the film with a Zen quality, which has aroused much conjecture among the critics. Her blissful expression suggests that Jen was able to let go of worldly attachment, achieving what Li Mubai had failed to accomplish at the beginning of the film when he tells Shulian that though he had entered a deep meditative state, he had not found joy. As Fran Martin (2005) writes, "Jen's flight—from her obligations in the moral world as well as from the field of vision of the film viewer—signifies an extension of the radical (and distinctly 1990s pop-feminist style) rebellion that has been her defining characteristic throughout the film. Instead of an expression of repentance, her magic flight might signify Jen's final, obdurate refusal to cleave to *any* of the social systems that structure the world of the living."

Despite its sweeping success and warm reception in the West, *Crouching Tiger, Hidden Dragon* met with a lukewarm response in Asia, particularly in China and Hong Kong. The contrast probably reveals different cross-cultural audience needs and different degrees of familiarity with the sword-fighting genre. The aestheticization of the martial-arts genre may account for the film's strong appeal to international audiences (Lu 2005). Furthermore, Lee's revisionist takes on what he called "a kind of dream of China, a China that probably never existed," incited polarized reactions among film critics. Salman Rushdie exalted the film as "an act of local resistance against the global domination of Hollywood" (Klein 2004, p. 20), whereas Derek Elley chastised it as "culturally inauthentic, asserting that its Asianness had been fatally corrupted by its absorption of Western cinematic conventions" (quoted in Klein 2004, p. 20). Schamus, the screenwriter and a financer for the film, made an "appeal that it be judged as a thing of beauty" (2004, p. 49).

SEE ALSO *Film Industry: Taiwan.*

BIBLIOGRAPHY

Chan, Kenneth. The Global Return of the Wu Xia Pian (Chinese Sword-Fighting Movie): Ang Lee's *Crouching Tiger, Hidden Dragon. Cinema Journal* 43, 4 (Summer 2004): 3–17.

Kim, L. S. Making Women Warriors: A Transnational Reading of Asian Female Action Heroes in *Crouching Tiger, Hidden Dragon. Jump Cut*, no. 48 (winter 2006). http://www.ejumpcut.org/archive/jc48.2006/womenWarriors/index.html.

Klein, Christina. *Crouching Tiger, Hidden Dragon*: A Diasporic Reading. *Cinema Journal* 43, 4 (Summer 2004): 18–42.

Lu, Sheldon. *Crouching Tiger, Hidden Dragon,* Bouncing Angels: Hollywood, Taiwan, Hong Kong, and Transnational Cinema. In *Chinese-Language Film: Historiography, Poetics, Politics*, ed. Sheldon Lu and Emilie Yeh, 220–233. Honolulu: University of Hawai'i Press, 2005.

Martin, Fran. The China Simulacrum: Genre, Feminism, and Pan-Chinese Cultural Politics in *Crouching Tiger, Hidden Dragon*. In *Island on the Edge: Taiwan New Cinema and After*, ed. Chris Berry and Feii Lu, 149–160. Hong Kong: Hong Kong University Press, 2005.

Schamus, James. Aesthetic Identities: A Response to Kenneth Chan and Christina Klein. *Cinema Journal* 43, 4 (Summer 2004): 43–52.

Chia-ju Chang

LEE TENG-HUI

SEE *Li Denghui (Lee Teng-hui).*

LEGAL TRAINING AND THE LEGAL PROFESSION, 1800–1949

Legal training in imperial China was a privilege as well as a duty for officials. During the nineteenth century, there were no schools in China that provided systematic legal education, and most officials acquired legal knowledge through self-study and on-the-job training. The published Qing Code was compulsory study material, and officials who failed to memorize the text or to interpret it correctly in an annual test were fined one month's salary. The Board of Punishment encouraged junior officials to study various annotations, commentaries, and casebooks in order to understand the implications of each clause of the code, the relationship among the stipulations, and the application of the law. Magistrates relied on handbooks (*guanzhen*) for practical knowledge of law.

Beginning in the early eighteenth century, undertrained magistrates who were busy with administrative duties increasingly relied on the assistance of private legal secretaries (*xingming muyou*), who were mostly lower degree holders trained through apprenticeship. Along with directing clerks to make necessary preparations for trials, legal secretaries advised magistrates on their judgments, although they never attended the court. Their duties also included drafting case reports for judicial review and responding to the refutations of superior officials; such judicial review and ratification (*shenzhuan*) of criminal cases were required by the Board of Punishment, and a stiff deadline (*shenxian*) was imposed for both criminal and civil cases. In the nineteenth century, legal secretaries became indispensable members of the magistrates' entourages.

Complicated property relationships caused by population growth and rapid commercialization during the nineteenth century led to a demand for court services. Such services were provided by litigation masters, who, like magistrates' secretaries, were legal experts. The government, however, saw litigation masters as a source of judicial backlogs and abuses, and repeatedly launched campaigns to eliminate them. Critics complained that litigation masters would make exaggerated accusations and pursue unwarranted appeals for their clients so as to be granted formal hearings and improve a lawsuit's chance of success. Local magistrates were unable to satisfy the demand for litigation. Many cases, especially disputes about adoption, marriage, property, and debts, which were formally classified as "trivial," were dismissed or left pending for long periods.

THE IMPACT OF LEGAL REFORM

Inspired by Japan's modernization of its legal system, which led to the abolition of extraterritorial privileges enjoyed by Westerners in Japan, the Qing government launched a movement of legal Westernization that brought about the rapid development of legal education in the early twentieth century. The reformers proposed a system in which judicial authorities would receive training in modern law and be allowed to process legal matters independently of the administrative sector. This system naturally raised a demand for law schools that trained qualified staff. After the Qing government founded the first law school in Beijing in 1906, more law schools were founded elsewhere. By the time of the collapse of the Qing regime in 1911, there was at least one public law school in each provincial capital. In addition, thousands of students went to Japan to study law in the first decade of the twentieth century. Many of these graduates became core members of China's judicial bureaucracy during the Republican era.

The legal reform of the early twentieth century led to the rise of Chinese lawyers. This development was also partly the result of the application of the British legal system in China. After China's defeat in the Opium War in 1842, the British Empire established consular jurisdiction in treaty ports and in the colony of Hong Kong. Subsequently, an increasing number of Western lawyers took up practice in China, especially in Hong Kong and Shanghai, where the two British Supreme Courts were situated. Chinese people soon learned how they could benefit from these lawyers' services.

British law also had an impact on legal reform in another way. Wu Tingfang (1842–1922), the commissioner of law revision (*xiuding falü dachen*) appointed by the Qing government in 1903, was the first Chinese person to qualify as a barrister in Britain. He had served in Hong Kong, and in 1906 Wu wrote the first Chinese Draft Code of Criminal and Civil Procedure (Xingshi Minshi Susongfa Caoan) on the British model. Though the code was shelved in 1907 because it did not conform with the actual conditions of China, efforts to establish a role for lawyers in the Chinese legal system continued. The legal reformers stressed that lawyers were defenders of civil rights, and they claimed a distinct identity for lawyers as opposed to litigation masters by emphasizing lawyers' formal legal education and state credentialing.

EXPANSION AND CONTRACTION

Unlike the ambivalent Qing court, the Republican government granted Chinese lawyers formal status as soon as the regime was established in 1912. However, lawyers could practice only in the areas under the jurisdiction of modern courts, according to the Forty-first Ordinance issued by the Ministry of Justice in 1913. For that reason, there were few lawyers in most of the hinterland counties even by the 1940s.

During the Republican period, the diploma acquired after three or more years of study at a specialized law school or law department of a university was the conversion certificate of a lawyer's license. A law-school diploma was also required before one could take the national judicial examination in order to qualify as a judge or prosecutor. Western-style legal education thus became an increasingly important avenue to success, especially during the Nanjing era. By 1934, thirty-one of seventy-six universities and independent colleges across China had established law departments. More than one-quarter of law schools were situated in Shanghai, where China's largest bar association was founded in 1930.

By the 1930s, the education policy makers of the Nationalist government had become concerned about an excess of law students. They believed that law was attracting students who might otherwise have pursued careers in science and technology, which were central to China's development. In addition, practicing lawyers in Shanghai and other large coastal cities often complained about the competition and growing misconduct caused by the oversupply of lawyers. Therefore, the nationalist government began to limit the enrollment of law schools in 1932. In 1935 both the Ministry of Justice and the Bar Association of the Republic of China proposed an internship system for lawyer candidates when they drafted a new lawyer's law. The internship system had not been enacted by the time the Nationalist government in mainland China fell in 1949, and law-school graduates continued to outnumber those in other disciplines in higher education.

SEE ALSO *Codified Law, 1800–1949; Customary Law, 1800–1949; Law Courts, 1800–1949.*

BIBLIOGRAPHY

Conner, Alison W. Lawyers and the Legal Profession during the Republican Period. In *Civil Law in Qing and Republican China*, ed. Kathryn Bernhardt and Huang Zongzhi (Philip C. C. Huang), 215–248. Stanford, CA: Stanford University Press, 1994.

Huang Zongzhi (Philip C. C. Huang). *Code, Custom, and Legal Practice in China: The Qing and the Republic Compared.* Stanford, CA: Stanford University Press, 2001.

Macauley, Melissa. *Social Power and Legal Culture: Litigation Masters in Late Imperial China.* Stanford, CA: Stanford University Press, 1998.

Ministry of Education of the Republic of China. *Zhongguo Jiaoyu Nianjian* [Chinese educational yearbook]. Taibei: Zhongqing Publishing Company, 1981.

Sun Huei-min. The Introduction of Western-Style Lawyers in the Late Qing. *Bulletin of the Institute of Modern History Academia Sinica* 52 (2006): 165–210.

Xu Xiaoqun. *Chinese Professionals and the Republican State: The Rise of Professional Associations in Shanghai, 1912–1937.* Cambridge, U.K.: Cambridge University Press, 2001.

Zhang Weiren (Chang Wejen). Legal Education in Ch'ing China. In *Education and Society in Late Imperial China, 1600–1900*, ed. Benjamin A. Elman and Alexander Woodside, 292–339. Berkeley: University of California Press, 1994.

Sun Huei-min

LEGGE, JAMES

1815–1897

James Legge was in many ways the greatest sinologist of the nineteenth century. First, as a Scots missionary-scholar, he undertook his heroic translation *The Chinese Classics* (1861–1872, revised in 1893–1895), and later, as the first professor of Chinese at Oxford University, he made valuable contributions to F. Max Müller's Sacred Books of the East (1879–1910). These works laid the foundation for Western understanding of the Chinese tradition and, as associated with Müller's Sacred Books, also gave rise to the fledgling discipline of the comparative study of world religions.

Legge was born in the small town of Huntly, Aberdeenshire, Scotland, on December 20, 1815. The youngest of the four sons of Ebenezer Legge, a prosperous Scottish merchant, James Legge was raised in the Scots evangelical tradition of Congregationalism. For his abilities in Latin translation, he won a First Bursary to King's College, Aberdeen University, where he graduated in 1835 with a master of arts degree and the Huttonian Prize as outstanding student of the year. After graduation, he found himself increasingly tormented by religious questions. These experiences culminated in his born-again conversion as a Christian and led in 1837 to his enrollment at Highbury Theological College in London. By the time of his ordination in 1838, he had already dedicated himself to the China missions conducted by the London Missionary Society and had started studying Chinese in London under the retired China missionary Samuel Kidd.

In 1839 Legge married Mary Isabella Morison (after her death he married a second time to Hannah Mary Willetts) and set out for Asia to take up a teaching position at the London Missionary Society school for Chinese students based in Malacca. After assuming the headship of the Anglo-Chinese College there, he became convinced of the importance of understanding and converting the Chinese through their classical literature and conceived of the idea of translating the Chinese classics. In 1843 he moved the Malacca operations to Hong Kong, recently annexed as a colony by Great Britain after the Opium War (1839–1842). For the next thirty years he played an active role in the religious, educational, social, and scholarly life of the new colony, nearly always championing liberal causes in the colony. He became embroiled in the divisive "term question" concerning the best translations of "God" and other terms for a definitive rendition of the Bible into Chinese. His famous and still largely standard translation *The Chinese Classics* was in fact an extension of his liberal "accommodationist" convictions that the ancient Chinese were aware of God and, as seen in the classics, possessed an authentic religious and moral sensibility. As a British scholar and missionary, he was unusual for engaging and acknowledging the help of outstanding Chinese scholars like Wang Tao in his translation project.

In 1873, after increased tension with conservative missionaries over his devotion to the Chinese classics, Legge permanently retired from the mission field and returned to Britain. Appointed in 1876 to the first professorship of Chinese at Oxford University, Legge embarked upon a second career as an influential non-Conformist scholar at Oxford and as the most famous sinologist in the Western world. Through his association with his Oxonian colleague F. Max Müller, Legge defined the Victorian Orientalist understanding of Confucianism and Daoism and participated in the emergence of the comparative science of religions. He died at age 82, several days after falling into a paralytic coma after his Chinese-language class. He is buried at Wolvercote Cemetery in Oxford.

Legge's passage from an early evangelical missionary career to the new, more secular academic fields of sinology and comparative religious studies epitomizes some of the most significant religious and intellectual changes during the Victorian era and the early twentieth century. Legge's indefatigable work as a translator helped to define a certain Protestant paradigm of "the pure and the corrupt" for interpreting Chinese texts and traditions. Legge was also a pioneering figure in liberal currents within the evangelical missionary movement and in the opening of Oxford University to Asian traditions and to the matriculation of women and non-Anglicans.

BIBLIOGRAPHY

Girardot, Norman J. *The Victorian Translation of China: James Legge's Oriental Pilgrimage.* Berkeley: University of California Press, 2002.

Pfister, Lauren F. *Striving for the "Whole Duty of Man": James Legge and the Scottish Protestant Encounter with China.* Frankfurt am Main, Germany: Peter Lang, 2003.

Norman Girardot

LEISURE

Leisure in China can be thought of in at least three distinct ways: as free time, as an activity distinct from work, and as an industry (see Yu Guangyuan 2005, pp. 19–20). Leisure in the latter two senses—as a specific kind of nonwork activity that is embedded in a large consumer industry—dominates contemporary discourse. China's recent history of unprecedented economic growth and social change has influenced leisure significantly. Whereas leisure thought of broadly as free time might include the traditional life of a scholar or poet, or the slack months of farm life, leisure in its dominant contemporary usage needs be understood in its relationship to culture and the economy (Yu Guangyuan 2005, p. 7). This relationship has developed through China's turbulent twentieth-century history, and is a key part of understanding leisure in China today.

FROM FREE TIME TO MORAL CAMPAIGN

Leisure in the broad sense of free time (*xian*) has a long history in China, with cultural roots that go back hundreds of years. The early twentieth-century scholar-ambassador of Chinese culture, Lin Yutang (1895–1976), wrote admiringly of traditional Chinese leisure pursuits in his 1935 book, *My Country and My People*, listing over fifty activities ranging from playing traditional games, to eating meals, to pursuing art and music (Lin Yutang 1935, pp. 322–323). These activities centered on food and family at home and in the neighborhood. Lin neglects to mention that leisure travel had also long been popular in China, and there is evidence that mass tourism in China may have predated that in Europe (Ward 2001, p. 21) and that less wholesome activities such as opium smoking, prostitution, and gambling were also very much a part of "traditional" leisure in China.

As the Qing dynasty (1644–1912) fell, however, China's leading reformers were primarily concerned with creating a modern nation. Social changes swept the country, influenced by both colonial powers and popular domestic movements. New movements in literature and art reflected reformist political agendas, as well as expanding literacy and interest in reading for enjoyment (Laughlin 2008). Urban vices and "traditional" leisure practices—teahouse life in eastern China, for example (Shao Qin 1998)—together came to symbolize the kind of backward tradition targeted by cultural elites seeking to modernize China. Some twenty years after the end of the Qing dynasty, Lin Yutang (1935, p. 323) was already lamenting the loss of China's traditional sense of leisure to the modern lifestyle taking root in Shanghai.

As it would be for most of the twentieth century, leisure in Republican China (1912–1949) became a focus of ideological and political debate, one with important economic implications. China's first modern entertainment services—cinemas and nightclubs, for example—flourished in and around the colonial concessions, as did less socially acceptable forms of leisure, such as prostitution, drugs, and gambling. Illegal leisure activities generated large profits, and by the late 1920s, the Nationalist

A family enjoying Chinese New Year, Tiananmen Square, Beijing, January 24, 2001. *Under Mao Zedong, the Communist Party limited leisure activities to those beneficial to the state, such as absorbing party propaganda through literature, cinema, or other collective activities. As restrictions eased in the 1970s, citizens have enjoyed many different types of leisure activities, including travel, recreation in public parks, and shopping.* AP IMAGES

government sought to regulate Shanghai's rapidly expanding entertainment districts, both as a way to prove their legitimacy and as a moral crusade (Wakeman 1995, p. 20). The vices that seemed to define "modern" Shanghai became the target of reform, and regulating the city's vices became the responsibility of the newly formed Public Security Bureau (Wakeman 1995, pp. 22–24). The deteriorating moral climate got worse during the Japanese occupation (1937–1945), and it would not be until the early 1950s, under the new Communist government, that the real cleanup began, and leisure became even more highly politicized (Wakeman 1995, pp. 34, 38).

THE MAO ERA (1949–1976)

In a sense, leisure disappeared in the Mao era, subsumed into the broader discussion of ideology and culture. Mao Zedong rarely spoke of leisure (*xian*), though he spoke often about culture (*wenhua*), which became a battleground for ideological reform and government control. The only providers of acceptable leisure services and products were organizations run by the Chinese Communist Party (Wang Ning 2005, p. 6). Leisure time was not free time, but rather time to recover from the day's work and rest for the following day's productivity—it was to be spent in public and put to proper ideological use in collective activity and political study (Wang Shaoguang 1995, p. 154). While leisure under Mao was tightly regulated and put in service of ideology, urban residents had more options for leisure activities than did those outside the cities—parks, stadiums, cinemas, and libraries (Wang Ning 2005, p. 6). "Workers' Cultural Palaces" and "Youth Palaces," for example, were among the few spaces for politically acceptable "leisure" activities, which included painting and calligraphy lessons, music and theater performances, and athletics. This urban disparity in leisure lasted through the Mao era, and once economic reforms began in 1979, China's cities were again the sites of unprecedented expansion of leisure choices for the masses.

THE EARLY REFORM ERA (1978–1993)

While leisure in China has been influenced by both Mao- and Republican-era policies, and by more traditional notions of leisure, leisure in the contemporary sense of *xiuxian* formed as economic reforms began in 1979. As China opened its economy, the state's attitude toward leisure changed. Private time and leisure activities, so long as they did not disrupt social stability, were not under public scrutiny as they were in the Mao era (Wang Shaoguang 1995, p. 156). As leisure activities became less overtly politicized and more a matter of individual preference, the state began to see the provision of leisure services as an opportunity for economic growth.

One of the major changes in leisure in the 1980s was the growth in entertainment services and technologies such as nightclubs, billiard halls, and bowling alleys, which developed concurrently with a mass-tourism infrastructure that catered to inbound foreign tourists (Sofield and Li 1998). These new leisure options became increasingly popular among Chinese, who had more leisure time available as political demands on private time diminished, work hours eased, and household chores were made easier through modern appliances (Wang Shaoguang 1995, p. 157). The increasing foreign influence on Chinese leisure through tourism and the growing market for foreign music, movies, and television spurred state organized campaigns against "spiritual pollution," which were aimed at combating the perceived negative foreign influences on an increasingly privatized life (Wang Ning 2005, p. 7). But while leisure remained a social battleground to some extent, the overall trend toward the depoliticization and privatization of leisure, along with the influence of a market more open to foreign influence, set the stage for the more intensified changes of the 1990s (Wang Shaoguang 1995; Wang Ning 2005).

THE CONTEMPORARY CULTURAL ECONOMY (1993–PRESENT)

Leisure, understood as a specific nonwork activity supported by a leisure industry, has its roots in the fast-changing social and economic context of the 1990s. The acceleration of economic reforms initiated by Deng Xiaoping in 1993

Families enjoying an indoor water park, Taiyuan, Shaanxi province, July 1, 1999. *Leisure time in China underwent significant changes in the twentieth century. Under Mao Zedong, the government suggested time away from work should be spent in service to the nation. By the end of the century, however, standardized work weeks and increased vacation time led to the development of other forms of entertainment, such as amusement parks, domestic tourism, and consumption of consumer goods.* © FRITZ HOFFMANN/CORBIS

focused on developing a socialist market economy, and put new attention to the economic importance of service industries (Wang Ning 2005, p. 8). Despite the uneven development between urban and rural areas, the loosening restrictions on internal migration and the growing popularity of domestic tourism meant increased mobility not only of people, but of new cultural practices and consumer habits (Schein 2001). Paralleling the changing consumer landscape of urban China (see Davis 2000), leisure in less urbanized areas has also been transformed, as rising incomes in the countryside are put toward leisure-related consumer goods.

As reforms were implemented, the state withdrew from its role as the primary provider of leisure services. It recognized the economic importance of leisure, and emerging leisure services grew into large-scale leisure industries (*xiuxian chanye*), from karaoke parlors and bathhouses, to cinemas and travel agencies. State policies encouraged the boom in leisure industries through the 1990s: Campaigns promoting leisure culture have been initiated by municipal governments and by state ministries (Wang Jing 2001, pp. 79, 87). In 1995 a national forty-hour workweek was established, and in 1999 a new national holiday calendar extended vacation time, spurring spending on tourism and consumer goods (Wang Jing 2001, pp. 74–75). These decisions increased the amount of leisure time available to individuals, and helped transform leisure into a central part of popular Chinese culture. The state's regulations on specific leisure services remained loose through this period, and, as it had throughout the twentieth century, the state continued to take a campaign-style approach to regulation (Wang Ning 2005, p. 11).

Leisure in contemporary China has exploded, and an unprecedented diversity of leisure choices—from traditional teahouses and exercise in public parks to cutting-edge cinema complexes and shopping centers—are available to increasing numbers of Chinese. And yet, leisure is not simply a matter of free time and rest from work. Especially since the mid-1990s, when leisure culture (*xiuxian wenhua*) became a buzzword in national media (Wang Jing 2001, p. 74), the broad sense of leisure as free time has become wedded to mass-market consumption. Leisure is a term that exemplifies the social and economic transformations of reform-era China, and a term that has itself been transformed by those very changes. Leisure in China has been depoliticized, privatized, diversified, demoralized, internationalized, commercialized, and differentiated among social groups (see Wang Shaoguang 1995; Wang Jing 2001; Wang Ning 2005). These characteristics speak of the intensified relationship between culture and economy, and between growing individual autonomy and shifting political and economic structures. Though leisure remains an important issue of governance—and of politics—for the state, China's culture industries have become the primary providers of leisure services. Likewise, it is individual Chinese pursuing diverse activities—whether for self-development, for status, or for any other purpose—that drive the consumption of leisure in China, a change no less dramatic than the transformations of the state or private industry.

SEE ALSO *Food and Drink since 1800; Games and Play; Music, Popular; Sports; Tourism.*

BIBLIOGRAPHY

Davis, Deborah S., ed. *The Consumer Revolution in Urban China.* Berkeley: University of California Press, 2000.

Laughlin, Charles A. *The Literature of Leisure and Chinese Modernity.* Honolulu: University of Hawai'i Press, 2008.

Lin Yutang. *My Country and My People.* New York: Reynal & Hitchcock, 1935.

Schein, Louisa. Urbanity, Cosmopolitanism, Consumption. In *China Urban: Ethnographies of Contemporary Culture*, ed. Nancy N. Chen, Constance D. Clark, Suzanne Z. Gottschang, and Lyn Jeffery, 225–241. Durham, NC: Duke University Press, 2001.

Shao Qin. Tempest over Teapots: The Vilification of Teahouse Culture in Early Republican China. *Journal of Asian Studies* 57, 4 (1998): 1009–1041.

Sofield, Trevor H. B., and Fung Mei Sarah Li. Tourism Development and Cultural Policies in China. *Annals of Tourism Research* 25, 2 (1998): 362–392.

Wakeman, Frederic. Licensing Leisure: The Chinese Nationalists' Attempt to Regulate Shanghai, 1927–49. *Journal of Asian Studies* 54, 1 (1995): 19–42.

Wang Jing. Culture as Leisure and Culture as Capital. *Positions* 9, 1 (2001): 69–104.

Wang Ning. From Leisure as Ideology to Leisure as Industry: Changing Leisure Policies in China. *World Leisure* 1 (2005): 5–11.

Wang Shaoguang. The Politics of Private Time: Changing Leisure Patterns in Urban China. In *Urban Spaces in Contemporary China: The Potential for Autonomy and Community in Post-Mao China*, ed. Deborah S. Davis, 149–172. Washington, D.C.: Woodrow Wilson Center Press, 1995.

Ward, Julian. *Xu Xiake (1587–1641): The Art of Travel Writing.* Richmond, U.K.: Curzon, 2001.

Yu Guangyuan. *Lun pubian youxian de shehui* [On the society of universal leisure]. Beijing: Zhongguo Jingji Chubanshe, 2005.

Travis Klingberg

LEISURE AND CULTURE FOR THE ELDERLY

Filial piety (*xiao*), a central value in Chinese culture, has defined individuals' positions and roles within the family for centuries. It not only enjoins children to respect and care for elders, but also articulates the expectation that the old maintain the harmony and stability of the family (Chow 1996).

Traditionally, older men, as the powerful patriarchs of the family, provided advice, knowledge, and wisdom to the young. Their advice and wisdom were respected and obeyed (Chow 1996). Older women, in contrast, continued to play an affective role by providing child care for grandchildren, passing on social and family rituals, and maintaining family networks. Essentially, they served as kin keepers for the family (Chang Xiangqun 1999).

While the traditional division of family roles still guides many elderly people's daily lives in modern Chinese society (Wu et al. 2008), new elderly lifestyles have emerged. With rising living standards, financial independence allows many Chinese elders (especially those with pension benefits) freedom from family responsibilities and enables them to enjoy a leisurely old age.

In 1996 the Communist Party passed the Laonianren Quanyi Baozhang Fa (Law for the Protection of Elders' Rights) (Falü Jiaoyu Wang). This law urges local governments, organizations, and communities to put more effort in enriching elders' social and psychological well-being through leisure activities and social engagement.

Since the enactment of the law, the number of senior facilities, such as senior-activity centers and continuing education for the elderly (*laonian daxue*), has increased rapidly in urban China. These facilities are funded mostly by local governments and communities (Jiang Xiangqun 2005). It is important to note that these facilities are often unavailable for elders in rural areas, especially impoverished rural areas, since most of the leisure facilities are funded by local governments and communities.

In these facilities, the elderly join groups such as dance clubs, bridge clubs, choir clubs, painting clubs, ping-pong clubs, according to their interests. They can also further their education in computer technology, foreign languages, history, arts, and music. Elders also participate in collective physical activities or exercises in the facilities. Qigong, taiji, and folk dancing are some of the most popular exercises among urban elders. Periodically, senior centers also organize such activities as traveling events, museum visits, and volunteer work (such as traffic directing). These facilities are consistently reported to have enhanced Chinese elders' self-confidence and life satisfaction (Guangzhou Laonian Xuehui 1998; Jiang Xiangqun 2005).

While senior facilities are becoming more and more popular in China, the majority of Chinese elders continue to spend much leisure time at home. Watching television at home is ranked as the foremost leisure activity among both rural and urban elders. In Guangzhou, 84.8 percent of urban elders and 63.33 percent of rural elders spend most of their daily leisure time watching television (Guangzhou Laonian Xuehui 1998). Playing such games as mahjongg and cards at home is also quite popular among older Chinese. Walking is the most popular daily exercise (82.2% of urban elders and 58.33% of rural elders). While 10 percent of urban elders participate in exercises such as taiji, qigong, and jogging, only 2 percent of rural elders participate in these activities (Guangzhou Laonian Xuehui 1998). Owing to the lack of pensions in rural China, rural elders may need to continue to work in the field or at home in exchange for support from their children. This may explain why significantly fewer rural elders enjoy leisure activities.

Man performing Tai chi exercises near the City Wall of Xi'an, March 14, 2008. *Often out of economic necessity, elderly rural citizens contribute to the running of a household by fulfilling traditional family roles, such as caring for grandchildren. Generally more prosperous, urban senior citizens frequently have less work obligations to their families, allowing them to take advantage of local recreation facilities offered by community and government organizations.* TIM GRAHAM/ GETTY IMAGES

SEE ALSO *Family; Filial Piety; Leisure; Life Cycle; Social Welfare.*

BIBLIOGRAPHY

Chang Xiangqun. "Fat Pigs" and Women's Gifts: Agnatic and Non-agnatic Social Support in Kaixianggong Village. In *Women of China: Economic and Social Transformation*, ed. Jackie West, Zhao Minghua, and Cheng Yuan, 156–174. London: Macmillan Press, 1999.

Chow, Nelson Wing Sun. Filial Piety in Asian Chinese Communities. *Hong Kong Journal of Gerontology* 10 suppl. (1996): 115–117.

Falü Jiaoyu Wang [Web for Chinese Law Education]. http://www.chinalawedu.com.

Guangzhou Laonian Xuehui (Guangzhou Gerontological Association). *Kua shiji de Guangzhou laonianren shenghuo* [The lives of the elderly in Guangzhou for over a century]. Guangzhou, China: Guangzhou Renmin Chubanshe, 1998.

Jiang Xiangqun. *Laonian shehui baozhang zhidu: Lishi yu biange* [The system of social guarantees for the elderly: History and changes]. Beijing: Renmin Daxue Chubanshe, 2005.

Wu, Bei, Iris Chi, Lee Ann Mjelde-Mossey, and Nina M. Silverstein. Gender Differences in Contributory Behaviors among the Oldest-Old Chinese in Shanghai. *Ageing International* 32 (2008): 65–77.

Baozhen Luo

LEXICOGRAPHY

Although textbooks for teaching Chinese characters are known to have existed in the Zhou (1046–256 BCE) and Qin (221–206 BCE) dynasties, the early traditions of lexicography were specialized character dictionaries preserving usage from earlier times. Hence, the earliest surviving text regarded as a dictionary is the *Erya* [Near to correctness] (third century BCE), which is largely devoted to preserving the meanings of characters as they were used in pre-Qin writings, especially Confucian classics.

The Han dynasty (206 BCE–220 CE) dictionary *Shuowen jiezi* [Explanations of simple and compound graphs] by Xu Shen (second century CE) was the first general dictionary in scope and introduced an innovative organization by identifying components of characters as "radicals" (*bushou*), under which various characters sharing a given component were grouped. Although the general method of categorizing characters that Xu Shen initiated would later be adapted to become a major feature of most Chinese dictionaries down to the present, Xu's purpose was more philosophical than practical. His method of identifying radical components of characters was designed to fit all characters into a formalistic set of numbers from metaphysics, and the characters that he analyzed were in the form of seal script from the Qin dynasty and earlier, rather than characters in the clerical script of his own time, all in an attempt to speculate on a systematic relationship between archaic script and cosmic order.

While the *Erya* organized its character entries by topic and the *Shuowen jiezi* by graphic radicals, a phonetic method did appear in rhyming dictionaries, compiled for composing poetry. The earliest surviving rhyming dictionary is the *Qieyun* (601 CE), in which the editors collated characters by adopting a system of spelling (*fanqie*) that used two different characters to represent the initial and final sounds of characters and their tones, and so group them. The meanings given for characters were not rigorously sourced, and although the *fanqie* spellings have provided valuable evidence for the language of the time, it remains uncertain whether the spellings were describing a common pronunciation or prescribing a pronunciation based on a particular status group.

Later dictionaries not only continued these traditions but also broadened the scope of lexicography—for example, to include common usage in the *Longkan shoujian* [Handy mirror of the dragon shrine] of 997—and combined and modified early methods. These advances culminated in the *Kangxi zidian* [Kangxi character dictionary] of 1716, so-named for the Kangxi emperor (r. 1661–1722) of the Qing dynasty (1644–1912), who ordered its compilation. Once corrected and supplemented, it provided entries for over 49,000 characters grouped under 214 radicals, giving variant forms, traditional *fanqie* spellings, and contemporary pronunciations through homophone characters, and meanings citing a wide range of texts. As such, the *Kangxi zidian* has provided a major source for modern dictionaries and is still used as a key reference. Indeed, this was the source for the first major dictionaries of the twentieth century: a revised and expanded edition of the *Kangxi zidian*, edited by prominent scholars, titled *Zhonghua da zidian* (1919), and the *Ciyuan* [Word source, 1915], edited by Lu Erkui (1862–1935), the first "word dictionary," with some 100,000 entries devoted to combinations of characters as well as solitary characters that provide words, modeled after the 1878 *Dictionnaire de la langue française* [Dictionary of the French language] edited by Émile Littré (1801–1881). Nevertheless, these dictionaries still remained focused almost exclusively on classical Chinese.

Another nineteenth-century French dictionary, the Larousse *Grand dictionnaire universal du XIXe siècle* [Great universal dictionary of the nineteenth century, 1865–1890], provided a model for the encyclopedic dictionary *Cihai* [Sea of words, 1936], first edited by Shu Xincheng, which included terms and names for many fields of modern knowledge and usage, and has been continually revised, expanded, and reissued to the present as a widely used reference work.

The needs of Chinese governments to promote a standard language have also resulted in dictionaries that are landmark texts, repeatedly revised and now also available online. The first of these is the *Guoyu cidian* (or *Gwoyeu tsyrdean*; Word dictionary of the national language), compiled for the

Republic of China in 1936 in three volumes, prescribing pronunciations for characters and words in the character-derived phonetic symbols known as *Zhuyin fuhao* and a romanization system termed *Gwoyeu romatzyh*. Entries for the online edition can be accessed in a variety of ways. The People's Republic of China promoted standard pronunciation first through the *Xinhua zidian* (New China character dictionary, 1953), edited by Wei Jiangong (1901–1980), which initially employed *Zhuyin fuhao* pronunciation guides, then adopted pinyin romanized spellings after they were approved by the state in 1958. With the adoption of simplified characters in 1958, the *Xinhua zidian* also revised the system of radicals by which characters are grouped, reducing the standard 214 radicals to 189.

While the compiling of comprehensive reference dictionaries was delayed in China during the Maoist era, the need was addressed in Japan by Morohashi Tetsuji (1883–1982) through his *Dai Kan-Wa jiten* (Great Chinese-Japanese word dictionary, 1958–1960), an unprecedented encyclopedic dictionary in thirteen volumes, which provided the standard reference work, especially for pre-twentieth-century Chinese studies, well into the 1980s. A similar Chinese-Chinese dictionary published in Taiwan, the forty-volume *Zhongwen da cidian*, supplemented but did not greatly expand the range of the Morohashi dictionary.

Following the Maoist era, however, teams in China simultaneously launched the most ambitious lexicographic projects to date, the *Hanyu da zidian* [Chinese-language comprehensive character dictionary, 1986–1989] under the editorship of Xu Zhongshu (1898–1991), with 54,678 character entries, and the *Hanyu da cidan* [Chinese-language comprehensive word dictionary, 1986–1993] under the editorship of Luo Zhufeng (1911–1996), with over 370,000 words formed from 23,000 characters. Both dictionaries revised once again the system of radicals used to organize entries, this time employing two hundred radicals. The model for these was the *Oxford English Dictionary*, so that whether from the point of view of lexical scope, etymological research, contemporary usage, or range of citations, these dictionaries now constitute the standard comprehensive dictionaries of the Chinese language. In addition, the seventy-four-volume *Zhongguo da baike quanshu* [Comprehensive encyclopedia sinica] appeared between 1980 and 1993, organized by fields of knowledge with a total of over 77,000 entries.

SEE ALSO *Language and Language Policy.*

BIBLIOGRAPHY

Huang Jianhua. Chinese and Western Metalexicography. In *Lexicography: Critical Concepts*, ed. R. R. K. Hartmann, Vol. 3, 391–404. New York: Routledge, 2003.

Norman, Jerry. *Chinese*. Cambridge, U.K.: Cambridge University Press, 1988.

Wang Ying. *Changyong hanyu cishu juyao* [Guide to frequently-used Chinese dictionaries]. Guiyang, PRC: Guizhou Jiaoyu, 1996.

Xue Shiqi. Chinese Lexicography Past and Present. In *Lexicography: Critical Concepts*, ed. R. R. K. Hartmann, Vol. 2, 158–173. New York: Routledge, 2003.

Edward Mansfield Gunn Jr.

LI AN

SEE *Lee, Ang.*

LI DENGHUI (LEE TENG-HUI)

1923–

Li Denghui (Lee Teng-hui) is the single most controversial figure in Taiwan's modern history. Some Taiwanese nationalists almost deify him as a "father of the nation," while for many Chinese nationalists he is regarded as a traitor. However, he played a critical role in Taiwan's democratization and move toward de facto independence in the 1990s.

Li was born in northern Taiwan in 1923, when Taiwan was a Japanese colony. He was an exceptional student, winning a scholarship to Kyoto Imperial University. Following the end of World War II (1939–1945), Li returned to Taiwan to complete his undergraduate education at National Taiwan University.

During the 1950s and 1960s, Li led an academic life. He earned a master's degree in agricultural economics from Iowa State University in 1953 and a Ph.D. from Cornell University in 1968. Between these degrees he taught at National Taiwan University and National Chengchi University and served as an economist for the Joint Commission on Rural Reconstruction.

Li entered government service soon after returning from Cornell to Taiwan, becoming the cabinet minister responsible for agriculture in 1972. He was later appointed mayor of Taibei (Taipei) in 1978 and provincial governor in 1981. President Jiang Jingguo (Chiang Ching-kuo) was impressed enough with Li's administrative performance to select him as vice president in 1984.

When Jiang Jingguo died in January 1988, Li automatically became president, although he was widely viewed as a stopgap president without a strong power base in the Guomindang (Nationalist) (GMD) party. Nevertheless, Li surprised many analysts by consolidating his position in the party and state. First, he overcame strong resistance from conservatives to win the powerful position of chairman of

Man holding a portrait of former Taiwanese presidents Li Denghui (left) and Chen Shuibian, Miaoli, Taiwan, February 28, 2004. *Taiwanese-born Li Denghui became the country's first democratically elected president in 1996, ending over forty decades of single-party rule. In his post-presidential years, Li has become an active member of his country's independence movement, looking to establish a Republic of Taiwan outside the authority of both the People's Republic of China and the Republic of China.* PATRICK LIN/AFP/GETTY IMAGES

the GMD. Another critical moment in his rise came in the spring of 1990, when he survived a challenge from the GMD's Non-mainstream Faction to win Taiwan's last indirect presidential election. At the same time, when facing pro-democracy student demonstrations, Li chose to meet the student leaders rather than send in tanks. In talks with the students, Li pledged to hold the National Affairs Conference, a consensus-seeking convention that set the direction of Taiwan's full democratization.

Li's dominant position was further strengthened when his last major rival, Premier Hao Bocun (Hau Pei-tsun), resigned in 1993 and many of his most outspoken critics from the Non-mainstream Faction split off to form the New Party. Li had won the inner-party power struggle by his strategy of political alliances. Li's Mainstream Faction incorporated mainly Taiwanese-elected politicians, many of whom had strong links with local GMD factions and big business. Although the alliance enabled the GMD to win post-transition elections, it was to have severe costs, as the GMD became increasingly vulnerable to accusations of political corruption.

Despite missile tests by the People's Republic of China (PRC) and the emergence of two rebel GMD candidates, Li won Taiwan's first direct presidential election in March 1996 with 54 percent of the vote. Li had become by far Taiwan's most popular politician; his popularity cut across party lines.

Li tapped into the Taiwanese desire for international recognition with his diplomatic offensives and his decision to apply for reentry in the United Nations. His unofficial visit to the United States in June 1995 was seen as a key diplomatic triumph. Li gained the support of many Taiwanese nationalists as a result of his willingness to promote Taiwan internationally and stand up to PRC military threats. He was also aware of the increasing unpopularity among Taiwanese citizens of the prospect of unification with China, so he tried to localize the regime, increasingly referring to the island as the Republic of China on Taiwan.

Although the direction of democratization adopted in the 1990s was set by the opposition Democratic Progressive Party (DPP), opinion polls in the mid-1990s showed that the credit largely went to Li, who was often referred to as "Mr. Democracy" by his supporters. Under Li, the pace of democratization was far more rapid than it had been under Jiang Jingguo. When Li became president Taiwan was still a semi-democracy, as the vast majority of Parliamentarians had been frozen in office since being elected on mainland China in 1947, and positions such as Taipei mayor were government appointees. During Li's tenure, Taiwan implemented full reelection of the national parliaments in 1991 and 1992, direct election for Taipei, Kaohsiung mayors and provincial governor in 1994 and presidential election in 1996.

In domestic policy, Li was skillful at appropriating popular opposition policy demands. For instance, though national health insurance was originally proposed by the DPP, it was introduced by the GMD government in 1995 and proved to be extremely popular, achieving approximately 97 percent coverage within a year of commencing operation.

Li's second term as president from 1996 to 2000 received a more mixed appraisal than his first. Li's victory in the presidential election gave him the mandate to continue democratic reforms. At the 1996 National Development Conference, important cross-party consensus was achieved on reforms such as scrapping the obsolete provincial government. Moreover, Li's discourse on "New Taiwanese" in 1998 was seen as encouraging ethnic reconciliation. Under Li's leadership, the GMD won a resounding victory in the 1998 legislative election.

Despite these achievements, Li's second term was marked by major setbacks. There was little progress on the diplomatic front, and PRC distrust of Li meant that cross-strait negotiations were stalled. Li's claim in 1999 that cross-strait relations should be categorized as "special state-to-state relations" heightened tensions with the PRC and damaged Taiwan's relations with the United States.

The greatest failure of Li's second term was the defeat of his protégé Lian Zhan (Lien Chan) in the 2000 presidential election. Instead of supporting the popular former provincial governor Song Chuyu (James Soong), Li backed his former premier, the uncharismatic Lian, as GMD candidate. Despite Li's active campaigning for Lian, a split GMD vote meant Lian only garnered 23 percent, while the DPP's Chen Shuibian (Chen Shui-bian) won the election with 39 percent of the vote.

After leaving office, Li remained politically active. He soon became alienated from GMD and in 2001 formed his own party, the Taiwan Solidarity Union, which cooperated with the ruling DPP. Li became more radical on the issue of Taiwan's independence after his retirement, and he came to be regarded as a Taiwanese nationalist. This may be one of the factors explaining his declining popularity in the post-2000 period.

SEE ALSO *Chen Shuibian; Taiwan, Republic of China: Democratic Progressive Party; Taiwan, Republic of China: Politics since 1945.*

BIBLIOGRAPHY

Dickson, Bruce, and Chien-min Chao, eds. *Assessing the Lee Teng-hui Legacy in Taiwan's Politics: Democratic Consolidation and External Relations*. Armonk, NY: Sharpe, 2002.

Lee Wei-chin, and T. Y. Wang, eds. *Sayonara to the Lee Teng-hui Era: Politics in Taiwan, 1988–2000*. Lanham, MD: University of America Press, 2003.

Tsia Shih-Shan, Henry. *Lee Teng-hui and Taiwan's Quest for Identity*. New York: Palgrave Macmillan, 2005.

Dafydd Fell

LI HONGZHANG

1823–1901

Li Hongzhang was an astute diplomat, an energetic and skillful politician, and a realistic practitioner who held high-ranking government positions and had widespread domestic and military responsibilities during China's period of early modernization. Li was among the foremost supporters of the Self-strengthening movement, and became involved at all stages of the development process, from planning and organization to pleading to the throne for approval and requisitioning funds to support many of the country's modernization projects.

EARLY LIFE AND CAREER

Li was born on February 15, 1823, in the village of Qunzhi in Modian Township, Anhui Province. He achieved the *jinshi* degree at the relatively young age of twenty-four. In 1853, with the Taiping Uprising (1851–1864) threatening his home district, he eagerly assisted local military defense forces. That same year, he quickly rose in prominence to become an important strategic adviser for the governor of Anhui. As early as 1843, Li had formed a teacher-disciple relationship (*mufu*) with Zeng Guofan, who had been a *jinshi* classmate of Li's father. Although the two did not always agree, it would appear they were very close. In 1859 Zeng, then the chief commander against the Taipings in Jiangxi, invited Li to join his personal staff. Later that year, Zeng made Li his chief secretary (Bland 1917, p. 42).

In 1861 Jiangsu gentry living in Shanghai urgently requested that Zeng send troops to Shanghai. On Zeng's command, Li put together an army—the Anhui Army (also known as the Huai Army), composed of men from his hometown area and also some of the newer (more vigorous) units of the Hunan Army. Seven British steamships were sent to Anqing to carry the army and the Huaiyang Navy to

Shanghai in March 1862. This episode marked Li's introduction to steamships and concurrently to the superiority of Western technology, paving the way for his later interest in "self-strengthening" (*ziqiang*).

EFFORTS TO STRENGTHEN CHINA'S MILITARY FORCES

To "self-strengthen" the Chinese forces fighting against the Taipings, Li arranged for Western advisers to train Chinese soldiers in the use of superior Western weaponry. By 1863, out of a force of forty thousand men, about ten thousand were using rifles, and many had also learned to use cannons. Li's "modern" forces began winning more battles, and were increasingly relied upon in the fight against the Taipings. Li also took measures to limit the direct help of Westerners, so that they always remained within Chinese control. For example, when he accepted the aid of British and French forces in an 1862 campaign near Shanghai, he insisted that the foreign forces stay within a thirty-mile radius of the Shanghai foreign settlement.

During this period, Li received valuable advice and formed friendships with several notable military leaders from the West. In letters to Li, the British army officer Charles George Gordon (1833–1885) provided valuable insight and suggestions, and the two are said to have chatted for hours on end. Frederick Townsend Ward (1831–1862), an American, was also an acquaintance, and at Li's suggestion Ward was made commander of the "Ever-Victorious Army," originally a band of foreign mercenaries hired by Shanghai gentry and merchants. Li was well-known for relying on his *mufu* relationships rather than official connections for getting things done, a practice that was not considered corrupt in China at the time. Li's relationship with Ward experienced many ups and downs (especially regarding pay), and impressed on Li the difficulties of working with Westerners. In 1864, after the Ever-Victorious Army was disbanded, Li hired many of its Western officers to work at the Fenghuangshan military camp, which had been founded for the purpose of training Chinese soldiers in Western military techniques (Chu and Liu 1994, p. 130).

In December 1862, Li was named governor of Jiangsu on Zeng's recommendation. In Shanghai, Li became acquainted with the presence of foreigners and polished his diplomatic skills. He understood that, economically and administratively, Shanghai was in Western hands. He also came to recognize the aggressive expansionist commercial interests of the Western powers and the importance of realizing "economic sovereignty" for China.

Li played a crucial role in the Self-strengthening movement (1860–1895), a wide-ranging effort aimed at preventing foreign encroachments. The quest to acquire Western technology for both military and commercial use was a major aspect of the movement, although few of its proponents ever seriously considered any corresponding political reforms. Li himself emphasized the need to maintain "good governance" within the framework of the traditional structure. In the reform of military, economic, and educational institutions, however, Li always tried to learn from Westerners without giving them too much power. He was fully aware of the West's expansionist intentions, and did what he could to limit Western involvement.

Chinese statesman Li Hongzhang, c. 1890. *Despite his notable losses during the Sino-Japanese War, Li Hongzhang nonetheless remains an important general in Chinese military history for his efforts at modernizing the Chinese army. As a viceroy for the imperial court, Li attempted to strengthen China's standing in the region through diplomatic ties with Western nations, hoping to balance Japan's rising power to the east.* HULTON ARCHIVE/ GETTY IMAGES

In 1865 Li founded Jiangnan Arsenal in Shanghai, which incorporated two smaller arsenals that Li had started earlier. In that same year, he also founded the Nanjing Arsenal by relocating equipment from the Suzhou Arsenal. These defense industries were soon followed in 1867 by the Tianjin Arsenal and the Fuzhou Navy Yard, created by Zuo Zongtang and managed by Shen Baozhen. All of these projects were officially approved and received funding from the court. Li was keen to build up China's military production industries, and, despite personal rivalries, he was generally supportive of those that others had founded because he recognized their importance to China's self-strengthening. These modern enterprises required sizable funding however, more than the state could provide. Beginning in 1868, after the Nian Uprising had been suppressed, the Qing government turned its attention to the suppression of the Muslim rebels in the northwest and to regaining control of land that the Russians, taking advantage of the chaos in the region, had seized (the Yili region). These expensive military campaigns were a blow to Li's plans for a substantial development of coastal defenses.

FOUNDING OF THE CHINA MERCHANTS' STEAM NAVIGATION COMPANY

In 1870 Li was made governor of Zhili, a position he kept for the next quarter century. Three months later, he became imperial commissioner for the northern ports, which included Tianjin, Zhefu, and Niuzhuang. While in those positions, he oversaw the founding of the China Merchants' Steam Navigation Company in 1872 to 1873. This was a groundbreaking project to be owned and primarily financed by Chinese merchants to compete with Western steamship companies in the carrying trade in Chinese waters. By 1877 the China Merchants' Steam Navigation Company owned twenty-nine steamships. The ships were used primarily for commercial purposes, but they also carried food relief during the famine in North China in 1876 and they sometimes transported military troops. With the success of the steamship company, Li turned to other commercial ventures, including the Hubei Coal Mining Company in 1875, the Kaiping Mining Company in 1877, and the Shanghai Cotton Textile Mill in 1878.

FOREIGN AFFAIRS AND DIPLOMACY

Li also worked closely with the Zongli Yamen (Office of General Management), and over time he had a major impact on foreign affairs. As a diplomat, Li strove to preserve China's territorial and administrative integrity under the unequal treaties. The threat from Japan became prominent in 1874 when, after signing a "nonaggression" treaty with China, meant to prevent Japan's collaboration with Western powers, Japan invaded Taiwan on dubious grounds—to seek recompense for the murder by Taiwan aborigines of shipwrecked Liuqiu sailors over whom Japan claimed suzerainty. Li's strategy was to negotiate peace while preparing for possible war. But, unaware of the strength of Chinese war preparedness on Taiwan, and poorly advised by the British minister Thomas Wade, Li acceded to Japanese demands and inadvertently lent support to Japan's claim over the Liuqiu Islands. The Japanese annexed the islands four years later.

Li also became concerned that either Russia or Japan would try to take control of Korea. To Li's relief, Korea and Japan signed a treaty in 1876 after the Jianghua Island Incident of 1875, in which a Japanese ship incited a defensive response from the Korean island. To thwart Japanese ambitions, Li advised Korea to also enter into treaty relations with Western powers, especially the United States. This way, the Western countries would defend Korea so as to protect their trade benefits. This Korea did, first with the United States in 1882, and later with European powers.

Only months later, however, a riot erupted in Seoul, in which several Japanese ministers were killed and the Japanese legation burned down. The Korean government that had signed the treaties was ousted, and three thousand troops from Li's Anhui Army were rushed to Korea just as Japan arrived with four warships and troops of its own. Thanks to the Chinese presence and Ma Jianzhong (1845–1900), a capable diplomat sent by Li, war was averted.

Finally, however, continued friction between Japan and China over Korea resulted in the Sino-Japanese War (1894–1895). Li, who by this time was more than seventy years of age, was the main military coordinator during the war, which resulted in total defeat. As with Li's many self-strengthening projects, insufficient and unreliable financing was a serious problem, and the Beiyang Fleet suffered from inadequate organization and obsolete equipment. Li was fully aware of these problems, and had to rely on a strategy of passive defense to avoid confrontation with the enemy's fleet. With military power inadequate to resist foreign aggression, security could be preserved only through diplomacy and through unavoidable compromises and concessions. In the end, Li's efforts proved to be in vain when the fleet was destroyed by the Japanese Navy in the Battle of the Yellow Seas. Li was blamed for poor leadership in the defeat, losing most of his political power.

A regionalist theory has been suggested in which Li's rapid fall was due to the devastation during the war of the Anhui Army, which was the basis of his extended hold on power. Li had been the unofficial leader of the most powerful of China's armies. This view is debatable, however, because it is clear that Li was very loyal to the court and never made a decision without consulting or considering the court's wishes. While the army protected the imperial court, stationed south of Tianjin in Zhili Province, Li had kept his position as governor-general for a notably long tenure. When ordered to relinquish the office, he did so without demur.

Despite his fall from grace, Li remained China's most experienced diplomat, and therefore the Qing government continued to request his service. In 1896 he was sent to Russia to attend the czar's coronation and finalize the Sino-Russian Treaty. He also traveled to Europe and the United States. He later became governor-general of Guangdong and Guangxi in 1899 and 1900. In 1901 he represented the Qing government in the humiliating 1901 Boxer settlement.

Li passed away on November 7, 1901, in Beijing, months after the Boxer settlement was finalized. The Qing government awarded him the title of Marquis Suyi of the First Class, and after his death this title was inherited by his grandson, Li Guojie.

SEE ALSO *China Merchants' Steam Navigation Company; Gordon, Charles; Liuqiu Islands; Qing Restoration; Shen Baozhen; Sino-Japanese War, 1894–1895; Wade, Thomas; Zeng Guofan; Zuo Zongtang.*

BIBLIOGRAPHY

Bland, John Otway Percy. *Li Hung-Chang*. New York: Holt, 1917.

Chu, Samuel (Zhu Changling), and Liu Kwang-Ching (Liu Guangjing), eds. *Li Hung-chang and China's Early Modernization*. Armonk, NY: Sharpe, 1994.

Douglas, Robert K. *Li Hungchang*. London: Bliss, Sands and Foster, 1895.

Folsom, Kenneth E. *Friends, Guests, and Colleagues: The Mu-fu System in the Late Ch'ing Period*. Berkeley: University of California Press, 1968.

Kennedy, Thomas L. *The Arms of Kiangnan: Modernization in the Chinese Ordnance Industry, 1860–1895*. Boulder, CO: Westview, 1978.

Li Hongzhang. *Li Wenzhong gong quanzhi* [The complete works of Li Hongzhang]. Nanjing, 1905.

Liu Kwang-Ching (Liu Guangjing). The Confucian as Patriot and Pragmatist: Li Hung-Chang's Formative Years, 1823–1866. *Harvard Journal of Asiatic Studies* 30 (1970): 5–45.

Mannix, William Francis, ed. *Memoirs of Li Hung Chang*. New York: Houghton Mifflin, 1913.

Rawlinson, John L. *China's Struggle for Naval Development, 1839–1895*. Cambridge, MA: Harvard University Press, 1967.

Spector, Stanley. *Li Hung-Chang and the Huai Army: A Study in Nineteenth-Century Regionalism*. Seattle: University of Washington Press, 1964.

Williams, F. W. Review of *Memoirs of Li Hung Chang*. *American Historical Review* 19 (1914): 633–635.

Lai Chi-kong

LI HUA

1907–1994

Best known for woodblock prints that portray China's twentieth-century political and social struggles with extraordinary emotional intensity, Li Hua devoted his artistic career to the development of the modern woodcut movement. Born in Panyu, Guangdong Province, to a merchant family, Li Hua studied oil painting at the Guangzhou Municipal Art College. After graduating in 1926, he then went to Japan in 1930 for further training in Western-style art and entered the Kawabata Painting School in Tokyo. Upon returning to Guangdong he took a teaching position at his alma mater.

Although Li Hua in his youth had absorbed the modernist painting styles of the Paris school, such as fauvism, he began making prints and became active in the woodcut movement in the early 1930s, eventually renouncing modernism. In 1934 he held a solo exhibition that led to his founding of the Modern Woodcut Society in Guangzhou. The purpose of this organization was to promote printmaking through publications, exhibitions, and workshops. Between 1934 and 1936 the group published eighteen issues of a biweekly journal, *Modern Woodcut*, for which Li was the editor-in-chief. The group sent a copy of each issue to the printmaker Lu Xun (1881–1936) in Shanghai. Lu was particularly impressed by the fourth issue and even suggested they send copies to artists in Japan and Russia, which they did. Lu Xun's friend Uchiyama Kanzō also was an enthusiast and sold their hand-printed journal in his bookstore in Shanghai.

Li Hua also demonstrated his skills as a curator of exhibitions for the society's monthly shows. The Modern Woodcut Society's successful first-anniversary exhibition displayed works by members as well as prints from Japan and Europe. In addition, Li and the society members took a major role in organizing the second National Traveling Print Exhibition, which opened at the Sun Yat-sen Municipal Library of Guangzhou on July 5, 1936.

Li Hua's relationship with Lu Xun had a significant impact on the creation of his prints, as well as on his curatorial and pedagogical commitment. In the summer of 1931, Lu Xun organized a workshop on woodcut prints in Shanghai for young students and gave a lecture on the history of prints from Japanese ukiyo-e through German expressionism. Uchiyama Kakitsu, brother of Uchiyama Kanzō, was invited to teach the technical aspects of the medium. Although not a member of the class, possibly because of his studies in Japan, Li Hua made a print illustrating a view of the workshop in which Lu Xun is depicted as presenting one of his collections to the students. Subsequently, Li Hua personally sent his prints to Lu Xun, and they continued their correspondence, exchanging their ideas about Chinese art, until Lu Xun's death in 1936. Thereafter, Li Hua carried on Lu's belief in the usefulness of art for the masses and the society, and led the development of the Chinese woodcut movement.

Li's work of the 1930s varies in style and content. His experiments range from cubism to expressionism, from lyrical polychromatic landscapes to still lifes in the style of the cubist master Pablo Picasso. His most representative piece of this period is *China, Roar!* from 1936. Reminiscent of German expressionism, the provocative depiction of a bound, blindfolded man screams out the distress of China under Japanese imperialism and internal political conflicts.

In the period between 1945 and 1949, Li's style tended to become more naturalistic and was accompanied by increasing technical refinement. His antigovernment prints, such as *When the Requisition Officers Leave*, offer easily readable narrative that clearly expresses his disgust with corruption and his opposition to the Nationalist authorities. In its style and content, *Arise, Suffering Slaves*, part of the "Tide of Anger" series from 1947, shows the influence of Käthe Kollwitz, the German artist who was Lu Xun's favorite. Kollwitz's expressionistic realism and sympathy for the hardships endured by the poor stimulated the creativity of many Chinese woodcut artists.

After 1949, under the Communist government, Li Hua devoted himself to printmaking in a socialist realist style and held several important posts, including vice president of the Central Academy of Fine Arts and vice chair of the Chinese Printmakers' Association. He taught printmaking at the Central Academy, where he is remembered for the rigor of his pedagogy, until shortly before his death in 1994.

SEE ALSO *Lu Xun; New Print Movement; Woodblock Printing (xylography).*

BIBLIOGRAPHY

Andrews, Julia F., and Kuiyi Shen, eds. *A Century in Crisis: Modernity and Tradition in the Art of Twentieth-Century China.* New York: Guggenheim Museum, 1998.

Danzker, Jo-Anne Birnie, Ken Lum, and Zheng Shengtian, eds. *Shanghai Modern, 1919–1945.* Ostfildern-Ruit, Germany: Hatje Cantz, 2004.

Sun, Shirley. *Modern Chinese Woodcuts.* San Francisco: Chinese Culture Foundation, 1979.

Mayumi Kamata

LI KERAN

1907–1989

The artist Li Keran, whose innovative work exemplifies a modernizer's mission to reform Chinese landscape painting, may be viewed as the most representative painter of the mainstream of Chinese art in the twentieth century. Li began to learn painting from Qian Songling (Shizhi, 1854–1927), a local painter in his hometown of Xuzhou, Jiangsu Province, and was taught by imitating paintings in the tradition of the Four Wangs, four landscape painters named Wang of the early Qing dynasty (1644–1912). In 1923 Li enrolled in the art education department of the private Shanghai Art Academy (Shanghai meishu zhuanke xuexuai), where he heard lectures by Kang Youwei (1858–1927) on three occasions and was exposed to both post-impressionist oil painting and ink painting of the epigraphic school. In 1929 he entered the recently founded West Lake National Art Academy (*Xihu guoli yishuyuan*) in Hangzhou, which was directed by the French-trained modernist Lin Fengmian (1900–1991). There he studied oil painting under the French professor André Claudot in an environment sympathetic to modernist schools of painting, ranging from impressionism and postimpressionism to cubism and German expressionism. In 1931 he joined a short-lived modernist painting society called the Eighteen Society, which brought him into contact with left-wing cultural circles. He exhibited a modernist oil landscape in the 1937 National Art Exhibition in Nanjing. Through the 1940s Li focused on painting oil portraits and landscapes in the impressionist style. He subsequently taught in Xuzhou for a number of years.

After the outbreak of the Anti-Japanese War (1937–1945), Li created woodblock prints and other images to assist the war effort. From 1938 to 1943 he worked under the scholar and government official Guo Moruo (1892–1978) in a propaganda section of the government. He moved inland first to Wuhan with the retreating government and eventually settled in Sichuan, where he began teaching at the reconstituted National Art Academy in Chongqing in 1943. Around 1942 he began painting intensively in ink. After the war, in 1946, Xu Beihong (1895–1953) invited Li to join the faculty of the Beiping National Art College (Beiping Guoli yishu zhuanke xuexiao). This move to the north gave him the opportunity to study ink painting with the venerable masters Qi Baishi (1863–1957) and Huang Binhong (1865–1955), which gave him the technical foundations for his later work.

Li Keran was the master in his generation of Chinese landscape painters at depicting effects of light, the inspiration for which, he claimed, was the seventeenth-century Dutch painter Rembrandt. Li promoted the practice of painting or sketching from nature on-site (*duijing xiesheng*), a practice that accorded with party-mandated arts policies of the 1950s, 1960s, and 1970s, but which in his own case produced remarkably vivid new ways of seeing and interpreting the landscape. Some good examples may be found among the landscapes of the last decade of his life, such as *Yellow Mountain in Mist and Cloud* (1982).

Li Keran was a rare artist in his embrace of both tradition and the modern, one who perhaps could have arisen only in his particular generation. Even as he accepted the influence of 1930s modernism and took part in the activities of left-wing art movements, he also studied intensively the techniques of traditional painting. Li was not only the successor of the leading reformists, such as Xu Beihong and Lin Fengmian but his creative accomplishments also matched those of prominent traditionalists, such as his mentors Qi Baishi and Huang Binhong. *Scratching the Back* (1947) is a work that shows Li's indebtedness to Qi. In a general sense, Li Keran, being a painter dedicated to reform, drew on Kang Youwei's notion of "synthesizing the Chinese and the Western" (*ronghe zhongxi*). Moreover, it was Kang who advised the use of the study of ancient inscriptions (*beixue*) in calligraphy and the use of realism in painting. In assimilating Chinese and Western painting style, Li Keran may be seen as retaining the spirit of traditional painting, and some part of its stylistic essence, while imbuing it with a modern sensibility.

The two main aspects that dominate Li's writings about art are the importance of the study of nature (*ziran*) and the study of tradition (*chuantong*). Li believed that artists should reexamine China's ancient heritage so as to increase their creativity and innovation. Li was also the first landscape artist to develop a new form of Chinese painting known as the epigraphic school of art, which incorporated the study of ancient inscriptions found on monuments or other relics. The flower painters Qi Baishi, Zhao Zhiqian (1829–1884), and Wu Changshi (1844–1927), with their powerful compositions based on both strong brushwork and artful contrasts between figure and ground, had earlier emerged as its representatives. Emulating the brush skill of Wu Changshi, Li creates a new monumental landscape style executed with strong contrasts of black ink, pale wash, and white paper. This heavy black ink, so effectively controlled, enables the artist to create majestic scenery with a feeling of great solidity. The blend of Eastern and Western art in his training, combined with a powerfully disciplined creative spirit, yielded a distinctive style that earned him renown as a Chinese landscape painting revolutionary. He was a leading figure in both major streams of twentieth-century Chinese art, traditionalism and reform, bringing them together in a unique way in his painting.

SEE ALSO *Calligraphy; Chinese Painting (guohua); Epigraphic School of Art; Guo Moruo; Huang Binhong; Kang Youwei; Lin Fengmian; Probaganda Art; Woodblock Printing (xylography); Wu Changshi (Wu Junqing); Xu Beihong.*

BIBLIOGRAPHY

PRIMARY WORKS

Li Keran hua yu [The quotations on paintings from Li Keran]. Shanghai: Shanghai Renmin Chubanshe, 1997.

Li Keran shu hua ji [Collected calligraphic works and paintings by Li Keran]. Taipei: National Museum of History, 1994.

Li Keran shu hua quanji [Album of Li Keran's calligraphy and paintings]. Tianjin: Tianjin Renmin Meishu Chubanshe, 1991.

SECONDARY WORKS

Wan, Qingli. *Li Keran pingzhuan* [The biography and criticism of Li Keran]. Taipei: Xiongshi Tushu Chubanshe, 1995.

Lin Su-hsing

LI RUI

1917–

Li Rui is one of the most outspoken liberals among leading Chinese Communist Party (CCP) intellectuals. His authority derives not only from his party position but also from his service as Mao Zedong's secretary in the 1950s.

Having lost his father, who was a congressman in Republican China, at five years old, Li Rui was raised in Changsha, Hunan, by his widowed mother until he went to Wuhan University to study engineering. Being one of the student leaders of the December Ninth movement that broke out in 1935 in Wuhan, he joined the Communist Party in 1937 at age twenty. After co-founding the newspaper *Qingqidui* (Light Cavalry), which satirized the dark side of Yan'an such as its hierarchy, he was put in jail from 1943 to 1944 in the rectification campaign. He had been falsely charged with being a secret agent from the Nationalist Party. His experience in prison propelled him to combat the ultra-leftism of the times.

In early 1958, Li Rui was invited to become Mao Zedong's secretary after he successfully persuaded Mao to postpone initiating the Three Gorges Project. Shortly thereafter, he was appointed vice minister of Water Conservancy and Electric Power. Before the Lushan Conference (1959), Li Rui petitioned Mao three times to reduce the quota for certain important industrial products, such as steel and iron, to solve problems in manufacturing. Although he was assigned to draft the minutes for the Lushan meetings, he was indicted as one of Peng Dehuai's cohorts and was branded an anti-party element and sent to a farm in Heilongjiang for reeducation through labor in 1960. After two years of labor, Li Rui worked at the Mozitan hydropower station in Anhui for several years.

From 1967 to 1975, Li Rui was incarcerated in Qincheng Prison, located in the suburb of Beijing, because he informed a special investigation team of his skepticism of the loyalty to the party of Chen Boda, then-head of the Central Cultural Revolution Group. In the wake of Deng Xiaoping's rehabilitation in 1975, Li Rui was released along with other party cadres. Nevertheless, he did not return to office until four years later when "Two Whatevers" was discredited.

Li Rui worked as vice minister of the power industry from 1979 to 1982 and the Organization Department of the CCP Central Committee from 1982 to 1984. In response to Deng Xiaoping's policy of rejuvenation of cadres, he resigned from his post as a member of the CCP Twelfth Central Committee in September 1984. Since then he has been active in advocating the eradication of the ultra-leftism of late Maoism by writing for the public and petitioning Jiang Zemin and Hu Jintao. Before the convening of the Sixteenth CCP National Congress in 2002, Li Rui openly appealed to the party to launch reforms of the political system. He called for the election of the general secretary and Politburo

Standing Committee members because, in his belief, democracy should begin with the CCP Central Committee. He also suggested drawing up laws to restrain CCP operation within the Constitution. In addition, he wrote numerous articles criticizing the personality cult of Mao Zedong.

SEE ALSO *Communist Party; Mao Zedong; Zhao Ziyang.*

BIBLIOGRAPHY

Li Pu and Ding Dong, eds. *Dazai! Li Rui* [Great! Li Rui]. 2nd ed. Hong Kong: Times International, 2005.

Li Rui. *Zhiyan: Li Rui liushinian de youyusi* [Opening out: Li Rui's suffering and pondering in sixty years]. Ed. Xue Xiaoyuan. Beijing: Jinri Zhongguo Chubanshe, 1998.

Li Rui. *Lushan huiyi shilu* [The memoir of the Lushan conference]. 3rd ed. Zhengzhou, PRC: Henan Chubanshe, 1998.

Shi Xiaoling

LI XIANGLAN

1920–

Renowned singer and film actress in occupied China during the 1930s and 1940s, Li Xianglan was the Chinese persona of Yamaguchi Yoshiko, whose identity was the subject of speculation during and after the Anti-Japanese War (1937–1945). Born to Japanese parents in Fushun, Manchuria, Yamaguchi learned Chinese from her father, an employee of the South Manchurian Railway Company who was fluent in Mandarin. His Chinese associates coined the names Li Xianglan and Pan Shuhua for the young Yoshiko. As a child, she took voice lessons from an Italian soprano, and in 1934 she was recruited by the Manchukuo radio station Hōten Kōha Dendai (Fengtian Broadcasting Station) to sing Chinese folk songs using her Chinese name Li Xianglan. She was sent to school in Beiping (later renamed Beijing), living with a Chinese family there and fully adopting a Chinese public persona. At eighteen she entered the Japanese-controlled Manshū Eiga Kyōkai (Manchurian Film Studios), starring in *Shina no yoru* (*Zhina zhi ye* [China night], 1940), *Soshū no yoru* (*Suzhou zhi ye* [Suzhou night], 1941), and other propaganda films touting Japanese-Manchurian friendship. Billed as Li Xianglan (Ri Kōran) and playing Chinese female lead roles, the actress was generally viewed as Chinese by audiences in Japan, China, and Southeast Asia, though occasional articles identifying her as Yamaguchi Yoshiko and her language skills led some to assume that she was of mixed Chinese and Japanese descent. In 1942 Li Xianglan began making films in Japanese-occupied Shanghai at the wartime studio Zhongguo Lianhe Zhipian Gufen Gongsi (China United Productions). Her first major film for Chinese audiences, *Wanshi liufang* (Eternity, 1942), was a costume drama about the Opium War in which Li sang theme songs such as "Jieyan ge" (The opium-quitting song). She became one of the major songstresses of the popular music scene in 1940s Shanghai, alongside Zhou Xuan and Bai Guang, recording such memorable hits as "Yelaixiang" (Tuberose). Lee Hsiang Lan, as she was also known, continued to perform in China until the end of World War II, when Chinese artists working in occupied zones were condemned as traitors.

The actress asserted her Japanese citizenship and left China in spring 1946. After her exit, the figure of Li Xianglan remained controversial in histories of wartime imperialism, occupation, and collaboration. In postwar Japan she initiated a new career on stage and screen as Yamaguchi Yoshiko, though her former reputation lingered, often shaping the roles she was offered, as in *Shanhai no onna* (A woman of Shanghai, 1952). Billed as Shirley Yamaguchi, she also worked in Hollywood and Broadway productions, including *House of Bamboo* (1955). From 1952 to 1956 Yamaguchi was married to the Japanese-American sculptor Isamu Noguchi. During this period she also made films for Shaw Brothers in Hong Kong. She retired from cinema in 1958 and married Ōtaka Hiroshi in Japan. Shifting into television work during the 1960s, she anchored her own talk show and reported from the warfronts of Vietnam and Palestine.

Ōtaka Yoshiko, as she became known, was elected in 1974 to the upper house of Japan's parliament, serving three terms until 1992 and participating in various international goodwill initiatives, including the Asian Women's Fund and visits to China. In a 1986 memoir detailing her youth and stardom in China, she expressed remorse for misleading Chinese about her true identity. Since then, television serials, films, album reissues, a stage musical, novels, and academic studies in Japanese, Chinese, and English have tracked her ambiguous legacy.

SEE ALSO *Anti-Japanese War, 1937–1945; Film Industry; Zhou Xuan.*

BIBLIOGRAPHY

Fu, Poshek. *Between Shanghai and Hong Kong: The Politics of Chinese Cinemas.* Stanford, CA: Stanford University Press, 2003.

Stephenson, Shelley. "Her Traces Are Found Everywhere": Shanghai, Li Xianglan, and the "Greater East Asia Film Sphere." In *Cinema and Urban Culture in Shanghai, 1922–1943*, ed. Yingjin Zhang, 222–245. Stanford, CA: Stanford University Press, 1999.

Yamaguchi Yoshiko and Fujiwara Sakuya. *Zai Zhongguo de rizi* [My days in China]. Trans. Jin Ruojing. Taibei: Linbo Chubanshe, 1989. A translation of *Ri Kōran: Watakushi no hansei* [Li Xianglan: Reflections on myself], 1987.

Kristine M. Harris

LIANG QICHAO
1873–1929

Together with Kang Youwei, Liang Qichao is known as a prominent leader in institutional reform in the waning days of the Qing dynasty (1644–1912). Born in 1873 to a humble gentry family in a village in Guangdong Province, Liang Qichao received a classical education, and his prodigious intellectual ability early on earned him the reputation of a child prodigy. Liang met Kang in 1890, and for Liang this meeting proved to be an intellectual awakening. As he later became Kang's student, Liang applied the new knowledge he learned from the latter to their agenda for transforming China. This scholarly association quickly thrust them into the national political spotlight, and they started a campaign to install a constitutional monarchy.

A concerned Confucian scholar, Liang Qichao applied classical and modern learning to the pragmatic management of the government, people, and society. He started his reformist activism with Kang while taking the metropolitan examination in Beijing in 1895. In the spring of that year China's defeat in the war with Japan resulted in a humiliating treaty, the Treaty of Shimonoseki. Kang and Liang roused the patriotic fervor of the 1,300 examination candidates to protest this unequal treaty signed by the Qing government with Japan and to petition the imperial court to begin institutional reform. While continuing to petition the Qing emperor and lobby court officials, Kang and Liang also organized study societies and published newspapers to communicate their reform agendas. The first organization of this budding movement was the Self-Strengthening Study Society (Qiang Xuehui), and its newspaper *Zhongwai gongbao* (Chinese and foreign news), with news and reviews of current affairs written by Liang himself, became popular among educated elites and officials in Beijing.

Liang and Kang succeeded in getting a hearing from the Guangxu emperor. Under the emperor's sponsorship they began a series of economic, political, and administrative reforms lasting 103 days from June to September 1898, known as the Hundred Days' Reform (Wuxu Bianfa). The reform focused on modernization, industrialization, political and institutional restructuring, and saving China from foreign threats. But as these reforms threatened the vested interests of the imperial house and court officials, the reformers and conservatives came into clash. The conservatives struck back with military force and destroyed the reformer group, and its members fled into exile in Japan.

POLITICAL THEORY

Removed from the political center and with much time for reflection during his exile in Japan from 1898 to 1901, Liang worked out a sophisticated political theory to guide action and articulated his nationalist ideas in the two well-known newspapers: *Qingyi bao* (Public opinion) and *Xinmin congbao* (New people's miscellany).

In the traditional view of the universal empire governing all under heaven (*tianxia*), China was the center of the world community with all people coexisting as a family. Liang departed from this Sinocentric world order toward the notion of modern nation-state. In his view, the Chinese nation-state would be a natural outgrowth of the renewed strength of its people. Traditionally, the monarch's rule received legitimacy through his care for the people. Liang, however, advocated the modern conception of government by the people. This new concept involves popular participation.

Liang developed a theory of the people as new citizens of the Chinese nation-state. Political reform was to transform individual Chinese into the Chinese people, forming a new citizenry. Citizens were to shed their narrow-minded loyalty to kin, family, and small communities and to cultivate public-mindedness and collective virtues. Public virtue cemented loosely connected individuals into a strong, cohesive group. The notion of public spirit also entails popular sovereignty—the people's power of self-rule and their consent as sanction for public authority. Modern citizens are to fulfill their public obligations to the government but also possess the right to criticize and reform the government. Traditionally, Chinese people were content with their inherited ways of life and valued harmony, moderation, and meekness. To Liang, this moral weakness was unfitting for a new nation confronted with a world of nation-states locked in a life-and-death struggle for survival. The new citizen was to cultivate a dynamic, adventurous, and competitive spirit. With public virtue and strong bonding, the Chinese nation would be able to compete with rival nation-states in the international arena. Only with a public-minded citizenry could China build a strong nation-state.

THEORY OF HISTORY

As part and parcel of his emphasis on struggle and competitiveness, Liang Qichao called for a new way of thinking and writing about history. He viewed the movement of history as a Darwinian struggle of the fittest. Liang pioneered the modern method of writing history and started a revolution in historiography. In a number of writings on history, the most important being *Zhongguo lishi yanjiu fa* (Methods for the study of Chinese history), he examined patterns of historiography through the ages. Traditional histories addressed only the rise and fall of dynastic houses, the loyalty of subjects, and the dramatization of exemplary figures. Missing was a notion of historical movement driven by people and social forces. The mission of modern history, in contrast, is to educate people into mature modern citizens and to bind them across ethnicity, occupations, and geography into a community. Traditional historiography blended classics, moral teaching, and historical events into one, and the narratives failed to suggest underlying reasons for historical movement. A succession of dynasties and rulers, for example, does not allude to any structure or logic. The movement of modern history, however, is a process motivated and driven by a people aspiring to be a nation. Modern history is about a people's identity, and it unfolds their destiny in time. It is not the record of private noblemen or individuals. Rather than serving as a forum for private individuals to air their opinions and preferences, modern history should provide a total picture of societal and national scope. History's public-minded perspective also entails the principle of objectivity. To be objective, historians should not hide the weaknesses and drawbacks of the people and whitewash their dark historical events. The good historian must promote the self-consciousness of the citizenry by narrating their past.

THEORY OF FICTION

As a reformer, Liang wrote on topics ranging from history and politics to anthropology, economics, and social theory. Yet Liang was also one of the most eloquent theorists of Chinese literature in modern China. He was something of a novelist himself and wrote fragments of fiction and drama propounding his ideas of nationalism and the new citizenry. His theory of literature flowed from his political and moral conceptions of the nation-state and the moral qualities desired in the citizenry.

Of his numerous writings on literature, the most famous is "Lun xiaoshuo yu qunzhi zhi guanxi" (On the relation between fiction and governance of the people). According to Liang, traditional fiction seductively sank readers into unhealthy frames of mind and morality. Under the influence of old fiction, the reading population inherited and engaged in corrupt morality, superstitions, parochialism, excessive sentimentality, and intrigues. These remnants of corrupt culture stood in the way of the people's moral improvement and were a source of ruin for China as a nation. On account of its power to improve or corrupt the moral profile of a people, public-minded authors and nationalist writers should take control of the power of fiction, Liang held. This is like taking control of nation-state sovereignty. The power of the nation comes from the power of a morally rejuvenated people.

Liang viewed fiction as a powerful medium for renovating the moral quality of the people by making aesthetic and emotional appeals to readers. Renewing the morality, religion, and politics of a nation hinges on a renewal of fiction. Average readers turn away from the dry teachings of classics written in inaccessible language. Yet fiction is effective in edifying the people's hearts and minds. Fictional works offer aesthetic pleasures and provoke emotional responses. Fiction also provokes the imagination, transporting readers to a more colorful, broader realm beyond their mundane day-to-day living. Realistic works tap into the reader's intimate unexpressed impressions and observations about the world. When drawn into the writer's finely depicted realistic world, readers experience a feeling of epiphany and resonance.

For Liang, fiction has four aesthetic components producing four effects. Fiction envelops the reader in the sensory ambience of a fictional world and makes the reader a part of it. Then it immerses the reader, so that fictional material seeps into the reader's mind, producing intoxication. Fiction works also provide shocks that send the reader along an emotional roller-coaster ride of exultant joy, deep sorrow, and sudden enlightenment. Finally, fiction lifts readers from the immersion and elevates them to a higher level of moral understanding. As part of the cultural approach to political and social problems, Liang's theory of fiction accounts in aesthetic terms for the emergence of a new people through moral, aesthetic education provided by fiction.

As activist, philosopher of history, and advocate of national literature, Liang Qichao is a major figure in the first political-reform movement in modern China. The debacle of the reform forced him to study and think deeply about political and cultural notions, both from Western and Chinese traditions, for the emergence of the new Chinese nation. Combining political activism with a theoretical, cultural and aesthetic reformist agenda, Liang was the modern avatar of the traditional scholar-official in the guise of the public intellectual. Sensitive to the intractable political reality of his times and hopeful for an alternative future, Liang was at once a realistic and utopian thinker—a trait marking the best tradition of the public intellectual in modern China.

SEE ALSO *Constitutionalism; Gong Zizhen; Hundred Days' Reform; Journalism; Kang Youwei.*

BIBLIOGRAPHY

Chang, Hao. *Liang Ch'i-ch'ao and Intellectual Transition in China, 1890–1907.* Cambridge, MA: Harvard University Press, 1971.

Huang, Philip C. *Liang Ch'i-ch'ao and Modern Chinese Liberalism.* Seattle: University of Washington Press, 1972.

Levenson, Joseph R. *Liang Ch'i-ch'ao and the Mind of Modern China.* Cambridge, MA: Harvard University Press, 1953.

Liang, Ch'i-ch'ao. *History of Chinese Political Thought during the Early Tsin* [*Qin*] *Period.* Trans. L. T. Chen. London: Kegan Paul, Trench, Trubner and Co., 1930.

Liang, Ch'i-ch'ao. *Intellectual Trends in the Ch'ing Period.* Trans. Immanuel C. Y. Hsü. Cambridge, MA: Harvard University Press, 1959.

Tang, Xiaobing. *Global Space and the Nationalistic Discourse of Modernity.* Stanford, CA: Stanford University Press, 1996.

Ban Wang

LIANG SICHENG
1901–1972

A pioneering scholar of Chinese architectural history, tireless defender of old Beijing, and influential founder of modern architectural education, Liang Sicheng looms large in twentieth-century Chinese architecture and urban planning. Paradoxically, he is remembered today as much for his bitter failure to save China's ancient capital from a government bent on remaking the city into a socialist industrial powerhouse filled with smokestacks as for his towering personal achievements.

Liang Sicheng, the eldest son of the late Qing scholar Liang Qichao, was born in Tokyo in 1901. Liang and his fiancée Lin Huiyin attended the School of Architecture at the University of Pennsylvania from 1924 to 1927. He was to regret occasionally that by studying in the United States, he had missed out on the modernist experiments then raging in Europe. He deeply appreciated, however, the solid training that he received at the University of Pennsylvania. The emphasis on rendering and the studies in period architecture proved invaluable to him as an architectural historian. Indeed, it was at the University of Pennsylvania that Liang discovered his interest in architectural history. Liang received his Bachelor of Architecture degree in February 1927 and his Master of Architecture degree in June of the same year.

While Liang was still on his homeward journey, his father secured him a teaching position at National Northeastern University (Guoli Dongbei Daxue) in Liaoning Province. Liang and his wife promptly founded and staffed the Department of Architecture, one of the nation's first and most influential. In addition to teaching, Liang formed a practice together with his colleagues. Within a short time the firm planned the campuses of two institutions of higher learning, Jilin University and a branch of Jiaotong University in Jinzhou, both in Manchuria, and designed teaching facilities and dormitories for the universities. In Manchuria, Liang began to apply and adapt the techniques that he had learned at the University of Pennsylvania to study and measure Qing-dynasty monuments in the region. Perhaps foreshadowing his later difficulties in preservation, his efforts to save historic monuments proved unsuccessful. Despite his pleas, the mayor of Mukden (present-day Shenyang) demolished the city's drum and bell towers.

The increasing Japanese military threat and Lin's failing health forced the couple to return to Beijing at the end of the 1930–1931 academic year. Putting aside his flourishing career as an architect and educator, Liang embarked on the next and arguably most influential phase of his professional life, his work as a historian of classical Chinese architecture.

Liang joined the little-known Society for Research in Chinese Architecture (Zhongguo Yingzao Xueshe), ensconced inside the Forbidden City. It was under the auspices of this organization that Liang and his colleagues made some of the most significant finds in Chinese architectural history. Liang combined modern empirical techniques with the traditional Chinese textual approach. He sought to date extant monuments as accurately as possible so that he could trace stylistic changes over time, a prerequisite for writing a coherent history of Chinese architecture.

Liang's first major discovery was the Liao-dynasty Buddhist temple Dulesi (built in 987) near Tianjin. The significance of Dulesi lies in the proximity of its construction to the date of the Song construction manual *Yingzao fashi* (Building standards), written in 1100. The temple thus corroborates some passages of that text. Other important buildings that Liang studied on site included the Song-dynasty temple Longxingsi (built in 1030), outside Shijiazhuang in Hebei Province. Yet Liang's most significant find was Foguangsi (built in 857), a Tang dynasty temple on Mount Wutai. It was the oldest wooden structure that Liang's team discovered. The ensemble of original Tang statues of the Buddha and attendant Bodhisattvas and the Tang mural segments make the building a rare exemplar of Tang art and architecture. The outbreak of the Second Sino-Japanese War (1937–1945) forced the society to retreat to the interior. Under extremely difficult wartime conditions Liang completed his *Zhongguo jianzhu shi* (A history of Chinese architecture) and *A Pictorial History of Chinese Architecture*, which he wrote in English.

Liang's profile was highest after the founding of the People's Republic of China in 1949. He and his wife were deeply involved in some of the most iconic designs for the new regime, including the new national flag, the national seal, and the Monument to the People's Heroes in Tiananmen Square. The Communist Party routinely sought Liang's advice on planning and preservation. Yet just as often, his opinion was ignored or criticized.

In 1950, together with the British-trained planner Chen Zhanxiang (1916–2001), Liang drafted a proposal to construct a new administration quarters outside Beijing's old city to accommodate the new bureaucracy, arguing that building a new city would also help keep the character of the ancient capital intact. Their plan, however, was out of step with the recommendations of Soviet advisers and the wishes of Chairman Mao. Liang's beloved old Beijing was irretrievably lost. Liang died in 1972, leaving behind a poignant legacy.

SEE ALSO *Architecture, History of; Imperial Palaces; Lin Huiyin; Xu Zhimo.*

BIBLIOGRAPHY

Fairbank, Wilma. *Liang and Lin: Partners in Exploring China's Architectural Past.* Philadelphia: University of Pennsylvania Press, 1994.

Liang Sicheng. *Zhongguo jianzhu shi* [History of Chinese architecture]. Beijing: Gaodeng Jiaoyubu Jiaocai Bianshenchu, 1954.

Liang Ssu-ch'eng. *A Pictorial History of Chinese Architecture.* Cambridge, MA: MIT Press, 1984.

Lin Zhu. *Dajiang de kunhuo* [Quandaries of a master]. Beijing: Zuojia Chubanshe, 1991.

Wang Jun. *Cheng ji* [Record of a city]. Beijing: Sanlian, 2003.

Yaohua Shi

LIAONING

Liaoning Province is located in the southern part of the northeast region of the People's Republic of China (PRC). It borders Jilin Province in the north and northeast, North Korea in the southeast, Inner Mongolia in the northwest, Hebei Province in the west, and the Bohai Sea and Yellow Sea in the south. Its southeastern part, the Liaodong Peninsula, overlooks Shandong Peninsula.

When the PRC was founded in October 1949 there were two provinces (Liaodong and Liaoxi) and five centrally administered municipalities (Shenyang [Mukden], Lüda, Anshan, Fushun, and Benxi). In August 1954 the two provinces were merged into Liaoning Province, with Shenyang as its capital. Liaoning covers an area of about 92,000 square miles (147,500 square kilometers), 1.5 percent of the total territory of China. Its population in 2006 was 42.71 million, making it the fourteenth-largest province in China in terms of population.

LIAONING

Capital city: Shenyang

Largest cities (population): Shenyang (7,040,000 [2006]), Dalian (5,720,000 [2006]), Anshan

Area: 145,500 sq. km. (56,950 sq. mi.)

Population: 42,710,000 (2006)

Demographics: Han, 84%; Manchu, 12.6%; Mongol, 1.6%; Hui, 0.6%; Korean, 0.57%; Xibe, 0.3%

GDP: CNY 925.1 billion

Famous sites: Mukden Palace, Wunu Mountain City, Anshan Jade Buddha, Bijia Mountain

HEAVY INDUSTRY

Liaoning initially was developed as a stronghold of heavy industry in China. During the First Five-Year Plan (1953–1957) Liaoning received 24 of 156 key projects in China. Liaoning's investment in all industries during the period 1953 to 1957 amounted to 4,640 million yuan, 18.5 percent of the national total; its investment in heavy industries was 4,360 million yuan, 20.5 percent of the national total investment in heavy industries. One of the 24 projects in the province, for instance, was Fuxin coal mine. Covering an area of more than 1,250 square miles (2,000 square kilometers), the coal mine was one of the four major producers of coal in the country in the 1950s. As a result, Liaoning became the most important region of heavy industry in China. Its gross regional product (GRP) was the highest in China in the late 1950s and the second highest in most years of the 1960s and the 1970s. In 1968, when the Liaoning Provincial Revolutionary Committee was formed under the leadership of Chen Xilian (1915–1999) and Mao Zedong's nephew, Mao Yuanxin (b. 1941), the province's GRP dipped to fourth in China. In 1983, however, Liaoning was again first in China in a number of industrial indicators. Its industrial enterprises had the largest fixed capital in the country, worth 53.1 billion yuan; its heavy industrial output was the highest; its railway passenger and cargo transportation was second to none; and it was first in production of steel, iron, electricity, cement, machine tools, paper, and washing machines.

THE RUST BELT

Coming into the 1990s, however, Liaoning faced economic crisis. Factories were closing down, workers were being laid off, and economic growth lagged behind other provinces. The number of industrial enterprises reached a peak of 33,703 in 1996, then declined to 31,893 in 1997 and 23,509 in 1998, the lowest level since 1986. Among those industries, the number of state-owned enterprises dropped from 5,379 in 1996 to only 2,835 in 1998, the lowest level since 1975. Industrial workers in Liaoning also declined from 8,274,000 in 1993 to 6,847,000 in 1998. Between 1994 and 1998, at least 1.4 million workers were laid off. The stronghold of heavy industry became the nation's rust belt. Paradoxically, few people in Liaoning emigrated in the late 1990s. Between 1995 and 2000, 800,000 immigrated to Liaoning and only half that number emigrated, producing a net gain of 400,000 people (Yan 2007, p. 72). The number of workers sent abroad was not large at first, but their numbers accelerated in the 1990s and 2000s. In 1991 Liaoning sent 8,232 workers abroad (*Liaoning Yearbook [1992]*, p. 210). The number increased almost fivefold in nine years, to 38,800 in 2000 (*Liaoning Yearbook [2001]*, p. 122). In 2006 the number of emigrants from Liaoning reached 76,490 (*Liaoning Yearbook [2007]*, p. 354). The main destinations are Japan, Russia, and South Korea (*Liaoning Yearbook [2007]*, p. 162). The workers sent abroad were organized by companies that had signed labor

contract agreements with foreign clients. In 2006, nine companies, including, for example, China Dalian International Cooperation (Group) Holdings, each sent more than 1,000 workers (*Liaoning Yearbook [2007]*, p. 162).

SHENYANG'S CORRUPTION CASE

Along with the economic decline, Liaoning was also hit by a corruption scandal in its capital, Shenyang. Mayor Mu Suixin and Vice Mayor Ma Xiangdong were discovered to have been involved in bribery and embezzlement. In October 2001 Mu was sentenced to death with two-year reprieve for taking bribes worth 6.6 million yuan, and Ma was sentenced to death for taking bribes totaling more than 3.4 million yuan. Ten other officials also were implicated, including a former president and two vice presidents of Shenyang intermediate court, a former president of Shenyang People's Procuratorate, and two former deputy secretaries-general of the Shenyang municipal government.

TRAINING GROUND FOR NATIONAL LEADERS

On the bright side, Liaoning has also served as a training ground for national leaders in the era of reforms. Li Changchun (b. 1944), a standing member of the Sixteenth and Seventeenth Politburos, was governor of Liaoning from April 1986 to June 1990; at forty-two, he was the youngest governor in China in 1986. He introduced the first bankruptcy law in China while he was party secretary of Shenyang and promoted enterprise reforms while he was governor of Liaoning. After having served in Liaoning, Henan, and Guangdong, he was promoted to Beijing in 2002. Bo Xilai (b. 1949), the son of Bo Yibo (a veteran revolutionary) and currently party secretary of Chongqing and a member of the Seventeenth Politburo, served as governor of Liaoning from January 2001 to February 2004, after his long tenure as mayor of Dalian. He opened Liaoning further for investment from other provinces as well as from abroad. He was transferred to Beijing in February 2004 as minister of commerce and was promoted to the Politburo in October 2007. Li Keqiang (b. 1955), executive vice premier and a standing member of the Seventeenth Politburo, had a stint as party secretary of Liaoning as well. He served in that capacity from December 2004 to October 2007, when he moved to Beijing as a rising political star. One of his legacies in Liaoning is the relocation of 1.2 million households from squatter settlements to new houses.

SEE ALSO *Manchuria; Shenyang.*

BIBLIOGRAPHY

Bo, Zhiyue. *Chinese Provincial Leaders: Economic Performance and Political Mobility Since 1949*. Armonk, NY: Sharpe, 2002.

Bo, Zhiyue. *China's Elite Politics: Political Transition and Power Balancing*. Singapore: World Scientific, 2007.

Finkelstein, David M., and Maryanne Kivelehan, eds. *China's Leadership in the Twenty-first Century: The Rise of the Fourth Generation*. Armonk, NY: Sharpe, 2003.

Liaoning Yearbook (1992). Beijing: China Statistics Press, 1992.

Liaoning Yearbook (2001). Beijing: China Statistics Press, 2001.

Liaoning Yearbook (2007). Beijing: China Statistics Press, 2007.

Yan Shanping. Zhongguo shengji renkou liudong de jizhiyanjiu [Inter-provincial migration and its determinants in the 1990s China]. *Chinese Journal of Population Science* 1 (2007): 71–96.

Schueller, Margot. Liaoning: Struggling with the Burdens of the Past. In *China's Provinces in Reform: Class, Community, and Political Culture*, ed. David S. G. Goodman, 93–121. London and New York: Routledge, 1997.

Zhiyue Bo

LIBERALISM

Chinese liberalism had its roots in translations from the West made at the end of the Qing dynasty (1644–1912). It found adherents during the Republican period (1912–1949) and was a significant element in Chinese thought and politics at that time, but was easily stifled by political circumstances.

INTRODUCTION THROUGH TRANSLATION

Liberal values and institutions had to be imported, through translation, from the West. Thanks to translators and writers such as Yan Fu (1853–1921) and Liang Qichao (1873–1929), liberalism became a popular creed in the Chinese intellectual and political world from the 1890s to the 1910s.

Yan Fu's translations introduced nineteenth-century Anglo-Saxon liberalism to those who would become New Culture liberals in the May Fourth period (after 1919). Yan Fu believed, however, that the individualism associated with liberalism was a means to attain wealth and power for the state, not the individual. In an age of Western and Japanese imperialism, Yan maintained the illiberal position that the freedom of the nation-state was more important than individual liberty.

The constitutional reformer Liang Qichao was strongly influenced by eighteenth- and nineteenth-century British liberal thinkers. The basis of his liberalism was the politically conscious and active "new citizen." Liang had to create a new vocabulary for liberalism, such as "ziyou" for "liberty." Influenced by Social Darwinism, he argued that individual freedom was to be valued because it strengthened the state. His writings before 1898 contained no mention of inalienable rights or of inviolable property rights.

NEW CULTURE LIBERALS

During the May Fourth intellectual movement, liberalism became popular in intellectual circles. Mao Zedong, the future Communist leader, admitted that during his early years he was passionate about "old-fashioned liberalism" (Chow 1960, p. 75). Liberalism's faith in the creative potential of individuals and its optimism about the future seized many intellectuals' minds. Although a few years before there had been no such Chinese term, now *liberalism* became a catchword among intellectuals (Chow 1960, p. 295). The New Culture Movement frequently issued liberal manifestos calling for the emancipation of the individual. Many Chinese intellectuals still argued, however, that liberating individuals was for national salvation, as well as the sake of the individual.

Hu Shi (1891–1962), undoubtedly the preeminent liberal of his time, vigorously stood for individual rights. At the same time, his thinking contained an element of "potentially antidemocratic elitism" (Grieder 1970, p. 196). Moreover, his appeal for unanimity of purpose revealed an illiberal bias, for liberal politics are characterized by a clash of vested interests. Many Chinese believed that because of its emphasis on the individual rather than the group, liberalism was a creed of divisiveness and selfishness, and clashed with the Confucian tradition of social harmony.

During the New Culture period (1917–1923), there were also many other liberals, such as Cai Yuanpei (1868–1940), Luo Longji (1896–1965), and Liang Shiqiu (1902–1987). Liberals were active in intellectual and professional circles and, with some exceptions, eschewed party politics. Despite the defense of liberalism by some of the liveliest minds of the May Fourth period, the noted liberal and educator Jiang Menglin (1886–1964) declared in 1924 that the liberalism that stood for the primacy of the individual was a failure.

LIBERALS AND THE GUOMINDANG AND CHINESE COMMUNISTS

Liberals of the illiberal 1920s and 1930s were united by their belief in reason, their support of a gradual and peaceful approach to China's problems, their desire to protect civil liberties, and their support for constitutional government. During the Republican era they had outlets for their ideas in independent newspapers and small liberal journals, but it was very difficult to be a liberal oppositionist. Moreover, because of the Japanese threat to national survival and the need for a strong state, many liberals became less critical of the Guomindang (Nationalist Party). It was telling that after 1933 the New Culture liberal Ding Wenjiang (1887–1936) advocated an enlightened dictatorship for China. Nor was he the only liberal who held such views.

Chiang Kai-shek (Jiang Jieshi), the Guomindang, and its Blue Shirts opposed liberalism. Chiang accused liberals of slighting tradition and blindly praising foreign ideas. The Blue Shirts (a clique within the Guomindang) particularly hated liberalism's individualism. The Guomindang expected the individual to sacrifice freedom for the nation. Instead of guaranteeing freedoms, the 1934 draft constitution restricted them. The Communist Party also rejected liberalism and its individualism, believing that the people would rather have good government than freedom.

During World War II, liberalism was kept alive by professors at the National Southwest Associated University in Kunming. Liberals organized the China Democratic League (Zhongguo Minzhu Tongmeng), which was the "closest thing to an organized political movement of Chinese liberalism" (Sheridan 1975, p. 281).

Following the war, there was a reaction against classical liberalism, with its laissez-faire economic policies and unrestricted individualism. The result was a "new liberalism," which included emphasis on economic and social rights. When General George C. Marshall departed China in January 1947, his attempt to forestall civil war through mediation a failure, he, like many Americans, regarded liberals as the potential saviors of China. In the end, though, the chaos and warfare of the late 1940s made liberalism untenable. During the civil war, the Democratic League, the embodiment of liberalism, was crushed between the two warring dictatorships. A large majority of Chinese liberals, influenced by nationalism and the return of a powerful government, supported the Communists after they won the civil war with the Nationalists.

THE FATE OF LIBERALISM

Chinese liberals bravely preached the importance of academic freedom, freedom of thought, the right to dissent, and the need for toleration. Yet Chinese liberalism was fatally flawed from the beginning, for individualism had shallow roots in a society built on the group and family. Moreover, Chinese liberals saw democracy as an attribute of the modern state rather than as an institution designed to protect individual rights.

Thus, there was Chinese liberalism but no liberal society or politics. This failure prevented self-government and parliamentary government, which cannot function in the absence of a liberal setting. "The liberals' faith in reason and legal processes could not resist dictatorship and militarism," wrote one historian. The "liberal alternative was no alternative at all" (Sheridan 1975, pp. 282–283).

The liberal program did not flourish in China, for several reasons. For one, China had a long-standing tradition of autocratic rule (especially one-man rule). For another, social harmony and order were highly valued over individualism. Also, in the twentieth century the military reigned supreme over civil society. Again, China's international situation in an imperialist age required a desperate quest for national salvation (*jiuwang* or *jiuguo*), rather than for personal freedoms, and the search for wealth and power was to save the country. Finally, China lacked a strong middle class. Although social democracy was an important element in Chinese liberal thought, liberals lacked the understanding, sympathy, and support of the Chinese populace. That is not surprising, for liberals, for the most part (except for such efforts as the Ding County experiment), failed to come to grips with the lives of the vast majority of Chinese and offer workable solutions to their problems.

In sum, in the Republican period, liberalism had influence but little power. It lost out largely because China lacked the prerequisites for liberalism. Instead, there was disorder, a populace that lacked understanding of liberal values, an environment in which force ruled over reason, and revolutionary violence everywhere.

SEE ALSO *Hu Shi; Lin Yutang; May Fourth Movement.*

BIBLIOGRAPHY

Chang Hao. *Liang Ch'i-ch'ao and Intellectual Transition in China, 1890–1907.* Cambridge, MA: Harvard University Press, 1971.

Chow Tse-tsung. *The May Fourth Movement: Intellectual Revolution in Modern China.* Cambridge, MA: Harvard University Press, 1960.

Fung, Edmund S. K. (Feng Zhaoji). *In Search of Chinese Democracy: Civil Opposition in Nationalist China, 1929–1949.* Cambridge, U.K.: Cambridge University Press, 2000.

Fung, Edmund S. K. (Feng Zhaoji). State Building, Capitalist Development, and Social Justice: Social Democracy in China's Modern Transformation, 1921–1949. *Modern China* 31, 3 (2005): 318–352.

Grieder, Jerome B. *Hu Shih and the Chinese Renaissance: Liberalism in the Chinese Revolution, 1917–1937.* Cambridge, MA: Harvard University Press, 1970.

Lubot, Eugene. *Liberalism in an Illiberal Age: New Culture Liberals in Republican China, 1919–1937.* Westport, CT: Greenwood Press, 1982.

Sheridan, James E. *China in Disintegration.* New York: Free Press, 1975.

Roger B. Jeans

LIBRARIES, ORIGINS AND EARLY DEVELOPMENT OF

In imperial China, book collecting was a continuous and phenomenal cultural activity following the invention of writing, paper, and printing technologies. Government, private, academy (*shuyuan*), and temple book repositories were the four major types of book repositories. Scholars had varying degrees of access to them: They were intended for preserving rather than using books, and the staff in charge of the collections assumed the role of custodians. International and domestic conflicts contributed to the destruction of traditional book repositories in the moribund Qing dynasty. Educational reform and the abolition of the civil service examination system accelerated their decline, which was further exacerbated by the deteriorating economy. In the later nineteenth and the early twentieth centuries, book repositories were replaced by modern libraries.

Academy book repositories were closely associated with the development of the civil service examinations (*keju*). After the abolition of the examinations in 1905 academies were converted into new style schools and their book collections taken over by those new schools. A number of public libraries also were founded on the old sites of academies or inherited the book collections previously stored there. For example, the Jiangnan Library (the predecessor of the Jiangsu Provincial Library) was founded on the old site of the Xiyin Academy (Xiyin shuyuan) in Jiangsu Province in 1907, before its new building was completed in 1909. The book collections of the Guangya Academy (Guangya shuyuan) went to the Zhongshan Library (Zhongshan tushuguan) in Guangzhou after the People's Republic of China was founded in 1949.

The establishment of modern Chinese libraries was a long and arduous process, lasting from the 1840s to the 1930s. Western learning, educational reform, missionary influence, the foreign threat, and the New Culture movement all contributed to their emergence. Western missionaries and educated Chinese were interested in modern libraries for different reasons. The missionaries founded missionary society and educational institution libraries, regarding them as an effective means of disseminating Western learning and facilitating evangelization. The Jesuit library at Xu Jia Hui in Shanghai, founded in 1847 with a collection of around 200,000 volumes, was an outstanding early example of a missionary library. The Chinese, while influenced by such examples, embraced the idea of modern libraries out of the need to advance modern education to ensure national survival. Yet, a nationwide modern library campaign failed to develop at an early date.

Enthusiasm for modern libraries strengthened in the last decade of the Qing dynasty, when Zhang Zhidong (1837–1909) assumed responsibility for the formulation of a new national education system. Zhang recognized the necessity of libraries in education relatively early, and he worked tirelessly to establish educational institutions and book collections during his lifetime. He searched for a way for China to survive in the modern world by accommodating Western learning while preserving Chinese traditional culture. He is credited with the founding of the Metropolitan Library of Beijing (Jingshi tushuguan)—the predecessor of the National Library of China—a few days before he died in office in September 1909.

A profound transformation of book repositories did not take place until the rise of the New Culture movement in the mid-1910s, which brought with it the New Library movement (1917–1927). The New Culture movement fostered the unprecedented growth of printed materials in the vernacular, challenging the traditional management style of book repositories and making knowledge more accessible to the general public than ever before in Chinese history. New Culture leaders advocated innovative ideas such as mass education, individual freedom, science, democracy, liberty, and equality. In addition, they were keen to reevaluate Chinese cultural traditions critically. Significantly, New Culture advocates such as Hu Shi, Cai Yuanpei (1868–1940), and Lu Xun, were also concerned with modern libraries.

The New Library movement criticized traditional book repositories and popularized the advanced librarianship that originated in the West, especially the United States. The launch and development of the movement owed a debt to missionary influence. Mary Elizabeth Wood (1861–1931), an American librarian, saw a firm link between librarianship and missionary enterprises in China, and she believed that God directed her to assist the Chinese in modernizing their libraries. She inspired Samuel Seng (Shen Zurong, 1883–1977), a poor young Chinese and converted Christian who

Students at the library of Communist North China Union University, April, 1946. *The development of modern libraries began in China during the mid-1800s, with the introduction of Western missionaries looking to expand their influence. Libraries in China prior to this time emphasized preserving material for posterity rather than developing a collection of books for circulation.* GEORGE LACKS/TIME & LIFE PICTURES/GETTY IMAGES

returned from the United States with an M.A. in library science to launch the New Library movement in 1917, aided by the Chinese Young Men's Christian Association (YMCA). Li Dazhao (1888–1927), later a founder of the Chinese Communist Party, was another active participant in the movement; as chief librarian, he transformed Peking University Library into a modern institution. Chinese libraries were modernized with new library technologies such as the open-shelf system, the card catalog, and the Dewey decimal classification. Moreover, they were opened to the public and equipped with different kinds of publications. Hence, the New Library movement completed the transition from book repositories to modern libraries as far as technology and management were concerned. In the Nanjing decade (1927–1937), when education was given an important place in national reconstruction, Chinese libraries were an agent of educational reform and were able to develop more extensively than before.

SEE ALSO *Education; Examination System, 1800–1905; Hu Shi; Lu Xun; May Fourth Movement; Missionaries; Zhang Zhidong.*

BIBLIOGRAPHY

Chen Yaosheng and Li Huizhen. Woguo tushuguan xue jiaoyu de huigu yu zhanwang [The retrospect and prospect of library science education in China]. *Tushuguan jianshe* [Library construction] 6 (2002): 1–4.

Cheng Huanwen. The Impact of American Librarianship on Chinese Librarianship in Modern Times (1840–1919). *Libraries and Culture* 26, 2 (Spring 1991): 372–387.

Ding Zhipin. *Zhongguo jin qishinian jiaoyu jishi* [The chronology of Chinese education over the last seventy years]. Nanjing: Guoli Bianyiguan, 1933.

Hu Sha. Beijing tushuguan de gaige yu zhanwang [Reform and prospect of the Beijing Library]. *Tushuguan xue tongxun* [Bulletin of library science] 4 (1985): 7–14.

Lai Xinxia. *Zhongguo gudai tushu shiyeshi* [History of book collections in ancient China]. Shanghai: Shanghai Renmin Chubanshe, 1990.

Liu Xun and Li Xinle. Zhongguo tushuguan: Jintian he mingtian de wenti [Chinese librarianship: The problems of today and tomorrow]. *Sichuan tushuguan xuebao* [Journal of library science in Sichuan Province] 4 (1985): 1–8.

Tang Jinhong. Tushuguan yuan juese bianqian tantao [Discussions on the changing roles of librarians]. *Tushuguan gongzuo yu yanjiu* [Library work and research] 1 (1994): 31–33.

Xiong Yuezhi. 1842 zhi 1860 nian xixue zai Zhongguo de chuanbo [The dissemination of Western learning in China between 1842 and 1860]. *Zhongguo jindaishi* [History of early modern China] 11 (1994): 16–34.

Zhou Hanguang. *Zhang Zhidong yu guangya shuyuan* [Zhang Zhidong and the Guangya Academy]. Taibei: Zhongguo Wenhua Daxue, 1983.

Jinhong Tang

LIFE CYCLE

This entry contains the following:

BIRTH

Childbirth in China is marked by customs reflecting beliefs about the birth process and celebrating the birth of a new family member. Childbirth usually took place in the father's home and was attended by a traditional midwife or by female relatives, in most regions from the father's side. Traditional midwives had considerable skills and experience but knew nothing of preventing infection. The cord might be cut with an unwashed implement and the umbilicus covered with a dirty cloth or mud. Infant and maternal mortality were high by modern standards. To make matters worse, as childbirth, and birth fluids in particular, were considered polluting, in some rural areas women were not allowed to give birth in the house but had to use outhouses.

After giving birth, the new mother was considered particularly vulnerable. In order to increase the inner yang of her body, and thus to recover quickly from childbirth and protect herself from illness, she needed to recuperate for a month (*zuoyuezi*). A woman who became ill during this month might never properly recover. During her month of recuperation, she rested at home, avoided bathing and washing her hair, and followed a special diet. This diet might include protein foods such as chicken and eggs, which poorer women rarely ate, or congee (rice porridge), perhaps reinforced with Chinese medicine.

The birth of a boy was always greeted with joy. In the case of a first birth, a girl would be welcome as a proof of fertility, and most families would be happy to rear at least one female child. However, no family wanted too many girls, and some might even resort to female infanticide.

The time of the birth was noted in an eight-character form (*bazi*), which could later be used in determining the child's horoscope and arranging marriage. A small celebration was held on the third day after the child's birth, but more important was the first-month birthday (*manyue*), when it was clearer that the child would live. At this stage the baby was ritually cleansed by washing and shaving its head, and the family received presents from both the father's and mother's families. A girl might have no first-month-birthday celebration, or one less elaborate than her brother's.

As early as the 1920s, reformers tried to reduce infant and maternal mortality not only by training modern midwives but, more important, also by giving short courses in hygiene to traditional village midwives. Simple precautions such as scrubbing hands and sterilizing instruments in locally distilled spirits were taught to traditional practitioners on a massive scale after 1949. In the cities, hospital births became the norm by the 1970s. In the countryside, women chose to give birth in a hospital or maternity station wherever there were facilities. Hospital deliveries were not only safer but, as an added bonus, also allowed the home to remain unpolluted. By the beginning of the twenty-first century, over two-thirds of births were taking place in a medical setting. Infant and maternity mortality have fallen dramatically, although rates in rural areas are still over twice as high as rates in cities.

Family-planning policy has affected childbirth in various ways. Couples are encouraged to delay both marriage and the birth of their first child. Most first-time mothers are now in their early twenties rather than their late teens. There are instances of third-trimester abortions where parents attempting to have a baby for which they have no permission are persuaded or coerced to abort. The use of modern scanning technology, combined with the traditional desire for sons, has resulted in the birth of disproportionate numbers of boys.

Studies also show the proportion of cesarean births rising steeply from the 1980s to a level of over one-fifth of all births by 2002. Medical reasons include an increased capacity for medical intervention and an increase in first births as a proportion of all births. Nonmedical factors include the beliefs that cesareans reduce the risks of birth complications, infant handicaps, and stillbirths, and that they help protect the baby's brain. Cesareans also allow parents to select an auspicious date for their baby's birth.

The concepts of *zuoyuezi* and *manyue* survive in Chinese society, though practices may be modernized or updated. Postpartum women expect to rest and eat carefully for a month. Among the bitterest grudges that women may list against their husbands is a failure to facilitate proper observance of a month of recuperation. In both mainland China and Taiwan, it is even possible to recuperate for a month in an institutionalized setting. In Beijing, Shanghai, Hong Kong, and Singapore, shops sell first-month-birthday hampers to present to the parents of one-month-old babies.

SEE ALSO *Family: Infanticide; Sex Ratio; Women, Status of.*

BIBLIOGRAPHY

Ahern, Emily M. The Power and Pollution of Chinese Women. In *Women in Chinese Society*, ed. Margery Wolf and Roxane Witke. Stanford, CA: Stanford University Press, 1975.

Callister, Lynn Clark. Doing the Month: Chinese Postpartum Practices. *American Journal of Maternal Child Nursing* 31, 6 (November/December 2006): 390.

Guo, Sufang, Sabu S. Padmdas, Zhao Fengmin, et al. Delivery Settings and Caesarean Section Rates in China. *Bulletin of the World Health Organization* 85 (2007): 733–821.

Hillier, S. M., and J. A. Jewell. *Health Care and Traditional Medicine in China, 1800–1982*. London: Routledge and Kegan Paul, 1983.

Wolf, Margery. *Women and the Family in Rural Taiwan*. Stanford, CA: Stanford University Press, 1972.

Delia Davin

INFANCY AND CHILDHOOD

In the 1930s China's great essayist and cultural critic Lu Xun (1881–1936) observed that Chinese children too often resembled "marionettes on strings or spiders without webs" (Lu Xun 1980). That is, parents had either controlled their children so tightly that they had little capacity for self-control and independence, or had so pampered them that they willfully trampled on the rights of others like petty tyrants. For Lu Xun, these over- and undersocialized children were human failures in Chinese dress; he wanted a different kind of children who as adults could advance China beyond a discredited tradition (Saari 1990, p. 107).

TRADITIONAL CHILDHOOD

In the late nineteenth century traditionalist neo-Confucians feared that children would not grow up to be moral beings. Not to be moral was not to be human, and *moral* meant acting correctly within the family according to prescribed roles, especially those that governed the relationships between fathers and sons, husbands and wives, and elder brothers and younger brothers. Ideally, this meant interdependence and mutuality, but in practice, obedience, loyalty, and deference were required of subordinate sons, wives, and younger brothers (Saari 1990). It was a strict and authoritarian family culture, especially for the small upper class, and especially within these prescribed relationships; among the peasants and in the less prescribed familial relationships (for example, father-daughter and grandfather-grandson) a looser interaction was often possible (Hsiung 2005).

Overall, the first six years of life were a respite from a harsh regime of learning to be moral (Saari 1990). Infants and toddlers (of both genders) did not yet *dongshi* (understand matters), so they were kept warm and fed and were not strictly disciplined. The slit pants of Chinese toddlers allowed for a leisurely approach to toilet training; similarly, nursing a child could be prolonged for years. Some writers of *jiaxun* (family instructions) had argued for centuries that this early indulgence was a mistake, and that mothers and fathers should intervene forcefully with toddlers to get them on the right moral path. Usually, though, this training did not start until schooling began for the young masters of the upper class, or working in field and home began for peasant boys and girls.

Schooling was meant to instill discipline and purpose, and understood as a serious apprenticeship in becoming a sage or ideal human being (Bai 2005). Elementary education occurred inside homes with private tutors. Pupils proceeded at their own pace, learning to recognize and write Chinese ideographs with ink and brush, and memorizing texts and primers in a classical written language they did not understand. They sat every day for hours on hard wooden benches, without recess or physical outlets. For gifted children this literary regimen was challenging, even fulfilling, but many youngsters struggled to box in their emotions. Eventually, after a few years, the difficult written language was mastered; words and texts could be understood, and competence promised a worthy career as a scholar or official, or at least a respected role as an educated gentleman in the countryside.

This sharp contrast between the two halves of childhood for schoolboys—birth to six, and seven to fourteen—left a lifelong ambivalence about authority. The first half was often remembered nostalgically as a time of warm caring and attentiveness to their needs by adults; the second half was a time of initiation—gently if possible, harshly via corporal punishment if necessary—into the conventional ways of the culture. The conventions of Chinese learning were narrowly moral and bookish, and demanded dependent behaviors and rote learning. In the Chinese life script, willpower was valued as long as it was attached to established values; willfulness, that is, persistence in one's own viewpoint, was dangerous, because it threatened to tear apart the web of relationships upon which the entire society rested.

GROWING UP IN CHINESE GROUPS

Consider the complex relationships within a large gentry family in Old China. Ideally, five generations of family members, along with servants—perhaps 100 or more persons—lived together within a large walled compound. It was a mini-universe. A child had to learn not just names but also what degree of respect and formality was required in each encounter. By the end of childhood a Chinese youngster was an amateur social psychologist, aware of all the nuances of social interaction. Children knew themselves not as individuals first, but as members of a human group within which their life stories and careers were to be played out. Nurturing harmony within the family group, even if it involved playacting and some falsehood, was a supreme virtue (Saari 1982).

This type of gentry family disappeared from history with Communist land reform in the early 1950s, but the emotional sensitivity fostered in the group, and especially the deference to superiors, persisted. The term that defines this fit within the group is *lian* (face). To have face is simply to be a decent human being within the group, but its essential quality is noted more by its loss in gradations of social disapproval (Saari 1982; Saari 1990, pp. 110–114). The anxieties of being "out" or "wrong" or "exposed," and the comforts of being "in" and "right," have no exact counterparts in European cultures. To lose face before others, both living and dead, was so shameful that one wished to disappear, and what small child could bear that prospect? For one's children to be shameless was the worst insult for a parent to bear. These emotions sit deep, grounded as they are in childhood experiences. In the twentieth century, expectations of deference from below and authoritarian leadership from above shadowed new non-kin groupings, whether they were peer groups in modern schools after 1905, political parties with armies in the 1920s, or collectives in the People's Republic of China (e.g., teams, brigades, and communes in the countryside, work units and neighborhoods in the cities). And woe be to those who would shame the big-family nation of China in front of outsiders.

GENDER AND ONE-CHILD FAMILIES

After the terrible convulsions of the decade of the Cultural Revolution (1966–1976), the family reemerged in a central way as refuge and primary identification, albeit as a smaller nuclear or three-generation stem family. But the new cultural phenomenon of one-child families revealed that some older patterns persisted. Introduced in 1979 to 1980 as state policy, limiting each family to just one child was intended to restrict China's burgeoning population growth (Greenhalgh 2008). An unintended consequence was the radical transformation of family dynamics by eliminating future uncles, aunts, and cousins, and concentrating all parental and grandparental energy and resources on a single child. This has led to the emergence of "little empresses" (*xiao gongzhu*) and "little emperors" (*xiao huangdi*), so called because they lord it over others, not just parents and grandparents but also teachers. Some observers welcome the new assertiveness of these children, arguing that in time they will become reform agents within the larger society, transforming interpersonal behavior within families, schools, and marriages in a more egalitarian direction (Ai 2008, pp. 49–51). Others criticize them as spoiled brats who have lost that Chinese feeling for fine-tuning or harmonizing their behavior with others: They are the latest version of Lu Xun's incompetent petty tyrants who have lost their essential humanness in an amoral society of consumerism and competitive individualism.

The odyssey of young girls over the past 200 years into the "little empresses" of today is remarkable. Traditionally, a girl was undervalued within the family, viewed as a "small happiness" as compared to her brothers. After all, she was destined to leave her natal family to join the family of her husband; raising her was regarded as "spilled water," a waste of resources and energy. Footbinding was a literal and symbolic mark of status; the painful practice (begun around age six or seven) reshaped a girl's natural feet into abnormal 3-inch pointed "golden lilies" that made her unfit for work outside the house but most desirable for marriage. Reformers and revolutionaries of all stripes ended this practice in the twentieth century, and unbinding women's feet was only the beginning. The Chinese Communists saw young women as an exploited group and worked to recruit them into their movement by ending practices such as concubinage and forced marriages. Women held up half the sky, was the Communist claim. But back in the villages, especially after 1979 when parents were pressured to have only one child, girl children were still disfavored. They were more likely to be abandoned or left to die after birth. With the introduction of prenatal ultrasounds to determine the sex of fetuses, girl babies were also more likely to be aborted, exacerbating China's unbalanced gender ratio. Old patriarchal preferences for sons die hard, because sons are still important for ritual continuity within rural families and as sources of support in old age.

THE PARAMETERS OF CHILDHOOD STUDIES

Today, Chinese infants have a vastly improved chance of surviving due to modern pediatric care. In 2007 China's infant mortality rate was twenty-two deaths per 1,000 live births (Central Intelligence Agency 2008); in 1800 probably one-third or more died before the age of one. In those earlier times Daoists believed that children had to pass through thirty dangerous barriers during the years of childhood; nine of these were in the first 100 days of life, when "soul-stealing devils" were particularly active. It was common not to name a child until his or her soul was believed to be safely locked into the body (Saari 1990, pp. 12–15). Modern science notwithstanding, what is remarkable is the hold of the traditional culture of childhood, embedded in China's language and deep beliefs about what it means to *zuoren* (be fully human). Instead of passing through a succession of distinct stages from tradition to modernity, as Western nations have, China has made subtle adjustments to a pervasive old pattern of social morality that is not so much "unmodern" as different and challenging to others' expectations (Hsiung 2008).

SEE ALSO *Education; Family; Footbinding; Lu Xun; Socialization and Pedagogy.*

BIBLIOGRAPHY

Ai, Bai. Corporal Punishment and China's Assertive Only Children. *China Rights Forum* 3 (2008): 49–51.

Bai, Limin. *Shaping the Ideal Child: Children and Their Primers in Late Imperial China.* Hong Kong: Chinese University Press, 2005.

Central Intelligence Agency. China. In *CIA 2008 World Factbook* 2008. https://www.cia.gov/library/publications/the-world-factbook/geos/ch.html.

Greenhalgh, Susan. *Just One Child: Science and Policy in Deng's China.* Berkeley: University of California Press, 2008.

Hsiung, Ping-chen. *A Tender Voyage: Children and Childhood in Late Imperial China.* Stanford, CA: Stanford University Press, 2005.

Hsiung, Ping-chen. Treading a Different Path? Thoughts on Childhood Studies in Chinese History. *Journal of the History of Childhood and Youth* 1, 1 (2008): 77–85.

Lu Xun. Shanghai Children (August 12, 1933). In *Selected Works*, trans. Yang Xianyi and Gladys Yang, vol. 3, 334–335. Beijing: Foreign Languages Press, 1980.

Saari, Jon L. Breaking the Hold of Tradition: The Self-Group Interface in Transitional China. In *Social Interaction in Chinese Society*, ed. Sidney L. Greenblatt, Richard W. Wilson, and Amy Auerbacher Wilson, 28–66. New York: Praeger, 1982.

Saari, Jon L. *Legacies of Childhood: Growing Up Chinese in a Time of Crisis, 1890–1920.* Cambridge, MA: Council on East Asian Studies, Harvard University, distributed by Harvard University Press, 1990.

Jon L. Saari

MARRIAGE

The Chinese state has enjoyed a tenure rivaled only by that of the Egyptian state. One of the many results was universal acceptance of a model specifying the nature of marriage. The bride and authority over her was transferred from her parents to her husband's parents. Her labor belonged to her husband and his parents, and they could rightfully claim all her children for their descent line. This was the only form of marriage mentioned in moralizing texts, the only form consonant with high status, the form assumed by marriage ritual, and, not incidentally, the most expensive form of marriage.

As expected in a steeply hierarchical society, Chinese weddings were shaped by status competition. The wealthy took advantage of this opportunity to display their wealth, while the poor made every effort to conceal their poverty. A wealthy family's daughter was carried to her husband's home in an elaborately decorated red sedan chair, accompanied by a band and festive lanterns. A poor family's daughter traveled alone in a simple black chair or walked.

Although women rarely inherited landed property, the great majority were given a dowry (*jiazhuang*) consisting of clothing, bedding, and household utensils. In North China the costs were borne by the woman's parents, while in the South the dowry (if it may be called that) was purchased with the brideprice (*pinjin*), paid by the groom's family. Poor parents sometimes pocketed the brideprice and sent their daughter off with nothing more than a small bundle of old clothing.

The traditional marriage model was prestigious but not prescriptive. All the rights and duties specified by the model were negotiable. Rather than surrendering their daughter to her husband's family, parents could arrange for her husband to live with them. And rather than allowing all of the daughter's children to take their descent from their father, the bride's family could insist that one or more sons take his descent from his mother. Even the timing of the bride's transfer was negotiable. Some brides were transferred to their husband's family as nursing infants, while others did not join their husband until five or more years after their wedding.

A wedding procession in Guangdong, c. 1870–1880. *Traditional Chinese wedding arrangements often involved a wedding procession to ferry the new bride to her husband's home. During this transition, a family displayed their wealth in the type of transportation selected for the bride, the amount of dowry that accompanied her, and the size of the wedding entourage.* © ALINARI ARCHIVES / THE IMAGE WORKS

The result was that marriages conforming to the model (what have come to be called "major marriages") were not the only form of marriage found in many communities. In some communities, they were outnumbered by a combination of what anthropologists call "uxorilocal marriages" (*ruzhui hun*) and "minor marriages." The most striking and most reliable evidence comes from southern Fujian and northern Taiwan, where major marriages accounted for less than 40 percent of all first marriages.

Men who married uxorilocally were expected to help support their wives' parents. Many also agreed to allow some or all of their children to take descent from their wives' fathers. Regardless, uxorilocal marriages were unstable. The wife's parents might be dissatisfied and drive the man out of the family. More often he could not tolerate their hectoring and fled. One early-twentieth-century magistrate claimed that "seven or eight of every ten civil cases" involved uxorilocal marriages.

The only difference between major and minor marriages was that a minor-marriage bride was transferred as an infant or small child, rather than as a young adult. It was, however, a critical difference. Couples raised in the same family commonly resisted marrying and often failed to consummate their unions. The fertility rate of minor marriages was abnormally low, and the likelihood of adultery and divorce abnormally high. The reason appears to be a sexual inhibition caused by early association. Young people say that marrying a childhood associate is "like going to see the same movie over and over again. It is uninteresting."

Institutions such as minor marriage existed only because of the extraordinary authority of Chinese parents, who enjoyed state-sponsored patriarchy. In return for staying in their place and paying their taxes, they were granted the right to use their children as they wished. It was the devil's pact that philosophers call Confucianism. The result was that any change that weakened the traditional state also weakened the traditional marriage regime.

In Taiwan this change was initiated by the Japanese occupation (1895–1945). In China proper it was initiated by the great campaigns of the 1950s—land reform and marriage reform. The latter included a deliberate effort to eliminate minor marriages and polygyny. The result was a reformed version of the marriage system envisioned by the traditional model. The forms of marriage most oppressive to the young were supp\ressed but many of the values of the traditional system were reaffirmed. Premarital sex and divorce were as strictly regulated by the People's Republic as they had been by its imperial predecessors.

The blow that finally destroyed the traditional marriage system was the birth-control program initiated in the late 1960s. Until then marriage in China followed the pattern found in all old agrarian empires. All women married, and they married at puberty if not before. The result was a fertility rate of approximately 6.0—the mean for populations without access to birth control.

Fertility fell during the chaotic 1940s but quickly recovered, fell again during the dislocations occasioned by the Great Leap Forward, but recovered in a matter of months. With infant and childhood mortality falling sharply at the same time, the result was a spurt of population growth that forced the government to abandon its anti-Malthusian stance and take vigorous birth-control measures.

The first step in what was to become the most successful birth-control program in history was to set a minimum age for marriage. In most provinces this was 23 for rural woman and 25 for urban women. This was followed by a series of measures limiting the number of births within a marriage. The upper limit was lowered by stages from four or five births to two or three births and finally to one birth. The unintended effect was almost as consequential as the intended effect. Because children became adults before attaining a marriageable age, parents could no longer arrange their children's marriages to suit their own best interests. The state had taken back the authority once given to parents.

The history of uxorilocal marriages illustrates the direction of recent changes. Before the uxorilocal marriages were discouraged by custom in North China and by officials everywhere. Officials disliked what they regarded as a heterodox arrangement with a potential for legal complaints. It would surprise if not appall them to learn that the state has recently mounted a national campaign promoting uxorilocal marriages. They are now seen as an inexpensive way of providing for elderly people whose only child is a girl.

The marriage model consolidated by centuries of central control still exists, but only as an ideological shadow. The reality is a developing compromise between young people's desires and the state's need to limit population growth and somehow to respond to the problems created by its efforts.

SEE ALSO *Confucianism; Domestic Violence; Family; Gender Relations; Marriage; Marriage Laws; Women, Status of.*

BIBLIOGRAPHY

Banister, Judith. *China's Changing Population*. Stanford, CA: Stanford University Press, 1987.

Diamant, Neil J. *Revolutionizing the Family*. Berkeley: University of California Press, 2000.

Stockard, Janice E. *Daughters of the Canton Delta*. Stanford, CA: Stanford University Press, 1989.

Wolf, Arthur P., and Chieh-shan Huang. *Marriage and Adoption in China, 1845–1945*. Stanford, CA: Stanford University Press, 1984.

Yan Yunxiang. *Private Life under Socialism*. Stanford, CA: Stanford University Press, 2003.

Arthur P. Wolf

OLD AGE

Any discussion of old age in Chinese society must begin by distinguishing between normative and empirical approaches to the topic. A normative approach focuses on norms or standards for correct behavior. Norms are expressed, for example, in texts, moral codes, and speeches by community leaders. Empirical approaches focus on actual behavior. Normative and empirical approaches also differ in their level of specificity, the former glossing over the impact of gender, wealth, and position on the experience of old age.

NORMATIVE DEPICTIONS

According to the conventional model of Confucian familism, old age is the stage of life in which the sacrifices that characterized the earlier stages are rewarded. Once parents have arranged the marriages of their children and seen the arrival of the next generation, they may cease toiling in the fields or shops. For the rest of their lives they are entitled to obedience, respect, support, and care from their children. Following death they are entitled to memorialization and "worship" as ancestors both daily and on special annual holidays. The familial ideal is epitomized by the expression "five generations under one roof." The father-son tie is considered the axis of the Confucian family, and filial piety the cement that holds it all together. Daughters marry into other families and transfer their filial obligations to their parents-in-law.

As an ideal, the Confucian model of familism has been under attack for nearly a century. Beginning in the 1910s and particularly during the May Fourth movement, young

Young Chinese girls learning traditional songs from elderly citizens, Guizhou province, March 25, 2008. *Traditional Confucian teachings emphasized respect for elders, with the oldest male in a family granted head of household status. Post-revolutionary China looked to eliminate this cherished status for the aged, however, transferring the balance of family power to younger generations.* LYNN JOHNSON/NATIONAL GEOGRAPHIC/GETTY IMAGES

people decried what they felt as oppression by the senior generation, particularly with regard to parental control of mate selection. Following the Communist Party's assumption of power in 1949, the Confucian family was redefined as the "feudal" family and slated for elimination, its gender and age hierarchies to be replaced by egalitarian principles. Old age could no longer command the obedience of the young; stripped of power the elderly were recast as dependents.

EMPIRICAL FINDINGS

The extent to which the Confucian model was ever realized is difficult to know because there are few systematic data sets that allow for before and after comparisons. Survey data are not available until the Republican era. The most readily accessible statistics deal with easily measured features such as family size, family structure (whether households are composed of nuclear, extended, or joint families), or residence patterns (whether newly married couples set up independent households or reside with the parents of the groom or, less frequently, of the bride). Statistics dealing with family dynamics (such as who has the power to make and enforce decisions) or sentiments (such as the relative strength of conjugal versus parent-child ties) are much more difficult to obtain.

Ethnographic studies of rural China, however, suggest that old age is not a favored stage of the life cycle. When interviewing older village residents in Zhejiang Province, Yachun Ku (1991) found that the elderly themselves described the life course as divided into three stages: first the stage of the monkey, next the ox, and lastly the dog. Village dogs are not pampered pets: Rather, in order to be fed, they must obey their owners. The elderly felt they too were like dogs—at risk of neglect or abandonment if they did not behave properly by making no demands.

Hong Zhang (2004), reporting from rural Hubei, found older parents choosing to move out of their sons' homes in order to shame them into providing support. These outcomes reflect both the general poverty of rural China and the utter lack of financial alternatives for the vast majority of village elderly once their labor power is gone—

they have no pensions, no savings, and no government-funded safety net. With the collapse in the early 1980s of the rural cooperative medical insurance scheme established during the Mao era (1949–1976), rural households once again became completely responsible for paying for members' medical treatment. A major health crisis can easily bankrupt a family.

With regard to finances, the urban elderly generally fare much better than the rural. Although pension payouts and health-insurance coverage have been eroding since the mid-1990s, most elderly do have an income and some form of medical coverage independent of their children. Compared with rural elderly, urban elderly have much more control over their own lives. Once out of the workforce, they may choose to maximize their role as grandparents, socialize with their peers in parks and restaurants, or participate in neighborhood committees. Higher incomes overall in the urban areas also mean that alternatives to family care of the elderly are available, such as live-in help or hourly workers. Increasingly, Chinese are coming to view institutional care—once reserved for those with no family to attend them—as a respectable option. Privately run homes now provide a full range of services, from independent and assisted living through twenty-four-hour nursing care. Given the rapidity with which China's population is aging and the large number of parents with only a single child, the need for a wide variety of services for the elderly will only increase over the next few decades.

SEE ALSO *Family: Roles of the Elderly; Filial Piety; Social Welfare.*

BIBLIOGRAPHY

Ku, Yachun. *Chinese Rural Elderly in the Post-Mao Era: Two Villages in Zhejiang Province*. Ph.D. diss., Case Western Reserve University, Cleveland, OH, 1991.

Zhang, Hong. "Living Alone" and the Rural Elderly: Strategy and Agency in Post-Mao Rural China. In *Filial Piety: Practice and Discourse in Contemporary East Asia*, ed. Charlotte Ikels, 63–87. Stanford, CA: Stanford University Press, 2004.

Charlotte Ikels

DEATH AND FUNERALS

Since the Bronze Age, people in China have believed in an afterlife and its continuity—in gender, status, and profession—with the present life. In the fourth to fifth centuries, Buddhism introduced the ideas of salvation, karmic destiny, and reincarnation. By the twentieth century, funerals reflected—without fully reconciling—the two sets of ideas. They were intended on the one hand to create a beneficent ancestor, and on the other to speed him or her through purgatory where underworld bureaucrats judged the good and bad deeds of a lifetime. More than any other ritual, funerals expressed filiality, a central Chinese value upheld by the Confucian classics, by the state, and by the emperor himself. They were, in other words, quintessentially Chinese. In the nineteenth century, frontier peoples choosing to assimilate Han ways in Taiwan and Yunnan proved their Chineseness by burying their dead Chinese style. In the early twentieth century, overseas Chinese in San Francisco and Chiang Mai, Thailand, demonstrated their ties to China and their local solidarity by holding public funerals in the Chinese manner. Under the People's Republic, funerals have been simplified without changing much of their basic logic.

FUNERALS IN MING AND QING

The task of mourners, led by ritual experts, was to manage the pollution of death and the flesh and move the soul through the underworld. The soul was kept with the corpse until the procession to the grave site; one aspect of it returned in the form of the altar tablet to the family house; the other stayed in the tomb, where it would be worshipped at Qingming (bright and clear) on the festival of tomb sweeping (April 4 or 5 in the Gregorian calendar).

Simultaneously with the funeral rituals, the soul in another form would be passing through the underworld courts, so that a lifetime of good and bad could be examined. One court of hell was traversed, with the help of Buddhist ceremonies, at the end of each seven days. The forty-ninth day for most ended the mourning period, but people in some places marked the eighth, ninth, and tenth courts on the one hundredth day after the death, the first-year anniversary, and the three-year anniversary. In southeast China, dealing with the pollution of death was not complete even then: it was the custom to dig up the corpse after five or ten years, clean the bones, store them in an urn, and eventually find a permanent place of burial. Food offerings appropriate to each phase were made, beginning soon after death and continuing at graveside.

The proper form for funeral rituals was debated for centuries. As practiced, they reflected the influence of local ritual experts; folk opera, notably the story of Mulian; and guides such as neo-Confucian reformer Zhu Xi's (1130–1200) *Family Rituals*. Efforts by officials to reform uncanonical local practices usually fell on deaf ears: the regional practices of buying water (to wash the corpse), delayed burial, and reburial persisted, as did the almost universal seven/seven Buddhist rituals, sundry styles of Daoist exorcism, the burning of paper houses and other goods for the use of the dead, the riotous send-off banquets, and the reliance on geomancers to site the grave. Educated locals often justified such officially disapproved practices as Confucian in spirit on the ground that they showed filial respect and a continuing sense of obligation.

Bones of a family ancestor, St. Michael's Cemetery, Macau, 1996. *Despite varying practices throughout the country, traditional Chinese culture displays a deep and enduring respect for the dead. In southeast China, some customs include caring for the bones of one's ancestors during the annual festival of Qingming, known in English as Tomb Sweeping Day.* © MICHAEL S. YAMASHITA/CORBIS

The reason why Ming and Qing reformers failed in the goal of simplification, despite a degree of standardization, was that funerals were a means of social competition, of face. Funerals, after all, were for the living even more than for the dead. They anointed the new family head (the elder son having the chief ritual role), distinguished agnatic relatives (who wore hemp), ranked the participants, and hosted distant relatives and neighbors. Because the rich and powerful needed to demonstrate their status, they had to have elaborate double coffins, expensive condolence gifts and all-night banquets, high literati to dot the spirit tablets, and kilometer-long processions with musical performances. Republican attempts to limit funeral expenditures and tomb construction failed for the same reason.

THE POLITICS OF DEATH

Disposal and commemoration of the dead have continued to be controversial in politics. In Beijing, the construction of a tomb for Mao Zedong in Tiananmen Square exposed all the ambivalences about the revolutionary leader's legacy. In such efforts, filiality and patriotism often intersect.

Take the case of cross-straits relations between the People's Republic and democratic Taiwan. The splendid mausoleum of Sun Yat-sen (Sun Yixian), father of the nation, overlooks the former Nationalist capital at Nanjing, dwarfing the tomb of the Ming founder. Sun's Guomindang successor, Chiang Kai-shek (Jiang Jieshi), has his own vast memorial in Taibei (Taipei or Taipeh), built by his son, Jiang Jingguo (Chiang Ching-kuo). Both father and son remain encoffined and unburied in temporary mausoleums, an unlucky state of affairs that folk belief blames for the deaths of Chiang's male descendants. The family cannot agree on their long-planned burial in a military cemetery, pending symbolic return to the ancestral seat in Zhejiang on the mainland, and (some say) prefer to wait for the election of a Guomindang president who will conduct the ceremony more fittingly.

Meanwhile Taiwan's politicians carry on their own politics of filiality and commemoration. Faced with the political ramifications of burial in Taiwan or the mainland, Chiang's widow, Song Meiling (Soong Mei-ling), asked to be buried in New York; on her death in 2003

SUICIDES

Suicide in Chinese societies has been exceptional in the high rate among young women. In Taiwan under Japanese rule (1895–1945), where traditional Chinese values and practices still prevailed and demographic records were meticulously kept, women were subjected to tremendous pressures. As a young wife, a woman had to meet high expectations from in-laws as household drudge and bearer of sons, and she came to the family as a stranger, without friends in the community. The pattern changed somewhat by 1940, reflecting widespread social change. There were half as many female suicides in the twenty to twenty-four age group in 1940 compared to 1905, but at 28.7 suicides per 100,000 women, the rate was very high. As Taiwan developed under the Japanese, suicides among the elderly became more and more common, especially among men. In the 1930s the total suicide rate for men overtook the rate for women.

Suicide in China by the late twentieth century continued to depart from international trends: in 1988, 1990, and 1992, the only years for which figures have been released, the suicide rate was three times higher among rural than urban dwellers, and rates for women were higher than for men wherever they lived. Chinese women fifteen to twenty-four years old are still more likely to kill themselves than women in other countries. Despite rapid social change, continuities in rural patrilocal marriage and the pressure to have sons may still play a role. But the peak suicide rate is now among those seventy-five and over. With age a key factor for both sexes, China has drawn closer to international patterns; in fact, though women still kill themselves more often than men, the imbalance, at 10 women for every 8 men, is far less than male over female suicide predominance in the United States, with 10 women for every 41 men, and in Japan with 10 women for every 17 men. China's most noticeable difference is its high overall rate of more than 17 suicides per 100,000 people, by one estimate 2.3 times higher than the world average.

China's high suicide rate is blamed on the stresses of the reform period, but no earlier figures exist for comparison, and continuing patterns of suicide point to a role for cultural factors in both commission and treatment. Unlike in the West, suicide is usually attributed to family or marital problems, not mental illness. Diagnosis and clinical treatment for depression are rare. Suicide attempts may more often succeed since pesticides are widely available (ingesting pesticide is the preferred mode), hospitals remote, and poison hotlines nonexistent. Individuals, especially young women, are expected to mold themselves to circumstances and not express their feelings. In the past, folk operas presented suicide not as a mental aberration but as a moral act to avoid dishonor or right a wrong. As a suicide ghost, one might bring redress or terrify one's persecutors, or following Buddhist notions of karma one might be reborn in a higher status. Some of these motivations may persist in rural China. At a desperate moment, suicide can still offer power and moral stature to the powerless, and inflict disgrace or embarrassment on the powerful.

BIBLIOGRAPHY

Hsieh, Andrew C. K., and Jonathan D. Spence. Suicide and the Family in Pre-modern Chinese Society. In *Normal and Abnormal Behavior in Chinese Culture*, ed. Arthr Kleinman and Lin Zongyi (Tsung Yi Lin), 29–47. Dordrecht, Netherlands: Reidel, 1980.

Ji Jianlin, Arthur Kleinman, and Anne E. Becker. Suicide in Contemporary China: A Review of China's Distinctive Suicide Demographics in Their Sociocultural Context. *Harvard Review of Psychiatry* 9, 1 (2001): 1–12.

Qin Ping and Preben Bo Mortensen. Specific Characteristics of Suicide in China. *Acta Psychiatrica Scandinavica* 103 (2001): 117–121.

Wolf, Margery. Women and Suicide in China. In *Women in Chinese Society*, ed. Margery Wolf and Roxane Witke, 111–142. Stanford, CA: Stanford University Press, 1975.

Donald S. Sutton

one of her relatives invited the Democratic Progressive Party president Chen Shuibian (Chen Shui-bian), who does not see Taiwan as part of China, to drape a Republic of China flag over her coffin. Invited to China in 2005, Song Chuyu (James Soong) of the People's First Party delighted his hosts by visiting in turn the tombs of the Yellow Emperor, progenitor of the Chinese, Sun Yat-sen, and his own maternal grandfather. Jiang Xiaoyan (John Chang), the natural son of Jiang Jingguo, made a similar cross-straits trip in his own personal search for parental and patriotic legitimacy. A filial son is always a son, and probably a patriot.

CONTEMPORARY FUNERALS

Recent patterns in the People's Republic show a marked urban/rural split. The standard funeral in the cities, except for smaller enterprises, is the officially preferred memorial meeting, often in the hospital; using Western forms, people wear armbands, give eulogies, and shake hands. It is focused on the individual and is conducted by and for his or her work unit, dwelling on contributions to it by the deceased. The family plays a distinctly secondary role, but is in charge of final disposal, which is usually by cremation. The continuing emotional sense of obligation to one's dead has been reflected in individual or local efforts to honor those persecuted in the Cultural Revolution, or to make good graves lost through land reclamation.

Some rural areas saw efforts to reform along the same lines, but the Maoist simplifications lasted for at most a decade. Even in the 1970s, refugees to Hong Kong reported continuing traditional practices, such as announcement and vigil, buying water, firecrackers, burnt paper offerings, drum and horn processions, and periodic memorial rites. Urban/rural differences are underlined by the information that only 15 percent of rural people are cremated, as against the 90 percent in the cities. Rural funerals and tombs, it is true, are simpler; lineage mortuary rituals are quite rare, and perhaps the sense of dependence on one's dead has weakened. However, an estimated sixteen billion yuan is spent on funerals annually. Qingming is still celebrated as tomb-sweeping day, despite a recent government effort to save money by doing it all in cyberspace. In 2001, 1.1 million people took the subway in Beijing to visit the family graves. Ancestral beliefs are much weakened, but evidently many Chinese still feel the need ritually to repay debts they owe to their parents. The channeling of parental love and effort in the standard one-child family makes that unlikely to change.

SEE ALSO *Buddhism; Chiang Ching-kuo (Jiang Jingguo); Chiang Kai-shek (Jiang Jieshi); Confucianism; Daoism; Family: Rituals; Festivals; Mao Zedong; Sun Yat-sen (Sun Yixian).*

BIBLIOGRAPHY

Brook, Timothy. Funerary Ritual and the Building of Lineages in Late Imperial China. *Harvard Journal of Asiatic Studies* 49, 2 (1989): 465–499.

Chau, Adam Yuet. Hosting Funerals and Temple Festivals: Folk Event Productions in Rural China. *Asian Anthropology* 3 (2004): 49–70.

Martin, Emily Ahern. *The Cult of the Dead in a Chinese Village.* Stanford, CA: Stanford University Press, 1979.

Oxfeld, Ellen. "When You Drink Water, Think of Its Source": Morality, Status, and Reinvention in Rural Chinese Funerals. *Journal of Asian Studies* 63, 4 (2004): 961–990.

Sutton, Donald S. Death Rites and Chinese Culture: Standardization and Variation in Ming and Qing Times. *Modern China* 33, 1 (2007): 123–153.

Watson, James L., and Evelyn S. Rawski, eds. *Death Ritual in Late Imperial and Modern China.* Berkeley: University of California Press, 1988.

Donald S. Sutton

LIN BIAO
1907–1971

Lin Biao (Lin Piao, Lin Yurong) was a Chinese Communist military and political leader. Lin Biao was born on December 15, 1907, in Linjia Dawan ("Big Village of Lin Family") in Huanggang County, Hubei Province. In his early years, he was heavily influenced by his two cousins, Lin Yunan (1898–1931) and Lin Yuying (1897–1942), who introduced him to Communist ideas.

In 1925 Lin Biao left home to attend Whampoa Military Academy, and he joined the Chinese Communist Party the same year. After the split of the Nationalist Party and the Communist Party in 1927, Lin Biao followed the defecting troops to Jinggang Mountain in Jiangxi Province, where the Communists set up their bases. Lin Biao was serving as commander of the First Red Army Corps when encirclements of the Nationalist troops forced the Communists to retreat in October 1934. Lin's troops were instrumental in breaking through the Nationalist encirclement, contributing significantly to the survival of the Red Army in its trek to northern China, a journey known as the Long March.

In June 1936 Lin Biao was appointed president of the Anti-Japanese Military and Political University (Kangri Junzheng Daxue) at Yan'an, but he returned to the battlefield within a year to fight the Japanese. He scored a victory at Pingxingguan Pass, successfully ambushing and annihilating Japanese general Itagaki Seishiro's (1885–1948) Fifth Division. In March 1938 a severe injury removed Lin from military duty, and he went to the Soviet Union for treatment.

When the civil war broke out after the Japanese surrender in 1945, Lin Biao was chosen to compete with the Nationalists for control of Manchuria, a strategically important region. Poorly equipped and outnumbered, Lin's troops initially lost a few battles. By late 1948, however, they emerged strong enough to engage the Nationalists in a large-scale offensive known as the Liaoshen Campaign, which cost Chiang Kai-shek (Jiang Jieshi) half a million of his best troops. Then, without rest, Lin's troops rushed back to interior China and were quickly embroiled in another major battle, the Pingjin campaign, which resulted in Communist control of Beijing (then known as Beiping) and Tianjin. Lin's troops continued marching south and gained control of a vast area from Manchuria to Hainan Island. Lin

Biao thus ranked as one the Communists' best strategists and generals. His Fourth Field Army, which numbered over one million troops, consisted of almost half of the entire People's Liberation Army. In 1955, at the age of forty-seven, he was awarded the title of marshal, the youngest of the ten men to be so honored.

For several years after the Communist victory, Lin Biao remained militarily and politically inactive. He did not command the Chinese Volunteers in the Korean War (1950–1953), though many of his troops were sent to Korea. Lin reappeared in public in 1959 when he replaced Peng Dehuai as defense minister. Between 1959 and 1965 Lin reoriented the focus of the People's Liberation Army, prioritizing political work in order to boost soldiers' morale. Under his leadership, the Department of General Politics of the People's Liberation Army compiled and published *The Quotations of Chairman Mao* and circulated it among the troops. The book, later known as the "little red book," became extremely popular during the Cultural Revolution. Mao was greatly pleased with Lin's efforts to enhance the cult of his personality, and this became an important reason for Lin's rise during the Cultural Revolution. In 1965 Lin gained international attention for an article bearing his name, "Long Live the People's War," published in the *People's Daily*. The article was believed to have delivered an important warning from the Chinese government concerning the Vietnam War (1957–1975) and contained Lin's theory of the people's war and world revolution.

The zenith of Lin's political career occurred during the Cultural Revolution, when he became the only vice chairman of the Communist Party in late 1966. He was known as Mao's "closest comrade-in-arms" and "Mao's best student," and the party constitution of 1970 officially recognized him as "Mao's heir." Lin's political career, however, ended abruptly in September 1971. According to the official explanation, Lin and his family were engaging in anti-Mao conspiracies, planning an assassination of Mao and a military coup d'état, and establishing a separate government in Guangzhou. After these alleged conspiracies were "exposed," Lin and his family were attempting to defect from the country when their plane crashed in the Mongolian Republic on September 13, 1971. Everyone aboard was killed, including Lin Biao, his wife, Ye Qun (1917–1971), and his son Lin Liguo (1945–1971). Chinese officials, however, have never provided convincing evidence to support their allegations against Lin Biao. His death in what is now known as the "Lin Biao incident" remains one of the biggest mysteries in the history of the People's Republic of China. After Lin's death, many of his top generals were purged. In 1980 and 1981, the government put Lin Biao and his wife posthumously on trial along with his generals, and declared them guilty.

Different interpretations of the Lin Biao incident have surfaced. His son may have been involved in certain anti-Mao dialogues, but there is no convincing evidence to associate these activities with Lin. Scholarly studies and eyewitness accounts suggest that Lin Biao was innocent of all the charges. Although the Chinese government has not rehabilitated Lin Biao in light of this new information, a subtle change in the official evaluation of Lin Biao seemed to occur when Lin's image was shown publicly side-by-side with other marshals in an exhibition at the Chinese Military Museum in Beijing to commemorate the eighty-year anniversary of the People's Liberation Army in August 2007.

SEE ALSO *Chinese Marxism: Postrevolutionary Marxism other than Mao Zedong Thought; Communist Party; People's Liberation Army.*

BIBLIOGRAPHY

Ding, Kevin, ed. *Chongshen Lin Biao zui'an* [Reevaluation of Lin Biao's criminal case]. Hong Kong: Mirror Press, 2005.

Jin Qiu. *The Culture of Power: The Lin Biao Incident in the Cultural Revolution.* Stanford, CA: Stanford University Press, 1999.

Kau, Michael Y. M. *The Lin Piao Affair: Power Politics and Military Coup.* New York: International Arts and Sciences Press, 1975.

Teiwes, Frederick C., and Warren Sun. *The Tragedy of Lin Biao: Riding the Tiger during the Cultural Revolution, 1966–1971.* Honolulu: University of Hawai'i Press, 1996.

Wu Faxian. *Suiyue jiannan: Wu Faxian huiyilu* [Difficult years: A memoir of Wu Faxian]. Hong Kong: Beixing Chubanshe, 2006.

Jin Qiu

LIN FENGMIAN
1900–1991

Lin Fengmian, a modernist who painted in both oils and Chinese ink, is recognized for his efforts to synthesize Chinese and Western art through expressive use of the Chinese brush and a Western sense of form, color, and composition. Educated in Paris, he established China's first national art academy, promoted art societies, and mentored a generation of free-thinking artists. In his painting, in Chinese art education, and in his published art theory, he made significant contributions to China's twentieth-century transition to cultural modernity.

Lin Fengmian was born in Meixian, Guangdong Province, into an artisan's family, and was taught traditional Chinese painting and calligraphy. After completing middle school in 1919, he traveled with his friend Lin Wenzheng (1903–1990) to Shanghai. They were fortunate to be chosen to go to France on a government-supported work-study program initiated by the eminent educator Cai Yuanpei, and arrived in Dijon in February 1920. While working as a sign painter, Lin began studying art at the École des Beaux-Arts in Dijon, and in September 1920 was admitted to the prestigious École des Beaux-Arts in Paris. He came under the tutelage of Fernand Cormon (1854–1924), with whom prominent, innovative painters such as Vincent van Gogh, Émile Bernard, and Henri de Toulouse-Lautrec had studied many years before, and who was famous for the free-spirited atmosphere of his atelier. Although Lin Fengmian's early work does not survive, it is believed that he painted oils in a fauvist style. During these years Lin also studied and copied works in the many museums and galleries in France.

In 1922 Lin traveled to Berlin, where devaluation of the German mark made it easier for a young artist to stretch his savings. He held a solo exhibition in Berlin in 1923 and there met an Austrian chemistry student, Roda von Steiner, whom he married. Tragically, she and their young child died of scarlet fever in 1924. During this time of misfortune Lin Fengmian continued to receive recognition in France, exhibiting in the Salon d'Automne in 1922 and 1924, and showing forty-two works in the Exhibition of Traditional and Modern Chinese Art organized by Chinese students and held in Paris and Strasbourg in 1924. He exhibited his paintings at the 1925 Exposition Internationale des Arts Décoratifs (International Exposition of Decorative Arts), held in Paris, for which he also helped Lin Wenzheng to organize the Chinese submission. That year Lin Fengmian married a French art student, Alice Vattant, who later returned with him to China.

In the course of the 1924 and 1925 exhibitions, Lin Fengmian's administrative abilities, as well as his art, came to the attention of Cai Yuanpei, who was then visiting Europe. Cai recommended that Lin Fengmian be appointed director of the Beijing Art Academy. Upon returning to China in 1926 to take up his new post, Lin invited a friend from Dijon, André Claudot, to join him on the academy faculty. The following year, Lin and Cai established the National Hangzhou Arts Academy on the banks of West Lake, with Lin as director, Lin Wenzheng as dean, and Claudot as painting professor. For a decade, until the outbreak of the war with Japan in 1937, Lin Fengmian served as director of the academy in Hangzhou, encouraging the same atmosphere of freedom that he had experienced in Paris. He was particularly committed to the possibilities of combining the subjectivity of Chinese painting with that of postimpressionist European painting, and saw no need for administrative divisions between Western-style (*xihua*) and National-style (*guohua*) painting within the curriculum. The academy, the most prestigious art institute in China until 1949, was particularly well-known for its French modernist styles. Like Lin Fengmian, some of its prominent graduates, including Li Keran (1907–1989) and Wu Guanzhong (b. 1919), worked in both oils and ink, ultimately developing personal styles that enriched Chinese painting with qualities absorbed from Western artistic practice. Other Lin Fengmian students, like Zhao Wuji (Zao Wouki; b. 1921), who emigrated to France, developed quite personal, and subjective, modes of abstract oil painting.

As did most professors, Lin Fengmian moved inland with his college during the Second Sino-Japanese War (1937–1945), leaving behind his oil paintings, which are believed to have been destroyed by the Japanese. The next few years brought dislocation. He gave up his directorship of the academy in a mandated reorganization and thereafter devoted himself to his painting. In the 1940s he exhibited in Hong Kong, Chongqing, and Paris. During the second half of his long life, Lin continued to write and paint, advocating a blending of Chinese and modern Western art, and painting primarily in water-based pigments and ink on Chinese paper.

Lin Fengmian moved to Shanghai in 1951. His modernist, subjective approach to teaching and practicing art was not valued by the art authorities in the newly established People's Republic of China, and he was virtually unemployable. Reportedly, it was only with the intervention of Premier Zhou Enlai, who had also studied in France, that he was awarded a governmental stipend. Over the next few decades, although he was granted several honorific titles in local cultural circles, Lin lived a secluded life, painting in comparative isolation and producing memory images that often have a rather gloomy feeling. He was denied an exit permit when his wife Alice and their daughter moved to Brazil in 1956, and he remained alone in Shanghai for the next two decades.

During a brief period of cultural liberalization in 1961, a solo exhibition of Lin Fengmian's work was held at the Shanghai Art Museum and Central Academy of Fine Arts Gallery in Beijing. In 1968, however, during the Cultural Revolution (1966–1969), he was arrested on unwarranted charges and jailed. In 1972, after his release from jail, his paintings were denounced by cultural arbiter Jiang Qing, the pseudonym of Mao's wife, and labeled "black paintings." This political attack generated another wave of mandatory criticism and caused great difficulties for the elderly artist. Once it became possible to leave China in 1977, Lin settled in Hong Kong, visiting his wife in Brazil almost every year until her death in 1982. In 1979 Lin Fengmian held one-man shows in Paris and Shanghai, and between 1988 and 1991 in Shanghai, Taibei, and Beijing. He died in Hong Kong in 1991. In an essay in tribute to the artist, Michael Sullivan noted the vigor and passion of Lin Fengmian's late works and praised his legacy of modern painting. "Passing from the lyrical, the decorative, the poetic at one extreme to the tragic, the violent, the melancholy at the other—what other modern Chinese artist has expressed such a range of feeling?" (Sullivan 1999, pp. 719–720).

SEE ALSO *Art Exhibitions Abroad; Art, History of: 1911–1949; Art Schools and Colleges; Chinese Painting (guohua); Modernist Art of the 1920s and 1930s; Oil Painting (youhua).*

BIBLIOGRAPHY

Lightfoot, Sonia. Harmonizing Eastern and Western Art. In *Lin Fengmian yu ershi shiji zhongguo meishu*, ed. Xu Jiang et al., 744–763. Hangzhou: Zhongguo Meishu Xueyuan Chubanshe, 1999.

Lin Fengmian huaji 林风眠畵集 (Collected paintings by Lin Fengmian). Shanghai: Shanghai People's Art Press, 1979.

Sullivan, Michael. A Modest Tribute to Lin Fengmian. In *Lin Fengmian yu ershi shiji zhongguo meishu*, ed. Xu Jiang et al., 716–720. Hangzhou: Zhongguo Meishu Xueyuan Chubanshe, 1999.

Xu Jiang et al., eds. *Lin Fengmian yu ershi shiji zhongguo meishu: Guoji xueshu yantao hui lunwenji* (林风眠与二十世纪中国美术：国际学术研讨会论文集) (The century of Lin Fengmian: International symposium proceedings). Hangzhou: Zhongguo Meishu Xueyuan Chubanshe, 1999.

Zheng, Chao. *Lin Fengmian yanjiu wenji* 林风眠研究文集 (Lin Fengmian in perspective). Hangzhou: Zhongguo Meishuxueyuan Chubanshe, 1995.

Christina Wei-Szu Burke Mathison
Julia F. Andrews

LIN HUIYIN
1904–1955

Born in Hangzhou, Zhejiang Province, on June 10, 1904, Lin Huiyin (also known as Phyllis Lin, Lin Whei-yin) came from a family of prominent scholar-officials from Fujian Province. She was raised by her grandparents in Hangzhou till the age of eight, when she attended elementary school in Shanghai. In 1916 the family moved to Beijing so that her father, Lin Changmin (1876–1925), could assume the post of minister of justice. In 1920–1921 she traveled to Europe with her father and attended school in London. Their English landlady was an architect, which instilled an interest in architecture in young Huiyin. She also met the poet Xu Zhimo (1897–1931) in London. They fell in love, but Lin decided to end the relationship because Xu was married at the time. The romance is memorialized in Xu's famous poem "Ouran" (A chance encounter).

In 1923 Hu Shi (1891–1962) and Xu Zhimo formed the Crescent Moon Society in Beijing, and Lin Huiyin became an active participant in its literary activities. In May 1924, in honor of the visit of the Nobel laureate Rabindranath Tagore (1861–1941), Lin and Xu played the lead roles in Tagore's play *Chitrangada*. A month later she and her fiancé Liang Sicheng (1901–1972), the eldest son of the leading intellectual Liang Qichao (1873–1929), went to the United States to study architecture. At the time, however, the University of Pennsylvania did not admit women to its Department of Architecture, so Lin enrolled in the School of Art but took many courses in architecture. She went on to do graduate work at Yale University, where she majored in stage design. In March 1928 Lin and Liang got married in Vancouver before returning to China, both to teach at Northeastern University (Dongbei daxue) in the city of Shenyang.

From 1930 to 1945 the couple traveled to more than two hundred counties in fifteen provinces to engage in field studies of ancient architectural sites. They collaborated on many scholarly articles, such as "Jin Fen gu jianzhu yucha jilue" (A preliminary investigation of ancient architecture in Shanxi, 1935) and *Zhongguo jianzhu shi* (History of Chinese architecture, 1942). Their work led to national, and even international, recognition of some hitherto unknown sites. After the War of Resistance against Japan (1937–1945), Lin taught at Tsinghua (Qinghua) University in Beijing, where Liang Sicheng was the founding chair of the Department of Architecture, a position he held till 1972. From September 1949 to June 1950 Lin was part of the team of architecture professors that designed the national emblem of the People's Republic of China. She also served on the Beijing Planning Committee and strongly advocated for the preservation of the old city walls. In 1951 she was involved in the design of the Monument to the People's Heroes in Tiananmen Square. Having always been frail since her youth, she passed away in Beijing on April 1, 1955.

Lin is primarily known as an architect and as a scholar of ancient Chinese architecture. In fact, she was the first female architect of China. She was also a writer throughout her life. She published her first poem in April 1931 and wrote fiction and drama as well. Lin was one of the first modern women poets in China, and her association with the Crescent Moon Society is manifest in the lyrical tenor and romantic flair of her poetry. She left behind a small corpus of poems, most of them expressing a longing for a peaceful life and speaking of remembrances. Lin has become a household name in China in recent years because of the popularity of the 1999 television drama series *Renjian siyue tian* (April in the human world), which depicts the three loves in Xu Zhimo's life. The title of the series is borrowed from Lin's poem. Lin's niece, Maya Ying Lin, also grew up to be an architect, best known for her design of the Vietnam Veterans Memorial in Washington, D.C.

SEE ALSO *Architecture, History of: Architecture to 1949; Liang Sicheng; Xu Zhimo.*

BIBLIOGRAPHY

Dooling, Amy D., and Kristina M. Torgeson. *Writing Women in Modern China: An Anthology of Women's Literature from the Early Twentieth Century*. New York: Columbia University Press, 1998.

Fairbank, Wilma. *Liang and Lin: Partners in Exploring China's Architectural Past.* Philadelphia: University of Pennsylvania Press, 1994.

Rowe, Peter G., and Seng Kuan. *Architectural Encounters with Essence and Form in Modern China.* Cambridge, MA: MIT Press, 2002.

Wong, Sidney. Lin Huiyin and Liang Sicheng as Architectural Students at the University of Pennsylvania (1924–27). *Planning and Development* 23, 1 (2008): 75–93.

Michelle Yeh

LIN YUTANG
1895–1976

Lin Yutang, writer and scholar, was the son of a Presbyterian minister in Banzi, rural Fujian Province. He received a bachelor of arts from St. John's University in Shanghai in 1916 and married Liao Cuifeng in 1919. She traveled with him overseas, where he received a master of arts in comparative literature at Harvard University (1921) and a doctorate in philology at the University of Leipzig (1923).

CAREER

After returning to Beijing, he was appointed professor of English philology at National Peking University and chair of the English Department at National Beijing Normal University for Women (1923–1926). During this time he joined the editorial board of the magazine *Yusi* (Tattler), founded by Lu Xun and Zhou Zuoren, and published studies on phonology. After condemning the government for killing students demonstrating against Japanese incursions on March 18, 1926, he joined other scholars in leaving Beijing and took a position at Xiamen University. In 1927 he briefly served as secretary to the Minister for Foreign Affairs of the newly established Republican government in Hankou. That same year he moved to Shanghai, where he taught English at Shanghai Dongwu University, composed English-language textbooks, and in 1930 was appointed research fellow and foreign-language editor of Academia Sinica (Zhongyang Yanjiu Yuan). In 1932 he established the journal *Lunyu* (Analects), in 1934 the magazine *Renjian shi* (The human world), and in 1935 the magazine *Yuzhou feng* (Cosmic wind).

Between 1933 and 1935 he wrote *My Country and My People* (*Wu guo yu wu min*) in English with the encouragement of Pearl Buck and her husband, Richard Walsh, and, upon the success of its publication in the United States, moved to New York City in 1936, where he continued to write on Chinese culture and current events until after the end of World War II. In 1948, after the commercial failure of his invention of a seventy-two-key Chinese typewriter, Lin moved to France, where he worked briefly for the United Nations Educational, Scientific, and Cultural Organization (UNESCO) as director of arts and letters, but he returned to writing until assuming the position of chancellor of the newly founded Nanyang University in Singapore in 1954. He soon returned to New York City and lived there until 1966, when he moved to Taiwan.

In 1967 the Chinese University of Hong Kong appointed him research professor in support of his project to compile *A Chinese-English Dictionary of Modern Usage* (1973), which employed an innovative system of encoding characters to order entries, and he soon began to divide his time living in Hong Kong and Taiwan. After the death in Taiwan of the eldest of three daughters, Adet (Rusi), Lin and his wife lived largely in Hong Kong, where their two younger daughters, Anor (Xiangru) and Taiyi (Meimei), lived and worked. Lin died in Hong Kong and was buried in Taiwan.

WRITINGS

During the 1920s Lin attracted attention as a writer of witty familiar essays largely associated with the social and cultural criticism of Lu Xun and his brother Zhou Zuoren, and aimed primarily at warlord leadership and the persistence of neo-Confucian culture. For Lin, this culminated in 1928 with a one-act closet drama "Zi jian Nanzi" (translated in 1937 as *Confucius Saw Nancy*), in which Confucius attempts to persuade the Duke of Wei to adopt Confucian ritual etiquette through his consort Nanzi. Nanzi, however, throws Confucius himself into doubt when she argues for a liberated individuality that recognizes the sensuous as the basis of the sentiments and culture that Confucius himself values.

Whereas Lu Xun turned from reform to furthering revolution, Lin used humor against politicized literary debates, which he believed were driving writers into dogmatic political positions. Lin's magazines of the 1930s, critical of the Nationalist government but not opposed to it, became extremely popular and cultivated a significant number of literary works and writers. By 1934 Lin's ambivalence toward both traditional culture and modernity resulted in his arguing that the unconventional literati of the Ming (1368–1644) and Qing (1644–1912) dynasties, by cultivating character (*xingling*) and thereby promoting an independence from the doctrines of their era, were an important source of modern individuality in China. These views also inform one of Lin's most successful books in the United States, *The Importance of Living* (1937; *Shenghuo de yishu*).

In pursuit of her project to forge a better understanding of China in America, Pearl Buck encouraged Lin to write for publication there. Such encouragement resulted in the book *My Country and My People* (1935), in which Lin sought in his cultural criticism of China to "demand from the past an answer to its present." He found in Chinese modernity the unintended consequences of Confucian teachings confronting a more aggressive, modern world in which law, which might reform China and adjust it to modern needs, was still ruled by "the three sisters" of "face, fate, and favor."

After the outbreak of the War of Resistance against Japan (1937–1945), Lin wrote *Moment in Peking* (1938; *Jinghua yanyun*). This episodic novel inspired by *Honglou meng* (*Dream of Red Mansions*) narrates the lives of some one hundred characters associated with three Beijing families in the tumultuous era beginning in 1900 and culminating in 1938, focusing on a woman who achieves through her father a Daoist-inspired emotional freedom from care about the frustrations of fate. In 1943 Lin published *Between Tears and Laughter* (*Ti xiao jie fei*), in which he implored the United States to rethink its strategic accommodation of British imperial power, trade, and racial discrimination and to support China more generously and overcome the "moral malignant tumor that is called twentieth-century culture." After travel to China he published *The Vigil of a Nation* (1944; *Zhen ge dai dan*) to support Nationalist leadership and argue against accommodating the Communists, explicitly going against prevailing views among American observers.

After the war, although Lin continued to write anticommunist prose, such as a critical survey of Soviet history (*The Secret Name*, 1958), he turned largely to translating premodern Chinese literature and writing innovative fiction. *Chinatown Family* (1948), initiated Chinese-American literature by presenting the patriotism and sense of dignity among Chinese immigrants. *The Unexpected Island* (1955; *Qidao*) is a futuristic utopian novel. *Lady Wu* (1957) is a historical novel, unusual for its time, portraying Empress Wu Zetian (r. 690–705) in a modern fictional form. *The Red Peony* (1961; *Hong mudan*), inspired by D. H. Lawrence, depicts a Chinese woman's search among several lovers for an ideal relationship. Thus, although Lin's career peaked in the 1930s, the scope of his varied creativity continued to attract attention in later years.

SEE ALSO *Interpreters of Things Chinese to the West; Literary Societies.*

BIBLIOGRAPHY

Laughlin, Charles. *The Literature of Leisure and Chinese Modernity*. Honolulu: University of Hawaii Press, 2008.

Lin, Taiyi. *Lin Yutang zhuan* [Biography of Lin Yutang]. Taibei: Lianjing Chuban Shiye Gongsi, 1989.

Qian, Suoqiao. *Oriental Modern: Lin Yutang Translating China and America*. New York: Routledge, 1999.

Shi Ping. *Lin Yutang: Wenhua zhuanxing de renge fuhao* [Lin Yutang: Signs of personality in cultural transformation]. Beijing: Beijing Daxue Chubanshe, 2005.

Wang Zhaosheng. *Lin Yutang da zhuan* [Comprehensive biography of Lin Yutang]. Beijing: Zuojia Chubanshe, 2006.

Edward Mansfield Gunn Jr.

LIN ZEXU

1785–1850

Lin Zexu is best known in the historical literature as the imperial commissioner whose relentless enforcement of the opium ban in Guangzhou led directly to open conflict with the British government and to the Opium War from 1839 to 1842. Historians now understand that his conviction and determination were shaped by a reform program that had been taking shape since the 1820s.

Lin Zexu, a native of Houguan County (Fuzhou City) of Fujian Province, obtained his *xiucai* degree at thirteen *sui* and the *juren* degree at twenty *sui*. He served in the private office (*mufu*) of Fujian governor Zhang Shicheng until he passed the *jinshi* examination on his third attempt in 1811.

After obtaining the *jinshi* and after a short posting at the Hanlin Academy in Beijing, Lin Zexu was appointed to the provinces. He rose rapidly through officialdom; by 1823 he was serving as Jiangsu Province surveillance commissioner, and from there on, he consistently held senior provincial appointments. After mourning for his mother in 1825, he returned to office in Jiangsu when he was appointed to the Provincial Administration Commission in Nanjing. He traveled home to mourn his father's death in 1827, but returned to office as Provisional Administration commissioner in Hubei in 1830, and in Henan and then Jiangsu (at Suzhou) in 1831. Later in 1831, he was appointed director-general of the Grand Canal, in which capacity he had charge of the transport of tribute grain to Beijing. By 1832 he was Jiangsu provincial governor.

The patronage of Tao Shu (1778–1839) is apparent in Lin's appointments. Tao was governor of Jiangsu from 1825 to 1830 and governor-general of Jiangsu, Jiangxi, and Anhui from 1830 to 1839. Lin's connection with Tao is interesting because during the Daoguan era Tao was at the center of a small coterie of officials who were keen on administrative reforms. It is possible to view the reform effort as having descended from the veiled references to dynastic decline of the Jiaqing era, but the reformers' state (*hukou*) craft (*jingshi*) approach had origins reaching back at least to the late Ming dynasty (1368–1644). While serving as Jiangsu governor, Tao Shu had taken credit for successfully organizing the transport of the tribute grain by sea in 1825. He had also been effective in introducing a tax license to replace hereditary salt-trading rights in the Huaibei salt administration. Lin Zexu's effectiveness in organizing famine relief, in managing river works in the Shanghai area, and in studying the feasibility of growing rice in Zhili Province were in line with the reform perspectives of statecraft. So was his interest in banning opium when increasing import of the drug in the 1820s and 1830s. The bullionist observation that payments for opium led to the outflow of silver and consequently economic depression, brought the issue to national attention.

Lin had been transferred to the governor-generalship of Hunan and Hubei in 1837 when the question of whether opium should be legalized was debated at the imperial court. Lin not only took part in that debate by memorializing the emperor on the ways and means of banning opium, but, as governor-general, he personally oversaw the burning of confiscated opium pipes at Wuhan. When he was called to Beijing in 1838 for an audience with the emperor, during which he was given his instructions as imperial commissioner to enforce the ban in Guangzhou, he was known as an effective provincial administrator deeply committed to the cause of the opium ban. He arrived in Guangzhou in 1839. Within a month, he was demanding the arrest of smugglers and admonishing the local garrisons and the *cohong* merchants for collaborating with them. Historian James M. Polachek (1992) suggests that Lin may have thought such measures would curtail the demand for opium in China, and so threaten its price that the foreign merchants who were shipping the drug would abandon the trade. Nevertheless, in another month, he had turned on the foreign community itself, threatening to halt all trade and arrest the culpable, and demanding the surrender of all opium held. The opium was duly handed over and destroyed. The vociferous opposition put up by the British merchants, followed by their eventual acquiescence, gave the impression in mid-1839 that Lin's high-handed treatment had worked. Lin did not seem to have anticipated the outbreak of war, which became apparent only toward the end of 1839. When the British expeditionary fleet arrived in mid-1840, blockaded Guangzhou, and turned north to attack Dinghai City in Zhejiang Province, the imperial court learned to its surprise the ferocity of British firepower. Lin Zexu, by then Guangdong-Guangxi governor-general, was removed from office in disgrace.

Lin was exiled to Yili for his inept dealings in Guangzhou. He emerged from exile in 1846, and served variously as governor of Shaanxi and governor-general of Yunnan and Guizhou. At the outbreak of the Taiping Uprising, he was appointed imperial commissioner and dispatched to Guangxi. Lin was already ill as he received the appointment, and died in 1850 on his way to the province.

While serving in Guangzhou, Lin Zexu embarked on a program to gather information about the West, which included translation of Western texts. He became one of the first senior officials to appreciate the power of Western armaments. Some of the translations produced under his aegis were passed on to Wei Yuan, who went on to produce the *Haiguo tuzhi* (Illustrated geography of the kingdoms from the sea), published in 1844.

SEE ALSO *Examination System, 1800–1905; Government Administration, 1800–1912; Grand Canal; Opium, 1800–1950; Opium Wars; Wei Yuan.*

BIBLIOGRAPHY

Chang Hsin-pao. *Commissioner Lin and the Opium War.* Cambridge, MA: Harvard University Press, 1964.

Lai Xinxia. *Lin Zexu nianpu.* Shanghai: Shanghai Renmin Chubanshe, 1981.

Mao Haijian. *Tianchao de bengkui.* Beijing: Sanlian, 1995.

Polachek, James M. *The Inner Opium War.* Cambridge, MA: Council on East Asian Studies, Harvard University, 1992.

Yang Guozhen. *Lin Zexu zhuan.* Beijing: Renmin Chubanshe, 1995.

David Faure

LINEAGE

The family was the basic building block of Chinese society. Though the origins of the lineage were social, the work of the state was made easier by dealing with a smaller number of families rather than a larger number of individuals, and making families even bigger was the logical aspiration of state and people alike. But there were physical constraints on expansion, and large numbers of people living together in one household generated tensions that led to members splitting away.

At the heart of the problem were the inheritance system and the relationship between brothers. While they stayed together in an undivided family, younger brothers were expected to be subservient to their eldest brother. But the law of inheritance laid down that brothers were to inherit equally from their father, so when the family estate was divided up, each brother became the absolute head of his own equal portion. For a younger brother, it was always tempting to press for division and gain equality and independence. Yet to do so was to offend against the universally accepted ideal of a united family.

In the mid-eleventh century, Fan Zhongyan, a high Song official, had the idea of setting up an ancestral trust (*zutang*) for the benefit of his descendants. The trust property was kept back from his heritable estate and registered in the perpetual ownership of his descent line, his lineage or clan (*zongzu*). It was called the Fan Shi Yizhuang (Fan Clan Charitable Estate). Brothers could take their shares of heritable property and set up independent families, but their membership in the lineage trust worked to create and maintain a permanent unifying focus. The idea quickly spread to other wealthy surname groups and eventually percolated down to those less well off.

LOCALITY

By the Ming dynasty (1368–1644), lineages were to be found all over China, and especially in the provinces south of the Yangzi River. Various reasons have been given for the predominance of lineages in the South, but it is likely that the need to control water resources in rice-growing areas gave these large social units an advantage there, and the greater prosperity of the region produced conditions favorable for lineage development.

Lineage members lived together, not in one household, but in separate families in one village or a cluster of villages. They were surrounded by the land they farmed, their exclusive territory. The man who first arrived in the area and founded the lineage was known as the founding ancestor (*shizu*), and his sons were counted as second generation, grandsons as third generation, and so on. In the New Territories of Hong Kong, a lineage of the Deng surname can be traced back to a founding ancestor who lived in the tenth century. It is still there more than thirty generations later, but at various times over the centuries members have moved away to other parts of the region to start new lineages. Each of them is a Deng lineage, taking its clan name from the area it lives in, such as the Deng Lineage of Xia Cun and the Deng Lineage of Longyuetou. In each case they began with a new founding ancestor.

Lineages could grow as large as the accidents of history and geography allowed. If there were no other settlements around them vying for space, they could continue to expand in landholdings and population size. At the other extreme, a small lineage might occupy only part of a village, sharing it with others of different surnames. Such mixed-lineage villages had a tendency to be riven with hostility, and the different groups might well seek to oust each other and have the settlement to themselves.

THE ANCESTRAL TRUST

The lineage held property in trust (usually land), and this land produced income used for the benefit of the group as a whole. Ceremonies of worship of lineage ancestors had first call on the income. Usually these rites took place in the spring, the autumn, and once a year at the grave of the founding ancestor. Worship involved expenditure on candles, incense, paper "spirit money," firecrackers, and considerable quantities of food, which was first offered to the dead and then consumed in a banquet for worshippers.

Surplus income could be used to improve living or working conditions for members, to support education for their children, to reward the deserving, to assist widows or other needy members, and to build communal halls. Most lineages maintained at least one ancestor hall (*citang*), in which the spirit tablets of the founding ancestor and other deceased members of importance were housed. Some lineages were sufficiently wealthy to make annual grants of grain or money to their members.

Membership in the trust had to be formally claimed, with fathers registering their newborn sons in the ancestor hall at New Year in a ceremony called lighting the lantern (*kaideng*). A lantern was lit before the altar to notify the ancestors, and a feast was given for lineage elders as the price of recognition of the newcomer. Details of births, marriages, and deaths were recorded in the lineage genealogy book (*zupu*), which enabled all living members to trace their lines back to the common founding ancestor.

LEADERSHIP

The lineage was organized on the same principles as the family, out of which it developed. Lineage leaders were those of higher generations and senior age. The lineage head (*zuzhang*) was the senior surviving male in the senior surviving generation. After him came the branch heads (*fangzhang*), who were the seniors of the branches (*fang*), sublineages composed of the descendants of the first set of brothers born to the line of the lineage founder. These men were aided by a body of elders (*fulao*), whose qualification, regardless of generation, was that they had reached a set age, usually 61 or 51, but perhaps only 41 in small lineages with few members. Women had no place in the organization and were forbidden to enter the ancestor halls.

Age and generational superiority were not necessarily the best qualifications for the strong leadership required by a lineage, particularly a large one of hundreds or thousands of members. Indeed, because poorer families tended to marry their sons late, they reproduced slower and had members of senior generations alive long after the richer families had. It was they who almost inevitably became the formal lineage leaders. Poor, ill educated, and without influence, they were capable of going through the ancestral rituals as figureheads, but were not well suited to political leadership.

Those who wielded real power in the group were the wealthy, the strong, and the educated, particularly if they were civil-service-examination-degree holders in the imperial era. Often they carried no formal lineage titles, but they had the means to get their way. The ancestral trusts that were the economic basis of lineage power were almost always under their management.

The lineage was, of course, ultimately subject to state law, but it was self-governing so far as possible. The lineage head, the elders, and the real political leaders looked after matters of internal discipline, passing judgment and carrying out punishments on unruly members, thieves, adulterers, and other offenders, according to well-understood values. Some lineages actually wrote their rules down in their genealogy books, but it was hardly necessary. Fines, beatings, confiscation of property, expulsion from the lineage, even death were meted out to offenders. Knowing that the state legal apparatus was uncertain, harsh, and unconcerned with the greater good of the lineage, few would object.

SUBLINEAGES

All males descended in the male line from the founding ancestor were members of the lineage and shared equally in the benefits from its trust. But the lineage was not an undifferentiated whole. As it grew larger over the generations, it developed sublineages, to which individuals could relate more closely.

The primary division was the branch, and the branch heads spoke for their members on matters of concern to the whole lineage. But the branches might not reproduce at the same rate. In one example, a lineage had three branches, with the branch descended from the second brother turning out to be much more numerous than the other two. The result was that a minority was represented by two branch heads, while the majority only had one. At the level of ritual leadership, this was no problem, but in political terms it was unsatisfactory. Ingeniously, the lineage chose to focus on the next generation down for political representation, because, while the eldest and third brothers each had only one son, the second brother had two, thus splitting the numerically overweight branch into two and producing four groups of more or less equal size.

In addition to the lineage trust, other trusts focused on later ancestors could be set up. Each new trust had a membership consisting only of the men descended from the ancestor concerned, but the members were still full members of the main trust. In richer lines of descent, the living might belong to trusts focused on all or most of the ancestors of each generation linking them with the founding ancestor. Setting up these later trusts was considered good filial behavior.

The proliferation of ancestral trusts had the effect of gradually reducing the amount of land in individual-family ownership. Where lineages were in existence for many centuries, a large percentage of the land around their settlements (up to 90% in some reports) would be held in trust, and this had the effect of tying lineage members even more firmly to the group, since as beneficiaries and tenants they were increasingly dependent on the lineage for their livelihood.

EXTERNAL RELATIONS

Lineages controlled life within their settlements and territories, but they could not live isolated from the rest of society. They had to deal with the state in matters of taxation; with commercial interests for the sale of surplus produce and the purchase of those goods they could not produce themselves; with providers of specialist services, such as doctors and religious practitioners; and of course with other lineages.

The lineage was expansionist. If it reproduced strongly, it needed more land to support its people. Inevitably, it would push out its boundaries until it met those of other similarly expansionist lineages, and intense rivalry would result. Sometimes this would be expressed in conspicuous consumption, each rival trying to outspend the others at local festivals. Disputes over rights of access to water were common, as were grievances over discriminatory treatment in markets where one lineage had control.

Problems would often escalate into skirmishing, open warfare, and long-term feuds. The possibility of battle (*xiedou*) was ever present, and lineages maintained stores of armor and arms (even cannons). If a member was killed in battle, his tablet was given a place of honor on a special "hero altar" in the ancestor hall, and his family was compensated from trust funds. Wealthier lineages would wall and moat their villages, these defenses serving to counter the attacks of either hostile lineages or predatory bandit gangs.

The state deplored lineage battling, but in rural areas tended to turn a blind eye. Meanwhile, the lineages had their own way of limiting bloodshed. In most cases, fighting was brought to a halt by the intervention of local peacemakers, negotiations were conducted to compensate for any imbalance in casualty numbers, and the trouble would be over until the next outbreak.

Chinese law and custom prohibited the marriage of two people bearing the same surname, but a lineage settlement housed men and women who all bore the same name, so it was unavoidable when seeking a spouse that there should be dealings with other lineages. Arranging a marriage with someone from a lineage that was a feuding opponent was difficult and was sometimes forbidden by the elders. Instead, it seems that many lineages deliberately sought spouses from lineages that were not immediate neighbors, thus securing in-law allies against their long-term enemies.

THE CONTEMPORARY LINEAGE

In China after the Communist victory of 1949, there was a thorough land reform, which obliterated overnight the ancestral trust holdings. Subsequent attacks on organized religion and the commandeering of ancestor halls, plus the well-grounded fears of reprisals against those who observed "feudal" practices during the Cultural Revolution, all worked to destroy lineages.

Single surname settlements still exist, and there have been reports of the rebuilding of ancestor halls and of a resurgence of "clannism," but it is unlikely that the lineage will ever again be a significant force in China.

SEE ALSO *Family.*

BIBLIOGRAPHY

Baker, Hugh D. R. *A Chinese Lineage Village: Sheung Shui.* Stanford, CA: Stanford University Press, 1968.

Chen, Ta. *Emigrant Communities in South China.* London: Oxford University Press, 1939.

Freedman, Maurice. *Chinese Lineage and Society: Fukien and Kwangtung.* London: Athlone Press, 1966.

Hu, Hsien-chin. *The Common Descent Group in China and Its Functions.* New York: Viking Fund, 1948.

Liu, Hui-chen Wang. *The Traditional Chinese Clan Rules.* New York: J. J. Augustin, 1959.

Potter, Jack. *Capitalism and the Chinese Peasant: Social and Economic Change in a Hong Kong Village.* Berkeley: University of California Press, 1968.

Twitchett, Denis. The Fan Clan's Charitable Estate, 1050–1760. In *Confucianism in Action*, ed. David S. Nivison and Arthur F. Wright, 97–133. Stanford, CA: Stanford University Press, 1959.

Hugh D. R. Baker

LING SHUHUA

1904–1990

Ling Shuhua—a writer, painter, and essayist whose career spanned six decades—was born Ling Ruitang on March 25, 1904, into a wealthy Cantonese family in Beijing. Her father was Ling Fupeng, an eminent poet in the classical style and high-ranking official (having served at one time as mayor of Beijing late in the Qing dynasty). Shuhua was the daughter of the fourth of his six concubines. Consequently, she received an elite education in Chinese classics and painting. She also studied English with the famous yet eccentric scholar Gu Hongming (1857–1928), and painting with Mou Suyun, Wang Zhulin, and Hao Ran.

In 1922 Ling entered the Department of Foreign Languages at Yanjing University, where she majored in English and French and minored in Japanese. She also began to publish short stories and prose. In May 1924, during the visit of the Nobel laureate Rabindranath Tagore, she met Chen Yuan (also known as Chen Xiying), who was the chair of the English Department at Peking University and editor of *Xiandai pinglun* (Modern review). In January 1925 Ling published "Jiu hou" (Flushed with wine) in this journal. The story has a simple plot. A young couple entertains a good friend, who is overcome with wine and falls asleep. As the wife admires his face, even more handsome from the wine, she has the sudden urge to give him a peck on the mouth. Although her husband admonishes her that the love between husband and wife is different from the love between friends, he gives in to her plea. Now that she has his permission, however, she hesitates and cannot bring herself to do it. Upon its publication, the story's subject matter of female sexual desire and its exploration of psychological nuance won critical acclaim. The playwright Ding Xilin (1893–1974) turned it into a play.

Ling continued to write throughout the 1930s and was closely associated with the Xiandai pinglun group and the writers and poets of Xinyue she (Crescent moon society). Her first collection of stories, *Hua zhi si* (Temple of flowers), was published in 1928, her second collection, *Nüren* (Women), appeared in 1930, and her third, *Xiao ger lia* (Little brothers), stories about children, in 1935.

In 1926, after graduation from college, Ling married Chen Yuan. In 1928 the couple moved to Wuchang to teach at Wuhan University, where Chen was also the dean of humanities and chair of the Department of Foreign Languages. Besides teaching, Ling edited *Wuhan wenyi* (Wuhan literature and art). She also began to write autobiographical essays in English. These were published, under the title *Ancient Melodies*, in London in 1953. Illustrated with Ling's own paintings, the book became a best-seller. It was not translated into Chinese, however, until 1990, in Taiwan. The year 1960 saw the publication of a collection of her stories and of a collection of essays titled *Aishanlu mengying* (Dreams from a mountain lover's studio). Her last story appeared in 1984.

In 1946 Chen Yuan was appointed as China's representative to the United Nations Educational, Scientific, and Cultural Organization (UNESCO) in Paris. The family of three—including their daughter Xiaoying—first lived in Paris and then settled in London. During this time Ling became acquainted with the British poet laureate Vita Sackville-West (who wrote the introduction to her *Ancient Melodies*) and the French scholar André Maurois. She also studied Impressionist painting in Paris. Life in Europe was far from easy, however, on Chen's modest salary. Ling helped out by teaching and giving lectures. From 1956 to 1960 she taught at Nanyang University in Singapore. During the next two decades she gave many lectures on Chinese literature and art at universities in Britain and Canada. An accomplished painter in the literati tradition, Ling held many exhibitions in London, Paris, Boston, and Singapore. Her work and her collection of paintings from the Yuan, Ming, and Qing dynasties were shown in Paris in 1962 and again in London in 1968.

In 1970 Chen Yuan died of a stroke in London. Ling stayed in London, although she maintained contact with her friends in Beijing and paid several visits to China in the 1970s and 1980s. In late 1989, already ill, she returned to China and passed away in Beijing on May 22, 1990. Her ashes were buried with those of her husband's at his hometown Wuxi in Jiangsu Province.

Although not a prolific writer—in addition to the short stories and essays, she also wrote twelve one-act plays—Ling Shuhua remains one of the best-known women writers of twentieth-century China. She is often mentioned along with such other writers as Chen Hengzhe (1890–1976), Bingxin (1900–1999), Feng Yuanjun (1900–1974), and Su Xuelin (1899–1999), but her work is distinguished by subtle representations of psychology, especially women's psychology. For her nuanced depictions, Ling has been compared to Katherine Mansfield (1888–1923) by Shen Congwen (1902–1988) and Su Xuelin.

In 1935 Ling met the Bloomsbury, London, poet Julian Bell (1908–1937), who was teaching English at Wuhan University as a visiting lecturer, and had an affair with him. Through Bell, she corresponded with his aunt Virginia Woolf (1882–1941), who encouraged her to translate her stories into English. Ling and Bell collaborated on the translations. In 1937 Bell volunteered in the Spanish civil war as an ambulance driver on the Republican side and was killed in the Battle of Brunete. In 1999 the London-based Chinese writer Hong Ying (b. 1962) published the novel *K*, a fictionalized account of the affair. ("K" was the name Bell used to refer to his mystery lover in his letters to family and friends.) Ling's daughter Chen Xiaoying, who also lived in London, filed a lawsuit in Beijing against Hong Ying for defamation of her parents and asked for a ban on the book and monetary compensation. The highly publicized case ended in 2002 with a victory for Chen. Hong Ying then rewrote the novel, which came out in 2003, under the new title *The English Lover*.

BIBLIOGRAPHY

Dooling, Amy D., and Kristina M. Torgeson. *Writing Women in Modern China: An Anthology of Women's Literature from the Early Twentieth Century*. New York: Columbia University Press, 1998.

Laurence, Patricia. *Lily Briscoe's Chinese Eyes: Bloomsbury, Modernism, and China*. Columbia: University of South Carolina Press, 2003.

Michelle Yeh

LINGNAN SCHOOL OF PAINTING

Lingnan literally means the region south of the five mountain ranges that separate the Yangzi River valley from the Pearl River valley, and refers almost exclusively to Guangdong Province. The Lingnan school or *Lingnan pai* refers to an early twentieth-century art movement initiated by three traditionally-trained Cantonese painters, the brothers Gao Jianfu (1879–1951) and Gao Qifeng (1889–1933), and Chen Shuren (1883–1948). Natives of Panyu, Guangdong, all three were first schooled in the painting style of the flower-and-bird painter Ju Lian (1824–1904), a popular local artist famous for realistic renderings of his subjects with highly decorative effects. The Lingnan school's innovations stem from Gao Jianfu's proposal for a new national painting (*xin guohua*), a revolution in Chinese painting that would synthesize the best elements of Chinese, Western, and world art and popularize it among a broader, modern audience. This idea of making art relevant to contemporary society is historically significant in China. Gao Jianfu is credited with being the first to propose and attempt to carry out a revolution in art parallel to China's Republican revolution.

Given Gao Jianfu's ambition to reform Chinese painting on a national level, the regional label attached to the school seems contradictory. Chinese scholars have debated this contradiction extensively, with no settled conclusion. Western art historians commonly consider the two Gaos and Chen as the founders of the Lingnan school and their art as the representative style of Guangdong.

In truth, the term *Lingnan school* was neither proclaimed by the three founders nor used commonly during their lifetimes but rather applied by later art critics and historians, such as Jian Youwen (1896–1979). Jian had a strong interest in promoting his native Guangdong and its culture, which he deemed particularly revolutionary and receptive to new ideas. In present-day scholarship on modern Chinese art, the Lingnan school label is generally understood to refer to the historical phenomenon, beginning with Gao Jianfu's proposal of new national painting principles in the 1910s, the development of his synthetic style, and its subsequent perpetuation and dissemination by his Guangdong disciples in the second half of the twentieth century. In the 1920s traditional artists in Guangdong, collectively known as the old-style school (*jiu pai*), attacked the artists of the Lingnan school, which was then called the new-style school (*xin pai*), for their alleged plagiarism of *nihonga* or Japanese-style paintings. The *xin-jiu* debates peaked during 1926 and 1928 and ended with the new-style school's victory, as it gained wider recognition on the national art scene.

EARLY DEVELOPMENT

The early stage of the school's development is marked by the founders' close connection to the Guomindang (Nationalist Party) and their direct involvement in politics. While studying art in Japan, all three joined the Revolutionary Alliance (*Tongmenghui*), which later became the Nationalist Party, led by Sun Yat-sen (Sun Yixian) in the first decade of the twentieth century. They were strongly attracted to *nihonga*, new-style Japanese painting that combined scientific observation with romantic, decorative effects. The rise of *nihonga* was a response to the Meiji government's intense Westernization. The three Chinese painters saw *nihonga* as fit for the Chinese situation partly because it would allow them to adopt Western realism while retaining their native Chinese painting traditions.

Throughout his painting career, Gao Jianfu adhered closely to his new national painting principles; his subjects, which were unprecedented, include such contemporary events as Japanese military aggression and its aftermath. His paintings of wild, fierce-looking animals are imbued with nationalistic messages. Though mostly decorative, his

Flying in the Rain *by Gao Jianfu, 1932.* GAO JIANFU/FOTOE

still lifes and flower-and-bird paintings sometimes make allegorical references to contemporary politics. While the elder Gao sought to combine his training in traditional Chinese painting with his enthusiasm for *nihonga*, the younger Gao immersed himself more thoroughly in the Japanese style, which remained his focus until his premature death at the age of forty-four. Chen Shuren's art, by contrast, is relatively individualistic and apolitical. His paintings are more self-expressive, and his subjects are consciously Guangdong-related. For example, one of his favorite subjects is the kapok tree, native to Guangdong. Chen, unlike the Gao brothers, did not engage in art education and left no disciples.

GOLDEN AGE

Gao Jianfu's national ambition to revolutionize Chinese painting was coldly received in the 1910s and 1920s, a time in which the Chinese art world remained dominated by two polarized groups: traditional-style artists and proponents of Western art. Gao's proposal finally had some impact on the national art scene in 1935 and 1936, when he was given a solo exhibition and a number of group exhibitions, with his disciples, in Shanghai. He also accepted an invitation from Xu Beihong, director of the art department of Nationalists' Central University, to become a visiting professor. But the 1937 outbreak of the war of resistance against Japan curtailed any further immediate impact of the Lingnan school on China. The flight of many of Gao Jianfu's disciples to British Hong Kong, and Gao's eventual settlement in Portuguese Macau, took the Lingnan school to these colonial cities.

SECOND GENERATION

In 1923 and 1929, respectively, Gao Jianfu and Gao Qifeng, both avid art educators, started their own art schools in Guangzhou. Through these two schools, Spring Slumber Studio (*Chunshui huayuan*) and Heavenly Wind Pavilion (*Tianfeng lou*), their numerous students continued to make contributions to the development of modern Chinese art and spread the influence of the Lingnan school. All the Gaos' students were natives of Guangdong and received their initial art training in their home province; most returned to Guangdong to pursue their artistic careers upon the end of the war of resistance in 1945. Gao Jianfu's most recognized students, Guan Shanyue (1912–2000), Li Xiongcai (1910–2001), Fang Rending (1901–1975), and Yang Shanshen (1913–2004), shared their teacher's synthetic approach toward modernizing Chinese painting as well as his advocacy for making art relevant to the masses by depicting contemporary subjects. However, their talents, specializations, and styles differed. For example, Guan is known for his realistic painting related to socialist ideals; Li for his realist landscapes suffused with atmospheric qualities; Fang for his descriptive figure paintings; and Yang for his paintings of wildlife and domestic animals.

Zhao Shaoang (1905–1998), Gao Qifeng's most successful disciple, was especially skilled at flower-and-bird paintings, attaining the expressiveness of literati painting (*wenrenhua*) and popular appeal through his use of bold colors. In 1948 he emigrated to Hong Kong, where he established a private art school, Lingnan Huayuan (Lingnan Studio). His students emulated his style so closely that it became almost formulaic, resulting in a negative stereotype of the Lingnan style. Nevertheless, in the period of the Lingnan school's greatest influence, during the 1920s and 1930s, Lingnan artists, particularly Gao Jianfu, played a crucial role in shaping the course of modern Chinese painting.

SEE ALSO *Literati Painting (wenrenhua); Xu Beihong.*

BIBLIOGRAPHY

Chu, Christina. The Lingnan School and Its Followers: Radical Innovation in Southern China. In *A Century in Crisis: Modernity and Tradition in the Art of Twentieth-Century China*, ed. Julia F. Andrews and Kuiyi Shen, 64–79. New York: Guggenheim Museum, 1998.

Croizier, Ralph. *Art and Revolution in Modern China: The Lingnan (Cantonese) School of Painting, 1906–1951*. Berkeley: University of California Press, 1988.

Gao, Meiqing, ed. *Lingnan san Gao hua yi* [The art of the Gao brothers of the Lingnan school]. Hong Kong: Hsiang'gang Zhong Wen Da Xue Wen Wu Guan, 1995.

Ho, Eliza. From Xin guohua (New National Painting) to the Lingnan School: Transformation of the Representations of Gao Jianfu and His Art in Twentieth Century Chinese Art. Master's thesis, Ohio State University, 2003.

Huang, Dade. Guanyu Lingnanpai de diacha ziliao [Investigation of the Lingnan school]. *Meishu shilun* 1 (1995): 15–28.

Sullivan, Michael. *Art and Artists of Twentieth-Century China*. Berkeley: University of California Press, 1996.

Eliza Ho

LITERARY SOCIETIES

After the literary revolution of 1917, the genre of New Literature (*xin wenxue*) was rapidly popularized through the activities of groups of young literary intellectuals working together in literary societies (*wenxue shetuan*). The popularity of literary societies harks back to traditional literati practices, but it is also directly connected to the popularity of magazine publication in China during the Republican period (1911–1949). Magazine publishers were interested in supporting active groups of young writers who could fill the pages of marketable magazines, catering to the needs of a predominantly young readership consisting of secondary school pupils and university students.

As the era progressed, some literary societies became institutions in their own right and gained considerable cultural power. Virtually all of the leading writers of the period were involved with societies and their publications, and magazine publishing was the predominant mode of publication for all literature of the time. After 1949, the significance of literary societies dwindled as writers were organized into the Writers' Union under Communist rule. From the 1980s onward, the literary system has gradually become market-led, and although literary societies are once again active on campuses and online, they no longer play a major role in publishing and they no longer hold any significant cultural power. The four main societies of the Republican period are briefly characterized below.

THE LITERARY ASSOCIATION

The first major literary society of the modern period was a group founded in 1921 in Beijing under the Chinese name Wenxue Yanjiu Hui. This means "literary research association," but the group itself later adopted the English name Chinese Literary Association. The name indicated the founders' interest in the new concept of *wenxue* (meaning "literature" in the Western sense, that is, the combination of poetry, fiction, [spoken] drama, and essays), as well as their intention to adopt a somewhat scholarly approach ("research"). The twelve founder members were Beijing-based scholars and students, as well as one representative of the Commercial Press in Shanghai, the largest commercial publishing house of the time. Through this representative, Shen Yanbing (1896–1981, later to become known as the novelist Mao Dun), the association gained access to the pages of the journal *Xiaoshuo yuebao* (Short story magazine), which was one of the most successful and most widely distributed literary journals of the time.

Association members published writings that broadly represented nineteenth-century Western views of literature, especially realism. The association soon relocated to Shanghai to be closer to the big publishing houses and the "literary scene" (*wentan*) and gathered over one hundred members. Apart from literary creation and writing about literature, association members also especially engaged in translation; one of its most successful projects was the publication of a series of books with the Commercial Press that consisted largely of translations of European literary works.

The association ceased its public activities in Shanghai after 1925, but a number of its core members continued to form a strong network throughout the Republican period. Apart from the already-mentioned Shen Yanbing (Mao Dun), other core members were Zheng Zhenduo (1898–1958), Ye Shengtao (1894–1988), and, especially in the early years, the brothers Zhou Zuoren (1885–1967) and Lu Xun (Zhou Shuren, 1881–1936).

THE CREATION SOCIETY

Founded by Chinese students in Japan in 1922, the Creation Society (Chuangzao She) was to become in many ways the Literary Association's nemesis. The young founders of the Creation Society, especially the then up-and-coming literary celebrities Guo Moruo (1892–1978) and Yu Dafu (1896–1945), who would remain its most famous members, were not very interested in comprehensive, scholarly approaches to literature and instead heralded romantic notions of creativity and heroism. Soon after returning from Japan they took the literary scene in Shanghai by storm, founding a number of different periodicals that were presented as being in direct competition with the publications of the Literary Association. Throughout the first half of the 1920s, the two organizations were involved in very public debates about the nature of literature and, especially, the quality of translations published in their respective series.

The Creation Society remained in existence throughout the 1920s and was responsible for a number of innovations in publishing. Its journals pioneered left-to-right printing and modernist illustrations. Its membership structure became essentially a shareholders structure, which enabled it to launch its own publishing house, independent from the existing commercial publishers. Because of the involvement of some of its members with the Communist movement, its publishing house and clubhouse were closed on government orders in 1930.

THE CRESCENT MOON SOCIETY

Founded in 1923 by a group of Beijing intellectuals, including the already famous Hu Shi (1891–1962) and the rising poets Xu Zhimo (1897–1931) and Wen Yiduo (1899–1946), this society's main activity until 1926 was the organization of social gatherings and literary events on the Beijing scene. After 1926, however, when many of its members had moved to Shanghai, the nature of its activities changed to producing and selling books and journals, following the example of self-funded publishing set by the Creation Society. Their main publication, the journal *Xin yue* (Crescent moon), was a professional-looking and expensive journal, similar in nature to the Western notion of a "serious" literary magazine.

As leftist writers become more vocal during the late 1920s and 1930s, the Crescent Moon group gradually came to be seen (and presented itself) as the representative of a more elitist view of literature and culture, with strong Anglo-American influences. Its main members also included the essayist Liang Shiqiu (c. 1902–1987). Its activities ceased after the untimely death of its main activist and fund-raiser, Xu Zhimo, in 1931.

THE LEAGUE OF LEFT-WING WRITERS

The League of Left-Wing Writers (Zuoyi Zuojia Lianmeng) was established as an underground organization by the Communist Party in 1930, with Lu Xun (1881–1936) as its chairperson, but with Qu Qiubai (1899–1935) as its main ideologue and driving force. Under the auspices of the league and its various cells, a large number of journals were published and distributed through unofficial channels, though some of the debate about the relationships between literature and revolution spilled over into regular literary magazines, where it was condoned by censorship authorities in part because of the economic interests of publishers, who were aware of the fact that there was a market for leftist writing. League members took an interest in rectifying what they considered to be the overly Europeanized writing style of the 1920s, advocating a simpler written vernacular that lies at the basis of present-day written Chinese. They also experimented with politically inspired genres such as reportage (*baogao wenxue*).

The league's leadership was marred by conflicts between writers and party representatives, and most of its publications were not long-lived. The novel *Ziye* (Midnight) by Mao Dun is generally seen as its most successful product, although it was typically published completely legally by a commercial publisher. Its most successful journal was *Beidou* (Big dipper), edited by Ding Ling (1904–1986), which also appeared aboveground although it was eventually banned. The league disbanded in 1936 amid internal strife and conflict.

SEE ALSO *League of Left-Wing Writers; Literature since 1800.*

BIBLIOGRAPHY

Denton, Kirk A., and Michel Hockx, eds. *Literary Societies of Republican China*. Lanham, MD: Lexington, 2008.

Hockx, Michel. *Questions of Style: Literary Societies and Literary Journals in Modern China, 1911–1937*. Leiden, Netherlands: Brill, 2003.

Wong Wang-chi. *Politics and Literature in Shanghai: The Chinese League of Left-Wing Writers, 1930–1936*. Manchester, U.K., and New York: Manchester University Press, 1991.

Michel Hockx

LITERATI PAINTING (*WENRENHUA*)

Historically speaking, the development of literati painting (*wenrenhua*) represents certain distinguishing characteristics of Chinese visual culture and came to define not only an art grounded in substantial erudition and creativity, but also a noncommercial, self-expressive ideal. In the modern period its main aspects were embodied in what was defined as *guohua* (national-style painting). The concept of literati painting originated in Chinese elite culture. When the earlier term for it, official-scholar's painting (*shifuhua* or *shidafuhua*), was coined in the Northern Song period (960–1127), three major aspects of it were notable: it was executed by amateur artists with established social status; it required a certain artistic talent; and its understood purpose was primarily *xieyi* (idea-writing, or self-expression). It thus stood in contrast to the more functional art commissioned for temples and palaces, and, within the critical value system of premodern China, was considered a superior art. By convention, such painting was not practiced for material gain.

Ever since, and especially since the Yuan dynasty (1279–1368), this special type of painting has gradually come to constitute the mainstream of Chinese pictorial art. A succession of great literati painters not only have established their distinguished styles, but also have formulated certain theoretical paradigms of painting. Dong Qichang (1555–1636), who proposed the theory of the Southern and Northern schools (*nanbeizong*), asserted that the literati should follow only the spontaneous style that he preferred. Dong was a great individualist himself, but he also codified the artistic practice of commenting upon earlier masterpieces in his own work, producing what has been called "historical art." Under his influence *wenrenhua* took two directions during the Qing dynasty (1644–1912).

On the one hand, Dong's disciple Wang Shimin (1592–1680), along with Wang Jian (1598–1677), Wang Hui (1632–1717), and Wang Yuanqi (1642–1715), known as the Four Wangs (*siwang*), won the imperial patronage of the Kangxi emperor (1654–1722). The amateur-like style for the first time became the officially recognized canon. This orthodox school therefore gained cultural significance, and was continued, with sharply declining originality, by the "minor Four Wangs" (*xiao siwang*) and the "later Four Wangs" (*hou siwang*), among many others. A variety of painting manuals widely circulated in China, Korea, and Japan accelerated its popularity. The republication in 1818 of *Jieziyuan huapu* (Mustard-seed garden manual of painting), for example, served as a reference for those wanting to practice *wenrenhua*. Because most extant early paintings disappeared into the court collection of the Qianlong emperor (p. 1736–1795), literati painters had no access to these masterpieces, and had to rely on copies, prints, and even fakes to keep that tradition alive. These circumstances ultimately led to *guohua*'s decline, and its weakened state was openly criticized when Westernization became overwhelmingly pressing in early twentieth-century China. Before and during the May Fourth New Culture movement in 1919 the reformist Kang Youwei (1858–1927) and the communist Chen Duxiu (1879–1942) launched an attack on the Four Wangs and their followers. According to Kang, the canonized spontaneity of *nanzong* (the Southern school) painting was incapable of depicting the world faithfully and confidently as Italian Renaissance oil painting had done, and, to him, was a tragic deterioration of the realistic painting styles of the Tang and Song periods.

On the other hand, those literati who lived far from the Manchu court enjoyed showing their individual painting styles in the growing art markets in Huizhou, Yangzhou, and elsewhere. Ironically, they had to be, in one way or another, professional amateurs. A group of such professionals in eighteenth-century Yangzhou, the Yangzhou baguai (Eight Eccentrics of Yangzhou), established signature styles to please their merchant patrons while at the same time downplaying the mercantile aspect of their paintings. Their versatile talents in painting, poetry, calligraphy, and seal-engraving created a new canon known as the Four Perfections (*sijue*) within the Chinese visual tradition. Certainly marketable, this aesthetic epitomized the individualist aspect of *wenrenhua* and left an enduring cultural heritage to modern China.

After the first Opium War (1839–1842) Shanghai grew rapidly as a cosmopolitan city and replaced Yangzhou as a center for the arts. The urban dwellers there adopted a different style of consumption from that of the merchant class in eighteenth-century Yangzhou. In order to survive and thrive in Shanghai, the professional literati organized various guilds and associations. Compared to professional painters in the same city, literati artists showed greater strengths in poetry, calligraphy, and epigraphic studies (*jinshixue*). The epigraphic movement merged into the main scholarly trend of late imperial China, utilizing an archaeological approach to antiquarianism such as collecting the rubbings of stelae, ancient seals, and bronze vessels. Through this learning, professional literati transformed their brushwork into an even more powerful expressive vehicle. In this light, Wu Changshi (1844–1927), Huang Binhong (1865–1955), Qi Baishi (1864–1957), and Pan Tianshou (1897–1971), to name only a few, made significant contributions to the modern development of *guohua*, with an emphasis on vision, intelligence, individuality, and idea writing. It echoed the rise of modernist art, especially the emergence of German expressionism, which fervently advocated the visual deliverance of human emotion. Soon after the criticism of the Four Wangs, Chen Hengque (1876–1923) translated *Bunjinga no fukkō* (*The Revitalization of the Literati Painting*) by Ōmura Seigai (1868–1927). In addition, Chen's essay "The Value of Literati Painting" (1921) reevaluates some principles of *wenrenhua*. These writings were a triumph, bringing about a brief renaissance of *wenrenhua* in China, though it was slowed by the deaths of Chen, Jin Cheng (1878–1923), Wu Changshi, and Yao Hua (1876–1930), all major players in *guohua* circles. In his *Huafa yaozhi* (Essential painting techniques, 1934), Huang Binhong took a much broader view of the development of *guohua* by defining *wenren* status (which includes poets and epigraphists) as a prerequisite to becoming a *mingjia* (famous painter) and finally a *dajia* (great painter).

Since 1949 *wenrenhua* as a genre has undergone many shifts in a dramatically changing world. Linked by its origins and by its very name with the educated elite, it has been marginalized or attacked during periods of greatest emphasis on popular art. Within the system of fine arts education in mainland China, it has been categorized as *xieyihua*, or *yibihua* (spontaneous style painting), in contrast to *gongbihua* (meticulous style painting), emphasizing its expressive characteristics. For *wenrenhua*, this is at once a curse and a blessing. When idea writing came to be associated with potential political protest, particularly during the Cultural Revolution (1966–1969), *wenrenhua* was cursed as "black painting" (*heihua*). At the same time, artists such as Shi Lu (1919–1982) in Shanxi, Lü Shoukun (1919–1975) in Hong Kong, and Zhang Daqian (1899–1983) in Taibei continued to assert the fundamental ideas of *wenrenhua* whenever the ideas were relevant to their artistic experimentation. Most recently, in the late 1980s in Nanjing, it has reemerged as *xin wenrenhua* (new literati painting) in connection with an art more similar to the modern Japanese practice of *nihonga* than to the literati painting (known in Japanese as *bunjinga*) that informed Chen Hengque's 1921 essay, a fashion with less interest in idea writing but more emphasis on visual effect.

SEE ALSO *Art, Japanese Influence on; Calligraphy; Chen Duxiu; Chinese Painting (guohua); Epigraphic School of Art; Kang Youwei; Pan Tianshou; Shanghai School of Painting; Wu Changshi (Wu Junqing).*

BIBLIOGRAPHY

Andrews, Julia. *Painters and Politics in the People's Republic of China, 1949–1979*. Berkeley: University of California Press, 1994.

Andrews, Julia, and Kuiyi Shen, eds. *A Century in Crisis, Modernity and Tradition in the Art of Twentieth-Century China*. New York: Guggenheim Museum, 1998.

Bush, Susan. *The Chinese Literati on Painting: Su Shih (1037–1101) to Tung Ch'i-ch'ang (1555–1636)*. Cambridge, MA: Harvard University Press, 1971.

Cahill, James. *The Painter's Practice: How Artists Lived and Worked in Traditional China*. New York: Columbia University Press, 1994.

Chen Shizeng and Omura Seigai. *Zhongguo wen ren hua zhi yan jiu* [Studies in Chinese literati painting]. Shanghai: Zhonghua Shuju, 1922.

Duo yun bian ji bu. *Qing chu si wang hua pai yan jiu lun wen ji* [Theses on research of the Four Wangs' painting in the early Qing dynasty]. Shanghai: Shanghai Shuhua Chubanshe, 1993.

Hong Kong in Ink Moods: Landscape Paintings by Lui Shou-kwan. Hong Kong: Fung Ping Shan Museum, 1985.

Shen Fu and Jan Stuart. *Challenging the Past: The Paintings of Chang Dai-chien*. Washington, DC: Arthur M. Sackler Gallery; Seattle: University of Washington Press, 1991.

Shi Lu shu hua ji [Shi Lu's painting and calligraphy]. Beijing: Renmin Meishu Chubanshe, 1990.

Sullivan, Michael. *Art and Artists of Twentieth-Century China*. Berkeley: University of California Press, 1996.

Wong, Aida. A New Life for Literati Painting in the Early Twentieth Century: Eastern Art and Modernity, a Transcultural Narrative? *Artibus Asiae* 60, 2 (2000): 297–327.

Xin Lu et al. *Wu Changshi, Qi Baishi, Huang Binhong, Pan Tianshou si da jia yan jiu* [Four leading masters of literati painting in twentieth-century China]. Hangzhou, China: Zhejiang Meishu Chubanshe, 1992.

Yu Sun and Ke Sun. *Chinese New Literati Painting.* Sydney: Art Gallery of New South Wales, 1997.

Zaixin Hong

LITERATURE OF NATIONAL DEFENSE

Literature of national defense (*guofang wenxue*), also *defense literature*, is a term borrowed from the Soviet Union. The notion was introduced by the Chinese Communist Party (CCP) in the mid-1930s to replace *proletarian literature*, which was deemed no longer suitable for the new policy of a united front between the CCP and the Guomindang (GMD, or the Nationalist Party). The term was first advanced by Zhou Yang (1908–1989), secretary of the League of Left-wing Writers (zuoyi zuojia lianmeng, March 1930 to March 1936), in "Literature of National Defense" (under the penname Qi), in the *Dawanbao* (Grand evening express) on October 27, 1934. At the time, the essay did not receive much attention because the united front had not yet been formulated. By the end of the following year, however, the term became a slogan promulgated avidly by the league. A chorus of essays appeared, notably Zhou Libo's (1908–1979) "About 'Literature of National Defense,'" published in *Meizhou wenxue* (Weekly literature), the literary supplement to the *Shishi xinbao* (New current affairs daily), on December 21, 1935. Similar terms such as *drama of national defense, poetry of national defense,* and *music of national defense* also were coined. According to Zhou Yang, literature of national defense was to be the central theme of all literary works in a time of national crisis, except those written by "traitors." Furthermore, because theme and style were inseparable, such literature should be written in the realist mode.

The slogan did not win universal support, however. Xu Xing voiced dissent early on, criticizing the slogan as a "cesspool of patriotism." Lu Xun's (1881–1936) marked silence on the slogan displeased Zhou Yang, who interpreted it as a gesture of disapproval. In the meantime, Feng Xuefeng (1903–1976) had returned to Shanghai after the Long March to pass on to the league Mao Zedong's united-front policy concerning literary activities. In Feng's meetings with Lu Xun and Hu Feng (1903–1985), the three decided to oppose literature of national defense because the slogan neglected the issue of class. On June 1, 1936, Hu Feng published the essay "Renmin dazhong xiang wenxue yaoqiu shenme?" (What do the masses expect from literature?) in the *Wenxue congbao* (Literary gazette), in which he proposed a new slogan: "literature of the masses of the national revolutionary war" (minzu geming zhanzheng de dazhong wenxue). Zhou Yang interpreted this as a challenge to his authority and mounted a counter-attack, thus raising the curtain on what came to be known as the "Polemic of the Two Slogans" (liangge kouhao de lunzheng).

Lu Xun finally broke his silence. On August 1, 1936, Xu Maoyong (1911–1977), who was executive secretary of the league at the time, sent a letter to Lu in which he accused his former mentor of making a mistake in introducing a leftist slogan into the united front. He also decried Hu Feng and Huang Yuan (1905–2003), both Lu's students, as "deceitful" and "toady." In his open letter to Xu, Lu replied that he did not consider the two slogans irreconcilable, but thought that the new one was more precise, meaningful, and substantive. He also criticized the League of Left-wing Writers under Zhou Yang's leadership and dismissed the unfounded charge that Hu Feng was a mole for the GMD.

The polemic revealed the disagreement between different approaches to literature as well as ideological divide, personal conflict, and power struggle among leftist writers. There was long-standing tension between Zhou Yang and Hu Feng and Feng Xuefeng, both of whom were close to Lu Xun. During Feng's absence in Shanghai, Zhou had taken control of the League of Left-wing Writers and alienated Lu. Equally important to the dispute was that Lu and his followers harbored a deep distrust of the united-front policy based on past experience. A split was inevitable. In March 1936 the League of Left-wing Writers was dissolved without any consultation with Lu, who was a founding member and the nominal head of the organization. In June Zhou founded the Association of Chinese Literary Artists (wenyijia xiehui) to replace the league in leading the united front in the cultural arena; its manifesto was drafted by Mao Dun (1896–1981) and signed by 111 writers. Although Lu Xun, Ba Jin (1904–2005), Hu Feng, Huang Yuan, and others were invited, none joined the new organization. In fact, the Lu Xun group presented a manifesto of its own. Drafted by Ba Jin and Li Liewen (1904–1972), "Manifesto of Chinese Literature and Art Workers" (Zhongguo wenyi gongzuozhe xuanyan) was signed by 65 writers on July 1, 1936, calling all writers to form a united front to save China, regardless of their ideological positions. Neither of the polemical slogans was mentioned in these manifestos.

The Polemic of the Two Slogans began to peter out by early October 1936. Feng Xuefeng withdrew from the CCP, and Lu Xun died of tuberculosis on October 19. In the Xi'an Incident (December 12, 1936) Marshal Zhang Xueliang (1901–2001) took Chiang Kai-shek hostage to extort a promise from him to form a united front with the

CCP against Japanese aggression. Hu Feng left Shanghai, and Zhou Yang went to Yan'an in 1937. In Yan'an, Zhou won the trust of Mao Zedong and was in charge of education in CCP-controlled areas; ironically, he was appointed vice president of the Lu Xun Academy of Art (founded April 1938) in 1939.

In 1954 to 1955, when Zhou was a powerful cultural bureaucrat, he orchestrated national campaigns against Feng Xuefeng and Hu Feng; their careers were terminated and their voices silenced for decades. During the Cultural Revolution (1966–1969) Zhou and his followers, in turn, were purged; their position in the Polemic of the Two Slogans was labeled rightist and criticized for ignoring the leadership of the proletariat. These are but some of the grave consequences of the feud between supporters of the literature of national defense and the literature of the masses of the national revolutionary war in the 1930s.

SEE ALSO *Ba Jin; Guo Moruo; Hu Feng; Lin Yutang; Lu Xun; Mao Dun; Zhou Yang.*

BIBLIOGRAPHY

Hsia, Tsi-an. *The Gate of Darkness: Studies on the Leftist Literary Movement in China*. Seattle: University of Washington Press, 1968.

Wong, Wang-chi. *Politics and Literature in Shanghai: The Chinese League of Left-wing Writers, 1930–36*. Manchester, U.K.: Manchester University Press, 1991.

Michelle Yeh

LITERATURE SINCE 1800

Literature in nineteenth-century China was structured around genres that favored writing in the classical language (poetry, essays, historiography, philosophy, textual exegesis), and that relegated vernacular literature (fiction and some drama) and folk performance to a lower status. It is not that the literati did not write fiction, but that fiction lacked the cultural prestige of more exalted classical genres like poetry and prose. Poetry was generally written in forms codified in the Tang (618–907) and Song (960–1279) dynasties, and by many accounts, the poetry of the nineteenth century is inferior in quality to that of earlier times; it is often said to be derivative and lacking in freshness, though that judgment reflects modern prejudices. Prose was centered on different schools, the most well known being the Tongcheng and Wenxuan Schools, the former promoting the pure prose style of the Tang and Song masters and the latter a more ornate style associated with the literature of the Wei, Jin, and Northern and Southern dynasties (220–589). Both schools sought for prose the function of upholding cultural and ethical values and cementing society together—a pressing concern, especially in the late nineteenth century, when the Qing court was in decline.

Although it has received relatively little attention from scholars in comparison to the great novels of the Ming (1368–1644) and early Qing (1644–1912)—such novels as *Journey to the West* (*Xiyou ji*), *Dream of the Red Chamber* (*Honglou meng*), *The Scholars* (*Rulin waishi*)—and also the fiction of the twentieth century, fiction flourished in the nineteenth century and was dominated by such genres as romances, court cases, chivalric cycles, exposés, and scientific fantasies. As David Wang argues, these novels were not just faint shadows of their early-Qing predecessors; rather, they should be seen as embodying elements of an indigenous Chinese modernity, though they were later denounced as "traditional" by May Fourth intellectuals because they did not conform to the literary expectations of Western-style realism.

THE LATE QING (1895–1911)

Although David Wang has sought to excavate an indigenous literary modernity from deep within the nineteenth century, most scholars see modern Chinese literature as having origins in the late Qing period. Indeed, late Qing saw many dramatic changes in its intellectual and literary scenes. With Western and Japanese imperialist threats and Qing internal weakness, intellectuals began to turn their eyes beyond their own tradition for solutions to their nation's woes. They introduced the values of the modern West to Chinese readers through translation and journalistic writing, published by new commercial presses. Much of the rhetoric of modernity that is associated with the May Fourth movement—nationalism, individualism, enlightenment—was introduced and formulated by late Qing intellectuals such as Liang Qichao and Yan Fu.

In conjunction with these dramatic changes in the intellectual sphere, poetry went through a revolution that encouraged the use of new forms and the incorporation of colloquial registers of language. Its leading proponents were Liang Qichao and Huang Zunxian, who famously wrote, "My hand writes what my mouth says." Despite these breaks with the classical past, poetry writing was dominated by the Tongguang style, a Song style in the manner of Huang Tingjian, promoted by Chen Yan and Chen Sanli.

Fiction began to be taken more seriously as a weapon for social exposé and for, as Liang Qichao put it, the "renovation of the nation." The late Qing period saw the publication—in serial and book form—of thousands of novels, including many satiric responses to contemporary social and political issues, but also novels about sentiment, detective fiction, and science fiction. Literary historians often identify the following as the four great masters of late-Qing fiction: Wu Woyao (1866–1910), Li Boyuan (1867–1906), Liu E (1857–1909), and Zeng Pu (1872–1935).

Perhaps the most significant late-Qing transformation was the changing notion of what it meant to be a writer. For perhaps the first time in Chinese literary history, a class of professional writers emerged, especially after the 1905 abolition of the imperial civil-service examination, which for centuries had been the principal route for the literati to advance socially and economically. This transition from literatus to professional writer was a difficult one, but it opened up a literary space independent of the state. Even so, throughout the twentieth century this intellectual autonomy would periodically be challenged by states seeking loyalty among the educated class.

THE REPUBLICAN PERIOD (1912–1949)

The early years of the new republic saw the rise of popular love stories, many written in an accessible form of the classical language. These appealed to urban readers in the uneasy political and cultural climate after the collapse of the Qing dynasty and the failure of democratic reforms. May Fourth intellectuals later scorned these love stories, along with other forms of popular fiction, for their lack of depth and their unconcern for social problems, mocking them as "mandarin ducks and butterflies fiction" (*yuanyang hudie xiaoshuo*), after the hackneyed Chinese symbols of love. Despite May Fourth efforts to eliminate it from the literary field, butterfly fiction continued to be popular among urban readers throughout the Republican era. These stories, not just a form of escape, offered readers a safe forum in which to negotiate the tensions between tradition and modernity that they felt in their lives.

In China, modern Chinese literature has conventionally been seen as the product of the larger May Fourth and New Culture movements. The New Culture Movement arose around 1915 and promoted a radical form of iconoclasm that targeted China's vaunted Confucian tradition, which the young, often Western-educated intellectuals saw as a hindrance to modernity. It then dovetailed with the political May Fourth movement, a protest movement against Western imperialism that exploded in 1919, first in Beijing and then in other urban centers around the country. One of the aims of the New Culture program was to bring an end to the hegemony of the classical language, which its participants saw as a vehicle for the propagation of Confucian ideology. In its place, polemicists such as Hu Shi and Chen Duxiu promoted the vernacular, a language that drew from the premodern vernacular, but would also incorporate elements of the syntax, rhetorical styles, and vocabulary of European languages and Japanese. This new vernacular would be the foundation of a truly modern literature.

Lu Xun is almost universally acknowledged as the first literary practitioner of this new vernacular, but his stories were actually preceded by experiments in vernacular poetry and short fiction by the woman writer Chen Hengzhe. However, no writer in the first half of the twentieth century matches Lu Xun in terms of the moral depth and formal innovation of his short fiction. "Kuangren riji" (1918; "Diary of a Madman") and "Yao" (1919; "Medicine"), for example, denounced tradition as cannibalistic, but at the same time they problematized the discourse of enlightenment and revolution used to attack that tradition. Like much of modern Chinese literature, Lu Xun's fiction is socially engaged, but it never succumbs simplistically to the demands of any political ideology.

The New Culture era (1915–1925) was generally a pluralistic period in which a variety of literary styles and literary ideologies competed. While the fiction of Lu Xun and Ye Shengtao is generally tagged as "realist," other writers such as Yu Dafu wrote in a more romantic mode emphasizing self-expression. Women writers, who emerged on a large scale at this time, were generally more concerned with female subjectivity than with topics of national concern. Representative here is Ding Ling's story "Shafei nüshi de riji" (1928; "The Diary of Miss Sophie").

The literary field in the late 1920s and early 1930s veered to the political left, with some critics going so far as to promote the idea that the writer should be a "gramophone" for the revolution. Having suffered defeats in the political and military realm, the Communist Party turned to culture as a vehicle for its revolutionary agenda. In 1930 it established the League of Left-Wing Writers as an umbrella cultural organization for writers on the left. The league sought to foster "revolutionary literature" and to encourage writers to embrace a Marxist worldview. Building on a utilitarian tendency in some May Fourth writing, leftists such as Mao Dun (1896–1981), a leading novelist, and Cao Yu (1910–1966), a dramatist, used their works for a specific political program, though it must be said that their works are complex and multifaceted and often exceed these political intentions.

The league was unable to impose its policies on the entire literary field. Many writers either ignored this politicization of literature or consciously rejected it. The New Sensationists (Xin Ganjue Pai), a group of Shanghai-based writers influenced by Western and Japanese modernism, for instance, rejected political literature in favor of explorations of the unconscious or experimentations in narrative form. Shen Congwen and Fei Ming wrote lyrical, almost nostalgic, fiction about the countryside, in sharp contrast to Lu Xun's depiction of rural China as stultifyingly oppressive or the leftist glorification of the noble peasant. A group of symbolist poets, including Dai Wangshu and Li Jinfa, generally shunned politics in their work. Essayists like Lin Yutang and Zhou Zuoren, writing in a genre called "little prose pieces" (*xiaopin wen*), which carried on the late-imperial literati tradition of a literature of leisure, preferred

Novelist Ba Jin, Shanghai, China. *In China's Republican period, prose attained a new level of importance in Chinese literature, with novelists such as Ba Jin writing in vernacular to reach a wider audience. Literary critics suggest modern Chinese literature first developed during this time, as artists influenced by the May Fourth movement rejected traditional Confucian themes and explored Western ideas for inspiration.*

humor, observations of everyday life, and personal matters to the grand political and cultural themes of the day. Still others, such as the female poet Lü Bicheng, bucked the vernacular tide altogether and wrote poetry in classical forms. Only very recently have scholars treated this kind of classical poetry as part of "modern" Chinese literature.

From its base in Yan'an during World War II, the Communist Party inherited and developed the literary platform of the League of Left-Wing Writers and promoted "national defense literature" (*guofang wenxue*). In 1942, partly in response to some writers who sought to uphold in Yan'an the Lu Xun–inspired spirit of critical realism, Mao Zedong gave a series of lectures to cultural workers in which he laid out a role for literature that was clearly subservient to politics and the Communist Party. Published as "Zai Yan'an wenyi zuotanhui shang de jianghua" ("Talks at the Yan'an Forum on Art and Literature"), these lectures became the canonical source of the party's official cultural policy after 1949. In areas under Nationalist control, however, writers continued to carry on the realist tradition (e.g., Sha Ding) or romantic tradition (e.g., Lu Ling) of the May Fourth movement. In areas under Japanese occupation, writers such as Zhang Ailing (Eileen Chang) balked at national defense literature and insisted in their works on the small concerns of everyday life and on turbulent relationships between men and women.

THE PEOPLE'S REPUBLIC (1949–PRESENT)

After coming to power in 1949, the Communist Party sought systematically to break down May Fourth notions of intellectual autonomy. It nationalized the publishing industry, centralized the book-distribution network, brought writers under institutional control through the Writers Union (Zuojia Xiehui), and implemented strict censorship. European and American literary influences waned dramatically, to be replaced by Soviet models. Socialist realism, which painted the new socialist society in a glowing light, dominated the literary scene. Popular were revolutionary history novels that glorified the Communist-led movement to liberate the

Chinese people from the shackles of feudalism and imperialism. Many novels, such as Yang Mo's *Qingchun zhi ge* (1958; *Song of Youth*), depicted the gradual ideological transformation of their protagonists from bourgeois individualists to committed Communist fighters willing to sacrifice themselves for the larger collective good.

During periods of relative liberalization, such as the short-lived Hundred Flowers movement (Baihua Yundong, 1956–1957), writers were emboldened to draw attention to social problems and criticize party policy. More often than not, though, they paid a heavy price. Literary theorist Hu Feng, who since the 1930s had been promoting subjectivism as a crucial ingredient in the creative process, was purged in a 1955 national campaign because his views seemed to threaten the hegemony of official party cultural policy.

Although subsequently portrayed as a cultural wasteland, the decade of the Cultural Revolution (1966–1976) had a thriving mass culture, which included "model theater" (*yangban xi*), posters, music, film, and fiction. These cultural forms, later often reviled as empty propaganda, had a profound influence on a generation of young people. Most exemplary of Cultural Revolution culture is *Bai mao nü* (*White-Haired Girl*), a ballet about a servant girl who flees the cruel oppression of an evil landlord for a cave in the mountains. The revolutionary army eventually liberates her from her dark and inhuman existence, restoring her from her ghostly life to humanity. Even as the effects of the Cultural Revolution dragged on into the 1970s, an antiofficial literature, especially poetry, circulated underground. With the recantation of the Cultural Revolution in the late 1970s, these underground poets would surface to become leaders in a startling literary revival.

With the death of Mao in 1976 and cultural liberalization in the late 1970s and early 1980s, the literary scene saw an unparalleled literary renaissance comparable to that of the May Fourth period. In the wake of the oppressive Cultural Revolution, literature spoke to a vast readership in new ways. Literature of the wounded (*shanghen wenxue*), which recounts the trauma inflicted on young people by the horrors of the Cultural Revolution, was immensely popular, as were the reportage writings of Liu Binyan (1925–2005), who exposed corruption within the party. Also widely read was obscure poetry (*menglong shi*), which presented a personal, lyrical style radically at odds with the epic, narrative poetry of the Mao era.

Over the course of the 1980s, Chinese literature became increasingly experimental and innovative. From the modernism of Wang Meng and Gao Xingjian to the root-searching literature of A Cheng and Mo Yan to the avant-gardism of Yu Hua, Ge Fei, and Su Tong, writers searched for new forms to capture a rapidly changing society. In the wake of the violent crackdown on the 1989 Tiananmen Prodemocracy Movement and the party's intensification of market reforms, this experimental spirit faded. In its place emerged a thriving commercial literature of entertainment, which, for some, marked the end of the literature of social relevance that dominated in the 1980s. Even some of the avant-garde writers of the 1980s, for example, Yu Hua with his novel *Xiongdi* (*Brothers*, 2005), were now said to have caved into the demands of commercial publishing. The pivotal figure in this transition to commercial literature is Wang Shuo, whose works of hooligan literature (*liumang wenxue* or *pizi wenxue*) were best sellers in the new book market.

Some poets reacted against this commercial culture by exalting poetry as a realm of pure aesthetics, while others tried to make poetry more accessible. Some fiction writers turned their attention to the social problems resulting from the market reforms: economic inequalities, the floating population (*liudong renkou*), pollution, globalization. Realism as a mode of social critique has made a comeback since the 1990s, with writers such as Chi Li, Fang Fang, and He Dun turning critical attention to urban social problems. Young dramatists have experimented with avant-garde forms even as they seek to make their plays relevant to the people experiencing these social problems. A group of young women writers—most notably, Wei Hui and Mian Mian—have focused on female subjectivity and sexuality in their controversial, sometimes banned, novels. While he does not write in the realist mode, the novelist Yan Lianke tackles difficult social issues, such as the HIV-AIDS problem, in his controversial *Dingzhuang meng* (Dreams of Ding Village).

Although it has not gained much attention from scholars in the West, the prose essay—ranging from the acerbically political to the lightly humorous—has been extremely popular among Chinese readers, in part because there is a long tradition of miscellaneous essay writing (*sanwen*) dating back at least to the Ming dynasty.

TAIWAN, HONG KONG, AND THE DIASPORA

Chinese-language literature has, of course, also flourished in Hong Kong, Taiwan, and the diaspora Chinese communities throughout the world, especially in Southeast Asia. Whereas mainland writers grappled with ways of expressing themselves through the strictures of censorship and the omnipresence of politics, Chinese writers in these other Chinese communities tended to pursue in their works questions of identity: What does it mean to be Chinese in colonial and postcolonial Hong Kong, or in Taiwan, successively occupied by the Dutch, the Japanese, and the Nationalists? Is there a specifically Taiwanese or Hong Kong identity separable from notions of Chinese identity? What does it mean to be a Chinese living in Malaysia?

Modern Taiwan literature developed under conditions very different from those on the mainland. Under Japanese colonial rule from 1895 to 1945, writers in Taiwan, though influenced by the new vernacular literature on the mainland, clung longer to writing in the classical language. During the War of Resistance against Japan (1937–1945), the Japanese imposed bans on writing in Chinese, and writers, many of whom had been educated in Japanese in Taiwan and Japan, wrote primarily in Japanese. This *kōminka* literature (literature written by Chinese in Japanese) has conventionally been scorned as collaborationist, but in recent years scholars have revisited this body of texts as an important part of the history of Taiwanese literature. With retrocession of Taiwan and Nationalist control in 1945 came the imposition of strict censorship against writing with even a modicum of leftist sensitivity. Writers in Taiwan were effectively cut off from the May Fourth tradition of socially engaged literature and generally sought models in Anglo-American modernism. If anticommunist novels dominated the 1950s, the 1960s saw the spread of Western-influenced modernist works in the hands of such writers as Bai Xianyong, Wang Wenxing, and Chen Ruoxi. In the 1970s and 1980s, there occurred a nativist Taiwanese reaction to this very foreign-sounding literature. Writers such as Huang Chunming, Wang Zhenhe, and Chen Yingzhen turned their attentions, mostly in realist styles, to Taiwan, its local culture, and its social problems.

After the end of martial law in 1987, writers, freed from Nationalist censorship, began to explore the colonial and Nationalist pasts and contemplated what it means to be Taiwanese in a nation unrecognized by most of the world's other nations and threatened by the constant possibility of mainland military aggression. Prominent among these writers are the sisters Zhu Tianwen and Zhu Tianxin.

An explicitly modern literature was slower to develop in Hong Kong, where writers identifying with tradition and writing in traditional forms dominated, perhaps as a reaction to British colonial rule. The development of a modern literature, it is often said, was sparked by the influx of cultural refugees from the mainland (especially during the War of Resistance against Japan, in the 1950s, and in the wake of the Tiananmen Prodemocracy Movement of 1989), but this is a Sinocentric view of Hong Kong literature. What really provoked the development of a literature concerned specifically with Hong Kong was the looming retrocession of Hong Kong to mainland control in 1997. From the 1980s, writers like Xi Xi, Dong Qizhang (Dung Kai Cheung), and Liang Bingjun (Leung Ping-kwan) wrote novels, essays, and poetry about what it means to live in the multicultural environment of Hong Kong. As Ackbar Abbas has argued, the culture of Hong Kong is "posited on the imminence of its disappearance."

Chinese writers in exile, such as the 2000 Nobel Laureate Gao Xingjian, have also used literature as a means for self-understanding, avoiding essentialized and nation-centered views of what it means to be Chinese. In recent years, scholars have started to reconceptualize modern Chinese literature in such terms as "Sinophone literature," which deemphasizes its relation to a particular nation-state and recognizes the complex cultural interactions among Asian nations that have a modern literature written in Chinese.

SEE ALSO *Avant-garde Fiction; Bingxin; Cao Yu; Chang, Eileen (Zhang Ailing); Ding Ling; Gao Xingjian; Hu Feng; Jia Pingwa; League of Left-Wing Writers; Liang Qichao; Lin Yutang; Literature of National Defense; Lu Xun; Mandarin Duck and Butterfly Literature; Mao Dun; Mo Yan; Plays (huaju); Poetry; Root-Searching Literature; Scar (Wound) Literature; Shen Congwen; Translation of Foreign Literatures; Wang Anyi; Women in the Visual Arts; Yan Fu; Yu Hua; Zhou Yang.*

BIBLIOGRAPHY

Abbas, Ackbar. *Hong Kong: Culture and the Politics of Disappearance.* Minneapolis: University of Minnesota Press, 1997.

Anderson, Marston. *The Limits of Realism: Chinese Fiction in the Revolutionary Period.* Berkeley: University of California Press, 1990.

Chang, Sung-cheng Yvonne. *Modernism and the Nativist Resistance: Contemporary Fiction from Taiwan.* Durham, NC: Duke University Press, 1993.

Chang, Sung-cheng Yvonne. *Literary Culture in Taiwan: From Martial Law to Market Law.* New York: Columbia University Press, 2004.

Chen, Xiaomei. *Acting the Right Part: Political Theater and Popular Drama in Contemporary China, 1966–1996.* Honolulu: University of Hawai'i Press, 2002.

Chi, Pang-yuan, and David Der-wei Wang, eds. *Chinese Literature in the Second Half of a Modern Century: A Critical Survey.* Bloomington: Indiana University Press, 2000.

Denton, Kirk A., ed. *Modern Chinese Literary Thought: Writings on Literature, 1893–1945.* Stanford, CA: Stanford University Press, 1996.

Dolezelova-Velingerova, Milena, ed. *The Chinese Novel at the Turn of the Century.* Toronto: University of Toronto Press, 1980.

Gunn, Edward. *Style and Innovation in Twentieth-Century Chinese Prose.* Stanford, CA: Stanford University Press, 1991.

Hanan, Patrick. *Chinese Fiction of the Nineteenth and Early Twentieth Centuries.* New York: Columbia University Press, 2004.

Hong Zicheng. *A History of Contemporary Chinese Literature.* Trans. Michael Day. Leiden, Netherlands: Brill, 2007.

Hsia, C. T. *A History of Modern Chinese Fiction.* 3rd ed. Bloomington: Indiana University Press, 1999.

Huters, Theodore. *Bringing the World Home: Appropriating the West in Late Qing and Early Republican China.* Honolulu: University of Hawai'i Press, 2005.

Kong, Shuyu. *Consuming Literature: Best Sellers and the Commercialization of Literary Production in Contemporary China.* Stanford, CA: Stanford University Press, 2004.

Kowallis, John. *The Subtle Revolution: Poets of the "Old Schools" during Late Qing and Early Republican China.* Berkeley: Center for Chinese Studies, University of California, 2006.

Laughlin, Charles. *The Literature of Leisure and Chinese Modernity.* Honolulu: University of Hawai'i Press, 2008.

Lee, Leo Ou-fan. *The Romantic Generation of Modern Chinese Writers.* Cambridge, MA: Harvard University Press, 1973.

Lee, Leo Ou-fan. *Voices from the Iron House: A Study of Lu Xun.* Bloomington: Indiana University Press, 1987.

Lee, Leo Ou-fan. *Shanghai Modern: The Flowering of a New Urban Culture in China, 1930–1945.* Cambridge, MA: Harvard University Press, 1999.

Link, E. Perry. *Mandarin Ducks and Butterflies: Popular Fiction in Early Twentieth Century Chinese Cities.* Berkeley: University of California Press, 1981.

Link, E. Perry. *The Uses of Literature: Life in the Socialist Chinese Literary System.* Princeton, NJ: Princeton University Press, 2000.

Liu, Lydia. *Translingual Practice: Literature, National Culture, and Translated Modernity, 1900–1937.* Stanford, CA: Stanford University Press, 1995.

McDougall, Bonnie S., and Kam Louie. *The Literature of China in the Twentieth Century.* London: Hurst and Co., 1997.

Mostow, Joshua, ed. *The Columbia Companion to Modern East Asian Literature.* New York: Columbia University Press, 2003.

Tang, Xiaobing. On the Concept of Taiwan Literature. *Modern China* 25, no. 4 (October 1999): 379–422.

Tay, William. Colonialism, the Cold War Era, and Marginal Space: The Existential Condition of Four Decades of Hong Kong Literature. In *Contemporary Chinese Literature: Crossing the Boundaries*, ed. Sung-sheng Yvonne Chang and Michelle Yeh, 141–147. Austin, TX: Literature East and West, 1995.

Wang, David Der-wei. *Fin-de-siècle Splendor: Repressed Modernities of Late Qing Fiction, 1849–1911.* Stanford, CA: Stanford University Press, 1997.

Wang, David Der-wei, and Carlos Rojas, eds. *Writing Taiwan: A New Literary History.* Durham, NC: Duke University Press, 2006.

Wu, Shengqing. "Old Learning" and the Refeminization of Modern Space in the Lyric Poetry of Lü Bicheng. *Modern Chinese Literature and Culture* 16, 2 (Fall 2004): 1–75.

Kirk A. Denton

LITHOGRAPHIC AND MODERN PRINTING

China has had a national book-reading public for centuries. Yet in the twenty-first century, the means by which books, newspapers, journals, and magazines reach a nationwide audience of hundreds of millions are those of a modern industrialized publishing industry. Its roots lie in the late Qing (1644–1912) and Republican (1912–1949) eras, but its greatest development has been achieved during the People's Republic of China (1949–present). From 1807 modern Western-style printing gradually (but not completely) replaced Chinese traditional woodblock printing by layering a new Western- and Japanese-inspired print culture onto China's millennium-old indigenous print world. It introduced new printing and publishing occupations to China and produced an important, but often neglected, technological backdrop to the upheavals from 1912 to 1949.

As with modern Western imprints, modern Chinese printing was made up of relief, planographic, and intaglio inked surfaces. The history of modern Chinese printing can be roughly divided into two overlapping periods, characterized by dominant technologies: the period of relief printing and letterpress (1807–1980s) and the period of lithography (1876–1905). In China, as in the West, over the course of the nineteenth and twentieth centuries, presses were increasingly powered by mechanical and industrial means. Since 1949 China has once again become one of the world's preeminent publishing countries, thanks to ongoing Chinese adaptation and dispersion of global printing technologies, most recently, digital ones.

The traditional Chinese printing and publishing industry was based on an inexpensive indigenous woodblock technology (xylography) dating from the seventh century. It was widely dispersed across the Chinese empire and had created a national print culture many centuries old by the time Western techniques loosely associated with Gutenberg's name began to arrive in the early 1800s. At that time, the Western system of printing technology was itself being transformed by the industrial revolution of the late eighteenth and nineteenth centuries. The new technology was introduced to China from Britain, America, and, to a lesser extent, France, Germany, and eventually Japan, via Macau, Guangzhou (Canton), Hong Kong, Ningbo, and then Shanghai. From 1807 to 1876 Protestant and Roman Catholic missionaries and their Chinese converts engaged in mechanical printing on China's southeastern coast, with Protestants typically favoring relief processes and Catholics preferring lithographic ones. In 1860 the Presbyterian printer William Gamble (1830–1886) adapted stereotyping to the Chinese language at Ningbo and then Shanghai, accelerating the creation of Chinese-language printing. Missionary efforts were supplemented by foreign newspaper publishers, led by the Shanghai-based *Huabei jiebao* (*North China Herald*, founded in 1850) and *Shenbao* (Shanghai journal, 1872). During these decades, however, expensive and technically demanding foreign mechanical-printing technology advanced relatively little against native technology.

From the 1870s Chinese, notably in Shanghai, began to acknowledge the advantages of modern industrial manufacturing, particularly for the honored cultural work of publishing. This work was motivated in part by the need to replace the books and libraries that had been destroyed during the Christian-inspired, anti-Confucian, and anti-Manchu Taiping Rebellion (1851–1864). Missionary printers became less significant in the transfer of printing technology to China and were replaced by Chinese investors pursuing their own logic of selection, adaptation, and invention.

The development of Shanghai's modern multivalent publishing enterprises from the 1880s to the very early Republican period can be traced to the reformist Chinese gentry and the contradictory influences that the imperial ethic of service and modern demand for adequate compensation for intellectual labor had on them. High start-up costs promoted an awareness of textual property, symbolized intellectually by the copyright and organizationally by the industrial trade association. Despite the high failure rate of early Chinese printing and publishing operations, this phase laid the groundwork for the industrial, commercial, and cultural bonanza that followed.

The conservative motivations of traditional Chinese publishers and booksellers were reflected in the golden age of Shanghai's lithographic industry (1876–1905). Lithography, not letterpress printing (i.e., printing with movable lead type), was the industry that brought about the transition from craft-based woodblock printing to mechanization. China's traditional publishing culture clearly influenced its modern technological choices in this important era. Despite their editorial conservatism, lithographers simultaneously raised treaty port Shanghai's intellectual profile and brought about new commercial forms and social categories of publications. They set the stage for the comprehensive lead-type printing and publishing industry that superseded lithography after the First Sino-Japanese War (1894–1895).

Established in 1897 by four upstart graduates of a Presbyterian missionary school, Shanghai's Shangwu Yinshuguan (Commercial Press) became preeminently important for promoting new printing machinery in China, both foreign and indigenous. Already by that time, numerous Shanghai-based Chinese-owned printing and publishing firms had replaced the missionary printers. Over the next decade or so, Chinese began to design and manufacture their own fonts and printing presses, and could thus provide domestic and overseas printers and publishers with an alternative to many lines of foreign-manufactured machinery. In time the success of Shanghai's machine makers contributed to the spread of China's Gutenberg revolution well beyond the confines of treaty port Shanghai, but not before the Chinese had gained a sense that they had sinicized this modern Western invention, which was itself rooted in the technology of medieval China. Almost simultaneously, the brutality of the trade in printing machines created conditions that radicalized its workers and those in the printing trade generally. As a result, large numbers of Shanghai printers gravitated toward the Communist Party after its establishment in 1921.

Owing to the centralization of print capitalism and modern printing technology in Shanghai, its Chinese-owned printing and publishing industry became the preeminent supplier of mass-produced books, newspapers, magazines, and visual images to Republican China's reading public. Pre-1937 Shanghai print capitalists set national agendas in educational and intellectual life, strongly influencing their own social environment and China's future in ways that traditional publishers could not have imagined. By 1931 the Commercial Press was the largest publisher in East Asia, and Shanghai's International Concession was home to Wenhuajie (Republican Shanghai's district for the publishing and selling of books, newspapers, and journals). Here leading printer-publishers—including the Big Three, the Commercial Press, Zhonghua Shuju (Zhonghua Book Co.), and Shijie Shuju (World Books), along with dozens of smaller firms—marketed their publications. Still, despite extraordinary efforts by its market-driven printer-publishers, China's printing and publishing lagged behind those of most major industrialized countries in absolute numbers of titles and imprints.

During its military assault on Shanghai in 1932, Japan deliberately destroyed the Commercial Press's printing plant and editorial library, then the largest in East Asia. Japan's invasion of the mainland from 1937 to 1945 and its occupation of Shanghai from 1941 to 1945 also proved disastrous to Shanghai's central position in modern Chinese publishing. After the People's Republic of China was established in 1949, Beijing was designated as the new printing and publishing capital of China, and Shanghai's physical plant was broken up and redistributed around the country in an attempt to advance modern printing in the inland provinces. The role played by market-driven entrepreneurs in advancing China's Gutenberg revolution was now taken over by the Communist Party, which guided the industry through its industrialization and cultural policies. Thus, in one of world history's most striking ironies, missionary printing technology, rather than missionaries' published religious messages, turned out to have the more lasting influence on China by contributing not to the creation of the nineteenth-century Christian kingdom of which missionaries dreamed, but to the twentieth-century People's Republic of China.

SEE ALSO *Publishing Industry; Woodblock Printing (xylography).*

BIBLIOGRAPHY

Reed, Christopher A. *Gutenberg in Shanghai: Chinese Print Capitalism, 1876–1937.* Vancouver: UBC; Honolulu: University of Hawaii Press, 2004.

Christopher A. Reed

LITTLE, ALICIA
1845–1926

Writer, traveler, and reform activist Alicia Little (née Bewicke), the daughter of Calverley Bewicke of Hallaton Hall, Leicestershire, England, was born in Madeira, and spent her young womanhood in London as a writer of novels. Beginning in 1868, she published nine novels under the name of A. E. N. Bewicke. In her works, she was critical of the social constraints imposed on women's lives and possibilities. In her most autobiographical novel, *Miss Standish* (1883), the heroine is highly interested in women's issues of the day; she supports women's suffrage, the right of married women to own property, and women's general participation in the "real world" beyond the narrow domestic role socially arranged for them.

In 1886 Alicia married Archibald John Little (1838–1908), a British merchant who had lived in China since 1859. In 1887 she went with her husband to Yichang (Ichang) and later to Chongqing, both of which were river ports in western China, where Archibald's business was based. While admiring many aspects of Chinese culture, Alicia Little was deeply upset by the custom of footbinding, which crippled Chinese girls and women. She devoted herself to uprooting this "evil practice" after living among the Chinese for several years. In April 1895, she gathered more than twenty women from various Western countries—most of whom were wives of diplomats, merchants, missionary-scholars, and other foreign-power elites in the Shanghai settlement—and founded the Natural Foot Society (Tianzu Hui), condemning footbinding as a cruel and injurious practice and calling for funds and friends to aid in creating a public sentiment against the practice.

Although the establishment of the society and its activities owed much to the help of missionaries, Alicia Little believed that the anti-footbinding movement should not become aligned with any one mission or with the evangelical movement. As a foreign resident in western China, where hostility toward Christians was widespread, she realized that if mission influence was prominent, natural-footed women might subsequently become the focus of antiforeign and anti-Christian violence. Besides, the missions were mainly associated with the poor and the humble, while the practice of footbinding was more popular among families of higher classes. Thus, Alicia Little made great efforts to secularize the anti-footbinding activities and to expand the scope of influence to non-Christian Chinese. What she pursued was a change from above rather than from below. The strategies she adopted included petitioning the court to legally prohibit the custom and looking for support from influential provincial governors.

Focusing on a political solution, the Natural Foot Society was not different from the Anti-footbinding Society (Bu Chanzu Hui) organized by indigenous reformers in 1897, also in Shanghai. Although these two anti-footbinding societies remained separate, there were clues about their interaction. Soon after the Anti-footbinding Society was organized, members of the Natural Foot Society wrote a letter to the reformer-run magazine *Shiwu Bao* [The Chinese progress] to celebrate this event. In 1897, when the reformers wanted to establish a girls' school, they invited these Western women to join a meeting with their female relatives who were going to be teachers and staff of the school.

At the turn of the century, the Natural Foot Society was the only active anti-footbinding group in China; indigenous efforts had been suppressed as a consequence of the failure of the reform movement, and church-based activities were diminishing due to the Boxer Uprising and the anti-Christian milieu. In the 1899–1900 period, Alicia Little set off on a tour to promote the movement, visiting major cities in the Yangzi Valley and on the southeast coast. In each city, she was introduced to both Chinese and British officials and community leaders. In the course of the existence of the Natural Foot Society (1895–1907), she organized meetings in over thirty cities, and she was the principal contributor to a total of 162 recorded meetings organized by the society. At the end of each meeting, a number of leaflets, tracts, placards, and pledges were distributed. By the end of 1906, over one million items of propaganda material had been printed and circulated from Shanghai, without counting those printed elsewhere.

Despite these documented activities, no evidence shows that the Natural Foot Society was successful in persuading Chinese women to unbind their feet, with the exception of a handful of Christian women under the influence of local churches. In fact, the direct impact of the late-Qing anti-footbinding societies as a whole was marginal. At a discursive and rhetorical level, however, these propaganda materials and Alicia Little's writings together played a key role in enlightening indigenous reform-minded intellectuals. It is also significant that the term *tianzu* (natural feet) was introduced into the Chinese language by the Natural Foot Society.

Alicia Little was an energetic person. She traveled all over China and wrote many books about her China experiences, including *Intimate China* (1899), *The Land of the Blue Gown* (1902), and *Round about My Peking Garden* (1905). These are still standard reference works for scholars working on this period of Chinese history. In 1907 she returned to England with her husband, then in poor health. After her husband's death in 1908, she remained based in England, where she continued to participate in movements for social reform. She also continued to travel, especially to Eastern Europe, where her elder sister lived. She died in 1926, at the age of eighty-one.

SEE ALSO *Footbinding.*

Bound foot of a woman from southern China, 1880s. *Arriving in China with her merchant husband in 1887, Alicia Little began an anti-footbinding organization after seeing the effects of this technique performed on young girls. The Natural Foot Society gained the support of other women from the West, giving lectures and distributing literature throughout China condemning the practice.* POPPERFOTO/GETTY IMAGES

BIBLIOGRAPHY

Croll, Elisabeth. *Wise Daughters from Foreign Lands: European Women Writers in China*. London: Pandora, 1989.

Oldfield, Sybil. *Women Humanitarians: A Biographical Dictionary of British Women Active between 1900 and 1950*. London: Continuum, 2001.

Yen-Wei Miao

LIU BINYAN

1925–2005

Liu Binyan is without doubt the founder of muckraking journalism in the People's Republic of China. Born in Changchun (Jilin Province) on February 7, 1925, to a father who, pushed by famine, had emigrated to Manchuria from his native Shandong, he was raised in Harbin. His father had spent seven years in the USSR and became an interpreter for the Trans-Manchurian Railway Company in Harbin. All through his childhood, Binyan heard his father praise the Soviet Union. He was only six when the Japanese invaded Manchuria, and this trauma, which caused his father to lose his job, made him a diehard patriot. Although Liu was obliged to interrupt his studies because of the family's lack of money, he managed to learn Japanese and Russian. It was out of patriotism that he joined the Communist Party in 1944 while in Tianjin. There, he took part in the underground political struggle against the Japanese. In 1946 Liu returned to Harbin, which was already ruled by the Communists, and thereafter he stayed in the "liberated" zones. He started to work in the Communist Youth League apparatus and witnessed the excesses of the land reform in Heilongjiang.

In the early 1950s, Liu often traveled to the USSR as an interpreter for delegations from *Zhongguo Qingnian bao* (Chinese youth), where he worked as a journalist. He established a solid friendship with Valentin Ovechkin (1904–1968), a famous Soviet writer of reportage literature, who exerted a strong influence on Liu. During a trip to Eastern Europe in the spring of 1956, he was deeply impressed by the situation in Poland and by the Soviet thaw that followed Nikita Khrushchev's report on Joseph Stalin's crimes.

most important oil painting society of the era, the Tianmahui (Heavenly Horse Society), founded by Ding Song, the Japan-trained oil painter Jiang Xin, and other members of the school faculty.

In his early years, Liu Haisu cut a dashing figure—fashionable, Westernized, and, most of all, modern. As an activist in the cultural circles of Shanghai and Beijing, Liu established personal relationships with numerous notable cultural figures, including prominent elders such as Cai Yuanpei (1868–1940), who served for many years on the academy's board of trustees, Liang Qichao (1873–1929), and Kang Youwei (1858–1927), as well as writers such as Xu Zhimo (1897–1931) and Hu Shi (1891–1962). Liu exhibited in Beijing, as well as in Shanghai, becoming one of the most prominent of the younger generation of Westernized painters in China. Exposure to the reformist *guohua* circles in Beijing and Shanghai convinced him of the value of modernizing ink painting, as well as oils, and he exhibited a number of such works in the mid and late 1920s. He made a point of obtaining inscriptions on his paintings by famous friends, men such as Cai Yuanpei, Wu Changshi (1844–1927), and Guo Moruo (1892–1978), thus forever embedding his works in the most progressive cultural networks of the day.

THE NUDE MODEL CONTROVERSY

Liu Haisu later claimed to have been the first in China to introduce the use of nude models to the art school curriculum. Although this claim to priority rightly rests with the Japan-educated Li Shutong (1880–1942), who taught life drawing in his art classes at the Zhejiang First Normal College as early as 1913, Liu's effective publicity for this practice ensured that it was identified with the institution he directed, and ultimately with him personally. In 1925, inspired by difficulties met by a former student living in the provinces, Liu Haisu began a vigorous campaign to publicize and advertise the use of nude models at the Shanghai Art Academy. Claiming to have been criticized ten years earlier by a prominent but recently deceased educator, whom he also blamed for coining the derogatory name "traitor to art" (*yishu pantu*) with which Liu signed his ink paintings in the period, he elaborated the progressive virtues and aesthetic value of drawing the nude in every possible public forum—giving a radio broadcast, publishing a long newspaper article on national day, and filling the newspaper with advertisements for his school.

This gambit produced controversy, and soon escalated into an exchange of insults in the press that ultimately resulted in lawsuits against Liu Haisu. Most important, appeals to the ruling warlord of the day, Sun Chuanfang (1885–1935), backfired and led to orders to close the Shanghai Art Academy. Liu finally complied by agreeing to cancel the nude model classes, a situation that was saved only by the overthrow and assassination of the warlord. Remarkably, in his subsequent retelling of the tale, Liu emerges as the victor, and has thus enjoyed a reputation as the initiator and defender of the liberal, Western practice of drawing the nude (Andrews 2005).

TRAVELS ABROAD AND EFFORTS TO INTEGRATE CHINESE AND WESTERN STYLES

The school was briefly closed following this and other debacles, but it reopened in the fall of 1927 under new leadership, while Cai Yuanpei arranged for Liu Haisu to travel in Europe. Although Liu had visited Japan twice, once in 1919 and again in 1927, and had good relationships with many of the Japanese art educators with whom his faculty members had studied, Liu himself was largely self-taught and had never studied abroad. However informal his pursuits in France may have been, his two years abroad, between 1929 and 1931, gave him the credentials that by the late 1920s were increasingly expected of experts in any modern field.

Despite competition with two national universities, the National Art Academy in Hangzhou, directed by Lin Fengmian (1900–1991), and the art department at National Central University, headed by Xu Beihong, by the 1930s the private Shanghai Art Academy had grown in size and influence, producing students in a wide range of art-related fields. The most academically talented students might use the Shanghai Art Academy as a preparatory program for entering the national art school, but those of more iconoclastic temperament used it to launch careers in such creative fields as film, drama, commercial art, graphic design, photography, printmaking, and journalism. The legacy of the Shanghai Art Academy's teaching and attitudes, and those of Liu Haisu, pervaded the Chinese art world throughout the twentieth century.

Liu Haisu's early experiences of traveling to Westernized Japan reinforced his belief in seeking solutions from the West. During the period between 1929 and 1935, Liu traveled and exhibited throughout Europe, serving as a cultural interpreter, lecturer, and unofficial ambassador. Through organizing a series of exhibitions, and giving lectures and demonstrations, Liu tried to convey to the European audience the most up-to-date information on Chinese modern art, as well as the value of China's traditional aesthetics. Yet, even before his trips to Europe, Liu had begun to conceive possible approaches for amalgamating Western and indigenous conventions, both theoretically and practically. A prolific writer of art history and aesthetics, Liu tried to construct a conceptual link between the two traditions. One of his most astonishing but influential articles is "Shitao and Post-Impressionism" (1923), which claims to find a theoretical consonance between painting by the nineteenth-century European painter Vincent van Gogh and the seventeenth-century Chinese painter Shitao. He also referred to van Gogh's genius as that of a "traitor to art," identifying himself quite directly with the stylistic model he chose for much of his own oil painting. The slight awkwardness in many of Liu's early paintings, such as the oil *Qianmen in Beijing* (1922) and the ink *Tomb of Yanzi* (1924), are viewed by admirers as manifestations of his effort to embrace Chinese and Western styles in both oil painting and Chinese ink painting, and further, to integrate the two traditions in his practice.

CHALLENGES AND REHABILITATION

After the outbreak of the War of Resistance in 1937, the Shanghai Art Academy, located in the French concession, was able to continue classes for a time in the protected "orphan island" on European territory. However, as the situation worsened, Liu traveled to Southeast Asia to raise funds for war-stricken China through sale exhibitions. He returned to Shanghai in 1943.

Following establishment of the People's Republic of China in 1949, the government undertook a major educational restructuring in 1952 that de-emphasized Shanghai's role as a cultural and artistic center. The Shanghai Art Academy was merged with two other schools and relocated, forming the East China Art Academy in Wuxi. Liu Haisu was given the title of director, but administrative authority passed to a new vice-director. The school moved again to Nanjing in 1958 and was eventually renamed the Nanjing Art Academy.

The outspoken Liu Haisu was declared a rightist in the political campaign of 1957. He was stripped of his position and other titles, and his wages were drastically reduced. He returned then to Shanghai, where he lived for the remainder of his life. The Cultural Revolution brought particularly serious difficulty to those labeled rightists—he was abused, his house was repeatedly raided, and he and his wife were later forced to move into the tiny attic garret of his old home, where he consoled himself by secretly painting. Ever energetic, even after suffering several strokes, he reemerged almost as soon as the Cultural Revolution was over, his frequent painting forays to local Shanghai parks attracting young admirers. By the late 1970s, a new generation of Shanghai artists had begun painting in the postimpressionist Shanghai Art Academy style that Liu Haisu had pioneered so many years earlier. He continued to paint, exhibit, and travel during his last years, enjoying the return of his reputation and the many titles, awards, and honors that came with it. The Liu Haisu Museum in Shanghai preserves many of his best surviving works.

SEE ALSO *Chinese Painting (guohua); Guo Moruo; Hu Shi; Kang Youwei; Liang Qichao; Lin Fengmian; Modernist Art of the 1920s and 1930s; Oil Painting (youhua); Wu Changshi (Wu Junqing); Xu Beihong; Xu Zhimo.*

BIBLIOGRAPHY

Andrews, Julia F. Art and the Cosmopolitan Culture of 1920s Shanghai: Liu Haisu and the Nude Model Controversy. *Chungguksa Yongu: Journal of Chinese Historical Researches* (Korean Society for Chinese History), Spec. issue: *Chinese History through Art* 35 (2005): 323–372.

Andrews, Julia F. The Heavenly Horse Society (Tianmahui) and Chinese Landscape Painting. In *Ershi shiji shanshuihua yanjiu wenji* [Studies in twentieth-century *shanshuihua*], ed. Lu Fusheng and Tang Zheming, 556–591. Shanghai: Shanghai Calligraphy and Painting Publishing House, 2006.

Sullivan, Michael. *Art and Artists of Twentieth-Century China.* Berkeley: University of California Press, 1996.

Xie Haiyan, ed. *Liu Haisu.* Nanjing: Jiangsu Meishu Chubanshe, 2002.

Yanfei Zhu
Julia F. Andrews

LIU HONGSHENG
1888–1956

Liu Hongsheng (O. S. Lieu) was a highly successful entrepreneur in Shanghai during the 1930s. He came from a Ningbo family—the Ningbo natives of Shanghai being well-known for their business acumen—and was educated at St. John's University in Shanghai. Thus he had the benefit of both the network of family connections and the best tradition in Western-style education. Liu became Shanghai comprador for the British-owned Kailan Mining operations in the 1910s, and by the 1920s he was running his own business.

Liu earned his comprador's position by first working as a salesman for the Chinese Engineering and Mining Company in 1909; he was promoted to comprador of its Shanghai Agent in 1911. In 1912, when the company's subsidiary, the Kailan Mining Administration (KMA), was formed, Liu became comprador of KMA's Shanghai Agent, a position he held for the next decade.

During World War I (1914–1918), Liu managed to make a handsome fortune by using the discretionary power of his compradorship to collaborate, often without KMA's acknowledgment, with local coal dealers in Shanghai and along the lower Yangzi region to build a network of partnerships for coal dealing and wharf operations. In December 1922, KMA made him the "Chinese representative" of its Shanghai Agent. After learning more about Liu's businesses related to coal, and hoping to promote business among Chinese customers, KMA formed a partnership with Liu and his principal collaborator, Nee Tai Shing Coal

Merchants, in 1924. This partnership, the Kalian Sales Agency, commenced business in 1925 for five years. In 1928 Liu secured another partnership contract with KMA on Kalian Sales Agency for another decade from 1930, but without Nee Tai Shing.

BUSINESS INTERESTS

Throughout the 1920s and 1930s, Liu Hongsheng's major business interests ranged from coal distribution (such as Kalian Sales Agency and Hongay Coal Company) and wharf operations (Nee Tai Shing Wharves, Coal Merchants' Wharf, and the Chung Hwa Wharf Company), to match manufacturing (Hong Sung Match and, later, China Match Company), cement making (Shanghai Portland Cement Works), coal mining (Liuchang Mining Company and East China Coal Mining Company), coal-briquette making (China Coal Briquette Company), woolen textiles (China Wool Manufacturing Company), and banking (China Development Bank) and insurance (China General Insurance Company). He also owned a considerable amount of land—used for residential purposes, factories, and wharf operations—within Shanghai's International Settlements.

ADVOCACY FOR SCIENTIFIC MANAGEMENT

During the 1920s and 1930s, Liu advocated "scientific management" by introducing Western-style bookkeeping and cost-accounting methods into his businesses. This process probably began in 1923 when he hired a Western-trained accountant, Hua Runchuan, to introduce cost accounting to Shanghai Cement. Some of his other companies that had been using Chinese methods of bookkeeping and accounting, such as the China Coal Briquette Company, were put under accounting reform in the late 1920s. In June 1930, Liu and others formed the China Institute of Scientific Management (Zhongguo Kexue Guanli Xiehui). After the formation of the China Match Company in 1930, Liu recruited another American-trained cost accountant, Lin Zhaotang, to design and implement "scientific management" for the new company. Liu even reformed the accounting system of his own accounts office in early 1932. The next year, Liu published a journal article to promote cost accounting, using experiences from his companies.

Despite his advocacy for scientific management, like most successful Chinese businesses of the time, Liu managed his business conglomerates through his private accounts office, the Lieu Ong Kee Accounts Office (Liu Hongji Zhangfang). In the 1920s, the office often acted as a financier for Liu's investment projects, as trade-credit provider for his companies, and sometimes as auditor of dubious accounts. Despite reforms within the accounts office and attempts to abolish it in the early 1930s, it survived until Liu passed away. Liu was also not above bending his companies' accounting policies to financial needs. In the 1920s, for example, he maneuvered the accounting term *depreciation* in Shanghai Cement to hide profits from its shareholders. In the 1930s, when Liu's China Coal Briquette Company failed to turn a profit, its board of directors simply ruled the stoppage of depreciation to mark up its profit figure. Such practices often drew criticism from auditors.

CONNECTIONS TO THE NANJING GOVERNMENT AFTER 1927

Liu's connections with the Nanjing government reached high-level personnel in the Chinese Nationalist Party. He was on good terms with Song Ziwen (T. V. Soong) and his brother Song Ziliang (T. L. Soong), who, like Liu, had studied at St. John's University. Material interest played a part in Liu's cultivation of connections with the Nationalist leaders. In particular, Song Ziliang helped Liu lobby Nanjing in 1929 for protective measures against foreign matches. In return, Song invested in Liu's China Match Company and East China Coal Mining Company.

During the "Nanjing decade," Liu was recruited as a promoter of several state-owned enterprises and banks, and he was appointed to positions in a number of important government agencies, including the National Economic Council. In late 1932, Liu was appointed to a three-year post as the general manager of China Merchants' Steam Navigation Corporation to implement much-needed reform in the sixty-year-old state enterprise. Liu's political connections partially enabled him, with government backing, to build a nationwide match cartel in 1936.

When war broke out in 1937, Liu left Shanghai and traveled via Hong Kong to the interior, leaving his eldest three sons to handle the family businesses in occupied Shanghai. Liu continued to hold positions in some state-own enterprises and government bodies after the end of the war. Following the Communist takeover, Liu returned to Shanghai, and stayed there until his death in 1956.

SEE ALSO *China Merchants' Steam Navigation Company.*

BIBLIOGRAPHY

Boorman, Howard L., ed. *Biographical Dictionary of Republican China.* New York: Columbia University Press, 1968.

Chan Kai Yiu. Capital Formation and Accumulation of Chinese Industrial Enterprises in the Republican Period: The Case of Liu Hongsheng's Shanghai Portland Cement Works Co. Ltd., 1920–1937. In *Chinese Business Enterprise: Critical Perspectives on Business and Management*, ed. Rajeswary Ampalavanar Brown, Vol. 2, 149–170. London: Routledge, 1996.

Chan Kai Yiu. *Business Expansion and Structural Change in Pre-War China: Liu Hongsheng and His Enterprises, 1920–1937.* Hong Kong: Hong Kong University Press, 2006.

Chan Kai Yiu. Minkokuki Shanhai no Chūgoku shihon kigyō niokeru seiyōshiki kaikei seido dōnyū mondai no shohoteki kōsatsu: Chūka Baikyū Kōshi no zirei wo chūshi tosite (1926–1936 nen) [A preliminary investigation of the transplantation of Western accounting system in Shanghai's Chinese-owned enterprises during the Republican period: The case of the China Coal Briquette Company (1926–1936)]. Trans. Yang Qiuli. In *Shakai sisutemu kenkyū* [Social system studies] 12 (March 2006): 173–193.

China Weekly Review, comp. *Who's Who in China: Biographies of Chinese Leaders*. 5th ed. Shanghai: Author, 1936.

Cochran, Sherman. Three Roads into Shanghai's Market: Japanese, Western, and Chinese Companies in the Match Trade, 1895–1937. In *Shanghai Sojourners*, ed. Frederic Wakeman Jr. and Ye Wenxin (Wen-hsin Yeh), 35–75. Berkeley: Institute of East Asian Studies, University of California, 1992.

Cochran, Sherman. *Encountering Chinese Networks: Western, Japanese, and Chinese Corporations in China, 1880–1937*. Berkeley: University of California Press, 2000.

Cochran, Sherman. Capitalists Choosing Communist China: The Liu Family of Shanghai, 1948–56. In *Dilemmas of Victory: The Early Years of the People's Republic of China*, ed. Jeremy Brown and Paul G. Pickowicz, 359–385. Cambridge, MA: Harvard University Press, 2007.

Liu Hongsheng. Wo weishenmo zuzhong chengben kuaiji [Why do I pay attention to cost accounting]. *Yinhang Zhoubao* [Shanghai bankers' weekly] 17, 14 (April 18, 1933): 3–8.

Shanghai Shehui Kexueyuan Jingji Yanjiusuo, comp. *Liu Hongsheng qiye shiliao* [Sources of the history of Liu Hongsheng's enterprises]. 3 vols. Shanghai: Shanghai Renmin Chubanshe, 1981.

Zhongguo Zhengxinxuo [Banker's Cooperative Credit Service, Ltd.]. *Shanghai gongshang renminlu* [Who's who in Shanghai's industry and commerce]. Shanghai: Zhongguo Zhengxinxuo, 1936.

Kai Yiu Chan

LIU KUO-SUNG

SEE *Liu Guosong (Liu Kuo-sung).*

LIU SHAOQI

1898–1969

Liu Shaoqi was born in Huaminglou village, Ningxiang County, Hunan Province, in 1898, the youngest in a rich peasant family of four boys and five girls; his father was a primary school teacher. After attending local primary and middle schools, he joined the New People's Study Society (Xinmin xuehui) recently established by Mao Zedong (1893–1976) and Cai Hesen (1895–1931), which sponsored a "work-study" program to enable students to continue their education abroad. In September 1919 he enrolled in Yude Middle School in Baoding (Hebei) as a work-study student, receiving vocational training with an orientation toward factory work (thus he was to make repeated proud references in later life to his proletarian origins). But the following year he withdrew and went to Shanghai, where he and Ren Bishi (1904–1950) joined the Socialist Youth League that had been organized in October by Comintern agent Grigory Voitinsky (1893–1956) and where he studied Russian for eight months.

COMMUNIST PARTY CAREER

In the early summer of 1921, Liu was one of eight students selected to study in the Soviet Union. He arrived in Moscow in July 1921 and studied about seven months at the Communist University of Toilers of the East. In the winter of 1921 to 1922, Liu joined the Chinese Communist Party (CCP) in the Soviet Union. Though a good student, he asked to be transferred home for "practical" work, and by the spring of 1922 he had been appointed to the secretariat of the Chinese Labor Unions (Zhongguo laodong zuhe shujibu), working with Zhang Guotao (1897–1979) and Li Lisan (1899–1967) to organize the coal miners of Anyuan at Pingxiang Xian (Hunan), part of the first major heavy industrial complex in China with some twelve thousand workers. At the Sixth CCP Congress (in Moscow, 1928), he became director of the CCP Labor Department, and in 1931 he became chairman of the All-China Labor Federation in Shanghai (and an alternate Politburo member).

Upon completing the Long March (where he supported Mao at the historic Zunyi conference with a critique of "leftist adventurism"), Liu became the leading organizer of the underground Communist base areas behind Japanese lines. He succeeded, by August 1945, in promoting a major expansion of CCP influence in some of the most populous and economically advanced regions of China, establishing the party machine in a territory stretching from the Yangzi River to Manchuria and from the China Sea to the Yellow River. Liu also spent several war years in the Yan'an base area as director of the Cadre Training Department, giving a series of lectures compiled as *How to Be a Good Communist* and drafting *On Inner-party Struggle,* both of which became leading training manuals in the party rectification movement (*zhengfeng*) of 1942 to 1944 and thereafter.

During the Sino-Japanese War (1937–1945), he supported Mao's interpretation of the second United Front and opposed the Wang Ming Line, which by subordinating the CCP to the Guomindang (GMD) would have greatly complicated underground organization in the White areas. At the Seventh Party Congress in 1945, the first to be held since disintegration of the first United Front in 1928, Liu in his report (*On the Party*) helped enshrine "Mao Zedong Thought" as the CCP's guiding doctrine and Mao himself as paramount leader; Liu was in turn appointed first vice

HOW TO BE A GOOD COMMUNIST

In 1938 Liu Shaoqi delivered a series of lectures to the Institute of Marxism-Leninism in Yan'an that were later compiled as *How to Be a Good Communist*, which eventually became one of the most influential and controversial tracts in the history of the Chinese Communist Party. Originally intended as a training manual for incoming party officials, the essay fuses "Communist ethics and Chinese tradition" (Nivison 1956), mixing quotations from Marxist and Confucian classics to promote the virtues of "steeling and cultivation" through "practical struggle," and "unconditional subordination of personal interests . . . to the interests of the Party," maintaining an appropriate balance between compromise and "principle." Liu quotes with approval the injunction from the *Book of Odes* that one should cultivate oneself "as a lapidary cuts and files, carves and polishes" (the Book of Odes or *Shi Jing*, a collection of more than 300 poems, was one of the "five classics" of traditional Confucian scholarship). "Any man can become a Yao or a Shun," he wrote, quoting Mencius (Mengzi, c. 371–289 BCE) in support of commitment to a bureaucratic career.

Among the manuals studied in the party rectification movement *(zhengfeng)* at Yan'an in 1942, *How to Be a Good Communist* was republished in at least six editions in several languages and widely circulated (especially the 1962 edition, copublished in *People's Daily* and *Red Flag*). During the Cultural Revolution it came under intensive polemical assault with the support of Mao Zedong himself, who criticized the book's excessive emphasis on top-down cadre discipline: "Since 1952, the masses have turned cold toward us. Party members in the past were isolated from the masses because of the influence of *How to Be a Good Communist*, held no independent views, and served as docile tools of the Party organs" (Mao 1967, p. 22).

Ironically, Liu's attempt to promote a life of unstinting party service by reassuring cadres that the organization would in turn see to their welfare was denounced as advocacy of selfish hedonism, for "merging" personal and collective interests. Nevertheless, following Liu Shaoqi's personal rehabilitation at the Fifth Plenum of the Eleventh Party Congress in February 1980, *How to Be a Good Communist* was absolved of all "revisionist" imputations, declared a "Marxist work of great significance," and republished, accompanied by a major promotion to popularize the book as a teaching manual for party cadres. Excerpts from this and other classic Marxist texts were given concurrent front-page coverage in national newspapers. Thus the book's significance lies not only in its normative impact on the party organization before and after the Cultural Revolution, but as a controversial symbol of enduring official and popular ambivalence about the dominant role of the party apparatus in Chinese society.

BIBLIOGRAPHY

Liu Shaoqi. *How to Be a Good Communist.* Peking, Foreign Languages Press, 1964.

Mao Zedong. Cited in *Asahi*, May 20, 1967, as translated in *Daily Summary of the Japanese Press*, May 23, 1967.

Nivison, David S. "Communist Ethics and Chinese Tradition." *Journal of Asian Studies* 16, 1 (1956): 51–75.

Lowell Dittmer

chairman of the CCP Central Committee. Though he had helped elevate Mao's Thought to its preeminent position as a model of peasant revolution for the third world, Liu became the CCP's organizational architect as well as a leading theorist, writing, for example, the 1952 tract *Internationalism and Nationalism* that justified the expulsion of Josip Tito (1892–1980) of Yugoslavia from the Communist International, ironically criticizing him for having taken the "capitalist road."

Although (according to subsequent accounts), Mao and Liu gravitated into opposing factional groupings after 1949, with Liu tending to support a more moderate pace of "socializing the means of production," Liu consistently supported Mao in leadership disputes (thus there was elite unity in the purge of Gao Gang [1902–1955] and Rao Shushi [1903–1975] in 1954 to 1955, Peng Dehuai and his associates in 1959, and even Peng Zhen [1902–1997] and his confederates in May 1966) and generally supported such major Maoist initiatives as the Great Leap Forward in 1958. However Liu (along with others within the leadership, such as Deng Xiaoping and Chen Yun) apparently became less useful to Mao when the latter sought to revive "class struggle" in the aftermath of the disastrous Great Leap Forward; thus even though Liu took a relatively hard line in the Socialist Education Movement or "Four Cleans," Mao also disagreed with this approach.

Propaganda poster titled* Resolutely Down with Liu Shaoqi!, *November, 1968. *Though an ally of Mao Zedong prior to the founding of the People's Republic of China, after 1949 Liu Shaoqi often suggested a slower, more conservative course toward making China a communist nation. Demoted from leadership positions shortly before his death in 1969, Liu did not live to see many of his ideas promoted by Deng Xiaoping after Mao's death.* **PRIVATE COLLECTION, © THE CHAMBERS GALLERY LONDON/THE BRIDGEMAN ART LIBRARY INTERNATIONAL.**

SEE ALSO *Classical Scholarship and Intellectual Debates: Debates, 1900–1949; Dissidents; Prodemocracy Movement (1989); Scar (Wound) Literature.*

BIBLIOGRAPHY

Béja, Jean-Philippe. Liu Xiaobo ou le retour de la morale [Liu Xiaobo or the return of morals]. In *La pensée chinoise aujourd'hui* [Thought in Today's China] ed. Anne Cheng. Paris: Gallimard. 2007

Liu Xiaobo. Reflections of an Anti-Traditionalist: The Revelation in New York. *China Perspectives*, 11 (1997): 24–27.

Liu Xiaobo. Reform in China: The Role of Civil Society. *Social Research* (China in Transition) 73, 1 (2006): 121–140.

Liu Xiaobo and Chen Maiping. Suffocating in the Chinese "Iron Box." Independent Chinese Pen Club (December 13, 2004).

The Philosophy of the Pig. *Dongxiang* 181 (September 2000): 29–36.

Solomon, Jon. The Sovereign Police and Knowledgeable Bodies: Liu Xiaobo's Exilic Critique of Politics and Knowledge. *Positions: East Asia Cultures Critique* 10, 2 (2002): 399–429.

Jean-Philippe Béja

LIUQIU ISLANDS

From 1372 the Zhongshan (Chuzan) kingdom of the Liuqiu (Japanese, Ryūkyū) Islands, located between Kyushu and Taiwan, paid tribute to the Chinese emperor, but from 1609 it also paid tribute (under political pressure) to the Satsuma domain of Tokugawa Japan. This seemingly contradictory dual-subordination status eventually precipitated a crisis between China and Japan in the 1870s.

After the Meiji restoration of 1868, a resurgent Japan challenged China's tributary state system by claiming the right to protect the lives of shipwrecked sailors from Liuqiu, a number of whom were killed by aborigines on Taiwan in 1871. At this time, Japan was already intent on taking over Liuqiu, and in 1872, having summoned the king of Liuqiu to Tokyo, the Meiji government unilaterally declared his kingdom a feudal domain of Japan, Ryūkyūhan. The dispute with China came to a head in 1874 after the Qing government initially refused to recognize Japan's interest in the Taiwan incident, on grounds that the sailors from Liuqiu were not Japanese subjects. In the agreement settling the dispute, the Chinese, by agreeing to pay compensation for the harm done to Japanese victims of the incident, implicitly acknowledged the right of the Japanese government to protect the shipwrecked sailors. The term *Liuqiu* or *Ryūkyū* was not mentioned in the agreement.

In the late 1870s, on the pretext of clarifying its political boundaries as defined by international law, the Japanese took steps unilaterally to annex the archipelago. Tribute payments to China were stopped, the king was forced to take up residence in Japan, and in 1879 Japanese officials were sent to oversee the transformation of Liuqiu into Okinawa Prefecture. The Qing government's protest at the annexation of Liuqiu came to little. Chinese minister He Ruzhang's (1838–1891) strongly worded letter of protest in 1878 furnished Japan with an excuse to refuse to discuss the Liuqiu question with China. Upon the advice of its French legal adviser, Gustave Boissonade (1825–1910), the Meiji government considered the Liuqiu affair an internal matter. Ulysses S. Grant (1822–1885), ex-president of the United States and on tour in Asia in 1879, was entreated by China to act as mediator in the dispute. Grant made an effort to prevent a possible Sino-Japanese war over Liuqiu. He succeeded in persuading the Japanese and Chinese to come to the negotiation table, but did not propose any concrete solution to the Liuqiu problem.

In 1880 Tokyo authorized Shishido Tamaki (1829–1901) to negotiate in Beijing with the Chinese Zongli Yamen on the Liuqiu issue. Draft treaties between the two parties were completed after the negotiations. The Qing government, however, refused to ratify the treaties. From the Chinese point of view, the dispute was never legally settled, but as far as the Japanese were concerned, the matter was closed. An important outcome of the dispute was that Taiwan—hitherto a prefecture of Fujian Province—was made a province in its own right in 1875, although twenty years later it too was annexed by Japan.

SEE ALSO *Japan, Relations with.*

BIBLIOGRAPHY

Kublin, Hyman. The Attitude of China during the Liu-ch'iu Controversy, 1871–1881. *Pacific Historical Review* 18, 2 (1949): 213–231.

Leung, Edwin Pak-wah. General Ulysses S. Grant and the Sino-Japanese Dispute over the Ryukyu Islands. In *Japan and Korea*. Vol. 2 of *Proceedings of the First International Symposium on Asian Studies*, 421–449. Hong Kong: Asian Research Service, 1979.

Leung, Edwin Pak-wah. The Quasi-War in East Asia: Japan's Expedition to Taiwan and the Ryukyu Controversy. *Modern Asian Studies* 17, 2 (1983): 257–281.

Leung, Edwin Pak-wah. Li Hung-chang and the Liu-ch'iu (Ryukyu) Controversy, 1871–1881. In *Li Hung-chang and China's Early Modernization*, ed. Liu Kwang-ching (Liu Guangjing) and Samuel Chu (Zhu Changling), 162–175. Armonk, NY: Sharpe, 1994.

Smits, George. *Visions of Ryukyu: Identity and Ideology in Early-Modern Thought and Politics*. Honolulu: University of Hawai'i Press, 1999.

Edwin Pak-wah Leung (Liang Bohua)

LOCAL GAZETTEERS

A local gazetteer (*difang zhi*) is a compendium of geographical, administrative, and biographical materials concerning the history and present conditions of a particular place. That place is most often an administrative unit: usually a county, less commonly a district, township, prefecture, or province, though even the entire country has been the subject of three "gazetteers of national unity" (*yitong zhi*) compiled in the Yuan (late 13th century), Ming (1461), and Qing (1746; revised in 1784 and 1820) dynasties. Gazetteers have also been published for topographical sites such as mountains, rivers, and lakes, and for institutions such as monasteries, schools, and government ministries.

In the traditional format, a gazetteer opens with several prefaces by the compiler (usually a local scholar) and his official patrons, which often helpfully reveal how and when the project to publish the gazetteer was organized, and how this edition relates to earlier editions. The front matter may also include prefaces to earlier editions, a table of contents, maps, and illustrations of local sights. The early chapters tend to address basic geographical and administrative matters; the middle chapters record the accomplishments of centrally appointed officials and local notables; and the later chapters reproduce documents and literary records by eminent locals and even more eminent outsiders.

Though prototypes appeared before the Song dynasty (960–1279), the genre was not incorporated into the state's textual regime until 993, when the court ordered every district to submit a copy of its local records every six years. This schedule of data collection quickly fell off, but standardization followed, as did the expectation that local officials would compile and later print gazetteers regularly, every sixty years if not more often. The state expected to see included such official data as records of state institutions, archives of taxation and corvée, and lists of those who passed the state exams and gained government appointments. So too it anticipated that a gazetteer should demonstrate conformity to official norms. A compliant compiler nonetheless made sure to record the best of what the locality had to offer, such as tourist-worthy scenic sights, local festivals, and life histories of the locally successful. Gazetteers thus show how the state was institutionally and ideologically present in local society, but also how distinctive local institutions and cultural practices shaped life in ways that were indifferent to that presence. Official values found expression alongside local identity and pride, allowing historians to draw on the evidence of both.

The structure and content of gazetteers have evolved over time as the state's self-conception has shifted and local priorities regarding the ordering of public life have changed. Thus gazetteers before 1911 attended to such official data as seasonal rites, filial sons, and abnormalities in the natural order portending moral or political collapse, whereas gazetteers thereafter recast local society according to such modern sociological categories as agriculture, industry, telecommunications, and now even environmental protection. The genre froze when the Communist Party came to power in 1949, but proposals to compile new gazetteers started to appear in 1956 and won the guarded support of Mao Zedong in 1958. A few were published, and a central working group was organized, but the initiative was blasted as a return to "feudal" historiography. Not until after the Third Plenum of the Eleventh Party Congress in 1978 did gazetteers reappear on the agenda of official publishing. Local offices of the Chinese People's Political Consultative Conference took up the task in the 1980s, generating a flood of redesigned gazetteers. The number of extant editions of gazetteers compiled before 1949—roughly eight thousand—has more than doubled since 1984. The most complete collection, close to twenty thousand, is in the Center for Documentation and Information of the Chinese Academy of Social Sciences in Beijing. Oxford's Bodleian Library holds the largest collection outside China.

BIBLIOGRAPHY

Brook, Timothy. *Geographical Sources of Ming-Qing History*. 2nd ed. Ann Arbor: Center for Chinese Studies, University of Michigan, 2002.

Dennis, Joseph. Writing, Publishing, and Reading Local Histories in Ming China. Ph.D. diss., University of Minnesota, 2004.

Timothy Brook

LOCUST PLAGUES SINCE 1800

China's premodern agricultural economy was periodically affected by plagues of insects, most commonly by locusts. Historical sources provide but scattered references to the various larvae, caterpillars, grubs, and bugs that threatened harvests. Only infestations by the oriental migratory locust (*Locusta migratoria manilensis* or *feihuang*) are relatively well documented. Migratory locusts breed twice a year and pass through different developmental phases, from the solitary to gregarious phase. The latter is the dangerous one, referred to in historical sources by descriptions such as "flying locusts darken the sky." A swarm of locusts could easily cover a thousand square miles in little time, and with each insect capable of eating the equivalent of its own body weight per day, a swarm could quickly consume enormous quantities of the tender leaves, stalks, and ears of rice, wheat, millet, and corn.

ORIGINS OF PLAGUES

Some authors have considered this scourge worse than floods and droughts, though in practice it might be difficult to separate the one from the other: Frequent floods producing swampy areas in a low-lying, normally dry environment provided the best breeding ground for locusts. The historical geographer Chen Zhengxiang (1922–2003) made probably the first attempt to map the occurrence of locust plagues based on records of temples devoted to Bazha (the insect god) and General Liu Meng (the protector against locusts) in local histories. This map clearly shows that the dry North China plain (the provinces of Hebei, Shandong, and Henan in particular), historically one of China's most flood-prone areas, was most vulnerable to locust plagues. The lower Yangzi (Chang) River area was affected to a lesser degree, whereas the southern parts of the country were rarely affected.

Conventionally the frequency of locust plagues is calculated as averages of occurrence. Daming county in Hebei Province, for example, experienced a locust plague serious enough to be recorded every ten years on average. National aggregate figures indicate that there was a locust plague every other year on average during the Qing dynasty (1644–1912). But such averages are misleading, as they gloss over clear concentrations of locust plagues, as between 1637 and 1641, the final years of the Ming dynasty (1368–1644), which were characterized by frequent and widespread locust infestations, devastating famines, and epidemics, or again, like the prolonged plague in North China in the years from 1647 to 1649 in the wake of the Manchu conquest. These two examples show that the occurrence of locust plagues is closely related to social unrest, warfare, and the lack of preventive measures.

The only other case of a widespread and prolonged locust infestation that might come near to the scope of these two examples is perhaps the plague of the ill-fated Xianfeng reign (1851–1861), which accompanied the disruptions brought about by the Taiping Uprising (1851–1864). In this plague cluster, locusts first arose in Guangxi (1852–1854), where the rebellion erupted, a region not commonly infested by locusts. In Zhili Province, locust plagues are recorded from 1854 to 1858; in Henan and Jiangsu, from 1855 to 1857. For the years 1856 and 1857, six more central and northern provinces have records of locust plagues. Not only the rebellion in the South but also the disruption in the North brought about by the Yellow (Huang) River, which had shifted course in 1855, made it difficult for officials and people alike to carry out the usual preventive measures.

METHODS TO FIGHT PLAGUES

In some places people believed that locusts were divine creatures that must not be touched, and that only devout worship of Bazha, the locust god, could prevent a plague. The fact that locusts could rest in fields without actually devouring the crops (because they were not hungry) contributed to the mystification of the insect. As their appearance did not necessarily mean a plague, the belief in the efficiency of worshipping the locust god became quite firm. The increasing number of locust infestations during the Kangxi reign seems to have motivated official sponsorship of the cult of General Liu Meng, a divine figure held to have actively expelled the locusts during the Yongzheng reign (1723–1735). Worship of General Liu Meng became an important court ritual, and existing Bazha temples were rededicated accordingly, although in practice Bazha continued to be worshipped. This process of the official appropriation of a popular cult reflects a twofold approach to fighting the plague: imploring the gods while simultaneously undertaking vigorous action.

In theory, local officials were obliged to report on plague conditions. But in practice, they often tried to conceal the actual situation so as to present their achievements in a better light. This seems to have worked in the case of the governor of Guangxi, who reported to the throne that in the winter of 1852/1853 "locusts passed through the area," that "locusts were caught" and "extinguished in time," and that "there was no harm done to the crops" (Li Wenhai et al. 1994). But alternative sources tell a different story of food riots due to drought, locust plagues, and famine. The governor of Zhili tried to do the same in 1856, but was less lucky. In this case the plague occurred right in front of the young emperor's eyes. Reports on the "strange sight" of locusts covering the sky evoked his curiosity, so he went to see for himself and discovered the true scope of the calamity. He then ordered a merciless war against the insects, regardless of whether they harmed the crops or not.

The reporting system was part of an elaborate catalog of plague-prevention measures that had become systematized by the early nineteenth century. These measures were set out in readily available handbooks and written regulations. The detailed descriptions of methods to fight the plague in the *Nongzheng quanshu* (1630) shows that at least since the Ming, and most likely much earlier, people also took an active approach to getting rid of the insects. During the plague of the 1850s, new manuals such as *Zhihuang quanfa* (Complete methods to control locusts) were compiled, and older ones were reprinted. The danger of locust plagues was taken seriously by the Qing rulers. The Kangxi emperor (r. 1662–1722), for example, once decreed that fields be ploughed to destroy the nymphs when abundant autumn rains followed by a relatively dry spring led to predictions of a plague. Digging out egg pods was also a common practice. Mostly, however, the emphasis in the manuals was on catching the adult insects and thoroughly destroying them, either by cooking or burning. The danger was not only that locusts destroyed the harvest; decaying insects in wells, cisterns, and reservoirs clogged the drains and poisoned the drinking water. According to Mallory (1926) the direct damage caused by locusts in China was less severe than that in other countries, but these indirect effects caused much harm.

We can be certain that many local plagues do not appear in the historical records, either because they were too insignificant or because people preferred to deal with them on their own, without the often disruptive intervention of officials and their potentially corrupt entourage. Once the local official took charge of the campaign, locust catching was organized in a quasi-military style, as described in the manuals. In severe cases, troops were sent to help, although they were often described as doing at least as much harm to the crops as the insects. The most common measure taken by officials was to establish bureaus where people could exchange the locusts they had caught for either cash or grain. This worked both as an instrument against the plague and as a method of famine relief. In addition, there are reports of locusts being used as famine food in North China from the late imperial and Republican periods. These observations seem to support the view that in times of peace and prosperity, insect plagues could be dealt with relatively well. The same applies to other causes of harvest failures. The disastrous locust plagues of the late Ming and the mid-nineteenth century corroborate the popular saying that locusts were born out of dead soldiers.

LOCUST PLAGUES IN THE TWENTIETH CENTURY

Although the most serious famine of the late nineteenth century (1876–1879) was only indirectly related to war, social and political disruption in the early twentieth century has to be blamed for the severe famines and the forceful resurgence of insect plagues during the Republican era. According to one source, only the years 1924, 1937, and 1948 have no records of locust plagues. Factors contributing to locust plagues during this period were the utter neglect of water control structures and large-scale deforestation, the latter often a consequence of warfare and certainly a more important cause of plagues than the often stated corruption and weakness of the Nationalist government. International efforts to control the plagues in the 1920s failed because of these factors. Important new insights in how to get rid of the locusts nonetheless came out of these international efforts. Measures discussed included introducing parasites to the insects, spraying swarms from airplanes, as well as possible industrial uses to which the dead insects could be put. Mallory wrote, "If useful products could be made from the carcasses of locusts so that they had a commercial value, a method of killing the insects would speedily be found" (1926, p. 161). The idea of introducing locust insurance, however, was deemed unrealistic by this author, because of the poverty of China's peasants. A resolution passed by the Pan-Pacific Food Conservation Conference held at Honolulu in the summer of 1924 advised that "accurate scientific surveys be made of lands which may constitute the permanent breeding grounds of these insects, . . . that they are scouted at frequent intervals, . . . in order to learn the prospects concerning approaching devastating flights, and in order to begin preventive measures at the earliest moment" (Mallory 1926, p. 162).

It might well be that these international activities formed the basis for the post-1949 ecological efforts aimed at destroying the breeding grounds of harmful insects. Enormous water-control and drainage projects, as well as scientific research on locust biology, carried out during the first decades of the People's Republic, no doubt helped solve the problem of insect plagues at the source. The pursued integrated control program included, apart from the application of insecticides, the use of such time-tested methods as driving ducks into infested fields to eat large amounts of locusts. After 1949 immense efforts were made with great dedication and massive labor input organized in the style of mass campaigns. Yet the implementation of this integrated program seems to have been overshadowed by the heavy use of insecticides from the beginning. Despite the success of these efforts—the affected areas have been reduced to less than one tenth of their premodern size—the problem has not been completely eradicated. Once the flight of gigantic swarms of locusts has started, little can be done to stop them. Nevertheless, plagues are far less deadly than in the past.

SEE ALSO *Medicine, Traditional; Rural Development, 1949–1978: Great Leap Forward.*

BIBLIOGRAPHY

Chen Zhengxiang. *Zhongguo wenhua dili* [China's cultural geography]. Hong Kong: Sanlian Shudian, 1981.

Committee on Scholarly Communication with the People's Republic of China. *Insect Control in the People's Republic of China.* Washington, DC: National Academy of Sciences, 1977.

Hsu, Shin-yi. The Cultural Ecology of the Locust Cult in Traditional China. *Annals of the Association of American Geographers* 59, 4 (1969): 731–752.

Hu Huifang. Minguo shiqi huangzai chutan [A preliminary exploration of locust disasters in the Republican period]. *Hebei daxue xuebao* 30, 1 (January 2005): 17–19.

Kolb, Raimund Theodor. Die ostasiatische Wanderheuschrecke und ihre Bekämpfung unter besonderer Berücksichtigung der Ming- und Qing-Zeit (1368–1911) [The oriental migratory locust and its control, with special emphasis on the Ming and Qing dynasties (1368–1911)]. Heidelberg: Edition Forum, 1996.

Li, Lillian M. *Fighting Famine in North China: State, Market, and Environmental Decline, 1690s–1990s.* Stanford, CA: Stanford University Press, 2007.

Li Wenhai, Chen Xiao, Liu Yangdong, and Xia Mingfang. Feihuang qi zai: Xianfeng nianjian de yanzhong huangzai

[Seven years of migratory locusts: The severe locust plague in the Xianfeng era]. In *Zhongguo jindai shi da zaihuang* [Ten great disasters in modern China], ed. Li Wenhai et al., 58–79. Shanghai: Shanghai Renmin Chubanshe, 1994.

Mallory, Walter H. *China: Land of Famine*. New York: American Geographical Society, 1926.

Needham, Joseph, ed. *Science and Civilisation in China*. Vol. 6, *Biology and Biological Technology*. Pt. 1, *Botany*, 519–553. Cambridge, U.K.: University of Cambridge Press, 1986.

Andrea Janku

LONG MARCH

After the breakup of the First United Front of the Nationalist Party and the Chinese Communist Party in April 1927, the Chinese Communists retreated to the countryside and managed to establish some revolutionary bases in Jiangxi Province through guerrilla war. There, at Ruijin, they founded the Soviet Republic of China in November 1931. Feeling threatened by the rapid Communist growth, Generalissimo Chiang Kai-shek (Jiang Jieshi) launched five encirclement campaigns to eradicate the Communists and their Red Army from 1931 to 1934. The Red Army successfully defended against the first four attacks of the Nationalists, but suffered heavy casualties in the fifth campaign. As a result, the Communists faced total annihilation.

On October 16, 1934, 86,000 people consisting mostly of troops of the central Red Army (also known as the First Front Army) and Communist officials started retreating from Yudu, in Jiangxi Province, toward the west. Their original plan was to link up in west Hunan Province with the Second and Sixth Corps (also known as the Second Front Army), led by He Long and Xiao Ke respectively. With heavy baggage of the exiled Soviet Republic of China—including archives, office supplies, and even currency printers—the Red Army moved slowly over rugged

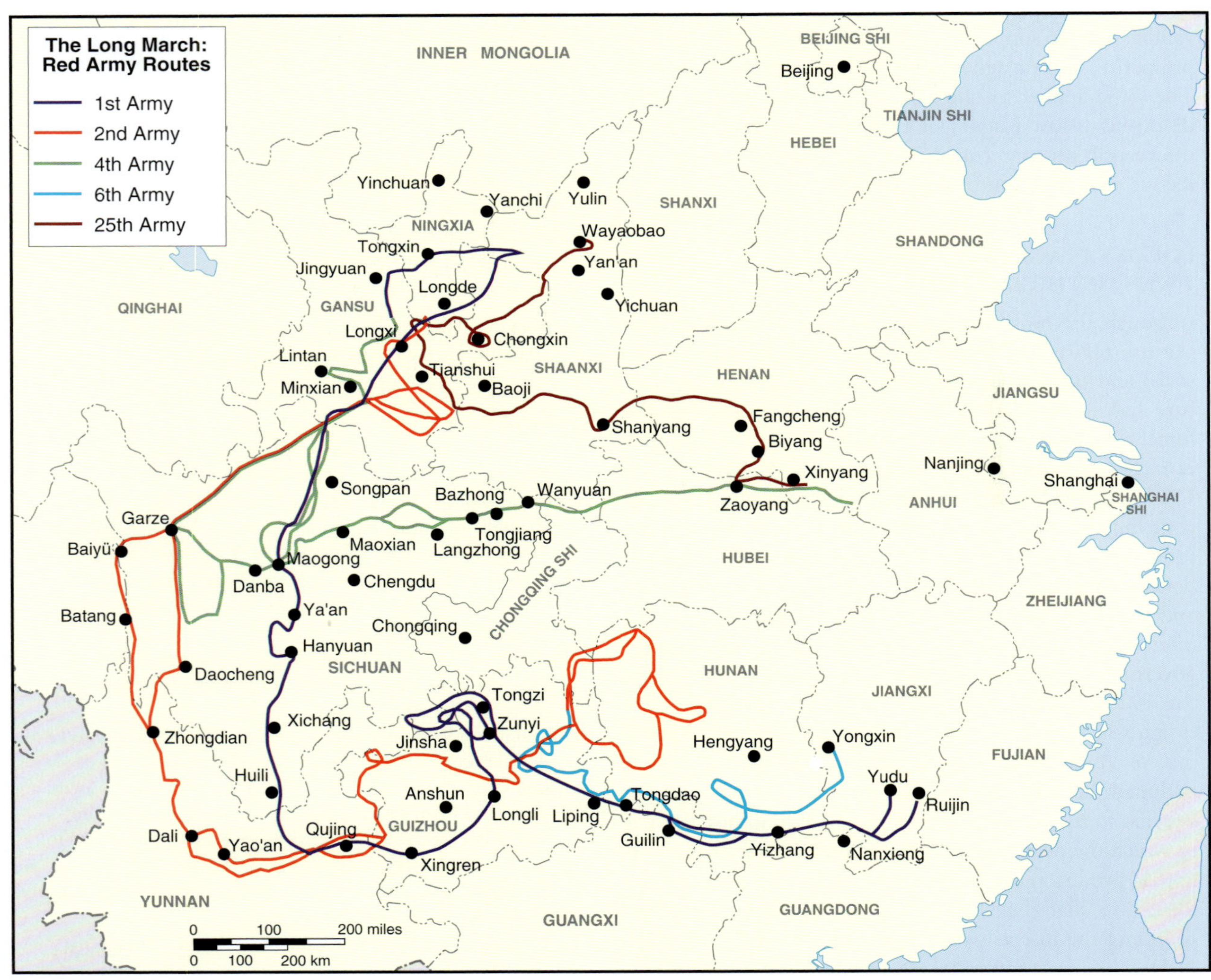

Followers of Mao Zedong on the Long March, October, 1935. *Several years after Nationalist and Communist forces split in 1927, Chiang Kai-shek engaged the Red Army, forcing Mao Zedong and the other communist generals to retreat. Chased by Chiang, the Communists suffered heavy losses while traversing the country in a two-year-long journey now referred to as the Long March.* THREE LIONS/GETTY IMAGES

mountains to avoid the Nationalist chase. During the first month, the Communist forces fought through the first three blockades by the Nationalists with few casualties. The local commander of the Nationalist force in Guangdong Province let the Communist troops by for fear that his own power would be weakened by Chiang should the battle between the Communists and Nationalists break out within the territory of Guangdong. The Red Army passed through Guangdong and reached the Guangxi-Hunan border in late November. Chiang deployed a large number of forces along the Xiang River, a tributary of Yangzi River, to reinforce the Nationalist defenses. From November 25 to December 1, 1934, the Red Army encountered severe attacks from the Nationalist Army along the Xiang River. Because of the equipment burden, the troops were unable to pass the river as quickly as needed. The Communists lost over 40,000 men in the bloody fight along the Xiang River. By the time that they crossed the river, the Red Army had been reduced to 30,000. They climbed over the mountains in Guangxi Province and entered Guizhou Province, where the local forces known as "double gun" troops—one gun for fighting and the other "gun" for smoking opium—were barely capable of defense. They easily occupied Zunyi on January 7, 1935.

Later, Zunyi became well known as a historically significant city during the Long March. From January 15 to 17, 1935, the Politburo held an enlarged meeting at Zunyi to discuss lessons from the retreat and where to head next. The resolutions adopted by the meeting, which pointed to the tactical mistakes of conventional warfare as opposed to more mobile warfare with small units, essentially reflected Mao Zedong's views. The upshot was Mao's election to full membership in the Politburo, which restored part, but not all, of his power within the Party and the Red Army. It was decided that the Red Army would go north and set up revolutionary bases in Sichuan Province. To shake pursuing Nationalist troops, the Red Army had to go back and forth over the Chishui River, a branch of the Yangzi, four times by the end of March. They entered Yunnan Province in late April. After passing over the Jinsha River, an intimidating natural barrier, around May 10, the Red Army broke through Chiang Kai-shek's encirclement. They then crossed an isolated Yi-minority area. On May 21 the Red Army was challenged by the Dadu River, where Shi Dakai, the Assistant King of the Taiping Rebellion, had suffered his final defeat in 1863. The Communist troops seized an iron-shackled bridge in Luding and crossed the natural barrier at the end of May. The Red Army reached the foot of Mount Jiajin, a snow-covered mountain. In the middle of June they climbed over the mountain and, in Maogong, met up with the Fourth Front Army led by Zhang Guotao, who in October 1932 had begun his retreat toward the west from the revolutionary bases in Hubei, Henan, and Anhui Provinces.

The union of the two Red Armies was joyfully celebrated. The Fourth Front Army had 45,000 troops, while the First Front Army numbered less than 10,000. Both were optimistic for the Red Army's future. But disagreement surfaced between the leaders of the two forces over the leadership of the Communist Party in general, and of the Red Army in particular. Zhang suggested a meeting to rectify the party's wrong political route and to reelect leaders. Mao and his supporters denied Zhang's proposal and insisted on sticking to the decision of the Zunyi meeting. The conflict resulted in separation: Mao led the First and Third Corps of the First Front Army to the north after two months of rest and struggle with Zhang. Zhang stayed and then headed south with the remaining forces. Mao and his followers suffered heavy losses trudging through the wild grasslands in Qinghai Province and eastern Tibet. On September 16 they took the Lazikou Pass. From there they opened a way to the north and reached a town called Wuqi in northern Shaanxi Province in November 1935. At the beginning of July 1936, the Second Front Army led by He Long joined the Fourth Front Army led by Zhang Guotao at Ganzi (in modern day Tibet). In October 1936 the Second and Fourth Front Armies arrived in Huining, Shaanxi Provience, welcomed by the First Front Army. The three Red Armies thus reunited and concluded the Long March.

The term *Long March* did not exist when the event actually started. The Long March was originally called "withdrawal" (*zhuanyi*) or "retreat" (*chetui*) even as late as the summer of 1935 after the Red Army finished two-thirds of its journey. The earliest record of the Long March on the Communist side *Suijun xixing jianwen lu* (Experiences of the march westward) by Chen Yun called it "expedition to the west (*xizheng*)." The earliest extant written use of the term *Long March*, dated September 12, 1935, appears in "Zhongyang guanyu Zhang Guotao tongzhi de cuowu de jueding" (Decision on Comrade Zhang Guotao's mistake). In October, after the Red Army crossed Mount Min, Mao Zedong wrote his spectacular poem "The Long March." Since then *Long March* has become the standard term for this event. Two months later Mao expounded on the significance of the Long March in a public speech later published under the title "On Tactics against Japanese Imperialism": "Speaking of the Long March, one may ask, 'What is its significance?' We answer that the Long March is the first of its kind in the annals of history, that it is a manifesto, a propaganda force, a seeding-machine."

SEE ALSO *People's Liberation Army.*

BIBLIOGRAPHY

Zhang Guotao. *Wo de huiyi* [My memoir]. Vol. 3. Hong Kong: Mingbao Yuekan Chubanshe, 1974.

Enhua Zhang

LOVE AND FRIENDSHIP

Scholars have long believed that there are fundamental differences between China and the West in the meanings and expressions of emotions within personal relationships such as love and friendship (Cheung Chan-Fai 1999; Sun Lung-Kee 1991). In Western countries, emotions are based on the concept of love, which is categorized into the eros-philia-agape schema (Joh 2007). Unlike the idea of *love* in English, *love* in Chinese culture is rooted within a rich and complex concept of *qing*. In the Chinese context, the scope of *qing* encompasses, but is not limited to, notions of care, empathy, fondness, camaraderie (friendship), forgiveness, and respect. *Qing* is so embedded in Chinese culture that it is often a sense of cultural pride; most Chinese hold the belief that *qing* is much more long-lasting, powerful, and transformative than love as defined in the West (Sun Lung-Kee 1991).

One of the most important components of the Chinese character *qing* 情 is the left part, which symbolizes the heart (心 *xin*). *Qing* is an intense and critical type of bond with the full devotion of an individual's heart. Descriptions of *qing* can be found in thousands of Chinese texts. One of the most prominent is *Qing shi* (A brief classification of stories about Qing) by the late Ming-dynasty author Feng Menglong (1574–1645). In *Qing shi*, Feng categorized *qing* into twenty-four different forms of relationships. According to Feng, *qing* saturates all kinds of relationships, including those between any two human beings, between human beings and animals, or any other type of being. This entry focuses on *qing* between two human beings.

EXPRESSION OF *QING*

Like love, *qing* is an intense and essential mode of bonding, but unlike love, *qing* is not openly expressed through verbal forms such as love letters, romantic phrases, vows of love, and so forth. Chinese are often considered the least expressive among cultures in terms of affection. The expression of *qing* is extremely indirect and subtle in traditional Chinese society (Gao Ge et al. 1996; Potter 1988). It is rare to see dating or married couples, or parents and children, holding hands, kissing, or hugging in public or even in private settings. Chinese individuals are embarrassed to say "I love you" to each other. However, scholars argue that, even with this low level of expressiveness, the commitment and assurance Chinese put into their relationships do not differ from those of Western counterparts (Yu Dehui and Gu Biling 1990).

The question thus arises: How, after all, do Chinese establish and maintain the bond of *qing*? In any relationship, whether romantic relationships or friendships, *qing* is achieved through helping and caring; "the [Chinese] expressive forms that validate the relationship are not enacted in anidiom of emotional love but an idiom of work and mutual aid" (Potter 1988, pp. 201–202). For example, cooking someone a meal, helping with housework, and teaching someone a skill are considered by many Chinese to be a more effective way of expressing emotions than simply saying "I love you." This is ironic, in that many Westerners feel that a direct statement of emotion is a more effective means of increasing the bond between individuals, and the lack of such expression would be considered abnormal.

ROMANTIC RELATIONSHIPS: LOVE

The concept of erotic love was completely absent in traditional Chinese society when referring to affection within a romantic relationship (Cheung Chan-Fai 1993). *Qing* symbolizes mutual good feelings and emphasizes mutual support and care, understanding, and consideration, with little emphasis on the erotic or sexual attraction. Unlike the Western notion of passionate and spontaneous love reflected in William Shakespeare's sixteenth-century play *Romeo and Juliet*, *qing* is often cultivated and nurtured over a period of time through mutual support rather than vows of love (Yu Dehui and Gu Biling 1990). The Chinese legend of Liang Shanbo and Zhu Yingtai (Liang-Zhu), also known as the Butterfly Lovers, is the best example of how *qing* fully saturates a "romantic" relationship. In the story of Liang-Zhu, there is no passion, struggle, mutual sexual attraction, or spontaneity, which are among the most essential elements of romantic love in Western culture (Cheung Chan-Fai 1999). There is, in addition, no promise or verbal expression of love. Romeo and Juliet fall in love at first sight, whereas the relationship of Liang and Zhu develops over seven years.

Family has played an important role in determining the striking difference between love as presented in *Romeo and Juliet* and the *qing* of Liang-Zhu. Unlike Western ideology, individual will and freedom were not recognized in traditional Chinese society. Like the love of Romeo and Juliet, the *qing* between Liang and Zhu is not permitted by their parents. However, unlike Romeo and Juliet's rebellious struggle against their parents, Liang and Zhu followed their parents' will, and their *qing* did not develop into marriage. For them, family obligation, the principal rule of *li* (ritual propriety), the foremost personal virtue, overrules the further development of *qing*.

Many Westerners believe that love is a necessity for marriage. However, in Chinese society, two individuals could marry each other without mutual attraction. Marriage was primarily a fulfillment of family obligation, a continuation of the family line, and an observance of *li* (Honig and Hershatter 1988). Marriages arranged by parents (*fumu baoban*) were the dominant form of "courtship." Mutual attraction, or *qing*, was not a consideration. After a couple married, they were encouraged to slowly cultivate *qing* through day-to-day interactions, in particular, through mutual care and help (Sun Lung-Kee 1991).

The Western notion of romantic love and marriage to a partner of one's choice emerged in China around the time of the 1911 revolution, when it was embraced and promoted by radical students and avant-garde writers during the May Fourth era. Influenced by Western ideology, these young pioneers advocated democracy and individual freedom, and the abolition of the old tradition of arranged marriage. Many popular novels from the May Fourth era depicted the spread of romantic love among the young and educated. These novels include *Shangshi* (Regret for the past) by Lu Xun (1881–1936), *Aiqing sanbuqu* ("Love" trilogy) and *Jiliu sanbuqu* ("Torrents" trilogy) by Ba Jin (1904–2005), and *Hulanhe* (Tales of Hulan River) by Xiao Hong

(1911–1942). It was not until the 1950s, however, that a new democratic marriage law officially abolishing arranged marriage was enacted. The law was amended in the 1980s to allow individual freedom to date and mate (Johnson 1983).

The concepts of love, passion, and romance have been flourishing in Chinese society as the door that China opens to the outside world becomes wider (Yan Yunxiang 2003), a process that has also occurred in Hong Kong and Taiwan. The Western concept of romantic (erotic) love has gradually become common. In popular media, stories of "passionate love" have become widely popular. The expression of the romantic vow "I love you" has also become more and more common among younger generations. The conception and expression of love and *qing* are thus experiencing major changes in contemporary Chinese society. Key elements of *qing* continue to be highly valued, however, even as the more expressive aspects of erotic love have become more widely accepted and emphasized in interpersonal relationships.

FRIENDSHIP

Friendship is another important form of relationship within the scope of *qing*. In China, friends were often described as "someone who knows my sounds" (*zhiyin*), "someone who shares my heart" (*tongxin*), or "someone who shares my life goal" (*tongzhi*). The importance of friendships in individual fulfillment and life satisfaction was greatly valued and appreciated in traditional Chinese society (Sun Lung-Kee 1991).

Traditionally, friendship was allowed only among males; women were separated and kept isolated from each other. Friendship among women, sisterhood, was unlikely to develop and impossible to maintain. Friendship among women was strictly prohibited and suppressed by the powerful (Mann 2000). For Chinese men, in contrast, establishing strong friendships was seen as a sign of masculinity and maturity. *San guo yan yi* (Romance of the three kingdoms) by Luo Guanzhong (1330–1400), *Shui hu zhuan* (All men are brothers) by Shi Naian (1296–1371), and *Xi you ji* (Journey to the west) by Wu Chengen (1500–1582) are the most famous Chinese novels that celebrate such intensive bonds (*qing*), in which men join for a common purpose. Sometimes, such bonds stimulated the formation of factions (*dang*) that sparked political action against the government (Mann 2000). That is why generations of dynasties and governments, including the Chinese Communist Party (CCP), kept a close watch on the formation of groups and brotherhoods.

Since the establishment of the People's Republic of China, the norms and behaviors of friendship have undergone major transformations under the leadership of the CCP, mainly through the replacement of friendship with "comradeship" (Gold 1985; Vogel 1965). Comradeship was seen as "a universalistic morality in which all citizens are in important respects equal under the state, and gradations on the basis of status or degree of closeness cannot legitimately interfere with this equality" (MacFarquhar 1966, p. 407). Friendship is a particular type of attachment where one is concerned about and helps only special individuals with whom one shares the bond of *qing*. Comradeship, in contrast, requires individuals to treat everyone equally, whether or not there is a bond of *qing*. Ezra Vogel (1965) stated bluntly that the CCP successfully achieved this transformation through a regime of fear. People were afraid that today's confidences might lead to tomorrow's sanction or punishment by the government. A sense of trust and commitment was almost impossible to establish because everyone was concerned about his or her own survival under the CCP regime. The paramount values of confidence and commitment through friendship were weakened, even though people continued to be friendly to each other through comradeship.

Since the end of the Cultural Revolution (1966–1969) and the start of economic reforms, comradeship as described above has become much less influential. Although people continue to maintain a cautious attitude when confiding with someone, friendship has regained its status as a vital part of personal relations. Chinese people value a small circle of close friends, with whom they can talk about anything (Gold 1985). However, there remains a common perception of the instrumental nature of friendship, expressed by the aphorism, "friendship is temporary; only self-interest is forever" (*pengyou shi zanshi de, liyi shi yongheng de*).

SEE ALSO *Life Cycle: Marriage; Sexuality.*

BIBLIOGRAPHY

Cheung Chan-Fai (Chan-fai Cheung). Eros and Qing: A Comparative Study of the Western and Chinese Concept of Love. In *Proceedings of the Second International Symposium on Comparative Studies of Eastern and Western Philosophy*, 293–304. Taibei: Chinese Cultural University, 1993.

Cheung Chan-Fai (Chan-fai Cheung). Western Love, Chinese Qing: A Philosophical Interpretation of the Idea of Love in *Romeo and Juliet* and *The Butterfly Love. Journal of Chinese Philosophy* 26, 4 (1999): 469–488.

Gao Ge, Stella Ting-Toomey, and William B. Gudykunst. Chinese Communication Processes. In *The Handbook of Chinese Psychology*, ed. Michael Harris Bond, 280–293. Hong Kong: Oxford University Press, 1996.

Gold, Thomas B. After Comradeship: Personal Relations in China since the Cultural Revolution. *China Quarterly* 104 (1985): 657–675.

Honig, Emily, and Gail Hershatter. *Personal Voices: Chinese Women in the 1980's*. Stanford, CA: Stanford University Press, 1988.

Joh, Wonhee Anne. Violence and Asian American Experience: From Abjection to *Jeong*. In *Off the Menu: Asian and Asian North American Women's Religion and Theology*, ed. Rita Nakashima Brock, Kwok Pui-Lan, Jung Ha Kim, and Seung Ai Yang, 145–162. Louisville, KY: Westminster John Knox Press, 2007.

Johnson, Kay Anne. *Women, the Family, and Peasant Revolution in China*. Chicago: University of Chicago Press, 1983.

MacFarquhar, Roderick, ed. *China under Mao: Politics Takes Command*. Cambridge, MA: MIT Press, 1966.

Mann, Susan. AHR Forum: The Male Bond in Chinese History and Culture. *American Historical Review* 105, 5 (2000): 1600–1614.

Potter, Sulamith Heins. The Cultural Construction of Emotion in Rural Chinese Social Life. *Ethos* 16, 2 (1988): 181–208.

Sun Lung-Kee (Lung-kee Sun). Contemporary Chinese Culture: Structure and Emotionality. *Australian Journal of Chinese Affairs* 26 (1991): 1–41.

Vogel, Ezra. From Friendship to Comradeship: The Change in Personal Relations in Communist China. *China Quarterly* 21 (1965): 46–60.

Yan Yunxiang (Yunciang Yan). *Private Life under Socialism: Love, Intimacy, and Family Change in a Chinese Village, 1949–1999*. Stanford, CA: Stanford University Press, 2003.

Yu Dehui (Dehui Yu) and Gu Biling (Biling Gu). Zhong guo ren de qing mian jiao lu [Chinese face concerns]. In *Zhong guo ren de mian ju xing ge: Ren qing yu mian zi* [China's mask character], ed. Huiqiu Zhan, 63–107. Taibei (Taipei): Zhang Lao Chi Chubanshe, 1990.

Luo Baozhen (Baozhen Luo)

LU XUN

1881–1936

A writer often called the father of modern Chinese literature, Lu Xun's centrality to the formation and development of modern Chinese literature has been nearly universally accepted. Only in recent years have intellectuals—some from a neoconservative perspective and others from a postmodern, postcolonial perspective—questioned Lu Xun's preeminence in the pantheon of modern Chinese writers. To be sure, Lu Xun studies have been a highly politicized affair from their inception. Even by the 1920s Lu Xun was fashioned into an icon of the May Fourth enlightenment and its iconoclastic attack on the "man-eating" Confucian tradition. After Lu Xun's death in 1936, Mao Zedong, the Communist Party, and Marxist literary critics became important agents in reshaping Lu Xun into a "Chinese Gorky," an icon of the revolution and the party. This image of Lu Xun dominated after 1949, and during the Cultural Revolution he became a poster boy for the radical leftists. In the post-Mao period, Lu Xun's role in the Chinese enlightenment was reemphasized and his humanism restored; he was recast as a voice of moral conscience and liberal disaffection. In reaction to his virtual deification in the Mao era, some scholars have sought to present him in a more human fashion, complete with faults, both personal and literary. A few—most famously the writers Wang Shuo and Feng Jicai—have gone so far as to suggest that his reputation as a writer is largely undeserved. Clearly, the struggle over the image and representation of Lu Xun has been a highly contentious one in which agents have appropriated Lu Xun for their own political, literary, or cultural agendas.

LIFE

Lu Xun was born into a scholar-gentry family from Shaoxing, Zhejiang province, Zhou Zhangshou is best known by his pen name Lu Xun. His courtesy name was Yushan, and during his student years in Nanjing, he used the name Zhou Shuren. In Marxist scholarship, Lu Xun's family is invariably described as "in decline," though no doubt the extent of this decline is exaggerated to emphasize his proper class consciousness. His first schooling was traditional and took place at a private clan school. From 1898 to 1902 he studied Western learning in two different Nanjing academies. He spent the next seven years in Japan, first studying Japanese in a language preparatory school in Tokyo, then pursuing a medical degree at a university in Sendai. Disenchanted with his medical studies, Lu Xun returned to Tokyo to pursue a literary career. There he wrote classical essays on a variety of modern topics—history of science, geology, and cultural criticism—and also translated with Zhou Zuoren, his younger brother, a collection of European short stories.

In financial straits and with his literary career going nowhere, Lu Xun returned to China, first to Hangzhou and then to his native Shaoxing, to take up teaching positions. In 1912 he moved briefly to Nanjing and then to Beijing for employment in the Ministry of Education of the newly established Republican government. Beijing would be his home until 1926. There he wrote the startlingly original and morally complex short fiction, prose poetry, and essays upon which his reputation as a writer is primarily based. Retaining his ministry position, Lu Xun also taught Chinese literature at various Beijing universities. In 1925, while married to a woman chosen for him by his mother, Lu Xun developed an intimate relationship with his student Xu Guangping, who would later become his common-law wife.

Finding the political situation of the warlord government oppressive, Lu Xun left Beijing. He taught for several months at Xiamen University, and then took up another short-term teaching position at Zhongshan University in Guangzhou, which was the center of the surging revolutionary movement. Lu Xun spent the final nine years of his life in Shanghai, where he would become the titular head of the League of Left-Wing Writers and publish numerous volumes of essays in the satiric miscellaneous (*zawen*) style. Lu Xun, the most famous writer in China, died of tuberculosis on October 19, 1936.

FICTION

Lu Xun's entire fictional output, for which he is most well known, is limited to one classical-language story and three volumes of stories in the modern vernacular: *Nahan* (1923; *Call to Arms*, also known as *Outcry* and *Cheering from the Sidelines*), *Panghuang* (1926; *Wandering*, also known as *Hesitation* and *Wondering Where to Turn*), and *Gushi xinbian* (1936; *Old Tales Retold*), a total of just thirty-four stories. While some have speculated that Lu Xun's personality inclined him toward brevity of form and concision of language and that he was fundamentally averse to the novel form, others have suggested that his intellectual interests were simply so diverse as to preclude sustained attention to longer narrative forms. The influence of the classical tradition, which favored brevity, is also apparent.

As Mao Dun first noted, Lu Xun played extensively and imaginatively with form and technique, and each of his stories is in some sense an experiment in genre. His fiction includes first-person autobiographical reminiscences, diaries, satires of intellectual pretension, allegories about the problem of the cultural tradition and the deficiencies of the Chinese national character, lyrical reminiscences, revisionist historical tales, and parodies of classical and popular genres. More than any other writer of the time, he explored the complex ironic possibilities of the first-person narrative mode. Frequently in the form of a reminiscence by a modern intellectual, these first-person stories often play ironically with that perspective, casting doubt on the moral integrity and enlightenment pretensions of the intelligentsia. His satirical portraits of high-minded, moralizing conservative scholars were heavily imitated in the 1930s.

Lu Xun's fiction was just as original in theme as it was in form. "Kuangren riji" (Diary of a madman, 1918) presents the diary of a delusional paranoid who thinks people are conspiring to eat him. Obviously allegorical, the story presents the madman as enlightened and denounces the Confucian social system as "cannibalistic." Often overlooked in Marxist scholarship, the story also problematizes the very notion of enlightenment by informing the reader in a framing preface in classical Chinese that the madman was eventually cured of his illness, that he chose the name of the diary, and that he is waiting to take up a position in the state bureaucracy. "Ah Q zhengzhuan" (The true story of Ah Q, 1921), Lu Xun's longest and most famous story, is centered on the figure of Ah Q, a homeless man who ekes out a living in a small town as a temporary worker. Ah Q is less a character who draws out the reader's sympathy than a symbol of what is wrong with the Chinese national character: jingoistic, living in an illusory world of self-deception, and spiritually and morally weak. At the end of the story, Ah Q is taken to the execution ground and the focus of Lu Xun's attack shifts from the now pitiable Ah Q to the spectators, who have come to enjoy the spectacle of his death. "Kong Yiji" (1919) and "Yao" (Medicine, 1919) similarly denounce tradition even as they pessimistically ponder the possibility of realizing an alternative.

Scholarship has often emphasized the foreign influences on Lu Xun's fiction (e.g., Guy de Maupassant, Nikolai Gogol, Henryk Sienkiewicz, Leonid Andreyev, Natsume Sōseki) and his themes (e.g., Nietzschean iconoclasm), but his debt to Chinese tradition is equally strong. One critic has drawn attention to the irony that the cultural approach to social transformation of Lu Xun and many of his May Fourth contemporaries is itself a product of that tradition.

The stories in *Wandering* tend to be less polemical and iconoclastic than the stories discussed above, all from *Call to Arms*. The best works in this collection are complex first-person stories, such as "Zhufu" (New Year's sacrifice, 1924), "Zai jiulou shang" (Upstairs in the tavern, 1924), "Guduzhe" (The misanthrope, 1925), and "Shangshi" (Regret for the past, 1925), whose narrators are all modern intellectuals. The stories tend to be less sanguine about the possibility of social transformation than those in *Call to Arms*. Characters in these stories are disillusioned, depressed, or caught between contending allegiances as they consider this possibility.

Lu Xun's third collection of fiction, *Old Tales Retold*, is markedly different from the first two. Here he reshapes ancient myths and legends—for example, the stories of Nüwa patching the sky, of Chang E stealing the elixir of immortality and fleeing to the moon, or of Yu the Great quelling the floods. Also featured in these tales are such traditional cultural heroes as the sage kings Yao and Shun, the hermits Bo Yi and Shu Qi, and the philosophers Mozi, Laozi, and Zhuangzi. As a whole, the tales present an irreverent view of China's cultural heroes. Laozi, for instance, is presented as an incurable talker who takes no action and whose ideas are nonsensical and socially irrelevant; Hou Yi, the legendary hero who saved the world from the ten suns that parched the earth, is henpecked and impotent. Lu Xun also inserts into these historical tales biting criticisms of his enemies in the contemporary cultural field, leading some critics to view the collection as unfocussed in intent and uneven in quality. Although this criticism is justified, the stories do show flashes of linguistic brilliance and thematic depth.

ESSAYS

Lu Xun published some eighteen volumes of essays, which thus outstrip by far his production in fiction. Yet, as in his fiction, the experimental nature of Lu Xun's essays is also pronounced. He wrote on a great variety of subjects and in an astounding array of forms and styles: longish treatises in classical language, essays in the form of letters, memorials to the dead, speeches to the living, parodies, aphorisms, polemics, caustic satires, autobiographical reminiscences, prefaces, random thoughts, etc. The essays make use of a broad range of rhetorical styles drawn from both the Chinese and Western traditions.

Lu Xun speaking at Beijing Normal University, November 27, 1932. *Considered a seminal figure in modern Chinese literature, Lu Xun published a variety of essays and short fiction after the establishment of the Republic of China. Even after his death from tuberculosis in 1936, Lu remained an influential figure in Communist China, with his publications satirizing the traditional elite promoted during the rule of Mao Zedong.* FOTOE

Many of the essays have an ironic tone that Lu Xun used to mock his enemies (Confucian moralists, reactionary politicians and their gentleman supporters, humanist intellectuals, self-professed revolutionary writers) and their intellectual failings. In Lu Xun's hands, the essay was an elastic and playful form to be used for cultural and political criticism.

Some of the essays are explicitly polemical and without much subtlety or artistry, but many of them are gems of prose that have transcended the particular historical context in and for which they were written. In his early vernacular random thoughts (*suigan lu*), he often targeted the proponents of "national essence," those who lamented that Western influence was tearing apart China's cultural fabric. For Lu Xun, the antidote to this kind of delusional national psychology was the strong individual who could speak truth to false consciousness. In "Lun zhengle yan kan" (On facing facts, 1925), Lu Xun criticizes the tendency in his cultural tradition to whitewash reality: "Afraid to look facts in the face, the Chinese resort to concealment and deceit to contrive ingenious lines of retreat, and think this quite right and proper. This shows the cowardice, laziness and cunning of our national character. Content to go downhill from day to day, we imagine we are advancing from glory to glory." In "Lun 'renyan kewei' " (On "gossip is a fearful thing," 1935), he attacks the popular media for its complicity in the oppression of women.

Like his stories, the essays also have a strong self-reflective quality. In "Da Youheng xiansheng" (In reply to Mr. Youheng, 1927), Lu Xun wonders if his own writing might not be contributing to social oppression:

> I have said before that since ancient times a man-eating feast has been set out in China, attended by the feasters and their victims. Those who are eaten have previously eaten others; those eating now will also be eaten later. But now I have discovered that I myself am helping set out this feast. You have read my works, sir, so let me ask you a question: After reading them, do you feel numbed or more clear-headed? Do they stupefy you or enlighten you? If you feel they do the latter, then my self-indictment is basically proved. Chinese feasts serve live shrimps steeped in wine. The more frisky the shrimps, the greater the eater's relish and enjoyment. I am one who helps prepare this dish by clearing the minds and intensifying the feelings of honest and innocent young people.

Lu Xun's essays—and his writing more generally—stand out in modern Chinese literature for their unique intermingling of social engagement with introspective soul searching.

OTHER CONTRIBUTIONS

Lu Xun contributed to the cultural scene of Republican China in a variety of other ways. His prose-poetry collection

Yecao (Wild grass, 1926), one of the first of its kind in China, presents twenty-four poems that are deeply personal yet resonate with important cultural and political issues of the day. Some critics consider them modernist in style because of their Symbolist quality. One poem, "Mujiewen" (Epitaph, 1925), for example, recounts a dream in which the dreamer comes to a tombstone on which is written the epitaph of a snake that ate its own heart. While Marxist critics in China have tended to interpret the poems as responses to particular moments in the political history of the day, their attention to alienation, psychological conflicts and trauma, macabre imagery, and dreamlike quality suggest more personal motivations.

Lu Xun was a prolific translator. He translated Japanese literary theory (e.g., Kuriyagawa Hakuson's *Symbols of Anguish*), Russian literary theory (Georgy Plekhanov), and Gogol's *Dead Souls*. He promoted, and was ridiculed in some camps for his advocacy of, literal translation that captured the essence of the style of the original, even if it resulted in language that was not smooth.

Lu Xun was also a scholar. His *Zhongguo xiaoshuo shilüe* (A brief history of Chinese fiction, 1925) is one of the first Chinese works of literary scholarship to describe and analyze the traditionally scorned genre of fiction. It is still widely cited today. Finally, Lu Xun also promoted the visuals arts, most famously, an avant-garde style of woodblock print, though he was also interested in less explicitly political forms of graphic art He collected such art, organized exhibitions, lent his support to woodblock-printing societies (e.g., the Eighteen Arts Society), and published catalogues and wrote prefaces for them.

Lu Xun was a central literary figure in the 1920s and 1930s. He actively participated in the literary debates of the time, edited or oversaw the editing of numerous journals and publishing projects, was the titular head of the League of Left-Wing Writers (1930–1936), and was an untiring patron of younger writers (among whom the best known are Xiao Jun, Xiao Hong, Duanmu Hongliang, and Rou Shi).

LEGACY

Even as they reacted against the Maoist politics that lionized Lu Xun, intellectuals and writers in the post-Mao period of liberalization continued to reread him, refer to him, allude to his work, and delve into the kinds of moral and cultural issues he raised. From the ironic realism of Gao Xiaosheng to the avant-gardism of Yu Hua, Lu Xun's presence can be seen in the writings of a host of contemporary authors in post-Mao China. Struggle over how best to conceive Lu Xun has been central to the literary history of modern China, and his image—both as enlightened individualist and Chinese Gorky—encapsulates the cultural problematic of modern China, caught between the discourses of enlightenment and national salvation.

In the West, Lu Xun has recently been cast in a new mold, perhaps equally problematic. The American Marxist Fredric Jameson has portrayed Lu Xun as a prototypical third-world intellectual and his short fiction as "third-world national allegories" par excellence. Lu Xun is the third-world "cultural revolutionary" who will awaken the soundly sleeping first-world intellectual caught in an "iron house" of literary irrelevance, Jameson asserts.

SEE ALSO *League of Left-Wing Writers; Li Hua; May Fourth Movement.*

BIBLIOGRAPHY

Foster, Paul B. *Ah Q Archaeology: Lu Xun, Ah Q, Ah Q's Progeny, and the National Character Discourse in Twentieth Century China*. Lanham, MD: Lexington Books, 2005.

Hsü, Raymond. *The Style of Lu Hsun: Vocabulary and Usage*. HK: Centre of Asian Studies, University of Hong Kong, 1979.

Jameson, Frederic. Third World Literature in the Era of Multinational Capitalism. *Social Text: Theory/Culture/Ideology* 15 (1986): 65–88.

Kowallis, Jon. *The Lyrical Lu Xun: A Study of His Classical Style Verse*. Honolulu: University of Hawaii Press, 1996.

Lee, Leo Ou-fan, ed. *Lu Xun and His Legacy*. Berkeley: University of California Press, 1985.

Lee, Leo Ou-fan. *Voices from the Iron House: A Study of Lu Xun*. Bloomington: Indiana University Press, 1987.

Lin, Yu-sheng. *The Crisis of Chinese Consciousness: Radical Anti-traditionalism in the May Fourth Era*. Madison: University of Wisconsin Press, 1979.

McDougall, Bonnie S. *Love-Letters and Privacy in Modern China: The Intimate Lives of Lu Xun and Xu Guangping*. Oxford, U.K.: Oxford University Press, 2002.

Pollard, David E. *The True Story of Lu Xun*. Hong Kong: Chinese University Press, 2002.

Pusey, James Reeves. *Lu Xun and Evolution*. Albany: State University of New York Press, 1998.

Semanov, V. I. *Lu Hsun and His Predecessors*. Trans. Charlers Alber. White Plains, NY: Sharpe, 1980.

Wang Shiqing. *Lu Xun, a Biography*. Trans. Zhang Peiji. Ed. Bonnie S. McDougall and Tang Bowen. Beijing: Foreign Languages Press, 1984.

Wang Xiaoming. *Wufa zhimian de rensheng: Lu Xun zhuan* [A life that cannot be faced directly: A biography of Lu Xun]. Taibei: Yeqiang Chubanshe, 1992.

Kirk A. Denton

LU ZUOFU
1893–1952

Lu Zuofu is now chiefly remembered as an entrepreneur and pioneer of Chinese shipping. The Minsheng Shipping Company (Minsheng Gongsi), which Lu founded in 1925, was revived in the 1980s by his son, Lu Guoji, and is now one of China's largest nonstate enterprises, with branches in major cities and ports along the coast and the Yangzi River. In addition to being an astute businessman, Lu Zuofu was a modernizer with a broad social vision. He worked to promote mass education, rural reconstruction, public health, and business management, which he believed were all essential elements of the modernization he so much desired. Lu was a Sichuanese with great pride in his native place, and he conducted extensive modernization projects there.

EARLY LIFE AND CAREER

Lu was born on April 14, 1893, in Hechuan County near Chongqing. He joined Sun Yat-sen's (Sun Yixian's) Tongmenghui in 1910. Despite an impoverished rural background, Lu acquired enough education to work as an editor, first of *Qun bao* (The masses) and later of *Chuan bao* (Sichuan newspaper), before becoming a mathematics teacher. He wrote articles on such issues as social backwardness and poverty. On trips to Shanghai in 1914 and 1922, he gained experience in long-distance river transport, and met reformers such as Huang Yanpei (1878–1965), a famous educator and advocate for rural reconstruction. These experiences inspired Lu to consider how Sichuan could emulate Shanghai.

Lu became an education official in Sichuan in 1921. Like many reformers, he regarded dirt and sickness as symptoms of China's backwardness; thus his first mass education experiment focused on hygiene and public health. In 1925 he became an adviser to the Sichuan warlord Liu Xiang (1890–1938), who subsequently appointed him director of Upper Yangzi Navigation. Lu began to put his reformist ideas into practice, establishing in quick succession an Academy of Sciences of Western China, middle schools, hospitals, factories, and mines. Influenced by Huang Yanpei's ideas on rural development, Lu built modern facilities, such as a library, museum, exhibition hall, and amusement park, in Beibei, a backward rural town close to his birthplace.

THE MINSHENG SHIPPING COMPANY

The resources for Lu's Beibei project came mostly from Minsheng, the shipping line he set up in 1925 to challenge the foreign domination of trade routes on the Upper Yangzi. The name *Minsheng*, meaning "people's livelihood"—one of Sun Yat-sen's Three People's Principles—reflected Lu's commitment to goals broader than his own business. Liu Xiang granted the company monopoly rights to shipping routes that connected Chongqing to Hechuan, Changshou, and Fuling. In 1930 Lu moved Minsheng's headquarters from Hechuan to Chongqing. A large percentage of the annual profit was invested in expansion, and by 1937 Minsheng was the biggest steamship company on the Upper Yangzi, with forty-six vessels.

Lu's interest in modern business was stimulated by a tour he made in 1930, visiting Shanghai, Nanjing, Nantong, Qingdao, Dalian, Tianjin, Shenyang, Harbin, Changchun, and Beijing. He was particularly impressed by Zhang Jian's modernizing project in Nantong. For Lu Zuofu, Minsheng's new business culture was part of his social reform project. He summed it up as "clean, orderly, classless, and with Chinese in command" (Reinhardt 2002, p. 278). The cleanliness of the steamers was supposed both to attract passengers and to teach them the principles of modern hygiene. The company employed educated Chinese rather than foreigners, and operated a system based on rewards and punishments that allowed hardworking staff at any level the possibility of promotion. It recruited new workers by open examinations in Chinese, English, math, record keeping, and general knowledge, and it conducted interviews and psychological and physical tests. Workers underwent several months of training before they took up their jobs. New workers were indoctrinated in the "Minsheng spirit" to actively and dutifully serve the company and the nation.

MINSHENG'S WARTIME EXPANSION

Lu was strongly committed to resistance to the Japanese. When the war began in July 1937, he played a vital role in the evacuation of the national government and its arsenals and industrial plants and equipment from the vulnerable seaboard provinces up the Yangzi, first to Wuhan and then to Chongqing. The company also assumed control of all the foreign-operated steamers in Sichuan waters. During this period, Minsheng expanded its fleet, while its rivals, the China Merchants' Steam Navigation Company and Sanbei, suffered because their interests had been concentrated in territory occupied by the Japanese. Shipping was crucial to the war effort and economic development, and the Minsheng Company became the major wartime transport company in Chongqing.

Lu's achievements were possible in part because of his talent for forging political relationships. He had first prospered under Liu Xiang's warlord regime in Sichuan. In 1936 he persuaded Liu Xiang to improve relations with the national government under Chiang Kai-shek (Jiang Jieshi). From 1938 to 1942, Lu served as assistant minister of communications in the Nationalist government, then based in Chongqing. He also headed the Food Management Bureau from 1940 to 1942. Both positions were relevant to his commercial interests. Throughout the war, the Minsheng Company, still under Lu's direction, held major government contracts for transporting military and food supplies. Having purchased several major industrial firms, it also emerged as the leading business group in

Chongqing, with interests in textiles, coal mining, and machine works. Lu became director of eleven major companies. After the war, Lu bought ships from the United States and raised a huge loan from Canada to finance the construction of more river steamers and Minsheng's expansion into the Pacific Ocean carrying trade. By 1948 the company operated 111 vessels totaling 63,174 tons.

AFTER 1949

When the new Communist government took power in 1949, Lu at first attempted to manage his business from Hong Kong but experienced great difficulties in servicing his loans. Overtures from the Communist government, anxious to secure the assistance of industrialists to revive the economy, tempted him back to Beijing, where he was made a member of the first People's Consultative Congress and was received by both Mao Zedong and Zhou Enlai. In Chongqing, Minsheng's close links to the Guomindang had led to its interests being confiscated by the Southwest Military and Administrative Committee (of which, however, Lu was made a member). Lu lost executive control over the company, and the Canadian debt remained unserviced.

Lu Zuofu was elected to the presidium of the People's Court in Chongqing in 1952. After his secretary of many years, who was in the courtroom during a trial, made political and financial accusations against Lu, it was decided that Lu himself should stand trial. The Five-Anti's campaign against bribery, tax evasion, theft of state property, cheating on government contracts, and theft of state economic information had just been launched, and private businesspeople were under great pressure. Lu took an overdose of barbiturates, and died that night.

Today, Lu is recognized in China as a patriotic figure who played a constructive role in society. Mao Zedong himself called Lu one of the unforgettable industrialists of Chinese history. Lu's collected works were brought out by the prestigious Beijing University Publishing House in 1999, and Minsheng has once more become a major shipping company.

SEE ALSO *China Merchants' Steam Navigation Company; Sichuan; Transport Infrastructure: Shipping since 1949.*

BIBLIOGRAPHY

Economist. Face Value: Lu Zuofu, an Old-Fashioned Chinese Capitalist. October 2, 1997.

Minsheng Industrial Group. History of Ming Sung Company. http://en.msshipping.cn/Html/Article_Show.asp?ID=13.

Reinhardt, Anne. Navigating Imperialism in China: Steamship, Semicolony, and Nation, 1860–1937. Ph.D. diss., Princeton University, 2002.

Zhang Jin. Hygenic Modernity: Beyond Rural Reconstruction? Lu Zuofu and the Public Health (Weisheng) Movement at Beibei. *Chinese Business History* 17, 3 (2007): 1–3.

Lai Chi-kong
Delia Davin

LUO GONGLIU
1916–2004

Luo Gongliu, born in Kaiping, Guangdong, was an artist and art educator distinguished by his rich experiences and fruitful artistic experiments. In 1936 he entered the National Art Academy in Hangzhou, a state-sponsored art college then directed by Lin Fengmian (1900–1991), who had become deeply interested in fauvist and cubist painting during his study in France. Like other students of the academy, Luo was exposed to the latest Western concepts as well as to traditional Chinese painting. The 1937 Japanese military invasion of China forced the school, like many educational institutions, to retreat inland to the wartime capital established in Chongqing, Sichuan, thus preventing Luo and his fellow schoolmates from graduating. Luo chose instead to travel to the Communist base at Yan'an in 1938 and involve himself in creating woodblock prints that served as wartime propaganda pictures. That same year he joined the Communist Party and was recruited into the Lu Xun Academy of Literature and Art in Yan'an. An active member of the academy's woodcut group, Luo participated in redesigning *nianhua* (rustic new year's prints), an effort aimed at counteracting the influence of Japanese propaganda prints that were based on Chinese folk print conventions. Particularly after Mao Zedong's Yan'an Forum on Literature and Art, Luo's woodblock works followed the party's preference for simple styles and rural subject matter that might appeal to the local populace, in contrast to the Europeanized woodcuts of the urban Shanghai woodcut movement. One frequently republished work from that period was his set of illustrations for Zhao Shuli's novel *Li Youcai Banhua* (The rhymes of Li Youcai, 1943). The illustrations were first published with the novel in *Jiefang ribao* (*Liberation Daily*) on June 26 and 27 and from June 29 to July 5, 1946.

Luo Gongliu's firsthand experiences of rural life and warfare benefited his career after liberation. In 1948 he moved with the Communist forces to Hebei and became a faculty member of the new North China United University. After the establishment of the People's Republic of China in 1949, Luo was designated a professor and later the chair of the painting department at the Central Academy of Fine Arts in Beijing. Luo and other wartime propaganda artists faced a new challenge with their mission to create large history paintings for the newly established Central Museum of Revolutionary History, which opened in 1951. As Julia F. Andrews observes in her 1994 study, as a result of Soviet influence the idea that oil paintings might have a patriotic function became widely accepted. Luo contributed two history paintings, *Tunnel Warfare* (1951) and *Mao Zedong Reporting on the Rectification in Yan'an* (1951), which were well-received and launched his return to oil painting.

In 1955 Luo was sent to the USSR and studied at the Repin Academy of Arts in Leningrad for the next three years. Through a curriculum specially designed for faculty members, which included copying masterpieces in museums and drawing from nature, his oil painting vocabulary, particularly his use of color, was greatly enriched. Upon returning to Beijing in 1958, Luo was appointed director of a history painting campaign that was unprecedented in its ambition. In 1958 and 1959 the city was in the midst of a construction project on a massive scale to celebrate the tenth anniversary of the new nation. A great many large history paintings were needed to ornament the new architectural projects, which were referred to collectively as the Ten Great Buildings. Newly commissioned works by artists called to Beijing from all over the nation filled the walls and storerooms of the new Great Hall of the People and the Museum of Revolutionary History. Luo himself painted *Mao Zedong at Mount Jinggang* in 1961 for the museum when he again served as director of a second history painting campaign. China's break with the Soviet Union in 1960 required a great deal of finesse on the part of Soviet-educated cultural administrators, and Luo successfully navigated a turn that took critical rhetoric in a more nationalistic, but slightly less restrictive, direction.

The mountain setting of *Mao Zedong at Mount Jinggang* appears to some viewers to incorporate a quotation from the fourteenth-century ink masterpiece by Huang Gongwang, *Dwelling in the Fuchun Mountains*. In any case, the work shows Luo's experimental approach in sinicizing oil painting or, in the terminology of the day, creating Chinese oil painting in a "national style." He sets Mao Zedong against a poetic, expansive landscape in the Chinese manner, and indeed his modeling of the distant mountains even suggests the appearance of the schematic "texture strokes" used in classical Chinese painting. In this successful experiment, he skillfully subdues his normally rich palette and expands the pictorial space in a way that evokes the aesthetics of ink painting without directly resembling one. Having the technical facility and education to invent a Chinese way of using the Western medium, he thus closely identifies Mao Zedong with China's long cultural tradition. The significance of the two history painting projects for codifying the standards of socialist realist painting, as well as giving visual form to the Communist historical narrative, cannot be overstated.

Luo Gongliu's career was that of a successful Communist artist and art administrator, and his own surviving art exemplifies the changing Chinese standards of socialist realism over its thirty-five-year history. At each stage he set an example for his students at the Central Academy of Fine Arts and those throughout the nation who hoped to join the mainstream art world and become the next generation of China's art leaders. During the decade of the Cultural Revolution (1966–1976), like many other artists and teachers who had served the country and the party, Luo Gongliu was maltreated and unfairly condemned. Nevertheless, he retained faith in the principles of Mao's Yan'an Forum—that art should serve the people and come from life—during and after the Cultural Revolution and until the end of his life. In his most widely disseminated effort, Luo also participated in designing the second (1955), third (1962), and fourth (1987) editions of China's currency, the renminbi.

SEE ALSO *Lin Fengmian; Oil Painting (youhua); Propaganda Art; Socialist Realism in Art; Woodblock Printing (xylography); Yan'an Forum; Zhao Shuli.*

BIBLIOGRAPHY

Andrews, Julia F. *Painters and Politics in the People's Republic of China, 1949–1979.* Berkeley: University of California Press, 1994.

Andrews, Julia F., and Kuiyi Shen. *A Century in Crisis: Modernity and Tradition in the Art of Twentieth-Century China.* New York: Guggenheim Museum, 1998.

Yanfei Zhu

M

MA YINCHU

SEE *Population Policy: Overview.*

MA, YO-YO

1955–

Preceding the swearing-in of the first black president of the United States of America on January 20, 2009, "Air and Simple Gifts," composed for the occasion by John Williams (b. 1932), was performed by a quartet of musicians who are masters of their instruments and also serve to illustrate the mood of change and openness that Barack Obama inaugurated with his presidency: Israeli American violinist Itzhak Perlman (b. 1945), South Side Chicago-born clarinetist Anthony McGill (b. 1979), Venezuelan pianist Gabriela Montero (b. 1970), and French-born Chinese American cellist Yo-Yo Ma. Although the musical integration of the Shaker tune "Simple Gifts" and Aaron Copland's *Appalachian Spring* clearly evoked an "American" sound, the quartet visually presented to the world a multicultural American identity that acknowledges its global roots. At the same time, the performance can be viewed as the epitome of Yo-Yo Ma's musical career and his views on the role and function of musical art. The cellist was chosen for this performance both for his exceptional mastery of his instrument and for his contributions to efforts to make music accessible to a wider audience. Moreover, his devotion to music education and to connecting musical traditions and musicians from different parts of the world make him an ideal representative of a culturally open and diverse America.

ARTISTIC DEVELOPMENT

Yo-Yo Ma (Ma Youyou) was born in Paris on October 7, 1955, into a Chinese family of musicians. His mother was the singer Marina Lu (b.1923), his father Hsiao-Tsun Ma (1911–1991), who had been a professor of music at Nanjing University until he left for Paris in 1936. Ma began to study the cello with his father at age four. Soon after, the family moved to New York. Ma studied with the Hungarian cellist János Scholz (1903–1993) and—on the recommendation of the violinist Isaac Stern (1920–2001), who had already heard Ma play as a young child in Paris—with Leonard Rose (1918–1984) in the precollege program of the Juilliard School of Music, New York. He complemented these studies with a traditional liberal arts education (including anthropology, history, and literature) at Columbia University, and graduated from Harvard University in 1976 with a bachelor's degree. In 1977 he married Jill Horner, with whom he has two children. In 1980 his career was threatened by a complicated spine surgery.

His stage debut at age four marked the beginning of his career as a child prodigy. In 1962 he performed for the Kennedy family with his elder sister, the violinist Yeou-Cheng Ma (b. 1952), who today works as a pediatrician and continues the work of their father with the Children's Orchestra Society. This concert was conducted by Leonard Bernstein (1918–1990) and broadcast on U.S. television. In 1964 Ma debuted at Carnegie Hall. Since then, Ma has given concerts on all continents. As an exclusive Sony Classical artist, he has recorded more than seventy-five albums that span a wide repertoire of mainstream classical, contemporary, popular, and crossover music. In these projects he cooperated with musicians and composers from all parts of the world and various musical traditions, including: Emmanuel Ax (b. 1949), Andrew Bird (b. 1973), Lynn Chang, Mark O'Connor (b. 1961), John

Corigliano (b. 1938), Richard Danielpour (b. 1956), Herbert von Karajan (1908–1989), Bobby McFerrin (b. 1950), Edgar Meyer (b. 1960), Ennio Morricone (b. 1928), Anne-Sophie Mutter (b. 1963), Seiji Ozawa (b. 1935), Kathryn Stott (b. 1958), Tan Dun (b. 1957), and John Williams.

From early in his career, Yo-Yo Ma moved beyond the strict confines of the mainstream classical repertoire. He has premiered many pieces of contemporary avant-garde music, some of which were commissioned for him. He has played cello on the soundtracks for several movies—*Seven Years in Tibet* and *Memoirs of a Geisha* (with music composed by John Williams), and *Crouching Tiger, Hidden Dragon* (music by Tan Dun). The album *Hush*, recorded in 1991 with Bobby McFerrin, was a move into the realm of improvisation. In 1993 Ma traveled to the Kalahari Desert to play for the inhabitants of the bush and to learn about their music. In 1997 he released the album *Soul of the Tango*, a homage to the late Argentine tango master Ástor Piazzolla (1921–1992), but also a technical experiment in which Ma performed "together" with recordings of Piazzolla.

THE SILK ROAD PROJECT

Ma's diverse activities aim at broadening both his own repertoire and his audience's, and at reaching out to potential new audiences through music education. These efforts culminated in 1998 with his foundation of the Silk Road Project, a not-for-profit arts organization inspired by the cultural traditions of the ancient Silk Road (which Yo-Yo Ma termed the "Internet of antiquity"). The project pursues several goals: undertaking academic research on the traditional and contemporary (musical) cultures of the countries along the Silk Road; preserving these traditions while at the same time commissioning new works that are performed at festivals and in concerts; fostering communication between musicians by bringing them together for concert projects; and reaching out to the wider community by providing teaching materials about these cultures. Although the project has been criticized on occasion for exoticizing foreign cultures when, for example, Central Asian musicians perform in traditional costumes while European and Chinese musicians dress in formal black suit, it has succeeded in raising awareness of musical cultures and encouraging multicultural exchange across continents.

HONORS AND AWARDS

His musical achievements as well as his dedication to the Silk Road Project have earned Yo-Yo Ma many international honors and awards. Among these are fifteen Grammy Awards in different categories for his musical recordings; the Avery Fisher Prize (1978); honorary doctorates from his alma mater Harvard University (1991), from the American University of Beirut (2004), and from Princeton University (2005); the Glenn Gould Prize (1999), the (U.S.) National Medal of Arts (2001); the Dan David Prize for his engagement with the Silk Road Project (2006); the Léonie Sonning Music Prize (2006); and the World Economic Forum's Crystal Award (2008). In 2002 Ma was appointed a culture connect ambassador by the U.S. Department of State, and in 2006 he was named a United Nations messenger of peace by Secretary General Kofi Annan, an appointment renewed in 2007 by Secretary General Ban Ki-Moon. In addition to playing for U.S. presidents John F. Kennedy and Obama, Yo-Yo Ma also has performed for Presidents Reagan, Clinton, and George W. Bush, played a duet with Secretary of State Condoleezza Rice on piano, and performed in 2002 during the memorial service for the victims of the terrorist attacks of September 11, 2001.

SEE ALSO *Music, Western and Russian Influence on; Tan Dun.*

BIBLIOGRAPHY

Silk Road Project Web site. http://www.silkroadproject.org/.

Ten Grotenhuis, Elizabeth, ed. *Along the Silk Road.* Seattle: University of Washington Press, 2001.

Yo-Yo Ma official Web site. http://www.yo-yoma.com/.

Lena Henningsen

MACAU

Macau, once notorious for opium dens and secret societies and now known as the Monte Carlo of the East due to its robust gambling industry, is a former Portuguese colony over which China resumed sovereignty in 1999. Macau is located 60 kilometers west of Hong Kong at the Pearl River estuary. In 2007 Macau's territory measured 28.6 square kilometers, although the land mass was expected to expand through reclamation for purposes of urban and economic development. At the end of 2007, Macau had a population of 531,400, including an estimated 80,000 migrant workers primarily from mainland China, Hong Kong, and the Philippines. Around 94 percent of the total population was ethnic Chinese, while Portuguese and Macanese (the descendants of Portuguese and Asian, mostly Chinese, parents) accounted for 1.3 percent.

RISE AND FALL AS A TRADING PORT

Macau was a fishing village before the Portuguese arrived. In 1535 Portuguese traders obtained the right of anchor at Macau, and the Portuguese became established in 1556 for trading and religious purposes, although China maintained sovereignty over the region. China permitted Portuguese to settle in Macau and administer its internal affairs because Chinese authorities hoped to benefit from the lucrative trade opportunities that the Portuguese and other foreign traders provided. Under Portuguese administration, Macau was transformed into a trading port connecting China, Japan, the Philippines, Latin America, and the Portuguese colonies in India and the Malay Peninsula.

MACAU

Area: 29.2 sq. km. (11.3 sq. mi.)
Population: 551,900 (2008)
Demographics: Chinese, 93.8%; Portguese, Macanese, and other, 6.2%
GDP: US$19.2 billion (2007); per capita, US$36,527 (2007)
Famous sites: Cotai strip, Macau Peninsula, Macau Tower, ruins of Sao Paulo Cathedral, Taipa Village, Colôane Village

In 1576 the See of Macau was founded with jurisdiction over Roman Catholic missions in China, Korea, and Japan. Many missionaries went to Macau for training in language, theology, and culture before preaching in other East Asian regions (Gunn 1996). The significance of Macau in East Asian trade and as a gateway to China invited the aggression of Spain, the Netherlands, and Britain. The latter two invaded Macau in the early seventeenth century, but were expelled by the Portuguese (Huang Hongzhao 1999).

Macau had begun to decline by the early seventeenth century when the rise of the Netherlands and Britain eroded Portugal's dominance over sea trade in East Asia. Strategic bases and settlements—such as Malacca on the Malay Peninsula and Colombo in Sri Lanka—were seized by other maritime powers. After the Opium War (1839–1842), Macau was eclipsed by Hong Kong as an important trading port. To salvage its economy, the Portuguese adopted a tolerant policy toward the coolie trade, opium, and gambling, all deemed immoral by most of the local population and by liberals in Portugal (Huang Hongzhao 1999, pp. 179–196).

BECOMING A PORTUGUESE COLONY

Before 1887, Macau was administered conjointly by the Chinese government and the Portuguese. The Chinese collected customs duties and shipping charges, arbitrated disputes among Chinese people, had the right to be consulted over law and order, and settled disputes between the Chinese and Portuguese. The Portuguese were responsible for other domestic affairs, initially within the walled city but eventually covering the whole Macau Peninsula and two outlying islands, Taipa and Coloanne (Huang Hongzhao 1999, pp. 130–159). Encouraged by the success of other Western powers in advancing their political and commercial interests in China, Portugal, wishing to regularize its position in Macau, negotiated hard for the Treaty of Friendship and Commerce with China in 1887. Thereby, Portugal gained the right of "perpetual occupation and government of Macau," making it a Portuguese colony (Gunn 1996, pp. 63–64).

WORLD WAR II AND COLD WAR ERA

During World War II (1937–1945), Japan did not occupy Macau so as to ease the spying activities of the Western allies in the East. The large Japanese population in Brazil—Portugal's ally—became potential hostages and played a role in deterring Japanese aggression.

In the Cold War era, the Chinese in Macau were divided between pro-Beijing and pro-Taiwan forces. On December 3, 1966, pro-Beijing forces, mainly composed of workers, street vendors, and students, responded to the Cultural Revolution in China and instigated riots, bringing Macau's economy to a halt. Portuguese colonial rulers had to yield to the demands of the pro-Beijing forces by expelling pro-Taiwan forces from the enclave. Thereafter, the Portuguese lost effective governance over Macau and had to co-opt pro-Beijing elements into the regime. The legacy of the pro-Beijing uprising was such that the pro-Beijing position became entrenched in later political development (Chou 2005a, pp. 191–206).

One of the most important figures in the post–World War II era was Ho Yin (He Xian, 1908–1983). Ho, a banker and the father of the first chief executive, Edmund Ho (He Houhua), was the leader of the most important interest group, the Macau Chinese General Chamber of Commerce, for more than thirty years. He played a liaison role between the Chinese and Portuguese governments, and between the Chinese community and the Portuguese administration in Macau. His political prowess became evident when he was appointed to the Standing Committee of National People's Congress of China and Legislative Assembly of Macau (Chou 2005a, p. 203).

Since the early 1970s, Macau has benefited from the economic prosperity of Hong Kong. Because Hong Kong prohibited casinos, Macau became a paradise for Hong Kong gamblers. In addition, many Hong Kong garment manufacturers took advantage of Macau's lower labor costs and lower price of export quota. The prosperity of Macau and the resulting labor shortage attracted numerous illegal workers from mainland China. Despite the social problems they caused, Macau's government granted citizenship to these workers because of their contribution to the booming manufacturing industry. They later became voters and tipped the balance of political power toward Beijing (Lo Shiu-hing 1995, pp. 55–116).

Macau's political development after the early 1970s was intertwined with the domestic politics of Portugal and China. After the 1974 coup in Portugal, the coup leaders formed a socialist government and considered returning Macau to China. But Chinese leaders were preoccupied with the Cultural Revolution, and unifying Macau without preparation would have destabilized the enclave and affected China's unification plans for Taiwan and Hong Kong. Chinese leaders thus asked the Portuguese to maintain the status quo.

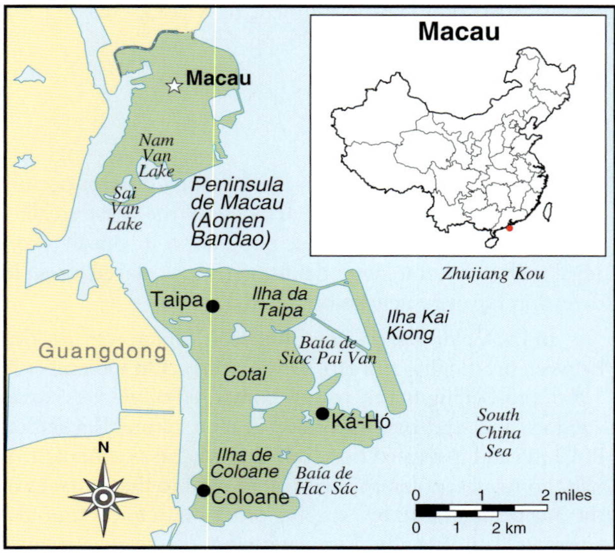

The left-leaning Portuguese leaders accordingly reformed Macau's political system, announced the Organic Law of Macau in 1976, and appointed a governor. As the head of the executive branch, the governor appointed a Consultative Committee to assist him making important decisions. The legislative branch—the Legislative Assembly—had earlier consisted of members appointed by the governor. The 1976 political reform introduced limited democracy. The number of seats returned by direct election (based on geographical constituencies) and indirect election (based on functional constituencies) increased gradually. Macau's judiciary became independent from the governor, with judges appointed by the Portuguese judiciary. This system became the basis of Macau's post-handover political system. The main difference is the shift of the appointment power from Lisbon to Beijing (Chan 2003).

At the beginning of Macau's democratization process, the franchise was limited to the ethnic Chinese and non-Chinese residents having resided in Macau for at least five years and seven years respectively. Since many ethnic Chinese were new migrants, they were unqualified and uninterested to vote. The Chinese community was therefore underrepresented in the Legislative Assembly. With the franchise extended to more Chinese residents in 1984, Macau's pro-Beijing forces became more significant, and contributed to the relatively smooth transition when sovereignty reverted to China (Chou 2007a; Lo Shiu-hing 1995, pp. 98–99).

THE TRANSITIONAL AND POST-TRANSITIONAL ERA

The year 1999 was chosen for the transfer of sovereignty because China's leaders wished to remove what they saw as a historical disgrace—in conjunction with the return of Hong Kong in 1997—before the end of the century. The Sino-Portuguese negotiations over Macau's retrocession were generally cordial, in contrast with the Sino-British entanglements over Hong Kong. On December 20, 1999, Macau joined Hong Kong to become China's second special administrative region. In both, the "one country, two systems" policy was applied, and the "capitalist" economy and way of life of the two cities are to be preserved. They also enjoy a high degree of autonomy over internal affairs, while the central government in Beijing is responsible for their defense and foreign affairs. In addition, Beijing appoints Macau's chief executives, which are first elected by committees. The nomination of principal officials by the chief executive also requires the approval of the central government.

Macau's post-handover political development was closely connected with the 2002 liberalization of the gambling industry. In that year, the hugely successful monopoly held since 1962 by Hong Kong businessman Stanley Ho (He Hongshen) and his Sociedade de Turismo e Diversões de Macau ended, and five new industry players were introduced. Thanks to the Chinese government's relaxation of rules regarding outbound tourists in 2003, the influx of foreign direct investment and tourists attracted by Macau's new casinos reversed the economic stagnation stemming from the macroeconomic adjustment of China and gangster warfare over casino interests. Macau's gross domestic product more than doubled between 2001 and 2007. In 2006 Macau became the number-one casino city in the world, with its gambling revenue exceeding that of Las Vegas.

The economic boom resulted in a labor shortage, and between 2003 and 2007 the number of migrant workers in Macau more than tripled, displacing some domestic unskilled and semiskilled workers. Those who were employed found their salaries suppressed. Because they are the Macau government's partners and the Beijing government's agents, the Macau Federation of Labor Unions and the Neighborhood Association—the two largest associations representing the working class—were reluctant to pressure the government to address these issues. The legitimacy of the government was further undermined by soaring property prices, maladministration, and corruption scandals involving high-ranking officials. As a result, widespread public discontent erupted in mass protests every Labor Day (May 1) and on December 20, the day commemorating the sovereignty retrocession. In view of that, the government has tapped its huge fiscal reserve for welfare and public housing programs, in an effort to boost its legitimacy. However, political reform to enhance the government's procedural legitimacy has not been on the agenda. Social tensions are unlikely to be alleviated before the appointment of a new chief executive in 2009 and a change in the economic climate.

SEE ALSO *Guangdong; Imperialism; Urban China: Cities and Urbanization, 1800–1949; Urban China: Organizing Principles of Cities; Urban China: Urban Planning since 1978.*

Gamblers in a Macau casino, February 15, 1999. *The first Western nation to gain territory in China, Portugal initially used the port city of Macau as a center of trade. However, to counter the rising commercial importance of British-controlled Hong Kong, the Portuguese liberalized laws against gambling in the mid-nineteenth century, turning Macau into a regional tourist destination.* AP IMAGES

BIBLIOGRAPHY

Chan, Ming K. Different Roads to Home: The Retrocession of Hong Kong and Macau to Chinese Sovereignty. *Journal of Contemporary China* 12, 36 (2003): 493–518.

Chou, Bill K. P. Interest Group Politics in Macao after Handover. *Journal of Contemporary China* 14, 43 (2005a): 191–206.

Chou, Bill K. P. Public Sector Reform in Macao and Hong Kong after Handover: An Examination of the Political Nexus Triads in the Two China's Special Administrative Region. *Public Administration and Policy* 14, 1 (2005b): 63–86.

Chou, Bill K. P. Hong Kong and Macau under One Country, Two Systems. In *Interpreting China's Development*, ed. Wang Gungwu and John Wong, 67–71. Singapore: World Scientific, 2007a.

Chou, Bill K. P. Macao's Lopsided Development. EAI Background Brief No. 341. Singapore: East Asian Institute, National University of Singapore, 2007b.

Gunn, Geoffrey C. *Encountering Macau: A Portuguese City-State on the Periphery of China, 1557–1999*. Boulder, CO: Westview Press, 1996.

Huang Hongzhao. *Aomen shi* [A History of Macau]. Fuzhou, PRC: Fujian People's Press, 1999.

Lo Shiu Hing. *Political Development in Macau*. Hong Kong: Chinese University Press, 1995.

Macao Special Administrative Region Government Portal. Fact Sheet: Geography and Population. 2007. http://www.gov.mo/egi/Portal/rkw/public/view/area.jsp?id=21.

Ministry of Foreign Affairs of the People's Republic of China. Basic Law of the Macao Special Administrative Region of the People's Republic of China. 2002. http://www.fmprc.gov.cn/eng/wjb/zzjg/tyfls/tyfl/2626/t15467.htm.

Yee, Herbert S. *Macau in Transition: From Colony to Autonomous Region*. New York: Palgrave, 2001.

Bill K. P. Chou

MAJOR, ERNEST

1841–1908

Ernest Major's impact on the modern Chinese public sphere and print culture was unmatched by any other foreigner's. Although Major was born into the modest household of a third clerk in the London War Ministry, a "financier" uncle provided entry to influential circles that

Chinese emperor Puyi with representatives of the Japanese military, c. 1935. *Using the bombing of Japanese-owned railroad tracks in Manchuria as a pretext, the Japanese military invaded the region, installing the last imperial Chinese emperor Puyi as the new emperor of Manchukuo, a puppet state controlled by Japan.* HULTON ARCHIVE/GETTY IMAGES

when the Republic had been inaugurated, Puyi, now a private citizen, accepted an invitation from the Manchukuo authorities to return as "emperor" of the new state. From 1934, the state was formally renamed Manzhou dadiguo, "The Great Empire of Manchuria," although Puyi found himself in the unusual position of being an emperor subservient to another emperor, the ruler of Japan. Puyi's reinstatement was regarded with little seriousness by most outside observers, although it was classed as treachery by the Chinese government, and engendered little popular enthusiasm within Manchukuo itself.

MANCHUKUO IN INTERNATIONAL CONFLICTS

The League of Nations, exercising its role as the arbiter of territorial disputes between member states, sent an investigation team to Manchukuo under the British politician V.A.G.R. Bulwer-Lytton, the second Earl of Lytton (1876–1947) in 1932. The Chinese government lobbied the commission with arguments about the violation of their sovereignty. The Japanese in turn used arguments that China itself was essentially a lawless state and that Japan had to take measures to protect its material investments in the region. The end report was a compromise and pleased no one. It dismissed the legitimacy of the new state, but also suggested that Japanese interests should be represented by some form of joint Sino-Japanese administration. The Chinese government expressed its feeling of betrayal, and the Japanese also refused to back down, and withdrew from the League of Nations in 1933 instead. Abandoning Manchukuo had become unthinkable for the Japanese, whose government had propagated the idea that the region was of central importance to the Japanese empire. The Tokyo government tried to use demographics to solidify its hold on Manchukuo, sending millions of migrants to Manchuria, although many returned home when they discovered conditions in the region were harsh and that the locals were unenthusiastic about the new arrivals. Meanwhile, a substantial community of Chinese exiles from Manchuria had built up in China south of the Great Wall after 1931, and they worked to fix the issue of Manchukuo in the minds of the Chinese public as a problem that must be solved.

The war years (1937–1945) meant that Manchukuo became part of a wider Japanese wartime empire that included much of occupied eastern and northern China. Chinese residents of Manchukuo were forced into labor service, and food became scarce. The end for Manchukuo came when the war ended abruptly on August 15 after the atomic bombings of Japan. During the period of Soviet occupation (1945–1946) and the civil war between the Nationalists and Communists (1946–1949), Manchuria once again became a center of conflict. The former emperor Puyi was captured by the Soviet Red Army in 1945, and testified in 1946 at the Tokyo war crimes trial, condemning Japanese treatment of him and of the region. He was sent to Communist China in 1950, and spent ten years in a "reeducation" camp, but was then released and died peacefully in 1967.

SEE ALSO *Anti-Japanese War, 1937–1945; Manchuria.*

BIBLIOGRAPHY

Duara, Prasenjit. *Sovereignty and Authenticity: Manchukuo and the East Asian Modern*. Lanham, MD: Rowman and Littlefield, 2003.

Matsusaka Yoshihisa Tak. *The Making of Japanese Manchuria, 1904–1932*. Cambridge, MA: Harvard University Asia Center, 2001.

Mitter, Rana. *The Manchurian Myth: Nationalism, Resistance, and Collaboration in Modern China*. Berkeley: University of California Press, 2000.

Smith, Norman. *Resisting Manchukuo: Chinese Women Writers and the Japanese Occupation*. Vancouver: University of British Columbia Press, 2007.

Young, Louise. *Japan's Total Empire: Manchuria and the Culture of Wartime Imperialism*. Berkeley: University of California Press, 1998.

Rana Mitter

MANCHURIA

Manchuria refers to northeast China, a huge region composed of over 422,000 square miles, slightly larger than France and Germany combined. In the north, where the Heilongjiang River marks much of the boundary with Russia, there are forests abundant with trees whose lumber is used for furniture and construction. Bears and tigers have been hunted for their fur and for the regional delicacy of bear paw. In the extreme west of the region is the Greater Khingan (Da Xing'an) Mountain Range separating Manchuria from Russia and Mongolia and from Chinese Inner Mongolia. In the southeast are the Changbaishan Mountains on the border with North Korea. This rugged and almost impassable range was for centuries known as a home for bandits. Much of Manchuria, especially its central and southern portions, consists of rolling plains. The soil is especially fertile, able to produce crops of all kinds, such as the tall-growing kaoliang (*gaoliang*) used for fuel, fodder, and wine; soy beans used for everything from pulp for insulation to oil for cooking and lubrication; and farm crops of barley, tomatoes, onions, potatoes, squash, watermelons, rice, grapes, apples, and flowers in hundreds of varieties. Falling largely within the latitudes of 48.43 degrees N and 53.30 degrees N, the climate is marked by extremes, from the brief hot summers of July and August, to bitter cold from November through March, when biting winds from Siberia freeze the ground and the breath from humans and animals.

THE RISE OF THE MANCHUS

In 1635 the horse-riding, animal-hunting Jurchen tribes that roamed the region formed themselves into a new ethnic confederation called the Manchus. The charismatic leader Nurhachi (1559–1626) inspired the process that organized the Manchus and began the momentum of their expansion toward China south of the Great Wall. The Manchus ruled China from 1644 until 1912 as the Great Qing dynasty, forming an effective government, based largely on Chinese bureaucratic models, which expanded China's borders to those of the present day. The Manchus tried to protect their homeland of Manchuria by prohibiting the Chinese from residing there, but in 1897 the prohibition was removed.

In the twentieth century, thousands of Chinese surged into Manchuria every year, some as migrants, others to farm, to work in the mines and factories, and to engage in trade. Today, the 110-million-strong population of Manchuria is largely Han Chinese, with Manchus comprising about 7.5 million persons. Because of this history, most of the world refers to this section of China as Manchuria, and the Chinese Post Office also used the term for its international mails before 1949. Within China, however, the area today is usually referred to as "the Northeast" (Dongbei). It has also been called the Three Eastern Provinces (Dongsansheng) for the provinces of Liaoning (formerly Fengtian), Jilin, and Heilongjiang.

FOCUS OF INTERNATIONAL RIVALRY

Throughout the twentieth century, Manchuria was a focus of international rivalry. To the north were the Russians, who managed to gain a foothold in central and south

Manchuria in 1896 following the Sino-Japanese War, including the important south Manchurian port of Dalian. Russia lost much of its regional influence following its defeat in the Russo-Japanese War of 1904 to 1905. But Russia retained a large cultural and important diplomatic presence in the north Manchurian city of Harbin. To the south were the Japanese, who occupied the Liaodong Peninsula, which they leased from China in 1906. Japan formally annexed Korea in 1910, meaning that Japanese influence over southern Manchuria was formidable. The

Travelers in a harbor station train depot, Dairen, Manchuria, China, c. 1930. *Situated in northeast China, Manchuria refers to the traditional region of the Manchus, an ethnic group that ruled the Chinese during the Qing dynasty. Because of the area's fertile farmland, abundant natural resources, and industrialized port city of Dairen, both Japan and Russia fought to control Manchuria in the late nineteenth and early twentieth centuries.* © JACQUES BOYER / ROGER-VIOLLET / THE IMAGE WORKS

Americans and the British also maintained crucial diplomatic offices in the region to gather political, economic, and military intelligence.

CHINESE-LED MODERNIZATION AND DEVELOPMENT

During the 1920s, the Chinese central government in Beijing was weak, and Manchuria functioned like a semi-independent kingdom. It was under the control of the Chinese warlord Zhang Zuolin (1873–1928), who allowed his chief civil official, Wang Yongjiang (1872–1927), to make the region a leader in modernization. Commercial highways were built, telegraph and telephone lines were strung, new rail lines were put into operation, and the provincial government made investments in trolley services, manufacturing plants, huge mining operations, and insurance and trading companies. From about 1917 on, the economy was booming and the regional currency, the Fengtian dollar (*fengpiao*) was stable into the mid-1920s. The Chinese business elite constructed what was probably the first integrated regional modern infrastructure in China that could sustain a highly industrialized and commercialized economy.

JAPANESE OCCUPATION

The Chinese-led regional economic boom ended in 1931, when the Japanese Guandong (Kwantung) Army, known as the Kantō Army in Japanese—influenced by the nationalist ideologue Ishiwara Kanji (1889–1949), who was an officer in the army—suddenly occupied the region. In 1932 the Japanese established the puppet state of Manchukuo (known as Manzhouguo in Chinese, and Manshūkoku in Japanese), and in 1934 the deposed last Manchu emperor, Puyi (1906–1967), was made emperor of the new country. All of the top officials were Chinese, but in fact all of the power holders were Japanese military officers and powerful bureaucrats. Some Japanese intellectuals conceived of Manchukuo as an idealized state, where the various ethnic races of the region (Chinese, Japanese, Korean, Manchu, and Mongol) would cooperate to create a stable and dynamic society. But in fact the Japanese officials in charge disdained the other ethnic groups, and as the wartime situation became dire in the 1940s, Japanese officials increasingly oppressed the resident Chinese and Koreans.

Nevertheless, under Japanese control the economic and industrial modernization continued, with the establishment of up-to-date smelters and steel plants, the efficient and much-admired South Manchuria Railway (formed in 1906) running through the heart of the region, modern ports with sturdy cranes, secure warehouses, and a distribution system the equal of any nation at the time. In the major cities, roads and sidewalks were paved and sewers laid, and large well-equipped hospitals offered the latest in medical care. The cities had well-stocked public libraries, modern hotels for travelers, banks, department stores, and movie theaters. In the largest cities were many vocational training schools and several large universities, while in the countryside thousands of Japanese farmers were sent in by the Japanese government to colonize the rural areas and exploit its agricultural wealth.

POSTWAR CHAOS

When Japan surrendered at the end of World War II in 1945, the region was plunged into chaos. Initially, Soviet forces swept in, removing much heavy machinery from the factories and arresting as many Japanese soldiers as they could find, using them as unpaid labor, and sending the machinery and the prisoners back to the Soviet Union. Then the Chinese Nationalist forces of Chiang Kai-shek (Jiang Jieshi), although engaged in a civil war with the Communists, sent Guomindang (GMD) troops to occupy the major cities of Manchuria. Using U.S. Navy ships and American-supplied planes, Nationalist units moved into all the major cities. But in the countryside, it was the Communist forces of Mao Zedong, led by the able general Lin Biao, that had the support of the people. The GMD troops became trapped in such cities as Mukden (Shenyang) and Changchun, while the Communists used their control of the rest of Manchuria to lay siege to the cities. As the GMD lost ground in its battles with the Communists throughout China, they surrendered the cities of Manchuria, and in 1949 fled to Taiwan.

In 1949 Manchuria, in spite of its empty and ruined factories, still had the most modern regional infrastructure in China and the most skilled labor force for heavy industry. This, combined with the region's wealth in minerals and ores and its strategic geographical location, with the Soviet Union, Korea, and Japan all nearly allowed Manchuria to continue as one of the most critically important regions of the People's Republic of China.

SEE ALSO *Manchukuo (Manzhouguo); Sino-Japanese War, 1894–1895.*

BIBLIOGRAPHY

Elliott, Mark C. *The Manchu Way: The Eight Banners and Ethnic Identity in Late Imperial China*. Stanford, CA: Stanford University Press, 2001.

Levine, Steven. *Anvil of Victory: The Communist Revolution in Manchuria, 1945–1948*. New York: Columbia University Press, 1987.

Suleski, Ronald. *Civil Government in Warlord China: Tradition, Modernization, and Manchuria*. New York: Lang, 2002.

Yamamuro Shin'ichi. *Manchuria under Japanese Dominion*. Trans. Joshua A. Fogel. Philadelphia: University of Pennsylvania Press, 2006.

Ronald Suleski

MANCHURIAN INCIDENT

SEE *Manchukuo (Manzhouguo).*

MANDARIN DUCK AND BUTTERFLY LITERATURE

The *mandarin duck and butterfly school* (*yuanyang hudie pai*) is a term invented in the late 1910s by May Fourth writers to deride the wave of popular fictional writings, mainly love stories, that flourished in Shanghai soon after the establishment of the Republic in 1911. Later, it came to be applied to various kinds of popular fiction, whether in classical or vernacular language, including social, historical, detective, and martial arts novels as well as love stories. If it is possible to identify common attributes of the writers of these works, they are that at a time when ideology flourished among intellectuals and the politically minded, these writers chose to appeal to the growing urban middle class with entertaining stories; and they experimented with a remarkable variety of narrative techniques and styles that combined native tradition with modern Western influence in novel ways.

The authors naturally did not accept the scoffing "mandarin duck and butterfly" taunt, nor the very idea that they formed a "school." Ironically, however, some of the writers themselves gave their May Fourth critics the idea for their scathing label. Under the influence of the age-old tradition of using mandarin ducks, other birds, and butterflies as images of ideal but highly vulnerable love, the writers incorporated the names for these animals in their pseudonyms; for instance *die* (butterfly) in Chen Xiaodie (1897–1989) and Chen Diexian (1879–1940), *yuan* (mandarin duck) in Zhu Yuanchu, and *juan* (cuckoo) in Zhou Shoujuan (1895–1968). The derisive label eventually proved devastatingly effective as their writings were increasingly and then totally rejected as frivolous and socially irresponsible entertainment.

The best that the less aggressive critics could say was that the "school" was a product of a modern industrialized society whose need for entertainment was being exploited for commercial purposes; and that its writings were dominated by Confucian themes and by traditional narrative modes, devices, and linguistic forms, though this misrepresents what these writers actually did.

POPULARITY AND REJECTION

The earliest representative work of the school is Xu Zhenya's (1889–1937) *Yü-li hun* (Jade pearl spirit, 1912), a novel about the conflict between love and familial obligations that touched the hearts of hundreds of thousands of readers when it was serialized in the *Minquan bao* (People's rights) magazine. The novel is written in a remarkably original adaptation of the old euphuistic style of parallel prose. Its great success set off a wave of fiction in parallel prose unlike any that had occurred before in Chinese literary history. The scholar C. T. Hsia wrote: "Far from being a commercial product exploitative of the sentimental clichés of the past for the amusement of the public, *Yü-li hun* owed its tremendous popularity to its astonishing emotional impact upon the educated readers of its time, and its equally astonishing literary virtuosity" (Hsia 1982, p. 201).

That was not the response of the May Fourth writers. In a lecture at Beijing University in 1918, Zhou Zuoren (1885–1967) remarked: "Most contemporary fiction uses the old forms. Its writers' views on life and literature remain the old ones . . . , [as in] the Mandarin Duck and Butterfly style of the *Jade Pearl Spirit* type of fiction" (Zhou 1935, pp. 292–293). A year later, Qian Xuantong (1887–1939) spoke of a "Mandarin duck and butterfly school" that included "black-curtain" (or scandal) fiction, which was poisoning young people with its depiction of licentiousness and the corruption of officials (Qian 1919, pp. 74–75).

A less biased look at these works reveals a large variety of subject matter and styles. The reason that *Yü-li hun*, for example, attracted tremendous attention was not only because of its love story but also for its innovative literary style. Other successful novels of the period reflected on important political and social events in a realistic idiom, among them Li Hanqiu (1873–1923)'s long novel *Guangling chao* (Tides of Yangzhou, 1909–1919). At the same time, martial arts and detective fiction were flourishing. The former genre has a long history in China; the latter was imported from the West.

Short stories became especially popular. They appeared in a striking variety of linguistic forms, notably the ancient *Qin-Han* (221 BCE–220 CE) style, as practiced by Lin Shu (1852–1924), the equally archaic *Wei-Jin* (220–420) style, and also the *Tang-Song* (618–1279) style. The influence of the latter is evident in Su Manshu's (1884–1918) *Duanhong lingyan ji* (The lone swan, 1912). Others developed the narrative features of *huaben* (a vernacular short story) from the Ming dynasty in original ways. This impressive transformation of traditional into new forms was achieved under the influence of Western narrative.

ECONOMIC AND SOCIAL CAUSES

These literary developments of the early republic had both economic and cultural causes. Having grown within a few decades from a small town into a major cosmopolitan center, Shanghai was at the forefront of Westernization, and its economic growth attracted a large influx of people from other parts of China. The city became a magnet that drew business entrepreneurs. As a place of new ideas and relative freedom, it also became a refuge for reformers, artists, and writers.

When the Qing government abolished the imperial examinations in 1905, thereby removing the conventional means of climbing the social ladder, educated people were forced to find new ways of establishing themselves financially and socially. Large numbers migrated to Shanghai, where they became contributors to and editors of cultural magazines and literary supplements. Those from Suzhou, such as Bao Tianxiao (1876–1973), Fan Yanqiao (1894–1967), and others, became especially active forces in the magazine world. Equipped with superior education in Suzhou's rich cultural tradition, they made Shanghai's commercial world more literate, and in doing so, they mediated the interaction between Shanghai's modernity and Confucian culture that characterized much of early twentieth-century literature. In this process, translations of Western literature begun by the late Qing reformers played an important role, which accounts for love becoming the prevailing theme. Lin Shu translated more than 100 works of fiction in a highly elegant classical language that became a model for imitation. Both Bao Tianxiao and Zhou Shoujuan began their literary careers with such translations.

CREATIVITY AND INNOVATIONS

Mandarin duck and butterfly writers carried still further the innovations begun by their immediate predecessors in the kinds of vernacular and classical idioms they used. As a result, the boundaries between *wenyan* (classical language) and *baihua* (vernacular language) became less strict; indeed, sometimes the two forms intermingled. Writers were moving toward a new language that retained the artistic qualities of classical Chinese but was infused with the lively vigor of the vernacular.

Their works became popular because their characters were so familiar to readers in large urban centers. For present-day literary historians, the writings are impressive in their depictions of a transitional period in China's progress toward modernity, particularly in how ordinary people adapted to the impact of Westernization on China's age-old traditions. This presentation of contemporary characters and nondoctrinaire social themes is conveyed by narrative devices introduced from the West that were strikingly new to China. These included limited third-person narrative, encountered in "Xiaoxue jiaoshi zhi qi" (The wife of a primary school teacher, 1911), a story written cooperatively by Bao and Xu Zhuodai (1881–1958); epistolary writing; and first-person narrative, as in "Siyuan" (A secret wish, 1915) by Zhou Shoujuan. New, too, was the use of dreams to reveal the protagonist's suppressed feelings, in Bao's "Qimeng" (Strange dreams, 1916).

In 1922 several Mandarin duck writers, among them Zhao Miamyun (1902–1948) and Fan Yanqiao, set up a new society in Suzhou, called Xingshe (Star society). Its members came to be regarded as the Mandarin duck school's society. It lasted fifteen years and published a newspaper as well as four books. The society's founding idea was *yi wen hui you* (making friends through literature). Its members' views on literature were markedly different both from those of the editors of the late Qing magazines, whose primary aim was to engage in nation building and the education of new citizens, and from those of followers of the May Fourth cultural movement, who were devoted to political enlightenment by rejecting tradition, particularly Confucianism. Mandarin duck writers emphasized that their works should be read for pleasure at least as much as for useful instruction, because they believed that education needed to be combined with refreshment.

EXCLUSION AND REEVALUATION

Yet the view first fostered by the May Fourth intellectuals—that Mandarin duck writers merely pandered to vulgar entertainment and crass commercialism—persisted for over half a century. It was only in the late 1970s that scholarly interest in them revived (notably fostered by E. Perry Link's 1981 study *Mandarin Ducks and Butterflies*). Since then, scholars in the West and from mainland China have begun to reevaluate positively the artistic qualities of the school's fiction (see especially works by C. T. Hsia, Leo Ou-fan Lee, and Fan Boqun). But there still has not been a clear and convincing definition of the school in terms of its period of coverage and its modernity in content and technique. There has been some disagreement as to whether certain late Qing dynasty writers should be included under the name: Some think the term should be confined to writers of the 1910s and early 1920s. A more widely accepted view is that some writers of the 1930s and the 1940s, such as Zhang Henshui (1897–1967) and Qin Shouou (1908–1993), warrant inclusion.

SEE ALSO *Literary Societies; Literature since 1800.*

BIBLIOGRAPHY

Chow, Rey. Mandarin Ducks and Butterflies: An Exercise in Popular Readings. In *Women and Chinese Modernity: The Politics of Reading between West and East*, 34–83. Minneapolis: University of Minnesota Press, 1991.

Fan Boqun 范伯群. *Libailiu de hudie meng* 礼拜六的蝴蝶梦 [A butterfly dream of the Saturday school]. Beijing: Renmin Chubanshe, 1989.

Fong, Gilbert Chee Fun. Subjectivism in Xu Zhenya (1889–193?) and Su Manshu (1884–1918): Chinese Fiction in Transition. Ph.D. diss., University of Toronto, 1981.

Hsia, C. T. Hsu Chen-ya's *Yü-li hun*: An Essay in Literary History and Criticism. *Renditions* 17–18 (1982): 199–240.

Lee, Leo Ou-fan. *Shanghai Modern: The Flowering of a New Urban Culture in China, 1930–1945.* Cambridge, MA: Harvard University Press, 1999.

Link, E. Perry. *Mandarin Ducks and Butterflies*. Berkeley: University of California Press, 1981.

Qian Xuantong 钱玄同. Heimu'shu (Books of "black-screen"). *Xinqingnian* 6, no. 1 (January 9, 1919): 74–75.

Wei Shaochang 魏绍昌. *Yuanyang hudie pai yanjiu ziliao* 鸳鸯蝴蝶派研究资料 [Research materials on the Mandarin duck and butterfly school]. Shanghai: Shanghai Wenxue Yishu, 1962.

Xu, Xueqing. The Mandarin Duck and Butterfly School. In *Literary Societies of Republican China*, ed. Kirk A. Denton and Michel Hockx, 47–78. Lanham, MD: Lexington Books, 2008.

Xu Zhenya 徐枕亚. *Yüli hun* 玉梨魂 [Jade pearl spirit]. [1912]. Shanghai: Minquan Chubanshe, 1914.

Zhou Zuoren 周作人. Riben jin sanshinian xiaoshuo zhi fada 日本近三十年小说之发达 [The development of Japanese fiction during the last thirty years]. In *Zhongguo xinwenxue daxi: Jianshe lilun ji* 中国新文学大系: 建设理论集 [A compendium of modern Chinese new literature: Construction of theory], ed. Cai Yuanpei, 292–293. Shanghai: Liangyou, 1935.

Xueqing Xu

MAO DUN
1896–1981

Born Shen Dehong (courtesy name: Yanbing) in Tongxiang County, Zhejiang Province, Mao Dun was one of twentieth-century China's most prominent fiction writers and cultural figures. He attended Peking University in 1913 to 1916, where he studied Chinese and Western literature, and later went to work as an English literature and translation editor at the Shanghai branch of the prestigious Commercial Press. At the time of the May Fourth movement, he became involved in student and radical causes, writing editorials for the Commercial Press's publication *Xuesheng Zazhi* (The student magazine). In 1920 he and some other young writers assumed control of *Xiaoshuo Yuebao* (Fiction monthly), a fiction magazine of the previous decade, and he became its chief editor. Mao Dun and his colleagues radicalized the content of the journal and used it to introduce prominent

Western writers such as Leo Tolstoy, Anton Chekhov, Honoré Balzac, Gustave Flaubert, and Émile Zola. These writers also greatly influenced Mao Dun's own fiction writing style, which is described as realist or, more narrowly, naturalist. Although the journal, best known in English as *The Short Story*, introduced the most prominent nineteenth-century European literary figures, Mao Dun was also responsible for a column introducing new international fiction. The journal, with its incisive original fiction by prominent progressive writers including Zheng Zhenduo (1898–1958), Xu Dishan (1893–1941), Wang Tongzhao (1897–1957), Bingxin (1900–1999), Ye Shengtao (1894–1988), and Zhou Zuoren (1885–1967), as well as Mao Dun himself, was a great success, selling as many as 10,000 copies per issue. Although in its early phase the journal had only about a dozen contributors, by 1928 it had attracted every distinguished name in Chinese fiction up to that time. In November 1920 Mao Dun and a group of socially committed writers established Wenxue Yanjiu Hui (the Literary Study Society, better known in English as the Literary Association). The society was dedicated to promoting quality translations of progressive Western literature, undertaking scientific research on traditional Chinese literature, and disseminating Western literary and intellectual knowledge. The society formally disbanded in 1932, though publications continued in its name until the late 1940s. Apart from *Xiaoshuo Yuebao*, the society also published *Wenxue Xunkan* (Literature trimonthly) as a newspaper supplement and, from 1922 onward, *Shi Yuekan* (Poetry monthly). Mao Dun's critical assessments of the writings of the other members of the Literary Association remain valuable contributions to Chinese literary history of the 1920s.

In 1921 Mao Dun joined a Chinese Communist Party cell in Shanghai and served as a liaison for the party. In that year he also became a faculty member of Shanghai University. In 1926 he took part in the Northern Expedition led by Chiang Kai-shek, until the Guomindang purged the Communists in 1927 to 1928. In 1927 Mao Dun became a columnist with *Minguo Yuebao* (National monthly), a newspaper for which he wrote a number of editorials that attacked Chiang Kai-shek for his betrayal of the Chinese revolution. In 1928, like a number of other progressive young Chinese, Mao Dun sought political refuge in Japan. Throughout 1928, 1929, and early 1930, Mao Dun wrote almost ceaselessly in Japan. On returning to China in 1930, Mao Dun joined the League of Left-Wing Writers. After the outbreak of the Sino-Japanese War in 1937, Mao Dun worked as a patriotic activist through his ongoing literary activities and eventually ended up in Hong Kong.

After acquiring a masterful knowledge of the craft of fiction, Mao Dun embarked on his first full-length work, *Shi* (Eclipse), a trilogy of novels—*Huanmie* (Disillusion, 1927), *Dongyao* (Vacillation, 1928), and *Zhuiqiu* (Pursuit, 1928)—that were serialized in the pages of *Xiaoshuo Yuebao* beginning in 1927. In 1929 he published his short-story collection *Ye Qiangwei* (*Wild Rose*). According to the literary scholar Yu-shih Chen (1979), the *Eclipse* trilogy and the short-story cycle *Wild Rose* represent the Great Revolution of 1926 to 1928 allegorically, and Mao Dun created protagonists whose relations symbolize the triangular (Chinese Communist Party–Guomindang–Comintern) political configuration he sought to document and interpret as a key player in these relations. The characters in *Shi* are young progressive intellectuals, but after publication the novels attracted criticism from some leftist intellectuals, including Qian Xingcun (1900–1977). Mao is better known for two later novels that provide a broad picture of urban society—*Hong* (*Rainbow*, 1929) and *Ziye* (*Midnight*, 1933). In *Hong*, Mao Dun again portrayed urban intellectuals; the novel is an allegory of May Fourth intellectual history presented through the life of the heroine. *Midnight* is a long novel presenting a panorama of urban bourgeois society in Shanghai. Its consummate portraits of bankers, landlords, and stockbrokers suggest parallels with the novels of Balzac. Mao Dun wrote *Midnight* after the Great Depression began to have a major impact in China.

Mao Dun has more than 100 publications to his name, but he is best known today for *Midnight* and for several of his novellas and short stories, including the highly acclaimed "Chuncan" (Spring silkworms, 1932–1933) and "Linjia puzi" (The Lin family shop), which was made into a movie of the same title by director Shui Hua in 1959. Although Mao Dun ambitiously planned to cover both town and country in *Midnight*, illness dictated that he curtail his plans and restrict himself to the city. Instead, Mao Dun turned his attention to rural themes in "Chuncan," and these he treats in a naturalistic manner.

Following the establishment of the People's Republic of China, Mao Dun was active on many cultural committees and served as one of Mao Zedong's secretaries and as minister of culture from 1949 until 1964, when he was dismissed. He survived the Cultural Revolution and was rehabilitated. In the 1970s he began working on his memoirs *Wo zouguo de lu* (The road I walked), which were serialized in the quarterly *Xin wenxue shiliao* (New literature materials), but he died in 1981 before their completion. After 1949 he served as chairman of the Chinese Writers Association, although the organization ceased to function during the Cultural Revolution. He held the post until his death, when he was succeeded by Ba Jin (1904–2005).

Mao's complete works, in fifteen volumes, were published between 1984 and 1987. Apart from long novels, novellas, and short stories, his writing included many essays on literary theory and works of criticism, travel writing, and reportage, including *Sulian jianwen lu* (Eyewitness account of the Soviet Union, 1948) and *Zatan Sulian* (Talks on the

USSR, 1949). He also published many translations, and a drama, *Qingming qianhou* (Before and after Qingming Festival, 1945). His correspondence has been published in two volumes under the title *Mao Dun shuxin ji* (The letters of Mao Dun, 1945).

Mao Dun had an enormous impact on twentieth-century Chinese literature through his writing, editing, patronage, and social activism. He used his royalties to establish an annual literary award for writers of fiction, the Mao Dun Literature Scholarship.

SEE ALSO *Ba Jin; Bingxin; League of Left-Wing Writers; Literary Societies; Literature since 1800; May Fourth Movement.*

BIBLIOGRAPHY

Chen, Yu-shih. Mao Tun and the Wild Roses: A Study of the Psychology of Revolutionary Commitment. *China Quarterly* 78 (June 1979): 296–323.

Chen, Yu-shih. *Realism and Allegory in the Early Fiction of Mao Tun*. Bloomington: Indiana University Press, 1986.

Galik, Marian. *Mao Tun and Modern Chinese Literary Criticism*. Wiesbaden, Germany: Franz Steiner Verlag, 1969.

Hsia, Chih-tsing. *A History of Modern Chinese Fiction*. 2nd ed. New Haven, CT, and London: Yale University Press, 1971.

Bruce G. Doar

MAO ZEDONG

1893–1976

Revolutionary leader and founder of the People's Republic of China (PRC), Mao Zedong was one of the most controversial world leaders of the twentieth century, although more spectacularly so outside China than within the country. Over his remarkable career he led the Chinese Communist Party from a seemingly hopeless position to nationwide victory. Over the next twenty-seven years, he was the absolute ruler of China, presiding over early successes but subsequently authoring the nation's two great disasters—the Great Leap Forward (1958–1960) and the Cultural Revolution (1966–1969) and its aftermath. It was these disasters that have led various analysts outside China to group Mao with Adolf Hitler (1889–1945) and Joseph Stalin (1879–1953) as one of the great monsters of the last century. Inside China, although there have been many conflicting views on his leadership, the predominant assessment has been that for all his faults he was, after all, responsible for unifying the country and raising China to its rightful place among the foremost world powers.

THE YOUNG REVOLUTIONARY

Born into a well-to-do peasant family in Hunan in central China, by his late teens Mao was caught up in the travails of China's transitional society. The imperial structure was crumbling and foreign intrusion was deeply resented, but foreign ideas were attractive because the traditional belief system proved inadequate. As political activist, student, writer, teacher, and entrepreneur, the young Mao sampled a variety of Western ideologies, including liberalism, anarchism, and utopian socialism, before settling on Marxism. In this period, Mao already demonstrated characteristics that would mark his leadership of the Communist Party—a passionate and strong-willed nature, a pronounced pragmatic bent, strong nationalist sentiments, a sweeping view of the changes required, appreciation of the need for organization and strong leadership, and an increasing awareness of the harshness of revolutionary struggle. It is more than likely that he also envisioned a leading role for himself in that struggle.

Mao was one of the twelve founders of the Chinese Communist Party at its first congress in 1921. Although a major party figure throughout the 1920s, he was not one of the highest leaders, a group that included the inaugural general secretary Chen Duxiu and later Zhou Enlai. Mao took a prominent role in the Comintern-mandated first United Front with the nationalist Guomindang party, but apparently was not close to the Comintern agents who played a key role in guiding the Communists. Mao's most notable contribution to inner-party debates was to argue the centrality of the revolutionary role of the peasantry in his 1927 *Report on the Peasant Movement in Hunan*, a document notable for its boldness in sidestepping the Marxist focus on the urban working class and for giving priority to Chinese conditions.

After the United Front collapsed in 1927 when Chiang Kai-shek (Jiang Jieshi) turned his forces on the Communists, in the late 1920s and early 1930s Mao became one of the party's key guerrilla leaders, first in Jinggangshan on the remote Hunan-Jiangxi border, and then in the larger Jiangxi base area. These fragile base areas survived largely due to other problems facing Chiang Kai-shek, but Mao earned a deserved reputation as a capable revolutionary leader. During this struggle for survival, Mao demonstrated political ruthlessness, notably during the 1930–1931 Futian Incident, when he authorized torture and executions to prevail over his local Communist opponents. Yet Mao was not unique in employing such methods in inner-party struggle during this fractious period, and he renounced them a decade later.

Paradoxically, Mao's power eroded during the early 1930s, despite his having "real power" in contrast to the party's central leadership, which scrambled to survive in the Shanghai underground. The problem was that the Shanghai center had Comintern support, and in turn enforced Moscow's "ultraleft" line, which was at odds with Mao's policies in Jiangxi. Basically, Mao was more pragmatic, if still radical, in promoting less extreme policies toward rich peasants and "intermediate classes," and he called for a flexible military strategy avoiding confrontation with superior enemy forces. These views were attacked as "rightist" by the Returned Student faction, which was supported by Zhou Enlai, and following the arrival of the Shanghai leaders in Jiangxi from 1931, Mao was marginalized. It was only during the Long March in late 1934, after the Communists were forced to leave Jiangxi, that Mao was able to restore his influence by criticizing the failed *military* policies of the central committee.

ACHIEVING VICTORY, 1935–1949

Although official sources date Mao's leadership of the party from the January 1935 Zunyi meeting in the midst of the Long March, this is a gross exaggeration. In policy terms, his views were largely accepted in the military sphere, while change was slower on political issues, and in organizational terms he had not yet gained the top party post. Yet he clearly was a key leader across the board from that point, before finally becoming unchallenged party leader in the early 1940s. Mao's political success derived from multiple factors: developing a successful strategy for dealing with both the Guomindang and the Japanese during the second United Front following the outbreak of the Sino-Japanese War in 1937; gaining Stalin's recognition in 1938 as the most capable leader of the Chinese party, despite his pursuit of a policy involving less cooperation with the Guomindang than Stalin desired; indoctrinating the party in a practical ideology, soon known as "Mao Zedong Thought," that combined loyalty to the party line and to the leader, while popularizing concepts that were relevant to Chinese conditions and easily understood; and unifying the party.

Unifying the party was critical to both Mao's personal success and that of the revolutionary struggle. In this, Mao acted in ways at variance with the common perception of him as a ruthless politician who advanced over the broken bodies of opponents. Instead, he realized that only a unified organization could survive and overcome stronger adversaries, and this in turn required drawing in all of the party's factions and giving them a stake in his leadership. The inner-party bloodletting of the recent past was denounced, even if party rectification in 1942 to 1944 involved intense psychological pressure and excesses. At the leadership level, Mao did not rely on a narrow clique of people personally loyal to him, but instead drew in leading figures from important party constituencies, including those like Zhou Enlai who had opposed him in the past. Even Mao's most important opponents, the Moscow-oriented Returned Student faction, still received official, albeit powerless, positions. None of this is to deny that Mao was determined to have the final say, something officially granted in 1943, but it does point to his recognition of the need to make use of talented individuals, consider their opinions, and often accept their advice.

Equally crucial was the formulation of strategies for a struggle in which the Communists were by far the weaker force. Under Mao's concept of "independence and initiative within the United Front," the party guarded its independence and engaged in sporadic conflict with its supposed nationalist allies. Crucially, the Communists developed large base areas behind Japanese lines, mobilizing support with a combination of flexible rural reforms and anti-Japanese appeals. Throughout the 1937–1945 conflict, and then during the 1946–1949 civil war, Communist forces adopted the same principle Mao had championed in Jiangxi of avoiding battles with superior enemy armies, in the civil war holding back until attacks could be directed against the overextended forces Chiang sent to northeast China. While the fact of the Japanese invasion, the American defeat of Japan, and the incompetence of the Guomindang were arguably more fundamental reasons for Communist success than Mao's policies, he formulated the strategies and tactics that allowed the party to take advantage of these developments. From the perspective of other leaders and the party generally, Mao had delivered an unimaginable victory that raised his already unchallengeable authority to an even higher level.

EARLY SUCCESS IN BUILDING SOCIALISM, 1949–1956

When Mao inaugurated the People's Republic in 1949, he was blessed with potent resources for building his new socialist regime. In addition to the unlimited authority that in effect made him the new emperor, Mao benefited from the rapid pacification of the entire country bar Taiwan; deep popular support generated by the combination of national unity and peace after three decades of civil and foreign wars; a disciplined, battle-tested party that provided the organizational basis for a new ruling structure; leading figures of the revolutionary struggle who assumed top positions overseeing the transition to socialism; and a broad leadership consensus on building the country on the Soviet model.

Together with his usual pragmatic approach to problems, Mao stressed the importance of the Soviet model, which provided a coherent blueprint for a planned economy. He further stressed the gradual collectivization of agriculture, the transition of the urban economy to state ownership, the imposition of socialist forms and totalitarian control over society, and the (often excessive) copying of Soviet practice in many spheres. While Mao undoubtedly bridled at excessive copying, and was clearly unhappy with having to accede to some of Stalin's demands, he nevertheless had no doubts that the Soviet path was the only one

involve Lin planning either to launch a military coup or to assassinate Mao as officially claimed. Indeed, Mao's downturn may have originated with emotional depression, hardly the reaction of someone having defeated a determined enemy, but rather one more plausibly reflecting disbelief that one of his favorite subordinates could have planned to flee China. Yet, almost immediately, he received U.S. president Richard Nixon (1913–1994), a crucial development in the Sino-U.S. rapprochement, during which Mao displayed striking mental acuity and enormous willpower.

Meanwhile, Mao's domestic concern was to preserve *his* Cultural Revolution, but with heavy emphasis on correcting what he described as the movement's 30 percent mistakes, a project assigned to Zhou Enlai in 1972 and Deng Xiaoping in 1975. In both cases, Mao came to believe Zhou and Deng were overstepping the mark and threatening the essence of the Cultural Revolution, leading to disruptive movements in 1974 and 1976 and the ousting but ongoing protection of Deng in the latter case. Throughout every change of course, Mao's directives were followed, and even as he slipped into a coma in mid-1976, his line and prestige were strictly upheld. Despite the existing disruption and bitter conflict with the radical "gang of four," two decades of major disasters, and Mao's decrepit state, the leadership and the broader elite obeyed his instructions. Various factors were involved, but ultimately Mao had moral authority as the person believed responsible for the victory of the revolution against incredible odds, a victory that gave meaning to the elite's life endeavors.

CHANGING PERCEPTIONS OF MAO

Reverence toward Mao was the dominant attitude of both the elite and a large part of the public in the period immediately following his death, notwithstanding widespread rejection of the Cultural Revolution and a recognition by the new leadership that a fundamental change of course was required. With the passage of time, more critical views emerged, leading to the official 1981 verdict declaring Mao a "great proletarian revolutionary" but the leader principally responsible for the disasters of his last two decades. This sanitized version hid even sharper reevaluations by individual leaders.

In society generally, as increasingly bitter reflections on the Cultural Revolution came to the fore, Mao's reputation suffered accordingly. Yet the public view remains complicated, with substantial nostalgia for the more egalitarian and less corrupt days of Mao's rule, the use of his image and views as indirect but obvious criticism of post-Mao leaders and their quasi-capitalist course, and Internet parodies balanced by the reverent display of Mao's photographs in many peasant households. Overall, despite his legacy of policy disasters and with many Chinese believing that Mao committed criminal acts, he is still regarded as a great man, as the father of the nation.

Internationally, Mao was regarded with fascination since the Communist Party's drive toward victory in the 1940s. As a victorious revolutionary in the underdeveloped African-Asian world, Mao represented a model for radical movements both within and outside the international communist movement. Radical groups in the West were also attracted by Mao's seemingly pure revolutionary posture in the 1960s, but many were driven away by demands for total obeisance during the Cultural Revolution, while state actors ranging from Vietnam to Albania were alienated by Mao's 1970s rapprochement with the United States. This did not stop many in both the West and third-world revolutionary movements, such as the Shining Path in Peru and the Indian Naxalites, from treating Mao as a guide and icon. Western students in the 1960s and 1970s often identified with Mao's radical rhetoric in the context of their rejection of the Vietnam War (1957–1975) and bourgeois values. Revolutionary movements adopted Mao's strategy of armed struggle in rural base areas as a prelude to urban attacks. More generally, many Maoist groups tended to universalize the Chinese experience, in sharp contrast to the pragmatic approach focused on concrete local conditions that produced the victory of 1949.

Assessing Mao is an inherently subjective exercise. While regarding someone who must bear personal responsibility for perhaps fifty million deaths as, in the words of the 1981 party resolution, a "tragic figure" seems perverse, in certain respects that view reflects reality. Mao was a revolutionary and a nationalist, someone driven by genuine visions of social transformation and national greatness. Supremely talented and profoundly willing to bend ideology to deal with real Chinese problems, Mao achieved a revolutionary victory that beggared imagination. He accepted great human costs as inevitable and had little sympathy for class enemies, or for leaders he perceived as enemies or as weak. But for tactical or other reasons, he limited violence, compared to other figures such as Stalin and Hitler. By the mid-1950s, Mao presided over a rapidly growing economy, a transformed social structure, and a nation that had earned considerable international respect. The following twenty years of failure, most gruesomely manifested in the massive starvation of the Great Leap, were the product of unchecked power, an erosion of the pragmatic instincts that were central to his earlier successes, and a hubris that meant he could not accept personal responsibility for failure. These failures drove him to blame others, and created horrific destruction for the Chinese people.

SEE ALSO *Communist Party; Communist Party History Revised (1981); Yan'an Forum.*

BIBLIOGRAPHY

Barmé, Geremie R. *Shades of Mao: The Posthumous Cult of the Great Leader*. Armonk, NY: Sharpe, 1996.

Li Zhisui. *The Private Life of Chairman Mao: The Memoirs of Mao's Personal Physician*. London: Chatto & Windus, 1994.

MacFarquhar, Roderick. *The Origins of the Cultural Revolution*. 3 vols. New York: Columbia University Press. Vol. 1: *Contradictions among the People, 1956–1957* (1974). Vol. 2: *The Great Leap Forward, 1958–1960* (1983). Vol. 3: *The Coming of the Cataclysm, 1961–1966* (1997).

MacFarquhar, Roderick, Timothy Cheek, and Eugene Wu, eds. *The Secret Speeches of Chairman Mao: From the Hundred Flowers to the Great Leap Forward*. Cambridge, MA: Harvard Council on East Asian Studies, 1989.

MacFarquhar, Roderick, and Michael Schoenhals. *Mao's Last Revolution*. Cambridge, MA: Belknap, 2006.

Pye, Lucian W. *Mao Tse-tung: The Man in the Leader*. New York: Basic Books, 1976.

Schram, Stuart. *Mao Tse-tung*. Rev. ed. Harmondsworth, U.K.: Penguin, 1967.

Schram, Stuart. *The Thought of Mao Tse-tung*. New York: Cambridge University Press, 1989.

Schram, Stuart, and Nancy J. Hodes, eds. *Mao's Road to Power: Revolutionary Writings, 1912–1949*. 7 vols. Armonk, NY: Sharpe, 1992-2005.

Short, Philip. *Mao: A Life*. New York: Holt, 2000.

Snow, Edgar. *Red Star Over China*. Rev. and enl. ed. New York: Grove, 1968.

Teiwes, Frederick C., with Warren Sun. *The Formation of the Maoist Leadership: From the Return of Wang Ming to the Seventh Party Congress*. London: Contemporary China Institute, 1994.

Teiwes, Frederick C., and Warren Sun. *The Tragedy of Lin Biao: Riding the Tiger during the Cultural Revolution, 1966–1971*. London: Hurst, 1996.

Teiwes, Frederick C., with Warren Sun. *China's Road to Disaster: Mao, Central Politicians, and Provincial Leaders in the Unfolding of the Great Leap Forward, 1955–1959*. Armonk, NY: Sharpe, 1999.

Teiwes, Frederick C., and Warren Sun. *The End of the Maoist Era: Chinese Politics During the Twilight of the Cultural Revolution, 1972–1976*. Armonk, NY: Sharpe, 2007.

Zhang Rong (Jung Chang) and Jon Halliday. *Mao: The Unknown Story*. London: Vintage, 2005. This study has been challenged on many fronts. See the collection of critical review articles in *China Journal* 55 (2006).

Frederick C. Teiwes

MARCO POLO BRIDGE INCIDENT, 1937

On July 7, 1937, a clash between local Chinese troops and Japanese soldiers garrisoned near the Marco Polo Bridge (Lugouqiao), some 50 kilometers from Beijing, provoked demands from the Japanese military for territorial concessions from the Nationalist government of China. The head of the government, Chiang Kai-shek (Jiang Jieshi), refused this demand, instead sending troops to confront Japanese soldiers in an attempt to curb further aggression. This decision expanded what had been a local incident into a full-scale war between China and Japan.

Late on July 7, soldiers of the Japanese North China Army took part in night maneuvers near the Marco Polo Bridge, so named by Westerners because it was thought to have been described by the Venetian traveler in his account of his journey to China. It appears that unidentified figures fired on the Japanese soldiers, and a subsequent roll call suggested that one man had gone missing. In fact, the errant soldier returned soon afterward, alive and well, but his commanders did not realize this and demanded to search the village of Wanping nearby. Local Chinese troops, part of the Twenty-ninth Army, refused this demand, and the Japanese forces began to shell the village in retaliation. Shortly afterward, the two sides clashed in a short battle.

The battle itself was little more than a skirmish, but it marks the beginning of the all-out war that would become the Second Sino-Japanese War (also known as the Anti-Japanese War or the War of Resistance against Japan), which lasted from July 7, 1937, to August 14, 1945 (although some recent Chinese historiography tends to date the war from the Japanese occupation of Manchuria in 1931).

Since 1935, the increasingly militaristic Japanese government gave strong indications that it wished to expand its power in North China. By 1937, there were significant Japanese garrisons in the area. In the immediate aftermath of the Marco Polo Bridge battle, the Japanese obtained certain concessions involving the withdrawal of Chinese troops around Beijing. Yet Chiang's central government made the decision that it could not allow the cession of the railway junction at Lugouqiao. If the junction was lost, railway transport in all directions from Beijing would be under control of the Japanese. Therefore, Chiang demanded that any settlement between local Chinese and Japanese forces must recognize the right of Chinese forces to go where they wished to. He also declared that any local political settlements must not change the composition of political bodies within North China to make them more pro-Japanese. At the same time, the Japanese government authorized the massive increase of troops into China from Manchukuo and Korea on July 12. Although the Incident was not preplanned on either side, it ended up as the trigger point for total war. The Japanese argued, technically correctly, that they were within their legal rights to act as they had done at Lugouqiao. This viewpoint ignored the wider issue identified by Chiang. It had become clear that even if this particular crisis were resolved, the Japanese would rapidly find some other *casus belli* to allow them to capture North China, and they would then be in a prime position to

FINDING MARRIAGE PARTNERS

Since the reform era, China has experienced a transformation in the methods used by young people to locate partners. Prior to the 1970s, the choice of a partner was rarely left to the individual. Parents and other respected elders in the community made the match. Sometimes, the Communist Party organization was involved in the matchmaking. In earlier times, the "matchmaker" played a vital role in people's marriages. A matchmaker was usually an elderly woman, who was financially involved in arranging the marriage. That is to say, the matchmaker was paid for her services by families of young men looking for wives. Her work usually depended on her local relationships and persuasive skills. There are still some professional matchmakers in rural areas of China today, and matchmaking is also undertaken voluntarily by middle-aged women of the locality who do not take fees for the task.

Arranged marriages are now thought to be old-fashioned. Individuals are much freer in the selection of potential marriage partners, although family and community pressures are still a factor. Relatives, friends, and colleagues often play a role in smoothing the way for a couple to meet. The Internet has become a popular mechanism for young people to meet partners. There are also countless marriage agencies in China's big cities. These agencies used to be frequented mainly by older persons who feared they could not find partners, but now they attract a growing number of young white-collar workers who choose this method to seek partners because of limited free time and small social circles.

MARITAL ARRANGEMENTS

From one point of view, Chinese society has long been monogamous. A man might take concubines, but a concubine was not his "wife," nor was she usually the mother of his children. In the early twentieth century, the practice of concubinage declined, and in 1949 a policy of monogamy was stipulated in China's constitution. Since then, bigamy has been seen as immoral and illegal. Bigamy was specifically prohibited under article three of China's new Marriage Law, which was put into effect in 2006. There have been some reports of bigamy among officials in recent years, but this behavior has had severe consequences.

Cohabiting was also frowned upon in earlier times, and during the Maoist era if couples were caught cohabiting they were subjected to reform through hard labor. Today, more and more young people see premarital sex and living together before marriage as acceptable. Many believe that cohabitation will help them find out whether they are suited for each other.

SOME IMPORTANT STATISTICS

The average age at first marriage in China has increased since the mid-twentieth century, from 19 for females and 23 for males in the 1950s, to 23.5 for females and 25.9 for males in 2005 (see Table 1). Moreover, there are major differences in the marriage-age patterns of urban and rural residents. In 2005 the average age at first marriage was nearly two years higher for people living in cities versus those living in rural areas. Also, urban residents are much more likely to be unmarried or divorced than are rural residents. Nationally, divorce is showing an upward trend. A divorce rate of one per thousand people at the beginning of the new millennium had risen to 1.5 per thousand by 2006.

Average age at first marriage by sex, 2005

Place of residence	Male	Female	Difference
Country	25.9	23.5	2.4
City	26.8	24.6	2.2
Town	25.8	23.6	2.2
Rural	25.1	22.6	2.5

SOURCE: 1% population 2005 Sample Survey of China, http://www.stats.gov.cn/tjsj/ndsj/renkou/2005/html/0604.htm.

Table 1

There are fifty-five minority nationalities in China in addition to the Han majority; minorities comprise over 8 percent of China's population. On average, minority peoples have a younger age at first marriage than the majority Han population. There are also higher percentages of Han people who are unmarried, remarried, and divorced compared to the minorities. It is likely that the contrast is a function of differences in urbanization and levels of education between the Han and non-Han. (According to 2000 census data, 24 percent of Han people and 12 percent of minority people were urban residents, while 4 percent of Han people and nearly 3 percent of minority people had at least some college education.)

A major challenge for the future will be the large number of extra bachelors resulting from China's unbalanced sex ratio at birth. In 2005 there were nearly twenty-five million extra males compared to females under age twenty. Males in rural areas account for more than two-thirds of the imbalance, but all places in China contain some surplus males except the cities of Tibet. Most of those males are concentrated in provinces that are characterized by large populations and greater son preference, such as Henan, Guangdong, and Anhui. Demographers have estimated that around thirty-two million boys in China will not be able to find Chinese women to marry. In adulthood, these men will likely resettle with other single men in "bachelor ghettos" in

Beijing, Shanghai, Tianjin, and other big cities, where commercial sex outlets will be prevalent. They will be more prone to crime than if they had married, and the risk of HIV/AIDS will be significantly enhanced.

SEE ALSO *Family; HIV/AIDS; Homosexuality; Life Cycle: Marriage; Minority Nationalities; Population Policy: Population Growth Projections; Prostitution, History of; Sex Ratio.*

BIBLIOGRAPHY

Cai Duoduo. A Study of Changes in Age at First Marriage and First Fertility of Chinese Women and Population Control. *Chinese Journal of Population Science* 4, 3 (1992): 224–237.

Laub, John H., and Robert J. Sampson. *Shared Beginnings, Divergent Lives: Delinquent Boys to Age 70.* Cambridge, MA: Harvard University Press, 2003.

National Bureau of Statistics of China. Average Age at First Marriage by Province, 2005. *Sample Survey of China.* 2005. http://www.stats.gov.cn/tjsj/ndsj/renkou/2005/html/0604.htm, http://www.stats.gov.cn/tjsj/ndsj/renkou/2005/html/0604a.htm, http://www.stats.gov.cn/tjsj/ndsj/renkou/2005/html/0604b.htm, http://www.stats.gov.cn/tjsj/ndsj/renkou/2005/html/0604c.htm.

Poston, Dudley L., Jr., and K. S. Glover. China's Demographic Destiny: Marriage Market Implications for the 21st Century. In *Fertility, Family Planning, and Population Policy in China,* ed. Dudley L. Poston Jr., Lee Che-Fu, Chang Chiung-Fang, et al., 172–186. London: Routledge, 2006.

Tucker, Joseph D., Gail E. Henderson, Tian F. Wang, et al. Surplus Men, Sex Work, and the Spread of HIV in China. *AIDS* 19 (2005): 539–547.

Zeng Yi. An Analysis of Changing Trends in China's Urban and Rural Households. *Chinese Journal of Population Science* 2 (1990): 187–199.

Dudley L. Poston, Jr.
Chang Yu-Ting
Danielle Xiaodan Deng
He Lei

MARRIAGE LAWS

Throughout Chinese history, marriage laws have served a number of purposes, including the regulation of sexuality and reproduction, the definition and establishment of kinship relationships, and the prescription of roles and duties for men and women within marriage and the family. The basic outline of the history of marriage law in modern China is one of progress, though progress that has been made in a variable and uneven pattern. Modern Chinese marriage laws have increasingly rejected patriarchal, patrilocal, and patrilineal norms and extended family ideals in favor of more egalitarian principles and nuclear families. The modernization of Chinese marriage law has also entailed strengthening the principle of monogamy, elevating the companionate marriage ideal, and increasing consideration for gender equality and women's (and to a lesser degree children's) rights within marriage and the family. Women have made extraordinary gains in terms of formal rights, but these gains have often meant the loss of traditional protections. Radical changes in marriage law, moreover, have not always translated into radical changes in marriage practices. The gap between law and practice remains a wide one, as does the lag between legal and attitudinal change, especially in rural China.

THE LATE IMPERIAL PERIOD

Late imperial marriage laws corresponded to Confucian ideas of marriage and the family. Accordingly, parents and grandparents had the authority to arrange and direct their children's marriages with the assistance of a matchmaker. In practice, however, there were several variations on traditional marriage patterns, usually created out of economic necessity, including uxorilocal marriage, polyandry, adopted daughter-in-law marriage, delayed-transfer marriage, postmarital dual residence, and outright marriage resistance.

Late imperial divorce provisions, moreover, reflected the subordination of a wife to her husband and in-laws. Based upon the "seven outs" (*qi chu*) dating back to the Spring and Autumn period (722–481 BCE), a husband could divorce a wife if she behaved in an unfilial manner toward his parents, failed to give birth to a son, committed adultery, expressed jealousy, suffered from an incurable disease, spoke too much, or stole. The "three limitations" (*san buqu*), however, protected a wife from divorce, if she had no other place to go, had observed three years of mourning for her in-laws, or her husband was poor at the time of marriage and had since prospered.

Divorce in late imperial law could also be mandated by the state, a process known as "breaking the bond" (*yijue*), applicable in certain situations, such as the killing of an in-law or other relative. More rarely, a wife (with the help of her natal family) could sue for a breakup of her marriage under late imperial law if her husband had abandoned her for a lengthy period, committed certain crimes, or seriously injured her. In addition, late imperial law (as well as modern Chinese marriage laws) provided for divorce by mutual consent, though with varying degrees of difficulty as a practical matter.

THE LATE QING AND EARLY REPUBLIC

The late Qing and early Republic were transitional periods for Chinese marriage laws. The first significant departures from late imperial marriage laws originated with late Qing judicial reform efforts, which produced a revised Qing Code (completed in 1909 and effective in 1910), a draft of a new civil code in 1911, and the establishment of the Daliyuan (the court with the highest authority to rule on appeals cases and provide interpretations of the law) in 1906. The draft of the new civil code was never promulgated, and the revised Qing Code (whose civil portions nominally remained the law of the land until 1930) retained the old code's provisions of marriage and divorce, but changes in marriage laws did come about through the rulings and interpretations of the Daliyuan. In the early Republic, for instance, the Daliyuan promoted the principle of monogamy (*yifu yiqi*), thus altering the legal position of concubines. Concubinage was no longer regarded under the law as a form of minor marriage, and concubines were no longer considered minor wives. The concubine-husband relationship was transformed, legally speaking, into a relationship between dependent and family head. Daliyuan decisions also loosened restrictions on divorce and generally expanded the property rights of daughters, wives, and widows.

THE NATIONALIST ERA

In 1930 the Guomindang (GMD) promulgated the portion of the Republican Civil Code that pertained to marriage (it became effective in 1931). These laws formally provided for greater freedom of marriage and divorce. Men and women were granted the right to determine their own marriages (though arranged marriage continued to be the prevalent practice in most areas), and GMD lawmakers lifted the restrictions that historically constrained a wife's ability to sue for divorce, giving women the right to initiate divorce. In keeping with the trend toward increasingly liberal divorce provisions, the Republican Civil Code also expanded the grounds upon which parties could seek a divorce to include bigamy, adultery, intolerable cruelty, a wife's cruelty to her in-laws, abandonment, attempted murder of a spouse, incurable physical disease, incurable mental disease, lengthy disappearance, and imprisonment or the commission of an infamous crime (these divorce provisions were modeled after the Swiss and German civil codes).

The availability of divorce on a wider, gender-equal basis in the Republic, however, did not necessarily mean that divorce itself became more readily available, as courts continued to demonstrate a strong preference for reconciliation and mediation over divorce. In general, the marriage and family law provisions in the 1930 Republican Civil Code contained remarkably modern passages, but these words had to contend with the persistence of customary attitudes, as well as sheer ignorance of the new laws in remote areas of the country.

THE MAOIST ERA

The 1950 Marriage Law of the People's Republic of China, built upon earlier regulations going back to the 1931 Jiangxi Soviet Marriage Regulations, accelerated trends toward the freedom of marriage and divorce. It was a showpiece designed to abolish the old "feudal marriage system" and to bring about the "New-Democratic marriage system." Despite the influence of feminists such as Deng Yingchao (1904–1992) and a nationwide educational campaign in 1953, the implementation of this marriage law met with fierce resistance, especially to the divorce provisions, by male peasants (and their mothers) and local cadres throughout the 1950s. The 1950 Marriage Law, moreover, lacked specific grounds for divorce, which allowed for wider latitude in interpretation. During the Maoist years, for instance, divorce (like marriage) could take on intensely political dimensions, as class background and "breaking with a class enemy" became newly established reasons for divorce.

THE POST-MAO ERA

The 1980 Marriage Law reaffirmed that marriage should be based upon individual free will, monogamy, and gender equality, and it introduced mandatory family planning, an important part of China's economic modernization in the post-Mao era. To further promote population control, the minimum age of marriage was raised from eighteen *sui* (a person is one *sui* at birth and two *sui* at the next New Year; therefore eighteen *sui* can refer to someone who is sixteen or seventeen) to twenty *zhousui* (*zhousui* corresponds to one's age in Western years) for females and from twenty *sui* to twenty-two *zhousui* for males (later marriage was thought to reduce fertility). Subsequent revisions in 2001 raised the minimum age of marriage by another two years for both men and women.

Revisions to the marriage law in 2001 responded in large part to the socioeconomic changes taking place in reform-era China. With the rapid economic transformation in postsocialist China, varieties of marital property have proliferated (intellectual property rights, partnership interests, and privately owned housing, among other types), the overall value of marital property has soared, and the complexity of property transactions between spouses and third parties has grown. These developments have given rise to increasingly detailed guidelines for spousal property ownership, debt liability, and monetary compensation.

Although parental decision making no longer carries the authority it possessed under late imperial marriage laws, parental involvement retains an important place in contemporary marriage decisions, with parents continuing to initiate matches themselves or to consent to or reject matches initiated by their children. In recent years, there have even been growing incidents of the reverse: adult children interfering with the remarriages of their parents (ostensibly for fear that marriage would adversely affect the children's inheritance rights).

China's ethnic minorities have been subject to the same basic marriage laws, though ethnic minority groups have been able to modify the general marriage laws to accord with custom.

SEE ALSO *Family; Filial Piety; Life Cycle: Marriage; Rape; Women, Status of.*

BIBLIOGRAPHY

Alford, William P., and Shen Yuanyuan. Have You Eaten? Have You Divorced? Debating the Meaning of Freedom in Marriage in China. In *Realms of Freedom in Modern China,* ed. William C. Kirby, 234–263. Stanford, CA: Stanford University Press, 2004.

Bernhardt, Kathryn. Women and the Law: Divorce in the Republican Period. In *Civil Law in Qing and Republican China,* ed. Kathryn Bernhardt and Philip C. C. Huang, 187–214. Stanford, CA: Stanford University Press, 1994.

Chen Mingxia. The Marriage Law and the Rights of Chinese Women in Marriage and the Family. In *Holding up Half the Sky: Chinese Women Past, Present, and Future,* ed. Tao Jie, Zheng Bijun, and Shirley L. Mow; trans. Amy Russell, 159–171. New York: Feminist Press, City University of New York, 2004.

Chu, David S. K., ed. One Hundred Court Cases on Marriage. *Chinese Sociology and Anthropology* 18, 1–2 (1985/1986): 10–179.

Civil Code of the Republic of China. Shanghai: Kelly and Walsh, 1930–1931.

Da Qing minlü cao'an [Draft civil code of the great Qing]. Beijing: Xiuding Falü Guan, 1911.

Da Qing xianxing xinglü [Criminal code of the great Qing currently in use]. Beijing: Xiuding Falü Guan, 1909.

Davin, Delia. *Woman-Work: Women and the Party in Revolutionary China.* Oxford, U.K.: Clarendon Press, 1976.

Diamant, Neil J. *Revolutionizing the Family: Politics, Love, and Divorce in Urban and Rural China, 1949–1968.* Berkeley: University of California Press, 2000.

Glosser, Susan L. *Chinese Visions of Family and State, 1915–1953.* Berkeley: University of California Press, 2003.

Huang, Philip C. C. *Code, Custom, and Legal Practice: The Qing and the Republic Compared.* Stanford, CA: Stanford University Press, 2001.

Johnson, Kay Ann. *Women, the Family, and Peasant Revolution in China.* Chicago: University of Chicago Press, 1983.

Meijer, Marinus Johan. *Marriage Law and Policy in the Chinese People's Republic.* Hong Kong: Hong Kong University Press, 1971.

Ocko, Jonathan K. Women, Property, and Law in the People's Republic of China. In *Marriage and Inequality in Chinese Society,* ed. Rubie S. Watson and Patricia Buckley Ebrey, 313–346. Berkeley: University of California Press, 1991.

Palmer, Michael. Transforming Family Law in Post-Deng China: Marriage, Divorce, and Reproduction. *China Quarterly* 191 (2007): 675–695.

Xue Yunsheng. *Du li cun yi* [Doubts from studying the substatutes]. 1905. 5 vols. Taibei: Chinese Materials and Research Aids Service Center, 1970.

Zhang Xipo. *Zhongguo hunyin lifa shi* [The history of Chinese marriage legislation]. Beijing: Renmin Chubanshe, 2004.

Margaret Kuo

MAY FOURTH MOVEMENT

The New Culture movement (Xin Wenhua yundong) of the mid 1910s and 1920s was a loose intellectual alliance that blamed the traditional Confucian way of life for China's weaknesses and determined to replace it with a new culture. On May 4, 1919, student demonstrators in Beijing protested the agreements at the Paris Peace Conference ceding German rights in Shandong to Japan, turning the cultural movement into political action. Orthodox histories long portrayed the 1919 demonstration, which became known as the May Fourth movement (Wusi yundong), as the start of the contemporary era when radical leaders ignited revolution, leading to the founding of the People's Republic of China in 1949. Recent scholarship finds a wider range of leaders who formulated and popularized earlier intellectual changes and left a legacy of both inspiration and frustration.

THE NEW CULTURE MOVEMENT, 1915–1919

The failure of the 1911 revolution to unite and reform China led concerned intellectuals to debate why the many changes had been to no avail: The self-strengthening movement and late Qing reformers had carried out technological, political, and institutional reforms; the abolition of the examination system in 1905 had ended state-sponsored Confucianism; the new system followed a broader curriculum; many students sought new learning in Japan, Europe, or the United States; new printing technologies made possible an explosion of inexpensive books, newspapers, and magazines for new urban middle-class audiences; and intellectuals searched Confucian reform thought as well as Western and Japanese constitutionalism, Darwinism, military thought, educational philosophy, socialism, and romanticism, to mention only a few.

The New Culture program was nurtured in several new institutions. When Cai Yuanpei (1867–1940), who had studied in Germany and France, became chancellor of Peking University in 1915, he introduced an almost romantic anarchist vision of a self-governing community of students and scholars. Cai's motto reflected his conviction that education independent of politics would best serve the nation: "The New Education Stands for Individual Development and Social Progress." Cai chose Chen Duxiu (1879–1942) to be dean of the faculty. Chen was not a deep philosophical thinker, but he had an iconoclastic mind, a facile pen, and an eye for diverse talent. He recruited such luminaries as Li Dazhao (1888–1927), university librarian, newly returned from Japan; Hu Shi (1891–1962) in philosophy; and Liang Shuming (1893–1988), a specialist in Buddhism and philosophy.

In 1915 Chen also founded the seminal journal *Xin Qingnian* (New youth), subtitled in French *La Jeunesse.* World events and contemporary thought appeared side by side with Chinese, Western, and Japanese poetry, drama, and fiction. These new reference points of global time and space redefined China as a nation among nations, not a universe unto itself. The idea that all societies progressed through the same stages of history also helped China's youth to identify with colonial youth around the world. Chen judged the Chinese people in reference to foreigners: "That we Chinese meet with insult wherever we set foot is not just because the country is moribund; it is because of our unclean ways.... Dirty and unwashed, Chinese stink worse than Western cattle, dogs, or horses." Yet Chen's remedy was implicitly Confucian: "I am a mad believer in education" (*Xin Qingnian,* 22 October 1916, quoted in Hayford 1990, p. 12).

Hu Shi, voted the most popular returned student in China, while still in the United States had called for a "literary revolution" to replace terse, allusive classical Chinese (*wenyan*) with vernacular "plain language" (*baihua*). "A dead language," he proclaimed, "cannot produce a living literature." In fact, vernacular language in New Culture publications used an artificial syntax and neologisms adopted from Japanese that made *baihua* difficult for less-educated readers to understand. But the new style defined what it meant to be "modern." Like Hu, Chen coupled literary reform with cultural change. He exhorted his readers to be "independent, not servile," "progressive, not conservative," "dynamic, not passive," "cosmopolitan, not isolationist," and "scientific, not merely imaginative." In each case, the first term was associated with the West, the second with China. In 1919 Chen urged that "Mr. Kong"—that is, Confucius—be replaced with "Mr. Sai En Si" and "Mr. De Mo Ke Lo Xi," that is, Mr. Science and Mr. Democracy, spelled out in Chinese characters chosen for their sound (Chow 1960, pp. 246, 259, 277).

In the pages of *New Youth,* Lu Xun (1881–1936) began to use vernacular fiction to diagnose China's cultural malady. His story "Diary of a Madman" (1918) portrayed a scholarly family, and by implication Confucian culture, as cannibalistic, but concluded with the lines "save the children." Young readers took to heart the sardonic "True Story of Ah Q" (1921), which caricatured a stereotypical Chinese as hapless, servile, and self-pitying. These writings and those of later writers, including Mao Dun (1896–1981), Ba Jin (1904–2005), and Ding Ling (1904–1986), helped young Chinese to envision themselves as part of a movement toward a modern and powerful China.

Among these calls for modern values, feminism was central, and the traditional family became a target. New Culture writers, themselves predominantly male, commonly portrayed women as helpless victims and objects of pity, not independent actors, but their writings undermined the legitimacy of patriarchal authority and ridiculed the neo-Confucian values of chastity and obedience. Some espoused free love or communal living. Especially in anarchist writings, the concept of "culture" expanded beyond literature and learning to include a "way of life," and it quickly came to seem self-evident that progress demanded the destruction of old ways, and that an intellectual elite should lead. Although Confucianism was in fact varied and resilient, these polemical attacks made it seem that nothing less than a New Culture would do.

THE MAY FOURTH DEMONSTRATION

Joy over U.S. president Woodrow Wilson's (1856–1924) wartime call for national liberation and open diplomacy turned to outrage with the revelation in 1919 of secret agreements to hand over Germany's colonies in Shandong to Japan. Students in Korea and Turkey had already marched in anti-imperialist protests when students at Beijing's leading universities planned a demonstration for May 7, National Humiliation Day, the anniversary of Yuan Shikai's acceptance of Japanese demands in 1915.

The demonstration was moved up to May 4 to avoid police suppression. By the early afternoon, more than three thousand students from thirteen schools and colleges gathered at Tiananmen, the Gate of Heavenly Peace. At first, the passion was limited to words: "China's territory can be conquered, but it cannot be given away," and "the Chinese people may be massacred but they will not surrender." The demonstrators marched steadfastly to legation quarter, the gated section that housed the foreign embassies, where they were refused entrance. Then a smaller number proceeded to the house of the foreign minister, whom they regarded as a traitor. Some students broke in, pummeled two of the minister's guests, threatened his concubine, and set the house on fire. Police finally established control, if not order, by arresting thirty-two students, one of whom died in police custody. Cai Yuanpei, as chancellor of Peking University, negotiated their release, but then resigned in frustration.

Student activists used new communication networks and skillful patriotic rhetoric to publicize these events across China and to the world. Workers and merchants joined demonstrations in Shanghai and other cities to turn the events of May 4, actually rather small in scale, into a popular nationalist movement.

THE MOVEMENT DEVELOPS AND DIVIDES, 1919–1923

Some students returned to the classroom, others—perhaps more impatient, perhaps more practical—wanted to organize and mobilize their countrymen into a larger force. The older generation, never uniform to begin with, likewise split. In his essay "Problems and Isms," published in the summer of 1919, Hu Shi criticized the lazy espousal of foreign ideologies or "isms" instead of thoughtful examination of practical problems. Paradoxically, Hu called both for gradual change, which would come "bit by bit, drop by drop," and also for "complete Westernization." Li Dazhao countered that the real challenge was not knowledge but action. He rejected gradual reform in favor of "fundamental solutions." While others felt anarchism offered a compelling model of mutual aid and radical equality, Li and Chen Duxiu, in their search for a power-building ideology, turned to Marxism. Yet New Culture elders—the generation of professors and literary men—still shared many values. As late as 1922, Li, Hu Shi, and Cai Yuanpei all signed a newspaper manifesto calling for "good government" based on "good men," a constitutional government, and a "government with a plan" (Chow 1960, pp. 218–220, 241).

The younger generation of activists implicitly criticized their elders for their elitism in offering cultural solutions to political problems and urban, imported solutions for an agrarian country. They adopted a rhetoric of populism in which national salvation would be achieved through uplifting and organizing the common people, not condemning them. Even for liberals, the search for organization was key. Y. C. James Yen (Yan Yangchu, 1890–1990) and Tao Xingzhi (1891–1946), both newly returned from the United States, adapted YMCA campaign models to organize mass literacy classes. With the slogan "new citizens for a new nation," they enlisted thousands of educated youth to volunteer as teachers. Among them was Mao Zedong and, like him, Yen and Tao soon moved their work to the countryside. Academics created university departments in such fields as sociology, political science, social work, folklore, and anthropology, part of whose rationale was to understand and organize the people scientifically. Young Chinese could reasonably see a way of building wealth and power in this liberalism. "If liberalism is to mean anything at all," wrote one young student returned from the United States, "it means first of all the possibility of rational control of social and national forces" (Hayford 1990, p. 31). While university graduates assumed that their middle-class roles as doctors, lawyers, and scholars would serve the nation, radical activists like Mao imported organizational techniques to mobilize the people and build a powerful state.

New Culture conservatives aimed to draw on China's past, not return to it, to modernize but avoid mere Westernization. For instance, Liang Shuming, an eclectic Confucian, argued that Western individualist philosophies did not apply to China's close-knit society, but that state control would destroy it. Rural reconstruction, he argued, would serve to implement, not jettison, Confucian social values. Wu Mi (1894–1978) and Mei Guangdi (1890–1945), American-trained literary philosophers, took another tack. Their New Humanism resisted the New Culture conscription of literature for political purposes, and ridiculed the vernacular language movement. They teamed Socrates with Confucius in their mission to elucidate and systematize Chinese learning and introduce and assimilate the best in Western civilization.

THE LEGACY OF NEW CULTURE

Within a few years, invasion and war made national political power, not cultural enlightenment, the central task for intellectuals. The Leninist orthodoxy of Mao's emerging revolution gave respect to New Culture principles but rejected foreign ideas as imperialist, condemned individualism as selfish, and defined free debate as bourgeois liberalism. Students of the 1930s and 1940s continued the May Fourth tradition of taking responsibility for political reform, but radicals in the cultural revolution of the 1960s reviled the New Culture leaders as liberals and cultural traitors.

Communist histories portrayed May Fourth as the starting point of Mao's revolution. They focused on radical New Culture leaders, cropping out cosmopolitan humanists, anarchists, and other rivals. The Tiananmen demonstrations of 1989 coincided with the seventieth anniversary of May Fourth; student leaders carried banners in English to welcome "Mr. Democracy" and "Mr. Science."

During the 1990s, China demonstrated that it could follow non-Maoist strategies to success, leading some to see May Fourth not as the origin of Mao's revolution but as the lost alternative to it. With little sense of paradox, the 1990s revived anti-Confucian New Culture, as well as Confucian traditions that now seemed rich, flexible, and usable.

Discussion among scholars in the West about the May Fourth movement also evolved, though for different reasons. Chow Tse-tsung's foundational study (1960) presented the

Wind in May, ***a monument to the May Fourth Movement, December, 2004, Qingdao, China.*** *After German concessions in China landed in the hands of Japan at the end of World War I, a small number of Chinese students opposed this continued foreign presence by leading organized protests in Beijing on May 4, 1919. Leaders of the resulting May Fourth Movement sought to end Confucianism's pull on China, blaming traditional teachings for the nation's weakened position.* © REDLINK/CORBIS

self-characterization of the movement as the turning point in modernizing China, but Benjamin Schwartz (1983) summarized new findings that the key intellectual shifts had taken place a generation earlier. Arif Dirlik (1991) showed that anarchism was at least as influential as Marxism, while studies on liberals, such as Y. C. James Yen, and conservatives, such as Liang Shuming, showed that they shared New Culture questions but not answers. Vera Schwarcz (1986) argued that rather than fulfilling Enlightenment programs, Mao's revolution betrayed them. Jeffrey Wasserstrom (1991) traced the uses of May Fourth examples in later student movements, while Erez Manela (2007) showed global parallels and interactions. Yu Yingshi, in Milena Doleželová-Velingerová's revisionist symposium (2001), reasoned that "Chinese Enlightenment" and "Renaissance" are European-derived terms that falsely imply that China had been stagnant, irrational and isolated, thereby justifying radical revolution.

SEE ALSO *Liberalism; Nationalism.*

BIBLIOGRAPHY

Chow Tse-tsung. *The May Fourth Movement: Intellectual Revolution in Modern China*. Cambridge, MA: Harvard University Press, 1960.

Dirlik, Arif. *Anarchism in the Chinese Revolution*. Berkeley: University of California Press, 1991.

Doleželová-Velingerová, Milena, Oldřich Král, and Graham Martin Sanders, eds. *The Appropriation of Cultural Capital: China's May Fourth Project*. Cambridge, MA: Harvard University Asia Center, 2001.

Hayford, Charles. *To the People: James Yen and Village China.* New York: Columbia University Press, 1990.

Manela, Erez. *The Wilsonian Moment: Self-Determination and the International Origins of Anticolonial Nationalism*. Oxford, U.K., and New York: Oxford University Press, 2007.

Schwarcz, Vera. *The Chinese Enlightenment: Intellectuals and the Legacy of the May Fourth Movement of 1919*. Berkeley: University of California Press, 1986.

Schwartz, Benjamin. Themes in Intellectual History: May Fourth and After. In *Cambridge History of China*, Vol. 12, pt. 1: *Republican China, 1912–1949*, 406–504. Cambridge, U.K.: Cambridge University Press, 1983.

Wasserstrom, Jeffrey N. *Student Protests in Twentieth-Century China: The View from Shanghai.* Stanford, CA: Stanford University Press, 1991.

Charles Hayford

MEDICAL CARE SINCE 1949

After the Chinese Communist Party came to power in 1949, it substantially transformed the system for delivering and financing medical care, and it extended state-run health services across China. The focus in the early years was on creating an extensive network of hospitals and clinics beneath the Ministry of Health. At the same time, employer-financed insurance systems were introduced that paid the medical costs of a growing proportion of urban dwellers. And from the late 1950s and then during the decade of the Cultural Revolution (1966–1976), there was a particular emphasis on extending and improving provision to rural dwellers through a combination of paramedic "barefoot doctors" (*chijiao yisheng*) and locally financed cooperative medical systems (*hezuo yiliao zhidu*, CMS) that provided a measure of risk-sharing. This system, as it developed from the 1950s until the late 1970s, is widely regarded as having provided low-cost basic preventive and curative care to the great majority of the population. It was partly credited with increasing life expectancy in that period and improving public health on other indicators, such as infant and maternal mortality.

But from the early 1980s, many of the earlier period's achievements in providing low-cost, preventive care and improving access to medical care were reversed. Rural CMS collapsed and health insurance for urban dwellers eroded. At the same time, the state's share of spending on medical care declined so that state hospitals (still the vast majority) and public-sector medical professionals relied increasingly on revenues generated from services and medicines. This resulted in the de facto privatization of much medical care, a declining focus on prevention, and rapidly growing inequalities in access. Although the central government from 2003 took a renewed interest in the health system and began to invest in reforming it, progress in turning around such an enormous and divided system is likely to be slow.

MEDICAL CARE, 1950s–1970s

After 1949, health policy focused on extending basic health services across China and particularly into rural areas. Despite consistently low shares of government budgetary spending for health, this was largely achieved. A significant urban-rural divide remained, however, with greater public spending on health in the cities, higher-quality services, and more-comprehensive health insurance. In this period, particularly in the late 1950s and during the Cultural Revolution, when Mao Zedong criticized the health system and Ministry of Health for its urban bias, policy emphasized extending and improving provision in the countryside. But there was no major shift in resources to rural health care, and instead policy emphasized low-cost preventive care and the use of inexpensive traditional Chinese medicine over more expensive "Western" drugs.

Rural Health System After 1949, a three-tier health system was set up across China's rural counties (the lowest level of government); communes (which replaced the township [*xiang*] after 1958), consisting of a number of villages; and "production brigades" (villages). Counties would usually have a general hospital, a maternal and child-health hospital, and an antiepidemic clinic—all beneath the county bureau of health. Communes would have a health center that provided referral services and supervised preventive work, while production-brigade clinics were staffed by barefoot doctors who had only basic training. This health-service network extended into almost all rural counties by the late 1950s.

In the three-tier system, there was state budgetary financing for the county and sometimes commune level, but little for brigade clinics. County-level service providers were funded entirely from the state budget, while commune health centers, often small hospitals, were funded from a combination of commune welfare fund, CMS, patient out-of-pocket payments, and subsidies from the county and provincial government. There was, however, great variety in the detail of local funding arrangements. Brigade clinics were financed by a combination of CMS contributions, the brigade's welfare fund, user fees, income from sales of medicinal herbs, and some government subsidies.

CMS consisted of locally funded schemes that provided some local health risk-sharing. The first were introduced experimentally from 1955 in Henan and Shanxi provinces, and by the mid-1970s some 90 percent of production brigades were usually reported to have had them. Although the schemes were sometimes subsidized by government budgets, CMS contributions were taken from rural communities' collective income, and the generosity of particular schemes depended on the wealth of the local collective economy. They often ceased to operate in times of economic hardship.

Through this extensive state-run but locally financed and managed system, access to health services was improved for many rural dwellers in the late Mao era. But for people living in remote areas, the nearest hospital could be beyond reach. Moreover, the quantity and quality of care was variable. Where CMS was in place, risk-pooling at the production-brigade level meant members probably had relatively equal access to basic outpatient care, but the amount and quality of that care was dependent on the amount of CMS money raised and the size of the brigade, commune, and county subsidies. And overall, care was significantly lower quality than in urban areas. Reliance on local financing meant low levels of spending across much of rural China.

Urban Health System In the cities after 1949, medical care was delivered within the Ministry of Health system through municipal, district, and small neighborhood hospitals. During the Cultural Revolution, there were clinics organized around residents' committees and staffed by supervised paramedics known as "red medical workers" who played a role in delivering preventive services and offered some very simple diagnostic and curative care. Separately, the army, some large state enterprises, and other public institutions, such as universities, ran hospitals and clinics for their personnel, employees, or students. Within the planned economy, local (mainly municipal and district) governments funded Ministry of Health hospitals, while military and enterprise hospitals were funded through their own budgets.

City and district governments financed medical care through budgetary allocations to hospitals, but from the early 1950s a growing number of urban dwellers' medical expenses were paid for by their employers, or work units (*danwei*). There were two programs of work unit–financed medical care: one for workers in state and collective enterprises as part of a "labor insurance" (*laodong baoxian*) system, and one for government and public-sector employees, such as officials, teachers, doctors, and students, called "publicly financed health insurance" (*gongfei yiliao baoxian*). Labor insurance was financed by enterprises, while public-sector health insurance was financed directly from local government budgets. Neither required individual employees to make contributions or significant direct copayments out of their own pockets, and patients often simply paid a small registration fee on arrival at a clinic or hospital, and then received treatment free at the point of delivery. Additionally, many enterprises paid half the medical costs of their employees' dependents.

This system delivered a relatively high level of health care to most people living and working in the cities, and higher levels of spending on medical care in urban areas in comparison with the countryside. Not only was government budgetary spending skewed toward the cities, but the urban-rural divide in insurance systems also resulted in more finance for the medical care of the urban population. In 1980, for example, labor and publicly financed health insurance together constituted almost 35 percent of total health spending for about 20 percent of the population resident in the cities, while the CMS system contributed only 17 percent for the 80 percent living in the countryside.

POST-MAO MEDICAL CARE AND MARKETIZATION

China's health system experienced enormous changes in the first two and a half decades of the post-Mao reform period. In the early 1980s, rural CMS collapsed extraordinarily quickly. In the late 1980s and 1990s, changes to the urban insurance system came more gradually as growing market competition meant many enterprises were unable to sustain generous health provision for their employees. At the same time, fiscal decentralization reduced redistribution in government spending and encouraged local governments to focus on investing in economic growth. With medical care a low government priority, policy shifted to allowing hospitals to generate income from selling medicines and charging fees for certain diagnostic services and treatments. Together with policies permitting private practice, these factors contributed to raising the costs of health care. This in turn contributed to increasing inequalities in provision and access to health services into the twenty-first century as more and more people paid for their medical care directly out of their own pockets. As a result utilization of services declined, particularly among the poor.

The Rural System The share of villages with CMS is estimated to have fallen from around 90 percent in the late 1970s to less than 5 percent by 1984. As a consequence, the vast majority of rural residents by the mid-1980s paid directly, out of their own pockets, for almost all their curative treatment, and often even for preventive services such as vaccinations and immunizations. With CMS funds either nonexistent or unable to pay them adequately, village health workers (as barefoot doctors were now called) were often forced to charge fees or sell medicines, were driven out of medical practice, or had to move to other areas. The result was a drop in the number of village clinics, and rural health services lost 3.7 million employees by the late 1980s.

Around this time, the problem of decline in rural residents' access to health services as a result of the collapse of CMS was recognized and central policy initiatives began to explore the alternatives. Until 2002, however, these initiatives did little to improve the affordability of health care and rural residents' access. From that time, prioritization of rural "new CMS," and injections of central government cofunding alongside local government funding and individual contributions, helped extend schemes across many rural areas.

A physician in rural China visiting patients, Yinchuan, November 12, 2006. *In the 1950s, Communist leaders used a system of "barefoot doctors," individuals trained in basic preventative techniques, to improve access to health care in rural areas. Though credited with increasing life expectancy and decreasing infant mortality, government funding for the system diminished in the 1980s, leaving a large number of poor residents in the countryside without adequate health services.* © LI ZHENG/XINHUA PRESS/CORBIS

The Urban System In the cities, the enterprise-based system of health insurance and financing was at first gradually eroded in the post-Mao reform era, in part by the rising costs of the health services it provided and in part by the competitive market pressures on enterprises that encouraged them to cut back on the health benefits they delivered to employees. Total spending on labor and government-employee health insurance rose almost fivefold in real terms between 1980 and 1990, from 670 million yuan to 3,236 million yuan. Many enterprises were genuinely unable to continue financing relatively generous health services and either introduced patient copayments or paid small annual or monthly lump sums to employees for health care, regardless of their actual health-care needs.

As local governments experimented with different arrangements, work-unit provision began to vary, and employees found increasingly that they had to pay directly for their own medical treatment. Thus, in the cities, too, the number of people paying directly from their own pockets for treatment grew during the 1990s. In addition, more and more people became self-employed or shifted to the private sector, where employers were much less likely to provide insurance. The 1993 and 1998 National Health Services Surveys revealed that the share of urban dwellers without health insurance had increased from 27 to 44 percent between the two survey years.

From 1999, the central government introduced a new national, compulsory, state-run, urban basic health-insurance system to replace the old urban labor and public-employee insurance. Under this new system, both employers and employees made contributions into insurance funds managed by urban governments. Although compulsory, participation in the system was slow to extend beyond the state sector and large private employers. At the turn of the twenty-first century, whether or not people had health insurance was primarily still dependent on whether or not they had work and if they did, on whether or not their employer provided such benefits. In addition, people without formal contracts, including rural migrants to the cities, were unlikely to be insured. Those most likely to have good access were still higher-ranking officials and people in public institutions, as well as workers with contracts in successful state enterprises. Private health insurance is used by a small minority of the population.

Decentralization and the Rise of Private Provision Alongside changes to CMS and urban employer sources of finance for health, some other shifts in health-system financing also affected the provision of medical care. First, fiscal decentralization meant that health services were financed and managed to a greater extent by lower levels of government than they had been in the past. Second, because local government officials were given incentives to prioritize economic growth through the inclusion of economic indicators in their performance targets, spending on health was relatively neglected. Third, another set of policies increased state hospitals' financial self-reliance. From the early 1980s, hospitals were permitted to generate income from sales of medicine and from certain diagnostic tests and treatments to subsidize government investment shortfalls. This created incentives for them to overprescribe medicines, perform unnecessary tests, and focus on curative care. It also contributed to a decline in government spending on health as a percentage of total health spending from 36 percent in 1980 to 15 percent in 2002.

Other transformations were the result of changing policy toward private practice. Prohibited in the Cultural Revolution period, private-sector health services were once again permitted from the early 1980s. Village (formerly production brigade) clinics, previously run and financed through CMS, were sold to private practitioners. In addition, doctors were allowed to provide services privately in the hours when they were not working their standard state-hospital shifts.

As a result of these policies, the share of doctors in private practice grew from 0 to 5 percent between 1980 and 1995, though the numbers of private hospitals grew much more slowly. In richer areas, provision expanded and better technology became available as more revenue was generated. But in poorer areas where incomes from medical practice were lower, doctors often left for wealthier locales where they could make a better living. Because they did not generate income, preventive programs, an internationally acclaimed feature of the pre-reform medical system, declined in many areas.

Health and Poverty Outcomes The collapse in CMS and erosion of urban health insurance in the 1980s and 1990s meant that access to medical care became increasingly dependent on people's ability to pay for it directly out of their own pockets. Within both countryside and cities, there are many who cannot afford treatment. Studies have shown that in both rural and urban areas many people who were referred to hospitals did not go for treatment because it was too costly. And other studies have shown rising interprovincial and rural-urban differences in life expectancy and infant mortality. Since ill-health may increase vulnerability to impoverishment, and poverty is thought to often contribute to ill-health, inequalities in access to medical care may be contributing to a vicious circle of deepening poverty and illness for some segments of the population. While medical care is not the only factor that impacts on health (other factors include diet, exercise, income, and environment), critics of China's health system have also noted that health gains in terms of life expectancy and improved infant mortality have slowed in the reform period as well as become more unequal across the country. Average life expectancy at birth increased by only two years, from sixty-eight to seventy years, between 1980 and 1998, while the infant mortality rate fell by only eleven points over the same period, much less than comparable countries internationally.

ONGOING REFORM

In the 1980s and 1990s, China focused on economic development, and state investment was channeled into increasing economic growth and raising living standards. As growth took off, the expectation was that marketization would solve China's problems, including bringing investment in the health system. The Ministry of Health, unable to win significant government budgetary spending for health, settled for allowing private practice and permitting hospitals to supplement their income with charges for certain services and medicines. Doctors and other medical professionals at first accepted this. But China's crisis over the outbreak of severe acute respiratory syndrome (SARS) in 2003 alerted leaders to the fact that long-term underinvestment had caused systemic problems, including neglect of infectious-disease prevention, poor disease-reporting systems, and unaffordable care for the poor.

Soon after, in 2005, a critical report by Chinese social scientists argued that the health reforms had been a failure and led the central government to order a reassessment of the health system and to formulate plans for its development. Doctors and medical professionals supported reform, not least because patient dissatisfaction had been at an all-time high and doctors' professional reputations and status had been undermined. The Chinese government has sought international, as well as domestic, expert advice on health-system reform, but there are no simple answers to setting up an affordable and equitable system. Even if there were,

A teenager at a weight-reduction hospital, Tianjin, July 12, 2007. *As incomes rise in urban China, so do rates of childhood obesity, as many families can afford an abundance of food and rely on automobiles for transportation. Youth residing in rural areas, however, generally have few of these advantages, often suffering from poor nutrition and limited access to health care.* © DIEGO AZUBEL/ EPA/CORBIS

the process of reforming a large, unequal system is both technically and managerially difficult, as well as politically fraught.

SEE ALSO *Employees' Health Insurance; Health Care, 1800–1949; Rural Cooperative Medical Systems.*

BIBLIOGRAPHY

Bloom, Gerald, and Gu Xingyuan. Health Sector Reform: Lessons from China. *Social Science and Medicine* 45, 3 (1997): 351–360.

Blumenthal, David, and William C. Hsiao. Privatization and Its Discontents: The Evolving Chinese Health Care System. *New England Journal of Medicine* 353, 11 (2005): 1165–1169.

Feng Xueshan, Tang Shenglan, Gerald Bloom, et al. Cooperative Medical Schemes in Contemporary Rural China. *Social Science and Medicine* 41, 8 (1995): 1111–1118.

Henderson, Gail E., and Myron S. Cohen. *The Chinese Hospital: A Socialist Work Unit.* New Haven, CT: Yale University Press, 1984.

Hillier, S. M., and J. A. Jewell. *Health Care and Traditional Medicine in China, 1800–1982.* London: Routledge & Kegan Paul, 1983.

Ho Lok Sang. Market Reforms and China's Health Care System. *Social Science and Medicine* 41, 8 (1995): 1065–1072.

Hossain, Shaikh I. *Tackling Health Transition in China.* Washington, DC: World Bank, 1997.

Lampton, David. *The Politics of Medicine in China: The Policy Process, 1949–77.* Boulder, CO: Westview, 1977.

Liu Yuanli, William C. Hsiao, and Karen Eggleston. Equity in Health and Health Care: The Chinese Experience. *Social Science and Medicine* 49, 10 (1999): 1349–1356.

Liu Yuanli. Reforming China's Urban Health Insurance System. *Health Policy* 60 (2002): 133–150.

Lucas, AnElissa. *Chinese Medical Modernization: Comparative Policy Continuities, 1930s–1980s.* New York: Praeger, 1982.

Pearson, Veronica. *Mental Health Care in China: State Policies, Professional Services, and Family Responsibilities.* London: Gaskell, 1995.

Rosenthal, Marilynn M. *Health Care in the People's Republic of China: Moving Towards Modernization.* Boulder, CO: Westview, 1987.

Sidel, Ruth, and Victor W. Sidel. *The Health of China.* Boston: Beacon Press, 1982.

Jane Duckett

MEDICINE, TRADITIONAL

Traditional Chinese medicine dates back to prehistoric times. Theories concerning its practice were formulated in the Spring and Autumn period (722–481 BCE). At that time, there were different medical specialties, and doctors began to use four diagnostic methods: observing, hearing, and smelling (called *wen* in Chinese, to include both senses), asking about background, and touching. Since then, a broad range of treatments have been used, including herbal medicine, acupuncture, and moxibustion, or the burning of various herbs on certain points of the body to stimulate blood flow.

In the Han dynasty (206 BCE–220 CE), *yin-yang* theory and five-elements theory were developed to explain physical symptoms. *Yin-yang* theory postulates a dualistic natural system based on a "yin" and a "yang" nature, with associated characteristics of each, while five-elements theory breaks down matter into five elemental building blocks: earth, metal, fire, water, and wood. During this period, Zhang Zhongjing (c. 150–219), known as the "sage of Chinese medicine," wrote *Shanghan lun* (Treatise on cold damage), a masterpiece of traditional Chinese medicine. Hua Tuo (c. 145–208) used anesthesia during surgery some 1,600 years before Europeans did so. Chinese people today describe a great doctor as "Hua Tuo reborn." During the Tang dynasty (618–907), Sun Simiao (581–682), known as "the king of medicine," compiled more than five thousand prescriptions for 232 diseases in his thirty-volume *Qian jin fang* (Essential formulas for emergencies [worth] a thousand pieces of gold).

After the Tang dynasty, Chinese medicinal theories and writings spread to Korea, Japan, the Middle East, and western Asia. Chinese medicine also influenced Mongolian and Tibetan medicine. Today, these traditional East Asian medical systems are called collectively "Oriental medicine."

The Chinese government established medical schools during the Song dynasty (960–1279). During the Ming (1368–1644) and Qing (1644–1912), the system of Chinese medicine became more complex. Li Shizhen's (c. 1518–1593) fifty-two-volume *Bencao gangmu* (Compendium of materia medica) remains the premier reference work for herbal medicine and has been translated into many languages.

By the late Qing, traditional Chinese medicine was challenged by imported modern Western medicine, leading to ongoing debates between practitioners and patrons of Western and Chinese medicine. The primary question for many was whether traditional Chinese medicine should be preserved or abandoned. For those students and scholars who had studied abroad in Japan, America, and Europe, the predominant view was of Western medicine as science and Chinese medicine as superstition. As a result, Chinese medicine lost its favor in hospitals, and patients began to choose Western medicine and therapies to treat their afflictions.

In 1914, the establishment of the Peking Union Medical College highlighted the transition to Western-based medicine in China. American physicians constituted the majority of faculty on the China Medical Board by 1928. The following year, against the advice of many intellectuals, the Nationalist government outlawed the practice of traditional Chinese medicine. Thirty years later, Mao Zedong commissioned ten top Chinese doctors to survey Chinese medicine and standardize its application. In the People's Republic of China, traditional Chinese medicine came to be widely practiced and taught in medical schools. From 1965 to 1981, primary health care in rural China was delivered through peasant farmers who were trained for up to eighteen months in the treatment of common illnesses. The arrangement came to be called the "barefoot doctor" system, in reference to the farmers who often worked barefoot in the rice paddies. The current health-care system in mainland China is delivered through a network of government-owned hospitals, including many hospitals utilizing the techniques of traditional Chinese medicine. Chinese medicine remains popular in mainland China, Taiwan, Hong Kong, and other East Asian countries.

THEORIES AND PRINCIPLES

There are three basic principles underlying traditional Chinese medicine. First, the *yin* and *yang* of the human body should be in balance. An imbalance of *yin* and *yang* causes illness, which must be treated by achieving the harmony of all the opposite elements. Second, all the parts, or all the organs, of the human body are seen as united and interconnected. The sickness of a certain organ must be treated with a view to the integrity of the whole body. Third, human beings have an intimate relationship with the environment. Therefore, the same symptom may be caused by different diseases related to different factors. Thus, diagnoses and treatments may vary from person to person. These three principles, that (1) the body is a holistic system, in which each part influences the health of the others, (2) this system is predicated on the continuing balance of *yin* and *yang* in the body, and (3) the body itself is dependent on a greater relationship with its environment, all underlie the five fundamental theories of traditional Chinese medicine: *yin-yang* theory, five-elements theory, *zang-fu* theory, *jing-luo* theory, and *qi* theory.

The notion of *yin* and *yang* is also basic to Chinese philosophy. *Yin* and *yang* represents the two opposing aspects of any phenomenon in the world, or in the human body. *Yin*, for example, might represent earth, darkness, or femaleness, while *yang* represents heaven, lightness, or maleness. *Yin* and *yang* are mutually rooted, can mutually transform, and can mutually wax and wane. In Chinese medicine, the harmony of *yin* and *yang* is essential to the normal balance of the body.

The five elements in Chinese philosophy are metal, wood, water, fire, and earth. They are not conceived as real substances but represent basic materials, phenomena, and universal processes. The five elements exist in two cycles of balance: a "generating" cycle and an "overcoming" cycle. In the generating cycle, wood feeds fire, fire creates earth, earth bears metal, metal carries water, and water nourishes wood. In the overcoming cycle, wood parts earth, earth absorbs water, water quenches fire, fire melts metal, and metal chops wood. In Chinese medicine, each element is associated with different organs, emotions, body parts, body fluids, tastes, and smells. For example, the five elements are believed to be related to various emotions; wood, fire, earth, metal, and water are believed to represent anger, happiness, yearning, sadness, and fear, respectively. These associations can be extrapolated even further: Metal represents the lung, and water represents the kidney. In the five elements theory, metal supports (or generates) water. So it is believed that when the lung is healthy, the *qi* (breath) will be efficient, which will improve the flow of water in the kidney.

Zang-fu theory can be understood alongside yin-yang theory and five-elements theory. *Zang* refers to the *yin* organs: wood, fire, earth, metal, and water represent the liver, heart, spleen, lungs, and kidneys, respectively. *Fu* refers to the *yang* organs: wood, fire, earth, metal, and water represent the gall bladder, small intestine, stomach, large intestine, and urinary bladder, respectively. *Zang xiang* is the visceral manifestation of the interaction between *zang* and *fu*.

Jing-luo theory refers to channels connecting organs, in which *qi* (breath, spiritual energy) and blood run through the whole body. *Jing* are the main vessels in the human body, and *luo* are small or branch vessels. There are twelve regular *jing-luo* channels, each nourishing and acting on a certain organ. Chinese acupuncture and *qigong* use the *jing-luo* map of the human body to treat diseases.

TRADITIONAL CHINESE MEDICINE IN CONTEMPORARY CHINA

In modern times, Western medical theories and techniques are dominant in the Chinese medical system. The ratio of hospitals and doctors of Western medicine relative to those of Chinese medicine is about six to one. Nevertheless, traditional Chinese medicine remains important in China. By the early twenty-first century, mainland China still had some 334,000 practitioners of traditional Chinese medicine, although the number was much higher in 1911 (800,000) and 1949 (500,000).

In 2008 thirty-two of mainland China's 136 medical universities were schools of traditional Chinese medicine. Students at these schools also study basic Western medical principles, pharmacology, technologies, and surgery, and they are thus able to diagnose and treat patients using Western approaches when necessary. In effect, their practice of traditional Chinese medicine is based on a broad knowledge of all areas of medicine.

There were also 3,072 hospitals of traditional Chinese medicine in mainland China in 2008, offering more than 330,000 beds for patients. In addition to these hospitals, most clinics include a department of traditional Chinese medicine. Traditional Chinese medical services are offered at the majority of county clinics, district medical centers, and other small clinics. According to data from 2006, nearly 300 million patients were treated using traditional Chinese medicine.

DIAGNOSTIC PRACTICES AND TREATMENTS

Modern diagnostic practices can be traced back to the four categories adopted in the Spring and Autumn period: observing signs and symptoms, examining the tongue, asking about a patient's background, and feeling the pulse. By feeling the pulse, a trained traditional physician may discern which organ is sick and what causes the sickness. According to literature of the Ming and Qing dynasties, male doctors were not permitted to touch female patients. They would hold a thread with one end tied to the woman's wrist, and thus determine whether the woman was pregnant. Unlike their teachers, modern practitioners of traditional Chinese medicine often combine traditional approaches with such Western methods as x-rays and laboratory tests to make a diagnosis.

Chinese herbal medicine is built on Chinese peoples' practical experiences over thousands of years. According to one count, there are 12,080 herbal medicines recognized in traditional Chinese medicine. Various parts of a plant can be used as an herbal drug, including the roots, twigs, leaves, flowers, fruits, and grasses. Insects, animals, and minerals can also be used as medicines. A prescription

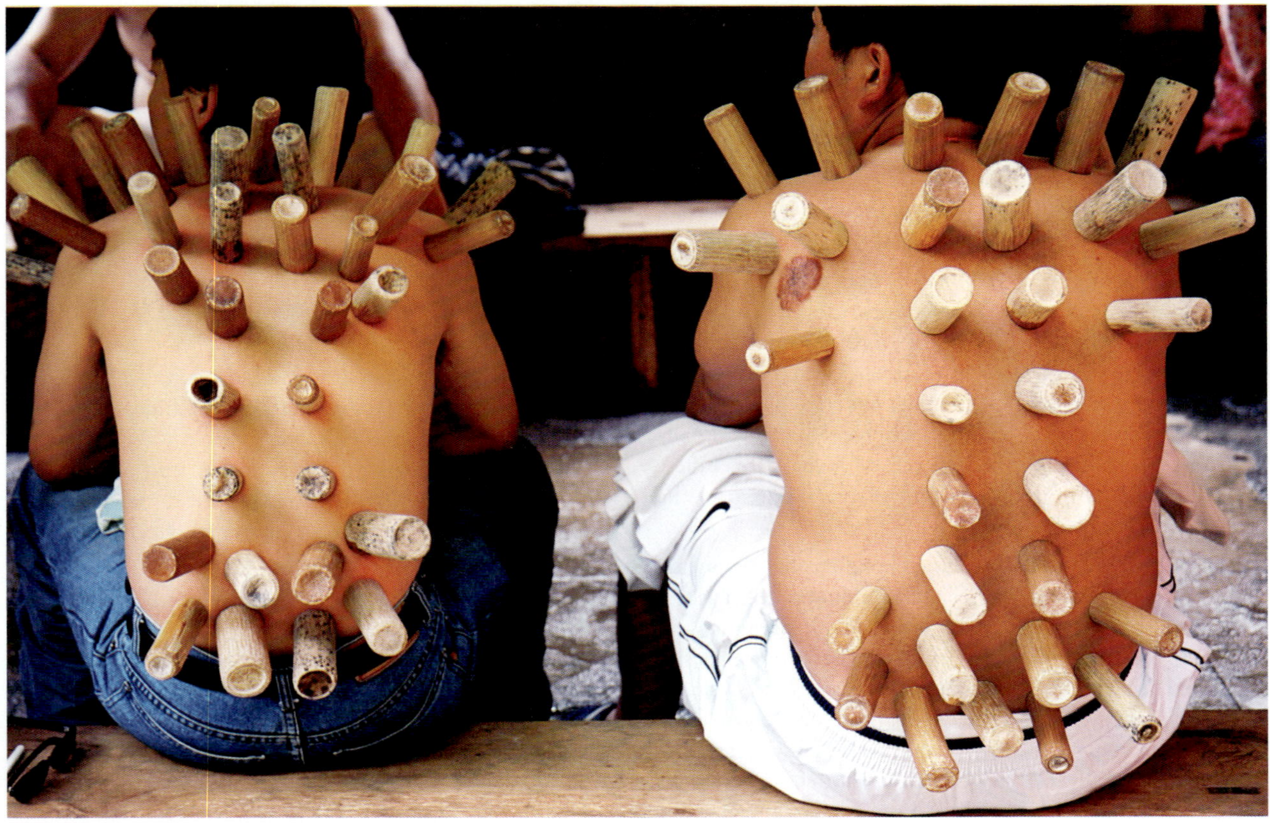

Patients receiving bamboo cupping treatment, Kunming, Yunnan province, January 17, 2005. *Theories regarding traditional Chinese medicine can be traced back to ancient times. While much of China has adopted Western medical practices, traditional medicine retains a strong presence throughout the nation with doctors blending both techniques to treat patients.* © TANG JIANG/EPA/CORBIS

is generally a combination of different kinds of medicines, and the amount of each medicine must be very precise.

In most cases, patients being treated with traditional medicines must go to a drugstore to collect the materials in the prescription, which they then prepare by boiling them at home. Today, most hospitals will prepare medicine for patients. The herbs and ingredients in many traditional medicines are now available as soluble granules and tablets, which are very popular.

Along with herbs, there are other traditional Chinese medical treatments, acupuncture being the most common. In acupuncture, the practitioner inserts a number of fine needles into the skin or the pockets of the body at precise points. Each point is associated with a corresponding visceral organ. Acupuncture is thought to influence the nervous system and perhaps the endocrine system.

In moxibustion, another common treatment, a practitioner places a small quantity of dried herbs, usually artemisia, on a patient's body or limbs. The herbs are then set alight, or the practitioner may use a paper tube to gently heat the herbs. Other treatments include cupping, *guasha*, massage therapy, Chinese food therapy, and *qigong*. To treat a disease, a doctor may use more than one therapy.

BRANCHES OF TRADITIONAL CHINESE MEDICINE

There are many branches of traditional Chinese medicine. Since the Han and Tang dynasties, the most prominent has been the Jingfang school, which relies on the oldest classics, *Huangdi neijing* (The medical classic of the Yellow Emperor) and *Shennong bencaojing* (Shennong's classic of materia medica). In the Ming and Qing dynasties, the Jingfang school was challenged by the Shifang school, which preferred to use prescriptions later than the Song dynasty. The competition between the two schools continues into the twenty-first century. Other branches of traditional Chinese medicine include the Wenbing school, which deals especially with febrile diseases; the Shanghan school, specializing in cold damage; the North school, popular in north China and combining the Jingfang and Shanghan schools of thought; and the South school, prevalent in South China and combining the Shifang and Wenbing approaches.

Physicians have been evaluating the efficacy and safety of Chinese medicine through clinical trials. Recent research suggests that Chinese medicine does indeed exert measurable therapeutic effects on many acute or chronic diseases, including cardiovascular diseases, diabetes, and stress-related disorders. Clinical evidence also suggests that acupuncture can grant a patient relief from pain, prevent nausea, and improve the success rates of conventional infertility treatments. In addition, *qigong* and dietary therapies are widely used to maintain patient health and prevent future disease.

Traditional Chinese medicine has a long history and is a central part of Chinese culture. For certain diseases, people may first try traditional Chinese treatments. However, cooperation between traditional Chinese medicine and Western medicine is a new trend, and most people will accept both types of treatment.

SEE ALSO *Acupuncture.*

BIBLIOGRAPHY

Bensky, Dan, Steven Clavey, Erich Stöger, et al., comps. and trans. *Chinese Herbal Medicine: Materia Medica.* 3rd ed. Seattle, WA: Eastland Press, 2004.

Lu, Henry C. *Traditional Chinese Medicine: An Authoritative and Comprehensive Guide.* Laguna Beach, CA: Basic Health, 2005.

Maciocia, Giovanni. *Diagnosis in Chinese Medicine: A Comprehensive Guide.* New York and Edinburgh, U.K.: Churchill Livingstone, 2004.

Maciocia, Giovanni. *The Foundations of Chinese Medicine: A Comprehensive Text for Acupuncturists and Herbalists.* New York and Edinburgh, U.K.: Churchill Livingstone, 2005.

Unschuld, Paul. *Medicine in China: A History of Ideas.* Berkeley: University of California Press, 1985.

Unschuld, Paul. *Chinese Medicine.* Brookline, MA: Paradigm, 1998.

Wong Kiew Kit. *The Complete Book of Chinese Medicine: A Holistic Approach to Physical, Emotional, and Mental Health.* Sungai Pentani, Malaysia: Cosmos, 2002.

Yiran Zheng

MEDICINE, WESTERN, 1800–1949

Portuguese and French Jesuits first brought Western medical concepts and texts to Macau and Beijing in the mid-to-late eighteenth century, but Protestant missionaries introduced Western medical practice and education in China. The first Protestant society to enter China, the London Missionary Society, sent Robert Morrison to Macau in the early 1800s. Morrison had only the limited medical training that prepared missionaries to survive in a setting without proper medical facilities, and he never practiced medicine. He did, however, see Western medicine as important to the Christian mission, and he established the first medical clinic of its kind in China.

The first medical missionary to arrive in the Far East was Peter Parker (1804–1888), who studied divinity and earned a medical degree at Yale University before going to Guangzhou (Canton) in 1834. The next year, Parker established China's first mission hospital, known as the Ophthalmic Hospital for Parker's outstanding ophthalmologic surgeries. In 1855 John Glasgow Kerr (1824–1901) relieved Parker, and in 1859 Kerr reopened the expanded hospital in a new location and named it as Boji Hospital, which became one of the best-known mission hospitals in China. The entire country then had only twenty-eight medical missionaries, but by 1905 the number had climbed to 301 working in 166 mission hospitals and 241 clinics (Zhu 1988, p. 66). Among them, women missionary doctors such as Mary Stone (Shi Meiyu, Shih Mei-yu, 1873–1954) and Ida Kahn (Gan Jiehou, 1873–1930) contributed to the medical training of women and the establishment of hospitals for women and children.

Medical missionaries soon realized that medical practice provided an entry into Chinese society. As one observed: "The medical missionary gains access at homes that are closed to other workers. He is called by all classes, rich and poor, high and low, and all classes come to the dispensary for consultation and medicine. He is able to make acquaintances and to gain friends, real friends, especially among the more educated and more progressive Chinese" (Choa 1990, p. 14). Deeply rooted in native medical theories and herbal medicine, however, most Chinese looked to Western medicine as a last resort. Despite the success of ophthalmologic and other types of surgeries in mission hospitals, the efficacy of Western medicine and the motives of its practitioners stirred suspicion among the Chinese. "The provision of free services would have engendered fresh antagonisms—either from literati who found yet another of their functions eroded, or from Chinese doctors who found their livelihoods threatened" (Spence 1974, p. 43). Nevertheless, Western medical practice and education developed rapidly in China, especially since the late nineteenth century.

In contrast to instruction at modern medical schools, Western medical training in China started with the master-apprentice method. The earliest such training occurred at Boji Hospital, which became the South China Medical College in 1904. In 1898, thirty-nine out of sixty mission hospitals provided medical training, with six hundred Chinese graduates (Zhu 1988, p. 67). The number of graduates and the quality of their training proved unsatisfactory, however. Eventually, formal medical schools were established. During the first half of the

A victim of the pneumonic plague, Manchuria, 1912. *In the late 1800s, Chinese men and women began earning medical educations at universities in the West, returning home to establish clinics, hospitals, and laboratories. An early Western-trained doctor, Wu Liande developed the Manchurian Plague Prevention Administration in 1912, responding to an earlier epidemic of pneumonic plague.* HULTON ARCHIVE/GETTY IMAGES

twentieth century, at least nine missionary medical schools officially registered and operated in large cities, including Saint John's University (Shanghai), Qilu University (Jinan), Xiangya Medical College (Changsha), and Lingnan University (Guangzhou). These schools became models of medical education in China, with a general standard requiring certain science and medical courses, as well as laboratories and teaching hospitals. Many Western medical books were translated for teaching.

The return of Chinese graduates from Western medical schools provided the mainstay of medical education and practice in China. Huang Kuan (Wong Fun, 1829–1878), the first Chinese doctor with Western medical training, taught medicine at Boji and later became its head. Jin Yunmei (Kim Yamei, 1864–1934) and Hu Yuying (Hu Kim-eng, 1865–1929) graduated from schools in the United States to become the first women doctors in China. Wu Liande (Wu Lien Teh, 1879–1960), a Cambridge University graduate, returned to head China's first governmental military medical school. In 1912 Wu established the Manchurian Plague Prevention Administration to fight pneumonic plague, and he eventually built some twenty hospitals, laboratories, and research institutions around the nation.

Western medical education and research reached its peak in China through the establishment of the Peking Union Medical College (PUMC). In 1915 the Rockefeller Foundation sought to export to China the most advanced laboratory-based medical science in an up-to-date institution for education and research. Influenced by the reform of medical education in early twentieth-century America, the PUMC was called a "transplant" of the Johns Hopkins University Medical School because it followed the latter's model closely. Over a period of thirty years, the Rockefeller Foundation gave the college a total of $45 million, and the PUMC developed into the best medical education facility in Asia. The college graduated 318 medical doctors and 168 master nurses, and over 2,000 doctors around the nation received advanced training there. These early professionals became leaders in Chinese medicine in the second half of the twentieth century.

The missionaries and the Rockefeller Foundation aimed to convert China to Western civilization, either through the Gospels or modern science. Undoubtedly, modern medicine and education served religious and political ambitions; yet China's search for modernity created the conditions for medicine's advancement. The reformer Liang Qichao praised the PUMC for its contribution to China's progress. He was convinced that China needed empirical methods of scientific research, and that medical science could help meet this need (Ma 1995, p. 197).

SEE ALSO *Education: 1800–1949; Health Care, 1800–1949; Medicine, Traditional; Missionaries.*

BIBLIOGRAPHY

Choa, G. H. *"Heal the Sick" Was Their Motto: The Protestant Medical Missionaries in China*. Hong Kong: Chinese University Press, 1990.

Gao Shiliang. *Zhongguo jiaohui xuexiao shi* [History of mission schools in China]. Changsha, China: Hunan Education Press, 1994.

Ma, Qiusha. The Rockefeller Foundation and Modern Medical Education in China, 1915–1951. Ph.D. diss., Case Western Reserve University, Cleveland, OH, 1995.

Spence, Jonathan. Aspects of the Western Medical Experience in China, 1850–1910. In *Medicine and Society in China*, eds. John Bowers and Elizabeth Purcell, 40–54. New York: Josiah Macy Jr. Foundation, 1974.

Zhu Chao ed. *Zhongwai yixue jiaoyu shi* [History of medical education in China and abroad]. Shanghai: Shanghai Medical University Press, 1988.

Qiusha Ma

MEDICINE, WESTERN, SINCE 1949

Since 1949, Western medicine in China has been characterized by rapid development, including professionalization, institutionalization, and scientization, as well as quick diffusion throughout the countryside. Chinese medicine was predominant in the medical domain in 1949, while Western medicine occupied only a marginal position. Medical education and research were key factors in its development as a completely new system of medical education took shape after 1949. This system trained a large number of doctors of Western medicine, who were assessed and promoted according to their proficiencies. Great strides were also made in every field of basic medical science and clinical medicine, and professional associations and journals were established for each field. Together, these developments contributed to the rapid professionalization of Western medicine in China. The founding of the Chinese Academy of Medical Sciences as the leading institute for medical research in 1956 was followed by the establishment of medical universities and research agencies in every province. Medical research was closely associated with the needs of disease prevention and treatment and emphasized the basic theories of medical science. Among the achievements of this work were developments in understanding the trachoma virus, in the reattachment of severed fingers, and in the treatment of extensive burns.

The use of vaccines, common medicines, and other pharmaceuticals made rapid progress, thanks to improvements in medical education and research. Faced with rampant epidemic and endemic diseases, the Chinese government launched a series of inoculation campaigns under the "prevention first" policy, beginning with a smallpox-inoculation campaign in 1950. By 1970, most of the population had been vaccinated for major acute epidemic diseases. The combination of effective vaccines and mass mobilization led to a drastic decline in the incidence and mortality rates of epidemic diseases (reaching their lowest levels in 1970), and the shift from an epidemic disease model to a chronic disease model.

In terms of medicines, including medical instruments, China made great progress thanks to industrial development. By 1965, the production of six basic medicines, including antibiotics and sulfamethazine, could meet the demands of disease prevention and treatment. Furthermore, the government reduced the price of medicine seven times from 1949 to 1984, so that the cost of medicine in 1984 was just 16.42 percent of what it had been in 1950. Due to mass production and the establishment of a complete commercial pharmaceutical network, Western medicines were quickly promoted, significantly improving China's standard of medical treatment and health care.

Medical institutionalization is a major characteristic of Western medicine. From 1949 to the mid-1960s, a complete range of modern medical systems was gradually formed at different levels of China's administrative system. Various medical institutions emerged, such as hospitals, clinics, and polyclinics, all of which adopted the institutional structures and management systems typical of Western medicine. Among these, the hospital was the most important institution. After 1949, China mainly developed general hospitals with certain specializations, while also establishing specialized hospitals. In 1949 there were only 2,600 hospitals and 80,000 beds in China. By 1985, the numbers had increased to 58,159 and 1,293,300 respectively. The popularization of hospitals also changed the traditional doctor-patient relationship and altered the health-seeking behavior of the masses. The doctor-patient encounter already moved from homes to hospitals, while hospitalization gradually became the common health-seeking behavior.

Developments in rural areas were crucial to the diffusion of Western medicine, because the peasantry accounted for the majority of China's population. After 1949, Western medicine gradually entered the villages. Ironically, rural practitioners of Chinese medicine played a major role in introducing Western medicine into villages, by participating in vaccination campaigns, prescribing Western medicines, and learning to use diagnostic instruments. The barefoot-doctor program that was implemented in rural China after 1970 quickly imposed a Western-influenced medical-knowledge structure across the countryside. Meanwhile, the establishment of medical stations in the villages completed a pharmaceutical sales network. Boosted by a drastic decline in prices in 1969, Western medicines flooded into the villages and were quickly accepted by the peasantry, even as Chinese and herbal medicines were promoted by the government in view of their low cost and easy availability.

The development of Western medicine greatly influenced Chinese medicine in terms of professionalization, institutionalization, and scientization, and led to the birth of "integrated Chinese and Western medicine." More importantly, the expansion of Western medicine ultimately brought about the marginalization of Chinese medicine. In 1949 there were 87,400 doctors of Western medicine in China, but by 1985 the number had increased to 1,075,021. In contrast, the number of doctors of Chinese medicine increased by only 21 percent between 1949 and 1985, from 276,000 to 336,224 respectively. Chinese medicine declined in popularity and authority, even while it obtained state legitimacy under the new regime.

Medical developments since 1949 have not been without shortcomings. Although the spread of Western medicine made tremendous progress after 1949, the problem of uneven access between the social classes, as well as between different regions and in urban versus rural areas, started immediately and has expanded steadily over the years. In China after Mao Zedong, rural reforms accomplished since the late 1970s, together with medical reforms and marketization implemented after 1998, have brought about high prices and seriously uneven levels of distribution of medical resources. The costs of medicine and medical services have become heavy burdens for many people. These widening disparities have attracted the attention of the Chinese government, which is working to adjust the country's uneven access to Western medicine. Meanwhile, Western medicine continues making rapid progress in China.

SEE ALSO *Health Care, 1800–1949; Medical Care since 1949; Medicine, Traditional; Medicine, Western, 1800–1949.*

BIBLIOGRAPHY

Dangdai Zhongguo Congshu Bianjibu [Editorial office of contemporary China book series]. *Dangdai Zhongguo de weisheng shiye* [Contemporary China's medical and health care]. Beijing: Zhongguo Shehui Kexue Chubanshe, 1986.

Dangdai Zhongguo Congshu Bianjibu [Editorial office of contemporary China book series]. *Dangdai Zhongguo de yiyao shiye* [Contemporary China's pharmaceuticals]. Beijing: Zhongguo Shehui Kexue Chubanshe, 1988.

Fang Xiaoping. Barefoot Doctors in Chinese Villages: Medical Contestation, Structural Evolution, and Professional Formation, 1968–1983. Ph.D. diss., National University of Singapore, 2008.

Scheid, Volker. *Chinese Medicine in Contemporary China: Plurality and Synthesis.* Durham, NC: Duke University Press, 2002.

Sivin, Nathan. Editor's Introduction. In *Biology and Biological Technology, Part VI: Medicine.* Vol. 6 of *Science and Civilization in China.* Cambridge, U.K.: Cambridge University Press, 2000.

Unschuld, Paul. *Medicine in China: A History of Ideas.* Berkeley: University of California Press, 1985.

Fang Xiaoping

MEI LANFANG
1894–1961

Mei Lanfang was twentieth-century China's greatest female impersonator (*nandan*) in Peking Opera. Brilliant exponent of traditional drama, yet reformer of his time, Mei Lanfang contributed more to twentieth-century Chinese opera, both domestically and internationally, than any other single person.

CAREER

He was born in Beijing to an acting family, his grandfather Mei Qiaoling (1842–1882) having achieved fame as another female impersonator. At ten he made his public début, enrolling three years later at the Xiliancheng Training School, then reputed to be Beijing's best and most progressive. His 1913 visit to Shanghai began a period of major fame. From then until his death he remained in demand all over China, and he made several overseas tours, in 1919, 1924, and 1956 to Japan, in 1930 to the United States, and in 1935 to Moscow, Leningrad, London, Berlin, and Paris.

Mei continued acting and teaching after 1949, also undertaking administrative roles, such as founding director of the China Peking Opera Institute (*Zhongguo Jingju Yuan,* established in January 1955). In 1954 he joined the National People's Congress and in 1959 the Chinese Communist Party. He took a leading role in Communist-inspired reform of drama. Mei Lanfang was the main one of the "four great famous female impersonators" (*sida mingdan*), the others being Cheng Yanqiu (1904–1958), Xun Huisheng (1899–1968), and Shang Xiaoyun (1900–1976).

Mei married twice. His first marriage, arranged in the traditional way, produced one son, who died young. About 1919 Mei took a concubine, Fu Zhifang, whom he married when his first wife died soon thereafter. Through his second marriage, which was lifelong, he had two sons and a daughter. The younger son, Mei Baojiu (b. 1934), achieved distinction as a female impersonator. Despite his fame, Mei Lanfang was modest in personality. He was extremely hardworking and firm of will. A brilliant teacher, he instructed some 115 individual students, the first being Cheng Yanqiu. He was also a good painter and calligrapher.

ARTISTIC CONTRIBUTIONS

Mei's main artistic innovations date from 1914 to the early 1930s. His distinctive style is called the Mei school (*Meipai*). His contributions ranged widely over the fields of music, costumes, and choreography. He innovatively fused the role-types of the demure young lady (*qingyi*), the coquettish female (*huadan*), and the military female (*wudan*). In music, he reformed singing styles and melodies and enlarged the accompaniment by adding the deeper and mellower *erhu* bowed fiddle to the preexisting *jinghu* bowed fiddle.

For operas set in contemporary times, he adopted realistic costumes, and for those of long ago, he often changed the practice of using Ming-dynasty costumes. In *Chang'e benyue* (Chang'e escapes to the moon), which premiered in September 1915 and is about a legendary woman who escapes to the moon after stealing the elixir of immortality, Mei decided to ignore the role's traditional costumes, modeling them instead on "the styles seen in ancient prints and paintings" (Scott 1971, p. 73). This highly controversial decision turned out to be very popular with the public.

An excellent example of Mei's choreographic brilliance is *Guifei zuijiu* (Guifei gets drunk), which premiered in 1914. The opera concerns the beautiful Yang Guifei, the favorite concubine of Emperor Xuanzong (r. 712–756). She plans to feast with the emperor, but he fails to appear. Mei's dancing, movements, and facial expressions showing expectation turning to anxiety and despair, then drunken stupor, were hailed as an artistic marvel.

POLITICS, SOCIETY

Living in Shanghai under Japanese occupation, he grew a mustache to betoken his refusal to act, symbolizing his patriotism. His plays also show his patriotism. An example is *Mulan congjun* (Mulan joins the army), which premiered in 1917. An old story, it concerns the heroine Hua Mulan, who disguises herself as a man to join the army and resist foreign aggression, the text of Mei's version emphasizing the patriotism of Mulan's action. In his last new opera, *Mu Guiying guashuai* (Mu Guiying takes command), which premiered in 1959, Mei took the traditional female-warrior title role. Set in the eleventh century, this opera too depicts resistance to aggression.

Another strong feature of Mei's plays and activities was his interest in women's issues. Though patriotism trumps gender in *Mulan Joins the Army* and *Mu Guiying Takes Command,* Mei consciously asserted feminist interests in these operas. Many of his operas, especially the early ones, emphasized gender. An excellent example is *Niehai bolan* (Waves of a sea of sin), which premiered about 1915, a long opera with a social message sympathizing with prostitutes.

Mei was in the vanguard in taking on female disciples, unprecedented in his time. Some of them became famous in their own right, including Du Jinfang (whose given name means "approaching Mei") and Li Yuru.

Mei was also at the forefront of a system of writing plays that Joshua Goldstein calls "part and parcel of the new cultural legitimation" (2007, p. 117). During the Republic, the playwright-theorist-impresario Qi Rushan (1877–1962), who strongly favored Western-style drama reform, advised Mei and wrote scripts for him from 1919 to 1931.

IMPACT ON WESTERN PERCEPTIONS OF CHINA

Mei Lanfang was a pioneer among Chinese actors in traveling to Europe and America, his performances significantly influencing images of Chinese culture and theater. Westerners formed an extremely positive impression of Mei Lanfang and, through him, of the art he represented.

Mei's 1930 visit to the United States was a triumphant milestone in Chinese-Western cultural relations. Mei won ecstatic praise from New York critics for his Broadway performances. He met and gained admiration from Charlie Chaplin (1889–1977) and other leading lights of the cinema world. Theater enthusiasts adored this master of a new and unfamiliar theatrical art.

In 1935 Mei won praise from the famous German Marxist dramatist Bertolt Brecht (1898–1956), who met Mei Lanfang and saw him act in Moscow. Brecht acknowledged that Mei's performance inspired his theory of "alienation effect" (*Verfremdungseffekt*), because for him Mei was the best at presenting an essential reality by making no attempt to do so. In a similar vein, though from a different standpoint, the great Russian actor-director-theorist Konstantin Stanislavsky (1863–1938) extolled Mei's acting as "an art full of poetic and conventionalized realism" (cited in the foreword to Mei et al. 1997).

SEE ALSO *Peking Opera and Regional Operas.*

BIBLIOGRAPHY

Goldstein, Joshua. *Drama Kings, Players, and Publics in the Recreation of Peking Opera, 1870–1937.* Berkeley: University of California Press, 2007.

Li, Siu Leung. *Cross-Dressing in Chinese Opera.* Hong Kong: Hong Kong University Press, 2003.

Mei Shaowu, Liu Zhanwen, Cheng Yuyan, et al., eds. *Mei Lanfang.* Trans. Hu Dongsheng. Beijing: Beijing Press, 1997. A pictorial biography in Chinese and English.

Scott, A. C. *Mei Lan-fang: The Life and Times of a Peking Actor.* Hong Kong: Hong Kong University Press, 1971. Originally published 1959 under the title *Mei Lan-fang: Leader of the Pear Garden.*

Wu Zuguang, Huang Zuolin, and Mei Shaowu. *Peking Opera and Mei Lanfang.* Beijing: New World Press, 1981.

Colin Mackerras

MIAO UPRISINGS

Descriptions of the Miao in the record of the Qing dynasty (1644–1912) give a misleading sense of a single, self-conscious ethnic group, and Western-language discussions of the mid- and late Qing revolts imply similar movements, even though one (1795–1797) was narrowly focused on west Hunan and the other (1854–1873) was dispersed over Guizhou Province. Yet both uprisings showed up late Qing vulnerability at the far-flung frontiers of the empire.

The term *Miao,* introduced by officials of the Ming dynasty (1368–1644), goes back to the prehistoric Three Miao (Sanmiao) mentioned in Chinese tales of the Yellow Emperor, but members of the several large language groups so described during the Qing do not seem to have used the term themselves or to have accepted the official designations (Hei [or black] Miao, Hua [or colored] Miao) based on the clothing that the men commonly wore. There is no evidence of a pan-Miao identity. But in west Hunan and spreading over the Guizhou and Sichuan borders, a population of several hundred thousand practiced settled agriculture rather than the swidden (slash and burn) farming more common in impoverished Guizhou and may already have been considered a community by 1795. They had had several generations of common experience since the early-eighteenth-century arrival of Qing administrators and an influx of Han settlers and garrison soldiers. They had close agnatic and affinal links through intermarrying surnames and shared distinctive customs, including worship of the White Emperor Heavenly Kings (Baidi Tianwang) and use of an informal oath-taking legal system. All these features distinguished the eastern Miao—who by at least the 1940s knew themselves as Khoxiong—from groups officially called Miao spread across the province of Guizhou.

The declared purpose of the 1795 uprising was publicly articulated in Chinese-language handbills: recovery of land lost to Han settlers in the previous sixty years, along with official positions for eastern Miao leaders. Though the draconian extermination of several hamlets a few years before had angered local eastern Miao people, the revolt was not directed at officialdom, for taxes and other dues and corvées had not been imposed. The start of the revolt, more or less coordinated over the three prefectures, involved mass possession trances, martial arts, the burning of Han settlements, and an attack on isolated Qing military columns and walled cities. A substantial part of the population was involved, some as a result of intimidation.

The Qing army suppressed the revolt, but only with a sizable army that, in cost, exceeded by far most of the ten accomplishments (*shiquan*) of the Qianlong reign that the emperor had celebrated in 1792. Led by his favorite Manchu generals Fukang'an and Helin, the suppression occupied much of the venerable emperor's attention for two years into his retirement. Hamlets were destroyed, local populations were put to the sword, but a policy of divide and rule won over many Miao and other locals. Hunan elites also played a role in reestablishing order. The difficult terrain was largely under official control by 1797, though mopping up continued for another eight years.

By contrast, in the misleadingly named Guizhou "Miao" Rebellion of 1854–1873, Miao represented only

one element, disgruntled Han Chinese being almost as numerous as the Miao, Muslims, and other ethnic minorities (such as the Bouyei and other Tai groups). Ethnic hostility played a role, but the principal motivations were desperate poverty, scarcity of land, excessive or unjust tax levies, and other official abuses. The disorder in Guizhou spread over a vast area to groups out of contact with each other. Religious sects and secret societies supplied the main basis for organization. The most famous rebel leaders were the Miao Gao He and (retrospectively) Zhang Xiumei, but many others had their own independent bands of followers. Thus Han, Miao, and other frontier people in this impoverished, mismanaged province joined the struggle against the government's representatives. The long delay before the government's recovery of the province must be attributed to Guizhou's low value to the center, its original forests having been felled and its land being poor. Leaders in neighboring provinces were busy enough recovering from other revolts, notably the ruinous Taiping Uprising (1851–1864), and it was not until 1873 that victory was declared. The "Miao" (or Khoxiong) of west Hunan, by then ruled with the help of a Miao constabulary, had never joined in.

The 1795 uprising was one of the first signs of difficulty at the frontiers. Influx and natural increase of the Han population had put great pressure on local resources. In the large-scale Guizhou uprising in the nineteenth century, the ethnic element was muted, all groups being united against the government. The long struggle in this second uprising displayed the Qing government's weakness and presaged a century of loose control in large areas of China's ethnic periphery. Historians of the People's Republic treat both episodes sympathetically as popular Miao movements. The west Hunan Miao are still inclined to see themselves as a distinct community, but there is a growing sense of Miao consciousness as China's fifty-five minorities compete for government attention and as diasporic Hmong/Miao assert the unity of all groups designated by these and similar terms.

SEE ALSO *Minority Nationalities.*

BIBLIOGRAPHY

Cheung, Siu-woo. Millenarianism and the Miao. In *Cultural Encounters on China's Ethnic Frontiers*, ed. Stevan Harrell. Seattle: University of Washington Press, 1995.

Elvin, Mark. *The Retreat of the Elephants: An Environmental History of China.* New Haven, CT: Yale University Press, 2004.

Jenks, Robert. *Insurgency and Social Disorder in Guizhou: The "Miao" Rebellion, 1864–1873.* Honolulu: University of Hawai'i Press, 1994.

McMahon, Daniel. Identity and Conflict on a Chinese Borderland: Yan Ruyi and the Recruitment of the Gelao during the 1795–97 Miao Revolt. *Late Imperial China* 23, 2 (2002): 53–86.

Sutton, Donald S. Ethnic Revolt in the Qing Empire: The "Miao Uprising" of 1795–1796 Reexamined. *Asia Major*, 3rd series, 17, 1 (2003): 105–151.

Sutton, Donald S. Ethnicity and the Miao Frontier in the Eighteenth Century. In *Empire at the Margins: Culture, Ethnicity, and Frontier in Early Modern China*, ed. Pamela K. Crossley, Helen F. Siu, and Donald S. Sutton. Berkeley: University of California Press, 2006.

Donald S. Sutton

MICROFINANCING

Although the term *microfinance* emerged in the international development community only in the late 1970s, organizations providing financial services to agricultural households date back to the 1920s and 1930s when the Chinese Communist Party experimented with rural credit cooperatives (RCCs) to eliminate usury. By the 1950s, an extensive national network of local RCCs provided farmers with savings and credit services. During the Great Leap Forward, the RCCs became fiscal institutions for communes. After 1962 an effort was made to separate the RCCs from the commune system by placing them under the management of the People's Bank of China, but RCCs were inactive during the Cultural Revolution. In 1970 the RCCs were revived and placed under the management of the People's Bank of China until 1979, when they were transferred to the Agricultural Bank of China.

In the early 1980s, the Ministry of Agriculture established a network of rural cooperative foundations (RCFs) to serve farmers, but the People's Bank of China never recognized them and in 1999 closed down about 18,000 RCFs with over five million depositors. The elimination of RCFs left about 44,000 RCCs at the township level (with about 280,000 village branches) as the only formally approved nonbanking financial institution meant to serve rural enterprises and households. In practice, RCCs' savings deposits are mostly transferred via the Agricultural Bank of China for industrial loans in urban areas.

The use of microfinance for poverty alleviation in China was initiated in 1994 by Professor Du Xiaoshan, an economist at the Rural Development Institute of the Chinese Academy of Social Sciences. With financial support from the Grameen Trust in Bangladesh and the Ford Foundation in Beijing, Professor Du and his colleagues established the Funding the Poor Cooperative (FPC) to provide microfinance in poor counties based on the Grameen Bank model. The latter relies on peer-based lending whereby a group of five people, typically women, are mutually responsible for loan repayment. FPC aims to charge sustainable interest rates to cover its operating expenses. By the mid-2000s, there were 260 different nongovernmental microfinance programs funded by a range of international and bilateral donors. With a total lending portfolio of thirty million dollars, the outreach of such nongovernmental programs numbered tens of thousands of clients.

Since the late 1990s, the Chinese government has also adopted the Grameen model in its poverty alleviation lending schemes. Administered through the Poverty Alleviation Office, the loans are distributed through the Agricultural Bank of China at the county level. Government microfinance programs have received one billion dollars in fiscal funding and serve hundreds of thousands of clients. In the early 2000s, the government also allocated thirteen million dollars to over 15,000 RCC branches to extend microloans to impoverished households.

International microfinance practitioners have criticized both the nongovernmental and governmental programs for relying on subsidized interest rates, which render such loans subject to capture by local elites and thwart prospects for building financially sustainable microfinance institutions. In 2005 the People's Bank of China and local governments in five provinces extended licenses for seven microfinance companies to provide financial services to middle- and lower-income clients in western China. In 2006 the China Banking Regulatory Commission authorized the establishment of village and township banks and launched a pilot program of village banks to engage in microfinance in thirty-six counties in six provinces. By the late 2000s, a number of international investors, foundations, and corporations were starting to donate or invest in microfinance programs.

SEE ALSO *Banking: Overview; Poverty; Rural Development since 1978: Agricultural Banking; Rural Development, 1949–1978: Credit Cooperatives; Social Policy Programs.*

BIBLIOGRAPHY

Findlay, Christopher, Andrew Watson, Cheng Enjiang, and Zhu Gang, eds. *Rural Financial Markets in China.* Canberra, Australia: Asia Pacific Press, 2003.

Park, Albert F., and Changqing Ren. Microfinance with Chinese Characteristics. *World Development* 29, 1 (2001): 3–62.

PlanetFinance: The Microfinance Platform. China: Country Overview. November 15, 2004. http://www.planetfinance.org/

Tsai, Kellee S. *Back-Alley Banking: Private Entrepreneurs in China.* Ithaca, NY: Cornell University Press, 2002.

Kellee S. Tsai

MIDDLE CLASS

SEE *Social Classes since 1978.*

MIDDLE EASTERN STATES, RELATIONS WITH

The relations of the People's Republic of China (PRC) with the Middle East can be divided into three periods: (1) the first twenty years, roughly 1950 to 1970, when the Middle East was of indirect importance for China, at best, and vice versa; (2) the next ten years, 1970 to 1980, a transition period from isolation to representation; and (3) the period from 1980, when China finally managed to establish full diplomatic relations with all Middle Eastern states.

ISOLATION AND BREAKTHROUGH

By the late 1960s, twenty years after the foundation of the PRC, Beijing had established official relations with only three core Middle Eastern governments (Egypt and Syria in 1956 and Iraq in 1958), two peripheral states (Yemen in 1956 and South Yemen in 1968), and a few Arab-African countries (e.g., Sudan and Morocco in 1958, and Algeria as soon as it gained independence in 1962). In 1967 Tunisia suspended its diplomatic relations with China (established in 1964).

Beijing's failure did not reflect any lack of interest. On the contrary, Chinese Communism has always regarded the Middle East as a crucial link and a stepping-stone in a U.S.-led Western attempt to encircle and threaten China. Getting rid of the foreign presence in the region became the cornerstone of China's policy in the Middle East. Yet this strategic-security consideration could not be translated into concrete and effective action for two main reasons. First, isolated from international organizations and many Western countries and being relatively backward, Beijing could offer the Middle Eastern states little in terms of political and diplomatic support, economic benefits, or military provisions. Second, for these reasons and others, the Middle Eastern states preferred to be associated with either the U.S.-led West (e.g., Israel, Turkey, Iran, Saudi Arabia, Jordan, and Lebanon) or with the Soviet-led East (e.g., Egypt, Syria, and Iraq). To win Arab goodwill, in the mid-1960s Beijing formed relations with the Palestinians and other insurgent groups, supplying them with revolutionary doctrines, military training, and light weapons. Promoting radicalism, the Chinese called for the settlement by force of Middle Eastern conflicts, notably the Arab-Israeli conflict, as a component of a common struggle against (Western) imperialism and (Soviet) social-imperialism. This policy failed as well.

China had begun to change course by the early 1970s following the end of the violent and chaotic phase of the Cultural Revolution, which enabled the restoration of domestic order and foreign policy, but primarily because of the improved relations with the United States, as well as China's admission to the United Nations in October 1971. In a complete about-face, by the late 1970s Beijing had established diplomatic relations with most Middle Eastern and Arab-African capitals, including Kuwait, Turkey, Iran, and Lebanon (all in 1971), Jordan (in 1977), and Oman and Libya (in 1978). Still ruled by the Gang of Four, Beijing was obviously displeased by the Arabs' use of terrorism and their association with the Soviet Union. A transition period in China's domestic and foreign policy, the 1970s witnessed a strange mix of revolutionary radicalism and bold reformism as power struggles and ideological debates continued.

Essentially, these struggles ended after Mao Zedong's death in 1976, which paved the ground for Deng Xiaoping's reform drive. These widespread economic and social reforms have affected China's relations with the Middle East. Unlike Mao's China, which had fostered instability to promote worldwide revolution based on strategic and ideological motivations, Deng's China systematically fostered international stability to enable China to modernize and grow based on economic, technological, and pragmatic motivations. This does not imply that the Middle East has ceased to be strategically important for China, but rather that the means used by the Chinese have changed.

ARMS AND OIL POLITICS

Because its international representation has increased, China can now offer political support, although Beijing still does not feel powerful enough to use whatever potential influence it may have and is still reluctant to become involved in Middle Eastern problems, let alone to mediate in them, for fear of antagonizing friendly countries. Yet, departing from their past practices, the Chinese began to sell arms to the Middle East, especially in the 1980s and mainly (around 90%) to Iran and Iraq. Chinese arms sales have, however, declined since the early 1990s because of

United Arab Emirates State Minister for Foreign Affairs Mohammed Hussein Al Shaali at the Sino-Arab Cooperation Forum, June 1, 2006, Beijing, China. *In the latter part of the twentieth century, China's primary interests in the Middle East were financial, becoming a major supplier of weaponry in the region. However, as China's economy grew, the country looked to secure new markets for natural resources and established relations with Iran and Saudi Arabia, in particular, to satisfy growing internal demands for oil.* © LUCAS SCHIFRES/POOL/EPA/CORBIS

U.S. criticism, the low quality of Chinese-made weapons, and the introduction of alternative, more reliable, arms. In fact, Chinese arms sales to the Middle East were motivated less by military, strategic, or political considerations and more by economic and commercial ones; arms sales were intended to generate more income. Economic means have indeed been the most important—and so far the least irritating—in China's "return" to the Middle East.

In Mao's time, China's economic relations with Middle Eastern countries were marginal and consisted of traditional trade and aid, mostly for political and strategic ends. Although these motivations still exist, they have become secondary. In addition to trade and aid, post-Mao China has launched new economic policies toward the Middle East, such as labor export, construction services, and large-scale investment, along with arms sales. Yet, the share of the Middle East in China's expanding international economic relations remains small, around 2 to 4 percent since the early 1990s, except for one commodity: oil.

Aware of the gap between its growing gross domestic product (GDP) and the relative stagnation of its oil output, China, then a net oil exporter, had begun to import oil in the 1980s, mainly from Southeast Asia. Persian Gulf oil suppliers were considered unstable, unreliable, and risky. However, by 1993, China had become a net oil importer, and Persian Gulf suppliers could no longer be ignored. Although China has tried to diversify its oil-import resources and acquire equity oil wherever possible in order to reduce its dependence on the Middle East, by 2007 about 55 to 60 percent of China's imported oil originated in the greater Middle East (including Arab-African countries). Because China's oil shares in other parts of the world are expected to decline, this percentage is expected to reach 70 percent or more in the future. This is one reason why China has cultivated relations with Iran and Saudi Arabia, which together provide around one-third of China's oil imports.

CONTRADICTORY PARTNERS

China's relations with Islamic revolutionary Iran began on the wrong foot, as PRC leader Hua Guofeng was one of the last foreign officials to visit the shah of Iran just before his 1979 downfall. To regain Tehran's goodwill, China began to supply weapons to Iran, which had been engaged since 1980 in a war with Iraq (which also received Chinese weapons). Yet China's interest in Iran is not just military; it is primarily strategic and based on a common hostility to the United States. In fact, the Chinese use Iran as proxy whenever they feel the need to react against U.S. policy in Taiwan. Oil was added later, and since 2001 Iran has become one of China's top oil suppliers. Iran has provided around 12 to 13 percent of China's oil imports. Still, China's relations with Iran should be regarded as a marriage of convenience, not love.

Beijing is implicitly concerned about President Mahmoud Ahmadinejad's perceived irresponsible behavior, which promotes regional—and global—instability, undermining the PRC's interests. While the Chinese explicitly accept Iran's claim that its nuclear program has a civilian purpose, they have joined, though reluctantly, all International Atomic Energy Agency and United Nations Security Council votes directed at Iran. Beijing can afford to do so and risk a possible Iranian retaliation because of its relations with Saudi Arabia.

The resumption of Chinese Muslim hajj missions to Mecca in the late 1970s signaled the restoration of unofficial relations between Beijing and Riyadh. These were given a boost in 1988 when China sold the Saudis a number of Dongfeng-3 intermediate range ballistic missiles, in defiance of the United States. This paved the ground for the establishment of diplomatic relations in July 1990, one week before Iraqi president Saddam Hussein (1937–2006) invaded Kuwait. Careful not to become directly involved, Beijing has begun to rely on Saudi Arabia as one of its leading oil suppliers, on occasion the leading supplier. Furthermore, in early 2006 Riyadh promised China that it would supply all its oil needs, even single-handedly, in case of disruptions (namely, sanctions against Iran). Thus, with a potential substitute, the Chinese can show more flexibility on Iran's nuclear issue.

In addition, since it was inconceivable that Sino-Israeli relations would precede Sino-Saudi relations, official Sino-Saudi relations paved the ground for official relations with Israel. Israel was the first country in the Middle East to recognize the PRC, which it did in January 1950, but diplomatic relations were delayed by forty-two years due to U.S. objections, Israeli difficulties, and China's preference for Arab and Muslim countries. As post-Mao China began to underline the need for a peaceful settlement of the Arab-Israeli conflict and the Palestine problem, unofficial explorations with Israel began in the late 1970s, leading to exchanges in agriculture, tourism, science and technology, and, not least, the military. Media reports suggested that Israel's arms supplies to China had reached $3 billion, yet this sum reflected, at best, a framework agreement. According to the Stockholm International Peace Research Institute, Israel's actual arms transfers to China through 2007 were valued at no more than $350 million, or nearly 1.2 percent of the total (Russia supplied nearly 88%).

The political turning point came in the late 1980s and early 1990s when Beijing realized that to play a more meaningful role in the Middle East it should establish official relations with Israel, particularly after some Arab countries had done so. Iraq's 1990 invasion of Kuwait expedited Sino-Israeli relations, because it caused Beijing to become aware that there are other conflicts in the Middle East that are no less violent than the Arab-Israeli conflict. In addition, Israel's restraint in the face of repeated Iraqi missile attacks prevented deterioration detrimental to China's interests. These realizations led, on January 24, 1992, to the establishment of diplomatic relations between the PRC and Israel. Unlike many other countries (e.g., Saudi Arabia), Israel did not have to cut off relations with the Republic of China (Taiwan) because Israel never recognized Taiwan, although the two have maintained unofficial economic, cultural, and even military relations all along. Paradoxically, while economic relations between Israel and the PRC have grown substantially, military relations have declined considerably since the establishment of diplomatic relations, due to uncompromising U.S. pressure and available Russian arms.

SEE ALSO *Foreign Trade since 1950; International Relations: Since 1949.*

BIBLIOGRAPHY

Bin Huwaidin, Mohamed. *China's Relations with Arabia and the Gulf.* London: Routledge, 2002.

Garver, John W. *China and Iran: Ancient Partners in a Post-Imperial World.* Seattle: University of Washington Press, 2006.

Garver, John W., and Jon B. Alterman. *The Vital Triangle: China, the United States, and the Middle East.* Washington, DC: Center for Strategic and International Studies, 2008.

Harris, Lillian Craig. *China Considers the Middle East.* London: Tauris, 1993.

Radtke, Kurt. China and the Greater Middle East: Globalization No Longer Equals Westernization. In *The Greater Middle East in Global Politics: Social Science Perspectives on the Changing Geography of the World Politics*, ed. M. Pavrizi Amineh, 377–404. Leiden, Netherlands: Brill, 2007.

Shichor, Yitzhak. *The Middle East in China's Foreign Policy, 1949–1977.* Cambridge, U.K.: Cambridge University Press, 1979.

Shichor, Yitzhak. *East Wind over Arabia: Origins and Implications of the Sino-Saudi Missile Deal.* Berkeley: Center for Chinese Studies, Institute of East Asian Studies, University of California, 1989.

Shichor, Yitzhak. China's Upsurge: Implications for the Middle East. *Israel Affairs* 12, 4 (2006): 665–683.

Shichor, Yitzhak. Competence and Incompetence: The Political Economy of China's Relations with the Middle East. *Asian Perspective* 30, 4 (2006): 39–67.

Sufott, E. Zev. *A China Diary: Towards the Establishment of China-Israel Diplomatic Relations.* London: Cass, 1997.

Yitzhak Shichor

MIGRANT WORKERS

From the 1980s onward, China has experienced one of the largest transfers of population from rural to urban areas in the history of economic development. Millions of rural people (*mingong* or *nongmingong*) sought jobs in the cities in order to obtain higher incomes, acquire skills, or simply to see something of life beyond their villages. The movement was stimulated by the rapid growth of China's economy. Established cities attracted migrants to work in manufacturing, in the service sector, on construction sites, and also as petty traders, while booming export industries in the coastal zones created a tremendous demand for assembly-line labor. Since the 1980s, economic inequality between the poor agricultural provinces of the interior and the industrializing coastal regions has increased, providing more incentives to migrate. According to the 2000 census, there were over 120 million migrant workers in Chinese cities. More recent estimates go as high as 200 million.

The scale of migration seemed particularly dramatic to the Chinese because population movement had been severely restricted since the 1950s. Under the *hukou* or household registration system, people were allowed to reside and work only where they had their *hukou*, and those with an agricultural *hukou* could not live in the cities. Few people moved at all, and rural to urban migration was particularly difficult. The system was enforceable because the state had a near monopoly over the necessities of life until the economic reforms of the early 1980s. Without proper papers, a migrant to the cities could not obtain rations, a job, or accommodation. After the reforms, as markets in unrationed food and accommodation developed, and as the demand for labor grew, the authorities began to relax the restrictions, and large-scale migration began.

MIGRANT LIFE IN THE CITIES

Even after migration was legally permitted, migrants continued to suffer considerable discrimination in the cities. Although most *mingong* have some high school education and tend to be better educated than the average for their own communities, they are looked down on in urban areas, where they are marked out by their regional accents and unsophisticated appearance. They are also readily identified by their rural *hukou*. There are many jobs for which they cannot apply, and they do not enjoy the subsidized health care or education to which urban residents are entitled. Their accommodation is often provided by their employer, construction workers being housed in shacks and factory workers in cheaply built dormitories. In other cases, *mingong* tend to congregate together in poor districts, often in the outskirts of towns. As most rely on friends or relations to help them find jobs and housing, they often live and work with people from their home region. In the early years, most migrants were young, single, and male. However, as migration chains became established, many women also went to the urban areas, usually either as factory or service workers.

Migrants' lives are hard and insecure. There is cutthroat competition in both the construction and manufacturing industries in China. Because the lowest bid tends to win the contract, employers want to keep their labor costs as low as possible. The result is that pay and conditions are poor, especially at the lowest level of subcontracting, and there is much compulsory overtime. Most factory workers are on the job ten to twelve hours a day, and many have no regular day off. Construction workers are not paid if the weather is too bad to work. In the worst cases, employers pay less than has been promised or do not pay at all. Health and safety standards are rarely enforced, and there is a high rate of work-related accidents and ill health. Migrants who are sick or injured usually must pay for their treatment themselves, and if they are unable to work, they return to their villages. Many migrants live so far from home that they can only afford to go home once every year or two, usually at the Chinese New Year, when many enterprises close down.

CIRCULAR VERSUS PERMANENT MIGRATION

Migrants endure these poor working conditions and long working hours in order to be able to send money home to their families or save for their futures. Successful *mingong* may earn in a month what they would receive in a year working on the land at home. When large-scale migration began, although some rural migrants dreamed of settling down in the cities, in reality, for the great majority it was too difficult. With little chance of secure employment or accommodation in which they could house a family, they tended to go home to get married. Afterward, if earning opportunities at home were scarce, one or both might "go out" again, leaving any child for grandparents to care for. Migration took an essentially circular form in which migrants moved backward and forward between rural and urban areas but regarded the village as home. As older migrants settled back in the villages, younger ones took their place in the urban workforce. There were complaints in migrant-exporting provinces such as Sichuan that they functioned as the nurseries and old people's homes, producing laborers whose productive years were spent elsewhere.

Although this circular form of migration is still the norm for the majority, reforms to the *hukou* system allow some successful migrants to settle in urban areas. Because each locality supervises its own registration system, the situation is not uniform across China. In general, however, big cities resist granting permanent residence to incomers unless they are highly qualified or exceptionally wealthy. Smaller cities and towns have more migrant-friendly policies, allowing long-term settlement for migrants who meet economic criteria, such as having a permanent job and buying their own apartment.

IMPACT ON THE RURAL AREAS

Large-scale migration has both negative and positive effects on the rural areas. In some regions, all those who can obtain nonagricultural employment do so, and there is concern that farming has been left to those who lack the

Migrants scanning job fair leaflets, Beijing, February 27, 2007. *Much of the economic growth in China has centered around large cities along the southern and eastern coasts, forcing a large migration of workers from rural to urban areas. Most job migration in China tends to be circular, with workers settling in urban areas only on a temporary basis, returning home once they have saved enough income.* GUANG NIU/GETTY IMAGES

initiative or skills to obtain other work. Migration distorts age and gender ratios in the sending areas and disrupts family life. There is a complete absence of people in their early twenties in some villages, while in others it is mainly men who are missing. Whichever group departs, burdens are transferred to those left behind. Old people and women have tended to become more heavily involved in agriculture, while many grandparents assume responsibility for their grandchildren.

Migration also has positive effects in the rural areas. Circular migration means that migrants maintain close touch with their families and ultimately return. It thus exerts a much stronger influence on the sending areas than permanent migration and is a real agent of social change. Migrant remittances increase the disposable income of farming families. They are invested in new housing, education, and small enterprises, thus raising living standards in the villages. New homes mark out the households whose members have migrated. Returning migrants may set up building firms, tailoring shops, restaurants, or other small businesses in the sending areas, using skills, entrepreneurial know-how, and contacts acquired during their time as a migrant. Migrants influenced by urban lifestyles also bring back new ideas. They press for electricity, running water, and improved sanitation, and they use mobile phones. They understand life beyond the village, have smaller families, and attempt to improve their children's life chances through education.

PUBLIC OPINION AND GOVERNMENT POLICY

Early reaction by urban residents to migration was negative, as was media discussion of the new phenomenon. Migration was described as a wave or a tide, and migrants were said to be flooding the cities. Terms used to refer to them, such as the "floating population" (*liudong renkou*) or "blind migrants" (*mangliu*), implied that their behavior was irrational. They were seen as a threat to social order, and there were complaints that they were dirty and dishonest. Migrants were frequently subjected to roundups, and if their papers were not in order they were trucked out of town.

However, the utility of rural migration was soon recognized by the authorities. A seemingly unlimited supply of cheap migrant labor made China attractive to foreign investors and kept the cost of manufacturing low. Migration also eased the problems of labor surplus and land shortage in the countryside. Through remittances, migration contributed to rural development and poverty alleviation. The state therefore began to develop policies intended to control rather than to prevent migration.

Rural people were encouraged to migrate, usually across comparatively short distances, to small and medium-sized towns where settlement was permitted. For those who went to the larger urban settlements, a system of temporary residence permits allowed the state to monitor migrant workers, and assisted urban planning and the maintenance of social order. Applicants for a permit have to supply a letter of introduction from their home area, evidence of employment, and a photograph. Permits have to be renewed regularly. There was official concern that rural migrants might undermine the success of the one-child family policy by coming to urban areas to have unauthorized births. Married women of childbearing age are therefore required to show "birth-planning cards" from their hometowns, which record their fertility history and the contraception they use.

Even after concessions were made to them, migrants remain disadvantaged compared to permanent urban residents. The best jobs are still open only to permanent urban residents. The government has ordered that migrant children who accompany their parents to the cities should be admitted to local schools, but this ruling is often ignored or migrant parents are asked for school fees higher than they can afford. The children of migrants in the large cities therefore tend to attend inferior segregated schools set up by migrant associations or nongovernmental organizations. Migrant workers still lack entitlements to medical care, unemployment allowances, or retirement pensions. The government justifies the discrimination in provision between them and urban residents with the claim that migrants have security through the right to a share of land in their villages when they return.

LABOR PROTECTION AND MIGRANT LABORERS

The state has demonstrated considerable ambivalence toward labor protection in relation to the migrant labor force. The Labor Law of 2005, further strengthened by a Labor Contract Law from January 2008, requires that every worker should have a contract, that the maximum work-week should be forty hours with one day off, that overtime should be paid, and that wages may not be delayed. Women workers have maternity rights, child labor is prohibited, and working conditions are required to be safe and sanitary. These laws are almost universally violated where migrants are employed, and there is little effort at enforcement. Newly arrived *mingong*, ignorant of their rights, will often work under almost any conditions. When workers protest, they can take their cases either to a mediation committee or to the official trade union. In some cases, such action has helped, but at other times official bodies have been unwilling to intervene on the side of the workers. Local protectionism opposes real changes in the system. Local governments benefit from investment in their areas and from the taxes and fees they levy on migrant workers. They do not wish to drive investment away to areas where easier labor regimes prevail.

Under pressure, some multinational firms have made efforts to ensure minimum wages and good working conditions at the factories from which they source their goods in China. But because export industries are characterized by much subcontracting, these codes are difficult to enforce. Moreover, the multinationals push subcontractors to produce at lower prices. Although some foreign companies welcomed the Chinese labor laws, others lobbied against them and threatened to take investment elsewhere. Local Chinese- , Hong Kong- , Korean- , and Taiwanese-invested enterprises tend to show the least interest in maintaining minimum pay and good working conditions. Chinese nongovernmental organizations such as the All-China Women's Federation and the Youth Federation, along with international ones such as the Asia Foundation and Oxfam Hong Kong, are increasingly involved in welfare, advice, and rights education work with Chinese migrant workers.

As a group, Chinese migrant workers remain systematically underprivileged. Given the size of China, its rural/urban divide, its underdeveloped transport networks, and its unequal economic development, a degree of regional economic inequality is inevitable. But inequalities have been exacerbated by limitations on the right of migrants to move and reside where they wish, and by the state's failure to ensure that migrants enjoy adequate labor and welfare rights.

SEE ALSO *Labor; Peasantry, 1800–1900; Poverty; Urban Employment and Unemployment since 1949; Women, Employment of.*

BIBLIOGRAPHY

Chan, Anita. *China's Workers under Assault: The Exploitation of Labor in a Globalizing Economy*. Armonk, NY: Sharpe, 2001.

Davin, Delia. *Internal Migration in Contemporary China*. New York: St. Martin's Press, 1999.

Gaetano, Arianne M., and Tamara Jacka, eds. *On the Move: Women and Rural-to-Urban Migration in Contemporary China*. New York: Columbia University Press, 2004.

Jacka, Tamara. *Rural Women in Urban China: Gender, Migration, and Social Change*. Armonk, NY: Sharpe, 2006.

Murphy, Rachel. *How Migrant Labor Is Changing Rural China*. Cambridge, U.K.: Cambridge University Press, 2002.

Solinger, Dorothy J. *Contesting Citizenship in Urban China: Peasant Migrants, the State, and the Logic of the Market*. Berkeley: University of California Press, 1999.

Delia Davin

MILITARISM

Militarism may be defined as the dominance of the military in politics or policy (which is usually deplored) and the ascendancy of military values and symbols in daily life (which in a vulnerable state or new nation may be highly prized). In China, shifts in the roles of generals and the social status of the military were sometimes linked, and sometimes not, during the turmoil of transition from empire to party-state.

PRO-MILITARY AND ANTIMILITARY THINKING

Confucian writings argued that persuasion and moral example were superior to brute force. Good men did not make soldiers. The government ranked military degrees, positions, and offices lower than civil equivalents and often utilized civilian generals in war. *Wen*, with its resonant meanings (the civil, writing, literature, culture, civilization) was held to be superior to (but inclusive of) *wu*, the military, and never more than in the fading years of the Ming dynasty (1368–1644). Whereas this nonmilitary official culture was set aside in a crisis, the familiar rhetoric could affect war preparation and the social status of the military. Yet there were other cultural strands that modern militarism could draw upon.

Popular thinking, in particular, did not share the Confucian aversion for war. Folk stories romanticized warfare, upholding military values of physical bravery, fraternal loyalty, and brilliant generalship. Folk religion gave pride of place to martial gods like Emperor Guan (the historical Guan Yu, 162–220 CE) and instilled a demonic view of a cosmos in which good and bad did battle, with Daoists and shamans brandishing weapons to exorcise demons and restore order. This pro-military counterculture, passed down on stage and translated in physical routines and swordplay, was ever available when the dynastic center weakened. The Taipings (1851–1864), the Boxers (1900), and other rebels drew on it. Later Mao Zedong and others of his generation recalled their fascination as children with these real-life rebels, with the adventures of the historical Zhuge Liang (181–234) and Guang Yu fictionalized in the *Romance of the Three Kingdoms*, and with the magical battles of Monkey (Sun Wukong) in the novel *Journey to the West*.

A new strain of military thinking appeared in the Qing dynasty (1644–1911). The Qianlong emperor (r. 1736–1796) worked to revive the martial spirit of the hereditary Manchu Eight Banners, which had led the conquest of China in the 1640s. He saw his generals' frontier campaigns as his greatest achievements, documenting ten of them in prose and poetry, engraved and on stone. He castigated Chinese pacifism and military ignorance. The emperor was no narrow militarist but rather a sort of one-man cultural conglomerate, with military perspectives a key part of the mix. As the empire slipped into chaos in the mid-nineteenth-century revolts, many Chinese admired the splendor of his reign, however strong their distaste for the Manchus. When Zeng Guofan (1811–1872), Hu Linyi (1812–1861), and other provincially based leaders led a dynastic Restoration against the rebels, they brought about a militarization of regional authority. Striving to inculcate military values in the forces they raised, they drew inspiration from the Qianlong's effort to raise military status, as well as from underappreciated Chinese generals of the past like Yue Fei (1103–1142) and Qi Jiguang (1528–1588). Their pro-military ideas, layered onto the Confucian value of loyalty, appealed to twentieth-century reformers like Cai E (1882–1916), whose work Chiang Kai-shek (Jiang Jieshi) in turn introduced to his cadets at the Soviet Russian–staffed Whampoa Military Academy in 1924 to 1925.

The third and most immediate influence on the generation of Chiang and Mao was foreign example, chiefly that of Japan's oligarchs, who in a generation had built a modern nation after winning a civil war. To young Chinese confronting the humiliations of the Sino-Japanese war (1894) and the Eight-Power invasion and Boxer protocol (1901–1902), it was time to "value the military" (*shangwu*) in what had become a Darwinian struggle for China's survival, time to shore up the defenses of the national polity and the physical strength of Chinese bodies. Among the ten thousand Chinese students who went to study in Meiji Japan in the years after 1902, as the Qing dynasty began its belated program of military modernization, many attended military schools. Some, sent by provincial leaders, returned to organize the New Army.

MILITARISM IN THE EARLY REPUBLIC

When the Manchu dynasty collapsed along with the imperial system in 1911, the returned students were among the agents of its demise. The semiprofessional military institutions they led, along with those of Yuan Shikai, initiator of the Western-style New Army in north China and the new Republic's president from 1912 to 1915, were the most modern creations of the former empire and became key bases of regional power. But militarization since the Restoration had produced a great variety of local armed forces. Whereas former New Army officers might be personally drawn to republican or Confucianist ideas, there was no national institution to focus their loyalty, pay them salaries, or offer them a regular bureaucratic career, and neither unified ideology nor road or rail system to assist their centralization. Even the better military units like Yuan Shikai's and the Yunnan provincial army steadily lost bureaucratic discipline, methodical training, and central financing in the pressure to survive and became little more than men with guns, titles, and connections. Far from being servants of the state in the patriotic spirit of the Song loyalist Yue Fei or the Italian unifier Giuseppi Garibaldi (1807–1882), the most successful generals were politicians clever at building—and feeding—armies personally loyal to themselves. Such warlords as Feng Yuxiang (1882–1948) and Wu Peifu

Students and Red Guard members parading in the streets of Beijing, holding volumes of Mao Zedong's* Little Red Book, *June, 1966. *During the Cultural Revolution, Mao Zedong relied on the support of young members of the Red Guard to bolster his standing after the failures of the Great Leap Forward. Chinese citizens accused of antirevolutionary sympathies faced persecution by the Red Guard, leading to the destruction of schools, libraries, and sites of historical importance.* JEAN VINCENT/AFP/GETTY IMAGES

(c. 1874–1939) had pretensions as reformers and skills in the Three Kingdoms mode but little military education and no link with public opinion or the masses. In the 1920s, newspaper-reading classes depressed by national weakness rejected ineffectual parliaments and local militarists, and began to look to parties that could mobilize new constituencies and build their own armies, based upon the legitimacy of the party itself as potential redeemer of the nation.

THE MILITARY AND CHINA'S MODERN PARTIES

The eventual leader of the reorganized and militarized Guomindang, Chiang Kai-shek, had been trained in Japan, though only in a military prep school, and shared the Confucian training and patriotic ideas of fellow students. Should Chiang be labeled a militarist? Certainly he rose to party power by military means, usually appeared in military uniform even as president, and spent at least 40 percent of revenue on the military; however, he identified himself with the nation, functioned as head of state, established at Nanjing (in 1928) the modern apparatus of national government, and kept his focus on broad national issues, such as the defeat of the warlords, the destruction of the Communists and their bases, and after 1936 survival in the war with Japan. Despite deploying modern weapons and military rhetoric, and employing German advisers to professionalize the army, he was never able to impose the centralized discipline and national idea that are the modern army's hallmarks.

The military wing of the Communist Party under Mao gained control during the epic Long March, but avoided the militarism of Chiang Kai-shek's forces, most of which were national armies only in name. In common with dynastic founders of the past, Mao Zedong understood that military force produced political power. Not only local strongmen but also opponents within the party's army, as in the Futian Incident (1931), must be brutally wiped out. The humblest soldiers, like the perhaps-mythical diarist Lei Feng, China's poster-soldier of the 1960s, must owe devotion to national purposes. Yet the Party drew on more than one military tradition. Its own hard-won Leninist discipline corresponded to the ideals of the modern military, and for all Mao Zedong's scorn for the "purely military viewpoint" among his early revolutionary colleagues, his characteristic later policies were variations on military themes. The Great Leap Forward of 1958, for example, militarized the entire country for production; and the quota-driven campaign against counterrevolutionaries (1950–1951) and the mass-led Cultural Revolution (1966–1969) labeled whole political classes as enemies of the people and authorized their members' persecution to death. The People's Liberation Army itself has remained under party control, but its proud history and its size, professionalism, and discipline make it a key political constituency that must be consulted on foreign policy as well as defense strategy. Two of its most celebrated leaders crossed Mao Zedong and were removed, Peng Dehuai for criticizing the Great Leap, and Lin Biao, Mao's designated successor, for moving troops in 1970 without Mao's authority. Twice, however, the PLA intervened to save the day for the party, once in the last stages of the Cultural Revolution and again in Beijing on June 4, 1989. Society pays respect to the military—for example, proud parents like to stick PLA hats on their infant sons' heads—but party leaders have seen to it that generals are not in a position to exercise independent power.

SEE ALSO *Army and Politics; People's Liberation Army: Overview; Warlord Era (1916–1928); Wars and the Military, 1800–1912.*

BIBLIOGRAPHY

Kuhn, Philip A. *Rebellion and Its Enemies in Late Imperial China: Militarization and Social Structure, 1796–1864*. Cambridge, MA: Harvard University Press, 1970.

McCord, Edward A. *The Power of the Gun: The Emergence of Modern Chinese Warlordism*. Berkeley: University of California Press, 1993.

Sutton, Donald S. *Provincial Militarism and the Chinese Republic: The Yunnan Army, 1905–25*. Ann Arbor: University of Michigan Press, 1980.

Swaine, Michael. *The Role of the Chinese Military in National Security Policymaking*. Rev. ed. Santa Monica, CA: Rand, 1998.

van de Ven, Hans, ed. *Warfare in Chinese History*. Leiden, Netherlands: Brill, 2000.

Waley-Cohen, Joanna. *The Culture of War in China: Empire and the Military under the Qing Dynasty*. New York: Tauris, 2006.

Donald S. Sutton

MILITARY, 1912–1949

In the last years of the nineteenth century, Qing authorities presided over the reorganization of China's military forces in order to protect China from further imperialist aggression and to support the dynasty. These forces increasingly utilized Western models of training, equipment, and organization, and served as the foundation for modern Chinese military forces during the Republican period. With the rise of nationalism, a heightened sense of urgency in the face of imperialist threats, and the abolition of the Confucian civil service exam in 1905, study in Chinese military academies took on a new prestige and attracted capable and ambitious young men. Others attended military academies in Japan or Europe, marking a transition in China's officer corps from Confucian scholar-officials to professional military men.

A 1903 plan called for the creation of a national military force called the *New Army*, composed of thirty-six divisions of approximately 12,500 men each. Individual provinces took responsibility for organizing, training, and financing one or more of the divisions that would make up the New Army. Two divisions from North China known as the Beiyang Army provided the first units of this national army and served as the strongest military force in China for the next decade. Revolutionary sentiment proved pervasive and elements of the Hubei New Army initiated the revolt of October 1911 that eventually led to the end of the Qing dynasty. Other provincial New Army divisions played important roles in local and national affairs for decades afterward.

Chinese cavalry in formation, c. 1926–1929. *After the collapse of the Qing dynasty, much of China fell into the control of regional warlords. As leader of the National Revolutionary Army in the late 1920s, Chiang Kai-shek began a military campaign to defeat these warlords, eventually uniting China under a central government based in Nanjing.* © ALINARI ARCHIVES / THE IMAGE WORKS

THE WARLORDS

In the wake of the 1911 revolution, Yuan Shikai assumed power by virtue of his command of the Beiyang Army. Yuan's death in 1916 initiated a power struggle among his subordinate generals, who fought each other in battles that were of short duration but caused significant destruction and dislocation. These generals, typically called "Beiyang warlords," commanded personal military forces and acted independently of central authority. As the Beiyang warlords jockeyed for position, making and breaking alliances in attempts to assert control over their rivals, other regional authority figures assumed local power in the various provinces of China. These regional warlords came from diverse backgrounds and some exhibited colorful characteristics, such as Zhang Zongchang (1881–1932), the "dog-meat general," who had a reputation for brutality and womanizing; Yan Xishan (1883–1960), the "model governor" of Shanxi Province, who promoted social reforms, including women's rights; and Feng Yuxiang (1882–1948), the "Christian general," who allegedly baptized entire units of his army with a fire hose. Each of these warlords depended on their military forces to maintain their positions and competed with others for resources. None proved capable of mustering enough force to defeat all the others and unify the country, and their battles continued throughout the decade of the 1920s, devastating the country and exhausting the people.

THE NATIONAL REVOLUTIONARY ARMY

In this atmosphere of competing military forces, Sun Yat-sen (Sun Yixian or Sun Zhongshan), the leader of the Guomindang (GMD), sought to create a national military force that could defeat the warlords, unify China, and establish a democratic republic. He accepted an offer of

WHAMPOA MILITARY ACADEMY

The Whampoa Military Academy was Republican China's renowned military officer training school. It was originally located at the Whampoa (Huangpu) Fort on Chengzhou Island downstream from the southeastern city of Guangzhou (Canton) in Guangdong Province. The academy was founded during the first United Front alliance between the Chinese Communist Party (CCP) and the Nationalist Party or Guomindang (GMD). Designed to prepare a patriotic and politically loyal officer corps for the GMD's military arm, the National Revolutionary Army, the academy was set up with money and weapons provided by the Soviet Union.

Sun Yat-sen (Sun Yixian), the "father" of the Republic of China (ROC) and GMD founder, officially opened the academy on June 16, 1924, for its first class of 645 cadets. He appointed Chiang Kai-shek (Jiang Jieshi) as the first commandant of the school, which was modeled on Moscow's Red Army academy. Liao Zhongkai (1877–1925), the pro-Communist GMD treasurer, became the academy's first political commissar. A second class with 449 new cadets started in August 1924, and a third class with 1,200 cadets began training four months later.

Altogether, more than 30,000 cadets were trained at the academy between 1924 and 1949. The first six classes consisting of 8,107 students were graduated at Whampoa. During the Northern Expedition (1926–1928), the academy followed the Guomindang government to the new capital at Nanjing, Jiangsu Province. It was officially renamed the Central Military Academy in March 1928. Following the Japanese invasion in 1937, the academy was relocated to Chengdu, Sichuan Province. The next seventeen classes, totaling about 25,000 students, were graduated at these two successive new locations, including 10,731 new officers graduated between 1928 and 1937.

The academy trained some of China's top military leaders, who fought in the Northern Expedition, the Second Sino-Japanese War (1937–1945), and the civil war. Among the more famous alumni were Nationalist commanders Xue Yue (1896–1998), Xie Jinyuan (1905–1941), Sun Yuanliang (1904–2007), Hu Zongnan (1896–1962), Chen Cheng (1897–1965), and Du Yuming (1903–1981), as well as Communist commanders Lin Biao (1907–1971), Xu Xiangqian (1901–1990), Zuo Quan (1905–1942), and Chen Geng (1903–1961).

Originally the Whampoa Academy had only one department, which provided students with basic infantry training. Later, five departments were established to teach military courses as well as revolutionary theory and propaganda. Some of the Chinese instructors had been educated at the Military Staff School in Tokyo, Japan, but most were graduates of Imperial China's Baoding Cadet Academy. Due to a shortage of native military experts at Whampoa, classes taught by Soviet instructors were the most popular among the cadets until all Soviet instructors left by the end of 1927. After the Communist victory in 1949, the academy was relocated to Fongshan in Taiwan under the name of the Chinese Military Academy (renamed the Military University in 2004).

BIBLIOGRAPHY

Jui-te Chang. The National Army from Whampoa to 1949. In *A Military History of China*, eds. David A. Graff and Robin Higham, 193–209. Boulder, CO: Westview Press, 2002.

Landis, Richard B. Training and Indoctrination at the Whampoa Academy. In *China in the 1920s: Nationalism and Revolution*, eds. F. Gilbert Chan and Thomas H. Etzold, 73–93. New York and London: New Viewpoints, 1976.

Li, Lincoln. The Whampoa Military Academy. In *Student Nationalism in China, 1924–1949*, 22–40. Albany: State University of New York Press, 1994.

Rossen Vassilev

assistance from Soviet Russia in return for a promise to allow members of the Chinese Communist Party (CCP) to join his party and army. In 1924 Sun and his Soviet advisers established the Whampoa (Huangpu) Military Academy near Guangzhou in order to train professional officers to lead men into battle against the warlord forces. Revolutionary ideology played a prominent role in the instruction, as political commissars lectured troops on the history of foreign imperialism in China and emphasized the importance of political awareness.

By June 1926, the initial force of soldiers and Whampoa Academy–trained officers had already won its first battles against warlord forces, and GMD leaders renamed it the National Revolutionary Army (NRA). Under the command of Chiang Kai-shek (Jiang Jieshi), the NRA divided into separate columns and attacked northward from

bureaucracy. Zeng was well aware of the problems plaguing the traditional forces, once lamenting that "If Yue Fei came back to life, he could probably train these soldiers to fight in half a year, but Confucius himself would need more than three years to change their evil habits!" (Cai 1999, p. 97). (Yue Fei, who commanded an army against the Jurchen-Jin during the Southern Song dynasty in the twelfth century, is one of China's most famous military heroes.) Contrary to contemporary popular wisdom that held that "good iron was not used to make nails and good men did not become soldiers," Zeng believed that men of good character in fact made the best soldiers. Accordingly, Zeng personally recruited young men from elite families to act as his officers. Zeng did not consider their lack of military experience a problem, for he assumed that those who possessed the character traits of a Confucian gentleman would also be able to command soldiers in battle.

The Chinese martial tradition holds that troops will always fight best for "those who know them," and historically the most effective armies were so-called family armies organized on the basis of personal ties. Zeng's officers were therefore required to recruit their soldiers from their home districts, thus ensuring that units were held together by both military discipline and affective bonds of personal and regional loyalty. The result was the Hunan Army's characteristic pyramid structure, with Zeng presiding over handpicked officers, who in turn commanded soldiers they had personally recruited. The bonds between officers and men were so close that the death or retirement of a commander necessitated the disbandment of his troops, for Zeng assumed they would never fight effectively under the command of an outsider. These tight bonds and narrowly focused loyalties were reflected in the old Chinese maxim "the troops belong to the general."

Zeng was a strict disciplinarian, for he understood that if his troops were little better than bandits in the eyes of the people, they would have great difficulty mobilizing the population against the Taiping rebels. Historically, the arrival of imperial armies had often prompted a mass exodus on the part of the local population, who saw little difference between bandits and soldiers, and the last thing Zeng wanted to do was drive peasants into the arms of the rebels. He insisted that recruits be men of good character with no vices, and he implemented harsh punishments for gambling, opium use, and crimes against civilians.

TOWARD A MODERN MILITARY, 1870–1911

The disciplined and well-trained regional armies organized by Zeng and others succeeded in turning the tide against the Taipings by the early 1860s. With the exception of the Hunan Army, which was voluntarily downsized by Zeng to assuage fears about his growing power, the regional armies remained largely intact throughout the remainder of the nineteenth century. The Qing authorities recognized that the regional armies had performed much better than the regular troops, but they refused to disband the traditional forces, opting instead to reorganize them by adopting more modern weapons and purging the ranks of those unfit for active service. However, military reform in the period 1870 to 1895 was characterized by a lack of central planning, little or no standardization, and wasteful duplication of effort on the part of regional and central forces. Moreover, foreign observers noted that by the 1890s even the regional armies were showing signs of decay, with rampant nepotism, irregular pay, and poor training increasingly the norm. In the end, China's halfhearted military reforms failed to prevent a Japanese victory in the Sino-Japanese War of 1894 to 1895. However, this humiliating defeat did finally prompt many Qing officials to call for the creation of a new national army organized, equipped, and drilled in the Western fashion.

One pressing problem identified by critics was the lack of qualified officers. In the period leading up to 1895, few officers had received extensive training in modern warfare, and the war with Japan made it clear that courage could not compensate for their inability to employ their men and weapons effectively. This belated realization led to a new emphasis on modern military education and the use of foreign instructors. Regional officials had made occasional use of European military advisers in the past, but after the humiliation of 1895 the court authorized the creation of new Western-style units and the employment of both European and Japanese officers as instructors and advisers. Despite the increased involvement by the court in the decade after the Sino-Japanese War, regional officials still controlled the bulk of China's military forces, and the pace and direction of modernization very much depended on their personal preferences and available funds. There was, however, one important exception. In late 1895 Yuan Shikai (1859–1916) was instructed by the court to create a model force organized, equipped, and trained entirely along Western lines. Yuan's initial brigade of 7,000 men eventually grew into the Beiyang Army, a six-division force that ultimately served as the model for the new national army created in 1905. Yuan handpicked his commanders, and the entire Beiyang Army was built around patron-client relationships that would have seemed very familiar to Zeng Guofan. Yuan did show a preference for officers who had received some training at one of the early Chinese military academies, such as the one operated by Li Hongzhang in Tianjin, so his commanders possessed a degree of technical proficiency that set them apart from their peers in the regional and Banner forces. The increasing professionalism of forces such as the Beiyang Army contributed to the general improvement in the status of soldiers in Chinese society and the growing popular support for military reforms.

THE RISE OF CHINESE MILITARISM

Some Chinese supported military reforms out of loyalty to the dynasty, but far more did so for patriotic reasons that had little to do with love for their Manchu rulers. Many Chinese expected further imperialist aggression, and called for the fostering of a national military spirit through the promotion of martial values and compulsory military training in schools. This new passion for soldiers and soldiering was especially evident among the young, who were at the forefront of the new nationalism sweeping China. Adding to this patriotic impulse was that in the years leading up to 1911 a military career offered new opportunities even as more traditional career paths were disappearing. The near simultaneous ending of the traditional civil service examination system and the creation of a new and socially prestigious professional army in 1905 ensured that large numbers of talented young men flocked to the military.

Even members of the literati who had previously viewed soldiers with disdain started to take an interest in issues of national defense. Liang Qichao (1873–1929) was representative of the patriotic intellectuals who took up the cause of military reform, and like many of his peers he harshly criticized the Chinese for their past weakness in the face of foreign aggression. Liang's attacks were aimed at goading his countrymen into embracing martial values such as courage, self-sacrifice, patriotism, and duty, but he was certainly not suggesting that they had to look abroad for a military ethos to emulate. In his essay "China's Bushidō" (*Zhongguo zhi Wushidao*), Liang argued that long before Japan developed a warrior culture, China was home to a martial race with its own warrior ethos: Centuries of soft living and Manchu domination had eroded China's original martial spirit, but it was still there if only his countrymen chose to look. This message had a significant impact on many young Chinese, including important military reformers such as Chiang Kai-shek (Jiang Jieshi). These men saw the new military as a vanguard institution in China's struggle to modernize, but they never forgot their own martial heritage. As Chiang noted, "A nation or an army must have as its basic elements its own spirit, way of thinking, and especially its own historical and cultural background. All of these elements come together to form a framework of tradition. Established on the basis of national history and culture, these traditions are in fact the crystallization of that history and culture" (Jiang Jieshi 1961, p. 1736).

THE WARLORD ERA AND THE WHAMPOA MILITARY ACADEMY

Much to the frustration of those who saw the modern military as a force for progress in China, the political chaos that followed the 1911 Revolution and Yuan Shikai's presidency eroded much of the public support for the army. The lingering regionalism and pervasive patron-client relationships within the partially modernized military establishment set the stage for the disunity and factional rivalry of the Warlord era (1916–1928). The decisive role played by the military in the 1911 Revolution propelled the soldiers to the forefront of national politics, and once in control they proved unwilling to step aside. Within a few years the new republic was torn apart by rival military cliques, and the recently revived prestige of the military took a distinct turn for the worse. Tragically, the biggest threat to the Chinese people in the years between 1916 and 1928 came not from the forces of imperialism, but rather from their own soldiers.

By the early 1920s the veteran revolutionary Sun Yat-sen (Sun Yixian) had concluded that defeating the major warlords and restoring national unity were necessary first steps in his campaign to free China from the yoke of foreign imperialism. However, his attempts to enlist the forces of local warlords for his campaigns had proven disastrous. These men were allies of convenience rather than Sun's ideological brethren, and frequently turned on him when he asked too much of them. In 1924, despairing of ever finding a reliable warlord ally, he moved ahead with plans to create a party army for the Guomindang (GMD, Nationalist Party) based on the Soviet Union's Red Army. This would be a force of soldiers motivated by a commitment to his ideology rather than their own self-interest. Such an army would require extraordinary officers capable of inspiring both their soldiers and the people of China, so Sun decided to create a military academy near his revolutionary base at Canton to train promising young men from across China.

With the founding of the Whampoa Military Academy (Huangpu Junxiao) in spring 1924, Chiang Kai-shek finally had the opportunity to repair the tattered image of the Chinese soldier and restore the reputation of the military. Chiang intended to distribute the Whampoa graduates throughout the GMD's allied armies in order to raise professional standards and spread the message of militant nationalism. In his speeches to the cadets at Whampoa, Chiang frequently reminded them of their intended role as models for both the army and the nation, and he made it clear that they were to be China's new *junzi* (Confucian superior men)—the men whose exemplary behavior would inspire the masses and transform them into the disciplined citizens China needed. Although the Comintern provided military instructors and the new Chinese Communist Party (CCP) dominated the Political Work Department at Whampoa, the martial ethos promoted through spiritual training at the academy was entirely Chinese. The core virtues promoted by Chiang were drawn from Chinese history and illustrated with examples taken from China's own pantheon of martial heroes. Zeng Guofan's writings on military leadership became required reading at the academy, for Chiang saw him as an example of the high ethical standards he expected of the Whampoa cadets.

THE NANJING DECADE AND THE WAR OF RESISTANCE

After the split with the Communists in 1927 and the completion of the Northern Expedition in 1928, Chiang continued to see the military as a vanguard institution in China's struggle to modernize, and he promoted militarism as an ideology of national development. He intended to make the GMD military into the most modern institution in the country, and German advisers were hired to upgrade his forces. The Germans helped to reorganize Chiang's core units, and oversaw their reequipping and retraining in accordance with German standards. Whampoa's successor institution, the Central Military Academy at Nanjing, was also upgraded with the assistance of the Germans, and in the years before 1937 it provided Chiang with a steady stream of professionally competent and fiercely loyal graduates. Despite the distractions posed by the ongoing campaigns against the remnants of the Communist Party and the occasional clash with political rivals, by 1937 Chiang had made considerable progress toward his goal of sixty German-trained divisions. However, his very success likely accelerated the onset of war with Japan, because the Japanese were not inclined to wait while Chiang built up his forces. The Anti-Japanese War (1937–1945) almost destroyed Chiang's forces, and quickly undid most of what he had accomplished during the Nanjing decade. Although he finished the war with a greatly expanded army equipped with the latest American weapons, the quality of the troops and officers was generally very low, and morale was poor. The CCP, in contrast, had prospered during the war, and emerged in 1945 with a much expanded army and a burning desire to resume the civil war with the GMD.

THE COMMUNIST RED ARMY AND THE PEOPLE'S LIBERATION ARMY

Comintern orders had prevented the CCP from organizing its own military force while it was still cooperating with the GMD in the period 1923 to 1927. The party paid a terrible price in blood for its obedience to Moscow's United Front policy when Chiang purged the Communists in 1927. Bloodied but not broken, the remnants of the party scattered, some going underground in cities such as Shanghai, while others fled deep into the countryside. The Chinese Red Army was born under these inauspicious circumstances in 1927, and its unique cultural traditions bear the imprint of its origins. The party's forces had to improvise, forging symbiotic relationships with the peasants in the countryside in order to survive. Chiang's forces gave them little respite, pursuing them relentlessly across China in a series of aptly named "extermination campaigns." Under these conditions, Communist commanders such as Zhu De (1886–1976) turned to the familiar tactics of Sun Zi's *Art of War* and the heroic Robin Hood–like bandits of the *Water Margin*. The much admired guerrilla tactics of the Chinese Red Army actually were part of a Chinese military tradition that stretched back over two millennia, and though Mao Zedong and the Communists might have updated them, the fundamental ideas were hardly their own.

Given their dependence on popular support for their very survival, the Communist forces were understandably concerned with civil-military relations, and great emphasis was placed on winning the hearts and minds of the people. Yet even this aspect of their strategy had precedents, and the party's guidelines for civil-military relations would have seemed quite familiar to a soldier in Zeng Guofan's Hunan Army in 1863. The Communist forces were very traditional in a number of other ways. For example, their reliance on moral exhortations and use of heroic role models situates them squarely within the Chinese military tradition. It is sometimes difficult to separate the Chinese wheat from the Communist chaff, but if one can penetrate the ideological smokescreen, the Red Army reveals itself to be first and foremost a Chinese force.

With the resumption of the civil war with the GMD after Japan's defeat, the Red Army was renamed the People's Liberation Army (PLA). The force that emerged from the Anti-Japanese War was vastly larger and much stronger than it had been in 1937, and it was reorganized to better suit the tasks it now faced. As guerrilla warfare gave way to large-scale conventional battles, the organizational culture of the PLA started to change as well. The old guerrilla "can-do" attitude lingered on, but the complexity and scale of operations now required a high degree of professional expertise. The period between 1946 and 1950 witnessed the transformation of the PLA from a guerrilla force into a conventional military organization largely structured along Soviet lines. This trend was reversed during the late 1950s when a combination of domestic political radicalization and deteriorating Sino-Soviet relations prompted a reintroduction of the "People's War" doctrine, with its emphasis on guerrilla warfare. Only with the introduction of Deng Xiaoping's Four Modernizations in 1978 did the PLA return to a conventional force structure and doctrine.

SEE ALSO *Army and Politics; Li Hongzhang; Liang Qichao; People's Liberation Army; Wars and the Military, 1800–1912; Yuan Shikai; Zeng Guofan; Zhu De.*

BIBLIOGRAPHY

Cai Songpo. *Zeng hu zhi bing yu lu* [A record of Zeng Guofan and Hu Linyi's writings on military leadership]. Taibei: Liming Publishing, 1999.

Jiang Jieshi. *Jiang zongtong ji* [Collected works of President Chiang]. Taibei: National Defense Research Institute, 1961.

Lary, Diana. *Warlord Soldiers*. Cambridge, U.K.: Cambridge University Press, 1985.

Li, Xiaobing. *A History of the Modern Chinese Army*. Lexington: University Press of Kentucky, 2007.

Powell, Ralph. *The Rise of Chinese Military Power, 1895–1912*. Princeton, NJ: Princeton University Press, 1955.

Van de Ven, Hans J. *War and Nationalism in China, 1925–1945*. London: RoutledgeCurzon, 2003.

Worthing, Peter. *A Military History of Modern China*. London: Praeger, 2007.

Colin Green

MILITIA

The history of militia in China can be traced back to the farmer-soldier armies fielded in the Warring States period (403–221 BCE). Traditional Chinese armies often bore militia-like characteristics as the state lowered military costs by relying on soldiers to supplement their own provisions. By the modern era, though, the form of militia more regularly seen was that of irregular forces organized at the local level for community self-defense.

At its simplest, Chinese local militia had their origins in crop-watching patrols and other ad hoc mobilizations of village or clan members for mutual defense against bandits or other marauders. While usually spontaneous and local, beginning with the Song dynasty (960–1279) the state often encouraged the more regularized organization of such local militia, linked to community mutual-responsibility systems (*baojia*), to maintain local order. In the late imperial period, militia leadership was usually assumed by local elites, including gentry and clan heads, whose social ties provided a means for broader cooperation in periods of broader unrest. Thus, local gentry easily collaborated in the rapid mobilization of village militia to resist British military incursions in the Guangzhou countryside during the Opium War (1839–1842).

State acquiescence to the organization of local armed forces outside its direct control could, however, be a two-edged sword. The Opium War mobilization of militia in Guangzhou also contributed to the militarization of local society and fed a cycle of intracommunity conflicts that lasted for decades. Such armed bands also served as a ready recruiting base for the series of rebellions that broke out in the early to mid-nineteenth century, culminating in the Taiping Rebellion (1850–1864). In response to the threat of these rebellions, and given the weakness of its regular armies, the Qing dynasty again acquiesced to the organization of militia (*tuanlian*) by local elites to defend their home communities against rebel forces. Even more important, these militia provided a model and a recruiting base for new regional armies that ultimately defeated the Taiping and other rebellions. Under these conditions, militia leadership became a new addition to the repertoire of local elite power. Nonetheless, with the defeat of the major rebellions, most militia forces were disbanded, though leaving a model to be revived as needed by later generations.

Local communities, including urban merchants as well as rural elites, again turned to militia for community self-defense during the 1911 revolution and in response to the outbreak of frequent civil war and banditry in the early years of the Republic. In the political and social turmoil of this period, militia organizations in many communities transitioned from ad hoc arrangements of volunteers to increasingly large standing forces of paid militiamen. In many places, existing elite structures were also threatened as militia leadership provided new routes to power for "local bullies" and even bandit chiefs whose bands were often incorporated into local militia as a shortcut to bandit "pacification."

Militia also played an important role in the struggle for political power between the Nationalist and Communist parties beginning in the mid-1920s. The Nationalist Party promoted elite-led militia as a tool in its Communist eradication campaign, even as it tried to bring these militia under greater state control. The Communists meanwhile first looked to the organization of "worker pickets" to build a base of armed power in Chinese cities. When forced to the countryside, the Communists also turned, with much greater success, to a massive organization of militia (*minbing*) to provide logistical support and reserves for its regular army. Ultimately numbering nearly two million men and women, militia organized by Communists behind Japanese lines during the 1937–1945 Sino-Japanese War played a key role in the expansion of Communist power and the defeat of the Nationalist government in 1949.

Militia have continued to be an important part of China's armed forces since 1949, though varying widely in both size and function under changing political situations. Initially, Mao Zedong promoted the idea of "a nation under arms" (*quanmin jiebing*) to bring nearly one-third of China's population into militia organizations, with an emphasis on providing support for the People's Liberation Army (PLA) and helping maintain local order. The role of militia expanded in the Great Leap Forward, as they were mobilized beyond security tasks to act as "vanguards of production." During the Cultural Revolution, some radical Maoist leaders sought to build up urban militia as an armed counterweight to the PLA itself. As a result, after the fall of the Gang of Four, militia organizations were drastically reduced in size and placed under direct PLA supervision. Nonetheless, at the beginning of the twenty-first century, some ten million Chinese men and women remained registered in militia organizations, where they are trained to aid in local relief and security operations and, in the case of the outbreak of war, provide logistical support and reserves for the PLA.

SEE ALSO *People's Liberation Army.*

BIBLIOGRAPHY

Kuhn, Philip A. *Rebellion and Its Enemies in Late Imperial China: Militarization and Social Structure, 1796–1864*. Cambridge, MA: Harvard University Press, 1970.

McCord, Edward A. Local Militia and State Power in Nationalist China. *Modern China* 25, 2 (1999): 115–141.

Perry, Elizabeth J. *Patrolling the Revolution: Worker Militias, Citizenship, and the Modern Chinese State*. Lanham, MD: Rowman & Littlefield, 2006.

Tien Chen-ya. *The Mass Militia System and Chinese Modernization*. Oakville, Ontario: Mosaic, 1982.

Edward A. McCord

MINES AND METALLURGY, 1800–1949

China entered the nineteenth century with a large mining industry using nonmechanized technology—the German geologist and geographer Ferdinand von Richthofen (1844–1905) estimated the output of iron in Shanxi alone at 160,000 tons annually in the 1870s. Several million tons of coal were also mined and used across the country. The copper mines in Yunnan, while having declined from their mid-eighteenth-century peak, still produced substantial amounts of copper. Modern technology only began to be introduced, however, late in the century: The Kaiping coal mine complex in Hebei, which began production in 1881, was the only really modern mine in China before 1895. For most of the latter part of the century, modern-sector demand for coal and iron was met by imports.

COAL MINING

As Table 1 shows, coal was the largest mining sector in the early twentieth century: The value of coal output was four times that of ferrous metallurgy and over twice that of all other minerals apart from salt. As shown in Figure 1, output by modern methods increased from 500,000 tons in 1901 to a pre-1949 peak of 58 million tons in 1942. Mining was heavily concentrated in northern and northeast China: In the 1927–1931 period, the provinces of Liaoning and Hebei alone accounted for 71.3 percent of output. Growth was heavily dependent on the health of the transport system, and the industry experienced considerable difficulties during the civil wars of the 1920s and the Anti-Japanese War.

Demand came from industrial and household users. In 1933 around 30 percent of coal was used in rural areas for domestic and industrial purposes; just over 20 percent was used by urban industry, particularly electric utilities, iron and steel, and textiles; around 15 percent was used for transport, either steamships or railway; and 13 percent was exported. The industry moved from import substitution to the beginnings of an export orientation, starting from the 1910s, when the war increased demand and modern Chinese coal mines began rapidly increasing their output.

Mineral and metallurgical output in China, 1933 (Ch$ million)

	Gross value of output	Net value added
Coal	142	99
Salt	66	41
Iron and steel	33	20
Tin	19	14
Limestone	10	9
Crude oil	13	8
Gold	11	8
Iron ore	9	7
Antimony	2	2

SOURCE: Liu Dazhong (Liu Ta-chung) and Ye Kongjia (Yeh Kung-chia). *The Economy of the Chinese Mainland: National Income and Economic Development, 1933–1959*. Princeton, NJ: Princeton University Press, 1965, p.569.

Table 1

FERROUS METALLURGY

Up to the seventeenth century, China had the world's most advanced iron industry, but in the nineteenth century, Chinese iron could not compete with imports on price or quality. The modern iron and steel industry originated in 1890, when Zhang Zhidong (1837–1909) started plans for an ironworks at Hanyang. Blast furnaces there began operation in 1894, earlier than their Japanese counterparts. The ironworks, together with the Daye iron mines, were later taken over by Sheng Xuanhuai (1844–1916) and, combined with coal mines at Pingxiang, were formed into the Hanyeping Company, a leading example of a "government-supervised merchant-managed" (*guandu shangban*) enterprise. From 1903 the company took out loans from Japan on terms that involved repayment in the form of iron ore at a fixed price, so it was able to benefit little from the substantial wartime rise in iron prices. In the early 1920s the collapse in demand for pig iron forced it to cease operations. Chinese nationalists held that the Japanese loans were the mechanism for preventing the development of an indigenous Chinese steel industry.

Later developments in iron and steel were mainly concentrated in Manchuria, where the Japanese-owned South Manchurian Railway Company began to develop the Anshan iron mines and to build the facilities that from the 1930s dominated China's iron and steel production, and remained a core part of the post-1949 steel industry.

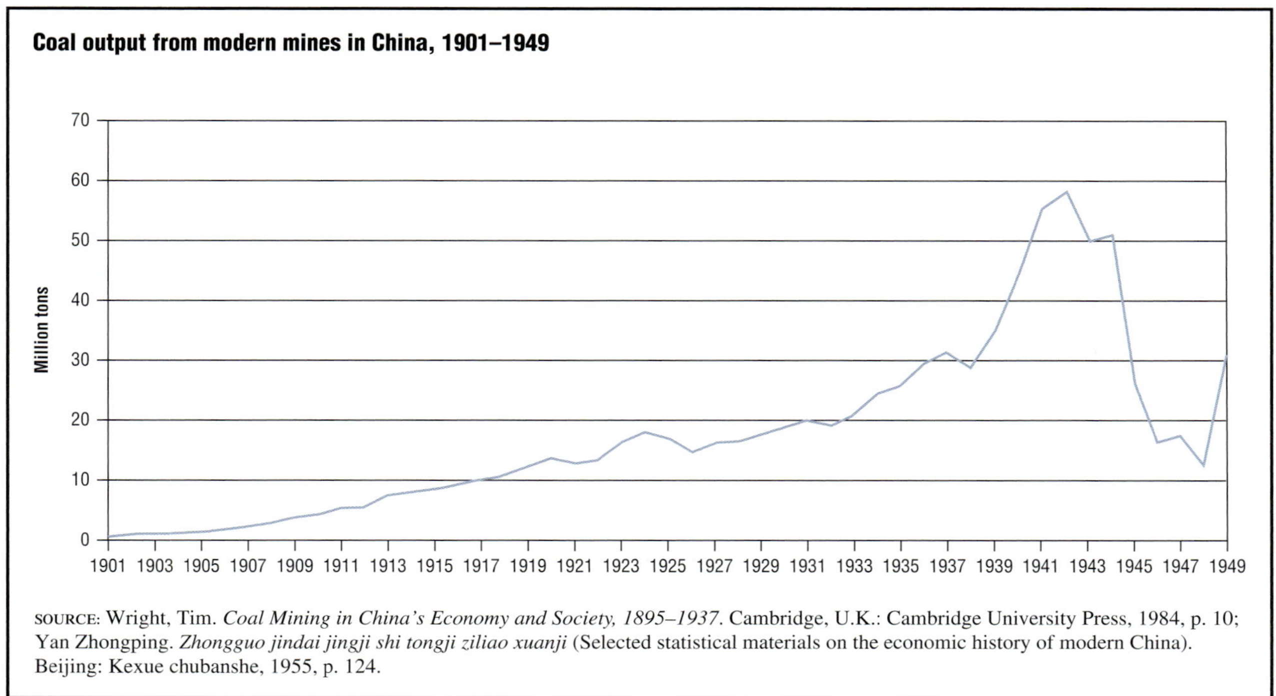

Figure 1

At its peak in 1942 and 1943, the Anshan Steelworks and other smaller producers in Manchuria produced around 750,000 tons of steel ingots, but thereafter production was seriously disrupted by American bombing.

NONFERROUS MINERALS

The Gejiu tin mines in Yunnan were the most important nonferrous metal mines. Run jointly with the French, these mines employed 80,000 to 90,000 workers directly or indirectly. Their output of between 5,000 and 10,000 tons annually between the 1910s and 1930s was shipped out by rail to Vietnam to be sold on the world market. These shipments made up more than 80 percent of Yunnan's exports, but had little broader impact on China's economy.

As for other metals, China had ceased to be a major producer of copper by the early twentieth century. Antimony (of which central Hunan was the world's largest producer in the 1910s) enjoyed a brief boom during World War I (1914–1918), when it was used in shrapnel shells. Tungsten enjoyed a similar boom. There was some gold production, particularly in northern Manchuria.

The other important extractive industry in China was salt, though that industry is not often given high prominence in mining history elsewhere. Salt was generally extracted from brine, from sea or lake water, or from deep wells or saline rock (mostly in southwest China). The great salt works at Ziliujing in Sichuan extracted about 200,000 tons of salt annually from brine wells in the 1920s and 1930s, with a workforce of up to 100,000 engaged directly in production and several hundred thousand depending on the industry.

MINING IN CHINESE POLITICS

In early twentieth-century China, mining was closely tied up with politics, particularly the impact of foreign powers. For most of the period, foreign-operated mines produced some 70 percent of China's coal. Mining, along with railway rights, was at the center of the "struggle for concessions" in the late nineteenth century and equally of the "rights-recovery movement" in the first decades of the twentieth. Later, Japanese plans to gain access to Chinese coal and iron lay behind their occupation both of Manchuria in 1931 and of north China in 1937.

In addition to Hanyeping, two other cases have played a major part in China's political history. The takeover of the pioneer Chinese coal mine, Kaiping, by an Anglo-Belgian consortium in the context of the Boxer Uprising in 1900 was thrown into question even by the British courts, but the court failed to restore control to the Chinese. A rights-recovery movement led by Yuan Shikai (1859–1916) forced the consortium to join with Chinese partners in a joint venture, the Kailuan (Kailan) Mining

Administration, but Kailuan remained dominated by the British up to the 1940s.

By far the most important case was the Japanese development of Manchuria. This originated from 1905 when Japan's victory over Russia enabled the Japanese to take over the Russian rights in south Manchuria. The South Manchurian Railway Company proceeded to build the coal mines at Fushun into the largest in China from 1922. After the occupation of Manchuria in 1931, other Japanese investment companies participated in a massive development of coal and iron production, which then fed into the Japanese military buildup. After the Japanese surrender, the Russian pillage of much of the industrial equipment left by the Japanese left a bitter legacy into the postrevolutionary period.

MINING TECHNOLOGY

By the 1920s, up to three-quarters of Chinese coal was produced using at least partially modern technology. It was possible, however, for unmodernized mines profitably to mine deposits close to the surface. In general, the advantages of modern technology lay less in lower costs and more in the ability to operate at a larger scale more suitable to the use of railway transport. Most other minerals were mined using nonmechanized methods.

Modern mining technology was transferred to China through the purchase of equipment, the training of Chinese engineers in the West or in foreign-operated mines, or the hiring of foreign engineers. Increasing numbers of trained Chinese engineers gradually reduced the need for foreign employees. For example, the Zhongxing Coal Mining Company in Shandong started off using German technicians but by the 1930s relied on Chinese expertise.

Most coal was mined underground, with the exception of the giant Japanese mines at Fushun, some of which ran on an open-cast basis, which allowed lower-cost operation. Even among modern underground mines, a range of technologies coexisted. At the minimum, mines were modernized only to the extent of replacing human with mechanical power in operating the winding engine. Later, the larger mines all employed some form of mechanical ventilation and pumping, while human labor, mules, or (the exception even in the 1930s) mechanical means were used for underground transport. In the prewar period, only a few mines introduced any mechanical cutting at the coal face.

MINING CONDITIONS AND SAFETY

Life in China's mines, as in most other areas of society, was hard and dangerous. Most miners were employed through labor contractors, adding an extra layer of exploitation. Unlike in Britain during the Industrial Revolution, female and child labor was the exception not the rule (though many young boys worked in appalling conditions in the Gejiu tin mines). Most labor came from the local farm population and, particularly in the earlier period and in smaller mines, labor supply was seasonal. Manchuria was the exception in its reliance on full-time, long-distance migrant workers on a large scale. Mining wages, although probably higher than those for agricultural laborers, were still low and subsistence precarious: The daily wage in the late 1920s even at the Sino-British mines at Kailuan, where conditions were better than average, was fifty cents, while the cost of living for a family of four was one dollar.

Although there were no national statistics, figures for eighteen large coal mines in the 1920s indicate a death rate of well over thirty per million tons extracted, almost twice the worst rate registered after 1949. China was also the site of the world's most serious mining disaster when 1,549 workers were killed in a coal-dust explosion at the Benxihu mine in Japanese-occupied Manchuria in April 1942.

SEE ALSO *Industrialization, 1860–1949.*

BIBLIOGRAPHY

Carlson, Ellsworth C. *The Kaiping Mines, 1877–1912.* 2nd ed. Cambridge, MA: East Asia Research Center, Harvard University, 1971.

Feuerwerker, Albert. *Studies in the Economic History of Late Imperial China: Handicraft, Modern Industry, and the State.* Ann Arbor: Center for Chinese Studies, University of Michigan, 1995.

Kinney, Ann Rasmussen. *Japanese Investment in Manchurian Manufacturing, Mining, Transportation, and Communications, 1931–1945.* New York: Garland, 1982.

Liu Dazhong (Liu Ta-chung) and Ye Kongjia (Yeh Kung-chia). *The Economy of the Chinese Mainland: National Income and Economic Development, 1933–1959.* Princeton, NJ: Princeton University Press, 1965.

Wagner, Donald. *The Traditional Chinese Iron Industry and Its Modern Fate.* Richmond, U.K.: Curzon, 1997.

Wright, Tim. *Coal Mining in China's Economy and Society, 1895–1937.* Cambridge, U.K.: Cambridge University Press, 1984.

Yan Zhongping. *Zhongguo jindai jingji shi tongji ziliao xuanji* [Selected statistical materials on the economic history of modern China]. Beijing: Kexue Chubanshe, 1955.

Zelin, Madeleine. *The Merchants of Zigong: Industrial Entrepreneurship in Early Modern China.* New York: Columbia University Press, 2005.

Tim Wright

MINORITY NATIONALITIES

This entry contains the following:

CULTURAL IMAGES OF NATIONAL MINORITIES
Thomas Heberer

ETHNIC MINORITY CULTURAL EXPRESSION
Mark Bender

BAI NATIONALITY
Zhao Yuzhong
Beth E. Notar

MOSUO AND NAXI NATIONALITIES
Eric D. Mortensen

OVERVIEW

The population of China consists of fifty-six nationalities. The majority of Chinese, more than 1.2 billion people, call themselves *Han*, although the Han are not a homogeneous nationality, but include different groups. The census of 2000 revealed 104.5 million people belonging to one of the fifty-five "national minorities" (*shaoshu minzu*), 8.4 percent of the entire population. Since the 1960s, the minorities' population has increased with a higher percentage than that of the Han.

The largest ethnic minority, the Zhuang in South China, comprised 16.2 million persons in 2000. The smallest group, the Luoba in Tibet, numbered 2,965. Only two groups, the Hui and the She, use the Han language and form of writing. The Yugur use two languages. In 1949 there were eleven written languages in regular use by China's ethnic minorities, and seven other languages saw sporadic use. Since then, twenty-five minority languages have been codified through the creation of new scripts, some based on Latin.

Since the 1950s, minorities in China have been granted "autonomy" defined by territory and nationality. In 2007 there were five areas with regional national autonomy at the provincial level (Inner Mongolia, Xinjiang of the Uygur, Guangxi of the Zhuang, Tibet, and Ningxia of the Hui), comprising thirty autonomous prefectures, 120 counties, and more than 3,000 townships. The autonomous regions cover 64 percent of the area of China.

Autonomy does not mean that these regions have the right to secede from the sovereign territory of the People's Republic of China, but they enjoy certain special rights compared to other administrative units. In these regions, the language(s) and writing of the autonomous nationality (or nationalities) can be used; administration shall be in the hands of officials from the minority population; and the regional governments may promulgate their own laws and regulations, administer local finances, and have their own security forces.

The central government also extends preferential treatment to China's non-Han nationalities, including official recognition of the existence of such ethnic groups, a prohibition on discrimination, and special laws for minorities passed in the 1950s and the 1980s. The government also provides aid to minority areas, as well as guarantees of representation in political institutions and other benefits in terms of population policy, university entrance examinations, freedom to choose one's ethnic identity, and so forth. Like the provinces the autonomous regions are represented in the National People's Congress. Moreover, the state's nationalities commission is at the central level in charge of ethnic issues. Concerning education, in autonomous areas nationalities' schools exist where children of ethnic minority origin could also learn the language of their nationality, albeit from the middle school onward priority is given to Chinese (Han) language.

Even today, however, traditional perceptions shape behavior and attitudes toward minorities and the expectations of how the minority population should behave toward the power center. These perceptions are related to more than two thousand years of centralized power in Chinese culture. Imperial China understood itself as the cultural center of the world and its culture as the culture of all humankind. In traditional conceptions, the existence of various peoples with clear-cut settlement areas was accepted, but there was only one people entrusted by heaven to be in charge of humankind. This people was regarded as the center of the world, as the "Middle Kingdom" (*Zhongguo*), and its emperors were seen as "sons of heaven." The people who represented the ancient river culture (later called Han) classified the peoples surrounding them as "barbarians," according to their direction (north, south, east, west) and distance from the center of the world (i.e., the court of the emperor) and their behavior toward this center. The emperor's court expected regular tributes from these groups, and the leaders of other peoples were regarded as tributary vassals. Relationships existed mainly with peoples assessed as weak and culturally inferior. Under conditions of far-reaching isolation for many centuries, the idea of superiority was always confirmed. The Han, who were farmers, were contemptuous of the peoples around them, who were hunters and gatherers or nomads and whom the Han believed to be culturally and technologically inferior. Confucianism, for centuries the state ideology, was the ideological fundament of the Han contempt of "barbarians."

These traditional hierarchical perceptions corresponded well with historic-materialistic concepts developed, for example, in the Soviet Union. Accordingly, the societies of all nationalities in history were classified into five categories: primitive, slave, feudal, capitalist, and socialist. In this way, every ethnic group had its fixed place in the hierarchy of nationalities and in its relationship with the "most advanced" people, the Han.

However, throughout Chinese history, minority groups have faced expulsion to remote areas and cruel punishments when they revolted. The Miao and the Hui and their treatment by the imperial court serve as examples. The uprisings of the desperate Miao in the eighteenth century who were

Chinese Muslims near sign reading "China's ethnicities are one family," Korla, Xinjiang province, May 29, 2002. *Ten percent of Chinese citizens belong to an ethnicity outside of the Han majority, some residing in autonomous regions where the government allows them to preserve their language, culture, and traditions.* AP IMAGES

driven away by the policy of the emperor who resettled those areas with Han or the uprisings of the Hui in Northwest and Southwest China against strong discrimination and eviction were punished by extremely cruel measures of retaliation that led to the obliteration of large shares of their population. These aspects of history are rarely mentioned in Chinese history books, and this one-sided perception of history is the reason such traumatic events are not critically reassessed, but simmer in the collective consciousness of an ethnic group and thus perpetuate tensions between nationalities.

Such traumatic events did not occur only during the time of imperial China or the Republic of China, but also since the People's Republic was established. The various political movements (e.g., against local nationalism in the 1950s, the Great Leap Forward, the Cultural Revolution) saw the worst excesses of suppression of nationalities, a history that cannot simply be erased from the memory of an ethnic group. Although the Cultural Revolution and other movements had an impact on every inhabitant of China, they were perceived by the Han as movements for which their own political leadership was responsible, but by non-Han as movements for which the Han and their party were responsible. For the Han, the Cultural Revolution is considered a political conflict; for China's minorities, it is seen as an ethnic conflict.

However, the experience of the Cultural Revolution made it clear that the integration of China's non-Han peoples could not be achieved through force, but had to be based on a broad consensus. The 1982 constitution reevaluated the status of China's minorities correspondingly, and the 1984 Autonomy Law formally extended to minority groups the widest-reaching freedoms since the founding of the People's Republic. But the Autonomy Law was so vaguely worded that it proved unimplementable in the absence of accompanying laws. It is a soft law that sets goals to be followed as much as possible by state policies, but it did not establish an effective system for the protection of autonomy nor legal measures for the implementation of such a system. The lack of implementable rights for self-rule, together with a gradual undermining of minority rights through Han migration into and environmental damage to minority areas are the nuclei of non-Han discontent.

Economically, the gap in development between the non-Han autonomous regions and the Han regions has grown despite the reform efforts. Although considerable materials flow from the center to the autonomous regions, nearly half of the counties classified as "poor" lie in minority areas. The Communist Party is not solely responsible for this development, because some of these areas are remote regions into which non-Han peoples have fled from Han expansion. Still, since the founding of the People's Republic, no development policy suited to these areas has been followed. The Great Western Development Scheme is by large sections of the ethnic groups concerned considered to be a strong menace, as it will be accompanied by a massive influx of Han Chinese in their areas and consequently might lead to a loss of their group cohesion and therefore their ethnic identity.

The main problem of China's cultural policy is that since the 1950s "healthy" and "unhealthy" customs and practices have been differentiated—unhealthy practices are to be eliminated or "reformed," while healthy ones should be preserved. Because this distinction between "healthy" and "unhealthy" has never been precisely clarified, it always leads to local interference in customary practices.

Exploitation of resources (forests, minerals, land) in minority areas, in-migration of Han, corruption, spatial mobilization, increasing unemployment, the growing gap between the Han and non-Han in income and economic development, increasing discrimination against non-Han, and the economization of minority cultures have led to new patterns of conflict. Modernization and social change have caused China's minority peoples to feel threatened, as they face the disintegration and decay of their cultures and communities. Although reform policies have brought about a more liberal treatment of minorities and have improved the lives of most of them, conflict continues.

SEE ALSO *Cultural Policy; Cultural Revolution, 1966–1969; Economic Development: Great Western Development Scheme; Language and Language Policy; Miao Uprisings; Provincial and Subprovincial Government Structure since 1949: Autonomous Regions; Regionalism.*

BIBLIOGRAPHY

Gladney, Dru. *Dislocating China: Reflections on Muslims, Minorities, and Other Subaltern Subjects.* Chicago: University of Chicago Press, 2004.

Heberer, Thomas. *Doing Business in Rural China: Lianghshan's New Ethnic Entrepreneurs.* Seattle: University of Washington Press, 2007.

Iredale, Robyn R., Naran Bilik, and Guo Fei, eds. *China's Minorities on the Move: Selected Case Studies.* Armonk, NY: Sharpe, 2003.

Mackerras, Colin. *China's Ethnic Minorities and Globalisation.* London and New York: RoutledgeCurzon, 2003.

Rossabi, Morris, ed. *Governing China's Multiethnic Frontiers.* Seattle: University of Washington Press, 2004.

Thomas Heberer

LARGE NATIONAL MINORITIES

The Qing empire comprised the five great nations: the Han, Manchu, Muslims, Mongols, and Tibetans. These nations were declared the foundation of the Chinese Republic in several statements in 1912 to 1913. The People's Republic of China undertook a more detailed exploration of nationalities in the 1950s, which ultimately led to the recognition of fifty-five national minorities, the largest of which are described here.

ZHUANG

The Zhuang are the largest of China's minorities, with a population of almost 15 million in 1990. They are concentrated almost exclusively in western Guangxi and eastern Yunnan. Over 90 percent of them live in the Guangxi Zhuang Autonomous Region (Kaup 2000; Ma 1994). The Zhuang are one of the more residentially segregated of China's minorities. They have their own language, which fits into the Chinese-Tibetan language family. The National People's Congress granted the Zhuang their own autonomous region in 1958.

The Zhuang are thought to be descendants of one of China's ancient ethnic groups, the Yue (China Handbook Editorial Committee 1985). In 221 BCE the Zhuang areas were conquered by China's central peoples, many of them Han, and people from other places were moved to this area to strengthen the control of the central government. In the rise and fall of the dynasties in succeeding centuries, a number of powerful clans emerged in the Zhuang areas. Backed by the central authorities, many of these clans governed most of the Zhuang areas from the Tang dynasty (618–907) through the Qing (1644–1912). One line of current research dealing with the Zhuang, however, holds that the group was given an explicit identification and legitimacy by the Chinese Communist Party (CCP) as recently as the 1950s (Kaup 2000).

During the Tang and Song (618–1279) dynasties the Zhuang clans practiced slash-and-burn cultivation while most of central China had irrigation systems. The Zhuang are still heavily agricultural; in 1990 almost 90 percent were employed in agriculture (Ma 1994).

MANZU (MANCHUS)

In 1990 the population of the Manzu nationality was 9.8 million, making it the second-largest minority group in China. The Manzu people are scattered all over China. The largest group, about 46 percent of the total, lives in Liaoning Province, and the rest are mostly in Jilin and Heilongjiang (the other two provinces in the northeast) and other parts of China.

The Manzu are descendants of the Sushen tribe, a people that lived in northeastern China about 2,000 years ago. The Sushen changed their tribal name to *Yilou*, *Huji*, *Mohe*, and *Nüzhen* in succeeding centuries. By the end of the Ming dynasty (1368–1644) the Nüzhen had accepted the name *Manzu*. In 1644 the Manzu troops took over China from the Han and established the Qing dynasty, which ruled China for over two hundred years.

The Manzu have their own oral and written language, which belongs to the Manzu-Tungusic group of the Altaic linguistic family. Beginning in the 1640s large numbers of Manzu gradually moved to the south and adopted Mandarin Chinese as their spoken language. Later, as more and more Han migrated to the north, many northern Manzu picked up Mandarin as well.

Compared with the other minority groups, the Manzu are relatively similar to the Han with respect to their population distributions in education, occupation, and industry (Poston and Shu 1987).

HUI

With a sizable population of 8.6 million, the Hui are the third-largest minority group in China. Over 70 percent of the Hui are in the Ningxia Hui Autonomous Region, and the rest are spread among Gansu, Qinghai, Henan, Hebei, Shandong, and Yunnan provinces, and in the Xinjiang Uygur Autonomous Region. Generally, of all the minorities of China, the Hui people are the most residentially integrated with the Han. (Poston and Micklin 1993). The term *Hui* in the Qing dynasty and in the Republican period indicated all Muslim groups in China, irrespective of other cultural, ethnic, and linguistic characteristics. After the various national minorities had been determined in the 1950s (including the predominantly Islamic Uygur, Kazakh, Dongxiang, Kyrgyz, Salar, Tajik, Uzbek, Bonan, and Tatar nationalities), the Hui remained as the residual group of Chinese Muslims.

The Hui are a Muslim people and employ an Arabic script. The name *Hui* is abbreviated from *Huihui*, a term that identified the peoples who resided in and around the large area of Xinjiang since the Tang dynasty (618–907); these people, however, were actually ancestors of today's Uygurs. The Hui ancestors also date back to the "Islamic-oriented peoples from Middle Asia, as well as Persians and Arabs" who migrated into China in the early periods of the thirteenth century.

Hui culture was developed mainly during the Mongol Yuan dynasty (1279–1368), when the Huihui obtained higher social positions than the Han. In the early Ming, they emerged as a distinct nationality. At first the Huihui used the Arabic, Persian, and Han languages, but as a result of intermarrying with the Han, the Mongolians, and the Uygurs, the Huihui language emerged. When the government introduced the Han language as a common language, the Hui assimilated by adopting the Han language (i.e., Mandarin), wearing clothing like the Han, and using Han names.

UYGUR

Among the fifty-five Chinese minorities, the Uygur are the fifth largest, with a population in 1990 of over 7.2 million (State Statistical Bureau 1993). The Uygur are one of China's ten predominantly Muslim groups.

The language of the Uygur belongs to the Turkic group of the Altaic language family (China Handbook Editorial Committee 1985). In 1990 virtually all of the Uygur (99.7%) resided in the Xinjiang Uygur Autonomous Region in far northwestern China, an area that includes about one-sixth of China's land mass (State Statistical Bureau 1993). The Uygur are mainly farmers, and their major products are wheat, rice, corn, and cotton (Ma 1994; Zhang and Zeng 1993).

According to their language, *Uygur* signifies "unity" or "alliance" (China Handbook Editorial Committee 1985; Zhang and Zeng 1993). Their origins date back to the Ding Ling nomads who lived in the third century BCE. The Uygur took the names *Tiele*, *Huihe*, and *Huigu* in succeeding centuries. Their descendants intermarried with people in southern Xinjiang and Tibet(an), Qidan (Khitan), and Mongol tribes (Ma 1994, p. 139). The nomadic Uygur settled into farming and related sustenance activities between the ninth and the twelfth centuries, and have over the centuries maintained strong relations with the Han.

In 1990 more than 84 percent of the Uygur were in agricultural jobs, and only 4.1 percent were professionals. They had an illiteracy rate of almost 27 percent, compared to 22.2 percent for the nation as a whole (State Statistical Bureau 1993).

MIAO

The Miao number almost 7.4 million persons and constitute the fourth-largest Chinese minority in 1990. The Miao have grown rapidly in recent decades, increasing by 47 percent in the 1982–1990 census interval, though much of this increase is due to ethnic reaffirmation.

Most Miao live in the mountainous areas of Guizhou (almost 50%) and Hunan (12.1%); the rest live mainly in Yunnan and Sichuan provinces and in the Guangxi Zhuang Autonomous Region (State Statistical Bureau 1993).

Historically the Miao were a migratory people. They were first found in areas around western Hunan and eastern Guizhou provinces about 2,000 years ago. During the third century they migrated to northwestern Guizhou and southern Sichuan. Over the centuries, the Miao have been widely dispersed and have interacted to a significant degree with the Han and some of the other minorities. The Miao language comprises the Miao-Yao branch of the Chinese-Tibetan language family; however, many Miao have adopted Han Chinese, Yao, or Dong as their spoken language (Poston, Chang, and Dan 2003).

The economic and social progress of the Miao society has been so slow that its earliest known forms of farming, weaving, and trade did not emerge until the time of the Eastern Han dynasty (25–220 CE). According to data from the 1990 census, 93 percent of the Miao are engaged in agriculture, and 42 percent of them (aged 15 and above) are illiterate or semi-illiterate (Poston, Chang, and Dan 2003; State Statistical Bureau 1993).

MONGOL

The Mongolian nationality numbered over 4.8 million in 1990; it is the eighth-largest minority in China. In 1990 about 70 percent of Mongolians lived in the Inner Mongolian Autonomous Region where natural resources are plentiful for both animal husbandry and farming.

The earliest Mongolians were known as Mongol Shiwei. By the twelfth century the Mongols had reached the upper limits of the Onon, Kerulen, and Tula rivers and into the Hentey Mountains. In the early thirteenth century the Mongol Empire was unified from several northern tribes. In 1272 Kublai Khan (1215–1294) founded the Yuan dynasty (1279–1368) and conquered the Southern Song (1127–1279), bringing all of China under the control of the Yuan dynasty for about one century (China Handbook Editorial Committee 1985; Khan 1995; Borchigud 1995).

The Mongolians believed in shamanism in ancient times. In the thirteenth century the red sect of Lamaism became popular among the Mongolian rulers; many feudal lords and herdsmen shifted to the yellow sect of Lamaism in the sixteenth century. Lamaism was later protected and encouraged by the imperial court of the Qing dynasty. Young people were encouraged to become lamas during the years of the Ming and Qing dynasties, which seriously impeded the development of production and the growth of the population. Lamaism is still the primary religion of Mongolians today.

The Mongolians originally had a nomadic lifestyle but are now almost entirely in permanent settlements (China Handbook Editorial Committee 1985). Compared with the other Chinese minorities, the Mongolians have a lower percentage in agriculture—70 percent in 1990, a figure just slightly higher than the 69.6 percent of the Han peoples.

TIBETAN

The Tibetan people, with a population of over 4.5 million, mostly live in the Tibet Autonomous Region. There are also Tibetan communities in Qinghai, Gansu, Sichuan, and Yunnan provinces.

At the beginning of the seventh century King Songzain Gambo (617–649) began to rule Tibet and made Losha (today's Lhasa) the capital. In the Tang dynasty (618–907) the Kingdom of Tibet began to have frequent contact with the Han, and in 641 Songzain Gambo married Princess Wencheng Gongzhu (d. 680) of the Tang. In 710 King Chide Zuzain married another Tang princess, Jin Cheng. The two princesses brought with them to Tibet the culture and advanced production techniques of central China, and they are credited with helping to introduce the Buddhist faith into Tibet. From that time, emissaries traveled frequently between the Tang dynasty and Tibet. These interactions helped to promote relations between the Tibetans and other ethnic groups in China and stimulated social development in Tibet.

The Tibetan language belongs to the Tibetan subbranch of the Tibetan-Myanmese language branch of the Chinese-Tibetan language family. According to geographical divisions, it has three major local dialects: Weizang, Kang, and Amdo. The Tibetan script, an alphabetic system of writing, was created in the early seventh century.

Lamaism, the major religion of the Tibetans, belongs to the Mahayana school of Buddhism. It was introduced into Tibet in the seventh century and developed into Lamaism by assimilating some of the beliefs and rites of the local religion, Bön. The Tibetan family is male-centered, and marriage is a strictly inner-class affair. Monogamy is the principal form of marriage. The husband controls and inherits the property of the family, and the wife is subordinate to the husband, even if he is married into a woman's family.

The areas where Tibetans live in compact communities are mostly highlands and mountainous country studded with snow-capped peaks. High in Tibet's mountains, yaks are the only form of transport. Known as the "boat on the plateau," the yak is capable of withstanding harsh weather and carrying heavy loads.

SEE ALSO *Inner Mongolia; Islam; Miao Uprisings; Provincial and Subprovincial Government Structure since 1949: Autonomous Regions; Tibet.*

BIBLIOGRAPHY

Borchigud, W. Transgressing Ethnic and National Boundaries: Contemporary "Inner Mongolian" Identities in China. In *Negotiating Ethnicities in China and Taiwan*, ed. M. J. Brown, 160–181. Berkeley: Institute of East Asian Studies, University of California, 1995.

China Handbook Editorial Committee. *China Handbook Series: Life and Lifestyles*. Beijing: Foreign Languages Press, 1985.

Kaup, K. P. *Creating the Zhuang: Ethnic Politics in China*. Boulder, CO, and London: Lynne Rienner Publishers, 2000.

Khan, A. Who Are the Mongols? State, Ethnicity, and the Politics of Representation in the PRC. In *Negotiating Ethnicities in China and Taiwan*, ed. M. J. Brown, 125–159. Berkeley: Institute of East Asian Studies, University of California, 1995.

Ma, Y. *China's Minority Nationalities*. Beijing: Foreign Languages Press, 1994.

Poston, Dudley L., Jr., and J. Shu. The Demographic and Socioeconomic Composition of China's Ethnic Minorities. *Population and Development Review* 13 (1987): 703–722.

Poston, Dudley L., Jr., and Michael Micklin. Spatial Segregation and Social Differentiation of the Minority Nationalities from the Han Majority in the People's Republic of China. *Sociological Inquiry* 63, 2 (1993): 150–165.

Poston, Dudley L., Jr., C. Chang, and H. Dan. Fertility Differences between the Majority and Minority Nationality Groups in China. *Population Research and Policy Review* 25 (2003): 67–101.

State Statistical Bureau. *Tabulation on the 1990 Census of the People's Republic of China*. Beijing: China Statistics Press, 1993.

Zhang, W., and Q. Zeng. *In Search of China's Minorities*. Beijing: New World Press, 1993.

Chiung-Fang Chang

CULTURAL IMAGES OF NATIONAL MINORITIES

Confucianism, for centuries the state ideology, was the ideological fundament of Han contempt for people whom they considered "barbarians." Non-Han peoples were held in contempt because, as the great Chinese historian Sima Qian (c. 145–86 BCE) stated, they knew nothing of *li,* the proper (Confucian) rules of life, and *yi,* the duties of life. To be different was understood by the Chinese as an expression of ignorance of the social structure of relations and of Confucian rites. Nevertheless, Confucianism did not advocate annihilating people who were different, but rather demanded their subordination to the emperor, as well as their integration into the Chinese Empire. The aim was "cultivation" by Confucian values, that is, a cultural, nonviolent assimilation. Even a "barbarian" could become an emperor, but only by fitting into the Chinese system and by giving up his previous identity. This traditional world image has been disintegrating since the middle of the nineteenth century, largely through Western influence and penetration. But its basic ideas have by no means disappeared.

Even in the twenty-first century, exoticism, paternalism, and idealized patterns characterize the official images of "minorities" among the Chinese public. China's minorities are usually depicted dancing, singing, laughing, in colorful garments, under palm trees, and in high mountain areas or bizarre landscapes. Their dances are wild, fires are blazing, and mythical images are presented, so that spectators perceive strangeness and sometimes feel suspicion and fright. Young minority women are usually depicted with features, figures, and motions that are similar to Han ideals of beauty, a tendency that can even include an eroticization of minorities.

Furthermore, a patriarchal kinship myth characterizes the official description of the relationship between Han and minority peoples, with the Han described as father figures or elder brothers. Surrounded by members of minority groups, the Han advise, teach, and instruct. This perspective is expressed by the term *big elder brother* (*Lao Dage*), which the Han have given themselves to describe their relationship with China's minority peoples.

Fathers and elder brothers have the task of educating children or younger brothers and sisters—a clearly Confucian element that also appears in other world regions. In China, this patriarchal concept finds its expression in the idea that the most advanced culture is that of the "father ethnic group," that is, the Han. Society as a whole is regarded as a homogeneous ethnic community, a closed unit like a family, where only a division of labor between the superior and the inferior exists. The head of the family (the Han) has the duty to protect the family, and to educate, instruct, and advise its members; the children (the minorities) are expected to be loyal and to respect the father of this family and his conception of education.

These traditional perceptions correspond well with historic-materialistic concepts developed, for example, by Joseph Stalin (1879–1953) in the 1930s. According to his "doctrine of socioeconomic formations," the societies of all nationalities in history could be classified into five categories: primitive, slave, feudal, capitalist, and socialist. This taxonomy fitted well into the traditional Chinese thinking of hierarchization. Even under socialism, the Han could retain their traditional position and what they saw as their function toward China's non-Han people. Because the national minorities were considered inferior to the Han, the culture of the Han remained the highest-ranking one. It was the duty of the Han to civilize and modernize the minorities' societies. The cultural "avant-garde," the representative and guardian of culture and civilization, was no longer the emperor's court, his officials, the gentry, and the traditional examination system, but the Communist Party with its functionaries and its education system. The duty of every nationality was to catch up with the Han as quickly as possible and to bring its economy and society into line with that of the Han. The patriarchal state in turn had to initiate suitable measures and policies. It decided what was useful for a minority group, what was advanced or backward, civilized or uncivilized, and which customs or habits were beneficial or harmful and had accordingly to be abolished or reformed. Even today, Chinese school students learn that ethnic minorities were economically and culturally more backward than the Han.

Yet there are other perceptions as well—for example, an idealization. Therefore, there are three "maps" of ethnic minorities in the minds of the Han: (1) *barbarian minorities* of stagnation and backwardness; (2) *sinicized minorities,* seen as latecomers to development that have to catch up with the Han, and (3) *delightful minorities* of prodigy, exoticism, and esotericism.

SEE ALSO *Confucianism; Cultural Policy.*

BIBLIOGRAPHY

Dodin, Thierry, and Heinz Räther, eds. *Imagining Tibet: Perceptions, Projections, and Fantasies.* Boston: Wisdom, 2001.

Guo Yingjie. *Cultural Nationalism in Contemporary China: The Search for National Identity under Reform.* London and New York: RoutledgeCurzon, 2004.

Harrell, Stevan, ed. *Cultural Encounters on China's Ethnic Frontiers.* Seattle: University of Washington Press, 1995.

Thomas Heberer

ETHNIC MINORITY CULTURAL EXPRESSION

In China in the early twenty-first century, cultural expressions of the ethnic minority groups include music, dance, folk art, literature, and fine arts, communicated in a variety of social contexts.

In the 1950s, local and national song and dance troupes were established to promote China as a big family of nationalities. As part of this program, ethnic dances and music in modified form, often promoting political agendas, soon became popular throughout China and were incorporated into school curriculums and workplace activities. The more popular traditions included the Mongolian, Uygur, Tibetan, and Dai traditions. Since the 1990s, provincial and state troupes provide highly choreographed spectacles for television broadcast during major festivals and performances worldwide.

Locally, folk song and dances are still strong traditions in many areas, though these traditions have often changed with the times. In many minority areas, large group dances and singing contests have become common at increasingly elaborate ethnic festivals, which often include participants from many ethnic backgrounds. In northwest China, a type of folk song known as "flower songs" (*hua'er*) is popular among the Hui and several other ethnic groups. Mountain songs (*shan'ge*), many on the theme of love, are still sung during planting and harvest festivals in ethnic areas throughout south and southwest China, including those of the Zhuang, Dong, Tujia, She, and Miao. Circle dances are performed in the street during the summer Torch Festival in Yi areas in Yunnan, Sichuan, and western Guizhou. Horse racing festivals, which include singing and dancing, are held throughout the summer in Tibetan and Mongolian areas. Since the 1990s a number of ethnic music bands, such as the Yi pop group from Sichuan known as Mountain Eagle and many Tibetan singers and bands, have emerged onto the popular-culture scene.

Among the many folk arts, weaving, embroidery, and batik are still practiced in many ethnic-minority areas today. One of the best examples is the intricately woven and dyed festive garments produced by Miao women in Guizhou Province, located in the southwest. Styles and technologies differ somewhat across Miao areas, but common features are the use of hemp, cotton, silk, and (occasionally) wool, as well as natural dyes derived from indigo. Decorative patterns embroidered or batiked on the garments (butterflies, fish, birds, and water plants) are primarily drawn from local mythology and nature. In some areas, geometric patterns prevail. The Miao are also known for their elaborate silverwork. During festivals, hundreds of young women don huge silver lockets and crowns, some with giant silver crescents and many with hundreds of smaller pieces of silverwork. Traditional ethnic clothing now sells for thousands of yuan and is much sought by collectors in China and abroad, and mass-produced ethnic-style clothing is now marketed in tourist venues throughout southwest China and elsewhere.

Films with ethnic-minority themes, especially those featuring young women resisting arranged marriages with evil overlords, became popular in the 1960s. The most enduring of these films include *Liu Sanjie* (Third sister Liu), a 1961 film about a young Zhuang woman who uses folk songs to duel with a go-between of the overlord, and *Ashima* (1964), based on a legendary heroine of the Sani people of Yunnan Province. Films featuring ethnic-minority themes have again become popular in recent years. Translations of traditional ethnic-minority folk songs and folk stories have been published for public consumption since the 1950s. Earlier collections tended to feature works with politically correct messages, though since the 1980s there has been more stress on cultural preservation. During the twentieth century up through the 1960s, many ethnic-minority writers and poets have risen to local and national prominence, including the Manchu novelist Lao She, the short-story writer Shen Congwen of Tujia and Miao ancestry, the short-story writer Mala Qinfu of Inner Mongolia, and the Zhuang poets Huang Yongsha and Sha Hong of

Guangxi. Since the 1980s, many younger writers have appeared, including the novelist Alai from the Tibetan areas of western Sichuan, the Bai poet and painter Liyuan Xiaodi from Yunnan, and the Yi poets Jidi Majia, Aku Wuwu, and Bamo Qubumo of southern Sichuan. Painting, sculpture, and mural art on ethnic-minority themes are an important part of museum exhibits and public art in many cityscapes.

The growth of ethnic tourism since the late 1980s and early 1990s has had a strong impact on traditional cultures throughout China, especially in the southwest. Yunnan Province has created a highway system that links major ethnic areas such as Xishuangbanna, the Stone Forest, Shangri-la, Dali, and Chuxiong to the capital Kunming. The ancient town of Lijiang, once a major stop on trade routes to the Tibetan Plateau, is a typical ethnic-tourism site. Its old town now features hundreds of shops offering ethnic-themed costumes, jewelry, wall hangings, paintings, song and dance compact discs, and knickknacks that cater to legions of tourists from all over the world. In Black Dragon Pool Park, ethnic music and rituals of the local Naxi people are performed daily, along with demonstrations of papermaking and pictograph writing used in Naxi rituals. Ethnic-minority art and performances are also prominent on tourist itineraries along the Silk Road of northwest China and the Tibetan Plateau.

SEE ALSO *Dance; Film Industry; Folk Art; Handicrafts; Lao She; Shen Congwen; Tourism: Domestic.*

BIBLIOGRAPHY

Bender, Mark. *Butterfly Mother: Miao (Hmong) Creation Epics from Guizhou, China.* Indianapolis, IN: Hackett, 2006.

Bender, Mark. China Overview. In *The Greenwood Encyclopedia of World Folklore and Folklife*, ed. William M. Clements, Vol. 2, 211–233. Westport, CT: Greenwood Press, 2006.

Corrigan, Gina. *Miao Textiles from China.* Seattle: University of Washington Press, 2001.

Mark Bender

BAI NATIONALITY

The Bai nationality, with a population of over 1.85 million (2000 census), is the fourteenth-largest minority in China. They live primarily in the Dali Bai Autonomous Prefecture (Dali Baizu Zizhi Zhou) of Yunnan Province, but many also live elsewhere in China, as well as in Southeast Asia and further abroad for work, trade, and study.

Bai refer to themselves as "speakers of Bai," a language with three main dialects: southern (Dali), central (Jianchuan), and northern (Bijiang). The language has been classified as part of the Sino-Tibetan language family, but whether it should be further classified as part of Loloish, Lolo-Burmese, Tibeto-Burman, or Sinitic is much debated. Similar debates exist over the origins of the Bai people.

In the early 1950s, when nationality identification was under way, scholars and officials argued over six different theories concerning the Bai's origins: (1) they are Tai/Shan; (2) they are descendants of the ancient Indian ruler Aśoka (d. c. 232 BCE); (3) they came from the Diqiang of northern China; (4) they are Han; (5) they are a mixture of many groups; or (6) they are indigenous to Dali. The first two theories were quickly dismissed. Since those who promoted the sixth theory of indigeneity were local intellectuals and officials in charge of nationality work, their theory prevailed. As diverse as the theories were, and despite the fact that anthropologist Francis L. K. Hsu (1909–1999) had described elite Bai in the 1940s (then referred to as the Minjia) as "typical Chinese," no one involved with nationality-identification work at the time doubted that the Bai should be recognized as a separate nationality according to Joseph Stalin's (1879–1953) definition. The Bai were believed to have been historically constituted since the rise of the Dali-based Nanzhao kingdom in 738 CE, yet in classifying the Bai as a nationality, their language and cultural characteristics were given priority. In June 1956, the central government approved the proposal to change the name *Minjia nationality* (Minjia *zu*) to *Bai nationality* (Bai *zu*), and in November, the Dali Bai Autonomous Prefecture was founded, along with some Bai autonomous counties elsewhere.

Since Dali has been an important crossroads on the old trade routes linking Chinese, Southeast Asian, and Tibetan areas since at least the Nanzhao and Dali kingdoms (738–1253 CE), and since Dali was conquered in the Yuan (1279–1368), Ming (1368–1644), and Qing (1644–1912) dynasties, there has been much outside influence on the Bai, and, it is now generally recognized, much historical Bai intermarriage with other groups.

Bai view themselves, and are viewed by others, as one of the most acculturated to Han society, and they have been one of the most economically, educationally, and politically successful of the minority nationalities. Since the early 1990s, some elite families have begun to rewrite their genealogies, claiming that their ancestors were indigenous, not Han, as formerly claimed.

Bai villagers practice a mix of Buddhism, Daoism, Confucianism, and local deity (*M. benzhu*) worship, and Bai craftspeople are famous for their wood and marble work that decorates temples. The biggest festivals in Dali are the Third Month Fair, Raosanling (Guersala), and the Torch Festival. Matrilocal marriage has been more common among the Bai than the Han, and Bai women have been remarked upon for their physical strength and marketing savvy. The Bai are renowned for their delicious and unique foods, including fried cheese, stewed fish with sour mango, and pork tartare with chili sauce.

SEE ALSO *Identity, Chinese.*

BIBLIOGRAPHY

Baizu jianshi bianxie zu. *Baizu jianshi* [A concise history of the Bai nationality]. Kunming, PRC: Yunnan Renmin Chubanshe, 1988.

Hsu, Francis L. K. *Under the Ancestors' Shadow: Kinship, Personality, and Social Mobility in Village China*. Rev. ed. Stanford, CA: Stanford University Press, 1967.

Wiersma, Grace. Yunnan Bai. In *The Sino-Tibetan Languages*, ed. Graham Thurgood and Randy LaPolla, 651–673. London: Taylor and Francis, 2003.

Xu Wei. "Bai zu" chengwei de laili [How the name of "Bai nationality" came into being]. *Yunnan dang'an* [Yunnan archives] 3 (2006): 14.

Yang Kun et al., eds. *Yunnan Baizu de qiyuan he xingcheng lunwen ji* [A collection of essays on the origin and formation of the Bai nationality of Yunnan]. Kunming, PRC: Yunnan Renmin Chubanshe, 1957.

Zhao Yuzhong
Beth E. Notar

MOSUO AND NAXI NATIONALITIES

The Naxi (or *Na-khi*) and the Moso (or *Mosuo*, or more properly, the *Na*) are together considered one of China's fifty-six officially recognized *minzu* (nationalities/peoples). Although the Naxi and the Moso are grouped together under the single term *Naxi*, in reality the two groups self-identify as having distinct cultural, linguistic, religious, and historical traditions. As is the case for many of the other *shaoshu minzu* (minority nationalities) communities in southwest China, the historical and ongoing relationships with neighboring *shaoshu minzu* peoples were and still are often more important to the Naxi and Moso than were their relationships to the Han Chinese. Although the borders of what constitutes being Naxi are ethereal and constantly renegotiated for any given individual, the Naxi's amplifying relationship with the Han was formalized with the classification and establishment of the Naxi minority nationality in the mid-1950s. Today there are over 300,000 Naxi and over 50,000 Mosuo.

Most Naxi live in southwest China, in northwest Yunnan Province, east of the Mekong River, and into the westernmost mountains of southwest Sichuan Province. There are a few Naxi communities as far north as the Tibetan Autonomous Region, and the southern reaches of the Naxi world essentially interface with the traditional Bai region. The center of the Naxi world is today the rapidly growing Lijiang City Prefecture, with over one million inhabitants, whereas historically the Naxi considered their most sacred sites and their heartland to be the area around the town of Sanba and surrounding villages on the northeastern arms of *Haba Xueshan* (Haba Snow Mountain). The Yangzi (locally called the *Jinsha jiang*, or Gold Sand River) bends twice through the pine forests and snow mountains of the center of the region historically most populated by the Naxi, descending over 1,000 meters in altitude in fewer than 1,000 kilometers. Most Moso live in Yunnan, in the area surrounding and to the west of Lugu Lake, to the east of Naxi areas. Traditionally, most Naxi and Moso were farmers and herders.

The ancestors of the Naxi and Moso migrated down the river valleys from the Tibetan Plateau several thousand years ago, as did other speakers of (primarily the Lolo subbranch of) the Tibeto-Burman languages, such as the neighbors of the Naxi and Moso: the Rekua, Meng, Muli Tibetans, Gyalthang Tibetans, Lisu, Nosuo Yi, Bai, and Pumi *minzu*. Prior to the establishment of *bka' brgyud* (Kagyu) Tibetan Vajrayāna Buddhism in the region by the fourteenth century, the Naxi and Moso both practiced a local religion more similar to traditional Yi, northern Lisu, Bai, and Gyalthang Tibetans than to the dominant religious traditions of either the Han or the central Tibetans. Naxi and Moso religion involved local mountain gods, *ssu* (Sanskrit: *nāga*; Tibetan: *klu*; Chinese: *long*; zoomorphic serpent spirits inhabiting springs), and other spirits and demons. Their ritual experts generally were bifurcated into two dual and gendered roles, but with the advent of writing and the partial collapse of Buddhism in the region, the Naxi male ritual experts, or *dongba* (Moso: *daba*; Naxi: *dto-mba*; Yi: *bimo*), came to be dominant. Today, they are famous, and Naxi *dongba* culture lies at the heart of the tourist-driven economic boom. Following the loss of many hues of traditional religious culture before and during the decade of the Cultural Revolution (1966–1976), and with the massive influx of Han settlers and millions of tourists into the region, few Naxi today practice or believe in their religious traditions, and only about a dozen (mostly elderly) *dongba* can read the Naxi pictographic script. The Moso religious and folkloric traditions have similarly undergone profound changes from the influence of *dge lugs* (Gelug) Tibetan Buddhism and Han culture. Today, few Moso *daba* still practice their tradition within what is an ostensibly *dge lugs* Buddhist religious culture, though both traditions suffered during the Cultural Revolution. The Moso are also famous for their somewhat matrilineal kinship system, wherein women run homes of extended family and wield significant economic power, and wherein paternity is not prioritized.

SEE ALSO *Buddhism.*

BIBLIOGRAPHY

Jackson, Anthony. *Na-khi Religion: An Analytical Appraisal of Na-khi Ritual Texts*. The Hague, Netherlands: Mouton, 1979.

Mathieu, Christine. *A History and Anthropological Study of the Ancient Kingdoms of the Sino-Tibetan Borderland—Naxi and Mosuo*. Lewiston, NY: Edwin Mellen, 2003.

Mortensen, Eric D. Raven Augury in Tibet, Northwest Yunnan, Inner Asia, and Circumpolar Regions: A Study in Comparative Folklore and Religion. Ph.D. diss., Harvard University, 2003.

Oppitz, Michael, and Elizabeth Hsu, eds. *Naxi and Moso Ethnography: Kin, Rites, Pictographs*. Zürich: Völkerkundemuseum Zürich, 1998.

Rock, Joseph F. *The Ancient Na-Khi Kingdom of Southwest China*. Cambridge, MA: Harvard University Press, 1947.

Eric D. Mortensen

MISSIONARIES

The modern missions movement in China began with Protestants, influenced by the dynamism of the evangelical revival in Great Britain and the United States, traveling to the China coast, hoping for entry into China itself. In 1800 there were almost no Christian missionaries in China: The previous missionary presence, all Roman Catholic, had been banned for decades, since 1724. The European Catholic missionaries, who had nurtured the growth of a Chinese Christian community of 300,000 between about 1600 and the early 1700s, now had to sneak into China from Portuguese Macau to administer the sacraments clandestinely to the faithful, who may have still numbered 200,000. Only a handful of elderly priests in the employ of the imperial court in Beijing as technicians were permitted to be in China, and they were forbidden to preach.

THE NINETEENTH CENTURY

Robert Morrison of the London Missionary Society was the first Protestant missionary to arrive, in 1807, in the narrow corridor between Guangzhou (Canton) and Macau where foreigners were permitted. Restrictions and frustrations were the norm for the missionaries; several of them spent considerable time working with overseas Chinese in Southeast Asia, pending access to China.

In the Opium War of 1839 to 1842, the missionaries (now nearly forty Protestants) unanimously saw the British defeat of China and imposition of the "unequal treaties" with their many special privileges for foreigners (e.g., extraterritoriality) as a divine mandate to "open" China. None asked if it was appropriate for Christianity to be tied so closely to the new imperialist system of Western political and military rights in China. After a second round of war from 1858 to 1860, missionaries became an integral part of the structure of Western power in China. In fact, provisions for unrestricted travel anywhere in China, and a special protectorate over Catholic missions of any nationality taken on by the French government, ensured diplomatic intervention in missionary affairs for decades to come.

While Protestants could not go beyond five coastal cities until 1860, Catholic missionaries had already started returning to the old surviving Catholic enclaves in the 1840s. At first welcomed back by the loyal Catholic communities, in some places they behaved so high-handedly and were so dismissive of the status and role of the few Chinese priests and many lay believers who had kept these communities functioning for over a century, that some Chinese Catholics protested to the Vatican. From the reimposition at this time of the control of European missionary priests, European hegemony prevailed in the Catholic Church until well into the twentieth century.

As late as 1860, there were still only about one hundred Protestant missionaries present in China. Dramatic increases in the number and variety of Protestant missionaries came after 1860. One trend was the proliferation of denominational missionary societies. Before the 1850s, Protestant personnel came largely from the two national interdenominational mission sending agencies, the London Missionary Society and the American Board of Commissioners for Foreign Missions. After 1860, these were joined by many denominational American societies, including both northern and southern Presbyterians and Methodists, and a few British dissenting groups, including the Wesleyan Methodists and British Baptists, in addition to the long-standing Church Missionary Society (Anglican). Hudson Taylor's (1832–1905) China Inland Mission began in the 1860s, structured as a "faith mission," that is, independent of any denominational control and entirely dependent on private contributions. Less than a half century after the breakthrough to the interior of China enabled by the 1858–1860 treaties, there were almost 3,500 Protestant missionaries from more than one hundred societies in China, over eight hundred alone from the China Inland Mission, which eschewed schools and hospitals and stressed evangelizing the hinterlands of the interior.

Between 1860 and 1905, several different missionary strategies were used in China. Many Protestants engaged in less direct evangelism and more medical and educational institution-building in urban areas, especially schools from the elementary level all the way (eventually, in the early twentieth century) to the collegiate level. Other Protestants, such as the China Inland Mission, continued a strong emphasis on preaching and religious conversion to Christianity. Catholic missionaries, who supervised many cohesive rural and semirural Catholic communities, also sought the creation of new communities by evangelism. As of 1905, there were about one million Chinese Catholics served by about 1,400 foreign Catholic priests, monks, and nuns who were members of religious orders and perhaps 250,000 Chinese Protestants served by nearly 3,500 missionaries.

Activities of a French missionary school, Shenyang, Liaoning province, 1911. *After the Opium Wars, Western missionaries enjoyed new access to China after decades of suppression by the Qing dynasty. At the beginning of the twentieth century, many Chinese looked to the missionaries for support in modernizing China, primarily through the education of a new generation according to Western standards.* BRANGER/ROGER VIOLLET/GETTY IMAGES

During these decades of the late nineteenth century, there were both positive and negative aspects of the foreign missionaries' residence and work in China. Underlying every development, however, was the bedrock reality of the legally privileged position of all missionaries in China—the fact that local or national Chinese authorities were unable to restrain their behavior or to control them in any way whatsoever. One of the most unfortunate recurring events was the series of *jiaoan* ("missionary cases") in this period. These were local riots or acts of violence perpetrated by commoners against foreign missionaries and their homes, chapels, churches, and schools, and sometimes against Chinese converts and their property. Often this violence was fomented by the traditional elite class, the "scholar-official" class or the "gentry." This class, though only 1 to 2 percent of the population, was educated, successful in the civil service examination system, and made up of self-conscious guardians of Confucian orthodoxy. Throughout the century, they regarded Christianity as a mortal threat to Chinese culture and traditional society, and the missionaries as threats to their own status as elites. This is not entirely surprising. Only a few years earlier, in the 1850s and 1860s, the Taiping Uprising, a movement originating in Christian ideas, attempted to overthrow the Qing dynasty (1644–1912) and replace it with an anti-Confucian and apparently Christian theocracy that would eliminate the old gentry class. The Taipings devastated the Lower Yangzi Valley, with twenty million or more deaths. The memory of the quasi-Christian Taipings hung heavy over the missionaries as an obstacle to their work until the end of the century.

Missionaries, withal, expanded the church in China in the late nineteenth century, and built some sound institutional foundations. Historians in China today especially note the modern education offered to both boys and girls in the mission schools, and the wider scope for recognition of a positive role for women in the churches. Yet with the exception of a handful (such as Timothy Richard [1845–1919] and Gilbert Reid [1857–1927]), missionaries remained on poor terms with officialdom and the scholar-official elite through century's end. This was manifested in the dramatic Boxer Uprising of 1900 in North China, a popular antiforeign mass movement aided and abetted by the imperial government, which killed hundreds of foreigners, almost all of them missionaries, as well as perhaps thirty thousand Chinese Christians.

THE TWENTIETH CENTURY

After the Boxer tragedy, which ended in China's humiliation under foreign military occupation, few would have thought that a "golden age" of missions was at hand. But China's sharp turn toward intellectual and political reform after 1900 elevated Chinese thinkers and officials who admired missionaries and wanted to emulate the Western nations' experience of national modernization. They saw Christianity as part of this Westernization, and this raised the influence of many missionaries, especially Protestants, who were active in education, health care, or social work. YMCAs and YWCAs became popular, and missionaries were active in reform projects, such as the anti-footbinding movement and the movement to eradicate the cultivation and importation of opium. Protestant prestige was never higher. When the Qing dynasty finally fell in 1912, a Christian, Sun Yat-sen (Sun Yixian or Sun Zhongshan), was the first president of the Republic of China. Protestant missions increased in personnel to eight thousand in 1925, their all-time high point. The missionary colleges, now thirteen of them, were models of modern education. And converts numbered a half million by the mid-1920s.

It appeared that missionaries were riding the wave of the future in China. Riding it with them were their Chinese protégés, a new generation of Chinese Christian leaders, well-educated (many with doctorates in theology or philosophy from the United States), dynamic, and articulate. Examples abound: Zhao Zichen (1888–1979), theologian; Cheng Jingyi (1881–1939), ecumenical church leader; Wu Yifang (1893–1985), the first Chinese woman college president; and Yu Rizhang (David Yui, 1882–1936), YMCA leader. These bright lights had more responsibility and visibility than their nineteenth-century forebears, and in fact shared in the leadership of what might be called the "Sino-foreign Protestant establishment." Chinese were actually a majority of those attending the great China Christian Conference of 1922, which created the National Christian Council and the Church of Christ in China, all Sino-foreign ecumenical monuments.

In fact, however, missionaries still held the real power, especially financial power. They failed to take advantage of this period when Christianity enjoyed a favorable image to permit a true "Chinese" church to emerge from the mission structures. In retrospect, this was their one historical opportunity to do so, and they did not seize it. Catholic missionaries were yet more openly jealous of European power in the mission than were Protestants. The European hierarchy in China was remarkably slow to ordain Chinese priests and give them real responsibility. Only vigorous intervention by the Vatican brought about, in 1926, the consecration of the first Chinese bishops since the 1680s.

Beneath the Protestant missionaries' radar screens were some new factors, now recognizable as harbingers of the future. By the 1920s were emerging new Christian movements that were out of missionary control or even influence. These independent churches, including the True Jesus Church, the Jesus Family, the movement led by Watchman Nee (Ni Tuosheng, 1903–1972) called "The Little Flock," and others, were outlets for Chinese talent that could not easily develop in the Sino-foreign world of the Protestant "establishment."

Due to the successes of the early twentieth century, many new missionaries came to China, including independent "faith missionaries" and those sent by new mission societies, often Holiness or Pentecostal in theology. Americans outstripped the British in personnel, as well as in financial support. But even as missionary numbers reached their highest level, eight thousand, in 1925, forces were brewing that would put an end to the missionary era in China. An increasingly powerful mass nationalism developed an active hostility to the position of Western imperialism. Its proponents lumped missionaries in with other "imperialists," and launched campaigns, some violent, against all foreigners in China. Almost all Protestant missionaries fled to the coast or went home in the late 1920s, and missionary numbers never were so high again. After this shock, in the 1930s the worldwide Great Depression decimated the budgets of the denominational mission societies, and more missionaries left. Yet more went when the Sino-Japanese War erupted in 1937, although many stayed at their posts and faithfully served as best they could. Some of those who stayed in the late 1930s were interned by the Japanese after the Pacific War began at the end of 1941; others retreated to the West with those Chinese still resisting the Japanese.

After Japan's defeat in 1945, even as many missionaries were returning to China in 1946 and 1947, China was plunging into civil war. Most missionaries, although bothered by the corruption and ineffectiveness of the Chinese Nationalist government, supported it against the Communists, partly because its leader, Chiang Kai-shek (Jiang Jieshi), was a Christian. Although the Communists won the civil war in 1949, many Protestant missionaries hoped that they could continue to serve in the new state established in late 1949. Catholics were more uniformly hostile to the new state, and were, in fact, ordered by the Vatican on the authority of the pope and under threat of excommunication not to cooperate with the Communist authorities. The opinions and hopes of foreign missionaries made no difference in the end. All missionaries, except for a handful who were imprisoned, were expelled from China during 1951 and 1952. Thus ended the century and a half of the modern missions movement in China (though several hundred resettled in Taiwan after 1949).

There are varied opinions about missionaries in China today. A few still endorse the claim first advanced in the 1920s that missionaries served the interests of the imperialist system in China. But since the 1980s, it has been increasingly common for Chinese of all walks of life to credit missionaries with bringing much good to China. Chinese alumni of Christian schools proudly display their diplomas. Perhaps most interesting of all, the Christian church has exploded in size and energy and is now probably fifteen to twenty times larger than it was when the missionaries left more than half a century ago.

SEE ALSO *Anti-Christian/Anti-Missionary Movements; Boxer Uprising; Catholicism; Education: Women's Education; Morrison, Robert; Protestantism.*

BIBLIOGRAPHY

Austin, Alvyn. *China's Millions: The China Inland Mission and Late Qing Society, 1832–1905.* Grand Rapids, MI: Eerdmans, 2007.

Bays, Daniel H., ed. *Christianity in China: From the Eighteenth Century to the Present.* Stanford, CA: Stanford University Press, 1996.

Fairbank, John K., ed. *The Missionary Enterprise in China and America.* Cambridge, MA: Harvard University Press, 1974.

Hyatt, Irwin T., Jr. *Our Ordered Lives Confess: Three Nineteenth-Century American Missionaries in East Shantung.* Cambridge, MA: Harvard University Press, 1976.

Latourette, Kenneth S. *A History of Christian Missions in China.* New York: Macmillan, 1929.

Lutz, Jessie G. *China and the Christian Colleges, 1850–1950.* Ithaca, NY: Cornell University Press, 1971.

West, Philip. *Yenching University and Sino-Western Relations, 1916–1952.* Cambridge, MA: Harvard University Press, 1976.

Xi Lian. *The Conversion of Missionaries: Liberalism in American Protestant Missions in China, 1907–1932.* University Park: Pennsylvania State University Press, 1997.

Yao Xiyi (Kevin Xiyi Yao). *The Fundamentalist Movement among Protestant Missionaries in China, 1920–1937.* Lanham, MD: University Press of America, 2003.

Daniel H. Bays

MO YAN
1955–

No literate Chinese and few foreigners who read about China will be unfamiliar with the name Mo Yan, having likely read his 1985 novel *Red Sorghum: A Novel of China* (*Hong gao liang jia zu*) or seen the 1987 Zhang Yimou movie based on the book. Widely referred to as post-Mao China's breakthrough novel, it was one of the most influential works from what is now referred to as the root-searching (Xungen) era, a period of exploration into the question of "Chineseness" by aspiring writers who had recently emerged from the catastrophic decade of the Cultural Revolution (1966–1976). As with nearly all his subsequent novels, *Red Sorghum* is set in the author's hometown of northeast Gaomi Township in Shandong Province, which has gained the sort of recognition afforded Yoknapatawpha County, the fictional locale of many novels by William Faulkner, Mo Yan's favorite Western author. After the groundbreaking effort of *Red Sorghum*, Mo Yan published prolifically. The quality and diversity of his fictional output, by any literary and popular measure, are extraordinary.

In 1988 Mo Yan followed *Red Sorghum* with *The Garlic Ballads* (*Tian tang suan tai zhi ge*), a passionate exposé of a heart of darkness represented by corrupt, venal local officials. It was removed from bookstore shelves during the 1989 Tiananmen Incident for fear that it might further incite the demonstrators. He then published the most uproarious and biting satire in the history of modern Chinese literature, *The Republic of Wine* (*Jiu guo*, 1992). In the style of the sixteenth-century French satirist François Rabelais, Mo Yan parodies unsavory aspects of Chinese society, including cannibalism and an obsession with food and alcohol as cultural commodities.

These and other early novels differ in style, content, and effects. Mo Yan has undertaken the ambitious project of chronicling twentieth-century Chinese history in blockbuster novels. *Big Breasts and Wide Hips* (*Fengru feitun*, 1996), narrated by the only son in a family of eight children, is by turns a brutally funny and graphically violent romp through the first half of the twentieth century and a bit beyond. His novel *Life and Death Are Wearing Me Out* (*Sheng si pi lao*, 2006), narrates the second half of the century, with all its tragic absurdities, and puts a human face on the Chinese revolution, replete with the dark humor, metafictional insertions, and fantasies that characterize Mo Yan's literary terrain.

Mo Yan is a master of diverse styles and forms—fable, magic realism (*Red Sorghum* is often compared to *One Hundred Years of Solitude*, by the Colombian writer Gabriel García Márquez), hard-core realism, and postmodernism. With striking imagery and richly appealing characters, his tales bewitch the reader. His literary stature, domestic and international, has been affirmed by numerous prizes and awards, critical acclaim, and a devoted readership.

SEE ALSO *Film Industry: Fifth Generation Filmmakers; Literature since 1800; Root-Searching Literature.*

BIBLIOGRAPHY

WORKS BY MO YAN IN ENGLISH TRANSLATION

Red Sorghum: A Novel of China. Trans. Howard Goldblatt. New York: Viking, 1993.

The Garlic Ballads. Trans. Howard Goldblatt. New York: Viking, 1995.

The Republic of Wine. Trans. Howard Goldblatt. New York: Arcade Publishing, 2000.

Shifu, You'll Do Anything for a Laugh. (Short stories.) Trans. Howard Goldblatt. New York: Arcade Publishing, 2001.

Big Breasts and Wide Hips. Trans. Howard Goldblatt. New York: Arcade Publishing, 2002.

Life and Death Are Wearing Me Out. Trans. Howard Goldblatt. New York: Arcade Publishing, 2008.

WORKS ON MO YAN

World Literature Today 74, 3 (Summer 2000), special issue. See Mo Yan, "My Three American Books," 473–476; Howard Goldblatt, "Forbidden Food: The 'Saturnicon' of Mo Yan," 477–485; David Der-wei Wang, "The Literary World of Mo Yan," 487–494; Shelley W. Chan, "From Fatherland to Motherland: On Mo Yan's *Red Sorghum* and *Big Breasts and Full Hips*," 495–500; M. Thomas Inge, "Mo Yan through Western Eyes," 501–506.

Howard Goldblatt

MODEL OPERAS AND BALLETS

During the decade of the Cultural Revolution (Wenhua dageming, 1966–1976), a period of strict censorship, Jiang Qing (1914–1991) spearheaded a collection of authorized performances known as model theater. The third wife of Mao Zedong and a member of the Gang of Four, Jiang was one of the most influential women figures in the People's Republic of China until the end of the Cultural Revolution. She began her career as an actress on stage and screen under the stage name Lan Ping in the 1930s. In 1963 she began promoting a new form of theater that combined Beijing opera (*jingju*) and ballet to dramatize proletarian themes. With Mao's support, she engaged in an attack on the Chinese intelligentsia that culminated in the Cultural Revolution, thereby profoundly altering China's cultural life.

The revolutionary model theater (*geming yangbanxi*) emerged as a state-endorsed, popular form of entertainment and propaganda tool, with class struggle as its central theme. These dramas featured dogmatic language, idealized circumstances, and idealized larger-than-life heroes and heroines. Performances of ballet dramas, such as *The White-Haired Girl* and *The Red Detachment of Women*, incorporated the highly symbolic body language of Beijing opera and ballet in revised and expanded form. Rigid plot structures and oral exchanges were supplemented by contemporary costumes, choreography, and exaggerated gestures. Performances were filmed for national release, creating models for filmmaking. The Beijing operas include *Shajiabang, The Red Lantern, Taking Tiger Mountains by Strategy, On the Docks, Raid on the White Tiger Regiment, Azalea Mountain*, and *The Song of the Dragon River*. *Shajiabang* was also performed as a symphony. The creation of the revolutionary model operas and ballets, which dominated Chinese stage and screen for a decade, was nothing less than a nationwide movement of theatrical experiment in China underwritten by the government. Following the success of the initial eight works promoted by the Chinese Communist Party in the spring and summer of 1967, Jiang Qing endorsed another ten revolutionary model works, known as the "second group," including the Beijing operas *Hongyu Hills* and *Boulder Bay*, piano concerto *Yellow River*, and ballet *Song of Nimeng Mountain*. Between 1976 and 1990, model theater was itself censored by the government when political correctness was redefined.

Model operas and ballets celebrated the victories of the revolution of the Chinese Communist Party and projected a bright future in the light of socialist ideology. One of the most important aesthetic principles of model operas and ballets is the polarizing "three prominences" approach (*san tuchu*): giving prominence to the most positive among all the characters; among the positive, to the heroic; and among the heroic, to the principal hero or heroine. The central character often functions as a symbol of his or her class.

Advocates for the model theater believed that the genre was exemplary in its reformation of existing performance practices and popular dramatic works of Beijing opera to meet the revolutionary ideals stated in Mao Zedong's 1942 "Talks at the Yan'an Forum on Literature and Art." Model operas and ballets were given the mission to educate the proletarian masses about the revolutionary cause and to indoctrinate them by presenting an idealized version of revolutionary history and class struggle. Thus model operas and ballets rehash revolutionary events and legends in oversimplified story lines and symbolic characters. *Taking Tiger Mountain by Strategy* (*Zhiqu Weihushan*), based on a play premiered in 1958 by the Shanghai Beijing Opera Theater, focuses on the war of liberation (1946–1949) and Yang Zirong, a People's Liberation Army scout. *The Red Lantern* (*Hongdeng ji*) is set during the war of resistance (1937–1945) against Japan.

Another prominent feature of model theater is a form of feminism that desexualizes the female body. For example, one of the most popular pieces, *The White-Haired Girl*, excises the rape and pregnancy of the peasant girl Xi'er from the 1945 script on which the ballet is based. The romantic relationship between Xi'er and Wang Dachun is also overshadowed, if not replaced, by brotherly love between fellow soldiers. Xi'er joins the Eighth Route Army and liberates the villagers from the throes of their evil landlord and Japanese invaders. Similarly, *The Red Detachment of Women* (*Hongse niangzi jun*), which was performed for U.S. President Richard Nixon during his visit to China in 1972, portrays the journey of a peasant's daughter from suffering at the hands of a despotic landlord to leadership of the Communist proletarian force of "Red Women" in the 1930s. In these plays class as a social category supplants gender or personal identity as the single most important defining factor in interpersonal relationships. Stripped of most feminine qualities (and the traditionally defined roles of daughter, wife, or mother), these heroines play the roles of fighters and military leaders. The heroic, gender-neutral, female characters are not intended to be sexually attractive; they rise to the challenges of class struggle by virtue of their new masculine identities.

Many in China argued that the model operas and ballets were created to satisfy Jiang's eccentric taste in Beijing opera. Despite their historically specific political messages, after the 1990s these productions gained renewed popularity for their nostalgic value.

SEE ALSO *Cultural Revolution, 1966–1969; Dance; Peking Opera and Regional Operas.*

BIBLIOGRAPHY

Clark, Paul. *The Chinese Cultural Revolution: A History*. Cambridge, U.K.: Cambridge University Press, 2008.

Huang, Alexander C. Y. Site-Specific Readings: Confucian Temple, Labor Camp, and Soviet-Chinese Theater. In his *Chinese Shakespeares: Two Centuries of Cultural Exchange,* 125–164. New York: Columbia University Press, 2009.

Mittler, Barbara. Cultural Revolution Model Works and the Politics of Modernization in China: An Analysis of *Taking Tiger Mountain by Strategy*. *World of Music* 45, 2 (2003): 53–81.

Roberts, Rosemary. From Zheng Qiang to Jiang Shuiying: The Feminization of a Revolutionary Hero in Maoist Theater's *Song of the Dragon River*. *Asian Theater Journal* 23, 2 (Fall 2006): 265–291.

Xiaomei Chen. *Acting the Right Part: Political Theater and Popular Drama in Contemporary China*. Honolulu: University of Hawai'i Press, 2002.

Alexander C. Y. Huang

MODERNIST ART OF THE 1920s AND 1930s

The paths by which Western styles of painting entered China naturally affected the Chinese art world's initial responses to them. In the early twentieth century one could study Western art in art schools in or near China's treaty ports, primarily Shanghai and Guangzhou. The next step for the adventurous aspiring artist would be study abroad. The majority of Chinese painters seeking to learn modern Western styles traveled to Japan, which offered the easiest access for Chinese students to modern science and culture, and, in that period, had a written language and Confucian culture that Chinese students could understand.

Beginning in the first decade of the twentieth century, successive waves of Chinese artists studied in Japan. One of the most influential such artists was Li Shutong (1880–1942), who studied at the Tokyo School of Fine Arts between 1905 and 1910. Upon his return, Li Shutong established a Western-style art curriculum modeled on that of the Tokyo School at the Zhejiang First Normal School in Hangzhou, which opened in 1912. A second wave of artists studied at the Tokyo School of Fine Arts and Kawabata Painting School in Tokyo roughly between 1915 and 1920. Among them were Chen Baoyi (1893–1945), Ni Yide (1901–1970), Guan Liang (1900–1986), Zhu Qizhan (1892–1996), and Guan Zilan (1903–1985).

Modern Western art also entered China directly from Europe, via the artists who studied in France, particularly in Paris. One of the most influential sources of French modernist styles was the prestigious Hangzhou National Art Academy, established in 1928 and headed by the French-trained Lin Fengmian (1900–1991). A proponent of individual creativity and modern styles, he assembled a like-minded faculty, including teachers from France and other countries, to create a lively, free-thinking academic atmosphere. The academically oriented artist who wielded the greatest influence in China was Xu Beihong (1895–1953). He was dispatched to Europe on a government scholarship in 1919 and spent eight years in France and Germany mastering an exquisitely detailed style of drawing and a highly romantic manner of oil painting. Upon his return to China, his oil-painting style softened and began to blend different elements in a quasi-impressionist style.

Although modernism may have had limited impact on the Chinese art world as a whole, in the late 1920s and early 1930s it enjoyed great popularity among artists in China's urban centers, particularly Shanghai, Hangzhou, and Guangzhou, and permeated the worlds of design, publishing, and architecture. This growing enthusiasm for modernism led to the formation of two art societies, the Storm Society and Chinese Independent Artists Association, in the early 1930s. Their activities formed the first Western-style avant-garde movement in Chinese history.

THE STORM SOCIETY

Pang Xunqin (1906–1985) had gone to Paris at the age of nineteen to study modernist styles at the Académie Julien. After his return to China five years later, he established a small modernist salon, and by 1931 had linked up with Ni Yide (1901–1970), who had been exposed to the Japanese avant-garde while studying at the Kawabata Academy in Tokyo in 1927 and 1928. They formed a Shanghai-based avant-garde and took the name Julanshe ("great wave"), which they rendered in English as the Storm Society. As Wang Jiyuan (1893–1975), one of the group's members, wrote, "we want to hit the rotten art of contemporary China with a powerful wave" (Wang Jiyuan, "Juelan [Storm] duanhe," *Yishu xunkan*, vol. no. 5 [Oct. 11, 1932], p. 10.).

Under the leadership of Pang and Ni, the group assembled like-minded young artists for a series of four exhibitions held in the first half of the 1930s. The first exhibition was held from October 9 to 16, 1932, at the China Society for the Study of Art in Shanghai's French concession. Works were exhibited in a variety of styles that reflected modernist currents in Europe, from post-impressionism and fauvism to cubism and the more avant-garde surrealism. The exhibitions were well received by the Shanghai art world, with special features published in pictorial magazines such as *Liangyou* (Young Companion), *Shidai* (Modern Miscellany), and newspapers of the day. The group's goal seems to have been to display work that reflected the many schools of painting then flourishing in Europe. In this they were successful, for the paintings that were reproduced in periodicals show a varied and more up-to-date range of artistic styles than was typical of earlier exhibitions.

Many of the society's works, including Ni Yide's, initially resembled European postimpressionist paintings. All the members strove to break through the barriers of representation. Pang Xunqin himself experimented with what he called "decorations," usually fragmented images of urban life, some of which comment on the modern condition. The Storm Society's only exhibition prize was awarded to a woman painter, Qiu Di (1906–1958), who had painted a highly stylized still life with red leaves and green flowers for the second group exhibition. The painting, published in 1933, apparently drew enough criticism from the realist camp that Ni Yide felt compelled to defend it in an article published the following year. Qiu Di had graduated from Shanghai Art Academy in 1928, then studied in Tokyo, and finally returned to Shanghai Art Academy as a graduate student in 1931. In the third exhibition she presented a crisply painted modern still life that demonstrated her interest in the formal beauty of everyday objects, many of which, such as a percolator and thermos bottle, were products of modern industrial manufacture.

THE CHINESE INDEPENDENT ART ASSOCIATION

The Chinese Independent Art Association was initiated in Tokyo in 1934 by a group of Chinese students. The founders included Liang Xihong (1912–1982), Zhao Shou (1912–2003), Li Zhongsheng (1912–1984), Li Dongping, Fang Rending (1901–1975), and Su Wonong. In that year the association held an exhibition called "Ten Chinese Painters in Japan." The works displayed in the show were for the most part in the styles of fauvism, surrealism, and cubism. Most members of the Chinese Independent Art Association returned to China in 1935. In February, Liang Xihong, Zhao Shou, Li Dongping, and Zeng Ming rejoined them in Guangzhou and decided to reorganize the association under the same name. In 1935 they published a journal for the association, *Duli Meishu* (Independent art).

The first exhibition of the Chinese Independent Art Association was held in the Guangzhou Education Center from March 16 to 25, 1935. Most of the paintings on display manifested modernist tendencies, including paintings with fauvist and surrealist styles. Some artists who were not members of the group but were active in Guangzhou, such as Ding Yanyong, Wu Wan, and Guan Liang, also participated in this show. Several Japanese painters, such as Senoo Masahiko (1901–1990) and Miyajima Saichirō (d. 1961) also participated in the exhibition. The second exhibition of the Chinese Independent Art Association, which included about sixty works and was held at the Chinese Literature and Art Society in Shanghai in October 1935, coincided with the Storm Society's fourth exhibition. This conjunction in schedules quickened the art world's interest in modernist art.

THE MODERNIST IDEAL VS. NATIONAL REALITIES

To the artists in both groups, modernism was a synonym for individuality. These artists were extremely enthusiastic about introducing Western modernist art to Chinese audiences, and especially advocated fauvist and surrealist art. Liang Xihong was the editor of two magazines, *Xin Meishu* (New art) and *Meishu Zazhi* (Art magazine), and wrote articles and criticism for other art journals, tirelessly explaining Western modern art to Chinese readers. Zeng Ming and Li Dongping edited and published an art journal, *Xiandai Meishu* (Modern art). Zeng Ming also edited a series of books titled *Xiandai Shijie Minghua Ji* (Master paintings of the modern world).

The six group exhibitions in quick succession between 1932 and 1935 prompted excitement in the Chinese art world as, for the first time, an innovative school of oil painting flourished simultaneously in China and in the West. China at the time, however, lacked the internal factors necessary for the growth of modern art. For one thing, it did not have the prerequisites for a modern industrial civilization. For another, it had not experienced the course of development from realism to antirealism that occurred in the art world of Europe; indeed, traditional values in art remained strong, and even most intellectuals, presumed to be open to new ideas, resisted modern art.

Furthermore, in the history of China, with its Confucian legacy, a strong and widespread consciousness of national peril inevitably became the social responsibility of intellectuals. Artists in twentieth-century China were looked upon not only as skilled artisans but also as intellectuals who must take the responsibility to rescue the country from national crisis. Therefore, as the Second Sino-Japanese War (1937–1945) began, bringing chaos to Chinese politics and society in general, Chinese intellectuals' greatest concern was to help the Chinese people. Modernism, with its strong focus on the individual imagination, became a luxury in the minds of all but a few Chinese. Art that manifested the slightest tendency toward modernism was regarded by Communists or Nationalists alike as displaying a "formalism" that was divorced from the people. It was impossible for the modernist artists, whose ultimate goal was individuality and pure art, to escape the heavy burden of social responsibility that required using their art as a means to rescue the country. Unwillingly, or possibly willingly, they accepted the dispersal of the avant-garde groups as fate.

Thus the first modernist art movement in China existed for about half a decade. Yet the modernist ambitions and vital energy of the artists of the Storm Society and the Chinese Independent Art Association have inspired a subsequent generation as it has sought to join the international art world.

SEE ALSO *Art Schools and Colleges; Art, Japanese Influence on; Li Hua; Lin Fengmian; New Print Movement; Pang Xunqin; Pictorial Magazines since 1880; Women in the Visual Arts; Xu Beihong.*

BIBLIOGRAPHY

Andrews, Julia, and Kuiyi Shen. *A Century in Crisis: Modernity and Tradition in the Art of Twentieth-Century China.* New York: Guggenheim Museum, 1998.

Croizier, Ralph. Post-Impressionists in Pre-War Shanghai: The Juelanshe (Storm Society) and the Fate of Modernism in Republican China. In *Modernity in Asian Art*, ed. John Clark,135–154. Sydney, Australia: Wild Peony, 1993.

Danzker, Jo-Anne Birnie, Ken Lum, Zheng Shengtian, eds. *Shanghai Modern, 1919–1945.* Ostfildern-Ruit, Germany: Hatje Cantz, 2004.

Pang Xunqin and Schudy. Nanjing: Jiangsu Education Publishing House, 2006.

Sullivan, Michael. *Art and Artists of Twentieth-Century China.* Berkeley: University of California Press, 1996.

Kuiyi Shen

MONEY AND BANKING, 1800–1949

Although China was a pioneer in the use of money and of paper representatives for money values, modern banks arrived there only at the end of the nineteenth century in the waning years of the Qing—and last—dynasty (1644–1912). It was then that, as part of an overall effort at modernization, Chinese officials and financiers founded banks based on Western models.

The financial system plays a critically important role in the activities of all economies. Without some form of capital and credit markets, societies are limited to little more than barter economies. Banking is the business of dealing with money and credit transactions. There is evidence of the beginning of banking activities in China as early as 2,000 years ago. By the Song dynasty (960–1279), Chinese financial institutions were already conducting all major banking functions, including deposits, loans, issuance of notes, and the exchange and long-distance remittance of money.

The Chinese term for bank is *yinhang*: *Yin* means silver, China's major currency until the 1930s; *hang* is a business institution larger than a small retail shop. When first used in the Tang dynasty (618–907), the term *yinhang* meant the guild of silversmiths or the market of silver traders. In the 1860s a Chinese-English dictionary adopted *yinhang* to refer to modern Western-style banks, to differentiate them from traditional Chinese financial institutions. The latter included "official money shops" (*guanyinhao*), silver smelter, retail finance stores, and especially *piaohao* and *qianzhuang*.

Piaohao (literally, "ticket store") first began as a method used by Shanxi Province's Xiyucheng Dye Company to transfer cash between its branches, often separated by hundreds of miles. China's primitive transportation system made cash transfers both expensive and dangerous, especially in rural areas prone to banditry. Instead of actual cash transfers, Xiyucheng devised a clever method whereby a branch manager would issue a paper draft that could be redeemed for cash in another branch. Other merchants soon asked Xiyucheng for the same service. In 1823 the company's remittance business had become so popular that its owner gave up the dye business altogether and reorganized his company into a special remittance firm named Rishengchang Piaohao.

In the 1860s the spread of unrest from the Taiping Uprising (1851–1864) led the Qing government to authorize provincial officials to use *piaohao* to remit their taxes. Gradually, *piaohao*'s government services expanded to the collection of taxes, managing foreign loans for provincial authorities, issuing notes, and advancing funds to officials. By the end of the nineteenth century, before modern banking was introduced, China's domestic remittances were the monopoly of a total of thirty-two *piaohao* with 475 branches, located mainly in the Yellow River valley.

Independent of the network of *piaohao* were small local banks called *qianzhuang* (money manor), which first came into existence well before 1776 in Shanghai. Whereas *piaohao* focused on government services and interprovincial remittances, and had high officials and big merchants as their main customers, *qianzhuang* were friendly neighborhood banks with fewer than 5,000 taels of silver in capital, serving the local business community. A customer could even knock at the door of his local *qianzhuang* at midnight for an emergency loan. In the late 1860s, as China was forced by the Western powers to open itself to the world, foreign and domestic trade burgeoned, resulting in a partnership between foreign banks and *qianzhuang*. The latter received promissory notes called *chaipiao* (chop loans) from the foreign banks, and then lent this money to Chinese merchants who used it to purchase goods from foreign firms. By the end of the nineteenth century there were 10,000 *qianzhuang* in China, concentrated in the south in the Yangzi Delta region.

As China's import and export trade grew, there was increasing need for specialized credit institutions as intermediaries between Western and Chinese merchants. Foreign banks quickly filled that void, the first being the British-Indian joint venture Oriental Bank. Other British banks followed, including the Hong Kong and Shanghai Banking Corporation (Huifeng Yinhang), which became the largest foreign bank in China.

For many years British banks enjoyed a virtual monopoly on modern banking in China. Then came other foreign banks, such as France's Comptoir d'Escompte de Paris and Banque de L'Indo-Chine, Germany's Deutsche Bank and Deutsch-Asiatische Bank, Japan's Yokohama Specie Bank, Ltd., and Russia's Russo-Asiatic Bank. Many went out of business after a brief period in operation, leaving nine foreign banks with forty-five branches in China's treaty ports at the end of the nineteenth century.

Unrestricted by the Chinese government's regulations by virtue of the Western powers' extraterritorial rights, foreign banks completely controlled China's international remittance and foreign trade financing. They also conducted other banking businesses—issuing banknotes, accepting deposits from Chinese citizens, and making loans to *qianzhuang*. The power of foreign banks greatly increased when the moribund Qing regime borrowed heavily from them to pay military expenses and war indemnities. The government had contracted its first foreign debt in 1853, followed by forty-three more loans totaling 64 million yuan from foreign banks and syndicates between 1853 and 1894. Between 1895 and 1896 the government borrowed another 350 million yuan to pay the Sino-Japanese War indemnities. As guarantees for the loans, special taxes or revenues were earmarked, which greatly compromised China's sovereignty and autonomy.

At the end of the nineteenth century the Chinese financial market was almost evenly divided among foreign banks, *piaohao*, and *qianzhuang*, which acted as "three kingdoms" that complemented and cooperated with each other. Foreign banks dominated the financing of China's import and export trade; *piaohao* monopolized the domestic remittance business; *qianzhuang* controlled the credit market for domestic trade throughout China.

THE BEGINNING OF MODERN CHINESE BANKS

On May 27, 1897, China's first modern bank, the Imperial Bank of China (IBC), opened in Shanghai. Chinese nationalism was the main reason for its creation. By that time, the Qing regime's coffers were depleted and its political legitimacy in tatters. Increasing numbers of Chinese intellectuals and officials recognized that China's very survival was imperiled if it did not modernize. The creation of modern Chinese banks was understood to be a critical component of economic modernization. As IBC founder Sheng Xuanhuai (1844–1916) said, "China would not be rich and strong without promoting modern industry; and modern industry would not be promoted without reforming China's financial institutions. … Should China not establish its own bank, [foreign powers] would seize all China's profit and power" (Linsun Cheng 2003, p. 24).

Established by a special imperial edict with the largest amount of capital a Chinese financial institution had ever possessed, the IBC was organized as a joint-stock firm for which shareholders assumed limited liability. Because China lacked modern banking skills, the IBC hired foreigners to staff its top positions, beginning with the British banker Andrew W. Maitland (1853–1906) as its first general manager. The Qing government granted the bank special protection and privileges, including the right to coin currency and issue paper notes. Chinese banknotes eventually replaced foreign banknotes in most of the country. The IBC also made loans to foreign trade firms and to develop a modern infrastructure of railway, steam navigation, telegraph, and iron and textile industries.

By the end of 1899 the IBC had branches in Hankou, Beijing, Tianjin, Canton, Fuzhou, Zhenjiang, Yantai, Shantou, Hong Kong, Baoding, and Chongqing. Both its deposits and loans increased 50 percent in only two years. But the Boxer Uprising broke out just as the bank's business was booming. Its Beijing and Tianjin branches were plundered and burned. Before the bank could recover, it was plunged into another crisis when Japanese-counterfeited IBC banknotes appeared in Shanghai. The resultant bank run on February 6 to 7, 1903—the first in the history of modern Chinese banking—inflicted nearly irreparable harm on the IBC's credit and reputation. The IBC also made the mistake of focusing only on the business of official remittances instead of attracting deposits from the general public. For all these reasons, the IBC never did become the engine of China's modernization.

In 1903 the Qing court conceded that dramatic reforms were needed if the dynasty were to survive. One reform was the creation of a central bank, Daqing Bank (DB). DB took over *piaohao*'s government tax remittance business and other official transactions, including the transfer of the Salt Surplus Tax, the government's diplomatic expenditures, the management of foreign loans, the payment of foreign indemnities, and the deposit and transfer of the customs tax in treaty ports. In just six years, DB's loans and deposits increased five and seven times, respectively, resulting in an annual stockholders' return of 13 to 34 percent.

The Qing government also undertook other banking initiatives. It founded the Bank of Communications (BOCO) in 1908; urged local officials to create or reorganize official silver shops into modern banks; encouraged citizens to create private banks; promulgated regulations giving banks legal status; and took all modern banks under its protection. Sichuan, Guangxi, Guizhou, and Zhejiang founded their own provincial banks. In all, eleven of the seventeen banks that appeared during the Qing dynasty were initiated by central and provincial governments as official or official-private joint ventures. Among the private banks founded by Chinese entrepreneurs were Xincheng Bank, National Commercial Bank, and the Ningbo Commercial and Savings Bank.

REPUBLICAN CHINA

In 1911 a revolution led to the collapse of the Qing dynasty. In the years after, the budding Chinese banking system experienced both boom and bust.

World War I (1914–1918) was a boon to Chinese industries and banks. Distracted and burdened by war, Western powers could not adequately supply consumer goods to the Chinese market. Chinese manufacturing industries quickly seized the opportunity, which created a need for financial services that was met by modern Chinese banks. Between 1912 and 1927, 266 new banks opened for business. Although half of them quickly failed, the deposits and loans of those that survived increased more than seven times between 1911 and 1927.

At the same time, however, those banks had to navigate an inhospitable environment of political instability, a short-lived monarchical movement, and the chaotic warlordism that followed. The warlords treated the provincial banks and money stores as their personal coffers. Most provincial banks were saddled with paper money for which there was no metallic reserve. Between 1916 and 1920 eight official banks folded. During the Northern Expedition of 1926 to 1927 another ten provincial banks went out of business or were forced to reorganize. Still, several special banks were created, such as the Yien Yieh Commercial Bank, the Sin-hua Trust and Savings Bank, and the Agricultural and Industrial Bank of China.

In the state-owned sector, DB was a casualty of the 1911 revolution when the political turmoil precipitated withdrawals in all of its branches. Some of DB's branches closed; others declared themselves autonomous. The new Republican government reorganized what was left into a central bank called the Bank of China (BOC); it also took over the BOCO. Official patronage became a curse for BOC and BOCO when they were forced to advance huge sums of money without sufficient security to a government constantly short of funds. By the end of 1915 BOCO was burdened with government debts that totaled more than six times its capital. The government then schemed to merge the two banks to obtain yet more funds. A leak of the conspiracy triggered a run on both banks, which eventually led to their privatization. Government ownership of BOC stock fell from 42 percent in 1918 to only 0.25 percent by 1924, and its share of BOCO decreased from one-third of the bank's total capital in 1921 to only 1 percent by 1927.

In effect, amid the political tumult, there was a decided trend toward the privatization of the Chinese banking system. Privately owned banks accounted for 90 percent of new banks between 1916 and 1925. The number of government banks among all Chinese banks declined dramatically from 65 percent in 1912 to 18 percent by the end of 1925. By that time, there were 132 private banks but only 26 official or official-private joint banks in China.

Along with privatization, the Chinese banking system also became increasingly concentrated. Those banks that survived the Darwinian competition became larger; the biggest were the Big Nine. All privately owned, they were the BOC, BOCO, the Southern Three Banks (Shanghai Commercial and Savings Bank, National Commercial Bank, and Zhejiang Industrial Bank), and the Northern Four Banks (Yien Yieh Commercial Bank, Kincheng Banking Corporation, Continental Bank, and China and South Sea Bank). By 1927 the Big Nine accounted for 35 percent of the capital, three-quarters of deposits and loans, one-third of paid-up capital, and 70 percent of the assets of all Chinese banks.

THE GOLDEN AGE

In 1927 China nominally was united under the Nationalist government in Nanjing. Although battles with warlords and the Communist Red Army continued, compared to the turmoil of past years, the Nanjing decade (1927–1937) was a golden age for China's modernization, when Chinese banks were the economy's success story. From 1927 to 1936 the total paid-up capital of Chinese banks increased by more than 240 percent. The Big Nine became even bigger, accounting for more than half of the deposits, loans, capital power, and total assets of all Chinese banks by 1935. The pace of bank privatization quickened. At the end of 1934 private interests made up 60 percent of paid-up capital, 85 percent of deposits, 87 percent of loans, and 82 percent of total assets of all Chinese banks.

The increase in the relative price of silver can be defined as a "silver premium," in that one had to pay for the privilege of holding silver. There was no evidence that this trend slowed down in the following decades.

In terms of monetary silver, the Ming-Qing government made no attempt to formulate any policy to regulate its supply and demand. Foreign silver entered China freely through trade and was circulated, by and large, in its original sizes, shapes, and finenesses. Only 7.7 percent of imported silver was melted down and refined to ingots of a higher quality, called *sycee*, which was done mainly by the private smelting sector (Hao 1986, p. 66). The Qing authorities made no effort even to standardize the silver weight system, allowing it to vary not only from region to region but also from department to department of the Qing government.

The Qing mint began to produce China's own silver coins during this period. In 1889 the "dragon dollars" (*longyang, dayang*), modelled after the Spanish-Mexican peso, were inaugurated. But both their production and issuing were decentralized: in 1894 in Hubei, in 1896 in Zhili, in 1897 in Jiangsu, and in 1898 in Fengtian, Jilin, Xinjiang, Anhui, Hunan, Fujian, Sichuan, and Yunnan. The actual number of Qing-minted silver coins remained largely unknown, although it was estimated that by 1913, 220 million coins (5,247 tons) had been issued (see *Yinhang Zhoubao* 1925). Worse still, dragon dollars did not gain status as the exclusive legal tender—they circulated together with numerous imports. The incentive for provinces to manufacture dragon dollars was rather unclear, because the seigniorage was likely to be minimal from a market where silver was used more or less in its bullion form.

Only a decade later, China's first quasi-central bank was established (1905). The sequence was wrong: The central bank should have come before the dragon dollars. There is no evidence that this bank ever played any significant role in centralizing and regulating China's money supply or exchange rate. In 1910 the imperial court finally issued currency regulations (*Bizhi Zeli*) that clarified the Qing silver standard and silver currency. The production of the new Qing silver currency was scheduled for the following May, but it was interrupted by the 1911 Revolution. All these delays are understandable because since 1850 the Qing regime had been living on borrowed time; priority was not given to a monetary reform.

The situation for the Qing legal tender, the copper coins, was no better. It was standard practice that each province supplied its own copper coins locally. Exporting local coins was never encouraged, and the output of provincial mints was never properly controlled by the central government. Even Beijing ran separate mints under the Ministry of Revenue and the Ministry of Works. Their outputs were determined by the supply of materials of copper and lead, not market demand (Sun Jia 1996, p. 245). Material scarcity in copper coin production produced strong incentives for the local authorities to block coin outflows, but if local coins could not move freely, there could be no monetary integration. The Qing market suffered from this lack of integration.

Qing retail price index measured in bronze and silver,[a] 1800–1850

Period	Coins *wen*	Silver *liang*	Ratio[b]	Index
1800–1804	96.0	100.0	0.96	100
1805–1809	100.0	104.6	0.96	100
1810–1814	106.8	101.2	1.06	110
1815–1819	104.2	90.4	1.15	120
1820–1824	101.6	84.6	1.20	125
1825–1829	99.0	78.6	1.26	131
1830–1834	97.2	73.8	1.32	138
1835–1839	108.5	78.0	1.39	145
1840–1844	100.0	61.5	1.63	170
1845–1850	117.0	55.0	2.13	222

[a] Five-year average; [b] bronze-silver price ratio.

SOURCE: Based on Lin Manhong, "Jiadao Qianjian Xianxiang Chansheng Yuanyin 'Qianduo Qianlie Lun' Zhi Shangque" ("On 'Over-supply of Inferior Currency' as the Causes of Devaluation of Money in China during 1808–1850"), in Zhang Bincun and Liu Shiji, eds., *Zhongguo Haiyang Fazhanshi Lunwenji* (Selected Essays on the Maritime History of China). Taipei: Academia Sinica, 1993, vol. 5, pp. 370–372.

Table 1

Although no one really knows just how much monetary copper was in circulation across the empire, the number of copper coins was huge. Their total value was estimated to be 622 million pesos (14,834.7 tons of silver) by 1910 (Hao 1986, p. 68). With a rough ratio of 2,000 coins to one *liang* of silver (or 1,274 coins per peso), the total number of copper coins was in the neighborhood of 792 billion, or 1,980 coins per head of the population.

It was worth noting that not all these coins came from official mints—a considerable percentage were counterfeits, due to the combination of the high returns from seigniorage, especially with debasement (i.e., the use of more lead in the alloy), and the technical easiness of faking them. In response to the corrupt copper coins, market prices inflated, and this inflation coincided with silver deflation. So, the data for the Qing retail price index shown in Table 1 illustrates the dual problem of copper coin inflation and silver deflation. The ultimate source of this dual problem was the lack of government monetary policy and control.

THE EARLY REPUBLIC, 1912 TO 1927

The period from 1912 to 1927 was marred by political fragmentation and instability. First, there was a north-south split between the Beijing military government and Sun Yat-sen's Guangdong city-state, each of which claimed legitimacy to rule China. Second, there were internal conflicts among Yuan's army generals after Yuan's death in 1916. These conflicts resulted in full-scale wars from 1920 to 1925 between three warlord factions, until Zhang Zuolin gained control over the Beijing government. Meanwhile, in 1924 Sun's southern Republicans declared war against Beijing. The southern Communists joined in. By early 1928 all the warlords either had been defeated or had come to an accommodation with the new Nationalist government. The country was reunited only nominally.

From this perspective, 1912 to 1927 can be regarded as a period of wartime economy in China. Nevertheless, in 1914 the Legal Tender Act (*Guobi Tiaoli*) was passed by the first democratically elected government under Yuan Shikai. This act represented the first modern monetary regulation in China's history, which aimed to standardize China's currency with a silver standard. According to the act, (1) all the silver coins in circulation were to be replaced by the Republican silver coins; (2) all the public spending was to be made by the Republican silver coins; and (3) the central government had the monopoly over the production of the Republican silver coins. Under the new law, between 1914 and 1916 a total of 71 million Republican silver coins (1,693 tons) were issued. But foreign coins were still on the loose on China's market. It was not until 1933 that the new Republican government under the leadership of Chiang Kai-shek was able to complete a long-delayed monetary reform by abolishing silver bullion and imposing the Chinese silver yuan (*fei liang gai yuan*).

SEE ALSO *Banking; Money and Banking, 1800–1949; Weights and Measures.*

BIBLIOGRAPHY

British Parliamentary Papers 37. London: Government of Great Britain, 1847.

Brook, Timothy, and B. T. Wakabayashi, eds. *Opium Regimes: China, Britain, and Japan, 1839–1952.* Berkeley: University of California Press, 2000.

Chen Feng. Qingdai Caizheng Zhichu Zhengche Yu Zhichu Jiegoude Biandong [Changes in Qing fiscal spending policy and structure]. *Jianghan Luntan* [Jianhan forum] 5 (2000): 67.

Deng, Kent G. Miracle or Mirage? Foreign Silver, China's Economy, and Globalisation from the Sixteenth to the Nineteenth Centuries. *Pacific Economic Review* 13, no. 3 (2008): 320–358.

Gong Yingyan. *Yapiande Chuanbo Yu Duihua Yapian Maoyi* [Spread of opium consumption and opium imports by China]. Beijing: Oriental Press, 1999.

Hao, Yen-p'ing. *The Commercial Revolution in Nineteenth-century China.* Berkeley: University of California Press, 1986.

Lin Manhong. Jiadao Qianjian Xianxiang Chansheng Yuanyin "Qianduo Qianlie Lun" Zhi Shangque [On "oversupply of inferior currency" as the cause of devaluation of money in China during 1808–1850]. In *Zhongguo Haiyang Fazhanshi Lunwenji* [Selected essays on the maritime history of China], ed. Zhang Bincun and Liu Shiji, vol. 5, 370–372. Taipei: Academia Sinica, 1993.

Li Yunjun, ed. *Wanqing Jingji Shishi Biannian* [A chronicle of late Qing economic history]. Shanghai: Shanghai Classics Press, 2000.

Messenger, J. A. *India and China (Exports and Imports).* London: Office of the Inspector-General of Imports and Exports, 1859.

Sun Jia. *Beijing Gudai Jingji Shi* [An economic history of premodern Beijing]. Beijing: Beijing Mount Yan Press, 1996.

Tang Xianglong. *Zhongguo Jindai Haiguan Shuishou He Fenpei Tongji* [Statistics of customs revenue and its distribution in modern China]. Beijing: Zhonghua, 1992.

Xu Ke. *Qing Bai Lei Chao* [Collection of antidotes of Qing times]. Book 4, vol. 18. Shanghai: Commercial Books, 1917.

Yinhang Zhoubao [Banking weekly] (Shanghai) 9, no. 8 (March 10, 1925), p. 25.

Kent G. Deng

MONGOLIA, PEOPLE'S REPUBLIC OF, RELATIONS WITH

Until 1949 every Chinese leader had laid claim to Mongolia, which by nature of its geography has great geopolitical importance to China, as well as to Russia. In 1950, while negotiating Soviet assistance, Mao Zedong, on behalf of the People's Republic of China, formally recognized Mongolian independence, thus ending a situation of Chinese suzerainty and Soviet control that had prevailed since 1924. Friendly relations during the 1950s allowed Mongolia to receive both Soviet and Chinese assistance in the transformation of its traditional herding economy. At its peak, some 13,000 Chinese workers were engaged in construction and infrastructure projects in Mongolia.

When Chinese-Soviet relations broke down in 1962, Mongolia resumed the position of a buffer state "between the Bear and the Dragon." Deployment of Soviet troops and the establishment of military bases in Mongolia led its relations with China to low points between 1969 and 1979, when the Soviet Union and China were on the verge of war. From the mid-1980s Mongolia showed an increasing self-interest in international relations; for instance, in 1983 the Mongolian government expelled the remaining 1,300 Chinese residents, an act that was met by strong Chinese protests.

Until the breakup of the Soviet Union and Mongolia's full independence in 1990, the country had remained a secluded Soviet satellite with foreign relations mostly emulating those of the Soviet Union. The withdrawal of Soviet troops, numbering as many as 75,000 and armed with nuclear weaponry, started already in 1987 as a result of normalization and finished in 1992. Since then, relations between China and Mongolia have normalized and treaties of mutual trust and cooperation have been signed. At the same time, Mongolia, as a nonaligned, nuclear-free country, has established closer ties with the United States, Europe, and Japan.

Economic collapse across Soviet Central Asia further drove Mongolia into closer cooperation with China, while for several years trade was hampered by a Mongolian state monopoly on the export of animal products and Mongolia's protection of old state industries. China has been Mongolia's largest trading partner since 1999, facilitated by the opening of a range of new trading points at the Mongolian-Chinese border. In 2008 bilateral trade was worth over US$2 billion. Particularly since the middle of the first decade of the 2000s, Chinese trade, investments, and economic assistance have contributed to high growth rates for Mongolia, potentially easing historical animosity and cultural divisions. However, new competition from China has been hard on Mongolia's traditional manufacturing of animal products such as cashmere, causing some resentment.

Since establishment of the independent and democratic state of Mongolia, "pan-Mongolian" nationalism has risen across all ethnic Mongolian areas. The fear of "splittism" in Inner Mongolia has spurred Chinese efforts to create economic dependency across Mongolian territories. At the same time, nationalist sentiments in both countries occasionally give rise to hostile outbursts in the media and literature. Many Chinese will claim that Mao Zedong wrongfully gave away Mongolia in return for Soviet assistance, while Mongolians may bear old grudges about Chinese exploitation and the cultural deprivation of Mongols in Inner Mongolia, fearing renewed colonization. The revival of Buddhism in Mongolia after independence is another source of conflict. Mongolia is historically linked to Tibet through adherence to the Gelugpa school of Tibetan Buddhism, with the Dalai Lama as its supreme head. The Fourteenth Dalai Lama, who is highly revered, has paid seven visits to Mongolia since 1979, each time accompanied by official Chinese protests.

BIBLIOGRAPHY

Bruun, Ole, and Ole Odgaard. *Mongolia in Transition: Old Patterns, New Challenges*. Richmond, U.K.: Curzon Press, 1996.

Rossabi, Morris. 2008. Between the Bear and the Dragon: Mongolia's Relations with China and Russia. Fathom Knowledge Network. http://www.fathom.com.

Soni, Sharad K. *Mongolia-China Relations: Modern and Contemporary Times*. New Delhi: Pentagon Press, 2006.

Ole Bruun

MONUMENTS

The Chinese traditionally employed steles (*shibei*), archways (*paifang* or *pailou*), and temples (*ci* or *miao*) as monuments and memorials. Steles, the most common form of Chinese monument, are inscribed stone tablets usually measuring between four and six feet in height but at times reaching over twenty feet and weighing over thirty tons. Typically, the purpose of the stele was to record the visit of a famous personage or to mark the completion of a significant building or restoration project. Archways, a more decorative form of monument, are used to show respect for an individual; to extol public values such as chastity, loyalty, or filial piety; or to enhance a scenic spot or tomb. Usually constructed of four or six timber or stone columns joined by engraved architraves, these structures once appeared in large numbers in both urban and rural settings and are recognized as a representative form of Chinese architecture. The greatest cultural and military heroes—such as Confucius, Yue Fei, and Zhuge Liang—could be honored with an architectural complex that included a temple, memorial steles and archways, elaborate halls, pavilions, and clay or wooden statues of the honorees.

Before the twentieth century, Chinese memorials and monuments followed established styles, with the engraved stele continuing as the preferred means to mark notable accomplishments. At the end of the nineteenth century, foreigners began to erect obelisk style monoliths within their treaty-port concessions to memorialize their own war dead, but the practice had little influence on the remainder of China. This situation began to change early in the twentieth century when the collapse of the Qing dynasty created a new type of political discourse and new forms of monuments. A few examples, such as the Song Jiaoren Memorial (1916) in Beijing, symbolized a decisive break with the past through their revolutionary subject matter and international architectural style. However, the fractured political circumstances during the next two decades deterred any coordinated program to create a network of national monuments. By the time the Anti-Japanese War moved south of the Great Wall in 1937, the only true national monuments were the Sun Yat-sen Mausoleum in Nanjing (1929) and the Sun Yat-sen Memorial Hall in Guangzhou (1931), both designed by the neoclassicist architect Lü Yanzhi.

After the defeat of Japan in 1945 and the Communist takeover of the mainland in 1949, the Chinese Communist Party took up the practice of erecting monuments and memorials. Memorials to martyrs began to appear in the late 1940s, but the boldest such statement was reserved for Beijing, where Tiananmen was reconfigured as a memorial square centering on the Monument to the People's Heroes (1958). During the late 1950s and 1960s, other monuments devoted to people's heroes and acts of anti-imperialism and anti-feudalism began to appear in urban centers across the country. By far the most common Mao-era monuments were statues of Chairman Mao himself, which began to appear in Beijing during the early stages of the Cultural Revolution and quickly spread across the country. In addition, Mao called

Monument to People's Heroes and Mao Zedong Memorial Hall, Tiananmen Square, Beijing, c. 2006. *After the birth of the People's Republic of China, Communist leaders erected many markers celebrating their victory. One of the most prominent, the Monument to People's Heroes, remembers China's path to independence through a ten-story marble obelisk situated in Tiananmen Square.* © LUCA DA ROS/GRAND TOUR/CORBIS

on the country's radical youth to destroy the Four Olds (old customs, old culture, old habits, and old ideas). As a part of old culture, China's historical monuments were targeted, and sites such as the tomb and temple of Confucius in Qufu, Shandong, and even the Song Jiaoren Memorial suffered irreparable damage in the late 1960s.

When Mao died in 1976, Tiananmen was altered again by the addition of the Mao Zedong Mausoleum, but with Deng Xiaoping's rise to power, much of the remaining Mao iconography began to disappear. In the 1980s Chinese authorities began to recognize and render into monumental form a wider array of Chinese heroes and definitive historical events. All of China's defeats of the nineteenth and twentieth centuries were reconfigured as struggles of resistance, and every step in the rise of the Chinese Communist Party was chronicled through museums, monuments, and memorials throughout the country. The most powerful of these representations relate to the Anti-Japanese War, most notably the Nanjing Massacre Memorial Hall (1985–2007) and Shenyang's 9-18 (Mukden) Incident Memorial and Museum (1999), both designed by the prominent museum architect Qi Kang. These and other monuments and memorials have become important tools in state-sponsored campaigns to address historical injustices and foster patriotism through education.

SEE ALSO *Archaeology, History of; Architecture, History of: Architecture, 1949–1978; Architecture, History of: Architecture to 1949; Gardens and Parks; Urban China: Urban Planning since 1978.*

BIBLIOGRAPHY

Denton, Kirk. Museums, Memorial Sites, and Exhibitionary Culture in the People's Republic of China. *China Quarterly* 183 (Fall 2005): 565–586.

Wang, Eugene Y. Romancing the Stone: An Archway in Shandong. *Orientations* 35, 2 (March 2004): 90–97.

Wang, Liping. Creating a National Symbol: The Sun Yatsen Memorial in Nanjing. *Republican China* 21, 2 (April 1996): 23–63.

Wu Hung. *Remaking Beijing: Tiananmen Square and the Creation of a Political Space.* Chicago: University of Chicago Press, 2005.

James Flath

MORALITY

The Chinese cultural tradition is one of the richest sources of moral thought in human history. Like all great traditions, it is filled with disagreements about what exactly is a good life and how one can attain it. Some of the main streams of this tradition include the teaching of the scholars, which takes its starting point from canonical writings of Confucius and Mencius (372–289 BCE); the teaching of the Dao; and the teaching of the Buddha. Within each of these streams there have been constant debates over the meaning of the tradition. Sometimes the three streams have worked against each other, but during many periods of Chinese history they have complemented one another in ways that produced a generalized vision of morality. In the Ming and Qing dynasties the official state ideology was based on neo-Confucianism, a system of ideas that mixed Confucian with Buddhist thought. Like any state ideology, though, the imperial ideology mummified many of the critical insights of Confucius and the Buddha, and used these ways of thought as a justification for the exercise of power.

Taken as a whole, the Chinese moral tradition is based on a complicated balance between universal aspirations and particular commitments. A key proposition is the Confucian version of the Golden Rule: Do not impose upon others what you yourself do not desire. This universal principle is given particular grounding by the principle of reciprocity: You should return an equivalent for what someone has given you, with the implication that those who give you more should get more in return. The core of the moral imagination is the family: Parents give their children the ultimate gifts of life and nurturing; children should give their parents complete loyalty and affection. Different family members have different roles to play: A husband's role is different from the wife's and these differences should be respected, although they should mutually support one another. This sensibility can be extended beyond the boundaries of one's immediate family: One's network of kin should be considered as part of an extended family, one's friends should also be thought of as kin, and one's ruler should be considered like a parent. To reconcile all of these relationships, one needs to cultivate certain virtues, the most important of which is *ren*, a concept difficult to translate into Western languages, but which basically means a respect for relatedness.

Overall, the Chinese moral tradition urges that conflicts be resolved by persuasion rather than force. Authority, whether of the paterfamilias or the ruler, should be respected, but not uncritically. If a ruler is harming a subject, the subject should remonstrate with the ruler, telling the ruler that he is not fulfilling the moral responsibilities of his role. Emperors, by contrast, often based their behavior on the realpolitik of the Legalist school of philosophy, by which they evoked the hierarchical principles of Confucianism while denying the critical imperatives embedded within Confucian teaching. There are stories of righteous Confucian officials who brought their coffins with them when they had an audience with an emperor whom they were prepared to criticize even though they were threatened with execution.

By the end of the Qing dynasty in 1911, Chinese moral discourse had become stagnant and formalistic, unable to respond constructively to the challenges posed internally by the increasing complexity of society and externally by foreign imperialism. During the May 4 period, in the decade after the dynasty collapsed, radical intellectuals and politicians called for an end to traditional culture and morality. Some of their most bitter attacks were aimed at the respect for hierarchy and for particularistic commitments that were at the core of the traditional family system. For the sake of building a strong country that could compete with Western powers, children should not defer to their parents, wives should not be subordinate to husbands, and subjects should overturn their traditional rulers. These ideas were based on a wide variety of Western ideas (usually subtly reinterpreted under the pressure of politics and culture), including utilitarianism, Kantian universalism, and Marxist dialectics.

The Marxist theory modified by Mao Zedong to be the ideology of the Chinese Communist Party emphasized universal class struggle over loyalty to family commitments. It also rejected the individualistic liberalism of the bourgeois West and denied the validity of romantic notions of universal love in order to mobilize a disciplined fighting force against class enemies.

After the Chinese Communists came to power in 1949 they continued to deploy this Marxist-Maoist moral rhetoric to justify ceaseless struggle against all manner of real or imagined enemies of the regime. This reached a crescendo during the Cultural Revolution (1966–1969). Even during that time, however, older ideas of morality seemed to persist. The Cultural Revolution was in fact touched off in 1966 by Mao's fury at the refusal of some high party officials to attack a play that had depicted a righteous Confucian official's courage in remonstrating against a tyrannical emperor during the Ming dynasty. During the Cultural Revolution, the premier Zhou Enlai seemed (to Mao at least) to be unduly influenced by Confucian ideals of using persuasion rather than violence to reconcile differences. One of the last campaigns of Mao's life was a campaign "against Confucius," which was really directed against Zhou Enlai. Mao cast himself in the image of the Legalist emperor Qin who used violent conquest and political manipulation to unify a vast empire, while executing Confucian scholars and burning their books.

In the early years of reform after the death of Mao, economic growth seemed to be the preoccupation of the entire country. Many Chinese commentators worried publicly that the country faced a moral vacuum; that all that counted anymore was the pursuit of wealth. By the beginning of the twenty-first century some Chinese intellectuals were urging a return to traditional roots to find the sources of a new social morality. The ideology of the regime of Hu Jintao is based on the notion of a "harmonious society," an echo of Confucian teaching, but as many emperors did in the past, the current (2009) regime has taken the critical energy out of the Confucian tradition, leaving a superficially attractive but empty ideological shell. Confucius said that true harmony was a peaceful reconciliation of differences, not a coercive imposition of conformity.

Meanwhile, after the Nationalist Party was defeated by the Communists in the civil war of the late 1940s, it set up a government on Taiwan that supposedly was based on Confucian moral values (as opposed to "godless Communism"). But these values were interpreted to emphasize the authoritarian rather than the critical aspects of the moral tradition. With the transition to democracy in Taiwan, there have been impressive attempts by Taiwanese religious and cultural leaders to reformulate Confucian, Buddhist, and Daoist traditions in ways that conform to a modern democratic spirit.

SEE ALSO *Buddhism; Confucianism; Family: Overview; May Fourth Movement.*

BIBLIOGRAPHY

Bell, Daniel A., ed. *Confucian Political Ethics*. Princeton, NJ: Princeton University Press, 2007.

De Bary, William Theodore. *Asian Values and Human Rights: A Confucian Communitarian Perspective*. Cambridge, MA: Harvard University Press, 1998.

Madsen, Richard. *Morality and Power in a Chinese Village*. Berkeley: University of California Press, 1984.

Pohl, Karl-Heinz, and Anselm Muller, eds. *Chinese Ethics in a Global Context*. Leiden, Netherlands: Brill, 2002.

Richard Madsen

MORRISON, GEORGE E.

1862–1920

George Ernest Morrison was a Beijing-based correspondent for *The Times* of London (1897–1912) and an adviser to Yuan Shikai and his successors (1912–1920). Arriving in Beijing in February 1897, Morrison quickly proved to be an enterprising, well-informed reporter of diplomatic developments at a time when China was a major field of international rivalry. His earlier life prepared him well for such a role.

LIFE BEFORE TRAVELING TO CHINA

Morrison was born in Geelong, Victoria, Australia. As a young man in Australia, he undertook several extensive solitary journeys on foot, one across the continent from north to south, and he served as a seaman on a "blackbirding" voyage, rounding up Pacific Islanders to work as near-slave laborers on the Queensland sugarcane fields. He wrote a series of articles describing and criticizing this trade, prompting official enquiries. Some newspapers then financed him on an expedition to the interior of New Guinea. There, he was wounded and forced to return with a sizeable spearhead in his side. Between these adventures, he had failed in his medical studies in Melbourne, so in March 1884 he set off for Edinburgh to seek expert surgery and renew his medical studies. Both objectives were achieved.

After graduation, he traveled to North America, the West Indies, and Spain, where he was medical officer at a mine for over a year. Returning to Australia, he worked in a country hospital, but after two years he set out on his travels again, first to the Philippines, where he unsuccessfully sought work on the strength of his knowledge of medicine and Spanish, then to Japan. There, he conceived the idea of another transcontinental journey, this time across China.

AN AUSTRALIAN IN CHINA

Dressed as a Chinese, in February 1894 Morrison traveled by boat to Chongqing and from there set off through Yunnan to Burma (Myanmar), hiring coolies and dodging bandits as necessary. He covered 3,000 miles in three months at a total cost, he estimated, of less than 30 pounds. After recovering in Calcutta from a near-fatal bout of fever, he returned home to write *An Australian in China*. Early in 1895, he took the manuscript to London for publication.

The book was well received, providing a graphic account of conditions in a part of China remote from treaty-port areas. Morrison insisted that his journey was "in no sense one of exploration... taken by one who spoke no Chinese, who had no interpreter or companion, who was unarmed but who trusted implicitly in the good faith of the Chinese" (1895, p. 1). He was ironically dismissive of missionary efforts, pragmatic, and sharp-eyed about Chinese practices, including opium production and consumption. "Edicts are still issued against the use of opium. They are drawn up by Chinese philanthropists over a quiet pipe of opium, signed by opium-smoking officials, whose revenues are derived from the poppy, and posted near fields of poppy by opium-smoking magistrates who own them" (1895, pp. 48–49). He went on to note the sale of "morphia pills" as a "cure" for the opium habit, which he suggested was like drinking methylated spirits instead of beer. Such direct observation interested many, including Moberley Bell (1847–1911), manager of *The Times*, who suggested Morrison go to China as its Beijing-based correspondent.

FIRST YEARS IN BEIJING

Before taking up the post, Morrison toured through Indo-China, reporting trenchantly on the French presence there. Soon after arriving in Beijing, he was on the move into Manchuria, eastern Siberia, and Mongolia, observing the Russian presence and ambitions. His report of their 1898 ultimatum demanding a lease on Port Arthur (Lüshan) was at first discounted but was soon proved accurate, prompting questions in Parliament and the excuse from Lord Curzon (1859–1925) that "the journalist whose concern is speed is sometimes likely to get the advantage of the diplomat, whose main concern is accuracy" (Pearl 1967, p. 98). Morrison's display of both attributes was further revealed in mid-1900 by his dispatches on the eve of the Boxer siege of the legations. He was severely wounded in the fighting, but at its end quickly sent off a 30,000-word account that *The Times* praised for its "transparent impartiality." Some months earlier, misled by a false report that the legations had been overrun, the paper had printed obituaries of Morrison, Robert Hart (1835–1911), and Claude MacDonald (1852–1915). All three survived; Morrison dismissed his obituary as "eulogistic to a grotesque degree" (Thompson and Macklin 2004, p. 198).

Over the next few years, Morrison's reputation as an outstanding journalist whose reports could influence policy makers was at its peak. He was a supporter of Japan in its rivalry with Russia to the extent that he was invited to accompany Japanese forces as they occupied Port Arthur in 1905. He was then sent by *The Times* to Portsmouth, New Hampshire, to report on the peace negotiations, in which he argued unrealistically that Japan conceded too much. The Russian negotiator, Count Sergei Witte (1849–1915), nevertheless felt it worthwhile to meet with Morrison. His reporting on this and other issues did not please all within *The Times*, but in 1907 Bell invited Morrison to become the paper's foreign editor. He rejected this position, and speculated about joining the Foreign Office or returning to Australia, but remained based in Beijing, though he was frequently absent for long periods.

In early 1910 Morrison set off on a journey through the far west of China, reporting that he was well treated "because I belong to a country which is known to sympathize with every movement in China that has as its object the advancement of the people....To me the suggestion is preposterous that British influence is waning in China" (Pearl 1967, p.203). Clearly Morrison had blind spots. Although consistently concerned for the future well-being of China as he conceived it, he was always fundamentally a spokesman for the British imperial presence there. In response to a request in 1914 to help fund a university in central China, using Boxer indemnity funds, Morrison refused, adding "I have never been able to accept the view that we have as a nation done China much harm" (Morrison 1976–1978, pp. 230–231).

LATER YEARS AS AN ADVISER

In 1912 Morrison married his secretary, Jennie Wark Robin, with whom he had three sons. By 1911 to 1912, Morrison was back in Beijing to report on the end of Qing rule and to support Yuan Shikai as leader of the new republic. At this time, he was dismissive of Sun Yat-sen (Sun Yixian or Sun Zhongshan) as unlikely to win international recognition. Now ready to leave *The Times*, in August 1912 Morrison accepted a better-paid appointment as one of Yuan's team of foreign advisers. In 1913 he approved of the controversial reorganization loan and was noncommittal about the assassination of Song Jiaoren (1882–1913), but he was soon frustrated at not being kept informed and consulted. Morrison advised against Yuan's monarchical ambitions, and in 1915, using his journalistic contacts, he publicized Japan's Twenty-one Demands, again facing skepticism.

By now, fearful of Japan's ambitions, although still seeing its modernization as a model for China, he favored China's entry into World War I (1914–1918) as a means of gaining international support. Not formally a delegate, he gave realistic advice to the Chinese representatives at Versailles in 1919, deploring the outcome. Disillusioned and in ill health, he returned to England, where he died on May 30, 1920.

Morrison's son Alastair became a colonial officer in Sarawak. Alastair's wife, Hedda (1908–1991), was a photographer in Beijing between 1933 and 1946, and her extensive collection of photos of the old city and its environs is now at the Powerhouse Museum in Sydney and the Harvard-Yenching Library at Harvard University. George Morrison's papers, including his diary, are held in the Mitchell Library in Sydney. His substantial library of Western books and pamphlets on China is housed in the Tokyo Toyo Bunko. An annual series of Morrison lectures on China began in 1932, and continues under the auspices of the Australian National University in Canberra.

SEE ALSO *Cixi, Empress Dowager; Li Hongzhang; Yuan Shikai.*

BIBLIOGRAPHY

PRIMARY WORKS

Morrison, George E. *An Australian in China: Being the Narrative of a Quiet Journey Across China to Burma*. London: Horace Cox, 1895.

Morrison, George E. *The Correspondence of G. E. Morrison*. Ed. Lo Huimin. 2 vols. Cambridge, U.K.: Cambridge University Press, 1976–1978.

SECONDARY WORKS

Morrison, Hedda. *A Photographer in Old Peking.* New York and Hong Kong: Oxford University Press, 1985.

Morrison, Hedda. Photographic Collection. Powerhouse Museum, Sydney, Australia. http://www.powerhousemuseum.com/heddamorrison/

Pearl, Cyril. *Morrison of Peking.* Sydney: Angus and Robertson, 1967.

Thompson, Peter, and Robert Macklin. *The Man Who Died Twice: The Life and Adventures of Morrison of Peking.* Crow's Nest, NSW, Australia: Allen & Unwin, 2004.

J. S. Gregory

MORRISON, ROBERT

1782–1834

Missionary and sinologist Robert Morrison was born in Northumberland, England, and grew up in Newcastle-on-Tyne. As a youth, he received a middling education and was apprenticed to his father, a bootblack. Inspired by the evangelical revival of the 1790s and its enthusiasm for foreign missions, Morrison became in 1807 the first Protestant missionary to reside in mainland China, representing the London Missionary Society (LMS). Morrison accomplished a variety of pioneering works in Guangzhou (Canton) and Macau. He also worked in Malacca (in present-day Malaysia), but his focus was always on China. Morrison was well known in England and was in his day the leading interpreter of China to Western nations. He was a major if not the foremost sinologist of his day, England's first really skilled interpreter in Chinese due to his many years working for the British East India Company in Guangzhou. He became the first to translate the entire Bible into Chinese and was the author of an excellent three-volume Chinese dictionary and dozens of other publications. Finally, as one of the driving forces behind the Ultra-Ganges Mission and the Anglo-Chinese College in Malacca, Morrison was an inspiration to aspiring missionaries to China and other places in the first decades of the nineteenth century.

A pious adolescent who underwent personal conversion and joined the Presbyterian Church in 1798, Morrison started to think seriously about foreign missions despite his family's initial opposition. He systematically prepared himself for his China mission by attending Hoxton Academy, North London, from early 1803, and the Missionary Academy at Gosport, Hampshire, the LMS missionary training school, in 1804. Accepted for assignment to China by the LMS, Morrison spent over two years preparing in London by studying Chinese (as best he could, with few resources except for a young Chinese tutor) and medicine. He showed immense capacity for hard work and self-deprivation, traits that he would have throughout his life. Commissioned as a missionary by the LMS in 1806, Morrison was formally charged to concentrate on learning Chinese and as soon as possible to translate the scriptures into Chinese. Finally ordained in early 1807, Morrison was unable to secure passage to China on a British East India Company ship because of the company's aversion to missionaries as potentially disruptive to trade; instead, he sailed on an American ship via the United States.

Morrison faced uncertainties after his arrival in Guangzhou and Macau, being essentially homeless for a time and having insecure legal and residential status. Despite the dangers to himself and his tutors (before 1842 it was illegal for foreigners to learn Chinese or for Chinese people to teach it to them), Morrison worked hard at language acquisition, and he made good progress, even starting his initial translations of the Bible. Within two years, his language skills earned him an appointment as official translator for the British East India Company. In early 1809 he married Mary Morton (1791–1821), the eighteen-year-old daughter of an East India Company surgeon. Morrison experienced much stress deriving from his wife's poor health and the division of his family between Guangzhou and Macau, as well as the tension between his missionary vocation and the pressing workload given him by the East India Company. He could not openly evangelize, or even translate and distribute tracts, without compromising the fortunes and the precarious position of the company in Guangzhou. He also remained alone in Guangzhou, his loneliness compounded by Mary's residence in Macau.

In the years after 1810, Morrison became well established as a translator and author. He published a grammar of the Chinese language, and continued his labors on both his Chinese-English dictionary (the first volume of three was published in 1815) and the translation of the scriptures. By this time, Morrison had several Chinese assistants. In 1813 he was joined by an LMS colleague, William Milne (1785–1822), who became an effective partner in several ventures, including the Bible translation and the initiatives in Southeast Asia, which resulted in 1817 in the opening of the Anglo-Chinese College. In the meantime, Morrison continued in public service. He was the official interpreter for Lord Amherst (1773–1857) in the latter's disastrous mission to Beijing in 1816 to try to persuade the emperor to liberalize the system of foreign trade on the China coast.

In 1815 Mary, ever in ill health, returned to England with their two surviving children, where she stayed until 1820 (she died in Macau in 1821). These years were the height of Morrison's trajectory as a missionary-scholar. He had already published a cobbled-together version of the New Testament in 1813. In 1819 he and Milne completed a translation of the entire Bible, which was published in 1823 in Malacca. The third volume of his dictionary was also published in 1823. That same year he returned to England with several thousand Chinese books, which eventually went to University College, London. He became a fellow of the Royal Society, and remarried, to Eliza Armstrong. They returned together to China in 1825, where, after publishing more translations and establishing in Guangzhou an English-language newspaper, *The Canton Register*, Morrison died in Macau in 1834. He is buried in the Protestant cemetery of Macau.

Morrison, well known to the British public in his day, is much less recognized today. His personality was not exciting; he was more pious and serious-minded than charming. Moreover, his Bible translation was not highly regarded by his successors; within a short time after its appearance, Walter Medhurst (1796–1857) of the LMS and Karl Gützlaff (1803–1851), an independent missionary, were pressing for a new, more readable translation. Yet Morrison remains a pioneer, and his dedication, perseverance, and capacity for hard work were admirable. His dictionary alone was a great achievement. So the many retrospective accolades that Morrison received during the 2007 bicentennial of his arrival in China were not undeserved.

SEE ALSO *Cantonese; Missionaries.*

BIBLIOGRAPHY

Hancock, Christopher. *Robert Morrison and the Birth of Chinese Protestantism.* London: Clark/Continuum, 2008.

Morrison, Eliza Armstrong, comp. *Memoirs of the Life and Labours of Robert Morrison.* 2 vols. London: Longmans, 1839.

Rubinstein, Murray A. *The Origins of the Anglo-American Missionary Enterprise in China, 1807–1840.* Lanham, MD: Scarecrow, 1996.

Daniel H. Bays

MOST-FAVORED-NATION TREATMENT

Most-favored-nation (MFN) status is a free-trade practice that commits all the members of the World Trade Organization (WTO) to reciprocal lowered tariffs and reductions of trade barriers. Prior to the formation of the WTO in 1995, only members of the General Agreement on Tariffs and Trade (GATT) could enjoy MFN status. During the Cold War era, MFN was an important foreign-policy instrument used by the U.S. government toward Communist countries that sought to trade with the United States. However, the 1974 Trade Act enacted by the U.S. Congress linked trade concessions to immigration. The Jackson-Vanik Amendment prohibited the U.S. government from entering MFN relations with Communist countries that did not allow free immigration, but it did empower the president to waive such immigration requirements if the president found that the country would substantially promote freedom of immigration.

China and the United States first entered into MFN relations when the two countries signed a trade agreement in 1979, shortly after normalization of diplomatic relations. Although the United States granted China MFN status, subject to the Jackson-Vanik Amendment, such MFN status needed to be renewed by the U.S. president every year (Tan Qingshan 1992, chap. 3). Three factors explain why the United States granted MFN status to China. First, economic interests could be served by expanding trade with China. Second, such a trade relationship could strengthen bilateral strategic relations in light of Soviet expansionism. Third, the United States, through MFN relations, intended to encourage Chinese domestic reform and transformation, including free immigration.

In less than seven years, the bilateral trade increased threefold. Increasing trade with the United States benefited China's economic reform and lent much support for Deng Xiaoping's open-door policy. Both countries established strategic cooperation to contain Soviet expansionism in Asia and Africa. In the late 1970s, China started to permit those who had relatives overseas to immigrate, and also sent students to study in the United States. By 1985 students no longer needed state approval to go abroad to study, as long as they obtained financial support.

After the 1989 Tiananmen crackdown, renewal of MFN status for China became the focus of political tensions between the U.S. executive and Congress (Tan Qingshan 1993, pp. 143–160). While President George H. W. Bush wanted to engage China by extending MFN status, Congress increasingly linked renewal of MFN status to China's human rights practices. Subsequently, Congress made yearly attempts to impose conditions on renewal, especially regarding human rights issues in China.

When President Bill Clinton took office in 1993, he initially incorporated congressional concerns over human rights into his MFN policy toward China. In an executive order issued on May 28, 1993, Clinton attached several conditions to the 1994 renewal of MFN, including improvements of human rights in the areas of immigration and prison labor, protection of Tibetan culture, and allowing foreign radio broadcasts. Clinton's initial MFN approach became a rallying point for liberal human rights advocates and Chinese overseas labor activists and political dissidents to push for greater changes within China (Sutter 1998). However, when the renewal of MFN became a battlefield for all forces interested in China, complicating U.S.-China policy making, Clinton reversed his MFN approach to China by delinking human rights from trade and granting China MFN status without conditions in 1994 (Jarrett 1996).

Clinton subsequently lost a battle to grant China permanent most-favored-nation (PMFN) status ahead of China's entry into the WTO, but the United States did annually renew China's MFN status until that time. Part of the rationale was that increased U.S.-China trade would promote economic freedom, which in the long run would spur the growth of political liberalization. A positive and constructive MFN approach to China on the part of the United States resulted in a tremendous surge in bilateral trade. With China's entry into the WTO in December 2001, MFN debates in the United States passed into history.

SEE ALSO *Foreign Trade since 1950; United States, Relations with.*

BIBLIOGRAPHY

Jarrett, Kenneth. Profits or Principles? Clinton's 1994 Decision to Delink China's MFN Status and Human Rights. Unpublished research paper, National War College, 1996.

Sutter, Robert G. *U.S. Policy toward China: An Introduction to the Role of Interest Groups*. Lanham, MD: Rowman & Littlefield, 1998.

Tan Qingshan. *The Making of U.S.-China Policy: From Normalization to the Post-Cold War Era.* Boulder, CO: Rienner, 1992.

Tan Qingshan. Explaining U.S.-China Policy in the 1990s: Who Is in Control? *Asian Affairs: An American Review* 20, 3 (1993): 143–160.

U.S. Congress. House. Committee on Foreign Affairs, Subcommittee on Economic Policy, Trade, and Environment. *China, Human Rights, and MFN: Joint Hearings before the Subcommittees on Economic Policy, Trade, and Environment; International Security, International Organizations, and Human Rights; and Asia and the Pacific of the Committee on Foreign Affairs, House of Representatives*. 103rd Congress, 2nd session, March 24, 1994. Washington, DC: U.S. Government Printing Office, 1994.

Qingshan Tan

MUSEUMS

When museums came into being one and a half centuries ago in China, there was no single term to denote the institution. *Bowuguan*, the conventionally agreed-upon Chinese equivalent of "museum," originally meant hall of science (*bowu* being the general term for all the objects of scientific study). Variations included *bowuyuan* (natural-science preserve) and *bolanguan* (hall of extensive collections). The first museums appeared in the late Qing, but development and expansion were difficult because of the political and social instabilities of the late Qing, warlord, and Republican periods. Nonetheless, a boom in the 1930s meant a total of seventy-seven museums nationwide by 1936. The Anti-Japanese War (1937–1945) not only slowed the development of museums but also caused collections to be moved away from areas of Japanese control. After the founding of the People's Republic in 1949, museums, now largely under state control, passed through roughly three stages of development: revival (1949–1965), low tide (1966–1976), and thriving development (1977–present).

EARLY MUSEUMS, 1868–1949

China's earliest museums were founded by foreigners. The first was the Shanghai Museum, established in 1857 by the North China Branch of the Royal Asiatic Society, a group of amateur naturalists, mostly British. French Jesuit priest Pierre Heude (1836–1902) served as adviser. The British government sponsored the building, located in the International Settlement, and society members curated the collections. Funding for the museum came from membership fees, visitor donations, and the Public Security Bureau from 1877.

Subsequently, in 1868, Father Heude founded the Xujiahui (Siccawei) Museum. Between 1882 and 1883 the museum was relocated from its original site on the western outskirts of the French concession to the Avenue Dubail (Chongqing Road South) in Shanghai. Funded by the Collegio Romano in Rome, Xujiahui Museum was organized and curated by Father Heude and two or three of his Jesuit colleagues. Chinese assistants managed the lithographic press. On Wednesday afternoons the museum was open for free admission to the public.

The first *Chinese* museum was Nantong Museum, established in 1905, in Nantong, Jiangsu, located approximately sixty miles northwest of Shanghai, on the north side of the Yangzi River. The founder, Zhang Jian (1853–1926), was inspired by the Shanghai treaty-port institutions mentioned above. Informed by the founder's vision of modern China, the museum was committed to maintaining culture and educating the public by presenting Chinese civilization, national identity, cultural legacy, and visual connoisseurship. The collections of Nantong Museum range from animal specimens to ancient vessels and classical art works of different periods. Privately funded and administered by Zhang Jian and his circle of elite associates, Nantong Museum primarily served the reformist gentry of Republican China during Zhang's tenure. The museum was closed down during the Anti-Japanese War, but was revived after 1949.

China's most famous museum is undoubtedly the Palace Museum in Beijing. In 1914, after the abdication of the last Qing emperor Puyi (1906–1967), the Guwu Chenlie Suo (Gallery of Antiquities), whose collections comprised treasures of the royal family, was set up in the front half of the Forbidden City. The collection was administered and funded by the Beiyang government. Eviction of the royal family from the Forbidden City in 1924 made way for the establishment of the Palace Museum, which took over the collection in the following year. Management of the Palace Museum frequently changed hands because of government instability. In 1928 the Republican government of Nanjing took over administration and funding of the collection. In 1933 a large quantity of artifacts in the Palace Museum were relocated to Nanjing in response to the Japanese aggression in the north. After the breakout of the Anti-Japanese War in 1937, they were relocated again to Sichuan, being returned to Nanjing at the conclusion of the war. Around one fifth of this collection, packed in nearly four thousand crates, was transferred to Taiwan in 1948, where it now comprises the core of the National Palace Museum collection in Taibei. In early 1949 the museum in Beijing, with its much depleted collection, was taken over by the authorities of the pending People's Republic.

Preparations for the construction of Shanghai Museum started in 1933 and the museum was opened to the public in Jiangwan in January 1937. In August 1937 the museum suffered partial destruction due to Japanese invasion and was forced to close. The museum did not reopen until mid-1946, and two-thirds of the looted collection was eventually recovered. The museum was taken over by the Shanghai People's Government in 1949 and in 1951 was incorporated into the Shanghai Museum Preparatory Committee. Shanghai Museum was established in 1952.

THE REVIVAL OF MUSEUMS, 1949–1965

The government of the People's Republic undertook substantial measures to revive twenty-one war-damaged museums inherited from the Republican administration, foreign powers, and private entrepreneurs. These measures included nationwide drives for donations of antiquities in 1950 and again in 1958–1960, a national campaign to study museum theory and develop expertise, and a national museum conference in 1956.

New museums were constructed, while old ones were renovated. Nantong Museum, for instance, resumed operations in 1951, was consolidated into Jiangsu Provincial Museum in 1954, but reverted to its original status in 1957. The National History Museum, established in 1926, was renamed the National Museum of Chinese History in 1949, relocated to its current structure built in 1959 on the east side of Tiananmen Square, and opened to the public in 1961. By 1957 a total of seventy-two new provincial museums, organized on the Soviet model, had been established, with museums lacking only in Tibet, Xinjiang, and Qinghai. Shandong Provincial Museum, the first comprehensive provincial museum remodeled in the Soviet fashion, was established between 1953 and 1956 by consolidating the Jinan Dao Yuan, built in 1921 with the Whitewright Institute, the latter initiated in 1940 by the Reverend John S. Whitewright (1858–1926) of the British Baptist Missionary Society.

In 1959 eight new grand museums were constructed, including the National Museum of Chinese History, Museum of the Chinese Revolution, Military Museum of the Chinese People's Revolution, National Art Museum of China, Ethnic Cultural Palace, Beijing Natural History Museum, National Agricultural Exhibition Hall, and Beijing Geological Museum. In the meantime, some substantial municipal museums were constructed. A good example is the Jingzhou Museum in Hubei, established in 1958 and now boasting a collection of well over 100,000 pieces including a number of national importance. The total number of museums in China reached 360 in 1958 and 480 in 1959. Although museum growth waxed and waned between 1958 and 1965 owing to the Great Leap Forward (1958–1960), during this first stage museums in China were not only restored but also enjoyed remarkable growth, laying a solid foundation for the future.

A LOW TIDE FOR MUSEUMS, 1966–1976

During the decade of the Cultural Revolution (1966–1976) museums were denounced as serving the bourgeoisie, and artifacts were destroyed as one of the four olds (*si jiu*). Many museums were closed and devastated despite protection efforts. The Palace Museum was closed for five years before reopening in 1971. The only highlight in this period was the exhibition in Hunan Provincial Museum in 1973 of the archaeological finds at Mawangdui Han tomb no. 1, which drew national as well as international attention.

THE REVITALIZATION AND PROLIFERATION OF MUSEUMS, 1977–PRESENT

Restoration and reconstruction after 1976 brought life back to China's museums. New museums were opened, including the Museum of Chinese Science and Technology (1988), the Zigong Dinosaur Museum (1987), the Guo State Tomb Museum (1984) in Henan, and the Tang'an Dong Ecological Museum (1995) in Guizhou. Museums multiplied in the early 1980s, a new museum appearing on average once every ten days between 1980 and 1985, peaking in 1984 with the addition of 151 museums, mainly specialized local institutions, small in scale. In addition, new types of museum made an appearance. Of the 558 museums inaugurated between 1983 and 1989, 55 percent were commemorative, 12 percent ethnic, 7 percent artistic, 6 percent archaeological, 5 percent natural history, 4 percent geological, and 3 percent local (county-level) (Su 2005,

A visitor examining a stone tablet at the Shanghai Museum, July 1, 1997. *During the Cultural Revolution, Red Guard units destroyed many museum collections throughout China. By the 1980s, however, the government made a renewed effort to restore many institutions, looking to educate citizens about China's past.* © FRITZ HOFFMANN/CORBIS

p. 38). Under China's policy of opening up to the outside world, Chinese museums started to became active in the international arena of museology.

The 1990s saw museum development in China switch from soaring numbers to the construction of large modernized museums. In 1991 Shaanxi History Museum, relocated and reconstructed, became the first modernized museum in China. The museum, founded in 1944, had been renamed the Northwest Cultural Relics Display Hall, then the Northwest History Museum, and then again the Shaanxi Provincial Museum. Other large modern museums include Shanghai Museum (1996), Fujian Museum (2002), Tianjin Museum (2004), Chongqing Sanxia Bowuguan (Chongqing Three Gorges Museum) (2005), and Shanxi Museum (2005).

In the first decade of the twenty-first century, museums have continued to diversify, with occasional amalgamations. In 2003 the National Museum of Chinese History and the Museum of Chinese Revolution were consolidated into the National Museum of China. In 2005, the Capital Museum, originally located in the Confucian Temple in the northeast of Beijing, was re-opened in a new five-story building that cost more than US $152 million. Private enterprise has contributed to the museum boom since the 1990s. Between 1949 and the late 1980s, all Chinese museums were publicly funded and administered, but there are now approximately 200 private museums in China.

By designating museums and memorials as patriotic educational bases (*aiguozhuyi jiaoyu jidi*), China has expanded the function of museums from knowledge education to moral education. Many museums, including Shanghai Museum, the Palace Museum, and the National Museum of Chinese History, are among the first one hundred listed patriotic educational bases. The United Nations Educational, Scientific, and Cultural Organization (UNESCO) now lists many of China's museums as World Heritage Sites. Foremost among these is the Mausoleum of the First Qin Emperor, listed in 1987. These museums while preserving world cultural heritage, also provide patriotic education to the Chinese public. From May 2004, public museums in China commenced offering free admission to the general public.

SEE ALSO *Art History and Historiography; Archaeology, History of; Art Museums; Heritage Protection.*

BIBLIOGRAPHY

Bai ge aiguozhuyi jiaoyu shifan jidi mingdan [List of the one hundred model patriotic educational bases]. *Dangjian* [Party Construction] 7 (1997): 38.

Bonneville, Patrick, and Phillipe Hémono. *The World Heritage: UNESCO's Classified Sites.* Saint-Hubert, Quebec: Bonneville Connection, 2006.

Chen Jinping. Zhang Jian yu Nantong Bowuyuan [Zhang Jian and Nantong Museum]. *Zhongguo Wenhua Yichan* 4 (2005): 14–16.

Claypool, Lisa. Zhang Jian and China's First Museum. *Journal of Asian Studies* 64, 3 (2005): 567–604.

Elliott, Jeanette Shambaugh, and David L. Shambaugh, *The Odyssey of China's Imperial Art Treasures*, Seattle: University of Washington Press, 2005.

Fan, Chunrong. *Shanghai shi bowuguan dashi jiyao (1933–1948)* [Chronicle of Shanghai Museum, 1933–1948]. *Zhongguo Bowuguan* 2 (1991): 77–84.

Fu Lianzhong. Guwu Chenliesuo yu Gugong Bowuyuan [Guwu Chenliesuo and the Palace Museum]. *Zhongguo Wenhua Yichan* 4 (2005): 22–26.

Guo, Changjian, and Jianzhi Song, eds. *World Heritage Sites in China.* Beijing: China Intercontinental Press, 2003.

Hu Jianzhong. Shanghai Bowuguan: Xiandaihua bowuguan de xianjin linian [Shanghai Museum: Advanced concepts of modernized museums]. *Zhongguo Wenhua Yichan* 4 (2005): 58–59.

Ji Bing. Dongbei Bowuguan: Xin Zhongguo diyi zuo bowuguan [Northeastern Museum: The first museum of new China]. *Zhongguo Wenhua Yichan* 4 (2005): 42–43.

Ji Dong. Shandong Bowuguan: Diyizuo shengji dizhi bowuguan [Shandong Provincial Museum: The first provincial local museum]. *Zhongguo Wenhua Yichan* 4 (2005): 44–45.

Jin Yan. Zhongguo bowuguan shiye de kaichuangzhe: Zhang Jian [An Initiator of Chinese Museums: Zhang Jian]. *Zhongguo Bowuguan* 1 (2005): 66–70.

Liang Jisheng. Zhongguo jindai bowuguan shiye jinian [Chronicle of modern Chinese museums]. *Zhongguo Bowuguan* 2 (1991): 68–76.

Liang Jisheng. Jindai Zhongguo diyizuo guoli bowuguan: Guoli Lishi Bowuguan [The first national museum of modern China: National History Museum]. *Zhongguo Wenhua Yichan* 4 (2005): 17–19.

Ma Zhenzhi. Shaanxi Lishi Bowuguan: Diyizuo xiandaihua bowuguan [Shaanxi History Museum: The first modernized museum]. *Zhongguo Wenhua Yichan* 4 (2005): 56–57.

Portal, Jane, ed. *The First Emperor: China's Terracotta Army.* Cambridge, MA: Harvard University Press, 2007.

Rawson, Jessica, ed. *Mysteries of Ancient China: New Discoveries from the Early Dynasties.* London: British Museum Press, 1996.

Shen Qinglin. Zhongguo Geming Bowuguan [The Museum of Chinese Revolution]. *Zhongguo Wenhua Yichan* 4 (2005): 50–52.

Song Xiangguang and Li Zhiling. Zhongguo dangdai sili bowuguan de fazhan ji tedian [The development and features of private museums in contemporary China]. *Zhongguo Bowuguan* 2 (2007): 12–20.

Su Donghai. Xin Zhongguo bowuguan shiye de fazhan, 1949–2005 [The development of new China's museum program, 1949–2005]. *Zhongguo Wenhua Yichan* 4 (2005): 30–41.

Sun Yu. Lu Xun de meishuguan [Lu Xun's viewpoint on the fine arts]. *Beijing wanbao*, January 18, 2007.

Tong Mingkang. Zhongguo de bowuguan shiye [The program of Chinese museums]. *Zhongguo Wenhua Yichan* 4 (2005): 5–7.

Wang Hongjun. Zhongguo bowuguan shiye de chuangshi he minguo shiqi de chubu fazhan [The initiation of China's museum program and its development during the Republican era]. *Zhongguo Wenhua Yichan* 4 (2005): 8–13.

Wang Hongjun. Zhongguo Lishi Bowuguan [The National Museum of Chinese History]. *Zhongguo Wenhua Yichan* 4 (2005): 52–53.

Zhen Shuonan. Beijing Ziran Bowuguan: Zuizao de zhuanti bowuguan [Beijing Natural History Museum: The earliest specialized museum]. *Zhongguo Wenhua Yichan* 4 (2005): 48–50.

Zhongxuanbu gongbu bai ge aiguozhuyi jiaoyu jidi [The Ministry of Publicity announces one hundred patriotic educational bases]. *Sheke Xinxi Wenhui* 10 (1997): 20.

Zhongguo renmin geming junshi bowuguan [The Military Museum of the Chinese People's Revolution]. *Zhongguo Wenhua Yichan* 4 (2005): 55–56.

Yu Luo Rioux

MUSIC, IMPACT IN THE WEST

For the longest time, Chinese music did not appeal to Western ears. Even the Jesuit missionaries who had a lot of good things to say about China and Chinese culture were much less favorable in their assessment of its music. The French composer Hector Berlioz (1803–1869) visited London in 1851 when the World Industrial Fair was held and heard some Chinese and Indian music performed. His reaction was devastated and devastating: "I shall not attempt to describe these wildcat howls, these death-rattles, these turkey cluckings, in the midst of which, despite my closest attention, I was able to make out only four distinct notes" (Berlioz 1956, pp. 249–250).

China and the Chinese had been represented in Western musics since the eighteenth century. The treatment of the Asian Other in, for example, Christoph Willibald Gluck's *Le cinesi* (*The Chinese*, 1754) and André Grétry's *Panurge dans l'île des lanternes* (1785), as well as in the parodistic *Ba-ta-clan* (1855) by Jacques Offenbach and still later works such as Béla Bartók's *Der wunderbare Mandarin* (*The Miraculous Mandarin*, 1918/1919) and Franz Léhar's *Das Land des Lächelns* (*The Land of Smiles*, 1923), is one of an often denigrating exoticism: The Asian appears as grotesque and childish, or, alternatively, as erotic and demonic. In all of the early ballets and operas with Chinese subjects (and for a while they were quite fashionable), Chinese local color appears mostly visually. The use of exotic (often not originally Chinese) instruments, too, served this purpose of visual appeal; the musical scores usually did not even mention them.

In the early twentieth century a number of European composers took a step away from what has been termed *naïve exoticism* to what one might call *intuitive exoticism* (Utz 2002, p. 45), recognizing some of the fundamental similarities between techniques found in Asian music and those later (re-)developed in Western new music, such as microtonalities, bruitism, sound melodies, polyrhythms and polytonalities, *Sprechgesang*, heterophony, and linearity. Compositions such as Claude Debussy's *Pagodes* (1903), Gustav Mahler's *Lied von der Erde* (*Song of the Earth*, 1908), and, later, Giacomo Puccini's *Turandot* (1928), which uses a number of Chinese melodies recorded in J. A. van Aalst's 1884 study *Chinese Music*, and Alexander Zemlinsky's *Der Kreidekreis* (*The Chalk Circle*, 1932), attest to the fact that new conceptions of and experiences with China's musical and philosophical heritage had influenced Western composers' musical imaginations. All of these compositions, which still remain within the boundaries of Western musical discourse, are characterized by their markedly different approach to the Asian Other.

Another significant change in the reception of Asian traditions in Western music is epitomized in the work of the composer John Cage (1912–1992), who translated Asian and Chinese philosophical traits into his revolutionary works (e.g., *Music of Changes*, 1952, and the silent piece *4.33'*, 1952). The recent international success of Chinese "new wave" composers such as Tan Dun (b. 1957), Qu Xiaosong (b. 1952), Guo Wenjing (b. 1956), Chen Qigang (b. 1951), and Bright Sheng (b. 1955), and the foundation of intercultural ensembles using not only European instruments, such as the Atlas Ensemble Amsterdam, have influenced the compositional styles of some upcoming Western composers and may introduce another method of integrating China and Asia, musically, in Western composition.

SEE ALSO *Tan Dun.*

BIBLIOGRAPHY

Berlioz, Hector. *Evenings with the Orchestra.* Trans. and ed. Jacques Barzun. New York: Alfred A. Knopf, 1956.

Cage, John. The East in the West. *Modern Music* 23 (1946): 111–115.

Gradenwitz, Peter. *Musik zwischen Orient und Okzident: Eine Kulturgeschichte der Wechselbeziehungen* [Music between East and West: A cultural history of interrelationships]. Wilhelmshaven, Germany: Heinrichshofen Verlag, 1977.

Revers, Peter. *Das Fremde und das Vertraute. Studien zur musiktheoretischen und musikdramatischen Asienrezeption* [The strange and the familiar: Studies in the reception of Asia in music theory and drama]. Stuttgart, Germany: Franz Steiner, 1997.

Stahl, Frank. China und die Entwicklung des Exotismus in der europäischen Musik—ein musikhistorischer Abriss [China and the development of exotism in European music: A draft history]. *Minima Sinica* 1 (1989): 39–53.

Stahl, Frank. Untersuchungen zum Chinabild einiger ausgewählter europäischer Kompositionen [Research into the image of China in selected European compositions]. *Minima Sinica* 2 (1989): 43–75.

Utz, Christian. *Neue Musik und Interkulturalität. Von John Cage bis Tan Dun* [New music and interculturality: From John Cage to Tan Dun]. Stuttgart, Germany: Franz Steiner, 2002.

Van Aalst, J. A. *Chinese Music*. 1884. New York: Paragon, 1966.

Barbara Mittler

MUSIC, POPULAR

The term *Chinese popular music* typically refers to music since the beginning of the twentieth century that is sung in Chinese and usually disseminated through the mass media as a commodity to a mass audience not confined to a particular locale. It circulates and is influenced by musical genres in the Chinese-speaking world, the Asian region, and beyond, particularly the United States and Europe. In Chinese, the term includes generic terms such as *liuxing yinyue* and *tongsu yingyue* (popular music) and subgenres such as rock music (*yaogun yinyue*). Popular music is construed in relation to other large musical categories such as classical, art, and folk music, which also may have widespread popularity. In modern China it is distinguished from Chinese traditional music.

The development of popular music is tied to changing economic structures and the growth of the media and related technologies and industries. Because the meanings associated with popular music differ in relation to ideologies and periods, there is considerable variation in the types of music included within the rubric. Some theorists consider popular music to be a top-down phenomenon and distinguish between market-driven and state-driven control over the production of music. Many consider popular music to be a commodity tied to entertainment industries and differentiate it from music associated with official politics and religion. Prominent topics in the discourse about Chinese popular music include the relation between the native and foreign, issues of authenticity, and the impact of commercialism. Studies of Chinese popular music have focused on such topics as musical style and lyrics; particular genres and musicians; interactions between popular music in China and other parts of the world; interfaces between music and politics; relations between music and identity; and the ways that popular music reflects contemporary society or acts as a generator of social change.

ORIGINS AND DEVELOPMENT OF POPULAR MUSIC

The beginnings of popular music in China are situated during the Republican era in the early twentieth century and within urban settings. By the 1920s, in cosmopolitan cities such as Shanghai, new technologies, a burgeoning media, and the growth of entertainment industries led to a concentration of musicians and music business activity. Dance halls and clubs provided venues for live performance, and music recorded by Chinese-owned and multinational companies, such as Pathé and EMI, was disseminated through radio and film. The music combined Chinese and foreign styles, particularly from Europe and the United States. Jazz musicians and big bands from the United States and musicians from Southeast Asia and Russia performed in Shanghai, and music circulated among urban centers on the mainland, Hong Kong, and other Chinese communities.

Among the most famous composers of popular music (*liuxing yinyue*) and modern songs (*shidaiqu*) in the late 1920s and 1930s was Li Jinhui (1891–1967), today called the "father of Chinese popular music." Modern songs, with lyrics focusing on love and other topics, were an entertainment genre that often combined characteristics of Chinese song styles with those of American jazz and dance music. Characteristic songs include Li's "Peach Blossom River" ("Taohuajiang") and "Drizzle" ("Maomaoyü"). A music activist and entrepreneur, Li established musical troupes such as the Bright Moon Song and Dance Troupe (Mingyue Gewutuan) and the first studio musician troupe for the Lianhua Film Studio (Lianhua Yingye Gongsi). Such groups launched the careers of actresses and singers such as Zhou Xuan (1918–1957), Bai Guang (1921–1999), and Bai Hong (1919–1992). The music and musicians had a wide fan base, promoted through a rapidly growing star apparatus system. Sometimes banned by the Nationalist government and criticized as decadent by leftists in the 1930s, Li's music was labeled as pornographic "yellow music" (*huangse yinyue*) and banned in the People's Republic of China (PRC) until the 1980s. The 1931 Japanese invasion of northeast China and the War of Resistance against the Japanese (1937–1945) spurred efforts to create music to mobilize people in social-political movements. Influenced particularly by Russian revolutionary music, leftist musicians promoted patriotism and national salvation through revolutionary songs (*geming gequ*), mass songs (*qunzhong gequ*), and mass music (*dazhong yinyue*). Although often presented as being in opposition to popular music, these genres were widely popular, commercially successful, disseminated through the mass media, and produced by some of the same companies.

Following China's victory in the Japanese war and of the Chinese Communist Party in the civil war, many musicians and companies moved to Hong Kong and Taiwan, which became sites for the development of popular music through the 1970s. In the PRC, music increasingly was used to promote socialism, and the mass media and private industries were nationalized. By the end of the 1950s, state-controlled media, educational institutions, and national song and dance troupes (*minzu gewutuan*) emphasized revolutionary and mass songs and revised music of the people, including folk and minority music. State-controlled institutions were avowedly anticommercial. Although often excluded from histories of Chinese popular music, this officially sanctioned music was disseminated through the mass media, including the national system of loudspeakers; some of the music was covered by popular musicians and included in anthologies of popular music after 1978.

POPULAR MUSIC IN THE POST-MAO REFORM ERA

The economic reforms beginning in 1978 led to what often is called the reemergence of popular music in China. The period from the late 1970s to the early 1990s is characterized by state control, coupled with the gradual privatization and growth of commercial recording and entertainment industries. The open-door policies of the late 1970s led to an increase in musical imports and the entry of foreign companies. Through the state-run music industry and media, the government supported new forms of popular music. Often labeled *tongsu yinyue* (popularized music), it included easy-listening light music (*qing yinyue*) and nationalized folk music (*minge*) and drew stylistically from genres associated with the commercial music industry outside China. The government cultivated popular music singers and sponsored competitions and television programs. Concerts by foreign musicians were officially sanctioned, among them the American singer John Denver in 1979 and the British-based group Wham! in 1985.

A less official opening came through increased access to foreign radio broadcasts and cassette technology, which increased private access to music production and reproduction. Often circulated underground, outside both the state-supported and commercial structures, imported music gained popularity among the youth. This included music from Taiwan and Hong Kong called *Gangtai yinyue* (Hong Kong–Taiwan music), which featured lyrical love songs and ballads sung in Mandarin (Mando-pop) and Cantonese (Canto-pop). Among those singers who influenced mainland musicians in the 1980s were Deng Lijun (Teresa Teng; 1953–1995), a Mando-pop singer from Taiwan, and Mei Yanfang (Anita Mui; 1963–2003), a Canto-pop singer from Hong Kong. Also influential was the music of singer-songwriters such as Luo Dayou (Lo

Ta-yu), whose music mixed influences from Taiwanese folk song and Euro-American popular music with social commentary. For instance, Luo's film theme song "Yes or No" ("Shifou") became popular in the mid-1980s through the underground circulation of cassettes. The mid-1980s also saw the development of the genre Northwest Wind (Xibeifeng) and Chinese rock music. Popular songs such as "Have Nothing" ("Yiwu suoyou") by Cui Jian and "Xintianyou" (named after a Shaanxi province folk song genre) were associated with both genres. Northwest Wind, which combined regional Chinese folk music with imported styles and instruments, was presented as a more "native" form than *Gangtai* music, particularly in relation to the roots-seeking (*xungen*) movement of the mid-1980s. Rock music drew more heavily on Euro-American rock styles and on rock understood as an expression—often oppositional and individualistic—of the youth subculture. First concentrated within Beijing, the rock music scene was situated in universities and private clubs and often supported by newly emerging private entrepreneurs. Performers included Cui Jian and groups such as Black Panther (Heibao), Breathing (Huxi yuedui), Cobra (Yanjingshe), and Tang Dynasty (Tangchao), all of which were subject to frequent government bans during the late 1980s.

The varied styles of imported music and their development within China resulted in an eclectic mix of styles. Diverse ideologies and rapidly shifting government regulations, along with subsequent transformations in singers and genres, also complicate the classifications of music of this period. For instance, Cui Jian, who has come to be associated with 1980s underground rock, initially gained fame in an official competition of *tongsu* musicians in 1986. Li Guyi, trained in a state-sponsored Flower Drum opera (*huaguxi,* a regional opera form from Hunan) troupe, was transferred to an official light music (*qing yinyue*) ensemble in the 1970s. In 1980 she was officially criticized for singing "Nostalgia" ("Xianglian"; "Longing for Home"), a song she then was invited to sing in the 1983 Spring Festival Program held by CCTV, the television network of China; she became the director of the Light Music Ensemble in 1986. Hou Dejian traveled from Taiwan to China in 1983, where he became popular through songs such as his 1978 "Descendants of the Dragon" ("Long de chuanren"), written originally as a response to the severing of U.S. official diplomatic relations with Taiwan. In 1989 Hou joined other Chinese rock and pop musicians to perform in the Tiananmen Square protest. In the early 1990s the state tightened its control over popular music. At the same time, revolutionary classics, such as music of the War of Resistance against the Japanese and of the decade of Cultural Revolution (1966–1976), were reformulated as popular music and issued through state and commercial companies.

POPULAR MUSIC IN THE 1990s AND EARLY 2000s

New economic and political reforms beginning in the early 1990s and China's entry into the World Trade Organization in 2001 propelled the privatization and growth of commercial music and related entertainment and consumer industries, along with other developments such as the diversification of musical genres; more extensive circulation of popular music within China, throughout Asia, and around the world; and the diversification of media and outlets, such as CCTV MTV (Zhongguo yinyue dianshi), commercialized karaoke, DVD and MP3 formats, and the Internet. Large multinational companies and independent recording labels became important players in music production. Music was promoted through a network of magazines, Web sites, marketing companies, educational institutions, and national and international awards. As a result of changes in regulations issued by the Ministry of Culture in the early 1990s, it became necessary for state-run music troupes to compete in the market. The state sponsors and makes money from popular music, as illustrated through activities surrounding the 2008 Beijing Olympics. And it continues to issue and lift bans on Chinese singers, both from inside and outside China, including Cui Jian and Zhang Huimei (A-mei; Gulilai Amit), an indigenous Taiwanese singer who gained famed in the late 1990s.

In the early twenty-first century, among the genres popular in China were pop, rock, heavy metal, rap and hip-hop, electronic dance music and experimental electronic music, and new popular folk and minority music. In addition to new voices, musicians from the 1980s remained on the scene, associated with new genres and institutions. Na Ying, earlier associated with Northwest Wind, signed with EMI. Liu Huan, who gained popularity in television dramas in the late 1980s and then through his performance at the 1990s Asian Games, signed with Sony Records and sang the official Olympics theme song at the 2008 Beijing Olympics. Tang Dynasty became known primarily as an experimental heavy metal band. He Yong, a late-1980s rock musician, became a punk musician in the 1990s. Mando- and Canto-pop musicians remained popular in China and throughout Asia, including musicians Wang Fei (Faye Wong) and 1990s Canto-pop musicians such as the "Four Heavenly Kings": Guo Fucheng (Aaron Kwok), Li Ming (Leon Lai), Liu Dehua (Andy Lau), and Zhang Xueyou (Jacky Cheung). Mandarin singers from Taiwan such as Zhou Jielun (Jay Chou), four-time winner in the Chinese category of the World Music Awards, also contributed to a pan-Chinese popular music that was prominently featured in the 2008 Olympics. New stars have emerged from new institutions such as the Super Girl contests (Chaoji nüsheng), which began in 2003 under the sponsorship of a dairy company; by 2004 it had became a nationwide phenomenon, producing megastars such as Jane Zhang (Zhang Liangying) and Zhou Bichang as well as associated products and consumer franchises.

The centers of production of popular music in China have also diversified. For instance, Shanghai reemerged as a center of new popular music as well as revivals of music from the 1930s. Singers such as Dao Lang, who sang covers of songs such as "In That Far Away Place" ("Zai na yaoyuan de difang") by Wang Luobin (1913–1996), reflect a broader trend of reformulating songs that formerly were considered "popular among the people" but not "popular music." Chinese ethnic minority music, such as that of singers such as the Chinese Mongolian Teng Ge'er and Siqin Gerile, also became important to the popular music scene in the early 1990s. Ethnic rock bands, such as the folk-rock band from Ningxia called Cloth (Buyi), make explicit ties to ethnicity and border provinces. The growth in the world music industry also has stimulated the growth and international recognition of Chinese popular, minority, and folk music. Within China, large-scale music festivals, such as Midi Modern Music and the Snow Mountain festivals, draw musicians from around the world. In 2008 China hosted its first World Music Festival, with support from the Chinese government.

SEE ALSO *Cui Jian; Film Industry; Gramophone and Gramophone Records; Music, Impact in the West; Music, Western and Russian Influence on; Zhou Xuan.*

BIBLIOGRAPHY

Baranovitch, Nimrod. *China's New Voices: Popular Music, Ethnicity, Gender, and Politics, 1978–1997*. Berkeley: University of California Press, 2003.

Fung, Anthony. Western Style, Chinese Pop: Jay Chou's Rap and Hip-Hip in China. *Asian Music* 39, 1 (2008): 69–80.

Huang, Hao. Voices from Chinese Rock, Past and Present Tense: Social Commentary and Construction of Identity in *Yaogun Yinyue*, from Tiananmen to the Present. *Popular Music and Society* 26 (2003): 183–202.

Jones, Andrew F. *Like a Knife: Ideology and Genre in Contemporary Chinese Popular Music*. Ithaca, NY: East Asia Program, Cornell University, 1992.

Jones, Andrew F. *Yellow Music: Media Culture and Colonial Modernity in the Chinese Jazz Age*. Durham, NC: Duke University Press, 2001.

Kloet, Jeroen de. Popular Music and Youth in Urban China: The Dakou Generation. *China Quarterly* 181 (2005): 610–626.

Li Hongji, ed. *Zhongguo yaogun shouce: Jilu Zhongguo yaogun 20 nian* [Encyclopedia of Chinese rock music: A twenty-year history of Chinese rock]. Chongqing: Chongqing Chubanshe, 2006.

Sue Tuohy

MUSIC, PROPAGANDA, AND MASS MOBILIZATION

Music has been employed as a communicative form and as a vehicle to rally people in support of national, revolutionary, and social-political movements throughout modern Chinese history. It has been used to raise awareness of problems, to gain support for particular ideologies, and to move people emotionally and physically. Broad patterns can be seen in the types of music associated with twentieth-century movements. Much music is based on styles historically associated with the West, including band music and hymns. Vocal music often follows a strophic form, with the lyrics of each stanza set to the same melody. A verse-and-refrain form, with stanzas alternating with a repeated chorus, has been a common form that facilitates the learning of songs by large numbers of people. Some movements have combined these features with musical characteristics of Chinese regional and folk genres. Subsequent movements have recycled or adapted music from prior movements, both Chinese and foreign. New lyrics have been set to preexisting tunes; images such as the Yellow River have been used repeatedly in song lyrics; and musical works from previous movements have been carried over into later movements.

Musical movements also have exhibited similar characteristics in their organizational strategies and philosophies. They have enlisted the participation of musicians and have fostered organizations of artists to promote the music and movement aims. They have composed and compiled music for live performance at venues associated with mass movements, such as demonstrations and rallies. They also have made use of available media to disseminate the music and to interpret it in relation to their goals. Movement organizers have published articles on the use of music to mobilize and educate the Chinese people. Many central leaders of the movements and in the national government have paid attention to the power of music, and have considered it to be an effective tool for changing people's minds, hearts, and behaviors. They also have utilized music's participatory nature as a strategy for organizing groups for collective action.

MODERNIZATION AND NATIONALISM, REFORM AND REVOLUTION

International events, internal reforms, and the creation of new institutions in the late nineteenth and early twentieth centuries contributed to the development of a repertoire of music, organizations, and strategies for using music to effect social-political change. Music was employed in movements ranging from anti-imperialism movements and late Qing reforms to the Xinhai Revolution (Xinhai geming) and the May Fourth movement (Wusi yundong). Whether aimed at reform or revolution, many were nationalist movements that called for a strengthening of China in relation to foreign imperialism, as well as for learning from the West to modernize China. Social-political reformers and government leaders included music in the arsenal of tools for social-political transformation, and modern media and educational institutions became important arenas for both movements and music.

Following the end of the first Sino-Japanese War in 1895, intellectuals set new lyrics to Western songs and Chinese folk tunes to rally the Chinese people in anti-imperialist demonstrations and boycotts of foreign goods. Lecture corps and speech clubs disseminated the songs orally, and the burgeoning modern press published the songs' lyrics. China's perceived weakness stimulated late Qing self-strengthening movements, and reformed institutions created the need for new music. Qing reformers such as Kang Youwei (1858–1927) advocated modern music to awaken and educate the people, and Yuan Shikai (1859–1916) hired German musical advisers to assist in the musical modernization of the reformed army. After the Xinhai Revolution and the overthrow of the Qing government in 1912, the new republic created national institutions and the need for national anthems. Chinese intellectuals formed research groups and magazines devoted to reform or revolution in the early 1900s. For instance, the Qing reformer Liang Qichao (1873–1929) considered both the press and music to be vehicles for education, and he included a column in *Xinmin congbao* (The New Citizen) to publish patriotic songs and articles on music. Members of his Music Discussion Society (Yinyue jiangxihui), such as Li Shutong (1880–1942) and Shen Xingong (1870–1947), studied musical modernization in Japan and applied the lessons to China. They created a new genre of school songs (*xuetang yuege*) based on military and choral styles from the West and Japan as well as popular Chinese music. Lyrics focused on topics such as patriotism, women's rights, and anti-imperialism. The Qing government establishment of a modern school system in 1905 provided an important venue for school songs, which functioned as a form of spiritual and moral education. Revolutionaries considered the songs useful in transforming Chinese people from imperial subjects into modern national citizens. The "Song of the Homeland" ("Zuguo ge"), "The Yellow River" ("Huanghe"), "Man of China" ("Zhongguo naner"), and "Geography and History of the Eighteen Provinces" ("Shibasheng dili lishi") promoted the idea of a unified Chinese people and territory.

By the mid-1910s some Chinese intellectuals were pushing for more radical changes. The New Culture movement (Xin wenhua yundong) called for the creation of a modern and national literature. Many musicians joined in movements to reform traditional music and to create a national Chinese music (*guoyue*); others searched for the musical equivalent of vernacular literature. Disillusionment grew with the Chinese government's weak response to the 1919 Treaty of Versailles, which transferred German concessions in Shandong to the Japanese. On May 4, 1919, students organized a mass protest in Beijing. The May Fourth movement developed into a broadly based cultural and nationalist movement that inspired composers of Chinese art songs, such as Zhao Yuanren (Yuen Ren Chao, 1892–1982), and of Chinese children's songs, such as Li Jinhui (1891–1967). The musicologist Wang Guangqi (1892–1936) joined Li Dazhao (1888–1927) and Mao Zedong (1893–1976) in the Young China Association (Shaonian Zhongguo xuehui), a social reform organization aimed at transforming individuals and society through both self cultivation and social activism. The movement also became the topic of commemoration in songs such as Xiao Youmei's (1884–1940) "Patriotic Song Commemorating 'May Fourth'" ("'Wusi' jinian aiguo ge," 1924) and Lü Ji's (1909–2002) "May Fourth Commemoration Song" ("Wusi jinian ge," 1939).

A number of musicians returned to China after studying overseas: Xian Xinghai (1905–1945) and Ren Guang (1900–1941) studied in Paris; Xiao Youmei and Wang Guangqi in Germany; Huang Zi (1904–1938) and Zhao Yuanren in the United States. Many of these musicians held positions at academic institutions that became important centers for publication and the organization of people and activities. Zhao Yuanren taught at Tsinghua University, and Liu Tianhua (1895–1932) and Wang Guangqi taught at Peking University, which had been reorganized by Cai Yuanpei (1868–1940). Xiao Youmei headed Peking University's Music Institute established in 1921; with Cai, he also founded the Shanghai Conservatory (formerly, National College of Music). Leading musicians published articles with theoretical and practical advice for using music to reach different types of people in China. The musical movements spread to rural areas, stimulated by calls to "go to the people" and organizations such as the Folk Song Research Society (Geyao yanjiuhui), which began publishing the *Geyao Zhoukan* (Folk Song Weekly) in 1922. Under a slogan of "from and to the masses," musicians went to the countryside to collect raw materials from which to compose new music and to teach movement songs to the rural populace. New progressive and proletarian music was emphasized by the Southern Society (Nanguoshe), established by Tian Han (1898–1968). Zhang Shu (1903–1938), composed music and adapted folk songs for theater. The establishment of the Chinese Communist Party (CCP) in 1921 also contributed to the development of revolutionary songs (*geming gequ*) and mass songs (*qunzhong gequ*). Musical organizers of the 1920s recycled lyrics and music from other movements, illustrating the transnational nature of Chinese nationalism. The "National Revolution Song" ("Guomin geming ge," 1926) of the Whampoa Military Academy was set to the melody of the French song "Frère

Jacques." "The Internationale" ("Guoji ge"), composed in France in the late 1880s and translated from Russian into Chinese by Qu Qiubai (1899–1935), was published in *Xin Qingnian* (New Youth) in 1921 and in revolutionary songbooks in the late 1920s.

JAPANESE AND CIVIL WARS, NATIONAL SALVATION AND THE YAN'AN MODEL

The Japanese and civil wars in the 1930s and 1940s further stimulated musical movements. Songs were performed in mass assemblies and were included in films, broadcast on the radio, published in song anthologies, and discussed in newspapers. The Japanese seizure of Manchuria following the Mukden incident on September 18, 1931, the battle between Japanese and Republic troops in Shanghai on January 28, 1932, and the December 9, 1935, Beijing student movement spurred musicians to organize large-scale musical movements in urban centers. These incidents also provided themes for commemorative events and songs, such as Huang Zi's "September 18th" ("Jiu-yi-ba," 1933), Lü Ji's "'January 28' Commemoration Song" ("'Yi-er-ba' jinian ge," 1936), and "On the Songhua River" ("Songhuajiang shang," 1936), a lament about the September 18 Japanese invasion of his homeland written by Zhang Hanhui (1902–1946).

Musicians formed numerous organizations to promote new music movements. Nie Er (1912–1935), Ren Guang, and Zhang Shu joined Tian Han in the music group of the Soviet Friends Society (Sulianzhiyou she yinyue xiaozu) in 1933 to produce revolutionary, proletarian, and mass music. They also participated in the left-wing arts movement, forming a music section under the leadership of Lü Ji. Movement organizers used new technologies to broadcast national defense music (*guofang yinyue*). Composers such as He Luding (1903–1999) and Lü Ji wrote music for film. Many of the compositions of Nie Er were theme songs for influential films, such as "The New Woman" ("Xinnüxing," 1934) for the 1935 film of the same title; "Song of the Big Road" ("Dalu ge"; lyrics, Sun Yu) and "The Pioneers" ("Kailu xianfeng"; lyrics Shi Yi) for the 1934 film *The Big Road* (*Dalu*); and the theme song of *Children of Troubled Times* (*Fengyun ernü*, 1935), "The March of the Volunteers" ("Yiyongjun jinxingqu"; lyrics, Tian Han), which later became the national anthem of the People's Republic of China (PRC).

Organizers worked to mobilize Chinese from all walks of life through musical activities. Lü Ji, who taught music in night schools for female workers, wrote theoretical articles on national defense music. Xiao Youmei wrote about Western nations that used music to unify citizens and promote nationalism. In a February 3, 1936, article in *Libao* newspaper, "The Mission of Composers in the Period of National Calamity," Sha Mei urged musicians to compose progressive folk songs and collective songs and music for the masses (*dazhong jiti geyue*). Sha's February 9, 1936, article in *Libao,* "Organizational Issues in the National Salvation Music Movement," outlined four types of organizations for the Singing for Resistance against Japan and National Salvation movement (Kang Ri jiuwang geyong yundong): performance groups to perform in factories and schools; education groups to teach songs to the masses; music groups to lead rallies and marches; and masses singing groups. By 1936 massive rallies such as the masses singing assembly (*minzhong geyonghui*) were held in major cities to raise awareness and funds for the National Salvation movements. Rallies featured songs such as Nie Er's "Graduation Song" ("Biyege"; lyrics, Chen Yu, 1934) and "Song of Advance" ("Qianjin ge"; lyrics, Tian Han, 1934) and Xian Xinghai's "Go to the Enemy's Rear" ("Dao diren houfang qu") and "Hot (Boiling) Blood" ("Rexue"; lyrics, by Tian Han). Newspapers published songs and commented on the role of music in stirring the emotions, using song lyrics to refer to the "boiling blood" of the Chinese people and the roaring sound of mass singing.

Much of the CCP relocated to Yan'an and concentrated its activity on rural areas from 1935 to 1948. Building on experiences from earlier social-political movements, the CCP developed its organizational strategies, emphasizing local and folk forms. In 1942 Mao Zedong set out the basic principles for the mass line in his "Talks at the Yan'an Forum on Literature and Art." The arts were to serve politics and the people, and music was to be used as a tool for uniting and transforming the people. Intellectuals were to learn from and teach the people; this work was to be done collectively, while living among the people. The Lu Xun Academy of Art (Lu Xun yishu xueyuan) was established in 1938 to train intellectuals, arts workers in the Eighth Route Army, and the local populace. Composers such as Xian Xinghai and Lü Ji taught in the music department. Folk songs were collected, revised, and disseminated back to the people, with the aims of mobilizing them to fight the Japanese, improving literacy, raising political consciousness, and instilling socialist ideas. Songs such as "Nanniwan"—composed by Ma Ke (1918–1976) and based on a northern Shaanxi folk tune, with lyrics by He Jingzhi—extolled the success of CCP agricultural policies in an impoverished area in Shaanxi. The concept of collectively composed music was developed, producing works such as opera *The White-Haired Girl* (*Baimaonü*, 1942). The *yangge* (rice seedlings) song and dance form was widely used. Xian Xinghai's *Yellow River Cantata* (*Huanghe dahechang*), based on a poem by Guang Weiren (1913–2002), was composed and performed in Yan'an in 1939 (revised in 1941). The centralized coordination of activities during the Yan'an period provided the basis for art and literature activities after 1949.

NATIONAL AND SOCIALIST CONSTRUCTION IN THE PRC

Music promoted and was impacted by national and socialist construction as artistic organizations were expanded under the control of the Ministries of Culture and Propaganda between 1949 and the early 1960s. Comprehensive literature and arts associations and individual arts associations were established, as were masses organizations and cultural units, from the national to village levels. This vertical and horizontal structure facilitated the national coordination of activities and the dissemination of policies. Following the Soviet model, the government sponsored musical troupes and festivals. State organizations founded arts magazines such as *Wenyi bao* (Literature and Arts Magazine) and controlled the broadcasting of music through mass-media technologies including the nationwide loudspeaker system. Music was to serve social-political purposes and "the people," but shifts in emphasis, leadership, and artistic policies resulted in frequent purges of leaders and musicians. The period saw the creation of new revolutionary favorites such as "Ode to the Homeland" ("Gechang zuguo"), composed by Wang Shen (1918–2007). The classic mobilization campaign was developed extensively and featured singing, dancing, and drama.

During the 1956 Hundred Flowers campaign Mao Zedong presented his "Talk to Music Workers" ("Tong yinyue gongzuozhe de tanhua"). Explaining that each nation had its own national style, he encouraged musicians to draw upon the best of the Chinese past and the foreign to develop a Chinese national style. The 1958 Folk Song Collecting movement (Caifeng yundong) sponsored teams to collect and edit songs for volumes such as *A Collection of Revolutionary Folk Songs* (*Geming mingeji*, 1958) and *Songs of the Red Flag* (*Hongqi geyao*, 1960). The 1958 Great Leap Forward also produced songs exhorting people to engage in industrial and agricultural production and extolling the party, the New Society, and collectivization campaigns. The Socialist Singing Campaign and the model opera movement of the early 1960s followed a three-pronged line in music: revolutionize, nationalize, and popularize (*sanhua*: *geminghua*, *minzuhua*, and *dazhonghua*). In 1964 new revolutionary song anthologies were published, such as the *Compilation of Revolutionary Songs* (*Geming gequ xuanji*), which included many songs from the 1920s and 1930s. A similar principle guided the creation of a performed anthology, *The East Is Red Song and Dance Epic* (*Dongfanghong yinyue wudao shishi*). "The East Is Red" song, based on a folk song that was rearranged during the Anti-Japanese War, was again transformed and became an unofficial anthem of the PRC. Other key events included the Festival of Peking Opera on Contemporary Themes in 1964, followed by a forum for opera workers and a series of articles and policy directives for creating revolutionary opera.

CULTURAL REVOLUTION

The period from 1966 to 1976 saw the continued expansion of organizational strategies, mass campaigns, and the use of the media to disseminate music and artistic policies. Music was interwoven into the contexts of the Cultural Revolution as performances accompanied massive political rallies in Tiananmen Square and criticism sessions. Musical works were made into movies, and famous characters from musical shows became the subject of posters. Songs such as "The Ode to the Great Proletarian Cultural Revolution" ("Gechang wuchan jieji wenhua dageming") encouraged wide participation in the complete transformation of society. Although post–Cultural Revolution histories often repeat the idea that music was limited to eight model works, music included symphonies and marching band pieces, folk songs and choral works, and regional opera. Ideological struggles over the arts led to purges, the dismantling of music education institutes, and the arrests and deaths of many musicians.

Much of the new music was produced by collectives of artists following the artistic guidelines of the cultural bureaucracy, led by Jiang Qing (1914–1991). With Mao Zedong Thought standing as the guiding principle for revolutionary undertakings, art was to be understood and appreciated by the masses. Artistic products should glorify peasants, and revolutionary leaders such as Mao should be portrayed as heroes for the people to emulate. Certain musical pieces were formally marked as models and carried the imprimatur of the cultural bureaucracy. Former leaders in the revolutionary arts, such as Lü Ji and Tian Han, were labeled bourgeois romantics and antirevolutionary revisionists; they were to be clearly portrayed as "bad elements," and their works were banned or their names were excluded from publications. The constant reinterpretation necessitated an interpretive discourse to clearly mark pieces as models or "poisonous weeds." *Renmin ribao* (People's Daily) and *Hongqi* (Red Flag) published songs and commentaries by national leaders such as Mao Zedong and Jiang Qing. From 1966 to 1968 Red Guard newspapers such as *Xinghuo liaoyuan* (A Single Spark Can Start a Prairie Fire) published songs with topical political themes, such as "Grasp Revolution, Promote Production" ("Zhua geming, cu shengchan") and "Pledge Your Life to Defend the Great Proletarian Cultural Revolution" ("Shisi hanwei wuchan jieji wenhua dageming"), as well as musical settings of quotations of Chairman Mao (*yuluge*). The late 1960s and early 1970s saw increased attention to the international dissemination of Cultural Revolution music and messages through magazines translated in many languages. The 1969 issue of the English-language version of *Chinese Literature* (vol. 10), for instance, published works such as "The Internationale," "The East Is Red," and "Sailing the Seas Depends on the Helmsman" ("Dahai hangxing kao duoshou").

A wide range of musical genres is evident in the serial *Wenyi jiemu* (Literary and Art Program), which began publication in 1972 under the Cultural Section of the State Council. The magazine often published music featured in officially sponsored festivals, including songs such as "I Love the Great Homeland" ("Wo ai weida de zuguo") and "Drink a Cup of Buttered Tea" ("Qing he yibei suyoucha"); regional opera versions of the model work *The Red Lantern* (*Hongdengji*); children's music and ballads; and Mongolian folk songs praising Chairman Mao. Some of the most orthodox works of the Cultural Revolution were rearrangements of earlier pieces. *The White-Haired Girl* of the Yan'an period was transformed into a revolutionary modern ballet (*geming xiandai wuju*) in 1966, revised in 1972 for live performance, and made into a feature film; it also became the basis of "The White-Haired Girl Impromptu" ("Baimaonü jixingqu"), from the *Youth Piano Concerto* (*Qingnian gangqin xiezouqu*) in the 1970s. The pianist Yin Chengzong (b. 1941) participated in the 1969 composition of the *Yellow River Piano Concerto* (*Huanghe gangqin xiezouqu*), based on Xian Xinghai's *Yellow River Cantata* composed in the Yan'an period.

FROM POST-1978 REFORMS TO THE OLYMPIC MOVEMENT

Music also signaled the end of the Cultural Revolution and beginning of the post-1978 economic reforms. Pieces and musicians that had been banned during the Cultural Revolution were rehabilitated. Music continued to be used to promote the CCP, government reforms, and nationalism, but the diversification of media organizations and the end of government subsidies for many arts organizations in the early 1990s led to increased privatization of the cultural industry. The state and private companies capitalized on the creation of musical products for national ceremonies and commemorations, contributing to the commercialization of revolutionary songs and their transformation into the genre of beloved old songs (*laogequ*). Protestors in Tiananmen Square in 1989 sang both Chinese rock songs and pieces from Chinese revolutionary history, including "The Internationale" and "The March of the Volunteers."

In the early 1990s Jiang Zemin launched a new patriotic education campaign that stimulated the production of textbooks for music education classes. Patriotic songs included those praising the party such as "Without the Communist Party There Would Be No New China" ("Meiyou Gongchandang jiu meiyou xin Zhongguo"), a rearranged folk tune written in 1943 and revised by Mao in 1950. Music appreciation classes on traditional and Chinese national music were intended to increase national pride. Provincial and national cultural bureaus organized patriotic song and karaoke competitions. The approach of the 1993 centennial of the Mao Zedong's birth prompted the reissuing of earlier revolutionary music, including Red Sun tapes published in the early 1990s such as *Hong Taiyang: Mao Zedong songge xin jiezou lianchang* (The Red Sun: A Medley of Mao Zedong Praise Songs Set to New Rhythms) and *Mao Zhuxi yuluge: Weiren songge yaogun lianchang* (Musical Settings of Quotations from Chairman Mao: A Rock 'n' Roll Medley of Praise Songs for a Great Man). The fiftieth anniversary of the end of the Anti-Japanese War in 1995 furthered this trend as songs from the 1930s National Salvation movement and from 1964's *The East Is Red Song and Dance Epic* were reissued in tape anthologies such as *Dadao xiang guizi toushang kan qu: Kang Ri gequ zhuanji* (Use the Sword to Cut Off the Heads of the Foreign Invader Devils: A Special Compilation of Songs of Resistance against Japan) and *Kang Ri zhanzheng gequ jingxuan* (Selection of Songs of the War of Resistance against Japan). In 1995 a 1,000-person chorus performed Xian Xinghai's *Yellow River Cantata* in a concert commemorating the war.

Preparations for the 2008 Beijing Olympics provided another opportunity to use music to mobilize the population to support the upcoming games. Pregame activities, including numerous concerts and annual festivals of culture and the arts, were extensive and pervasive, occurring over the course of several years. Participation also was encouraged through competitions for official theme songs for the Olympics. Promotional marketing of the games and of official commercial sponsors was also extensive, with officially produced Olympics products such as DVDs and CDs. The opening and closing ceremonies, directed by Zhang Yimou, were a mass production, with an estimated 30,000 people involved in the production and performance. Among the featured works were the *Yellow River Piano Concerto*, "Ode to the Motherland," and "The March of the Volunteers."

SEE ALSO *Kang Youwei; Liang Qichao; Model Operas and Ballets; National Flags and National Anthems; Nationalism; Propaganda Art; Yan'an Forum; Yuan Shikai; Zhang Yimou.*

BIBLIOGRAPHY

Clark, Paul. *The Chinese Cultural Revolution: A History*. New York: Cambridge University Press, 2008.

Hung, Chang-tai. *War and Popular Culture: Resistance in Modern China, 1937–1945*. Berkeley: University of California Press, 1994.

Jones, Andrew F. *Yellow Music: Media Culture and Colonial Modernity in the Chinese Jazz Age*. Durham, NC: Duke University Press, 2001.

Kraus, Richard Curt. *Pianos and Politics in China: Middle-Class Ambitions and the Struggle over Western Music*. New York: Oxford University Press, 1989.

McDougall, Bonnie S. *Popular Chinese Literature and Performing Arts in the People's Republic of China, 1949–1979*. Berkeley: University of California Press, 1984.

Mittler, Barbara. *Dangerous Tunes: The Politics of Chinese Music in Hong Kong, Taiwan, and the People's Republic of China since 1949.* Wiesbaden, Germany: Harrassowitz, 1997.

Tuohy, Sue. The Sonic Dimensions of Nationalism in Modern China: Musical Representation and Transformation. *Ethnomusicology* 45 (2001): 107–131.

Zhonggong Shanghai shiwei, Dangshi ziliao zhengji weiyuanhui, ed. *"Yi'er jiu" yihou Shanghai jiuguohui shiliao xuanji* [Shanghai National Salvation assemblies after the December 9th movement: Collection of historical documents]. Shanghai: Shanghai Shehui Kexueyuan Chubanshe [Shanghai Social Science Academy Press], 1987.

Zhongyang yinyue xueyuan, ed. *Zhongguo jinxiandai yinyueshi jiaoxue cankao ziliao* [Educational reference materials for Chinese modern music history]. Beijing: Renmin Peoples Music Press, 1987.

Sue Tuohy

MUSIC, WESTERN AND RUSSIAN INFLUENCE ON

One of the most distinctive qualities of China's musical tradition is its ability to absorb outside influences. Some typical "Chinese" instruments, such as the lute, *pipa*, and the fiddle, *erhu,* are foreign imports from Central Asia and Mongolia. (Indeed, the two characters that comprise the term *erhu* mean "two-stringed foreign instrument.") Traditional Chinese music is based on melodic and rhythmic patterns transmitted orally; it does not know the "composer." The exclusive reign of this type of music in China ended around the turn of the twentieth century, with the arrival of foreign missionaries, foreign armies, and foreign merchants. In the wake of foreign invasion, a new type of Chinese music arose. It makes use of violins, organs, pianos, and clarinets, it is performed according to strict notation, and it is linked with the name of a particular composer.

NEW MUSIC IN THE TWENTIETH CENTURY

Military music was an integral part of General Yuan Shikai's formation of his New Army in the final years of the nineteenth century. Music education as practiced in missionary schools was taken as an example for the national educational reforms initiated in 1902. Among the first "compositions" of Chinese new music were *xuetangge* (school songs), some of which were based on foreign tunes, some of which were first attempts at composition in a new, foreign style. Some had simple harmonies, and others aspired to the romantic art song tradition. The first two decades of the twentieth century saw the establishment of a growing number of music societies that promoted both the practice of traditional Chinese music and the practice of foreign instruments. In the wake of the iconoclastic May Fourth movement of 1919, when foreign values were firmly established as superior to Chinese, first attempts were made to "improve" Chinese instruments. The strings for stringed instruments were no longer made of silk but of metal, in order to make the sound more sonorous to fill the newly built, large concert halls. The *erhu,* a two-stringed, high-pitched fiddle, was provided with an entire family in the alto, tenor, and bass range. Chinese orchestral performances were given in specially built concert halls where no one was allowed to talk or eat, as had been common practice before, when music was performed in traditional teahouses. In 1927 the Shanghai Conservatory was founded, introducing the professional training of musicians on both foreign and Chinese traditional instruments. Among the teachers in the composition department were many foreigners, including two Jewish students of the Austrian composers Alban Berg (1885–1935) and Arnold Schönberg (1874–1951), as well as, temporarily, the Russian composer Alexander Tcherepnin (1899–1977). The composer, conductor, and pianist Sergei Rachmaninoff (1873–1943), and the violinists Jacques Thibaud (1880–1953), Jascha Heifetz (1901–1987), and Fritz Kreisler (1875–1962) all performed in Shanghai. All of these Western musicians were important influences in the development of new Chinese music (Melvin and Cai Jindong 2004).

Whereas the earliest pieces of new Chinese music were all songs, the 1910s and 1920s saw the creation of the first instrumental works, such as Huang Zi's (1904–1938) orchestral overture *Huaijiu* (*Remembering,* 1929), the first large-scale symphonic and polyphonic piece to be composed in China. The 1930s also brought the first international recognition of new Chinese music: In 1934 Alexander Tcherepnin inaugurated a competition for piano pieces in the Chinese style. The first and second prizes went to two of He Lüding's (1903–1999) little pentatonic character pieces for piano. One of Tcherepnin's students, the Taiwanese-born composer Jiang Wenye (1910–1983), won a first international composition prize at the Berlin Olympics in 1936 for his orchestral piece *Taiwan wuqu* (*Taiwan Dance*). He was successful again in 1938 at the Fourth International Contemporary Music Festival in Venice with his *Wushou sumiao* (*Five Sketches for Piano*). His music is clearly influenced by the teachings of Tcherepnin, who advocated that the Chinese ought not to burden themselves with learning all about foreign nineteenth-century compositional styles, but rather to concern themselves with the study of contemporary foreign music, which was just as alien to them, but more progressive. Accordingly, the percussive sounds of Béla Bartók (1881–1945) on the one hand and the fragile impressionism of Claude Debussy (1862–1918) on the other, as well as the pentatonicism from Chinese melody, have influenced Jiang's style.

In the 1940s there were a few more "modernists" such as Tan Xiaolin (1911–1948), a student of the

German composer and violinist Paul Hindemith (1895–1963), and an influential composition teacher at the Shanghai Conservatory. At the same time, however, a greater number of composers chose a different road: Ma Sicong (1912–1987) composed Chinese-style music in the grand manner of Pyotr Ilich Tchaikovsky and Sergey Rachmaninov, whereas Xian Xinghai (1905–1945), the "People's Composer," used the same techniques to compose music that served the masses and the revolution. Xian Xinghai had grown up among the fishermen of Guangdong Province. Despite his lowly background, he studied music in Paris and at Chinese universities and was thought to be able to synthesize in his music the sentiments of both the intellectuals and the mass of workers and peasants. This made him an ideal teacher at the Lu Xun Academy in Yan'an, where he taught the young cadres how to compose songs and organize or conduct choral groups. During his years in Yan'an, between 1938 and 1940, Xian wrote *Shengchan yundong dahechang* (*Production Movement Cantata*); a theatrical, *Junmin jinxingqu* (*The Soldiers Advance*); and his most famous composition, the anti-Japanese *Huanghe dahechang* (*Yellow River Cantata*, 1939).

In 1949, with the Communist victory won, the history of new Chinese music splits into three: There are separate developments in new music produced in the People's Republic of China (PRC), in the Nationalist Republic on Taiwan, and in British colonial Hong Kong. In all three regions, in spite of different political systems and directions, pentatonic romanticism, a style that employs the functional harmonic framework established in the musical language of the late nineteenth century to accompany pentatonic melodies, remained a dominant style.

HONG KONG'S MUSIC SINCE 1949

Although it was a British colony and thus unimpeded by direct political interference, Hong Kong's music did not immediately take off in the early period. Hong Kong was dominated by business interests and therefore, during the 1950s and 1960s, cultural developments were not particularly significant and did not find sponsorship. Lin Shengshih (1915–1991) and Shi Kumpor (b. 1932), both of whom wrote music in a pleasant pentatonic idiom, were the most significant Chinese composers active in Hong Kong at the time. It was only during the governorship of Murray MacLehose (1971–1982) that cultural production picked up. In the 1970s the Hong Kong Philharmonic turned professional, the Hong Kong Chinese Orchestra was founded, the Hong Kong Music Office and the Hong Kong Arts Centre were inaugurated, and a number of cultural venues were built. Some composers who had studied abroad returned to Hong Kong and brought back with them new compositional techniques. Modernist compositions by Doming Lam (b. 1926), Law Wing-fai (b. 1949), and Tseng Yip-fat (b. 1952) scandalized largely conservative audiences.

Hong Kong composers cannot live from their art alone. All of them either teach or supplement their incomes by writing pop and film music. Thus, even though they were for the most part politically unbound (at least before 1997), Hong Kong composers were influenced by the demands of the market, a circumstance that has become more and more a reality even in Communist China today. Instead of the politicians railing against unintelligible music in Hong Kong, it is the lack of sophistication of the Hong Kong audiences that has driven Hong Kong composers to write music in more conservative styles.

TAIWAN'S MUSIC SINCE 1949

When the Nationalists under Chiang Kai-shek moved to Taiwan, the musical infrastructure they found was already well established. In 1945, the Japanese had left an educational system in full working order. The Nationalists simply took over the positions once held by the Japanese, and accordingly, the tension between Japanese and Taiwanese was simply substituted by a tension between Mainlanders and Taiwanese. Composers in Taiwan were subject to constant government supervision and propaganda. The two most important aims of all art until the late 1970s consisted of demonizing the "Communist bandits" and strengthening the reign of Mainlanders over Taiwanese. At the same time, the Nationalists wanted to surpass the Communists in preserving their national heritage (the iconoclastic Communists were said to have destroyed it). This root-seeking prescribed by the Taiwanese government was primarily interested in Mainlander Chinese culture. The choreographer, the producer, and the composer thus were caught between the Scylla of not being able to use mainland material (suspected of Communism) and the Charybdis of not being allowed to quote from Taiwanese traditions (suspected of calling for Taiwan independence).

This ambiguity in government cultural policy was prevalent throughout the 1960s and 1970s. The Sunflower Group (Xiangrikui yuehui), a composers' association that organized performances of Chinese new music in the late 1960s, had to change their name because sunflowers were too closely associated with Mao. The Yayin opera ensemble Yayin Xiaoji, founded in 1979, which made modern adaptations of Peking Opera, was at first accused of copying the Communist-model works produced under Jiang Qing's supervision during the Cultural Revolution (1966–1969).

Government policies to support new—but Chinese-style—arts produced a paradox: It was less dangerous to simply use foreign themes and techniques than to try to capture "Chinese traditions." Music education in Taiwan reflected this dilemma: Until the late 1970s, textbooks for the study of music were based on Western music history alone. A rather moderate musical modernism with minimal references to Chinese tradition was the result of political safe-play by Taiwan composers, although it was not easy to find an audience in the 1960s and 1970s. At the same time, politically condoned compositions—those that won national prizes, or were composed for official events—were all written in the style of pentatonic romanticism. Increased politicization in the 1970s and 1980s somewhat diminished fears of facing up to ambiguous government policy. A *xiangtu* (homeland) movement spread from literature to the other arts. Folk singers tried to express their Taiwanese experience. Composers such as Xu Changhui (1929–2001) and Shi Weiliang (1925–1977) began ethnomusicological fieldwork in the Taiwanese countryside. In 1975 Lin Huaimin (b. 1947) founded what later became one of the most successful cultural endeavors in Taiwan, the Cloud Gate Theater ballet troupe (Yunmen wuji), to perform to "music by Chinese, choreographed by Chinese, for Chinese to enjoy."

Since the 1980s, Taiwan folk opera and the Taiwanese language have regained a "new nobility." On university campuses, clubs devoted to the study of Taiwanese history and the Taiwanese language have sprung up. Taiwanese schools and universities have likewise begun to include China's and Taiwan's musical traditions in their curricula. This relaxation of government policies was partly due to the softening of the radical denial of Chineseness in favor of exclusive Taiwaneseness prevalent in the *xiangtu* movement, especially since travel to and contact with mainland China has become possible. In the late 1980s a *xungen re* (roots fever) began to endorse the ancestral mainland. Accordingly, Taiwanese composers now turn more and more frequently toward their own heritage.

MUSIC IN THE PRC SINCE 1949

On the mainland, musical education was influenced by the Soviet model. The Soviet Zhdanov Doctrine of 1946, which condemned musical modernism as formalist, determined the educational style not just in the Tchaikovsky Conservatory in Moscow, where many Chinese musicians were trained, but also in China's own conservatories. The Chinese music journal *Renmin yinyue* (People's music) openly castigated compositions by Igor Stravinsky (1882–1971), Arnold Schönberg, and Paul Hindemith. During the anti-rightist campaign in 1957 many Chinese modernists such as Jiang Wenye (and also composers who were not modernists but had lived and worked in Nationalist areas during the 1930s and 1940s, such as Ma Sicong) were criticized. The celebrations of the ten-year anniversary of the PRC saw the composition of many colossal symphonic works, praising the victory of the revolution. These compositions established pentatonic romanticism as the orthodox musical language for Communist China. Ding Shande (1911–1995) in his *Changzheng jiaoxiangqu* (*Long March Symphony*) employed folk songs from the Yao minority, working them into a patchwork of functional romantic harmonies. A similar method was used by Chen Gang (b. 1935) and He Zhanhao (b. 1933) in their famous *Liang Shanbo yu Zhu Yingtai* (*Butterfly Violin Concerto*), one of the best-known pieces of new Chinese music, based on the melodies of a Shaoxing opera.

During the early 1960s contacts with the Soviet Union were broken off. Even more than before, Chinese composers and musicians were required to write and perform music by Chinese rather than foreign composers, and preferably music in the officially approved "national style" (pentatonic romanticism). The ensuing Cultural Revolution was a period of many restrictions on the arts, including music. During this time, the production of *yangbanxi* (model works)—ten operas, four ballets, and four symphonic/instrumental works—further perpetuated pentatonic romanticism.

For China's musicians and composers, the end of the Cultural Revolution meant a reopening to the world; the official visits by a number of Western symphony orchestras during the period of ping-pong diplomacy that began in 1971 can be considered a prelude (Mittler 2007, p. 35). Music students once again had the chance to listen more frequently to music by Franz Schubert and Ludwig van Beethoven, by Felix Mendelssohn and Johannes Brahms, and they soon learned that musical developments had moved on from the days of Rachmaninov and Tchaikovsky.

In the late 1970s the conservatories opened their doors again. Alexander Goehr (b. 1932), a British composer and educator, was invited to the Central Conservatory in Beijing in 1980 to teach modern compositional techniques to select students from Shanghai and Beijing. Old musical scores from the 1930s and 1940s were rediscovered by a new generation of students. Ideas silenced since the late 1940s could be heard, thought, and composed again. The mid-1980s saw the rise of the *xinchao* ("new wave" composers). The music of this group is characterized on the one hand by a distinct familiarity with and exploration of modernist and avant-garde techniques and sounds from the West, and on the other hand by a particular approach to Chinese tradition that sets them apart, in style if not in method, from earlier attempts to compose "national music," and in particular from works in the style of pentatonic romanticism.

PRODUCING "CHINESENESS"

In different parts of China—Hong Kong, the PRC, and Taiwan—there is the constant presence of pentatonic romanticism. It makes use of Chinese raw material such as pentatonic melodies from folk song and opera and stylizes them by transferring them onto Western instruments and by pressing them into a (foreign) system of notation. Chinese folk song and operatic singing, however, are

Elvis Presley impersonator Melvis Kwok Lam-sang, Hong Kong, July 30, 2002. *After China's reacquisition of Hong Kong in 1997, Western-influenced music reached a broader audience on the mainland, though the Communist Party continues to promote patriotic music reinforcing revolutionary themes.* AP IMAGES

characterized by a changing irregular meter, and make use of elaborate ornamentation and tonal inflections that are difficult to notate in the foreign five-staff system. These idiosyncrasies are lost in stylized composition. *Xinchao* composers took a very different approach to Chinese melody. Their alternative was also in vogue in the 1940s, when Sang Tong (b. 1923) wrote his now famous piano piece *Zai na yaoyuan de difang* (*In That Place, Far Far Away*), which he later renounced. It is polytonal and constantly changes meter, as Sang Tong attempted to capture the rhythmic as well as the tonal idiosyncrasies of Chinese folk song. Chinese composers today have become even more radical in their translation of these idiosyncrasies into sound.

In addition to Chinese melody, Chinese instrumental techniques, too, have been used frequently by Chinese composers to mark their Chineseness. Again, there is the stylizing approach that simply transfers a Chinese instrumental technique onto a foreign instrument, and the more radical approach, found particularly among new wave composers, that changes the foreign instrument into one that is essentially Chinese. If *erhu* music is translated onto the cello, for example, the strings need to be lowered by a full octave; only then do they create the same kinds of background noises produced by playing the *erhu* used in the countryside, where resin is dropped directly onto the body of the instrument and the bow scrapes at it every time it is drawn.

Yet another approach to "Chineseness" that was taken up by many twentieth-century Chinese composers was to draw on Chinese myths and literature or to translate Chinese philosophical ideas into sound. Musically speaking, compositions that fall into this category appear in a great variety of styles. Not only John Cage but also Chinese composers have taken up the ideas of the *I Ching* (*Book of Changes*) and designed entire compositional systems based on them. The emphasis on single sounds (derived from the aesthetics of *qin* playing) and on silence is derived from the teachings of Daoism, where the greatest sound is said to be "rare, unhearable," and the best instrument a *guqin* without strings (for the political context, see Mittler 2000). This approach is epitomized in Tan Dun's *Circle with Four Trios, Conductor, and Audience* (1992), where a bar of complete silence is marked with a crescendo and a decrescendo. Silence is perhaps one of the most powerful and frequently heard elements in much new Chinese music today, and although it is not yet considered orthophonic by Chinese governments on either side of the Taiwan straits, perhaps it will supplant pentatonic romanticism to become the dominant style of new Chinese music in the twenty-first century.

With these last examples it is clear that some of the techniques described here as traditional and Chinese—the bruitism (from *erhu* playing), the microtonal practices (from Chinese operatic practice), the silences (from *guqin* playing)—are actually typical trademarks in works of Western new music. As these techniques were introduced after the Cultural Revolution to Chinese composers eager to learn about new music in the West, they often had a feeling of déjà vu. They saw mirrored, in the works of foreign contemporary composers, their own tradition. This merge can be explained in part by a strong Western interest in Asian culture since the beginning of the twentieth century: Composers such as Debussy, Cage, Karlheinz Stockhausen (1928–2007), Benjamin Britten (1913–1976), and Lou Harrison (1917–2003) were fascinated by the sounds, the instruments, and the philosophies of Asia. And yet the fact that fundamental Asian concepts and practices in music are unobtrusively integrated into the mainstream of Western contemporary music cannot be explained by the strong Western interest in Asian culture alone. Rather, there are fundamental similarities, certain affinities between Eastern old and Western new techniques.

The breakdown of Western harmony was the first step in creating new music in the West. Conventional vertical structure made way for a more linear, horizontal structure, and this type of structure is indeed typical of Chinese traditional music. The concept of sound compositions emphasizing single sounds rather than melodic developments, a technique prevalent in new music and exemplified in compositions by György Ligeti (1923–2006), Witold Lutostawski (1913–1994), and Giacinto Scelsi (1905–1988), among others, is a common feature of traditional Chinese music. Aleatoric approaches soften the concept of the unchanging opus and the dictatorial position of the composer, a concept never inherent in China's musical tradition. Complicated and polyrhythmic structures, another of the "discoveries" of new music, are customary in China's tradition, and even the use of speech-voice is similar to some of the vocal effects of Chinese opera.

Since the Cultural Revolution, new Chinese music no longer seeks only to improve Chinese musical traditions and instruments by bringing them up to foreign standards, as efforts at stylization and reform of Chinese instruments would do, but instead to redevelop, to renew, and to reinvigorate traditional Chinese music. The merging of the techniques of new music and Chinese tradition makes it possible to do two things at the same time: to redevelop and to restore the traditional heritage.

SEE ALSO *Model Operas and Bullets; Peking Opera and Regional Operas; Tan Dun; Yuan Shikai.*

BIBLIOGRAPHY

Melvin, Sheila, and Cai Jindong. *Rhapsody in Red: How Western Classical Music Became Chinese.* New York: Algora, 2004.

Mittler, Barbara. *Dangerous Tunes: The Politics of Chinese Music in Hong Kong, Taiwan, and the People's Republic of China since 1949.* Wiesbaden, Germany: Harrassowitz, 1997.

Mittler, Barbara. Ohrenbetäubende Stille: Chinas musikalische Avantgarde als Politikum. *Berliner China Hefte* 19 (2000): 65–76.

Mittler, Barbara. Sound Patterns of Cultural Memory: Wound/Scar Music and Its Making in Contemporary China. *World New Music Magazine* 17 (2007): 33–54.

Utz, Christian. *Neue Musik und Interkulturalität. Von John Cage bis Tan Dun* [New Music and Interculturality: From John Cage to Tan Dun]. Stuttgart, Germany: Franz Steiner, 2002.

Barbara Mittler

MUSLIM UPRISINGS

From the mid- to late nineteenth century, outbreaks of violence and social disorder spread over vast areas of Muslim-populated China. In the borderlands of the northwest, the disturbances stretched across Shaanxi and Gansu (including present-day Ningxia and parts of Qinghai). By 1864 unrest had reached the already volatile region of Xinjiang. The immediate causes of the Great Muslim Rebellion (1862–1877) were localized incidents. Thus the aims and objectives of the leaders varied considerably, with no one centralized, coordinated movement. Nevertheless, certain prevailing conditions were conducive to the rapid spread of violence. Qing forces, preoccupied in suppressing the Taiping Uprising (1851–1864) and Nian Uprising (1851–1868), were overstretched and demoralized, while the formation of local militias to defend against the rebels encouraged a culture of violence. Social dislocation had resulted in a loosening of central control and corruption and extortion by local officials compounded a heavy tax burden and entrenched poverty. To this may be added, among the community of Sino-Muslims (Tungan or Hui) and Turkic Muslim Salars, an increasing sense of discrimination by the state and Sufi revivalism.

SHIFTING ALLEGIANCES AND SPREADING VIOLENCE

Traditionally, China's Muslim community belonged to the non-Sufi mosque-based *gedimu* tradition, but in the early eighteenth century Ma Laichi (1681–1766) returned

to Gansu from the Muslim heartlands and founded the Khafīya order of Naqshabandī Sufis. Some fifty years later, Ma Mingxin (1719?–1781), who had studied in Mecca and Yemen, also returned to the region and founded another Naqshabandī order, the Jahrīya. Characterized by devotion to one leader, the desire to purify ritual practice, and a leaning toward political and social activism, both orders garnered large numbers of adherents and by the late 1760s were vying for dominance. As tensions grew, fueled by disputes over ritual (notably the vocalization of *dhikr*, an act of devotion involving repetition of the names of Allah), the distribution of finances, and hereditary succession, the Qing authorities purported to tolerate adherents of the "Old Teaching" while suppressing those of the "New Teaching." Yet, just as the former did not refer exclusively to the Khafīya and non-Sufi Gedimu tradition, the latter was not synonymous with the Jahrīya. The definition of the rebel blurred as allegiances shifted; nor was the feuding limited to these two orders. Suborders also clashed, and ultimately many of those involved in violence against the imperial government were neither Sufis nor indeed, in some cases, Muslims.

By the early 1860s, with Shaanxi under pressure from the approaching Taiping and Nian rebels, communal violence became more acute and people looked to military and religious leaders for security. The Jahrīya leader, Ma Hualong (d. 1871), made his headquarters at Jinjibao south of Ningxia city; Ma Zhan'ao, a Khafīya leader, was based at Hezhou; to the west, Ma Guiyuan marshaled troops in Xining; and Ma Wenlu based himself in Suzhou out along the Gansu Corridor. The first full-scale military confrontation with Qing troops, often identified as the onset of the Northwest Muslim Rebellion (1862), occurred when Muslim militias besieged the city of Xi'an. The siege continued for over a year. In the bloody aftermath, a large number of Muslim refugees from Shaanxi fled west to Gansu. There they formed the Eighteen Great Battalions and continued their struggle against the imperial troops. Elsewhere, Muslims controlled substantial parts of Shaanxi until 1868, while in Gansu the main centers of resistance, Jinjibao and Suzhou, held out until 1872 and 1873 respectively.

Similarly, after a century of Qing rule in Xinjiang, by the 1860s high taxes and maladministration by both the *begs* (native officials) and Qing officials had alienated large segments of the predominantly Turkic Muslim population, as well as the Sino-Muslims. In the south the hardships inflicted by the repeated incursions of the *khwājas*, the descendants of local Turkic Muslim leaders who had been ousted from the southern region of Altishahr during the conquest, had only added to the suffering. Fired by rumors carried from Gansu of a wholesale massacre of Muslims, the Sino-Muslims were the first to resort to violence against the imperial government. In the summer of 1864 disturbances spread throughout the entire region, involving both Sino-Muslims and Turkic Muslims.

In Kucha the uprising was headed by the Turkic spiritual leader, Rāshidīn Khwāja (d. 1867), who attempted to extend his control across the Tarim Basin; in the north a Sino-Muslim military officer, Tuo Ming (Tuo Delin, d. 1872) led the revolt. One by one, the major cities of the north were captured until with the fall of Yili (Ili) in 1866, Qing rule of the region collapsed. Initially Qing resistance had been stronger in the oasis cities of Altishahr; but in 1865 the rebels received assistance from the khanate of Khokand (periodic sponsors of the *khwājas*), in the form of troops headed by Buzurg Khwāja and the Khokandi military commander Yaʿqūb Beg (Yakub Beg, 1820–1877). Within less than two years, Yaʿqūb Beg had removed Buzurg, overthrown Rāshidīn Khwāja's regime at Kucha, and established an Islamic state throughout the south of Xinjiang. In 1870 he moved north and wrested power from the Sino-Muslim leaders. With the exception of Qumul (Hami) in the east and the Yili region, seized by Russia in 1871, he was to rule Xinjiang until 1877.

SUPPRESSION AND ITS AFTERMATH

In December 1868, having assisted in the suppression of the Taipings and the Nian rebels, the Qing general Zuo Zongtang (1812–1885) began his meticulously executed campaign against the northwest. In the ensuing bloodbath, thousands of Muslims were killed and thousands more were exiled to different parts of China. Zuo's troops then moved west to Jinjibao, where they besieged Ma Hualong for sixteen months before advancing toward Hezhou. Ma Zhan'ao surrendered his stronghold in 1872, and with the recapture of Suzhou and the mopping-up of resistance in the Gansu Corridor, Zuo completed his campaign.

From 1874 to 1875 the question of the retention of Xinjiang was famously debated by Zuo and Li Hongzhang, governor-general of Zhili. Zuo's success in the northwest had been won in the face of a constant struggle for funds. Now Li argued against the recovery of Xinjiang on the grounds that the court needed to focus its limited resources on coastal defense. Despite the persistence of doubts in certain circles, Zuo's conviction persuaded the court that, in keeping with the domino theory, the security of the entire north of China, including Beijing, depended on the retention of Xinjiang. The campaign against Xinjiang was approved. Within a year much of the north had been retaken and Zuo's troops were heading south. In early summer 1877 Yaʿqūb Beg died, and torn by internal disputes, the Muslim defense swiftly collapsed. With the fall of Kashgar and Khotan in early 1878, the Qing reconquest was complete, notwithstanding the Yili region's remaining in Russian hands until the Treaty of Petersburg in 1881.

Among the far-reaching repercussions of the uprisings, two stand out: First, Beijing tightened its control of the northwestern borderlands, adopting social, political, and economic policies of integration that sought to bind the frontier firmly to the emerging nation-state; second, although Islam had not united all the factions of the Muslim community, it had served to unify Muslims against the state and thus was to be recognized in China as a powerful political force.

SEE ALSO *Li Hongzhang; Nian Uprising; Taiping Uprising; Zuo Zongtang.*

BIBLIOGRAPHY

Kim, Hodong. *Holy War in China: The Muslim Rebellion and State in Chinese Central Asia, 1864–1877*. Stanford, CA: Stanford University Press, 2004.

Lipman, Jonathan N. *Familiar Strangers: A History of Muslims in Northwest China*. Seattle: University of Washington Press, 1998.

Zhu, Wenzhang (Chu Wen-djang). *The Moslem Rebellion in Northwest China, 1862–1878: A Study of Government Minority Policy*. The Hague: Mouton, 1966.

Laura J. Newby

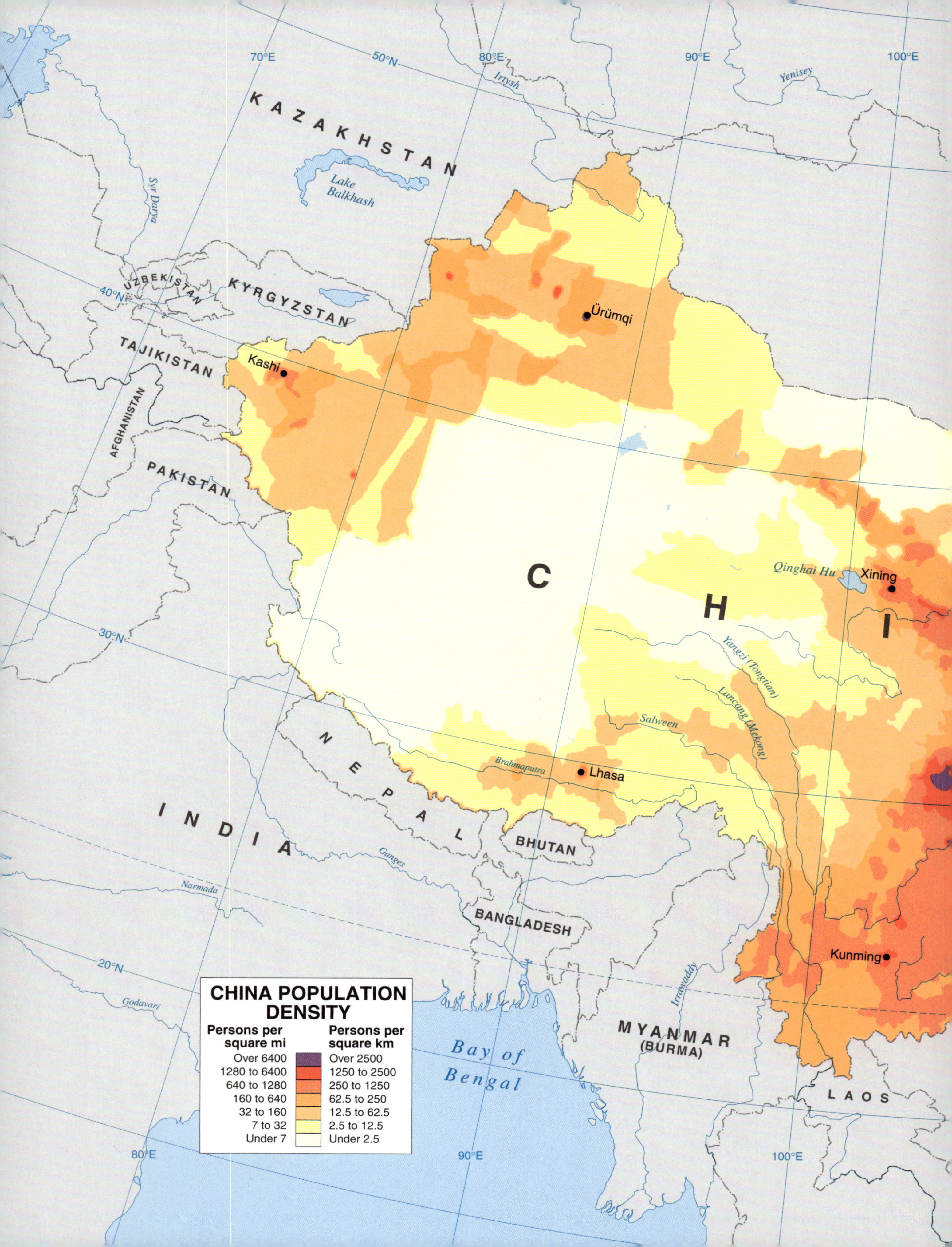

CHINA POPULATION DENSITY
Persons per square mi
Over 6400
1280 to 6400
640 to 1280
160 to 640
32 to 160
7 to 32
Under 7
Persons per square km
Over 2500
1250 to 2500
250 to 1250
62.5 to 250
12.5 to 62.5
2.5 to 12.5
Under 2.5
KAZAKHSTAN
Lake Balkhash
UZBEKISTAN
KYRGYZSTAN
TAJIKISTAN
AFGHANISTAN
PAKISTAN
INDIA
NEPAL
BHUTAN
BANGLADESH
MYANMAR (BURMA)
LAOS
CHI
Kashi
Ürümqi
Lhasa
Xining
Kunming
Qinghai Hu
Yangzi (Tongtian)
Lancang (Mekong)
Salween
Brahmaputra
Irrawaddy
Ganges
Narmada
Godavari
Syr Darya
Irtysh
Yenisey
Bay of Bengal
70°E
80°E
90°E
100°E
50°N
40°N
30°N
20°N